ATLAS OF THE INDIAN TRIBES
OF NORTH AMERICA
AND
THE CLASH OF CULTURES

Nicholas J. Santoro

Kansas City, Missouri

iUniverse, Inc.

New York   Bloomington

ATLAS OF THE INDIAN TRIBES OF NORTH AMERICA AND THE CLASH OF CULTURES

iUniverse books may be ordered through booksellers or by contacting:

iUniverse
1663 Liberty Drive
Bloomington, IN 47403
www.iuniverse.com
1-800-Authors (1-800-288-4677)

ISBN: 978-1-4401-0795-5 (pbk)
ISBN: 978-1-4401-0796-2 (ebk)

Printed in the United States of America

iUniverse rev. date: 1/2/2009

On the cover: Man and Woman of Laguna Pueblo, New Mexico.
Ben Wittick, Photographer. Courtesy National Archives, photo no. 530898.

Contents

Introduction

The most common trait of all primitive peoples is a reverence for the lifegiving earth, and the native Americans shared this elemental ethic: the land was alive to his loving touch, and he, its son, was brother to all creatures. His feelings were made visible in medicine bundles and dance rhythms for rain, and all of his religious rites and land attitudes savored the inseparable work of nature and God, the master of Life. During the long Indian tenure the land remained undefiled save for scars no deeper than the scratches of cornfield clearing or the farming canals of the Hohokams of the Arizona desert.

Stewart Lee Udall, *The Quiet Crisis* (1963)

This *Atlas* was written to provide a compact resource on the identity, location, and history of the American Indians and the Native American tribes of North American with particular emphasis on those tribes that have inhabited the lands that we now refer to as the continental United States since the beginning of what is generally referred to as the historical period. It was also written as a salute to the heart and spirit of the American Indian.

It is hoped that this book will serve as a convenient resource to inform and assist equally the casual reader, the researcher and the teacher and student alike. It is also hoped that the book will awaken interest, foster greater understanding, and encourage further study and involvement in the affairs of the Native American population of the United States. The text lists the Native American tribes of the continental United States and answers to the extent possible the three basic questions of who, where, and when. Regrettably, the information on all too many of the tribes is extremely limited. For some, there is little more than a name. A brief synopsis of their tribal history is also provided, expanded where deemed of particular historical interest and to address specific issues.

I have searched to find and use the best scholarship available. Discrepancies in the literature have been noted wherever possible. Hopefully, I have not been careless in repeating information that subsequent scholarship has judged to be erroneous, but I alone am responsible for any errors.

For too many years, the native population of America has been a people ignored. I hope that this book will help serve as a reminder to all that the history of the American Indian is America's history; it is our history. In the words of Daniel Richter, "...native history belongs to us all."[1] Native American history, in all its aspects, is part of America's cultural heritage. By seeing something of who we were, we all may be better able to define who we need to be. To the extent that the format of the book permits, I have tried to recount the impact of European settlement, westward expansion, government policy, and public attitudes on their lives and culture of America's first people.

A member of the Editorial Board of the *Kansas City Star* recently published an essay titled "A History Ignored" that decried the fact that not one of the new state quarters issued by the U.S. Mint, with the exception of the buffalo depicted on the quarter piece of the state of Kansas, even remotely attempted to recognize America's Indian heritage.[2] Since that article was written the new state quarter has been issued

---

1   Daniel K. Richter, Facing East from Indian Country: A Native History of Early America, 10
2   Lewis W. Diuguid, "A History Ignored," *Kansas City Star*, January 13, 2006, 12.

for the state of North Dakota that features two bison grazing at sunrise on the North Dakota Badlands.[3] The issue, however, is not the bison or what they do or do not represent. What is important is that the history of the American Indian as well as dire circumstances under which many Native American people presently exit on the American reservations has been ignored.

The *Atlas* consists of three parts. Part One provides a brief overview of Native Americans history. Part Two is an annotated alphabetical listing of the Indian tribes of North America, specifically those tribes that have occupied the continental United States and constitutes the body of the text. Part Three contains supplemental information, including an extensive set of notes and sources, a selected bibliography, and addenda on the role of American Indian tribes in the American Civil War and the role played by American Indians in the Military Service. The reader's attention is called to Appendix A which contains a master list of some 4,700 of the names that have been used over the years to identify the various Indian tribes. It is my hope that the *Atlas* will prove both interesting and a continuing source of reference to the casual reader and the student alike.

The Indians of North America within the contiguous forty-eight states are commonly referred to as American Indians or Native Americans. My attempts to discern a preference among the native peoples themselves have found both terms equally acceptable. The Bureau of Indian Affairs uses the name American Indian (AI). I have employed both names interchangeably. (The BIA uses the term American Native (AN) for the native Indian tribes of Alaska.)

A note on phraseology. The words "tribe" and "nation" are often a source of confusion and misunderstanding. The word tribe is most commonly used to define an aggregate of people of the same descent. That decent, however, can take the form of blood relation, custom, tradition, or adherence to the same leader. The term is also used simply to indicate a division within a larger aggregate or group. A check of most dictionaries, however, will give roughly the same definition for the word nation. Often, the problem arises because for some the word nation appears to carry greater prestige, its omission portrayed as a negative. The *Random House Dictionary of the English Language* defines the word nation both as "a tribe of an Indian confederation" and as "an aggregation of persons of the same ethnic family."

Into the lexicon of the Native Americans comes not only the meaning associated with the words nation and tribe, but also with the words division, subdivision, sub-tribe, band, group, people, village, clan, and family. Into the mix are thrown the words league and confederation. These words challenge the writer and reader alike and make identification and classification of the American Indians somewhat difficult. For example, the word family almost always connotes an extended family although the bounds ascribed by the term are not always easily discernable.

For the most part, I have used the word tribe to designate any separate, independent unit capable of sustaining itself, the members of which have a common bond. I have employed the word "nation" rather sparingly to designate a larger entity comprised of a number of tribes or large divisions that are traditionally sub-divided into one or more separate and distinct sub-units. The Apache and Sioux are prime examples. For example, the name Sioux can be subdivided to include the Lakota which can be subdivided to include the Oglalla which can be further subdivided to include the Miniconjous.

I have treated those groups separately that common usage has treated separately; but, where applicable, I have attempted to place the group within the appropriate organizational structure. Where the literature treats of divisions or subdivisions, the meaning is more circumspect. The terms may refer to independent tribes or sub-tribes, or to bands, a cluster of villages or other geographical alignments. In identifying the

---

3   French for Badlands, *les mauvaises terres a traverser* or "bad lands to travel through." For the Sioux, the Badlands was the "place where the hills look at each other." The principal locations were along the Little Missouri River in North Dakota and along the White River southeast of Rapid City, South Dakota.

various units, I have used my best judgement based on what I was able to discern from the literature, taking into account the roles that pride and prestige play in modern-day accounts. If I have slighted any individuals or group, I apologize.

Grammar can also cause a problem when referring to individual tribes and the members of the respective tribes in the aggregate. Use of singular form and the plural form of the tribal names appear equally acceptable although use of the plural form appears somewhat more common. I have found myself using both forms depending on the circumstances but generally favoring the singular form as used by historian Keith Algier writing on the Crow creation myth, "The Crow, because their hearts were strong, found themselves inhabiting lands surrounded by jealous enemies."[4]

An extensive set of notes and sources is provided. I have adopted a modified style for online resources that I hope is fully communicative and gives full credit to the originator. It is my sincere hope that I have not failed to properly acknowledge any of the hard work of others.

This book provides only a brief glimps in to the lives of the Native Americans that have inhabited the forty-eight states since the beginning of the historical record. While it attempts to answer the who, where and when and in some cases the how and the why the reader must look further to gain some insight into the culture and heart of the American Indian. May I suggest Joseph M. Marshall, III, *The Journey of Crazy Horse*. Marshall's work is not a historical account in the traditional sense; nor is it a biography. More than either, it gives the reader a sense of time and space in the lives of America's Indians during the critical fifty-year span between 1825 and 1875. Written of the Lakota, it could have been written just as appropriately of, by and for the Pueblo, the Shawnee or the Delaware and others.

As George Catlin wrote, before proceeding, it is suggested that the reader first "divest himself, as far as possible of the deadly prejudices which he has carried from his childhood."[5] For my part, I have tried to be sensitive to the words of John Joseph Mathews, writing of Major Laban J. Miles, for many years the caring and dedicated agent for the Osage on their last reservation in Indian Territory: "He thought there was nothing more sickening than the 'trash' that had been written about the Indian, the 'poor Indian,' and his treatment by the government...represented as blundering, ignorant and soulless. He was afraid of books which mentioned the 'noble red man,' and made no distinctions among the vastly different tribes... attributing to all of them the same characteristics and tendencies."[6]

We'-a-hnon — "Thank you." (Osage)

Nicholas J. Santoro
October 20, 2008

---

4   Keith Algier, *The Crow and the Eagle: A Tribal History from Lewis & Clark to Custer*, 19.
5   George Catlin, *North American Indians*, 4.
6   John Joseph Mathews, *Wah'Kon-Tah: The Osage and the White Man's Road* , 79.

The American Indian World of Yesterday and Today

Only to the white man was nature a "wilderness"
and only to him was the land "infested"
with "wild" animals and "savage" people.

To us it was tame.

Earth was bountiful and we were surrounded
with the blessings of the Great Mystery.

Not until the hairy man from the east came
and with brutal frenzy heaped injustices upon us
and the families that we loved
was it "wild" for us.

When the very animals of the forest began fleeing from his approach,
then it was that for us the "Wild West" Began.

—Luther Standing Bear, Chief of the Oglala
Land of the Spotted Eagle (1933)

Early European explorers, traders and settlers from Spain, France, and Great Britain encountered Native Americans tribes throughout the North American continent. Everywhere they traveled, Native Americans were already there, along the shores of Nova Scotia, the wetlands of the Floridas, the deserts and mountains of Mexico and the southwest, and the waters of Canada and the northwest. Theories about the arrival of the first Americans abound, but that subject is best left to others. This work picks up the story of Native Americans about the time of the arrival of the first Europeans.

Among the Native Americans, there was the natural migration in search of food and improved living conditions. Although there had always been displacements among the tribes of American Indians, the arrival of the Europeans gave a whole new meaning to the process. When displacements proved insufficient, inadequate, or too slow, the Europeans resorted to forced removals. For those tribes east of the Mississippi River, movement was generally from East to West and generally along the same latitude. For those on the west coast, migration patters generally flowed west to east and in some cases from west to east and back again. For those living in the high plains and the northwest, migration was for the most part from north to south. A few, more by chance than any beneficial concern on the part of the Europeans, were allowed to remain on or in the general vicinity of their traditional homeland.

Displacements from along the Atlantic coast were the more prevalent. Each successive push by the Europeans as well as European intrusions upon Indian society precipitated a series of subsequent moves as one tribe displaced another. Concepts of land tenure, private property, and accumulation of wealth set Indians and Europeans apart. Yet, no one in an Indian village ever went hungry if there was food to be had. If one ate they all ate, though it might be only crumbs. To share and share-alike was not an act of charity; it was not a habit to be developed; it came as natural as breathing. It was as sure as the rising and setting of the sun. Writes Daniel Denton of the Long Island Lenapes of 1670: "They are extraordinarily charitable to one another, one having nothing to spare, but he freely imparts it to his friends, and whatsoever they get by gaming or any other way, they share to one another, leaving to themselves commonly the least share."[7] And across the country a century and half later, "Back at the encampment, they [Crazy Horse and is brother Little Hawk] distributed the fresh meat first to those who had nothing to eat but kept only a little for their family."[8] Mari Sandoz possibly summed it up best, writing of the Cheyenne in their flight north in 1878, "It seemed better to follow those who lived in the old Indian way, where everyone would have meat for the coals if anyone did."[9]

Generally speaking the French traders and settlers made the greatest accommodation to the native peoples that they encountered, followed by the English and the Spanish. Initially, the English colonists *as traders*—particularly those from Pennsylvania and Virginia—tried to compete with the French by distributing gifts to the Native American tribes along the Ohio River and Great Lakes.

Competition between European nations for Indian favor ceased following the end of the French and Indian War, and the Indians suffered accordingly. American colonists not only believed that the Native Americans were infringing on *their* lands but also that they were their subjects. The British commander in the Colonies, General Thomas Gage remarked of the Iroquois, who had fought and sacrificed as British allies, "As for the Six Nations having acknowledged themselves subject of the English, that I conclude must be a very gross mistake and am well satisfied were they told so,...they would on such an attempt very soon resolve to cut our Throats."[10] Over a half a century later, John Roebling, that German immigrant who would design the Brooklyn Bridge reflected on the life of the American Indians as his ship entered Delaware Bay. He wrote in his *Journal* of the Indians who had once lived "quietly on the property inherited from their ancestors" before "interrupted by the all-disturbing Europeans."[11]

With the ouster of the British rule following the War for Independence, citizens of the new confederated colonies expected free access to the Indians lands that had been denied them by Royal Proclamation—the threat to colonial liberty less spoken of and less written about but possibly as significant as the issue of taxation without representation.[12] Those who defended Indian rights, in the words of Alan Taylor, "betrayed the racial hierarchy favored by the Patriots." Thomas Jefferson, for his part some twenty years later, naively believed that the Louisiana Purchase could be used to resettle the Native Americans displaced from the east thereby opening the land east of the Mississippi exclusively to white settlers.

American Indian and Alaskan Native Population and Geographic Divisions

Before the great American Indian relocation that took place in the first half of the nineteenth century, the Native American Indian population in the lower forty-eight states could be placed into one of six or seven basic geographic groupings:

- Woodland, Eastern Woodland, and Great Lakes Tribes, including the tribes of Southeastern Canada.

   The Woodlands or Eastern Woodlands as it is often referred to covered the lands from the Atlantic west to the Mississippi River and just beyond and from the Kentucky-Tennessee border north beyond the Great Lakes into Canada.[13]

---

7   Edwin G. Burrows and Mike Wallace, *Gotham*, 12, from Daniel Denton, *A Brief Description of New York* [1670] (New York, 1966).
8   Joseph M. Marchall, III, *The Journey of Crazy Horse*, 152.
9   Mari Sandoz, *Cheyenne Autumn*, 17.
10   Alan Taylor, *The Divided Ground*, 34, 416n70. Remarks made October 7, 1772.
11   David McCullough, *The Great Bridge*, 46, 569.
12   Taylor, *op. cit.*, 79.
13   Indiana Historical Bureau, State of Indiana, "Finding Our Way Home: The Great Lakes Woodland People," *The Indiana Historian* (September 2001), no. 7052, available at http://www.in.gov/history/files/findourwayhome.pdf.

- Southeast Tribes, excluding the Carolinas

  The more noted tribes of the Southeast—i.e., those most often written about by Anglo-Americans, include the Cherokee, the Choctaw, the Seminole, and the Creek.

- Plains Tribes stretching into Saskatchewan and Alberta, Canada divided between the Northern Plains and Southern Plains roughly at the South Platte River.

  The larger tribes of the Plains to the north included the many divisions of the Sioux or Dakota, the Northern Cheyenne and Arapahoe, Ponca, the Crow, Assiniboine, and the Shoshone, with the Chippewa and the Iowa to the Northeast that presses our common definition of the Plains. To the south rode the more populous Southern Cheyenne and Arapahoe, the Pawnee, and the Ute at the western limits of the region. Among the smaller tribes were the Omaha, Piute, and Ponca. In a large chunk of land on the Southern reaches of the Plains, beyond the Arkansas, settled the Comanche and the Kiowa, the Kiowa-Apache, and the Plains Apache.

- Southwest Tribes includes all the desert lands between the Rockies and the Sierras but often subdivided into a subgroup, the Plateau Indians.

  The mountainous regions of the Southwest were home to the Apache, the Pueblo, the Navaho, with the Caddoan in the eastern limits. The tribes of the Plains and the Southwest are the most easily recognized thanks to the motion picture studios of Hollywood and their depiction of life in the West during the 1870s and 1880s.

- North Pacific tribes including the plateaus of the Columbia River Basin

  Probably the most noted of the Northwest tribes were the Nez Percé, the Flathead, and the Walla-Walla.

- California or South Pacific coast tribes

  Probably the least familiar to the to the vast majority of American readers are the tribes of California and the coastal regions of the Northwest.

Census Figures and Tribal Entities

American Indians (AI) have been counted in government census figures beginning with the 1860 census. However, those living on reservations and in the Indian Territory were not counted until 1890. Alaska Natives (AN) were included in the totals beginning in 1880 and listed separately beginning in 1940. Eskimos and Aleuts were first counted separately in all states in 1980. Up until then they had only been counted separately in Alaska.

Year	AIAN Population	In the West	Total Population
1860	44,021*		31,443,321
1900	237,196*		75,994,575
1960	795,110	271,036	179,323,175
1970	798,119	379,214	203,211,926
1980	1,364,033	670,655	226,545,805
1990	1,878,285	865,522	248,709,873
2000	2,475,956		281,421,906

Including Eskimo and Aleut; no breakdown by region.

It was not until the census of 1980 that the person being counted was permitted to select his or her race. Among others, the options included "American Indian," "Alaskan Native," and "American Indian or Alaskan Native *and* Another Race." In the 2000 Census the combined American Indian (AI) and Alaskan Native (AN) population of 2,475,956 made up 0.88% of the total U.S. population of 281,421,906 States (including Hawaii, Puerto Rico, and the District of Columbia) compared to 12.32% for Blacks and African Americans; 3.64% for Asians; and 12.55% for Latinos or Hispanics. A total of 910,527 or 36.8% lived on a reservation or on off-reservation trust lands.

Including those individuals of the American Indian or Alaskan Native race combined with another race, the total population jumps to 4,119,301 or 1.5% of the total population. Of the total, 1,047,770 or 25.4% lived on one of the many reservations or trust lands.

A breakdown of the populations by state is provided in the Appendices.. The five states with the highest population were, in descending order, California, Oklahoma, Arizona, New Mexico, and Texas. Together, they included nearly half the population of native peoples in the United States (46.6%). Rounding out the top ten were North Carolina, Alaska, Washington, New York, and South Dakota—all but two of the top ten were west of the Mississippi. Reservation population figures are also given in the Appendices.

Indicative of their state of health, Native Americans have the lowest percentage of persons 65 years of age and older (5.6%) except for Native Hawaiians and Other Pacific Islanders (5.2%)—less than half the ratio of the white population over 65 (14.4 %) and 12.2% for the population as a whole.

Supporting the population were 561 tribal entities recognized by the federal government in 2005, 334 of which were within the contiguous forty-eight states and 227 within the state of Alaska. By definition, tribal entities are eligible to receive services from the Bureau of Indian Affairs. The word entity is an administrative term and does not necessarily denote separate tribes or nations. For example, the list includes the Sac & Fox Tribe of the Mississippi in Iowa; the Sac & Fox Nation of Missouri in Kansas and Nebraska; and the Sac & Fox Nation, Oklahoma. For a listing of the tribal entities recognized in 2005, see the Appendices.

The ten largest tribal groupings to come out of the 2000 Census were Cherokee, Navajo, Latin American Indian, Choctaw, Sioux, Chippewa, Apache, Blackfeet, Iroquois, Pueblo. The Navajo had the highest percentage of people (90%) reporting only one race or tribal grouping, whereas the Cherokee had the lowest percentage (39%).[14]

The Early Period

Europeans arrived in what is now the continental United States in five waves from the early fifteen hundreds to the late sixteen hundreds:

---

14   U.S. Census Bureau, Census 2000 Summary File 1 (Series of Tables); Becca Jones, "Executive Summary: American Indians and Alaska Natives: A Demographic Perspective" (Washington, DC: Population Resource Center, July 2003) at http://www.prcdc.org/summaries/amindiansaknatives/amindiansaknatives.html [September 16, 2006].

- Spanish into the Floridas and the southeast from South America and the Caribbean islands

- Spanish into Texas, the desert Southwest, and California from Mexico

- English with landings along the Atlantic seaboard

- French into the Great Lakes region and Mississippi Valley from Canada

- French and Spanish with landings along the Gulf Coast

To the Europeans it was a new world; it was not The New World. It had been home to the Native Peoples for thousand of years. The early explorers gave way to hunters and traders. They, in turn, gave way to missionaries and settlers. In the next hundred years or so, the Spanish and the French gave way to the English, and the English gave way to those who took the name Americans for their own. These new Americans pushed west and pushed the Native Americans out ahead of them, ever farther until finally, except for a small minority left on reservations, they were pushed beyond the Mississippi.

Reservations were established for these immigrant Indians from the east along what is the now the eastern borders of Nebraska, Kansas, and Oklahoma—what became known as Indian Territory. Their removal west also brought them into conflict with the Indians of the Plains and the Southwest who themselves were pushed this way and that by an influx of white traders, farmers, and miners, as were those Indians along the Pacific Coast. Native who were driven from their homes by the white horde.

A series of successive steps transformed a free people into managed liability over a period of less than one hundred and fifty years:

- French and Indian War (1763)
- American Revolutionary War and Treaty of Paris (1783)
  - Battle of Fallen Timbers and the Treaty of Greenville (1794-1795)
- Louisiana Purchase (1803)
- Indian Removal Act and the Trail of Tears (1830-1835)
  - End of the Black Hawk War (1832)
- Manifest Destiny (1845)
- War with Mexico (1846-1848)
- California Gold Rush (1849-)
- Kansas-Nebraska Act (1854)
- Transcontinental Railroad (1862-1869)
- Battle for the Black Hills and the Battle at the Little Big Horn (June 17, 1876)
- Wounded Knee (December 29, 1890)

Spain took possession of the Louisiana Territory from the French following the end of the French and Indian War. At the same time, the British took possession of the "western lands" between the Alleghenies and the Mississippi River and tried to establish a coherent policy for dealing with the Indian situation. With the Royal Proclamation of 1763, the British government decreed the land west of the Alleghenies-Appalachians as Indian territory, prohibiting white settlement. But the Prohibition Line as it was called became meaningless before the ink was dry on the parchment. What transpired over the next forty years was nothing short of a white invasion. The new government of the United States gained formal control of the western lands with the end of the Revolutionary War, and the Louisiana Purchase brought on was a sudden and chaotic rush to explore and settle the trans-Mississippi west. By 1810 white settlers numbering almost a million persons occupied the states of Kentucky, Tennessee, and Ohio and the territories of Michigan, Indiana, and Illinois that heretofore had been the sole possession of Native American Peoples.[15]

In the words of Oneida Chief Gwedelhes Agwelondongwas (Good Peter to the American colonists), a man held in high esteem by Indians and colonists alike:

> *It is just so with your People. As long as any Spot of our excellent Land remains, they will covet it, and if one dies, another will pursue it, and will never rest till they possess it.*[16]

Early Government Policy

On July 13, 1787, the Continental Congress passed the Northwest Ordinance that contained a provision popularly titled the "Utmost Good Faith Law" that read:

> Article the Third. ... The utmost good faith shall always be observed towards the Indians, their lands and property shall never be taken from them without their consent; and in their property, rights and liberty, they never shall be invaded or disturbed, unless in just and lawful wars authorised [sic] by Congress; but laws founded in justice and humanity shall from time to time be made, for preventing wrongs being done to them, and for preserving peace and friendship with them.[17]

The new federal government of the United States continued a relatively conciliatory position with respect to rights the Native Americans compared to the Confederation of Colonies, albeit short-lived. The first of the Indian laws to emerge from the US Congress was the act of July 22, 1790 dealing with trade. The Indian Trade and Intercourse Act required commercial licenses and established rules for punishing white men guilty of crimes committed in Indian country. The law also prohibited private land purchases. There followed the law of March 1, 1793, that, in addition to strengthening the earlier law, authorized funds to encourage civilization among the tribes and the appointment of federal agents

Still trying to find a satisfactory solution for dealing with trade with the Indians, the factory system was established by law April 18, 1796. Its dual role was to offer Native Americans fair treatment in commerce and help offset the inroads made by the French, English, and Spanish traders. (The next generation of Americans would demand unfettered freedom of westward expansion unencumbered by the restrictions of the factory system. The law of May 6, 1822, sponsored by Missouri Senator Thomas H. Benton, discontinued the system altogether. New laws were put on the books in 1822 and 1824 that increased the bond for licenses traders and required that traders designate the legal places where trade would take place. The system soon led to domination of Indian trade by a few large companies.)

The issue was not so much a matter of trade as it was of land—expansion. Just as the proclamation of 1763 attempted to enforce a boundary between Indians and whites, so did the law of May 19, 1796, passed by the American Congress. And, just as the proclamation directed British soldiers to expel violators, so Congress empowered the president to expel violators. Neither was realistic; neither was successful; both were rendered mute before they were written.

Enforcement of Indian laws became an ongoing battle between States' Rights and what was considered the best interests of the national government. Governor George Clinton and the state of New York

---

15 John Sugden, *Blue Jacket: Warrior of the Shawnees*, 30, 35, 36-37.

16 Alan Taylor, *The Divided Ground*, 183, 450n39. Remarks made September 20, 1788. The Oneida was a member of the Iroquois League.

17 Roscoe R. Hill, ed., "Northwest Ordinance, Article the Third," *Journals of the Continental Congress, 1774-1789* (Washington, DC: US Government Printing Office, 1936), vol. xxxii. 1787, January 17 - July 20, pp. 340-341 available from Library of Congress at http://memory.loc.gov/ammem/amlaw/lawhome.html [October 10, 2007].

championed the fight for state control. The fight was not just political. It was also financial. Indian lands meant hard, cold cash to the states, and they were not about to give it up. As an example, a land speculator named Peter Smith leased 45,793 acres of land in New York state from the Oneida Indians of the Iroquois group. Believing themselves to have been cheated, the Oneida appealed to the state. New York abrogated the lease and purchased 132,000 acres of land that included the tract in the Smith lease for fifty cents an acre from the Indians; sold the original tract back to Smith for $3.53; and sold the remainder of the lands to other parties. The state got rich. Smith and the others got richer.

Timothy Pickering, federal Indian Agent under Washington and later Secretary of War, summarized the situation:

> They [state authorities] pretend to a great deal of generosity and provide a plenty of liquor: and when your hearts become cheerful, and your heads grow giddy, then they make their bargains with you, and get your Chiefs to sign their papers. But as soon as you are sober, you find, to your sorrow, that your beds have slipped from under you. Another misfortune, Brothers, attends these bargains, that true interpretations are not always given of the papers you sign. Perhaps sometimes the interpreters purposely deceive you, at other times the interpretations are not exact because you have no words in your language by which the meaning of the English can be expressed.[18]

Progress on federalizing Indian affairs was agonizingly slow during the administrations of George Washington and John Adams, but there were efforts to establish diplomatic recognition with the Indian nations and to recognize Indian sovereignty at the national level. Beginning with the eight years of the Republican administration of Thomas Jefferson, such efforts came to halt. Henceforth, Indian relations would be the purview of the individual states, subjecting the Indians to state laws. By the time Thomas Jefferson took office in 1803, the Indian confederacy had been broken and the tribes of the Northeast tribes had, for the most part, been pushed west. Their interests were of little concern to the Americans. Jefferson wrote, "As to their fear, we presume that our strength and their weakness is now so visible that they must see we have only to shut our hand to crush them."[19] Three years later, Jefferson not so subtly reminded the members of an Indian delegation at the White House of the relative strengths of the white man and the Indians: "We are strong, we are numerous as the stars in the heaven, & we are all gunmen."[20] Historian Joseph Ellis goes on to write, "'the seeds of extinction' for Native American culture were sown under Jefferson."[21]

Jefferson's early attitude towards Native American was ambivalent at best. In several instances in his letters and in his *Notes on the State of Virginia*, he praised and defended the noble spirit and capacity of the Indian as an individual; but, as for the Indian race as a valued culture, he had little use. As a representative of the Virginia colony to the Continental Congress, he was responsible for the words of condemnation imparted to the Indians in the Declaration of Independence in his list of "injuries and usurptations" assigned to the king: "he has endeavored to bring on the inhabitants of our frontiers and merciless Indian savages, whose known rule of warfare is an undistinguished destruction of all ages, sexes, & conditions of existence."[22] Only minor changes were made in Jefferson's original draft to produce the final version. Regardless of the accuracy of the charge against the king, which for the most part were

---

18 Alan Taylor, *The Divided Ground*, 300, 477n9. Memorandum of October 12, 1794.

19 Jefferson's in a letter to William Henry Harrison, territorial governor of Ohio, February 27, 1803. Joseph J. Ellis, *American Sphinx*, 201; Alan Taylor, *The Divided Ground*, 321; Landon Y. Jones, *William Clark and the Shaping of the West*, 151, 349n6.

20 At the White House, January 4, 1806. Landon Y. Jones, *William Clark and the Shaping of the West*, 151, 349n9, from Donald Jackson, *Letters of the Lewis and Clark Expedition, with Related Documents, 1783-1854* (Urbana: University of Illinois Press, 1978), 1, 280-283.

21 Ellis, *op. cit.*, 201.

22 Pauline Maier, *American Scripture*, 106, 119-121; Appendix C, 239; 250n42, 259n55.

false, Jefferson's choice of words can only be interpreted as a reflection of a deep-seated prejudice of the Indian race.

In a related issue, not just Jefferson, who penned the charges against the king, but the colonies, their representatives and their citizens all for the most part resented the fact the king and his ministers sought to deny to the colonies the lands of the trans-Appalachia west with the Proclamation of 1763 and the Quebec Act of 1774. Jefferson's seventh charge read: "he has endeavored to prevent the population of these states; for that purpose obstructing the laws for naturalization of foreigners; refusing to pass others to encourage their migrations hither; & raising the conditions of new appropriations of land."[23] The new land Jefferson referred to was Indian land. The Quebec Act was regarded as one of the Intolerable Acts, but it had none of the features of the other acts. It was not coercive nor punitive, nor it infringe on colonial rights or liberties. It was an administrative measure that designated the lands north and west of the Ohio River as part of the province of Quebec.

The king's earlier Proclamation had been more expressive on the issue of Indian lands:

> [T]he several nations or tribes of Indians, with whom we are connected, and who live under our protection, should not be molested or disturbed in the possession of such parts of our dominions and territories as, not having been ceded to, or purchased by us, are reserved to them.[24]

Historian Stephen Ambrose writes that as president Jefferson "stole all the land he could from the Indians east of the Mississippi while preparing those west of the river for the same fate...Americans had but one Indian policy—get out of the way or get killed—and it was nonnegotiable."[25] His strategy was to develop among the Indians such an appetite for white goods that it forced them into debt beyond their means of ever paying if off and then to retire the debt by a cession of lands.[26] To William Henry Harrison on February 27,1803, Jefferson wrote:

> We shall push our trading uses, and be glad to see the good and influential Indians...run into debt, because we observe when these debts get beyond what the individual can pay, they become willing to lop them off by a cession of land. In this way our settlement will gradually circumscribe and approach the Indians, and they will in time either incorporate with us as citizens of the United States, or remove beyond the Mississippi. The former is certainly the termination of their history most happy for themselves but, in the whole course of this, it is essential to cultivate their love.[27]

Contrary to general thinking and Hollywood depiction, the bloodiest of the Indian wars did not occur on the plains in the trans-Mississippi west during the nineteenth century but in the east along the Atlantic coast during the seventeenth century as the woodland and coastal tribes fought to hold on to their lands against the ever-increasing numbers of English colonists.[28]

The Louisiana Purchase

The Louisiana Purchase changed the picture entirely. Jefferson naively believed that he could persuade the early pioneers in Upper Louisiana to exchange their holdings for land in Illinois thus freeing the trans-Mississippi west for conversion into one vast Indian reservation-—albeit if only temporary.

---

23 *Ibid*, 12, 118, text from Appendix C (7th provision), 237; Robert Middlekauff, *The Glorious Cause*, 231, 239, 280.

24 Daniel K. Richter, *Facing East from Indian Country*, 208, 210-211, 214, 216-217. Excerpt from Proclamation from p. 208.

25 Steven E. Ambrose, *Undaunted Courage*, 338.

26 Joseph E. Ellis, *American Sphinx*, 337n54, on forcing the Indians into debt.

27 Quoted in Landon Y. Jones, *William Clark and the Shaping of the West* (New York: Hill and Wang, 2004), 151, 349n6, from Andrew A. Lipscomb and Albert E. Bergh, eds., *The Writings of Thomas Jefferson*, (Washington, D.C.: Thomas Jefferson Memorial Association, 1905), vol. 10, 269-70, quoted in Seal Wilentz, ed., *Major Problems in the Early Republic, 1787-1848: Documents and Essays* (Lexington, MA: D.C. Heath, 1992), 130-131.

28 T. R. Fehrenback, *Comanches*, 269-270.

Jefferson understood better than most that nothing was going to stop the inexorable flow of American pioneers from moving ever westward where good, cheap land was readily available for the taking. He fully understood that this vast reservation was to be only temporary. The Indians, once removed, would become fully assimilated into the white man's culture or they would become extinct. There was no place for a mixed society of diverse cultures in the world he envisioned for America. "[I]t is impossible not to look forward to distant times, when our continent, with a people speaking the same language, governed in similar form, and by similar laws; nor can we contemplate with satisfactory either blot or mixture [Indians as well as Blacks] on that surface." Jefferson spoke even more bluntly at his Second Inaugural Address four years later. American society of the future will not countenance a native population that clings to tribal mores or holds "a sanctimonious reverence for the custom of their ancestors."[29]

The European population of the present-day state of Missouri that was sitting at 900-1000 in 1765 jumped to some ten thousand by the time the Louisiana Purchase was signed in 1803. The population doubled to 20,845 in 1810 and rose to more than twenty-five thousand in 1814. By 1820 when Missouri became a state, the population had surpassed sixty-six thousand persons. The population grew to over one million seven-hundred thousand by the time of the 1870 census fifty years hence (1,721,295).[30] The growth came primarily from Kentucky and Tennessee, followed by Virginia and the Carolinas. After the Civil War, many Union soldiers from Ohio, Illinois, and Indiana also settled in the state, for the most part following the same tract as the Native Americans who were pushed west. The soldiers, however, were free to choose.

Pioneers and settlers poured across the Appalachians and then across the Mississippi. The rush accelerated with the end of the Black Hawk War as settlers from the Atlantic states gorged themselves on lands in northern Illinois and Wisconsin. Coming out of this period was the ruling by the United States Supreme Court in *Johnson v. M'Intosh*, in the opinion written by Chief Justice John Marshall that the American Indians did not own the land in the traditional sense of the word and therefore could not dispose of the land except to the federal government.[31] Private purchases of Indian lands, therefore, would not be recognized. Putting aside the multitude of underlying legal issues raised by the decision, the Chief Justice saw the decision as a way of protecting the Indian tribes from unprincipled land speculators. The decision had a profound impact on the way Americans claimed property and the way the government treated Native Americans.

The Presidency and the Policy of Indian Removal

> *Lo, the poor Indian! whose untutored mind Sees God in clouds, or hears him in the wind; His soul proud Science never taught to stray Far as the solar walk or milky way; Yet simple nature to his hope has giv'n, Behind the cloud-topped hill, an humbler heav'n.*
>
> —Alexander Pope, "An Essay on Man," 1733-1734

Twenty-three men held the office of President of the United States in the hundred years from 1789 until the damming experience of Wounded Knee in the winter of 1890. But the very soul of the American Indian, collectively if not individually, east as well as west, north as well as south, was wrenched from the body and effectively destroyed during the relatively short seventy-five year period beginning with the administration of Thomas Jefferson and ending with the administration of Ulysses S. Grant.

---

29   Joseph J. Ellis, *American Sphinx*, 202; quotes taken from a letter to James Monroe, November 24, 1801, and from his Second Inaugural Address, March 4, 1805. For the full address, see Thomas Jefferson, *Writings* (New York: Library of America, 1984), 518-523; quote appears on p. 520. Jefferson writes that the Indians must overcome "the habits of their bodies, prejudice of their minds, ignorance, [and] pride" to become something more than they are.

30   Eugene Morrow Violette, *History of Missouri*, 18, 67, 74-75, 81, 443.

31   *Johnson v. M'Intosh*, 21 U.S. (8 Wheaton) 543, 591 (1823).

	President	Years in Office
1	George Washington	1789-1797
2	John Adams	1797-1801
3	Thomas Jefferson	1801-1809
4	James Madison	1809-1817
5	James Monroe	1817-1825
6	John Quincy Adams	1825-1829
7	Andrew Jackson	1829-1837
8	Martin Van Buren	1837-1841
9	William Henry Harrison	1841-1841
10	John Tyler	1841-1845
11	James Knox Polk	1845-1849
12	Zachary Taylor	1849-1850
13	Millard Fillmore	1850-1853
14	Franklin Pierce	1853-1857
15	James Buchanan	1857-1861
16	Abraham Lincoln	1861-1865
17	Andrew Johnson	1865-1869
18	Ulysses Simpson Grant	1869-1877
19	Rutherford Birchard Hayes	1877-1881
20	James Abram Garfield	1881-1881
21	Chester Alan Arthur	1881-1885
22	Grover Cleveland	1885-1889
23	Benjamin Harrison	1889-1893

During those intervening years, there was a concerted effort to remove, if not eliminate, the Native American population from the land coveted by the white man. Some had lived on the land for nearly three hundred years by the time the white man arrived within the historic period alone. Constantly driven into the Indian consciousness was the idea that the President of the United States was the Great White Father; they, his children. That in itself tells much of the attitude of the whites towards the American Indians.

During Jefferson and Madison's time in office, fifty-three treaties for land cession were extracted from Indians. But in the year 1825 alone during the administration of John Quincy Adams, the 68,736 square miles (44,000,000 acres) that that made up the state of Missouri were effectively cleared of all Native American claims.

Thomas Jefferson's casual approach to the confiscation of Indian land for white settlement became axiomatic by the time of Andrew Jackson. In 1803 Jefferson wrote William Henry Harrison, who as governor of the Ohio Territory and as President, would hoist the same banner.

> To promote this disposition to exchange lands which they [the Indians] have to spare and we want, for necessaries which we have to spare and they want, we shall be glad to see the good and influential among them in debt, because we observe that when these debts get beyond what the individuals can pay, they become willing to lop them off by a cession of lands.[32]

---

32   Merrill D. Beal, *"I Will Fight No More Forever": Chief Joseph and the Nez Percé e War*, 24.

One hundred and forty-six treaties with the Indians were recorded before 1829, almost all of which included the cession of Indian homelands. These treaties pushed the woodland tribes ever father west until their backs were at the Mississippi. In the Southeast, the treaties at first constricted the tribes into a narrower and narrower belt until they too were pushed west up to and across the Mississippi.

The early removals from the East and Southeast to the West began around 1814, mid-way into Madison's second term, and continued for the next ten years through the two terms of the James Monroe. For his part, Monroe attempted to do justice to the Indian cause and prevent white encroachment onto Indian lands, especially in the burgeoning Southeast and the Ohio Country. Monroe's position, at least initially, was pro-Indian.

From several of the Indian tribes inhabiting the country bordering on Lake Erie purchases have been made of lands on conditions very favorable to the United States, and, as it is presumed, not less so to the tribes themselves. ... In this progress, which the rights of nature demand and nothing can prevent, marking a growth rapid and gigantic, it is our duty to make new efforts for the preservation, improvement, and civilization of the native inhabitants.[33]

At one point Monroe, through Secretary of War William Crawford, ordered Maj. General Andrew Jackson to remove by force all settlers on public lands—specifically Indian lands, within his Southeast District of Tennessee, Mississippi, and Louisiana—an order analogous to the Royal Proclamation of 1763 following the end of the French & Indian War. To Jackson, the order was contrary to the best interests of the country, and any actions to implement it would be ineffectual. The notion was quietly dropped.

First of the Indians to be resettled outside of their original homelands was a band of Cherokees from Georgia under Tahlonteskee followed by a band of Shawnee from Ohio under Quitewepea who were settled in Arkansas. The moves were followed by the removal of the Piankeshaws, and the Weas, the Kickapoos, and the Delawares who on their own had drifted into Arkansas and Missouri. These were to be followed by the removal of the Wyandots, Senecas, Miamis, the Eel River Indians, and the Illini. Although pursued rather hesitantly at times, the plan was to sweep Ohio and Indiana clean of Native Americans, followed by Illinois, onto lands ceded by the Osage and Kansa in Missouri and Arkansas.

John Quincy Adams succeeded Monroe in 1825. Adams was not as hesitant as Monroe. During 1825 and 1826, Adams forced treaties on the Dakotas, Osages, Kansas, Chippewas, Sacs, Foxes, Winnebagoes, Miamis, Ottawas, and Potawatomies by which they agreed to immigrate west. Senator Benton of Missouri did not think much of the idea of what he called dumping the Indians on Missouri. He pushed for their removal further West to Oklahoma, clearing both Missouri and Kansas.

On March 4, 1829, when the man the Choctaws of Mississippi called "the Devil," was inaugurated President, Indian removal had already been a matter of government policy. Andrew Jackson made it a campaign issue and the primary focus of his two-term administration, interrupted by a fight over the U.S. Bank, a depression, and a secession crisis.[34] Jackson, if any thing, was straight forward and direct in his handling of the issue. He had laid out his philosophy twelve years earlier on March 4, 1817 in a letter to President Monroe:

> I have long viewed treaties with the Indians as an absurdity not be reconciled to the principles of our Government. The Indians are *subjects* of the United States, inhabiting *its territory* and acknowledging *its sovereignty*. Then is it not absurd for the sovereign to negotiate by treaty with the subject? I have always thought that Congress had as much right to regulate by acts of legislation

---

33 "The Messages and Papers of the Presidents: Washington - Taft (1789-1913)," *American Presidency Project.* Home Page at http://www. presidency.ucsb.edu/index.php [October 10, 2007].

34 Gloria Jahoda, *Trail of Tears*, esp. 32-33, 36, 39; quote taken from p. 39.

all Indian concerns as they had of Territories. There is only this difference: that the inhabitants of Territories are citizens of the United States and entitled to the rights thereof; the *Indians are subjects* and entitled to their protection and fostering care. ...I would therefore contend that the Legislature...[has] the right to prescribe their bounds at pleasure...[35] [emphasis added]

Jackson went on to write that whenever the government believed it necessary, it had "the right to take [the land] and dispose of it" as it sees fit.

To Jackson there was no doubt that the lands east of the Mississippi were destined to be for the exclusive use of the white race and that the Indians should be removed beyond. In his first annual message to Congress on December 8, 1829, Jackson acknowledged that the native peoples had been forced "to retire from river to river and from mountain to mountain, until some of the tribes have become extinct and others have left but remnants..." Although he appears to offer a measure of sympathy for the their plight, he reminds the Congress that the Indians are savages and speaks of the fear that their names had brought to earlier generations. Jackson states flatly that the Choctaw, Cherokee, and Creek of the Southeast must leave their homes if they are to survive, but notes that their removal would be entirely voluntary. He goes on to say that should they fail to accede, however, they will be doomed "to weakness and decay" and suffer the fate of the Narragansett and the Delaware.[36]

Although he would couch his words in charity and benevolence towards the Indian race, in his succeeding messages to Congress, Jackson made it very clear that he would pursue policy of removal with all the authority of his office , and with a force and determination few men could equal. If it were not so pathetic, the hypocrisy of the Jackson's second annual message of December 6, 1830, would almost be laughable.

> It gives me pleasure to announce to Congress that the benevolent policy of the Government, steadily pursued for nearly 30 years, in relation to the removal of the Indians beyond the white settlements is approaching to a happy consummation. ... With a full understanding of the subject, the Choctaw and the Chickasaw tribes have with great unanimity determined to avail themselves of the liberal offers presented by the act of Congress, and have agreed to remove beyond the Mississippi River. Treaties have been made with them...In negotiating these treaties they were made to understand their true condition, and they have preferred maintaining their independence in the Western forests to submitting to the laws of the States in which they now reside. These treaties, being probably the last which will ever be made with them, are characterized by great liberality on the part of the Government. ... The present policy of the Government is but a continuation of the same progressive change by a milder process. The tribes which occupied the countries now constituting the Eastern States were annihilated or have melted away to make room for the whites. The waves of population and civilization are rolling to the westward, and we now propose to acquire the countries occupied by the red men of the South and West by a fair exchange, and, at the expense of the United States, to send them to a land where their existence may be prolonged and perhaps made perpetual.

> Doubtless it will be painful to leave the graves of their fathers; but what do they [do] more than our ancestors did or than our children are now doing? To better their condition in an unknown land our forefathers left all that was dear in earthly objects. ... In the consummation of a policy originating at an early period, and steadily pursued by every Administration within the present century -- so just to the States and so generous to the Indians...[37]

---

35 H. W. Brands, *Andrew Jackson*, 319-320.

36 *Ibid*, 435-436.

37 "President Andrew Jackson's Message to Congress 'On Indian Removal' (1830)," 100 Documents that Shaped America (Washington, DC: NARA et al., n.d.) at http://www.ourdocuments.gov/doc.php?flash=true&doc=25.

In Jackson's Third Annual Message to Congress of December 6, 1831, he addresses the situation in the State of Ohio. He expresses his hope that very soon "Ohio will be no longer embarrassed with the Indian population" and reports that within a few years the government will have extinguished "the Indian title to all the lands lying within the States" of the Union. The following year, he reports to Congress on the "hostile incursions of the Sac and Fox Indians" in what was called the Black Hawk War and the fact that they were "entirely defeated, and the disaffected band dispersed or destroyed." He goes on to reiterated that government action was necessary to deal with "their unprovoked aggressions." In conclusion he admits to some remaining loose ends dealing with the remnants of the Cherokees in Georgia. The loose end was the 1832 Supreme Court decision that held that state law, in this case Georgia, that conflicted with federal treaties governing relations with the Cherokee was unconstitutional and therefore null and void. Other than for the purposes of the brief, circumspect remarks in this annual message, Jackson ignored the Court's decision and the case itself.

In his fifth message to Congress on December 3, 1833, as the first year of his second term was coming to a close, he reported that except for the "remaining difficulties" with two Southern tribes, the events over the past years have been a confirmation of his policy of removal. Jackson then proceeds to define in unequivocal terms his low opinion of the Native American peoples and their prospects for the future:

> They have neither the intelligence, the industry, the moral habits, nor the desire of improvement which are essential to any favorable change in their condition. Established in the midst of another and a superior race, and without appreciating the causes of their inferiority or seeking to control them, they must necessarily yield to the force of circumstances and ere long disappear. [38]

It was an opinion to which most whites wholeheartedly subscribed, hidden if you would in the policy that "might makes right." A "Trail of Tears" only begins to describe the suffering, the torment, and injustices suffered by the Indian race that would not abate for the next fifty years and before taking on a new form.

It was not until well into the presidency of Rutherford B. Hayes that began in 1877 that the attitude of Whites towards the American Indians began to moderate to a noticeable degree. When the government ordered the Poncas were forcibly removed from their homelands on the Missouri River to Baxter Springs in eastern Oklahoma and then to Ponca City in north-central Oklahoma in May 1877 without their consent and without the government "having first made some provision for their settlement and comfort," their grievance found a receptive audience in Washington and with the public. The President ordered a thorough investigation of the matter in December 1880 and on February 1, 1881, in a special message to Congress, he not only recommended remedial legislation to aid the Ponca, which Congress was uncharacteristically quick to enact, but he also set forth those principles that he believed should control all future dealings between the government and the Indians and put renewed emphasis on the assimilation of Indians into mainstream of white culture. As to the incident itself, the President accepted full responsibility:

> I do not undertake to apportion the blame for the injustice done to the Poncas. Whether the Executive or Congress or the public is chiefly in fault is not now a question of practical importance. As the Chief Executive at the time when the wrong was consummated, I am deeply sensible that enough of the responsibility for that wrong justly attaches to me to make it my particular duty and earnest desire to do all I can to give to these injured people that measure of redress which is required alike by justice and by humanity.

---

38 "Andrew Jackson…In His Own Words" (TNGenNet Inc, 2002) at http://www.tngenweb.org/cessions/jackson.html. See also H. W. Brands, *Andrew Jackson*, 488-493.

More generally in stunning contrast to previous presidents, "[N]othing should be left undone to show to the Indians that the Government of the United States regards their rights as equally sacred with those of its citizens. The time has come when the policy should be to place the Indians as rapidly as practicable on the same footing with the other permanent inhabitants of our country."[39]

Senator Henry Dawes of Massachusetts immediately wrote the President: "Will you permit me to express to you personally, what I shall embrace the first opportunity to say publicly in the Senate, my great gratification in the Ponca message just read to the Senate. Every word of it meets my hearty commendation, and is worthy of your high office and high character. In my opinion it will pass into history as a great state paper, marking an epoch in our dealings with the weak and defenseless more conspicuous and grand than any other public expression from the head of the nation for many years."

In 1887, the same Senator Dawes sponsored the *General Allotment Act* better known as the *Dawes Severalty Act* that was designed to promote the assimilation of Indians into American society. While good intentioned, the result has generally been judged less than successful. The Dawns Act provided for each head of an Indian family to be given 160 acres of farmland or 320 acres of grazing land. The remaining tribal lands were to be declared surplus and opened up for settlement. Land allotments to individual Indians was soon controlled by non-Indians. Native Americans lost much of their land and received inadequate payment at best and then, often as not, quickly spent all that they received leaving them destitute. In addition, the reservation system was nearly destroyed. The reader will see the act played out in the Annotated Tribal Listing to follow.

Treaty Language

As noted previously, Andrew Jackson thought the treaty process with the Indians was absurd, but absurd was not the word for the process—not from the point of view of the Indians. The documents that proscribed the Indian cessions of land and removals used variations of the same familiar words and phrases. The documents were presented to the tribal chiefs and headmen (sometimes only selected chiefs) for their signature only after they had been fully *persuaded* that the new territory proffered in exchange offered their only hope for a permanent and peaceful home. In almost all cases, the treaties declared that the policy of the government of removing the Indians was humane and that the President "was anxious to promote the peace, prosperity and happiness of his red children." The treaties further declared that the policy was being carried out with utmost "justice and liberality" and stipulated that the Government would provide a new home in perpetuity plus compensation in goods and moneys. In the end the Indians were told to appreciate the fact that it was in their best interests to accept the terms set forth without delay.

Where is my home-my forest home?
the proud land of my sires?
Where stands the wigwam of my pride?
Where gleam the council fires?
Where are my fathers' hollowed graves?
my friends so light and free?
Gone, gone, — forever from my view!
Great Spirit! can it be?[40]

---

39   James D. Richardson, "Executive Mansion, February 1, 1881. To the Senate and House of Representatives" *Messages and Papers of Rutherford B. Hayes*, Part 6, from FullBooks (Flossmoor, IL: Advameg, 2006) at http://www.fullbooks.com/Messages-and-Papers-of-Rutherford-B-Hayes6.html [November 28, 2006]. Senator Dawes words taken from *Diary and Letters of Rutherford B. Hayes*, vol. iii, chap. xxxviii, 590-650, available from Ohio History Online (Columbus: Ohio Historical Society, 2006) at http://www.ohiohistory.org/onlinedoc/hayes/chapterxxxviii.html [November 25, 2006].

40   Writer unknown. Taken from Samuel G. Drake, *The Aboriginal Races of North America...* (New York: Hurst & Company, 1880), 4.

Hypocrisy and condescending phrases marked the treaty process from the days of the first colonists through the nineteenth century and into the twentieth. The words of T. R. Fehrenbach describe the government's policies and practices with regard to the negotiation and execution of treaties between the government—in all its various forms—and the native peoples they encountered. Fehrenbach's words also succinctly express the confusion, frustration, and sorrow of the American Indians with regard to these treaties.

> The greatest of all travesties...was the incessant seeking and signing of peace pacts or treaties with the different peoples. ...The British had used the same approach, but the American republic carried the practice to ridiculous extremes. ...While no nation or people was more eager to solve problems by negotiation, no government on earth had a poorer record of keeping its ratified agreements. The problem was inherent in the Anglo-American form of democracy. ...Unpopular treaties could not be enforced without political repercussions [especially from]... powerful pressure groups.
>
> Any agreement that provided the tribes with rights, privileges, or territory was inevitably challenged—sooner or later—by some part of white society... [The government of Canada on the other hand] made pragmatic arrangements with the tribes, gave them certain rights, then rigidly enforced the rights they granted. Although the end result was the same—the Amerindians were engulfed—the Canadian conquest was carried out with a maximum of justice, good faith, and rationality, and almost without bloodshed or lingering psychic trauma. The inability of the American government...to enforce treaty provision on white citizens was historic.[41]

Peace treaties were offered as placebos for the Indians to delay the inevitable day of reckoning as the whites grew stronger and the native peoples weaker. The natives would be removed from the march of white civilization. Timing was the only issue. In addition, input from the Indians during the "negotiations" was ignored in the preparation of the written document they could not read and on which their "representatives" could only make a mark with a pen to signify their signature that was affirmed by the white man. (Although it rendered negotiations almost impossible, war chiefs or other "representatives" had no authority within the Indian political structure to speak for anyone but himself or to agree to any conditions in the name of others of the band or tribe. As a consequence the treaties that were signed were rarely binding on all members of the tribe.) But treaty-making became a cherished end in and of itself although boundaries remained unspecified and stipulations wholly impractical or unenforceable. The final insult was the failure of the government to deliver on its promises of material support and to protect the Indians from profiteering. "But peace was rarely cheaply purchased; whatever treaties were signed, the final peace was paid for in bloodshed..."[42]

Treaty language ceased to be an issue after 1871, at least as far as any new treaties were concerned. More for political reasons than anything else, the Indian Appropriation Act of 1871 barred the federal government from negotiating any future treaties with the country's Native American Indians—Chief Justice John Marshall's sterling argument of "domestic dependent nations" aside.[43] Treaties were supplanted by "agreements" that were the same in all but name only and the fact that the U.S. House and the Senate now shared responsibility equally at the Congressional level.

Post-removal Life West of the Mississippi

The travail of the woodland and eastern Indians did not end with their removal beyond the Mississippi. It only entered a new phase, a phase that now paralleled the lives of the western tribes. They were lives first shaped and then destroyed by westward migration that began in 1840, the concept of Manifest Destiny

---

41 T. R. Fehrenback, *Comanches*, 368-369.
42 *Ibid*, 372.
43 Robert M. Utley, *The Indian Frontier of the American West*, 134; *Cherokee Nation v. Georgia* in 1831.

that raised its head in 1845, the war with Mexico in 1846, the California gold rush of 1849, passage of the Kansas-Nebraska Act in 1854, and finally construction of the transcontinental railroad, completed in 1869. In that morass came statehood for Iowa, Texas, California, Kansas, Nebraska, preceded by Missouri and Arkansas, and followed substantially later by Oklahoma.

At first the Eastern tribes were to find a semblance of peace and solitude in Missouri, Arkansas, and Texas (unofficially); then Iowa, Kansas, and Nebraska; and finally Oklahoma. It was to these six trans-Mississippi states that thousands of Native Americans from the east, displaced at least once previously, were to find their "permanent" homes. Instead, the six states became mere weigh stations in route to further anxiety, frustration, and despair. Once the lands to the east were consumed by the white man, they looked to a new frontiers beyond the Mississippi. Americans continued to push west through the prairies and into the plains and on to the Pacific. They found that the Great American Desert was no desert at all. What they found were new treasures, new opportunities, and ever-important new lands. The ever-progressing white frontier soon surrounded the Indians on all sides as the strings were drawn tighter and tighter. Although "free to roam and hunt" as provided for in the white man's treaties, their freedom became more and more constricted as the land given to them was reclaimed.

Events put a stranglehold on the Native American Indians west of the Mississippi. By 1875, new homelands were an illusion and the seizure and destruction of native homelands was an irreversible fact. The "fall" of Oklahoma added only bitter poison to the Indian diet of governmental largesse.

Manifest Destiny

Manifest Destiny, not put into those words until 1845, defined a nation and the roles of the white man and the Indians. The phrase *Manifest Destiny* entered the American lexicon thanks to John Louis O'Sullivan. It was during the 1844 election campaign for Democrat James Polk that the Democratic press hit on that phrase that would resonate in Washington and throughout the nation for years to come. O'Sullivan, wrote in The *United States Magazine and Democratic Review* of July-August 1845 that it was America's "manifest destiny" was "to overspread the continent allotted by Providence for the free development of our yearly multiplying millions."[44]

Before O'Sullivan, there was John Quincy Adams, who in 1819 after his negotiations with Spain for the Floridas, declared to the cabinet that America's proper domain was the "continent of North America."[45] And before O'Sullivan and before John Quincy Adams, there was John Jay. In 1787, Jay wrote in *Federalist II*:

With equal pleasure I have as often taken notice, that Providence has been pleased to give this one connected country to one united people; a people descended from the same ancestors, speaking the same language, professing the same religion, attached to the same principles of government...[46]

The story of what came to be accepted as the country's "manifest destiny" reflected the vision, the determination, and the greed of those who shaped the land we know as the United States of America—to occupy all the lands from the Atlantic to the Pacific and from the Canadian border to its border with Mexico and, as it turned out, to points beyond. Historian Michael Holt writes that O'Sullivan

---

44 David Haward Bain, *Empire Express*, 22. Bain refers the reader to the *United States Magazine and Democratic Review*, August 1845. It should be noted that the *Democratic Review* was a bimonthly publication; thus, July-August 1845. This was the first published use of the expression that he reused in an editorial in support of American's claim to the Oregon Territory in the December 27, 1845, issue of the New York *Morning News*. America's claim, he wrote, was "by the right of our manifest destiny to overspread and to possess the whole of the continent which Providence has given us for the...great experiment of liberty." See Arthur M Schlesinger, Jr., *The Age of Jackson*, 427, who cites Frederick Merk, *Manifest Destiny and the Mission in American History: A Reinterpretation* (New York, 1963).

45 Jack Shepherd, *The Adams Chronicles*, 265.

46 Max Beloff, ed., *The Federalist or, The New Constitution*, 5-9. John Jay, Federalist II.

permanently grafted expansionism to the Democratic platform by coning the phrase to justify the nation's territorial designs.[47] McPherson writes that the Democrats "pressed for the expansion of American institutions across the whole of North America whether the residents—Indians, Spaniards, Mexicans, Canadian—wanted them or not."[48]

Beyond the issues of geography and nationalism, lay something else, something deeper. John Jay spoke of it first, in more politic terms. The issue was the doctrine of white supremacy.[49] Illinois Senator Stephen A. Douglas saw only an Americanized continent from ocean to ocean. "Indian control over plains between Missouri and the Rockies seemed to him a travesty on white men's Manifest Destiny. … To Douglas, removing the 'Indian barrier' and establishing white government were 'first steps' towards a 'tide of emigration and civilization.'"[50]

The Big Horn Association of Cheyenne had the perfunctory to attribute white supremacy and the extermination of the Indian to God's design:

> The rich and beautiful valleys of Wyoming are destined for the occupancy and sustenance of the Anglo-Saxon race. …The Indians must stand aside or be overwhelmed by the ever advancing and ever increasing tide of emigration. The destiny of the aborigines is written in characters not to be mistaken. The same inscrutable Arbiter that decreed the downfall of Rome has pronounced the doom of extinction upon the red men of America.[51]

Walter Colton, a traveler in the West, may have best summed up the dominant racist attitude of the American populous in his succinct description of California emigrants and their vision of their own ethnic superiority: "They seem to look upon this beautiful land as their own Canaan, and the motley race around them as the Hittites, the Hivites, and the Jebusites, whom they are to drive out."[52]

Trails West and the Transcontinental Railroad

In regard to these Indian difficulties,
I think that if great caution is not exercised on our part,
there will be a bloody war.
It should be our policyto tryand conciliate them,
guard our mails and trains well to prevent theft,
and stop these scouting parties that are roaming over the country,
who do not know one tribe from another
and will kill anything in the shape of an Indian.
It will require only a few more murders on the part of our troops
to unite all these warlike tribes.[53]

—Major T. I. McKenny to General Curtis

---

47   Michael F. Holt, *The Rise and Fall of the American Whig Party*, 232.

48   James M. McPherson, *Battle Cry of Freedom*, 48.

49   Desmond King, *Making Americans: Immigration, Race, and the Origins of the Diverse Democracy*, 12. King cites R. Horsman, *Race and Manifest Destiny: The Origins of American Radial Anglo-Saxonism* (Cambridge, MA: Harvard University Press, 1981), 219-221.

50   William W. Freehling, *The Road to Disunion*, 546. Freehling quotes Robert W. Johannsen, *Stephen A. Douglas* (New York, 1973), 399-400.

51   Dee Brown, *Bury My Heart at Wounded Knee*, 189, 456n9, *Cheyenne Daily Leader*, March 3, 1870.

52   Frank McLynn, *Wagons West*, 10, 447n10. McLynn cites Walter Colton, *Three Years in California* (New York, 1850), 118.

53   Quoted in George Bird Grinnell, *The Fighting Cheyennes*, 147. Written in late spring of 1864 from Ft. Larned on the Arkansas River east of Cimarron Crossing in present-dayKansas. At the time, General Samuel R. Curtis commanded the military district that included Kansas and the Indians of the southern Plains but who was deeply immersed in the Civil War being waged along the border.

The trails west, followed by the transcontinental railroad, put life in the phrase *Manifest Destiny*. There were three principal trails westward from Missouri that also included a number of branches and cutoffs. They also went by a number of different names. For the most part the trails began along the border between Kansas and Missouri.[54]

SANTA FE TRAIL

The granddaddy of the trails was the Santa Fe Trail. The trail ran southwest of the Big Bend of the Missouri to Gardner, Kansas; through Council Grove, Fort Zarah (present-day Great Bend—established by General Samuel R. Curtis and named for his son), Fort Dodge (Dodge City), Wagon Bed Spring or Lower Spring, Kansas; and through the northwestern corner of the present Oklahoma Panhandle to near Springer, New Mexico, and finally into Santa Fe. This route was called the Cimarron Route or Cutoff Branch—also the Dry Route and the Desert Route.

The Santa Fe Trail was surveyed for the government by the Sibley (George C.) Commission (1825-1827), creating a national highway. The survey was no more than a marking of trail. A treaty was signed with Osage to obtain their consent for the passage of a road "from the Western frontier of Missouri to the confines of New Mexico." Forts and trading posts quickly followed. The first trading post on the road was established in 1847 by Seth M. Hays of Westport on the site of the treaty grounds at Council Grove, one hundred and fifty miles west of Independence. A hunter with the party, Ben Jones, found a flowing spring of fresh water just west of Council Grove on August 11, 1825. The survey team marked the spring naming it Jones Spring. On a return visit in June 1827, Sibley renamed it Diamond in the Plains—as contrast to Diamond in the Desert from the tale of a spring in the Arabian Desert. One of the best known springs on the Trail, it was subsequently renamed Diamond Springs.

An alternate route, the Mountain Branch or Wet Branch, ran west out of Fort Dodge along the Arkansas River into Colorado through the site of Bent's New Fort (Fort Lyon No.1, originally Fort Wise) and Fort Lyon No. 2 to Bent's Old Fort and La Junta; and south through Raton Pass into Santa Fe. Approximately 780 miles.

The first successful trading expedition from Missouri to Santa Fe originated from the town of Franklin in Howard County, Missouri, in Boone's Lick country as it is called, in September 1821. It was the feat of William Becknell, with twenty to thirty associates. Three more trips were made the following year—one of which was by Becknell. Becknell's second trip was a huge financial success. It was also especially noteworthy because it established a more direct route to Santa Fe and because it made use of wagons for the first time. It was because of his second trip that Becknell was accorded the honor of being called the father of the Santa Fe Trail.

The trail from Franklin began as an extension of the Boonslick Road (Osage Trace) to Arrow Rock in Saline County, Lexington, and to a point less than two miles south of Fort Osage. The trail then crossed the Little Blue River at Blue Mills and ran south and west to Independence in eastern Jackson County.

The trail developed very rapidly after 1822. Later wagons would almost double the capacity of Becknell's early wagons; and by 1829 traders learned that oxen were better adapted to the heavy work required than mules or horses. The early expeditions were made by individual traders who traveled together, often organized as a joint stock company. By the mid-thirties, the arrangement change to that of trader-owner and employees. Profits generally ran from twenty to one hundred percent, but even higher yields were not uncommon.

---

54   David Dary, *The Oregon Trail*, esp. 289, 292 on the Smokey Hill Route; Frank Doster, "Eleventh Indiana Cavalry in Kansas," *Kansas Historical Collections* (Topeka: Kansas State Historical Society, 1921), vol. xv, 1919-1922, 527; David Hayward Bain, *Empire Express*, 346-347, 684; Eugene Morrow Violette, *History of Missouri*, 187-203; William Y. Chalfant, *Cheyennes and Horse Soldiers*, 10-15, 78n, 83-91.

The original eastern terminus at Franklin was repeatedly moved westward step-by-step until it finally reached Independence in eastern Jackson County in 1829. Still later the terminus was moved twelve miles further west to the town of Westport on the Missouri-Kansas border, Westport Landing near the mouth of the Kansas River, and finally the town of Kansas itself. By 1857, Kansas City had become the trail's main eastern terminus. From Jackson County, traders, settlers, and later prospectors crossed the border into Kansas.

(The town of Franklin was completely washed away by the Missouri River in 1826-27. The original site is north of the present Missouri River channel and about one-half mile west of the Boonville bridge on Missouri Highway 87. By 1833, the Missouri River had also destroyed the Blue Mills steamboat landing used by city of Independence.)

Between 1821 and 1880, the Santa Fe Trail was a commercial highway that connected Missouri and Santa Fe, New Mexico. For its first twenty-five years, it was also an international highway used by Spanish, Mexican and American traders. When the United States War with Mexico began in 1846, the Army of the West followed the Santa Fe Trail to move troops south. When the Treaty of Guadalupe-Hidalgo ended the war in 1848, the Santa Fe Trail became a national road connecting the United States to its new southwest territories. The Civil War and construction of the railroads sealed the fate of the Santa Fe Trail. (The trail was designated a National Historic Trail by Congress in 1987.)

OREGON TRAIL

The trail that had the greatest impact on the Indian population of the West was the Oregon Trail that includes both the California Trail and the Mormon Trail. The Oregon Trail, which had its roots in the fur trade, ran west, north-west from Westport on the Kansas-Missouri border, crossing the Big Blue River at Alcove Springs in northeast Kansas; through Fort Kearny (for Stephen Watts Kearny) on the Platte River; past Courthouse Rock, Chimney Rock, Scott's Bluff to Fort Laramie along the south bank of the Platte River and the North Platte rivers; through Emigrant Gap, past Independence Rock (an oval outcropping of granite 2,000 feet long by 700 feet wide), through Devil's Gate, across the Continental Divide over South Pass, southwest to Fort Bridger, northwest to Fort Hall, Fort Boise (built inn 1863), and Fort Walla Walla to Fort Vancouver and the Willamette Valley. The prime travel period was April to September. Leaving on or about mid-April would put emigrants into Oregon's Willamette Valley by early September. The Oregon Trail, over twice the length of the Santa Fe Trail at about 2020 miles, was never surveyed. By 1843 the trail was well-defined.

The first party of travelers from the east whose destination was Oregon Territory consisted of seventy missionaries and traders (Wyeth, Lee & Sublette). They left Independence, Missouri, April 28, 1834 and headed west. The party constructed Fort Hall on the Snake River and raised the flag what was the first permanent U.S. settlement west of the Divide on August 4, 1834. On September 15 the party reached Fort Vancouver of the Hudson's Bay Company. The first loaded wagons arrived in central Wyoming in 1830 (Sublette). The year 1832 marked the first time loaded wagons crossed over South Pass (Bonneville); but it was not until 1840 that wagons were brought all the way to Oregon (Newell & Meek).

The earliest Overland routes to Oregon were established with the exploration of Lewis and Clark (westbound, 1803-1805; eastbound, 1805-1806); the journey of Wilson Price Hunt (westbound, 1810-1812); and David Stuart (eastbound, 1812). It was Stuart's trek that plowed the ground for what became the Oregon Trail, and it is to Stuart goes the discovery of the Oregon Trail.

Throughout the forties, a number of cutoffs and branches were added to the Oregon Trail to shorten the route. With the discovery of gold in California, the California Cutoff was established from Fort Hall southwest to the Humboldt River, around Lake Tahoe, and into Sacramento, California, and Sutter's Fort.

Later the Hastings Cutoff left Fort Bridger passing south of the Great Salt Lake before connecting with the Humboldt. From 1849 forward the Oregon Trail would become known as the Oregon-California Trail.

At first the Oregon-bound wagon trains originated in Independence and Westport, Missouri. Other sites on the Missouri River soon began to compete, from Weston to St. Joseph to Council Bluffs (Kanesville until the name was changed in 1853). Emigrants leaving from Council Bluffs more often than not took to the north bank of the Platte and the north fork of the Platte to Fort Laramie, especially the Mormons who began their migration west in April 1847. The route soon became known as the Mormon Trail.

Leaving from points higher up the Missouri, settlers exchanged what some considered the more dangerous crossing of the Kansas River in the vicinity of present-day Topeka for a crossing of the Missouri. Also, by 1847 the lower stations of Independence, Westport, and Town of Kansas that served as the eastern terminus of the Santa Fe Trail were congested by military activity associated with the Mexican War.

The Santa Fe Trail and the Oregon-California Trail followed the same route out of Missouri and into Kansas where they diverged southwest of present-day Gardner, Kansas, in Johnson County. The Oregon Trail began to decline with the joining of the Union Pacific and Central Pacific railroads on May 10, 1869.

Relations with the Native American along the trail remained relatively good, and conflict was minimal until their lives became threatened by whiteman's diseases and their hunting grounds became threatened by the whiteman's craving for gold found, especially following the discovery of gold in eastern Oregon and in present-day Montana in July 1862.

John Butterfield's Overland Mail (Stage) Company began in May 1848 ran a southern route from St. Louis across Arkansas, Texas, New Mexico and Arizona to California in order to avoid possible delays because of winter weather farther north. The company ceased operations June 30, 1861, with the advent of the Civil War. A competitor, the Central Overland California & Pike's Pak Express ceased operations almost as soon as it began. The company was purchased by Ben Holladay and renamed the Overland Stage Line.

Originally the Overland Stage left Atchison, Kansas, headed northwest until it joined the Oregon Trail then headed west across Wyoming to Salt Lake City and California. As conflict with the Indians increased in the sixties, a more southerly route was taken departing from the Oregon Trail at Julesberg into Greeley Colorado (originally Latham), through Virginia Dale (Colorado) and Tie Siding (Wyoming) northwest to the Laramie Plains, across Bridger's Pass, rejoining the Oregon Trail at Fort Bridger. Emigrants also took the stage route to avoid encounters with the Indians, thus resurrecting the original name Overland Trail for what had been called the Oregon Trail.

SMOKY (SMOKEY) HILL TRAIL

The third of the principal trails was the Smoky (Smokey) Hill Trail that took its name from the Smokey Hill River that runs through central Kansas west from Salina into Colorado. The trail ran through Fort Riley (Manhattan), Fort Hays (Hays), and Fort Wallace (Sharon Springs, southwest of Colby) in Kansas into Colorado and Denver. The route generally followed the route taken by Zebulon Pike in 1806 and mapped by John W. Gunnison in 1853 from Fort Leavenworth along the 38 parallel of north latitude .

It was the Smokey Hill Trail that was at the heart of the conflict between the Central Plains Indians and the white man. It ran straight through the rich buffalo hunting grounds of west-central Kansas and east-central Colorado, much of which was included in the reservation provided for in the 1861 treaty concluded at Fort Wise, to Denver in Colorado Territory where new gold fields were discovered in 1859. There were also reports of huge coal and iron-ore deposits in the Smokey Hill region. (Gold-seekers previous traveled the Oregon Trail to the juncture of the South Platte, following the southern branch into Colorado Territory.)

It also became the proposed route of the Kansas Pacific Railroad (formerly the Leavenworth, Pawnee, and Western and later the Union Pacific, Eastern Division). Indian attacks, though sporadic, continued, driven primarily by the Cheyenne Dog Soldiers and various bands of Sioux.

TRANSCONTINENTAL RAILROAD

There were four possible routes: the Northern Route between the 47th and 49th parallels; the Pacific Railroad Route along the 42nd parallel out of Chicago to Council Bluffs and from Omaha to Sacramento; the Buffalo Trail or Missouri Railroad Route between the 38th and 39th parallels from St. Louis through Kansas City along the Santa Fe Trail and through the Rockies ending in northern California (a great central path); and the Southern Route between the 32nd and 35th parallels out of Memphis across Texas to San Diego.

On May 9, 1869, the Central Pacific from the West and the Union Pacific from the East met at Promontory Point Summit north of Salt Lake City, Utah. The transcontinental railroad was a reality. With railroad came the death of the Oregon and California trails. The railroad also nailed shut the coffin of the Indians of the Northern Plains.

WESTERN POPULATION GROWTH

By 1880, the population of Oregon was approximately 175,000. Over the decade of the eighties, it nearly doubled to 300,000.

American Indian Culture

As one reads the literature on the native peoples, one is struck by the fact so many of the tribes refer to themselves by words meaning some variation of the "People" as with *Nermernuh* by the Comanches and *Hum-a-luh* by the Skagits. The name Narraganset means "people of the small point"; the name Abnaki, for "eastern people;" Lenni Lenape, the Delaware's own name, meaning "true men"; and Pipatsje, the Maricopa's own name, again signifying "people" In the Northwest and Pacific Coast many of tribal names end with the syllable, -ish, meaning "people." What did the names signify; what were the People trying to say? Possibly, something like we are who we are; we are who we were; we are unique unto our selves; we are at peace with the earth. Whatever the full meaning, it was far from how the white man saw them. As Blacks were chattels, Indians were savages, animals, certainly less than equals.

The white man has made much of what he judged as the barbaric and savage nature of the American Indian as if Indian passions and emotions, feelings and frustrations, loves and desires, contentment and anger, fears and triumphs were any different from those of the white man a thousand years earlier. Seventeenth and eighteenth and even nineteenth century whites most often viewed the American Indian with eyes only of the moment, without thought given to the white man's own tumultuous history of fighting hunger and of grappling with the elements of nature and of centuries of conflict between one band and another and between one race and another. In 54 B.C., Caesar recorded his description of the British islanders that he encountered. They lived, he wrote, "on milk and flesh and clothe themselves in skins... [and] dye themselves with woad, which produces a blue colour, and makes they appearance in battle more terrible. They wear long hair, and shave every part of the body save the head and the upper lip. Groups of ten or twelve men have wives together in common, and particularly brothers along with brothers, and fathers with sons."[55] Their mode of fighting was no different from that of the Native Americans the English encountered sixteen

---

55   Julius Caesar, *Caesar: The Gallic War*. Translated by W. J. Edwards (Cambridge, MA: Harvard University Press. Loeb Classical Library, 1986), v. 12, p. 253.

hundred years later. New World settlers and their descendants gave no thought to that past, no though to how the Romans later viewed the Huns and the Visigoths; how the English viewed the Irish; how the Anglo-Saxons viewed the Normans and vice versa; and how half the known world viewed the Vikings.

Historic white man, both individually and communally, has been to varying degrees savage and barbaric, content and threatening, aggressive and defensive, as influenced by time and place and concern for his own survival. Man changes, learns, and progresses as he finds reason, opportunity, and example.

For the most part, the American Indian society hand lived a unique communal existence that also exhibited a general openness to strangers and foreigners with a level of innocence one finds hard to fathom, even today. All along the Atlantic coast, Europeans were almost universally welcomed by the native inhabitants. They not only welcomed the white man, but in many cases freely fed him, clothed him, guided him, and protected him from nature's elements and man's enemies. For the most part they welcomed and encouraged explorers along the Gulf Coast, up and down the Mississippi, up the Missouri, and across the Great Lakes and along the Pacific Coast and into the deserts of the southwest. Their trades for food, goods, and services were always eminently fair, as far as they understood the worth of a given item. They never thought to cheat. Many of those that stole horses and frying pans, colored cloth and beads were as children stealing candy from the store counter.

Even the great westward migration that began in 1840 initially met with at worst passive acceptance. Of the ten thousand deaths of settlers and pioneers that occurred between 1840 and 1860 on the trek West, only 362 have been directly attributed to the Indian hostilities (against 426 Indian deaths during the corresponding period related to the westward migration). The vast majority of the deaths were the result of accidents, drownings, and guns, plus the deaths of the old, the very young, and the weak who succumbed to the elements and the lack of food and water. The Shoshoni and others traded salmon and berries to starving travelers, and Cayuse warriors guided Oregon-bound settlers over the Blue Mountains and down the Columbia rapids. If it was not for the Indian, many more would have died along the way. As historian Frank McLynn writes, the Sioux "had to be pushed into confrontation with the whites by blatant provocation and exploitation." Of the English at Roanoke, Edmund Morgan writes, "the Indians, though hospitable, were not prepared for the company that came to stay." Soon, they had had enough of their "grasshopper guests." [56]

There were exceptions of course demonstrated by the inherent savagery of the Comanches and Kiowas that was loosed on the sedentary tribes of the Plains and the white inhabitants of northern Mexico and the Texas frontier. The Comanches took bestiality to a new level, seemingly for its own sake, while the Kiowa were known for their proficiency in inflicting torture. Emotions rising from the blood feud on the Texas frontier, however, unjustly influenced the subsequent treatment by whites of the Nez Percé, the Sioux, and other tribes on the northern Plains. The Comanches, however, cannot be blamed for the actions of the whites that drove the Cherokees and others from their homes east of the Mississippi and stripped the Omaha, the Osage and others in the trans-Mississippi west of their heritage and led to the near extermination of the Native Americans of California.

Cochise and Juh and their respective bands of the Chiricahua Apaches were another exception. Juh is largely unknown; but thanks in large measure to Hollywood publicists, Cochise has escaped much of condemnation that has been leveled against the Comanches and Kiowas. Cochise the avenger led his people on a war of death and mutilation that lasted ten years during which time he sought to terrorize his enemies by killing "every White Eye that fell into his hands." Only human, he was hardly unique in seeing events only from his own perspective, but he allowed himself to be totally consume by those

56 Frank McLynn, *Wagons West*, 433, 434, 440; quote taken from 440. Quotes taken from Edmund S. Morgan, *American Slavery, American Freedom*, 39-40, 40.

events, often with tragic results. Long after others had thrown down their guns, he fought on—to make the whites suffer for what they had done. He was a strong and capable leader but at times stubborn and wrong-headed, and his methods were often times counterproductive. But for nineteen years, he "protected his family and served his people... What more could a man do?"[57] Nothing he did was in his own self-interests nor to advance his people beyond where nature had placed them.

On a broader front, however, the near total destruction of the native peoples of America was rooted in self-righteous arrogance and greed on the part of whites that was born of an all-consuming passion for individual self-interest. Anglo-Americans as a group cared little about the differences between one Indian and another and between one tribe or band and another, and they exhibited the same utter disregard for their own culpability as the Comanches did for their actions. The clash of cultures was exasperbated by the callous treatment netted out to the Indians once they had been reduced to life on the reservations.

The Inhumanity of Man

The modern age continues to wrestle with the concept of cruel and unusual punishment. Back in 1594 at the time the colonists were establishing their homes in the New World, an attempt on the life of Henry IV of France resulted in the guilty party being torn limb from limb by four horses. Not long afterward the English Protestants of Massachusetts saw the work of Jesuit Sebastian Rasle among the Abenaki Indians of Maine as an unwelcome intrusion of Canadian Catholics into the Protestant community. Fr. Rasle was killed; his body horribly mutilated; and his scalp brought back to Boston in triumph.[58] Burning victims alive at the stake had been common practice in Europe, and the practice was readily accepted in America for condemned "witches" and others.

It is especially difficult to separate acts of cruelty from military tactics during time of war, which by its nature is inhuman. But the ability to distinguish between the two is what separates civilized beings from animals. The purpose of military tactics is to achieve a strategic goal. Wanton acts of destruction; wanton acts of killing without regard to age, sex, participation or involvement (guilt or innocence); and wanton acts of mutilation of the human body that do not serve to achieve a strategic objective but death and destruction for their own sake are cruel and inhuman. In some cases, judgment hangs on words like "premeditated" and "intent." No race of men is immune from the dangers arising from the use of cruel and unusual punishment, torture, mutilation, and base veniality.

In 1761 during the French & Indian War, the British attacked and destroyed a Cherokee village. Only a few Indians were killed in the fighting, but to some the attack and the aftermath made a lasting impression.. Then lieutenant of militia Francis Marion in the service of the British army recorded his observations on the attitude taken by some of the soldiers in a letter to a friend.

> We proceeded, by Colonel Grant's orders, to burn the Indian cabins. Some of the men seemed to enjoy this cruel work, laughing heartily at the curling flames...Poor creatures...we surely need not grudge you such miserable habitations. ...Who without grief, could see the stately stalks [of corn] with broad green leaves and tasseled shock, the staff of life, sink under our swords with all their precious load, to wither and rot untasted in their mourning fields?

> I saw everywhere around, the footsteps of the little Indian children, where they had lately played under the shade of their rustling corn. When we were gone, thought I, they will return, and peeping through the weeds with tearful eyes, will mark the ghastly ruin where they had so often

---

57 Peter Aleshire, *Cochise*, "every White eye" from 136; "protected his family" from 288-289. See also pp. 42, 47, 130-138, 148, 152, 192.
58 Jonathan Wright, *God's Soldiers: A History of the Jesuits* (New York: Doubleday Image, 2004), 108.

played. "Who did this?" they will ask their mothers, and the reply will be, "The white people did it, - the Christians did it!"[59]

Nearly two hundred years later in the South Pacific, not a lot had changed. Admiral William F. Hulsey, who "professed to delight in sinking Japanese barges full of troops, who on a few occasions were shot in the water. 'It was rich, rewarding, beautiful slaughter.'" At one point, Halsey's Chief of Staff, Admiral Robert Carney, told reporters, "[I]t would seem to be an unnecessary refinement to worry too much about" sinking Japanese hospital ships because "they are caring for Nips which we failed to kill in the first attempt."[60]

The Indian practice of scalping their fallen enemies has also received much attention. To the American Indian, an enemy scalp was a hard-won prize, a trophy, a token of victory—just as it was for many other races. In an account of the Rogue River War in Oregon, it was noted, "Scalping natives was not an atrocity unfamiliar to Oregon pioneers." According to the Scottish Field Archery Association, the practice was introduced into the Americas by Scotsmen. A report describes the technique and notes that the palm-sized scalp, or larger in some cases, was "dried, often ornamented and preserved, being highly valued as a trophy, by the victor." The report goes on to state that "scalping was not calculated of itself, to take life."[61]

For Americans on the other hand, who put cash bounties on scalps—as they would for wolves and other predators to home and livestock, the scalp was verification of a life taken. American colonies and European powers condoned the practice and were not in the least hesitant to pay for the scalps of their enemies. In the years prior to 1703, the colony of Massachusetts offered to pay its Indian allies a premium of twelve pounds for each enemy scalp. The bounty was raised to one hundred pounds in 1722. In the mid-1800s in California, it was common practice for towns to offer bounty hunters cash for every Indian scalp *or head* taken. Five dollars for a head and 25 cents for a scalp were the going rates.

Battle accounts of the American Civil War contain numerous references to the high price paid in human lives to have the regimental colors carried ever forward into the heat of battle—a price closely matched by the lives expended by the other side to capture those same colors. A typical account reads, "The combat became hand-to-hand, and several men from each side fell fighting for the 7th colors."[62] Successful capture of the enemy's colors produced a wave of euphoria and immense sense of pride in the achievement. The new prize was put on display for all to see.

An enemy scalp was the equivalent of capturing the regimental colors on a personal scale. In different times and in different cultures, a person's hair and hair style took on a special significance, whether it be the "Mohawk," the pony tail, the pigtail, or the braids. One's hair was a sign of strength, of virility, of honor. At times in some lands, it was also a sign of piety, servitude, and submission. One need not look far to see the importance given to hair. Consider the Chinese *queue* (pigtail) that began with the conquest of China by Manchuria in 1644. It was not officially abolished until the Chinese revolution of 1911. Consider the traditional Han ethic hair style where one's long hair is tied up atop the head. Consider the hair of the Jewish men as they stand before the Wailing Wall. Look at today's fashions and the lengths (no pun intended) we go to make a statement with our hair. To take an enemy's scalp was to sap his

59 George Ellison, "Cowee Mountain's wartime history," *Smoky Mountain News*, January 1, 2001 at http://www.smokymountainnews.com/issues/1_01/1_10_01/back_then.shtml and Jerry Trivette, *Appalachian Summit: A Documentary History, 1540-1900* (2001-2006), chp. 12, at http://appalachiansummit.tripod.com/chapt12.htm#_edn10 [December 20, 2006]. From John P. Brown, *Old Frontiers*, 111.

60 Evan Thomas, *Sea of Thunder: Four Commanders and the Last Great Naval Campaign 1941-1945* (New York: Simon& Schuster, 2006), 107-108.

61 Joel Palmer, " Rogue River War" (Corvallis, OR: Community Pages, n.d.) at http://www.corvalliscommunitypages.com/Americas/US/Oregon/OregonNotCorvallis/roguewarleft.htm [September 15, 2006].

62 Seven E. Woodworth, *Nothing but Victory*, 52 , writing of the 7th Iowa at the Battle of Belmont.

strength. It was not the hideous, bloody process that it is often made out to be. It was in fact a fast and convenient acknowledgement of success on the field of battle.

Mutilation of the human body presented another and more serious charge leveled against the American Indian. Mutilation, as it occurred in the collective, was at best a warning; at worst, a form of revenge. One of the worst occurred at Fort Mackinac in 1763. There the Ojibwas distracted the British garrison with a ball game between themselves and stole past the sentries into the compound. The surprise and the killing were near total. The scalpings and mutilations committed were horrendous and grew with the telling, all the more to serve the purpose of the Indians—to terrify the settlers along the Ohio frontier. Indians as a race never reveled in death, least of all, cruelty and multination. The most grievous acts were acts of individuals, as in the case of Chief Juh, a Nde-nda-i Chiricahua Apache, who roamed the southwest between Mexico, Arizona and New Mexico before his death in the 1880s.[63] His sadistic nature was unique among Native Americans, East to West.

To give perspective, consider the of conduct of the Puritans of Plymouth who professed to be both civilized and stewards of God and who in 1637 mounted the head of a Massachusett war chief on a pole above the roof of their fort and replaced the banner of St. George's cross on their flag pole with the blood-stained linen with which they had wrapped the head.

Regrettably, all to many persons of every age, sex, and culture came not only to accept mutilation and other forms of sadistic behavior but to revel in it. Following an incident involving the gang rape of two young white sisters by six white men that occurred in the town of Ladore in southeastern Kansas, the editor of the local newspaper attempted to give some perspective to the issues of the day: "The Citizens of Ladore deserve the thanks of every decent person, for hanging these vile scoundrels who by their acts have thrown the atrocities of the savage Indians into the shade."[64]

War-making Proclivity

Many American Indian tribes, but certainly not all, had a passion for war—as they defined war. Cherokee chiefs complained when treaty provisions mandated inter-tribal peace. "We cannot live without war. Should we make peace with [one enemy]...we must immediately look out for some others with whom we can be engaged in our beloved occupation.[65] It was no different a half a century later with the signers of the first Fort Laramie Treaty with the Sioux and other tribes of the northern plains. Contrast the words of the Cherokee chiefs to the words of another chief: "Should there be a war, this will be a handsome theater for our enterprising young men and a certain source of acquiring fame."[66] The words of Maj. General Andrew Jackson speaking of the Spanish possessions of Santa Fe and Mexico. Jackson thrilled to the idea of war as he did to the duel of honor.

Another American president also spoke of the glories of war, "No triumph of peace is quite so great as the supreme triumphs of war. He was accused by many of seeking war for war's sake. His former professor at Harvard, believed that to him, "one foe...[was] as good as another."[67] That president was Theodore Roosevelt. But the difference between Jackson and TR was that Roosevelt was much more complex an individual. When it came to relations with other nations, he was acute manager of events and a master of diplomacy. Bluntness and boast were saved for the circuit. Whether he believed his every pronouncement

---

63 James L. Haley, *Apaches*, 346, 370, 381.

64 *Southern Kansas Advance*, May 18, 1870, quoted in John N. Mack, "Law and Order on the Southeastern Kansas Frontier, 1866-1870, *Kansas History: A Journal of the Kansas Plains* (Topeka: Kansas State Historical Society, Winter 2007/2008), vol. 30, no. 4, 250. Ladore is located in south-central Neosho County.

65 T. R. Fehrenback, *Comanches*, 84.

66 *Ibid*, 119-120.

67 Nathan Miller, *Theodore Roosevelt*, 255.

of fire and brimstone is arguable. The responsibility of office led to reflection, and reflection led to the formulation of peaceful solutions. Yet TR's words expressed the feelings of many Americans.

As Assistant Secretary of the Navy, Roosevelt was instrumental in the taking of the Philippines from Spain in 1898 although his boss, President McKinley, saw little purpose in holding the islands following the end of the Spanish-American War. But a force bigger than Roosevelt and McKinley combined drove the issue—a new sense of power. Americans were bent on flexing their muscle. If blood-letting was the result, so be it. A writer for the Washington Post reflected at the time:

> A new consciousness seems to have come upon us—the consciousness of strength—and with it a new appetite, the yearning to show our...ambition, interest, land hunger, pride, the mere joy of fighting whatever it may be, we are animated by a new sensation. ...The taste of empire is in the mouth of the people even as the taste of blood in the jungle. It means an imperial policy.[68]

Pursuit of "the supreme triumphs of war" was not unique to the American Indians. It was not even unique to Americans. But Native Americans held a more constricted concept of war. Kiowa Chief Satank (Sitting Bear), recognized as one of the most formidable warriors of the Plains, remarked, "We have warred against the white man, but never because it gave us pleasure."[69]

Before the Europe of the history books, there was martial race of men for whom "[r]aiding was endemic"; men "who craved war" for the sake of war; who launched "plundering attacks" and "children carried off in bondage." They were the Helvetii, ancestors of the modern Swiss, who ranged throughout the region about 60 B.C.[70]

Later Europeans fought over territory, power, distant colonies, pride, and politics. The Indians fought for their very survival, for their right to exist as men. Colonists fought for independence; Native Americans fought to *remain* independent. Chief Cornstalk of the Shawnee lamented the plight of a once mighty nation that had been reduced to a handful; that once possessed "land almost to the seashore, not now have hardly enough ground to stand upon. ...It is plain that the white people intend to extirpate the Indians."[71] He asked where it was not better to die as warriors that to waste away inch by inch.

Americans also fought and died for the gold of the Black Hills, California, Colorado, and Wyoming—the Indians called gold the white man's god. But before there was gold, there was something more disruptive to the lives of America's native peoples and their traditional homelands—though seldom spoken of or written about, wars of extermination.

Americans fought wars of extermination years before the phrase "ethnic cleansing" became popular—years before the Holocaust, the Armenians, and the Balkans, and years before Rwanda and Darfur. Of the early American Period of California, anthropology professor Charles Smith writes:

> The first 50 years of the American Period was a horrible time for the Native Californians, given the sheer magnitude of what happened during that half century: scalpings of men, women, & children; incarceration in jails with the only way out being enforced indenture to whites for unspecified lengths of time; the kidnapping & sale of Indian children; the massacres of entire Indian villages; the military roundup of Indians and their enforced exile on military reservations where even the most basic of living amenities were lacking; their complete legal disenfranchisement. The outcome of all this was that during the first two decades of the American

68 David Halberstam, *The Coldest Winter: America and the Korean War* (New York: Hyperion, 2007), 109, taken from Stanley Karnow, *In our Image: America's Empire in the Philippines* (New York: Random House, 1989), 96.
69 Angie Debo, *A History of the Indians of the United States*, 247.
70 Adrian Goldsworthy, *Caesar: Life of a Colossus* (New Haven: Yale University Press, 2006), 206, 213, 214.
71 H. W. Brands, *Andrew Jackson*, 86.

occupation, the native population of California plummeted by 90 percent - in short, a California version of the WWII Holocaust.[72]

Other cases were less catastrophic. In the late 1830s, the crops and villages of peaceful Caddo, Cherokee, Delaware, Shawnee, Kickapoo and other eastern tribes, the "rats' nest" of east Texas as it was called, were burned out by the army of the Republic of Texas. Those who thought that they had finally found peace were driven from the land now coveted by whites.[73] And in Kansas—once called Indian Territory—the land was summarily ordered cleared of Indians following the passage the Kansas-Nebraska Act in 1854.

White atrocities were by no means all mob influenced. Many were born of an unconscionable singular attitude of hatred exhibited by thousands of individual whites. An American volunteer in the Black Hawk war of 1832 shot a Sac papoose strapped to piece of bark floating on the river "while reciting the proverb, 'Kill the nits and you'll have no lice.'"[74]

A pitched battle to the death or a battle between warring tribes that might bring death to tens or hundreds of their people was anathema to Native Americans. The words war and enemy did not have the same connotation to the American Indians as it did to the Europeans who had grown accustomed to the death and destruction of the likes of the Hundred-Years War, the War of the Roses, the Seven-Years War, the march to and the retreat from Moscow, the Crusades, the wars of succession, the wars of religion, the wars for territory. For the American Indian, raids were launched for survival—raids to steal food, raids to steal horses, attacks to protect their hunting grounds. Conflicts were also tests of manhood and tests of skills. Each tribe menaced the other in a game of tit for tat with little major harm done to either party.

An old man of the Lakota tribe spoke of wars and the killing to the young of the tribe.

> The Snakes, Crows, and Pawnees have been our enemies for longer than anyone can remember. So we know them, where they live, how they fight, and how they think. When we meet them on the field of battle, sometimes their medicine is stronger and other times ours is. That's how things are. The whites don't understand war. They don't understand that the power of an enemy is a way to strengthen our fighting men. They are killers. A killer does not respect something or someone he knows he can kill, or must kill. Therefore he does not measure victory by the strength of his medicine. He measures his victories by how many he has killed. If we are to defeat this kind of people, we must come to know them in every way. It is not a pleasant thought, but it is necessary.[75]

The common attitude towards the Indians among the British was one of contempt. For the most part, in historian Brands' descriptive phrase, the Indians were considered "savages beneath regard by civilized men." At one point during Pontiac's Rebellion in 1764, James Amherst, the British commander in North American, approved Colonel Henry Bouquet's plan to distribute blankets infested with smallpox to the Indians. Further, he told Bouquet, "[y]ou will do well...to try every other method than can serve to extirpate this execrable race."

Joseph Marshall writes of how the Lakota "understood the philosophy of being a warrior, that defeating one's enemy didn't always depend on taking his life. Defeating one's enemy meant being better on a given day, overpowering his mind and spirit with the strength of your own being and the power you

---

72   Charles R. Smith, "An Introduction to California's Native People: American Period" (Aptos, CA: Cabrillo College, n.d.) at http://www.cabrillo.edu/~crsmith/anth6_americanperiod.html [May 26, 2006].
73   T. R. Fehrenbach, *Comanches*, 227, "rats' nest"
74   Gloria Jahoda, *The Trail of Tears*, 137.
75   Joseph M. Marshall, *The Journey of Crazy Horse*, 118.

carried in your own spirit. Such victories were honorable. ...whites didn't understand honor...they only understood killing."[76] Following the massacre of over four hundred men, women and children of the Pequot of southeastern Connecticut by Puritans of the Massachusetts Colony and their allies, the sachem or chief of one their own reluctant allies, Miantonomi of the Narraganset, angrily retorted, "[I]t is too furious, and slays too many men."[77] There was no honor.

It was the words of General Phil Sheridan that encapsulated the feelings of the white settlers in the West and the generations that followed, "The only good Indians I ever saw were dead," or its more modern variation.[78] It was in those words that Sheridan addressed Toch-a-way, a Comanche Chief, at Fort Cobb, Indian Territory, in January 1868 after the chief introduced himself saying that he was a "good" Indian.

Sheridan's boss, General William Sherman, while never as colorful in words or actions as his subordinate, made it clear that the extermination of the fighting Indians was the only practical solution to the Indian problem. Both generals applauded the actions of George Custer at the 7th Calvary on the upper Washita River in western Oklahoma in the early morning hours of November 27, 1868, that left the Cheyenne chief, Black Kettle, who continually fought for peace, and his wife and some forty women and children dead. The calvary had tracked a raiding party that rode into Black Kettle's camp the day before from the north. Custer was following the army's new campaign strategy—hit the Indian camps where found, fast and hard, survivors to be driven onto the reservations. [79] Two years earlier on December 28, 1866, after learning of what became known as the Fetterman Massacre, Sherman had been unequivocal in writing still General in Chief of the Army Ulysses S. Grant, "We must act with vindictive earnestness against the Sioux, even to their extermination, man, women and children."[80] Eight months later in the wake of the Cheyenne attack on the Union Pacific construction trains near Plum Creek station, Sherman wrote, "The more we can kill this year the less ill have to be killed the next year, for the more I see of these Indians the more convinced I am that all have to be killed or be maintained as a species of paupers."[81] For the most part, Americans did both.

Had it not been for President Grant and the humanitarian efforts of secular and religious groups in the East, proposals that arose from several quarters for the unqualified extermination of the last of the fighting Indians might have become a reality, ostensibly to secure peace.[82] But there was little public outcry to those actions that went on day after day that produced the same results but which for the most part did not involve the army. There was no remorse a generation later when Theodore Roosevelt wrote, "[T]he rude, fierce settler who drives the savage from the land lays all civilized mankind under a debt to him."[83]

Politicians also wanted wars of extinction. About twenty miles east of Julesburg on the Union Pacific line in northeast Colorado, an excursion train came to the end of track on June 6, 1867. Senator George Francis Train was among the dignitaries. When it was his turn to utter words of wisdom to the crowd, he spoke not of the new age of travel but of war, war with the Indians: "Most of the frontier towns like war. It makes good trade; hence traders and military men become active....Help me cheat the Indians and I will give you one half! The officers on small salary say 'extermination' and the war bugle is sounded."[84] Even General Sherman had to walk away in disgust.

Two hundred-plus years earlier in 1637, John Robinson, spiritual minister to the Pilgrims of Plymouth who had remained behind in Europe, wrote William Bradford, governor of Plymouth, regarding the raid and

---

76 *Ibid*, 178.
77 Nathaniel Philbrick, *Mayflower*, 179, "too furious."
78 *Bartlett's Familiar Quotations*, 610:4.
79 Benjamin Capps, *The Indians*, 188, 190-191.
80 David Haward Bain, *Empire Express*, 311.
81 Steven E. Ambrose, *Nothing Like in the World*, 223, 396n41.
82 Benjamin Capps, *The Indians*, 200.
83 Daniel K. Richter, *Facing East from Indian Country*, 190, from TR, *The Writings of the West*, 4 vols. (1889-1896).
84 David Haward Bain, *Empire Express*, 353.

massacre of Massachusett Indians at Wessagusett: "It is...a thing more glorious, in men's eyes, than pleasing in God's or convenient for Christians, to be a terror to poor **barbarous** people." He saw the wanton murder as an ominous sign of what the future held for the Indians of America as he continued, "And indeed I am afraid lest, by these occasions, others should be drawn to affect a kind of ruffling course in the world."[85]

In the 1865 annual report of the Department of the Interior submitted to the Present Andrew Johnson, Secretary James Harlan, who took charge of the department May 15 of that year, summarized not only the status of the affairs of the department but also the attitude of the American people towards the Indian population and offered recommendations for reaching a state of relatively peaceful coexistence between whites and Indians. The total population of the Indian race at that time he put at three hundred and fifty thousand; and, either in total ignorance of the situation on the ground or in political deference to the President and the Congress, he began by stating that a number of tribes had been in "flagrant violation" of the provisions of existing treaties that the government had observed "with scrupulous good faith."

The evidence aptly demonstrates that that was hardly the case. The issue of the treaties aside, the Secretary provided a succinct statement of the issues:

> The terrible massacre of the white inhabitants in the year 1862 [by the Santee Sioux in Minnesota] is fresh in the memory of the country. The intense exasperation which followed led in that State to a policy, which has also prevailed to some extent in several of our organized Territories, inducing a personal predatory warfare between the frontier citizens, emigrants, and miners, and isolated bands of Indians belonging, in many instances, to tribes at peace with our Government. This awakens a spirit of retaliation inciting atrocious acts of violence, which, oft repeated, result in irreparable disasters to both races.

The Secretary goes on to direct the President's attention to "[t]he policy of total destruction of the Indians [that] has been openly advocated by gentlemen of high position, intelligence, and personal character" and states unequivocally that "no enlightened nation can adopt or sanction it without a forfeiture of its self-respect and the respect of the civilized nations of the earth."

Harlan goes on to state that, in the first instance, such a policy would cost too much and would be impractical before ending on a higher tone. "Such a policy is manifestly as impracticable as it is in violation of every dictate of humanity and Christian duty." Although he almost seems to imply that the one incident in Minnesota precipitated white retaliation across the country, he attempts to put the situation somewhat in focus, namely that the rights and properties of the Indians must be protected from "encroaching settlements springing up in every organized Territory." Specifically, "[t]he occupation of their hunting grounds and fisheries by agriculturists, and even of their mountain fastnesses [*sic*] by miners, has necessarily deprived the Indians of their accustomed means of support and reduced them to extreme want." Harlan goes on to warn that "[if] the deficiency to occasioned should not be supplied, it is not to be expected that a savage people can be restrained from seeking, by violence, redress of what they conceive to be a grievous wrong."[86]

Native Americans of California

Beyond the scope of the 1865 report of the Secretary of the Interior were the efforts by the state and citizenry of California to bring about the utter destruction of the Native American population within the confines of that state. The settlement of California had its roots in the Spanish mission system. Along with

---

85   Nathaniel Philbrick, *Mayflower*, 156, "I am afraid."

86   "Appendix to the *Congressional Globe*, Message of the President of the United States," First Session Thirty-ninth Congress, *Congressional Globe*, December 4, 1865, pp. 28-29 of 4310, available online at http://memory.loc.gov/ammem/amlaw/lwcg.html. The *Globe* was the predecessor of the *Congressional Record*.

the missions, came the presidios or garrisons. It was not until much later that the first pueblo or secular township was established. The Spanish granted the rights to settle California first to the Jesuit religious order. The Jesuits had the money and the people that Spain had in short supply. In addition, the well-educated Jesuits exhibited the requisite fervor and dedication necessary to accomplish the job assigned to them. They began in the Baja peninsula where the first mission was established in 1697, dedicated to Our Lady of Loreto. The Jesuits were also given rights to Ala (upper) California. Within the next half century, eighteen Jesuits missions had been established on the peninsula. At the same time, Jesuit missions were also being established on the "mainland" north through Sonora into what is now southern Arizona and west to the border with California at the confluence of the Gila and Colorado rivers.

Political issues in Europe and a power struggle within the Catholic church brought an end to the Jesuit missionary activity in New Spain. In 1768, the job settling California was given to the Franciscans from the College of San Francisco in Mexico city. Mission San Diego de Alcalá was established July 16, 1769. Nine more missions were founded quickly thereafter. The first pueblo, San José de Guadalupe, was established November 29, 1777.[87] For the next seventy-five years, the role of the Spanish mission system along the coast was to settle California and evangelize the Native American population—whether they wanted evangelization or not. Albeit replete with good intentions, the system (twenty-one missions in all) wrought death and devastation on the indigenous peoples of California from Spanish diseases and the mental trauma of dislocation and chronic sexual abuse of native women. One-time plans to secularize the missions and assign them to the Indians living on the mission lands never came to fruition.

By the mid-nineteenth century, evangelization had been replaced by Mexican independence, the American War with Mexico, the American agitation and finally conquest of California, the discovery of gold, and a stampede of emigrants onto lands that for generations had belonged to the Indians. The Native Americans of California were hit with a new wave of devastation fueled by greed and the lure of riches.

> *The love of money has infused others*
> *to act for their own employment*
> *even at the destruction of `the Indians*
> *and no measure was considered too unjust or fraudulent*
> *to engage in to accomplish their aims.*[88]

Money accelerated the process of destruction. The fact that, as Fred Rosen wrote, "[l]ike all 'foreign' enemies, the red Indians had become dehumanized" made it all that much easier.[89] Yet it was the Indians, working side by side with the whites of the Mormon Battalion, that James Marshall put to work at the state's first gold strike at Sutter's Mill on the American River in Coloma, California, January 24, 1848. A short time later, Indians would be banned from working the mines.

California had no sooner become a state amidst the controversy over the extension of slavery in 1850 than the governor called for a "war of extinction" against the Indians.[90] He declared that its complete destruction was "the inevitable destiny of the Race." That same year over a million dollars in state funds were budgeted to fund the predatory warfare alluded to in Harlan's 1865 report. A bounty was put on

---

87   For a concise, one volume history of California, see Kevin Starr, *California, A History* with a summary of Native American tribes on pp. 12-16.

88   Methodist Missionary Rev. George Bradley from his 1870 Journal, quoted in "The Aftermath: Land, Lumber and Money," Clarke Historical Library (Mount Pleasant, MI: Central Michigan University, mod. 2005) at http://clarke.cmich.edu/nativeamericans/reservation/4-aftermath.htm [May 30, 2006].

89   Fred Rosen, *Gold!*, 138.

90   Peter Burnett, "Governor's Message" (Annual Message to the Legislature), *Journals of the Legislature of the State of California at its Second Session* (San Jose, 1851), 15; full text appears on pp. 11-37. Burnett, the first governor of California, took office on December 20, 1849 and resigned on January 8 amidst of the furor over his inaugural speech. He was succeeded by Lt. Governor John McDougall, who served from January 9, 1851 until 1852.

Indian scalps. Massacres and murders became common place. They died simply because they were who they were—Indians.[91] If whites could not get to the Indians directly, they destroyed their food source with indiscriminate killing of game and destruction of fields and water supplies. Those that were not killed outright were enslaved. California Indians were even more vulnerable that their brethren to the east. By nature, they were more placable. They were fisherman, farmers, gatherers, and small game hunters who existed in their own small, individual worlds. They had never developed the fighting prowess of the likes of the Comanche and the Sioux.

On April 22, 1850, the California legislature adopted "An Act for the Government and Protection of Indians" that despite its high-sounding rhetoric created the status of indentured servant for California Indians and legalized child labor. Californians traded slavery for forced labor, Indian labor. An amendment passed in 1860 raised the ages of majority of indentured children from eighteen and fifteen for males and females, respectively, to twenty-five and twenty-one.[92] Some traders in human flesh did not even bother with the procedures provided under the statute. Indians, particularly women and children, were kidnapped and sold outright. Authorities looked the other way. The law was not revoked until 1867.

Prior to the rush for gold, the estimated Indian population in California was 150,000. Just twenty years later, in 1870, the population had been reduced to 31,000. Over one hundred thousand were killed; the rest died of starvation, disease, and overwork.[93] Whole tribes had been wiped out forever.

In 1904, Galen Clark wrote of the travail of the Indians of the Yosemite Valley of California:

> The Indians of the Yosemite are fast passing away. Only a handful now remain of the powerful tribes that once gathered in the Valley and considered it an absolute stronghold against their white enemies.

> Their miserable, squalid condition of living opened the way for diseases of a malignant character, which their medicine men could not cure, and their numbers were rapidly reduced by death.

> At the present time there are not in existence a half-dozen of the old Yosemites who were living, even as children, when the Valley was first discovered in 1851; and many of the other tribes have been correspondingly reduced.[94]

From California to Massachusetts, from Minnesota to Texas, it varied by degrees; yet it was the same. Major General John Pope may have best expressed the tragic situation that existed.

> The Indian, in truth, no longer has a country. He is reduced to starvation or to warring to the death. The Indian's first demand is that the white man shall not drive off his game and dispossess him of his lands. How can we promise this unless we prohibit emigration and settlement?...The end is sure and dreadful to contemplate.[95]

We could have done better.

Native Americans' Status in the Modern World

Beginning in 1953, the federal government pursued the policy of "termination" whereby the special legal and political relationships that heretofore existed between tribal governments and the federal government

---

91 Robert M. Utley, *The Indian Frontier of the American West*, 51-52.

92 Chapter 133, *Statutes of California*, April 22, 1850; Amendments to Act of April 1850, Chapter 231, April 18, 1860.

93 Fred Rosen, *Gold!*, 203-205; Kevin Starr, *California*, 99.

94 Galen Clark, *Indians of the Yosemite Valley and Vicinity: Their History, Customs and Traditions* (1904), ix, 14, available from Project Gutenberg Literary Archive Foundation (2003-2006) at http://www.gutenberg.org/etext/16572 [September 17, 2006].

95 Steven E. Ambrose, *Nothing Like in the World*, 173, 393n13.

were eliminated. At the same time the government terminated federal benefits and support services to tribes.[96] From 1953 to 1962, Congress "terminated" over one hundred Indian tribes. The tribes were directed to distribute tribal property to their members and dissolve their governments. An integral part of the termination policy was the enactment of Pub. Law. 280 that transferred criminal jurisdiction over Indian lands to individual state courts. The forced assimilation that resulted was a disaster to the American Indian tribes.

On July 8, 1970, President Richard Nixon submitted a Special Message to the Congress on Indian Affairs, as a consequence of which Indian tribal self-determination became the foundation of federal policy. The *Indian self-determination and Education Assistance Act* passed in 1975 gave tribal governments maximum flexibility in administering federal programs and services for their members. In the Declaration of Policy, Congress recognized "the obligation of the United States to respond to the strong expression of the Indian people for self-determination by assuring maximum Indian participation in the direction of educational as well as other Federal services to Indian communities so as to render such services more responsive to the needs and desires of those communities."[97] The act authorized of the Secretary of Health and Human Services or the Secretary of the Interior to contract with tribal organizations for the planning, conduct and administration of programs or services that were otherwise provided to Indian tribes and their members under existing Federal law.

The policy has been affirmed by each succeeding president. With Executive Order 13084 of May 14, 1998, President Clinton directed continuous and on-going consultation and coordination between executive departments and agencies with Indian tribal governments in the development of regulatory practices in order to reduce the imposition of unfunded mandates and to streamline the application process for services and increase availability where applicable.

Within the last twenty-five years or so, Native Americans have begun to reach a level of acceptance in the American community and enjoy some of the fruits of American citizenship after years of thankless contributions to the American way of life exemplified by their participation in the First and Second World Wars, the Korean War, and the Vietnam War. Many Americans of Indian ancestry have broken the ethnic bounds that kept them segregated and have gained recognition in the white man's world and advanced into the twenty-first century on near-equal footing. The National Museum of the American Indian, long overdue, has opened in Washington, DC[98]

American Indian tribes are also tapping into the white man's largess with sovereignty-based gaming enterprises.[99] There are presently about four hundred casinos operated by some two hundred-plus federally recognized Indian entities.

The multi-million dollar casino gaming phenomenon for the most part has been good to some Indian tribes, certainly to their states, local communities, and local school districts that would be hard pressed to replace the income stream. Gaming income has paid for new health facilities and educational programs, disease prevention and wellness programs and provided funds to improve the infrastructure, promote business expansion, and increase community services for many tribal units across the country.

---

96 "The Enduring Validity of Indian Self- Determination," *Senate Committee on Indian Affairs Briefing Booklet* (January 11, 1999) available at http://www.senate.gov/~scia/106brfs/selfd.htm [September 10, 2006].

97 Public Law 93–638. 25 U.S.C. 450.

98 W. Richard West is a Southern Cheyenne and member of the Cheyenne and Arapaho tribes of Oklahoma and director the Smithsonian's National Museum of the American Indian. Director West officially opened the doors of the museum on September 21, 2004. The curving lines of the sandstone structure that houses the museum, which is oriented towards the east, echo those of circular Indian structures. The museum's Cultural Resource Center in Maryland houses hundreds of thousands of tribal pieces. Only eight thousand items are on display in the museum. The collection includes both historic and contemporary artifacts from 900 tribes throughout the Americas. See Lyric Wallwork Winik, "'To Reconcile a Tragic Past,'" *Parade*, September 5, 2004, p. 10.

99 In 1988, Congress passed the *Indian Gaming Regulatory Act* that permitted casinos on land controlled by Native American tribes.

On the other hand, there have been problems of corruption, mismanagement, profiteering by investors, and undue political posturing, but not to the extremes argued by some.[100] There is also the problem of the haves and have-nots, some by choice; others by circumstances—as was the case of those Indians that ended up on oil-rich land while others scratched at rocks. And, as in baseball, there are the big-market teams and the small-market teams. With improved financial security, more thought should be given to revenue sharing and philanthropy among the Indian tribes of the United States. Millions of dollars have been spent lobbying members of Congress. While Indian nations have as much right to lobby legislators as the automotive industry, the tobacco industry, the oil companies, and the pharmaceutical and insurance industries, that in itself does not make it a laudable endeavor. And, while car manufacture is a one hundred percent profit-making enterprise by definition, the question arises whether a reasonable portion of Indian lobby money is earmarked to improve the lot of the Indian people vs. increased gaming concessions. And, in the background, is the lingering question of the morality of the gaming business that has interjected, as a minimum, a measure of discomfort to some if not outright condemnation.

That said, what is most interesting is the impact on the relationship between Native Americans and the non-Indian community in the light of sovereignty-bases gaming. Gaming has fully engulfed the American scene thanks to horse racing, dog races, off-track para-mutual betting, lotteries, bingo parlors, and now the internet. Casino gambling, however, had been limited for over thirty years to the state of Nevada, followed later by Atlantic City.[101] Next came riverboat gambling. With the additional access now provided by sovereignty-based gaming, patrons have convenient access to gaming facilities almost right around the corner, any corner.

This role for Native Americans as a purveyor of gaming has generally been well received if not wholeheartedly accepted and indorsed by the non-Indian community. In addition to the gaming opportunities provided individual patrons, sovereign-based gaming has been a financial boon to state and local authorities. Millions of dollars are now available to public entities that otherwise would have gone elsewhere. In addition, gaming draws tourist dollars to local businesses. Politically, revenue from sovereign-based gaming is preferable to that provided by the traditional sin taxes on liquor and cigarettes. Many see it as a win-win situation. The question arises, what if the legal basis for sovereign-based gaming were expanded to include other products and services in competition with public and private enterprise? What would be the attitude of the non-Indian community? For now, Indian tribes offer access to a service not otherwise commonly available within the local community.

Although there have been significant gains in the lives of Native Americans, particularly at the individual level, and an infusion of cash to the casino tribes, Native Americans as a race continue to fight prejudices, stereotypes, and biases. For the most part, those with American Indian blood coursing through their veins are often left beholden to the white man not only for their few gains, limited successes, and hard-fought concessions, but for the abject poverty, inordinately high unemployment, poor educational opportunities, inadequate health care, marginal living conditions, higher infant mortality rates, and a shorter life expectancy—all of which can be reduced if not eliminated. The only element that has been missing is a non-Indian community that truly cares.

---

100 Donald L. Barlett; James B. Steele, "Special Report/Indian Casinos," *Time*, Two Parts, December 16, 2002, and December 23, 2002, beginning on p. 47 and p. 52, respectively.

101 The Nevada legislature legalized gambling in 1931 partly as a recovery measure following the collapse of the national economy. See Daniel J. Boorstin, *The Americans: The Democratic Experience* (New York: Random House, 1973), 73. The state of New Jersey legalized gambling in Atlantic City in the 1977, and other states followed under a myriad of conditions and restrictions, beginning with riverboat gambling in Iowa in 1989.

Death Keel of a Culture

Little Turtle, Chief of the of the Miamis, on his visit to Philadelphia not long after the signing of the Treaty of Greenville, August 3, 1795, laments:

> Here I am deaf and dumb. When I walk through the streets I see every person in his shop employed about something. One makes shoes, another hats, a third sell cloth and everyone lives by his labor. I say to myself, which of all these things can you do? Not one. I can make a boy or an arrow, catch fish, kill game, and go to war, but not of these is of any use here...I should be a piece of furniture, useless to my nation, useless to the whites, and useless to myself.[102]

It took less than a century for White America to destroy a culture. In some respects it may have been inevitable, but there is no question that much more could have been done, that much more should have been done.

---

102 Quoted in Landon Y. Jones, *William Clark and the Shaping of the West* (New York: Hill and Wang, 2004), 86, 343n104, taken from Sword, *President Washington's Indian War*, 335, in Samuel Gardner Drake, *Book of Indians of North America* (Boston, 1834), 56-57.

American Indian Tribes of North America

va'ôhtama!
"Welcome"
(Cheyenne)

This section includes some thirteen hundred separate American Indian tribal names from the continental United States, from Abenaki to Zuñi. They include entities identified as tribes, sub-tribes, divisions, nations, and "peoples," with the number of sub-groups limited to those that are commonly treated separately in the literature in order to keep the *Atlas* to a manageable size. For corresponding name variations, synonyms, and names derived from the use of accent marks and hyphens, foreign names given to the tribes by the French and Spanish, and the names given to one tribe by another tribe or by the Federal government, refer to the list of names in Appendix B.

Also included in this section are formal and informal confederacies of tribes and groups based on geography and other select criteria plus those Canadian and Mexican tribes that had a close association with the tribes of the United States and the state and federal governments.

Ethnologists have assigned each tribe and sub-tribe to thirty different language families and some six hundred dialects—about the same number of dialects as their are distinctive tribes. Ethnology has allowed us to identify members of tribal groups, to learn of their migration patterns, and to delve into their history. The classifications, to the extent that they have been determined, are included in the narratives.

———————··········———————

ABENAKI

The Abenaki or Abnaki (People of the Northern Lights or Wababun) were a tribe of the Algonquian linguistic group of the Eastern Woodlands. They inhabited New Hampshire, Vermont, and western Maine, where the main body was located in the valleys of the Kennebec, Androscoggin, and Saco Rivers. They could also be found in Massachusetts, Connecticut, New Brunswick, and southeastern Canada.

At times the name was used to include their neighbors, the Malecite, Penobscot, and Pennacook. The name, which means "those living at the sunrise," was taken as "those leaving at the east" or "easterners." Thus the name was mistakenly used for the Delaware. The Abenaki were also known as the Tarranteens (Tarratines), the name given to them by the early Pilgrims. Swanton lists nine major subdivisions or sub-tribes and thirty villages.

DIVISIONS
- Amaseconti, on Sandy River, Franklin County, Vermont
- Arosaguntacook, on the lower course of Androscoggin River
- Koasek or Cowasuck, Newbury, Vermont, and Haverhill, New Hampshire; earlier about Quebec. Also written as Koasekiak, Coos, Cohass, Koas.
- Part settled with the Pennacook of Massachusetts
- Missiassik or Mazipskwik (the Abenaki word for Missisquoi),
- in the valley of Missisquoi River, Franklin County, Vermont
- Norridgewock, on Kennebec River
- Ossipee, on Ossipee River and Lake in Maine and New Hampshire
- Pequawket or Pigwacket, on Lowell's Pond and the headwaters of Saco River,
- Maine and New Hampshire
- Rocameca, on the upper course of Androscoggin River
- Sokoki, on the Saco River and adjacent parts of Cumberland and York counties
- Wawenoc, on the seacoast of Sagadahoc, Lincoln and Knox counties
- Penobscot, generally considered to be a division or sub-tribe of the Abenaki; commonly treated as a separate, distinct tribe.

Hutchins (1769) listed them as Abenakics located on *Trois-Rivières** in Quebec. Bouquet (1764) listed them as the Abenaquis and classified them as one of the St. Lawrence River Indians along with the Chalas, Michmacs (Micmac), and Amalistes (Ameliste).

ABENAKI WAR

The Treaty of Utrecht in April 1713 ended Queen Anne's War (2nd French and Indian War) but not the lingering animosity between the English colonists and the Indians. Queen Anne's War came on the heels of King Philip's War in which the Abenaki again came out on the loosing side, though never beaten, while absorbing many of those who fled from Cape Cod and the surrounding area to the south.

Abenaki resistance to the continued encroachment of English settlers up the Atlantic coast of Maine and into their homelands in the Connecticut Valley of southern Vermont and New Hampshire broke out in a series of individual battles and skirmishes that became known by several names, including the Abenaki War, Dummer's War, and Lovewell's War, among others. The fighting continued on and off for five from 1721 through 1725. It was not until 1727 that relative peace was finally established. Complicating the situation on the frontier at the time was the uneasy truce between France and England and the all-too-common animosity that existed between French Catholics and New England Protestants. The Abenaki were supported, at least in spirit, by the French in Canada, and in the east they were administered to a Jesuit missionaries, most notably Father Sebastian Rasles.

The Abenaki war operated on two fronts, one to the east and one to the west. There was also an Abenaki element in Canada. Early talks between the two parties were fruitless. The Indians wanted the white men out; the colonists wanted the Indian land. Abenaki chief Gray Lock directed the war in western Massachusetts from his base in the village of Missisquoi, near present-day Swanton, Vermont, on the northern end of Lake Champlain. He successfully conduced raids against English towns in the Connecticut Valley, including Northfield, Hatfield, Deerfield, and Northampton. In an effort to protect their western lands, the Massachusetts government built Fort Dummer in 1724 near what is now Brattleboro, Vermont. The fort did nothing to stop the raiding or bring Gray Lock to task. He continued to elude the soldiers at every turn. Colonial forces never threatened Missisquoi. (William Dummer was the Lieutenant Governor and acting Royal governor at the time. Governor Samuel Shute had gone to London two years earlier to attempt to explain the difficult situation that existed with the Indians in the Massachusetts colony. He did not return.)

To the east in Maine the Abnaki of the Kennebec River region were urged by their Jesuit mentors to resist white settlement and retake their lands. In July of 1722, the Indians destroyed the new settlement at Brunswick and attacked the fort on the lower St. Georges River near present-day Thomaston, but with little success. They followed-up later in the year with attacks on Arrowsic (present-day Georgetown) and renewed attacks on Fort St. George, again with little success. In February 1723, the English burned the Abenaki village on the Penobscot River to the ground, but the Indians had previously fled the area.

Father Rasles was killed, along with fifty to a hundred Indians, in a surprise attack by the English in 1724 that and burned the village Norridgewock on the upper Kennebec River, and his body mutilated—an act which threatened to bring the French Canadians actively into the war. Survivors of Norridgewock fled to Canada. In April 1725, following two relatively successful bounty expeditions in the Winnipiscogee lake region and at Tamworth, New Hampshire, Capt. John Lovewell and his cohorts were met and defeated at Fryeburg Pond, Maine. Among the dead lay Lovewell, one of the several who gave their name to the war.

Beaten down by years of almost continuous fighting, the Penobscot and other eastern groups agreed to peace in 1725 and 1726. The first treaty was signed December15. The Abenaki from Canada made peace in 1727. Gray Lock, who was never defeated, never surrendered nor agreed to terms nor even agreed to negotiate terms. The fighting to the west just stopped, and Gray Lock for all practical purposes disappeared. (In tribute, the citizens of Massachusetts gave his name to the highest peak in the Berkshire Mountains in Massachusetts.)

The death toll over five years for both sides was low, but the results of the Abenaki War were the same as for all other Indian wars—removal.

---

* *Trois-Rivières* (Three Rivers), located about mid-way between Quebec and Montreal, takes its name from the Saint-Maurice River that divides into three island-separated channels before flowing into the St Lawrence River.

MASSACRE AT FORT WILLIAM HENRY

Massacre at Fort William Henry as it is called developed from the siege of the English fort by French troops and their Indian allies during the French and Indian War (1754-1763). Fort William Henry was situated at the southern tip of Lake George, New York (Lac du Saint Sacrement to the French), and was the northern outpost of the British in North America. The next closest British post was Fort Edward on the banks of the upper Hudson River to the southeast. Fort Carillon, located between lakes Champlain and George, was the southernmost outpost of New France. Fort William Henry lay in between. In August 1857 a French force of over 7,000 soldiers and their Indian allies under the command of General Louis-Joseph de Montcalm laid siege to Fort William Henry under the command of Lieutenant Colonel George Monro (spelled Munro in some accounts). Monro had some 2,200 soldiers, but only about 1,600 in any condition to fight. Also within the fort were a number of women and children, families of the soldiers, their servants and a few friendly Indians. Realizing that no reinforcements were forthcoming from Fort Edwards, Monro surrendered on August 8.

In soliciting support from the Abenaki, Ottawa, and Potawatomi Indians, Montcalm had agreed to award the Indians the pillage from the fort following the British withdrawal. On the morning of August 9, the British marched out with all their personal possessions, less their arms, per their agreement with Montcalm. The Indians believed that they had been tricked and lied to and attacked the helpless women and children as well as the sick and wounded soldiers and others who were at the back of the train. They were shot, scalped and bludgeoned to death. The general consensus appears to be that, at least initially, French soldiers did nothing to stop the carnage. Within a very short time it was all over. Accounts of the number of those killed range from a low of 70 to a high of 1500 from contemporary accounts that typically exaggerated the true situation. The number of deaths most likely actually fell between 180 and 200. A number of women and children were also taken captive, but most were later rescued by the French. After the French soldiers escorted the survivors to safety at Fort Edwards, they returned to Fort William Henry and burned it to the ground. The battle, and slaughter that followed, was one of the most well-known but ugliest blotches of the decade-long war for supremacy in America. The incident was repeatedly used to dramatize the savagery of the Indian race as justification for seizing their lands. (Of the soldiers scalped, a number were sick with smallpox, which quickly spread among the Indians.)

Of Note

The events at Fort William Henry were made famous by James Fenimore Cooper's 1827 novel *The Last of the Mohicans* and the subsequent movie.

FRENCH AND INDIAN WARS

First French & Indian War

The 1st French & Indian War or King William's War ranged from 1688-1699. In Europe it was known as St Castin's War of the League of Augsburg and the War of the Grand Alliance.

Second French & Indian War

The 2nd French & Indian War or Queen Anne's War raged from 1702-1713. In Europe it was known as the War of the Spanish Succession. The Treaty of Utrecht or Peace of Utrecht was signed in the Netherlands in April 1713 ending the war. France gave up most of Acadia (modern Nova Scotia and New Brunswick), but not Cape Breton (renamed Île Royale), and Newfoundland. They retained several islands and the St. Lawrence Peninsula and the St. Lawrence River. In Europe, France was forced from Spanish Netherlands; and England acquired Gibraltar and Minorca and the island of St. Kitt's in the West Indies. The French also recognized the British claim to the Hudson Bay territory.

Third French & Indian War

The 3rd French & Indian War or King George's War or Governor Shirley's War raged from 1744-1749. In Europe it was known as the War of the Austrian Succession.

Fourth French & Indian War

The war most commonly known as the French & Indian War raged in Europe and American from 1754-1763. It was actually the Fourth French & Indian War. In Europe it was known as the Seven Years' War. Following the Seven Years War, the Treaty of Paris or Treaty of Peace (February 10, 1763) ceded all French lands and all claims to lands east of the Mississippi to the British, namely what would become West Florida. Prior to beginning negotiations with Britain, France had secretly signed the Treaty of Fontainebleau (November 3, 1762) that ceded all French lands west of the Mississippi to Spain. The Treaty of Paris affirmed the provisions of the Treaty of Fontainebleau and recognized the boundaries of the British as extending west to the Mississippi and north to the Canada border. In addition, Spain, France's ally in the war, relinquished her claims to Florida (East Florida). (With the Treaty of San Ildefonso October 1, 1800, Spain transferred the vast territory west of the Mississippi back to France in what was termed a retrocession.)

On taking possession of Florida, Britain created two colonies, East Florida and West Florida. East Florida included the peninsula and the land along the coast to the western border of present-day Georgia. The colony or province of West Florida included the territory along the Gulf Coast from the Chattahoochee/Apalachicola River westward to the Mississippi River and the border with Louisiana. Shortly thereafter Britain arbitrarily moved the northern boundary of West Florida to a line running from the mouth of the Yazoo River about thirty miles north of Jackson, Mississippi, east to the Chattahoochee, incorporating roughly half of the present states of Mississippi and Alabama into West Florida.

ABIHKA

The Abihka was a sub-tribe or subdivision of the Muskogee and a member of the Creek Confederacy. They constituted the Coosa or Abihka branch of the Upper Creeks that inhabited the area along the Coosa River of Alabama.

ABÓ PUEBLO

The Abó Pueblo belonged to the Tompiro group. It was situated east of the Los Pinos mountain chain in New Mexico. Abó was reportedly first occupied around the year 1300. It is believed that the Spanish mission was built sometime around 1620. It has been abandoned now for over three hundred years, dating back to the 1670s. The Abó Pueblo, Grand Quivira Pueblo, and Quarai Pueblo now comprise the Salinas Pueblo Missions National Monument.

ABOTIREITSU

Abotireitsu was a subdivision of the Shasta that lived in Shasta Valley in California. For more see Shasta

ACCOCESAW

The Accocesaw principal location was on the west side of the Colorado River about 200 miles southwest of Nacogdoches, Texas. Earlier they had lived near the gulf of Mexico. Fish and oysters were main staples. Their language was apparently unique to them. At one time around 1750 they were served by a Spanish Mission that later moved to Nacogdoches.

ACCOHANOC

Accohanoc was a member of the Powhatan Confederacy and inhabited parts of Accomac and Northampton counties in Virginia and into Maryland.

ACCOMAC

The Accomac belonged to the Algonquian linguistic group and inhabited the southern parts of present Northampton County, Virginia, principally about Cheriton on Cherrystone Inlet. (Parts of the Nanticoke inhabited present Accomac County on the eastern shore of the Chesapeake.) Present in very small numbers with the arrival of the first Europeans in 1607, there was no reference to them in the 1669 Virginia census of Indian tribes.

Shoolcraft classifies the Accomac as a sub-tribe of the Nanticoke of Maryland. Swanton classifies them as a subdivision of the Powhatan of Virginia and makes no reference to the Nanticoke. Both write of the village in Northhampton County and their listing in Jefferson's enumeration of 1801.

ACHOMAWI

Part of the large Hokan family of the tribes, the Achomawi inhabited the area from around the juncture of the Pit River and Montgomery Creek in Shasta County, California, to Goose Lake on the Oregon border. They were also known as the Pit River Indians and the River People. They were very closely related to the Atsugewi.

ACOLAPISSA

The Acolapissa belonged to the Muskhogean linguistic group. They originally lived on the Pearl River about 11 miles above its mouth in Louisiana. They moved just after the turn of the century and settled on the north side of Lake Pontchartrain on present Bayou Castine (Castembayouque). Some ten to fifteen years later they moved to the east side of the Mississippi River and settled upriver about thirty-five miles from of New Orleans. Around 1722 their homelands on the Pearl River were occupied by the Biloxi.

By 1739 the Acolapissa, the Houma, and the Bayogoula formed what was in effect one settlement. Later members of the three tribes merged together and enjoyed the same fate. For more see Houma.

ACOMA PUEBLO

Acoma (Ako-me) or Anacona were of the Western (Sitsime or Kawaiko) dialectic group of the Keresan or Keres linguistic stock with the Laguna. At one time they numbered about 6,000 persons who inhabited a number of villages spread over several acres of west-central New Mexico sixty miles west of the Rio Grande River. The Acoma Pueblo dates to before the twelfth century. It sits on a mesa 357 feet high with a commanding view of the countryside of Valencia County. Accordingly, it was called Sky City. The Hopi villages of Walpi and Oraibi and Acoma's Sky City are reportedly the three oldest continuously inhabited towns in the United States. The name means People of the White Rock.

Spanish explorer and the first governor of New Mexico, Juan de Oñate, defeated the Indians of the Acoma Pueblo in the winter of 1598-1599 in what is sometimes referred to as the Acoma Indian War that is more misnomer than fact. The killings that took place on January 22 and 23. The battle came in retribution for the what is generally considered the unprovoked killing of one of Oñate's lieutenants (Zutacapán) and twelve members of his party in early December. Although utterly defeated the Acoma refused to surrender. In the end, according to the official count, 600 to 800 Acoma were killed. The Spanish took another seventy to eighty warriors captive along with 500 women and children. In February, the Acoma were tried before a Spanish court. Men over the age of 25 had their right foot cut off and given twenty years of slavery. Men and women over the age of twelve were also sent into slavery for twenty years. Children under twelve were assigned as servants v. slaves to Spanish families, of which sixty girls ended up in slavery in Mexico.

No riches were found in the new Spanish colony of Nuevo México, and day-to-day existence remained harsh for both Indians and Spaniards alike. Although Oñate led historical explorations to the coast and to lands of Quivera, his administration was fraught to failure. He resigned under pressure in 1607 and returned to Mexico City two years later where he was tried and convicted of lying to authorities in his reports and the brutal treatment of the Indians of Acoma, among other crimes of omission and commission. He was fined, stripped of his title, and shunted aside to die a lonely death in Spain.

In 1629, thirty years after Oñate had handed down his sentence, the Indians of Acoma were allowed to begin rebuilding their pueblo. Today six thousand Acoma live in several villages on a 400,000 acre reservation, principally Acomita, McCarty, and Anzac. Less than fifty people live in Sky City.

The Acoma pueblo is the home of the Franciscan mission church of San Estevan del Rey (Saint Stephan) that was established in 1629 on the south edge of the mesa. The church, with its twin bell towers, was constructed of adobe brick under the direction of Fray Juan Ramírez. Construction began immediately when the Acomas were allowed back on their pueblo. It took eleven years to complete. For some inexplicable reason, the church of San Estevan survived the wholesale destruction of Catholic churches by the Indians during the Pueblo Revolt of 1680. The two resident Franciscan priests, however, were hurled to their deaths. The feast of San Estevan continues to be celebrated annually on September 2 to this day.

In the years of reconquest from 1692-1699, Acoma served as a refuge for those that escaped the fighting to the east, including those from Santo Domingo, Jemez, and Cochiti. Differences over religion, culture, and politics led a group of Indians to secede from the pueblo and form a new, separate and distinct pueblo, Laguna, fourteen miles to the northeast. By the end of the first decade of the 1700s, both Laguna had a population of somewhat less than 350, about half that of Acoma.

ACOPSELES

The Acopseles was listed by Farther Ortiz in his memorial to the king of Spain sometime after February 14, 1747, cited by Bolton in "Missions on the San Gabriel," but no additional information about the tribe is known. It was most likely a band or village or possibly a variation in the spelling of an unknown tribal name.

ACQUINTANACSUAK

The Acquintanacsuak was one of the nine divisions of the Conoy and lived on the west bank of the Patuxent River in St. Marys County, Maryland. For more see Conoy Peoples.

ACUERA

The Acuera were of the Timucuan or Timuquanan division of the Muskhogean linguistic group and inhabited the area about the headwaters of the Ocklawaha River in Florida. They were first noted by De Soto and later in French journals, but by the mid-1700s they had lost their identity.

ACURAG-NA

Acurag-na or Akura-nga was a sub-tribe of the Tongva of California that inhabited the area about La Presa. For more see Tongva.

ADAES

The Adaes (Atais, Atayos, or Adai—used by Swanton) was an independent Caddoan tribe with a divergent dialect. They constituted one of the five major groups of the Caddo Peoples. The tribe lived about the Red River north of present Natchitoches, Louisiana. Pierre le Moyne d'Iberville, in 1699, called them Natao—a variant recognized by Swanton. The San Miguel de Linares de los Adaes Mission was established for them in 1716. It was destroyed in 1719 and restored in 1721. The Adaes were also found at San Francisco de los Tejas Mission. Swanton suggests that they appeared to have had a more primitive culture than the other Caddoan tribes of the area.

The Adaes, under the name Atai, was listed by Farther Ortiz in his memorial to the king of Spain sometime after February 14, 1747. For more see the Caddo Peoples.

ADERO

The Adero (Ardeco) is listed in the journal of La Harpe's expedition in Oklahoma in 1719, but no additional information has become available.

ADIRONDAK

The Indians who lived on north banks of the St. Lawrence in French Canada during the latter part of the 16th century were called the Adirondak or Adirondack by the Iroquois (Mohawk). The French called them Algonquin. The first definitive record was in 1724 by the Jesuit missionary Father Joseph-François Lafitau who called the Indians "Rontaks" although there were references to the Indians in Dutch writings a century prior. (The Adirondack mountain range is in the northeastern part of New York State.)

AFFAGOULA

The Affagoula was a small village of Indians in Louisiana that lived near Point Coupe on the Mississippi River in the late 1700s.

AGAIDEKA SHOSHONI

The Agaideka (Agaidika, Agaid ika) or Salmon Eaters were a subgroup of the Northen Shoshoni that have often been treated separately. They lived about the principal spawning grounds of the Salmon River. For more see the Shoshoni.

AGAWOM

The Agawom was a tribe of southern New England near Wareham, a subdivision or village of the Wampanoag that is treated separately in the literature. For more see Wampanoag.

AHANTCHUYUK KALAPUYA

The Ahantchuyuk were also called the Pudding River Indians and the French Prairie Indians. They belonged to the Kaloapooian linguistic stock and inhabited the area of the Pudding River, a tributary of the Molalla River in western Oregon, near Aurora where it flows through the lower Willamette Valley. For more see Kalapuya Peoples.

AHTENA

The Ahtena or Copper River Indians belonged to the Athapascan linguistic group of Indians of Alaska. They lived in the basin of the Copper River. The Ahtena are included in this section because the synonym Copper River is often mistaken for one of the tribes of the lower forty-eight.

AIONAI

The Aionai was listed in the preamble of the Treaty of May 15, 1846, that was signed at Council Springs in the county of Robinson, Texas, near the Brazos River, and in Kappler, "Revised Spelling of Names." The tribe is not included in signature section of the treaty. No other information is known.

AIS

Possibly of Muskhogean stock and related to the Calusa, Ais was a small tribe that lived along the Indian River on the east coast of Florida, whence the name of the river. They disappeared from history towards the beginning of the eighteenth century, most probably absorbed into the Calusa. Generally speaking, by 1763 when Florida passed from the Spanish into the hands of the English, the original aboriginal life in Florida had all but disappeared.

AKAITCHI

It is believed that the Akaitchi was a band or sub-tribe of one of the Plateau tribes of southeast Washington and northeast Oregon that belonged to the Shahaptian linguistic family.

AKAWANTCA'KA

Akawantca'ka was one of the three tribes or subdivisions of the Tuscarora confederacy.

AKOKISA

The Akokisa was the name given to the Atákapa that inhabited the coastal regions of East Texas but whose speech was identical to the Atákapa of Lake Charles and distinctly different from that of the Eastern Atákapa. They are generally treated separately.

ALABAMA

One of the Upper Creek tribes of the Creek Confederacy, the Alabama (Alibamu) originally inhabited the upper course of the Alabama River. With the movement of the southeast tribes following the end of the French and Indian War in 1763, some headed west into Louisiana and settled along the Mississippi before moving inland into Calcasieu and St. Landry Parishes and then on to present Polk County, Texas, where they were joined by members of the Kosati (Cosshatte). A few ventured into Florida and joined the Seminole; others accompanied the Kosati to the Tombigbee River before returning to their homeland.

All those who remained in Alabama participated in the Creek-American War in 1813 and suffered accordingly. With the Treaty of Fort Jackson (1814), the Alabama were removed to Indian Territory along with the rest of the Creeks. Those that migrated into Texas and joined with the Koasati have since been referred to as the Alabama-Coushatta. See the Koasati.

People of the eastern tribes who fled to the southwest and settled in the fertile lands of East Texas soon found themselves at the mercy of the Anglos who had supplanted first the Spanish and then the Mexicans. In the late 1830s, the crops and villages of peaceful eastern tribes, the "rats' nest" of east Texas as they called, were burned out by the Republic of Texas and driven from the land. Those that attempted to flee to Mexico were caught and brought back. A few escaped into the Plains. Considered too small to be of concern, only the Alabama-Coushatta were permitted to remain in east Texas but were removed to less fertile lands.

ALBIVI

The Albivi was one of the minor tribes of the Illinois Cluster of tribes for which there is only passing mention. For more see Illinois Cluster.

ALEUPKIG-NA

Aleupkig-na was a sub-tribe of the Tongva of California that inhabited the area about Santa Anita. For more see Tongva.

ALGONQUIN

There is an ongoing controversy whether there was an Algonquin tribe or whether the name was used solely to identify the members of the Algonquian linguistic group. The weight of reason, as well as the testimony of their descendants, support the presence of a distinct Algonquin tribe.

In the October 2004, the editors of AAA Native Arts were quite emphatic in response to a question from their readers: "Algonquin (or Algonkin) is often used in reference to a tribe. However, Algonquin is not a tribe, it is a language group." Swanton lists an Algonkin tribe of Canada that lived on the northern tributaries of the Ottawa River, but otherwise does not embroil himself in the controversy specifically. He identifies them as the easternmost group of the Chippewa, who were of the Algonquian linguistic stock. It appears reasonable to this author to conclude that Swanton's Algonkin (and Drake's) was the Algonquin proper.

Random House describes the Algonkin as a member of a group of North American Indian tribes of the Ojibwa dialect of the Algonquian linguistic group, who lived along the Ottawa River and the tributaries of the St. Lawrence.

In geological time, Algonkian identifies the period from 600,000,000 to 1,000,000,000 years ago.

ALGONQUIN GROUP

The Algonquin tribes were members of the Algonquian (Algonkian) linguistic family or language group. Their territory ranged from Virginia along the Atlantic coast north through New England and into Nova

Scotia and New Brunswick and west across Lake Huron and Lake Superior and down the western shore of Lake Michigan through Illinois, Michigan, Ohio, and parts of Kentucky. With many dialects, It was the largest native language group in North America.

ALGONQUIAN LINGUISTIC GROUP

Abenaki	Menominee	Nipmuc
Arapaho	Miami	Ojibwa
Blackfoot	Micmac	Ottawa
Cheyenne	Mohegan	Pequot
Cree	Mohican	Piscataway
Delaware	Montagnais	Sac
Fox	Montauketts	Shawnee
Gros Ventres of the River	Munsee	Tête de Boule
Kickapoo	Narragansett	Wampanoag
Maliseet	Naskapi	
Massachuset	Nauset	

King Philip's War (for chief Metacom of the Wampanoag) effectively brought Algonquin power in the Northeast to an end.

ALLAKAWEAH

The name Allakaweah (Al-la-ká'-we-áh or Paunch Indians) was used by Lewis and Clark to identify a tribe located on Yellowstone and Bighorn rivers in Montana, with 800 warriors and 2,300 souls. It is quite probably that the Allakaweah was a band of the Crow whom the Hidatsa referred to as the "people who refused the paunch."

ALLIKLIK

Located on the Santa Clara River in California, the Alliklik belonged to the Shoshonean division of the Uto-Aztecan linguistic stock that included the Kitanemuk, Vanyume, Kawaiisu, and Serrano.

ALSEA

The Alsea (also, Alsé or Alsi) belonged to the Yakonan linguistic stock that is sometimes referred to as the Alsean group. "Alsi" was the Alsea name for peace. Others of the group that lived along the rivers of the central Oregon coast were, from north to south, the Yaquina on the Yaquina River near present-day Newport, the Alsea, the Siuslaw on the Siuslaw River near Florence, and the Kuitsh or Lower Umpqua on the lower Umpqua River near Reedsport. The Siuslaw spoke a dialect that was considerably different from the others of the group. The Alsea, inhabited the area around what is now known as the Alsea River and Alsea Bay—in their language, the Wusi River. The Alsea are believed to have had as many as twenty villages along the Alsea River and the coast from Seal Rock to Ten Mile Creek, nine north of the main village and eleven to the south. They were used on a rotating basis during the year. The Yackats are believed to have been a semi-autonomous band of the Alsea to the south.

The Alsean group is believed to have numbered about 5,000 in the late eighteenth century. As all Native American peoples, they soon suffered the rages of decease and depravations hurled at them by the white man in the form of settlers and miners. More were lost to the Rogue River wars of the 1850s. Remnants were placed on the Alsean Sub-Agency where many died from lack starvation and disease and then later to the Siletz Reservation. The 1910 census put the total for the group less than one hundred. They were subsequently organized as the Confederated Siletz Indians of Oregon.

ALTAMAHA

The Altamaha was a sub-tribe (one of the Lower Towns) of the Yamasee that is sometimes treated separately in the literature. Its location in Georgia is unknown, but the "Province of Altamaha" was mentioned by Ranjel, the chronicler of De Soto, in 1540. For more see the Yamasee.

AMACANO

The Amacano was a band or possibly a village in Florida that may have been connected with the Yamasee of the early Spanish period. Language-wise they were likely of the southern division of the Muskhogean stock. They were placed on the Spanish mission of San Luis on the Apalachee coast in 1674 with the Camparaz and Chine—together all three numbered only about three hundred people.

AMAHAMI

Amahami or Mahaha inhabited the south bank of the Knife River along the Middle Missouri in North Dakota adjoining the Metaharta. They were very closely related in language and culture to the Hidatsa to the extent that their village is generally considered a village of the Hidatsa; however they are frequently treated separately in the literature because they maintained an independent tribal structure. They are found in the literature under a number of names, in addition to Mahaha, including the Anahaway or Ahnahaway and Ahwahaway. The Amahami village was destroyed by a Sioux raiding party in 1834. For more see the Hidatsa and Metaharta.

AMASECONTI

The Amaseconti was a subdivision of the Abnaki. They lived on Sandy River, Franklin County. Villages were located at Farmington Falls and New Sharon. For more see Abenaki.

AMELISTE

The Ameliste or Amaliste was an Algonquian tribe listed in Jefferson's *Notes on the State of Virginia*. They lived on the St. Lawrence River and had a reported population of 550 warriors. For more see "Aborigines," Appendix D.

AMIMENIPATY

The Amimenipaty was a sub-tribe of the Unalachtigo division of the Delaware. They lived near Edgemoor, Delaware. For more see Unalachtigo and Delaware.

AMONOKOA

The Amonokoa was one of the minor tribes of the Illinois Cluster of Tribes for which there is only passing mention. For more see Illinois Cluster.

ANADARKO

The Anadarko was one of the thirteen principal tribes of the southwestern or Hasinai Division of the Caddo Indians or Hasinai Confederacy. The Anadarko lived northwest of Nacogdoches in Rusk County, Texas. For more see Hasinai Confederacy and Caddo Peoples.

ANASAZI

Anasazi, the ancient ones, was a proto-civilization of a thousand years hence that left ruins and potsherds scattered across the desert country of the southern Colorado Plateau and the upper Rio Grande drainage area of northeastern Arizona, northwestern New Mexico, southeastern Utah and southwestern Colorado.

Before AD 500, Anasazi Basketmaker groups took shelter in caves and rock overhangs within canyon walls. Between 500 and 600 they began to make and use pottery. The Anasazi Pueblo peoples took their place about 700 and gave rise to the "Chaco Phenomenon" around a ten-mile segment of northwestern New Mexico's Chaco Canyon. Over time their villages became ever larger and more permanent and set in clusters around plazas. From semi-subterranean kivas, they advanced to masonry surface structures which continued to increase in size and complexity.

By the middle of the 12th century, the Chaco population scattered throughout the region, probably in a series of migrations. One of the last know sites was located on the banks of Animas River, a few miles below the Colorado border.

Another group, the San Juan/Mesa Verde people, occupied southeastern Utah and southwestern Colorado building small scattered pueblos on mesa tops and talus slopes. Beginning in the 13th century, they built pueblos with strangely shaped towers at the heads of canyons in Utah and "cliff dwellings" in the great stone alcoves of Mesa Verde. By the late 13th century, the Mesa Verde system collapsed, and the population migrated to new areas. The Kayaenta branch of the Anasazi, who inhabited northern Arizona into southern Utah and southeastern Nevada, also dispersed in the late thirteenth century.

Immigrants from the declining Chaco and Kayenta regions apparently migrated south and settled the Hopi villages in northeastern Arizona and the Zuni, Acoma and Laguna villages in west-central New Mexico. Others from Chaco and Mesa Verde went east of Chaco Canyon to the area of the upper Rio Grande drainage and were responsible for pueblos of northwestern Arizona and western New Mexico. They not only survived but continued to increase in population and were there to greet the Spanish expeditions into the Southwest in the 16th century.

ANASITCH

The Anasitch, also called Cookkoo-oose, was a tribe of the Kusan linguistic family (Coast Oregon Penutian). They lived on the south side of Coos Bay in western Oregon. The Kusan and Yakonan tribes were placed on the Siletz Reservation in Oregon. For more see Coos.

ANATHAGUA

The Anathagua (Anatagu) was listed by Farther Ortiz in his memorial to the king of Spain sometime after February 14, 1747, cited by Bolton in "Missions on the San Gabriel," but no additional information about the tribe is known. It is believed that the Anathagua lived in east central or southeastern Texas. It was most likely a little known band or village or a variation in the spelling of a name.

Campbell suggests that it is possible that the Anathaguas were the same as the Quanataguos that Swanton places in the Coahuiltecan group. (Swanton makes no reference to the Anathagua.) The Quanataguos were reported at San Antonio de Valero Mission at San Antonio in the 1720s. If the Pastates are same as the Postito Indians, that would place two Coahuiltecans tribes in Father Orgiz's list. Campbell also notes that the Anathagua bear some resemblance to Quiutcanuaha.

The Four Corners Institute lists the Anathagua in the Coahuiltecan linguistic family, but no additional information is provided.

ANCHOSE

The Anchoses was listed by Farther Ortiz in his memorial to the king of Spain sometime after February 14, 1747, cited by Bolton in "Missions on the San Gabriel," but no additional information about the tribe has become available. It is believed that the Anchose lived in east central or southeastern Texas.

APACHE

The name Apache (uh-pach'-ee) may have come from the Yuma word for "fighting men" or a Zuni (Puebloan) term Apachu meaning "enemy" that was applied to the Navaho. A number of over derivatives have also been suggested. As was common among Native tribes, the Apache called themselves Tin-ne-áh: "The People" or the common variant, Indé.

Major General George Crook, who spent eight years trying to subdue the Apaches, wrote that "the greed and rapacity of the vultures who fatten on Indian wars have been a greater obstruction in the path of civilization than the ferocity of the wildest savages who have fought them."

The Apache belonged to the southern branch of the Athapascan linguistic family. (Alaska is the homeland of the Athapascan Indian proper.) The several branches of the family located throughout the southwest all went by different names and dialectical variations, as Tindé and N'de (Nde) and Dinë. It is also quite probable that the same tribes went by different names, depending on the locale. The Dinë became better known to the white man's world as the Navaho. The name Apache has also been applied to unrelated Yuman tribes, the Apache-Mojave (Yavapai) and Apache-Yuma.

It is believed that the Apache migrated into the Southwest and the Southern Plains from Canada and Northwest along the eastern slope of the Rockies between 1000 and 1400.

Some of the smaller bands of the Athapascan that moved south stopped and spread out into western Nebraska, western Kansas, and eastern Colorado. The French referred to those of Kansas and Nebraska as the Padouca. At some point in the trek south, either in eastern Colorado or northeastern New Mexico, the branch of the Athapascan that came to be known as the Navajo broke off and headed west-southwest while the others continued south. They remained forever separated from their Athapascan relatives and have always been regarded as a separate tribe and are treated separately by historians.

It was the four survivors of the 1528 expedition of Pánfilo de Narváez, led by Núnez Cabeza de Vaca, who were the first Old World people to encounter the Apache. It was in the autumn of 1535 in the plains of west Texas. Six years later in the summer of 1541 the nomads of the prairie encountered the people of the Old World for the second time. This time it was an advance contingent of the expedition of Francisco Vásquez de Coronado in the Texas Panhandle—perhaps, Terrell writes, in Tule Canyon. The name Apache, referring to the Plains Apache, appears to have first been used in the official records by Don Juan de Oñate around 1598 as he took an expedition of Spanish soldiers into the Rio Grande valley to subjugate the Pueblo.

By the late 1600s the Apaches were a powerful people, raiding their Spanish and the Native American neighbors, particularly the Pueblo, with impunity. Their aggressive behavior naturally created enemies. By 1700, the Apaches were being pushed further south and west into New Mexico, Arizona and Texas by the Comanche, the Wichita, and others. Those that moved into Central Texas and Northern Mexico collided with the Spanish. The Spanish mounted several expeditions against the Apache in the early seventeen hundreds, principally the Faraon—all mostly ineffective. The Spanish in New Mexico were being hit on all four sides at once—from the south by the Western Apache, from the west by the Navaho, from the north by the Ute and Comanche, and from the east by the Lipan, Faraon, other Plains Apache.

All the southern Athapascan were a nomadic people until around the 1700. The Apache in general lived almost exclusively off hunting, primarily deer and antelope. They became early masters of the horse, but were not committed to the horse as were many of the other tribes: and, in general, they were able to better maintain their cultural purity. Their measured attachment to the horse allowed them greater flexibility in meeting the horse-borne calvary of the U.S. government. Off the horse and in the rocks, the fight was one-on-one.

By the mid-1700s, the Lipan and others had been almost destroyed first by the combined raids of the Ute and the Comanche and later by combined strength of the Comanche, Kiowa, and Kiowa-Apache. Those that survived were driven either south into the far reaches of Texas or west to join the Western Apache. When the Spanish began to see the Comanche as their real enemy, they asked for help from the Lipan, which they gladly provided, all to no avail. Later the Americans would use the Comanche against the Apache.

Those Native Americans that we recognize today as Apaches were divided into two major groups or divisions, the Eastern or Plains Apache and the Western Apache, separated for the most part by the Rio Grande running down the heart of present-day New Mexico.

Terrell lists twenty-two identifiable tribes or bands of the Eastern group of Apaches that occupied the Plains from Nebraska to Texas. One of the tribes was the Gattacka that became better known but misnamed as the Kiowa-Apache that initially ranged north of the Padouca in Nebraska.

The Plains Apache included the Jicarilla or Prairie Apache and the Lipan. The Jicarilla was a large group that ranged through the prairie and grasslands from central Colorado around the Arkansas River south across the eastern part of the Colorado-New Mexico border and into northern New Mexico as well as parts of western Oklahoma and the panhandle of Texas. The Jicarilla ranged with the Kiowa and later formed an alliance with the Ute. After almost being destroyed as a viable entity in 1750, the Jicarillas grew stronger and attacked settlers and travelers across the Plains for the next hundred year. Those around the Arkansas were hit with a smallpox epidemic in the winter of 1854-1854. The Lipan, also a relatively large group, ranged from eastern New Mexico into Texas and southeast as far as San Antonio. They are almost exclusively treated as a separate tribe. (The Kiowa-Apache and the Lipan are treated separately in this work.)

The Western group included the Chiricahua; the Mescalero; and multiple bands of the San Carlos or Gileño, the White Mountain, the Tonto, and the Cibicue that were grouped together under the name Western Apaches—leading to still greater confusion. The Chiricahua lands included southwestern New Mexico and southeastern Arizona and across the border into Mexico. They were comprised of three bands: the Nde-nda-i or Nednhi (actually a sub-band); the Tci-he-nde Mimbre or Chihenne; and the Tsoka-ne-nde or Chokonen. To their east across New Mexico were the Mescalero.

The Mescalero ranged throughout southeastern New Mexico and across the border to the southeast into Texas. In 1811, the Spanish were preoccupied with the Mexican War of Independence; and as a consequence the Mescalero (and the Lipan) raided into both Texas and Mexico with impunity.

The tribes and bands referred to as Western Apache of the Western group inhabited an arc with its apex on the Arizona-New Mexico border and stretching northwest to near present-day Prescott and southwest to Tucson, generally northwest of the Chiricahua. The Navajo inhabited northeast Arizona and northwest New Mexico. The Spanish names Querecho, Vaquero, and Llanero were often applied to the Apache in general. Their camps or villages were referred to as rancherias.

Among the noted leaders of the Apaches were Cochise of the Tsoka-ne-nde Chiricahua, the one they called the Great Chief; Mangas Coloradas and Victorio of the Tci-he-nde Mimbre; Diablo (Heske-hldasila) of the White Mountain Apache; Chato of the Chiricahua, who subsequently joined the Apache Scouts and worked for the government; Juh and Gerónimo of the Nde-nda-i Chiricahua.

THE 1850s

The eighteen fifties were arguably the most eventful years for the Apache in terms of their relations with the Mexicans and the Anglos. Politics and international relations were also potent elements during this period and served to exacerbate a difficult situation. The following events set the stage.

In 1836 Texas declared its independence from Mexico.

On December 29, 1845, Texas officially became the twenty-eighth state. On February 19, 1846, the flag of the Texas Republic was hauled down, but the boundary dispute with Mexico continued. With Texas statehood, the Federal government assumed responsibility for Indian relations.

On May 13, 1846, President Polk signed the bill that officially declared a state of war with Mexico.

On February 2, 1848, the Treaty of Guadalupe-Hidalgo was signed ending the war with Mexico. (See more below)

On August 9, 1850, the bill was passed in Congress that set the Texas boundary with New Mexico Territory. As a result, one-third of New Mexico was surrendered to Texas. September 7 and 9 produced the last votes on the bills creating New Mexico Territory and the Utah Territory.

On June 30, 1854, President Pierce executed the Gadsden Treaty with Mexico by which the United States purchased an area of approximately 30,000 square miles in northern Mexico. (See more below)

At this time the land of the Mexican Cession held some 40,000 American Indians belonging to a number of different tribes out of a total population of about 100,000. The principal tribes included 2,000 Utes; 10,000-12,000 Navajos; and 6,000-8,000 Apache. Also during these years, an administrative battle raged in Washington over which department should manage the Native population, the War Department or the Interior Department.

For the Apache the decade of the fifties was a time of small victories, numerous defeats, depravation, and starvation. Raids and atrocities continued on by sides. Raids into Mexico were the stock of the Chiricahuas along the Continental Divide and the Western Apache proper, most notably the White Mountain Apache. The white man's diseases and alcohol, particularly among the Jicarillas, also took a heavy toll. Men died, peace treaties were signed, and reservation lands were set aside. It was also during these years that the Apache seriously turned to the soil for the first time. Surprisingly, the Mangas Mimbre were the most successful. For the most part the Apache benefited from hard-working, conscientious, and dedicated Indian agents, most notably James S. Calhoun, Michael Steck.

By 1850, the raids had become more and more deadly in response to the increasing white encroachment on the Indian lands. More significant was the attitude of the white man who enveloped the area. Elsewhere, as the Indians were pushed across the country from east to west and west to east, the attitude of the white man had generally been, "anywhere but here." In the lands of the Apache, however, as it was in adjoining California, the white man's goal for the most part was extermination of the Indian race. The intensity of the relations between the white settlers and the Indians continued to escalate throughout the decade of the fifties.

James S. Calhoun, governor of New Mexico territory and superintendent of Indian Affairs, negotiated the first peace treaty with the Apaches in April 1851. The treaty was made with Francisco Chacón of the Jicarillas. Calhoun also signed treaties with Lobo and Josecito of the Mescalero. These treaties were never approved by Congress; but Calhoun, on his own authority and from his own operating funds, provided goods and supplies to the tribes. Throughout their history, the Apaches were signatories of very few treaties compared to other Native American tribes.

The first approved peace treaty was signed by seven Chiefs and headmen, including Mangas Coloradas, at Santa Fe on July 1, 1852. In accepting the treaty, the chiefs acknowledged the authority of the United States government; agreed to end all hostilities; agreed to desist from making unlawful incursions of a into and Mexico; and granted the people of the United States free and safe passage through their lands. The boundaries of their lands, however, were not specified; only that the government would designate their territorial boundaries sometime in the future at the government's convenience. In a letter of July 31, 1852, John Greiner, who succeeded Calhoun, wrote that scarcely a complaint had been lodged against the Indians and that people would be unmolested if the people of New Mexico would leave them to lead their lives, but that was not to be.

Raids, particularly into Sonora, Mexico but elsewhere as well, were a way of life for the Apache. The raids were not vicious nor especially violent. In another time might simply be called stealing. They stole to survive in a harsh land. Their only other means were farming and hunting. Only a small percentage of the land was suitable to farming, and even there the annual water supply was far from reliable. Hunting also was limited. There were not the thousands upon thousands of deer and antelope as there were the buffalo of the plains. And, as the Mexican-American populations grew, the range became ever smaller and smaller. Cochise came to prominence among the Tsoka-ne-nde Chiricahua, who are most often simply referred to in the literature as the Chiricahua, in the early 1850s. By the beginning of the sixties, Cochise became inflamed by what he considered acts of deceit and treachery inflicted on his people, especially his family, at the hands of the whites.

APACHE WARS

The series of Apache Wars erupted in 1861 following the death of Cochise's brother, Coyuntura. (Coyuntura was tricked into giving himself and then held pending the release of a young boy that had been capture earlier by Apaches. Cochise did not have the boy but took captives to trade for his brother. Coyuntura was hanged by the soldiers after Cochise allowed the captives to kill and mutilate the bodies of the four captives.) Cochise's war raged across both Northern Mexico and Arizona and continued for ten years. Throughout 1861 and 1862, he joined forces with his father-in-law, Mangas Coloradas; but in 1863 Mangas was tricked into attending a parley and executed gangland style by his guards—the grievest of wrongs in Cochise's eyes, testifying to the morality of the white man and intensifying Cochise's hatred for all whites. Later he often rode with Victorio, Nana, Gerónimo, Juh, and Francisco of the White Mountain.

Although Cochise is often portrayed as a man wronged and a man of peace, his peace was as often as not a peace of strategic convenience, not attitude. He sought peace from Sonora to have an outlet for goods taken from Chihuahua and vice versa, and he sought an early peace with the Americans lest he be called to fight both Mexicans and Americans at the same time. Even later during peace negotiations with the Americans regarding a suitable site for a reservation, one of the factors utmost in his mind was "a place to quietly dispose of plunder brought back from Mexico." It was not until 1872 following negotiations with President Grant's special envoy General Oliver Otis Howard that Cochise finally agreed to peace.

Under the agreement reached on October 12, 1872, at Dragoon Springs in the Dragoon Mountains, Cochise's favorite hideaway, Howard agreed to Cochise's request for a Chiricahua reservation in southeastern Arizona. in their home lands. Cochise's trusted blood brother, Tom Jeffords, was to be made the agent. President Grant confirmed the terms in an executive order of December 14. Cochise kept the treaty and maintained the peace until his death. The Great Chief died June 8, 1874, after a protracted illness. His body was taken into the mountains where it was walled up in one of the crevices at the foot of the western face of Signal Peak. The hidden burial place has never been discovered.

This was Howard's second peace mission. The first began in the early months of 1872, following the massacre at Camp Grant. He was the second peace envoy sent into the region. The first was Vincent Colyer from the Department of Indian Affairs. Colyer established interim reservations at Camp Apache, McDowell, Verde, Date Creek and Beale Springs in addition to the irregular activities at Camp Grant. The agencies continued to serve the needs of the Indian population for many years. Colyer also held successful councils with the Pimas at Camp McDowell and the Yavapai at Camp Verde.

An army lieutenant, Charles Drew, had helped set the stage for Coyler's success with the Tci-he-nde Mimbre. By 1870 some five hundred Mimbre under Victorio, Nanna, and Loco had come in to Drew's agency at Ojo Caliente (sometimes translated as Hot Springs; other times as Warm Springs). Within two years the number has swelled to twelve hundred, including the Tsoka-ne-nde Chiricahuas from Cochise's band. Whites forced the Bureau to move the agency sixty miles northwest to Tularosa—a place nobody wanted. The Indians fanned out rather than move: the Mimbre east to the Mescaleros and Cochise south to his home range in the mountains. When Howard arrived, he got the Mimbre to come in to Tularosa with the promise that if Cochise came in they would all be moved to the agency at Cañada Alamosa. When Howard later agreed to terms with Cochise, he unwittingly left Victorio and Loco high and dry.

Meantime, Indian raids by different tribes and bands, some by reservation Indians, continued unabated. General George Crook, who had been given command of the military in the region in May 1871, saw his plans for wars of repression but on hold as Colyer and Howard attempted to work magic. An incident in November 1871 in which a stagecoach was attacked by Indians nears Wickensburg ignited more retributions and counter-retributions. In the attack, seven of the eight persons were killed outright or mortally wounded. As with most events in the history of American Indian relations, any act by one was an act of all leading to indiscriminate killings.

It was in May 1863 during the period of the first Apache wars that gold was discovered in central Arizona. The influx of prospectors led to the establishment of the city of Prescott bringing on the inevitable clash with the Indians—this time with the Tonto Apache of the Western Apache. These events led to the story of the "pinole (cornmeal) treaty" in which the Indians were called to parley and were treated to pinole laced with strychnine that killed twenty-five. The supposed perpetrator was an Australian native known as King Woolsey. Folklore or true, no one is sure. The weight of evidence leans toward folklore.

The Mescaleros surrendered in 1863. On June 13, 1863, Henry Connelly, Governor of New Mexico, wrote to Secretary of War Stanton, "General Carleton has reduced the whole Mescalero Apache tribe to a state of peace..." Eight months earlier, on October 12, 1862, Brig. Gen. James H. Carleton, commander of the Department of New Mexico, issued an order to Col. Christopher Carson, commanding the First New Mexico Volunteers: "All Indian men of that tribe [Mescaleros] are to be killed whenever and wherever you can find them; the women and children will not be harmed, but you will take them prisoners..." until further orders. The order applied equally to "all other Indians you may find in the Mescalero country." The Mescaleros were placed on a reservation established in southwestern New Mexico midway between the Pecos and Rio Grand near present White Sands. The Jicarillas followed Mescaleros five years later in 1868. A reservation was established for the Jicarillas in northern New Mexico on the Colorado border just east of the Continental Divide. In 1887 they were allotted land in severalty.

The Navaho also felt the sting of the white man. Kit Carson and his California volunteers under orders from Brig. Gen. James Carleton waged a march of destruction that ravaged the Navaho country. Eight thousand Navaho were rounded up and placed on the small, poorly-suited Bosque Redondo reservation astride the

Pecos in east-central New Mexico adjoining Fort Sumner that Carleton had established for five hundred Mescaleros in March 1863. Animosity between the two tribes was rampant on land barely large enough for the Mescalero alone. In addition crops repeatedly failed. Finally, in November 1865, Mescaleros simply disappeared to the four winds. They remained hidden for seven years. In 1868, General Sherman gave orders for the Navaho to be allowed to return to their native homeland in northern Arizona.

On the plus side, relations improved considerably between the powerful White Mountain Apache tribe led by Diablo (Heske-hldasila) and the army in 1864.

CONCENTRATION POLICY

No sooner had life at San Carlos begun to stabilize than Washington decided that all Apaches, not just the Western Apaches, but all Apaches and "associated" tribes throughout Arizona and New Mexico should be concentrated at San Carlos—the concentration policy.

The first move involved bringing 1,500 Yavapai and Walapai from Camp Verde February 27, 1875. The move was anything by acrimonious. And, although the Yavapai got along with several of tribes of the Western Apache, the Walapai were traditional enemies of the group and had to be separated to the extent possible.

The next move was that of the White Mountain and Cibicue from Camp Apache. One of the biggest problems was the stubbornness of the local Army commander that made cooperation between the army and Indian agent virtually impossible. General August V. Kautz, who had different ideas on the handling of Apaches, had replaced General Crook as commander of the Arizona Department. When the move was completed, the population of San Carlos had grown to over four thousand—still a new rancheria for the Tca-tci-dn clan (Red Rock Strata People) had been left behind.

On May 3, 1876, instructions were received to close down the Chiricahua reservation on the Mexico border and move the Cochise's Chiricahuas to San Carlos. Taza, Cochise's son and hereditary chief of the Tsoka-ne-nde, reluctantly agreed to move. Taza, who died later that same year, and about 325 Tsoka-ne-nde headed for San Carlos in June.

A small renegade band under Skinya and his brother Pion-se-nay remained in the mountains and continued their raids into Mexico. Apache police brought Pion-se-nay in and turned him over to the sheriff at Tucson from whom he promptly escaped. The Tci-he-nde Mimbre, who had been using the reservation as a springboard for their raids into Mexico, headed northeast back to Ojo Caliente. There was also the Nednhi band of the Nde-nda-i Chiricahuas under a violent chief named Juh and a group of Bedonkohe under a still minor chief at the time named Gerónimo. Together they totaled four hundred warriors. For the army it would be like trying to coral four thousand.

VICTORIO

Orders were received in 1877 to arrest the renegades using Ojo Caliente as a base for raids and bring the Tci-he-nde Mimbre under Victorio back to San Carlos. Seventeen Nde-nda-i Chiricahuas, including Gerónimo were captured. On May 1, the agent headed for San Carlos with 110 of Gerónimo's Nde-nda-i and 343 of Victorio's Tci-he-nde and arrived three weeks later. Two months later, 310 Apaches consisting mostly of Victorio's Tci-he-nde Mimbre bolted the reservation for Ojo Climente. Gerónimo remained. Some two hundred of Victorio's band surrendered at Fort Wingate and were taken to Ojo Climente. Victorio himself came in voluntarily in February. Efforts made to allow them to stay at their sacred home site were eventually rebuffed by the government and on October 1, 1878, troopers arrived to escort them back to San Carlos.

Victorio bolted again taking about eighty warriors with him. Another twenty soon followed. Attempts to track him down were unsuccessful. The troopers returned to Ojo Climente and assembled the 170 or so women and children left behind for the trip to San Carlos. They left for Fort Apache in December at the beginning of an unusually cold winter. From Camp Apache they traveled on foot to San Carlos. (The post surgeon at Fort Apache was a young Walter Reed.)

In February 1879, Victorio came in and told the authorities that he would go anywhere they liked but San Carlos. The authorities sent word in April that he was to be sent to the Mescalero Reservation at Tularosa. Victorio had second thoughts and fled again but showed up at Tularosa on June 30 stating his good intentions. All plans dissolved when Victorio was indicted by civilian authorities for horse stealing and murder in July. Believing that they came to arrest and hang him two months later in September, Victorio escaped taking sixty warriors with him. Thus began two of the bloodiest years in the annals of the Southwest. During that time, Victorio's band increased at one point to some 350, including his own Tci-he-nde Mimbre, the Tsoka-ne-nde Chiricahua, disgruntled Mescaleros, and even some Lipan and possibly a few Comanches.

Victorio and his men were tracked back and forth across the desert by General Edward P. Hatch, Major Albert P. Morrow, Lieutenant Charles B. Gatewood, and Colonel Benjamin H. Grierson from Fort Davis in Texas. The troopers were from the all black 9th and 10th Calvary regiments. (Over the years Fort Davis, one of the most desolate posts in the west-southwest, was the home of one or more of the two black calvary regiments and the two black infantry regiments, the 24th and the 25th.) Because Victorio was using Tularosa as one of his bases, the 320 reservation Mescaleros there were disarmed and dismounted, except for thirty to fifty that took to the hills to join Victorio. Victorio was finally surrounded and killed in the Tres Castillos Mountains of Mexico by the Mexican army under the command of General Terrazas on October 15, 1880. Sixty warriors and eighteen women and children died that day. Seventy prisoners were also taken. There has been some debate as to whether Victorio was actually killed that day, but all the evidence supports that conclusion.

NANA AND THE WHITE MOUNTAIN

A small group of Victorio's followers escaped the battle and rallied around the old chief Nana. Two members of the group were Nana's daughter and the wife of Gerónimo and their son Robert. Nana and his followers took revenge on Mexicans citizens and soldiers wherever the opportunity presented itself. By late November or December, the group came upon a band of Nde-nda-i Apaches led by Gerónimo. (Gerónimo had escaped from San Carlos in April 4, 1878 and joined with Juh and his followers.) Six months later, Nana and Gerónimo separated, and Nana led a blistering six-week campaign of bloodletting in a one thousand-mile trek across New Mexico, after which he faded back into the Sierra Madre of Mexico. When almost all of the Chiricahuas were on the reservation, Nana was still hiding and raiding in Mexico.

That April of 1881, new trouble began with the White Mountain Apaches at San Carlos under a new prophet named Nakai-doklini. At the end of August, General Eugene Carr with a force of 117 regulars and scouts arrested Nakai-doklini and were taking him back to the post when they were attacked at their camp on Cibicue Creek resulting in several deaths on both sides. Soon the troop was surrounded by upwards of a thousand braves from throughout the area, but they soon just faded back into the wilderness. Nakai-doklini was killed in the fighting, and his death became a bitter memory for the White Mountains that brought on depredations and killings around Fort Apache over the next several months. The Wheel Dance that Nakai-doklini instituted on.

BREAK OUT FROM SAN CARLOS

Because of the continuing confusion and misunderstanding that existed in the relations between the Apaches and the white man, more problems erupted in October 1881 from the Camp Goodwin sub-agency of San Carlos that housed the Chiricahuas. Seventy-four warriors and many of their families bolted from the reservation and fled to Mexico. They included the Tsoka-ne-nde led by Cochise's second son Naiche and the Nde-nda-i led by Juh and Gerónimo and a separate band led by a lesser chief named

Chato. (See the movie Chato's Land with Charles Bronson, 1972.) Old chief Loco, who commanded the largest single contingent of Chiricahuas consisting of some seven hundred Tci-he-nde, remained on the sidelines during the outbreak. The others not only wanted him and his warriors, but they needed them if their renegade existence was to survive. They went back to San Carlos in mid-April 1882 to get Loco to join them and were willing to do whatever it took to gain his cooperation. The renegades in effect kidnapped Loco and all his followers, including some White Mountains, and herded them off the reservation like cattle with little resistance.

On the way south, the combined force raided, killed, mutilated, and tortured in some of the most inhumane ways ever seen—believed to be mostly the work of Juh. They also fought one inconclusive battle with the army under Lt. Col. George Forsyth's command in Horseshoe Canyon before decimating a tent city of prospectors in the Chiricahua Mountains and fading into the Sierra Madre. Two regiments of calvary stationed nearby, the 6th Calvary under the command of Capt. Tullius C. Tupper and the 4th Calvary under the command of Capt. William A. Rafferty immediately struck out in pursuit and followed them into Mexico itself. The troopers attacked the Apache camp about twenty miles inside the border. That night the troopers fell back to regroup and were joined by the force under Col. Forsyth. When the Apaches broke away, they ran into an ambush set up by Mexican authorities and lost seventy-eight killed, mostly women and children, and thirty-three captured, all women and children. Tupper's men had killed six to ten warriors. The Apaches moved up into the mountains, and the army was told to return to U.S. territory. The renegades held out for almost two more years.

WARS COME TO AN END

Back at San Carlos in July 1882, Na-tio-tish broke out with some sixty White Mountain warriors and also went on a rampage. Within a week an overwhelming force, with the aid of White Mountain scouts, attacked and killed sixteen to twenty-seven of the renegades, including Na-tio-tish. The rest slowly drifted back to the reservation. It was called the Battle of Big Dry Wash. Except for the continuing battles with the Chiricahua and Mimbre, it was the last battle with the Apaches fought by the army.

In 1882, General George Crook was recalled to Arizona and assumed command on September 4. At about the same time, Carl Schurz was appointed Secretary of the Interior and instituted a thorough house cleaning of the Bureau of Indian Affairs, beginning with the Commissioner. Crook's first step was to initiate what Haley (358) labeled a "good-faith-oriented Indian policy." He also received approval to move the White Mountains from San Carlos to outer reaches of Fort Apache.

Mexicans had taken Gerónimo's wife and Chato's family along with others in the summer of 1882 who were either killed or sold. The Mexican state of Chihuahua suffered even more than he previously. The Mexican employed civilian militia to augment the army. In an attack by a local militia in early, Juh lost face when his wife and about twelve others were killed and thirty of his followers were taken captive. He went off to live by himself and shortly thereafter died, leaving leadership of the Chiricahuas to Gerónimo, Chato, Benito, and a chief named Chihuahua. At one point Chato took a band of the renegades rampaging into southeastern Arizona around Tombstone in the spring of 1883 just as Crook was making plans to move into Mexico. One of Chato's men, Tzo-e or Peaches as the soldiers called him, quit the band and went into San Carlos. He subsequently agreed to lead Crook's force into Mexico.

Crook mounted his campaign to bring in the Apaches in the Sierra Madre setting out on May 1 with one troop of 42 men and 192 Indian scouts. A limited "hot-pursuit" treaty had been signed with Mexican authorities on July 29, 1882, and Crook duly notified Mexican authorities. By May 19, Crook had received into his camp Chihuahua and some one hundred of his followers who wanted to surrender. A few days later Old Nana came in with a small band as did Loco and Benito. By the end of the month some 375 Apaches had voluntarily turned themselves in as talks continued with Gerónimo. Crook returned to San Carlos with his prisoners on June 23.

In late December and into February 1874, first individual warriors, then Chato with nineteen, and then finally Gerónimo himself crossed voluntarily into the United States giving themselves up as had been agreed upon in May. They were quickly escorted to San Carlos in order to avoid any contact or conflict with the civilian populace. The last stragglers finally made to San Carlos in mid-May. Chato was subsequently made a sergeant of scouts.

Gerónimo bolted again from San Carlos on May 17, 1885, with 134 followers that included upwards of forty-two warriors and chiefs Mangus, Naiche and Chihuahua. After fighting, dodging, and raiding for almost a year, Gerónimo, Naiche and Chihuahua, and Old Nana met with Crook just south of the border at Cañón de los Embudos on March 28, 1886 and agreed to surrender. They would follow Crook at their own pace.

Crook had agreed that if they were imprisoned in the East that it would not be for more than two years. When he advised General Sheridan, the agreement was submitted to President Grover Cleveland who rejected the plan. The only terms were unconditional surrender. Before he could do anything about his new instructions, Crook learned that Gerónimo and Naiche had bolted again. Chihuahua's followers came in to Fort Bowie on April 3 and set up a new rancheria nearby. Nana, Ulzanna and Cut-le were also safely in and accounted for. Crook was ordered to ship all seventy-seven prisoners, including the families of the Gerónimo and Naiche, by train to prison in Fort Marion in St. Augustine, Florida. Sheridan disparaged Crook's efforts and his plans to try to capture Gerónimo.

Crook requested that he be relieved of command of the department and reassigned. Sheridan assigned Crook to command the Department of the Platte and replaced him with General Nelson A. Miles who reported for duty at Fort Bowie on April 11. It was believed that Gerónimo had seventeen warriors, including Naiche; Mangus, three warriors. Bellying his boasts that the Apaches could be subdued by white troops, Miles included twenty Indian scouts with thirty-five handpicked calvary and a company of infantry. He also adopted Crook's use of pack mules instead of wagons.

Gerónimo again agreed to end the fighting and surrendered for the final time to General at Skeleton Canyon near the international border in Arizona on September 3, 1886. Fearful for his life, Naiche belatedly came in and joined the others. Gerónimo's followers had been reduced to less than forty including, about half women and children.

Gerónimo and Naiche and their followers were entrained to Florida on September 8 although civilian authorities wanted the men tried and executed in Arizona. At Fort Apache in the White Mountains, 382 Chiricahuas were rounded up, disarmed, and on September 12 also entrained for Florida. The warriors were sent to Fort Pickins; the families to Fort Marion. It is estimated that up to a third died of disease and the climate. Some of the children were set to the Indian school at Carlisle, Pennsylvania. Some went on to prosper; some died of cold; and others lived the remainder of the lives in depression. (For more on the American Indian Boarding Schools, see below.)

Later the families were reunited at Mt. Vernon barracks in Alabama. There were more deaths from tuberculosis and other diseases. The final move was to Fort Sill in 1894 on land given up by the Kiowa and Comanche. Nana died at Fort Sill in 1896. Gerónimo died there February 17, 1909. In 1913, the Chiricahua prisoners were allowed to leave Fort Sill and return west but only as far as the Mescalero reservation in eastern New Mexico. A few who had established roots in Oklahoma remained behind. For more see Camp Grant Massacre and Tonto War.

APACHE NATIONS (21st Century)

White Mountain Apache Tribe
Whiteriver, Arizona

Apache Tribe of Oklahoma
Anadarko, Oklahoma

San Carlos, Apache Tribe
San Carlos, Arizona

Yavapai Apache Nation
Camp Verde, Arizona

Jicarilla Apache Nation
Dulce, New Mexico

Tonto Apache Nation
Payson Arizona

Ft. McDowell, Yavapai Nation
Ft. McDowell, Arizona

Ft. Sill Apache Tribe
Ft. Sill, Oklahoma

Mescalero Apache Nation
Mescalero, New Mexico

Lipan Apache Tribe
San Antonio, Texas

Chiricahua Apache
Albuquerque, New Mexico

TREATY OF GUADALUPE HIDALGO

The war with Mexico took the lives of nearly thirteen thousand American soldiers—casualties of both combat and disease, and another four thousand wounded. Mexican casualties were considerably higher. The treaty signed February 2 reached the White House just over two weeks later on the on the nineteenth and was approved by the Senate on March 10. Ratifications were exchanged between the two countries on the May 13, 1848 but not officially approved by Congress until July 6.

Mexico agreed to sell America not only the land south to the Rio Grande as the boundary of Texas but also California and all the territory in between, south of the 42nd parallel—a total of one-half million plus square miles. With the agreement, Mexico ceded the New Mexico Territory (present states of Arizona, New Mexico, Utah, Nevada, a small corner of present-day Wyoming, and the western and southern portions of Colorado) and Upper California (present state of California) in what was called the Mexican Cession. In addition to provisions regarding the payment of claims of American citizens, the treaty also provided those Mexican captives in the hands of the Apache would be returned to Mexico. This last provision was to derail future negotiations with Mangas.

In his message to Congress, President Pope wrote, in part, "The results of the war with Mexico have given the United States a national character which our country never before enjoyed." In historian William Seale's picturesque description, the "garden of democracy stretched from the Rio Grande to the Pacific ocean." To Native Americans, it was anything but. Among the terms of the treaty, the Santa Fe Trail became a national road connecting the United States to its new southwest territories and the native peoples of California were to become U. S. citizens and guaranteed of all the rights of citizenship, including property rights. They received no rights.

GADSDEN PURCHASE

On June 30, 1854, six years after the Treaty of Guadalupe-Hidalgo, President Pierce executed the Gadsden Treaty with Mexico by which the United States purchased an area of approximately 30,000 square miles in northern Mexico.

Prospects for construction of a transcontinental rail line across the southwest and the necessity of an all-American wagon route to California, Cooke's Road, were major factors in prompting the administration to initiate negotiations. For ten million dollars, the U.S. obtained the semiarid desert land in what is now southern Arizona south of the Gila River and the southwest corner of New Mexico bounded by the Rio Grande and the Gila. The purchase included the Spanish town of Tucson with a population at the time of about 800 persons. The treaty put aside the boundary established with the Treaty of Guadalupe-Hidalgo. The actual transfer of land took place in 1856.

AMERICAN INDIAN BOARDING SCHOOLS

Introduced in the early 1840s American Indian boarding schools became official government policy under President Grant's Peace Policy or Quaker Policy as it was called of 1869. The system, which at one time included more than 400 such schools continued well in the 20th century. Most of the schools were operated by church groups and religious orders. The schools, which took children as young as five years old forcibly from the arms of their parents, focused on the acculturation and assimilation of Indians into white society rather than on Indian education and training under a strict disciplinary regimen. By the mid-twentieth century, operation of the schools was being increasingly turned over to the tribes themselves.

Two of the earliest schools were the Shawnee Methodist Mission and Indian Manual Labor School in western Kansas that opened as a boarding school in October 1839 and the mission and boarding school at Bellevue, Nebraska, established in 1846 for the Otoes and Omahas by the Board of Foreign Missions of the Presbyterian Church. When the Omaha moved to their reservation in 1855, the Presbyterians went along with them "to tell them how to live and how to die." Hicksite Friends came to the Omaha reservation in 1869 as part of Grant's new policy although a year earlier the Omaha chiefs had requested the closing of the boarding school. The result for the Omahas was the destruction of their government and social structure. For more on the Shawnee Methodist Mission, see the Shawnee.

The largest and most well-known Indian boarding school was located at Carlisle Barracks, Pennsylvania. In 1875, Lt. Richard Henry Pratt was assigned to Fort Marion, Florida where he established a prison school for the Apache Indian prisoners. On their release in 1878, Pratt organized an Indian Branch of the Hampton Normal and Agricultural Institute in Virginia, later called the Hampton Institute, that had opened in 1868 under the auspices of the American Missionary Association. Hampton became the first American school to accept Indian students. The experiment, which included a program taught by Booker T. Washington, was less than successful. That same year Pratt obtained permission to convert a portion of Carlisle Barracks in Pennsylvania to an Indian school. The school opened in October 1879 with 82 Sioux children and was formally recognized by Congress in 1882. Pratt's philosophy of Indian education articulated in a 1892 speech was "Kill the Indian in him, and save the man." In its first twenty-five years, some five thousand Indian children from more than seventy tribes passed through the doors at Carlisle.

Two noted graduates of Carlisle were Charles Albert (Chief) Bender and James Francis (Jim) Thrope. Bender, whose mother was a member of the Ojibwe tribe, was born the White Earth Reservation in Minnesota. Discovered by Philadelphia Manager Connie Mack, Bender left Carlisle in 1903. He pitched for the Philadelphia Athletics in the first two decades of the 1900s and was admitted to the Baseball Hall of Fame in 1953. Thorpe was born in Indian Territory of mixed Indian blood. He attended the Haskell Institute, and went on to Carlisle, ten years behind Bender. Thorpe, an all-around athletic, demonstrated his athletic prowess in football, baseball, and track. He was forced to return the gold medals he had won (pentathlon and decathlon) in the 1912 summer games at Stockholm because he had played baseball at the professional level forfeiting his amateur status.

One of the early successes in Indian education and training outside the mission system was the United States Indian Industrial Training School that opened in Lawrence, Kansas, in 1884 with twenty-two students in grades one through five. Open to all American Indian and Alaska Native people from across the United States, enrollment continued to increase as the academic program expanded beyond the elementary level to the secondary (1927) and the junior college (1970) levels. The school became Haskell Indian Nations University in 1993.

APALACHEE

The Apalachee, also called the Tallahassee and Palache, belonged to the Muskhogean linguistic group. They inhabited the area around present-day Tallahassee in western Florida and the Upper Gulf coast. They were first encountered in Florida by the Spanish in the 1500s. Many were baptized Catholics as a result of the encounter. The name Tallahassee was derived from the Apalachee word for the "old fields" that once encompassed the area

The Apalachee were defeated by the Creek in 1702, and an expedition from South Carolina two years nearly destroyed them. Some fled to Mobile, other were captured and taken to South Carolina. Some later returned to Florida and settled around Tallahassee and Pensacola. When Florida passed from England in 1764, the Apalachee and others migrated into Louisiana and settled along the Red River. Their lands were sold in 1803, and they subsequently disappeared from history—generally by 1763 when Florida passed from the Spanish into the hands of the English the original aboriginal life in Florida had all but disappeared. Many of those that had been baptized left with the withdrawing Spanish.

APALACHICOLA

The Apalachicola were one of the tribes of Lower Creeks of the Creek Confederacy. They inhabited of the coastal region of the northern Gulf. With the Chiaha, they moved into northern Florida and established a town called Mikasuki where they became strong and prospered. They gave their name to the river that flows through the panhandle of Florida to the Gulf.

APAPAX

The Apapax was listed by Farther Ortiz in his memorial to the king of Spain sometime after February 14, 1747, cited by Bolton in "Missions on the San Gabriel," but no additional information about the tribe is known. It is believed that the Apapax lived in east central or southeastern Texas. There is a possibility that the Apapax may be the same as the Apayxam that Swanton includes in the Coahuiltecan group.

APPOMATOTOX

The Appomatotox (Appomattoc) inhabited colonial Virginia. In September 1675, a number of Appomatotox were seized by Nathaniel Bacon for allegedly stealing corn. For more see Bacon's Rebellion.

AQUACKANONK

The Aquackanonk was a sub-tribe of the Unami division of the Delaware. They lived on the Passaic River in New Jersey and on the tract of land called the Dundee. For more see Unami and Delaware.

AQUASCOGOOC

The Aquascogooc is believed to be of the Algonquian linguistic group and has been described as a sub-tribe of the Secotan, but available information on its status is limited. Their village is believed to have been located on the Pungo River near Sladesville, North Carolina, in Hyde County. It was burned to the ground by the Roanoke colonists in 1585. The name contains the common shellfish suffix, "ooc."

ARAPAHO

The Arapaho was of the Algonquian linguistic stock originally from the valley of the Red River of the North. They migrated west and south across the Missouri just ahead of the Cheyenne. (Nester writes that the Indians that became known as the Arapaho split off from the Hidatsa of the Middle Missouri in the late 1500s.) Some writers associate the Arapaho principally with northeastern Wyoming where a large portion of the tribe settled for many years, ranging at times into Montana. Another large group moved farther south as did a large group of Cheyenne following on their heels. The southern branches of the two tribes formed an alliance—the Arapaho being initially the more numerous. Of all the alliances made between the native American Indians tribes, that between the Arapaho and Cheyenne was one of the most enduring and most successful. Together they became a formidable force throughout the plains.

Early scholars recognized five main divisions within the Arapaho: the Northern Arapaho (Nákasine'na or Báachinena); the Southern Arapaho (Náwunena); and the Atsina or Gros Ventre of the Prairie (Aä'ninena or Hitúnena) that is now generally treated as a separate and distinct tribe. The two other divisions (the Bäsawunena and the Hánahawunena or Aanú'nhawa) remained with or were incorporated into the Northern Arapaho. Some writers also refer to the Northern Arapaho as the Arapaho proper; others, the Southern Arapaho.

Construction of the Kansas Pacific Railroad encroached into to the heart of the Arapaho's food preserve in western Kansas, eastern Colorado, and southern Wyoming. A few joined the Cheyenne to fight the Iron Horse. Others joined Sitting Bull to live in the Yellowstone country outside of reservation control only to find railroad surveyors laying out a route for the Northern Pacific across the Yellowstone in 1871 and 1872. Two years after Sitting Bull surrendered in 1881, his nemesis, the Northern Pacific Railroad, was completed.

The Northern Arapaho ended up on a reservation on the Wind River in Wyoming with the Shoshoni; the Southern Arapaho and the Southern Cheyenne were placed on a reservation in Indian Territory; and the Atsina shared the Fort Belknap Reservation in northcentral Montana with the Assiniboin.

The reservation in the Indian Territory was established with the treaty of October 14, 1865, executed at the council-ground on the Little Arkansas in Kansas. The tribes agreed to accept the reservation as their permanent home and relinquish all claims or rights to any portion of the United States or its territories and especially those of their former lands, the boundaries of which were delineated in the treaty. The original reservation was replaced by another with what is commonly referred to as the Medicine Lodge Treaty (on Medicine Lodge Creek, seventy miles south of Fort Larned in the State of Kansas) on October 21, 1867.

ARAVAIPA

Aravaipa Apache lived in the canyon of Aravaipa creek, a tributary of the Rio San Pedro, in southern Arizona. About 1872 they were removed to San Carlos Agency and subsequently put under the San Carlos and Fort Apache agencies on the White Mountain reservation. For more see Apache.

ARIKARA

The Arikara were called the Rees by the Americans and Europeans. They are also referred to as the Recares. The Arikara belonged to the Caddoan linguistic group and are believed to have been closely related to the Skidi Pawnee if not originally of the same people. From archaeological evidence it is known that they migrated north from Nebraska at an early stage to what became their home land in the region of the Upper Missouri in the western half of North Dakota and the eastern quarter of Montana where they cultivated the land.

Hyde reports that the Arikara were driven out of northeastern Nebraska, apparently by the Padouca Apache, around 1700 to land about the mouth of the Big Sioux River where by 1725 they were settled on the north side of the Missouri. The Omaha and Iowa lived just below them. The Arikara moved again establishing new settlements on both banks of the Missouri from a spot near present Chamberlain north to Pierre between 1730 and 1740 where they were joined for a brief time by the Ponka. It was here during the middle of the eighteenth century about 1760 that the Arikara first encountered the Oglala and Brulé Teton Sioux as immigrant settlers on the Upper Missouri and helped them through a period of rough times. Evidence indicates that the Arikara had a very large and heavily fortified village below the Great Bend of the Missouri, on the east bank near the mouth of Crow Creek—about seven miles south of Pierre, South Dakota..

Across the river, on the site of Old Fort George, opposite present DeGrey and just above the mouth of the Bad River were three more villages. The population in the area was estimated at some 20,000. Although primarily an agricultural society, the Arikara were well-supplied with horses and metal weapons by 1760, thanks to the Spanish. They conducted two buffalo hunts a year into the Black Hills region and eastward and were no longer terrified of the Sioux. As a result, the Sioux, who lost their primary source for guns and ammunition with the French defeat in the French and Indian War, found their way west blocked by the Arikara.

Between 1772 and 1780, the Arikara were hit by three epidemics of smallpox that decimated the tribe and weaken them to the point that the Sioux were able to move forward after destroying the large Arikara village below Pierre. The Oglala were the first to cross the Missouri below the Great Bend near the mouth of Crow Creek, to be followed by the Brulé. The Arikara, for their part, consolidated and moved slowly up river where by 1786 they had settled on the west bank of the Missouri near the mouth of Cheyenne River. The new location, however, put them in the path of the Saone Tetons, and they were forced to withdraw farther north in 1795, after which they were hit by another smallpox epidemic.

In 1810 they had two strong, well-fortified villages just north of the Grand River in the Middle Missouri. The Hidatsa, the Mandan, and the Arikara dominated the region and the route to the Upper Missouri and thus the trade and economy of the entire region. The Arikara were possessive of their lands and the more warlike of the three tribes. However, they had generally maintained relatively friendly relations with the white man, but in May of 1823 they attacked the Missouri Fur Company post of Fort Recovery. The following month they attacked a trapping expedition of William Ashley (later to become the Rocky Mountain Fur Company). Twelve men from Ashley's trapper brigade were killed and eleven sounded. Two died later. It was the beginning of the very brief but economically and culturally significant Arikara War.

Ashley retreated down river to Fort Akinson near present Omaha and procured the assistance of Colonel Henry Leavenworth. Leavenworth assembled an expedition of 230 soldiers with cannon, 750 Teton Sioux warriors, and over fifty trappers. On reaching the Arikara territory, Leavenworth attacked both villages but refused to press the attack. His actions were to be a show of force, not a campaign of extermination much to the consternation of the assembled trappers and the Sioux.

The Arikara asked for peace, and a treaty was signed on August 11, 1823. The Arikara War—the first Plains Indian War—had come to an end. The trappers ignored the treaty and pressed for vengeance and retribution. For their part the Arikara slipped away from camp during the night and fled into the prairie, leaving some fifty Indians dead. Economic power of the region changed forever.

The Arikara headed south to Nebraska to join the Skidi Pawnee, the beginning of fourteen years of wandering the prairie. Whenever they settled with or near another tribe, they were invariably asked to leave after a short time. At the same time the Oglala moved onto the Upper Platte in force and defeated the Arikara in a stunning battle while Colonel Henry Dodge and his command were moving up the Platte. By 1837 the

Arikara were back in the Upper Missouri beyond their old villages above the mouth of the Grand River, and on April 28, 1837, two hundred and fifty lodges joined the Mandan near Fort Clark. Twenty joined the nearby Hidasta. Soon thereafter the region was hit with the smallpox epidemic and nearly wiped out all of the tribes. The Arikara population was halved. Animosity resurfaced between the Arikara and the Mandan, and the Mandan moved across the Missouri River. The Arikara moved downriver and then in the spring returned to occupy the deserted Mandan village near the Knife River on March 20, 1838.

In 1839 the Mandan and Hidasta moved upriver, but by 1855 the three depleted, mound-dwelling tribes were again living together. In 1862 they all moved to Fort Berthold. On July 13, 1880, President Rutherford Hayes signed a document that extinguished title to thirty thousand square miles of land belonging to the Arikari, Hidatsa, and Blackfeet making it available to the Northern Pacific Railroad while at the same time creating the Fort Berthold Reservation.

The Arikara was one of the most belligerent, hostile and most universally disliked tribes of American Indians, by both whites and Indians alike. They were particularly bitter against all whites and they instilled that bitterness and hatred in their children at an early age. They were also looked down on for their personal and social habits. Many later volunteered to scout for the Army against the Sioux, Cheyenne, and Arapaho.

YELLOWSTONE EXPEDITION

The purpose of the government's Yellowstone Expedition was to both show the colors so to speak and negotiate peace treaties with the Indian tribes of the Missouri Country. President James Monroe signed the authorizing legislation for a peace commission to the Indians on May 25, 1824. Henry Atkinson and Benajmin O'Fallon were appointed joint peace commissioners.

On May 16, 1825, the expedition left Fort Atkinson for its journey up the Missouri. It arrived at the Arikara village near the mouth of the Grand River on July 15 and the mouth of the Yellowstone on August 17, where Cantonment Barbour was built. Continuing up river the expedition reached the Porcucline River on August 24, and three days later turned around and headed back downriver reaching Fort Atkinson on September 19. The expedition met with sixteen tribes and signed peace treaties with twelve. Not one man was lost from hostilities or accident. Signing treaties were the Arikara, Cheyenne, Crow, Hidatsa, Mandan, Oglala, Saone, Yankton, and Yanktonai.

ARMOUCHIQUOIS

The Armouchiquois lived in southern Main south to Cape Elizabeth. The name is believed to be a French corruption of Alemousiski (land of the little dog) given to them by the Abnaki, but the French applied the name to several tribes in the area. The English apparently included them in with the Massachusettes. Reportedly, the name was also used collectively for several Algonquian tribes of New England, to include the Mohegan, Pequot, Massachuset, Marraganset—which was generally consistent with the French and English usage. They have also been called the Penobscots and Maliseet.

AROSAGUNTACOOK

The Arosaguntacook was a division of the Abnaki located near present-day Lewiston, Maine. It has been treated as a separate tribe in the literature. For more see Abenaki.

ARRENAMUSE

The Arrenamuse, with a population of 120 men in 1818, lived near the mouth of the San Antonio River in Texas.

ARROHATTOC

Arrohattoc was a member of the Powhatan Confederacy and inhabited parts of Henrico County, Virginia.

ASHEPOO

The Ashepoo was a subdivision or sub-tribe of the Cusabo (South). They lived on the lower Ashepoo River of South Carolina. For more see the Cusabo.

ASOMOCHE

The Asomoche was a sub-tribe of the Unalachtigo division of the Delaware. They lived on the eastern bank of the Delaware River between the cities of Salem and Camden, New Jersey. For more see Unalachtigo and Delaware.

ASSINIBOIN

Linguistically of the Siouan group, the Assiniboin, also spelled Assiniboin, inhabited an area of about 20,000 square miles along the Upper Missouri from the region of the Milk and Missouri rivers in the northern half of North Dakota and Montana to the Saskatchewan and Assiniboin river valleys in Canada. The Assiniboin had migrated northwestward from their homeland around the headwaters of the Mississippi to the Lake of the Woods and towards Lake Winnipeg. The first written record of the Assiniboin comes from the Jesuits who reported that the Assiniboin split off from the Yanktonai Sioux sometime prior to 1640.

Theirs was a roving/hunting society of active traders. According to Denig, they were always looking for a good deal. Some eight hundred Assinuboins died in the smallpox epidemic of 1837. In later years they gathered under the Fort Belknap and Fort Peck agencies. The Fort Peck Reservation in Montana became the home of the Sioux as they fled from the U.S. Calvary.

Jesuit Father De Smet described the Assiniboin, which are referred to as the Assiniboin of the Forest, as "filthy beyond description" and the most "adroit and incorrigible rogues to be found in the forest."

ASSUNPINK

The Assunpink was a sub-tribe of the Unami division of the Delaware. They lived on Stoney Creek near present Trenton, New Jersey. For more see Unami and Delaware.

ASUCSAG-NA

Asucsag-na or Asuksa was a sub-tribe of the Tongva of California that inhabited the area about Azuza. For more see Tongva.

ATÁKAPA

The Atákapa (quite common without the accent) or Attakapa as they are frequently identified in the literature, are now believed to have belonged to the Tunican linguistic stock. They lived in southern Louisiana, with a large concentration around Lake Charles. At one time it was believed that the Atakapa, along with the Bidai or Bedies, Orcoquiza, and Deadose constituted the Attacapan linguistic family. The Karankawa and several other tribes were included in the same group. Their name, meaning "man-eater," was given to them by their Choctaw neighbors to the east.

The Atákapa also lived in northeast Texas around Trinity Bay and the lower course of the Trinity River. The Trinity River people came to the knowledge of the Spanish, who called them the Akokisa, about 1528. Their speech was identical to that of the Atákapa of Lake Charles, both distinctly different from the Eastern Atákapa.

By 1805 the principal village of Akokisa of Trinity Bay was located some two hundred miles southwest of Nacogdoches on the west side of the Colorado River. Others settled between the Neches and the Sabine. The Calcasieu band of the St. Charles region on Indian Lake or Lake Prien held together well into the mid-1800s or later before becoming absorbed into the general population.

A historical marker was dedicated in 2003 memorializing the Atakapas-Ishak located at the Junction of US Hwy 190 and LA Hwy 111, between Merryville and DeRidder, Louisiana, in what was a part of their ancestral homeland in present-day Beauregard Parish. Ishak came from their own name, Yuk'hiti- ishak.

ATÁKAPA , EASTERN

The Atákapa belonged to the Tunican linguistic stock but with a distinctly different dialect from the Atákapa at Lake Charles and Trinity Bay. There were two bands, one along Vermilion Bay and one on the Mermentou River in Louisiana. The two bands provided braves to the Spanish (Galvez) in their expedition against the English forts on the Mississippi River. Those of the eastern group on Vermilion Bayou continued to live there well the 1830s.

ATANUM

The Atanum or Atanumlema was a sub-tribe of the Yakima that lived on the Oregon plateau. For more see Yakima.

ATASACNEUS

The Atasacneus was listed by Farther Ortiz in his memorial to the king of Spain sometime after February 14, 1747, cited by Bolton in "Missions on the San Gabriel," but no additional information is available. It is believed that the Atasacneus lived in east central or southeastern Texas.

ATASI

The Atasi was a sub-tribe or division of the Muskogee and a member of the Creek Confederacy that inhabited Alabama. For more see Creek Confederacy.

ATCHATCHAKANGOUEN

The Atchatchakangouen or Miami proper was one of the six major divisions of the Miami that inhabited parts of present-day Indiana. They later lost their identity. For more see the Miami.

ATFALATI KALAPUYA

The Atfalati, also known as the Wapato Lake Indians and the Tualatin, belonged to the Kaloapooian linguistic stock. They lived along the Tualatin River, a tributary of the Willamette River, and inhabited the Atfalati plains and the area about Forest Grove and Wapato in Oregon, possibly venturing as far as the site of present Portland to the east. For more see the Kalapuya Peoples.

ATIASNOGUE

The Atiasnogue was listed by Farther Ortiz in his memorial to the king of Spain sometime after February 14, 1747, cited by Bolton in "Missions on the San Gabriel," but no other reference has been found. It is believed that the Atiasnogue lived in east central or southeastern Texas.

ATSINA

The Atsina or more commonly the Gros Ventre of the Prairie, as distinct from the Gros Ventre of the River, was of Algonquian linguistic stock and originally part of the Arapaho around the Red River of the North. (The words *gros* and *ventre* constitute the proper French spelling of the two words for large belly. In the literature, *ventre* is commonly written in what appears to be the plural form as "ventres"; and, occasionally, the English spelling "gross" is used for *gros*.) The French had misinterpreted the sign language for the name Water Falls People.

The Gros Ventre inhabited the area of the Milk River in present-day Montana and ranged northward into Canada. They were subsequently classified as a separate and distinct tribe. The Atsina are also called the Minnetaree of the Plains, Minnetaree of the Prairie, and Minnetaree of Fort de Prarie to avoid confusion with the Hidatsa of North Dakota called the Minnetaree or Minitari of the River and Water Falls People. The Atsina are also called the Fall Indians (as were the Clowwewalla).

The Gros Ventre of the Prairie were allied with the Blackfeet and the Sarcee or Sarci in the Blackfeet Confederacy, but broke from the Blackfeet as a result of an incident in 1861 precipitated by the Pend d'Oreilles west of the Rockies. The Gros Ventre allied themselves with their former enemies the Crow in a war with the Piegan that lasted for five years. In the summer of 1866, the war ended with the death of over three hundred Gros Ventre and Crows following their an attack on a Piegan camp. A number of women and children were also taken captive. It was the worst defeat for the Gros Ventre in memory. The Gros Ventre were placed on the Fort Belknap Reserve in Montana along with Assiniboin.

ATSUGEWI

The Atsugewi and the Achomawi were originally thought to constitute the Palaihnihan or eastern group of the Stastan stock, but have been subsequently placed in the HoKan family. They lived on Burney, Hat, and Horse creeks in California.

ATTIKAMIGUE

The Attikamigue lived north of the Canada River but were reportedly destroyed by a plague or epidemic in 1670.

AUCOCISCO

The name applied to those Abnaki Indians that occupied territory about Casco Bay and the Presumpscot River in the area now included in Cumberland County, Maine. Because the area was settled by whites at an early date, the name soon dropped out of use as applied to the Indians, or rather it was changed to "Casco."

The proper form of the word is Uh-kos-is-co (crane or heron) for the birds that still frequent the bay. Reportedly it was the Indian name of Falmouth (Portland), Maine.

AUGHQUAGA

Aughquaga or Aughquàgah was name of a village on the Susquehanna River inhabited by a number of disaffected Indians from the Six Nations. It was called by some and "Aboriginal Port Royal." The population in 1768 has been given as one hundred and fifty warriors.

AVOYEL

The Avoyel, also spelled Ayogel, was of the Natches group of the Muskhogean linguistic group and lived in the area of present Marksville, Louisiana. They had a very close relationship to the Taensa; and, as a result, the Avoyel were also called the Little Taensa. The tribe was extinct by the 1800s.

AWIG-NA

Awig-na (or Awig) was a sub-tribe of the Tongva of California that inhabited the area about La Puente Valley. For more see Tongva.

AXION

The Axion was a sub-tribe of the Unami division of the Delaware. They lived on the eastern bank of the Delaware River between the Rancocas Creek and Trenton, New Jersey. For more see Unami and Delaware.

AYUTAN

The Ayutan was reportedly a very large tribe of about 8,000 warriors in 1820 that lived southwest of the Missouri River near the Rocky Mountains. . The name was listed in Drake's enumeration, but no additional information is available The Ayutan may have been the Utes. See Drake in the Appendices.

BACKHOOK

Backhook was small tribe that reportedly lived along the Pee Dee River in South Carolina at the turn of the eighteenth century. It is believed that they were of the Siouan linguistic group. According to one account, the Hook, the name by which they were commonly known, were enemies of the Santee.

BANNOCK

The Bannock belonged to the Shoshonean branch of the Uto-Aztecan linguistic stock. Formerly a branch of the Northern Paiute, they ranged through Idaho, Utah, Colorado, western Wyoming, and southern Montana, but the principal center was southeastern Idaho. The Shoshoni in general and the Northern Shoshoni in particular, the Bannock, and Northern Paiute are often confused. The Bannock consisted of several subdivisions that included the Kutsshundika or Buffalo-eaters, Penointikara or Honey-eaters, and Shohopanaiti or Connonwood Bannock; also, the Warrarica or Sunflower Eaters.

The Bannock were first mentioned by Bridger in 1829, but contact increased significantly in 1834 with the construction of Fort Hall. Twenty years later in 1853, they suffered a smallpox epidemic that took a heavy toll. On August 9, 1862, the Bannock ambushed a wagon train of emigrants on the Oregon Trail in modern-day Idaho at what became known as Massacre Rock west of American Falls killing ten. In 1869 they were assigned to the Fort Hall Reservation with the Shoshoni, and in 1875 the Lemhi Indian Reservation was set aside by President Ulysses S. Grant for Shoshoni, Bannock, and Tukuarika. Frustrated by loss of buffalo herds and lack of support by the government, the Bannock rebelled, but the uprising was put down by General Oliver Howard in the Bannock War of 1878. They should not be confused with the Bannock Creek Shoshoni or Kamdüka, a subdivision of the Northern Shoshoni, also known as Chief Pocatello band.

BANNOCK WAR

The Bannock had been placed on the Fort Hall Reservation in Idaho (est. June 14, 1867) by the Fort Bridger Treaty of July 3, 1868. Ten years later, they were suffering from severe famine. They, had not received promised rations from the government, and what rations they did received served for only three days. In addition they were angry because cattle, horses and hogs of the white men encroached on their lands destroying the camas roots. About two hundred Bannock warriors led by Chief Buffalo Horn escaped from Fort Hall in May 1878 and conducted a number of raids throughout the area. Farms and ranches were burned, and cattle and horses stolen, and a number of whites were killed. The incident that brought everything to a head was killing of two white ranchers by two Bannock Indians.

At Big Camas Prairie the Bannock where they were joined by a few Paiutes and Columbia River Indians (Umatilla and Cayuse) already there. Also assembled were Bannock from the Lemhi Agency and Northern Shoshoni. Later they joined Northern Paiutes from the Malheur Agency led by Chief Egan and Medicine Man Oytes of the Snake River Paiutes, Egan reluctantly. There may have been upwards of fifteen hundred to two thousand Indians involved at one time or another, including women and children. General Oliver Otis Howard, who had been enroute to attempt to resolve some of the problems, was ordered to suppress the uprising. Most of the fighting took place in Oregon and Idaho.

Buffalo Horn, who was leading a band of about sixty warriors, was killed in a skirmish at the small settlement of South Mountain on June 8 by one of the friendly Paiute scouts leading a company of volunteers from Silver City. The volunteers quit the field, and the Indians led by Oytes pushed onward to Juniper or Stein Mountains to join the Malheur Paiutes.

There was another encounter with the between the Indians and the volunteers on July 6; and on the 8th, a battle was fought between the Indians and regular troops under General Howard at Birch Creek that resulted in very casualties. On the twentieth the advance element came upon the rear guard waiting in ambush in the canyon of the north fork of the John Day River. Before the soldiers could deploy, the Indians mounted and fled. Some days later, the Umatilla, from the agency, near Pendleton, Oregon, killed Chief Egan and brought his head in to the army for identification. The Bannock headed east; the Paiutes headed south.

During August and September, several small Bannock bands were captured. Oytes and the Northern Paiutes surrendered August 12 and were held at Camp Harney in Oregon and later sent to the Yakima Reservation. A final party of Bannocks and Shoshoni were captured in northwestern Wyoming in September. The Bannocks were held through the winter and returned to their reservation on the Upper Snake River in Idaho.

The Bannock War, which lasted approximately four months, was the last of the Indian wars to qualify for the name. The total number of casualties was quite low by normal standards of comparison. (The literature includes a claim of a massacre of 140 Bannock men, women and children at Charles' Ford in present-day Wyoming, but no data has become available to collaborate the claim.)

BANNOCK CREEK SHOSHONI

Bannock Creek Shoshoni or Kamdüka was a subdivision of the Northern Shoshoni and should not be confused with the Bannock Indians that broke off from the Northern Paiute that were later placed on the Fort Hall Reservation with the Shoshoni. The Bannock Creek Shoshoni was also known as Chief Pocatello Band. Their principal village was near Kelton, Idaho.

BARBAREŃO CHUMASH

The Barbareño were one of the eight dialectic and geographical divisions of the Chumash of the Southern California coast. The Barbareño Chumash lived about present Santa Barbara on the coast from Point Conception to near the Ventura River. For more see the Chumash.

BAYOUGOULA

The Bayogoula, whom some reports identify as a sub-tribe of the Houma, was of the southern Muskhogean division in speech They lived along the Mississippi River near the present town of Bay in Iberville Parish, Louisiana. The Bayogoula occupied the same town as the Mogoulacha (Mugulasha) whom they destroyed in 1706 only to be nearly destroyed in turn by the Taensa who were themselves fleeing the Yazoo and Chickasaw.

Iberville met them first at the village of the Biloxi when they were east on a hunting trip. The chief of the Bayogoula served as Iberville's guide up the Mississippi where they met the Houma in March 1699 at what is now the site of the Louisiana capital of Baton Rouge. There French, Houma, and Bayogoula celebrated before Iberville continued his exploration, returning to his ships anchored in the Mississippi Gulf Coast by an alternate route told to him by the Indians.

On his return to France, Iberville brought with him a young Indian boy given to him by the Bayogoula whose mission it was to learn French. After returning to the America in October 1699, the boy died of a throat disease while at the Bay of St. Louis before ever reaching his own people.

Following their destruction by the Taensa, the remnants settled around New Orleans for a short time before moving north to Ascension Parish where they settled between the Houma and Acolapissa around 1739. After that, the three tribes merged and became one, all passing into history soon after the turn of the century. See the Houma.

BEAR RIVER INDIANS OF CALIFORNIA

The Bear River were a small tribe that belonged to the Athapascan linguistic family. They were closely associated with the Masttole, Sinkyone, and Nongatl to the south and east of their home along the Bear River in present Humboldt County, California. (There has been reference to them as the Bear River Indians of Utah.)

BEAR RIVER INDIANS OF NORTH CAROLINA

The Bear River Indians of North Carolina were a small tribe associated with the Algonquian tribes and may have been part of the Machapunga. They have also been placed with the Pamlico of North Carolina. They have also been called the Bay River Indians, but very little is known about the tribe except, according to one writer, the name of their town was Raudauqua-quank.

BEAVER INDIANS

The Beaver were an Athapascan-speaking people that inhabited the area of the Peace River of British Columbia and Alberta in Canada. It was a name given to them by early explorers after the name of a local group, the tsa-dunne, who call themselves Dunneza (real people) in British Columbia and Dene dháa in Alberta. Many were converted by Jesuit Missionaries after 1850. Although they had some interaction with tribes that inhabited the United States, the Beaver remained in Canada.

BEOTHUK

The Beothuk (also Beothunk), a Canadian tribe in an independent linguistic group, inhabited the island of Newfoundland. They were noted for their great use of the color red. The Micmac name for them was Macquaejeet or Ulno Mequaegit, meaning "red man," a name picked up by the Europeans that became applied to all Indians.

BIDAI

At one time the Bidai were thought to be in an independent Atakapan linguistic stock with the Atakapa and Deadose, and probably the Opelousa of Louisiana, but the Atakapa have since been assigned to one family with the Chitimacha and probably the Tunican group on the Mississippi of the Tunican stock. Where that leaves the Bidai is uncertain. They lived about the middle course of the Trinity River at Bidai Creek in Texas. They reportedly served as intermediaries in the sale of guns between the Spanish and the Apache.

Nearly half the Bidai were destroyed in the epidemic of 1776-1777 but continued an independent existence into the mid-1800s. The San Ildefonso Mission was established for the Bidai, the Deadose, and the Patiri; but the Bidai were never converted. They have since disappeared from history.

BILOXI

The Biloxi belonged to the Siouan linguistic family and settled on the lower course of the Pascagoula River. The Moctobi and Capinans may be branches of either the Biloxi or the Pascagoula, or they may be synonyms for the tribal name.

Iberville first landed on the shore of the Mississippi Gulf Coast in February 1699 where he encountered the Biloxi (Bilocchy). With them were members of the Moctoby (Moctobi) and Pascagoula who had villages on the Pascagoula River. They were later joined by the Bayogoula and the Mugulasha who were from the same village along the Malbanchya River (the Mississippi/Myssysypy—Palisade to the Spanish) and had traveled east on a hunting trip.

Iberville went on to discover the mouth of the Mississippi, explore the lower Mississippi, and found the colony of Louisiana. Before returning to France, Iberville established a fort on Biloxi Bay, Fort Maurapas, which is often referred to as Fort Bilocchy.

On his return to America in October 1699 Iberville renewed his acquaintances with the Indians, reprovisioned Fort Biloxi and resumed his explorations of the area around present-day Pascagoula. On his journey up the Pascagoula River, he came to the original village of the Biloxi only to find it devastated by disease.

A few soon after moved to a small bayou near New Orleans but by 1722 returned to modern Mississippi and settled along the Pearl River in the former land of the Acolapissa. When French control east of the Mississippi came to an end in 1763, members of the Pascagoula group and the Pearl River group moved to Louisiana and settled near Marksville, later moving up the Red River to Bayou Boeuf, the same route taken by many of the other tribes of the region.

In the early nineteenth century the Biloxi sold some of their lands in Louisiana and moved to Texas in Angelina County. Later they returned to Louisiana or settled in Oklahoma. Descendants of those that remained on the Red River were found living Rapides Parish up into the 1950s, but the tribe as a distinct entity had long disappeared. See the Houma and Bayogoula.

BLACKFEET

The Blackfeet called themselves Soyi-tapix (prairie people). Swanton identifies them under the name Siksika. John Evers refers to them as the Blackfoot (pl. Blackfeet). Other writers use the name Blackfeet in both the singular and the plural—the convention adopted in this book. The Blackfeet were comprised of three divisions or tribes, each composed of a number separate bands. They three were the Piegan (or Pikuni) to the south; the Kainai, commonly known as the Blood tribe, in the middle; and the Siksika (Siksiká) or Blackfeet proper to the north. Linguistically related to the Cree and Gros Ventre of the Prairie, all three tribes spoke the same Algonquin language with only slight variations in dialect

Blackfeet land encompassed the area from the North Saskatchewan River and its major tributary, the Battle River, in Alberta, Canada, south to the headwaters of the Missouri in Northern Montana. In the nomadic period, they allied themselves with the Sarcee and the Gros Ventre of the Prairie or Atsina, forming what was commonly called the Blackfeet Confederacy. They have also been referred to as the Alliance Indians.

The Blackfeet acquired the horse and the gun about the same time around 1750. It was probably about that time or somewhat earlier that they encountered their first white man, most likely French traders on the lower Saskatchewan. Trade with the Cree or Assiniboin middlemen to with the French traders in Montreal and the English of the Hudson's Bay Company brought the first guns. They very likely also traded for their first horse, but from whom is unknown. The Piegan first sighted the horse in their encounters with their Shoshoni enemies to the southwest and, to a lesser extent, the Flathead. The Shoshoni and Blackfeet populations were devastated by a smallpox epidemic that struck in 1781. The Blackfeet, unlike the Shoshoni, recovered relatively quickly, due primarily to their polygamous living arrangements. In the beginning, the Blackfeet were friendly and receptive to the intrusion of the white man into their territory, but as the number of whites increased, they became fiercely resistant. By the end of the first decade of the nineteenth century, the Blackfeet had become the dominant force among the Indians of the northwestern plains.

In the spring of 1810 trappers from the new Missouri Fur Company established a post at the Three Forks of the Missouri to serve as a supply center for their activities in the Rocky Mountains. The Blackfeet attacked killing twenty trappers and kept the rest of their party bottled-up in the fort until autumn. When the Blackfeet pulled back, the trappers headed across the Divide and set up a new post called Henry's Post for the group's leader Andrew Henry. The site on the Snake River became known as Henry's Fork. It was the first American post west of the Divide. Thirteen years later on May 4, 1823, the Blackfeet attacked Fort Henry and killed four trappers and again bottled-up the rest forcing them to abandon their traps, and again on May 31 Piegan killed seven and wounded four under the leadership of Michael Immell and Robert Jones of the Missouri Fur Company in addition to taking their furs, supplies, and horses and killing another four trappers who had previously deserted the brigade. When Henry abandoned Fort Henry for another on the Bighorn River, that too was attacked by the Blackfeet or the Assiniboin. The Blackfeet persisted in their attacks which almost succeeded in closing off the entire region from hunters and trappers. General Henry Atkinson's 1825 Yellowstone Expedition failed to make contact with the Blackfeet or the Assiniboin. In 1831 Astor's American Fur Company established Fort Piegan up the Missouri near the Marias River to work the Blackfeet trade.

The smallpox epidemic of 1837 took almost half the Blackfeet population bringing it to a low of about 6300. In the fall of 1845 Jesuit priest Peter John De Smet sought out the Blackfeet. First to introduce them to Christianity and second to attempt to bring peace between them and the Flatheads. De Smet and his party traveled north from their base at Saint Mary's Mission among the Salish to the Rocky Mountain House (est. 1805) of the Hudson's Bay Company on the Saskatchewan River. (Enroute, they passed Lake Columbia, the source of the Columbia River, about 40 miles north of the 49th parallel in present-day British Columbia.) A number of Blackfeet braves appeared at the Rocky Mountain House on the twenty-fifth of October to trade and invited Fr. De Smet to their village to speak to the tribe of the Master of Life. Abandoned by his interpreter, Fr. De Smet was unable to locate the Blackfeet village until the following year.

Frs. De Smet and Nicholas Point arrived at the principal village of the Blackfeet on a large island on the Missouri River near Fort Benton in September 1846 and on the 25th they brokered a peace between the Blackfeet, led by Chief Big Lake, and the Flathead. The previous year, the Flathead had defeated their enemy the Crow. (See the Salish.) The Blackfeet attributed the Salish victory to the power or intercession of the Black Robe with the Master of Life on behalf of the Flathead. Nearest neighbors to the Flathead was the Small Robe band of the Piegan Blackfeet that hunted near the three forks of the Missouri. The Blackfeet asked Fr. De Smet to share the words of the Great Manitou (Master of Life) with the Blackfeet as he had the Flathead. At the Flathead mission on Christmas Day 1841, the chief of the Small Robes and his family of five were baptized by Father De Smet. They were the first Blackfoot Indians to adopt the Christian teaching. The chief took the Christian name Nicholas and later helped spread the word of Christianity to the Indians of the Plains. An attack by the Crows in the summer of 1846 nearly wiped out the Small Robes, and the band never again regained its prominence in the tribe.

Using the American Fur Company's Fort Lewis post as his headquarters, Fr. Nicholas Point worked among the Blackfeet until May of 1847 when he returned East. It was not until 1859 that the Jesuits returned to establish Saint Peter's Mission for the Blackfeet on the Teton River near present Choteau. The Jesuits subsequently moved the mission to the Little Belt Mountains out of the way of the gold prospectors and was finally abandoned in 1866 with little to show for the time and effort.

The Blackfeet were not a part to the Ft. Laramie Treaty of 1851. Their turn came in October 1855 just below the mouth of the Judith River in Montana. The government's treaty commission was headed by Governor Stevens. In addition to the three tribes of the Blackfeet, delegations from the Flathead, Pend d'Orielle, Nez Percé, and one chief from the Cree were also present to sign what became known as Lame Bull's Treaty out of respect for the venerable chief of the Piegans on October 17. As with the Fort Laramie treaty, the treaty called for intertribal peace and assigned territories to each tribe in exchange for annuities. It was ratified by Congress the following year, but two subsequent treaties signed by the Blackfeet in 1865 and 1868 never received Congressional approval—a concept beyond the understanding of the Indians. The failure of the government to follow through on what had been promised during the negotiations and to which their chiefs had made their mark became a constant source of bitterness and frustration to the Indian tribes of United States.

On July 13, 1880, President Rutherford Hayes signed an order that extinguished the title to thirty thousand square miles of land belonging to the Arikara, Gros Ventre, and Blackfeet making it available to the Northern Pacific Railroad. (With nearly fifty million acres of federal land rich in natural resources in its coffers, the Northern Pacific's transcontinental line across the north country was completed August 23, 1883, when construction crews working from either end met at Independence Gulch, near Dear Lodge, Montana, southwest of Helena. A golden spike ceremony was held up the line about twenty miles west at Goldcreek on September 8.)

BLACKFEET CONFEDERACY

The Blackfeet, more particularly the Piegan Blackfeet and the Blood tribe; the Sarcee or Sarci, and the Gros Ventre of the Prairie (the Atsina or Minnetaree) were allied during the nomadic period prior to white settlement forming what has been referred to as the Blackfeet Confederacy. There are some writers, however, that refer to the three tribes or divisions of the Blackfeet as comprising the Blackfeet Confederacy. For more see Blackfeet and Atsina.

BLACKFOOT SIOUX

The Blackfoot Sioux was a subgroup of the Western Division (Lakota) of the Sioux Nation. They were also known as the Sihasapa or Siksika (blackfoot) and often confused with the Siksika Blackfeet. For more see Sioux and Lakota.

BLEWMOUTH

Nothing is known about the Blewmouth Indians except that the name appears in early literature of southeastern United States. The strongest evidence suggest that they lived in southern Georgia about the time the colony was founded in 1733. Another source, however, states that they were "a nation of Indians on the other side of the Messasippi," presumably the west bank. Blewmouth was very likely the name given to a small, local band of Indians. It has no known connections in the later history of the region.

BODEGA MIWOK

The Bodega Miwok, which are sometimes treated separately, was a subdivision of the Coast Miwok and spoke one of the seven distinct Miwok dialects. They inhabited a number of villages in the area on and about Bodega Bay. There was no Bodega proper. For more see Miwok.

BOHICKET

The Bohicket was a subdivision or sub-tribe of the Cusabo of South Carolina. For more see the Cusabo.

BOTHENIN

The Bothenin or Pathenin was associated with the Saponi and Tutelo of Ontario, Canada. They are thought to be identical to the Occaneechi. See Occaneechi.

BROTHERTON

The Brotherton or Brothertown were Indians of a number of tribes of the Algonquian linguistic group that had been Christianized but displaced by the American colonists. The state of New Jersey created the first Indian Reservation at Brotherton in Burlington County around 1758 that began with a population of two hundred. Rev. John Brainerd, an Indian missionary, supervised the reservation from 1758 to 1774, after which it began to decline. In 1796, the Oneida tribe of New Stockbridge, New York, invited the Brotherton tribe to join them. (In 1801, the state of New Jersey sold the reservation and distributed the proceeds to the those members of the Brotherton who had remained. At the time there were fewer then eighty-five.)

The Brothertown project was established in New York in Oneida country by Samson Occom in 1774. The settlement lay between the Oneida and the settlers in the Mohawk Valley. Between 1774 and 1788, with a break for the War of Independence, Brothertown attracted Indians from the Mohegan, Groton, Niantic, Pequot, and Farmington of Connecticut; the Narraganset of Rhode Island; and the Montauk of Long Island. The Mohegan became the largest single group. Some of the Wappinger also dissolved into the Brotherton. Stockbridge Mohicans refugees from New England resettled nearby to the south on lands given to them by the Oneida, a place they called New Stockbridge.

A Brothertown Indian was tried for murder in 1801 and executed March 26, 1802 in Oneida County (formed from Herkimer County). The man was guilty of the crime, but of far greater significance was the fact that he was the first Indian executed by the State of New York. The case was also momentous for the fact that the state Supreme Court had ruled—but without universal application to all tribes—that the state had murder jurisdiction over the Brothertown Indians. Several months later a Seneca Indian was tried for murder. The Seneca chief Red Jacket challenged the state's legal jurisdiction and asserted federal supremacy in Indian affairs, citing the Treaty of Canandaigua. Thomas Jefferson and federal authorities of the new Republican Party refused to intervene bowing to the doctrine of States' Rights. Previously, the Federalists under John Adams had been willing to stand behind Indian sovereignty.

The Seneca, called Seneca George, was tried and found guilty on February 22, 1803, and sentenced to be executed. But the jurors cited extenuating circumstances, and Governor Clinton petitioned the state Legislature to issue a pardon which was granted providing that Seneca George leave the state forever. Although fear of an Indian uprising drove events, a legal precedent had been established. Nevertheless, both incidents had occurred on New York soil. The question of crimes committed on reservation land remained unsettled until 1822 when the New York State legislature passed a law giving the state sole and exclusive jurisdiction. So the situation remained until successfully challenged by the federal government.

The Brotherton remained with the Oneida until the early 1800s when they were removed to Wisconsin with the Stockbridge.

BRULÉ

The Brulé or Sicangu was one of the major seven subgroups of the Lakota or Teton Sioux or Western Division of the Sioux Nation. The "Tetons of the Burnt Woods" was the name used by Lewis and Clark. The Wazhazha Brulé band to which Scattering Bear belonged is sometimes treated separately. (It has been found listed among the Oglala bands.) For more see Sioux and Lakota.

GRATTAN MASSACRE AND THE BATTLE OF BLUE WATER CREEK

Relations between whites and Sioux had been generally peaceful, so much so that the number of troopers at Fort Laramie had been reduced down to one infantry company under an inexperienced Lieutenant named Fleming. With a less-than-minor incident in August of 1854, Indian relations in the northern Plains took a drastic reversal.

A band of Brulé Sioux was camped eight miles east of Fort Laramie waiting to receive government provisions. On August 18, a single, lame cow belonging to an immigrant Mormon party traveling the Oregon Trail nearby wandered off towards the Indian camp and was taken and slaughtered by a Miniconjou warrior who had been camped with the Brulé. The Mormons lodged a complaint at the fort. Although Lt. Fleming was inclined to ignore the matter, 2nd Lt. John L. Grattan convinced him to make an example of the to the Indians. The next day Grattan led a detachment of twenty-nine men, including himself and an interpreter, to the Sioux camp to arrest the person responsible. Four Sioux chiefs accompanied the soldiers at the urging of a white trader to try to smooth things over, but the Indians refused to give the man up. Grattan ordered his men to fire—at what is uncertain. The soldiers wounded one of the chiefs and his brother. The Indians struck back and killed all the soldiers except one who was critically wounded and died soon thereafter. They then ransacked the nearby trading post of James Bordeaux and pillaged the P. Chouteau Jr. & Company trading post three miles upriver called Fort John and took the government annuity provisions stored there as well, but the employees were left unharmed.

Much of the blame for the Grattan Massacre as it was called was left at the foot of an arrogant lieutenant and a drunken interpreter. But Washington accepted no mitigating circumstances and demanded retribution. No differentiation was made between the guilty and the innocent, nor between the warlike and the peaceful. Thus began the First Sioux War that was to last two years.

Following the Grattan incident, several bands of Sioux began attacks up and down the Oregon Trail from Fort Laramie. On November 13 a Brulé war party attacked a mail stage on its way to Fort Pierre, killed three employees, and wounded a passenger while making off with $10,000 in gold. The following

February on the 13th, a Miniconjou party raided the trading post of Ward and Guerrier northwest of Laramie and drove off sixty-five horses and mules. As events unfolded, P. Chouteau, Jr. & Company sold its Fort Pierre trading post "Without Fences" to the army in the spring of 1855. The landing at Fort Pierre was quickly put to use to receive troops brought in to meet the escalating situation.

A troop of six hundred soldiers, including infantry, light artillery, and calvary under Lt. Col. Philip St. George Cook, under the command of Brvt. Brig. Gen. W. S. Harney left Fort Leavenworth on August 4 and followed along the Oregon Trail to Fort Kearney where they arrived on the 20th. After rest and resupply, what became known as the Sioux Expedition, moved off on August 24.

Learning of a Brulé encampment six miles north of Fort Kearny near the mouth of Ash Hollow, Harney planned a surprise. As the infantry moved into position, the calvary circled around behind the camp. On the morning of September 3, the attack was launched, and the Sioux were caught in a deadly crossfire.

Eighty-six Indians, including many women and children were killed. Reports of the number women and children taken prisoner vary from forty to seventy. The soldiers suffered nine casualties: four killed, four wounded, and one missing. The incident came to be called the Battle of Blue Water Creek, a tributary of the North Platte; also the Battle of Ash Hollow and Harney's Massacre.

(About the time of the Grattan incident, an immigrant party of nineteen persons led by Alexander Ward were killed by a band of Yakima Indians twenty-five miles above Fort Boise. All these incidents were lumped together in the Eastern press.)

FORT LARAMIE

The similarity of names and the numerous changes among the ranks of the private trading companies in the Northwest country and Upper Plains have caused a certain amount of confusion regarding the history of Fort Laramie that was located at the confluence of the Laramie and North Platte rivers, about fifty miles northwest of Scottsbluff, Nebraska. Clustered within a short distance of one another in 1841 were Fort John, Fort William, and Fort Platte. Best evidence suggests the following scenario.

Messrs. William Sublette and Robert Campbell obtained a trading license in 1834 that referred to "Laramais' Point" in present-day eastern Wyoming. On May 30, 1834, they laid the foundation for Fort William. In 1835 they sold Fort William to Jim Bridger, Thomas Fitzpatrick and Milton Sublette, who within less than a year were bought out by Pratte, Chouteau and Company, the company managed by Pierre Chouteau, Jr. (Some reports give 1838 as the year Fort William was sold.) The Chouteau company, B. Pratt & Company, had purchased the American Fur Company's Western Department as it was called in 1834 when John Jacob Astor retired from the fur trading business and called it Pratte, Chouteau & Company. (The Northern Department was sold to another party with ties to Chouteau but retained the American Fur Company name.) Pratte, Chouteau & Company was dissolved following the 1839 trading season.

In 1840 Chouteau formed P. Chouteau Jr. & Company and in 1841 built a new large complex of adobe brick about three miles upriver that he named Fort John for John B. Sarpy, one of the partners in his new firm. Fort John was built in response to the competition from the new trading post known as Fort Platte that was built on the North Platte in 1840-1841. The small, deteriorating Fort William was abandoned. Fort William, and later Fort John, had both come to be popularly known as Fort Laramie, which has caused a great deal of confusion. Fort John was also known as "Without Fences" and "Gratiot House(s)," a misnomer. J. P. "Bunyun" Gratiot was Chouteau's cousin and the *bourgeois* or chief trader at Fort John.

In 1849 Lieutenant Daniel P. Woodbury of the Army Corps of Engineers purchased what is believed to have been the abandoned Fort William, referred to as Fort Laramie, on June 26 from Bruce Husband, Chouteau's agent, for $4,000. Thus commenced the long history of the site as a military post. At this time James Bordeaux, who at one time managed Fort John for Chouteau, operated his own trading post about eight miles southeast of Fort Laramie near the site of the Grattan Massacre. The losses at Fort John were initially estimated at over thirteen thousand dollars. Subsequent estimates put the loss at possibly twice that much. At the same time trade with the Indians nearly came to a standstill. In response to the deteriorating situation, the Army was looking for a suitable facility on the Missouri River as a base of the influx of soldiers. In the spring of 1855, Chouteau sold Fort Pierre in the heart of Sioux country on the Missouri River at the mouth of Teton, the site of the present-day capital of South Dakota, to the Army for a renegotiated price of $36,500. By 1865 P. Chouteau Jr. & Company had lost its license to trade with the Indians.

"WOMAN KILLER" AT THE SICANGU ENCAMPMENT

General William Harney attacked Little Thunder's Sicangu (Brulé) encampment on the Blue Water River near where it joins the North Platte River (the Shell to the Lakota) on September 3, 1855, gaining for himself the name "Woman Killer." Harney had been ordered to take prisoners and punish the Lakota for the Grattan affair. The attack occurred while most of the warriors were out hunting. The dead included both women and children—all scalped or mutilated in one fashion or another. A few escaped into the hills. About one hundred were taken captive and marched to Fort Laramie. The village was burned. Spotted Tail, whose own Sicangu camp was nearby, was seriously wounded in the fighting. He had been talking to General Harney, having come forward under a while flag, when a second troop attacked the encampment.

BUENA VISTA YOKUTS

The Buena Vista was one of the seven subdivisions of the Yokuts Group of Indians of California with villages on Buena Vista Lake, Kern Lake, and the Kern River. For more see Yokuts.

BURT WOODS CHIPPEWA

The Burt Woods Chippewa or Bois Forte (Fr. wood, forest) was one of the more well-known of the small bands of Chippewa. They lived on the Brois Brule River near the west end of Lake Superior in northern Wisconsin. For more see Chippewa.

CADDO PEOPLES

The Caddo Indians, Caddo Peoples, or Caddo Tribes referred to distinct but closely affiliated Indian groups clustered around the Red River in Texas, Arkansas, Louisiana, and Oklahoma. At one time the Caddoan Hasinai were the most numerous of all the native peoples of Texas.

CADDO GROUPS

Adaes or Adai of Louisiana
Natchitoches Confederacy of Louisiana
Eyeish of Texas
Hasinai Confederacy of Texas
Kadohadacho Confederacy of Texas

Although the Caddo acquired the horse around the beginning of the eighteenth century, they had little use for them; and they were careful to stay out of the lands of the Comanche to their west. Epidemics hit the Caddo hard between 1691 and 1816 greatly reducing the population and bringing them to the verge of extinction. At the same time, the Caddo became active in trade with Europeans and with other tribes of the region.

Members of some of the tribes whose homes had been east of the Mississippi fled to the southwest and settled in East Texas but soon found themselves at the mercy of the Anglos who had supplanted first the Spanish and then the Mexicans. In the late 1830s in, the crops and villages of peaceful Caddo and others, the "rats' nest" of east Texas as they called, were burned out by the Republic of Texas. Those who attempted to flee to Mexico were caught and brought back. A few escaped onto the Plains.

By the early 1840s most of the Caddo Peoples had been pushed south and west to the area of the Brazos. There they remained until they were placed on the Brazos Indian Reservation in 1855. Four years later, they were removed to the Washita River in Indian Territory in present-day western Oklahoma.

To avoid the conflict of the Civil War, most of the Caddo groups fled to southern and eastern Kansas and moved back to the Wichita after the war in 1867. By 1874 the boundaries of the Caddo reservation were defined, and the separate Caddo tribes agreed to unite as the unified Caddo Indian Tribe. Under the General Allotment Act of 1887, the Caddo reservation was partitioned in 1902 with 160-acre allotments going to each enrolled Caddo. The remaining lands were opened for white settlement. The Caddo continue to live in western Oklahoma, outside Binger in Caddo County. For more see Nations of the North and the respective Caddo groups.

CAHINNIO

The Cahinnio was a Caddoan tribe and one of the six subdivisions of the Kadohadacho Confederacy. They lived in the area around the Ouachita River in Arkansas. For more see Kadohadacho Confederacy and Caddo Peoples.

CAHOKIA

The Cahokia was a tribe of the Illinois Confederacy or Illinois Cluster of Tribes that lived about the modern city of Cahokia, on the southwest edge of present-day East Saint Louis. They were often associated with the Tamaroa, another tribe of the cluster. The Tamaroa Mission, later changed to the Cahokia Mission, was established by Jesuit missionaries in 1698 to serve both tribes. The mission was situated on the east side of the Mississippi across from St. Louis near the Cahokia village. The remnants of the Illinois tribes were removed to Indian Territory in 1820 where they were all consolidated under the name Peoria. For more see the Illinois.

Of Note

Cahokia was once a thriving regional metropolis of pyramid builders and mound builders during the Mississippian Period from about 800 C.E. to 1600. At its pinnacle in the 1300s, it had a population of some twenty thousand. In pre-European history, the Mississippians followed the Hopewell Indians who replaced the Adena.

CAHUEG-NA

Cahueg-na was a sub-tribe of the Tongva of California that inhabited the area about Cahuenga. For more see Tongva.

CAHUILLA

The Cahuilla, also spelled Cahuila or Kawia, belonged to the southern California group of the Shoshonean division of the Uto-Aztecan stock. The Takic-speaking peoples were also known as the California Desert People. Comprised of three divisions, Desert, Mountain and Pass, the Cahuilla inhabited the inland basin between the San Bernardino Range and the range extending southward from Mount San

Jacinto in California. They were initially placed on the Colorado River Reservation with the Mohave and Chemehuevi. On May 15, 1876, President Grant issued an executive order creating the Cabazon Reservation in Indio, California. It was named for Chief Cabazon, a leader of the Desert Cahuilla from the 1830s into the 1870s. Today, most of the descendants reside on a number of California reservations.

CALAPOOYA KALAPUYA

The Calapooya belonged to the Calapooya dialectic division of the Kalapooian linguistic stock. They inhabited the area along the Calapooya (Calapooia) River, a tributary of the Willamette River, near present Crawfordsville and Brownsville, Oregon, and the headwaters of the Willamette including the McKinzie, Middle, and West forks.

The Calapooya had five subdivisions or bands: Ampishtna, east of the upper Willamette River; Txanchifin located on the site of modern Eugene City; the Tsandlightemifa, at Eugene City; Tsankupi, at Brownsville in Lynn County; and the Tsawokot north of Eugene City. A variation in the spelling of the tribal name is commonly used to apply to all the Kalapooian peoples of western Oregon. For more see Kalapuya Peoples.

CALASTHOCLE

The Calasthoele was the name of a division or associated band of the Quinalt of the Salishan linguistic family identified by Lewis and Clark. They inhabited the Pacific coast and the Quinault River Valley of Washington. Lewis & Clark estimated the population at the time (1805) as two hundred men.

CALCEFAR

The Calcefar was a sub-tribe of the Unami division of the Delaware. They lived between the Rancocas Creek and Trenton in New Jersey. For more see Unami and Delaware.

CALLIMIX

The Callimix lived on the Pacific coast about forty miles north of the Columbia River in Washington.

CALUSA

The Calusa, a tribe warlike by nature, inhabited the west coast of Florida south of Tampa Bay and the Florida Keys. Those Indians of the interior about the Everglades and Lake Okeechobee, though distinct, may also have been Calusa. It appears likely that they were of the Muskhogean linguistic stock, related to the Apalachee and Choctaw. It also appears that they may been represented by if not absorbed into the Choctaw by the mid-1700s and incorporated into the Seminoles that were removed west. Some may have fled to Cuba when the Spanish relinquished the Floridas to the English in 1763. By the 1800s the Calusa had passed into history.

CANARSEE

The Canarsee or Carnarsie was a tribe of the Unami division of the Delaware. They lived in Kings County, Long Island, and a part of Jamaica and on the southern tip of Manhattan Island. They also inhabited the eastern end of Staten Island, New York. Their principal village was the Flatlands on Long Island.

CANAWAGHAUNA

The Canawaghauna or Conawaghruna was a Canadian tribe located near the Falls of St. Louis below the site of Montreal.

CANCEPNE

The Cancepne was listed by Farther Ortiz in his memorial to the king of Spain sometime after February 14, 1747, cited by Bolton in "Missions on the San Gabriel," but no additional information is available. It is believed that the Cancepne lived in east central or southeastern Texas.

CAOUITA

The Caouita was listed in Jefferson's *Notes on the State of Virginia.* Jefferson noted that they lived east of the Alabama and had a warrior population of some seven hundred. For more, see "Aborigines," Appendix D.

CAPARAZ

The Caparaz was a small band or tribe that lived along the coast of Florida that may have been the survivors of the Capachequi that were encountered by De Soto in 1540. They were likely of the southern division of the Muskhogean stock. They were placed on the Spanish mission of San Luis on the Apalachee coast in 1674 with the Amacano and Chine—together they numbered only about three hundred people.

CAPE FEAR INDIANS

The Cape Fear Indians may have belonged to the eastern division of the Siouan linguistic family. It is not known whether they were an independent tribe or a branch or division of another tribe, but it is known that they were closely associated with many eastern Siouan tribes. One opinion is that they were a part of the Waccamaw of the Waccamaw River because they lived along the Cape Fear River in North Carolina close to the head of the Waccamaw. First reference to them is from a New England colony on Cape Fear in 1661 that was subsequently driven off. Two other settlements were started but failed. The Indians were visited by Captain William Hilton in 1663, and in 1665 they asked for and received protection from Governor Archdale. Shortly thereafter they rescued 52 persons from a wrecked New England ship that subsequently formed Christ Church Parish North of Cooper River.

A few of the Cape Fear Indians accompanied the British in the Tuscarora expedition in 1711-12. They acted as both scouts and guards for Port Royal. Following the Yamasee War they moved to South Carolina and settled inland from Charleston. Remnants of the Cape Fear joined the Pedee in the Parishes of St. Stephens and St. Johns. By the early 1800s they were extinct as a separate entity. Some may have been absorbed by the Catawba.

CAPICHÉ

The literature contains one known reference to the Capiché of the Caddo division of the Caddoan linguistic group and one of the three allied member of the Natchitoches Confederacy of Louisiana, but the claim is unsupported. For more see Natchitoches Confederacy and Caddo Peoples.

CAPINANS

The Capinans belonged to the Siouan linguistic family and lived about the lower course of the Pascagoula River. The Capinans may be a branch of either the Biloxi or the Pascagoula, or the name may be a synonym for the tribal name. In the 1764 enumeration, the Capinans are combined with the Pensacola, Biloxi, Chatot, Washa, and Chawasha.

CAPOTE UTE

Capote was a subdivision of the Ute that inhabited the Tierra Amarilla and Chama River country of northcentral New Mexico, west of the Rio Grande.

CAREE

The Caree reportedly lived on the Pacific coast between the Nuáces and Rio del Norte in California.

CARRIER

The Carrier (most often used in the plural, Carriers) or Dakelh of Canada were of the Athabascan or Athapascan linguistic family who inhabited British Columbia. There were three subdivisions: Southern Carrier, Northern Carrier, and Babine. They lived about Eutsuk, Francis, Babine, and Stuart lakes and the headwaters of the Frazer River south to near Quesnel in British Columbia. They were also popularly known as the Taculli (pl. Tacullies), Takulli or Takahli.

CASCANGUE

The Cascangue may have been a tribe related to the Muskogee or Hitchiti. It may also only been another name for the Icafui used by the Creeks or Hitchiti. Literature on the Icafui refer to the Cascangue, but little else is known.

CASO

The Caso was listed by Farther Ortiz in his memorial to the king of Spain sometime after February 14, 1747, cited by Bolton in "Missions on the San Gabriel," but no additional information about the tribe is known. It is believed that the Cancepne lived in east central or southeastern Texas. It has been suggested that the Caso Indians were the same as the Caxo of the Hasinai division of the Caddoan linguistic family that had been reported in a Spanish missionary report from eastern Texas over fifty years earlier in 1691.

CASTAHANA

The Castahana lived between the sources of the Padouca Fork (North Platte River) and the Yellowstone in Wyoming.

CATAWBA

The tribe popularly known as the Catawba was new tribe formed from two independent tribes, the Catawba and the Iswa, that merged completely. They belonged the Siouan linguistic family. The Catawba was soon joined by the remnants other tribes of the Carolina piedmont that had been devastated by inter-tribal wars, wars with the English setters, and disease. Together, they represented four linguistic families: Siouan, Iroquoian, Muskhogean, and Algonquian. By the time the colonists began to talk of independence, the Catawba, who had became fearsome fighters, were able to obtain modern arms from Virginia traders and thus hold their own against the Iroquois and Tuscaroras, who had not yet joined the Iroquois Confederacy. They also managed to stay on relatively good terms with their white neighbors.

The Catawba (who would also give their name to a local university) lived in York and Lancaster counties in South Carolina but ranged into other parts of the state and into North Carolina (southwestern parts near Catawba River, to which they gave their name), and Tennessee.

CATHLACOMATUP

The Cathlacomatup was a subdivision or sub-tribe of the Multnomah. They belonged to the Chinookan linguistic family and lived on the sluice that connects the Wappatoo inlet with the Multnomah Channel in the Portland Basin of Oregon. For more see Multnomah.

CATHLACUMUP

The Cathlacumup was a subdivision or sub-tribe of the Multnomah of Oregon that has generally treated separately. They belonged to the Clackamas division of the Chinookan linguistic family and lived on the west bank of the lower mouth of the Willamette River near the Columbia River in Washington State. (Drake calls it the Wallaumut River.) They claimed as their territory all the land south to Deer Island, Oregon. Lewis and Clark estimated their population at 450 in 1806.

CATHLAKAHECKIT

The Cathlakaheckit belonged to Chinookan linguistic family. They lived at the Cascades of the Columbia River in Washington State. In 1812, the population was estimated at 900.

CATHLAMET

The Cathlamet or Kathlamet were part of the Chinookan linguistic stock. They inhabited an area along the south bank of the Columbia River near its mouth in Washington State. Present-day city of Cathlamet is the county seat of Wahkiakum County. Lewis & Clark encountered both the Cathlamet and Wahkiakum

CATHLANAQUIAH

The Cathlanaquiah was a subdivision or sub-tribe of the Multnomah of Oregon that has generally treated separately. They belonged to the Clackamas division of the Chinookan linguistic family. They lived on the southwest side of Sauvies Island (also spelled Sauvies) near Vancouver, Washington. Drake names the place Wappatoo Island. The tribe was decimated by an epidemic that hit in 1830, probably malaria.

CATHLAPOTLE

The Cathlapotle or Cathlahpotle belonged to the Chinookan linguistic stock. They lived along the Lewis River in Washington State and the southeast side of the Columbia River in present Clarke County.

CATHLASKO

According to Drake, the Cathlasko lived on the Columbia River, opposite the Chippanchikchiks.

CATHLATH

The Cathlath lived on the Willamette River in Oregon about sixty miles from its mouth. In 1843, Father John Paul De Smet picked a site on the Willamette River near Oregon City, south of Portland, for the new Jesuit Mission that he named Saint Francis Xavier. Construction of the new complex began immediately on what was to become the mother house and supply center for the Jesuit missions in the Oregon Country. The administrative center, however, would remain at the Salish mission. Father De Vos from the Kalispel mission was assigned to and take charge of Saint Francis Xavier.

After ten years, the series of Jesuit Indian missions in the Northwest had not proved successful. The failure can be attributed to the policy or system of "reduction" as it was called—a system that proved successful for the Jesuit missions in South American but totally impractical in California and the upper Northwest. First it required a complete change of life style and movement to an agrarian economy. It also required total isolation from the white man. Situated as the Indians were on lands rich in agricultural promise, precious metals, and fertile grasslands, isolation was simply not possible. The Jesuits also faced financial pressures to keep the missions operating. More disheartening possibly was the fact that Protestants accused the Jesuits of precipitating if not instigating the attacks to drive the Protestants out of the country.

In 1853 Rocky Mountain Mission was renamed the Oregon Mission and combined with the California Mission, under the direction of Father Nicholas Congiato. They were separate again in 1858.

CATHLATHLALA

It is generally believed that the Cathlathlala was a subdivision of the Watlala, but there is also some thought that it may be an separate tribe. They belonged to the Clackamas dialectic group of Chinookan linguistic stock and lived just below the Cascades in Oregon. For more see Watlala.

CATSKILL

The Catskill was a sub-tribe of the Munsee division of the Delaware and one of the five tribes of the Esopus group. They lived on Catskill Creek just north of Esopus Creek in Green County, New York

CATTANAHAW

The Cattanahaw lived between the Saskatchewan River and Missouri River, a huge area that essentially encompasses the northern third of the state of Montana and the southern portion of the Canadian province of Saskatchewan.

CAUGHNEWAGA

Caughnewaga was an independent Christian village of the Iroquois Confederation in Canada at Sault St. Louis (St. Regis) on the St. Lawrence River in Quebec Province. It was inhabited mostly by the Mohawk and the Akwesasane. For more see Mohawk.

CAYUGA

The Cayuga of upper New York State was a member of the federation of Iroquois-speaking Indian nations known as the League of Great Peace. They lived about Cayuga Lake. The Cayuga adopted the Saponi and the Tutelo. For more see Iroquois.

CAYUSE

The Cayuse, a relatively small tribe, constituted a branch of the Shapwailutan linguistic family or, along with the Molalla, the Waiilatpuan division of the Shapwailutan linguistic family, and they called themselves the Waiilatpus. The Cayuse and the Molalla lived together, but the Molalla were driven west by wars and hostile tribes into the Willamette Valley of western Oregon. The more aggressive Cayuse inhabited the lands about the heads of the Walla Walla, Umatilla, and Grande Ronde rivers from the Blue Mountains to the Deschutes River in Washington and Oregon. They acquired the horse from their enemies the Snakes (Northern Paiutes) to the south in the late 1700s.* The Cayuse became accomplished horsemen and passed the horse on to their neighbors that included the Nez Percé. With their close association with the Nez Percé, over time they began to adopt the Nez Percé dialect of the Shapwailutan language. As was common among some of their neighbors, the Cayuse held to the practice of flattering the heads by tying a child's head tightly with cords passed over folded hides rather than a board. The process also produced something of an edge around the top. To the casual white observer, the broad, flat back head with its edge was grotesque.

The Cayuse first came to the attention of the white man with the expedition of Lewis & Clark and became very familiar to the white hunters, settlers, and explorers who ventured in the Northwest Territory. From that time on, the proud and arrogant Cayuse, to the point of being haughty, became embroiled in the clash of cultures exasperbated by the fact that the Oregon Trail ran through their territory and the mighty Columbia was at their door. They demeaned women, practiced polygamy, and believed themselves superior to many of their neighbors, especially the Walla Walla. An aggressive, warring tribe, the Cayuse took and kept slaves as slaves not in the sense that other tribes took captives. Like many tribes along the Pacific coast and in the northwest country, possessions were important to increase individual and family status not in the communal sense as was typical of the tribes of the Great Plains to the east.

Suspicious and embittered by perceived grievances and unquestionably the most unfriendly tribe, relations between the Cayuse and whites were never amiable. It all came together in late November 1847 in an event that has come down in history as the Whitman Massacre that, in turn, precipitated the Cayuse War. (See Whitman Massacre below.)

The Cayuse, Walla Wall, and Umatilla signed the Treaty of June 9, 1855, but under duress. The chiefs were told by Governor Stevens of Washington that if they did not sign the treaty, they would "walk in blood knee deep." The tribes were placed on one of two reservations to be established on the lands of the Nez Percé and the Yakima. The Cayuse, Umatilla, Walla Walla, and Spokane were to live on Nez Percé lands that had been taken for the Umatilla Reservation. Most of the other tribes were to live with the Yakima on the Yakima Reservation (Also called Simcoe, for Fort Simcoe, established in 1856). A Nez Perce Reservation was also established along the border of western Idaho near the junction of Washington, Oregon, and Idaho. Indian hatred for whites had been building for the previous two years as a result of the ever-increasing influx of immigrants. The 1855 treaty brought matters to a head, and fighting broke out again in the fall of 1855 in what has been called the Yakima War in which the Cayuse were one of the principal antagonists. The Yakima War was followed by the short-lived Spokane War in 1858 in which the Cayuse were only in a position to offer moral support.

The 1855 Treaty was not ratified by the Congress until March 8, 1859. In December 1960 the Cayuse were moved to the Umatilla Reservation—except for the few that headed north or joined the holdouts from other tribes along the Columbia. A few braves from the reservation joined Chief (Young) Joseph in the Nez Percé war that broke out in June 1877, but many more volunteered as scouts for the Bannock War and the Sheepeater Campaign in 1878. The Allotment Act of March 3, 1885, reduced the reservation by about one-forth.

WHITMAN MASSACRE AND THE CAYUSE WAR

Dr. Marcus Whitman established the Whitman Mission for the Cayuse about twenty-five miles east of Walla Walla, Washington, in 1838. A smallpox epidemic that hit the tribe in 1847 brought fomenting anger to erupt. The Cayuse believed the missionaries were responsible. Within a few minutes on November 29, 1847, in a carefully planned and coordinated attack, a group of Cayuse had killed Dr. Whitman, his wife and eleven others at the mission and took fifty-four women and children captive. In January 1848, Peter Skene Ogden, the factor at Fort Vancouver, was subsequently able to negotiate the release of all but three older girls who were taken as wives.

What has been called the Cayuse War began at the end of November 1847 with the Whitman Massacre. The killings at the mission were followed of a series of raids and reprisals and a number of fights with members of the Oregon militia hat continued intermittently over the next two years. At the time, the entire Cayuse tribe numbered only from 400 to 800 souls. As a result, they recruited and threatened to fill their ranks. Those among the Walla Walla, Mollalah, Nez Percé, Umatilla, Palouse, and others who for a time joined them quickly fell away leaving the Cayuse on their own. Soon the renegades were on their own abandoned by the rest of the tribe who nevertheless continued to provide passive assistance until one Cayuse chief, Tauitau, stood up and was instrumental in the capture of those deemed to have been the ringleaders. By that time the Nez Percé stood firmly against the Cayuse and on the side of the government. The war, such as it was, effectively ended with the hanging deaths in the summer of 1850 of those believed to be responsible for the massacre.

(Oregon Territory was established August 14, 1848; and U.S. jurisdiction became effective on March 3, 1849, when the Oregon territorial government took over from the Provincial government. Federal troops arrived in late summer.)

General Joseph Lane, fresh from the Mexican war, was appointed governor of Oregon Territory in 1849 and determined that it was his responsibility to bring the guilty parties to justice and bring peace to the region. The trial of the five Cayuse leaders held responsible for the crimes began May 22, 1850. They were found guilty, sentenced, and hanged June 3, 1850. The Great Grave Memorial was erected above the site of the Whitman mission.

According to author Helen Jackson, three principal men of the Cayuse tribe, but innocent men, voluntarily agreed to accompany the Governor Lane and the soldiers of the Mounted Rifles to Oregon City where they knew they would be tried and hanged for the Whitman murders for the guilt of others of their tribe who had committed the crimes. The five men were duly found guilty and hanged on June 3, 1850. Jackson also writes that retribution for the murders had previously be wrought upon the Indians by white settlers who had killed many more Indians than had been killed at the mission. Rudy and Brown made no such assertion other than writing of the wretched condition of the Cayuse as a result of the war.

Author David Dary, on the other hand, writes that five guilty men were surrendered to the authorities for trail based on the first hand account of the U.S. Marshal Joseph Meek who directed the executions. Frank McLynn writes that three men entered the mission and killed Whitman and that his death signaled the beginning of the massacre that followed. He goes on to write that the five ringleaders surrendered to be hanged but provides no specifics.

Angie Debo's account is slightly different from Dary's. She writes that five guilty leaders surrendered in order to make peace with the white man and includes a quote from one of the men that he surrendered "to save our people," but she does not give a source. Rudy and Brown, who give an extended account of the proceedings, including several of the different arguments, as well as events leading up to their capture, expand on the quote, citing Herbert Howe Bancroft. The truth will never be known with any degree of certainty.

------

*According to a brief filed before the U.S. Claims Commission, the name Snakes as used by the Cayuse referred to the Northern Paiutes not the Shoshoni.

CECILVILLE INDIANS

Cecilville Indians constituted a division of the Shasta, lived about Cecilville, California, and spoke a distinct dialect. They are also call Haldokehewuk.

CHABANAKONGKOMUN

The Chabanakongkomun was a subdivision or band of the Nipmuc. They lived about Dudley, Massachusetts, and were placed on the Dudley Reservation. They were also called the Dudley Indians and the Pegan band (listed in Drake as Pecan). For more see Nipmuc.

CHAFTAN

The Chaftan was a band or sub-tribe of Indians that lived west of the Cascade Mountains in Oregon. Their name is listed in the U.S. Code, but no additional information is available. Also see Western Oregon Indians.

CHAKANKNI MOLALLA

The Chakankni was one of the three divisions of the Molalla. They lived on the on the headwaters of the Rogue River in western Oregon, northwest of Klamath Lake and were later absorbed by the Klamath and others. For more see Molalla.

CHAKCHIUMA

The Chakchiuma spoke a dialect closely related to the Choctaw and Chickasaw and were closely related to the Houma but separated from them. They lived along the Yalobusha River at its mouth on the Yazoo River in Mississippi. At one time their lands extended to the head of the Yalobusha and east to West Point. According to tradition, the Chakchiuma came east at the same time as the Chickasaw and Choctaw.

At the time of De Soto, the Chickasaw reportedly sent an expedition against the Chakchiuma, but the circumstances are unknown. In retribution for killing a French missionary, the French encouraged attacks on the Chakchiuma by their neighbors, which further weakened the tribe. Later, however, they assisted the French after the Natchez outbreak.

It is generally thought that the Chakchiuma were destroyed as a distinct people by the Chickasaw around 1739 and that remnants were absorbed into the Chickasaw and Choctaw. But it has also been suggested that a part may have joined the Chickasaw prior to 1733 and that the rest joined the Choctaw. The Chakchiuma had an estimated total population of only 150 in 1722 and dwindling.

CHALA

The Chalas was listed in Jefferson's *Notes on the State of Virginia*. Bouquet (1764) reported a population of 130 warriors. Their location is given as the St. Lawrence River and they are listed as one of the St. Lawrence Indians along with the Abenaquis (Abnaki); Michmacs (Micmac); and Amalistes (Ameliste). For more see "Aborigines" in the appendices.

CHALAOKLOWA CHICKASAW

The Chalaoklowa Chickasaw were a group of Chickasaw that avoided removal to Indian Territory in the eighteen hundreds and generally remained out of sight and out of mind until legal discrimination against Indians ended. In 2005 the tribe gained official recognition by the state of South Carolina. They are now headquartered in Indiantown, South Carolina, reportedly their historic homeland. Swanton makes no mention of Chalaoklowa and refers to Indian Town only in reference to the Cusabo.

CHAMNAPUM

The Chamnapum was one of the two branches of the Wanapam tribe. For more see Wanapam.

CHASTACOSTA

Chastacosta (also written Chasta Costa and Shasta Costa and simply as Chasta) were a Athapascan people who lived in Oregon on the lower course of the Illinois River and on the Rogue River near its confluence with the Illinois. It difficult to differentiate in the literature between the Chastacosta, identified as Chasta, and the Shasta, spelled Chasta, which is a common occurrence.

CHATO

The Chato was a Matagalpa or possibly a Lenca tribe of Honduras in Central America, not to be confused with the Chatot of Florida.

CHATOT

The Chatot belonged to the southern division of the Muskhogean stock. They inhabited the area west of the Apalachicola River in Florida. They were first mentioned by the Spanish in 1639. Under the constant threat of attack by larger, and more powerful tribes, they escaped to Mobile around 1707. Following the end of the French and Indian War in 1763 in which Mobile was ceded to the English, the Chatot moved to French Louisiana and settled on Bayou Boeuf and later on the Sabine River. Other than roomers, nothing more was heard of them as a people.

CHAWASHA

The Chawasha belonged to the Chitimacha division of the Tunican linguistic family. They lived along Bayou La Fourche (or Lafourche) in Louisiana and eastward to the Gulf and across the Mississippi River. The Indians that attacked De Soto on the Mississippi may have been the Chawasha and the Washa. Bienville moved them to the west side of the Mississippi near English Town.

Sometime before 1722 they crossed to the east side of the river, and in 1730 they were attacked by black slaves in order to insure that there was no repeat of the likes of the Natchez uprising in New Orleans. The last record of the Chawasha was in 1758. At the time they constituted one of the villages of the Washa, but they could have continued as a distinct people considerably longer.

CHEEGEE

The Cheegee were reported at living in Kentucky in 1783. Swanton lists only five tribes in Kentucky, all five of which had their homelands elsewhere. It appears most likely that Cheegee was a village of the Cherokee. It may have been the village Swanton calls Chagee on the border with South Carolina. Drake refers to the Middle Settlements of the Cherokee.

CHEHALI

The Chehali (meaning "sand") belonged to the coastal division of the Salishan linguistic family. There were two principal subdivision or tribes that spoke distinct yet related Salish languages and maintained close ties with one another, the Upper Chehali and Lower Chehali. They lived along the course of the Chehalis River and on the south side of Grays Bay or Grays Harbor in Washington Territory. The village of the Chehalis proper was located on the south side of Grays Harbor near the present city of Westport, Washington. In later years the Chehalis occupied the territory about Willapa Bay that at one time had been the home of the Chinook.

The Lower Chehalis, whose principal livelihood came from the sea, were closely affiliated with the Copalis, Wynoochee and Humptulip tribes. The Satsop were also affiliated politically with the Lower Chehalis although their dialect was more similar to Upper Chehalis. The Upper Chehalis, of which there were at least five bands, maintained a river-based economy augmented by edible roots and berries from the land. Major villages were located at the mouths of Lincoln Creek, Scatter Creek, Skookumchuck River, Black River, Cedar Creek and at Grand Mound. By the close of the eighteenth century, they had the horse.

The four thousand-plus acre Chehalis Reservation was selected by the government in 1860 to serve both the Upper and Lower Chehalis. The Chehalis also received allotments, on petition, from the Quinault

Reservation in Washington State with the Chinook and other "the Fish-Eating Indians of western Washington."

CHELEMELA KALAPUYA

Chelemela (also spelled Chelamela) or Long Tom Creek Indians were of the Central Division of the Kalapooian linguistic stock who lived along the Long Tom Creek or River , a western tributary of the Willamette River, between Eugene and Corvallis, Oregon. Long Tom Creek Indians are referred to in the definitions listed in the U.S. Code. For more see Kalapuya Peoples.

CHEMAPOHO KALAPUYA

Chemapoho, Chemapho, or Maddy was of the Central Division of the Kalapooian linguistic stock. They lived west of the Cascade Mountains in western Oregon. The name "Maddy" is listed in the U.S. Code under the definitions of tribe. For more see Kalapuya Peoples.

CHEMEHUEVI

The Chemehuevi were part of the Paiute and with the Paiute and the Ute, they constituted one subdivision of the Shoshonean Division of the Uto-Aztecan linguistic stock. They originally inhabited the eastern half of the Mohave Desert of Arizona; latter on Cottonwood Island, in the Chemehuevi Valley; and a number of locations on the Colorado River. The Chemehuevi were placed on the Colorado River Reservation with the Mohave and Kawia.

CHEPENAFA KALAPUYA

The Chepenafa or Mary's River Band belonged to the Calapooya or Central Division of the Kalapooian linguistic stock. They were at times considered a division of the Luckamiut. They inhabited the forks of St. Mary's River near present Corvallis, Oregon. For more see Kalapuya Peoples.

CHEPOUSSA

The Chepousssa was one of the minor tribes of the Illinois Cluster of Tribes for which there is only passing mention. For more see Illinois Cluster.

CHERAW

The Cheraw have been placed in the Siouan linguistic group. They lived originally near the head of the Saluda River in present Pickens and Oconee Counties of South Carolina before moving to North Carolina at a early date. They are believed to have been the Indians referred to indirectly by De Soto in 1540. By 1700 they were on the Dan River near the southern border of Virginia later moving southeast where they joined the Keyaswee.

The Cheraw were accused of widespread depredations along the Santee River. The Cheraw subsequently moved to the upper course of the Great Pee Dee River near the line between North Carolina and Virginia and in the Cheraw District of South Carolina. A 1760 map refers to a "Lower Saura Town" and an "Upper Saura Town."

Between 1726 and 1739 the Cheraw were incorporated into the Catawba as protection against the treat of attack by the Iroquois. Although according to some reports the Cheraw were noted for their hostility to the English, they joined the English in an expedition against the French at Fort Duquesne in 1759.

CHEROKEE

The Cherokee or Tsalagi (Tsa-La-Gi) nation was a distant members of the Iroquoian linguistic family and was known as one of the "Five Civilized Tribes" of southeast. From the earliest of times, they lived about the southern tip of the Appalachia Mountains in Tennessee and North Carolina and parts of Virginia, South Carolina, Georgia, and Alabama. They were known, in fact, as the mountaineers of the South. Their lands extended generally from the Carolina Broad River on the east to the Alabama River on the west. There were three Cherokee dialects that generally corresponded to the three geographical divisions of the Cherokee nation: Lower Settlements, Middle Settlements, and Over-the-Hills and Valley Settlements or Overhill Settlements, each with their own subdivisions and villages. There were also a significant number of independent villages.

LOWER SETTLEMENTS

Estatoee, Keowee, Kulsetsiyi, Oconee, Qualatchee, Tomassee, Toxaway, Tugaloo, and Ustanali

CHEROKEE, MIDDLE SETTLEMENTS

Cowee, Coweeshee, Ellijay, Itseyi, Jore, Kituchwa, Nucassee, Stikayi, Tawsee, Tekanitli, Tessuntee, Itkaleyasuni, Watauga, and U=Yunsawi

OVER-THE-HILL AND VALLEY SETTLEMENTS

Chatuga, Chilhowee, Cotocanahut, Echota, Hiwassee, Natuhli, Nayuhi, Sitiku, Tahlasi, Tallulah, Tamahli, Tellico, Tennessee, Toquo, Tsiyahi, and Ustanali

Accommodations made to the English and the countervailing presence of the French encouraged trade and kept relations between Cherokees and whites civil if not amiable. The establishment of the colony of Georgia in 1733 and the incursion of land-hungry whites west of the Appalachia about the same time changed the dynamics of relations in the region that grew steadily worse until the complete removal of the Cherokee west of the Mississippi a century later.

Like all Native American tribes, particularly those in the lands west of the Appalachian Mountains, the Cherokee were nearly destroyed by the French and Indian War and the British victory in 1763. In late 1759 Carolinians launched an attack into Cherokee country that ended in a draw. In the following months, the Cherokee not only beat back a second attack but inflicted a heavy toll on the borderlands of the Carolinas and Virginia. By then the successive victories of the British at Fort Frontenac on Lake Ontario, Fort Duquesne/Fort Pitt, Quebec, and Montreal had cut the source of French trade goods on which the Cherokee and other tribes depended. A third expedition was launched against the Cherokee by some 2,500 British regulars and colonial militia in 1761 that destroyed fifteen villages and left the crops in ruin. The peace agreed to by Attakullaculla (Little Carpenter) came at the price of a large tract of land. The defeat of the French left the Native Peoples wholly at the mercy of the British colonial governments that were not disposed to even a feigned policy of coexistence.

The Cherokee signed a treaty with the Continental government on November 28, 1785, at Hopewell, South Carolina (since abandoned), on the Keowee River. The treaty set the boundaries of Cherokee lands generally along the Tennessee and Cumberland rivers. The treaty also contained a provision to the effect that squatters on Indian lands could be expelled and punished. All Indian treaties generally contained similar language, whether it was the Cherokee of Georgia and Tennessee or the Sioux of South Dakota. For all intents and purposes, the words were meaningless. Hopewell was just the first of many treaties with the Cherokee over the next fifty years by which their lands would be methodically taken from them.

The federal government up through the presidency of President Monroe held to the policy that Indian tribes were sovereign nations legally capable of selling or otherwise transferring title to their lands. (The policy was attacked Andrew Jackson, among others.) On March 30, 1802, the Congress passed an act entitled "An act to regulate trade and intercourse with the Indian tribes, and to preserve peace on the frontiers." The law recognized the several Indian nations as distinct political communities, having territorial boundaries and the right to all the land within those boundaries and, further, that within those boundaries their authority was exclusive. The state of Georgia itself negotiated a contract of cession with the Cherokee in 1802 by which it acquiesced in that basic constitutional premise. In addition, the legislature and officers of the state repeatedly issued a number of resolutions and proclamations during the first two decades of the 1820s that acknowledged the independence of the Cherokee nation and the exclusive authority of the United States government—a position that would be short lived. In addition, such independence merely established the legal basis for the transfer of title to which the Indians were, for the most part, forced to agree.

In the early 1800s, the Cherokee Nation was one of the strongest Indian tribes in the United States. By 1819 it began to unravel. A band of Cherokees led by Tahlonteskee relinquished their rights to their lands east of the Mississippi and moved west to lands in Arkansas and Missouri that had been ceded to the government by the Osage. They were the first of the great removal. Soon there were six thousand Cherokees living along the banks of the Arkansas River. Primarily farmers who wore white man's clothes and lived in permanent structures, the Cherokee quickly came into conflict with the Osage who were primarily horsemen and hunters who ranged across the plains. Fort Smith was charged with maintaining the peace.

To the east, as the 1820s drew to a close, there was an onslaught of land-hungry white settlers who squatted on Cherokee land, stole their livestock, and burned their towns. Beginning in December 1828, the state of Georgia, through a series of new laws, took the position that the Cherokees were mere tenants living on state land. The Cherokee took their case to the Supreme Court. In *Cherokee Nation v. the State of Georgia*, the Supreme Court held that native tribes could be treated as wards of the federal government rather than as foreign nations.

Two years later the Georgia legislature passed a law that prohibited whites from living on Indian territory after March 31, 1831, without a license from the state in order to state authority to remove white missionaries who were helping the Indians resist their removal. The Cherokee again appealed to the Supreme Court. In *Worcester v. Georgia*, the Supreme Court ruled in favor of the Cherokees and the missionaries reversing its earlier position. In *Worcester* the court held the Cherokee had the right to self-government and declared Georgia's extension of state law over them to be unconstitutional.

In an opinion delivered by Chief Justice John Marshall, the "treaties and laws of the United States contemplate the Indian territory as completely separated from that of the states; and provide that all intercourse with them shall be carried on exclusively by the government of the union." Chief Justice Marshall argued, "The Cherokee nation, then, is a distinct community occupying its own territory in which the laws of Georgia can have no force. The whole intercourse between the United States and this nation, is, by our constitution and laws, vested in the government of the United States." Thus acts of the individual states that interfere with the federal government's authority are therefore unconstitutional.

The state of Georgia refused to abide by the court's decision, and President Jackson refused to intervene to enforce the court order. Jackson's attitude toward Native Americans was much the same as Thomas Jefferson's, paternalistic and condescending. They were all as small children to the Great White Father in Washington—a symbolism that marked all future dealings between the government and the Native American Indians. As their Great White Father, he was saving them from the encroachments and depredations of the white man. That they would have their new lands in perpetuity was as meaningless as the earlier provisions for the removal and punishment of squatters on Indian lands. It was a common practice that dated back to colonial American for state governors to secure the agreement of minor chiefs with which to bind whole nations. That such treaties were disavowed by a council of major chiefs as illegitimate was irrelevant. It was not new wisdom to government officials that even in the most tightly woven tribal unit, no single chief ever spoke for all members of the unit. That fact was conveniently ignored.

On March 14, 1835, President Jackson secured the signature of a relatively minor Cherokee chief, named the Ridge or Major Ridge, to the Schermerhorn Compact. With his signature, Ridge willingly agreed to relocation. The compact was formally disavowed by over 15,000 Cherokees led by the mix-blood Principal Chief of the Cherokee, John Ross, who was seven-eighths Scottish. Nevertheless, the Treaty of New Enchola, Georgia, was executed December 29, 1835, following new negotiations and a meaningless vote of some five hundred Indians at the most from a population of over twenty-one thousand based on the 1835 census. The treaty was ratified by Congress May 23, 1836, over the objections of Daniel Webster and Henry Clay, two members of the Great Triumvirate; and when the case was brought before the Supreme Court, the Court sided with the government.

On the basis of the Schermerhorn as it was called, the Cherokee were given two years to migrate voluntarily or they would be forcibly removed by the military. By 1838, only two thousand left of their own accord. Some sixteen thousand, followers of Chief John Ross, remained. Seven thousand federal troops and Georgia militia were brought in to round them up into stockades preparatory to the move west. They were given no chance to gather their belongings; they would take with them the clothes on their backs and no more. What followed was the march west that came to be known as the Trail of Tears (nu-na-hi du-na tlo-hi-lu-i, the "trail where they cried") in which 4,000 Cherokees died of cold, hunger, and disease. Although accounts vary from 13,000 to 17,000 on the number of Cherokees removed in the autumn of 1838, they all agree on the number that died along the way. There were also reports of possible bribes paid to John Ross and others to facilitate the move, but the claims have not be substantiated. See the full account in Gloria Jahoda, *The Trail of Tears*.

No sooner had they left than thousands of white settlers descended upon the Coosa River Valley. The homes they left behind were looted, and heir lands and goods were auctioned off. Within five years of the date of the treaty, the Alabama plantation system was firmly anchored on former Indians lands, poised to exploit another non-white race.

THE SITUATION IN THE WEST

Three separate groups of Cherokees emigrated West: the Old Settlers under Tahlonteskee several years before the Great March; the Treaty Party under Ridge, his son John Ridge and Watie; and the Late Immigrants under John Ross (White Bird). A few Cherokee had escaped into the hills of North Carolina. Some of the early emigrants continued west and settled on the fertile lands of east Texas, but by in the late 1830s their crops and villages were burned and they were driven out by the new Republic of Texas.

Ridge and the Treaty Part of some 650 settled near Honey Creek on the Cherokee line that defined the border between Missouri and Arkansas in relative ease and comfort. The Late Immigrants settled in the southeast part of the present-state of Oklahoma. (Confusion often arises regarding the boundaries of the present-state of Arkansas and the Arkansas Territory of the 1830s. In 1819 when Missouri first applied for statehood, the Arkansas Territory included the present states of Arkansas and Oklahoma, excluding the panhandle. Arkansas became a state in 1836, and Oklahoma became a state in 1907.)

When Ross and his followers agreed to live under the government that had been set up by the Old Settlers, they met at Double Springs near present-day Tahlequah to sign a pact; but arguments erupted over who would be the principal chief, and no agreement was signed. Tensions also erupted into bloodshed between the Treaty Party and the Late Immigrants who were considered traitors because of their stand on the Schermerhorn Treaty. Ridge and his son were among the first to die.

During the American Civil War, Stand Watie, one of the leaders of the Treaty Party, and his group fought side by side with the Confederates. Watie himself rose to the rank of brigadier general and was the last Confederate general to surrender on June 23 at Doaksville in Indian Territory. John Ross at first remained neutral then on October 7, 1861, he signed a treaty with the Confederacy acceding to what appeared to be the majority sentiment of the tribe in order to try to preserve unity. The Cherokee suffered from the decision. Following the defeat of the pro-Confederate Cherokee under Stand Watie at Honey Springs on July 17, 1863, Ross's faction repudiated the treaty with the Confederacy and returned to he Union fold. Following the war the Cherokee united behind a full-blooded chief named Louis Downing.

More than 100,000 Cherokee now live in parts of Oklahoma. Over the years, many have moved elsewhere. Beginning in 1953, the Cherokee Nation celebrated the Cherokee National Holiday to commemorate the signing of the 1839 Cherokee Constitution. The Labor Day Weekend event has grown over the years into one of the largest events in Oklahoma.

The Qualla Boundary in North Carolina, midway between Atlanta, Georgia, and Charlotte, North Carolina, is the homeland of the Eastern Band of Cherokee Indians with 13,079 enrolled members. Another federally recognized entity is the United Keetowa Band of Cherokee Indians in Oklahoma.

Note: The Jackson administration removed 46,000 Native American people of the Five Nations from their lands east of the Mississippi by 1838. The removal opened 25 million acres of land to white settlement and to the extension of slavery.

INDIAN REMOVAL ACT OF 1830 AND THE TRAIL OF TEARS

President Andrew Jackson took office in March 1829. The following year he pushed the Indian Removal Act described as "An Act to provide for an exchange of lands with the Indians residing in any of the states or territories, and for their removal west of the river Mississippi." Passed by the Twenty-first Congress on May 26, 1830, the act was signed into law by President Andrew Jackson on May 28. The bill passed the House by the narrow margin of 102 to 97.

The act gave the president the power to negotiate removal treaties with Indian tribes living east of the Mississippi. The Indians were to give up their lands in exchange for lands to the West, beyond the states of Missouri and Arkansas. The act appropriated the relatively meager sum of $500,000 to carry out the provisions of the law. Indians who wished to remain in the East would be required to become citizens of their home state. The tribes of the Southeast were the most affected, but the legislation applied to all Indians living in the East. Little thought was given to the other people already living on the lands to the West. Intercourse Act of 1834 attempted to control the removal process and gave a location for the Indian lands as "that part of the United States west of the Mississippi, and not within the states of Missouri, Louisiana, or the Territory of Arkansas."

In the eyes of Jackson and the Congress, the act would make removal both voluntary and peaceful. In actuality, it was something entirely different. For those that agreed to relocate, the process was relatively peaceful. Those that resisted were removed by force.

The government forced the Indians east of the Mississippi to move out of the lands that they had lived on for generations and to move to land given to them in parts of Oklahoma. President Jackson was quoted as saying that this was a way of protecting the Indians allowing them time to adjust to the white culture. Most affected in terms of numbers were the Five Civilized Tribes: Cherokee, Creek, Seminole, Choctaw, Chickasaw. On September 27, 1830, the Choctaw signed the Treaty of Dancing Rabbit Creek, Mississippi, by which they ceded all their lands east of the Mississippi to the federal government, 10,423,130 acres. It was the first removal negotiated among the five tribes under the new act. Because of their extensive land holdings and the large number of Indians involved, the five tribes were Jackson's first priority. Some five thousand Choctaw were involved in the first move. In addition, gold had been discovered on the Cherokee land in 1829. To the north, there were dozens of smaller tribes along the upper reaches of the Mississippi, the Great Lakes, and along the Ohio River. A series of treaties were executed with the Menominees, Senecas, Shawnees, Ottawas, and Wyandots beginning in February 1831.

Within ten years of the passage of the act, more than 70,000 Indians had moved across the Mississippi. Many Indians died on the journey that came to be known as the "Trail of Tears." The term was given to several different trails used by the members of the Creeks and Cherokees and Choctaws to reach their new lands in the west. They had wept on leaving their homes in the Southeast. They were promised title of the "as long as grass shall grow and rivers run," but by 1906 they were forced to move to other reservations. The phrase "Trail of Tears" has been subsequently used to refer to all forced removals. The Potawatomi called it the "Trail of Blood." See the painting *Trail of Tears* by Robert Lindneux, Woolaroc Museum, Bartlesville, Oklahoma. In 1906, the Cherokees were granted U.S. citizenship.

SEQUOYAH

On December 27, 1980, the U.S. Postal Service issued a 19-cent stamp honoring Sequoyah (also know under his white name, George Guess), who invented the Cherokee syllabary. Ceremonies were held at Tahlequah, Oklahoma. He is believed to have been born around 1773 in that portion of the Cherokee Nation in the present state of Georgia. He devised a set of written characters and symbols that could be used to represent spoken syllables in the Cherokee language. His syllabary made possible a written constitution and newspaper, the *Cherokee Phoenix*. Sequoyah was part of the group of Cherokees that had migrated to Arkansas in 1822. He died near San Fernando, Mexico in 1843.

CHEROKEE NATION V. STATE OF GEORGIA 30 U.S. 1 (5 PET. 1831)

Mr. Chief Justice MARSHALL delivered the opinion of the Court.

"This bill is brought by the Cherokee nation, praying an injunction to restrain the state of Georgia from the execution of certain laws of that state, which, as is alleged, go directly to annihilate the Cherokees as a political society, and to seize, for the use of Georgia, the lands of the nation which have been assured to them by the United States in solemn treaties repeatedly made and still in force.

"If courts were permitted to indulge their sympathies, a case better calculated to excite them can scarcely be imagined. A people once numerous, powerful, and truly independent, found by our ancestors in the quiet and uncontrolled possession of an ample domain, gradually sinking beneath our superior policy, our arts and our arms, have yielded their lands by successive treaties, each of which contains a solemn guarantee of the residue, until they retain no more of their formerly extensive territory than is deemed necessary to their comfortable subsistence. To preserve this remnant, the present application is made. "

CHESAPEAKE

The Chesapeake, a member of the Powhatan Confederacy, belonged to the Algonquian linguistic stock. They lived in the Cape Henry region, the southern headland at the opening of Chesapeake Bay in Virginia in Princess Anne County. It was the Chesapeake who first encountered the English in 1607 Jamestown and drove them back to their ships. Jamestown was sixty miles inland on the James River, formerly the Powhatan River.

The Chesapeake are assumed to be the Cheseppiooc Indians, the name meaning Expanse of Waters (Big Water) where shellfish are found or where Great Shellfish Water People live.

CHESKITALOWA

The Cheskitalowa was reportedly a band of the Seminole that lived on the west side Chattahoochee River.

CHETCO

The Chetco belonged to the Athapascan linguistic stock. They lived on each side of the mouth and up the Chetco River in Oregon and along the Winchuch River and south just inside the California border.

CHETLESSINGTON

The Chetlessington was a band or sub-tribe of Indians that lived west of the Cascade Mountains in Oregon. No additional information is known. Also see Western Oregon Indians.

CHEWELAH

The Chewelah, a division of the Kalispel, inhabited the land west of the Calispell or Chewelah Mountains in the upper Colville Valley of Idaho.

CHEYENNE

The Cheyenne became the most westerly of the Algonquian linguistic family. History first encountered the Cheyenne, or the Cheyenne first encountered history, around 1680 on the east bank of the Mississippi when a group of Chaa (Cheyenne) visited La Salle as he and his men were building Fort Crèvecoeur on the Illinois River. But the first record was their appearance on the Marquette-Juliet maps of 1673 that places the "Chaiena" living above the mouth of the Wisconsin River and north of the Sioux (Dakota).

The maps of French fur traders of the next decade placed the Cheyenne in the valley of the Minnesota River on its western reaches in present south-central Minnesota between the Iowa to the east and the Otoe to the south and west. During the next quarter century the Cheyenne continued their migration west and north up the Minnesota between Big Stone Lake and Lake Traverse and ultimately to the Sheyenne River of present North Dakota. As in many cases, migration is the result of pressures from others. In the case of the Cheyenne, pressure came from the Sioux, the Cree, or the Assiniboin—any one or all three. Most scholars believe the major push came from the Sioux; Grinnell believes strongly that it was the Assiniboin.

The Cheyenne lived peacefully on the Sheyenne River until well into the mid 1700s. There they acquired the horse, traded with neighboring tribes, cultivated crops of beans, corn and squash, and hunted buffalo. Apparently the Cheyenne left the Sheyenne sometime between 1770 and 1790 following a devastating attack on the principal village by a large band of Chippewa that escaped into Canada. The Cheyenne moved on westward and took up residence on the Missouri River near the boundary of the present North and South Dakota. A large village was located on Porcupine Creek in North Dakota. Groups also began moving down the Missouri into South Dakota and Grand River.

By the early 1800s, the Cheyenne had begun a more nomadic life, expelled from the Missouri by the Sioux. They ranged over the plains east of the Black Hills southwest of the Missouri and subsequently moved further south and west into the central and southern plains of southeast Wyoming, southwest Nebraska, eastern Colorado, and western Kansas between the North Platte River on the north and the Arkansas on the south.

The Cheyenne of modern history was made up of the descendants of two distinct, independent yet related tribes, the Tsistsistas or Cheyenne proper, the Omissis being the single largest band, and the Suhtai who joined the Cheyenne after they crossed the Missouri River. West of the Missouri, the two tribes pitched them camps adjoining one, the Suhtai to the north of the Cheyenne to the south. Although some researchers believe that the Suhtai may have crossed the Missouri somewhat earlier than the Cheyenne, Grinnell suggests that the relative position of their camps may have had "some reference to the order in which the three tribes crossed the Missouri." (South of the camp of the Cheyenne proper were the Arapaho who crossed the Missouri first.) At times the two tribes separated from one another only to come back together again later. Throughout the early years they continued to maintain separate identities and dialects camps until around the 1830s when they became fully integrated into the single tribe popularly known as the Cheyenne nation. For more see the Suhtai. Two cherished talismans, sacred to the Cheyenne, were the medicine arrows (*Mahuts*) and the buffalo hat (*Issiwun*), sometimes referred to as the sacred hat. They were handed down from generation to generation to insure good health, a long life of plenty, strength, and courage and were carried into battle with them. The medicine arrows were brought to the Cheyenne by the Tsistsistas; the buffalo hat by the Suhtai—but both were revered by all.

The Cheyenne are generally considered to be comprised of ten primary bands and a number of lesser bands. Grinnell notes that in the earliest times, there were three divisions (*) from which all other bands emerged. The following lists are taken from Chalfant and Swanton, who took his lists from Moody (1928). The identity of the primary bands is the same with one exception. It will also be noted that the spelling of the names is different in almost every instance.

PRIMARY (Chalfant)
*Hevataniu (Hair Rope Men)
    associated with the village named Chaguyenne
*Omissis or Quify or Ouisay/Ouisy (Eaters)
    Ouisay/Ouisy were names given for the Omissis village
*Suhtai or Sutaio or Chousa (Buffalo People of the Suhtai Tribe)
    Chousa being the name for their village
Hofnowa (Poor People)
Hotamitaniu (Dog Men)
Issiometaniu (Hill or Ridge People)
Iviststsinihpah or Heviqsnipahis (Burnt Aorta)
Ohktounna (Protruding Jaw People)
Oivimanah (Scabby)
Watapiu (Eat with the Sioux)

LESSER BANDS (Chalfant)
Anskovinis (Narrow Nose Bridge)
Honisku (meaning unknown)
Mohkstahetaniu (Ute People)
Moisiyu (the band of mixed Cheyenne-Sioux incorporated into the tribe)
Nakoimanah (Bear People)
Notamin (Facing the North—possibly of Arapaho descent)
Wohkpotsit (White Crafty People)

PRIMARY (Swanton)
Havhaita'nio
Heviqs'-ni"pahs
Hisiometa'nio

Ho'nowa
Masi''kota
Moiseyu
Oi'vimana
O'mi'sis
Oqtoguna
Sutaio
Wu'tapiu

SECONDARY (Swanton)
Anskowinis
Black Lodges (near Lame Deer)
Half-breed Band
Mahoyum
Moqtavhaita'niu
Na'kuimana
Pi'nutgu'
Ree Band
Totoimana (on Tongue River)
Woopotsi't
Yellow Wolf Band

Of the lesser bands was the Mahsihkota band that joined the Hotamitaniu en masse and together became known as the Dog Soldiers or the Dog Soldier Military Society. (For more on the Dog Soldiers, see below.) Other smaller bands were the Anskovinis (Narrow Nose Bridge); Mohkstahetaniu (Ute or Mountain People); Moisiyu (from the Moisiyu Sioux Tribe who had intermarried with the Cheyenne); Nakoimanah (Bear People); Wohkpotsit (White Crafty People); Notamin (Facing the North); and Honisku (unknown).

In time the Cheyenne divided into the Northern Cheyenne or Northern Bands and the Southern Cheyenne, but the two divisions considered themselves one people. Individuals, families, and whole bands frequently crossed from north to south and south to north and back again. At times the entire Cheyenne nation closed ranks. The Suhtai constituted a major part of what became separately known as the Northern Bands or Northern Cheyenne that remained north of the Platte/North Platte River. The Southern Cheyenne to the south of the Platte and north of the Arkansas were more numerous. They were firmly established by the end of the 1830s. Bent-St. Vrain and Company established trading posts on the upper Arkansas in 1832 and on the south bank of the South Platte between 1834 and 1839 to service the Cheyenne trade. William Bent, on the Arkansas, married a Cheyenne woman and would remain their friend and support up until his death. (See more under William Bent and Bent's Fort.)

By 1875, after two military campaigns, the Southern Cheyenne were removed to a reservation in Indian Territory. The Northern Cheyenne, for their part, fought beside the Sioux; but by the spring of 1877 they too had been forced to surrender and were removed to the reservation in the south. Little more than one year later, a small group of Northern Cheyenne headed home. They embarked on what became the Cheyenne Trail of Tears—the Cheyenne Autumn. (See below.)

Cheyenne and the Mandan maintained close ties in the early years before the Cheyenne move to the central and southern plains. With the migration to the plains, the Cheyenne established a formidable alliance with the Arapaho, north and south. Their relationship with the Sioux, however, remained tenuous at best. At times they joined together against a common foe, as against the Crow; but until about the mid-1850s, the Sioux remained a constant nemesis if not a threat.

As noted previously, the Cheyenne remained close to their kinsmen, the Suhtai (Sutaio) throughout the migration from the woodlands to the prairie to the plains. In the early years, the Cheyenne also maintained friendly relations with the Arikara, but that relationship became strained as time went on. While the Northern Plains were dominated by the Sioux, the Central Plains came to be dominated by the Southern Cheyenne and Arapaho; the Southern Plains below the Arkansas by the Comanche, Kiowa, and Kiowa Apache. The Pawnee dominated the lands east of the Cheyenne; the Osage south and east. They all made maximum use of the horse. Alliances between the tribes, however, went back and forth over the years; but by 1840 intertribal peace took hold in large part as a result of the white unbending surge across Texas. The Cheyenne signed their first treaty at the mouth of the Teton River on July 6, 1825, in which they acknowledged the sovereignty of the United States and its right to regulate trade.

When the whites came, they hit with both fists—guns and disease. The Cheyenne escaped the smallpox epidemic of the thirties, but in the summer of 1849, emigrants brought cholera to the Plains Indians. Berthrong writes that the Pawnee "were swept off like 'chaff before the wind.'" More than eleven hundred died that summer. As the Cheyenne moved south, the land between the Platt and the Arkansas was strewed with the bodies of men, women and children ravaged by disease. The unknown enemy claimed their shadows. Before the disease ran its course, the Cheyenne lost half their people. The Kiowa and Osage were also hit but, farther east and south, escaped the devastation of the northern tribes.

In 1851 the Cheyenne, the Arapaho, the Sioux and others signed the Fort Laramie Treaty or Horse Creek Treaty. It was a great event. (It was also called the Big Treaty and the Fitzpatrick Treaty for agent Thomas Fitzpatrick of the Upper Platte Agency.) Everyone was pleased. Although lands were identified for each tribe, there were no restrictions. In the end it was all illusion. First there were the wagon trains and the settlers traveling on to points farther west. They were followed by the telegraph and the railroads and the buffalo hunters. With them came soldiers who staked out new Army posts. With time more and more whites decided to stay and claimed the lands that had belonged to the Cheyenne. It was as if a noose had been placed around the necks of the Cheyenne and other Plains tribes and slowly tightened until there was no breathing room left.

In early April 1856, the conflict between the Cheyenne and the whites came into sharp focus. It occurred three miles northeast of present Casper, Wyoming, at a bridge crossing used by immigrant trains. It began as a minor issue over the dubious ownership of a single horse. It ended with the killing of one Cheyenne; the wounding of another who managed to escape; and the capture of a third who subsequently died while imprisoned at Fort Laramie—the reported cause, the effect of imprisonment. When the wounded man managed to get back to camp, the entire band quickly gathered up what belongings they could carry and rushed off into the Black Hills fearing greater reprisals at the hands of the soldiers. The soldiers came and burned everything in sight. In retribution, Cheyenne war parties combed the region committing acts of vengeance upon those they encountered. More violence followed, at Fort Kearny, Grand Island and along the Platte. A council of chiefs and leaders on October 16 led to an agreement to end hostilities. The Cheyenne wars had begun. The agreement produced only a short lull.

It was in 1856 that plans for an expedition against the Cheyenne began to coalesce in the War Department, but the seeds were planted the year before when the Cheyenne agent reported to Washington that the Cheyenne and other Plains tribes needed of a "sound chastisement" to ensure that they stayed in line. In the eyes of the agent and some of the military, the Cheyenne, believing themselves to be free men, did not demonstrate the proper deference to their betters. The Cheyenne population at the time numbered about 4,500 persons.

The War Department issued the necessary orders in late October. Troops for the Cheyenne Expedition were assembled at Fort Leavenworth under the command of Col. E. V. Sumner. With all necessary preparations completed, the command moved out in two columns in May 1857. One column led by

Sumner, with Pawnee scouts as guides, followed the Platte River and Oregon Trail to Fort Kearny and on to Fort Laramie and then south to the site of Fort St. Vrain. The second column, under Maj. John Sedgwick, with Delaware scouts as guides, followed the Arkansas River and West Branch of the Santa Fe Trail to Bent's New Fort and then north to St. Vrain. The two wings formed up east of St. Vrain along the South Platte (*Witaniyohe* or Fat River to the Cheyenne) and on July 13 began the march that would take them east-southeast into northwest Kansas and up the Solomon River for the first major battle on the Southern plains between the Cheyenne and the U.S. Army. Together, Sumner's command included six calvary companies of the First Calvary, each with an effective strength of about fifty men, and three infantry companies. (In August 1861, the First Calvary was redesignated the Fourth Calvary.)

The Battle of Solomon's Fork took place on the afternoon of July 29, 1857 on the South Fork of the Solomon River (*Mahkineoche* or Turkeys Creek) in northwest Kansas, about mid-way between the Smoky Hill River to the south and the Republican River to the north. About three hundred Cheyenne were arrayed in a line for battle. Among the leaders of the was Dog Soldier chief Tall Bull. The Cheyenne were confident that Maheo's medicine (Cheyenne's Supreme Being) would protect them from guns and bullets, but what they saw rushing at them was the flashing steel of the military sabers (long knives) of the First Calvary—the infantry and the artillery had been left behind. It was the first time they had seen such a site. They were defeated before the battle began. The Cheyenne fired a bevy of arrows; then broke and scattered.

Fighting continued on the run until the horses on both sides gave out. The Expedition counted two men dead and nine wounded. First estimates of Cheyenne causalities were nine dead and a great number wounded. Later, Cheyenne accounts reported four braves killed. After the soldiers fell back to rest and refit, the Cheyenne headed straight for their village where the women and children and the old waited and grabbed all they could carry. Most headed south to the Arkansas and beyond to the relative safety of the large camps of the Comanche and Kiowa. Others headed north across the Platte while a few Dog Soldiers remained in the general vicinity and continued raids against the whites.

After the men and horses had rested, the wounded cared for, and the dead buried, the soldiers followed the Cheyenne south until they came upon the now abandoned village. The soldiers burned and otherwise destroyed everything they could not use. The men of the Cheyenne Expedition and the Cheyenne never crossed paths again. By the middle of September, the soldiers had new assignments. Although casualties on both sides were extremely light, it took two years for the Cheyenne to begin to recover what was lost with the destruction of their village on the Saline River. During those years, the Cheyenne lived in a state of utter privation.

Solomon's Fork was much more than a single military battle, it was a "confrontation between the people of two cultures." Robert Utley described the conflict in the forward of *Chalfant's Cheyennes and Horse Soldiers* as one "of human beings caught up in historical forces beyond their comprehension." With the Treaty of Fort Wise in 1861, the Southern Cheyenne and Arapaho ceded back to the government all the lands given to them in the Treaty of Fort Laramie except for a reservation on which they were expected to remain if they were to receive government annuities although not all Cheyenne bands were represented. The reservation was oriented around the mouth of Sand Creek on the Arkansas River. Berthrong put the situation succinctly, "the days of freedom were at an end."

Discontent and unrest among the Cheyenne continued to build for the next three years. During the spring and summer of 1864, Indian forays that included murder and other depredations became common as travel through the buffalo range increased and as land-hungry immigrants vied for valuable Colorado lands that belonged. Isolated ranches and travelers on the Platte and Santa Fe trails were the principal targets. The attacks were the work of youthful warriors of both the Cheyenne and Arapaho, north and south, but punitive military scouting parties and the clamor of vigorous retaliation that led to clashes between the military and peaceful Indians only made the situation worse. Mistaken acts of retribution perpetrated by both parties led to rumors of an all-out war that inflamed emotions.

A council was held at Camp Weld near Denver September 28, 1864, that was attended by elder, peaceful chiefs of the Cheyenne and Arapaho, Governor Evans of Colorado Territory, Colonel John M. Chivington, and others. The Indians offered proposals for peace. The military answered by relieving Major Wynkoop, whose efforts brought about the conference, of his command. Chivington saw glory in the military destruction of the Indians; Evans saw land cessions; and General Curtis, the senior officer in command in the West with headquarters at Fort Leavenworth wanted punishment for the ringleaders and full restitution. No effort was made to reach out for the branch of peace.

Indian unrest was becoming more and more widespread as the attacks increased in number and intensity, feeding upon itself. The four confederations who occupied the Central and Southern Plains began to look to each other for support: the Northern Cheyenne and Northern Arapaho; the Southern Cheyenne and Southern Arapaho; the Comanche and Kiowa and Kiowa-Apache south of the Arkansas; and the various bands of the Sioux in the central and upper Plains.

It all led to one defining event, the massacre of a camp of predominantly peaceful Cheyenne at Sand Creek, twenty-five miles from Fort Lyon on November 29, 1864. Colonel Chivington led a force of 700-750 troopers, mostly Colorado volunteers. They surrounded the encamped Indians and ruthlessly murdered all those that could not escape. Chivington estimated that five to six hundred Indians were killed, animals captured, and lodges and equipment destroyed. He insisted that the greater number of women and children had escaped before the attack and that he faced some seven hundred warriors. Chivington's unsupported fabrication was supported by no one. There was no actual count of the number of Indians killed. Estimates ranged from 137 to 300 Indians killed with estimates of fifty to ninety percent women and children. One account gives the number of warriors killed at twenty-six out of a total of the less than one hundred warriors present. A number of military and Congressional investigations followed.

Sand Creek led to a confederation of Plains tribes and all-out war of hit and run. Those that escaped Sand Creek joined there kinsmen, and together they were by the Arapaho and the Sioux. The incident also brought the Cheyenne Dog Soldiers and the mainline Cheyenne closer together than they had ever been. Attacks and raids were carried out north and south of the Platte throughout 1865. Major Wynkoop was recognized as a potential healing force and sent out as a special commissioner of peace by Washington. Peace conferences were held first with the Comanche and Kiowa and Kiowa-Apaches; then with the Arapaho and Cheyenne. Traders and scouts also played a big part in bringing both sides together to produce the Treaty of the Little Arkansas near Wichita, Kansas, on October 14, 1865.

The Cheyenne and Arapaho ceded their lands in Colorado that had been granted in the Treaty of Fort Wise in 1861 back to the government for a reservation south of the Arkansas yet to be defined with rights to hunt north of the river in areas not occupied by whites. The treaty also repudiated "the gross and wanton outrages" of Sand Creek and offered reparation payments for surviving kin. The Arapaho and seven chiefs and leaders of the Cheyenne signed the treaty; but they represented only a part of the Cheyenne Nation. The Cheyenne north of the Platte were not aware of what was transpiring to the south. In February 1866, Wynkoop met with the Cheyenne, Kiowa, and Kiowa Apache living on Bluff Creek and managed to secure their marks of acceptance, and on April 4 he secured the acceptance of the last of those from the north. Another hurdle was presented by a Senate amendment that decreed that the new reservation must be entirely outside of the boundaries of the state of Kansas. The crucial amendment, along with others, was accepted by the Cheyenne chiefs at Fort Zarah on November 13-14, 1866—thus seemingly ending the conflict, but it was only the beginning of another.

Of the trails West, it was the Smokey Hill Route through the heart of Kansas Territory that sharpened the conflict between the Indians of the Central Plains and the whites. Attacks, though sporadic, continued, driven primarily by the Cheyenne Dog Soldiers and several bands of Sioux. (See Trails West in this work.)

Although the army was more than willing to clear the path for the railroad with force, Washington was under pressures to conclude a permanent peace with the western tribes. A Blue Ribbon peace commission was appointed, and on the October 28, the Arapaho and Cheyenne signed what is commonly referred to as the Medicine Lodge Creek Treaty. A new reservation was established in Indian Territory that replaced the reservation stipulated in the treaty of October 1865. It did not take long, however, for the old problems to resurface. It was clear by the spring of 1868 that the Cheyenne and Arapaho were not happy with the provisions of the latest treaty as some two hundred Cheyenne Dog Soldiers along with a few Sioux and Arapaho continued the fight against the Iron Horse. Adding to the turmoil was the long-standing intertribal enmities between the Cheyenne and Arapaho on one hand and Kaw, the Osage, and the Utes, singly and together on the other.

Sherman was determined to quell all resistance and assigned the task to General Phil Sheridan. What followed was the Battle of Washita that had all the markings of a second Sand Creek massacre, but this time there were no fact-finding committees or recriminations. Government policy had changed. It did not help the Indians' situation any that responsibility fell to two popular and respected military figures, Sherman and Sheridan. For more see Battle of Washita. Following Washita, twenty-one chiefs and leaders of the Cheyenne and Arapaho met with Sheridan at Fort Cobb on December 31. He stated his position simply as one of total war or total surrender. Within the first three weeks of January 1869, a number of bands of Cheyenne and Arapaho voluntarily came into Fort Sill (formerly Fort Wichita) and surrendered.

Over the next several months other bands came into Fort Sill and Camp Supply. By the first week in April, most of the Arapaho had been accounted for as the search for the last of the Cheyenne continued. On July 11, 1869, three hundred troopers of the Fifth Calvary and a battalion of Pawnee scouts under the command of Major Eugene A. Carr surprised a band of five hundred Cheyenne Dog soldiers and Sioux warriors led by Tall Bull at Summit Springs, near Sterling in Logan County, Colorado. Over fifty Indians were killed, including Tall Bull himself. Those that survived either fled north or were captured. With the Battle of Summit Springs the history of the Southern Cheyenne and the Arapaho upon the lands between the Platt and Arkansas came to an end.

Some of those who escaped joined the Northern Cheyenne and Sioux to the north. Others drifted quietly into existing Cheyenne villages at Fort Supply a few at a time. Both the military and the civilian authorities pretended to take no notice of their arrival. Accepting their life as it was now handed to them, the Dog Soldiers rejected invitations by Santana of the Kiowa to join the Kiowa, the Comanche, and the Kiowa-Apache for raids into Texas. Those that attempted to remain in the Republican Valley were chased out by the military. Their attempt to turn and attack a detachment of troopers led to the discovery and destruction of a large Brulé village with whom they were living.

Lives for the Southern Cheyenne and Arapaho began anew on the reservation under the auspices of the Quakers (Society of Friends). But the two tribes refused the land provided in the Treaty of Medicine Lodge Creek—rancid water, no timber, poor soil, adjoining the Osage, on the Kansas border etc. President Grant, by executive order, established a new reservation for them of 4,297,771 acres. Nonetheless, some of the Cheyenne were reluctant to move. Two bands headed north to join the Sioux, but by late 1871 they had returned to the agency. By then a few of the Arapaho were beginning to settle into a life of agriculture—a life that the Cheyenne continued to resist.

The Plains remained relatively quiet for three or four years. Although the Kiowa were poised for war, the Cheyenne continued to resists overtures to join them. At the same time, outside pressures and constant change were turning the Cheyenne away from reservation life. There were legal issues to settle regarding the reservation lands. In 1872 the Arapaho signed a treaty relinquishing the lands set aside in the Treaty of Medicine Lodge Creek, and plans were laid for the establishment of two separate reservations, one for the Arapaho and one for the Cheyenne. The agent in charge also decided to move the agency itself. Two Cheyenne bands remained with the Kiowa rather than move with the main villages. A major factor was the continued indiscriminate killing of buffalo by white hunters. At first the supply seemed inexhaustible, but the effect was soon felt, and there was inadequate beef to fill the gap. It has been estimated that 7,500,000 buffalo were slaughtered just for their hides between 1872-1874. There was also the ever present and increasing destructive effect of illicit whisky. In addition, the reservation tribes were themselves becoming the victims of horse stealing on a grand scale.

Writing to the governor of Kansas, General Pope remarked on the "violent and inexcusable outrages upon the Indians" committed by hunters and traders. As the grievances increased, so did the grumbling. The Cheyenne moved out of the reservation. As the number of incidents increased, they also grew in intensity. The most publicized was the attack on traders at Adobe Walls on June 9, 1874, by 250-300 Indians representing all five Plains tribes, but mostly Cheyenne and Comanche. Four columns of soldiers were sent out from four directions. They were to pursue the hostiles and bring them in or destroy them. Mid-October saw the first surrender of a small party of Dog Soldiers. Although there were few deaths, the military for the most part captured Indian horses and destroyed foodstuffs and supplies.

Individuals, families, and whole bands threw up their hands in surrender though the end of the year, but it was estimated that upwards of fifteen hundred Cheyenne remained off the reservation in hostile camps. The majority surrendered to Colonel Miles from Camp Supply on January 2. Others also began moving to the reservation. Small groups surrendered to the army throughout January and February, then on March 6, 1875, eight hundred and thirty-one surrendered at the agency. Still others from the south held back in the north with Northern Cheyenne and the Sioux. Then in early April a large group bolted from the reservation, and a chase and fight ensued. The majority were captured or, after a time, returned voluntarily. Ringleaders of the Cheyenne's final war of 1874-75 were identified and shipped off to prison at Fort Marion, Florida. By May it was thought that 678 Cheyenne were still absent from the agency, but the count was probably closer to three hundred.

Soon all had returned from the north except for a that remained to fight with Sitting Bull, Crazy Horse, and the Northern Cheyenne under Chief Morning Star (Dull Knife). The times also pitted Indian against Indian. The anti-government Indians consisted of the Oglala, Hunkpapa, Miniconjou, and Sans Arc and Northern Cheyenne, with some support from the Santee and Yanktonai Sioux and the Arapaho. The pro-government Indians serving as scouts and auxiliaries were the Crow, the Arikara, the Shoshoni, the Ute, the Pawnee, the Bannock and the Nez Percé. Primary support came from the Crow and Shoshoni.

The Powder River Expedition was formed in 1876 under the command of Maj. Gen. George Crook and headed out from Fort Fetterman on November 14 to bring the anti-treaty Indians led by led by Crazy Horse to terms. Final preparations were made at Cantonment Reno for the push north into Yellowstone country. Crook's command numbered more than 1,750 officers and men of the calvary, infantry and artillery plus a civilian packtrain and Indian auxiliaries. When joined by ninety-one additional Indians, mostly Shoshoni, in route, the Indian contingent totaled more than 350 out of a the total force to more than twenty-one hundred.

In what is referred to as a "target of opportunity," Crook received word from scouts that a large band of Northern Cheyenne led by Dull Knife was nearby. Crook sent Colonel Ronald S. Mackenzie with eleven hundred men, a third of whom were Indians, to find the camp and destroy it. The large camp of Dull Knife and Little Wolf was located in a canyon on the Red Fork of the Powder River in northern Wyoming (present Johnson County). The camp held nearly the entire population of the Northern Cheyenne of upwards of 1,300 inhabitants with some 300 warriors. The surprise attack of the calvary and Indian auxiliaries out of the east end of the canyon on the morning of November 25 and the subsequent destruction of the village broke Cheyenne military power in the north forever and induced others among the Lakota to surrender.

Mackenzie's troop suffered six killed and twenty-two wounded, one mortally, plus one Shoshoni scout by friendly fire. Reports of the number of Indian casualties vary. Best estimates are about 30-40 killed and twice that number wounded. Survivors of the battle escaped out and over the west end of the canyon and almost literally dragged themselves north to the Sioux camp. Meanwhile the units of the Powder River Expedition received new orders. The expedition organized to punish the Sioux had destroyed the Cheyenne.

The refugees moved north against the cold wind to the Oglalla camp but received little aid before being told to leave as soon as possible. What was left was a band of scavengers. A band under Two Moon surrendered to Colonel Miles on April 22, 1877. Others under White Hawk joined Lame Deer's Miniconjous on a tributary of the Rosebud. The camp was attacked and destroyed by Miles attacked in May. Survivors surrendered to the agencies and turned in their weapons and horses. Elsewhere over 1,200 Miniconjous from other bands and San Arcs surrendered to General Crook at Camp Sheridan on April 14. A week later Dull Knife and some five hundred Cheyenne came into the Red Cloud agency and surrendered.

The Northern Cheyenne were placed on the Cheyenne-Arapaho Reservation at Darlington, Oklahoma, with the promise that they did not have to stay if they did not like it. Nine hundred and eighty made the trek south. Nine hundred and thirty-seven arrived. Some died enroute; some took off on their own. No one made an accounting. The new arrivals put increasing pressures on the scarce food supply at the agency. Men, women and children went hungry; forty-one died the first winter.

SOLDIER OR WARRIOR SOCIETIES

The soldier societies, also referred to as military societies and warrior societies, were comprised of warriors from across bands. These societies were responsible for tribal defense and internal security, enforcement of tribal law, raids, and leadership during the time of war—war leaders or war chiefs, as distinct from the peace chiefs who were responsible for religious as well as administrative and organizational activities.

The Dog Soldier Society, also referred to as the Dog Men, was one of the four original military or warrior societies. It was the largest and strongest that in fact constituted a small division of the tribe in and of itself. The names of the others were the Kit Fox or Swift Fox Society or Fox Soldiers and the Crooked Lance or Elk Horn Scraper Society, also referred to as Elk-horn Scrapers. Later, because of an accident that burned a number of the warriors, they picked up the name Blue Bellies which they in turn converted to Blue Soldiers following the killing of a number of troopers and donning their uniforms. The name "Fingers" has also been associated with the Elk-horn Scrapers. The last of the four was; and the Red Shields or Bull Soldiers. Two additional military societies were subsequently formed, the Bow Strings Society, also written Bowstrings, or Wolf Soldiers and the Crazy Dogs Society. A seventh band, the Chief Soldiers, consisted exclusively of the forty-four chiefs of the tribe. Always listed first among the bands and claimed by some as the best was the Kit Fox. Other tribes like the Kiowa and Blackfoot also had their warrior societies. First among the Blackfoot soldier bands was also reportedly based on the kit fox which is surprising because the kit fox, the smallest of the fox family, is associated with the drier, warmer climate to the south.

Beginning in the 1860s, the Dog Soldiers became more and more aggressive towards whites and the U.S. military in particular. As time progressed, they stood alone in the battle for the plains, often standing with their allies the Sioux as the other Cheyenne bands fell to the overwhelming might of their white adversary.

The name Strong Hearts has been given to a warrior association comprised of both the Cheyenne and the Dakota and embodied in the fox.

SAND CREEK

The Sand Creek Massacre took place November 29, 1864, in southeastern Colorado about fifteen miles east of Bent's New Fort, the trading post of William Bent. Approximately five hundred volunteers of the Third Colorado Regiment and two battalions of the Colorado First Regiment under the command of Colonel John Chivington attacked a peaceful camp of Cheyenne killing men, women, and children indiscriminately. Reports of the number killed range from 150 to 500. William Bent's son George, who was there with his brother Charles, sister Julia, and their Cheyenne step-mother Island, estimated that 163 Indians had been killed and that 110 of those killed were women and children. One writer gives the totals as 133 and 105, respectively; another puts the number of bodies at three hundred, of which only 26 were warriors. Chivington, in his official report, claimed 400-500 dead *warriors*. He made no mention of women and children. Bent's son Robert was made an unwilling accessory to the events, having been forced to guide the soldiers to the encampment unaware of their intentions. Unbeknownst to him, William Bent's ranch on the Purgatoire River was surrounded by soldiers to prevent him from giving any warning.

The events of November 29 sent repercussions all the way to Washington. George Bent provided an eyewitness account of the massacre to the Sand Creek Commission that met in 1865. His brother Robert also testified. Although condemned by military and Congressional committees, many officials, military and civilian, were ambivalent. General Sherman remarked that regrettably, it was an "inglorious war." Chevington declared no remorse whatsoever for his actions. That warriors died in battle was expected; however, Chevington had not only committed atrocities but he violated the code—the village was under a truce. With Sand Creek, relations with the Indians took a tragic turn across the Plains.

In mid-April 1867, soldiers led by General Winfield Scott Hancock and Colonel George Armstrong Custer attacked a large camp of Cheyenne and Sioux about forty miles west of Fort Larned on the Pawnee Fork but found the camp deserted. The Indians had fled northwest to the Smoky Hill country from what they believed would have been a repeat of Sand Creek.

BEECHER'S ISLAND FIGHT

On orders from General William Sherman, General Philip Sheridan formed a special company of citizen scouts at Fort Hays with orders to hunt down and kill any Indians sited near the construction of the Kansas Pacific Railroad across Kansas. In mid-September 1868, the scout company of 51 men under the command of Colonel George A. Forsyth moved out from Fort Wallace. They tracked a large band of Cheyenne Dog soldiers to the Arikaree Fork of the Republican River, seventeen miles south of Wray, Yuma County, Colorado, about five miles west of the Kansas border. On the night of the September 16, the scouts camped on the north bank of the Arikaree opposite a small island.

The next morning they awoke to find themselves staring at several hundred Indians on the hills above them. Colonel Forsythe gave orders for the men to make for the island. The Cheyenne charged across the water individually and in small groups throughout the day. The next several days were broken only by the sound of intermittent sharpshooting. There were no more attacks. After the fifth day the Indians withdrew. After the sixth day, they dried meat gave out and were forced to eat their dead horses. On the ninth day, a relief column of regulars arrived under the command of Captain Louis H. Carpenter. Lieutenant Frederick Beecher—a nephew of Henry Ward Beecher—was among the dead, giving rise to the name of the battle site as recorded in the official records of the U.S. Army. Casualties among the Americans were put at five killed and about twenty-five wounded. Cheyenne war chief Roman Nose was among those killed on September 17. As a consequence, the Cheyenne called the battle the Fight When Roman Nose Was Killed. What followed was Sheridan's winter campaign and the Battle of the Washita.

BATTLE OF THE WASHITA

General Phil Sheridan, who commanded the district that included Missouri, Kansas, Indian Territory of Oklahoma, and New Mexico, was given the responsibility for putting a stop to all Indian agitation over the Medicine Lodge Treaty— specifically, to mussel the Cheyenne. A force of seven hundred soldiers of the Seventh Calvary and Kansas Volunteers and Osage guides under the command of Armstrong Custer came upon the unsuspecting Cheyenne village of Chief Black Kettle on the banks of the Washita River. Troopers surrounded the village on the morning of November 27, 1868, and attacked while the warriors and their families lay asleep.

Black Kettle, who survived Sand Creek, did not walk away from the Washita this day. Custer reported one hundred and three warriors killed but made no mention of women and children. Other accounts put the count at 9-20 warriors and 18-40 women and children; others at 103 killed, including women and children and another 53 taken prisoner. With large villages of Cheyenne, Arapaho, Comanche, and Kiowa in the vicinity, Custer withdrew from the field. Some have asserted that the Battle of Washita was a second Sand Creek. Sheridan was unapologetic. For him, there was nothing but a military solution to the Indian situation. When Sheridan returned to the site of the battle on December 7, he found the mutilated bodies of Major Joel Elliot and his men who had be cut off from the main body plus some white prisoners.

JULESBURG RAID

Julesburg, Colorado, with Fort Sedgwick two miles away, was twenty miles west of the end of track for the Union Pacific Railroad in June 1867. About fifty Cheyenne struck the town in a Hollywood-style raid on June 10. Five men were wounded by arrows; and two whites were killed, scalped, and mutilated—one believed to have been shot through the neck with an arrow after he lay on the ground. One Cheyenne was killed, and two wounded. It was a minor raid, but another strike by the Indians in their continuing struggle against the railroad. Later that month on June 23, a large Sioux war party of some three hundred attacked a survey party consisting of engineer Percy Browne, an assistant, and five soldiers in south-central Wyoming about mid-way between Laramie and Green River. Browne, wounded in the attack, died within days. The Sioux did not press the attack taking satisfaction in taking the party's horses.

SAPPA CREEK FIGHT (MASSACRE AT CHEYENNE HOLE)

The incident took place on April 23, 1875, along Middle Sappa Creek (called by the Cheyenne, "Horse Stealing Creek") in northwest Kansas. The Cheyenne had fled April 6 after the Sandhill Fight east of Ft. Reno because of trouble over ironing prisoners to be sent to prison in Florida. Forty troopers of Company H of the Sixth Calvary under the command of Lt. Austin Henely and some twenty-five buffalo hunters caught up with them at Sappa Creek. What happened after has been highly controversial.

According to reports, the troopers and buffalo hunters savagely murdered from sixty to upwards of one hundred and twenty Cheyenne men, women, and children, mostly women and children, as they waved white flags of surrender. Reports declare that everything and everyone were thrown upon a huge fires and that babies were pulled from the hole where their mothers lay, clubbed, and thrown into the fires as well. Reports appear to agree that most of the deadly work was that of the buffalo hunters and that the troopers held back, although Henely participated in the cover-up. The official count, submitted by General Pope, was 27 Indians killed, nineteen men and eight women and children, and two troopers. Black Horse and few others were said to have watched silently from a distance.

Reportedly among the dead was Medicine Arrow, Keeper of the Arrows; but that too is controversial. According to Sandoz, the Sacred Arrows were retrieved from Medicine Arrow's body by his wife and divided between a young brave and his wife whom she sent scurrying away to safety with their brethren to the north—each taking half of the arrows. Sandoz goes on to write that days later they found each other at the camp of Dull Knife and Little Wolf on the Powder River. Monnett writes that Sandoz was misinformed about the presence of Medicine Arrow at the fight, but other than pointing out that stories are embellished in the retelling and challenging the presence of Medicine Arrow, Monnett does not appear to question the basic contention that a significant number of women and children were killed and that the camp was burned.

The University of Oklahoma Press describes Chalfant's recent book:

"Cheyennes at Dark Water Creek tells the tragic story of the southern bands of Cheyennes from the period following the Treaty of Medicine Lodge through the battles and skirmishes known as the Red River War.* The Battle of Sappa Creek, the last encounter of that conflict, was a fight between a band of Cheyennes and a company of the Sixth Cavalry that took place in Kansas in April 1875. More Cheyennes were killed in that single engagement than in all the previous fighting of the war combined, and later there were controversial charges of massacre-and worse. William Y. Chalfant has used all known contemporaneous sources to recount the tragedy that occurred at the place known to the Cheyennes as Dark Water Creek. In Cheyenne memories, its name remains second only to Sand Creek in the terrible images and the sorrow it evokes."

*For the Red River War, see under the Comanche (224).

BENT'S FORT

William Bent (*Skay-Ah-Veho*, Little White Man), while maintaining strong ties at the head of the trails in Kansas City/Westport, Missouri, became one of the most widely known and highly respected men of the West. He was a fur trader, scout, Indian agent, interpreter, and confidant and friend of Indians and white men alike. He gained renown for his trading posts in western Colorado, known as Old Bent's Fort and New Bent's Fort, and his knowledge and understanding of the Plains Indians—especially the Cheyenne and Arapaho.

Popularly known as Bent's Fort (Bent's Old Ford) was located 530 miles west of Independence, Missouri, on the north bank of the Upper Arkansas River in southeastern Colorado, east of present Rocky Ford and La Junta, Colorado, above the mouth of the Purgatoire River. Bent's trading post was situated on the Mountain Branch of the Santa Fe Trail in Unorganized Territory (Missouri Country). Bent's Old Fort was abandoned and later destroyed, and Bent constructed a new post thirty-eight miles down river that he subsequently leased to the Army in 1859.

Bent helped secure the Peace of 1840 that reduced the enmity, if it did not secure total peace, between the Southern Cheyenne and Arapaho to the north of the Arkansas River and the Comanche, Kiowa, and Kiowa or Prairie Apache to south of the river. Bent brought the tribes to see a common purpose.

The massacre at Sand Creek in the fall of 1864 changed life forever on the Upper Arkansas with reverberations across the Plains, north and south. In his forty years among the Indians of the Upper Arkansas for forty years, nothing so destroyed Bent's hopes for the future.

Of Note

During the wars on the Plains, scouts from the Delaware, the Osage, and the Kaw and the Arapaho as well as the Pawnee and a few Sioux and Cheyenne guided the military commanders and fought beside them. At times the military also used braves from the Seminole and Tonkawa.

CHIAHA

The Chiaha was a one of the tribes of the Lower Creek and a member of the Creek Confederacy. They belonged to the Muskhogean linguistic family, but some have classed them in the Hitchiti group. In the earliest period they inhabited Burns Island in the present state of Tennessee and in eastern Georgia near the coast. Later they lived about the middle course of the Chattahoochee River. At times they also lived in South Carolina near the Savannah River and in Florida at a town known as Beech Creek. The Mikasuki of northern Florida are believed to have once been a part of the Chiaha.

CHIAKANESSOU

The Chiakanessou was listed in Jefferson's *Notes on the State of Virginia*. At the time it was estimated that they had a population of 350 warriors. It has been suggested that they may have been a member of the Creek Confederacy. For more see "Aborigines," Appendix D.

CHICAGO

Nothing has been found to indicate the existence of a separate tribe called the Chicago. Best evidence suggests a village called Chicago inhabited by members of one of the tribes of the Illinois Cluster of Tribes or one the Miami group of tribes. A chief, identified as an Illinois and named Chicagou (Che-cau-gou), accompanied Etienne de Véniard, sieur de Bourgmont and other Native American chiefs to Paris in 1724 thus establishing for recorded history a band or tribe popularly known as the Chicago.

The name Che-cau-gou is also found to refer a village of the Illiniwek (Illinois) on the southern tip of Lake Michigan. The name, which was also given to the small river that flowed from its source near the Illinois River to Lake Michigan, reportedly derived from the odor of wild onions that were so prevalent in the area. It is not uncommon to find a village name after a local chief, but it would be highly unusual to have a river named after one. Swanton makes no entry for the Chicago Indians but lists an Indian village on the site of present-day Chicago that was probably occupied by the Wea, who at the time were generally considered to be one of the major divisions of the Miami. Jesuit priest and explorer, Father Jacques Marquette, founded a mission on the site on Illinois River on December 4, 1674. Seen years later in his 1681-1682 expedition the French explorer, René Robert Cavelier, Sieur de La Salle, crossed from the mouth of the St. Joseph River in Michigan to the Illinois River using the short land bridge called the Chicago Portage, referred to as Chicago's "Plymouth Rock." The portage linked the Chicago River to the Illinois River via the Des Plaines River, thus connecting Lake Michigan to Mississippi River system.

At the Treaty of Greenville, August 3, 1795, the Wea ceded to the United States "One piece of land six miles square, at the mouth of Chikago river, emptying into the southwest end of lake Michigan, where a fort formerly stood." (Article 3, ¶2, Item 14). For more see the Illinois Cluster of Tribes and the Miami.

CHICHIMICI

The Chichimici was an early tribe of northern Mexico. They were reportedly led by a escaped Negro slave in attacks on the Spanish in the sixteenth century.

CHICKAHOMINY

The Chickahominy belonged to the Algonquian linguistic stock and was a member of the Powhatan Confederacy. They lived on the Chickahominy River in Virginia. Their homes and crops were burned by the early inhabitants of Jamestown in 1611 under the orders of the Governor Dale for the apparent disrespect shown him by Chief Powhatan A century and a half later, Englishman William Stitch, in his history of colonial Virginia, claimed that the Chickahominy disdained Powhatan. Whether his claim was based on any hard evidence or just wishful thinking to support is theories on government and the dangers of prerogative power is unknown. It is known, however, that Powhatan apparently achieved his position as head of the Confederacy by force.

CHICKAMAUGA

Chickamauga was a subgroup of Cherokee independent of the three geographical subdivisions sometimes and generally separately. They lived at a temporary settlement on Chickamauga Creek near Chattanooga,

CHICKASAW

The Chickasaw constituted the war-like element of the Choctaw Nation. They came from the Pacific Coast and migrated East across the Mississippi with the Choctaw settling in upper Mississippi and Alabama and southern Tennessee. They spoke the Muskogee dialect of the Choctaw. Jahoda writes, "Abruptly, the Choctaws severed these braves, called Chickasaws, into a separate nation." Early in the eighteenth century, the Chickasaw joined forces with the last of the Natchez Indians.

As in the case of the Choctaw, the treaty with the Chickasaw of January 7, 1786, at Hopewell guaranteed the boundaries of Chickasaw lands in Mississippi and Alabama that at the time were in the possession of the Creeks. The Chickasaw and the Choctaw had continuing disputes with the settlers in Mississippi and saw their removal as inevitable. As with other nations during the Jefferson administration, Indian debt was encouraged—encouraged to the point that they could only pay with land. Their holdings were soon reduced to a corner of northeastern Mississippi and a half-million acres in northwestern Alabama.

Concurrent with white migration, land was ceded to the government piecemeal from 1805 to 1818. In each instance, select individuals received pecuniary payments and tracts of land that might well be considered payoffs. But, in a treaty proposed to both the Chickasaws and Choctaws in 1826, they both flatly refused to cede their lands in Mississippi in exchange for lands west of the Mississippi or for money compensation. But six years later, the Chickasaw signed the Treaty of Pontotoc, Mississippi, by which they sold six million acres of land. The government was to provide them with suitable western land and protect them until the move, but failed on both accounts. The Chickasaw were forced to pay the Choctaws a half-million dollars for the right to live on part of their western allotment.

The first of the Chickasaws migrated west reaching the banks of the Mississippi in July 1837. With the crossing into Arkansas, they encountered the same problems as had the tribes that came before them: cold, hunger, disease. At the same time four thousand of those who remained in Alabama and Mississippi were forced into camps prior to their journey west. A few, mainly women and children, who had been assigned white guardians were left behind. By October the long column reached Memphis and headed across Arkansas into Oklahoma.

The arriving Chickasaw were assigned the fertile Washita Valley that, in turn, brought resentment from Shawnee and Kickapoo and the Kiowa and Comanche to their immediate west. Finally the Chickasaw settled on the Clear Boggy River, 120 miles south of Fort Coffee on the Arkansas River. Dysentery and malnutrition were constant companions, and a smallpox epidemic broke out taking some five hundred lives. As was the case with other tribes, many merchants and suppliers cheated them out of their food allotments.

The present territory of the Chickasaw Nation includes 7,648-plus square miles of south-central Oklahoma and encompasses all or parts of thirteen counties: Grady, McClain, Garvin, Pontotoc, Stephens, Carter, Murray, Johnston, Jefferson, Love, Marchall, Bryan and Coal.

CHICORA

The Chicora of South Carolina appeared prominantly in the annals of the Spanish exploration. It is likely that they are the same as the Shakori. They gave their name to the Province of Chicora in South Carolina. The Chicora/Shakori have also been linked with the Sissipahaw. For more see the Shakori.

CHIHEELEESH

According to Drake, the Chiheeleesh lived forty miles north of the Columbia River in Washington State.

CHIKOHOKI

The Chikohoki was a sub-tribe of the Unalachtigo division of the Delaware. They lived on the west bank of the Delaware River near its junction with the Christanna River. For more see Unalachtigo and Delaware.

CHILLATE

The Chillate lived along the Pacific coast north of the Columbia River beyond the Quieetso in Washington State.

CHILLUCKITTEQUAW

The Chilluckitequaw belonged to the Chinookan linguistic stock. Lewis and Clark reported them along the north shore of the Columbia River in present Klickitat and Skamania counties in Washington, but they may also have had settlements on the south side of the river. Remnants lived near the mouth of the White Salmon River until 1880 when they were removed to the Cascades. Accordingly, some writers have suggested that the Chilluckitequaw might have been identical with the White Salmon River Indians or the Hood River Indians or both.

CHILUCAN

The Chilucan was a small tribe found enumerated with the Indians in the Spanish missions in Florida in 1726. There may have been a Timucuan connection.

CHILULA

The Chilula, the Hupa, and the Whilkut formed one group of the Athapascan linguistic stock. They are also known as the Yurok Tsulu-la (people of Tsulu), but with no connection to the Yurok tribe of Algonquian stock. The Chilula inhabited an area near lower Redwood Creek and Minor Creek in California.

CHIMAKUM

The Chimakum, popularly called Port Townsend Indians, lived on the peninsula between Hood's Canal and Port Townsend in Washington State. They belonged to the Chimakuan linguistic stock with the Quileute and the Hoh, very likely connected with the Salishan linguistic family.

CHIMARIKO

The Chimariko are in the Hokan linguistic family. They lived on the canyon of the Trinity River from the mouth of New River to Canyon Creek in California.

CHIMBUIHA MOLALLA

The Chimbuiha was one of the three divisions of the Molalla. They lived on the lived on the headwaters of the Santiam River. For more see Molalla.

CHIMNAPUM

It is believed that the Chimnapum was a band or sub-tribe of one of the Plateau tribes of southeast Washington and northeast Oregon that belonged to the Shahaptian linguistic family. The Chimnapums lived at the mouth of the Yakima River. It is very likely that they were a sub-tribe of the Wanapam or Yakima.

CHINE

The Chine was a small tribe or band of Florida, possibly a band of the Chatot. They were likely of the southern division of the Muskhogean stock. They were placed on the Spanish mission of San Luis on the Apalachee coast in 1674 with the Camparaz and Amacano—together they numbered only about three hundred people.

CHINKO

The Chinko was one of the minor tribes of the Illinois Cluster of Tribes for which there is only passing mention. For more see Illinois Cluster.

CHINOOK

The Chinook or Flatheads belonged to the Lower Chinook division of the Chinookan linguistic family. They inhabited lands in present-day southwest Washington State along the Columbia River where they were encountered by the Corps of Discovery. The site is today's city of The Dalles, Washington. Later they joined the Chehalis. They were called Flatheads because of the manner in which they deformed their heads, a custom followed by a number of tribes of the Northwest. The Salish, on the other hand who were also called Flatheads, left their heads natural.

It was a Chinook village at present Doug's Beach on the Columbia River in Washington State that Lewis & Clark referred to as the "Friendly Village."

CHIPAYNE

Chipayne (Chilpaine or Chipainde) was the name applied to the Plains Apaches as a group and the name from which Lipan probably evolved although some reports appear to threat the Chipayne as a separate, early Lipan band. In early Spanish writings, the Plains Apaches were variously called variously Chipaynes, Limitas, Trementinas, or Faraones as if they were all one and the same. For more see Lipan, Limita, Trementina.

CHIPEWYAN

The Chipewyan tribe of Canada formed a dialect of the Athapascan linguistic stock. They claimed the land in the far northern reaches of the province of Saskatchewan. See Montagnais.

CHIPPANCHIKCHIK

The Chippanchikchik lived on the north side of the Columbia River about 220 miles from its mouth.

CHIPPEWA

The Chippewa (Ojibwa, Ojibway and Ojibwe) was a very large migratory tribe that belonged to the Central Division of the Algonquian linguistic family closely related to the Algonquin proper, the Ottawa, the Cree, and the Potawatomi. They were one of the largest Native American tribes north of Mexico with population estimates going as high as 35,000. By the mid-eighteenth century, their bands and villages were spread across over a thousand miles. For their size they had very little history, measured in terms of "being in the news." The Chippewa took the side of the French in the French and Indian War and the side of the English in the Colonies' War of Independence and in the War of 1812, but generally maintained peaceful relations with the government thereafter. (The government determined that a total of thirty-seven tribes took the side of the British in the War of 1812.)

The name Chippewa has been established as the tribe's official name in the United States; Ojibwa and Ojibway in Canada, Anglicized versions of Ojibwe, preferred by the people themselves. The Algonquian name derives from Outchibou, the 17th-century name of a group living north of Sault Ste. Marie, Ontario. They were one of several closely related but distinct groups residing between northeastern Georgian Bay and eastern Lake Superior to whom the name Ojibwa was later extended. Where Swanton employs the latter, he uses the spelling Ojibwa. The people called themselves the Anishinabe (An-ish-in-aub-ag), which is interpreted as "first men." They accepted the name Ojibwa but had a fervent dislike for the name Chippewa and all it stood for. The name Chippewa came from the French interpretation or misinterpretation of Ojibwa. The Chippewa were also recognized by a number of different names in addition to Ojibwa and its derivatives.

As to organization, the Ojibwe were comprised of twelve generally recognized major subdivisions, a number of smaller subdivisions or bands, and numerous villages. Swanton, who generally follows Willam Warren, *History of the Ojibway People*, lists ten major subdivisions, omitting the Ojibwe in Michigan, western Minnesota and westward, and all of Canada. Reaman, for his part, divides the Chippewa into four distinct groups: the Ojibwa proper, the Potawatomi, the Ottawa, and the Chippewa of the Mississippi (not to be confused with the Mississauga). Most writers, however, classify the Potawatomi and the Ottawa as separate and distinct from the Chippewa, although they were probably formed out of the same large group that migrated west.

MAJOR SUBDIVISIONS
Mississippi River
Bad River
Pillager (Minnesota)
Lake Winibigoshish
Swan Creek
Lake Superior
Mississauga
Black River
Leech Lake (may be identical to Pillager)
Saulteaux (Sault Chippewa)
Sandy Lake
Mille Lacs
12

Of the smaller bands, the Burt Woods Chippewa may be the best known.

Beginning around 1640, many of the Ojibwa moved or were driven westward from the area about Sault Ste. Marie, Ontario, where they had been primarily hunters and fishermen. Some turned south into the Lower Peninsula; others continued west. It was in the Upper Peninsula of Michigan that the Chippewa encountered their first Europeans and became active in the fur trade with the French. It was the Jesuit missionaries that made first contact with the Chippewa sometime after 1660.

Between 1680 and 1800, Ojibwa settlements were established in Michigan, Wisconsin, and Minnesota, the northeast corner of North Dakota, and Canada. These settlement comprised four geographic divisions: Southwestern Ojibwa, the Northern Ojibwa , the Plains Ojibwa, and the Southeastern Ojibwa. The Southwestern bands, armed with French weapons, moved along the river system south of Lake Superior into Wisconsin and Minnesota, displacing the Dakota, the Sac, and the Fox. The Northern bands ranged throughout the area of northern Ontario. After 1780 some shifted to Manitoba, Saskatchewan, and North Dakota, becoming the Plains Ojibwa or Bung. The Southeastern Ojibwa moved into south-central Ontario and the lower Michigan Peninsula.

Those that congregated on the southeastern outlet of Lake Superior about Sault Ste. Marie, in Canada and Michigan were called the Saulteaux. They were also located across northern Michigan; and throughout the Great Lakes regions A treaty with Canada established the Saulteaux reservation in northern Saskatchewan. For more see the Sault Chippewa.

In Michigan, the Chippewa joined the Ottawa and Potawatomi in the Three Fires or Three Brothers Society, and in Wisconsin the allied with Menominee, who migrated west about the same time and settled in southern Wisconsin, to dominate the state.

In treaties executed between 1837 and 1864, the various bands of the Chippewa ceded all their lands to the government and were collected on reservations located primarily in Minnesota, Wisconsin, and North Dakota—all within their original territory. At the same time some of their lands were carved out to make a home for the Oneida from New York. The Swan Creek and Black River Chippewa sold their lands in southern Michigan in a treaty executed May 9, 1836, and settled with the Munsee in Franklin County, Kansas. In 1866 they agreed to join with the Cherokee in Indian Territory.

There are currently thirteen federally recognized Chippewa entities that reflect the reservation system adopted for the Chippewa.

1. Bad River Band of the Lake Superior Tribe of Chippewa Indians of the Bad River Reservation, Wisconsin
2. Chippewa-Cree Indians of the Rocky Boy's Reservation, Montana Grand Traverse Band of Ottawa and Chippewa Indians, Michigan
3. Lac Courte Oreilles Band of Lake Superior Chippewa Indians of Wisconsin
4. Lac du Flambeau Band of Lake Superior Chippewa Indians of the Lac du Flambeau Reservation of Wisconsin
5. Lac Vieux Desert Band of Lake Superior Chippewa Indians, Michigan
6. Minnesota Chippewa Tribe, Minnesota (Six component reservations: Bois Forte Band (Nett Lake); Fond du Lac Band; Grand Portage Band; Leech Lake Band; Mille Lacs Band; White Earth Band)
7. Red Cliff Band of Lake Superior Chippewa Indians of Wisconsin
8. Red Lake Band of Chippewa Indians, Minnesota
9. Saginaw Chippewa Indian Tribe of Michigan
10. St. Croix Chippewa Indians of Wisconsin
11. Sault Ste. Marie Tribe of Chippewa Indians of Michigan

12. Sokaogon Chippewa Community, Wisconsin
13. Turtle Mountain Band of Chippewa Indians of North Dakota

Canadian Ojibwa occupy reserves in four areas. For more see the Three Fires Confederacy, the Sault Chippewa, and the Mississauga Chippewa.

CHIRICAHUA

The Chiricahua was a tribe of the Western Division of the Apache nation. It was comprised of three large bands or sub-tribes: the Chiricahua proper or Tsoka-ne-nde, the Tci-he-nde Mimbre and the Nde-nda-i. The Tci-he-nde were the most easterly group of the three, clustered about west-central and southwestern New Mexico around Santa Rita del Cobre, and the Nde-nda-i lived to the southwest of the Tsoka-ne-nde, almost wholly within the Sierra Madre of Mexico. For more see Apache and the Tci-he-nde Mimbre and Nde-nda-i, respectively.

The Mescaleros of the Western Division lived to the east of the three Chiricahua sub-tribes; and the Western Apache—the group that included the White Mountain Apache, lived to their west.

The Tsoka-ne-nde or Chiricahua proper were also popularly referred to as the Chokonen (middle or real). They lived southwest of the Tci-he-nde and north of the Nde-nda-i about the Dragoon, Chiricahua, and Dos Cabezas mountain ranges in southeastern Arizona. Their principal leader or *natan* was Cochise, who succeeded his father Pisago Cabezón. Cochise was born between 1800 and 1810 and led his people for nineteen years before he died. He had successfully negotiated with President Grant's special envoy, General Oliver Otis Howard, for a reservation that embraced both the Dragoon and Chiricahua mountain ranges with the agency for dispensing rations to the Chokonen near Ft. Bowie to the west of Tucson. Cochise died of natural causes June 8, 1874, in his camp on the on the reservation and was buried in his beloved Dragoon Mountains. Although a good leader of men who had been groomed by his father to take his place, Cochise's son Taza did not have the stature to prevent the resumption of raiding and infighting. The resumption of the raiding brought an end to the reservation that Cochise had fought so long and hard for. Taza died of natural causes on his way to Washington, DC For more see Apache.

CHISKIAC

The Chiskiac was a subdivision of the Powhatan and a member of the Powhatan Confederacy. They lived about the Piankatank River in Gloucester, Virginia, and parts of York County.

CHITIMACHA

The Chitimacha was of the Tunican linguistic stock and the original inhabitants of the Mississippi Delta area of South Central Louisiana. As a language group they were related to the Chawasha and Washa. There were two main geographic divisions, those on the upper end of Bayou La Fourche (or Lafourche) and the other on Grand Lake. The Yagenachito or more properly Yakna-Chitto may have been a sub-tribe of the Chitimacha.

Their first major contact with the Europeans was with Iberville in 1699. In 1706, Taensa, allies of the French, captured some Chitmacha and enslaved them. Later the Chitimacha killed a French missionary and three others. That action precipitated a war with the French that lasted for twelve years until 1718. It was also at this time that many of the Chitimacha were enslaved by white colonists of Louisiana. In the peace agreement, those to the east agreed to resettlement along the Mississippi near present Plaquemine but moved to the south and later disappeared from history. Others found a home near Clarenton well into the late 1800s.

195 CHO-BAH-AH-BISH

A sub-tribe or band of western Washington under the name Cho-bah-ah-bish was listed as a party to the Point Elliott Treaty of January 22, 1855. No other information has become available.

CHOCTAW

The Choctaw were known by a number of different names, including Flat Heads because of their custom of flattening the heads of their infants. The Choctaw began life When the Sun falls into the Water, the Pacific Coast. They migrated South and East searching for the holy place towards the sunrise. They came upon the wide, brown Mississippi that they named *Mish Sipokni* (beyond the ages; the father of all its kind). Never before had they seen inland water so wide. They inhabited the land bordering the Gulf of Mexico and extending west of the Creeks to the Mississippi.

In the 1500s the Choctaw faced the Spanish conquistadors under Hernando De Soto. Next came the French, the Spanish, and finally the English. They separated into two groups, the central group that later would ride into battle beside General Jackson and the second group that lived across the Tombigbee River in Alabama.

The treaty of January 3, 1786, concluded at Hopewell, established the boundaries of Choctaw lands. By 1816 the Choctaw had sold all their land east of the Tombigbee. It was at that time when the Choctaw, along with the Chickasaw, were having almost continuous encounters with white settlers in Mississippi. In 1820 they signed away their southern lands for western lands between the Red River on the South and the Canadian River on the North near the home of the Cherokee. However, together with the Chickasaws, they refused a treaty in 1826 that would trade their lands in Mississippi for lands west of the Mississippi.

Chief Moshulatubbee (although the title and position had been banned under a new Mississippi law) regretfully finally signed the Choctaw's removal treaty in September 1830. The Choctaw was the first nation to sign a removal treaty under the terms of the 1830 Indian Removal Act. In the fall of 1831 the great migration began. Some four thousand Choctaws left their homes in Mississippi and marched through Louisiana and Arkansas. Sickness and death accompanied them. Cholera was single most destructive force they had to deal with. They were also cheated by traders and plied with whisky.

They finally reached their destination, that portion of the Arkansas River that flowed through the future state of Oklahoma and bounded on the south the Red River. They built houses and planted their first crops that fell to the raging Arkansas in flood and were forced to begin again.

Some of the Choctaw chose to stay as citizens of Mississippi under the terms of the Removal Act. But land-hungry whites squatted on Indian land and cheated them out of their holdings. The War Department did make some modest but inadequate to protect them. Before long most of those that had remained sold their land and followed their brothers west.

It was the Choctaw Indian Allen Wright that gave the one-time Indian Territory its name. The Choctaw word for red was *houma*; for people, *okla*.

INDIAN TERRITORY

The first Indian Territory to house of the Indians removed from the East was the present-day state of Kansas. It was already the home of People of the South Wind (Kansa), who had migrated from the Ohio Valley; the Wichita and Pawnee, also recent migrants; and the Osage, who had been forced to cede their Missouri lands for land to the west. The fact that, in 1820, Major Stephan Long had labeled the

Great Plains the Great American Desert and unfit for human habitation solidified the thinking in the upper echelons of government. (Zebulon Pike had described it as sandy deserts devoid of vegetation and unsuitable for cultivation.) Forts were built to maintain control and mark the boundary of this new Indian Territory. Fort Gibson, established, on April 20, 1824, was situated near the confluence of the Verdigris, Neosho and Arkansas Rivers. A month later, Fort Towson was established on month later six miles north of the Red River; and on May 8, 1827, Colonel Henry Leavenworth established a fort that bears his name on the western bank of the Missouri River. With the passage of the Kansas-Nebraska Act in 1854, Kansas was designated Kansas Territory with boundaries that extended west to the summit of the Rocky Mountains. (Kansas was admitted to the Union on January 29, 1861.)

All Indians were ordered cleared from Kansas, and the present state of Oklahoma to the south, thinly settled and in little demand by white settlers was subsequently designated by the government as Indian Territory. The territory of some 19,525,966 acres, less the Panhandle, was originally divided among five tribes removed from the east with the Indian Removal Act of 1830. The Choctaws received 6,953,048 acres in the southeast part of territory; the Chickasaw, over 4,707,903 acres west of the Choctaws; the Cherokees, 4,420,068 acres in the northeast; the Creek, 3,079,095 acres southwest of the Cherokees. The Seminoles purchased 365,852 acres from the Creeks. (The Chickasaw and the Choctaw owned their lands jointly because they were so closely related, but each tribes exercised jurisdiction over its own territory.) The five original tribes soon became fifty-five plus.

CHOKISHG-NA

Chokishg-na was a sub-tribe of the Tongva of California that inhabited the area about the Saboneria. For more see Tongva.

CHOULA

The Choula was a small tribe on the Yazoo River that may have been a sub-tribe or offshoot of the Ibitoupa of Mississippi.

CHOWANOC

The Chowanoc or Chowan belonged to the Algonquian linguistic family. Although Swanton lists the names Chowan and Chomanoc separately, they are almost certainly the same tribe. They inhabited the area along the Chowan River in North Carolina near the junction of the Meherrin and Blackwater rivers. They first encountered the Europeans in 1584-85. At thee time they were possibly the leading tribe in northeastern North Carolina. In 1663 they signed a treaty of friendship with the English but renounced the treaty in 1675. A year of war followed. The Chowanoc were defeated and forced to cede their this northern tribal lands to the Lords Proprietors and were restricted to a reservation on Bennett's Creek. They sided with the colonists in the Tuscarora War; yet in 1723 a reservation of 53,000 acres was set aside for them and the Tuscarora. Ten years later they were given permission to incorporate with the Tuscarora and were effectively extinct by 1755.

CHOWCHILLA YOKUT

The Chowchilla (Chochilla) was a member of the Northern Group of the Valley Division of the Yokut that is generally treated separately. They lived along the several channels of the Chowchilla (Chauchilla) River at the southern end of the San Joaquin Valley in present Madera County, California. John Frémont referred to them as the "Horse-thief Indians" in his memoirs of 1844. Known as fierce warriors, the Chowchilla were featured prominently in the Mariposa War. There were few deaths, but the scorched earth campaigh destroyed their valuable food stores. The Chochilla held out until the death of their chief José Rey.

CHOWIG-NA

Chowig-na was a sub-tribe of the Tongva of California that inhabited the area about Palos Verdes. For more see Tongva.

CHOYE

The Choye (Chaye), a Caddoan tribe, was possibly one of the three allied tribes of the Natchitoches Confederacy of Louisiana., but they may have been associated with the Yatasi. For more see Natchitoches Confederacy and Caddo Peoples.

CHUGNUT

The Chugnut was reportedly a dependent tribe of the Iroquois. They attended the Fort Stanwix treaty conference of 1768.

CHUMASH

The Chumash, also commonly referred the Santa Barbara Indians, were generally considered members of the Hokan linguistic family, but the placement is not universally accepted. They inhabited the three northern islands of the Santa Barbara group, the coast of Malibu Canyon to Estero Bay, and inland areas to include portions of the valley of the Santa Maria River and along the Santa Ynez River, and the drainage areas of the Ventura River, the Calleguas Creek, and the Santa Clara River—generally the Malibu area of Los Angeles County and parts of Ventura and Santa Barbara Counties.

Except for the Island group, the eight Chumash divisions in some ninety villages were named after the Spanish-language places where they lived. Each spoke a different dialect and is treated separately in this work to recognize the relative size of the Chumash nation and the different dialects and to facilitate future identification. For the most part the Chumash were seafaring people and accomplished fishermen. They were also respected for their artistic talents. In 1824 a Chumash revolt seized missions at Santa Barbara, Santa Inez, and La Purisma Concepcion.

The Chumash population went from an estimated 10,000 in 1770 to a mere 14 persons in the 1930 census. One report indicates that there may have been upwards to 22,000 when the Spanish missionaries first arrived in the early seventeenth century. Today, about 2,000 people living primarily in Ventura and Santa Barbara Counties claim their Chumash ancestry.

MAJOR SUBDIVISIONS
Barbareño
Cuyama
Emigdiano
Island
Obispeño
Purisimeño
Santa Ynez
Ventureño

CIBICUE

The Cibecue Apache was a subgroup of the San Carlos Group or Western Apache that also included the White Mountain, San Carlos proper or Gileños, and the Northern and Southern Tonto. The Cibecue consisted of the Canyon Creek Band on Canyon Creek in Gila and Navajo counties; the Carrizo Band on Carrizo Creek in Gila County; and Cibicue Band proper on Cibicue Creek between the Canyon Creek Band and the Carrizo Band. For more see Apache.

BATTLE OF CIBICUE CREEK

On August 28, 1881, Col. Eugene Asa Carr left Fort Apache with two cavalry troops and a company of White Mountain Apache scouts to arrest a Cibecue Apache medicine man or Prophet as he was called, Nochaydelklinne (Nock-ay-det-klinne), for inciting his followers against whites in the area. Although the arrest itself proved uneventful, Carr and his men were attacked by Nochaydelklinne's followers at Cibecue Creek, on the White Mountain Apache Reservation about 40 miles west of Fort Apache, as they camped for the night. The entire company of scouts, less one, joined the Cibecue Apaches in the attack in what is recorded as the only mutiny of an entire troop of Indian scouts in the history of America's Indian wars. When the battle was over, six soldiers were dead; another man later died of his wounds; and one was missing. Nochaydelklinne himself was killed Accounts. Various accounts also include his wife and son among the dead. The following day, the Apaches made repeated attacks against Fort Apache but were repulsed each time. With the arrival of reinforcements, the Indians scattered into the hills and south into Mexico. By the time it was over, eighteen scouts were dead, but there was no count of other casualties. Three of the scouts were tried for mutiny. (Several accounts give the date of the incident as August 30, 1881.)

CLACKAMAS

The Clackamas (used both in the singular and plural) were of the Clackamas or Upper Chinook division of the Chinookan linguistic family. They inhabited the area along the Clackamas River but claimed lands as far east as the Cascade Mountains. For more see Chinook.

CLAHCLELLAH

It is generally believed that the Clahclellah (Clah-clel-lah) was a subdivision of the Watlala, but there is also some thought that it may have been an separate tribe. They belonged to the Clackamas dialectic group of Chinookan linguistic stock and lived at the foot of the Cascades of the Columbia River in Oregon. For more see Watlala.

CLALLAM

The Clallam (strong and clever people) or Sklallam (S'Klallam) was a tribe of the coastal division of the Salishan linguistic family. They lived along the south side of the Strait of Juan de Fuca between Port Discovery and the Hoko River in Washington State. They also shared territory at Port Gamble and Port Townsend with the Chemakum and seasonal sites along Hood Canal. A small group lived on the lower end of Vancouver Island. The S'Klallam were one of the signatories to the Point No Point Treaty of 1855.

Seventeen bands or villages have been identified that include the Lower Elwah at the mouth of the Elwah River, sometimes referred to as the Lower Clallam; the Upper Elwah at Sestietl; Huiauuick on the site of modern Jamestown, sometimes referred to as the Jamestown band; and the Port Gamble band.

CLATSKANIE

The Clatskanie (or Clatsanie) were part of the Athapascan linguistic family. They inhabited the prairies bordering the Chehalis River in Washington at the mouth of the Skookumchuck River. Later they crossed the Columbia River into Oregon and settled about the mountains surrounding the Clatskanie River. By the 1850 they had effectively lost their identity as a tribe.

CLATSOP

The Clatsop was a small tribe of the Chinookan linguistic stock and inhabited lands in what is today southwest Washington State on the southern bank of the Columbia River where they encountered the Corps of Discovery. Captains Lewis and Clark named their 1805-1806 winter camp in their territory Fort Clatsop. The tribe was hit very hard by a smallpox epidemic around 1800 that took several hundred lives.

CLOWWEWALLA

The Clowwewalla were of the Clackamas division of the Chinookan linguistic stock. They lived about the falls of the Willamette River in Oregon. Because of their location, they were called the Fall Indians (as were the Atsina).

COAHUILTECAN TRIBES

The name Coahuiltecan, also known as Tejano, comes from the Mexican state of Coahuila. The associated tribes inhabited the eastern part of the province of Coahuila and Texas west of the San Antonio River and Cibolo Creek. The tribes belonged to the Coahuiltecan linguistic family. They may also be related to the Tamaulipecan family of México; also the Karankawan and Tonkawan. The confederation of tribes was comprised of a large number of small tribes or bands. Swanton lists 224 but gives no assurances that he had the names of all. To confuse the matter more, some of those listed may actually have had other affiliations; and some of the names may be synonyms of others. The 1690 total estimated population given by Mooney (1928) was 15,000; yet some tribes or bands were represented by only a single individual. According to Swanton, there were no known descendants in the Texas by 1952, and it might be reasonable to conclude that they had completely passed into history by the beginning of the twentieth century. The Aranama of Texas, extinct by 1843, are generally considered to be among the affiliated tribes of the Coahuiltecan, but they also have listed among the Karankawan and Tonkawan. They lived in the area about ten miles inland from the Gulf coast.

It is believed that the Coahuiltecan were succeeded by the Karankawan tribes on the Gulf coast who have been shown to have been very close connected linguistically. Further north they were displaced by the Apache and Comanche.

COAPITE

The Coapite was one of the five principal Karankawan Tribes of Texas. For more see Karankawan Tribes.

COAQUE

The Coaque, also known as the Capoques, Cocos or Caoco, was one of the five principal Karankawan Tribes of Texas. They inhabited Galveston Island and the mouth of the Brazos River. According to Bolton, the Cocos lived on the lower Colorado and Gulf coast. For more see Karankawan Tribes.

COAST YUKI

The Coast Yuki or Ukhotno'm have been placed linguistically close to the Yuki; however, they are not Yuki Indians of the interior living on the coast. The Coast Yuki was a separate and distinct tribe who considered themselves an offshoot of the Huchnom. The name "Yuki," given to the Yuki (of the interior) simply meant "stranger." The Yuki, in turn, applied the name to those strangers living by the ocean, thus Coast Yuki. They lived along the coast from Cleone to near Rockport, California, and inland to include the area about Ten Mile River, Warren Creek, and in the Sherwood Valley. For more see Yuki. and Huchnom.

COCHITI PUEBLO

The Cochiti (also spelled Cochita) were of the eastern dialectic group of Keresan or Keres linguistic stock. They lived along the Rio Grande River in north central New Mexico, between the Rio de los Friholes and the Rio Jemez and along the Rio Jemez from the Pueblo of Sia (Zia) to its mouth. For more see Pueblo.

COCOPA

The Cocopa belonged to the Yuman branch of the Hokan linguistic stock. They inhabited the area around the mouth of the Colorado River in Arizona. Their history dates to the Spanish of the 1500s. Most of the Cocopa territory was in Mexico. Those of the population in the United States were subsequently assigned to the Colorado River Reservation. In some reports the name is Cocopah for those living in the United States and Cocopa for those in Mexico.

COEUR D'ALÊNE SKITSWISH

The Coeur d'Alêne (awl heart) belonged to the inland division of the Salishan family. They lived about the Coeur d'Alêne Lake and Coeur d'Alêne River of northern Idaho and the Spokane River. The Coeur d'Alêne constituted two divisions of the Skitswish: the Coeur d'Alêne Lake Division and Spokane River Division and the Coeur d'Alêne River Division. The name is also popularly used applied to all Skitswish.

In the 1840s, Father Peter John De Smet established a permanent mission for the tribe and assigned Father Nicolas Point as its director. Fr. Point named it the Mission of the Sacred Heart of Jesus, but in Father De Smet absence, the temporary superior changed the name to the Saint Joseph Mission. Fr. De Smet reversed the decision as soon as he learned of it.

The Coeur d'Alene War broke out in May 17, 1858, when a combined force of twelve hundred Coeur d'Alene, Palouse, Spokane, and St. Joe River Skitswish Indians defeated Colonel Edward Steptoe in a direct confrontation near Colfax, Washington, at the village of To-ho-to-nim-me. Colonel George Wright, in turn, defeated a combined force of hundreds of Coeur d'Alene and Spokane in two bloody engagements in August and September ending the war. Thirty-three of the natives were taken prisoner as hostages and imprisoned at Fort Walla Walla. Later that year the commandant of the fort released them to the custody of Father De Smet, much to the chagrin of Col. Wright.

They were subsequently placed on a reservation in the area that was given their name. For more see Skitswish.

COFITACHEQUI

The Cofitachequi or Cofitachiqui, which appears quite common, occupied a number of sites in South Carolina from the Savannah River to the Pee Dee River; within the Santee River watershed from St. Stephens to Camden; and near the confluence of the Wateree and Congaree rivers.

The Cofitachequi were first described in the journals of the De Soto expedition. Juan Pardo visited the Cofitachiqui in 1566 and 1567, but all references to them seems to have disappeared about 1685. Swanton noted that the Kasihta, a Muskhogean people and the most important division of the Muskogee, may have been the Cofitachequi of De Soto; but Waddell, after an exhaustive study of the subject, has stated that all the evidence supports the conclusion that Confitachequi were the Catawba (a Siouan people) and that they and their Siouan allies were given another name by tribes to the south. For more see the Catawba.

COHARIE

The Coharie descended from the Neusiok who lived along the south side of the lower Neuse River in present Craven and Cartaret counties of North Carolina. Inter-tribal conflicts that arose with the arrival of the Europeans on the Carolina shores caused a split within the tribe. A group of Indians that became known as the Coharie removed from the main body and settled along the Little Coharie River in present-day Sampson and Harnett counties in southeast North Carolina sometime between 1729 and 1746. From that time forward they have lived as a separate and independent tribe, currently governed by the Coharie Intra-Tribal Council.

The modern Coharie community is comprised of four settlements located at Holly Grove, New Bethel, Shiloh, and Antioch. The Coharie Indian Tribe was recognized by the state of North Carolina in 1971. The petitioning process for Federal recognition has been underway since the nineteen eighties. For more see the Neusiok.

COHUNNEWAGO

The Cohunnewago was listed in Jefferson's *Notes on the State of Virginia*. Jefferson gives no location but gives a population of 200 warriors. For more see "Aborigines," Appendix D.

COIRACOENTANON

The Coiracoentanon was one of the minor tribes of the Illinois Cluster of Tribes for which there is only passing mention. For more see the Illinois Cluster.

COLUMBIA

The Columbia people were named for their prominent association with the Columbia River where the largest bands had their homes. The Columbia belonged to the inland division of the Salishan linguistic family. They were closely related to the Wenatchee and Methow. They were also called the Sickiuse, a name applied a number of neighboring Salish tribes. Traders also gave them the name Isle-de-Pierre.

The principal bands lived on the east side of the Columbia River from Fort Ikanogan to the near Point Easton. The Columbia Reservation was created for them By the 1950s the Sinkiuse-Columbia were under the jurisdiction of the Colville Agency. The Moses-Columbia band was located in the southern part of the Colville Reservation.

COLVILLE

The Colville name was taken from Fort Colville, a Hudson Bay Company post at Kettle Falls, in honor of a governor of the company. The Colville were part of the inland division of Salishan linguistic family and lived along the Colville River and along the Columbia River at Kettle Falls. In 1845, Father John Paul De Smet established the Saint Francis Regis Mission below Fort Colville and the Saint Paul Mission to the north on the 49th parallel overlooking Fort Colville.

COMANCHE

The Eastern or Rocky Mountain Shoshoni split into different cultures at the close of the seventeenth century although they were linguistically identical,. The Northern Shoshoni remained in the mountains. Those who would become the Comanche of the southwest began migrating south into eastern Colorado and western Kansas in search of the buffalo, beneficiaries of the horse herds left behind by the Spanish who were forced to abandon their settlements in New Mexico by the Pueblo Revolt of 1680. It was not a mass movement, but a slow, steady progression.

The Comanche began their move to the south from the country of the Platte River about 1700. A small party of Comanche first appeared in New Mexico with a band of mountain Utes in 1705 to whom they were related and with whom they would maintain perpetual enmity. They also maintained perpetual enmity with the Pawnee and Wichita, but they had an unbridled hatred for the Apache or Athapascans, so much so that they formed an uneasy truce with the Utes against Apache.

In the migration south the Utes had called their companions Koh-mahts (those who are always with us). The Spanish wrote the word as Comantz and Comanche. The Comanche called themselves Nermernuh, or the "people" as did almost all tribes in their respective languages. The Comanche continued further south and across the Arkansas River. By 1725 the Comanche controlled most of lands that stretched from the foothills of the Rockies in New Mexico south to the Pecos River east through central Oklahoma and Texas, including all of the panhandle, north to the Arkansas River and Santa Fe Trail and south to near the source of the San Antonio River, a range that covered some covered six hundred miles from north to south and four hundred miles from east to west. The Spanish called the land Comanchería. By 1750 Comanche domination of the land was total.

The sedentary Eastern Apaches were entirely driven off the southern plains by the 1740s, and the whites along the Spanish-American frontier and northern Mexico were subject to continual attack by Comanche war parties. The Ute remained secure in their Colorado mountains as were the Pawnee and Wichita who maintained a mobile life style equal to the Comanche. The Tonkawa and Caddo just stayed out the way, but the Lipan and Tonkawa took their revenge some hundred years later when they acted as scouts for the Texas Rangers.

According to Fehrenbach, the Comanche Nation was comprised of up to thirteen bands or sub-tribes, but the structure evolved as groups combined and broke apart. Five major sub-tribes (*) are considered to have played a significant roles in Comanche history. *Our Comanche Dictionary* lists nineteen bands, and Swanton lists nine and acknowledges six others. Attempts to correlate the three lists has met with less than success, notwithstanding the variations in spelling.

FEHRENBACH
Eeh-tahtah-oh
Hois (timber people)
Jupe (or Hupene, Yupini)
Kotsoteka* (or Caschotethka, Koocheteka, Kotsai) (buffalo eaters)

Kwahada* (or Kwahadi, Kwahari, Kwaharior, Quahada) (antelopes)
Parkeenaum (water people)
Nahmah-er-nuh
Nokoni* (or Detsanyuka, Naconee, Nakoni, Nawkoni, Nocony) (people who return)
Pehnahterkuh* (wasps)
Tahneemuh (or Dehaui, Tanima, Tevawish, Yanimna) (liver eaters)
Tenawa (or Tahnahwah, Tenahwit) (those who stay downstream)
Widyunuu (or Widyu Yapa) (awl people)
Yamparika* (or Yamparack, Yapparethka) (root or Yap eaters)
13

OUR COMANCHE DICTIONARY
(published by the Comanche Language and Cultural Preservation Committee)
Hanitaibo (Corn People)
Kuhtsutuuka (Buffalo Eaters)
Kwaharu (Antelope Eaters)
Kwahihuu ki (Back Shade Comanche)
Kwaru (or Kwa?aru Nuu) (Loud Speaking People)
Nokoni (or Nokoninuu) (They Travel Around)
Noyuhkanuu (or Noyukanuu) (Wanderers)
Numu (Comanche Person, singular)
Numunuu (Comanche People, plural) (crawling on belly like a snake)
Ohnonuu (or Ohnononuu, Onahununuu) (Comanche Clan from Cyril area)
Parukaa (or Padouka) Name given by the Sioux.
Pekwi Tuhka (Fish Eaters)
Penatuka (or Penanuu, Pihnaatuka, or Penatuka Nuu) (Honey Eaters; also, Quick Striking)
Pikaatamu (Buckskin Sewing)
Saria Tuhka (or Sata Teichas) (Dog Eaters)— Generally believed to be an Arapaho group that was accepted into the Comanche sometime after 1800. Other variations of the name include Särĕtĭka, Sarh Rikka, Sarritecha, and Charitica
Taninuu (Liver Eaters, south of the Peace River in Texas)
Tutsanoo Yehku (Comanche Band)
Wianu (or Wianuu, Wia?nuu) (Band from the Walters Oklahoma area)
Yaparuhka (or Yapai Nuu, Yapainuu, Yapuruhka) (Root Eaters)
19

SWANTON
Detsanayuka or Nokoni
Ditsakana, Widyu, Yapa or Yamparika
Kewatsana
Kotsai
Kotsoteka, Kwahari or Kwahadi
Motsai
Pagatsu
Penateka or Penande
Pohoi (adopted Shoshoni)
Tanima, Tenawa or Tenahwit
Waaih
9

Guage-johe
Ketahto
Kwashi
Muvinabore
Nauniem
Parkeenaum
6 (15)

Their mastery of the horse made the Comanche unique. What others considered a skill to the Comanche was an art. With that very special weapon, they quickly became masters of the Plains or, as some writers have referred them, "Lords of the Plains." The Comanche not only used the horse as did other Plains tribes but they also understood the Spanish Mustang and learned to breed it successfully. They also developed the fighting and hunting skills that took full advantage of the capabilities the horse offered. The Pawnee called the Comanche the "Horse People." The horse empowered all the major tribes of the Central and Southern Plains, the Comanche, the Southern Cheyenne, the Arapaho, the Kiowa, the Pawnee, and the Kiowa Apache—the Comanche and Kiowa remained south of the Arkansas River. The "horse soldiers" of the north, across the Platte, were the Dakota and Northern Cheyenne. Smaller but equally mobile and capable were the Wichita and Osage. The Comanche maintained herds of tough, durable horses that numbered in the thousands. The Kiowa first appeared between the Platte and Arkansas in the 1780s and, traveling with them, those the Anglos called the Kiowa-Apache. They became lasting allies of the Comanche.

Comanche raids across the Spanish-American frontier and into northern Mexico for a hundred-plus years generally between 1735 and 1835 were endemic. Murder, mutilation, stealing (particularly horses), and burnings became common. They carried off captives first to humiliate, then to force them into slavery or to put on the trading block. Young male children were often adopted into the tribe. Peace was finally negotiated in Spanish New Mexico in 1786 thanks to the efforts of Don Juan Bautista de Anza. It was not a treaty of co-existence between the parties. Every where else terror reigned. With peace in New Mexico arose the Comancheros, civilian traders and ranchers who were allowed into Comanche camps.

THE 1800s

The first thirty-five years of the new century brought numerous changes precipitated by a series of national and international events: the recession of the Louisiana Territory from the Spanish back to the French in 1800; the Louisiana Purchase in 1803; Anglo-American settlement in east Texas beginning in 1821; the war of Mexican independence that culminated in 1821; and Texas independence in 1835. By 1835 there were 30,000 Americans living in Texas compared to 3,500 Mexicans. The following year began a forty-year war between the Comanche and the Texans (or tejanos) that would ultimately lead to the defeat and removal of the Comanche from the Plains. In addition, the Comanche, the Kiowa, and the Kiowa-Apaches were hit by a smallpox epidemic in the summer of 1839 that decimated the tribes.

The following year on March 19, 1840, the Pehnahterkuh band of the Comanche suffered the Council House Tragedy in which 33 chiefs, women and children were killed and 32 women and children, many wounded, were thrown into jail.. Retributions followed along with an ongoing war of raids in force. The Pehnahterkuh, however, received only vocal support from the other bands.

Prior to the Council House fight, Texas Anglos had determined to rid the frontier west of all Indians. Using the raids by the Comanche and the Kiowa as an excuse, President Lamar and the Rangers launched a war of extermination from 1836-1840. The Texans turned their attention first to the peaceful and sedentary tribes of east Texas. Before the 1830s came to a close, the Cherokee, Delaware, Shawnee, Caddo, Kickapoo, Creek, and Seminole and remnants of other eastern tribes were burned out of and off the lands on which they had settled.

When Sam Houston again became president in 1841 and reinstated his policy of peace between Indians and whites that, at this stage, was totally unrealistic. The Comanche had continued to raid in Mexico while they skirted the settlements in Texas. But Houston's peace initiatives reopened the door to further confrontations. In 1844 the southern Comanche agreed to attend a peace council at Tehuacana Creek. The result was a promise by Houston to establish trading posts in return for an agreement from the Comanche to halt raiding in Texas. Houston had authority to grant nothing more. For the most part, the treaty was ignored by the majority of the Comanche who did not participate in the sessions.

Texas was officially annexed to the Union on December 29, 1845, although the Lone Star flag was not lowered until the following February 19. With annexation, the federal government took over the administration of Indian affairs and established a line of military forts to serve as a cordon between the two races. (To the Comanche, these forts were manned by Americans, the americano, or the white man—"tahbay-boh" vs. the "tejanos" or Texans.) For their parts, the settlers and Indians assumed their traditional roles—encroachment and seizure followed by depredations. To exacerbate the situation still further, the federal government and the state government worked at cross purposes. On the one side the goal was marginal coexistence and peace through negotiation; on the other, extermination. The Comanches and others were also hit hard by diseases, both cholera and smallpox, against which they had no weapons.

In the spring 1846 the southern Comanche agreed to attend a peace council along with chiefs from the Wichita, the Caddo, the Tonkawa, and others. The resulting Butler-Lewis Treaty called for peace and trade, but the commissioners lacked the authority to establish a permanent boundary between the two nations within the borders of Texas. That failure in itself guaranteed that their would be no lasting peace. Peace or war became mute issues with the epidemic that hit the southern plains in the summer of 1849, killing half of remaining Pehnahterkuh and destroying the once formidable cohesion between the bands. Only he remote Antelope clan survived in tack.

A treaty was concluded between with the northern Comanche, the Kiowa, and the Kiowa Apache inhabiting the territory south of the Arkansas River at Fort Atkinson, Indian Territory, in July 1853. In exchange for a stop to the raiding and a return of captives, the Indians were to be given an annuity in cash, goods, and merchandise. Both parties failed to deliver, but this time the primary blame fell on the Indians. From their subsequent actions, it was apparent the treaty talks were no more than a game.

Under legislation passed by the Texas Legislature, some seventy thousand acres were made available for use by the Bureau of Indian Affairs as reservations for Texas Indians. The legislature was finally made to understand that unless definitive boundaries were established there would be no peace. Two reservations were established in 1854, one on the upper Brazos near Fort Belknap, designated the Brazos Reservations for the Waco, the Ioni, the Anadarko, the Tawakoni, and other Wichita-Caddoan remnants. The second, a 23,000-acre reservation, was established on the Clear Fork of the Brazos, in what is now Throckmorton County. It became home to some the Pehnahterkuh Comanche. Out of some one thousand Pehnahterkuh in Texas, 431 were brought into the reservation. The rest rode across the Red River to make new homes with the northern bands.

The Army established Camp Cooper in 1856 to police the reservations and maintain order, but the endless war with the Texans, disease, and the reduction in the buffalo herds had weakened them to the point of utter destruction. The indiscriminate slaughter of the buffalo, the life blood of the Plains Indians that began in 1870, ended in 1881. They were no more.

Raids into Texas by members of other southern Indians continued. And, although the reservation Indians were blameless, they were made to suffer thanks to bigots like John Baylor who would not rest until all Indians were out of Texas. On September 1, 1859, the reservation Indians were removed to Indian Territory leaving all that they had built and worked for. They were given a tract of land near the Anadarko and assigned to the Wichita Agency. Indian Agent Robert Neighbors wrote to his wife comparing the Indian removal to the Exodus of the Jews out of Egypt.

CIVIL WAR PERIOD

On March 10, 1860, army headquarters ordered the Comanche-Kiowa Expedition to take place that summer. The three-prong search and destroy mission that began May 15 from Fort Riley, Fort Cobb, and Fort Union was for the most part a failure except for one undeceive engagement with the Kiowa between the Republic and the Solomon in July.

Throughout the period of the Civil War, the Indian situation took a back seat to more pressing issues at the Federal level. The Plains Indians took advantage of the respite and wrought havoc along the frontier. What ensued was a period of bloody guerilla warfare between whites and Indians across the Plains from Minnesota to Texas.

For the war itself, some of the Indian bands, particularly from the east, joined the war effort. The Choctaw, the Chickaway, the Seminole, and the majority of the Cherokee took the Confederate side. The Creek, the Shawnee, the Delaware, and others of the Cherokee joined the Union. An extension of the "civil war" erupted between the Indian tribes themselves.

LATER TREATIES

A treaty was concluded with the Comanche and Kiowa in 1863 that reaffirmed the provisions of the 1853 treaty, but it was never ratified by the Congress. As a result, the Indians, not understanding the process, felt betrayed when their promised disbursements did not arrive leading to renewed outbreaks of war.

In October 1865, a treaty was concluded with the Apache, Cheyenne, and Arapaho at the council-ground on the Little Arkansas, in Kansas. The treaty united the bands and tribes of Apache with those of the Cheyenne and Arapaho dissolving their confederation with the Comanche and Kiowa from the treaty of 1853.

Two years later on October 21, 1867, at the Council Camp on Medicine Lodge Creek, seventy miles south of Fort Larned in Kansas, another treaty was concluded between the Apache, the Kiowa, and the Comanche tribes of the Upper Arkansas. The Apache, at their request, were again confederated with the Kiowa and Comanche nations, accepting as their permanent home the reservation specified in the original treaty and relinquishing all rights in the confederation of the Arapaho and Cheyenne from the 1865 treaty.

The 1867 Treaty of Medicine Lodge Creek in present Barbour County, Kansas, the last treaty made with the Comanches, established a reservation for the Comanche, Kiowa, and Kiowa Apache in southwestern Indian Territory between the Washita and Red rivers. The reservation had originally been assigned to the Choctaw and the Chickasaw but was taken back by the government. Six bands of the Comanche participated in the one-sided negotiations. The Comanches refused to stay on the reservation and joined those who remained free on the Plains. They continued with wanton raids into Texas and elsewhere until warriors attacked buffalo hunters with their long-range Sharp's rifles at Adobe Walls in Hutchinson County. The unsuccessful attack destroyed the Indians' faith in their Medicine Man and brought retribution from the government.

FINAL CAMPAIGN

In 1874 the U.S. army began a campaign against the Indians known as the Red River War. As part of a concerted five-pronged attack that was launched in the Panhandle, forces under the command of Col. Ronald [Randall] S. Mackenzie surprised a Comanche camp in Palo Duro Canyon and completely destroyed their horse herd. Although the campaign resulted in very few Indians deaths, their will and their ability to wage war were effectively destroyed. To survive the winter on the plains, they were forced to enter the reservation. Quanah, the last chief of the Comanche, a half-breed, and one who some say was their greatest chief, surrendered unconditionally at Fort Sill in June 1875. Fort Sill, located within the 5,546-square-mile-reservation provided for in the Treaty at Medicine Lodge, had been established in February 1869 as the agency for the Comanche, the Kiowa, and the Kiowa Apache after it was moved farther to the interior to avoid contacts between the Comanche and their allies and the Cheyenne and the Arapaho.

RED RIVER WAR

The Medicine Lodge Treaty of 1867 established two reservations in Indian Territory, one for the Comanche and Kiowa and the other for the Southern Cheyenne and Arapaho. Ten chiefs endorsed the treaty, and many tribal members moved voluntarily to the reservations. The Comanches, particularly, hated and feared the reservation. They would slip silently away, strike out in anger against the white settlements, and return to the reservation. Their strikes were the last gasps of a once proud, independent people. And so it continued until the spring of 1874.

Typically, the government had been slow in delivery of goods and supplies as promised in the treaty, and what food that reached the Indians was often of poor quality. Meanwhile settlers and commercial hunters decimated the once plentiful herds of buffalo herds on Indian hunting grounds. That spring, many of the Comanche broke from the reservation and returned to the open plains of Texas where they talked of war. They were led by Isa-tai, a Comanche medicine man, and Quanah of the Quahadi (Kwahadi/Kwerhar-rehnuh), the principal war chief. The first strike was to be against the buffalo hunters.

On June 27, 1874, an alliance of upwards of seven hundred Comanche, Kiowa, Arapaho, and Cheyenne warriors led by Quanah as principal war chief attacked the camp of buffalo hunters at Bent's abandoned trading post at Adobe Walls on the Canadian River in the Texas Panhandle. What amounted to a seige continued until July 1. With the firepower of their long-range Sharps rifles, the twenty-eight hunters and one woman not only held off the attackers they completely demoralized them. The Indians withdrew with recriminations among them that led to the dissolution of the alliance—for the most part the Cheyenne and Arapaho went their way; the Comanche and Kiowa, theirs. Except for a Lone Wolf and a few others, the Kiowa returned to the reservation on the own. On July 12, Lone Wolf, with a small band of fifty Kiowa warriors, engaged a force of Texas Rangers of the Frontier Battalion in the Lost Valley Fight near Jacksboro. Two rangers were killed, and the rest escaped under the cover of darkness.

Lieutenant Frank D. Baldwin was chief of scouts for Colonel Nelson A. Miles. On August 20, 1874, at a stream he named Chicken Creek in the eastern Panhandle, Baldwin's scouts were the first military to draw blood in the War. Just over two months later on November 8, 1874, Baldwin led an attack on Chief Grey Beard's Cheyenne encampment of a hundred lodges on McClellan Creek in Gray County, Texas, with two companies of soldiers without waiting for reinforcements as might reasonably have been expected against superior numbers in a strong defensive position. The men recovered two young white girls that had previously been taken captive, Julia Germaine, age 7, and Adelaide Germaine, age 5. For his gallantry in action, Baldwin was awarded the Congressional Medal of Honor. It was his second. Baldwin is one of only nineteen servicemen ever to be awarded the Medal of Honor twice. (The first was awarded for his actions during the Civil War. Both Medals were presented on December 3, 1891.)

One hundred and ninety whites died in a series of violent, vicious attacks that continued throughout the summer months. What sympathy there was for the Indian cause disappeared. President Grant ordered a military expedition to quell the attacks and subdue all the Indians that became known as the Red River War. It also ushered in an new government policy for dealing with the Indians across the country—complete and total subjugation at the hands of the military.

The offensive employed five columns that were to converge on the upper tributaries of the Red River in the Panhandle of Texas and encircle the entire region. Colonel Nelson A. Miles moved southward from Fort Dodge; Lieutenant Colonel John W. Davidson marched westward from Fort Sill; Lieutenant Colonel George P. Buell moved northwest from Fort Griffin; Colonel Ranald S. Mackenzie marched northward from Fort Concho; and Major William R. Price marched eastward across the Panhandle from Fort Union. The Tonkawa scouted for the army.

On September 28, 1874, Colonel "Bad Hand" Mackenzie with Tonkawa scouts attacked and defeated a large force of Comanche and Kiowa party and a few Cheyenne at Palo Duro Canyon (the 2nd). Two days earlier, Mackenzie had defeated the Cheyenne at Tule Canyon. In the first battle at Palo Duro, Colonel Miles had fought a running, but inconclusive battle with a force of Cheyennes from August 27 through 31, before the Indians dispersed. A detachment from Mile's column destroyed a large Cheyenne camp at the headwaters of McClellan Creek on November 8, 1874, and rescued two white captives. In all, there may have been twenty or more engagements between the Army and the Southern Plains Indians across the region of Texas Panhandle. It was Mackenzie's fight at Palo Duro on the 28th that destroyed the Indians' will and the capacity to continue their resistance. Only a handful of Indians were killed; but as typically happened, the army destroyed the Indian villages and food stores and, this time, slaughtered over a thousand Indian ponies.

From the standpoint of the Army, the Red River War was a huge success. There were holdouts, but by December, the war was effectively over. Lone Wolf and Mama'nte and the last of the Kiowa warriors turned themselves in at Fort Sill on February 26, 1875, along with 180 women and children. Meanwhile Colonel Miles continued to press the fight against the Southern Cheyenne. In April 1876 Stone Calf surrendered. (The Southern Cheyenne had sent their Sacred Arrows to their brothers to the north for safety.)

The war officially came to an end June 2, 1875, with Quanah's surrender to Mackenzie at Fort Sill. By that time, many of the leaders had been exiled to Fort Marion, Florida, and were not allowed to return to the reservation until 1878. Lone Wolf and a few others were sentenced to prison for murder.

COMMENTARY

Once numbered in the thousands, the Comanche population had been reduced to 1,597 according to an 1875 reservation census. Within ten years the number was down to 1,382. With the total restructuring of Comanche society, its cultural values and its beliefs, the Comanche possibly suffered more from reservation life than most. The reservation period came to an end in 1901 when the Comanche reservation was broken up into allotments in severalty. The 1910 census put the total population at 1,171.

Of all the American Indian tribes, the Comanche, and secondarily the Kiowa, might be the last to warrant feelings of remorse. They were masters of their lives on the southern plains as they were masters of the Plains themselves. Their early migration from the north was voluntary; and, once settled in the southern plains, having driven the original inhabitants out, they moved about freely throughout the southwest and northern Mexico. If they did not precipitate, they welcomed intertribal wars; and long before they or their lands were ever threatened by the whites (whether the Spanish, the French, or the Mexicans and Anglo-Americans), the Comanche went on the aggressive, robbing, stealing, killing, mutilating, and burning across Texas and parts of New Mexico and Colorado, and northern Mexico—far beyond their own immense territory. They took captives, both Reds and whites; used them and sold them. And empathy for their victims, even basic compassion, appears to have been totally beyond their nature. In many instances atrocities and depredations they committed were as much in sport and acts of pride as anything.

Their geographical position would unquestionably have led to the same fate as that of other native peoples, but the consequences of their forty-year war with the Anglo-Americans, their ultimate destruction as a people, was as much of their own doing as the Anglo-Americans campaign of extermination. It is argued that not only did their actions rain down ruin on themselves but also indirectly contributed to the deaths of peaceful Indians elsewhere and that their actions turned public opinion and official response against all Indians in the trans-Mississippi west. Fehrenback writes, "The tragedy within the tragedy was that the intransigence of the southern predators brought revenge down upon the Sioux and the Nez Percé, and, in fact, all remaining American Indians."

That their own actions contributed significantly to their very destruction there is little doubt. That their actions were directly or indirectly responsible for the treatment netted out by the white man to others of their race is, in the opinion of this writer, highly questionable.

In the 1830s, the citizens of the new Republic of Texas were determined to clear out what they called the "rats' nest" of east Texas that had been settled by remnants of a number of peaceful, sedentary tribes from the east. It was not the actions of the Comanches to the west that precipitated the wanton destruction of the their homes and crops; it was the white man's envy and greed for the fertile lands of the east Texas, arguably the most fertile lands in all of Texas. Just as actions of the Comanche had no bearing on the removal of the eastern tribes westward, it was not the actions of the Comanche that were responsible for the war of extermination in California brought on by the discovery of gold; nor were they responsible the seizure of the Black Hills from the Sioux or the Sand Creek massacre or the mutilation by civilians of the bodies of the Cheyennes killed by troopers during the breakout from Ft. Robinson or the Camp Grant massacre. It is a lengthy list.

The Comanche were a large, powerful tribe. As fighters they were among the best. They were capable; they fought tenaciously; they were hardened; and they were not easily subdued. And they never backed down. They simply fought to the last. Unquestionably their actions garnered little sympathy and turned the opinion of some against all Indians and hardened the positions of others. But I question whether their actions were in any way responsible for the meanness and the greed and the hatred exhibited by many whites towards the Indians. The atrocities committed against the American Indians were for the most part the work of civilians, however labeled, to feed their own sickness and their own purposes without regard to what the Comanche did or did not do. Such men were responsible for their own actions.

For more on the Comanche, see Red River War, Council House Tragedy, and Nations of the North.

COMBAHEE

The Combahee was a subdivision or sub-tribe of the Cusabo proper (South). They lived on the lower Combahee River of South Carolina. For more see the Cusabo.

CONCOW MAIDU

The ConCow Maidu or ConCow (Concow) was a sub-tribe of the Maidu sometimes treated separately. The ConCow was of the Penution language stock and lived in the drainage of the Feather River in the KonKow Valley about twenty miles north of present day Oroville, in Butte County, California. Swanton calls them Konkau and lists them as a sub-tribe or village of the Northwestern division of the Maidu inhabiting the lower course of the North Fork of the Feather River.

The ConCow encountered trapper, guide, and explorer Jedediah Smith in 1828 whose party stayed with the ConCow for six months during the winter of 1828-29. For the next five years, the ConCow village welcomed independent trappers and employees of the Hudson's Bay Company, but in 1833 the village was decimated by a malaria epidemic killing an estimated 800 people.

With the discovery of gold, the ConCow territory was overrun, and food sources became scarce as conflicts arose between the Indians and the white man. On August 1, 1851, a treaty was signed at the Bidwell Rancho on Chico Creek with Indian Agent Oliver Wozencraft that created a reservation of over two hundred square miles from Chico to Nimshew to Oroville. The state of California objected to this prime land being given to the Indians, and the following year the U.S. rejected the treaty. (A number of treaties were signed with California tribes in 1851 and 1852, all of which were rejected by Congress.)

In early 1850s the Concow were hit by bouts of pneumonia, influenza, tuberculosis, small pox, malaria or cholera that took nearly another thousand lives. In 1854, Thomas J Henley, Superintendent of California Indians, established four reservations: Fresno; Nome Lackie Reserve in the Upper Sacramento Valley; on Klamath River; and below Cape Mendicino on the coast. The Tejon Reservation in southern California was established in 1853. In 1856, Round Valley was designated as "Nome Cult Valley" by the state. Nome Cult Farm was an extension of the Nome Lackie Reserve and later became the Round Valley Reservation.

On September 4, 1863, 471weekened and distressed ConCow Indians that had been previously corralled at a camp near Chico, California, were marched under military escort to Round Valley, a distance of approximately 100 miles. Many died along the road in their own Trail of Tears, recorded in the literature as "Death March," before the main group reached Round Valley on September 18. There is an annual walk along the Nome Cult Trail as it is called to commemorate and remember.

On April 8, 1864, the Round Valley Reserve was officially established at Covelo, California, in Mendocino County. Six years later the entire reserve was designated as a reservation for Indians with President Grant's Executive Order of March 30, 1870. The Round Valley Reservation became home to the ConCow, Nomalaki Pomo, Littlelake (Little Lake, Miton Pomo), Yuki, and Pit River (Achomawi) Indians. For more see the Maidu. (The present city of Concow is located in northcentral California in Butte County.)

CONEJERO

The Conejero (or Conexero) "rabbit people" was a band of Plains Apache, possibly an early band of the Lipan, that ranged across the valley of the Canadian River in northeastern New Mexico and the Panhandle of Texas, as well as western Kansas and southeastern Colorado, during the seventeenth century. They have been an early band of Lipan Apaches. It reported that the Conejero had some contact with the French in the Mississippi valley and the Spanish in 1706 in the vicinity of present Cimmaron, New Mexico. The Conejero disappear from recorded history by the mid-1700s, most likely destroyed and scattered by the invading Comanche with remnants absorbed into the Jicarilla.

CONGAREE

The Congaree were most likely of the Siouan linguistic family. The lived about the Congaree River in Richland and Lexington counties and in the vicinity of present-day Columbia, South Carolina (originally known as Congaree). They had an estimated population of 800 in 1600. They fought the colonists in the Yamasee War of 1715-1716 and were drastically reduced with over half the population captured and enslaved. Remnants later joined the Catawba to whom they were related.

CONOY

The Conoy proper or Piscataway was one of the nine divisions of the Conoy and lived in the southern part of Prince George County in Maryland, on the west shore of the Patuxent River flowing parallel to the west side of Chesapeake Bay. Although they generally remained on the Maryland side of the Potomac, the Piscataway, the Susquehanna, and the Doeg (Nanticoke) became involved in the Rebellion of 1676 or Bacon's Rebellion in colonial Virginia. For more see Conoy Peoples. The Piscataway name came from a village on Piscataway Creek that was home to the Conoy chief.

Confusion has arisen because the name Piscataway has been reported as an alternate name for the Pennacook Piscataqua, two distinct and independent Algonquian tribes.

CONOY PEOPLES

The Conoy (Canawese and Ganawese) or Kanawha belonged to the Algonquian linguistic stock and inhabited colonial Maryland and parts of present-day New Jersey, and Pennsylvania. They were comprised of nine principal divisions, including the Conoy proper or Piscataway (Piscataway). The Jesuits established missions among the Conoy in 1634. The colonial government of Maryland gave the Conoy a fort on Metapoint Creek, east of the Potomac River, as a refuge against hostile tribes. The Conoy made their way north from Maryland by the mid-1700s; but by the end of the century, the remnants had been absorbed by the Mahican and Delaware.

PRINCIPAL SUBDIVISIONS
Acquintanacsuak
Conoy or Piscataway
Mattapanient
Moyawance
Nacotchtank
Pamacocack
Patuxent
Potapaco
Secowocomoco

COOKKOO-OOSE

Little is known about the Cookkoo-oose except that they possibly lived about Coos Bay in western Oregon.

COOPSPELLAR

The Coopspellar, as reported by Drake, lived on an unnamed river falling into the Columbia, north of Clark's River. With no other information available it is difficult to ascertain the tribe's probable location at the time.

The Clark Fork River, Clark's River in some accounts and previously the Flathead River, is formed in Montana by the Flathead River from the north and the Bitterroot River from the south. It drains an extensive region of the mountains of western Montana and northern Idaho as it flows northwest through a long mountain valley emptying into Lake Pend Oreille (ear pendant in French) in the far northern handle of Idaho. From the western outlet of the lake into Washington State and north to its mouth on the Columbia, the river is called the Pend Oreille River. It is the main northern tributary of the Columbia River. The Pend Oreille River joins the Columbia above the 49th parallel just over the U.S.-Canadian border in British Columbia in northeast Washington.

The river that Lewis had previously called Clark's River with it's three principal sources in mountains Hood, Jefferson and the Northern side of the Southwest Mountains he renamed the Towannahiooks River (as called by the Eneshur).

(What the explorer's called Lewis's River, we know as the Snake or Kimooenem River. It is the main southern tributary of the Columbia with its mouth in Washington.)

COOS

The Coos or Kusa spoke the Hanis dialect of the Kusan linguistic family, to which they gave their name. They inhabited the central and south central Oregon coast in an area that included the Coos Bay and Umpqua and Siuslaw estuaries. Traditionally they lived in plank-slab houses; gathered berries, roots and nuts; and harvested salmon and other fish and shellfish. They used cedar trees and deer and elk skins were for everything from clothing to dug-out canoes. Baskets were woven using a variety of materials, including conifers and grasses—nearly everything had a spirit. (The Smithsonian Institution Museum of Indian artifacts is learning to treat items with that concept in mind.)

The 1855 treaty that confederated the Coos, Lower Umpqua and Siuslaw was never ratified. In 1856, the Coos, Umpqua and Siuslaw were rounded up and put in Fort Umpqua on the Umpqua River. In 1860, they were moved to the Alsea subagency at Yachats. When the agency was turned over to white settlement in 1876, the tribes were reassigned to the Siletz Reservation. Many declined to move.

The present federally recognized Confederated Tribes of Coos, Lower Umpqua and Siuslaw Indians live on less than ten acres. (Federal recognition of the Confederated Tribes was terminated in 1956 and restored in 1984.)

COOSA

The Coosa or Kusso or Kussah was of the Muskhogean linguistic family, one of the two principal subdivisions of the Cusabo, and one of the four foundation members of the Creek Confederacy. They were first encountered by De Soto in 1540. The Coosa inhabited the valleys of the Coosawhatchie, Ashley, Edisto, Ashepoo, Combahee, and Salkehatchie rivers inland from the South Carolina coast. They were effectively destroyed by English colonists in 1671. Those that survived were enslaved. For more see the Cusabo and Creek Confederacy.

COPALIS

The Copalis belonged to the coastal division of the Salishan linguistic family. They lived along the Copalis River and the Pacific Coast of Washington between Joe Creek and Grays Harbor where Lewis and Clark encountered them. They were closely affiliated with the Lower Chehalis whose dialect they spoke.

CORCHAUG MONTAUK

The Corchaug or Cochaug was a division of the Montauk and a member of the Algonquian linguistic group. They lived on Long Island, New York, in Riverhead and Southold townships. For more see Montauk Peoples and Delaware.

COREE

One opinion is that the Coree were affiliated with the Algonquin; another that they belonged to the Iroquois group. They inhabited the peninsula south of the Neuse River in present Carteret and Craven counties in North Carolina. They were greatly reduced by intertribal war in 1699, but they sided with the Tuscarora in the war with the colonists. The remnants were placed on a reservation on Mattamuskeet Lake in present Hyde County with the remnants of the Machapunga although a few remained with the Tuscarora.

COSTANOAN

The Costanoan, from the Spanish for "coast people," formed a separate division of the Penutian linguistic stock. They ranged the coast of California from San Francisco Bay to Point Sur and inland possibly to the Mount Diable Range. Over two centuries, the Costanoan population was effectively wiped out—from and estimated 7,000 in 1770 to none in the 1930 census.

COW CREEK UMPQUA

The Cow Creek Indians were a subdivision or band of the Umpqua that inhabited southwestern Oregon. They are often treated separately. Swanton refers to them as the Umpqua on Cow Creek. Cow Creek Umpqua were one of the first Oregon tribes to negotiate and sign a treaty with the government on September 19, 1853. Over 800 members of the tribe were placed on the Grand Ronde Reservation. They later challenged the value of the lands that they were forced to cede in 1853.

(The Grand Ronde Reservation was established by treaty arrangements in 1854 and 1855 and an Executive Order of June 30, 1857. The reservation of over 60,000 acres was located on the eastern side of the coastal range on the head-waters of the South Yamhill River, about 60 miles southwest of Portland and about 25 miles from the ocean. In 1901 a 25,791 acre tract of the reserve was declared surplus and sold by the government for $1.16 per acre. The Grand Ronde became home to a number of tribes of western Oregon and northern California, including the Rogue River, Umpqua, Chasta, Kalapuya, Molalla, Salmon River, and Tillamook.

COWETA

The Coweta was a major sub-tribe or division of the Muskogee and a member of the Creek Confederacy. They first appeared on the upper Ocmulgee and later on the west bank of the Chattahoochee River in Russell County, Alabama, near the Falls, after driving the Chickasaw from the land. They also inhabited a number of settlements in the region. Roger's *History of Chattahoochee County* states that the Coweta and Cusseta settled on either side of the river; that Cassette was the more populated site; but that "Coweta was always the head town of the Nation." A small band of Coweta under Secoffee may have been one of the first of the Creeks to remove to Florida.

COWLITZ

The Cowlitz were of the coastal divisions of the Salishan linguistic family. They inhabited the lower and middle course of the Cowlitz River in Washington Territory that empties into the Columbia at Kelso near Longview.

COYOTERO

The Coyotero Apache was a geographic division that was comprised of the White Mountain Apache and Pinal Apache. For more see Apache.

CREE

The Cree or Montagnais were of Algonquin (Algonquian) linguistic stock, originally part of the same group from which the Chippewa nation emerged. The name originated from a group of natives that lived near James Bay. The name was first recorded by the French as Kristenau (Christenaux) but later contracted to *Cri* in French and Cree in English. Although the home of the Cree was in Canada, they conducted raids against the Dakota, Blackfeet and other tribes in the U.S. In the early twentieth century, a small number settled in Montana and in other northern-tier states, including a few as far south as Kansas.

When and why the Cree and Chippewa separated is lost to history, but the separation likely dates to very early times. In the seventeenth century, the numerous bands raged in the forests along the Athabaska, Slave, Rainy and Great Bear Lakes between Lake Superior and Hudson Bay without ever reaching the latter. The Hudson Bay company armed them with guns sometime prior to 1690. They in turn armed the Assiniboins with whom they formed alliance. (The Chippewa at the time were spread out towards Lake Superior, Lake of the Woods, and as far south as Lake Michigan and Prairie du Chien.)

The Cree and their new ally moved out from the forests and onto the plains to the west and still farther west and southward ahead of Sioux and their enemies, the Blackfeet until they finally settled in the valley of the Upper Missouri and the upper Saskatchewan around 1800. The Cri inhabit areas from Alberta to Québec making it the largest geographic distribution of any native group in Canada. Those to the west and south—to the north and south of the Assiniboin River and west of the Red River—were referred to as the Plains Cree, further categorized as the River Cree and the Lowland Cree. Their ally, the Assiniboin, moved still further south along the Missouri and Yellowstonerivers along the border between Canada and present-day Montana and North Dakota. The Cree that lived north of the Saskatchewan and east of the Red River of the North were referred to as the Woodland Cree. (The Red River empties into the Assiniboin south of Lake Winnipeg.)

CREEK CONFEDERACY

The Creek Confederacy as we have come to define it came under the general heading of Mobilian tribes. Their territory was second only to that of Algonquins in size. It stretched some six hundred miles along the Gulf of Mexico from the Atlantic to the Mississippi River and up the Mississippi to the mouth of the Ohio, and along the Atlantic coast to the Cape Fear. The territory comprised a greater portion of the present-day state of Georgia, part of South Carolina, all of Florida, Alabama, Mississippi, and portions of Tennessee and Kentucky. Within the Mobilian classification, there were three grand confederacies, the Muskogee or Creek, the Choctaw, and the Chickasaw.

The organization of associated tribes that came to be known as the Creek Confederacy was assembled about the dominant Muskogee tribe and its sub-tribes and divisions.

CREEK CONFEDERATED TRIBES

Abihka	Kan-hatki	Pawokti
Alabama	Kasihta	Pithlako
Apalachicola	Kawita	Sawokli
Atasi	Kealedji	Tali
Chiaha	Koasati	Tawasa
Coosa	Kolomi	Tukaabahchee
Coweta	Muklasa	Tuskegee
Eufaula	Muskogee (Creek)	Wakokai
Fus-hatchee	Okehai	Wiwohka
Hilibi	Okmulgee	Yamasee
Hitchiti	Osochi	Yuchi
Holiwahali	Pakana	

CREEK WAR

The War of 1812 between the British and the United States was declared June 18, 1812. The Cherokee sided with the United States as did the majority of the Creek. One large band of a thousand warriors called the Red Sticks under William Weatherford (mostly white, but wholly committed to the Indian cause and hostile to the whites) supported the British. The division of support for the parties of the War of 1812 erupted into a civil war among the Creeks themselves. The Creek War or the Red Stick War as it called broke out in 1813, but it could justifiably be considered a subpart or an extension of the War of 1812.

The first clash of note between the Red Sticks and the Americans was the Battle of Burnt Corn in southern Alabama about eighty miles north of Pensacola, Florida, on July 27, 1813. Soldiers from Fort Mims surprised and scattered a group of Red Stick who were returning with guns and ammunition that they had received from the Spanish governor at Pensacola, allies of the British. While the soldiers were distracted looting the Red Stick camp, the Red Sticks launched their own surprise counter attack and scattered the Americans.

On August 30, 1813, the Red Sticks attacked a community of white settlers numbering over five hundred at Fort Mims at Lake Tensaw, Alabama, north of Mobile. Fort Mims was more a civilian enclave where settlers had assembled for their mutual protection rather than a military fort in the normal sense of the word. The result was a slaughter of several hundred settlers, mostly women and children, that put the Southeast into a justifiable panic (see more below). In response, Jackson, who held the rank of Major General of the Tennessee state militia, assembled a militia force from West Tennessee of some 2,500 infantry and calvary and established a forward post at Fort Strother along the Coosa River in the eastern part of Mississippi Territory that would become the state of Alabama. The original plan was for Jackson to meet up with a similar force from East Tennessee under Major General William Cocke that did not arrive until December 12.

Three significant battles were fought in November 1813. Jackson order General John Coffee to take one thousand dragoons and attack the Creek village at Tallasahatchee in Alabama. (See below) Six days later on November 9, in response to a request for assistance from friendly Creeks, Jackson attacked and destroyed the village of Talladega to the south of Tallasachatchee. Reports of hostile Creeks killed vary from three hundred to over four hundred against compared to 15-17 lives of Tennesseeans and about eighty-plus wounded.

On November 29, General John Floyd leading a force of about one thousand Georgia militia and several hundred friendly Creeks crossed the Chattahoochee and attacked the village of Auttose south of Talladega, about in the center of the state. An estimated two hundred hostile Creeks were killed. Floyd's losses were eleven killed and fifty-four wounded, plus Floyd himself. After the first of the year, Floyd marched out of Fort Mitchell with a somewhat larger force of Georgia militia and friendly Creeks and set up camp at Calibee Creek, just southwest of Auttose. On January 29, the Red Sticks attacked his camp, but the attackers were successfully driven off after considerable hard fighting. Casualty figures were about twenty militia and friendly Indians killed and about 150 wounded against an estimated forty Red Sticks killed. No estimate was made of the number of wounded.

The end of the Creek War came in the early spring of 1814 as Jackson launched what he called his final offensive against the Red Sticks. Weatherford had established a fortified camp on the Horseshoe Bend of the Tallapoosa River north of its junction with the Coosa, with water on three sides. Jackson launched an attack with Tennessee militia consisting of both infantry and calvary, and aided by friendly Creeks and 150-200 Cherokees, on March 27, 1814, that broke the Red Stick defensive perimeter. The battle continued into the next day. In the end the Red Sticks were totally destroyed. Five hundred and fifty-seven Indian bodies were counted at the site of the battle itself, and it was estimated that some 250-300 more bodies lay in the river. Raids on nearby Red Stick villages found them deserted. The few survivors faded into the Spanish Floridas and the ranks of the Creek Nation.

Weatherford was not at the camp the day of the attack but surrendered to Jackson shortly thereafter. As Tippecanoe put an end to all Indian hopes in the Old Northwest, Tallapoosa put an end to the Creek War and all Indian hopes in the Old Southwest.

Following his victory at the Battle of Talapoosa, Jackson was commissioned a Major General of the regular army and given the command of the Southwest District that included Tennessee, Louisiana, and Mississippi territory. In his first official act in his new position, he dictated the terms of the Treaty at Fort Jackson on August 9, 1814, that officially ended the Creek War. In the process he treated friendly and hostile Creeks all alike, thereby causing considerable bitterness and resentment. With no foreseeable alternative, most tribal leaders signed the treaty. The Creek Nation ceded 23 million acres—half of Alabama and part of southern Georgia to the government, including 1.9 million acres claimed by the Cherokee, who had also allied themselves with the Americans.

(A few Creek headed south hoping to receive supplies from British ships in the Gulf. Jackson set up his headquarters at Mobile, Alabama. His plan was ostensibly to pursue the hostile Creeks into Spanish Florida. His real objective was the removal of the Spanish from Florida.)

FORT MIMS MASSACRE

Chief Tecumseh's efforts to draw allies inspired a minority faction of the Creeks called the Red Sticks led by Chief William Weatherford in what began as a intra-tribal rift that eventually led to the Creek War with the Americans. The early conflict between the Creek factions drove the settlers in the outlying areas to seek safety. They gravitated to the outpost of Samuel Mims, called Fort Mims. Governor Claiborne of Orleans Territory ordered 170 militia to provide protection for the area about Fort Mims. About 120 were sent at Fort Mims itself.

Some one thousand Red Sticks attacked the fort the morning of August 30, 1813. They killed every white person they could find as well as their black slaves and Indians believed to be friends of the whites in a fit of utter, uncontrolled mayhem that Weatherford himself was unable to control. Reportedly there was a total of 553 people in the compound. The number of deaths was somewhere between 247 and 400, including settlers and militia, although one account states that only thirteen survived. Many of those killed were women and children who were reportedly butchered and mutilated without restraint. A few slaves were also killed, but reports suggest that that between 100 and 175 slaves were taken captive, and possibly a few women and children. It has been suggested that upwards of 200 Red Stick Creeks may have been killed in the fighting, although some accounts put the number between 300 and 400. A new period of uncontrolled violence began. President Madison activated the Tennessee militia with Andrew Jackson in command. The war came down to three key battles: Talluschatchee, Talladega, and Tallapoosa.

TALLUSHATCHEE

Maj. General Andrew Jackson ordered a Tennessee calvary brigade under the command of General John Coffee, for with David Crocket served as scout, to destroy the Red Stick Creek town of Tallushatchee, about fifteen miles from Fort Strother. Dividing his force into two columns, Coffee surrounded the village and drew the Indians out into the open before launching his attack on November 3, 1813. Reportedly, at one point, a woman pretended to be surrendering and shot an arrow that killed one of the militia. In retribution, the soldiers shot and killed the group of women she was with. A building where some forty-six warriors had barricaded themselves was burned to the ground killing everyone inside. It was all over in less than an hour. Reports of the number of Red Sticks killed vary from 176 to 200, including some women; the number of prisoners taken from eighty to one hundred, mostly women and children. The boast "shot like dogs," attributed to Crocket, was used to describe the carnage. This day Andrew Jackson took an Indian child named Lyncoya, who was left an orphan by the battle, home to the Hermitage and his wife Rachel as his own. American losses have been put at five killed and about forty wounded.

CROATAN

The Raleigh colonists reportedly took refuge with the Croatan Indians of North Carolina. They may be the same as the Indians that came to be known as the Hatteras of Hatteras Island of North Carolina. Swanton writes that the name has been erroneously applied to the Indians of Rebeson County (see below). It is thought that the Waccamaw of South Carolina united with the Croatan and that the Croatan later joined the Mattamuskeet (Machapunga) at Lake Mattamuskeet in Hyde County.

The words "Cro" and "Crotan" were carved on trees and fence posts at the Roanoke Colony site. Smith writes that Croatan was the Indian name for "Hatteras." In 1914 the Secretary of the Interior stated that the Indians of Robeson and the adjoining counties of North Carolina that were recently declared by the Legislature of North Carolina to be Cherokees were formerly known as Croatans.

Of Note

The USS *Croatan* (CVE-25; previously AVG-25 then ACV-25) was a Bogue class escort aircraft carrier launched August 1, 1942, by Seattle-Tacoma Shipbuilding Company.

CROW

The Crow or Absaroka (Absároke), a roving/hunting society, inhabited northwestern Wyoming and south central Montana centering principally on the three southern tributaries of the Yellowstone River—the Powder, the Wind, and the Big Horn. They were also known as the Bird People. The Crow belonged to the Siouan linguistic stock and at one time they were part of the Hidatsa on the Missouri River where they maintained a relatively sedentary existence. It is believed that sometime around the mid-to-late 1700s, a large group of Hidatsa migrated west from the Missouri to the Rocky Mountains where they became known as the Absároke and took up a more nomadic life. (Nester puts the date in the late 1500s.) The Absaroka Mountains formed the western boundary of their territory and the Yellowstone River and the North Platte River the northern and southern boundaries, respectively. An imaginary north-south line from the Missouri River to the Powder River marked the eastern limits. Jean Baptiste Trudeau, a fur trader, first mentioned them by name in his journal of 1795.

It was the French that translated Absároke as "Crow" or "sarrowhawk" or "bird-people." Variations appear in modern place names: Absaraka, Absaroka, and Absarokee. The Crow openly practiced abortion and infanticide until around the mid-1800s when such acts were deemed unacceptable and brought disgrace on both the father and the mother. Those early practices plus the ravages of wars and disease, especially the smallpox epidemics in the Northern Plains and an outbreak of influenza in 1849, kept growth of the Crow population in check and by the 1860s had reduced it by half from a high of some sixty-five hundred. From the early 1800s the Crow had split into two and later three branches as a result of rivalry between chiefs. By the mid-to-late 1800s, the three branches had evolved into two separate divisions, the River Crow along the Upper Missouri and the Mountain Crow. Slowly over time the two division drew back together.

Their Sioux neighbors to the east began to chip away at the Crow's traditional homelands in the mid-1860s; then with the Treaty of 1868 the Crow were removed to a reservation composed of lands lying between the Yellowstone River and the southern boundary of the present state of Montana east of Billings to the 107th degree of longitude, generally on a line with the present town of Busby, Montana. With the discovery of gold and the introduction of cattle on a commercial scale in Montana in the 1860s, the *Montana Post* in a January 26, 1867, issue called for abandonment of the reservation system and adoption of an Indian policy that would "wipe them out." In 1870, the Sioux were back and forced the Crow to abandon their reservation lands east of the Big Horn River. The decade of the seventies also saw a large swath of Crow reservation land was taken by the Northern Pacific Railroad in clear violation of the 1868 treaty. The main line of Yellowstone division of the Northern Pacific, encompassing 546 route miles, ran from Mandan, North Dakota, to Billings, Montana, and from Billings to Livingston, Montana. The ground on which the 1876 Battle of the Little Bighorn took place falls on Crow reservation land, land that the Sioux still consider theirs. It was not until the summer of 1877 that the Crow felt free to ride across their own lands without fear of attack by the Sioux.

Of Note

What has come to be known as the Crow Creek Massacre is believed to have occurred about 1325. The attack by unknown parties left some five hundred men, women, and children dead at a Crow Creek village site on the Missouri River in Buffalo County in central South Dakota. It is believed that the Village Farmer People as they were called had recently moved west from the central plains and were probably attacked by people indigenous to the area, who are generally referred to as the Middle Missouri Tradition People.

CUCAMOG-NA

Cucamog-na was a sub-tribe of the Tongva of California that inhabited the area about Cucamonga Farm. Also spelled Cucamonga. For more see Tongva.

CUPEÑO

The Cupeño belonged to the Luiseño-Cahuilla branch of the Shoshonean division of the Uto-Aztecan linguistic family. They inhabited the mountain area on the headwaters of San Luis Ray River in California. Antonio Garrá, chief of the Cupeño, attempted to form a union of tribes in 1851 to drive the white settlers out of California but was betrayed by the Cahuilla. For the Pauma Massacre and the Garra Revolt, see the Luiseño.

CUSABO

The Cusabo inhabited the southernmost part of South Carolina between Charleston Harbor and the Savannah River and the valleys of the Ashley, Edisto, Ashepoo, Combahee, Salkehatchie, and Coosawhatchi rivers. They belonged to the Muskhogean linguistic family. They are generally divided into two major divisions, the Cusabo proper, of which there was a northern group and a southern group, and the Coosa, those that lived inland in the valleys of the rivers mentioned. A band from the southern Cusabo group joined the colonists against the Tuscarora in 1711-1712 and the Island of Palawana was granted to them. Later, others joined in the governor's expedition against Spanish at St. Augustine.

SUBDIVISIONS OF THE CUSABO PROPER
(North)
Etiwaw
Wando
Kiawa (not to be confused with the Kiowa)
Stono
(South)
Edisto
Ashepoo
Combahee

Wimbee
Excamacu
(Others)
Bohicket
Cusso
Escamacu
Wappoo

CUSSO

The Cusso was a subdivision or sub-tribe of the Cusabo of South Carolina. For more see the Cusabo.

CUTTATAWOMEN

Cuttatawomen was a member of the Powhatan Confederacy and inhabited parts of King George County, Virginia.

CUYAMA CHUMASH

The Cuyama were one of the eight dialectic and geographical divisions of the Chumash of the Southern California coast. The Cuyama Chumash lived in the Cuyama River Valley and the valley of the upper Santa Maria River. For more see the Chumash.

CWAREUUOOC

Nothing is known of the tribe or village named Cwareuuooc other than the reference in Willard. Presumably of North Carolina or Virginia, the name contains the suffix "ooc" referring to shellfish and a large body of water. There may have been an association between the Cwareuuooc and the Lost Colony and also with an Indian site named Pekernickeack, possibly in Carteret County near present Sea Level, North Carolina.

DAKOTA

The Dakota (sometimes spelled Dacota) or Isanyati (Dwellers at the Knife Lake in Minnesota), also called the Santee, composed the Eastern Division of the Sioux Nation or People (Oyate). Later, the Dakota name came to represent all the tribes of the Sioux nation and is the name preferred by the native peoples themselves vs. the name Sioux given to them by the white man. The Dakota Oyate consisted of four subgroups. For more see Sioux.

SUBGROUPS
Wahepkute (Shooters among the Leaves)
Sisiton or Sisseton* (People of the Fish Ground)
Wahpeton* (Dwellers among the Leaves)
Mdewahaton* (Spirit Lake People)

---

*Often found spelled with the "wan" suffix.

SPIRIT LAKE MASSACRE

Members of the Wahpekute band of the Santee, led by Inkpaduta, attacked and murdered a number of white settlers in Dickinson County in northwestern Iowa on March 8-9, 1857. It was one of the bloodiest events in the early history of the state and gave Inkpaduta the reputation as the most brutal of the Sioux leaders.

There was no one cause for the massacre save years of pent-up frustration and humiliation. Contributing was the brutal murder in 1852 of Inkpaduta's brother Sintomnaduta and his family of nine women and children. Protestations by Inkpaduta to the U.S. Army produced nothing but increased bitterness towards whites. Reservation life and failed government promises only made matter worse. Five years later following the harsh winter of 1856-1857 that led to widespread starvation among the Santee, Inkpaduta left the Minnesota reservation and headed south into Iowa. Relatively minor depredations committed by both whites and Indians alike and the fact that Spirit Lake was sacred to the Santee as a dwelling place for the gods led to the events in northwestern Iowa in the spring of 1857.

It is generally believed that a total of twenty settlers were killed the first day of the massacre with one female taken captive. Four families were destroyed the next day and two more women were taken captive. A few days later another white man was murdered and his wife taken captive. In all 33-38 men, women and children were murdered in the raids. Reports also differ on the number of warriors in Inkpaduta's party and the number that might have been wounded and killed. Of the four women captives, two were killed by the raiders, and two were subsequently sold into freedom. Inkpaduta headed west after the Minnesota Uprising of 1862 and joined his Lakota brethren. He was present at the Battle of the Little Big Horn and later accompanied Sitting Bull north into Canada.

MINNESOTA SIOUX UPRISING

The Santee Sioux in Minnesota, many starving and desperate, rebelled against all whites in August 1862 in what has been called the Minnesota Sioux Uprising or the Minnesota Massacre. Government annuity payments were late in arriving, and the Indians were no longer paid in gold. To make matters worse, traders refused them credit. The rebellion began on August 17, 1862, with the killing of four whites near Litshfield. The next day, forty-four whites were killed at the Redwood Agency, sixteen more the following day at New Ulm. In all more than 450-500 whites were killed over the next several months. Many were taken captive, some tortured and mutilated. In addition, many whites were left homeless. Some missionaries and teachers and their families escaped the rampage after having been warned by friendly Indians. Some whites, known to be friendly to the Indians, survived unharmed.

The army under the command of Colonel Henry Sibley took over twelve hundred Dakota men, women and children into custody. Another eight hundred surrendered, and about sixty died resisting. Thousands of the Indians fled into the Dakotas where they joined the Lakota. Three hundred and twenty-three were convicted of murder and sentenced to be hanged. All but thirty-eight had their sentences commuted by President Lincoln at the urgings of Episcopal Bishop Henry Whipple. The executions were conducted December 26, 1862.

DAKUBETEDE

The Dakubetede belonged to the Athapascan linguistic stock in a group with the Taltushtuntude. They lived along the Applegate River in Oregon and beyond the northern California border. They are also known by the names Applegate River and Applegate Creek Indians.

DASEMUNKEPEUC

The Dasemunkepeuc is believed to be of the Algonquian linguistic group and has been described as a sub-tribe of the Secotan, but available information on its status is limited. It is known that on June 1, 1585, Roanoke colonists under the leadership of Ralph Lane attacked the Dasemunkepeuc Indian village. Map studies have suggested that the village was near Mann's Harbor, North Carolina and has probably washed into the Croatan Sound. For more see Secotan.

DEADOSE

The Deadose was a part of the Atakapa of Louisiana and Texas. They lived on the lower Trinity River above the Bidai. The Franciscan mission of San Ildefonso west of the Trinity River in Texas was founded for the Deadose, the Bidai, the Patiri, and the Akokisa.

DELAWARE

The Delaware or Lenape (Lenapé or Lenni Lenape) was belonged to the Algonquian linguistic stock. They inhabited all of New Jersey, the western end of Long Island, Manhattan and Staten islands, lands west of the Hudson River, eastern Pennsylvania, and northern Delaware. Those that lived along the Delaware River were given the name Delaware for the governor of Jamestown colony, Lord de la Warr. Soon the name was applied to all the Lenape. Kraft (1986) identified two main dialects, Proto-Munsee in the upper Delaware River (including North Jersey) and Proto-Unami in the lower Delaware River (including South Jersey). The Encyclopedia of North American Indians assigns a separate dialect to each of the three major subdivisions. (See divisions below)

The Delaware had early contact with Dutch, English, and Swedish explorers and settlers. It was people of the Munsee and Unami divisions of the Delaware who encountered Henry Hudson in his epic-making voyage of 1609 for the Dutch West Indies Company in search of the Northwest Passage. (It was almost a century after Giovanni de Verranzano sailed along the Jersey coast and anchored off Sandy Hook in 1524. In 1525 Portuguese explorer Esteban Gomez sailed up the Hudson, the river that he named Deer River, and seized fifty-seven Indians to sell on the slave market in Lisbon. These Indians may very well have been Delaware.)

After venturing into Delaware Bay and up the Delaware River (that the Dutch would call the South River), Hudson realized that it could not be the entrance to the passage that would take him to the other side of the world. On putting ashore, it was then that he and his men encountered the Delaware. After his friendly and cordial meeting with the Delaware, Hudson returned to the mouth of the bay and sailed up the coast to what came to be called the Hudson River and Manhattan Island. By this time the Delaware had become excellent farmers. The principal crops were beans, squash, and maize (corn).

The Delaware were also known as the Loup "wolf" by the French. They were also mistakenly called the Wabanaki for "Easterners" in relation to other Algonquian tribes. The name Wabanaki was, in turn, corrupted into Openaki, Openaji, Abnaki, Wapanachki, Waupenocky, Wappinger, Abenaquis, Apenakis, and Abenakis—all names that would be used for related but separate tribes in the Northeast that has resulted in much confusion even to this date.

Traditionally, the Delaware, by far the largest of the Algonquian-speaking tribes, was comprised of three major divisions based on differences in dialect and location: Munsee or Minsi (wolf) in northern New Jersey and adjacent portions of New York; Unalachtigo (turkey) in northern Delaware, southeastern Pennsylvania, and southern New Jersey; and the Unami (turtle) in the central region between the two. The French, however, called the Indians of all three clans or divisions "wolves" (Fr. Loup).

The three divisions were comprised of a number of subgroups. In addition, Swanton lists over one hundred villages from the Handbook of American Indians (Hodge, 1907, 1910) that he states would be impractical to attempt to separate into one of the three divisions. In time, the Munsee (Christian) were treated as separate and distinct from the Delaware.

Burrows & Wallace described the Delaware as comprised of a number of groups of Indians living between eastern Connecticut and central New Jersey, to include the Raritan, Hackensack, Tappan, Rechgawawanche, Wiechquaesgeck, Siwanoy, Matinecock, Massapequa, Rockaway, Merrick in addition to "other tribes of Long Island." These would include the Canarsee and the remaining divisions of the Montauk: the Montauk proper, Nissequoge, Secatoag, Seatauket, Patchoag, Corchaug, Shinnecock, and Manhasset. Burrows & Wallace wrote that the majority spoke the Munsee dialect. Swanton places the Raritan, Hackensack, Tappan, and the Rechgawawanche in the Unami division. He places the Siwanoy with the Wappinger vs. the Delaware; treats the Montauk separately; and refers to the Wecquaesgeek (Wecksquaesgek) as a division of the Wappinger. In all likelihood Swanton's Wecquaesgeek are the same as the Wiechquaesgeck of Burrows & Wallace.

ARRIVAL OF EUROPEANS

The first Dutch settlers of the West Indian Company arrived in 1624 and established a post on the east bank of the Delaware (South) River and the Hudson (North) River. In May or June 1626, Director Peter Minuit began a program of purchasing the lands of the Lenape. Records indicate that he bought Staten Island on August 10, 1626 for some iron kettles, cloth, axes, drilling awls, and other miscellaneous trade goods. Seven years later in 1633 the Delaware were hit with their first smallpox epidemic that lasted into 1635. Settlers from Sweden arrived in Delaware Bay in 1638 and contested the Dutch for the land until the Dutch drove them out in 1655.

The original colony of New Jersey that had been established by the Swedish in 1638, fell to the Dutch, then to the British who sold it to the Quakers who, in turn, divided the land into East Jersey and West Jersey. When the Quakers surrendered the land to the English Crown in 1702, the two parts were rejoined. The Proprietors of what was then organized as West Jersey first purchased lands from the Delaware in 1676.

On March 4, 1681 William Penn obtained the charter for Pennsylvania and the following year obtained the rights to Delaware. The legendary or mystical chief of the Delaware, Tamamend, is reported to have met William Penn on his arrival in America in the fall of 1862—in addition to the carving out Niagara Falls. (The Society of St. Tammany, variously translated as "affable" or "deserving," was founded in his honor in New York City in 1789, and in tome Tammany societies arose throughout the Eastern seaboard.)

Shortly after his arrival Penn negotiated the first of many treaties with the Delaware at the village of Shackamaxon. Penn returned to England in 1684 and did not return to Pennsylvania until 1699. He purchased a large piece of land on the Susquehanna River in 1701 when the Susquehannock Indians moved back to their old homes at Conestoga. He returned to England permanently shortly thereafter. The Delaware also came out on the short end (literally and figuratively) of the 1737 treaty that gave Pennsylvania "the land between the junction of the Delaware and Lehigh Rivers as far west as a man could walk in a day and a half " that was variously estimated at some forty miles. Pennsylvania hired the fastest man they could find, and as a result the Lenape lost most of the Lehigh Valley, about 80 miles.

CONFLICT AND TREATIES

Conflict between the Lenape and the settlers became more and more common in the late 1630s and early 1640s until an all-out war broke out that did not end until the summer of 1645 with the deaths of some sixteen hundred Indians and scores of colonists. Renewed fighting broke out in 1655. In 1656 a Massapequa sachem (chief) named Tackapousaha signed a treaty with Governor Peter Stuyvesant on behalf of a number of Lenape groups, including the Canarsee (Unami) and Rockaway, vowing peace.

Stuyvesant purchased more and more Delaware land until by the mid-1660s European colonists owned virtually all of present Kings and Queens counties.

The first treaty between the colonists and the Delaware was concluded September 17, 1778. The language and provisions of the treaty were formed on the model of those treaties that had been executed between the crowned heads of Europe. The treaty, thus, treated the Delaware as a sovereign nation. Among its provisions, the treaty guaranteed the Delaware their territorial rights. The first official encroachment on those lands came with the Treaty at Fort M'Intosh in 1785. In exchange for their lands, the Wyandot and Delaware were granted exclusive rights to lands along the Miami or Ome River and the south shore of Lake Erie to the mouth of the Cayahoga.

GNADENHÜTTEN MASSACRE

Killings, even to the level of massacres, and mutilation perpetrated by both Indians and whites became all too common events in the Ohio Country in the last half of the 18th century, but the gruesome, sickening events at Gnadenhütten (Huts of Grace) crossed all bounds of humanity. On March 8 and 9, 1782, some sixty men of the Pittsburgh militia of Washington County, some former Paxton Boys, under the command of David Williamson methodically bludgeoned twenty-eight men, twenty-nine women, and thirty-nine children to death in what became known as the Gnadenhütten Massacre. (Other accounts put the numbers at forty-two men, twenty women and thirty-four children.)

The victims were all innocent Christian Indians, mostly Delawares, of the Moravian Mission at Gnadenhütten in present-day Tuscarawas County, Ohio, founded by David Zeisberger. The previous August a party of Wyandot warriors and a British agent forced the neutral Moravians of Gnadenhütten and nearby Salem to move to the pro-British Indian settlement on the Sandusky River for their own protection. In the spring the Moravians returned to their deserted towns to gather up their weather-beaten corn that stood in the fields along the Muskingum River. The Pennsylvanians, with promises of protection, convinced them to give up all their weapons and gathered them all into a building in Gnadenhütten. The next morning the militiamen marched the Indians in pairs into two houses and systematically slaughtered each one. One of the former Paxton Boys bragged of the murder of fourteen with a cooper's mallet before turning the weapon over to another because his arms grew weary.

Their crimes, as if that would have justified their slaughter, were raids into Pennsylvania that had resulted in several deaths and kidnappings. And, if they themselves were not guilty, surely they must have collaborated with the guilty parties; and if they did not collaborate in these instances, then surely at some time they must have blundered white settlements, else where would they have gotten pots and pans and axes and other whiteman's goods. (The raids were very likely perpetrated by a band of Wyandots.) The perpetrators expressed no remorse, and no remorse appeared in the published account in the April 17 edition of the *Pennsylvania Gazette*. There was none of the condemnation of Conestoga Massacre of nineteen years earlier. Benjamin Franklin was in France.

DRIVEN FROM THEIR HOMES

In the first hundred years, the white man's diseases—smallpox, typhus, measles, and diphtheria—decimated the Lenape reducing the population to ten percent of what it had been before the Europeans arrived. Conflict did the rest, exacerbated by guns and alcohol. With the combined pressure of the Europeans from the coast and the members of the Iroquois League to the north, the Lenape were soon driven from their homelands. According to Labadist missionary Jasar Danckaerts, the few Lenapes that were left soon simply disappeared. These were most likely the Unami. Legend has it that the last Lenape died in Canarsie in 1803.

The Lenape were soon forced to give up their lands in the rich Ohio River country of Ohio and Indiana for lands in Missouri, Arkansas, and Kansas before finally being settled in Indian Territory—Oklahoma.

In the early years of the Louisiana territory of Missouri, there were only two settlements, Ste. Genevieve and St. Louis. During the period of Spanish rule, as new settlements emerged, the Spanish grouped them into five districts (N to S): St. Charles, St. Louis, Ste. Genevieve, Cape Girardeau, and New Madrid. The first permanent white settlement in the Cape Girardeau District was Cape Girardeau, founded by Louis Lorimier 1795. He had been an Indian trader, first in Ohio and then in Vincennes, Indiana, and had been in the area as early as 1787. At the insistence of Spanish officials, Lorimier brought with him a band of Shawnees and Delawares as protection against the Osages who, according to reports, were considered less civilized than the Indians to the east of the Mississippi. The two tribes settled along Apple Creek and other small tributaries of the Mississippi. By 1812 they were located along the Whitewater River as well as the Mississippi.

In response to frequent Indian attacks in Boone's Lick country in September 1814, General Henry Dodge took a troop of volunteers and forty or fifty Shawnees and Delawares to suppress the attacks. They located the hostile Miamis in Saline County and captured 153 who were promised that their lives would be spared.

KANSAS TERRITORY

Wyandotte County, Kansas, originally land of the Kansa Indians, came to the United States in the Louisiana Purchase of 1803. In a treaty with the Kansa of June 3, 1825, the government acquired all their lands and placed the Kansa on a reservation. On October 3, 1818, the Delaware Indians on the White River in east central Indiana (near present Muncie) ceded their lands in Indiana for lands in the West "yet to be described," effective in 1825.

In the interim they joined other members of the Delaware who lived on the Whitewater River in southeast Missouri that had been awarded to the Shawnee and Delaware under a grant from the Spanish government. A supplementary article to the 1818 treaty was executed September 24, 1829, by which the lands in Missouri were given up in exchange for land at the confluence of the Missouri and Kansas (Kaw) rivers west of the Missouri state line that extended far up the Kansas. The Delaware Reserve included all of present Wyandotte County, Kansas, north of the Kansas River. (The area south of the river was part of the Shawnee Reserve that was established in 1825.) The principal Delaware settlements were in what is now western Wyandotte County and southern Leavenworth County to the north. The eastern portion of the reserve that includes the present city of Kansas City, Kansas, remained largely uninhabited.

With an agreement signed December 14, 1843, the Delaware sold the eastern portion of the reserve comprised of thirty-six sections to the Wyandot for the sum of $46,080 and gave the Wyandot another three sections in appreciation for Wyandot assistance back in Ohio. The Wyandot Purchase included all the land between the Kansas and Missouri rivers west to a line drawn from the village of Muncie north. The transaction was approved by the government July 25, 1848.

In 1830 Isaac McCoy, a Baptist missionary and surveyor, was hired by the secretary of war to survey a boundary for the Delawares who were soon to immigrate to the new Delaware Reserve west of Missouri. He took two of his sons, Rice and John Calvin, as well as two other white men as chain carriers and a black man as a cook. The following year he established a Baptist mission on reservation lands for the Delaware and Shawnee. The Baptists were joined by the Mormon missionaries on the Shawnee and Delaware reservation that same year. The Rev. Thomas Johnson had earlier established the first Shawnee Methodist Mission at the request of a group of Shawnee led by a white chief, Chief Fish. The mission served the Shawnee and Delaware continuously until 1862. The manual school that Johnson established was closed in 1854.

On May 6, 1854, Commissioner of Indian Affairs George Manypenny negotiated a treaty with the Delaware by which the Delaware Nation ceded to the United States all of the land provided in the Treaty of 1829, except eighty acres reserved for each tribal allottee, for the central route of the transcontinental railroad. Article 12 of 1854 treaty provided that the railroad companies, when their lines necessarily passed through the diminished reservation, should have a right of way on payment of a just compensation.

They were subsequently forced to surrender all their land along the central route and retreat to Indian Territory. Article 3 of the Delaware treaty of May 30, 1860, typifies the rationale presented by Commissioner Manypenny to the Central Plains Indians.

> The Delaware tribe of Indians, entertaining the belief that the value of their lands will be enhanced by having a railroad passing through their present reservation, and being of opinion that the Leavenworth, Pawnee, and Western Railroad Incorporated by an act of the legislative assembly of Kansas Territory, will have the advantage of travel and general transportation over every other company proposed to be formed, which will run through their lands, have expressed a desire that the said Leavenworth, Pawnee, and Western Railroad shall have the preference of purchasing the remainder of their lands after the tracts in severalty and those for the special objects herein named shall have been selected and set apart, upon the payment into the United States Treasury, which payment shall be made in six months after the quantity shall have been ascertained, in gold or silver coin, of such a sum as three commissioners, to be appointed by the Secretary of the Interior, shall appraise to be the value of the said land.

What the Potawatomi and Delaware got was the appraised value of $1.25 per acre for "surplus" land that had a market value of ten dollars per acre. The tribes were swindled out of exclusive rights to hundreds of thousands of acres of tribal land by the Leavenworth Railroad with the collusion of corrupted officials within the U.S. Office of Indian Affairs.

END OF THE JOURNEY

The Delaware that marched west from Indiana into Kansas, is now centered about Bartlesville, Oklahoma, with a population of some ten thousand plus under the name Delaware Tribe of Indians.

Several bands of Delaware took a different track out of Indiana. Crossing Louisiana, they settled on the fertile lands of east Texas. They soon found that they were unwelcome and at the mercy of the Anglos who had supplanted first the Spanish then the Mexicans. In the late 1830s they were driven from the land, and their crops and villages were burned. A few escaped onto the Plains, and those that attempted to flee to Mexico were caught and brought back. The Western group as it was called was finally settled in western Oklahoma about Anadarko under the name Delaware Nation. Descendants of the early Delaware can also be found throughout the forty-eight states, but primarily in Pennsylvania and New Jersey. The Indians of the Munsee division for the most part lived on three Indian reserves in Western Ontario, the largest at Moraviantown, Ontario, where the first arrivals settled in 1792. For more see Montauk, Manhattan and Susquehanna. Also see the Shawnee.

(In 1833 with an eye on the Indian annuities and the Santa Fe traders on their way from Independence, college-educated surveyor John Calvin McCoy (1811-1889) returned to Jackson County and acquired land near his father Isaac's house. He went into business with J.P. Hickman and J.H. Flourney. He became a tradesman and trading post operator, real estate investor, and town father.)

BATTLE OF BUSHY RUN

Fort Pitt had been under seige by the Indians as part of Pontiac's Rebellion, but after a time the Indians abruptly withdrew. Colonel Henry Bouquet, who was leading a relief force to Fort Pitt, was attacked enroute by Delaware, Mingoe, Shawnee, and Wyandot Indians at Bushy Run (Creek) east of present-day Pittsburgh on August 5, 1763. The following day the Indians withdrew. The number of casualties is not reported but included two prominent Delaware chiefs.

MANYPENNY TREATIES AND THE TRANSCONTINENTAL RAILROADS

George W. Manypenny became commissioner of Indian Affairs in 1853 under President Franklin Pierce. He set out immediately to negotiate new treaties that would give the Indian tribes "permanent" new lands in the West in order to clear way for the transcontinental railroad. Manypenny concerned himself with only with the two of the proposed routes, the central routes through Nebraska and Kansas. He did not visit the tribes of the Southwest nor those of the Northwest that might have been uprooted by the Southern and Northern routes. The Central Plains Indians ceded title to some eighteen million acres of 19,342,000 acres, most of which fell between the 40th and 45th parallels. Manypenny treaties were negotiated with the Omaha, Sac and Fox, Iowa, Kickapoo, Otoe, Delaware, Shawnee, Kaskaskia, Peoria, Wea, Piankeshaw, and Miami.

In 1885, Manypenny saw things quite differently:

> When I made those treaties I was confident that good results would follow. Had I not so believed I would not have been a party to the transactions. Events following the execution of those treaties proved that I committed a grave error. I had provided for the abrogation of the reservations the dissolution of the tribal relation, and for the lands in severalty and citizenship, thus making the road clear for the rapacity of the white man....Had I known then as I now know...I would be compelled to admit that I had committed a high crime.

MORAVIAN MISSIONARIES

The Moravians missionaries first came to America in 1735. The majority of their work was among the Delawares, but they also administered to the Creeks and Cherokees of Georgia (and later in Oklahoma) and the Mahicans of New York and Connecticut. The Moravians followed the Delaware from Pennsylvania to Ohio, Canada, Indiana, and then into Kansas. Moravian David Zeisberger was the first into Georgia in 1740. John Ettwein arrived in from Germany in 1754. He also traveled as far south as Georgia, preaching and establishing missions. Ettwein later became the head of the Moravian Church in the United States. Although their number of Indian converts was relatively low, they continued their work until 1900.

DIEGUEÑO

The Diegueño or more properly Kumeyaay* belonged to the Central division of the Yuman linguistic group. There were two major geographical divisions and a population of some 3,000 in 1770. The Northern Diegueño inhabited eastern San Diego County south into Baja California. The Southern Diegueño inhabited the present districts of Campo, La Posta, Manzanita, Guyapipe, and La Laguna and some territory in Baja. The name Diegueño was derived from the Spanish Mission of San Diego. For the Pauma Massacre and the Garra Revolt, see the Luiseño.

*More fully, Kumeyaay Kumiai Diegueño Ipai-Tipai Diegueno-Kamia.

DINONDADIES

The Dinondadies was one of the tribes of the Tionontati (Petuns or Tobacco Indians). Other tribes were the Tionnontates proper, the Etionnontates, and Khionnontatehronon. In several instances, the name Dinondadies is used interchangeably for the Tionantati as a whole.

The killing of several ambassadors of the Five Nations the Dinondadies in 1688 led an attack on Montreal on July 26 of that year by 1,200 warriors of the Five Nations that resulted in the deaths of a thousand French men, women, and children, and a number of prisoners who were later burned alive. The French retaliated by making incursions into the Indian country and burning the villages. Not long thereafter the Dinondadies, with the Huron, the Ottawawa, or Ottawa, were driven from Canada by the Iroquois. For more see Tionantati, Huron, and Wyandot.

DOTAME

The Dotame was a very small tribe that inhabited the upper plains. They spoke the Comanche language and have been identified with the Kiowa. They have also been referred to by some writers as a possible division of the Comanche. Lewis and Clark recorded information on the tribe that they learned from informants.

DOUSTIONI

The Doustioni or Souchitioni or Dulcinoe was of the Caddo division of the Caddoan linguistic group and one of the four principal divisions of the Natchitoches Confederacy of Louisiana. It was a small tribe that inhabited the area about present Natchitoches. For more see Natchitoches Confederacy and Caddo

DUWÁMISH

The Duwámish belonged to the Nisqually branch of the coastal division of the Salishan linguistic stock with close connections to the Suquámish. They were comprised of five subdivisions or villages in Washington State. Seattle was the chief of both tribes.

SUBDIVISIONS
Duwamish River w/ 8-10 separate villages
Black River w/ 2 villages
Green River w/6 villages or clusters of homes
White River village
Lake Washington w/ 3 villages

EASTERN MONO

The Eastern Mono was a tribe of the western division of the Northern Paiute that occupied parts of California. They belonged to Shoshonean branch of the Uto-Aztecan stock.

ECHELOOT

The Echeloot, Eloot, or Eskeloot belonged to the Upper Chinook division of the Chinookan family. They lived along the Columbia River in Oregon. The journals of the Lewis and Clark expedition contain several entries regarding the Echeloot.

EDISTO

The Edisto was a subdivision or sub-tribe of the southern group of the Cusabo proper. They lived on Edisto Island in South Carolina. For more see Cusabo and Coosa. The present-day Edisto Group of South Carolina is comprised of the Coosa (identified as Kusso) and the Natchez .

EEH-TAHTAH-OH

The Eeh-tahtah-oh (burnt meat) was one of the sub-tribes or bands of the Comanche. For more see Comanche.

EEL RIVER OF INDIANA

The Eel River Indians, who took their name from the Eel River in northern Indiana, were of the Algonquian linguistic group. They inhabited primarily northwestern Indiana during the late 1700s and the early 1800s. With the signing of the Treaty of Greenville in 1795, the Eel River Indians were absorbed into the Miami. Because of typographical/transposition errors, the name is frequently found spelled Ell. Corruption of the French produced the name Isle River; thus Isle-river Indians and Long-isle Indians. The Eel River was also called the White River. They should not be confused with the Indians that lived about the Eel River in coastal northern California.

ELK MOUNTAIN UTE

Elk Mountain Ute was a subdivision of the Ute that lived in the Elk Mountains of Colorado.

ELWHA KLALLAM

Elwah was a Clallam village at the mouth of the Elwah River of Washington generally treated separately. A Lower Elwha Klallam tribe is listed as a member of the Northwest Indian Fisheries Commission in the Tribal Natural Resource. For more see Clallam.

EMIGDIANO CHUMASH

The Emigdiano were one of the eight dialectic and geographical divisions of the Chumash of the Southern California coast. The Emigdiano Chumash were an inland group that lived beyond the coastal range at the southern of the San Joaquin Valley. Unlike their coastal relatives the Emigdiano avoided contact with European explorers and settlers and were never brought into one of the Spanish missions or incorporated into the Tejon Farm/Reservation (Sebastian Indian Reservation).

TEJON FARM

Edward F. Beale, appointed Superintendent of Indian Affairs for California in April 1852, requested funds for the establishment of an Indian reservation to help counter the neglect and depredations that had been inflicted upon the Native Americans of the California. In early 1853 he established a farming operation for Indians at Tejon and the San Joaquin River that was called Tejon Farm. In March Congress appropriated funds for five reservations, and in September, Beale expanded the Tejon Farm into the first California reservation. The reservation, commonly known as the Tejon Indian Reservation, was located in the southern end of the San Joaquin Valley. The official name was the Sebastian Indian Reservation for the Chairman of the Indian Affairs Committee, Senator William Sebastian. Beale was replaced in July 1854. Although Beale had reported that some 2,500 Indians had been gathered on the reservation, his successor noted the presence of only 800 with fewer than 350 at any one time. Fort Tejon was established to protect and control the Indians on the reservation and to protect white settlers in the area from Indian raids. The fort was garrisoned from August 10, 1854 to September 11, 1864.

In November of 1856, the reservation was reduced to 25,000 acres, and in June 1864 the reservation was ordered closed. The Indians on the Tejon Farm, about two hundred in number, were removed to the Tule River farm. One of the reasons that Tejon was closed was that it was located on a Mexican land grant rather than on public land which severely restricted investment in the property. Beale chose Tejon because of the presence of mission-trained Indians with agricultural skills were deemed more likely to succeed on a reservation. The Emigdiano, having not been brought into the Mission system, were not considered good candidates for the conversion from food gathering to settled agriculture.

EMUSA

The Emusa was a small band of the Yamasee. They lived on the on Chattahoochee River in Seminole County, Georgia, which lies in the far southwest corner of the state between Alabama and Florida. The population number only 20 people in 1821. Swanton writes of the Emusas with quotations around the name but gives no explanation.

ENESHER

The Enesher, Eneshur, Enneshuh, Eneesher or Eneshure was a tribe of the Upper Chinookan peoples of the Pacific Northwest. Their village was located at the great falls of the Columbia [Celilo Falls] in the vicinity of Wishram tribe. The Enesher called the Deschutes River of Oregon the To-wannahiooks. Lewis and Clark wrote of their experiences with the Enesher in April 1806 negotiating for the sale of horses.

Of Note

Celilo Falls in Oregon, also called Wyam, was located at the eastern end of the Columbia Gorge, 12 miles east of The Dalles and about a hundred miles from Portland. It was inundated and flooded with construction of The Dalles Dam in 1957. The small Celilo Village fishing community was called Oregon's oldest town.

ENO

It is believed by some that the Eno were of the Siouan linguistic stock. Their nearest relatives were the Shajori. They lived along the Eno River in present Orange and Durham counties in North Carolina. They had previously lived along the Enoree River in South Carolina. They were first mentioned by Governor Yeardley of Virginia. In 1701 they were living with the Shakori in the town of Adshusheer. The two tribes began a movement northward toward the settlements in Virginia about Albermarle Sound around 1714 in conjunction with the Tutelo, the Saponi, the Occanecchi, and the Keyauwee that drew resistance. The Eno moved to northern South Carolina in 1716 and in all likelihood merged with the Catawba.

ENQUISACO

The Enquisaco inhabited Texas, but little else is known about the tribe or whether it was a tribe, sub-tribe, subdivision, band or village.

ERIE

The Erie belonged to the Iroquoian linguistic family and inhabited northern Ohio, northwestern Pennsylvania, and western New York. They are also known as the Cat Nation, from the translation of their Iroquois name, "long tail." Swanton refers to the Erie several times as the Erie Nation, which is rather unusual. Apparently, at one time, there were several subdivisions. Little is known of the Erie until their almost complete destruction in a war with the Iroquois League that raged between 1653 and 1656. Remnants were most likely absorbed into the Seneca.

Of Note

Lake Erie, named for the Erie Indians, was the last of the Great Lakes to be discovered by the Europeans. The French had explored the upper lakes as early as 1615 but avoided the region to the south because of the Iroquois. In 1669, Louis Jolliet entered Lake Erie from the Detroit River and followed the north shore eastward. The final link was added to the mighty inland waterway so vital to Michigan's history.

ERIWONEC

The Eriwonec was a sub-tribe of the Unalachtigo division of the Delaware. They lived in the area about Old Man's Creek in Salem and Gloucester counties of New Jersey. For more see Unalachtigo and Delaware.

ESCAMACU

The Escamacu or St. Helena Indicns was a subdivision or sub-tribe of the Cusabo of South Carolina. For more see the Cusabo.

ESOPUS

The general consensus is that the Esopus (Espachomy) was not a single, independent tribe of the Delaware nation but rather a group of four or five distinct tribes of the Munsee division of the Delaware that occupied the same general area of New York State identified as Esopus County. A search of the literature will find the name spelled both Esopus and Esophus. The present town of Esopus is north of Poughkeepsie on the west side of the Hudson River across from Hyde Park. Esopus Creek empties into the Hudson River as it flows south about mid-way between present Albany and New York City where the channel deepens.

It is generally believed that the Esopus group was comprised of five distinct sub-tribes: Catskill, Wawarsink, Mamekoting, Waranawonkong, Minisink. Each is treated separately in this work. The reports that identify only four sub-tribes omit the Minisink. A minority opinion holds that the Esopus group was separate and distinct from the Munsee but spoke the Munsee language.

During the Dutch period, a contingent of 60-70 settlers from Fort Orange (Albany) moved south down the Hudson and established a village that they named Esopus after the Esopus Creek in the heart of the maize (corn) fields of Esopus Country. Peter Stuyvesant, the Dutch director-general or governor, recognized the strategic advantages offered by the location and built a stockade there in 1657 for the protection of the settlers. He renamed the village Wiltwyck The Dutch knew that the land belonged to the Esopus. David de Vries reported meeting the them as early as 1640 and noted their fields ripe for harvest. Inevitably, the conflict that began with the arrival of the settlers in 1652 erupted into the Esopus Indian Wars of 1658-1663. Peter Stuyvesant issued a formal declaration of war March 25, 1660. A peace treaty was signed March 16, 1664. The Hackensack and Nyack of New Jersey also signed the treaty as allies of the Dutch, agreeing to insure the good behavior of the Esopus. Shortly thereafter in September 1664, Stuyvesant was forced to surrender New Netherland to the English. (For the involvement of the Esopus the Peach War of 1655. See the Wappinger.)

The English changed the name of the village again in 1669 to Kingston. It was there that American colonists declared a new, free state of New York, and Kingston became the seat of the State legislature. Shortly thereafter in October 1777, the village and all the stores that had been collected there were destroyed by English troops.

The Esopus signed a contract in 1677 by which they agreed to sell much of their land to Huguenots; and between 1683 and 1685, Livingston was able to acquire some 100,000 acres from the Wappinger and the

Esopus for Livingston Manor. The last known Esopus lived on Rondout Creek above the city of Kingston and died in 1830.

ESPEMINKIA

The Espeminkia was one of the minor tribes of the Illinois Cluster of Tribes for which there is only passing mention. For more see Illinois Cluster.

ESQUIMAUX

The Esquimaux was a Canadian tribe that lived about Hudson's Bay, Labrador and Newfoundland. Because of the complexion of the skins and facial hair, it is believed that the Esquimmaux Indians were not native to America but originally mixed blood descendent from Europeans.

ESSELEN

The Esselen are part of the Hokan linguistic group. They lived along the upper course of the Carmel River, the Sur River, and the coast from Point Lopez to near Point Sur in California. A small tribe, it became extinct sometime prior to 1900.

ETCHEMIN

Although the two tribes maintained their individual political identities, the French called both the Passamaquoddy (Openagoes or Quoddy) and the Maliseet (or Malecite) tribes by the same French name, Etchemin, which is also spelled Echemin and Etechemin.

There is much confusion in the literature between the tribal names Malecite, Etchemin, Abnaki, Quoddy, and Tarratines (Tarrrateens). Into the mix is added the common name, Canoe men or Canoe-men.

In his text, Swanton lists Etchemin as an alternate name for the Malecite. The Index, on the other hand, gives Etechemin as "possibly" an alternate name for the Passamaquoddy in addition to referring the reader to the text on the Malecite. Swanton also notes that one writer, Maurault (1866), makes a distinction between the Etchemin and Malecite. And, although he finds no basis for that conclusion, the evidence would tend to indicate otherwise.

Another writer asserts that all that remains of the original Etechemin inhabitants of the area about Camden, Maine, and westward were two small tribes, the remnants of the Tarratines (Tarrateens) or "canoe men" at Oldtown and a few Quoddy Indians in the eastern part of the state. Swanton, on the other hand, gives the name Tarrateens as another name for the Abnaki. Conversely, the Malecite are frequently placed under the general name Abnaki. For more see Maliseet and Abnaki.

ETIWAW

The Etiwaw was a subdivision or sub-tribe of the Cusabo proper (North). They lived on the Wando River of South Carolina

ETOHUSSEWAKKE

The Etohussewakke was reportedly a band of the Seminole that lived on the Chattahoochee River, three miles above Ft. Gainer in Florida

EUFAULA

The Eufaula was a sub-tribe or division of the Muskogee and a member of the Creek Confederacy. The Eufaula of Alabama was the first to settle into Florida, some distance from Tampa on the west cost of the peninsula

EXCAMACU

The Excamacu was a subdivision or sub-tribe of the Cusabo proper (South). They lived between St. Helena Sound and the Broad River of South Carolina. For more see Cusabo and Coosa.

EYEISH

The Eyeish or Háish was an independent tribe that belonged to the Caddoan linguistic family that was closely related to the Adai. They appear on Father Marquette's 1673 map as the Aiaichi—other forms are Ahiahichi and Ayiches. They constituted one of the five major groups of the Caddo Peoples.

The Eyeish lived in northwest Louisiana and along Ayish Creek in northeastern Texas between the Sabine River and the Neches. It was there that they were first encountered by the Spanish in 1542. They may have also at some point lived in southern Arkansas and southeastern Oklahoma, which might help explain the reference on Marquette's map. Later their villages were located near the road between the French post at Natchitoches and the Spanish post at Nacogdoches. But situated near the principal route between the French and Spanish was hardly conducive to tribal life and they moved farther west between the Brazos and Colorado rivers.

Sometime after 1828 they joined the other Caddoan tribes and disappeared from history as a separate unit. For more see the Caddo Peoples.

FALL INDIANS

According to the Canadians, the Fall Indians of Canada were located between the Saskatchewan River and South Branch. For Drake, the Fall Indians, for their location at the falls of the Kooskooskee River (Clearwater River), was an alternative name for the Alansar or Alannar, who he placed at the headwaters of the branches of South fork of the Saskatchewan with an estimated population of 2,000 in 1804.

The Fall Indians should not be confused with the Atsina (about the Milk River in Montana) and Clowwewalla (about the falls of the Willamette River in Oregon) who are also called by the alternate name Fall Indians; also, according to Drake, the Sauteur (Fr. literally, leaping), about the falls of St. Mary. Neither the Alansar nor the Sauteurs have otherwise been identified in the literature to date.

FARAON

Faraon or Faraón (Pharoah, Pharaones or Pharoaha) was an early name given to the Mescalero Apache. The Faraon is variously treated as a separate, independent tribe and as an early band of Lipan. Other reports indicate that the Mescalero were formed from part of the Faraon. Swanton describes the Faraon (or Apache Band of Pharoah as he also refers to it) as the southern division of the Mescalero.

FERNANDEŃO

The Fernandeño belonged to the Shoshonean Division of the Uto-Aztecan linguistic stock. They inhabited the valley of the Los Angeles River above the city of Los Angeles. Of some 5,000 in 1770, they were nearly extinct by 1950.

FIVE CIVILIZED TRIBES

The Five Civilized Tribes was the name given to five Native American nations of Southeastern United States, the Iroquoian-speaking Cherokee and the Muskogean-speaking Chickasaw, Choctaw, Creek, and Seminole because they had adopted many of the white customs and had generally maintained peaceful relations with their white neighbors. In the early decades of the nineteenth century, they went to great lengths to emulate the white man's way of life hoping that their efforts would save their lands and their culture. They did not bargain for the extent of the white man's greed. In 1820, the Choctaw were induced to vacate their tribal homes to the east and resettle in Indian Territory to the west.

The forced removal of the other four tribes from their traditional homelands and resettlement in Indian Territory followed enactment of the Indian Removal Act of 1830, each subsequent removal fraught with ever-increasing internal strife, resentment, and bloodshed. In the years following enactment of the Indian Removal Act of 1830, all five tribes, with minor exceptions, were forcibly removed from their traditional homelands and resettles in Indian Territory to the west. They occupied lands which the Osage and Quapaw had previously ceded to the government. Each tribe duly organized an autonomous state modeled after the federal government, developed a writing system patterned on the system devised by the Cherokee, and in 1859 formed a loose confederation under the name "Five Civilized Tribes."

The appellation drew resentment from other Native American tribes, the implication being that all others were less than civilized—savages. The five nations remained independent until 1907, when statehood was granted to Oklahoma and the territory was opened to white settlement. For more, see the individual tribes; Indian Removal Act of 1830 and the Trail of Tears; and the appendix, American Indians in the Civil War.

FOX

The Fox (also written Foxes, though sing.) belonged to a group of the Algonquin linguistic family. French missionaries found them in 1670 in the vicinity of Lake Winnebago and along the Fox River in Wisconsin, but they had heard of the Fox some thirty years earlier. Some reports have them originally from the northeastern United States. Other reports state that it is very probable that they once lived about Saginaw Bay in Michigan while others believe that they lived in northern Wisconsin and were pushed south by the Chippewa. The Fox River is an outlet of Lake Winnebago, first named for the *Puants*, the Winnebagoes. With the arrival of the Outagami about 1680, it became known to the French as *Riviere des Renards* and to the English as Fox River.

Outagami or Outagamie was the original name for the Foxes until the French nicknamed them *les renards*, meaning foxes. (The name of the Wisconsin county is spelled Outagamie in honor of the Indians.) The Jesuits reported the Outagami as a large nation believed to have been on Wolf River, somewhere in Waupaca or Outagami County, Wisconsin. Other members of their linguistic group were the Sauk (Sac), the Kickapoo, and Mascoutin.

The name Mesquaki (or Meshkwa kihug; also Meskwaki) is found in the literature listed as a sub-tribe of the Sac and Fox. It is actually the Fox name for themselves, meaning "red earth people." It is the preferred name of the group of Fox that broke away and migrated to Iowa. For more on the subject, see the Sauk.

The Fox were continually at war with the Chippewa, which led them into conflict with the French. An attack on Fort Detroit in 1712 was nearly successful; and a bitter four-year war with the French between 1729 and 1733 brought the Fox heavy losses as well as the Sauk who had allied with them. Around 1746 the Fox were driven south down the Wisconsin River by the French to a point twenty miles from its mouth where they settled on the north bank.

During the mid-1700s, the Fox joined the Sauk to drive the Illinois tribes from the northwestern part of the Rock River Country and settled on the lands they had vacated. In 1780, in an alliance with the Dakota, they attacked the Chippewa at St. Croix Falls and were defeated. Early in the nineteenth century, the Fox separated form the Sac and settled in Iowa. Over the next half century, the Fox and Sac would rejoin and separate again. At one point, the two tribes would locate hold the territory between the Missouri and the Mississippi rivers as far north as the headwaters of the Des Moines and Iowa rivers.

The Fox and Sac are often treated in the literature as a single group because the confederation of the two tribes was so thorough and complete, the Sac being the more numerous of the two. See the Sauk (Sac) for a more detail account of the two tribes during the last half of the eighteenth century and the first half of the nineteenth century.

FREMONT

The name Fremont has been used to describe scattered groups of hunters and farmers that inhabited vastly different landscapes of the American west. Thus there were a wide variety of lifestyles represented with minimal social organization between them. As a result the Fremont were once thought to be an lower or inferior branch of their neighbors, the Anasazi.

The Fremont are now considered to be a distinct and unique prehistoric culture that once inhabited the western Colorado Plateau and the eastern Great Basin of California from about 400 to 1350 AD. The Great Basin sites tend to be larger and more village-like that the Plateau sites.

Having thrived for some fifteen hundred years, the Fremont culture disappeared between 1250 and 1500 AD As with all pre-history peoples, theories abound with the reasons for their disappearance as a separate entity. The most likely causes are the weather, food source, and wars or at a minimum encroachment by other peoples. It appears likely that they were absorbed into the tribes of the region including the Numic speaking Western Shoshoni, Ute, and the Northern and Southern Paiute.

The Fremont Indian State Park in Clear Creek, south-central Utah, protects the largest Fremont site ever excavated in Utah. Other notable sites include those found in Dinosaur National Monument and Zion and Arches National Parks.

FRENCH CHAOUANONS

The French Chaouanons are believed to be a branch of the Shawnee and that they inhabited the Susquehanna Valley of Pennsylvania in the late 1600s.

FRESH WATER INDIANS

The name French Water Indians or *Agua Dulce* was applied to the Indians of seven to nine neighboring tribes in eastern Florida between St. Augustine and Cape Canaveral. They belonged to the Timucuan or Timuquanan linguistic division of the Muskhogean linguistic family. The vast majority, if not all, were converted to Christianity early in the seventeenth century.

FUS-HATCHEE

The Fus-hatchee was a sub-tribe or division of the Muskogee and a member of the Creek Confederacy that inhabited parts of Alabama.

GACHWECHNAGECHGA

The Gachwechnagechga was a sub-tribe of the Unami division of the Delaware. They lived on the Lehigh River in Pennsylvania. For more see Unami and Delaware.

GALLINOMERO POMO

The Gallinomero or Southern Pomo were one of the seven divisions of the Pomo nation generally treated separately. They lived inland from the northwestern coast of California all along the area between Cleone above Fort Bragg on the north and Duncan's Point in northern Sunoma County on the south and about Clear Lake. The Southern Pomo people are from the Sebastopol area. For more see the Pomo.

GEOTE

The Geote was listed by Farther Ortiz in his memorial to the king of Spain sometime after February 14, 1747, cited by Bolton in "Missions on the San Gabriel," but no additional information about the tribe is known. It is believed that the Geote lived in east central or southeastern Texas.

GIG HARBOR

The Gig Harbor Indians lived about Puget Sound in Washington Territory and are now considered extinct. Reportedly, when the first settlers, including an Indian woman from Canada, arrived at Gig Harbor there was already a Indian village at the head of the bay. No additional information is available.

GILA

The name Gila or Xila has been given a number of different meanings. Generally speaking, the name refers to the Tci-he-nde Mimbre (Mimbreño) Chiricahua Apaches of southwest New Mexico and southeastern Arizona.

The "Indians of Arizona" identifies the Gila as the Apaches living west of Socorro in southwestern New Mexico, embracing the Mimbreño, Mogollon, and Warm Springs Apaches and then later that part of the Arivaipa and Chiricahua living along the Gila. The text further identifies the Mogollon as associated with the Mimbre and living about the Mogollon mesa and mountains in western New Mexico and eastern Arizona.

Haley makes no reference to the Gila as a separate group, only the 1857 Gila River Expedition against the Mimbre; nor does he refer to the Mogollon as a separate group but writes of the Apaches living in eastern Arizona south of the Mogollon Rim. For Haley, the Warm Springs Apaches was simply another name imparted by the white man for the Mimbre, some of whom were clustered near the hot springs on the west bank of the Rio Grande near Santa Rita de Cobre. For more see Apache.

GILEÑOS

According to Haley, the Gileño Apaches and San Carlos Apaches (Apache Peaks, Arivaipa, Pinal, and San Carlos proper) were one and the same and together with the Cibicue, White Mountain, Northern Tonto, and Southern Tonto subgroups were collectively called Western Apache—not to be confused with the Western Division.

To Swanton, the Gileño Apaches and San Carlos Apaches were separate and distinct entities. For Swanton, the Apache nation consisted of two major groupings, the San Carlos Group that included the San Carlos proper (w/ same bands listed by Haley), the White Mountain, Cibecue, Southern Tonto, and Northern Tonto subgroups—again the same subgroups Haley includes in the Western Apache, and the

Chiricahua-Mescalero Group that included the Gileños (Chiricahua proper, Mimbreño, Mogollon, and Warm Spring) and Mescalero subgroups. Both Haley and Swanton refer to Goodwin (1935).

According to "Indians of Arizona," the name San Carlos has little or no ethnic significance, and the writer notes that the name has been applied officially to the Apaches living on the Gila River and they are sometimes referred to as Gileño, or Gila Apache. The name Gileño has also been used to designate the Pima that lived along the Gila River in Arizona. The one fact that all the writers appear to agree on is that no group of tribes has caused greater confusion when it comes to the identification and use of the popular names of individual tribes.

In the modern day, the name San Carlos Apache refers to the Apaches of the San Carlos Reservation. For more see Apache.

CAMP GRANT MASSACRE

Camp Grant was originally established as Fort Arivaipa about sixty miles northeast of Tucson in 1859 and suffered through several name changes. It was subsequently be moved and renamed Fort Grant. About five hundred Pinal and Arivaipa (Gileños Apache) had gathered around Camp Grant by the spring of 1871 under the unofficial protection and support of a senior lieutenant Royal Emerson Whitman.

Their leader of the group was Eskiminzim, a Pinal, who had married to an Arivaipa. On the morning of April 30, 1871, a mob of fifty-four civilians—forty-eight Mexicans and six other civilians from Tucson—and ninety-four Papago Indians attacked the Indians around the camp. It happened so quickly that the army was unable to respond. It has been estimated that one hundred and twenty-five lives were taken, of which only eight were men. Twenty-nine other children were taken captive. Two later escaped; five were taken to Tucson; and twenty-two were sold in Sonora.

By the time General Oliver Howard arrived in Arizona, those that had escaped the massacre had for the most part filtered back into camp. Howard agreed to move the reservation from Camp Grant north to what became the San Carlos Reservation. Howard also managed to locate and return the five children from Tucson. His responsive actions helped to diffuse an exceeding deadly situation.

GOSIUTE SHOSHONI

The Gosiute (also Gushute among a number of other variations) was a small etholinguistic group of Western Shoshoni commonly classified as a division of the Western Shoshoni. More often than not, however, they are treated separately. Swanton acknowledges their somewhat unique status. The Gosiute inhabited the region about the Great Salt Lake in northern Utah. At one time they were thought to be a mixture of Ute and Shoshoni. In fact they are sometimes identified as Goshen Utes or Goship-Utes. (In 1928 they were enumerated with the Ute.) The state of Utah identifies the Gosiute as one of the five tribes that inhabited the state, the others being the Paiute Bands in Southern Utah, the Northwestern Band of Shoshoni in Northern Utah, the Dine', and the Ute.

It has been frequently written of the Gosiute that they lived an isolated, wretched life style in the desert—but the statement as often as not is immediately qualified as probably an exaggeration.

The treaty of 1863 defined their lands as lying "[o]n the north by the middle of the Great Desert; on the west by Steptoe Valley; on the south by Tooedoe or Green Mountains; and on the east by Great Salt Lake, Tuilla, and Rush Valleys."

GOWANUS

Gowanus or Gowanas was not a separate tribe, although it is sometimes found treated separately, but a settlement or village of the Canarsee of the Algonquian linguistic group of Delaware who inhabited what is now Brooklyn, New York, on Long Island. The Canarsee also had settlements in present-day Sheepshead Bay, Flatlands, and Canarsie.

The Indian name of Gowanus was applied to all the land fronting on Gowanus Bay and traversed Gowanus Creek. There is a land patent from 1636 that Messrs. Bennet and Bentyn purchased from the Indians a tract of 930 acres of land at Gowanus but no information on the Indians themselves. The patent is generally considered the first step in the founding of the city of Brooklyn. For more see Canarsee.

GRAN QUIVIRA PUEBLO

The Grand Quivera Pueblo belonged to the Tompiro group. It was established about 800 in the Manzano Mountains southeast of Albuquerque and prospered as a trading center. (Manzano means apple in Spanish.) Originally called Pueblo de Las Humanas by the Spanish, the pueblo did not receive its current name until after it had been abandoned. (The name Quivera represented the place of riches beyond he horizon—one of the mystical Seven Cities of Gold.) The Indians of Quivera were first visited by Coronado in 1540, but it was not until almost a century later in 1636 that the first mission was built. A second, San Buenaventura, was begun in 1659 but never completed. The population, which at its peak numbered well over 2,000, was decimated by disease and the famine brought on by persistent draught. To the natural hardships were added Apache raids and the harsh treatment the Indians received as de facto slaves to the Spanish. By the mid-1670s, Quivera and Abó Pueblo to the north were abandoned by the survivors, believed to have numbered from five to eight hundred. Some went to Isleta Pueblo where they spoke the same language; others went south to El Paso. The Grand Quivira Pueblo, the Abó Pueblo, and the Quarai Pueblo now comprise the Salinas Pueblo Missions National Monument. The name "salinas" refers to the nearby salt beds.

GRAND PAWNEE

Grand Pawnee or Chaui were one of the four subdivisions of the Pawnee. They lived about the Platte River in Nebraska. For more see the Pawnee.

GRANDE EAUX

The Grande Eaux or Grandes Eaux meaning Big Waters was listed in Jefferson's *Notes on the State of Virginia*, taking his information from Bouquet (1764). He gives a population of 1,000 warriors. For more see "Aborigines," Appendix D.

GRAVE CREEK UMPQUA

The Grave Creek or Grave is believed to have been a band or sub-tribe of the Umpqua that lived on Grave Creek, a northern tributary of the Rogue River in western Oregon. (The name of the creek came from the fact that it was site of the "grave" of Martha Leland Crowley, a sixteen year old girl who died of Typhoid Fever in 1846.) The name Galice Creeks also appears to have been given to them. The Grave Creek were the targets it what has been called the Massacre at Grave Creek in the summer of 1851 that killed eleven and nearly exterminated the male population. Also see Western Oregon Indians.

GRIGRA

The Griga, probably of the Tunican linguistic group, inhabited St. Catherines Creek in Mississippi and were subsequently adopted by the Natchez with whom they appear as the "Gray Valley." It is believed that they may have lived at one time on the Yazoo River. The Grigra (Gris or Gras) are mentioned as one of the anti-French faction.

GUACATA

The Guacata was a small tribe of south Florida. It is believed that they may have emigrated to Cuba in 1763.

GUALALA POMO

The Gualala or Southwestern Pomo were one of the seven divisions of the Pomo sometimes treated separately. They lived along the California coast at the southern end of the Pomo range near what was Duncan's Point in northern Sunoma County. For more see the Pomo.

GUALE

The Guale tribe was of Muskhogean stock. Part may have been Creeks or Muskogee. They inhabited the area on the coast of Georgia between St. Andrews Sound and the Savannah River. Guale history dates to the 1500s, and the villages have been classified as belonging to one three groups: Northern, Central, and Southern. Guale proper was a village of the Northern group but not on the island of that name. Locations of the Northern group included St. Catherines Island and Ossabaw Island; of the Central group, Tulufina and Sapello Island; of the Southern group, St. Simons Island.

Sometime before 1600 the Guale had moved to Florida where there was a general Indian insurrection in 1573. Guale towns and granaries were burned, and by 1601 the insurrection was over. Under attack by northern Indians, many of the Guale moved inland; others settled or were removed to the islands north of St. Augustine.

Another small group may have gone to South Carolina. Those who remained mounted another general insurrection in 1702 under the leadership of the Yamasee and joined the group in South Carolina. The Guale came together, except for those with the Creeks, with the outbreak of the Yamasee War of 1715. The last record of the Guale appeared in 1726.

GUASCO

The Guasco was one of the thirteen principal tribes of the southwestern or Hasinai Division of the Caddo Indians or Hasinai Confederacy. In 1686 they were living near the headwaters of the Neches River what is now Houston County, Texas. Little is known of For more see Hasinai Confederacy and Caddo Peoples.

HACANAC

The Hacanac were of the Caddoan group first encountered in 1542 in northeastern Texas and the adjacent parts of Arkansas and Louisiana. It is possible that they were the same as the Lacane, a name that has been regarded as an early name for the Nacaniche or Nacanish of the Hasinai Confederacy.

There is one school of thought that suggests that the Hacanac, Lacane, Nacachau, Nacau, Nacaniche, Nacono, and Nakanawan Indians were fragments of the same Caddoan tribe. There is no documentary evidence to substantiate that hypothesis, but the Nacachau, Nacanish, Nocomo, and Nacau (Nacao) were members of the Hasinai Confederacy, and the Nakanawan could very likely could have been, which would leave the Hacanac and Lacane. For more see Hasinai Confederacy, Caddo Peoples, and Nacanish.

HACKENSACK

The Hackensack was a tribe of the Unami subdivision of the Delaware. They lived in the Hackensack, Raritan, and Passaic river valleys of New Jersey. On March 6, 1660, the Hackensack, Nyack, Haverstraw, Wecquaesgeek (Weschester), and Western Long Island Indians accepted a peace treaty with the Dutch that isolated the Esopus who signed a peace treaty March 16, 1664 ending the Esopus Indian Wars. The Hackensack and Nyack of New Jersey also signed the treaty as allies of the Dutch, agreeing to insure the good behavior of the Esopus. For more see Esopus and Wickquasgeck.

HAINAI

The Hainai was one of the thirteen principal tribes or subdivisions of the southwestern or Hasinai Division of the Caddo Indians or Hasinai Confederacy. They lived in eastern Texas west of Nacogdoches on the Neches and Angelina rivers. For more see Hasinai Confederacy and Caddo Peoples.

HALCHIDHOMA

The Halchidhoma belonged to the Yuman branch of the Hokan linguistic stock. Closely related to the Maricopa and speaking the same language as the Yuma, they inhabited various point along the Colorado River near the mouth of the Gila. Around the late 1700s they moved farther north with the Kohuana but were soon driven back south by the Mohave. They were eventually absorbed into the Maricopa on the Gila

HALYIKWAMAI

The Halyikwamai belonged to the Yuman linguistic stock. Around 1600 they lived on the Colorado River below the mouth of the Gila River, and by 1760s they inhabited a fertile plain up river on its eastern bank. It was this group of villages that Father Garcés named Santo Rosa in 1771. By 1775 they had moved to the west side of the river. It is believed that they may been absorbed by the Cocopa or another Yuman tribe.

HAMMONASSET

The Hammonasset was a sub-tribe of the Quinnipiac of the Wappinger of Connecticut. They lived west of the Connecticut River at its mouth. For more see Quinnipiac and Wappinger.

HANIS

The Hanis formed one dialectic group of the Kusan linguistic family. The other was the Miluk dialect. They lived along the Coos River and the north and south sides of Coos Bay in Oregon.

HANNAKALLAL

According to Lewis and Clark the Hannakallal lived on the seacoast of Washington State to the south of the Coos. They reportedly spoke the Killamook language. Their estimated the total population at the time at some 600 people. Drake describes their location as on the Pacific coast south of the Columbia River, next beyond the Luckkarso.

HANO PUEBLO

The Hano was a member of the Northern division of the Tewa group. They were of the Tanoan linguistic family, now Kiowa-Tanoan stock. They lived in the area from near Santa Fe north to the mouth of the Rio Chama in northcentral New Mexico.

HARASG-NA

Harasg-na (possibly Haras-nga) was a sub-tribe of the Tongva of California. No location has been identified. It has been suggested that it might be the name of a village near San Pedro or of San Clemente Island. For more see Tongva.

HASINAI CONFEDERACY

The Hasinai Confederacy constituted one of the main divisions of the Caddoan linguistic family. The other divisions or groups were the Kadohadacho Confederacy, Natchitoches Confederacy, and the independent Adai and Eyeish tribes. The Hasinai comprised thirteen known tribes or bands and six affiliated tribes about which little is known. A seventh is also referred to in the literature that may have been only a local group. The members of the Hasinai inhabited an area in northeastern Texas between the headwaters of the Neches and Trinity rivers.

At one time the Caddoan Hasinai was the most numerous of all the native peoples of Texas. They first appear in written history in the chronicles of the De Soto expedition of 1542. They led a sedentary, agricultural life in an organized community structure. The Hasinai continued to live in their traditional East Texas homeland into the 1830s. For more see Caddo Peoples.

PRINCIPAL TRIBES	ALLIED TRIBES
Anadarko	Naansi
Guasco	Nabeyeyxa
Hainai	Nadamin
Nabedache	Natsshostanno
Nacachau	Neihahat
Nacanish	Tadiva
Nacao	Kayamaici (possibly a local group)
Nacogdoche	
Nacono	
Namidish or Nabiti	
Nasoni	
Nechaui	
Neches	

By the 1790s disease, alcoholism, cultural decline, and the intrusion of white settlers and Indians from other regions reduced their numbers. The Hasinais were forced out of their homeland at the end of the Cherokee War in 1839. With the Caddo and others they migrated to the west and northwest and eventually settled in near Fort Worth before being eventually removed to present-day Caddo County in Oklahoma in 1859.

HASSANAMISCO

The Hassanamisco or Hassanameisit was a sub-tribe of the Nipmuc of Grafton, Massachusetts that is sometimes treated separately.

HASSINUNGA

The Hassinunga was a sub-tribe of the Manahoac of Virginia or as sometimes referred to, the Hassinunga Confederacy. They lived on the headwaters of the Rappahannock River. Other members of the confederacy were the Ontponea, Shackaconia, Stegaraki, Tanxnitania, I'egninateo, and Whonkentia.

HATTERAS

The Hatteras, also spelled Hattaras, belonged to the Algonquian linguistic family. They lived among the sandbanks of Cape Hatteras east of Pamlico Sound in North Carolina and frequented Roanoke Island. They may be the Croatan Indians with whom Raleigh's colonists supposedly took refuge. They disappeared as a separate tribe soon thereafter and united with the mainland Algonquian.

HAVASUPAI

The Havasupai, Hualupai or Supai were of the Yuman branch of the Hokan linguistic stock and closely related to the Walapi. There is some thought that may have come from the Walapi. They inhabited Cataract Canyon of the Colorado River in northwestern Arizona. They were comprised of seven divisions. Although they had earlier contacts, not much was learned about them until the middle of the nineteenth century.

DIVISIONS
Mata'va-kopai
Soto'lve-kopai
Ko'o'u-kopai
Nyav-kopai
Hakia' tce-pai or Talta'l-kuwa
Kwe'va-kopai
Hua'la-pai, Howa'laa-pai

HAVERSTRAW

The Haverstraw was a sub-tribe of the Unami division of the Delaware. They lived on the western bank of the lower Hudson River in Rockland County, New York. On March 6, 1660, the Hackensack, Nyack, Haverstraw, Wcquaesgeek (Weschester), and Western Long Island Indians of New York accepted a peace treaty with the Dutch that isolated the Esopus.

HELLWITS

The Hellwits lived in northwest Oregon not far from present Rainier. Drake identified them as living along the north side of Columbia River, from the falls upward.

HERRING POND

The Herring Pond Indians were a Wampanoag settlement in the southeastern part of Plymouth, Massachusetts. In an Indian deed executed in 1664, the land was called Kawamasuhkakamid. The Herring River Watershed reportedly contains the remains of what is believed to be the principal habitation area for the Herring Pond Indians of the late seventeenth century. Over sixty Herring Pond Indians were members of Captain Thomas Tupper of Sandwich's 1693 congregation. He had built a combined mission, church, and meeting house near Herring Pond.

In an act passed by the Massachusetts Legislature in 1859, John Milton Earle of Worcester was appointed to conduct a census and investigate the social conditions of Native Americans in the state and make recommendations regarding their status in the Commonwealth. Earle enumerated just under 150 Herring Pond and New Bedford Indians, the names appear to used interchangeably. For more see Wampanoag.

HIDATSA

The Hidatsa or Gros Ventre of the River (*Gros Ventre de la Rivière*) were of the Siouan linguistic stock and distinct from the Gros Ventre of the Prairie, the Atsina. Their closest relations were the Crow. The Hidatsa were also called the Gros Ventre of the Missouri and the Hidatsa of North Dakota. They are also commonly referred to as the Minnetaree or Minitari and other variations. Catlin translates the name as "people of the willows"; Swanton as "they crossed the water." The Hidatsa inhabited villages in the Middle Missouri on both banks of the Knife River near the mouth of the Little Missouri a few miles above the Mandan.

Swanton reports that Lewis and Clark gave the names of three Hidatsa villages as Amatiha, Amahami or Mahaha, and the Hidatsa proper. According to De Voto, Lewis and Clark reported that the Hidatsa occupied three villages or rather two villages and a third that was inhabited by their close relation who maintained an independent structure that they called the Anahaways or Wattersoons. Lewis and Clark named one of the two Hidatsa villages Meteharta and identified Black Moccasin as the name of its chief. They did not name the second village but identified Little Wolf's Medicine as the tribal chief. The second village would have been the larger Hidatsa proper. Catlin (185, 187) writes of three Hidatsa (Minataree) villages but does not name them. He does write of the patriarchal chief Black Moccasin who by Catlin's time in the early 1830s had counted "more than a hundred *snows.*" All the variations of the names of the two villages, in addition to the Hidatsa proper, can be found here under the names Amahami and Meteharta.

From their original homeland to the northeast of their middle-Missouri location, the Hidatsa were taken in by the Mandan, maintained very close relations with them over they years, and adopted many of their customs and practices, including the use of earth-covered lodges. Arguably, their greatest claim to fame is the guidance and support they gave to Lewis and Clark and the Corps of Discovery on their upriver. The Hidatsa were also continually at war with the Shoshoni and Assiniboin to their west until they finally made peace in 1844. They among the tribes devastated by a violent smallpox epidemic in 1837. Remnants consolidated into one village which they moved to a location near Fort Berthold in 1845.

On July 13, 1880, President Rutherford Hayes with a stroke of the pen extinguished the title to thirty thousand square miles of land belonging to the Arikara, Gros Ventre, and Piegan Blackfeet making it available to the Northern Pacific Railroad. The route was completed in 1883.

HIERBIPIAMES

The Hierbipiames tribe is cited in Bolton, "Missions on the San Gabriel," but no additional information is known.

HIETAN

The name Ietan or Hietan was more properly an alternate name for the Ute of Colorado, but it found wide use for all Indians of the Shoshonean stock, especially the Comanche. Indian agent Dr. Sibley, Drake, Lewis & Clark, and others used the name Hietan to refer to the Comanches. For more see Ute and Comanche.

HIHIGHENIMMO

The Hihighenimmo was one of the northwest tribes enumerated by Lewis & Clark. They reportedly lived on what was called the Lastaw River from its mouth up to the forks in northeast Washington. The Lastaw is the what we know as the Pend Orielle River with its mouth on the Columbia just across the U.S.-Canadian border in northeastern Washington State. What exactly was meant by the "forks" is unknown. The Pend Orielle flows from east to west and then south to north after emptying the Pend Oreille Lake in northern Idaho. One possibility if the junction of Sullivan Creek where it empties into the Pend Orielle just north of Metaline, Washington. (Lewis & Clark refer to the Pend Orielle Lake as Wayton Lake.)

HILIBI

The Hilibi was a sub-tribe or division of the Muskogee and a member of the Creek Confederacy that lived in Alabama.

HISCA

The Hisca was listed by Farther Ortiz in his memorial to the king of Spain sometime after February 14, 1747, cited by Bolton in "Missions on the San Gabriel," but no additional information about the tribe is known. It is believed that the Hisca lived in east central or southeastern Texas.

HITCHITI

The Hitchiti were noted in the chronicles of De Soto as the Ocute living at the time on the Ocmulgee River near present Macon, Georgia. After 1715, they inhabited the land in present Chattahoochee County, Georgia. When the original tribes of the peninsula were destroyed with their help, a group of Hitchiti moved onto the Alachua Plains in present Alachua County, Florida, and became the nucleus of the Seminole Nation. The Hitchiti language was spoken by the great number of Seminole until the mass migrations occurred, and the Hitchiti dialect of the Muskhogean language was replaced by a language almost identical to the Muskogee of the Creek. The Hitchiti, a member of the Creek Confederacy of Lower Creeks, lost their identity by the end of the Seminole wars, and remnants merged into the Creeks. For more see Seminole.

Fort Scott is located on a protected site on the shores of Lake Seminole in Southwest Georgia.

HOCHELAGAN

The Hochelagan of Canada were of the Iroquoian linguistic stock and inhabited the village of Hochelaga, the site of present-day Montreal. They are generally believed to have been a branch of the Huron-Iroquois race, the general consensus being that they were of the early Hurons, most often referred to separately. The Hochelagan were first encountered by French explorer and navigator Jacques Cartier during his second voyage in 1535. By Samuel de Champlain's first voyage in 1603, they had disappeared. For more see the Huron.

HOH

The Hoh lived along the Hoh River on the west coast of Washington State. They belonged to the Chimakuan linguistic stock, and were often considered part of the Quileute because they spoke the same

HOHOKAM

Hohokam (Huhugam and Huhukam) meaning "vanished ones" or "those who have gone" were of the prehistoric period ending around 1450. Some writers, as well as the Indians themselves, believe may be the ancestors of the Pima and Papago. The name itself was given to them by the Pima. Hohokam farmed the Salt River Valley and had a distinct cultural identity rich in arts and architecture, including an elaborate and innovative canal system to irrigate their desert lands—the system, now modernized, is still used today. Member of the group constituted the Hokan linguistic division of the Uto-Aztecan stock that today includes the Yuma and the Pima. It is believed that they came north from Mexico around 300 BC and inhabited the middle Gila River and lower Salt River drainage areas of southwestern Arizona and northern Mexico and centered around the present-day cities of Phoenix and Tucson. Their descendants are believed to be the Papago.

The Hohokam Pima National Monument is located near Coolidge, Arizona. Hohokam Stadium in Mesa, Arizona, is the spring training ground for the Chicago Cubs baseball team, and their name was given to an elementary school in Scottsdale among their many connections to the modern world.

HOIS

The Hois or Hoh'ees (timber people) was one of the sub-tribes or bands of the Comanche. The Hois is generally listed as a separate tribe, but Fehrenbach gives the name as an alternate for the Pehnahterkuh. For more see Comanche.

HOLIWAHALI

The Holiwahali was a sub-tribe or division of the Muskogee and a member of the Creek Confederacy. For more see Muskogee.

HONNIASONT

The Honniasont belonged to the Iroquoian linguistic family and inhabited the upper Ohio River and its branches in western Pennsylvania and neighboring parts of West Virginia. Although once allies of the Susquehanna in war, they were subsequently destroyed by the Susquehanna and Seneca with the remnants settling among the Seneca.

HOPI

The Hopi or Hopituh Shi-nu-mu, the Peaceful People, lived principally on three mesa in northeast Arizona. A with all Puebloans, the Hopi built their villages or pueblos on mesas or flat mountains that rose above the low altitude deserts of the Southwest for protection. They were particularly vulnerable to raids by the Navajos, Apaches, and Utes. The Hopi shared with the Zuni and other Pueblos to the east in New Mexico a basic culture; yet their language constituted a unique dialect of the Shoshonean division of the Uto-Aztecan linguistic stock. Also, to a large extent they were virtually ignored by the Spanish because of the great distance; nevertheless the Franciscan friars were quire active. The Hopi did not have a single group identity as such, but rather were comprised of a number of independent towns or villages.

VILLAGES
Awatovi, Antelope Mesa nine miles east of Walpi
Jongopavi, Second or Middle Mesa (DR)
Hano, First or East Mesa (DR)
Homolobi, near Winslow
Kisakobi, northwest base of East Mesa

Kuchaptuvela, terrace of East Mesa
Mishongnovi, Second or Middle Mesa*
Oraibi, Third or West Mesa*
Shipaulovi, Second or Middle Mesa*
Shumopovi or Shongopovi, Second or Middle Mesa*
Sichomovi, First or East Mesa*
Walpi, First or East Mesa*

---

*Principal villages. Kisakobi and Kuchaptuvela were successively occupied prior to the building of Walpi. Hano was founded in 1700 by Tano emigrants from Puebloan villages in the Galiesteo Basin in New Mexico that included San Lázaro, San Cristóbal, and Galisteo. (DR) from David Roberts, *The Pueblo Revolt.*

The Hopi were first visited by Coronado at Awatovi in 1540, and it was there that the first church was built in 1629. (It is destroyed in the Pueblo Revolt of 1680.) Following the Spanish reconquest, Awatovi again became the focal point of the renewed effort to bring Christianity to the Hopi. In 1700, the village was destroyed by their Puebloan kinsmen. The men, women, and children were massacred—young and old alike. Of those women and girls taken captive, most of whom were later killed. The common consensus is there was causal relationship between the village's acceptance of Christianity and its destruction. Christianity was never again installed in any Hopi village.

One story has it that Awatoni had reached such depths of sinfulness and debauchery that destruction was the only recourse and that the headman pleaded with the leaders of other villages to do what was necessary although it was against all their beliefs. As the story goes, the Oraibi finally agreed.

The Hopi Reservation is located in northeastern Arizona. For more see individual villages.

HOPOKOHACKING

The Hopokohacking was a sub-tribe of the Unalachtigo division of the Delaware. They lived in the area about the modern city of Wilmington, Delaware. For more see Unalachtigo and Delaware.

HOSTAQUA

The Hostaqua or Yustaga belonged to the Timucuan or Timuquanan division of the Muskhogean linguistic group that inhabited parts of northwestern Florida. For more see the Utina.

HOUMA

The Houma (literally "red" and an abbreviation for *saktci homma*, "red crawfish") spoke Muskhogean. Also called Houmas and Oumas, they inhabited an area inland from the Mississippi-Louisiana border possibly near present-day Pickney, Louisiana, above Baton Rouge. It is believed that they separated from the Chakchiuma. The Houma diet consisted of corn, beans, squash, melons and sunflowers that they grew themselves, augmented by hunting and fishing. They used the dugout canoe for travel on the rivers.

Rene Robert Cavelier, Seiur de La Salle, French explorer and fur trader, reported that he heard of the Houma in his exploration down the Mississippi in 1682. The French explorer/soldier Henri de Tonti visited with them four years later as did Pierre le Moyne d'Iberville, the soldier, sailor, explorer, and colonizer who founded the French colony of Louisiana. Iberville celebrated his exploits with the Houma in March 1699 at the boundary between the Houma and the Bayogoula that was marked by a large red pole adorned with skulls of animals that is now the site of present day Baton Rouge and the mouth of the Red River. (Remnants of the Quynypyssa were living with the Houma at the time of Iberville's visit.)

In returning to his ships anchored at Ship Island at the site of present-day Gulfport, Mississippi, on the Gulf Coast, Iberville passed across two lakes that he named "Lake Maurapas" and the larger, "Lake Pontchartrain," after the French Minister of Marine, Louis Pontchartrain.

Driven from their home by the Tunia they settled on Bayou St. John near New Orleans but soon moved back up river to Ascension Parish near the Bayogoula and Acolapissa. In 1805 following the Louisiana Purchase some moved west to Lake Charles, Louisiana, where they joined the Atakapa. The others drifted away into Louisiana, mixing with Creole and Negro. The Houma gave their name to the Creole town about thirty-five miles southwest of New Orleans. (The city of Daigleville near Houma was the site of the first Indian High School in the State of Louisiana, established in 1959.)

RENÉ-ROBERT CAVELIER, SIEUR DE LA SALLE

In his 1681-1682 expedition, La Salle traveled the length of the Mississippi River to the Gulf of Mexico. When the party reached the "grand rivière des Émisourites" (Missouri River), they encamped on the west bank of the Mississippi near its confluence with the Missouri. La Salle mistakenly believed the grand rivière flowed southwest rather than northwest. La Salle noted the large number of Native American villages along the Missouri but made no specific mention of contact. On completing his journey down the Mississippi, in an elaborate ceremony on April 9, 1682, La Salle claimed the entire Mississippi River valley for France under the names New France and Louisiana.

Henri Tonti, 1649-1704, a Canadian fur trader and explorer, traveled with La Salle as his trusted scout and second in command. Tonti's writings were a rich source of information on the early years of exploration.

HOUSATONIC

The Housatonic or Westenhuck was a subdivision of the Mahican and occupied the Housatonic Valley of Connecticut and Massachusetts. See the Mahican Group.

HOUTG-NA

Houtg-na was a sub-tribe of the Tongva of California that inhabited the area about Ranchito de Lugo. For more see Tongva.

HUALAPAI

The Hualapai (pronounced Walapai, thus the variations on the spelling) were of the Yuma branch of the Hokan (Hohokam) linguistic stock and were closely related to the Havasupai. They inhabited the middle course of the Colorado River in Arizona, between Sacramento Wash and National Canyon and inland to near Bill Williams Fork. The Hualapai had little contact with western civilization until the 1840s, when trappers and prospectors moved into their territory. Their history is much the same as the other Yuma tribes of the Southwest. The Hualapai now occupy a reservation on the south rim of the Grand.

HUCHNOM

The Huchnom are of Yukian stock. They inhabited the valley of the South Eel River from Hullville to near its mouth and the valley of the Tomki as well as the lower course of the Deep (Outlet) Creek in California.

HUHAMOG-NA

Huhamog-na was a sub-tribe of the Tongva of California that inhabited the area about Rancho de los Verdugos [Pasadena-Arroyo Seco]. For more see Tongva.

HULIWAHLI

Huliwahli or Holiwahali was a subdivision of the Muskogee (Creek). They lived on the north bank of the Tallapoosa River in Elmore County, Alabama. For more see Muskogee

HUMPTULIP

The Humptulip inhabited the Humptulip River and part of Grays Harbor in Washington State. They belonged to the coastal division of the Salishan linguistic family and were closely affiliated with the Lower Chehalis whose dialect they spoke.

HUNKPAPA

The Hunkpapa was a subgroup of the Western Sioux, Teton (Lakota). Hunkpapa comes from Hunupatina, referring to Hunu-pa-paha, or what is known today as Devil's Tower. For more see Sioux and Lakota.

IMAGES OF AMERICAN INDIANS ON U.S. CURRENCY

The term currency refers to both bills and coins. The image of Chief Running Antelope of the Hunkpapa Lakota Sioux, ca. 1851) appeared on the 1899 series U.S. Five Dollar Silver Certificate (oversized bill). He was the only Native American other than Sacagawea years later to be featured on U.S. currency. The image portrayed the Chief in a Pawnee headdress rather than his Sioux tribal headdress that added to the animosity between the Pawnee and the Sioux. In 2000, A U.S. Gold Coin in the denomination of one dollar was struck with the image of the young Sacagawea who traveled with the Corps of Discovery.

The Indian Head nickel, also known as the Buffalo nickel, was minted from 1913 to 1938. It was designed by sculptor James Earle Fraser. It was modeled using the images of three different individuals: Iron Tail (Sinte Maza) of the Oglala; Two Moons (Ishi'eyo) of the Northern Cheyenne; and Big Tree of the Seneca. The model for the American bison was named Black Diamond, then living in Central Park Zoo in New York City.

HUPA

The Hupa were of the Athapascan linguistic stock and closely related to the Chilula and Whilkup. They inhabited the middle course of the Trinity River and its branches, including the Hupa Valley; also the New River.

HURON

The Huron were of the Iroquoian linguistic stock and inhabited the area of the St. Lawrence Valley in Canada and the territory of the present province of Ontario on the north side of Lake Ontario across to Georgian Bay. During his exploration of the St. Lawrence River on his second voyage to America in 1535, French explorer and navigator Jacques Cartier found two Indian villages, Hochelaga and Stadacona, that occupied the sites of present-day Montreal and Quebec, respectively. (Cartier made three voyages to North America between 1534 and 1543.)

It is generally believed that the villages Cartier came across were inhabited by a branch of the Huron-Iroquois race, with the emphasis on the Huron. It was their first contact with Europeans. Although the Huron and the Iroquois were related linguistically, they were bitter enemies. The home lands of the Iroquois group (Mohawk, Oneida, Onondaga, Cayuga and Seneca) were south of Lake Ontario, principally in present-day New York State. Cartier was followed several years later by Samuel de Champlain, who made his first voyage in 1603. By that time Hurons had disappeared, and throughout the area Champlain found wandering groups of Algonquin Indians. Champlain explored the coast during his second voyage in 1604-1607, and on his third voyage in 1608 he founded the city of Quebec.

Early estimates put the Huron population at near thirty thousand at the turn of the seventeenth century before the white man's diseases reduced their numbers by a third. The Huron were willing converts to Christianity. Armed with French weapons, the Hurons turned back the armies of the Iroquois League near the end of the sixteenth century. Around the mid-1600s, armed with Dutch weapons, the Iroquois attacked and almost totally annihilated the Hurons. In 1649 and 1650, they destroyed over thirty Huron villages. Many of the survivors were adopted by the Five Nations; a number escaped and settled near Quebec under the protection of the French; and others fled to the area of present Detroit, Michigan, and Sandusky, Ohio, where they became known as Wyandot.

It is as the Wyandot that the Huron have come down in American history. The name Huron, given to them by the French from *quelle hures* (meaning "what heads!" referring to their wild hair) continues in Canada. In early written history, several tribes living in southern Ontario referred to themselves as Wendat, meaning "island people" or those living on a peninsula. The various pronunciations of the name Wendat by their allies and enemies alike came out as Guyandot, Guyandotte, Ouendat, and Wyandot with various spellings.

In 1668 Farther Jacques Marquette, S. J. set up a mission at Chequamegon Bay near the western end of Lake Superior where he worked with the Huron/Wyandot. After repeated Sioux attacks, they fled west. Fr. Marquette followed and moved the mission to the northern shore of the Straits of Mackinac (between Lake Michigan and Lake Huron). For more see the Wyandot.

HUTUCG-NA

Hutucg-na was a sub-tribe of the Tongva of California that inhabited the area about Santa Ana [Yorbes]. For more see Tongva.

IBITOUPA

The Ibitoupa belonged to the Muskhogean stock and were closely related to the Chackshiuma, Chickasaw, and Choctaw. They lived along the Yazoo River in Mississippi in present Holmes County. It is believed that they united with the Chickasaw soon after the Natchez War of 1729.

ICAFUI

The Icafui were a small tribe of the Timucuan group in Florida and southeastern Georgia. They were first encountered by Franciscan missionaries. In the literature the Icafui are referred to as Cascangue. Whether Cascangue was another name for the Icafui or a matter of confusing identities is unknown. See Utina on the history of the group.

ILLINOIS

An Illinois proper is not listed among the Illinois Cluster of Tribes provided by Swanton, but it appears reasonable that there should have been such a tribe. The name appears quite frequently in the literature. One source puts them on the Illinois River two hundred miles above the Ozaw. It would appear that those reports that them on the Vermilion River to the east are in error. The clearest evidence for the existence of the Illinois proper is the account of an unnamed chief of the Illinois who accompanied Etienne de Véniard, sieru de Bourgmont and other chiefs to Paris in 1724 where they were received by the Duke and Duchess of Bourbon. For more see the Illinois Cluster of Tribes, Chicago, Osage, and Vermilion.

ILLINOIS CLUSTER OF TRIBES

The Illinois Cluster or Tribes or Illinois Confederacy tribes belonged to the Algonquian linguistic group. Their historical homeland was the area along the Illinois and Mississippi rivers in present Illinois, Iowa, and Missouri, with one group as far south as northeastern Arkansas. The Illinois were a loose cluster of thirteen or more related major and minor tribes or subdivisions. The journals of Nicholas La Salle mention four more. The minor tribes receive only passing mention in the literature. Although one would expect that one of the tribes of the cluster would have been called the Illinois proper, there is some debate as to whether there actually was an Illinois proper. The name is frequently found in court records and in the popular texts where it is clearly used to identify one particular tribe.

MAJOR TRIBES	MINOR TRIBES
Cahokia	Albivi
Kaskaskia	Amonokoa
Michigamea	Chepoussa
Moingwena	Chinko
Peoria	Coiracoentanon
Tamaroa	Espeminkia
*Illinois (Illiniwek)	Tapouaro

The Illinois migrated from the Pacific coast to the shores of Lake Michigan around AD 900. They migrated southwest perhaps in the hundred years before European contact. Jesuit missionaries made their first contact with the Illinois in 1667.

Father Jacques Marquette, S.J., encountered the Illinois on his journey south. in his exploration of the Mississippi River from the Great Lakes to the mouth of the Arkansas River in 1673. The Illinois were reportedly so pleased to have the French visiting them that they provided Marquette and fellow travelers with a peace pipe to use for the remainder of the journey. In 1680 La Salle made contact with the Illinois at the village of Pimitoui, ear Peoria. He built Fort Crèvecoeur (Broken Heart), which was later destroyed, after which he built Fort St. Louis, north of Crèvecoeur. The later years of the seventeenth century saw the Illinois at war with the Iroquois to the East and the Sioux to the West.

It was a Kaskaskia brave that murdered Chief Pontiac of the Ottawa in 1769 and brought the wrath of the northern tribes down on all the Illinois reducing them to just a fraction of their former strength. Disease also took a heavy toll. The Sauk and the Fox, themselves driven south out of Green Bay; the Kickapoo; and the Potawatomi dispossessed the greater part of those who remained. Remnants settled near Kaskaskia until they were removed to Kansas in 1832 where Jesuit missionary Fr. Charles Felix van Quickenborne made contact with them in 1835. (The Illinois relinquished all claims to land in present Indiana in the Treaty of Greenville in 1795.) What few of the Illinois that survived in Kansas were consolidated with the Wea and Piankashaw in 1867 in Indian Territory.

IONI

The Ioni inhabited Palo Pinto County or Anderson County, Texas. They have been often treated separately, and their name has several modern-day connections, for example, the Ioni Creek runs through Palo Pinto and Stephens counties and another, through Anderson County. No information is available on the Ioni other than the references in the *Handbook of Texas Online* and the fact that they were one of the eleven signatories (Chief Bead Eye) to the Tehuacana Creek Treaty of October 9, 1844, with the Republic of Texas. They were included in the treaty at Council Springs, Texas, on May 15, 1846, with the U.S. government.

IOWA

The Iowa spoke the Chiwerian dialect of the Siouan language group as did the Otoe and Missouri. All three tribes once belonged to the Ho-Chunk or Winnebago Nation in the Great Lakes region. At some point a large group separated themselves and migrated south. One group, the Iowa, settled along the Mississippi River. The Missouri settled along the Missouri River, and the Oto settled farther west. Chiwere was the common language.

The first reported contacts with the Iowa was in the late 1600s near the present village of Trempeleau, Wisconsin. They hunted in the valley of the Iowa River and in prairie west towards the Missouri. Well known to Canadian fur trappers, an Iowa delegation appeared in Montreal in the mid-1700s. The Iowa were also mentioned briefly in the journals of William Clark in 1804.

About 1815, the Iowas were located on the Chariton River in Missouri at the time that white settlers were pushing into central Missouri. Two years later the town of Chariton was laid out on the banks of the river just upstream from its confluence with the Missouri about thirty miles up river from Franklin, the center of white civilization in Missouri west of the Mississippi that soon thereafter moved west to Kansas City. (Chariton County was organized out of Howard County in 1821.)

IROQUOIS

George Catlin is one of the few known reporters who writes of a separate Iroquois tribe; and the one matter of which he was quite certain, "the Iroquois tribe did not belong to the Confederacy." He declares that the Mohawks were at one time a branch of Iroquois tribe and had become a important member of the Confederacy but the Iroquois proper moved their settlements farther to the north and east from the shores of the St. Lawrence to avoid the continual wars of the nations of the Iroquois Confederacy and that by the mid-1830s they were nearly extinct. Swanton makes no mention of an Iroquois proper and uses the name only in reference to the Iroquois Leaque or Confederacy of Nations.

Catlin gives as their original lands a vast tract of country on the St. Lawrence River between the banks of the river and Lake Champlain and that at one time they claimed all the lands to the shores of Lakes Erie, Michigan, and Huron. Catlin painted a full-length portrait of the chief of the Iroquois, *Not-way, The Thinker.*

IROQUOIS LEAGUE

Both the origin of the name Iroquois and the formation of the league have multiple versions. The name Iroquois originated from French adaptations of various Indian words. The most likely was the combination of the Ojibwe/Algonquian words *irin* (meaning real) and *ako* (meaning adders–i.e., enemies or snakes) that the French wrote as "Irinakhoiw" or "Iriakoiw" with the addition of the French *-ois* termination.

As to the formation of the Iroquois League, the Iroquois Confederacy or the Five Nations Confederacy, the most popular legend centers of the efforts involving Deganawidah (De-Kah-Na-Wi-Da), a Huron prophet and philosopher, who was aided in his work by Hiawatha. As the story goes, Deganawidah, also written Deganawi:dah, wondered among the Iroquois-speaking peoples of upper New York State preaching a gospel of unity, brotherhood and equality. Around 1570 he founded the League of the Great Peace. Historians Glatthaar and Martin write that "Iroquois storytellers described the formation of the league as the work of Mohawk named Deganawi:dah, assisted by an Oneida named Odatshehdeh (Quiver Bearer)." Deganawidah has also been described as a Huron by birth and a Mohawk by adoption (prevailing view) and an Onondaga by birth and Mohawk by adoption. Hiawatha, an Onondaga by birth, was also adopted by the Mohawk.

The league, later referred to as the Iroquois League or the Five Nations, stretched from the Niagara River at Lake Erie on the west to the Hudson River on the east, south of the Adirondack, south of Lake Ontario, and north of the Kaatsbergs (Catskill). The five tribes (later six) were of the Iroquoian linguistic stock. East to west from the Hudson River valley were the Mohawk, Oneida, (Tuscarora), Onondaga, Cayuga, and Seneca. The Seneca were by far the most numerous and occupied the largest stretch of land; the Mohawk the smallest.

The League or Five Nations was also referred to as the Confederated Indians or Canton Indians. The Iroquois were one of the largest and, arguably, one of the most important Native American groups in U.S. history. It was also important to the British in Canada. Reports put the population of the Iroquois League at some forty thousand at its peak. A mid-eighteenth century estimate puts the population of about ten thousand. The Confederacy was unique feat of democratic government based on the separation of political power and anchored in diplomacy and oral discussion, so much so that its structure served as an example for the colonists as they formulated the new Federal Constitution.

There was no Iroquois tribe proper. Anthropologically, the term also includes the Huron, their enemy to the north; the Petuns or Tobacco Indians; the Neutrals to the west; the Erie of New York; and the Susquehanna or Susquehannock of Pennsylvania. In 1712 they were joined by the first wave of the Tuscarora from North Carolina to whom the five were related—thus, the Six Nations or Haudenosaunee. Successive migrations of the Tuscarora continued through 1722. The remainder of the Tuscarora migrated north in 1802.

The Iroquois were a sedentary, agricultural people as were the Huron, the Tobacco, and the Neutral in contrast to the Algonquin and Chippewa. The antagonism between the Iroquois and the Huron arose because of their respective alliances with the European powers—the Iroquois allied with the English; the Huron, the French. Religion was also a factor. The Huron were open to the Christianity of the French Jesuit Missionaries; the Iroquois were adamantly opposed. Economic competition was another factor.

FIRST ENCOUNTERS

The Iroquoian-speaking tribes first encountered the Europeans in the 1530s in what became French Canada or New France about the site of present Quebec. The first record is found in the chronicles of explorer Jacques Cartier in 1534 followed by others including Samuel de Champlain in 1603 to whom credit is given for establishing the first true relations with the Iroquois. At this time the Hurons were in the area of Georgian Bay, and the Iroquois were in their historical homes in New York State having move down from the north.

Champlain took the side of the Huron and Algonquins. He fought alongside the Huron in 1609 and shot and killed two Iroquois chiefs. From that time on the Iroquois and Huron and their French allies were mortal enemies. Wars continued throughout the first half of the seventeenth century until the Iroquois launched a major expedition against the Huron in 1649-1650 that almost destroyed the Huron Nation. Many Huron survivors were adopted by the Five Nations; others roamed from one place to another before finally moving west and south where they became known as the Wyandot. A number settled about the French fort at Quebec under the protection of French guns. The Iroquois carried the war to the French throughout Canada and to the Tobacco and the Neutrals, almost destroying both tribes.

Armed with guns supplied by the Dutch at Albany, Iroquois war parties, sometimes numbering a thousand warriors or more, ranged as far west as the Mississippi River and south into Virginia and the Carolinas and east and north into New England. Between 1675 and 1677 after the English displaced the Dutch, the Five Nations formed an alliance with the English that has been called the Covenant Chain. The English agreed to support the Iroquois against the Algonquins along the coast, and in return the Iroquois agreed to attack the Algonquins in New England and to join with the English against the French in Canada. Each was to respect the other's sphere of influence, the Iroquois to the west and the English to the east.

In the Battle of Sandy Point, Ohio, in the late 1600s, the Iroquois defeated the Shawnee, staking claim to all of Kentucky. The Treaty of Ryswick in 1696 (1697) brought about a general peace and acknowledged the Iroquois' right to their western conquests, but at the 1744 Treaty of Lancaster, Pennsylvania, they were forced to cede all their lands in present West Virginia to the colony of Virginia. The Iroquois Confederacy's presence in the Ohio River Valley was severely reduced as a result.

SEVENTEEN HUNDREDS

In 1752 at Logstown on the Ohio, the Shawnee and other western tribes confirmed the Lancaster treaty and sold their claims to the country south of the Ohio. The peace treaty ending the Seven Years War or the French and Indian War as it was called in North America between the French and the British was signed in February 1763. The war brought the British to ascendancy in North America, and Indian relations with the white man took a dramatic turn. Trying to diffuse the an already tense situation and to head-off future conflict between the colonists and the Native Americans, the British King established by Royal Proclamation the western boundary beyond which white settlement was prohibited.

With the 1768 Treaty of Fort Stanwix, the by now Six Nations ceded their claim to Kentucky and Western Pennsylvania. The treaty also, in effect, replaced the 1763 Royal Proclamation Line with a new boundary between Indians and whites at the Ohio, Susquehanna, and Unadilla rivers. Over thirty-one hundred Indians attended the conference, three-quarters of whom were Iroquois. Other tribes represented were the Chugnut, Conoy, Delaware, Minisink, Nanticoke, Shawnee, and Tutelo. With the treaty the British also allowed (or encouraged, accepted, or demanded) the Iroquois cession of the Ohio Valley lands belonging to the Delaware, Shawnee, and Mingo. They, in turn, vowed to fight to retain their rights. To put it another way, the British simply ignored the rights of the other tribes in order to obtain the concessions they wanted from the Iroquois in the north. Regardless, the new boundary line was a porous as the previous Proclamation Line to the settlers of Virginia and Pennsylvania. (Similarly, with the Treaty of Camp Charlotte in October 1774 one group of Shawnee signed over most of what is now the state of Kentucky to the colony of Virginia without the approval of the rest of the Shawnee and without any regard for the Cherokee, whose land it was.)

AMERICAN REVOLUTIONARY WAR

The Albany Conference of 1775 confirmed the alliance between the Six Nations and the colonies, but only as neutrals. As the War for Independence unfolded, the Mohawk, Seneca, Cayuga, and Onondaga sided with the British; the Oneida and their dependents, the Tuscarora, sided with the colonists—primarily because they resented the favoritism the British had shown to the Mohawk and to Chief Thayendanegea (Joseph Brant) in particular. As a consequence, the war that secured American independence from Britain destroyed Iroquois power forever.

In the course of the Revolutionary War, George Washington ordered the Iroquois Campaigns of 1778-1779 that ended with the Iroquois Expedition commanded by Maj. General John Sullivan in 1779. The 4000-man expeditionary force that included several Oneida scouts covered 500 miles. Before it returned to its base at Elmira, forty Iroquois towns had been destroyed. The expedition fought the bloody Battle of Newtown as it was called on August 29 against a combined force of one thousand Loyalists and Indians led by Chief Joseph Brant. The colonials matched the cruelty and brutality of the Indians one for one. It may be said that they outdid them. The campaign was the climax of the ongoing conflict between the Iroquois and the American colonists that would have come sooner or later. A generation of warriors was lost; and, as the war came to a close, the Iroquois found themselves homeless. For more see below.

The British set aside land for them on the Grand River in Ontario, due west of the western tip of the lake, primarily for the Mohawk and their leader Joseph Brant. Brant so dominated the community that it became known as Brant's Town. Another postwar site was set aside on Buffalo Creek at the northeast tip of Lake Erie at the Niagara River. A cluster of villages was laid out that soon became the political hub of the Iroquois Nation—primarily Seneca, Cayuga, Onondaga. Eventually, many returned to their homelands to the south. Allies of the colonies in the fight for independence the Oneida and their dependents, the Tuscarora, were allowed to remain on their home lands in perpetuity, or so they thought.

Over the next twenty-five years, Iroquois lands were systematically stolen from them by settlers and the colonial governments, particularly that of Governor George Clinton of New York. The Indians were given reservations just a fraction of the size of their home lands. The Oneida and Tuscarora fared no better than the others. The Oneida were reduced to a 250,000-acre reservation; the Cayuga and Onondaga, 64,000 acres each. During this period, there was the continuing contest between land speculators, individual settlers, swindlers, and the states of New York, Pennsylvania, and Massachusetts over who would take the most from the Indian tribes first. Even Christian ministers joined the fray. There was also an ongoing political battled between the state governments and their States' Rights supporters like Clinton and Thomas Jefferson and the federalist administrations of Washington, Adams, Hamilton, and Knox.

One of the most glaring thefts of Indian lands was encapsulated in the Treaty of Fort Schuyler of September 22, 1784, by which the state of New York, in the mask of a benevolent rescuer, acquired some five million acres of land from the Oneida. On February 25, 1789, a few minor chiefs from a small community of Cayuga signed away the entire Cayuga homeland that had stretched from the New York-Pennsylvania border to Lake Ontario. Representatives of the Cayuga main bodies on Buffalo Creek and Grand River were not invited to participate.

FINAL SETTLEMENT

The Oneida and Tuscarora were eventually settled near Green Bay. The majority of the Mohawk remained in Canada. The nineteenth century Seneca of Oklahoma included remnants of all the Iroquoian-speaking tribes. For more see the respective members of the League.

WESTERN EXPEDITION AGAINST THE SIX NATIONS

As news of depredations and killings by the Iroquois allied with the British reached General George Washington, he diverted troops from the eastern battlefront to reduce the Indians in a scorched-earth campaign. Washington sent four separate forces into the field. Colonel Goose Van Schaick left Fort Schuyler in April and attacked the main Onondaga village. He destroyed the village, killed twelve, and took thirty-three prisoners although most of the warriors were away at Niagara at the time. The soldiers were also accused of raping and killing captured women.

As spring turned to summer, Colonel Daniel Broadhead moved against Seneca villages in the Allegheny Valley from his base at Pittsburgh; General James Clinton led a brigade from the Mohawk River Valley down the Susquehanna to Tioga Point; and General John Sullivan marched up the Susquehanna from Wyoming to join Clinton at Tioga on August 22. The combined force of some 4,000 men moved out into Indian territory. Throughout the Allegheny Valley, about the Finger Lakes, and in the Genesee River Valley, Iroquois villages, crops, and orchards were systematically destroyed.

Sullivan's main force turned back on September 15, reaching Tioga again on September 30. Sullivan claimed the destruction of forty villages, including Kanadasega, and at least 160,000 bushels of corn. The neutral Mohawks at Tiononderoge were also dispossessed and thrown into prison until Washington ordered them freed. Their lands, however, were quickly claimed by envious settlers. The soldiers themselves had made mental note of the fertile lands of the Seneca for future reference.

A British relief column from Canada found 5,000 Iroquois refugees at Niagara on October 5. The Iroquois, for their part, angered by the destruction of their villages, resumed their raids on the white villages and their Oneida and Tuscarora allies in the Spring 1780 causing a sizable number to defect to the British. The Oneida villages of Kanaghsoraga and Old Oneida were abandoned, and Kanonwalohale was destroyed. A few Oneida surrendered, but over four hundred Oneida took refuge at Fort Schuyler and moved their families to Schenectady. The Americans vacated Fort Schuyler in the spring of 1781 leaving the area vulnerable to raids. By the end of 1781, the Iroquois and loyalist raiders had destroyed most of the American settlements in the Mohawk valley, reportedly leaving 2,000 orphans and 380 widows.

JAY TREATY

At the end of November 1782, the Americans and the British reached a settlement that produced the Treaty of Paris or the Treaty of Peace as it was often called that was signed September 3, 1783, officially ending the American War of Independence. Of critical importance to both nations and to several thousand American Indians in the region was the establishment of the northern boundary between the United States and Canada. The Six Nations of the Iroquois believed that they were betrayed by the British. The new boundary left the Iroquois on the American side of the border leaving them alone to fight the onslaught of settlers into their lands and the machinations of state authorities, particularly the state of New York, to take their lands from them.

Yet the British did not withdraw from Fort Niagara and the other border outposts as promised in the 1783 treaty. Nor did they use the posts to protect the Iroquois or support their interests. The northern reaches became a form of limbo, but that in itself slowed the advancing Americans. At least it made the advancing hordes hesitate. The status lasted for eleven years. It was not until the treaty negotiated by John Jay(Treaty of Amity Commerce and Navigation) in November 19, 1794 that the British finally agreed to withdraw. It was not until August 1796 that American forces occupied Fort Niagara. The Jay Treaty, along with other events of the day, established new bounds and new rules that shackled the once proud Confederacy of Nations.

Of Note

Following the War of 1812, several dozen Iroquois braves traveled west to Oregon country with fur traders from the North West Company. Many of them had previously been Baptized by French Jesuits at missions along the St. Lawrence River. Among the group was Ignace la Mousee. His name was taken from that of Saint Ignatius of Loyola, the founder of the Society of Jesus. Ignace and many of the others joined the Flathead (Salish) and became the first to introduce the western Indians to Christianity—the first Indian missionaries.

Iroquois Land Cessions

The following list of selected land cessions involving the Iroquois present a vivid an example of the machinations of the white man in securing Indians lands.

-Annexation of 1782. All Cayuga and Onondaga lands were annexed by the New York state legislature.

-Federal Cession, October 22, 1784, Fort Stanwix. Attended by Oneida and their allies and dependents: Akwesasne, Kahnawake, Mohican, Tuscarora, Brotherton plus a nominal representation from the Cayuga, Mohawk, Onondaga, Seneca under the "protection" of one hundred armed militia. The Indians ceded a tract of land around Fort Stanwix at Oswego; a four-mile strip of land along the Niagara River; and all lands west of the mouth of Buffalo Creek. The Six Nations council at Buffalo Creek disavowed the treaty, but the government ignored the disavowal. (The treaty of 1794 established the boundaries for the individual tribes.)

-Pennsylvania Cession, October 23, 1784. The state of Pennsylvania procured all remaining Iroquois lands in the state for $5,000 in goods.

-Fort Herkimer Cession, near German Flats, June 23-June 27, 1785. The state of New York paid $11,500 for 460,000 Oneida acres . Within two years it had sold 343,594 acres for $125,955.

-Livingston Lease, at Kanadasetga, November 30, 1787. Speculators leased thirteen million acres of Seneca, Cayuga, and Onondaga land for $20,000 plus $2,000 annually for 999 years.

-Butler Lease, Buffalo Creek, 1787.

-Livingston Lease at Kanonwalohale, January 8, 1788. Speculators leased five million acres of Oneida land for 999 years.

-Oliver Phelps & Nathaniel Gorbam Purchase, July 8, 1788. From the Livingston and Butler leases, twelve million acres of the land were divided into three sections. The western third west of the Genesee River, Seneca land, was relinquished. The middle third between the Genesee and Seneca Lake went to Phels and Gorbam. The speculators retained the rights to eastern third but would have to fight the state of New York over the title.

-Onondaga Cession, 1789.

-Treaty at Fort Harmar on January 9, 1789, renewed and confirmed the 1784, Treaty at Fort Stanwix. The Shawnee were given no say in the matter. To the outside world they had lost all claim to the land to the Iroquois. (In 1775 the Cherokee ceded most of their claims to Kentucky.)

-John Richardson & Squatters Lease, 1791. Speculators leased 99 square miles of the 100 square miles of the Cayuga Lake Reservation for $500 annually for twenty years, payable half in cattle.

-June 1798 and 1820. Oneida ceded 30,000 acres and 11,000 acres, respectively to the state of New York for $500 and $900 plus annuities. The two cessions reduced the Oneida reservation to 75,000 acres or two percent of the postwar lands.

-October 1794. Over sixteen hundred Iroquois assembled at Canandaigua to the west of the Finger Lakes and south of Lake Ontario to treat with Timothy Pickering the federal treaty commissioner. It was the largest assemblage of the Six Nations since Fort Stanwix in 1768. The Treaty of Canandaigua was concluded November 11. The Iroquois relinquished all claims to the Erie Triangle to the state of Pennsylvania and in return received most of the Niagara River tract and one million acres above Buffalo Creek. It was the first and only treaty by which the Iroquois actually recovered land. The treaty was ratified in January 1795.

> The Erie Triangle was a tract of land of 800,000 acres on the western edge of the state of Pennsylvania lying between the Pennsylvania-New York boundary and the southern shore of Lake Erie. The state had purchased the tract from the federal government in September 1788, having paid $2,000 to Iroquois Chief Cornplanter at Fort Harmar in January 1789 to extinguish the Iroquois claim. The problem was that Cornplanter did not speak for the Buffalo Creek and Grand River chiefs, who denied the validity of the purchase. Canandaigua cleared the issued.

-Peter Smith-New York State Cession, September 15, 1795. Oneida ceded 120,000 acres.

-Big Tree Cession of September 16, 1796. For a lowly $100,000, the Seneca ceded all but 200,000 acres of the four million acres of Seneca land.

IRUSITSU

The Irusitsu was a subdivision of the Shasta. They lived in Scott Valley, California. For more see Shasta.

ISANTHCAG-NA

Isanthcag-na was a sub-tribe of the Tongva of California that inhabited the area about Mission Vieja. For more see Tongva.

ISLAND CHUMASH

The Island Chumash was one of the eight dialectic and geographical divisions of the Chumash of the Southern California coast. The Island Chumash lived on the San Miguel, Santo Rosa, and Santa Cruz islands. For more see the Chumash.

ISLETA PUEBLO

The Isleta or Ysleta Pueblo (Little Island) belonged to the Tiwa Pueblo of the Tanoan linguistic family now part of the Kiowa-Tanoan stock. Isleta and the Sandia formed one of the three Tiwa divisions. Isleta, established in the 1300s, was located about fifteen miles southwest of present-day Albuquerque in the Rio Grande valley. It was first entered by Coronado in 1540 and in 1582-3 by Espejo. Saint Augustine church was built on the plaza between 1612 and 1630 following the conquest of New Mexico by the Spanish. The pueblo was so named by the Spanish because was located on a projection of land.

With the Pueblo Revolt in 1680, many Isleta fled to the Hopi in Arizona; others accompanied the Spanish south to El Paso. The pueblo was used as a base camp by Governor Otermín in his failed attempt to retake New Mexico from the Puebloans in November and December 1681. Otermín returned to El Paso with 385 loyal people from Isleta who would very likely have been killed had they been left behind. For more see Pueblo Peoples and Tiwa Pueblo.

ITAZIPCO

The Itazipco or San(s) Arc "Without Bow" was a subgroup of the Western Sioux, Lakota Titunwan. For more see Sioux and Lakota.

ITHKYEMAMITS

The Ithkyemamits was of the Lower Chinook division of the Chinookan family that inhabited coastal Oregon. Whether the Ithkyemamits was an independent tribe, sub-tribe, or village is unknown.

IWAI

Iwai was a village of the Yaquina located on the north side of the Yaquina River in Oregon that has generally been treated separately. For more see Yaquina.

JAMECO

The Jameco or Yamecah "beaver" were of the Algonquian linguistic group. They lived along Beaver Stream and about Beaver Pond on Long Island, New York, and inhabited the northern shore of Jamaica Bay in the Queens Borough to which they gave their name as well as to the town of Jamaica that became the colonial capital of Queens. The Jameco may have been a sub-tribe of the Canarsee.

JEAGA

The Jeaga lived about the present Jupiter Inlet on the east coast of Florida and were probably of Muskhogean stock. It is believed that they merged with the Ais or Tequesta or others from the east coast

JELAN

The Jelan was the name recorded by Drake for a band of Comanche that lived on the sources of the Brazos and Del Norte rivers in Texas.

JEMEZ PUEBLO

The Jemez (pronounced "Hay-mess" or traditionally as "He-mish") and Pecos constituted a distinct group within the Tiwa Pueblo of the Tanoan linguistic stock that is now part of the Kiowa-Tanoan stock. Tu'-wa was their own name. The Jemez came from the north and lived in twenty-nine villages along the north bank of the Jemez River about twenty miles west of Bernalillo in north central New Mexico. By 1622 they were concentrated into the pueblos of Giusewa or Gyusiwa and possibly Astialakwa.

Astialakwa was located on a mesa that separated the San Diego and Guadalupe canyons. Giusewa, which was located on a bend of the Jemez River a mile north of Jamez Hot Springs, was relatively small in size compared to Pecos or Gran Quivera. The original mission of San José de los Jemez was established about 1600 by Fray Alonzo de Lugo, who served all the Jemez people scattered among at least eleven villages. He left a year later and was followed by a succession of priests. The San José mission was built Fray Zarate Salmeron in 1621-1622. The mission and pueblo now constitute the Jemez State Monument. Fr. Salmeron subsequently established a second mission, San Diego de la Congregacion, at the site of modern Jemez Pueblo.

The Jemez were among the leaders of the Pueblo Revolt of 1680 against the Spanish. In 1694 they were attacked by the Spanish who destroyed their pueblos, killed 84 Indians and took 361 prisoners. Those that survived lived in the Jemez pueblo. Following a 1696 revolt, the Jemez fled to the Navaho country where they remained for a time before returning to their own land. There they joined the Navajo in the repulse of Roque Madrid's attack on August 12, 1705. A portion of the Jemez homeland now lies it what has been since 1905 the Santa Fe National Forest.

JICARILLA

The Jicarilla (hek-a-REH-ya) belonged to the Athapascan linguistic stock and with the Lipan constitute the Eastern Division of the Apache nation although some reports incorrectly classify the Jicarilla as distinct from the Apache proper. Although they at times ranged across parts of Kansas, Oklahoma, and Texas, their home land was in southeastern Colorado and northern New Mexico on either side of the Rio Pueblo (Pueblo River).

It is believed that the Jicarilla were among the Querechos whom Coronado met in 1540-1542. Later Spanish explorers knew them as Vaqueros. They were not mentioned by their own name until 1733 in Taos, New Mexico. In the mid-1700s they lost much of their lands to the Comanches to the east, the Ute to the north, and the Navajo to the west. The Senate refused to ratify a 1853 treaty with the Jicarilla who responded by going on the warpath until defeated by the army in 1854.

The Jicarilla lived on the Maswell grant in northeastern New Mexico until it was sold. Although assigned to Fort Stanton, most were permitted to go to Tierra Amarilla on a 900 square mile reservation set aside in 1874. A new reservation was established for them on the Navajo River in 1880 where they remained until 1883 when they were transferred to Fort Stanton. In 1887 they were given a new reservation by executive order in the Tierra Amarilla region. Dating back to 1845, the Jicarilla tribe never numbered more than eight hundred. For more see Apache.

Note

Apache Stone Bluff was the big stone bluff on the south bank of the Arkansas River across from Bent's New Fort four miles below Mud or Boggey Creek. It was there in holes and crevices that the bodies of the Jicarilla Apaches who died in the smallpox epidemic of 1854 were buried. It may be the same site referred to as Point of Rocks.

JOSHUA

The Joshua or Chemetunne was a band of the Tututini that lived just north of the Rogue River in Oregon that is generally treated separately.

JUANEÑO

The Juaneño were of the Shoshonean Division of the Uto-Aztecan linguistic family. They inhabited the area generally from the coast of California to the crest of the southern continuation of the Sierra Santa Ana. The name was derived from the mission of San Juan Capistrano.

JUPE

The Jupe (or Hupene, Yupini; also known as People of the Timber) was one of the sub-tribes or bands of the Comanche. For more see Comanche.

KA'TE'NU'A'KA'

The Ka'te'nu'a'ka' (People of the submerged pine tree) was one of the three tribes or subdivisions of the Tuscarora confederacy.

KADAPAUS

The Kadapaus inhabited the Catawba-Wateree Valley of North Carolina. Other inhabitants of the valley included the Sugerees and Esaws. Consolidated they became known as the Catawba. For more see Catawba.

KADOHADACHO

The Kadohadacho proper was a Caddoan tribe and gave their name to the Kadohadacho Confederacy of which they constituted one of its six subdivisions. They lived on the north side of the Red River near where it reaches the Arkansas-Oklahoma border.

The Kadohadacho moved off the Red River in the 1790s to avoid the Osage depredations and slave-raiding and settled between the Sabine River and Caddo Lake, generally along the boundary between the territory of Louisiana and what was then the province of Texas. Most of the Kadohadachos remained in the Caddo Lake area until about 1842, although with the cession of Caddoan lands in Louisiana in 1835 and ever-increasing white settlement, others moved to the Brazos River in north central Texas.

The Kadohadacho and their allies signed a treaty in 1835 by which they gave up their lands for land in Texas near the Hasinai. Thereafter the fortunes of the two groups followed closely together under the name Caddo. Some united with the Cherokee; some with the Chickasaw. A reservation was setup for the Caddo in Texas along the Brazos River in 1852. In 1859 they were removed to Indian Territory. For more see Kadohadacho Confederacy, Hasinai Confederacy, and Caddo Peoples.

KADOHADACHO CONFEDERACY

The Kadohadachho Confederacy was one of the main divisions of the Caddo Peoples. From the abbreviation of their name comes the name Caddo. Their home land was in northeastern Texas and southwestern Arkansas at the Great Bend of the Red River. Later the occupied the region around Caddo Lake. The confederacy was comprised of six principal tribes or subdivisions.

PRINCIPAL TRIBES
Kadohadacho Proper
Cahinnio
Nanatsoho
Upper Nasoni
Upper Natchitoches
Upper Yataas

KAH MILT-PAH

The Kah milt-pah was a sub-tribe of the Yakima that is sometimes referred to separately. In the 1855 Yakima treaty at Camp Stevens, the Kah milt-pah ceded all their lands to the government and settled on the Yakima Reservation. For more see Yakima.

KAHANSUK

The Kahansuk was a sub-tribe of the Unalachtigo division of the Delaware. They lived in the area about Low Creek in Cumberland County, Delaware. For more see Unalachtigo and Delaware.

KAHOSADI SHASTA

The Kahosadi was a subdivision of the Shasta that lived on the affluents of the Rogue River in California. For more see Shasta

KAIBAB

The Kai'vav-wits or Kaibab was village of the Southern Paiute in the vicinity of Kanab or the Kaibab Plateau. It has also been classified as sub-tribe or subdivision of the Paiute.

KAINAI BLACKFEET

The Kainai or Kainah or Blood Indians constituted one of the three tribes of the Blackfeet Nation that spoke a dialect of the basic Algonquian language. They inhabited the middle ground between the Sisika group to the north and Piegan to the south. By the mid-19th century, the Blood had moved farther south to the Pakowki Lake, Belly River, and the Teton River regions and often ranged far into Montana. Bull Back Fat (2nd), Chief of the Blood, made peace with the Americans in 1831, permitting them to open trading posts on the Upper Missouri River. Aided by their Piegan brothers, the Kainai defeated a large force of Cree and Assiniboin warriors who had attacked their camps on the Oldman and St. Mary rivers on October 18, 1870, thanks primarily to use of the newly acquired repeating rifle that they had received from traders Healy and Hamilton at trade at Fort Woop Up.

The Blood signed Treaty No. 7 with the Canadian government September 22, 1877, and were given a reserve adjacent to the Northern Blackfeet on the Bow River. In 1880 they moved to a new site between the St Mary River and Belly River at what became the largest Indian Reserve in Canada. The Blood launched a successful ranching industry. After the turn of the century, they became large-scale farmers. By 1996, the population was 8,338. For more see Blackfeet.

KAIQUARIEGAHAGA

Little is known about the Kaiquariegahaga except for a reference that suggests that they may have been a subdivision or clan of the Susquehanna. For more see Susquehanna.

KALAPUYA PEOPLES

The Kalapuya Peoples (also Calapooya, Calapooia, or Kalapooia) formed the Kalapooian (also Kalapuyan) linguistic family that inhabited western Oregon. They are generally regarded related to the Penutian linguistic stock. The Kalapuya Indians were the first people to settle in the Willamette Valley. The also inhabited the valley of the Umpqua River in present Douglas County, Washington.

The Kalapuyan included eight recognized tribes and thirteen groups divided into three linguistic divisions: Northern Kalapuya, Central Kalapuya, and Yocalla or Southern Kalapuya. The following breakdown is taken from Native American Tribes of North America.

NORTHERN GROUP
1. Tualatin
2. Yamhill

CENTRAL (Calapooya) GROUP
3. Chafan
4. Long Tom (Chelamela)
5. Luckiamute
6. Mary's River (Chepenefa)
7. Mohawk
8. Muddy Creek (Chemapho)
9. Pudding River (Ahantchuyuk)
10. Santiam
11. Tsankupi
12. Winefelly

SOUTHERN GROUP
13. Yoncalla

LISTING FROM *SMOKE SIGNALS*
1. Tualatin (Wapato Lake)
2. Yamhill
3. Ahantchuyuk (Pudding River)
4. Luckiamute
5. Santiam
6. Mary's River Band (Chepenafa)
7. Chemapho (Maddy Band)
8. Tsankupi
9. Tsanchifin (McKenzie)
10. Mohawk River
11. Chelemela (Long Tom River)
12. Winnefelly
13. Yonkalla (Umpqua Kalapuya) - Northern

The Kalapuya as a people were devastated by a malaria epidemic in 1831-1834 that took upwards of seventy-five percent of their population. A measles epidemic in 1848 also hit them extremely hard. Those that survived were forced to cede their lands to the government in the treaties of 1854 and 1855 and were placed on the Grande Ronde Reservation.

KALISPEL

The Kalispel or Pend d'Oreilles (because they wore large shell earrings) were part of the interior division of the Salishan Family. They inhabited the area about Pend Oreille River and Lake, Priest Lake, and the lower course of the Clark's Fork in Washington, Idaho and Montana. They may also have ranged as far as Thompson Lake and Horse Plains and over the Salmon River Country in Canada. There were three major divisions: Upper Kalispel (Pend d'Oreilles); Lower Kalispel (Pend d'Oreilles) or Kalispel Proper; and Chewelah.

The Kalispel met Lewis & Clark in 1805, and a trading post was established on the Pend Oreille Lake by the Northwest Company with another on Clark Fork (Salish House). The American Fur Company also courted them, and in 1840s Catholic missionaries arrived. In the late fall of 1841, Jesuit John Paul De Smet visited the Kalispel camp on a bay of Lake Pend Oreille and again in the spring of 1842. Later that year, the Jesuits established Saint Michael's Mission on the Pend Oreille River near the present-day town of Albeni Falls, Idaho, directed by Father Peter De Vos. In 1845, Fr. De Smet relocated the mission up the Pend Oreille River at the Bay of the Kalispels, a more isolated location that would help avoid contact with white settlers. He renamed the mission Saint Ignatius Loyola.

The Kalispel ceded all their lands to the government in 1855 except for an area about Flathead Lake that became the Jocko Reservation where the greater part of the Kalispel settled. Others joined the Okanagon, Colville, and others on the Colville Reservation.

KAMIA

The Kamia were of the Yman Division of the Hokan family. A very small tribe, they inhabited portions of the Imperial Valley and the banks of the sloughs that connected it with the Colorado River.

KAMMATWA SHASTA

Kammatwa or Wiruhikwairuk'a was a subdivision of the Shasta that lived on the Klamath River in California. For more see Shasta.

KAN-HATKI

The Kan-hatki was a sub-tribe or division of the Muskogee and a member of the Creek Confederacy that inhabited parts of Alabama.

KANAWAKE

Kahnawake (also spelled Kahnawá:ke and Kanawaké) or Kanienkehaka "People of the Flint" (also known as the Caughnawaga) was a early community of Catholic Indians, primarily Mohawks and Oneidas. They are generally treated separately in the literature. The Kahnawake Catholic mission was established on the Saint Lawrence River opposite Montréal in 1667 by Iroquois converts to Christianity and French Jesuit missionaries. Kahnawake was populated mostly by Mohawks, but there were also many Onondagas and Oneidas and few captured English colonists. The Mohawk language was spoken, and Mohawk customs followed or modified to reflect their new Catholic faith.

The purpose of the mission was to consolidate Christian families to protect them from temptations and persecution. As the population of Montreal increased, the site was moved farther upstream to minimize interactions with the whites. This second site was the scene of the life and death of the Blessed Catherine Tekakwitha (d. 1680). In 1890 a granite monument was erected on the site in her memory.

The years 1689 and 1696 found the mission community at new locations. The fifth move in 1716 brought the inhabitants to the present site of the Kanawaké Mohawk Reservation located on the south bank of the St. Lawrence River about ten miles above Montréal. With a population of approximately 8,000, it is one of seven communities that comprise the Mohawk Nation. It is also known as the Caughnawaga or Sault (Rapids) St. Louis Reservation.

The original Caughnawaga village was in the valley of the Mohawk on the south bank of the Mohawk River near the site of present Auriesville, New York, forty miles west of Albany. The site was variously known as Ossernenon, Gandawaga and Caughnawaga. It was from here that Christian families removed to Kanawake. Kateri, the Lily of the Mohawks, was born at Kanawake in 1656, the daughter of a Christian

Algonquin mother and a non-Christian Mohawk chief. It was also the site of the murder of three early missionaries.

The Kanawaké distinguished themselves in the War of 1812 as they allied themselves with the British in defeating the invading Americans. For more see Kateri (Catherine) Tekakwitha and the Saint Regis.

KANSA

The Kansa Indians or Kaw, also known as the South Wind People, were of the Dhegiha Siouan language group. Modern history found them east of the Mississippi River between 1500 and 1600 possibly at the confluence of the Ohio and Wabash rivers. Over the next hundred years they moved or were pushed steadily westward, first across the Mississippi then across the Missouri into Kansas Territory. In 1673, Farther Marquette noted the "Kansa" on his map as one of the Missouri River tribes. Throughout their existence as a free people, they would be continually surrounded by more powerful neighbors. At their peak, they numbered about 1,600 and lived in pole-frame lodges covered with bark.

Having crossed the Missouri by the early 1700s, the Kansa inhabited the area at the juncture of the Kansas and Missouri rivers (Kawsmouth). They cultivated corn, pumpkins, beans and melons and went on buffalo hunts twice a year. They also hunted beaver, otter and deer. Efforts to covert them to white man's ways and the white man's religion over the years proved futile as the Kansa remained a proud people clinging to their traditional ways in spite of hardships they suffered even after their removal.

Their first contacts with the white man were the early French fur traders and explorers who ascended the Missouri River hoping to trade goods with the natives. A Frenchman who was to have a profound impact on the Missouri River tribes, Éttienne de Véniard, sieru de Bourgmont, surveyed the Missouri and later constructed a post that he named Fort d'Orleans in honor of the Duke of Orléans on the bank of the Missouri River near villages of the Little Osage and the Missouri tribe near present-day Brunswick in Clariton County. It was the western-most French post in Upper Louisiana. (See more on Bourgmont in the Osage.)

Bourgmont led a party of Osage and Missouri Indians and French soldiers for a visit to the Kansa village at Doniphan in 1724. His dual mission was to establish trade relations with the Kansa and to broker a peace settlement between the Osage, Kansa, Missouri, and Padouca The Padouca were often the victims in the Indian slave trade practiced by the Kansa. They all assembled in October 1724 at the Grand Village of the Padouca (Plains Apache) near present-day Ellsworth, Kansas, some ten days journey west of the main Kansa village. In name at least, Bourgmont was successful, returning to Fort d'Orleans in that November.

Because of the importance of the lower Kansas River Valley to the fur trade and the location of Kansa Indians near the juncture of the Kansas and Missouri rivers, the French established Fort de Cavagnial (Cavagnolle), named for the new French governor of Louisiana, in 1745 near the principal Kansa village at the northern boundary of the present-day Fort Leavenworth Reservation. The French evacuated the fort in 1764.

Over the ensuing decades, the Kansa were nearly decimated by outbreaks of smallpox and cholera and continual warring with their neighbors, especially the Black Pawnee on the Republican River and later the Platte and with the Otoe to the north. Often portrayed as the victim because of their relatively small population, the Kansa were far from innocent. One member of the St. Louis Missouri Fur Company wrote in 1809, "The Cansas have long been the terror of their neighboring tribes, their temerity is hardly credible…" Another observer considered them "the greatest scoundrels of the

Missouri." One incident, "so destitute of honor," was the massacre of some sixty women and children in December 1840 in a village of the Republican Pawnee about ten days ride from their home at Medicine Creek. On the other hand they could be overly generous, giving away the food they had so little of to "most any tribe" that asked.

The Kansa gave their name to the Kansas River and to the towns of Kansas City, Missouri, and Kansas City, Kansas. Father Nicholas Point, S.J., who drew a map of the Town of Kanzas or Frenchtown in 1840, mistakenly labeled his map Plan de Westport (Missouri). Other names for the "town" were Kawsmouth, Kansasmouth, Chouteau's, and Westport Landing and finally Kansas City. The Kansas or Kaw river that we know today was the Kanzas, written in French as *Rivière des Kanzas*.

The Spanish map of tribal Locations produced in 1775 showed the Kansa near the mouth of the Kansas River. Pushed out of Kawsmouth by white settlers and more powerful tribes, the Kansa relocated along the lower Kansas River Valley between the mouth of the Big Blue (Earth) River and Stranger Creek.

In September of 1818 the Kansa agreed to cede all rights to a portion of the lands they claimed in Missouri in exchange for an annuity. The treaty was never ratified. Congress and the administration wanted the Kansa out of Missouri territory all together. In a treaty agreed to in June 1825, the Kansa ceded claims and title to all lands within the State of Missouri and all lands west of Missouri in exchange for a Kansas reserve thirty miles wide beginning twenty leagues (about 60 miles) west of the mouth of the Kansas River and extending west to the present Kansas-Colorado border, a considerable expanse of territory.

The reserve defined in the treaty of 1825 was ceded to the United States in a treaty concluded in 1846 that provided a significantly diminished reserve of 256,000 acres in the Upper Neosho Valley south of Fort Riley that included the town of Council Grove. (The town took its name from the site of a meeting held in 1825 between the Osage and the government commissioners to negotiate passage across what was then Osage lands for what was to become the Santa Fe Trail.) In August 1825 the commissioners had concluded a treaty with the Kansa for the same purpose to insure free use of the trail.

With the passage of the Kansas-Nebraska Act of 1854, all of Kansas Territory, including the land of the Kansa, were overrun by squatters, land jobbers, and speculators. By 1857, with a total population of about 1,000, they were totally dependent on the government for their very existence. The last step before being expelled from the state was the treaty concluded in 1859 that ceded to the government in trust 176,000 of the 256,000-acre Kansa reserve, leaving the Kansa only 80,000 acres that was divided into individual 40-acre plots. After abortive attempts to conclude a removal treaty in 1864, 1867, and 1869, Congress approved the sale of the diminished Neosho reserve in small tracts in 1872. The Kansa were to give up their last small foothold in the Neosho Valley. On June 4, 1873, the Kansa began their trek to a 100,137 acre reserve on the southern border of Kansas that constitutes a portion of Kay County, Oklahoma, east of the Arkansas River. They purchased the land from the Osage in 1874. By the end of the month the removal of the Kansa had been completed without incident. The Neosho land was in turn sold between 1874 and 1876.

The Osage, the Kansa, the Ponca, and Otoe-Missouri successfully fought to hold onto their four reserves in Indian Territory in the face of the Cherokee Commission's aggressive campaign conducted between 1890 and 1893 to clear the Native Americans from western Oklahoma. (Indian Territory became Oklahoma Territory on May 2, 1890.) Eleven other tribes had agreed to sell their lands totaling fifteen million acres back to the government opening the way for white settlement. The reserves of the four holdouts formed a compact area on the southern border of Kansas just west of the 96th meridian and west from the site of present Bartlesville, Oklahoma.

The history of the Kansa, like many other Native American tribes, can be summed up in the words of their last government agent in Kansas in 1870. He declared that the Kansa "have been so badly dealt with in former years—that they have but little confidence in white men of any class." Today the Kaw Nation is located in Kay County in north central Oklahoma. Of the population of 2,084 tribal members, about 25 percent reside in and around Kay County.

KARANKAWA

The Karankawa proper or Carancaquaca was one of the five principal Karankawan Tribes. Comprised of several bands, they lived on Matagorda Bay in Texas. Although they were only one of five, all five were often grouped together under their name. There are also instances in the literature where the Karankawa are listed as two separate tribes, Karan and Kawa. Although there have been attempts to qualify the term, the Karankawa were cannibals. They ate captured enemy warriors to obtain the magic power of the dead. The practice was not uncommon among the tribes of Texas and Mexico, especially in the pre-historic period. Overall, the reputation that has come down through history has not been good—whether wholly justified or not is subject to debate.

Their first contact with Europeans was Spanish explorer Cabeza de Vaca who became shipwrecked on Galveston Island in 1528. In 1685, La Salle built Fort St. Louis which the French maintained for two years before being driven out by the Spanish under De Leon. Over the ensuing years, many Karankawa were captured and enslaved by the Spanish. Mission Rosario, four miles west of Goliad, that was founded in 1754 by Franciscans from the College of Zacatecas in Mexico to serve them, but they never took well to the Spanish mission system. The Karankawa began to disappear in the early 1800s, and by 1850 they appear to have disappeared completely.

KARANKAWAN TRIBES

The Karankawan tribes of Texas constituted an independent division of the Caddo linguistic family. The five principal and four allied tribes lived along the Gulf coast between Trinity Bay and Arkansas Bay. They are all commonly referred to in the literature as Karankawa. The Indians were pushed into the Gulf marshes and islands and racked by European diseases first by the Spanish and then by the Anglo-Texan settlements that sprung up along the coast. By 1850 they were extinct.

PRINCIPAL TRIBES (Swanton)
Coapite
Coaque (Cocos)
Karankawa proper
Kohani
Kapok (Copanes)

ALLIED TRIBES (Swanton)
Pataquilla
Quilotes
Tiopane
Tups

OTHER TRIBES OR VILLAGES
(probably Karankawan)
Cujames
Ebahamo
Emet
Kouyam
Meracouman
Quara
Quinet
Toyal

INHABITED THE SAME AREA
(unknown whether linguistically connected)
Ahehouen
Ahouerhopiheim
Arhau
Chorruco
Doguenes
Kabaye
Kiabaha
Kopano
Las Mulas
Mariames
Mendica
Mora
Ointemarhen
Omenaosse
Pataquilla
Quevenes
San Francisco
Spichehat

KAROK

The Karok were of the Hokan family. They occupied the middle course of the Klamath River its branches in California, except for the upper course of the Salmon. They were situated between the Yurok and the Shasta.

KASIHTA

The Kasihta (or Cusseta) was a large sub-tribe and one of the most important divisions of the Muskogee. A member of the Creek Confederacy, they inhabited Georgia about the Falls of the Chattahoochee after driving the Chickasaws from the land. At one time it was believed that Cusseta and the Casiste of De Soto (date, 1540) may have been one and the same, but that has generally been disproved to satisfaction of most writers. Likewise, it had been suggested that Cofitachequi visited by De Soto were Cusseta, but that also has been disproven. For more see Creek Confederacy, the Muskogee, and the Cofitachequi.

KASKASKIA

The Kaskaskia was one of the major tribes of the Illinois Cluster of Tribes. Before 1700 they lived near present Utica in La Salle County and later about the Kaskaskia River in southern Illinois near the present town of Kaskaskia. They were joined by the Michigamea. For more see Illinois Cluster.

KASKINAMPO

The Kaskinampo were of Muskhogean stock and spoke the language of the Koasati, very probably the Coste of De Soto, with whom they were closely related and through them to the Alabama and other of the Muskhogean stock. They lived along the lower end of an island in the Tennessee River, believed to be what is known today as Pine Island. The Coushatta (Koasati) lived at the upper end. There was also a report that they may have lived upon the Cumberland River at one time, possibly near its mouth on the Ohio. Their first encounter with Europeans was with De Soto in 1541 possibly at what is now Helena, Arkansas, in Phillips County. They appear in the journals under the names Casqui, Ecasqui, and Casquin; also as Quizquiz (pronounced Keys-key), Quizqui, and Chisca, the latter sounding the same as the "Chiska," the Muskogee name for the Yuchi. Quizquiz, is claimed to be a Tunica village in the southwestern corner of Coahoma County, Mississippi, and the capital of a rich province of thousands of Tunica Indians conquered by De Soto. The Casqui, on the other hand, are also identified in the literature as a tribe of Southern Indiana. This is an excellent example of the names of tribes, bands, villages, and prominent chiefs all becoming intertwined, with politics thrown in.

The Kaskinampo Fr. Jacques Marquette in 1673. On Marquette's 1673 autograph map, they appear under the name Kakinonba, a name with a number of variants that include Kakinouba, Kaskinonba, and, erroneously, Kanawha. Kanawha is a synonym for the Conoy tribe of Maryland, but not to be confused with the Kanawake. Jesuit missions had been established for the Conoy in 1634. Other reported variants of the name are Kasquinampo, Kakinonba, and Koskinempo. Little is know of the Kaskinampo after the beginning of the eighteenth century. It is most likely that they united with the Koasati.

KATHLAMINIMIN

The Kathlaminimin was a subdivision or sub-tribe of the Multnomah of Oregon generally treated separately. They belonged to the Clackamas division of the Chinookan linguistic family. They lived on the south end of Sauvies Island. Reportedly, they later joined the Cathlacumup subdivision of the Multnomah and the Nemoit. For more see Multnomah.

KATO

The Kato belonged to the Athapascan linguistic stock but had a dialect unique unto themselves. They lived along the uppermost course of the South Fork of the Eel River in California..

406 KAVIAWACH UTE

The Kaviawach or White River was a subdivision of the Northern Ute.

KAWAIISU

Inhabitants of the Tehachapi Mountains in California, the Kawaiisu belonged to the Shoshonean division of the Uto-Aztecan linguistic stock that included the Kitanemuk, Vanyume, Alliklik, and Serrano.

KEYSVILLE MASSACRE

By 1863 the anger and resentment of the Indians of the Kern River Valley and adjacent areas of south-central California reached a point where the Kawaiisu chief in Walker Basin, Old Jesus, called for a war council with the Owens Valley Indians. Up to this point there had been random thefts of cattle and at least one death of a miner. On April 12, 1863, Captain Moses A. McLaughlin from Camp Babbitt near Visalia, with an attachment of twenty-four, rode into Kernville (Keysville) to punish the Indians. The Kern River runs from the slopes of the High Sierra near Mt. Whitney more than 100 miles to the San Joaquin Valley, near Bakersfield, California. On the morning of April 19, the soldiers surrounded the camp, separated out thirty-five Tehachapi men, and either shot or ran them through.

(In May 1856, five innocent Tejon Indians had been killed at Keyesville by several dozen settlers that called themselves the Tulare Mounted Volunteers.)

KAWCHOTTINE

The Kawchottine was a Canadian tribe of the Athapascan linguistic family. They lived west and northwest of Great Bear Lake. They were comprised of seven subdivisions.

KAWITA

The Kawita or Coweta was a band of Muskogee that have been generally treated separately. They lived in Russell County, Alabama. Before 1715 the Kawita had their villages on Ocheese Creek (Ocmulgee River above Macon, Georgia). There is a possibility that they may be the same as the Oconee. For more see Creek Confederacy and Muskogee.

KAYAMAICI

The Kayamaici may been one of the six or seven allied tribes of the southwestern or Hasinai Division of the Caddo Indians or Hasinai Confederacy. Swanton believes that it may have possibly been only a local group on the Kiamichi River. For more see Hasinai Confederacy and Caddo Peoples.

KEALEDJI

The Kealedji was a sub-tribe or division of the Muskogee and a member of the Creek Confederacy that inhabited Alabama.

KECOUGHTAN

Kecoughtan was a member of the Powhatan Confederacy and inhabited parts of Elizabeth City County, Virginia.

KERESAN PUEBLOS

The Keresan linguistic stock of Pueblo Indians was comprised of two groups, the Eastern Group (Queres) that included the San Felipe, Santa Ana, Sia, Cochiti, and Santo Domingo and the Western Group (Sitsime or Kawaiko) of the Acoma and Laguna, and their outlying villages.

KEYAUWEE

The Keyauwee or Key Auwee is of the Siouan linguistic family. They inhabited areas around present Guilford, Davidson, and Randolph counties in North Carolina. The earliest European contact was not until 1701. The Keyauwee began a movement northward toward the settlements in Virginia about Albermarle Sound around 1714. They subsequently moved to South Carolina and settled along the Pee Dee River with the Cheraw, and possibly the Eno and Shakori. It is likely that they ultimately united with the Catawba. Soon descendants, miscalled Croatan, were represented among the Robeson County Indians.

KEYCHIE

The Keychie was a member of the Natchitoches Confederacy of the Southern Caddoan Indians of Louisiana. They lived west of the Yatasi (Yattassee) on the Sabine River and the east branch of the Trinity River. For more see Natchitoches Confederacy and Caddo Peoples.

KIAWA

The Kiawa (not to be confused with the Kiowa of the Plains) was a subdivision or sub-tribe of the Cusabo proper (North). They lived on the lower course of the Ashley River of South Carolina. For more see Cusabo and Coosa.

KICHAI

The Kichai (commonly, Keechi) were of the Caddoan stock, most likely of the Wichita Group. They can be found in the literature identified simply as a band of the Wichita. The Kichai were also called the Quitsei(s). They inhabited the upper waters of the Trinity River west and northwest of Nacogdoches, Texas. Although they may have lived north of the Red River in Oklahoma at one time, by 1701 they were at the home site on the Trinity and counted among the Nations of the North. In 1855 the Kichai were assigned to a reservation on the Brazos River with several other small tribes, but in 1858 they fled to Oklahoma and joined the Wichita. For more see Nations of the North.

KICKAPOO

The Kickapoo belonged to the Algonquian linguistic stock in a subgroup that included the Fox and Sauk. It is believed that the Kickapoo originally inhabited the area about present Columbia County, Wisconsin, and the lower peninsula of Michigan. It was there that they were evangelized by the Jesuit missionaries from Canada in the 1600s. Over time they continued to migrate south until they settled about Peoria, the Sangamon River, and the Wabash and Vermilion rivers of Illinois and took part in the Black Hawk War of 1812. They ceded their lands in Illinois to the government in 1809 and 1819 and removed to Missouri.

A 1832 treaty extinguished Kickapoo claims to land in Missouri, and they were pushed across the border into Kansas—the original Indian Territory. After the passage of the Kansas-Nebraska in 1854, about half of the Kickapoo in Kansas were removed to a reservation in Oklahoma.

The first Indian mission west of the Mississippi was established in 1836 the for the members of the Kickapoo tribe eight miles north of Fort Leavenworth, Kansas. Later they established a mission school. By the beginning of the 1860s they had maintained and educated four hundred children under contract to the Bureau of Indian Affairs. The Jesuits continued to serve the Kickapoo until well into the late 1800s.

When the Kickapoo were being pushed out of Illinois, a group choose to settle on the lands of East Texas along with members of other eastern tribes. They soon found themselves unwelcome. In the 1830s their homes and crops were burned, and they were driven out of Texas into Indian Territory. A few escaped into the Plains and Mexico. By 1852 there was a rather large group in Mexico that became known as the Mexican Kickapoo. They were later joined by others, but a part was induced to return to Indian Territory in 1873. Those that remained in Mexico received a reservation in the Santa Rosa Mountains of eastern Chihuahua.

By 1833 title to all Indian lands in Missouri—some thirty-nine million acres—had been ceded to the government.

KIGENE

The Kigene reportedly lived on the Pacific coast. Drake gives the name of the chief as Skittegates.

KIKIA'LOS

The Kikia'los, for which there are numerous spellings, was a subdivision of Swinomish and a member of the coastal division of the Salishan linguistic family. The Kikia'los or Kikiallus were generally treated separately. They lived on Skagit Bay from the South Fort at the Skagit River to the north tip of Camano

Island, in the Skagit River Valley. They also had a village at the mouth of Carpenter Creek and another called Atsala'di at Utsalady on Camano Island. They were among the original inhabitants of the Skagit River Valley. They were one of the signatories to the Point Elliott on January 22, 1855.

KIKSADI TLINGIT

The Tlingit inhabited most of the coast and the islands of Alaska from Yakutat Bay southward. They were comprised of sixteen subdivisions, each with a number of villages. Several of the subdivisions have often been treated separately. One of those was the Kiksadi Tlingit. They are often referred to in the literature on the Indians of the lower forty-eight.

The Kiksadi or Sitka were the original inhabitants of the present-day city of Sitka, Alaska. The city is located in southeastern Alaska about 95 miles southwest of Juneau. The Tlingit settlement, called Shee Atika, was located on the seaward or Pacific side of the Baranof Island, the word Shee meaning "outside" or "facing our." Sitka is a contraction of Shee. Russian explorers arrived in 1741 and built a fort in 1799 (Old Sitka or Fort Michael). Three years later the Tlingit attacked and destroyed the fort and killed its Russian occupants and their slaves. The site was renamed New Archangel in 1804 when it became the headquarters for the Russian-American Fur Company. The name was changed to Sitka in 1867.

KILATIKA

The Kilatika or Kilatak belonged to the Algonquian linguistic stock. They were one of the six major divisions of the Miami. They subsequently lost their identity.

KILLASTHOKLE

The Killasthokle was a village of the Chinook, probably on Willapa Bay, that is treated separately. For more see Chinook.

KILLAWAT

The Killawat or Killamuck was reportedly a large Indian town on the Pacific coast east of the Lukton. They were included in William Clark's enumeration of western Indians.

KINGS RIVER YOKUTS

The Kings River Indians were one of the seven subdivisions of the Yokut Group of Indians of California in villages on the Kings River, Mill Creek, Hughes Creek, Big Dry Creek, Little Dry Creek, and in Squaw Valley and Auberry Valley. For more see Yokut.

KINKIPAR

Kinkipar was a sub-tribe of the Tongva of California that inhabited the area about San Clemente Island. For more see Tongva.

KIOWA

The Kiowa (Kai-o-wa), meaning "principal people" in their language, spoke a Tanoan language similar to the Pueblo of New Mexico. Originally from the Kootenay Region of British Columbia, Canada, they migrated south to the region of the headwaters of the Missouri River in Montana where they were neighbors of the Flathead, then into the Black Hills country where they joined the Crows who reportedly taught them how to ride. The earliest written mention of the Kiowa was in 1682.

Finally, during the eighteenth century, they were pushed southwestward into the southern plains by the Arapaho, Cheyenne, and Dakota Sioux. What became their historic range was located along the headwaters of the Arkansas, Cimarron, Canadian, and Red rivers in Nebraska, Kansas, Oklahoma, and Texas. In their migration southwest, they were joined by a small detached tribe of Athapascan stock, commonly known as Kiowa-Apache, that used a different language. Otherwise, for all intents, they were Kiowa. The two spoke to one another, as did all the American Indian tribes, through sign language, at which the Kiowa were the acknowledged experts.

Although first contenders for the same range, the Kiowa formed an early bond with the Comanche during the late seventeen hundreds that continued strong throughout the coming years. The Kiowa, nomadic buffalo hunters who lived in portable skin-covered lodges, owned many horses and became expert horsemen. They also gained a reputation for being extremely warlike. Together with the Comanche, they raided into Texas and Mexico driving the Apache before them.

The most decisive years in the modern history of the Kiowa were the decades of the 1860s and 1870s. Principal chiefs during this time were Lone Wolf, Santana, and Stumbling Bear. Santana signed the October 1867 Medicine Lodge Treaty* that established the Kiowa reservation between the Washita and Red rivers surrounding in southwestern Oklahoma. Lone Wolf did not sign. But the Kiowa continued their nomadic, hunter existence and never stepped foot on the reservation until defeated by Sheridan and Custer on the Washita River in southwestern Oklahoma on November 27, 1868. Following the battle, Santana and Lone Wolf approached Custer under a flag of peace on December 17 and promised to surrender their people. The two chiefs were grabbed and taken hostage and a message was sent to the Kiowa advising them that if they did not come into the Fort Cobb agency immediately the two chiefs would be hanged. Although accounts differ on the contents of the message sent to the Kiowa, the incident dramatically illustrated the change in tactics adopted by the army under Sherman and Sheridan in 1868.

(It was at this time that Sheridan decided to close Fort Cobb and move to another site to the south near Medicine Creek and the Wichita Mountains. The new site that was named Camp Wichita became Fort Sill, Oklahoma on January 7, 1869, in honor of General Joshua W. Sill, killed in the Civil War Battle of Stone River on December 31, 1862.)

The Kiowa soon resumed their raids on white settlers and ranches in Texas. In a pattern that continued for the next several years, war parties bolted the reservation, conducted raids into Texas, and return to the reservation, sometimes under arrest. Among the most noted raids during this period were the ambush of a wagon train along the Butterfield Stage Route on the Salt Creek Prairie in May 1871, referred to by some as the Warren Wagon Train Massacre, and the attack on white buffalo hunters at Adobe Walls on June 27, 1874. The last precipitated what was called the Red River War.

Santana was tried and convicted of murder in 1873, but he his sentence was commuted and he was paroled back to the reservation. He again bolted and led raids into Texas until forced to surrender in October 1875. Santana, who was also noted for his skills as a negotiator and orator, was returned to the Texas State Penitentiary in Huntsville where he died in 1878. Lone Wolf surrendered at Fort Sill in late February 1875 and was sent to prison at Fort Marion, Florida. After more than three years, he was returned to Fort Sill where he died in the summer of 1879. Stumbling Bear died peacefully at Ft. Sill in 1903. A frame house was built for Stumbling Bear on the Kiowa Reservation in 1878 because of his efforts to dissuade the more militant Lone Wolf and Santana in the years following the Medicine Lodge Treaty.

BUFFALO WAR

The Buffalo War is a continuing twenty-first century clash between American Indians, ranchers, government officials, the Montana Department of Livestock, and environmentalists over the killing of wild buffalo that migrate from adjoining Yellowstone National Park onto public lands in Montana used by ranchers for grazing cattle. Ranchers and Montana state officials charge that the buffalo carry a disease (brucellosis) that poses a threat to livestock. One thousand were killed in the winter of 1996-'97. None were killed in 1999-2000, but the war continues.

> *The buffalo is more than animal. It is the sun's shadow. Our lives are bound to it.*
> *If it lives, we live. If it dies, we die. It is our life and our living shield - Kiowa*

---

*The Medicine Lodge Treaty executed at the Council Camp on Medicine Lodge Creek seventy miles south of Fort Learned in southern Kansas consisted of three separate treaties. The first was signed October 21, 1867, by the Kiowa and Comanche (led by Ten Bears). The second, with the Kiowa-Apache, the same day, and the third with the Cheyenne and Arapaho on October 28.

KIOWA APACHE

Kiowa Apache, known as Gattacka (Gáta'-ka) in French chronicles, was a small band of Athabascan (Apachean)-speaking people from the region of the eastern base of the northern Rockies in the McKenzie River basin that had a north and south division. The Kiowa Apache migrated south and eventually into southwestern Oklahoma and the Panhandle of Texas during the 1780s. Except for the language difference, they were very similar to the Kiowa, to whom they attached themselves in every respect. They communicated with the Kiowa through sign, a skill which the Kiowa may have been the most proficient of all America Indian tribes. Anglo Americans gave them the name Kiowa Apaches because they spoke a dialect similar to the Apache. For more see the Kiowa and the Comanche.

KITANEMUK

Located on the upper Tejon and Pasco creeks in California, the Kitanemuk belonged to the Shoshonean division of the Uto-Aztecan linguistic stock that included the Alliklik, Vanyume, Kawaiisu, and Serrano.

KITCHAWANK

The Kitchawank was a subdivision or sub-tribe of the Wappinger and lived in the northern part of Westchester County beyond Croton River and between Hudson River and the Connecticut. For more see Wappinger.

KITCHIGAMICH

Referred to in two volumes of *Jesuit Relations* but not yet identified. The name Kitchigamich means "people of the great lake," and refers to a tribe living on or near Lake Michigan. It is known that they were of the Algonquian linguistic stock and spoke the same language as the Kickapoo and Mascoutin.

[Source: Shea, John Gilmary. "The Indian Tribes of Wisconsin." Collections of the State Historical Society of Wisconsin, v.3]

KLAMATH

The Modoc and the Klamath constituted the Lutuamian division of the Shapwailutan linguistic stock. They lived along Upper Klamath Lake, Klamath Marsh, and the Williamson and Sprague rivers in Oregon. Believing the Klamath to have been responsible for the deaths of three of their party while camped on the of Klamath Lake, Kit Carson, under orders from Captain John Charles Frémont to punish the Indians, attacked a peaceful Klamath settlement at Dokdokwas in May 1846 while most of the men were away. Carson and the ten men in his party killed twenty-one according to one report. The Delaware Indians who were with them then sought out and slaughtered the Klamath who run into the hills to hide. It The massacre has been referred to as "a perfect butchery." Not that such an attack would have been justified in any case, but it was later determined that it was the Modoc not the Klamath who were responsible for the original attack. On the trek around the lake and their return to California, "they continued to kill Indians in a desultory fashion, in ones and twos."

KLICKITAT

The Klickitat (also spelled Klikatat and Klikitat) belonged to the Shahaptian division of the Shapwailutan linguistic family. They were originally from south of the Columbia River in Washington State. Lewis and Clark found them on the Yakima and Klickitat Rivers. Owing to the geographic position, the Klickitat were great traders. They joined in the 1855 Yakima treaty at Camp Stevens in which they ceded all their lands to the government and were assigned to the Yakima Reservation where most eventually settled. They are often classified as a part of the Yakima nation rather than as a independent and distinct tribe.

KLINQUIT

The Klinquit was a sub-tribe of the Yakima. In the 1855 Yakima treaty at Camp Stevens, the Klinquit ceded all their lands to the government and settled on the Yakima Reservation. For more see Yakima.

KOASATI

The Koasati (pronounced "koh-uh-sah-tee") or the Coushatta, their more common name, belonged to the southern division of the Muskhogean linguistic group. Cooshatta is another of the other more common names among the several variations. Coushatta is used by the Coushatta themselves and the BIA. The Koasati were a member of the Creek Confederacy of Upper Creeks and inhabited the area around the junction of the Coosa and Tallapoosa Rivers in Alabama. Although Alabama was their historic homeland, they are believed to have lived on the Tennessee River between about 1500 to the end of seventeenth century. There is also evidence to indicate that the Koasati were the Coste, Acoste, or Costehe referred to in De Soto's chronicles.

The Koasati were related to the Kaskinampo. Both tribes moved south into Alabama and settled on the Tallapoosa, although it is likely that at least one group remained behind. The Koasati became closely associated with the Alabama.

Following the French and Indian War in 1763, a large group moved to the Tombigbee River but later returned to the Tallapoosa. Towards the end of the eighteenth century, a group moved into Louisiana and settled along the Red and Sabine rivers as did so many other tribes from the Southeast during this period. Some continued west as far as the Neches and Trinity rivers in Texas. A few of the Texas bands joined the Alabama in present Polk County, Texas, and have since been referred to as the Alabama-Coushatta. The Alabama had made the same trek west. Most of the Koasati, however, returned to Louisiana and settled in an area northeast of Kinder just outside of New Orleans. The city of Coushatta is the seat of Red River Parish, Louisiana. The Coushatta Tribe Reservation is located three miles north of Elton. While some went west into Louisiana, a small band went east into Florida and joined the Seminole, but little else is known of them.

A report in the literature indicates that the Alabama-Coushatta, along with a large number from other tribes, participated in a 1817 retaliatory raid on the Osage. The force arraigned against the Osage that supposedly included the Shawnee, Delaware, Comanche, and Cherokee among others is also most too much to fathom. The Alabama-Coushatta were subsequently established on a reservation in present Polk County. The Koasati that remained in Alabama joined the Creeks in the removal to Indian Territory.

When the other eastern tribes were burned out of east Texas in the 1830s, the Alabama-Coushatta were permitted to remain as too insignificant to bother with, but they were removed to less fertile lands.

KOHANI

The Kohani or Kohanis was one of the five principal Karankawan Tribes of Texas and inhabited the area about the mouth of Colorado River. For more see Karankawan Tribes.

KOHUANA

The Kohuana belonged to the Yuman branch of the Hokan linguistic stock. They were closely related to the Halyikwamai and spoke the dialect of the Cocopa. The Spanish mentioned them as the Coana in 1540. They lived on the east bank of the Colorado River below the mouth of the Gila, next to the Halyikwamai. They then seemed to move from place to place until they joined the Yuma for a period before ultimately merging with the Maricopa.

KOLOMI

The Kolomi was a sub-tribe or division of the Muskogee and a member of the Creek Confederacy.

KONAGEN

The Konagen inhabited Kadjak Island, Alaska, at Latitude 53°, Longitude 152° West, discovered by Russian explorer S. Glotov in 1763. (Often confused with Kodiak Island located about 57° 44' N Latitude, 152° 24' W Longitude)

KONOMIHU

The Konomihu belonged to the Shastan group of the Hokan linguistic family. They lived about the forks of the Salmon River in California.

KOOTENAY

The linguistic relationship of the Kootenay or Kutenai is uncertain. They have been placed in a distinct linguistic stock called Kitunahan. They are also regarded as distantly related to the Algonquians and Salishans. They were comprised of two general geographic divisions, the Upper Kutenai to the east and the Lower Kutenai to the west. Thy lived on the Kootenay River and Lake, Arrow Lake, and the upper course of the Columbia River of northwestern Montana, northeastern Washington, and the northern tip of Idaho, plus southeastern British Columbia. It is believed that they first lived east of the Rocky Mountains and as far north as MacLeod, Alberta. First contact was likely from the Northwest Company. The Kootenai House, a trading post for the North West Company located near Lake Windemere was established in 1807. The modern Kootenai House is a unique art, furnishings, and clothing store in Eureka, Montana. The establishment of the international boundary through their lands was very disruptive.

The bands to the West (Lower division) lived primarily off fish and other aquatic sources. The Upper division to the East were hunters and undertook annual bison hunts over the Continental Divide after acquiring the horse which put them in contact with Plains Indians. As a result, they adopted much from the Plains culture after 1800. The Kootenai on the Saint Regis River were first visited by Jesuit missionaries in the form of Fr. John Paul De Smet in the spring of 1842. The Kootenay were a party to the treaty of July 16, 1855, that also included the Flathead and Upper Pend d'Oreilles Indians.

KOPANO

The Kopano, Kopanes or Copanes was one of the five principal Karankawan Tribes of Texas and inhabited the area about Copano Bay. For more see Karankawan Tribes.

KOROA

The Koroa belonged to the Tunican linguistic group. Early in their history they lived on the banks of the Mississippi River and the inland in Louisiana, but they are generally associated with their later home along the lower course of the Yajoo River in Mississippi. The tribe appears on Marquette's map of 1673 although mistakenly much higher up the Mississippi. La Salle listed two tribes by the name Koroa, one on the Mississippi and one below Natchez, the later elsewhere called the Tiou. In all likelihood the Koroa were absorbed by the Chickasaw and Choctaw after the Natchez outbreak in which the Kora joined the Natchez and the Yazoo against the French. Choctaw chief Allenn Wright claimed to be of Koroa decent.

KOSO SHOSHONI

The Koso Shoshoni or the more commonly the Panamint Shoshoni were a subdivision and California famiily of the Western Shoshoni, but they are more commonly listed as a separate California tribe associated with the Shoshoni only by language. They ranged between the Sierras and Nevada border in southeastern California, including Owens Lake, the Coso, Argus, Panamint, and Funeral Mountains and valleys. It was a large geographical area for a tribe of less than five hundred. See Numic Languages.

KOSUNAT UTE

The Kosunat was a subdivision of the Northern Ute. They were placed on the Uintah Reservation in 1873. For more see Ute.

KOTSOTEKA

The Kotsoteka (or Caschotethka, Koocheteka, Kotsai, Kuhtsoo-ehkuh) "buffalo eaters" were one of the five major sub-tribes or bands of the Comanche. For more see Comanche.

KOWASAYEE

The Kowasayee (or Kow-was-say-ee) was a sub-tribe of the Tenino that is generally treated separately. They lived on the north bank of Columbia River nearly opposite the mouth of the Umatilla in Oregon. In the 1855 Yakima treaty at Camp Stevens they were listed as the Kow-was-say-ee and classified among other signatories as a subdivision or sub-tribe of the Yakima. By the treaty the Kowasayee ceded all their lands to the government and settled on the Yakima Reservation. For more see Tenino and Yakima.

KUITSH

The Kuitsh, also known by the popular name of Lower Umpqua and Umpwua, should not be confused with the Umpqua proper or Upper Umpqua. The Kuitsh were distantly related to the Yakonan linguistic stock. Swanton noted one report that placed them in an independent group, the Siuslawan. An unknown reference placed in the Athapascan group. They lived along the Lower Umpqua River on the Oregon coast. Their lives and history ran parallel with that of the Coos. For more see the Coos.

KUSOTONY

The Kusotony was a band or sub-tribe of Indians that lived west of the Cascade Mountains in Oregon listed in the U.S. Code. No additional information is available. Also see Western Oregon Indians.

KUTZADIKA'A

The Kutzadika's or Kutzadika'a People or Mono Lake Kutzadika'a or Monachie (fly people), shortened to Mono, were the early inhabitants of the Mono Lake Basin located in the Long Valley Caldera of California east of Yosemite near the Nevada border. They date back some five thousand plus years. The Kutzadika'a became absorbed by and are now more commonly referred to as Mono Lake Paiutes or Yosemite-Mono Lake Paiutes; also as the Northern Paiute Indians from the Mono Lake region and Mono Lake Kutzadika. (The large yet shallow alkaline terminal lake that is fed by springs of the Eastern Sierra Nevada is one of the oldest lakes in North America.). For more see Paiute and Mono.

KWAHADA

The Kwahada (or Kwerhar-rehnuh, Kwahadi, Kwahari, Kwaharior, Quahada) "antelopes" was one of the five major sub-tribes or bands of the Comanche. It was the smallest of the major bands and the most fierce. The band's leader, Quanah (Parker to Texans), is certainly the most famous of the Comanche chiefs and regarded by many as the greatest Comanche warrior. The Kwahada (Quahadi) lived deep in Palo Duro and Tule canyons and the high plains of the Llano Estacado. For more see Comanche and Red River War.

KWAIAILK

The Kwaiailk belonged to the coastal division of the Salishan linguistic family. They lived along the upper course of the Chehalis River in Washington State and are commonly known as the Upper Chehalis, with whom they subsequently became assimilated.

KWALHIOQUA

Inhabitants of the area on the upper course of the Willopah River and the southern and western headwaters of the Chehalis River in Washington State, the Kwalhioqua belonged to the Athapascan linguistic family.

KWATAMI

Kwatami was a band of Athapascan Indians that lived near the Sixes and Elk rivers in the southwest corner of the present state of Oregon. The Kwatami were a coastal people who actively engaged in trade.

L'ANSE

The L'Anse was a band of Lake Superior Chippewa Indians generally treated separately. The L'Anse Federal Indian Reservation of 54,000 acres in Baraga County, Michigan, was set aside under the 1854 Treaty of LaPointe. Along with the Vieux Desert and Ontonagon band, the three comprise the Keweenaw Bay Indian Community of Michigan. For more see Chippewa.

LA JOLLA LUISEÑO

La Jolla near Palomar is one of six recognized tribes of Luiseño. The La Jolla originally inhabited the area around San Diego but were displaced by the Kumeyaay. In 1875 President Ulysses S. Grant signed an Executive Order that establish reservations for the Pala, La Jolla, and Rincon. In 1891 the Mission Indian Relief Act made the Rincon, La Jolla, Pauma, Pala, reservations permanent. For more see Luiseño Peoples.

LAC COURTE OREILLE

Lac Courte Oreille was a band of Chippewa that lived on Lake Courte Oreille at the headwaters of the Chippewa River in Sawyer County, Wisconsin. It is sometimes referred to an independent tribe. For more see Chippewa.

LACANE

The Lacane were of Caddoan stock, first encountered in 1542. They lived in northeastern Texas and the adjacent parts of Arkansas and Louisiana. One theory is that they may have been the same as the Hacanac; another, the same as the Nacaniches; another, a band of yet another Caddoan tribe.

LACOPSELE

The Lacopsele was listed by Farther Ortiz in his memorial to the king of Spain sometime after February 14, 1747, cited by Bolton in "Missions on the San Gabriel," but no additional information about the tribe is known. It is believed that the Lacopsele lived in east central or southeastern Texas.

LAGUNA PUEBLO

The Keresan-speaking Laguna Pueblo of the Western (Sitsime or Kawaiko) dialectic group was comprised a number of villages spread over several acres in west-central New Mexico along the south bank of the San José River in Valencia County. In their native language, spelled Ka-waikah or Kawaik, the name means Lake People. Laguna was the only pueblo founded after the Pueblo Revolt. It was founded in 1696 by a group of one-time refugees of the Spanish reconquest from Acoma, and some disgruntled Acomans as well, who seceded from the Acoma Pueblo. By 1707, Laguna had a population of 330. For more see Pueblo Peoples and Acoma.

LAKOTA

The Lakota (also spelled Lakhota and Lacota) or Teton comprised the Western Division of the Sioux nation. The French had several names for the Lakota generally referencing meadows and prairies. The Lakota Oyate (the people) or Teton Sioux (Tetonwan, "Dwellers of the Plains") consisted of seven major groups or Seven Tents (Ti Sakowin).

MAJOR GROUPS

Oglala	Scatter their Own
Sicangu or Brulé	"Burnt Thigh," Brulé in French
Miniconjou	Plant Beside the River
Oohenonpa or Oohenumpa	Two Boils Kettle or Two Kettle(s)
Itazipacola or Itazipco	Sans Arc, "Without Bow"
Sihasapa	Blackfeet Not to be confused with Algonquian Blackfeet of Montana and Canada
Hunkpapa or Uncpapa.	Lived west of a northern plains fringe near the Minnesota woodlands. The name comes from Hunupatina, referring to Hunu-pa-paha or Devil's Tower.

Each division was subdivided into bands (tiyospaye) that, in turn, consisted of a number of smaller family camps (tiwahe). The word "tiyospaye" is also used to refer to lodge groups or cluster of families.

The Lakota had moved onto the central Dakota plains including the Black Hills by the early 1700's. The Black Hills of South Dakota (known as the heart of all things) were traditional home of the Lakota and the location that generally give as their place of origin. The Oglala have been the designated caretakers. Among the leaders of the Teton were Sitting Bull of the Humkpapa, Crazy Horse of the Oglala, and Spotted Tail of the Brulé. Much of the modern history of the Sioux Nation derives from history of the Lakota and these three men and the time of the Great Sioux War.

FIGHT FOR THE POWDER RIVER COUNTRY (OR RED CLOUD'S WAR)

The Bozeman Trail (for John M. Bozeman from Georgia) ran from Fort Laramie, Wyoming, to Virginia City, Montana, through the Powder River hunting lands of the Oglala. In March of the Bozeman crossed the Gallatin Valley and cut through a pass that would become known as the Bozeman Pass into the valley of the Yellowstone River. (The traditional route was the Oregon Trail over South Pass to Fort Bridger and north past Fort Hall into Montana Territory.) Known as the Powder River Trail by the Lakota, the Bozeman Trail was protected by three forts: Fort Phil Kearny, Fort C. F. Smith, and Fort Bufford.

In the summer of 1865, now Maj. General Patrick Connor with 2,600 men and a company of Pawnee Soldier-Scouts began what was called the Powder River Expedition to punish the Indians who had been attacking travelers along the Oregon Trail. As the expedition moved north, it established a new route for the Bozeman Trail from the North Platte near present day Douglas, Wyoming, to just south of Buffalo, Wyoming. Where the trail crossed the Powder River, Connor constructed Fort Connor (later renamed Fort Reno). The expedition actually accomplished very little. The soldiers attacked a band of Sioux and Cheyenne and killed about thirty. They also attacked a camp of peaceful Arapaho north of the Tongue River and drove off a large herd of horses and mules. (A second Powder River Expedition was formed under General George Crook in November 1876. For more see Cheyenne and Sioux.)

A peace conference was held with the Sioux in June 1866 at Fort Laramie to discuss the Bozeman. It was attended by about 2,000 Brulé and Oglala under Spotted Tail and Red Cloud, respectively. While peace was being discussed in Laramie, Colonel Carrington made plans to secure the trail. He reestablished Fort Connor as Fort Reno east of present day Kaycee, Wyoming, and established new posts—Fort Phil Kearny northwest of Buffalo, Wyoming, and Fort C. F. Smith and near Hardin in southwest Montana.

Believing that he was being lied to, Red Cloud, left the conference and began a campaign of harassment, pillage and murder along the Bozeman that came to known as Red Cloud's War. (Spotted Tail remained and agreed to terms.) The war continued for almost two years from 1866 into the spring of 1868. It had one goal—to drive the white man from the Powder Hill country and close the Bozeman Trail into Montana. Just in the months from August through December 1866, Red Cloud led the Ogalala in over fifty encounters with the white man, resulting in the deaths of one hundred and fifty-four persons.

The Fetterman Fight near Fort Phil Kearny, the Hayfield Fight at Fort C. F. Smith, and the Wagon Box Fight at Fort Phil Kearny were fought over the Bozeman. At the same time Sitting Bull and the Hunkpapa waged a determined campaign against Fort Bufford on the Upper Missouri at the mouth of the Yellowstone. (Bufford was established in the summer of 1866.) In the spring and summer of 1867, Sioux hunting parties also joined the Cheyenne and Arapaho in raids in Kansas along the stretch of track of the Kansas Pacific Railroad that crossed Indian hunting grounds between Ellsworth and Fort Hays.

Red Cloud set the minimum conditions for peace. The Army had to abandon the forts on the Bozeman and in the Powder River Valley. The battle for the Powder River Country gained public attention and won sympathy, forcing the government to finally agree to terms. A peace treaty was concluded at Fort Laramie in Wyoming Territory on May 25, 1868, with the Brulé, Oglala, Miniconjou, Yanktonai, Blackfeet, Cuthead, San(s) Arc, and Santee Sioux and a band of Arapaho. Some chiefs and headmen signed on April 29; others on November 6.

The Fort Laramie Treaty of 1868, sometimes referred to as the Great Fort Laramie Treaty, gave the Sioux all of the present-day state of South Dakota north of the Missouri River, including most of the Black Hills. In addition, the treaty confirmed the occupation and use of the existing reservations on the east bank of the Missouri River. More importantly, the treaty provided that the land north of the North Platte River (north of the Oregon Trail) and east of the summits of the Big Horn Mountains "shall be held and considered to be unceded Indian territory." The treaty further stipulated "that no white person or persons shall be permitted to settle upon or occupy any portion of the same; or ...pass through the same." (Article 16) And, in accordance with the conditions laid out by Red Cloud, the government agreed to abandon all military posts established within the territory and to close "that the road leading to them," the Bozeman Trail

Red Cloud withheld his signature until the soldiers actually left and Fort Phil Kearny was burned to the ground. The Indians had won one round. It was the failure of the government to enforce these provisions of the treaty precipitated the Great Sioux War a decade later.

FETTERMAN FIGHT

The Fetterman Fight or the Fetterman Massacre as white men called it was a hard fought battle waged by several hundred Lakota and Cheyenne warriors and a few Arapaho. Most of the Lakota warriors were Miniconjou and Oglala plus a few Sicangu. Eighty soldiers were lured into an ambush about five miles from Fort Phil Kearny in the foothills of the Big Horn Mountains in the frigid cold of the winter of 1866-67. Captain William J. Fetterman, brevet lieutenant colonel, led a column of soldiers into the ambush in pursuit of a small party of Indians led by Crazy Horse that severed as decoys. Fifteen warriors were killed, and many were wounded. The Indians called the battle of December 21, 1866, the Battle of the Hundred in the Hand—from the "vision" of a Miniconjou medicine dreamer. (Some texts refer to it as the Hundred-Soldiers-Killed-Fight.) The deaths and mutilations that followed were in direct response to Sand Creek Massacre to the south.

HAYFIELD AND WAGON BOX FIGHTS

The Hayfield and Wagon Box fights took place August 1 and 2, 1867. In each instance, largely outnumbered whites with new Springfield breechloaders (breech-loading carbines) held off the attacking Indians with minimal casualties. The Indians, on the other hand, lost heavily. Arrows were no match for the hail of fire produced by the Springfields. On August 1, some five hundred Sioux, Cheyenne, and Arapaho attacked a haying party of nineteen soldiers and six civilians from Fort Smith along the Big Horn River under the command of Lieutenant Sigismund Sternberg. Three soldiers were killed with three wounded.

The following day, Red Cloud, with Crazy Horse and High Backbone, led a large band of a thousand Oglala Sioux that struck a wood cutting party about six miles from Fort Phil Kearny on Buffalo Creek under the command of Captain James W. Powell. (Marshall writes that the Miniconjou led the attack.) Three whites were killed, and two were wounded from Powell's force of 28 soldiers and four civilians. (Other accounts put the number of soldiers at 30 with no count of civilians; another at 31 total.) Indian casualties totaled sixty killed and 120 wounded. The Sioux managed only to drive off a large number of horses and mules. Crazy Horse attributed many of the Indian deaths were the result of foolish bravery. (Although both sides claimed victory, statistically it was a draw; but as in the case of many Southern victories and defeats during the Civil War, the South could not afford the loss.)

WOUNDED KNEE

Wounded Knee signaled the close of the struggle for freedom of the American Indians and defined a tragic era in American History. Ironically, coming at the end of the struggle as it did, it typified the remorseless conflict that had been waged in hundreds of locales from north to south and from east to west across the nation and the systematic plunder of the Indian race inflicted by whites. It was no battle in any sense of the word, even the word massacre comes up lacking.

On the 28th of December 1890, troopers of the 7th U.S. Calvary Regiment under the command of Colonel James W. Forsyth caught up with a destitute band of some 350 Lakota Sioux under Chief Big Foot on a open field at Wounded Knee Creek in South Dakota—twenty miles from their destination at the Pine Ridge Reservation. The next day, December 29, the troopers exterminated almost every man, woman, and child in one of the most spectacular acts of Indian genocide inflicted by the white man. "[T] hey shot us like we were buffalo." The first shot was fired by an Indian of the Crow Dog Band, Black Coyote, one of five bad Indians who the chiefs had repeatedly asked to be arrested and confined to prevent trouble. The harmless shot came unexpectedly after the Indians has surrendered their weapons, and the soldiers were completing a search of the camp for more guns that they believed remained hidden—they found two. Having been formed into a square, the soldiers were caught in the crossfire that raked the camp. Casualties among the soldiers totaled twenty-five killed and thirty-nine wounded, most of them from bullets and shrapnel of their own making.

Estimates place the number killed at three hundred or so of the original 350 who were making their way to safety at Pine Ridge. After the troop march off, a detail gathered the wounded survivors into wagons for the journey to Pine Ridge. Arriving after dark on the 29th, four men and forty-seven women stumbled from the wagons. (One account puts the number of men at five.) The survivors, several of whom died of their wounds, were left in the cold to fend for themselves as a half-hearted attempt was made to find a place to put them. Finally, they were moved into the shelter of an Episcopal mission from which the benches were removed and replaced with straw.

WHITE BUFFALO

In Lakota mythology, the White Buffalo (Tantanka) is a sacred animal, a sign of rebirth and the harbinger of peace and harmony as foretold by the White Buffalo Calf Maiden, a sacred woman of legend who on her visit (Canupa Wakan) gave the Lakota their Seven Sacred Rituals:

Nagi Gluhapi	- The Keeping of The Soul
Inipi	- The Rite of Purification
Hanbleceya	- Crying For A Vision
Wiwangag Wachi	- The Sun Dance
Hunkakaga	- The Making of Relatives
Isnati Awicaliwanpi	- A Girl's Coming of Age
Tapa Wankaye	- The Throwing of The Ball

LASSIK

The Lassik were of the Athapascan linguistic group and were connected to the Nongatl who lived to their south. The Lassik lived along the Eel River from the near the mouth of the South Fork to near Kekawaka Creek and along Dobbins Creek, Soldier Basin at the head of the North Fork, and the headwaters of Mad River in California.

LATGAWA

The Latgawa (also spelled Latagawa) and the Takelma proper constituted the Takilman linguistic family affiliated with the Shastan stock. They lived along the Upper Rogue River eastward around Table Rock and Bear Creek near present Jacksonville, Oregon.

LEMHI SHOSHONI

The Lemhi of Mountain Lemhi lived in area from the Beaverhead country of southwest Montana to the Salmon River, in western Idaho, and along the Boise and Bruneau rivers. The Lemhi have been subdivided four subgroups:
Lemhi Subgroups
Boise/Weiser Rivers Shoshoni
Bruneau River Shoshoni
Snake River Shoshoni
Mountain Shoshoni

At one time, Bear River or Northwest Bands were included. The Lemhi have also been identified as the Salmon Eaters, and the Salmon Easters and the Sheepeaters have been identified as subbands of the Lemhi. References to the Northern Shoshoni, without any further description, generally refer to the Indians of the Lemhi subgroup.

Sacagawea (or Sacajawea), the young wife and mother and the invaluable guide to the Corps of Discovery, was a member of the Lemhi Northern Shoshoni. For more see Shoshoni.

On February 12, 1875, the Lemhi Reservation was established by Executive Order for the Lemhi, the Bannock and the Sheepeaters. On May 14, 1880, an agreement was reached with Shoshoni, Bannock, and Sheepeaters to cede Lemhi Reserve to the government. In the same agreement, the Shoshoni and Bannock agreed to cede portions of the Fort Hall Reservation to the government and to accept the Lemhi at Fort Hall. In July of 1881 the Shoshoni and Bannock were forced to give up more of their land for the railroad. For more see the Shoshoni.

LEZAR

The Lezar was listed in Jefferson's *Notes on the State of Virginia* from Croghan (1759). They had a reported population of 400 warriors and lived from the mouth of Ohio River to the mouth of Wabash River. For more see "Aborigines," Appendix D.

LI-AY-WA

The Li-ay-was was a sub-tribe of the Yakima that is sometimes referred to separately. In the 1855 Yakima treaty at Camp Stevens, the Li-ay-wa ceded all their lands to the government and settled on the Yakima Reservation. For more see Yakima.

LIAYWA

It is believed that the Liaywa was a band or sub-tribe of one of the Plateau tribes of southeast Washington and northeast Oregon that belonged to the Shahaptian linguistic family.

LIMITA

The Limita (Lemita) Indians were a band of Plains Apache, possibly an early band of the Lipan, that ranged over eastern New Mexico and adjoining portions of western Texas, generally south of the Canadian River.

In the face of the invasion of the Comanche from the north, it is believed that the Limita likely merged with the Mescalero. For more see Lipan, Chipayne, Trementina. It has also be suggested that the Limita and the Tremintina may be one and the same, and both name are sometimes equated with Chipayne.

LINWAY

The Linway was listed in Jefferson's *Notes on the State of Virginia* from Croghan (1759). They had a reported population of 1000 warriors and lived on the Mississippi River. For more see "Aborigines," Appendix D.

LIPAN

The Lipan or Lipanes (Spanish name) or Lipan Apaches were of the Athapascan linguistic group to which the general name Apache was applied. The relatively small group of twelve or more bands called themselves the Ipa'Nde or "Ipa's People," the followers of a great war chief. The name Tindi has been applied to both the Lipan and the Jicarilla who constituted the Eastern Division of the Apache or Eastern Apache. Some writings include the Kiowa Apache among the Eastern Apache, but that appears to be a minority position. The Lipan lived east of the Rio Grande and ranged over the Llano Estacodo of eastern New Mexico and northwest Texas (Texas Panhandle) and the Colorado River Valley of Texas. The Jicarilla were to their north; the Mescalero to the west.

The Lipan were a sedentary people who took their livelihood from the soil. As a consequence, they were no match for the Horse People when they arrived on the Plains. By 1740 the Lipan had been driven from their homelands by the Comanche. The Lipan retreated into central Texas and northern Mexico. Three missions were established for the Lipans by the Franciscan missionaries in the mid-1700s, but the missions enjoyed only limited success. The San Saba mission was destroyed within a year by a combined force of Comanches, several bands of Wichita and other tribes; the other two were abandoned.

Their livelihood taken from them, the Lipan became predators of the border region—taking out their vengeance on the whites. The raids picked up in intensify when the Spanish became preoccupied with the Mexican War of Independence that began 1811.

In 1839 the Lipan took the side of the Texans against the Comanche, taking revenge for what was done do them a century before. Six years later on October 9, 1844, the Lipan, Comanche, and other tribes signed the Tehuacana Creek Treaty that stipulated that the Indian hunting grounds were to be protected from white encroachment. The Indians also agreed to make no treaty with any other nation, namely Mexico, which was at war with the Texas, and that they would trade exclusively with the people of Texas. On December 29, 1845, Texas officially entered the Union. But over the next ten years the Lipan suffer severely at the hands of Texans who drove most of the Lipan into Mexico where they joined remnants of the Kickapoo.

The federal government forced the Lipans on a reserve near Fort Mason in 1852 and on a reservation along the Brazos River in 1854. Many escaped and fled into Mexico. In 1853, the Lipan had signed a treaty of peace with the Mexican government. Throughout the 1860s and 1870s, the Kickapoo and Lipan conducted raids into Texas, often joining the Mescalero in Mexico.

In 1873, Col. Ronald MacKenzie took four hundred troopers and crossed the Rio Grande River into the Mexican state of Coahuila and attacked and killed many and Kickapoo and Lipan warriors, putting a stop to the raids. Those that survived dispersed throughout the countryside. The captured were placed on the Mescalero Reservation that had been established in the Sacramento Mountains of New Mexico in 1855. Remnants still in Mexico at the beginning of the 1900s were allowed to reenter the United States and were also placed on the Mescalero Reservation. A few joined the Tonkawa and the Kiowa Apaches in Indian Territory. For more see Apache and the records of Plains Apaches listed below. (The Mescalero Reservation also became home to some Kiowa and Chiricahua Indians and a few Comanche.)

MISSIONS

San Saba Mission de la Santa Cruz
  —established April 1757; destroyed Mar. 1758

Nuestra Señora de la Candelaria del Cañón Mission on the Nueces River
  —established February 1762; abandoned about 1767

San Lorenzo de la Santa Cruz
  —established January 1762; abandoned prior to 1771

NAMES OF PLAINS APACHES ASSOCIATED WITH THE LIPAN
Teya
Faraon
Limita
Chipayne
Trementina
Conejero

LITTLE ALGONKIN

The Little Algonkin was listed in Jefferson's *Notes on the State of Virginia*. They had a reported population of one hundred warriors and lived near *Trois-Rivières* in Michigan. For more see "Aborigines," Appendix D.

LOHIM

The Lohim (also referred to as Snake Shoshonean) were of the Shoshonean linguistic stock who lived on Willow Creek, a southern affluent of the Columbia River, in Oregon in the middle of a group of Sahaptians, the Umatilla. It is believed that they entered Oregon late, sometime after the mid-1850s. Swanton lists the Lohim both as a distinct and independent tribe and as an isolated Shoshonean band of Northern Paiute. They have also been identified as a band of Lemhi, from the Bannock, who arrived from Idaho. They have also been identified as a group of renegades who at one time belonged to the Umatilla Reservation. By the twentieth century the name had disappeared from official reports. One source states that the name Lohim applied to the Yakima. They were never recognized by the Federal government. Even their very existence has been questioned.

LONG ISLAND, NEW YORK, INDIAN TRIBES

When Long Island was first settled by Europeans, it was inhabited by thirteen distinct and independent tribes.

SOUTH SHORE	NORTH
Canarsee	Matinecock
Rockaway	Nesaquake
Merrick	Setalcott
Marsapeague	Corchaug
Secatogue	
Unkechaug	EAST END
	Shinnecock
	Manhasset
	Montauk

LONGWHA

The Longwha cannot be identified except for its inclusion in the preamble of the Treaty of May 15, 1846, that was signed at Council Springs in the county of Robinson, Texas, near the Brazos River. The tribe is not included in signature section nor in the title/heading of the treaty.

LOWER CREEKS

The Lower Creeks lived about the lower Chattahoochee and Ocmulgee rivers. For more see Creek

LOWER PEND D'OREILLES

The Lower Pend d'Oreilles or Lower Kalispel or Kalispel proper, a division of the Kalispel, included several minor bands. They inhabited parts of Idaho from Thompson Falls to Clark Fork, Pend Oreille Lake, Priest Lake, and Pend Oreille River almost to the border with Canada.

LUCKIAMUTE KALAPUYA

Luckiamute or Lakmiut Kalapuya were of the Calapooyan dialectic division of the Kalapooian linguistic stock and inhabited the area about the Luckiamute River in Oregon. For more see Kalapuya Peoples.

LUCKKARSO

Luckkarso has been identified with Kosothe, a former village on the Tututni between Port Orford and Sixes Creek on the Pacific coast of Oregon, perhaps on Flores Creek. Lewis and Clark listed them on the Oregon coast above the Hannakallal tribe south of the Kusan. Drake identified as on the coast south of the Columbia River beyond the Shallalah.

LUISEÑO PEOPLES

The Luiseño belonged to the Shoshonean division of the Uto-Aztecan linguistic family. They occupied the far southern part of California from the coast inland. Their territory included the upper, lower, and middle course of the San Louis Rey River, parts of the Santa Margarita River northwest of Temecula, Elsinore Lake, and the area around Escondido and Pala. The Luiseño was also called Ghecham or Khecham.

Swanton treats the Luiseño as a single tribe with over forty villages, but uses the term "peoples" at least once. There are also six recognized tribes that all spoke the same language. Luiseño was the name given by the Spanish to those tribes of Indians (the payomkowishum—"people of the west") living in the territory served by Mission San Luis Rey de Francia that was founded in 1798 as Sanluiseños or San Luiseño or Luiseños for short.

BANDS OR TRIBES
Pechanga or Temecula
Soboba (Sovovo), near San Jacinto*
Pauma (Pauma), in the Pauma Valley*
Rincon, near Valley Center
La Jolla, near Palomar
Pala Remnants*
*also listed as villages

PAUMA MASSACRE

During the Mexican War, some Luiseño, Diegeño and Cupeño bands, raided Californio ranches. Although the Californios believed the raids were inspired by the Americans, the majority were probably the work Indians taking advantage of the chaos after years of depredations. A major event was the Pauma Massacre in which eleven Californians that had taken refuge in an adobe house on Rancho Pauma owned by José Antonio Serrano were taken prisoner and subsequently killed in December 1846 by Luiseños led by Manuelito Cota. (War was declared in May 1846.) The massacre was possibly instigated by William Marshall, an American.

A force of twenty-two Californios with a force of friendly Cahuilla Indians, all led by José del Cármen Lugo, tracked and ambushed the Luiseño force and killed more than a hundred. They also took twenty captive who were later killed by their Cahuilla.

The Pauma Massacre occurred a few days after the controversial Battle of San Pasqual, in what is now San Diego, in which Brigadier General Stephen Watts Kearney engaged a band of Californios led by General Andres Pico. Of fifty or so Americans that entered involved in the action, twenty-one died and seventeen were seriously wounded. The American occupation of San Diego lasted from July 29, 1846 until the first week in October.

GARRA REVOLT

Information on the Garra Revolt is sketchy at best. A revolt in name only, it was named for Chief Antonio Garra who called the Indians to arms. The short-lived revolt broke out in late 1851 in lower California and along the Colorado River of the adjoining parts of Arizona. It came after years of pent-up resentment against the white man and pressures from new taxes on this cattle, stirred to a frenzy by the likes of an American adventurer named William "Bill" Marshall. By this time the missions had been closed, and Federal troops had withdrawn from the area. Involved were the Cupeño, Diegueño, and Luiseño Indians, and a few Cahuilla who lived about San Diego and the Yumas and Cocopas along the Colorado River. In began with an attack on a southern California range on November 27. After four chiefs were taken and executed in December, the revolt or what there was of it began to unravel. In January 1852 Maj. Gen. Joshua Bean, the first American mayor of San Diego and a commander of the state militia, captured Garra who was found guilty of murder and theft on January 17, 1852, and executed. (Previously, on December 13, 1851, Bill Marshall were hanged in San Diego for his part in the uprising.) The revolt resulted in few deaths. About the only thing that changed was that defenses against Indian attacks were reorganized. The Cahuilla led by Juan Antonio took the side of the whites.

LUKAWI

According to Drake, the Lukawi lived west of the Rocky Mountains, but no additional information is available.

LUKTON

According to Drake, the Lukton reportedly lived west of the Rocky Mountains. The Luktons are also referred to in Drake's note on the Killawat to provide geographic orientation, but no additional information is known. (Drake notes that the Killawat lived on the Pacific coast, "E. of the Luktons.")

LUMBEE

The Lumbee is a modern Indian nation that traces its roots to the North Carolina Algonquian bands (Pamlico, Hatteras, Croatan) and Siouan band (Cheraw). They also intermarried extensively with whites, the Blacks, and the Cherokee people. Although the tribe was recognized by the state of North Carolina in 1885, it is not recognized by the Federal government because of the high degree of mixed blood. With a twenty-first century population of some 40,000, they live as private citizens primarily in Robeson, Hoke and Scotland counties of North Carolina.

LUMMI

The Lummi belonged to the coastal division of the Salishan linguistic family. They were the Coast Salish people and lived on the upper part of Bellingham Bay near the mouth of the Nooksack River and on the San Juan Islands. The San Juan Islands, 172 in number depending on how they are counted, are located in the northern reaches of Puget Sound. The four largest islands are San Juan, Orcas, Lopez, and Shaw Islands. The Lummi had villages and fishing stations on Orcas and Shaw islands among others. A confrontation between the United States and Britain over the ownership of San Juan Island, precipitated by the killing of a pig in 1859, almost came to war, the "Pig War." The issue was finally settled under arbitration by the German Kaiser in the US's favor in 1872.

The Lummi were covered in the Point Elliott Treaty of 1855, although they were not listed in the Preamble. Executive Order of November 22, 1873, placed them on the Lummi Reserve of 15,000 acres in western Whatcom County, Washington. Some 12,000 acres currently remain under Indian control. The Samish were also placed on the Lummi Reservation.

Fourteen Chiefs, Sub-chiefs, and Warriors signed the Point Elliott Treaty, an unusually high number for one nation given that they fell under the category of "other allied…tribes."
Chow-its-hoot, Chief of the Lummi and other tribes
Seh-lek-qu, Sub-chief Lummi tribe
S'h'-cheh-oos, or General Washington, Sub-chief of Lummi tribe
Whai-lan-hu, or Davy Crockett, Sub-chief of Lummi tribe
She-ah-delt-hu, Sub-chief of Lummi tribe
Kwult-seh, Sub-chief of Lummi tribe
Kwull-et-hu, Lummi tribe
Hwn-lah-lakq, or Thomas Jefferson, Lummi tribe
Cht-simpt, Lummi tribe
Tse-sum-ten, Lummi tribe
Klt-hahl-ten, Lummi tribe
Kut-ta-kanam, or John, Lummi tribe
S'hoolk-ka-nam, Lummi sub-chief
Ch-lok-suts, Lummi sub-chief

MACAPIRAS

Macapiras or Amacapiras was a small tribe of southwest Florida. They were brought to the Spanish Mission at St. Augustine in 1726, but after 1728 there is no record.

MACHAPUNGA

The Machapunga or Mattamuskeet or Attamuskeet were of the Algonquian linguistic stock. They lived in present Hyde County, North Carolina, and possibly also in Washington, Tyrrell, Dare, and Beaufort counties. The Machapunga had only one village by 1701, at Lake Mattamuskeet. Swanton writes that the Secotan may also have been a village of the Machapunga. Other reports indicate that the Machaunga adopted the Secotan, but no date or other information is recorded; also, that the Croatan joined the Mattamuskeet. The Machapunga took part in the Tuscarora War against the colonists. By 1775 there were only a handful left, equally on the mainland and on the off-shore banks, the latter may have combined with the Bear River Indians.

MACHECOU

The Machecou was a tribe of the Ohio River valley. They were referred to as a "little band of Machecoux" in a letter from Pierre Chouteau to General James Wilkinson, April 12, 1806, regarding the presents and provisions provided to the Indian tribes by lieutenant governor of Upper Louisiana. They were also listed in Jefferson's *Notes on the State of Virginia*, citing Bouquet (1764) where they were reported to have had a population of eight hundred warriors.

MACHEPUNGO

The Machepungo or Machapunga inhabited the Eastern Shore of the Chesapeake Bay in Virginia colony. Later they adopted the Secotan.

MAHICAN

The Mahican proper was the most northern subdivision of the Mahican Group. See the Mahican Group.

MAHICAN GROUP

The Algonquian-speaking Mahicans of New York lived on the banks of the upper Hudson River from Catskill Creek to Lake Champlain and east to the valley of the Housatonic River in Litchfield County, Connecticut.

James Fenimore Cooper made the Mahican famous in "Last of the Mohicans." At the same time, he also effectively erased them from memory having confused their name and history with that of the Mohegan of eastern Connecticut. (The confusion arises because the two names are varieties of the same word and because the Mahican also lived in parts of Connecticut.) The error continues to this day.

The Mahican Group was comprised of five subdivisions or bands: the Mahican proper, Mechkentowoon, Wawyachtonoc, Housatonic or Westenhuck, and Wiekagjoc.

The Mahicans, that became later known as the Stockbridge Indians, were placed on a reservation in Shawano County, Wisconsin. They received the name Stockbridge Indians from the name of a mission into which the Mahicans living in the Housatonic Valley were gathered in 1736. Although the name was initially applied only to those Indians of the valley, it was subsequently applied to all Mahicans, that is to the remnants of the Mahicans that were moved west.

In 1626, the Mohawk ambushed a party of Algonquin-speaking Mahicans and Dutch settlers from Fort Orange (present Albany). The Mohawk killed the fort commander, Daniel Van Crieckenbeeck, three of his men, and twenty-four Mahicans, including their tribal leader Monemin. Three Dutchmen and a few of the Mahicans escaped. By 1635, Fort Orange became the center of the Mohawk trade.

One of the first Dutch settlers in 1624 was Bastiaen Krol. After successfully performing various assignments in New Netherland, he returned to Amsterdam and was hired by a wealthy diamond merchant, Kiliaen Van Rensselaer. He returned in the 1630s and purchased the land surrounding Fort Orange from the Mahicans. What Krol created for his employer and patron was a colony-within-a-colony called Rensselaerswyck. The land stretched along both sides of the river for nine miles and "two-days' journey" inland. Over the next several years the colony was steadily enlarged by buying additional tracts of land from the Mahicans. It eventually covered several hundred thousand acres along both sides of the Hudson completely surrounding Fort Orange. In 1641, there were some one hundred settlers within this sub-colony. That same year Van de Donck arrived as "schout." He was hired by Van Rensselaer in the position of sheriff and public prosecutor to maintain order within the colony. But Donck, who got along quite well with the Indians of the region, considered the idea of establishing his own colony to the west. Before he could put his plan in motion, Van Rensselaer sent another agent to New Netherland who acquired the tract of land called the Catskill from the Indians, presumably also from the Mahicans, thereby extending the colony by several thousand acres.

The Dutch and Mahicans around Fort Orange were insulated from the ravages of the Indian wars that were going on to the south.

MAIDU

The Maidu was of the Penutian linguistic family and inhabited the drainage areas of the Feather River and American River in California. They were one of the larger tribes of California with an estimated population of 9,000 in 1770, probably somewhat of a liberal estimate. The Maidu were divided into three dialectic groups: Nishinam or Southern Maidu, Northeastern Maidu, and Northwestern Maidu. The Southern division was the largest.

The Northeastern Maidu, with less than ten villages, was the smallest. They lived on the upper reaches of the North and Middle Forks of the Feather River. The Northwestern Maidu lived below the High Sierra; in the foothills where the South, Middle, North, and West branches of the Feather River converge; on the upper Butte and Chico creeks; and in the open Sacramento Valley along the lower courses of the Butte and Chico. Individual village names were sometimes applied to all the Maidu. There were also several independent villages. By the 1930 census, the entire population numbered only ninety-three.

MAIDU MASSACRE

Captain John C. Frémont was in command of a newly established California Battalion of Mounted Riflemen in 1846, aching for a fight that would give California to the United States. On March 5, he was ordered out of California by José Castro, Mexican Commandant of California. Frémont's command included a contingent of Delaware Indians and Kit Carson as chief of scouts. With him was Marine Lieutenant Archibald Gillespie, messenger from Washington traveling with Commodore Robert Field Stockton's naval squadron that was anchored off the coast at Monterey. By April Frémont his men had moved into southern Oregon, and two months later he was back in California as part of his undeclared War with Mexico. Under one pretext or another, murderous attacks on the Indians about Klamath Lake in Oregon and the Sacramento River in California became commonplace. An untold number of Indians were killed, and hundreds more were left homeless. Tribes affected were the Kalmath, Maidu, Wintu, and Yana among others. The Maidu Massacre was one incident. Reportedly hearing that the Spanish had encouraged the local Indians to attack white settlers, Frémont ordered an attack and slaughtered the inhabitants of a Maidu village that left upwards of one hundred and seventy-five Indians dead. Whether the people of the village or any Indians were involved in planning an attack on whites is purely conjecture. Also see the Klamath. (The United States declared war on Mexico on May 13, 1846, unbeknownst to Frémont.)

MAKAH

The Makah or Maha belonged to the Nootka branch of the Wakashan linguistic stock and inhabited the area about Cape Flattery in Washington Territory. They claimed the lands from the Hoko River to Flattery Rocks. Mayhill writes that the Makah were 735 miles up from the mouth of the Missouri River on the Mahas (Big Sioux) River. With the treaty of 1855, they were placed on the Makah Reservation.

MALISEET

The Maliseet, Malecite, Marechite, Etchemin or Echemin were of the Algonquian linguistic family and occupied much of what is now considered the eastern border between the U.S. and Canada in northern New England, primarily in northeastern Maine. They are closely related to the Passamaquoddy, Penobscot, and Abenaki and shared the same fate. In early times the territorial boundaries of the three tribes overlapped.

There is much confusion in the literature between the tribal names Malecite, Etchemin, Abenaki, Quoddy, and Tarratines (Tarrateens). Into the mix is added the common names, Canoe men or Canoe-men. For more see Etchemin and Abenaki. The Maliseet were members of the Wabanaki (or Eastern) Confederacy that included the Abenaki, from which the confederacy received its name. Additional confusion has arisen because the Micmac and the Maliseet collectively referred to themselves as Wabanaki, and some material on the two tribes appears in the literature under the Wabanaki name, but they are not Abenaki.

The Malecite Reservation community in Canada is located on a tongue of land at the confluence of the Tobique and Saint John rivers. The Woodstock First Nation reserve was established in May 1851. On June 24 in 1604, the Feast Day of St. John the Baptist, Samuel de Champlain and Pierre de Monts named the river "St. John." The Maliseet had called it *Woolastook* or Good River.

MAMEKOTING

The Mamekoting was a sub-tribe of the Munsee division of the Delaware and one of the five tribes of the Esopus group. They lived west of the Shawangunk mountains in the Mamakating Valley in New York

MANAHOAC

The Manahoac or Mahock belonged to the Siouan linguistic stock and were closely related to the Monacan, the Moneton, and the Tutelo. They inhabited northern Virginia between the Potomac and North Anna rivers north and south. Eight sub-tribes have been identified, together sometimes referred to as the Manahoac Confederacy: Hassinunga, Manahoac proper, Ontponea, Shackaconia, Stegaraki, Tanxnitania, I'eginateo, and Whonkentia. The remnants united with the Tutelo and Saponi.

MANAMOYICK

The Manamoyick tribe was of the Algonquian linguistic family. They lived south of Cape Cod on the Atlantic coast about modern Pleasant Bay (then, Manomoyick Bay). Their lands included the present city of Orleans, Massachusetts, on the outer cape inland from the bay. Mattaguason, the Manamoyick sachem, traded with the settlers of the Plymouth Colony in the early sixteen hundreds. It was from Mattaguason that settlers purchased the rights to Orleans. European history began in 1642 with the arrival and settlement of Nicholas Snow and his family.

MANDAN

The Mandan or Pheasant People were of the Siouan linguistic stock and lived on the Middle Missouri between the Heart and Little Missouri rivers at the northern edge of the territory of the Dakota Sioux.

The first encounter between the Mandan and whites was Vérendrye in 1738. At the time they were living in nine villages near the mouth of the Heart River at the upper limits of the Middle Missouri, about 60 miles downstream from they first encountered Lewis & Clark.* They were a charitable and friendly race and welcomed Lewis and Clark and the other members of the Corps of Discovery on their way up the Missouri and again on their return. They have been uniquely described as "the polite and friendly Mandans." George Catlin also writes of their good hearts but describes them "a very peculiar people" from the "very numerous and striking peculiarities in their personal appearance—their customs—traditions and language" and poses the argument that White blood courses through their veins. For more see the Welsh Indians.

A smallpox epidemic in 1782 nearly devastated the tribe. Reduced in numbers, they were forced to move upstream sometime around 1790 to avoid the Sioux migrating from the east. By the 1800s, wars with the Sioux, Assiniboin, Arikara and others reduced their presence to two large villages, Mupta and Mitutak. Though generally peaceable cultivators of the soils in contrast to their more warlike neighbors who preferred the hunt to the plow, their religious rituals bordered on the sadistic. In 1837 the Mandan almost became extinct as the result of a massive smallpox epidemic. Remnants called themselves Numakaki, meaning "people," and Métutahanke for the name of their old village.

*The 2341-mile Missouri River (or *Mni Sose* in the Lakota language) is generally divided geographically into three regions: the Upper Missouri, the Middle Missouri, and the Lower Missouri. From its source at the Three Forks in Montana north and east some 800 miles to the mouth of the Little Missouri in North Dakota is regarded as the Upper Missouri. The next 1100 miles south to the mouth of the Platte River in southeastern Nebraska is regarded as the Middle Missouri; and from the Platte south to the mouth of the Kansas River at Kansas City and east to its mouth on the Mississippi at St. Louis, the Lower Missouri. The Missouri River basin is now home to people from 28 Native American tribal entities, ten states, and a small part of Canada.

MANHAHOAC

The Manhahoac (also spelled Mahahoac) or Mahock belonged to the Siouan linguistic family and lived in northern Virginia. They may have had an early home in the Ohio Valley. The Mahohoac were noted by Captain John Smith in 1608. After some movement around the colony, remnants were apparently absorbed into the Saponi and Tutelo.

MANHASSET

The Manhasset or Manhansick was a division of the Montauk and a member of the Algonquian linguistic group. They lived along the north shore of Long Island, New York, and on Shelter Island. For more see Montauk Peoples and Delaware.

MANHATAN

The Manhatan was a tribe of the Algonquian linguistic stock that inhabited Manhattan Island of present New York State, a finger of land encompassing 33.8 square miles, that took it name from them. Some writers classify the Manhatan as a sub-tribe of the Delaware; others as a member of the Wappinger Confederacy. This author could find no specific reference to the Manhatan in Swanton. He states (49) only that the Delaware "occupied...all of Staten and Manhattan Islands" and (55) that "their tribes occupied Manhattan Island and the shores of New York Harbor at the arrival of the Dutch." He also states flatly (48) that the Wappinger occupied much of mainland of what is today Greater New York, "but not Manhattan Island." He makes only two references to tribes on the island, the Canarsee on the southern end and the Reckgawawanc on the upper part of the island and names no villages. Elsewhere throughout the literature, the Manhatan tribe appear numerous times with little or no classification indicated.

Shorto, however, puts the Wickquasgeck (which may be the Wecquaesgeek of the Wappinger that Swanton (45) places between the Hudson, Bronx, and Pocantico rivers) on the mainland to the north of the island with the Manhatan principally occupying the island itself, particularly the southern reaches. He writes, "Wickquasgeck was the name of a tribe that inhabited portions of the mainland just to the north of the island [present Yonkers], as well as some of the northern forests of Manhattan. The Manhattan Indians used the Wickquasgeck name for the path they took through the center of the island to these northern reaches." (60) Beczak Center appears to agree. Shorto's position appears consistent with events. On pages 163-164, he writes of land purchases from the Indians to the north adjacent to Manhattan that he identifies as Yonkers, but does not identify the tribe of Indians.

Burrows & Wallace note that the early writings reflect that only few hundred of the "old Manhatans" still lived on the island in 1628. They go on to write that Minuit purchased the island from the "Lenapes" (Delaware) and that the Wappinger drove the original inhabitants from the banks of the East River.

Under the employ of the Dutch West India Company, Henry Hudson make a epic journey in 1609 an attempt to discover the Northwest Passage aboard his ship the Half Moon (*Halve Maen*). He entered what came to be known as Delaware Bay and sailed up the Delaware River that was called the South River by the Dutch. He soon realized that the Delaware was not the portal to the elusive passage to the East. He retraced his steps and sailed up the Atlantic coast into New York harbor and up the Hudson River (the Dutch called it the North River). The territory was subsequently charted for the Dutch by Adriaen Block.

The Delaware Indians called the east side of the river Mannahatta or hilly island. (Recorded variations of the Delaware name were Manados, Manahata, Manahtoes, Manhattos.) Robert Juet, Henry Hudson's first mate, recorded the name "Manna-hatta" in his report. The Mohawk called it Gänóno (place of reeds). It came down in history as Manhattan Island. A report of the secretary of Dutch New Netherland in 1626 referred to them as the Manhatesen. He wrote that they numbered two to three hundred under different chiefs that were called Sackimas (Sachems).

On his return to Europe, Hudson docked at Dartmouth, England, rather than proceeding immediately to Amsterdam to make his report to the company but forward his by way a Dutch agent in England. The Dutch immediately announced Hudson's discovery of the north country and staked their claim on the territory that would be called New Netherland. The land lay between the colonies of the Puritans and the Pilgrims to the north, with French Canada beyond, and the Virginia colony to the south.*

The Dutch West India Company was satisfied with the commercial prospects for Hudson's discovery in the new world and with its location as a counter to the English to the north and south for the trade routes to the Caribbean. Hudson, however, was not. He was determined to uncover the passage to the East and secured the backing of three wealthy English aristocrats for a return trip in the spring of 1610. His route took him and his crew through what would come to be called Hudson Bay. Henry Hudson did not return from that voyage. The crew mutinied against the cold, against the pack ice, and against the frozen sails. They abandoned Hudson, his young son, and those of the crew still loyal to him in the southern reaches of the bay to freeze to death. To save themselves from hanging on their return, they lied and reported that Hudson and indeed discovered the passage and that they alone knew the location of the portal.

Although a few traders followed Hudson, the first settlers (Walloons from French-speaking Belgium) did not arrived until 1624. Small communities were established on Nut Island (today Governor's Island) just to the south of the tip of Manhattan; on the South River; and near the north end of the Hudson river at Fort Orange (today Albany). Peter Minuit (pronounced Min-wee) succeeded to the position of commander of New Netherland two years later. He purchased Manhattan Island from the Manhatesen for the equivalent of sixty Dutch guilders worth of goods (translated as 24 dollars American) in the summer of 1626.** Minuite consolidated the Dutch settlers from the three communities who had been spread across hundreds of miles of New Netherland onto Manhattan Island.

Minuit established a community that he called New Amsterdam at the southern the tip of the island, constructing Fort Amsterdam at the southwest point of the island near the future site of the old Customs House. By 1635 Fort Orange, the center of the growing Mohawk trade, was becoming a thriving settlement. The colony of New Netherland, however, suffered from poor management in spite of the accomplishments of a few individuals. In 1638 William (Willem) Kieft was appointed director (governor), and two years later in 1640 the West India Company ended its monopoly on trade within the company and concentrated on the profitable role as middle-man from its base on Manhattan.

A private, colony-within-a-colony, more of a fiefdom called Rensselaerswyck was established to the north around Fort Orange in the 1630s by a wealthy diamond merchant from Amsterdam, Kiliaen Van Rensselaer. (See the Mahican) Sweden also sought a toehold in the territory claimed by the Dutch, establishing a colony within a colony on the South River in March 1638. (See the Susquehanna) Encroachment into Dutch territory also came from English colonists of the Massachusetts Colony beginning in 1636. They established a settlement called Hartford on the Connecticut River (Fresh River).

The Indian tribes in the region of New Amsterdam included the Tappans, the Hackinsacks, the Wickquasgecks, the Raritans, and the Manhattan. To the north were the Mahicans and the Mohawk. Governor Kieft, ignoring the common will of the citizens of New Amsterdam, embarked on an war with the Indians of the lower valley in what came to be known as Kieft's War. (See the Wickquasgeck) Adriaen van der Donck, who had been hired to provide law and order for the Rensselaerswyck colony to the north, came to Manhattan when his three-year contract expired and helped prepare a petition of grievances against Kieft that eventually led to Kieft's recall. Nevertheless Van Donck assisted Kieft in negotiating treaties with the Indians around Fort Orange.

In payment for his services, Kieft awarded him a large tract of land on the mainland adjacent to Manhattan on the north in July 1645. The land that continued along the river for twelve miles and east to the Bronx River totaled twenty-four thousand acres and became much of what is now the Bronx and the southern portion of Winchester County. Van Donck, in turn, purchased the land from the Indians. The area immediately around his home has come down in history as Yonkers (an extraction from Jonker, Dutch for squire or gentleman of property).

Peter Stuyvesant, who arrived from Amsterdam on May 11, 1647, succeeded Kieft as governor. (He had been sworn in the preceding July.) Kieft set sail on August 16 for his return to Amsterdam and died in a shipwreck off the coast of Wales. Bigoted, intolerant, and autocratic, yet a conscientious and capable administrator, Stuyvesant was the last and most famous of the Dutch governors. It was a time marked by battles with the English and the Swedes and wars with the Indians. In addition, Stuyvesant and Van Donck, once allies, split over the issue of representative government.

The Hartford Treaty of 1650 settled the boundary dispute between New Netherland and New England, but in 1653 a wall was constructed across Manhattan Island (Wall Street) to defend against future intrusions by the English from New England. In 1655 Stuyvesant conquered New Sweden and brought the region back under Dutch control. Dutch settlers were brought in and the settlement was renamed New Amstel. Today, it is New Castle, Delaware. Stuyvesant also became embroiled in two Indian wars: the Peach War (1655) and Esopus Indian Wars (1658-1663). See the Susquehanna and the Esopus, respectively, in this work. Van Donck died sometime between September 1655 and January 1656; some believe that he was killed in the mayhem of the Peach War.

An English naval force under the command Admiral Richard Nicolls, who became the first English governor of New York, captured New Netherland in a surprise attack in 1664. Stuyvesant was forced to surrender without a fight. The terms of negotiated surrender handled by agents of the principals on September 6. The Dutch commissioners negotiated what was in effect the first Bill of Rights. The English commissioners, including John Winthrop (younger), governor of Connecticut, accepted. Stuyvesant was ordered home to explain. Eventually he received permission to return to New York. By that time Fort Amsterdam had become Fort George. Stuyvesant died peacefully in 1672.

The Dutch period lasted just over fifty years from 1609 to 1664. In 1664 there were some fifteen hundred residents of New Amsterdam and some ten thousand residents of the colony of New Netherland. In August 1673 the Dutch recaptured New York, but the Peace of Westminster in 1674 returned it to the English. In a strange twist of fate, William and Mary assumed the throne of England as King and Queen February 13, 1689, succeeding Roman Catholic James II—who succeeded his brother Charles II in 1685. William, who ruled as William III, was Willem of Orange, Stadtholder of the Netherlands; Mary, the daughter of James II.

Reports on the fate of the Manhatesen vary, but 1680 referred to their presence on Manhattan in the past tense. Some reports are that they died out; others that they were driven away by the Wappeno (Wappinger); still others that they moved north into the what became the Bronx. Stuyvesant continued to live on Manhattan until his death in 1672. It is generally believed that by 1700 ninety percent of the one populous Native Americans of the Hudson River Valley had been lost by death and migration and that all their lands in the valley were in the hands of whites by 1758.

*New Netherland occupied the territory from Albany, New York, in the north to Delaware Bay in the south that comprised all or a portion of the states of New York, Pennsylvania, New Jersey, Connecticut, and Delaware. There were three principal river systems within the territory: the Delaware (South River), the Hudson (North River), and the Connecticut River (Fresh River).

**Before he was recalled to Amsterdam in 1632, Minuit had purchased Staten Island (August 10, 1626) and huge tracts of land along the Hudson River and around the Delaware Bay from the Indians. In addition he forged an alliance with the Mohawk to the north.

Of Note

The source of the Hudson River is in the Adirondack Mountains at Lake Tear of the Clouds 4,293 feet up Mt. March (Marcy), the tallest peak in New York State. The River flows 315 miles from its source to its mouth on the Atlantic at the southern tip of Manhattan.

MANSO

The Manso belonged to the Tanoan division of the Kiowa-Tanoan linguistic stock. They lived about Mesilla Valley in New Mexico near present Las Cruces. The Mission of Nuestra Señora de Guadalupe de los Manso was founded among them in 1659 by Fray Garcia de San Francisco. Remnants of the Manso joined the Tiwa and Piro Pueblo.

MANTA

The Manta was a sub-tribe of the Unalachtigo division of the Delaware. They lived in the area about Salem Creek in Delaware. For more see Unalachtigo and Delaware.

MARICOPA

The Maricopa or Pipatsje or Xalychidom Piipaash (People who live toward the water) belonged to the Yuman linguistic stock of the Hokan family. They were composed of a number of small bands that lived along the lower Gila and Colorado rivers in Arizona. Their first encounter with Europeans was with Juan de Oñate in 1604-1605. In the early 1800s they migrated toward Pima villages, and the two tribes formed a strong, mutually-supportive relationship. Both tribes were habitually at war with the Yuma and generally friendly to whites. Although a treaty was never signed with the Maricopa, a reservation near Phoenix was established for the Maricopa and the Pima by Congress February 28, 1859. Now known as Salt River Pima-Maricopa Indian Community, it was enlarged by an Executive Order by President Hayes June 14, 1879 and again on May 5, 1882 and November 15, 1883.

MARSAPEAGUE

The Marsapeague or Massapequa inhabited Long Island. For more see Long Island, New York, Indian Tribes.

MARSHEWTOOC

Nothing is known of the tribe or village named Marshewtooc other than the reference in Willard. Presumably of North Carolina or Virginia, the name contains the suffix "ooc" referring to shellfish and a large body of water.

MASCOUTIN

The Mascoutin or Mascouten, along with many variants of name, belonged to the Algonquian linguistic group. They were first encountered by French missionaries in southern Michigan. The French used their Huron name, Assistaeronon and its variants, meaning "Nation of Fire" or "Fire Nation." It is believed that the Mascoutin were the original people at and around Mackinac, and early French accounts represent them as the dominant tribe in the area, waging war on the Ottawa and other tribes in the area. Early Jesuit missionaries later placed them on the Wolf River, a stream emptying into Lake Winnebago, in Wisconsin. Later in 1670, Father Marquette placed their town on the Fox River, nine miles from the Wisconsin River, at Portage.

The Mascoutins were closely related in language and in interests to their neighbors the Kickapoo, and the two tribes appear to have moved from place to place in unison. One group of Mascoutin that settled on the St. Joseph River in Ohio was nearly destroyed by the Ottawa in the early 1700s. Another group settled with the Fox and the Kickapoo on the Rock River near Chicago; and another, around Detroit where they were attacked and defeated by a body of French-allied Indians about 1712. Later accounts put some of them on the Wabash River and on Lake Michigan.

Swanton, whose description is limited to just one sentence in his tribes of Wisconsin, states only that the name *Mascouten* was applied both to the Prairie Band of the Potawatomi and to the Peoria Band of the Illinois that at one time lived near the Kickapoo, more often the latter. In his tribes of Indiana on the other hand, he lists *Macousin* as a Potawatomi village located on the west bank of the St. Joseph. He also notes that the Potawatomi were sometimes called the Fire Nation, for "people of the fire" or "people of the place of the fire" by the Ojibwe and the Huron. What exactly that they were referring to is unknown.

What might appear to be confirmation of Swanton's description, the generally accepted history of the Potawatomi tribe states that in the 1700s the Potawatomi were comprised of three major groups, one of which was the Prairie Potawatomi, further identified as the Mascoutin or Council Bluffs Band, located in northern Illinois.

It can be argued whether the Mascoutin were a separate, independent tribe or a village or band of the Potawatomi, but the weight of the evidence suggests that the Mascoutins constituted an organizationally independent tribe. They were treated separately by the Jesuit Missionaries and listed separately as the Màscoutens by Jefferson in his *Notes* and as the Mascoutins by Drake in his Enumeration as well as by Shea's "Indian Tribes of Wisconsin." A possible explanation for the confusion and the identification of the Mascoutin as another name for the Prairie Band of the Potawatomi comes from name itself. The word "mascoutin" is a descriptive term derived from the word Muskortenee meaning "prairie." The Iowa Indians were also known as Maskoutens, prefaced by the word Nadouessioux, meaning "Dakota of the Plains."

As far as the name Mascoutin being applied to the Peoria Band of the Illinois, it is known that in 1719 the Mascoutin, along with their allies the Fox and the Kickapoo, were at war with the Illinois. Ten years later the French made peace with the Mascoutin and the Kickapoo. They disappeared from the records about the mid-1700s, the remnants most likely absorbed into the Kickapoo.

Of Note

- The Mascoutin Society of Chicagoland that promotes the culture of the American Indian in the Chicago area adopted for their use the name Mascoutin, but society has no direct connection to the Mascoutin Indians as described here nor, in fact, to any one American Indian tribe.

- There are some that attribute the derivation of the name of city of Muscatine, Iowa, to the Mascoutin Indians, who were reportedly driven westward across the Mississippi and settled on sandy bottomland south of the present site of the city on the Mississippi River in southeastern Iowa. Erected in Muscatine's Riverside Park is a statue of an American Indian. The plaque reads, "Presented to the city by the Muscuitine Tribe #95, Improved Order of Red Men" and "dedicated to the Mascoutin Indians in 1926." Native Americans had nothing to do with the statue. According to David Schweingruber, "Although presented in 1926 by 'Muscuitine Tribe' and dedicated to 'Mascoutin Indians,' no such tribe existed in Muscatine then." White-built monuments to Indians were often used to justify the white conquest of Native Americans by honoring Indians as a "vanishing race," as was the case with the Red Men, a white fraternal organization "devoted to inspiring a greater love for the United States of America and the principles of American liberty."

  Nothing has been found to indicate that the Mascoutin tribe as described here ever settled in eastern Iowa. The Prairie Potawatomi settled for a time in western Iowa. The only tribal groups known to have inhabited eastern Iowa south of present-day Muscatine to the mouth of the Des Moines River at Keokuk were the Fox, the Sauk (Sac), the Iowa, and the Moingwena of the Illinois Cluster of Tribes. As noted previously, members of the Iowa tribe were also known as Maskoutens, further evidence of the common use of the Indian word for "of the prairie," but not necessarily indicative of a separate entity.

MASEQUETOOC

Nothing is known of the tribe or village named Masequetooc other than the reference in Willard. Presumably of North Carolina or Virginia, the name contains the suffix "ooc" referring to shellfish and a large body of water.

MASHPEE WAMPANOAG

The name Mashpee traces its origin to the aboriginal name Massippie, "Land of the Great Cove." Also called the "South Sea Indians" by the colonists of the Plymouth Colony, they lived on Cape Cod generally between what are now the Santuit and Childs rivers, about the present-day town of Mashpee. The early town was settled in the mid-1600s by Wampanoag Indians driven from their lands elsewhere on the Cape by white colonists. In 1665 two Wampanoag chiefs deeded the land in and around Mashpee to the Indians of the town in perpetuity. A few years later, the town became a refuge for survivors of King Philip's war from southeastern Massachusetts.

By the eighteenth century, the few Native Americans still living on Cape Cod and the surrounding islands in southern New England were located on reservations on Cape Cod at Mashpee (Barnstable County), Massachusetts, and at Aquinnah on the very southwestern tip of Martha's Vineyard. In 1763 the General Court incorporated Mashpee as a "plantation" or district belonging to the Indian residents, but with White overseers. The Mashpee were officially recognized by the federal government in 1822 but subsequently removed from the list, apparently as a result of bureaucratic error. The Mashpee Revolt or Woodland Revolt of 1833, that might be more appropriately referred to as passive resistance or civil disobedience, political freedom, that is, freedom to manage their own affairs. The Mashpee were stirred to action by a Pequot Methodist minister named William Apess who took their cause to the Boston newspapers. In 1834 the Massachusetts legislature acquiesced and passed the Mashpee District Act that granted the Wampanoag greater autonomy to govern themselves.

WILLIAM APESS

Apess (also spelled Apes) was born January 31, 1798, in Colrain, Massachusetts, the son of a Euro-Indian father and a mother who he claimed was Pequot but may have been of mixed blood or African ancestry. Deserted by his parents at the age of four while the family was living in Connecticut, he was sent to live with his maternal grandparents and later bound as an indentured servant to three successive white families. The experience enable him to acquire some formal schooling. He escaped to Manhattan in 1813, enlisted in the U.S. Army as a drummer boy in the War of 1812, and saw action in upstate New York. Out of the army in 1815 (accounts differ as to whether he mustered out or deserted because he did not receive his promised enlistment bonuses), he wondered about upper New York and southern Canada for a time before making his way back to Connecticut. Religion hit a positive chord with Apess. As he was growing up, he had attended religious services of both the Calvins and the Methodists. Back in Connecticut, he resumed attending Methodist services, was baptized, and became a licensed Methodist "exhorter" but was denied ministerial ordination. That did not stop him. He traveled throughout southern New England and the Hudson River Valley preaching primarily to Indians, African Americans, and mixed-bloods. In 1829 a break-away Methodist Protestant group formally licensed him as a preacher, and he continued to exhort his audiences and to write.

Apess wrote in the English language, clearly and coherently, and became one of the most prolific Native American authors of all times. He wrote of politics, of history, and of religion. A new collection of his works was compiled and published as recently as 1992 (O'Connell). Among his writings was an autobiography, *A Son of the Forest* (1831). In addition to clarity of his writings, his work on the Mashpee Revolt also won praise for its legal scholarship, *Indian Nullification of the Unconstitutional Laws of Massachusetts, Relative to The Marshpee Tribe: Or, The Pretended Riot Explained* (Boston: Press of J. Howe,1835; reprinted in 1979). Arguably, his most famous work was *Eulogy on King Philip*, which he delivered as a speech in Boston in 1836 and which he subsequently self-published as a pamphlet in 1836 and 1837, *Eulogy on King Philip, as Pronounced at the Odeon, in Federal Street, Boston*. The *Eulogy* compared King Philip (Metacom) to George Washington and King Philip's War with the American Revolution. He wrote and spoke of Native Americans, of their relationships with whites and their struggles and hardships and of what might have been and what could be. He gave Native Americans a renewed sense of identity, a renewed sense of dignity, and a renewed sense of self-worth

Apess attacked prejudice and challenged the biased versions of historical accounts proffered by white authors and speakers, including Daniel Webster, with his own only somewhat less biased versions. Apess was not anti-White; he was pro-justice and pro-Indian-White accord. He died in April 1839 of natural causes in New York.

MASSACHUSETT

The Massachusett, who gave their name to the state, belonged to the Algonquian linguistic stock. They formed one language group with the Narraganset, the Niantic (East and West), and the Wampanoag and possibly the Nauset. They lived to the north of the Wampanoag about Massachusetts Bay between Salem and Marshfield-Brackton including the modern city of Boston. The Massachusett were comprised of six main divisions or bands known by the names of their chiefs.

Band of Chickataubut
Band of Nanepashemet
Band of Manatahqua
Band of Cato
Band of Nahaton
Band of Cutshamakin

It is believed that their first contact with Europeans may have been with John Cabot in 1497. Captain John Smith mentions them frequently in conjunction with his exploration of the New England coast in 1614. Within ten years three-quarters of the population had been destroyed by disease. Warned by Massasoit of the Pokanoket and believing that the Massachusett had targeted the English colony at Wessagussett and Plymouth Colony for a surprise attack, Miles Standish and seven Plymouth men and a Pokanoket warrior took the war to them at Wessagussett. After luring three of the leaders to eat with them inside the fort, Standish and others jumped the three and killed them; another was hanged; and word was sent out to the English to kill all Indians that they came in contact with, resulting in three more deaths. The Massachusett sachem led his warrior in an attack that failed before it got started, suffering one man wounded and the others disappearing into the woods.

Three Englishmen that were then living with the Indians were executed. Standish cut off the head of the warrior who had been primarily responsible for instigating the attack and carried it back to Plymouth where he placed it atop a pole. The Massacre at Wessagussett gained the Plymouth men the acclamation "cutthroats."

The events of the winter of 1623 changed the dynamics of the region and Cape Code in particular. The Massachusett sued for peace; and Wessagussett was abandoned. The all male population headed north to Maine. For their part, the Indians fled their villages in panic and scattered throughout the area, believing that their lives and their villages might be next. Their movements picked up and spread diseases amongst all, and by summer of 1624 hundreds had died. In addition, political alliance between the Indians and between the Indians and the English were forever altered.

MASSACO

The Massaco was a subdivision or sub-tribe of the Wappinger and lived in the present towns of Simsbury and Canton on Farmington River, Connecticut Menunkatuck, in the present town of Guilford, Connecticut. For more see Wappinger.

MASSAPEQUA

The Massapequa or Marsapequa or Matinecocwas a division of the Montauk and a member of the Algonquian linguistic group. They lived on eastern Long Island, New York, in the southern part of Oyster Bay and Huntington townships. Burrows & Wallace place them with the Delaware. For more see Montauk Peoples and Delaware. Some writers equate the Massapequa to the Maspeth; however, Maspeth was the name of an early Dutch settlement on Long Island that took its name from the Mespat.

MATHLANOB

The Mathlanob lived on an island at the mouth of Willamette River where it joins the Columbia in Oregon, near the modern city of Portland.

MATINECOCK

The Matinecock proper was a division of the Montauk and a member of the Algonquian linguistic group. They lived on Long Island, New York, in the townships of Flushing, North Hempstead, the northern part of Oyster Bay and Huntington, and the western part of Smithtown. For more see Montauk Peoples and Delaware.

MATO POMO

Mato Pomo was a sub-tribe of the Northern Poma sometimes treated separately. They lived northwest of Sherwood, California, north of the Noyo River.

MATTABESIC

The Mattabesec or Mattabesec were of Algonquian stock and reportedly the largest and most important village of the Wangunk division of the Wappinger. They occupied both banks of Connecticut river from Wethersfield to Middletown, Connecticut. Some writers have included the Pyquaug village of the Wangunk, also near Westerfield, as part of the Mattabesic. Swanton lists the Pyquaugs separately. For more see Wappinger and Wangunk.

MATTAPANIENT

The Mattapanient was one of the nine divisions of the Conoy and lived on the Patuxent River in St. Marys County, Maryland. For more see Conoy Peoples.

MATTAPONI

Mattaponi (also Mattapony) was a member of the Powhatan Confederacy and the area along the Mattapony River in Virginia. They were divided into the Upper Mattapony and the Lower Mattapony.

MATTOLE

The Mattole constituted one of the divisions of the Athapascan stock of California. They lived in the drainage areas of the Bear and Mattole rivers and on the Eel River near its Van Dusen Fork.

MAUG-NA

Maug-na was a sub-tribe of the Tongva of California that inhabited the area about Rancho de los Felis. For more see Tongva.

MAYEYE

The Mayeye lived inland north or northwest of Matagorda Bay, probably between the Colorado and Brazos rivers in Texas. The Mayeye was counted among the Nations of the North and appear to be the same tribe as the Maquies and possibly the Mayes on St. Gabriel Creek at the mouth of the Guadalupe River in Louisiana. For more see Nations of the North.

MDEWAHATON

The Mdewahaton or Mdewahatonwan (Spirit Lake People) was a tribe of the Eastern Division of the Sioux Nation or People. Other spellings are Mdewkanton and Mdewakanton.

MDEWAKANTON

Mdewakanton, also Medawah-Kanton, was of the Siouan linguistic family and a sub-tribe of the Dakota Oyate or Eastern Division. Most of the Mdewakanton people were exiled from the Minnesota to Nebraska in 1863 following the 1862 Minnesota Sioux War. In Nebraska they became part of a collective entity known as the Santee Sioux of Nebraska. Those that remained in Minnesota were redefined during the 1880s as the Minnesota Mdewakanton Sioux. There has been a continuing struggle over the official identity of Mdewakanton Sioux. Without a thorough knowledge of the situation and all the particulars, any judgement is subject to question; but the Mdewakanton argument appears on the surface to be reasonable and justified. Much of the basis for the contrasting positions appears to be the result of the use and misuse of the name Santee. Readers of this work will recall that Santee is generally taken as a common or popular name for the Dakota Sioux (or the Eastern Division) tribes of the Sioux—understanding that the name Dakota is also used to represent the Sioux Nation as a whole. The Mdewakanton village of Red Wing, Minnesota, was also known as Khemnichan. For more see Sioux and Dakota. For more see Sioux and Dakota.

MECHKENTOWOON

The Mechkentowoon were a subdivision of the Mahican and lived on the west bank of the Hudson River above Catskill Creek. See the Mahican Group.

MEHERRIN

The Meherrin belonged to the Iroquoian linguistic family. They lived along the Meherin River on the Virginia-North Carolina border. They first appeared in 1650. In one report all the members of the tribe were said to be Conestoga. The only basis for the assertion would appear to be if a body of Conestoga from Pennsylvania who were fleeing the Iroquois in 1675 joined the Meherrin. The Meherrin were living on the Roanoke River in 1761 along with the southern bands of the Tuscarora and Saponi, and the Machapunga moving north in 1802.

MELETECUNK

The Meletecunk was a sub-tribe of the Unami division of the Delaware. They lived in Monmouth County, New Jersey. For more see Unami and Delaware.

MELUKITZ

The Melukitz was a tribe of the Kusan linguistic family (Coast Oregon Penutian). They lived on the north side of Coos Bay in western Oregon. The Kusan and Yakonan tribes were placed on the Siletz Reservation in Oregon. For more see Coos.

MEMANKITONNA

The Memankitonna was a sub-tribe of the Unalachtigo division of the Delaware. They lived in the area about Nasman's Creek near present Claymount, Delaware. For more see Unalachtigo and Delaware.

MENGAKONKIA

The Mengakonkia of the Algonquian linguistic stock was one of the six major divisions of the Miami. Later they lost their identity.

MENOMINEE

The Menominee or "Wild Rice Men" as they were called were of the Algonquian linguistic family and lived on and near the Menominee River in Wisconsin. The subdivisions that have been recorded appear to me at the band or settlement level or named for their chiefs. One band, Wi'skos Se'peo Win'niwuk (Wisconsin River People), that lived on the Mississippi near the Wisconsin River, gave their name to the future state.

The Menominee, Chippewa, and Winnebago drove the Sac and Fox from Wisconsin, and in the 1830s the Menominee and the Chippewa ruled eastern Wisconsin. Portions of their land were carved out to make a home for the Oneida of New York State. Earlier they had given refuge to a few Stockbridge Indians from Massachusetts. The senior chief of the Menominee, Oshkosh, agreed to allow the Oneida five hundred thousand acres of Menominee land south of the Fox River. Soon they too would immigrate west in the Great Removal.

MENTO

The Mento (Menton and Mentou) is believed to be the Matora that appears on Father Jacques Marquette's 1673 map. Variations in the spelling that have been found in the literature are Matoua, Matora, Mathora, Mantona, and Mathorha. Delanglez places the tribe in the Arkansas Group (No. 42), and the Tonti Letters places them on the north bank of the Arkansas River about forty leagues or about 120 miles from the village of the Wichita.

MENUNKATUCK

The Menunkatuck was a subdivision or sub-tribe of the Wappinger and lived about the present town of Cuilford, Connecticut. For more see Wappinger.

MERRICK

The Merrick, or Meroke, Merikoke, Meracock was a division of the Montauk and a member of the Algonquian linguistic group. They lived on Long Island, New York, in the eastern part of Hempstead Township. Burrows & Wallace place them with the Delaware. For more see Montauk Peoples and Delaware.

MESCALERO

The Mescalero were one of the three groups of the Western Division of the Apache nation with their homeland in New Mexico's Sierra Blanca. Swanton describes the Mescalero (Group) as comprised of two subdivisions, the Mescalero Band, that lived mainly between the Rio Grande and Pecos rivers in New Mexico, and the Faraon or Apache Band of Pharaoh, a southern division of the Mescalero. The Mescalero life style showed significant traces of the Plains Indians. For more see Apache.

MESPAT

The Mespat inhabited the headwaters of Newton Creek on Long Island, New York, and gave their name to Maspeth, a neighborhood in west central Queens. Maspeth was the first European settlement in Queens County (Dutch New Netherland, 1642) but was attacked by the Indians in 1643 and abandoned a year later but later revived by the English.

MESSASAGU

The Messasagu or Messesague or River Indians was listed in Jefferson's *Notes on the State of Virginia*. They lived about Lake Huron and Lake Superior and had a reported population of 2,000 warriors. For more see "Aborigines," Appendix D.

METEHARTA

The Meteharta or Metaharta inhabited the south bank of the Knife River along the Middle Missouri in North Dakota adjoining the Amahami. They were closely related to the Hidatsa in culture and language; and, although they have been referred to separately in the literature, they were unquestionably a village of the Hidatsa. They are found in the literature under a number of names, including the Minnetwees Metaharta and the very confusing name, Amatiha. The Metaharta village was destroyed by a Sioux raiding party in 1834. For more see the Hidatsa and Amahami.

METHOW

The Methow belonged to the interior division of the Salishan linguistic family. They inhabited the area along the Methow River in Washington State.

MIAMI

The Miami belonged to the Algonquian linguistic stock and were closely related to the Delaware, the Ottawa, and the Shawnee. The Miami were made up of six major divisions.

DIVISIONS
Wea
Piankashaw or Piankashaw
Pepikokia or Pepicokia
Kilatak or Kilatika
Atchatchakangouen or Miami Proper
Mengakonkia.

The Wea and Piankashaw were later recognized as independent tribes, and it is believed that the Pepikokia were absorbed into the Piankashaw. The other three divisions lost their individual identities.

The Miami originally inhabited the area about Green Bay, Wisconsin, but by 1670 they were located at the headwaters of the Fox River. Soon thereafter, they settled at the lower end of Lake Michigan and on the Kalamazoo River in Michigan, parts of Indiana, Illinois, and southern end of Lake Michigan at Chicago (Wea) and on the St. Joseph River. The Miami were pushed from the northern lake country by the Potawatomi, the Kickapoo, and other northern tribes and settled about the Maumee River Valley of Ohio around 1700, quickly becoming the most powerful Indian tribe in Ohio before being pushed west into Indiana. (The Maumee River begins at Ft. Wayne, Indiana, and travels more than 130 river miles to Lake Erie, 105 miles of which are located in Ohio.)

With the intrusion of white settlers into the Ohio Territory following the end of the French and Indian War in 1763, many Indians abandoned Ohio to the Shawnee and moved west into Indiana. The Miami, who had allied themselves with the French, chose the British side in the American War of Independence. After the defeat of the British, the Indians continued their fight against the Americans.

Little Turtle, the arguably the greatest chief of the Miamis, led a combined force of Miamis and other Ohio tribes in the defeat of the army of General Josiah Harmar in 1790 (Harmar's Defeat) and the defeat of the army of General Arthur St. Clair in 1791 (St. Clair's Defeat). Following Harmar's defeat, three Seneca chiefs, Cornplanter, Half Town, and Great Tree, offered to help resolved the conflict between the Miami and the United States, but nothing came of the offer.

In accepting their offer of assistance in the matter, President George Washington responded, "By this humane measure, you will render these mistaken people a great service, and probably prevent their being swept off the face of the earth. The United States require only that these people should demean themselves peaceably. But they may be assured that the United States are able, and will most certainly punish them severely for all their robberies and murders."

Peace failed, and General Anthony Wayne defeated the Miamis and other Ohio Indians at the Battle of Fallen Timbers in 1794. It put an end to the War of the Wabash Confederacy or Wabash Tribes, that is, those tribes living along the Wabash River. With their defeat, the Miami surrendered most of their lands in Ohio with the signing of the Treaty of Greenville (1795). A few Miami moved west and settled in central Missouri. In response to frequent attacks in was called the Boone's Lick, General Henry Dodge took a troop of volunteers and forty or fifty Shawnees and Delawares in September 1814, located Miamis in Saline County, and captured over a hundred and fifty.

In the Treaty of St. Mary's (1818), the Miami were forced give up their reservation in Ohio, and most resettled in Indiana. In 1838 and 1840, they ceded all of what remained of their lands east of the Mississippi except for one small tract of land in Indiana that was held back for the Meshingomesia. (It was divided among their descendants in 1872.) The remainder of the Miami were assigned lands west of the Missouri in Kansas (Indian Territory prior to the 1854 Kansas-Nebraska Act). Jesuit missionaries began visiting the Miami in Kansas about 1847. The Miami were subsequently removed to Indian Territory (northeastern corner of Oklahoma) in 1867 with the Illinois.

HARMAR'S DEFEAT

Josiah Harmar was the commander of the American army in the Northwest Territory, stationed at Fort Washington (present-day Cincinnati). Henry Knox, the Secretary of War, ordered Harmar to suppress the Indian threat in western Ohio. Harmar commanded a force of 320 regulars and about 1,100 poorly trained and poorly equipped militiamen—primarily from Pennsylvania and Kentucky. He planned to attack the Miami and other Indians in western Ohio wherever he found them and to destroy the Indian village near present-day Fort Wayne, Indiana

On October 20, a combined force of Miami, Shawnee and Delaware Indians led by Little Turtle ambushed a detachment from Harmar's force led by Colonel John Hardin that consisted of several hundred militiamen and a few regular soldiers and inflicted heavy losses. Two days later Little Turtle's warriors attacked another column, again inflicting heavy losses. Harmar retreated to Fort Washington. One hundred and eighty-three regulars and militia had been killed or missing. Harmar was accused of wrongdoing during the campaign, but a court marshal found him not guilty. He retired from the army on January 1, 1792.

ST. CLAIR'S DEFEAT

Major General Arthur St. Clair expected to succeed where Harmar had failed. In 1791, he led a second offensive into the Ohio country. St. Clair left Fort Washington on September 17, 1791. Enroute to the Wabash River, St. Clair constructed Fort Hamilton about 25 miles west of present-day Cincinnati and Fort Jefferson about 45 miles north of Fort Hamilton, in what is now western Ohio. On October 24, he engaged in a skirmish with some Miami Indians and November 3 he arrived on the banks of the Wabash River, near several Miami villages.

On the morning of November 4, 1791, Little Turtle led a force composed of one thousand warriors from the Wyandots, Ojibwas, Ottawas, Potawatomies, Cherokees, and Six Nations in an attack on the American camp of about 1,400 regulars and militia, again poorly trained and disciplined. With the party were a number of wives of the soldiers. When the Indians withdrew, over six hundred soldiers lay dead, including a number of women. One account puts the number of women killed at fifty-six. Some accounts put the number killed at over nine hundred, which appears highly exaggerated. Other women and children were reportedly taken prisoner. The number of Indian deaths was very likely less than fifty. St. Clair retreated, retracing his steps to Fort Jefferson and then back to Fort Washington. President George Washington demanded St. Clair resignation from the army, but St. Clair remained governor of the Northwest Territory. The largely unknown Battle on the Wabash River was the worst defeat of an American force by Native Americans in the country's history. Fort Recovery, Ohio, in West Central Ohio was built by Anthony Wayne in March 1794 on the site of St. Clair's Defeat.

FALLEN TIMBERS

Following the defeat of General Arthur St. Clair, an expedition under the command of Major General Anthony Wayne was ordered across the Ohio River to suppress the Indians of the Ohio Valley and open the western lands for settlement. Wayne's advance followed the failed negotiations at Sandusky on Lake Erie in the winter of 1793-1794. Following a major victory at Fort Recovery on June 30, 1794, the expedition won the decisive battle of the campaign at Fallen Timbers on August 20, 1794, defeating the Ohio confederacy of Shawnee, Miami, Wyandot, and Delaware led by Weyapiersenwah (Blue Jacket) of the Shawnee and Michikinikwa (Little Turtle) of the Miami. Fallen Timbers was located near the Maumee River about three miles southwest of the present-day City of Maumee in Lucas County, Ohio. Indian casualties were relatively low, but their homes and crops were destroyed. Appeals to the British at Fort Miamis for assistance were ignored. The War of the Wabash Confederacy had come to an end. The battle broke the back of the confederacy and the hearts of the Indians of the Ohio Valley. It meant the end of the life as they knew it. The Treaty of Greenville followed. Also see Western Indian Confederacy.

TREATY OF GREENVILLE (AUGUST 3, 1795)

With the Royal Proclamation of 1763 all the land west of the original thirteen colonies and east of the Mississippi River from the Canadian border to Spanish Florida was designated Indian Territory. The territory went to the British following the end of the third French Indian War in 1763. The British government immediately issued the Proclamation of 1763 that designated all land west of the demarcation line draws at the crest of the Alleghenies and east of the Mississippi River from the Canadian border to Spanish Florida as Indian Territory. British soldiers were unable to stem the tide of migration. In 1783 the United Colonies obtained the land from Britain by the Treaty of Paris following the Revolutionary War, and the rate of immigration accelerated.

The land to the south of the Ohio River soon began to fill with emigrants from Maryland and Virginia. The land to the north, designated the Old Northwest Territory, was defined in 1787 and consisted of the land south and west of the Great Lakes, north of the Ohio River, west of Pennsylvania, and east of the

Mississippi River and included all of modern-day Ohio, Indiana, Illinois, Michigan, Wisconsin, and part of Minnesota. (The name Old Northwest Territory was used to differentiate it from the New Northwest Territory acquired with the Louisiana Purchase in 1803.) The Ordinance of 1787 set up the machinery for the organization of the Northwest Territory and prohibited slavery within its borders. There were some forty-thousand Native Americans north of the Ohio at the time. In 1800 Congress divided the land creating the Ohio Territory and the Indiana Territory.

Following the successive defeats of generals Harmar and St. Clair by the Native American tribes in the Northwest Territory, a federal force of some three thousand was organized into a Legion under the command of the Major General Anthony (Mad Anthony) Wayne. Wayne's Legion, which included 1,400 mounted militia from Kentucky, met and defeated a combined force of some two thousand American Indians and a small contingent of white Canadians in the Battle of Fallen Timbers on the site of modern-day Toledo, Ohio, on August 20, 1794.

The Indians on foot with bows and arrows were no match for the mounted soldiers with muskets and bayonets. Appeals by the Indians to the English at nearby Fort Miami for help fell on deaf ears. The bitter fighting with atrocities committed by both sides resulted in approximately fifty Indian deaths and some one hundred wounded. Wayne's casualties were somewhat less. After the brief battle, the Wayne's Legion traversed the nearby countryside destroying villages and burning crops. Although reports differ somewhat on the identity of the participating tribes, the weight of available evidence indicates that the combined Native American force consisted of members of the Shawnee, Wyandot, Delaware, Miami, Potawatomi, Chippewa, and Mingo tribes. They were led by Chief Blue Jacket (Weyapiersenwah) of the Shawnee, Chief Turkey Foot of the Ottawa, and Chief Little Turtle (Michikinikwa) of the Miami.

The Battle of Greenville was one of the most significant events of the early republic. Some authors have put on par with the Battle of Lexington and the Battle of Gettysburg. Although the battle was significant in the history of the United States, the fact that the outcome was inevitable—whether this day or next— would tend to question the climatic nature of the event itself. Debates over semantics aside, the battle effectively closed the door on the history of the American Indian in the Northwest Territory, including those who had previously migrated west to escape the white man along the Atlantic seaboard.

The battle was also significant because it precipitated the end of British occupation in North America below the U.S.-Canadian border—the Jay Treaty of 1796. (A little-known provision of the Treaty of Paris of 1783 between the United States and Great Britain that recognized the independence of the American colonies permitted the British to occupy the western lands east of the Mississippi until relations between the federal government and the Native Americans were resolved. The Battle of Fallen Timbers brought a final resolution to the heretofore contentious relationship, not an end to the hostilities.

Representatives of the "western" Native American tribes met with General Wayne at Fort Greene Ville in January 1795 to hammer out an agreement. Eight months later on August 3, 1795, the Treaty of Greenville was signed. Representatives of the following tribes signed the treaty: Wyandot, Delaware, Shawnee, Ottawa, Chippewa, Potawatomi of the River St. Joseph, Potawatomi of Huron, Miami, Eel River, Wea (for themselves and for the Piankeshaws), Kickapoos, Kaskaskias, Delawares of Sandusky, and Reyntueco of the Six Nations living at Sandusky. (Although there were multiple listings for the Ottawa, the Miami, and the Eel River, there was no specific reference to either the Mingo or the Chianti.)

The Indians were forced to cede claim to the land south and east of a boundary that began roughly at the mouth of the Cuyahoga River, southward to Fort Laurens, westward to Fort Laramie and Fort Recovery, and southward to the Ohio River—approximately 25,000 square miles within the present states of Indiana, Illinois, Michigan, and Ohio.

The treaty pushed the Indians into the far northwest corner of Ohio, opening the lower two-thirds of Ohio that ran along a line from Celina to Canton for white settlement. The new Indian Territory would remain Indian territory in name only. In return the Indians received $20,000 in of goods "suited to the circumstances of the Indians" initially and $9,500 in similarly useful goods every year thereafter. Seven tribes, including the Chianti, were to receive one thousand dollars in goods each; the other five, five hundred dollars each. (This was the only reference to the Chianti(s). The name may have referred to the Miami.)

With the large influx of white settlers into southern and eastern Ohio and part of Indiana, Ohio achieved statehood just eight years later in 1803. Native American leaders like Tecumseh and the Prophet emerged in the early 1800s in an attempt to regain their lost lands, but by then Manifest Destiny had become a sacred right. The land in northwestern Ohio that would give rise to fourteen new Ohio counties was acquired from the Wyandot and other Indian tribes with the Treaty of Maumee Rapids signed September 29, 1817.

Of Note

News of the Wayne's victory helped reduce tensions associated with the Whiskey Rebellion in Western Pennsylvania and Virginia by showing the disaffected that the federal government could do something *for* them as well as *to* them.

MICAL

The Mical were a branch of the Pshwanwapam of the Shahaptian linguistic family of Washington State and inhabited the area on the upper course of the Nisqually River.

MICHIGAMEA

The Michigamea or Mitchigamea was one of the major tribes of the Illinois Cluster of Tribes. It is believed that they lived on Big Lake, between the St. Francis and Mississippi rivers, in northeastern Arkansas having migrated south from the Illinois territory. It was visited in Farther Marquette in 1673 in his decent down the Mississippi. The Michigamea were subsequently driven back north by the Quapaw or Chickasaw and united with the Kaskaskia. For more see Illinois Cluster of Tribes.

MICHIGAN POTAWATOMI

In 1850 the Michigan Potawatomi removed to the reserve in Kansas adjoining the Potawatomi of the Woods and the Prairie Potawatomi. For more see Potawatomi and Potawatomi of the Woods.

MICMAC

The Micmac was a Canadian tribe and one of the first Native Peoples to have regular contact with Europeans. They were of the Algonquian linguistic group who originally inhabited Nova Scotia, eastern New Brunswick, most of southeastern Canada, and northern Maine. (Swanton makes no mention of Micmac villages in the state of Maine.) The Micmac survived by fishing and hunting. Although the first recorded contact was made in 1497 by John Cabot, there are some who believe that first contact may have occurred between the Micmac and Viking explorers and settlers as early as the 11th century or possibly with Basque fishermen around the Grand Banks in the fifteenth century. Cabot took three Micmac with him when he returned to England. During his second voyage, Cabot disappeared in the same area. The Micmac were members of the Wabanaki (or Eastern) Confederacy that included the Abenaki, from which the confederacy received its name. Confusion has arisen because the Micmac and the Maliseet collectively referred to themselves as Wabanaki, and some material on the two tribes appears in the literature under the Wabanaki name, but they are not Abenaki.

Their skill at splint-ash basket making was well known in colonial America. Today's Canadian Micmac population is estimated at over 25,000 in twenty-eight separate groups in sixty villages and reserves.

There is one recognized group of Micmac in the United States, the Aroostook Band of Northern Maine with more than 700 members. It is also believed that some 2,000 descendants live in Boston and New York City. The state of Maine formerly recognized the Micmac in 1973. But Federal recognition did not come until 1991. The Micmac of Maine were able to purchase 5,000 acres of their old lands with the funds allocated by Congress in conjunction with Federal recognition.

MIDDLE MISSOURI TRADITION PEOPLE

The Middle Missouri Tradition People was a name given to the Indians that inhabited the area about south-central South Dakota in the mid-1300s. See the Crow.

MIKASUKI

The Mikasuki or Miccosukee, which appears to be the more common form of the name, was a tribe of the Hitchiti-speaking branch of the Muskhogean linguistic family. Hitchiti was one of two languages spoken by the Seminoles, the other being Muskogee (or Creek). It is generally believed that the Miccosukee originally branched from the true Hitchiti or the Chiaha, the latter being more generally accepted. They first appeared by name in 1778. They lived about a lake to which they gave their name, Miccosukee Lake, in Jefferson and Leon counties in northern Florida (Old Milasuki). They subsequently divided, part going to New Milasuki near Greenville in Madison County and part to the Alachua Plains of Alachua County. The name given to the latter was Alachua Talofa or John Hick's Town. Andrew Jackson burned Old Milasuki in 1817. The Miccosukee claimed the center of the state from Gainesville to Okeechobee under the 1823 Treaty of Moultrie Creek; and under an 1839 agreement with the commander in chief of the U.S. Army, Maj. Gen. Alexander Macomb, they claimed the land south of Okeechobee. For over one hundred years lived they have on lands in the Everglades, some of which were established as a Reservation.

One group "accompanied" the Seminole to Indian Territory where they maintained their own identity. Their name in the form Mekusuky was given to a village in Seminole County, Oklahoma. Swanton writes that those that remained in Florida retained their identity as the Big Cypress band of Seminole. They are now known unofficially as the Miccosukee Tribe of Seminole and officially (BIA) as the Miccosukee Tribe of Indians of Florida. They identify themselves as the Miccosukee Seminole Nation. For more see the Seminole.

MIKONOTUNNE

The Mikonotunne (also spelled Mikonotuni) or Mac-qua-noot-na was a band of Tututni that inhabited the north side of the Rogue River in southern Oregon fourteen miles from the mouth of the river.

MILUK

The Miluk or Kus or Mulluk or Lower Coquille Indians were of the Kusan linguistic family and remotely related to the Yakonan stock. They spoke a different dialect from the other tribes of the Kusan family. The Miluk lived on the north side of Coquille River in western Oregon, around its mouth. For more see Coos.

MINDAWARCARTON

The Mindawarcarton or Keenkesah was one of the ten separate tribes or Sioux bands identified by Lewis and Clark. It was the principal tribe of the Dakota or Eastern Division of the Sioux. They lived on both sides of the Mississippi River about the Falls of Saint Anthony that is situated near the modern city of Minneapolis. The tribe reportedly numbered about 300 at the time.

The falls were named in honor of St. Anthony of Padua by a French missionary, Fr. Louis Hennepin, in 1683. Hennepin County, Minnesota, was named in his honor. The falls and its islands were sacred to the Indians of the area. The town of St. Anthony, established in 1849 on the east side of the Mississippi near the falls, was joined with the city of Minneapolis in 1872.

MINGO

The Mingo or Mingwe was a small group of Native Americans related to the Iroquois or Six Nations group of Indians. It was considered by some as a multi-cultural group rather than as a separate tribe. They were sometimes called the Ohio Seneca and Ohio Iroquois. They were also referred to as the Ohio-based Shawnee. Like many other Native Americans, they lived east of the mountains but were pushed west into eastern Ohio and western Virginia by the arrival of European settlers. A 1753-54 map of Ohio Country shows Mingo Town about twenty miles below present Pittsburgh near Steubenville. A later report puts them on the Scioto River in Ohio near Columbus.

By the 1800s, the Mingo Indians had villages along the Sandusky River as well as at Lewistown and later began to live with other tribes, primarily the Miami and the Shawnee. In 1831, the Mingos were forced to sell their lands and move to reservations in the West. Logan was the noted chief of the Mingo Indians. For more see the Iroquois League and the War for Kentucky and the Mingo leader Tachnedorus (John Logan) in the section on the Shawnee.

MINICONJOU

The Miniconjou (Miniconju or Minneconjou) was a tribe of the Teton (Lakota) Division of the Sioux Nation. For more see the Sioux and Lakota.

MINISINK

The Minisink (the place of the Minsi) was one of the principal sub-tribe of the Munsee division of the Delaware and generally considered one of the five tribes of the Esopus group. They lived in the hill country on the headwaters of the Delaware River in southwestern Ulster and Orange Counties of New York and the adjacent lands of New Jersey and Pennsylvania. Thus the name Minsi that signifies "people of the stony country."

MINNAKENOZZO

The Minnakenozzo or Tetons Minnakenozzo were identified by Lewis and Clark as one of the ten separate Sioux tribes or bands. For more see Sioux.

MISCÒTHIN

The Miscòthin was listed in Jefferson's *Notes on the State of Virginia*. They had a reported population of four thousand. For more see "Aborigines," Appendix D.

MISHIKHWUTMETUNNE

The Mishikhwutmetunne, also commonly knows as Coquille or Upper Coquille, was of the Athapascan linguistic stock. Located on the upper Coquille River in western Oregon, they were particularly close to the Tututni. In 1854 they were massacred by Oregon civilian volunteers.

Of Note

In 1854, the Oregon legislature barred testimony of "Negroes, mulattoes, and Indians, or persons one half or more of Indian blood" in proceedings involving a white person.

MISHONGNOVI HOPI

Mishongnovi was a Hopi village on the Second or Middle Mesa. It is frequently referred to as an independent tribe. For more see Hopi.

MISSIASSIK

The Missiassik was a subdivision of the Abnaki. They lived on Lake Champlain in the valley of Missisquoi River at its mouth in Franklin County, Vermont. For more see Abenaki.

MISSISSAUGA CHIPPEWA

The Mississauga or Missisauga of Canada was of the Algonquian linguistic family and a major subdivision of the Chippewa. They lived by hunting, fishing, and gathering on the lands between the St. Lawrence River to the east and Lake Huron to the west, the Ottawa River to the north and Lake Erie, Lake Ontario, the Credit River Valley of Ontario to the south where they became known as the "Mississaugas of the River Credit Indians." One-time enemies of the Iroquois, they were forced to share the lands with the pro-British Iroquois following America's War of Independence. Some of the land was also given to the British loyalists (Tories). The Mississagi River area was on the North Shore of North Channel at the head of Lake Huron. To these Ojibways, the French gave the name of the River. They should not be confused the Mississippi River Chippewa. The first Mississauga land cession came in 1781. Purchases of much larger tracts were made in 1805 and 1806. From the later came today's city of Toronto. The present-day town of Mississauga is a suburb of Ontario. The 1923 treaty between the Mississauga and the Canadian government placed the Mississauga on Rice Lake, Mud Lake, Scugog Lake and Alderville. For more see the Chippewa.

MISSISSIPPI CHIPPEWA

The Mississippi Chippewa or Mississippi River Chippewa was a sub-tribe or subdivision of Chippewa that is generally treated separately. The Mississippi Chippewa were comprised of a number of sub-bands that inhabited the headwaters of the Mississippi River and its tributaries. For more see the Chippewa.

MISSISSIPPI RIVER

When including the Mighty Missouri, the Mississippi River is the third longest river system in the world and drains all or parts of 31 states and two Canadian provinces. The Mississippi itself stretches approximately 2350 miles from a small creek at Lake Itasca in Minnesota to the Gulf of Mexico, building momentum as it draws water from tributaries in Minnesota, Wisconsin, Illinois, and Iowa, followed by the waters of its two principal tributaries, the Missouri at St. Louis and the Ohio at Cairo, Illinois. Before running past New Orleans to empty its fresh currents out into the Gulf through the unusual, finger-like extensions that constitute its mouth, the larger tributaries of the lower Mississippi—the Tennessee, the Arkansas, and the Red—add their waters to the flow.[103]

---

103 Henry R. Schoolcraft discovered the true source of the Mississippi in 1832. At the mouth of the Mississippi River in the Gulf of Mexico there is an area of 5,000-8,000 square mile called the "dead zone" where the oxygen has been severely depleted because of contaminants and an overabundance of nutrients, including fertilizers and decaying plant matter, carried downstream.

Spanish explorer Hernando de Soto is credited with being the first white man to discover the Mississippi River in the spring of 1541 at a village the chroniclers called Quizquiz (pronounced Keyskey), located just south of present-day Memphis.[104] Alvarez de Pineda, who explored the Gulf from Florida to Vera Cruz in 1519, had referred to the tidal flows of a river into the Gulf, but his river that he called *Rio del Espiritu Santo* may have been the Mobile River, east of the Mississippi. If any of the earlier explorers of the likes of Christopher Columbus or Americo Vespucci or Panfilo De Narvaez saw the Great River before De Soto, the event went unrecorded. Three members of the De Soto expedition chronicled their adventures, recording the event. [105] In addition, Garcilaso de la Vega, compiled the most carefully document account of the expedition several years later from the information given to him by members of the original party.

Jesuit missionary Jacques Marquette and Canadian trader Louis Jolliet rediscovered the Mississippi on June 17, 1673. Following Marquette and Jolliet, French explorer Rene' Robert Cavelier (Sieur de La Salle) left Canada and traveled the length of Mississippi into the Gulf of Mexico and on April 9, 1682, took possession the country watered by the Mississippi and its tributaries and claimed it for France, in the name of Louis XIV. It was La Salle that Christened the land New France and Louisiana. In the course of his expedition, La Salle also discovered the mouth of the Mississippi, but the problem of locating the mouth from the Gulf of Mexico remained. On March 2, 1699, Canadian explorer Pierre LeMoyne (Sieur d'Iberville) picked up where La Salle left off.

> *When drawing near to the rocks to take shelter, I became aware that there was a river (!!!!!). I passed between two of the rocks in 12 feet of water, the seas quite heavy. When I got close to the rocks, I found fresh water with a very strong current. These rocks....made me know that here was the Palisade River, which appears to me to be rightly named....I found the mouth of the river 28 leagues south of the place where the ships are. The water from the river does not blend with the salt water for 3/4 of a league to seaward...where there is 18 to 20 fathoms (fathom is about 6 feet)...Ships can come and anchor at the mouth...and take on fresh water without any risk.* [Iberville appears to interpret the name Palisade differently than the way in which the Spanish used the word. He may be referring to the large cottonwood trees that grew in abundance on the lower passes of the river. He makes no mention of obstructions.]

The Spaniards of the De Soto expedition only called the river the Rio Grande (the Great River). Later, other Spaniards, unable to penetrate the Mississippi from the south because of a "palisade" of huge logs and snags that were washed down-stream during high water and lodged in the outlet fingers collecting rocks and mud, named the river Rio de la Palizada. Other names were the Rio Escondido (Lost River); Rio del Espiritu Santo (River of the Holy Spirit); and Rio Grande del Florida.[106] De Vega wrote that he was told by one of the old men of De Soto's expedition (Juan Coles) that in the language of the Indians the river was called the Chucagua. (Interestingly, this is the same name given to the Chicago River by Indians living around the southern tip of Lake Michigan. See the Chicago. Use of the name in relation to the Mississippi could possibly lend some credence to one the later theories on the route taken by the De Soto expedition.)

---

104 A mural depicting the scene by A. Alaux adorns a wall of the Mississippi State Capital., a painting by William Powell hangs in the capital in Washington. The route of the De Soto expedition was first established by a Federal Commission in 1939. The De Soto expedition came ashore near Tampa Bay on the west coast of the Florida peninsula in 1539, marched north-northeast, and then struck out to the west. In recent years, there has been considerable debate as to how far west the expedition traveled, the route taken from that point forward, and when and where the Mississippi was discovered. Tunica County, Mississippi, claims to be the site of De Soto's discovery of the Mississippi River. The honor is also claimed by Coahoma County to the south and Memphis, Tennessee, to the north (see C. Hudson, p. 6). Coahoma County claims that the De Soto expedition crossed the Mississippi River on June 18, 1541, at a point in northwestern Mississippi between Sunflower Landing in Coahoma County to the south and Bass Landing in De Soto County to the north. Other writers have presented completely difference theories. The AIM puts Quizqui at present-day Clarksville in north central Tennessee near the Kentucky border.

105 Fernandez de Biedma, Rodrigo Rangel, A Gentleman of Elvas (Portugal).

106 During the late Colonial period, Spain's Florida territory was reorganized creating two colonies, East Florida and West Florida. East Florida included the peninsula and the land along the coast to the western border of present-day Georgia. The colony of West Florida included the territory along the Gulf Coast from the Chattahoochee/Apalachicola River westward to the Mississippi River and the border with Louisiana. At the time of DeSot0, however, it included all lands south of Virginia and west to Spain's Mexican providence.

In the early Colonial period, over two hundred different Indian tribes made their homes on or near the Mississippi. The great waterway was both a barrier and an avenue of trade; it both protected and gave enemies ready access; and it both nourished the soil and destroyed crops and villages. The river came to known to the Indians by many names. The Dakota called the river "Hahawakpa" (River of the Falls) in reference to the falls now called the Falls of St. Anthony that gave birth to the twin cities of Minneapolis-St. Paul. The place where the Minnesota River meets the Mississippi River was called "Makoce Cokaya Kin" by the Mdewakanton Dakota, meaning "Center of the Earth"; also, "M'dota," a Dakota word used to name the present-day city of Mendota. On the lower Mississippi, the Bayogoula and the Mugulasha were said to live along the Malbanchya River.

To other tribes it was known as Tamalisen; by others, the Tapata; and where it entered the Gulf, the Ri. Among the other known names given to the river by the Gulf Indians were Sassagoula, Malabanchia, and Iser. Later the French gave it the name "Colbert" for the French Finance Minister Jean Baptiste Colbert; "St. Louis" (Iberville, 1699); "R. de La Conception" (Marquette, 1673); and "Riuiere Buade" for Louis de Buade de Frontenac, the French governor of Canada (Jolliet, 1674). The latter was subsequently changed by other writers to "Riuiere Colbert"; and "R. Mitchisipj ou Grande Riviere"; and "Riviere de Messisipi" (1674-1678). The Choctaw and Chickasaw, early migrants from the west called the river Misha sipokni (beyond age), "the idea of something ancient." Some writers have equated "ancient" to father.[107]

Yet, the name may be in fact a European derivation of what many writers believe was the true Ojibwe name, Maesi-sipu or Mamese-Sipou meaning "river of fishes" or "river of many fishes." The highly romanticized Father of Waters it was not, not at least in the early days of the white man although the words may have had an Indian origin. But it was the name Messipi or Mechacebe that stuck. (Mechacebe came from the Latinized form of the two Indian words for Great River, Mecha and Ceba.) It was the Indian names Mee-zee-see-bee and Mechasipi (a contraction of Meact and Chassipi) that some have been interpreted as Father of Waters for *receiving* water from its many tributaries, though one would expect a Father to be *giving* rather than receiving. It was Mee-zee-see-bee in combination with Messipi (Mechacebe) that gave us the name Mississippi.[108]

MISSOURI

The Missouri or Mintache or Missouria spoke the Chiwerian dialect of the Siouan language group as did the Otoe and the Iowa. All three tribes once belonged to the Ho-Chunk or Winnebago Nation in the Great Lakes region. At some point a large group separated themselves and migrated south. One group, the Ioway, settled along the Mississippi River. The Missouria settled along the Missouri River, and the Otoe settled farther west. The Otoe and Missouria, both relatively small in number, were very closely related, both in family genes and in cultural practices.

The Missouri Indians ("people having wooden or dugout canoes") appear as the We-messouret on Farther Marquette's 1673 map. The river he labeled as the Pekitanoui. Around 1690, French trappers encountered a group of Indians, who called themselves the Mintache, camped at the mouth of the Missouri. "Missouri" was the Mintache name for the river. The French adopted the name and also called the Mintache the Missouri because they were the first Indians they had seen on the Missouri River. Another group of

---

107 The name that has come down through history is generally attributed to the Algonquian-speaking Ojibwe of Northern Central United States. They reportedly called the river Messipi (literally misi or missi, "big"; sipi, "water") for Big River or Large River.. The corollary in the Creek language is micco, taken to mean "chief" when used as a noun. The "Michi" of Lake Michigan comes from the same word.

108 There are some that believe, with justification, that the Mississippi is misnamed altogether, at least after it confluence with the Missouri or the Ohio. The Missouri in its own right was longer than the Mississippi (2,466 v. 2,330 or 2,723 v. 2,470, regardless of who is counting) and arguably had a greater flow than the Mississippi. And by any measure, the Ohio had a greater flow than the combined Missouri and Mississippi. When the Mississippi was charted and named, the Missouri was an unknown entity. The Ohio begins in Pittsburgh with the confluence of the Allegheny and Monongahela rivers. Possibly the Allegheny, longer than the Mississippi to Cairo, deserved to have its name carried to the Gulf.

French traders, accompanied by Kaskaskia Indians, visited the Missouri and the Osage in May 1693; and by 1700 French exploration up the Missouri had become routine.

Etienne de Véniard, sieur de Bourgmont, surveyed the Missouri River for the French and constructed a post that he named Fort d' Orleans in honor of the Duke of Orléans on the bank of the Missouri near villages of the Little Osage Indians and the Missouri near present-day Brunswick in Clariton County. In his account of his travels, Bourgmont called the Missouri an ally of the French. A chief of the Missouri and one Missouri woman accompanied Bourgmont and other chiefs to Paris in 1724 where they were received by the Duke and Duchess of Bourbon. Earlier that year, about one hundred Missouri accompanied on his peace and trade mission to the Kansa and Padouca.

Otos and a few Missouris were the first American Indians encountered by the Lewis and Clark's Corp of Discovery in 1804. The Indians approached the campsite of the explorers on the west bank of the Missouri on August 2, 1804. Lewis and Clark invited the Indians to bring their chiefs to a meeting the following day at their campsite at the bottom of a bluff near the present town of Fort Calhoun, about fifteen miles north of Omaha. The campsite came to be known as "council bluff." The Missouri River now runs well east of the bluffs, and the bluffs today are the site of Fort Atkinson State Historical Park. Down river and across from Omaha emerged Council Bluffs, Iowa, that took its name from the council meeting site.

In 1812 the Missouri were located north of the Missouri River along the Grand River, a tributary of the Missouri. They were later dispersed by the Sac and the Fox. An Indian conference was held in May 1815 at Portage de Sioux. The town got its name as a result of the war between the Missouris and the Sioux ranged to the north. To avoid an ambush set up by the Missouris at the mouth of the Missouri River, the Sioux crossed the Mississippi River just north of the confluence of the two rivers at the site of the town and carried the canoes to the Missouri. The victorious Sioux escaped with their spoils of war.

Between 1817 and 1841, the Otoe lived about the mouth of the Platte River in Nebraska. The Missouria, decimated by wars, rejoined the Otoe there around 1829. From that time on, the combined Otoe-Missouri was treated as a single tribe, although the Missouri continued to serve their own chiefs and traditions. During the 1830's, Baptist missionaries established a school for the Otoe. A son born to the missionaries may have the first child born to white settlers in the Nebraska territory. The school, however, lasted less than a decade. With the Manypenny Treaty of 1854 signed in May and modified by a second treaty signed that December, the confederated tribes of the Otoe and the Missouri ceded almost all their lands west of the Missouri River and south of the Platte River in eastern Nebraska to clear the route for construction of the transcontinental railroad. In return a small strip of land ten miles wide and twenty-five miles long in southeast Nebraska Territory was retained as a reserve.

With growing pressure from whites during the 1870s, the Coyote band favored an immediate move to Indian Territory where they believed they could maintain and perpetuate their tribal traditions in peace. The Quaker band wanted to stay where they were in Nebraska even if it meant selling a portion of their reserve. By the spring of 1880, about half of the Otoe-Missouri had left the Big Blue Reservation and joined the Sac and Fox in Indian Territory. By 1881 the Otoe-Missouria were forced to sell their entire Big Blue Reservation and purchased a new reservation of 129,000 acres in the Cherokee Outlet in the Indian Territory in what is presently Noble and Pawnee Counties in northern Oklahoma. Within a few years the tribe was together again in Oklahoma. In 1899 and 1906, the entire reservation was allotted to tribal members in severalty. They instituted a formal constitutional government in 1984 based in Red Rock, Oklahoma.

Of Note

In 1964, after more than a decade of legal argument, the Indians Claims Commission awarded the Otoe-Missouri a million dollar in compensation for the fraudulent way in which the government sold their tribal lands. The award was a landmark in federal claims because it was the first time that an aboriginal title, in lieu of written treaties and deeds, was accepted as legal proof.

MITOM POMO

Mitom Pomo was a sub-tribe of the Northern Pomo that is treated separately. They lived in the area of the Little Lake Valley near Willits with Big River to the west. They claimed the coast of California from south of the Noyo River at present Fort Bragg south to just north of the Navarro River. The Mitom called their coastal village "Bool-dam" or Buldam "big holes" for the blowholes on the headlands at Mendocino and Russian Gulch. The Mitom made Buldam their permanent home about 1850 with the influx of white settlers into Little Lake Valley.

Swanton uses the name Buldam for the name of the band and identifies the village as located at the mouth of the Big River. He also identified another band, Bakau, at Little Lake north of Willits. All references to the Round Valley Reservation refer to the Little Lake tribe.

This writer has found no direct evidence, but it appears the Mitom Pomo had two villages, Bakau at Little Lake and Buldam on the coast at the mouth of the Big River, and that the two Indian names and one American name for the two sites are used interchangeably to identify the same band or tribe.

MIWOK

The Miwok or Mewuk of California were a separate subdivision of the Penutian linguistic family. There were seven different dialects among the bands or villages that were grouped geographically into the Lake Miwok, Coast Miwok, and Valley Miwok—with a population at one time of some 11,000 Indians.

The main body or Valley Miwok was further subdivided between the Plains group, the Northern group, the Central group, and the Southern group. They inhabited the western slope of the Sierra Nevada Mountains between the Fresno and Cosumnes rivers, including the deltas of the San Joaquin and Sacramento rivers, the upper valleys of the Mokelumne and Calaversas rivers, the upper valleys of the Stanislaus and Tuolumne, and along the headwaters of the Merced and the Chowchilla rivers and about Mariposa Creek.

The Coast Miwok lived in the area from the Golden Gate north to Duncan's Point and inland to Sonoma Creek, to include the area about San Rafael, Novato, Bolinas Bay, Freestone, Petaluma, and Bodega Bay. During a December 15, 2007, Mass, at the Church of St. Raphael in San Rafael, retired Bishop Francis A. Quinn of Sacramento apologized to the Coast Miwok for the Catholic church's mistreatment of them two centuries earlier. The Miwok had helped the Spanish priests build and maintain the mission there in 1817 only to be rewarded with the destruction of their spiritual practices and severe punishment for failure to accept European Catholicism.

The Lake Miwok lived in the basin of Clear Lake and the deltas of the streams and creeks flowing into the lake and the southern bank of Cache Creek, including Coyote and Pope valleys.

MAJOR SUBDIVISIONS AND DIALECTS
Lake Miwok
    Lower Lake
    Headwaters of Putah Creek
    Pope Valley

Coast Miwok
    Bodega (sometimes treated separately)
Valley Miwok
    Plains
    Northern
    Central
    Southern

MIWOK REVOLT

In 1829, a former mission Indian named Estanisláo from Mission San José led some four hundred Coastal Miwok of California in a revolt against the Spanish. From their base camp in the San Joaquin Valley they conducted raids against the Spanish missions and ranches in the area, including the Mission San Rafael Arcángel (est. 1814) and Mission San Francisco Solano (Sonoma, 1823), both located north of San Francisco. A company of soldiers from the Presidio at San Francisco sent to capture the Miwok in the spring of 1829 was defeated after of three days of fighting and was forced to return to the presidio empty handed in early May.

A second expedition was launched by Mariano Guadalupe Valleejo on May 29. This time the soldiers were largely successful in destroying all the rebellious Indians except Estanisláo and few others. The battle on the edge of the present-day city of Ripon was called the Spring Creek Massacre. The survivors joined others led by Chief José Jesus and continued their raids of the nearby missions and ranches until they finally signed a peace treaty with the German immigrant and pioneer, Captain Charles M. Weber, that ended the uprising. In gratitude, Weber acquired a Spanish land grant of over 49,000 acres of land on which he founded the city of Stockton (originally, French Camp) in 1849. Estanisláo gave his name to the Stanislaus River (formerly Rio Laquisimes), one of the largest tributaries of the San Joaquin River, on the banks of which Estanisláo and his band made their camp.

Of Note

In 1863, President Abraham Lincoln signed an act declaring the twenty-one missions in the former Spanish California mission chain to be the property of the Catholic Church, and they have remained so since that time.

MOACHE UTE

The Moache or Muache was a subdivision of the Southern Ute that lived in southwest Colorado and northwest New Mexico. For more see Ute.

MOBILE

Mobile was French for the Indian village Mabila in Spanish.. The Indians are referred to both as the Mabila and the Tascaloosas, members of the Tascaloosa Chiefdom (later changed to Tuscaloosa). They spoke a language similar to the Choctaw and lived on the west shore of the Mobile River just below the junction of the Alabama and Tombigbee rivers. They first encountered by the De Soto in 1540. The battle that ensued, led by Chief Tascaloosa, took the lives of some 2,500 Indians. According to Spanish documents, the Mobile were at war with the Pensacola around 1686. The French found them in the same location. After being decimated by wars and disease, it is believed that the Mobile were absorbed into the Choctaw sometime following the end of the French and Indian War in 1763. The village passed to the Creeks.

MOCOCO

The Mococo belonged to the Timucuan division of the Muskhogean linguistic stock and inhabited the area around Hillsbora Bay in Florida. Their connection to De Soto, who landed near the Mococo town, gives them their place in history.

MOCTOBI

The Moctobi belonged to the Siouan linguistic family and lived about the lower course of the Pascagoula River. The name appears in the narratives of the first settlement of Louisiana in 1699 living near the Biloxi and Pascagoula. The Moctobi (also spelled Moctoby) may be a branch of either the Biloxi or the Pascagoula, or the name may be a synonym for the tribal name. For example, it has been suggested that Moctobi is the name used by the Biloxi for the Pascagoula.

MODOC

The Modoc and the Klamath constituted the Lutuamian division of the Shapwailutan linguistic stock. They lived about Little Klamath Lake, Modoc Lake, Tule Lake, the Lost River Valley, and Clear Lake in Oregon, ranging at times to Goose Lake. They did not come into contact with the whites until comparatively late. As a consequence, there were frequent conflicts with atrocities committed by both sides. In 1850 over ninety emigrants on the Oregon Trail, including men, women, and children, were attacked and massacred by a band of Modoc in what has been called the Bloody Point Massacre. The attack occurred in California about three miles from the Oregon border in present Modoc County, In 1864 the Modoc and Klamath were forced to cede their land and were placed on the Klamath Reservation.

Oppressed with their situation on the reservation, a group of some 150 warriors led by Captain Jack (Chief Kintpuash or Kentipoos) left their reservation to return to their homelands in the California border area and refused to return to the reservation. Thus began the Modoc War of 1872-73 with the Modoc retreating to the lava beds of northern California in Siskiyou County. Vastly outnumbered, the Modoc were finally overcome, and five of their leaders were hanged in October, including Captain Jack. Eighty-three U.S. soldiers were killed, including Brigadier General Edward R. S. Canby, head of a truce commission, who was brutally murdered by Captain Jack. Some of what the Americans considered recalcitrants were shipped off to the Quapaw Reservation in Indian Territory. The remainder were returned to the Klamath Reservation. With the end of the Modoc War came the end of Indian resistance in California.

MOGOLLON

The Mogollon Apaches were a subgroup of Apache closely linked to the Mimbreño. They lived about the mesa and mountains of the same name in western New Mexico and eastern Arizona that were named in honor of Juan Ignacio Flores Mogollon, the governor of New Mexico from 1712–15. They were placed under the Southern Apache agency, New Mexico, in 1868; the Hot Springs agency in 1875; and subsequently under the Fort Apache agency. Although the name is now commonly associated with the Apache, the name Mogollon has been used to identify one of three distinct cultural groups of Southwest prehistory, the other two being the Anasazi and Hohokam. The name has also been used in the collective for all prehistory people identified by brownware pottery.

MOGOULACHA

Mogoulacha or Mugulasha inhabited parts of Louisiana on the lower course of the Mississippi and were destroyed by the Bayogoula in 1706. There are reports that they may have been identical to the Quinipissa; other reports indicate that the Mogoulacha absorbed the remnants of the Quinipissa.

MOHAWK

The original homeland of the Mohawk (Kanien:keha'ka) was the middle of the Mohawk River Valley of upper New York State and extended from Schoharie Creek upriver to East Canada Creek. Their hunting range, however, extended well beyond into the Adirondack Mountains in the north and near Oneonta to the south. They lived principally in two villages: Tiononderoge (later Fort Hunter) and Canajoharie. The Mohawk nation was a member of the federation of Iroquois-speaking Indian nations known as the League of Great Peace or the Five (Six) Nations. The smallest of the six confederated nations, the influence of the Mohawks far exceeded their size, in large part because of their position adjoining the European settlements. Their influenced was further enhanced by the reputation of one of their chiefs, Thayendenegea (Joseph Brant).* As the most easterly of the nations of the Iroquois Confederation., they were the first to have their lives and culture influenced by the New Englanders. The Mohawk also received preferential attention from the colonists under the mistaken idea that so goes the Mohawk, so goes the Iroquois and so goes the Iroquois, so goes the native tribes of the Great Lakes and the Ohio Valley.

In 1626, the Mohawk ambushed a party of Algonquian-speaking Mahicans and Dutch settlers from Fort Orange (present Albany). The Mohawk killed the fort commander, Daniel Van Crieckenbeeck, three of his men, and twenty-four Mahicans. Three Dutchmen and a few of the Mahicans escaped. Following the incident, Dutch settlers were regrouped on Manhattan Island, but soldiers were stationed at Fort Orange. In the early years of the decade of the 1630s, Peter Minuit, the leader of the Dutch New Netherland, made peace with the Mohawk and established an enduring alliance. Both the French in and the Dutch in New Netherland contended for trade with the Mohawk. In general the Mohawk favored the Dutch because the French had established an alliance with their enemy the Huron. Dutch trade was directed through the growing settlement at Fort Orange. Furs were collected and shipped downriver to Manhattan to be loaded on ships for Europe.

In late 1634, the Dutch launched an expedition into the interior, led by a young Harmen Myndersz van den Bogaert. The three-man party visited Mohawk villages north and west as far as Oneida Lake, near Lake Ontario, before returning to Fort Orange in January 1635. Van den Bogaert's journal included the first-ever dictionary of the Mohawk language. It also included the first reference to the Five Tribes of the Iroquois League. Present at one of the Mohawk villages was chief from the Oneida tribe. Some two centuries later, the Erie Canal followed Van den Bogaert's route.

Willem Keift, Dutch director-general of New Netherland, with the help of Gysbert van der Donck, negotiated a peace treaty with the Mohawk in 1643.

In 1676 the Mohawk, under the terms of the Convenant Chain with the English, destroyed a major Algonquian encampment in Connecticut thus putting to an end the uprising against the English. The French later made peace with the Mohawk who joined in the Raid of Deerfield, Massachusetts, on February 29, 1704 during Queen Anne's War. Fifty-six English men, women, and children were killed, and more than one hundred residents were driven on a forced to Canada, twenty-one died along the way. After more than a year, some sixty prisoners of war returned to Massachusetts, but some remained in Canada.

The Mohawk sided with the British in the American War of Independence, and the British rewarded them with a compound on the Grand River in Ontario in compensation for the destruction of their homes and the loss of their lands in the Mohawk Valley. Henceforth, the Mohawk would for the most part remain on the Canadian side of the border. The Grand River community that became known as Brant's Town for Chief Joseph Brant became the future home of the majority of the Mohawk principally those formerly of the Canajoharie village. The former inhabitants of Tiononderoge (Fort Hunter) assembled at Tyendinaga at the Bay of Quinte under Chief John Deserontyon. Joseph Brant personally made several trips to

England and remained active in League affairs, but he was more influential with the British than with the brethren of the League who did trust his high living style and his familiarity with the English. Between 1795 and 1797, over 380,000 acres of Grand River lands were sold.

A bronze statue of a Mohawk praying to the Great Spirit, "Hail to the Sunrise," is located in Charlemont, Massachusetts, along the Mohawk Trail (MA Highway 2) in western Massachusetts. The Trail runs from Lexington in the east to the New York State line in the west. For more see Iroquois Confederacy.

*Alan Taylor (4) writes: "Although only about 400 people, the Mohawks derived extra clout from belonging to a broader Iroquois confederacy..." He goes on to record that "the Senecas composed about half of the Iroquois total of 10,000 population." On the other hand, Glatthaar and Martin (18) write: "The two largest nations, the Mohawks and the Senecas, controlled the extremities of Iroquoia." Swanton (40) does not break down the Iroquois population by nation until the 1910 census.

BLESSED KATERI (CATHERINE) TEKAKWITHA (TEGAKOUITA/TEGAKWITHA/TAKWITA)

Native American Catholics pray to Blessed Kateri Tekakwitha (Gah-da-LEE Dey-guh-DWEE-ta) in times of fear and times of challenge, even in times of hope. They pray to the woman they believe will be Rome's first Native American Saint. Kateri, the Lily of the Mohawks, was the daughter of a Christian Algonquin mother and a non-Christian Mohawk chief. She was born in 1656 on the south bank of the Mohawk River in a village known as Ossernenon (present-day Auriesville), New York, forty miles west of Albany.

Kateri was orphaned by a smallpox epidemic that decimated her village and killed her family. Smallpox also left her face disfigured and partially blind. She was Baptized in 1676 by Father Jacques de Lamberville, a Jesuit missionary. She pledged a vow of chastity in 1679, an act that alienated her from her fellow tribe members. Kateri fled their torments traveling some 200 miles through the wilderness to reach the Christian village of Sault Sainte Marie in upper Michigan that was also home to the Sault Indians. The Jesuits founded the mission of Sault Sainte (Ste.) Marie in 1668. It was Fr. Jacques Marquette who named the city and mission in honor of the Virgin Mary. With the Sault (Rapids) mission as their base, the Jesuits evangelized the adjacent country.

Kateri lived an austere life of spirituality caring for the sick and teaching prayers to children until she died of illness at the early age of 24. She died during Holy Week on April 17, 1680, at Caughnawaga, Canada (Kanawaké, Québec). Her last words were reportedly, "Iesos Konoronkwa" (Jesus, I love you). In 1890 a granite monument was erected on the site in her memory. Kateri was declared Blessed by Pope John Paul II on June 22, 1980. The Native Americans of the Catholic faith anxiously await her beatification. Her Memorial Day is celebrated July 14.

The earliest known painting of Kateri, an oil painting on canvas 41"x 37" painted by Father Chauchetière between 1682-1693, hangs in the sacristy of St. Francis Xavier Church on the Kanawaké Mohawk Reservation on the south bank of the St. Lawrence River near Montréal, Québec.

The Tekakwitha Conference is held annually. The conference focuses on Catholic and Native American spirituality and offers educational and spiritual enrichment opportunities. The 65th annual conference was hosted by the Tigua tribe of Texas and the Diocese of El Paso July 28 - August 1, 2004. The latest census conducted by the U.S. Conference of Catholic Bishops indicated that over 500,000 Native Americans were Catholics. Kateri was one of the nine patrons of World Youth Day held in 2002 in Toronto. For more see Kanawake (also spelled Kahnawá:ke and Kanawaké); the Saint Regis; and Sault in this work.

MOHAWK RIVER KALAPUYA

Using the classification of the *Native American Tribes of North America*, the Mohawk River Kalapuya was a group within the of the Central Division of the Kalapooian linguistic stock along the Mohawk River in Oregon. Swanton does not identify a distinct tribe as the Mohawk Kalapuya but refers to a band of the Luckiamute (Lakmiut) living along the Mohawk River. The Luckiamute was also a group within the Central linguistic division of Kalapuya. Several sources also refer to the Winefelly-Mohawk dialect and the Winefelly who also lived along the Mohawk River. See Kalapuya

MOHEGAN

The Mohegan and Mahican (the names are varieties of the same word) are two distinct Algonquin tribes with different locations about a hundred miles apart and with distinctly different histories. The Mohegan or Moheeconneuch were of the Algonquian linguistic family and inhabited the region east of the Thames or Massachusetts River and its branches in eastern Connecticut. James Fenimore Cooper confused the two tribes in the writing of the *Last of the Mohicans* (1826). He was referring to the Mahican of the upper Hudson Valley rather than the Mohegan of Connecticut.

The Mohegan, led by sachem Uncas, allied with the English Puritans against the Pequot in 1637. The alliance brought them unprecedented power and prestige in the region. Those Pequot that were not killed at Mystic River in the Pequot War were placed under Uncas. Narraganset sachem Miantonomi organized a plot to assassinated Uncas in 1643, but the plot failed. He then led an attack on the Mohegan with a force of one thousand warriors that also failed. Instead, Miantonomi was captured and killed in September 1843.

At the peak of the power, the Mohegan claimed authority over some of the Nipmuc and the Connecticut River tribes, and Pequot territory west of the Massachusetts River. Catlin refers to them as the Pequot of Massachusetts. When the Mohegan no longer served the English purposes, they were forced to cede their Connecticut land to the colonies. For more see Pequot War and King Philip's War.

MOINGWENA

The Moingwena, also called the Moingonan, was one of the major tribes of the Illinois Cluster of Tribes. They lived in present state of Iowa near the mouth of the Des Moines River in the southeast corner of the state at present-day Keokuk, Iowa. See the Illinois Cluster.

MOISEYU

The Moiseyu or Moiséyu belong to the Siouan linguistic family. They are believed to have inhabited the lake district of northwestern Minnesota before relocating to the banks of the Missouri in the Dakotas. Swanton and some classifies them as a band of the Cheyenne and occupying one of the "well-recognized places" in the camp circle. Grinnell does not list them, unless under an unrecognized name or spelling. It appears that they were a distinct, independent Siouan tribe that became closely associated with the Cheyenne after the move west and that a number of intertribal marriages created a small Moiseyu band within the Cheyenne, but the great majority moved back north. For more Cheyenne.

MOJAVE

The Mojave (Mohave) belonged to the Yuman division of the Hokan linguistic family. They inhabited Arizona and into California alongside the banks of the lower Colorado River. The Mojave were a sedentary, farming tribe that grew beans, corn and pumpkins. They also fished the river and hunted small animals. The Mojave did not encounter the white man until about 1775. Less than one hundred years later in

1859 the Mojave placed on were combined with the Chemehuevi on the Colorado River Reservation in La Paz County in west-central Arizona which stretches into two counties in California Following the Second World War, a substantial number of Hopi and Navajo were relocated to the California River Reservation. Today, the Chemehuevi, Mojave, Hopi and Navajo Indians collectively form a geopolitical body known as the Colorado River Indian Tribes, headquartered in Parker, Arizona.

MOLALLA

Molalla or Mollalah and the Cayuse constituted the Waiilatpuan division of the Shapwailutan linguistic stock. The Molalla lived together with the more aggressive Cayuse in the valley of the Deschutes River but were driven west by wars and hostile tribes into the valleys of the Molala and Santiam rivers and also to the headwaters of the Umpqua and Rogue rivers. There were three subdivisions: Chakankni, Chimbuiha, Mukanti. They were referred to as the Molel in the treaty of December 21, 1855. The "Definitions" in the U.S. Code refer to the Southern Molalla and the Northern Molalla. The were subsequently placed on the Grande Ronde Reserve.

MONACAN

Monacan or Manakin lived along the upper waters of the James River above the falls at Richmond, Virginia. They were of the Siouan linguistic stock. Captain John Smith learned of them in 1607, and they were visited the following year. The Monacan town of Mohemencho was taken over by the Huguenots in 1699, but most of the Indians had been previously driven away by then. The remnants were apparently absorbed in the Saponi and Tutelo. One writer (Mooney, 1928) identifies the Saponi and Tutelo as the remnants of the Monacan.

MONETON

The Moneton belonged to the Siouan linguistic family. It is believed that they inhabited the area on the lower course of the Knawha River in West Virginia. Their name first appeared in the historical records in 1671, but 1674 was the last reference to them as an independent tribe, possibly absorbed into the Siouan people of the Piedmont.

MONO

The Mono, Western Mono, Monache, or Mono Lake Paiute was a tribe of the western division of the Northern Paiute that occupied the slopes of the Sierra Nevada range in California. They were also called the Mono Lake Kutzadika'a and Kutzadika'a People. They belonged to Shoshonean branch of the Uto-Aztecan stock. Some reports refer to the language as being of the Western Numic group of the Uto-Aztecan language stock.* Official government reports refer to the Mono Lake Kutzadika Paiute Indian Community that speaks a Paiute dialect.

Although there was reportedly a Eastern Mono, most reports generally combine the Western and Eastern into one. No reference has been found of the Eastern Mono except in Swanton. The Mono lived about Mono Lake and the mountain streams that fed the lake, a large but shallow and alkaline terminal lake of about seventy square miles in the Eastern Sierra of California about thirty miles north of Mammoth.

There are reports that Paiutes called the Kutzadika'a lived off Mono Lake and the surrounding Mono Basin for over five thousand years (Fletcher). The Kutzadika'a Community in California is now working to obtain federal recognition of their tribe. There are other reports (Resendes) that the Western Mono may once have occupied the Colorado Plateau before inhabiting the slopes of the Sierra Nevada to join the ancestors of the Yokuts about the year 900. Six divisions of the Western Mono have been reported:

DIVISIONS OF THE WESTERN MONO
Balwisha. On the Kaweah River
Holkoma. Big Burr and Sycamore Creeks near where they join the Kings River
Northfort Mono. North Fork of San Joaquin River (w/ numerous hamlets)
Posgisa (Poshgisha). Big Sandy Creek
Waksachi. On Limekiln and Eshom Creeks and North Fork of Kaweah River
Wobonuch. Head of Mill Creek—one of the five major streams that feed Mono Lake
The 1850s brought the rush of gold miners and new towns along with the white diseases. Their streams were polluted, and much of their lands were taken from them along with their way of life. Today there are two Western Mono rancherias, the North Fork Rancheria and the Auberry or Big Sandy Rancheria.

*NUMIC LANGUAGES
The Numic languages were spoken by Native Americans in Nevada, Utah, and portions of California, Oregon, Idaho, Wyoming, Arizona, Colorado, and Oklahoma. They were formerly classified as Plateau Shoshonean. There are seven Numic languages classified in three groups.

CENTRAL NUMIC LANGUAGES
Comanche
Panamint (Koso, Timbisha)
Shoshone

SOUTHERN NUMIC LANGUAGES
Kawaiisu
Ute-Southern Paiute

WESTERN NUMIC LANGUAGES
Mono
Northern Paiute

MONOMOYICK

The Monomoyick lived about Lower Cape Cod in Massachusetts. After the failure of the Indian plot to wipe out the English at Plymouth and Wessagussett in 1623, the Monomoyick Sachemry became the most powerful on the local tribes because it was the only one of the larger tribes on the Cape not implicated in the conspiracy. It therefore escaped the destruction that befell the other tribes whose sachems were killed, died of disease, or went into exile.

MONTAGNAIS-NASKAPI

The Montagnais-Naskapi was a Canadian tribe that belonged to the Algonquian linguistic stock. They lived between the St. Maurice River and the hinterland of Labrador and from the River and Bluff of St. Lawrence to James Bay.

MONTAUK

The Montauk proper was a division of the Montauk and a member of the Algonquian linguistic group. They lived on Long Island, New York, in Southampton Township. The village was located above Fort Pond in Suffolk county. For more see Montauk Peoples and Delaware.

MONTAUK PEOPLES

The Montauk or Meotac belonged to the Algonquian linguistic family and spoke a dialect similar to the Wappinger. They are generally placed within the Delaware communion of nations.

The Montauk are believed to be the same as the Metoac (also spelled Meotac) of other writers although the number of subdivisions reported vary from twelve to sixteen. In some writings preference is given to the name Metoac v. Montauk. The name Sewanakie was synonymous with the names Meotac and Montauk, but the references give no collaborative information—one reference merely cites the other. It is the opinion of this author that the name Sewanakie most likely originated from the Dutch word *seawan* (sewan or siwan) for wampum for which the Montauk were well respected producers.

The Montauk inhabited the eastern and central parts of Long Island (Paumanok), New York. The Montauk were decimated by a smallpox epidemic in 1658 that reportedly killed two-thirds of the inhabitants of Long Island. A century later, disease struck again. They also suffered a series of attacks by the Narraganset and Wappinger, who regularly conducted raids on Montauk villages. At the same time European settlers were destroying the local animals and their habitats that the Montauk relied on for survival. By the late eighteenth century, there were virtually no native people left on Long Island. Remnants removed to the mainland where they joined the Brotherton.

Long Island was regarded as the source of the best wampum—purple clamshells, and the Montauk were leaders in its manufacture. Each summer the Metoac harvested clam shells from the eastern shores of Long Island that were fashioned into small beads they called "wampompeag" that became shortened to wampum. Wampum was used as a form of currency during the Dutch Period as were furs and pelts. Wampum even found its way into the collection plates at Sunday services. In addition to the color, the grade, quality and condition of the seawan differed dramatically. The best were polished; others were more likely dirty and unpolished. At one point, there was an official exchange rate of six unpolished to four polished. Quality seawan consisted of four polished beads strung. Wampum became a universal language for the different native tribes. For more see Delaware.

SUBDIVISIONS (Swanton)
Corchaug
Manhasset
Massapequa
Matinecock
Merric
Montauk proper
Nesaquake
Patchogue
Rockaway
Secatogue
Setauket
Shinnecock

Population figures have been reported under the names Montauk; Patchogue, a village; and Shinnecock, a division, as if they were three separate, but confederated tribes. (There is at least one reference in the literature to a Montauk Confederation.) None of the other subdivisions of the Montauk are listed separately in the population figures. Descendants are recognized as a tribe by the State of New York under the name Shinnecock.

MONTESANO

The Montesano (healthy mountain) reportedly lived about Puget Sound in Washington Territory and may have been related to the Chehalis of the Salishan linguistic family. The tribe is now considered extinct. Although there is almost no information available, the name is preserved in a number of organizations and institutions throughout the region, including the city of Montesano in Grays Harbor County.

MOOSEHEAD LAKE INDIANS

The Moosehead Lake Indians was a band or subdivision of Penobscot that lived on Moosehead Lake in Maine that separated for a time from the Penobscot. They lived on Moosehead Lake. For more see Penobscot.

MORATOK

The Moratok belonged to the Algonquian linguistic stock. They lived along the north side of the Roanoke River, up river from the Roanoke colony. The only written record is from the Raleigh expeditions.

MORATUOOC

Nothing is known of the tribe or village named Moratuooc except for the reference in Willard. The village was located at the convergence of Welsh Creek and the Roanoke River near Plymouth, North Carolina. The name contains the suffix "ooc" referring to shellfish and a large body of water.

MORAUGHTACUND

Moraughtacund was a member of the Powhatan Confederacy and inhabited parts of Lancaster and Richmond counties.

MOSILIAN

The Mosilian was a sub-tribe of the Unami division of the Delaware. They lived on the eastern bank of the Delaware River about the city of Trenton, New Jersey. For more see Unami and Delaware.

MOSOPELEA

The Mosopelea were originally an Ohio tribe that was also called the Ofo or "Dog People." They were of the Algonquian linguistic family. They were first noted by the French (Tonti) when living in southwestern Ohio. They abandoned the site some time before 1673, possibly driven out by the Iroquois. They settled along the Cumberland River. They subsequently descended the Mississippi to just below the mouth of the Ohio on the western side before continuing on south. Their best-known location was on the lower Yazoo River near the Yazoo and Koroa where Iberville encountered them in 1699. They refused to join their neighbors in the Natchez uprising and joined the Tunica who were allied with the French. Around 1739 they settled close to Fort Rosalie where they remained until 1758. In 1784 they were living along the western bank of the Mississippi above Point Coupée. No more was heard of them until one survivor was located in Marksville, Louisiana, in 1904.

MOSQUITO

The Mosquito or Miskito inhabited an area along the Caribbean Coast of present-day Nicaragua that came to be known as the Mosquito Coast.

The Mosquito concluded a Treaty of Friendship and Alliance with the British in 1740, followed by the appointment of a resident Superintendent in 1749. Soon an formal protectorate was established. The Mosquito allied with the British against the French and Spanish in the American Revolutionary War. The British were forced to subsequently withdrawal from the coast in 1787.

MOYAWANCE

The Moyawance was one of the nine divisions of the Conoy and lived on the west bank of the Potomac River. For more see Conoy Peoples.

MUCKLESHOOT

The Muckleshoot belonged to the Nisqually dialectic group of the coastal division of the Salishan linguistic family. They lived along the White River in Washington State from Kent east to the mountains and about the Green River. According to Swanton, there were three principal subdivisions: the Sekamish on the White River; the Skopamish or Skopamich on the upper Green River; and the Smulkamish or Smalkamish on the upper White River. A fourth division, the Dothliuk at South Prairie, is sometimes added. It is believed by this author that the Sekamish of Swanton was the same as the Stkamish of White River history. Members of the tribes or sub-tribes were subsequently placed on the Muckleshoot Reservation in Kings County.

The name Muckleshoot came into use following the January 22, 1865 treaty at Point Elliott. Muckleshoot was the name given to the native people of the White River area because their reservation was located on Muckleshoot Prairie at the site of Fort Muckleshoot, later changed to Fort Slaughter with the death of Lt. William A. Slaughter who was killed by Indians December 4, 1855. The name was gradually adopted by the people themselves.

591 MUHHUHWAU

The Muhhuhwau reportedly lived in Lower Cape Cod, in Massachusetts and that were most likely a band of the Monomoyick, Nawset, or Sauquatucket. They also reportedly fought with the French in the French and Indian War and may have been influenced to do so by the Scattahook.

Nickerson writes that the Muhhuhwau were also called the Orondock, which appears to be an error because of reference to an Orondoc tribe in Michigan; however, the information available on the two tribes is insufficient to render a final judgment.

MUKANTI MOLALLA

The Mukanti was one of the three divisions of the Molalla. They lived on the western slope of the Cascade Mountains. For more see Molalla.

MUKLASA

The Muklasa was a member of the Creek Confederacy of Upper Creeks. They lived along the south bank of the Tallapoosa River in Montgomery County, Alabama, and moved to Florida following the Creek war.

MULTNOMAH

The Multnomah or Multnomash or Multnomach belonged to the Clackamas or Upper Chinook division of the Chinookan linguistic family. They lived on and near Sauvies Island on the lower Columbia River in Oregon and at the mouth of the Willamette. The subdivisions or sub-tribes are often treated separately in the literature. Drake and others refer to the Wappatoo Island, now called Sauvie (or Sauvies) Island. It is one of the largest river islands in North America.

SUBDIVISIONS
Cathlacomatup, on the south side of Sauvie Island on a slough of Willamette River.
Cathlacumup, on the west bank of the lower mouth of the Willamette River.
They claiming as their territory the bank of the Columbia from there to Deer Island.
Cathlanaquiah, on the southwest side of Sauvie Island.
Clahnaquah, on Sauvie Island.
Claninnata, on the southwest side of Sauvie Island.
Kathlaminimin, at the south end of Sauvie Island.
It was reported that later they became associated with the Cathlacumup and Nemoit.
Multnomah proper, on the upper end of Sauvie Island.
Nechacokee, on the south bank of Columbia River a few miles below Quicksand (Sandy) River.
Nemalquinner, at the falls of the Willamette but with a temporary house on the north end of Sauvie Island.
Shoto, on the north side of Columbia River, nearly opposite the mouth of the Willamette.
They also lived on Vancouver Island.

MUMMAPACUNE

The Mummapacune was a member of the Powhatan Confederacy and inhabited parts of York County.

MUNSEE

The Munsee, under a number of name variations, belonged to the Algonquian linguistic group and originally inhabited northern New Jersey and adjacent portions of New York west of the Hudson River. Swanton and others describe them as major subdivision of the Delaware. Elsewhere they are treated as separate and distinct from the Delaware. Over time they began to be treated separately by all writers. The Munsee (Wolf) inhabited the northernmost territory of the Delaware beyond the Unami (Turtle) and the Unalachtigo (Turkey) to their south. The Munsee were comprised of five sub-tribes or major subdivisions that are often treated separately in addition to a number of villages. Some reports note a correlation between the Munsee and the Esopus Group in what appears to be a minority position. Four and more often five of the sub-tribes collectively constituted the Esopus Group. With four, the Minisink were omitted.

SUB-TRIBES
Catskill
Mamekoting
Minisink
Waranawonkong
Wawarsink

Swanton credits the Munsee and the Unami and Munsee with having the first contact with the Henry Hudson in 1609. The Munsee fled to the Great Lakes region and participated in Pontiac's Rebellion in 1763.

They were pushed west with the other Woodland tribes and in 1854 ended up on 2,571 acres located two miles from the town of Leavenworth, Kansas, that had been part of the Delaware Reserve. (At the same time the Delaware surrendered their rights to the land around Leavenworth distancing themselves from the white settlement leaving the Munsee alone in the area.

Following the passage of the Kansas-Nebraska Act in 1854, white settlers streamed into Kansas. Leavenworth was a growing "metropolis" along the Missouri River, therefore highly attractive to white settlement. By 1857 fifteen squatters and speculators settled on the Munsee land. In violation of the Intercourse Act, offers were made to buy the remaining tract of land, which proved a tempting offer the unwary Munsee. The squatters also subsequently tendered offers—all refused by the George Manypenny, Commissioner of Indian Affairs, and the Secretary of the Department of the Interior. At the same time attempts to buy Kansas half-breed lands on the north bank of the Kansas River were denied by President Pierce. Charges and counter-charges regarding the issue of slavery in the territory entered into the debate.

The land was targeted for construction of competing western railroads: the Leavenworth, Pawnee and Western Railroad (later known as the Union Pacific, Eastern division, and still later as the Kansas Pacific) and Missouri River and Rocky Mountain Railroad. To get around legal obstructions imposed by the Intercourse Act, investors got Congress to patent the Munsee title to their four tracts of land in May 1857, thereby placing the investors in a position to negotiate for sale of the lands directly with the Indians. Eight days after the patent was issued, the investors got the Munsee to sign a contract of sale for all 2,571 acres for $43,400. In order to secure a clear title, it was first necessary for the investors to prevent ratification of a treaty pending in the Senate that would have authorized the proposed sale of 120 acres of the land to the Church of the United Brethren. The treaty failed, and the investors pressed for confirmation of the sale by the land office.

In October 1858 the issue was closed thanks to more highhanded work by territorial officials. The sale to Andrew J. Isaacs was the first instance of the transfer of an important tract of Indian land directly to an individual or group and marked the end of the George Manypenny's influence in the plight of the Indian, and opened up a new avenue for speculators and promoters to get control of Indian lands before they became a part of the public domain.

MUNSEL CREEK

The Munsel Creek was a band or sub-tribe of Indians that lived west of the Cascade Mountains in Oregon. The tribe was listed in the ""Definitions" provided in the U.S. Code. It is believed that they may have lived near present-day Florence, Oregon. Also see Western Oregon Indians.

MUS-QUAH-TA

The Mus-quah-ta reportedly inhabited the St. Joseph River valley in Michigan. The only reference to the tribe that can be found is in conjunction with a report of the Three Brothers Federation by Ms. Silliman. She writes that the tribe was almost exterminated when it challenged the Ottawa. For more see Three Fires Confederacy.

MUSKOGEE

The Muskogee, Muscogee, Ochesee, or Creeks and its sub-tribes and divisions were the dominant tribes of the Creek Confederacy. The Muskogee constituted one division of the Muskhogean language that Swanton calls Northern. The Muskogee had towns and villages throughout the southeast from the Atlantic coast of Georgia and the area about the Savannah River to central Alabama and parts of Florida, Louisiana, and Tennessee.

SUB-TRIBES AND DIVISIONS

Abihka	Kasihta
Atasi	Kealedji
Coosa	Kolomi
Coweta	Okehai
Eufaula	Pakana
Fus-hatchee	Tukabahchee
Hilibi	Wakokai
Holiwahali	Wiwohka
Kan-hatki	

The first historical records date to De Soto's time around 1540. The name "Creek" was first given to a group of Muskogee that inhabited the area around Ocheese (Ocmulgee) CREEK in present-day South Carolina by the colonists.

The confederated Creek tribes spanned across the Carolinas, Florida, Georgia, and Alabama. They were divided geographically into two parts that had no significance other than geographic. The Upper Creeks were located on the Coosa (Abihka) and Tallapoosa rivers with two sub-branches corresponding with the two rivers. The Lower Creeks lived about the lower Chattahoochee and Ocmulgee rivers. Including the Muskogee and the several sub-tribes or divisions of the Muskogee, the Confederacy included some thirty-five tribes.

A division of the Muskogee, the Eufaula, were the first to settle into Florida, some distance from Tampa on the west cost of the peninsula around 1761. A few more drifted in until the great migration following the Creek-American War of 1813-1814. What is referred to as the Seminole language is Muskogee. It replaced the Hitchiti language.

A treaty with the Creek Nation was concluded in New York City in 1790 that set the boundary between the Creeks and the white inhabitants of the United States and established the means and the method of identifying and marking the boundary. But the treaty meant little to those who coveted Creek lands. The Creek fight to hold their lands in the face of hungry settlers was doomed to failure.

WAR, TREATIES AND REMOVAL

Andrew Jackson (known to the Creek as Jacksa Chula Harjo) commanded the U.S. military in 1814 that defeated the Creeks led by Red Eagle. Jackson was helped by the Choctaws and the likes of David Crockett. Battles, which were little more than a series of Indian slaughters, occurred at Burnt Corn Creek, Fort Mims, Black Warriors' Town, Tallussahatchee, Talladega, Horseshoe Bend of the Tallapoosa River. At the conclusion, the Creeks lost 22 million acres of land in southern Georgia and central Alabama.

Eleven treaties were negotiated between 1814 and 1824, a period of voluntary migration, that divested the southern tribes of their eastern lands in exchange for lands in the west, but only a small number of Creeks, as well as Cherokee and Choctaws—traditional enemies of the Creeks—actually moved to the new lands in the west. Early Creek emigrants West settled on the Arkansas River in Oklahoma near present-day Tulsa. In all, the U.S. acquired over three-quarters of the states of Alabama and Florida, as well as parts of Georgia, Tennessee, Mississippi, Kentucky and North Carolina.

By agreeing to the treaties, the Creek hoped to appease the government with the hopes that they would be able to retain some of their land. They also believed that the treaties would protect them from white harassment. In acts of further appeasement, they adopted Anglo-American cultural and economic practices such as large-scale farming and education. They also acquired slaves. Their efforts gained them the designation Civilized Tribe, but it only increased white resentment.

In *Johnson v. M'Intosh* (1823), the Supreme Court ruled that Indians could occupy lands, but the Court held that the Indian "right of occupancy" was subordinate to the government's "right of discovery." The decision put a halt to all Indian land sales.

Having surrendered their lands in Florida (Tallahassee) and Georgia, the Creek continued to hold some 5,200,000 acres in Alabama, but in March 1832, they agreed to a treaty that opened a large portion of the land to white settlement in exchange for government protection of their ownership of the remaining portion divided among the leading families. That approach also failed.

The passage of the Indian removal act marked the beginning of the period of forced migration. By the summer of 1834, only 630 Creeks signed up to immigrate. A year later those remaining in Alabama were defrauded out of their land and left destitute. They stole to survive, and committed acts of arson and murder in retaliation for the brutal treatment they received. Some fled to the Cherokees in Georgia only to be hunted down and murdered by the Georgia militia. In 1836 the Creeks led by Neamathla were forcibly removed by the military, many dying of disease, including cholera and dysentery, and privation in route. The Creeks in the west were nervous and anxious with the coming those from the East, but they were soon overcome with pity for their plight as they witnessed the arrival of the manacled, weakened, and destitute that had been driven west.

The journey west was hazardous at best. In one incident in 1837, the aged steamboat Monmouth carrying six hundred and eleven Creeks struck the barge Trenton on the Mississippi River as it was being towed downstream. The Monmouth broke in two and sank. Three hundred and eleven Creeks were drowned. By 1837, approximately 15,000 Creeks had been driven west on a route that took them south to Mobile and by steamboat up the Mississippi to Memphis where they crossed the river for the overland journey west. The Creeks had never signed a removal treaty.

Some of those from the Eastern tribes fled to east Texas but soon found themselves at the mercy of the Anglos who had supplanted first the Spanish and then the Mexicans. In the late 1830s, the crops and villages of Creeks and other eastern tribes, the "rats' nest" of east Texas as it was called, were destroyed and the Indians driven into Oklahoma. Those that attempted to flee to Mexico were caught and brought back. A few escaped into the Plains. For more see Creek Confederacy, Creek War, and Indian Removal Act of 1830.

MUSQUAKI

The Musquaki tribe was listed in Jefferson's *Notes on the State of Virginia*. They were reported by Croghan (1759); Bouquet (1764); and Dodge (1779) with a population of 200-250 warriors. No location was given. For more see "Aborigines," Appendix D.

MYNONÀMI

The Mynonàmi tribe was listed in Jefferson's *Notes on the State of Virginia*. They lived near Puans Bay on Lake Michigan. For more see "Aborigines," Appendix D.

NAANSI

The Naansi was one of the six or seven allied tribes of the southwestern or Hasinai Division (Hasinai Confederacy) of the Caddo Indians. For more see Hasinai Confederacy and Caddo Peoples.

NABEDACHE

The Nabedache was one of the thirteen principal tribes of the southwestern or Hasinai Division (Hasinai Confederacy) of the Caddo Indians. They lived in eastern west of the Neches River and near Arroyo San Pedo, close to the San Antonio road, at a site that became known as San Pedro. For more see Hasinai Confederacy and Caddo Peoples.

NABEYEYXA

The Nabeyeyxa was one of the six or seven allied tribes of the southwestern or Hasinai Division (Hasinai Confederacy) of the Caddo Indians. For more see Hasinai Confederacy and Caddo Peoples.

NACACHAU

The Nacachau was one of the thirteen principal tribes of the southwestern or Hasinai Division or Hasinai Confederacy of the Caddo Indians, but it may have been a part of the Nacanish. They lived on the east side of the Neches River. For more see Hasinai Confederacy and Caddo Peoples.

NACANISH

The Nacanish (Nacaniche or Nacanish) was one of the thirteen principal tribes of the southwestern or Hasinai Division or Hasinai Confederacy of the Caddo Indians. They lived in eastern Texas north of the Hainai. For more see Hasinai Confederacy and Caddo Peoples.

NACAO

The Nacao or Nacau was one of the thirteen principal tribes of the southwestern or Hasinai Division or Hasinai Confederacy of the Caddo Indians, but it may have been part of the Nacanish according to Swanton. For more see Hasinai Confederacy and Caddo Peoples.

NACAUG-NA

Nacaug-na was a sub-tribe of the Tongva of California that inhabited the area about Carpenter's Farm. For more see Tongva.

NACOGDOCHE

The Nacogdoche was one of the thirteen principal tribes of the southwestern or Hasinai Division or Hasinai Confederacy of the Caddo Indians. They lived at the present site of Nacogdoches. For more see Hasinai Confederacy and Caddo Peoples.

NACONO

The Nacono was one of the thirteen principal tribes of the southwestern or Hasinai Division or Hasinai Confederacy of the Caddo Indians. They lived southeast of the Neches and Nabedache. For more see Hasinai Confederacy and Caddo Peoples.

NACOTCHTANK

The Nacotchtank was one of the nine divisions of the Conoy and lived on the eastern branch of the Potomac River in the District of Columbia. For more see Conoy Peoples.

NADAMIN

The Nadamin was one of the six or seven allied tribes of the southwestern or Hasinai Division (Hasinai Confederacy) of the Caddo Indians. For more see Hasinai Confederacy and Caddo Peoples.

NAGUIDIS

According to Bolton, "Missions on the San Gabriel," the Naguidis was a little known branch of the Hasinai of East Texas. No additional information is known.

NAHMAH-ER-NUH

The Nahmah-er-nuh (obscene) was one of the sub-tribes or bands of the Comanche sometimes treated separately. For more see Comanche.

NAHYSSAN

The Nahyssan belonged to the Siouan linguistic family. Their earliest known location was on the left bank of the James River upstream from present Wingina (Nelson), Virginia. They were first reported in the mid-1600s. By 1675 they had settled on an island near the junction of the Staunton and Dan rivers. Around 1700, they followed the Saponi and Tutelo to the headwaters of the Yadkin. The histories of the three tribes run together thereafter.

NAKANAWAN

The Nakanawan, identified as a tribe of the Caddoan group, was first referred to in 1870. Some believed that it was another name for the Hainai, but it appears more likely that the name referred to some other group that had been previously absorbed by the Hainai, who had absorbed the remnants of several Caddo tribes.

There is one school of thought that suggests that the Hacanac, Lacane, Nacachau, Nacau, Nacaniche, Nacono, and Nakanawan Indians were fragments of the same Caddoan tribe; however, there is no documentary evidence to substantiate the claim.

NAKASA

The Nakasa was a Caddoan tribe and possibly one of the three allied tribes of the Natchitoches Confederacy of Louisiana., but they may have been, which appears more likely, a sub-tribe of the Yatasi. For more see Natchitoches Confederacy and Caddo Peoples.

NAKOTA

The Nakota (also spelled Nacota) or Wiciyela composed the Middle Sioux or Middle Division of the Sioux Nation. It was comprised of two groups:

> Yanktonai or Ihanktonwana "Lesser Campers/Dwellers at the End"
> Yankton or Ihanktonwan "Campers/Dwellers at the End"

They continued to speak the dialect as the Yanktonai, believed to be the senior of the two tribes. There are several interpretations of the structural history of the Nakota.

According to Swanton, the Yanktonai was divided into the Upper Yanktonai and the Lower Yanktonai, also called Hunkpatina. Elsewhere in his writings, he does not use the qualifier "lower." Other writers refer to the Hunkpatina or Hunkpati and the Yanktonai as two related but distinct groups; others refer to the Hunkpatina as a band of the Lower Yanktonai—with no mention of an Upper Yanktonai. Still others call the Upper Yanktonai "Ihanktonwana" (Little End Village) and Lower Yanktonai "Hunkpatina" (Campers at the Horn or End of the Camping Circle).

It is generally believed that at one time the Yankton and Yanktonai and Assiniboin constituted one tribe with three subdivisions, possibly with multiple bands. The Assiniboin or Stone Indians (Stonies), more restless, separated from the other two in the mid-1600s to join the Algonquian Cree to the west. Others believe that they separated from the Wazikute band of the senior Yanktonai.

The Yanktonai and Yankton migrated from their eastern homes north of Mille Lac, Minnesota, in the early 18th century. The Yankton moved west-southwest into Minnesota and South Dakota while the Yanktonai followed the Teton towards the west. The Yanktonai lived at the headwaters of the Sioux, James, and Red rivers and between the James and Missouri rivers as far north as Devil's Lake. They diplaced the Mandan, Hidatsa, and Arikara, forcing them to move upstream. The consensus is that the Yanktonai were comprised of two sub-tribes, the Upper Yanktonai and Hunkpatina or Lower Yanktonai, the latter name falling out of use. The Yankton lived on the James, Des Moines and Sioux rivers.

The Yankton was first mentioned by La Sueur in 1700, without reference to the Yanktonai. It was not until Lewis & Clark in 1804 that both tribes appear in the historical record. The explorers called the two tribes the Yanktons of the Plains and the Yanktons. Presumably, the Yanktonia were the Yankton of the Plains or Big Devils (vs. the Yanktons) described by Lewis & Clark. Drake enumerates the Big Devils, who he places at the head of the Red River (Red River of the North). He assigns the Big Devils to the Youktons (Drake's spelling).

In 1865 separate treaties were made with the government by the Upper and Lower Yanktonai. Subsequently, the Upper Yanktonai were placed mostly at the Standing Rock Reservation and partly at Devils Lake, North Dakota; the Lower Yanktonai (Hunkpatina) mostly on the Crow Creek reservation in South Dakota and partly at Standing Rock and Fort Peck Reservation in Montana. For more see Sioux.

NALTUNNE

The Naltunne or Naltûnnetûnne (Naltunnetunne) was a small tribe of the Athapascan linguistic stock of Oregon sometimes included under the Tututni. Swanton uses all three variations of the spelling of their name.

NAMBE PUEBLO

The Nambe was a member of the Northern division of the Tewa Pueblo Group of the Tanoan linguistic stock. They lived about sixteen miles north of Santa Fe on the Nambe River, a tributary of the Rio Grande, near Nambe Falls. They were the "People of the Round Earth."

NAMIDISH

The Caddoan-speaking Namidish or Nabiti or Amediche was one of the thirteen principal tribes of the southwestern or Hasinai Division of the Caddo Indians or Hasinai Confederacy. They lived on the Angelina River north of the Hainai. For more see Hasinai Confederacy and Caddo Peoples.

NANATSOHO

The Nanatsoho was a Caddoan tribe and was one of the six subdivisions of the Kadohadacho Confederacy. They lived on the south side of the Red River near where it meets the Arkansas-Oklahoma border. For more see Kadohadacho Confederacy and Caddo Peoples.

NANDAKOE

The Nandakoe was a member of the Natchitoches Confederacy of the Southern Caddoan Indians of Louisiana. They lived west of the Yatasi (Yattassee) on the Sabine River. For more see Natchitoches Confederacy and Caddo Peoples.

NANIABA CHOCTAW

The Naniaba was a sub-tribe of the Choctaw that inhabited parts of Alabama, often associated with the Mobile. By 1758 there were only a few warriors left.

NANSEMOND

The Nansemond was a member of the Powhatan Confederacy. For more see Powhatan and Powhatan Confederacy.

NANTAUGHTACUND

Nantaughtacund was a member of the Powhatan Confederacy and inhabited parts of Essex and Caroline counties. For more see Powhatan and Powhatan Confederacy.

NANTICOKE

A separate and distinct tribe, the Nanticoke or Doeg, as they were commonly referred to in the literature, belonged to the Algonquian linguistic group and were one of the Woodland tribes of southern Delaware along the Nanticoke River and the eastern shore of Maryland where they were known as the "Tidewater People." Swanton writes that their name derived from Nenetgo, a variant of the Delaware name Unechtgo or Unalachtigo, the name given to the southern division of the Delaware (Lenape) who were neighbors of the Nanticoke.

The name Doeg may have been a generic term for the Indians of colonial Maryland that included the Piscataway and several other tribes. Under the name Doeg, this instance the Nanticoke, participated in Bacon's Rebellion with the Piscataway and Susquehanna.

The Nanticoke history states that with the migration of late 1600s, the Nanticoke moved north, some as far north as Canada. One group joined the Lenni-Lenape then living in New Jersey where they continue to find their home and refer to themselves as the Nanticoke Lenni-Lenape of New Jersey. There is no specific mention of the when or why they adopted the Lenape name. Swanton tells of the Nanticoke migration into the old Northwest Territory in the early 1700s, but makes no mention of the settlement in New Jersey.

BACON'S REBELLION

Nathaniel Bacon was a colonist and planter whose lands bordered the James River in Virginia. Bacon's Rebellion or Virginia's Rebellion as it is sometimes referred to was the rebellion of Nathaniel Bacon against the established authority of the colonial government under Governor Sir William Berkeley who continually cautioned restraint. During this time, the colonists were suffering the effects of adverse weather on their crops, declining tobacco prices, increasing competition from Maryland and the Carolinas, and rising prices for goods purchased from England. Not that they needed much of an excuse, the colonists blamed their troubles on the local Indians. It took only one relatively small incident to ignite the situation.

In July 1675 the Nanticoke or Doeg raided the plantation of Thomas Mathews in the Northern Neck section of Virginia near the Potomac River in a dispute over the alleged nonpayment for some items

Mathews had apparently obtained from the tribe. Several of the Indians were killed, but the colonists demanded retribution. The militia, one led by Giles Brent and George Mason were ordered out to track down the Nanticoke and punish them. One group led by Giles Brent caught up with the Doeg and asked for a parley. When the Doeg came forward, Brent and his men killed the chief and ten warriors. The second group under George Mason came upon a group of Susquehanna and killed fourteen before they realized that he had the wrong Indians—whether on purpose or by accident is unknown.

The Susquehanna took sanctuary at the fort of the Piscataway. Five chiefs came out of the fort to treat for peace with the leaders of the militias. They were captured and murdered on September 26, 1675. During the siege of the fort that lasted for several weeks, the Indians killed several of the sentinels and escaped and began a campaign of guerrilla warfare on the widely dispersed population. Fearing extermination by a confederation of Indians who seemed to be everywhere, the colonists called on the government to do something. Nathaniel Bacon entered the picture.

In dealing with the situation, Bacon followed his own agenda of extermination, ignoring Berkeley's orders. By April of 1676 he had begun a crusade "against all Indians in general for that they were all Enemies." He assembled a few neighbors who thought as he did and began a march through Virginia. He gathered supporters. Before long he had a large contingent of malcontent, impoverished freemen (former indentured servants who had fulfilled their obligation to their masters with little to show for it). Although their frustrations lay with the upper class, they too blamed the Indians. He even offered freedom to servants and slaves of loyalist masters, and his relations with the governor became more and more acrimonious. Incident followed incident.

In May 1676, Bacon marched south to a fort held by the friendly Occaneechi on the Roanoke River near the present border with North Carolina. The Occaneechi had captured several Susquehanna. Bacon killed the prisoners, then he turned his guns on the Occaneechi. Later he attacked a party of peaceful Pamunkey and took a number of prisoners. At one point, Berkeley pardoned Bacon for his misdeeds; and Bacon was allowed to take his seat in the assembly. The feigned peace did not last long.

On July 30, 1676, Bacon issued his "Declaration of the People" that declared Berkeley corrupt for playing favorites and protecting the Indians for his own selfish purposes. Bacon also required his followers to swear loyalty to him, but by this time his authority was beginning to unravel. In his last act of defiance he burned Jamestown to the ground on September 19. The rebellion ended with Bacon's death on October 26, 1676.

Berkeley hanged, twenty-three persons were hanged for their part in the rebellion and seized rebel property. Authorities in England conducted an investigation, and Berkeley was relieved of his position of governor. He returned to England where he died a year later.

The amount of blood spilled by the rebellion was minimal, and the escaped servants and slaves were easily recaptured, but the white population came away from the experience with a profound hatred of the "unwhite."

NANTUXET

The Nantuxet was a sub-tribe of the Unalachtigo division of the Delaware. They lived in parts of Pennsylvania and Delaware. For more see Unalachtigo and Delaware.

NAPOCHI

The Napochi belonged to the southern division of the Muskhogean and lived along the Black Warrior River in Alabama. They first appear in the accounts of the Spanish in the 1550s. A group of mounds at Moundville (Hale), Alabama, has been connected to the Napochi; otherwise nothing has come down in history after the first accounts. There is speculation that the Napochi may be the Napissa mentioned by Iberville in 1699. There is also some thought that the Acolapissa or the Quinipissa of Louisiana may be the surviving branches of the same tribe.

NARATICON

The Naraticon was a sub-tribe of the Unalachtigo division of the Delaware. They lived in the area about Raccoon Creek in southern New Jersey. For more see Unalachtigo and Delaware.

NARCOTAH

The Narcotah is believed to be a small tribe of the Siouan linguistic stock that inhabited the north county of the upper Mississippi.

NARRAGANSETT

The Narragansett belonged to the Algonquian linguistic family (n-dialect). They inhabited parts of the present states of Connecticut and Massachusetts as well as the greater part of Rhode Island west of Narragansett Bay between the Providence and Pawcatuck rivers. They were the largest and strongest tribe of the region and continually at odds with the Pokanoket (Wampanoag) and Nauset. They befriended Roger Williams in 1636, and with their help he was able to lay the foundation for the colony of Rhode Island. Three years earlier the tribe was hit by a smallpox epidemic that took some seven hundred lives.

The Narragansett, led by sachem Miantonomi, were reluctant allies of the Massachusetts Bay Colony in the Pequot War of 1637 and the massacre at Mystic River. In addition to destroying the Pequot, the power and prestige of the Mohegan were on the ascent. In 1642-1643, Miantonomi attempted to assemble a confederacy of tribes to drive the English out of New England. He began with an attack on their staunch ally, the Mohegan. An attempted assassination on the Mohegan sachem, Uncas, in 1643 failed. Miantonomi subsequently led an attack on the Mohegan with a force of one thousand warriors. The attack also failed, and Miantonomi was captured and in September 1643 killed by Uncas' brother.

In King Philip's war (1675-1676), the Narragansett suffered almost one thousand casualties, both killed or captured in the battle at Kingston.. Remnants joined the Mahican and Abnaki. Some of those who fled to Canada returned and joined with Eastern Niantic—the combined tribe was called the Narragansett.

NASHUA

The Nashua, of the Algonquian linguistic family, inhabited the upper course of the Nashua River near present Leominster, Massachusetts. They were a subdivision of the Pennacook of New Hampshire that were sometimes said to be Nipmuc. The Nashua bartered skins and furs with the early settlers of Groton in the 1600s. Supplied with arms and ammunition by the Canadian French and New York Dutch, they fought against the English in King Philip's War. Remnants escaped to St. Francois in Canada.

NASONI

The Nasoni was one of the thirteen principal tribes of the southwestern or Hasinai Division of the Caddo Indians or Hasinai Confederacy. One of their villages was in the Kadohadacho Confederacy. They lost their individual identity by the late 1800. For more see Hasinai Confederacy and Caddo Peoples.

NASONI, UPPER

The Upper Nasoni was of the Caddo division of the Caddoan linguistic group and one of the six divisions of the Kadohadacho Confederacy. They lived on the south side of the Red River nearly opposite present Ogden, Texas. For more see Nasoni, Kadohadacho Confederacy and Caddo Peoples.

NASONI, UPPER

The Upper Nasoni was a Caddoan tribe of northeastern Texas and was one of the six subdivisions of the Kadohadacho Confederacy. They lived on the on the south side of the Red River. The "Lower" Nasoni, in contrast, was a part of the Hasinai Confederacy. For more see Caddo, Kadohadacho Confederacy, and Hasinai Confederacy.

NASUMI

The Nasumi was a tribe of the Kusan linguistic family (Coast Oregon Penutian). They lived on the south side of Coquille River in western Oregon. The Kusan and Yakonan tribes were placed on the Siletz Reservation in Oregon. For more see Coos.

NATCHEZ

The Natchez were remotely related to the Muskhogean family and spoke the same dialect as the Taensa and Avoyel. They lived along St. Catherines Creek just east of the present day city of Natchez, Tennessee. D'Iberville visited the Natchez on his second voyage to America in October 1699 as he explored the regions of the Mississippi River north of Baton Rouge in Louisiana. He listed nine villages. The Natchez adopted the Grigra who passed into history as a separate tribe. They also had a presence in Alabama among the Abihka Creeks near the Coosa River after 1731; North Carolina along the Hiwassee River with the Cherokee; South Carolina at Fort Hole Springs, leaving in 1744; and Tennessee with the Cherokee after being driven from Mississippi and Louisiana. The Natchez accompanied the Creeks and Cherokees to Indian Territory in the removals of the eighteen-hundreds.

NATCHEZ WAR

The Natchez War in 1729 has been referred to as the Natchez Massacre, Natchez Uprising, and the Natchez Revolt. Resentful of the treatment they were receiving from the French commandant they attacked the post and settlement at Fort Rosalie on November 28, 1729; massacred 229-237 men, women, and children; and took an equal number or more of captives, mostly black slaves but also a number of women and children. They followed with a massacre at Fort St. Pierre, overlooking the Yazoo River near present-day Redwood, Mississippi, as the revolt continued to spread throughout the area. A French force of 1,400 from New Orleans and their allies the Choctaw drove the Natchez from their Grand Village near Fort Rosalie and continued to press the Indians over the next two years, pursuing them into northeastern Louisiana. The Natchez had received some limited support from the Chickasaw but were essentially on their own but were joined by some escaped black slaves.

A few escaped to join the Chickasaw, but some four hundred Natchez finally surrendered in 1731 and were sent into slavery in Santo Domingo. Of the remnants, one group merged with the Upper Creeks, eventually settling near Eufaula, Oklahoma. The others joined the Cherokee, becoming known as the Cherokee Natchez, and eventually settling in Indian Territory.

NATCHITOCHES

The Natchitoches (pronounced Nack ă tish) proper belonged to the Caddo division of the Caddoan linguistic group and one of the four principal divisions of the Natchitoches Confederacy of Louisiana. It inhabited the area near Natchitoches. For more see Natchitoches Confederacy and Caddo Peoples.

NATCHITOCHES CONFEDERACY

The Natchitoches Confederacy constituted one of the major divisions of the Caddo Peoples and the Caddo division of the Caddoan linguistic group. They lived in northwestern Louisiana on the Red River in the vicinity of the French post of Natchitoches established in 1714 (Fort St. Jean Baptiste aux Natchitos). Members were first placed on the Brazos Indian Reservation (Young County, Texas) and later in 1858 removed to the Indian Territory. For more see Caddo Peoples.

PRICINPAL TRIBES	ALLIED TRIBES
Doustioni	Capiché
Natchitoches proper	Nakasa
Ouachita	Choye
Yatasi	

NATCHITOCHES, UPPER

The Upper Natchitoches was of the Caddo divisions of the Caddoan linguistic group and one of four principal tribes of the Natchitoches Confederacy. They lived on the south side of the Red River between the Nanatsoho and Nasoni. The "Lower" Natchitoches was a member of the Natchitoches Confederacy. For more Natchitoches Confederacy and Caddo Peoples.

NATEOTETAIN

According to Drake, the Nateotetain lived on a river of their name, west of the Facullies. but no additional information is available. The Facullies were the Northern Carrier Indians of British Columbia, Canada.

NATICK

The Natick or "Praying Indians" was a village of the Massachusett Indians that had been converted to Christianity by Rev. John Eliot in the mid-1600s. Protestant missionary John Eliot was considered the Apostle to the Indians. In 1649,he founded the oldest Protestant foreign missionary society. Joining those at Natick by Indians from various tribes in eastern Massachusetts and emerged as a separate tribal unit. They lived near the present town of Natick, Massachusetts, in Middlesex County west of Boston.

During King Philip's War, the Natick Indians were removed to Deer Island, located in the inlet to Boston harbor from Massachusetts Bay, where many died of disease, cold and starvation. Several, however, joined the British as scouts and trackers. The Natick village was destroyed during the war and never recovered. Their lands were sold off to the white settlers, and by 1725 most of the Natick Indians had drifted from the area. For more see Praying Indians and King Philip's War.

NATIONS OF THE NORTH

Nations of the North or Norteños (northerners) was the name coined by the Spanish of the mid-1700s to identify the Indians of North Central Texas that were enemies of the Apaches. One or more reports include the following tribes, sub-tribes or bands among the Nations of the North, often the same tribe under several different names.

NORTEÑOS
Caddo (name was used as the collective term for the linguistic group)
Comanche
Kitsai (Wichita Group)
Macheye (Tonkawa Group)
Osage
Ovedsita
Queissei
Tancague

Taovaya (Wichita Group)
Tawakoni (Wichita Group)
Tuacane
Vidai
Wichita (name was used in the collective sense)
Xaramane
Yacovane
Yscani (Wichita Group)

Reference to the Wichita was used as a collective term for the Wichita proper and its sub-tribes and divisions whereas the name Caddo appears to have been used in the collective sense for the linguistic group.

The Norteños waged an ongoing war with Spanish authorities in Texas until a temporary peace was finally established with treaties executed in 1771 and 1772 by Baron de Ripperdá, governor of Texas. Accounts attributable to the "Nations," however, cannot be assumed to include any one or all of the individual tribes. The word Nations was used in the generic sense for enemy.

Most notable of the incidents was the attack and destruction of the Mission Santa Cruz de San Sabá by some two thousand Norteños in March 1758. The mission was situated about four miles downstream from the Presidio de San Saba (originally Presidio San Luis de las Amarillas) that was established as an outpost of San Antonio in April 1757. It was located on the outskirts of is presently the town of Menard, Texas, at the western edge of the Texas Hill Country. The mission was subsequently rebuilt and combined with the presidio itself. A retaliatory expedition in 1759 led by Don Diego Ortiz Parrilla against the Norteños in a Taovaya stronghold was a failure. The name San Sava found in some reports is a typographical error. Also some reports mistakenly refer to an attack on the presidio itself rather than on the mission. Also see Lipan in this work.

It is reported that in 1760 a number of the Norteños petitioned Padre Fray Josef Calahorra to intercede for them to secure peace and to establish a mission or them on their territory. It would still be twelve years before peace was restored. In 1772 the presidio was officially abandoned, and the buildings fell into the possession of the Indians until the American settlers moved into the area in the 1850s.

NATSSHOSTANNO

The Natsshostanno was one of the six or seven allied tribes of the southwestern or Hasinai Division of the Caddo Indians or Hasinai Confederacy. For more see Hasinai Confederacy and Caddo Peoples.

NAUDI

The Naudi was listed by Farther Ortiz in his memorial to the king of Spain sometime after February 14, 1747, cited by Bolton in "Missions on the San Gabriel," but no additional information about the tribe is known. It is believed that the Naudi lived in east central or southeastern Texas.

NAUSEGOOC

Nothing is known of the tribe or village named Nausegooc except for the reference in Willard. The village is depicted on many maps and it thought to be located near the Neuse River in Carteret County, North Carolina. The name contains the suffix "ooc" referring to shellfish and a large body of water.

NAUSET

The Nauset belonged to the Algonquian linguistic stock and were probably in the same linguistic group or dialect as the Massachusett and Narragansett. They inhabited all of Cape Code in modern Massachusetts except for the western end. As a result they are popularly called the Cape Indians. The Nauset felt the sting of the Europeans early in modern history. In 1614, a English ship's captain, Thomas Hunt, abducted about twenty Nausets to sell as slaves in Spain. Hunt commanded one of the ships in John Smith exploratory expedition into New England waters. In New England tribal politics, the Nauset were allied with the Wampanoag and the Massachusett against the Narragansett.

They were one of the first tribes to encounter the settlers from Mayflower in 1620-1621. The settlers stole from their store of corn and rifled their graves, but later made amends through the intervention of the Wampanoag. Many died of fever in 1710. The Nauset were joined by remnants of other tribes over the years.

NAVAJO

The Navajo or Navaho or Nabijo were of the southern division of the Athapascan linguistic group that included all the Apache. There own name, which is quite common in the literature, is Diné (written Dîné and sometimes as Déné). Diné was a variation of Indé, meaning "the people" by which the Apache referred to themselves. The Athapascans migrated south from the Mackenzie River Basin of Canada along the eastern slope of the Rockies sometime between 1000-1400, descendants of those first who had first crossed the land bridge from Siberia. As the main group of Apaches continued south into Texas, the Navajo broke off from their blood brothers in eastern Colorado or northern New Mexico and headed west-southwest into their historical homeland in the canyons of northern Arizona and northern New Mexico. It is believed that they settled the area about 1500. The first mention of them in the historical record came as "Apaches de Nabaxu" in a 1626 report by Father Zarate Salmeron, a Franciscan friar at Jemez. (Swanton gives the year as 1629 and hyphenates the friar's name.)

The Navaho maintained ongoing wars with the Pueblos to the east, the Utes to the north, and the encroaching Mexican and Anglo-American settlers to the south. By the dawn of the eighteenth century the Navajo economy had become almost wholly dependent on the raising of sheep and goats introduced into the region by the New Mexicans in the 1500s, augmented by selective farm crops. The bloody raids that began against the Mexican settlements continued unabated following the ascension of the United States. Terms agreed to at Bear Springs on November 21, 1846 with Col. Alexander Donipahn and 1848 was not worth the paper it was written on. The second round of talks ended in disaster. Following an row over a stolen horse that took place during peace negotiations on September 9, 1849 between Lt. Colonel John M. Washington, Governor of New Mexico, and James Calhoun, the Indian agent, and three Navajo headmen including the aged but still revered Norbona, seven Indians were killed. Norbona was one of the seven. Manuelito, the proud son-in-law of Narbona and a hothead who hated Americans and Mexicans alike, rose to the position of headman. The bloody raids continued with a vengeance, the Navajos stealing children, women, and sheep, with almost total impunity. The 1861 massacre at Fort Fauntleroy under the command of Colonel Manuel Antonio Chaves ended whatever slight hope for peace that there might have been. Twenty men, women and children were killed; many more were wounded, and well over one hundred were taken prisoner. The depredations continued until the outcry from the settlers became such that they demanded a final solution.

Beginning in early July of 1863, a New Mexican militia force of nearly one thousand men under the command of Colonel Christopher "Kit" Carson crossed the Navajo lands from east to west in a scorched-earth campaign that left no crops or hogans standing and no animal alive. Carson set up outposts at Fort Wingate and the old Fort Defiance that he renamed Fort Canby. As the soldiers moved west, the Navajo dispersed. Many took refuge in the great sandstone chasm of Cayon de Chelly, over three hundred atop Fortress Rock deep within the canyon itself. Nevertheless, the winter of 1863-1864 took a deadly toll. Once they learned that Carson was not on a mission of extermination, but rather relocation, they surrendered voluntarily—first by the tens, then by the hundreds in such numbers as to overwhelm the facilities of Fort Canby. Eight hundred had arrived by the first week in February. The fighting such as it was produced twenty-three killed and thirty-four prisoners. Utterly defeated and half-starved, they began what they called the "Long Walk" to the Bosque Redondo (Round Forest) Reservation on the Rio Pecos in eastern New Mexico guarded by troops stationed at Fort Sumner. They traveled in groups throughout 1864 and into 1865. Depending on the weather, the "Walk" took about three weeks. It was not only the weather and hunger that they had to contend with. It was undisciplined soldiers and both New Mexicans settlers and Comanche raiding parties who swooped down stealing women and children. Some nine thousand Navajo were marched out from their lands to the west, five hundred or more died or disappeared enroute. Manuelito managed to keep out of sight of government informants until late 1866 when he and about two dozen of his followers turned themselves in at Fort Wingate to be taken to Redondo.

The Navajo's first winter was particularly harsh. They not only had to deal with the weather but also with an insect infestation that destroyed three thousand acres of corn. The Navajo were kept from starvation only through the extraordinary efforts of General James Henry Carlton to secure food and supplies to feed the mass of starving Indians. It was Carlton who had ordered the relocation of the Navajo to put the greatest distance possible between them and the Anglo and Hispanic settlement and to facilitate the assimilation of the Navajo children into American culture. Carlton saw no hope in transforming the adult population. It was also Carlton who had selected the Redondo site for the experimental project to which he became obsessed. A further troubling issue was the friction caused by the presence of the Mescalero Apaches from southwestern New Mexico who had been rounded up and placed on Redondo in late 1862. The problem finally resolved itself when all four hundred Mescaleros bolted the reservation in mass in November 1864.

Carlton's project was finally recognized as an economic and social failure. Four years after the first Navajos arrived at Bosque Redondo, the Navajo were allowed to return to a reservation established for them on their home lands. Only 7,300 Navajos remained. Although the reports of the numbers vary, more than one in four of those imprisoned at Bosque Redondo died there. A new treaty was signed June 1, 1868, by the U.S. Peace Commissioners led by Lt. Gen. William T. Sherman and Barboncito and Manuelito for the Navahos. The new treaty gave the Navajo all that they might have hoped for. On June 18, they began their walk home.

The Navajo reservation occupies some 26,110 square miles (17 million acres) in Arizona, Utah, and New Mexico. Approximately 165,000 Navajo now live within its borders, and another one-hundred thousand plus live off the reservation primarily in the same three states. With a total population of some 270,000, the Navajo are the most populous of the Native American tribes. The reservation, with its capital at Window Rock, Arizona, constitutes one-third of all Indian lands in the lower forty-eight states. But a failing infrastructure and a lack of basic services coupled with limited education and employment opportunities continue to siphon off the population.

NAVASINK

The Navasink was a sub-tribe of the Unami division of the Delaware. They lived on the Navasink highlands and from the Barnegat River to the Raritan in New Jersey. For more see Unami and Delaware.

NDE-NDA-I

The Nde-nda-i was one of the three major bands or sub-tribes of the Chiricahua. They lived a more nomadic life style southwest of the Tsoka-ne-nde, almost wholly within the Sierra Madre of Mexico.

They were considered the more predatory of the three bands. Noted leaders included Juh (pronounced Hwu) of a sub-group called the Nednhi, one of the most vicious of all the Apaches, and Gerónimo of the sub-group Bedonkohe. The names Nednhi and Nde-nda-i are sometimes used interchangeably.

Gerónimo or Goyathlay (ca.1829-1909) was of the Bedonkohe group of the Nde-nda-i. He was the di-yin or shaman for war rather than a hereditary chief. For more see Apache.

(The shaman was part priest, part healer—more mental than physical, part mystic, part magician. He was the link to the spirit. He was a "medicine man" who believed strongly in the power of the inner self. He was also a man of vision and a man with a forceful personality and a strong sense of purpose and self-worth. Shamans also became involved in political issues and participated in treaty-making.)

NEBADACHE

The Nebadache was a member of the Natchitoches Confederacy of the Southern Caddoan Indians of Louisiana. For more see Natchitoches Confederacy and Caddo Peoples.

NECHACOKEE

The Nechacokee was a sub-tribe of the Eloot or Echeloot and belonged to the Upper Chinook division of the Chinookan family. They are often found treated separately. They inhabited the area about present Blue Lake in Oregon. The journals of the Lewis and Clark expedition contain an entry dated April 3, 1806, that notes passing a Nechacokee village on the Columbia. Decimated by disease and white encroachment, the tribe was extinct by the mid-nineteenth century. For more see Echeloot.

NECHACOLEE

The Nechacolee or Nechacokee was a subdivision or sub-tribe of the Multnomah. They belonged to the Chinookan linguistic family and lived about the headwaters of the Columbia River Slough along Blue and Fairview Lakes in Oregon's Portland Basin. For more see Multnomah.

NECHAUI

The Nechaui was one of the thirteen principal tribes of the southwestern or Hasinai Division of the Caddo Indians or Hasinai Confederacy. Some scholars, however, believe that the Nechaui may have been a more southern group of the Neche, but that assertion has not been proved. Their principal village was located southeast of the Nebedache near the Nacono on the Neches River in what is now southern Cherokee County, Texas. In the 1700s any remaining members of the tribe were in all likelihood absorbed by one or more neighboring Hasinai tribes. For more see Hasinai Confederacy and Caddo Peoples.

NECHE

The Neche (often written as Neches for both singular and plural) was one of the thirteen principal tribes of the Caddoan-speaking tribes of the southwestern or Hasinai Division or Hasinai Confederacy. They lived along the Neches River in present-day Cherokee and Houston counties in Texas during the seventeenth and eighteenth centuries. Their main village was about three miles east of the Neches River, west of Nacogdoches. It was from their name that the Neches River received its name. They lost their ethnic identity among the surviving remnants of Hasinai tribes that were placed first on the Brazos Indian Reservation (1855) and four years later removed to Indian Territory. For more see Hasinai Confederacy and Caddo Peoples.

NEEKEETOO

The Neekeetoo reportedly lived on the Pacific coast south of the Columbia River in Oregon, beyond the Youicone.

NEHALEM TILLAMOOK

The Nehalem of the coastal division of the Salishan linguistic family was a subdivision of the Tillamook. They lived on the Nehalem River of Oregon

NEIHAHAT

The Neihahat was one of the six or seven allied tribes of the southwestern or Hasinai Division of the Caddo Indians or Hasinai Confederacy. For more see Hasinai Confederacy and Caddo Peoples.

NEPONSET

Neponset was a sub-tribe or village of the Massachusett Indians that lived on the Neponset River about Stoughton that is generally treated separately. At one time they claimed what is now the Walpole area and surrounding territory, adjoining the town of Dedham. For more see Massachusett.

NESAQUAKE

The Nesaquake was a division of the Montauk and a member of the Algonquian linguistic group. They lived on Long Island, New York, in the eastern part of Smithtown and the land to the east. For more see Montauk Peoples and Delaware.

NESHAMINI

The Neshamini was a sub-tribe of the Unalachtigo division of the Delaware. They lived on Neshaminy Creek in Bucks County, Pennsylvania. For more see Unalachtigo and Delaware.

NESPELIM

The Nespelim or Nespelem was of the Salisham linguistic family and a major division of the Sanpoil that is generally treated separately. They lived on the Nespelem Creek, a tributary of the Columbia in northeastern Washington about 40 miles above Fort Okinagan. The division should not be confused with one of its villages, Nspilem, on the Nespelem. The Nespelim were placed on Washington's Colville Reservation.

NESTUCCA TILLAMOOK

The Nestucca, one of the distinguishing flathead tribes, was a subdivision of the Tillamook. They lived on Nestucca Bay and the streams flowing into the bay in present Tillamook County, Oregon. They were one of the largest groups of the Salishan linguistic family south of the Columbia River.

NEUSIOK

The Neusiok were related linguistically to either the Algonquian or the Iroquoian families. Opinion is divided. Reed suggests the Iroquoian linguistic group because of their closeness to the Tuscarora. The Neusiok lived along the south side of the lower Neuse River in present Craven and Cartaret counties of North Carolina. They were first spoken of in 1584. Their numbers fell quickly after contact with the Europeans. It was during the first half of the eighteenth century that a group of Indians that became known as the Coharie removed from the main body and settled in southeast North Carolina. Remnants of the Neusiok may have united finally with the Tuscarora. For more see the Coharie.

NEUTRALS

The Neutrals or Neutral Nation were of the Iroquoian linguistic stock and originally inhabited present New York State. They got their name, not because they were necessarily peaceful, but because they tried to stay out of the continuing war between the Five Nations and the Huron. At one time the Neutrals were believed to have twenty-eight villages, the names of only five have survived. One name, Ongniaahra, that was located at the present site of Youngstown, New York, gave a form of its name to Niagara Falls between New York and Ontario. They were destroyed by the Iroquois in 1650-1651, but an independent group of some 800 survived in Detroit until subsequently incorporated with the Wyandot and Iroquois.

NEUUSTOOC

Nothing is known of the tribe or village named Neuustooc other than the reference in Willard. Presumably of North Carolina or Virginia, the name contains the suffix "ooc" referring to shellfish and a large body of water, referring to the Chesapeake.

NEZ PERCÉ

The Nez Percé (French for pierced nose) constituted the principal branch of the Shahaptian linguistic family. The Nez Percé (pl. Nez Percés) was comprised of numerous bands in western Idaho and the adjoining lands of Oregon and Washington states, including the lower Snake River and its tributaries the Salmon, Clearwater, and Grande Ronde and from the Blue Mountains of Oregon on the west to the main divide of the Bitterroot Mountains to the east. One of the largest and most important bands was the Willewah [Wallowa] of the Wallowa Valley in Oregon. (Drake reported that the Soyennom was either another name for or a band of the Nez Percé.)

As did many of the Native Americans tribes, the Nez Percé referred to themselves as "the people," in their language variously as Nimipu, Kamuinu, and Tsutpeli. Legend has it that French-Canadian trades pinned the name Nez Percé on a delegation that was visiting St. Louis in the early 1830s. The misnomer, which the tribesmen accepted without the French pronunciation, stuck. Thus, the name is most often spelled without the acute accent over the final "e."

The Nez Percé encountered the Corps of Discovery in 1805. It was Lewis and Clark that applied the name Chopunnish. Two Nez Percé chiefs, Twisted Hair and Tetoharsky, guided and translated for the Lewis and Clark until they reached the Snake-Columbia junction where they met the Wanapam and Yakima Indians. In June 1806, the Corps camped at Camp Chopunnish on the Kooskooskee (Clearwater) River, near present Kamiah, Idaho. Drake estimated the population at 4,300 at the time.

The Nez Percé and whites maintained good relations up through the mid-1850s, but the Nez Percé were not blind to the wars of subjugation that hit the Yakima, the Rogue River, and the Cayuse following the Whitman Massacre 1847.

With the arrival of the Isaac I. Stevens as Governor of the Washington Territory in 1853, the lives of the Native Peoples of the region began to change. Stevens was determined to relocate all Native Americans to reservations, a task to which he became wholly committed. In May 1855, he arranged the Walla Walla Conference with the Indians of the Columbia Plateau. The council was attended by the Nez Percé, the Cayuse, the Yakima, the Umatilla, and the Walla Walla among others. Although the Indians were permitted to speak and offer their thoughts, it was not so much a council as a declaration of purpose.

Three reservations were established. One was to be on the upper drainage of the Yakima River for the Yakima, the Klickitat, the Palouse, and their kindred tribes and bands. The second, a tract of land of some three million acres on the north side of the Snake River, the valleys of the Clearwater and Salmon rivers on the east of the Snake, and the lower Grande Ronde, Wallowa, and Imnaha valleys on the west. It was to be the home of the Nez Percé. The third reservation was established at the headwaters of the Umatilla River in the Blue Mountains for the Umatilla, the Cayuse, and the Walla Walla. The treaty was singed by the Nez Percé on June 11.

The ink was barely dry before settlers began to drift onto reservation lands; then, in 1860, gold was discovered in the region. Miners came and went; farmers and ranchers stayed. The Nez Percé generally remained relatively patient throughout all this. A new treaty was presented in 1863, amended in 1868. The 1863 treaty significantly reduced the limits of the reservation from five thousand square miles to six hundred square miles. Old Joseph, who had grudgingly signed the 1855 treaty, refused to sign. He was not alone. The treaty produced a split in the Nez Percé tribe and the emergence of the group that came to be known as the non-treaty Indians. No immediate attempt was made by the government to resolve the issue. As the years came and went, civilization continued to close in on the Nez Percé. By 1876, the situation was such that it could no longer be ignored.

Old Joseph was converted to Christianity in the 1830s. It was at that time that he and his son were given the Christian name Joseph. When Old Joseph walked out on the 1863 treaty negotiations, he not only tore his copy of the treaty to shreds but he also destroyed his New Testament. He died in 1871, taking with him a pledge from his son, who now became chief at the age of thirty-one, not to sell their beloved Wallowa Valley. The non-treaty Indians or Lower Nez Percé were now came to be identified by the man who has come down through history simply as Chief Joseph.

NEZ PERCÉ WAR

Throughout the winter and early spring of 1877, General Howard and the chiefs of the non-treaty Indians held discussions on their removal to the reservation at Lapwai. An agreement was finally reached in mid-May, and the Indians returned to their villages to gather their belongings for the move. About the middle of June a few of the young braves grew restless and, fortified by alcohol, rode out into White Bird Canyon to take reprisals on a white man who maliciously killed a young Indian boy. Not finding the one they sought, they took their revenge on another, and one raid followed after another. By the time they returned to camp, at least fourteen white settlers in White Bird Canyon were dead.

The young braves and a few of the elders and their families rode out to the base at White Bird Cayon to await the reaction from the military, not knowing exactly what to expect—whether it would be punishment for the guilty or war. As each day passed, more and more of the tribe assembled in the canyon. Chief Joseph had been away from the main camp and was unaware of recent events. On his return, he too joined those waiting.

Hearing the reports, General Howard ordered out two companies of calvary of some ninety-plus men. What exactly their orders were is not known. But, reportedly, the general had dismissed all hope of peace with the Nez Percé. If true, the question arises why he mounted only a relatively small troops of men, although the troop did pick up a few civilian volunteers in route. The troop reached the plateau three thousand feet above the Indian camp. In the early morning hours of June 17 they began their decent to the canyon floor where they fanned out. They were met by a truce party under a white flag (according to Indian reports although the military account is silent on the matter).

First shots were reportedly fired by a military scout. The Nez Percé, who fielded a well-positioned force of an estimated seventy warriors, responded. Within a short time, what was left of the troop of calvary was in full retreat. They left thirty-four dead on the field. Only two Nez Percé were wounded, and the Nez Percé War of 1877 had begun.

General Howard assembled a large force some four hundred plus a number of volunteer companies and moved on White Bird Canyon in pursuit and ordered a troop of calvary to arrest Chief Looking Glass and neutralize the members of his band. The Looking Glass Band had not been at the Canyon and had hoped to remain at peace with the white man. The troop failed to arrest Looking Glass. Instead, they killed one youth, wounded two braves, burned and pillaged the village, and trampled the gardens. Looking Glass and his warriors now joined the Joseph. The end came four months later. It was a grueling four months between two skilled forces, neither brilliant, both determined.

Chief Joseph surrendered to Colonel Nelson A. Miles following the Battle of Bear Paws in northcentral Montana, just forty miles short of the Canadian border, on October 5, 1877. Miles was in the Department of the Dakota commanded by General Alfred Terry but assigned to cooperate with Howard and the troops from the Department of the Columbia to block the Indians' path north. Howard was on hand for the negotiations but allowed Miles to take the surrender following a four-day siege. (Howard went to lead American forces in the Bannock War of 1878; Miles' subsequent promotions would eventually bring him to the position of chief and staff and the rank of lieutenant general. The Bannock served as scouts to Miles in the Nez Percé War.) It was that day in upper Montana that Chief Joseph, in his formal speech of surrendered, spoke the words that have resonated down through history, "From where the sun now stands, I will fight no more tomorrow."

Four hundred and eighteen Nez Percé surrendered that day under the belief that they would be returned to their reservation in the spring. Some two hundred escaped to Canada—some would be caught; some would return voluntarily. The war had been fought across Idaho, through the Yellowstone country, and into Montana to its conclusion at Bear Paws. Official military history summed up the war: "In 11 weeks, he [Chief Joseph] had moved his tribe 1,600 miles, engaged 10 separate U.S. commands in 13 battles and skirmishes, and in nearly every instance had either defeated them or fought them to a standstill. General Sherman rightly termed the struggle 'one of the most extraordinary Indian Wars of which there is any record.'"

The number of reported causalities from the Nez Percé War vary, but it is reasonable to say that some three hundred were killed and another two hundred and fifty wounded, in total, about equally divided between Indians and whites.

AFTERMATH

Contrary to the promises received from Miles and Howard, who were overruled by higher authorities as was frequently the case, the prisoners spent the winter of 1877-78 at Fort Leavenworth and in the spring of 1878 were placed on the Quapaw reserve in Kansas Territory before being relocated in the fall within the Ponca agency near present Tonkawa, Oklahoma, that became known as the Oakland Reservation. It is estimated that twenty or more members of the tribe died that winter at Fort Leavenworth, but the burial ground in what is now considered a remote area of the installation has yet to be located. By 1885, the Nez Percé eventually secured a home in their beloved Northwest county thanks in no small measure to the then General Miles and influential Congressmen, but to the great displeasure of many white settlers in Idaho, Oregon and Washington. On November 19, 2004, Fort Leavenworth was formally certified as a site along the Nez Percé National Historic Trail, part of a continuing effort to tell the full tribal story rather than to have it end with their defeat in north-central Montana.

The exiled survivors, who numbered less than three hundred, were divided into two groups. Two of the original three bands (White Bird and Looking Glass) were to go to the Lapwai Reservation in Idaho; the third, Chief Joseph's, was assigned to the Colville Reservation in Washington. They all accepted this as an interim arrangement although they hoped someday to return to the Wallowa Valley in Idaho—it would never come to pass.

Chief Joseph died September 21, 1904, a continuing inspiration to whites and Indians. Yet there were some who, as late of 1939, still considered him a outlaw. On June 12, 1956, the Chief Joseph Dam on the Columbia River in Washington was officially dedicated to "a man of true magnanimity." The travail of the Nez Percé has been and continues to be an inspiration for freedom to all of mankind, regardless of race or ethnicity.

NIANTIC

The Niantic or Nehantic tribe was of the Algonquian linguistic family. They lived in the New England in modern Connecticut and Rhode Island and gave their name to the town of Niantic, Connecticut. They were split into two divisions by the Pequot: the Eastern Niantic of Rhode Island and Western Niantic of Connecticut. During King Philip's War, the Niantic took the side of the English, after which they were joined by large numbers of Narragansett.

NIANTIC, EASTERN

The Eastern Niantic lived along the western coast of Rhode Island and the neighboring coast of Connecticut. They were joined by large numbers of the Narragansett following King Philip's War. The amalgamated tribe at Charlestown was called the Narragansett. For more see Niantic.

NIANTIC, WESTERN

The Western Niantic were located on the coast from Niantic Bay to the Connecticut River. They subsequently allied with the Pequot and fought in the Pequot war of 1637. Those that were not killed or enslaved following the war, numbering about one hundred, were put under the control of the Mohegan. Later they joined the Brotherton living in the land of the Oneida in New York State and shared the fate of the Brotherton when they were removed to Wisconsin. For more see Niantic.

NICARIAGA

According to Drake the Nicariaga once lived about the French trading post Michilimakinac at the junction of Lake Huron and Lake Michigan and joined the Iroquois in 1723 as seventh nation. Drake is possibly referring to the Ottawa Nation. There is nothing to support the contention that a seventh nation joined the Iroquois League. There was a Canadian confederation of Catholic Indians called The Seven Nations (see St. Regis). The name Mackinac as used in Mackinac Island in the Straits of Mackinac is a derivation of the Indian "Michilimackinac." The British converted the French post to a fort.

NICOLEÑO

The Nicoleño (from San Nicolas) of California belonged to the Shoshonean Division of the Uto-Aztecan linguistic family. They inhabited the most eastward of the Santa Barbara islands. Their population numbers were included with the Gabrielino and Fernandeño for enumeration purposes.

NIPISSIN

The Nipissin or Nipissing were of Algonquian linguistic stock. They lived in northern Ontario presumably about Lake Nipissing, 175 miles due north of Toronto, east of Lake Huron's Georgian Bay. In the mid-1700s, there was a reported population of some 400 warriors. Jesuit Father René Ménard, the Jesuit superior in the New World, labored among the Nipissin and others in the region from 1640 until his death in 1661 somewhere about the Black River in Wisconsin. His body was never found.

JESUIT MISSIONARIES IN THE NEW WORLD

Almost continuously from 1611 onward, Jesuit missionaries spread out across Canada from Acadia and the St. Lawrence fifteen hundred miles west, north to James Bay, and south down the Mississippi to Louisiana from their base at Quebec. In time they spread across the United States. During those early years, few tribes within several hundred miles of Quebec were unaffected by their unique presence, most especially, the Five Nations of the Iroquois, the Montagnais-Naskapi that took a wide swath of eastern Canada, the Ottawa to the west, and the Huron. One hundred and fifteen Jesuits labored in New France and the British colonies during the Jesuits' first century in the New World. Jesuits learned the languages, established schools and hospitals, and established seminaries to train new ministers of the faith from within the native population itself. Overall the Jesuits were remarkably successful. In 1805, two dozen members of the order assembled in Maryland to begin building the Catholic Church in the United States. During the American Civil War, the Jesuits as well as other ministers were subject to the federal draft with passage of the Enrollment Act by the third session of the Thirty-seventh Congress on March 3, 1863. The law applied to all able-bodied males between the ages of twenty and forty-five.

NIPMUC

The Nipmuc (also Nipmuck and Nipnet) were of the Algonquian linguistic family and inhabited the central plateau of Massachusetts, particularly southern present Worcester Country, and parts of Connecticut and Rhode Island. Swanton lists twenty-nine subdivisions, bands, or villages. Many are treated separately in the literature.

SUBDIVISIONS
Acoomemeck
Attawaugan, Killingly, Connecticut
Chabanakongkomun, Dudley, Massachusetts
Chachaubunkkakowok
COWESET, northern Rhode Island west of the Blackstone River (Regarded as Nipmuc proper)
Hassanamesit, Grafton, Massachusetts (Referred to by Drake)
Magunkaquog, Hopkinton, Massachusetts
Manchaug, Oxford, Massachusetts
Manexit, Thompson, Connecticut
Mashapaug, Union, Connecticut
Medfield, Medfield, Massachusetts
Menemesseg, New Braintree, Massachusetts
Metewemesick, Sturbridge, Massachusetts
Missogkonnog
Muskataquid
Nasbobnh, Magog Pond, in Littleton, Massachusetts
Nichewaug, Petersham, Massachusetts
Okommakamesit, Marlborough, Massachusetts
Pakachoog, Worcester, Massachusetts
Quabaug, Brookfield, Massachusetts
Quadick, Thompson County, Connecticut
Quantisset, Thompson, Connecticut
Quinebaug, Thompson, Connecticut
Quinetusset, Thompson in northeast corner of Connecticut
Segunesit, northeastern Connecticut
Tatumasket, southern Worcester County

Wabaquasset, about the Quinebaug River, south of Woodstock, Connecticut (Sometimes regarded as independent)

Wacuntug, west side of Blackstone River, Uxbridge

Wenimesset, New Braintree

The Coweset is sometimes written of as the Nipmuc itself. From time to time the Nipmuc attached themselves to other, more powerful tribes. Those in northwestern Rhode Island were under the domination of the Narragansett. In 1674 there were seven villages of Christian Indians among the Nipmuc, but in 1675 they fled to Canada and among the Indians of the Hudson river after taking the part of King Philip of the Wampanoag in the war against the colonists (King Philip's War).

NISHINAM MAIDU

The Nishinam or Southern Maidu lived about the whole of the drainage of the American River and the drainage of the Bear and Yuba rivers in California. They were of the Penutian linguistic family.

NISKAH

The Niskah, or Naas Indians, was a Canadian tribe that lived in the vicinity of the mouth of the Columbia and had their main camp on the Naas river in British Columbia. George Catlin (Letter No. 48) writes of them under the name "Na-as" in conjunction with northwestern tribes of the United States, including the Chinook, Chehalis, and Klickitat.

NISQUALLY

The Nisqually gave their name to one dialectic division of the coastal division of the Salishan linguistic stock. They inhabited the area about the Nisqually River above its mouth and on the middle and upper courses of the Puyallup River in western Washington Territory.

Following a second trail, Chief Leschi of the Nisqually was hanged for the "murder" of Colonel A. Benton Moses in the Indian wars in the region in 1855. The first trial ended in a hung jury. The judge in the second trial refused to instruct the jury that the killing of Col. Moses in war, if in fact the killing was committed by Chief Leschi, would not be classified as murder. On appeal the court refused to hear new evidence that showed that Chief Leschi was miles away at the time. A seven-judge panel of a historical court exonerated the Chief in a unanimous decision handed down December 10, 2004.

NISSEQUOGE

The Nissequoge or Nesaquake or Missaquogue were a division of the Montauk and were a member of the Algonquian linguistic group that were generally treated separately. They lived on Long Island, New York. For more see the Montauk and the Delaware.

NOCHPEEM

The Nochpeem was a subdivision or sub-tribe of the Wappinger and lived in the southern part of Duchess County, New York. For more see Wappinger.

NOGATL

The Nogatl (commonly written as Nongatl) were of the Athapascan linguistic group and closely connected to the Lassik. They inhabited the territory drained by three affluents of the Eel River—Yaker Creek, Van Dusen Fork, and Larrabee Creek—and the upper waters of the Mad River in California. The permanent villages of this relatively small tribe were located near present-day Bridgeville. Nearly the entire population was killed or removed from the area within fifteen years after the arrival of white settlers. The remnants all disappeared entirely within 60 to 70 years.

NOKONI

The Nokoni (people who return or turn back) was one of the five major sub-tribes or bands of the Comanche. They were the most nomadic and farthest ranging or the bands. For more see Comanche.

NOMALAKI

The Namalaki was a tribe of the upper Sacramento Valley in California. The tribe was placed on the Round Valley Reservation—originally named Nome Cult, a Nomalaki name for "west place" or "west dwellings," established in June 1856. Between the late fifties and the mid-1860s, California Indians were driven from their homes by vigilantes and literally marched to Nome Cult, many dying along the way. The trek was referred to as a Death March. Others removed to the reservations on their own seeking sanctuaries from assault by Californians. The results were the same. For more see ConCow and Mitom.

NOMLAKI

Nomlaki was the central division of the Penutian-speaking Wintun Indians of the Sacramento Valley region that inhabited parts of what are now Tehama and Glenn counties. They are apparently the same as the Nom-laka (Nom-kewel) referred to in Swanton. In 1854 the Konkow Reservation was established as the Nome Lackee Reservation in Tehama County between Corning and Red Bluff on Stony Creek, but dissolved in 1863. Residents were moved to the Round Table or Covelo Reservation in the Mendocino Valley near Paskenta in a forced march, many dying and killed along the way, including women, children, and the aged.

NOOKSACK

The Nooksack belonged to the coastal division of the Salishan linguistic family. Thy lived along the Nooksack River on present Whatcom County, Washington. They reportedly separated from the Squawmish of British Columbia. They were closely related to the Lummi. The Nooksack were established on their reservation of one acre of land at Demming in 1971 and given full federal recognition.

NOOK-WA-CHAH-MISH

A sub-tribe or band of western Washington under the name Nook-wa-chah-mish was listed as a party to the Point Elliott Treaty of January 22, 1855. No other information has become available.

NOO-SEH-CHATL

The Noo-Seh-Chatl belonged to the Nisqually Branch of the coastal division of the Salisham linguistic family of Washington Territory about Puget Sound. They would later become a subdivision of the Squaxin Island Tribe and lived about Henderson Inlet of Squaxin Island. See the Squaxon.

NOO-WHA-HA

The Noo-Wha-Ha lived about Puget Sound and the rivers flowing from the Cascades in Washington State. The Noo-Wha-Ha was always referred to as the Noo-Wha-Ha Band, but no additional information has been located. The Noo-Wha-Ha was a signatory to the Point Elliott Treaty of 1855. It is known that the remnants were absorbed into other tribes. The Noo-Wha-Ha is not currently recognized by the Federal government or the state of Washington.

NOQUET

The Noquet (Nouquet, Nouket) are believed to have been related to the Menominee of the Algonquian linguistic family. They lived about Big Bay de Noquet and Little Bay de Noquet of Michigan and across the northern peninsula of Michigan to Lake Superior and into Wisconsin. In 1659 the tribe was attached to the mission of St. Michael. It is thought that they were absorbed very early into the Menominee or Chippewa.

NORRIDGEWOCK

Norridgewock was a subdivision of the Abnaki on the Kennebec River of Maine. They were subsequently destroyed. For more see Abenaki.

NORTHERN CHEYENNE

The Northern Cheyenne or Northern Bands of the Cheyenne were comprised of those bands and families that remained north of the Platte/North Platte River, the original Suhtai being a major part. For more see Cheyenne.

SLIM BUTTES

On September 9, 1876, one hundred and fifty men of the Third Calvary under the command of Captain Anson Mills attacked a camp of Northern Cheyenne and Lakota Sioux at Slim Buttes on the Great Sioux Reservation in Dakota and drove the Indians from their camp. Before any sort of a counterattack could be launched, Capt. Mills was quickly reinforced by troops from General Crook's main force.

The victory was significant because it introduced the government's new policy of "disarm and dismount." Soldiers were directed to enter government agencies in Dakota and Nebraska and disarm and dismount all warriors to prevent them from giving aid and substance to Indians that continued to resist, some of whom came into the agencies to rest and recoup before continuing the fight. The new policy came in conjunction with the transfer of responsibility for Indian submission from the Interior Department to the War Department.

At the Red Cloud Agency in Nebraska two weeks later on September 26, 1876, the Oglala, Cheyenne, and Arapaho were forced to ceded large portions of their April 29, 1868, treaty lands to the government, allowing the land to be officially opened to settlers and prospectors. The Indians were to be moved south to Indian Territory within one year. Although all the chiefs signed, many swore that they would never move. The agreement was ratified by Congress February 28, 1877.

CHEYENNE AUTUMN

The Northern Cheyenne under head chief Little Wolf and the aging Dull Knife vowed to bring their people back home up north. Two hundred and eighty-four people that included 87 men, counted from age thirteen, stole away their guarded camp on the reservation during the night of September 8, 1878, undetected and headed north. They included the old, the sick, and the new born. Their fifteen hundred mile, seventy day journey became known as the Cheyenne Autumn. A few of the Southern Cheyenne headed north with the cousins from the north, mostly young braves who soon turned back unaccustomed to Little Wolff's harsh regimen and his rule that the Cheyenne would only kill soldiers and only after the soldiers shot first. There was to be no wanton killing of civilian settlers, but civilians manning government way stations and the like, suffered if they resisted. The Cheyenne needed horses. The need became acute around the Arkansas as the army began to close in on all sides. Desperate measures drove the Cheyenne to extremes, and Little Wolf regrettably allowed his rule to be problem, but no women and children were to be harmed. But it was not the Cheyenne way, and soon the rule was reinstated.

Across the Platte after about a month of pain, hunger and death with soldiers all around and with winter fast approaching, Dull Knife declared that it was foolish to attempt to make it all the way to the Yellowstone. He counseled for the Red Cloud Agency, not knowing that it had been closed and that the new reservation was at Pine Ridge, but that would be of little matter. Little Wolf stood for the country of the Yellowstone. With heavy hearts, the Cheyenne went their two ways. About half followed Dull Knife as he led out from camp: 46 men, 61 women, and 42 children—149 people in all with 131 horses, and nine mules. Dull Knife and those with him were captured in late October and interred at Fort Robinson, Nebraska. Told they were to be returned south, they broke free on the night of January 9, 1879. (Their food, water, and heat had been cut off for their refusal to accede to the move.) They were 130, including 44 men counting eleven year olds. The rest women and children—no horses, no mules, a few scraps of food, old blankets, and a couple of rifles and few revolvers that they had hidden, into the cloudless winter night through a broken window. Thirty died and 35 were captured, mostly wounded, that same night within hours of the break.

Over the next days, troopers brought in more bodies, more wounded, and a few more prisoners. Some were never found. The last fight and the last killings took place January 22 at the Last Hole as it was called on Warbonnet Creek or Hat Creek. The seventy-eight people that were left when it was all over were brought together at Ft. Robinson. Fifty-eight, including forty-eight women and children, were sent to Pine Ridge with the Lakota. Dull Knife and a handful of others had already managed to make their escape to the Sioux agency where they were kept hidden until the arrival of the others from Robinson. The Cheyenne head men, however, accompanied by their families, were put in irons and sent to Ft. Leavenworth to be tried for the murders committed in Kansas in the trek north. They were found innocent for lack of evidence and sent to the agency in the south. Later they were allowed to return north to the Pine Ridge Reservation. In the meantime, the Tongue River Reservation was established for the Northern Cheyenne on the Rosebud and Tongue rivers near Miles City, Montana, by Executive Order of President Chester A. Arthur, dated November 26, 1884. There they were all allowed to come together. Dull Knife did not live to see that day. He died at the Pine Ridge Reservation in 1883.

Little Wolf had with him 40 men, 47 women and 39 children—126 people when the two groups separated. He led them north until they found shelter in a hidden valley where they were able to hunt, rest, and gather strength out of sight of the patrolling soldiers. After the worst of the winter months had passed, Little Wolf led his people off again towards the Powder River country. They found a secure place to camp about fifty miles from the Yellowstone and waited. Scouts from the soldiers, following the tracks, came and they talked. On March 25, 1879, troopers from the command of Colonel Miles rode into the Cheyenne camp. The Cheyenne followed the soldiers to Fort Keogh (previously Tongue River Cantonment). There would be no more fighting and killing. The Cheyenne trail of tears had come to an end. They now numbered 114, including thirty-three men. They remained at Ft. Keogh, and some of men enlisted as Scouts to track Sitting Bull. With the establishment of the new reservation, those who were left of the two groups that had left the south in September 1878 were again united. They were home. (For the complete account, see *Cheyenne Autumn* by Mari Sandoz.)

NORTHERN GROUP OF THE FOOTHILLS YOKUTS

The Northern Group of the Foothills Division was one of the seven subdivisions of the Yokuts Group of Indians of California. They lived in villages on Fine Gold Creek, Coarse Gold Creek, Picayune Creek, Cottonwood Creek and along the San Jaoquin. For more see Yokuts.

NOTHERN PAIUTE

The Northern Paiute or Paviotso was not properly a tribe but constituted one dialectic division of the Shoshonean Branch of the Uto-Aztecan stock that includes a detached group, the Bannock. Some reports refer to the language as being of the Western Numic group. The Northern Paiute inhabited western Nevada; southeastern Oregon, where they were also called Snake; and small portion of California east of the Sierra Nevada divided by the Sierra Nevada Mountains into an large, widely dispersed eastern division and a small division consisting of the Eastern Mono and the Western Mono of California. For more see the Paiute.

NORTHWEST INDIANS FISHERIES COMMISSION (NWIFC)

Listed here are the member tribes of the Northwest Indians Fisheries Commission.

Hoh Indian Tribe	Quileute Indian Tribe
Jamestown S'Klallam Tribe	Quinault Nation
Lower Elwha Klallam Tribe	Sauk-Suiattle Tribe
Lummi Indian Tribe	Skokomish Tribe
Makah Indian Tribe	Squaxin Island Tribe
Muckleshoot Tribe	Stillaguamish Tribe
Nisqually Indian Tribe	Suquamish Tribe
Nooksack Indian Tribe	Swinomish Tribe
Port Gamble S'Klallam	Tulalip Tribe
Puyallup Tribe	Upper Skagit Tribe

NOTHERN GROUP OF THE VALLEY YOKUTS

The Northern Group of the Valley Division was one of the seven subdivisions of the Yokuts Group of Indians of California in villages on the San Joaquin near Herndon , Weshiu, Gawachiu and Millerton; on the Fresno River; and the Chauchilla River. For more see Yokuts.

NOTTAWAY

The Nottaway belonged to the Iroquoian linguistic group. They lived along the Nottaway River in southeastern Virginia. It may have been a band of the Nottaway that appeared on the northern frontier of South Carolina in the mid-1700s. Although not large in numbers or politically prominent, they existed as a tribe long after the other tribes in the region had become extinct. They were living on a reservation in Southampton County in 1825.

N'QUENTL-MA-MISH

A sub-tribe or band of western Washington under the name N'Quentl-ma-mish was listed as a party to the Point Elliott Treaty of January 22, 1855. No other information has become available.

NTLAKYAPAMUK

Ntlakyapamuk was a large Canadian tribe that belonged to the interior division of the Salisham linguistic stock. They inhabited British Columbia with a few southern bands in Washington State. They were called the Knife Indians by the Hudson's Bay Company.

NUMNI

The Numni reportedly inhabited Washington State, but no supporting information has been found.

NYACK

The Nyack was a sub-tribe of the Delaware. On March 6, 1660, the Hackensack, Nyack, Haverstraw, Wecquaesgeek (Weschester), and Western Long Island Indians accepted a peace treaty with the Dutch that isolated the Esopus. The Esopus Indians signed a peace treaty March 16, 1664 ending the Esopus Indian Wars. The Hackensack and Nyack of New Jersey also signed the treaty as allies of the Dutch, agreeing to insure the good behavior of the Esopus. For more see Delaware and Wickquasgeck.

OBISPEÑO CHUMASH

The Obispeño were one of the eight dialectic and geographical divisions of the Chumash of the Southern California.. The Obispeño lived about present San Luis Obispo on the coast from just north of the Santa Maria River. For more see the Chumash.

OCALE

The Ocale or Etocale belonged to the Timucuan or Timuquanan division of the Muskhogean linguistic family. They lived in present Marion County or Levy County, Florida, north of the bend of the Withlacoochee River.

OCCANEECHI

The Occaneechi or Ocaneechi was of the Siouan linguistic family. They lived in parts of Virginia, Maryland and North Carolina, including near the site of present-day Clarksville, Mecklenburg County, Virginia.. The also occupied the largest island in the Roanoke River. that was located just below the confluence of the Staunton and Dan rivers in Mecklenburg County. They first came to attention in 1650. Over the years they were highly regarded as traders. Around the turn of the century, they moved to an area along the Eno River in Orange County, North Carolina. They subsequently united with the Saponi and Tutelo and reportedly took the name of the Saponi. The Occaneechi allowed themselves be drawn into Bacon's Rebellion of 1676 in Virginia in which a large group were massacred.

OCHECHOTE

The Ochechote was a sub-tribe of the Yakima that is generally referred to separately. In the 1855 Yakima treaty at Camp Stevens, the Ochechote ceded all their lands to the government and settled on the Yakima Reservation. For more see Yakima.

OCONEE

The Oconee or Oconi inhabited central Georgia. They were driven east-southeast into Florida and joined in the formation of what became the Seminole Nation.

OGLALA

The Oglala (Ogallala) was one of the seven major subgroups of the Lakota (Teton) or Western Division of the Sioux Nation. The Oglala are most commonly subdivided into seven bands, but listings of eight and up to eleven bands are not uncommon. They were the Hunkpatila (also written Hunkpitila); the Kiyuksa, also subdivided into two groups; the Itesica or Ite Sica or, more commonly, "Bad Face" band of Red Cloud; the Oyuhpe, also subdivided into groups; the Payabya; the Tapisleca or "Spleen"; and the

Wagluhe or "Loafer." The Payabya derived from the Hunkpatila; therefore, based on the time frame, both may not be listed. The Wazhazha band has been found listed among both the Brulé and Oglala bands. For more see Sioux and Lakota. The Hunkpatila band to which Crazy Horse belonged is sometimes treated separately as a tribe or division of the Lakota, parallel with the Oglala and Hunkpapa, confusion arising from the similarity in the spelling between Hunkpapa and Hunkpatila may have been the cause.

PLATTE RIVER BRIDGE AND RED BUTTES

The Battle of the Platte River Bridge Station near present-day Casper, Wyoming, fought July 26, 1865, was little more than a route by warriors from an assembled force of more than a thousand Sioux, Northern Cheyenne, and Southern Cheyenne and a detachment of the U.S. army troopers under the command of Lieutenant Caspar Collins. Five soldiers were killed, among them Lt. Collins; and twelve or more men were wounded. One account put the total number of Indians at three thousand. The Southern Cheyenne, led by Roman Nose, were north seeking revenge for Sand Creek. Other leaders were Red Cloud, Dull Knife, and Crazy Horse.

Louis Guinard had built the bridge and a trading post on the cite in 1859. It soon developed into an overnight stagecoach station and telegraph office. Platte Bridge Station became Fort Casper and later the site of the town of Casper, Wyoming, name in honor of Lt. Collins. (On November 21, 1865, Major General John Pope changed the name of Platte Bridge Station to Fort Casper, misspelling the lieutenant's first name. Fort Collins in Colorado was named after Caspar's father.) The Indians followed-up later that day with a wagon train at Red Buttes about five miles from Platte River Station. The wagon train was bound for Sweetwater Station near Independence Rock. Twenty-four soldiers of the 11th Ohio and Sgt. Amos J. Custard of the 11th Kansas Cavalry were killed. Three escaped. The Indians had also burned some buildings at Rocky Ridge Station near South Pass and had left some scalped and mutilated bodies.

BATTLE OF WOLF MOUNTAINS

Oglala Sioux led by Crazy Horse and a number of Cheyenne under White Bull attacked men of the Fifth and Twenty-second Infantry under Colonel Nelson A. Miles on January 8, 1877. Fierce fighting continued for several hours marked by charges and counter-charges until the worsening winter weather brought on a cease fire. The Indians withdrew to their camp on the Tongue River, and the troops returned to their cantonment on the Yellowstone at the mouth of the Tongue. Casualties on both sides were minimal but, coupled with the destruction of the Cheyenne camp at the Red Fork of the Powder River in November, the battle reinforced the fact that whatever the outcome of any one battle the Indians could not win.

OHONGEEOQUENA

Little is known about the Ohongeeoquena except for a reference that suggests that they may have been a subdivision or clan of the Susquehanna. For more see Susquehanna.

OKAHOKI

The Okahoki was a sub-tribe of the Unalachtigo division of the Delaware. They lived on Ridley and Crum creeks in Delaware County, Pennsylvania. For more see Unalachtigo and Delaware.

OKANAGON

The Okanagon or Okinagon was of the interior division of the Salisham stock, related to the Sanpoil, Coolville, and Senijextee. The Okanagon lived in Washington State along the Okanagan River above the mouth of the Similkameen north to the Canadian border and along the shores of Okanagan Lake in British

Columbia. It was comprised of two major divisions, the Okanagon proper and the Similkameen Okanagon. Steadily moving north, they displaced the Shuswap, an Athapascan tribe, and part of the Ntlakyapamuk from the Similkameen Valley. The Sinkaietk or Lower Okanagon are also sometimes counted among the Okanagon. Jesuit John Noboli administered to the Okanogan north of the 49th parallel in the 1840s and fifties.

The Okanagon proper was divided into four bands and a number of separate villages: Douglas Lake Band; Komaplix or Head of the Lake Band; Penticton Band; Nkamip Band. The Similkameen were comprised of the Upper Similkameen, Ashnola, and Lower Similkameen, each with a number of villages.

OKANDANDA

The Okandand or Tetons Okandandas was one of the ten separate Sioux tribes or bands identified by Lewis and Clark. For more see Sioux.

OKATIOKINANS

The Okatiokinan was a band of the Seminole that lived near Fort Gaines on the east side Mississippi River

OKEHAI

The Okehai was a sub-tribe or division of the Muskogee and a member of the Creek Confederacy. There were six Okehai villages in Alabama.

VILLAGES

Alsilanabi, on Yellow Leaf Creek in Shelby County
Lalogalga (Fish Pond), on the a branch of Elkhatchee Creek in Tallapoosa or Coosa county
Okchai proper, on the lower Coosa in Elmore County and on Okehai Creek in southeast Coosa County
Potcas Hatchee, most likely on the upper course of Haatchet Creek in Clay or Coosa county
Tcahki Lako, on the Chattachoochee River
Tulsa Hatchee, location unknown

OKELOUSA

The Okelousa belonged to the Muskhogean family of Louisiana. They were constantly on the move. The most discernable location was on the west side of the Mississippi back of and above Pointe Coupée. It is believed that the Okelousa or descendants of them were the Caluça visited by De Soto. It has been reported that the Okelousa at one time were allies of the Houma. They are also noted as being allies of the Washa and the Chawasha. The Okelousa merged with the Houma, the Acolapissa, or one of the other Muskhogean tribes.

OKMULGEE

The Okmulgee tribe was a member of the Creek Confederacy. The tribe was one of the Lower Creeks that inhabited the area around Ocheese (Ocmulgee) Creek in South Carolina. It was the Indian tribe that the local colonists knew best and they conferred the "creek" on them and their confederacy.

OKWANUCHU

The Okwanuchu were of the Shastan Division of the Hokan linguistic stock. They lived along the upper Sacramento River in California from around the Salt and Boulder creeks to its headwaters; also on the McCloud River and Squaw Creek.

OMAHA

The Omaha were of the Dhegiha (pronounced They-geé-hah) Siouan linguistic group that included the Kansas, Osage, Ponca, and Quapaw. They inhabited the area near Pipestone Quarry in Pipestone County, Minnesota, about fifty miles from the present city of Sioux Falls, South Dakota. The quarry was source of red stone and stone pipes used for ceremonial smoking. It has been suggested that Dhegiha group at one time lived as single nation east of the Mississippi River—possibly around the lower Ohio. The Omaha were driven out of Minnesota into South Dakota by the Sioux around the turn of the century.

The Omaha ("those going against the wind") moved westward to west bank of the Big Sioux River near present-day Sioux Falls, South Dakota, and eventually into northeastern. By that the time the Ponca, who had been part of the Omaha, had separated but later rejoined them on the Lower Missouri. The Omaha ranged along the Missouri in eastern Nebraska from the mouth of the to Dakota County in northeast Nebraska. By the late seventeen hundreds, the Omaha and Ponca had firmly established themselves in northeastern Nebraska, had obtained horses, and were equipped with metal weapons and guns thanks to traders. From their vantage point on the Lower Missouri, the Omaha controlled access upriver and soon began to receive visitors. James Mackay, a Scottish trader and explorer, visited the Omaha in 1795. (Lewis and Clark used what has been referred to as the Mackay Map.) The Omaha were almost wiped out as a people in a smallpox epidemic that hit in 1800.

Another visitor was Manuel Lisa of the Missouri Fur Company, possibly the most noted of the early fur traders on the Missouri. He was born of Spanish parents probably in New Orleans and made his way to St. Louis by 1790. He took an Omaha woman for his wife who greatly helped fortify his position among the various tribes. Lisa was a master conciliator and easily earned the good will and friendly relations of the Indians of the Missouri. He was also instrumental in getting many of the tribes to agree to treaties of friendship and alliance with the government following the close of the War of 1812. Here Lisa died in 1820.

During the first half of eighteen hundreds, the Omaha lived in deadly fear of Yankton and Santee Sioux to the North, an animosity between the tribes that apparently carried over the days that the Omaha lived in Minnesota. Sioux raids hit their peak in the 1840s.

In the treaty of March 16, 1854, the Omaha sold all their lands in eastern Nebraska along the Missouri north of the Platte, to the government except for a reserve on the west bank of the Missouri about 150 miles north of present-day Omaha, called Black Bird Hills, highly prized by settlers and investors alike. In 1865 the Omaha they gave up the northern part of their reserve for the Winnebago who abandoned the barren Crow Creek reservation in South Dakota. In 1874 they sold additional land to the Winnebago, and at the same time the Winnebago and Omaha agencies were consolidated in a government economy move. In 1882 the Omahas were awarded their land in severalty in a test case of the virtues and benefits of allotment (the Omaha experiment). Observers saw what they wanted to see, and the process went forward with the passage of the Dawes Act in 1887 that made allotment and citizenship official government policy. In 1887, the Omaha too became citizens, wholly unaware and unprepared for what that entailed.

Ethnologist and self-proclaimed Omaha expert Alice C. Fletcher declared the Dawes Act "the Magna Carta of the Indians of our county." It was her belief that making each Indian a U.S. citizen and guaranteeing him a homestead made him free of what she called "tribal tyranny." She was oblivious to the fact that the average Indians was wholly unprepared in temperament, discipline, and knowledge to manage his own affairs without assistance. She all but ignored the provision of the law that opened surplus reservation lands to white settlement; the effect of leasing unalloted lands to outsiders; the conflicts that arose between tribal members over citizenship and land use; and the rapacious greed of whites who all but stole the allotments from the Indians through "premature and unregulated leasing" that left the Indians idle and with just enough coin in their pockets to buy illegal liquor from greedy townfolks and bootleggers. (For more, "Manypenny Treaties and the Transcontinental Railroads" under the Delaware, 257)

Christianity had entered the world of the Omaha in the 1840s. The Board of Foreign Missions of the Presbyterian Church established a mission and school for the Omaha and Otoe at the Bellevue agency just south of present-day Omaha in 1846. When the Omaha moved to their reservation in Black Bird Hills in 1855, the Presbyterians went with them and began a serious program of acculturation. In 1869, under President Grant's new Indian policy, Hickite Friends were assigned as agents to the Omaha, a policy that brought only conflict between the Quakers and the Presbyterians with the Omaha in the middle. In September 1869, the Presbyterian school contract was cancelled.

Omaha homelands were across the Missouri River from Council Bluffs, Iowa, the spot President Lincoln had designated for the start for the transcontinental railroad. The town of Omaha quickly overshadowed its neighbor to the east and became the headquarters of the Union Pacific Railroad. The Omaha tribe, on the other hand, teetered on the brink of extinction.

ONATHEAQUA

The Onatheaqua was one of the two tribes of Timucua that inhabited parts of northwestern Florida.

ONAWMANIENT

Onawmanient was a member of the Powhatan Confederacy and inhabited parts of Westmoreland County, Virginia.

ONEIDA

The Oneidas or the Granite People or People of the Standing Stone of upper New York State were members of the federation of Iroquois-speaking Indian nations known as the League of Great Peace (see the Iroquois). Oneida lands lay between the Mohawk to the east and the Onondaga to the west. Around 1730 the Oneida established the village of Oquaga on the Susquehanna River near the Pennsylvania border. Migration to the area continued over the years until what was at first a single town became four peopled by Oneidas, Tuscaroras, Mohawks, Delawares, and a few others. As a group, the population of this mixed enclave came to known independently as the Oquagas.

The Oneida fought on the side of the colonists in the American War of Independence. Of the Six Nations of the Iroquois League, the Oneidas were the only nation to stand solidly behind the rebels. Participation gained them nothing but a few kind words. Some two hundred lives were lost in the fighting; their homes and lands were destroyed; and they "emerged from the conflict as a people confused about, and in come cases, divorced from their cultural and political foundations." By 1790 Oneida lands that had been measured in the millions of acres were measured in the thousands—in 1788, the state of New York walked away with 5.5 million acres for a paltry $5,500 and a $600 annuity. By the early twentieth century, the Oneidas that remained in New York held a mere thirty-two acres of land. With the Treaty of Fort Stanwix (formerly Fort Schuyler), signed October 2, 1784, the Six Nations had surrendered their home lands around Niagara and Oswego as well as their claims in Ohio country. The Oneidas that remained loyal to the Crown removed to Canada where they established permanent residence and were compensated with £520 by the British government for their losses.

A treaty concluded December 2, 1794, compensated the members of Wolf Clan and Turtle Clan of the Oneida and some members of Tuscarora for their individual losses and for their services during the war and provided funds to replace a church that was burned. The treaty also compensated a member of the Kaughnawauga and a few Stockbridge Indians as well. In the early 1820s, the Oneidas began their migration west to the Green Bay of Wisconsin. Through the machinations of the War Department, their new home was carved out of lands belonging to the Menominee, Winnebago, and Chippewa. Others headed south of the Thames River in the province of Ontario in Canada. By 1845 less than two hundred Oneidas remained in New York.

After a series of negotiations, the Oneida were given five hundred thousand acres of Menominee land on the west side of the Fox River by the Menominee-Oneida treaty. It was subsequently revised to make provision for the Stockbridge, Brotherton, and Munsee refugees as well. The Federal government subsequently offered the Wisconsin Oneida land in Missouri in exchange for their lands in Wisconsin. Their Wisconsin claims were slowly eroded to a strip of land near Green Bay eight miles wide and twelve miles long. For more see Iroquois League.

Of Note

Congress passed the Indian Nonintercourse Act in 1790 that the federal government exclusive rights to negotiate with Indian tribes. The intent was to protect Indian lands from unscrupulous land speculators and greedy state authorities. In 1970, almost two hundred years later, Oneida descendents sued Madison and Oneida counties in New York alleging that the sale of one hundred thousand acres of land to New York in 1795 was in violation of the act, as amended. Related litigation continued into the early 21st century.

ORISKE

In August 1777, seven hundred British soldiers and loyalists and eight hundred Seneca, Cayuga, Onondaga, and Mohawk under the command of St. Ledger marched south from Canada for an attack on Fort Schuyler (formerly Fort Stanwix). The American garrison included braves from the Oneida and Tuscarora. Receiving intelligence that a relief column of seven hundred Americans and sixty Oneida under the command of General Nicholas Herkimer were moving to reinforce the garrison, the British ambushed the column on August 6 at the Oriske village of the Oneida. Two hundred men of the relief column met their death in a fierce battle before retreating. Fifty Iroquois were also killed. Not accustomed to pitched battles and the resulting casualties, the Iroquois wanted no more and returned to their villages to bury their dead. Another relief column under Benedict Arnold was sent out, but before they could reach their objective, the British had retreated north to Canada.

HAMILTON-ONEIDA ACADEMY

In January 1793, a charter was issued for a new school being established in upstate New York to educate both white and Native American students. Alexander Hamilton, then Secretary of the Treasury, was enthusiastic over the project and agreed to join the board of trustees of the school. The cornerstone of the building was laid the following year by Revolutionary War stalwart Baron von Steuben, acting as Hamilton's ambassador. The school received a broad new charter in 1812 and was renamed Hamilton College.

ONEOTA

The Oneota was northern group of trans-Mississippi tribes that included the Iowa, Missouri, Oto, and Winnebago.

ONONDAGA

The Onondagas of upper New York State were one of the five (later six) members of the federation of Iroquois-speaking Indian nations known as the League of Great Peace or Iroquois Confederacy and functioned as the league's administrative head and preserved the council fire. The several villages were located principally along the Onondaga and Salmon rivers in Onondaga, Madison, Onondaga, and Oswego counties situated between the lands of the Oneida and the Cayuga and centrally located in Iroquoia. In 1747, the Catholic mission of Oswegatchie was established at what is now Ogdensburg, New York, that drew from the Onondaga, Cayuga, and Oneida. See more under the Saint Regis.

The Iroquois Confederacy prospered over the years because the Six Nations were of one mind both in words and in deeds. The American Revolutionary War changed the dynamics of the relationship forever. The Oneidas along with the majority of their Tuscarora dependents preached strict neutrality while at the same time their actions drew them closer and closer to the side of rebels. The Mohawks, especially the faction under the leadership of Joseph Brant, openly supported the English. The Senecas, whose lands lay far to the west, were content to remain neutral but began to see greater benefits to be gained in supporting the British. The Cayugas for their part followed the lead of the Senecas. The Onondagas were stuck in the middle geographically and politically. For all of the Six Nations, however, the situation was far from black and white. A turning point was reached in January 1777 with the announcement by the Onondagas that the Great Council Fire of Onondaga was extinguished. Each nation was henceforth free to pursue it own course. In the end only the Oneida stood solidly with the rebels. (The British surrendered October 19, 1781.) For more see the Iroquois League.

ONTARIO

There were a number of native peoples that originally fell into the category of Ontario Indians. They were classified into four groups employing thirteen different languages.
Three Fires Confederacy Languages: Odawa, Ojibwe, Potawatomi (Firekeepers)
Six Nations Confederacy Languages: Cayuga, Mohawk, Oneida, Onondaga, Seneca, and Tuscarora
Cree Family: Cree, Oji-Cree
Other: Algonquin (Golden Lake), Delaware
The Ojibwe, Mohawk, Cree, Oji-Cree, and the Algonquin (Golden Lake) languages were the most widely used.

ONTONAGON

The Ontonagon was a band of the Lake Superior Chippewa Indians that was sometimes treated separately. For more see Chippewa.

ONTPONEA

The Ontponea was a sub-tribe of the Manahoac of Virginia or possibly a distinct and independent tribe and member of the Manahoac Confederacy that lived in Orange County.

OPELOUSA

It is believed that the Opelousa were of the Atakapan family, separate and distinct from the Okelousa. They led a wandering life throughout parts of Louisiana, mostly about the present city of Opelousas west of Baton Rouge. They were mentioned by Bienville as one of the tribes of the Mississippi. A small tribe, they managed to maintain a distinct existence into the first quarter of the nineteenth century.

ORAIBI HOPI

Oraibi was a Hopi village on the third or West Mesa. The Pueblo of Old Oraibi, reportedly established in 1050, is considered the oldest continuously inhabited settlement in North America. There was a supporting farming village forty miles northwest at Moenkapi. Oraibi was the only Puebloan group to resist the Spanish reconquest mounted by Governor Vargas in 1692.

The Hopi village of Oraibi in Arizona should not be confused with the satellite settlement of the Isleta Pueblo by the same name in New Mexico.

ORCOQUISAC

The Orcoquisac lived along the Texas coast and the upper reaches of Galveston in what is now Liberty County. They initially got along well with the early white settlers tribe but were soon ravaged by the white man's diseases. An east-west trail on their foraging expeditions became the La Bahia or lower road in the 18th Century and later the Opelousas Road that was used for the large cattle drives. The Spanish outpost of El Orcoquisac (1765-71) was located on the present site of Wallisville in present Chambers County on the east side of Galveston Bay.

ORONDOC

An Orondoc tribe was listed in Jefferson's *Notes on the State of Virginia* based on information supplied by Hitchins (1769). He notes that they lived near *Trois-Rivières* in modern Michigan. The name may also be spelled Orondock. There is a report that a tribe on Cape Cod , the Muhhuhwau, was also called the Orondock which would appear to an error, but the information on the two tribes is insufficient to render a final judgment.

OSAGE

The Osage or Wazhazhe as they called themselves was the most prominent tribe of the Dhegiha Siouan language group that included the Omaha, Kansa, Ponca, and Quapaw. The word Osage was a French corruption of their own name. An exceptionally tall tribe of hunters, they were also known as the Anahou and Bone Indians. The Osage were also the largest of the Missouri River tribes and generally warlike in nature. The combination made them the gatekeepers of the American West. It also put them on a short list for extermination by both the Spanish and the Jefferson administration. It was Jefferson's proposal to subsidize the eastern tribes in a war of extermination against the Osage. None of the proposals were ever put into action, thanks in large part to Pierre and Auguste Chouteau.

It is believed that the Osage first emerged as a separate tribe around 1500, but the first archeological evidence dates from around 1700. The Osage ranged over the present-state of Missouri and across most of the southern half of Kansas and the northern halves of the present states of Oklahoma and Arkansas. At some unrecorded time in their early history, a disastrous flood struck the region that legend has it was responsible for dividing Osage into two groups or tribes, the Little Osage (Petit or Down-Below People) and the Big Osage (Giant, Grand, or Up-Above People). The Little Osage located to the north along the Missouri River in central Missouri near the village of the Missouri Indians. The Big Osage located farther south along the Osage River.

Father Jacques Marquette and trader Louis Jolliet traveled up the Missouri River in 1673 to where it is joined by the Osage River just east of present-day Jefferson City, Missouri. Marquette and Jolliet were very possibly the first white men to encounter the Osage. Father Marquette's 1673 map shows the locations of the Big Osage and Little Osage villages. Contact with Europeans from the settlements in Illinois Country became common place in the early 1700s. The white man that made the most significant early impact was the Frenchman Éttienne de Véniard, sieru de Bourgmont.

Bourgmont, the former commandant of Fort Detroit, deserted his post in 1712 to marry an Indian girl from among the members of the Missouri tribe who were working with the French at Detroit and became an unofficial explorer of the Midwest. In 1714, he surveyed the Missouri River upriver as far as the mouth of the Platte River in Nebraska. There are indications that he may have ascended the Missouri as far up as the Arikara villages near Pierre, South Dakota, well above the Platte. He mapped his route and published it with supportive information on the country in *Carte de la Louisiane et du Cours du Mississippi* and *Exacte Description de la Louisianne* in 1717. The success of Bourgmont's exploration of the Missouri brought him a pardon and official recognition plus appointment as commandant of the Missouri River in 1720. His job was to implement French plans for expansion in the Louisiana territory.

He returned to Osage country in 1723-24 to establish Fort d' Orleans in honor of the Duke of Orléans on the bank of the Missouri near villages of the Little Osage and the Missouri Indians near the mouth of the Grand River. It was the western-most French post in upper Louisiana. (See more on Fort d'Orleans below.) Five years before the establishment of Fort d'Orleans, Claude-Charles DuTisné made the first official contact with the Osage in spring of 1719. Traveling up stream from Kaskaskia, Illinois, his mission was to explore the Lower Missouri and make treaties with the Osage, the Paniouassa (Black Pawnee), and the Padouca. DuTisné traded with the Osage and got as far the Black Pawnees with whom he also completed a trade agreement. Because of the animosity between the Osage and the Pawnee on the one hand and the Plaines Apaches on the other, he got no further and returned to Kaskaskia. (Antoine de La Mothe, sieur de Cadillac, governor of Louisiana, had explored the lead region of southeastern Missouri in 1715.)

On July 3, 1724, he Bourgmont set out overland with a small detachment of troops on a trade and peace mission to the Kansa and the Padouca west of the Missouri River accompanied by over one hundred and fifty Osage and Missouri Indians. Boatloads of gifts were sent upstream a week earlier. The Kansa and the Missouri River Indians, particularly, the Osage, were mortal enemies of the Padouca whose Grand Village was located near present Ellsworth, Kansas. After meeting with the Kansa at their village at Doniphan near where Independence Creek joins the Missouri, a peace council was held with the Padouca in October some ten day's march from the banks of the Missouri. Not only did the Padouca pledge their friendship with the French and guarantee their safe passage to Santa Fe, the parties all agreed to live in peace; but the settlement was tenuous at best. (At one time it was thought that the Padouca were Comanche, the name deriving from the Penatuka Comanche. More recent evidence suggests that the Padouca were Plains Apache. The North Platte River was known as the Padua Fork as late as 1805.)

Bourgmont returned to Paris that same year leading a delegation of Indians from the Midwest. The party included one chief each from the tribes of the Osage, Missouri, Illinois, Oto, and Chicago and the daughter of the principal Missouri chief. They arrived in France on September 20 and were received by the Duke and Duchess of Bourbon and presented to the king Louis XV in a highly-successful visit. A short time after their return, Fort d'Orleans was abandoned and in 1726 Bourgmont himself was recalled to France.

The Osage did not adapt well to peace and tranquility as envisioned by the French, nor later by the Spanish and Americans. The Americans would be forever trying to domesticate them. Auguste Chouteau called them "unmanageable" and stated that they he scarcely knew a tribe to be "more barbarous." The Osage were continually at war with one tribe or another, including the Otos, Quapaws, Panis noir, Panis piqués, and all the Missouri River nations with the possible exception of the Missouri. Although the names of the tribes would change, the warring would continue over the next three quarters of a century. Some elements were also continually involved in raids that included robbery and murder against both the white man and the red man throughout Missouri, Arkansas, eastern Illinois, and Kansas. The stealing and violence increased with the France cession of the Louisiana Territory to the Spanish following the end of the French and Indian War in 1763. The influx of white settlers onto their lands only exasperated the situation. One group of the Big Osage, the Les Cheniers, that regularly hunted along the Arkansas River to the south were particularly troublesome to the Spanish. They were led by a man called Le Chenier.

With the establishment of St. Louis post in 1764 by Pierre Laclède, the Laclède-Chouteau family became the masters of the Osage nation. Laclède received an exclusive seven-year license to trade with Osage. Laclède died in 1778 and was succeeded in business by his stepson Auguste son Pierre, both of whom at times lived with the Osage and took Osage wives. The intimate connection between the Osage and the Chouteaus endured for four generations and the Osage affinity for the French nearly twice as long. Until well past the exploration and settlement years, French was the only white man's language that the Osage people chose to learn. The Little Osage and the principal group of the Big Osage hunted across a wide range of the midland from their villages along the Missouri and Upper Osage rivers in Missouri. Reaching an agreement with Spanish authorities in New Orleans in 1794, the Chouteau brothers received a monopoly to trade with Osage good for a period of six years and constructed a fortified trading post they named Fort Carondelet for the Spanish governor on the Osage River in the heart of Osage country. The government was to station a small contingent of soldiers at the fort and absorb some of the costs of operation.

In June 1802 the Chouteau trade monopoly with the Osage was cancelled and given to Manuel Lisa—but only for the trade on the Missouri River and its tributary. Instrumental in the governor's decision was the fact that Lisa agreed to pick up the cost of garrisoning troops at Fort Carondelet. That, however, was never to be. In the fall when the Chouteaus vacated the fort, it was ransacked by the Indians and fell into ruin and was never used again.

About 1800 the Les Cheniers made a permanent move two hundred miles south to the banks of the Arkansas where they wrecked havoc on the countryside with raids, robberies and occasional murders. About this same time, a schism that had been growing among the Big Osage in Missouri between the hereditary chief, Clermont, and a rising new leader called Cheveux Blancs (White Hair or Pawhuska in the Osage language) broke wide-open. Clermont led his followers into Oklahoma Territory and settled along the Arkansas where they became known as the Southern Band of Osage, Clermont's Band, or the Arkansas River Osages.

The fine print of Lisa's license gave the Chouteaus an opening that moved immediately to exploit by encouraging another band of the Big Osage led by Grande Piste (Big Track) to leave the land of the Missouri and Osage rivers and join the Clermont's group on the Arkansas River at the juncture of the Neosho and Verdigris rivers in modern Oklahoma call the Three Forks, about four miles northeast of Muskogee. By the second decade of the eighteen-hundreds, there were four groups of Osages: a group of Big Osages on the traditional Osage lands on the Osage River in Missouri; a group of Big Osage Indians on the Arkansas River in northeastern Oklahoma; a group of Little Osages on the Osage River in Missouri; and a group of Little Osages on the Neosho River on land that would be crossed by the Santa Fe Trail in present-day southeastern Kansas. (Arkansas Territory that was separated from the Missouri Territory in 1819 included the modern state of Oklahoma except for the Panhandle. The Arkansas territory was reduced twice before the present boundaries of the state of Arkansas were established in 1824. Arkansas was admitted to the Union in 1836.)

On October 1, 1800, with the secret treaty of San Ildefonso, the Spanish ceded the Louisiana Territory back to France who in turn sold it to the United States in 1803. With that the world of the Osage changed forever. As Lewis and Clark were heading upriver in 1804, Pierre Chouteau was escorting a contingent of twelve Osage chiefs and elders and two Osage boys to Washington, DC to meet President Jefferson. In the party that left on May 19, 1804, were Chouteau's son and nephew who were to attend the new West Point Military Academy on recommendation of Meriwether Lewis.

While trees were being felled for construction of Fort Osage, William Clark negotiated a treaty with the Osage in September 1808 in which the Little Osage and the Great Osage ceded claim to all land north of the Missouri River and east of a line running from Fort Osage south to the Arkansas River in exchange for an annuity in goods and specie. The treaty of September 14 was the first treaty that "bought" land from the Indians within the Louisiana Purchase. The Arkansas Osage objected because they had not been a party to the negotiations, and several chiefs of both the Little Osage and the Great Osage also objected. The treaty was never ratified. On hearing of the objections, Meriwether Lewis, on his own initiative, modified the treaty and directed Osage Indian agent Pierre Chouteau to bring it to the Missouri Osage and have it signed. There was to be no discussion, no options. The new treaty was adopted on November 10, 1808. Under the new treaty, the Osage ceded their claim to all land north and south of the Missouri River and east of the north-south line passing through Fort Osage to the Arkansas River—effectively all of Missouri except for the tier of counties south of the Missouri River and east of the Missouri-Kansas border that encompassed their Marais de Cygnes homeland. (For more on Fort Osage, see below.)

The year 1812 saw several Indian tribes living within the present boundaries of the state of Missouri. Besides the Osage and Missouri, there the Sac, Fox, Shawnee, and the Delaware had all been driven west. The Osage, who were by far the most numerous, lived primarily along the Osage River a tributary of the Missouri River in the southwest. It is estimated that there were some eight thousand of them in the area in 1819. In the meantime, the first of the Cherokee from the southeast were moved onto land in Arkansas that had been ceded to the United States in the treaty of 1808. And in a meeting with the Cherokee agent in July 1816, the Osage agreed to sell a section of land in northwestern Arkansas and northeastern Oklahoma for the use by Cherokee, making further interaction and friction inevitable.

After the War of 1812 there was a surge in the white population in Missouri. People moved farther up the Missouri River to the Osage Indian boundary at Fort Osage and on west until by 1820 they nearly reached the proposed state boundary at the Kansas River. The Franklin land office in Boonslick country began land sales on February 8, 1819. The fourth decennial census of the United States in 1820 on the eve of Missouri's admission to statehood counted 66,586 persons including 10,222 slaves and 347 free Blacks. With native Americans, the total population was estimated at 71,000.

The earliest Catholic sacramental records from the Diocese of Kansas City-St. Joseph and western Kansas are those of Fr. Charles de la Croix, 1822, who witnessed the Osage treaty of 1822; Fr. Benedict Roux, 1834-1835; Fr. August Saunier, 1848-1849; and Fr. Charles Felix Quickenborne, who became superior of the Missouri Mission in 1823. Ten years later, the Missouri Mission was assigned responsibility for all Indian mission activity in the United States west of the Mississippi River. The earliest entries were for the Indians of Missouri and later the Indians of the newly established reservations in Kansas and Oklahoma. Jesuit missionaries, with their headquarters in Florissant, Missouri, outside of St. Louis, were very active in the region up until 1875.

From 1824 to 1831, the Jesuits operated Saint John Francis Regis Seminary for Osage Indians boys on the grounds at Florissant. The school, the first Roman Catholic institution established in the country for the higher education of Native Americans, opened May 11, 1824. Father John Shoenmakers established the Osage Mission in Kansas in 1847 and remained with the tribe until his death in 1883. At the time the Osage were generally concentrated in Neosho and Labette counties in southeast Kansas. Missionaries from United Foreign Missionary Society came to Missouri at the request of the Osage in 1821 and established a mission and school that served the Osage until 1836.

A number of treaties were signed by the Osage between 1815 and 1870. With the treaty of 1808 the Osage lost practically all their lands in Arkansas and Missouri. In the intervening years to 1870, the treaty of June 2, 1825, was the most significant. The Great and Little Osage tribes not only ceded their homeland in Missouri but all lands and all claims to lands in Missouri, the Territory of Arkansas, and west of the state of Missouri and south of the Kansas River—basically anywhere west of the Mississippi that Osage might have a land claim. In return they were given a reserve fifty miles wide and one hundred and twenty-five miles long along the border between Kansas and Oklahoma in Kansas beginning twenty-fives west of the Missouri-Kansas border. Included in the cession was the western tier of counties in Missouri to include Jackson, Cass, Bates, Vernon, Jasper, Newton, and McDonald. Before the ink was dry on the parchment, pioneers began pouring into the western counties. A land office opened, and soon Anglo names overshadowed French names in the plat books.

Also include in the cession were the Osage villages in the vicinity of what is now Osawatomie in Miami County, Kansas, on its eastern border with Missouri. The town Osawatomie about 45 miles SW of Kansas City on the Missouri Pacific rail line was settled around 1854 by colonists sent by the New England Emigrant Aid Company and was platted in 1855. The name was coined from the names of the Osage and the Potawatomi tribes.

The final removal treaty was signed July 15, 1870, by which the Osage were expelled from Kansas and relocated to lands in the Indian Territory in the present state of Oklahoma (96th meridian on the east to the Arkansas River on the west). In some ways, it turned out to be the best that thing to have happened to Osage over the preceding century of dealing with the white man. Oil and natural gas were found on the land in 1894, and since 1896 the Osage have been referred to as the oil-rich Indians. In 1906 the Osage National Council agreed to give up joint ownership of the land, and the Osage Allotment Act of 1907 established individual ownerships. For more see Missouri, Kansa (Kaw), and Nations of the North. Also the painting by George Fuller Green of early Fort Osage.

FORT D'ORLEANS

Reports differ on the exact location and history of Fort d'Orleans. One report has the fort was located 106 leagues up the Missouri River from its mouth on the north bank of Missouri River in Chariton County at Tetsau Bend about two miles above the outlet of the Wakenda River. (A league is 2.76 miles and refers to leagues by waterway not by land.) A historical marker stands on U.S. Highway 24 near Brunswisk. Other reports have the fort was located on the south bank of the river at Malta Bend in Saline County. As to it demise, various accounts indicate that the fort was attacked and burned by Indians in 1726; that it was simply abandoned for political reasons in 1726; and that it was abandoned in 1728 or 1729. The greater weight of evidence suggests the latter date. Nester writes that the French war with the Fox and Natchez Indians forced them to abandon d'Orleans and pull back to Cahokia. During the short history of the fort, the French supplied the Osage with guns and bullets and swords and hatchets and an assortment of household items including scissors, needles, pots, bells, and wire.

FORT OSAGE

Originally called Fort Clark and at times referred to as Fort Point, Fort Osage was a fortified trading post or "factory" run by a factor or government agent vs. a private trader. The fort was located on a 70-foot cliff above the Missouri River twenty-four miles down river from the mouth of the Kansas River in a place known as Fire Prairie. George Champlain Sibley was appointed factor. Meriwether Lewis, the recently appointed governor of Louisiana territory (v. the territory of New Orleans), submitted a proposal for the fort to Jefferson's Secretary of War, Henry Dearborn, in July 1808. William Clark, the new government agent for all the Indians west of the Mississippi, with the exception of the Osage, had noted the site on his journey west with the Corps of Discovery. It fell to him to see to the construction of the fort that was to serve all the tribes of the watershed of the Missouri River valley. The fort operated continuously from 1808 until the spring of 1813 when it was closed. The fort was the site of the first treaty between the Osage and the government concuded in August 1808 and signed November 10 of that same year. The treaty is remembered in a mural that adorns the Missouri State Capitol in Jefferson City.

The factory reopened again in 1815 only to be closed permanently in 1822. Although subsequent events overcame the best of intentions, the fort played a significant role in the westward growth of the nation. Every mile coming and going from Santa Fe was measured from Fort Osage, and it was from Fort Osage that the first traders embarked in 1816-17. The site of the reconstructed old fort, dedicated in 1948, can be found three miles north of Buckner, Missouri, about 23 miles east of Kansas City.

George Sibley, the only factor at Fort Osage, was subsequently appointed by President John Quincy Adams as one of the three commissioners to survey the Santa Fe Trail in 1825 that brought him into contact with the Osage yet again. As it turned out the route required an easement through the Osage reservation in Kansas. Sibley would later appear prominently in Indian affairs in Louisiana and Texas. The Missouri town of Sibley located near the site of Fort Osage was named in his honor.

OSOCHI

The Osochi were part of the Creek Confederacy of Lower Creeks thought to have originated in Florida as part of the Timucua and moving north in the early eighteenth century to the area of the bend of the Chattahoochee River in Russell County, Alabama, near the Chiaha. Retaining their own identity they were removed with the Creeks to Indian Territory. After a time they were absorbed by the Creeks.

OSSIPEE

The Ossipee was a subdivision of the Abnaki. They lived on Ossipee River and Ossipee Lake in Maine and New Hampshire. For more see Abenaki.

OSWEGATCHI

The Oswegatchi was listed in Jefferson's *Notes on the State of Virginia*. He took his information from Hutchins (1769) who reported a population of one hundred warriors who lived near Swagatchy on the St. Laurence River. For more see "Aborigines," Appendix D.

OTO

Oto or Otoe spoke the Chiwerian dialect of the Siouan language group as did the Missouri and the Iowa. All three tribes once belonged to the Ho-Chunk or Winnebago Nation in the Great Lakes region. At some point a large group separated themselves and migrated south. One group, the Ioway, settled along the Mississippi River. The Missouria settled along the Missouri River, and the Otoe settled farther west. The Otoe and Missouria, both relatively small in number, were very closely related, both in family gens and in cultural practices. (See the Missouri)

The treaty that spelled the end of the Otoe was signed in 1854. Theirs was one of the Manypenny treaties from 1854 to 1857. For more see Missouri.

Of Note

It was the Oto that gave the state of Nebraska its name, the Oto Indian word *nebrathka*, meaning flat water, referring to the Platte River.

OTTAWA

The Ottawa were a migratory tribe of the Algonquian linguistic group. They lived originally along the Ottawa River in eastern Ontario and western Quebec The Ottawa were allies of French in their wars with the British. The French alliance joined them with the Potawatomi, Delaware, Abenaki, Miami, and Shawnee against the Iroquois and Wyandot, allies of the English. The Ottawas were evangelized by

Catholic missionaries in the 1600s. In 1668 Father Jacques Marquette was sent as a missionary to the Ottawa, spent a winter at Sault Ste Marie, and in 1669 reached the La Pointe Mission on Chequamegon Bay.

Fear of attack by the Sioux drove the Ottawa and Huron to Mackinac. Marquette accompanied them to Mackinac where he founded a new mission on Point St. Ignace near the Straits of Mackinac in present-day Michigan. In the spring of 1673 the Ottawa provided guides for Father Marquette and Louis Jolliet from St. Ignace to the Mississippi River and down the Mississippi past the mouth of the Missouri to the Arkansas River.

The Ottawa moved into northern Ohio along the Cuyahoga, Maumee, and Sandusky Rivers around 1740. Twenty years later Pontiac's Rebellion broke out led by the famous Ottawa chief. Missionary priest Gabriel Richard, a Sulpician, made contact in 1821 when the tribe was living on Lake Michigan. The nation was relocated for a time in the region of the confluence of the Kansas (Kaw) and Missouri rivers where Jesuit missionaries began visiting the tribe again in 1839.

PONTIAC'S REBELLION*

The French and English officials and American colonists used the Indians to weigh the balance of power to their side. The Indians, for their part realizing their situation, cheered both sides. Chief Pontiac of the Ottawas, who fought on the side of the French against the British and the Iroquois in the Seven Years War or the French and Indian War or as it was called in North America, was the first to foresee what would happen if one side or the other prevailed. When the fighting stopped in 1763, he knew the only chance the Indians had was to assemble a coalition, attack swiftly, and drive the English, who were at their ascendancy, from their lands back across the Appalachian Mountains.

The Ottawas attacked Fort Detroit above Lake Erie in May of 1763. It was the beginning of Pontiac's Rebellion. The Battle of Bloody Run was fought on July 31, 1763, in an attempt by the British to break the siege of Fort Detroit. Two hundred and fifty British troops attempted a surprise attack on Pontiac's encampment; but, possibly alerted by French settlers, the British were met and defeated at a creek two miles north of the fort. The creek, or run as it was called, was said to have been awash in the blood of the 20 dead and 34 wounded British soldiers. However, Pontiac did not achieve his principal goal, the complete destruction of this British force, that he believed would have greatly demoralized the British and dissuade future British efforts.

The coalition of Shawnee, Munsee, Wyandot, Seneca, and Delaware raided British settlements in the Ohio Country and western Pennsylvania. By late fall they had killed or captured more than 600 Pennsylvanians. Fort Sandusky, Great Britain's only garrisoned fort in the Ohio Country, fell to the Ottawas that same year, and thirteen soldiers inside were killed.

Soon, the Indians controlled the entire region west of Fort Pitt at the forks of the Ohio River. They had killed some two thousand settlers and another four hundred plus British soldiers—unmercifully in some cases as the massacre at Fort Machinaw by the Ojibwe fully demonstrated.

But in the autumn of 1764, Col. John Bradstreet and Col. Henry Bouquet each launched expeditions into the Ohio Country from Pennsylvania and easily defeated the Indian population. Most of the Wyandots and Ottawas, except Pontiac, surrendered to Bradstreet in September. Bouquet forced the surrender of the Senecas, Shawnees, and Delawares a month later. Pontiac's Rebellion came to an end. In early November, Bouquet's army marched to Fort Pitt with more than 200 former captives, several of whom fled back to the natives while enroute. The march to Fort Pitt is often labeled Bouquet's Expedition. It is Bouquet who distributed smallpox infested blankets to the Indians, with General James Amherst's blessing.

Pontiac did not formally surrender to the British until July 1766. By then he had lost face for having failed, and in 1769 he was murdered by a Illinois Indian of the Kaskaskia tribe. (Brands writes that he was killed by a member of the Peoria tribe at a trading post on the Mississippi.)

To avert the costs of further Indian uprisings in both lives and treasury, the British monarch issued the Proclamation of 1763 on October 7 that established the Appalachian Mountains as the boundary between Indians and whites. In a pattern that would stretch over the next hundred-plus years, white settlers ignored the act and soon moved beyond the mountains into the Ohio Country. Virginians, who twenty years before had settled in the Kanawha Valley and were driven out by the Indians, were the first to cross the mountains in what began a steady migration into western Virginia, Maryland, southwestern Pennsylvania, and then northwestern Penns1ylvania. These settlers were all bitterly resentful of the British soldiers who tried to prevent the movement west. (The act also established the colonies of Quebec, West Florida, and East Florida.)

*Also see the Massacre at Fort William Henry under the Abenaki.

ROYAL PROCLAMATION OF 1763

Following Pontiac's Rebellion, the King issued the Royal Proclamation of 1763 in October of that year that established what was referred to the Proclamation Line that was to separate settlers and colonists from the Indians. The proclamation reserved by the Native Peoples the land west of the Appalachian Mountains. Before the proclamation was issued, it was no avail. Settlers, colonists, land speculators, and hunters and trappers had already penetrated the line and there would be no going back regardless of the best efforts of the British soldiers to enforce the ban.

FATHER JACQUES MARQUETTE AND LOUIS JOLLIET (Jolliet is an acceptable spelling)

In the spring of 1673 the Ottawa of Canada provided guides for Father Jacques Marquette and Louis Jolliet down the Mississippi River past its junction with the Illinois River and past the mouth of the Missouri (or Pekitanoui) River on south to the Arkansas River. Marquette correctly located several native tribes on his map of the Missouri River Valley, including the Osage (Ouchage), the Missouri (Ouemessourit), the Kansa, and the Pawnee (Paniassa).

In his journal, Father Marquette wrote, "we heard the noise of a rapid, into which we were about to run. I have seen nothing more dreadful. An accumulation of large and entire trees, branches, and floating islands, was issuing from The mouth of The river pekistanouï, with such impetuosity that we could not without great danger risk passing through it. So great was the agitation that the water was very muddy, and could not become clear. Pekitanouï is a river of Considerable size, coming from the Northwest, from a great Distance; and it discharges into the Mississippi. There are many Villages of savages along this river..."

Tribal names as written on Father Jacques Marquette's 1673 map (usual form in parentheses, as known)

Moingwena
Pe-warea (Peoria)
Ilinois (Alliniwek and Illinois)
Miscousing (Wisconsin)
Kachkaskia (Kaskaskia)
Maskoutens
Kanza (Kansa)
Ouchage (Osage)
We-messouret (Missouri)
Aiaichi (Ayiches)

Tanik-wa (Tonica)
Matora (Mento)
Atotchasi (Southouis)
Monsoupelea
Wabous-quigou (Wabash)
Kakinonba (Kanawha)

OUACHANON

The Ouachanon lived on the Wabash River in present Union County, Ohio.

OUACHITA

The Ouachita belonged to the Caddo division of the Caddoan linguistic stock and was one of the four principal members of the Natchitoches Confederacy. They inhabited the Ouachita River near present Columbia in northwestern Louisiana.

When Iberville's brother Bienville (Jean-Baptiste LeMoyne de) explored west of the Mississippi into the Red River basin that comprises the present-day New Iberia, Lafayette and Morgan City in late 1699 and the spring of 1670, he was accompanied by six Taensa and one Ouachita guide. The Taensa, however, deserted the party after only a few days. Bienville traveled as far as Yatasi before returning to Biloxi. Generally by the end of the eighteenth century, the Ouachita and other divisions of the Natchitoches Confederacy has lost their identity. For more see Natchitoches Confederacy and Caddo Peoples.

OUANAKINA

The Ouanakina was listed in Jefferson's *Notes on the State of Virginia*. They had a reported population of 300 warriors. For more see "Aborigines," Appendix D.

OUIÀTONON

The Ouiàtonon lived on the banks of the Wabash River near Fort Ouiatonon. Croghan (1759), Bouquet (1764), Hutchins (1768) and Dodge (1779) reported population figures of between 200 and 400 warriors.

OUISCONSING

According to Bouquet (1764), the Ouisconsing lived on the Ouisconsing River in Wisconsin He reported a population of 550 warriors. For more see "Aborigines," Appendix D.

OUSASOY

The Ousasoy was listed in Jefferson's Query XI of his *Notes on the State of Virginia* as "Ousasoys. Grand Tuc." His information was taken from Croghan (1759) who reported that they lived on White Creek, a branch of the Mississippi River, and that they had a population of 400 warriors. No additional information has become available.

Speculation is that the Ousasoy was one of the Woodland Tribes living east of the Mississippi between Kentucky and Michigan.

OUTIMAC

The Outimac was listed in Jefferson's *Notes on the State of Virginia*. No population figure or location was given. For more see "Aborigines," Appendix D.

OVEDSITA

The Ovedsita lived on the Salk Fork of the Brazos River in central Texas and was counted among the Nations of the North, but no additional information has been uncovered. For more see Nations of the North.

OWASSISSAS

The Owassissas was a village of the Seminole Indians of Florida that is generally treated separately. They lived on an eastern branch of St. Mark's River, probably near its head. For more see Seminole.

OWENS VALLEY PAIUTE

The Owens Valley Paiute were a group or subdivision of the Northern Paiute that inhabited the area about Owens Lake in California. Also see the Koso.

OZAW

The Ozaw (possibly Osaw) reportedly lived on the Ozaw River, an unidentified tributary of the Mississippi in Kentucky, 200 miles below the Kaskaskia. They were possibly related to the Usuchee (Yuchi) of the Upper Creeks. Drake gave them a population of 2,000 in 1750.

OZETTE

The Ozette lived along the Ozette River and Ozette Lake in present Clallam County, Washington. They belonged to the Nootka division of the Wakashan linguistic family with the Makah, of which they were a

OZIMIE

According to Drake, the Ozimie lived on the eastern shore of Maryland and Virginia during the early colonial period.

PADOUCA

At one time it was thought that the Padouca were Comanche, the name deriving from the Penateka Comanche (Swanton). More recent evidence suggests that the Padouca or Pahucah were Plains Apache. The North Platte River through Scottsbluff, Nebraska, to North Platte was known as the Paduca Fork as late as 1805. For more see Osage.

PADOWAGA

Drake states that Padowaga was the name used by some people when referring to the Seneca of New York, but whether it was actually another name for the Seneca is uncertain.

PAGUATE PUEBLO

Paguate was a Laguna Pueblo village of the Eastern Keresan Group. For more see Pueblo.

PAHMAP

Lewis and Clark encountered the Pahmap Indians at the mouth of the Potlatch River in Idaho on their return trip.

PAHVANT UTE

The Pahvant, a subdivision of the Northern Ute, inhabited Pahvant Valley in west-central Utah. They reportedly worked farms on the east side of Sevier Lake near present Filmore, Utah. In 1853, Chief Walkara and his band of Pahvant Indians were on the warpath in what has been called the Walker War. An old Indian attempting to trade with settlers headed for California was killed. The old man was a member of the band of Chief Kanosh, Walkara's brother. What ensued in October 1853, was the Gunnison Massacre. The Pahvant were subsequently placed on the Goshute Agency in Utah.

GUNNISON MASSACRE

What has been called the Gunnison Massacre occurred in Utah Territory, October 26, 1853. In 1853, Congress authorized the Corps of Topographic Engineers to conduct a survey of potential rail routes between the Mississippi River and the Pacific. Captain John W. Gunnison led the survey party that mapped the "central" route at the 38th and 39th parallels across Kansas, Colorado, and Utah. He was assisted by Lt. Edward G. Beckwith. Gunnison and seven others, including Richard H. Kern, the topographer and survey party artist, were attacked and killed by a band of thirty Pahvant (Ewtaws) Indians of Chief Walkara along the Sevier River in central Utah. The dead were plundered and mutilated. The killings were reportedly in retaliation for the killing of a Pahvant Indian man the month before by a group of white travelers.

Other accounts attribute the killings to Pahvant Ute Chief Moshoquop and forty of his warriors; others to the work of Mormon militia masquerading as Utah Paiutes angry because of a book, *The Mormons*, Gunnison had written critical of the Mormons. (Beckwith took command and explored the "northern" route at the 41st parallel that would generally lay out the route to be followed by the first transcontinental railroad.)

PAILSH

According to Drake, the Pailsh lived on the Pacific coast north of the Columbia River beyond the Potoash.

PAIUTE

The name Paiute (also written Piute and Pah-Ute) refers to two different but related groups of American Indians, the Southern Paiute and the Northern Paiute, although the Northern Paiute was not a tribe in the true sense. The two groups were distinguished by their language. According to Swanton, the Northern Paiute language was of a dialectic group of the Shoshonean branch of the Uto-Aztecan family. The Southern Paiute belonged to the Ute-Chemehuevi that included the Ute.

The state of California lists the "Paiute (Mono Paiute/Kutzadikaa) (Owens Paiute)" language group as including the Northern and Owens Valley Paiutes who lived along the eastern slope of the Sierra Nevada mountains from Oregon to Owens Valley who spoke a Shoshonean dialect and the Southern Paiutes who lived along southeastern California who spoke Numic. (Numic is a branch of the Uto-Aztecan language family, and Chemehuevi is a Numic dialect.) California also lists separately the "Western Mono/Monache" who lived within the south-central foothills of the Sierra Nevada and spoke Shoshoni.

Both the Northern and Southern Paiutes were also known by a number of different names that were sometimes used interchangeably between the two groups. Swanton and other writers treat the two groups separately, but the two groups are commonly written of under the name Paiute, without a qualifier.

McLynee writes that Paiutes went on the warpath in 1860 in the area of northwestern Nevada, southern Oregon and northern California and ambushed an army detachment under the command of Maj. William Ormsby and killed between forty-six and sixty soldiers and that a large force of eight hundred soldiers was sent against the Paiutes that killed forty to fifty braves. And, it will be noted that the Central Pacific Railroad, in building the transcontinental railroad east from Sacramento, negotiated special treaties with the Paiutes and Shoshoni granting rights to ride the trains whenever they wished. (Both male and female Indians worked alongside the Chinese in railroad construction).

There is a certain amount of confusion in the literature as to the identity of the Indians who occupied the Mono Lake Basin of California and the adjacent lands both before and after the recorded history of the region. There are references to the Kutzadika'a, Mono Lake Kutzadika'a, Mono Lake Paiute, the Mono, Western Mono, and Eastern Mono. Swanton reports the1925 classification (Kroeber) of the eastern division of the Northern Paiutes of California as being composed of the Western Mono and the Eastern Mono but gives no additional information on their locale.

Swanton cites the 1910 census figures for the Paiute that give the population of the Mono—assumed to include all other Northern Paiute and possibly some Southern Paiute. Among the other names for the Northern Paiute is the Mono-Paviotso, Mono coming from the Maidu name Monozi. (The Maidu was a California tribe.) Several reports in the literature treat the Paviotso as a group distinctly different from the Northern Paiute.

The Paiute bands that lived in the area of Lake, Harney, and Malheur counties in Oregon eventually settled at Warm Springs and now, along with bands of Walla Walla (later called Warm Springs) and the Wasco, comprise the Confederated Tribes of Warm Springs, Oregon, formally organized in 1938. The settlement of the Paiutes at Warm Springs began in 1879 when thirty-eight Paiutes moved from the Yakama Reservation. For more see Northern Paiute, Southern Paiute, Mono, Eastern Mono, and Owens Valley Paiute.

MOUNTAIN MEADOWS MASSACRE

Approximately one hundred and twenty men, women, and children were massacred at Mountain Meadows in southern Utah on September 11, 1857. They were members of a wagon train known as the Fancher Party en route from Arkansas to California that was led by Capt. Alexander Fancher and John T. Bakerwas. The attack was carried out local Mormon settlers and members of the Iron County militia aided by some Paiute Indians. (Some reports suggest that the attack was organized with the approval of Bringham Young himself, a charge he vehemently denied.)

The brutality of the event stunned and shocked the nation. What made the attack and deaths all the more disheartening was the fact that it carried out under a act of subterfuge. Seventeen children between the ages of two months and seven years were spared—only because it was determined that they were too young to bring evidence against the perpetrators. Other reports suggest that Mormon law forbade the murder of children up to the age of eight.

Early Mormon accounts but the blame on the Paiutes as leaders of the attacking party and responsible for the slaughter that followed whereas, in fact, the killings were a part of the ongoing war between the Mormons and Federal Government over polygamy. Major James H. Carleton issued a scathing indictment of the Mormons following his investigation of the incident in the summer of 1859. John D. Lee, Bringham Young's adopted son, who gave the orders, was tried and found guilty in a second trail.

On March 23, 1877, he was executed on the very spot of the Mountain Meadows Massacre. (The first trial miscarried.) No members of the church hierarchy nor any other members of the party nor those who originated the plan were ever brought to trial.

PAIUTE (PAH-UTE) WAR

The Paiute War erupted in western Nevada in May 1860. It began with attacks on Pony Express stations and nearby settler homes located below the Great Bend of the Carson River on May 7-8 by some 150 Northern Paiutes who lived about Carson Valley, in what is sometimes referred to separately as the Massacre in Carson Valley. Twelve or thirteen white men were killed. The raiders were soon joined by another three hundred of their brethren, threatening an all out war that never developed. Back in January, the Indians killed a white man on Willow Creek. Whites demanded the Paiutes surrender those responsible. Old Winnemuca countered with a demand for reparations for the loss of their hunting grounds and the piñon nut trees that had been cut down. There, negotiations, for lack of better word, stood until May.

A militia force of over one hundred led by Major Ormsby tracked the Indians but soon found themselves trapped on May 12. What amounted to a massacre followed. One account puts the number of whites killed at forty-six men, including Ormsby. A much larger militia force was subsequently assembled from Nevada and California to deal with the Indians. They were joined on May 31 by a detachment of 207 regular soldiers—together they totaled 754 men. Militia Colonel Jack Hays assumed command of the combined force. The Battle at Truckee that followed on June 2 left several Indians killed and wounded—the numbers reported in the various accounts: 3-4, 26, 46, and 160 killed, plus wounded. Best evidence suggests that twenty-six or fewer Indians were killed in the fighting. After Truckee, the Indians refused to engage the army and militia head on. Indian agent Frederick Dodge was finally able to negotiate a settlement with chiefs Young Winnemuca, Oderkoo, and Truckee. Full scale war was averted although sporadic raids continued over the next year. By the first of July 1860, life for Indians and whites in western Nevada were reasonably back as it was before the fighting.

PAKANA

The Pakana or Pacana (also called Pakana Creeks) was a division of the Muscogee that lived in Alabama and on the Calcasieu River in Louisiana. A few found their way to Texas, near Livingston, in the nineteenth century. For more see Muscogee and Creek Confederacy.

PALA LUISEÑO

The Pala was one of six recognized tribes of Luiseños. In 1875 President Ulysses S. Grant signed an Executive Order that established reservations for the Pala, La Jolla, and Rincon. In 1891 the Mission Indian Relief Act made the Rincon, La Jolla, Pauma, Pala, reservations permanent. For more see Luiseño.

PALACHE

According to the Drake, the Palache was reportedly an early tribe of Florida long since extinct.

PALOUSE

Palouse, Paloos or Pelloatpallah lived about the Palouse River in Washington State and Idaho and a portion of the Snake River to near Moscow, Idaho. They belonged to the Shahaptian division of the Shapwailutan linguistic stock. They were closely connected to the Nez Percé and are also said to have separated from the Yakima, which appears quite probable.

Although included in the 1855 Yakima treaty at Camp Stevens as a member of the Yakima Confederation, they refused to recognize it and refused to lead their lives on the on the Yakima Reservation. For more see Yakima.

PAMACOCACK

The Pamacocack was one of the nine divisions of the Conoy and lived about the mouth of Mattawoman Creek and Pomonkey Creek in Charles County, Maryland. For more see Conoy Peoples.

PAMLICO

The Pamlico belonged to the Algonquian linguistic family. They lived along the Pamlico River in North Carolina and were first mentioned by the Raleigh colonists in 1585-1586 under the name Pomouik. A smallpox epidemic in 1696 nearly destroyed the Pamlico. They were down to a single small village by 1710. It is reported that the Tuscarora under treaty with the English were bound to destroy the Pamlico who had been their allies. Remnants may have been taken by the Tuscarora as slaves.

PAMPTECOUGH

The Pamptecough are believed to have been part of the early history of the colony of North Carolina. The only reference to the Pamptecough, who were allies of the Tuscarora, was found in Reed. It may have been only the name of a village.

PAMUNKEY

The principal city of the Pamunkey, Werowocomoco, was located on the Pamunkey River, land that later became Gloucester and Mathews Counties, Virginia. Wahunsonacock (1547-1618), whom the English gave the name Powhatan was the chief of the Pamunkey and became the leader of the Powhatan Confederacy or Powhatan Nation. (See Powhatan in this work.)

The Pamunkey, the Piscataway, the Susquehanna, and the Doeg became embroiled in the Rebellion of 1676 or Bacon's Rebellion. In the early fall of 1676, Bacon attacked the peaceful Pamunkey in the Great Dragon Swamp between the Mattapony and the Pianketank rivers in New Kent county, Virginia, and captured forty-five and most of the tribe's goods and supplies. See more on Bacon's Rebellion under the Piscataway.

PANACA

Panaca or Pioche was a band of Indians, believed to be Paiute, that lived about present Lincoln County, Nevada, but no supporting information has been found.

PANAWICKY

The Panawicky or Panauuaiooc took their name from the name of their village along the coastal region of North Carolina believed to have been located on or near Rice Creek on the headwaters of the Pamlico Sound near the site of the present town of Chocowinity. The Panawicky village appears on the 1588/1618 Theodore deBry map, but little else is known about them. But there are seven variant spellings of this name in the literature. The suffix "ooc" refers

PAPAGO

The Papago (now known as the Tohono O'odham Nation) belonged to the Piman branch of the Uto-Aztecan linguistic stock and were closely related to the Pima. They lived in the area south and southeast of the Gila River in Arizona, especially south of Tucson; in the valleys of the Santa Cruz River and its tributaries; and west and southwest across the Papaguería into Sonora. There were over eighty separate subdivisions or bands and villages, all believed to be descendants of the Hohokam. The first known European contact was with Spanish missionary and explorer Farther Eusebio Kino in 1694. The Papago were generally friendly to whites and their native Indian neighbors.

PARAJE

Paraje was a Laguna Pueblo village of the Eastern Keresan Group that has been treated separately. For more see Pueblo.

PARKEENAUM

The Parkeenaum (water people) was one of the sub-tribes or bands of the Comanche. For more see Comanche.

PASCAGOULA

The Pascagoula were probably of the Muskhogean family but closely associated with Biloxi of Siouan stock. They lived above the mouth of the Pascagoula River in Mississippi. The Pascagoula came to Iberville's attention in 1699 when he established the first French settlement in Louisiana.

PASECG-NA

Pasecg-na was a sub-tribe of the Tongva of California that inhabited the area about San Fernando. For more see Tongva.

PASINOG-NA

Pasinog-na was a sub-tribe of the Tongva of California that inhabited the area about Rancho del Chino. For more see Tongva.

PASPEHEAN

The Paspehean or Paspahegh was a member of the Powhatan Confederacy and were of the Algonquian linguistic stock. They lived in Virginia not far from the English settlement at Jamestown. Under the orders of the Governor Dale because the apparent disrespect shown him in the summer of 1611 by Powhatan, the head of the Powhatan Confederacy, George Percy was instructed to take revenge upon both the Paspehean and the Chickahominy, who of the several local Indian tribes lived the closest to Jamestown. Percy and a group of soldiers killed fifteen or sixteen of the Paspehean and captured the queen and her children. On their return, the children were thrown into the river and shot. Although some wanted her burned, Percy had the queen led away and stabbed to death.

PASSAMAQUODDY

The Passamaquoddy (People of the Dawn) were of the Algonquian linguistic stock and inhabited the southeastern corner of the state of Maine and a tract of land in southwestern New Brunswick on Passamaquoddy Bay across from Nova Scotia, commonly referred to as the Quoddy Loop area. They are also known as the St. Croix Indians and the Unchechauge or Unquechauge. As a result there is considerable confusion between the Passamaquoddy or Unchechauge and the Unkechaug (with its various spellings) of Long Island, New York.

Passamaquoddy Bay is an inlet of the Bay of Fundy at the mouth of the St. Croix River. The town of Qonasqamkuk on St. Croix was the tribe's traditional capital and the sacred burial ground for Passamaquoddy chiefs . Although distantly related to the Abnaki, the Passamaquoddy were not a sub-tribe of the Abnaki as been reported in the literature. Swanton writes that their early history was identical to that of the Malecite.

Their first encounter with Europeans was with the expedition of some eighty men led by Pierre Dugua de Monts (Sieur de Monts) and Samuel de Champlain on St. Croix Island in 1604. The island became the first French colony in North America, albeit a temporary one. The harsh winter following their arrival took the lives of thirty-five men from scurvy, and the settlement was moved to a sheltered inlet at Port-Royal south of present Annapolis Royal and north of Digby, Nova Scotia. There the survivors spent the next two winters.

(On a subsequent expedition in 1608, Champlain established the first permanent settlement north of Florida at what became the city of Québec, twelve years before the English at Plymouth, Massachusetts, in 1620; one year after the English at Jamestown, Virginia, in 1607; but well after the Spanish settlement at St. Augustine, Florida, in 1565. The official date is recorded as July 3.)

The Passamaquoddy allied themselves with the colonists in the American War of Independence, but offered the escaping British Loyalists a sanctuary on their land. As a consequence, they found their fertile lands literally taken from them. The majority settled in the area at the far southern end of Passamaquoddy Bay in present Washington County, Maine, between Perry and Eastport. The location subsequently became a Passamaquoddy Reservation known as Sipayik. Other members of the tribe settled inland from St. Croix in Indian Township north of Princeton that also became a reservation. Still others remained in Canada. Their former capital became St. Andrews in 1785.

The boundary between the state of Maine and New Brunswick, ending a decades-long controversy that began with Article II of the Treaty of Paris in 1783, was finalized with the Webster-Ashburton Treaty (Treaty of Washington), August 9, 1842. The boundary of the St. Croix River that was accepted by both the United States and Great Britain without any thought to the Passamaquoddy or other locals sliced through their tribal lands leaving St. Croix Island and Qonasqamkuk/St. Andrews in New Brunswick.

PASSAYONK

The Passayonk was a sub-tribe of the Unalachtigo division of the Delaware. They lived on the Schuylkill River in Pennsylvania and along the western bank of the Delaware River extending into the state of Delaware. For more see Unalachtigo and Delaware.

PASTATE

The Pastate was listed by Farther Ortiz in his memorial to the king of Spain sometime after February 14, 1747, cited by Bolton in "Missions on the San Gabriel," but no additional information about the tribe is known. It is believed that the Pastate lived in east central or southeastern Texas. Campbell suggests that it is possible that the Pastates are the same as the Postito Indians, who were generally thought to be Coahuiltecans that inhabited the region west of San Antonio.

PATAQUILLA

The Pataquilla was one of the four allied tribes of the Karankawan Tribes of Texas. For more see Karankawan Tribes.

PATAUNCK

Pataunck was a member of the Powhatan Confederacy and inhabited the area along the Pamunkey River.

PATCHOAG MONTAUK

The Patchoag or Patchogue or possibly Onechechaug was a division of the Montauk and a member of the Algonquian linguistic group that were generally treated separately. They lived on Long Island, New York. For more see Montauk and Delaware.

PATCHOGUE

The Patchogue was a division of the Montauk and a member of the Algonquian linguistic group. They lived on Long Island, New York, on the southern coast from Patchogue to Westhampton. For more see Montauk Peoples and Delaware.

PATIRI

The Patiri was a part of the Atakapa language group of Louisiana and Texas. The Franciscan mission of San Ildefonso west of the Trinity River in Texas was founded for them and the Deadose, the Bidai, and Akokisa.

PATÔUVOMEK

The Patôuvomek lived on the Potomac Creek (River) in Stafford and St. George counties in Virginia. They reportedly had a population of some 200 warriors.

PATUXENT

The Patuxent was one of the nine divisions of the Conoy and lived in Calavery County, Maryland. For more see Conoy Peoples.

PATWIN

The Patwin were of the Penutian stock and are now generally considered the southern division of the Penutian-speaking Wintun Indians of the Sacramento Valley region. The Patwin inhabited the western side of the Sacramento Valley in from roughly San Francisco Bay to Willows and both sides of the Sacramento River from its junction with the Feather River. There were two major divisions, the River Patwin of which there were three distinct dialects (Colusa, Grimes, Knight's Landing) and the Hill Patwin. Swanton identifies the groups within each division as "tribelets" and villages.

PAUGUSSET

The Paugusset was a subdivision or sub-tribe of the Wappinger and lived in the eastern part of Fairfield County, Connecticut, as well as the western edge of New Haven County. For more see Wappinger.

PAUMA LUISEÑO

Pauma in the Pauma Valley is one of six recognized tribes of Luiseños. Pauma, composed of two clans, was located at the foothills of Palomar Mountain. Pauma Band of Mission Indians was officially established 1886. In 1891 the Mission Indian Relief Act made the Rincon, La Jolla, Pauma, Pala, reservations permanent. For more see Luiseño.

PAVOGOWUNSIN UTE

The Pavogowunsin was a subdivision of the Northern Ute and lived on the upper Sevier River in Utah. For more see Ute.

PAWISTUCIENEMUCK

Drake describes the Pawistucienemuck as a small tribe that lived in the prairies of Missouri, but no further information has become available. It is uncertain whether Drake was referring to Missouri Territory or the lands traversed by the Missouri River.

PAWNEE

The Pawnee or Paunies were of the Caddoan linguistic stock. The tribe spoken and written of as the Pawnee was actually comprised of four sub-tribes or divisions. They are also written of as the Panis, which causes confusion with the name more commonly used for the Wichita. Some writings place the Pawnee as a subdivision of the Wichita under the name Panis piques (Prickled Panis), one of the names given for the Wichita.

The word Pani, which has become synonymous with Pawnee means or is equivalent to the word slave or subjected to a state of bond. It was reportedly from the Pawnee that the Algonquian tribes from the great lakes obtained many of their slaves; thus the name.

DIVISIONS

Chaui or Grand Pawnee, Nebraska
Kitkehahki or Republican Pawnee, Kansas
Pitahauerat or Tapage Pawnee, Nebraska
Skidi or Skiri Pawnee (Loos, Loup, Wolf), Nebraska

The Grand, Republican, and Tapage spoke the same dialect and were more closely related. The Pawnee inhabited the area along the middle course of Platte Rive and the Republican fork of the Kansas River, principally in Kansas and Nebraska. They were also known as the Padani and Panana. They name Pawnee that was also used as a descriptive term to identify other tribes not related to the Pawnee.

Their first encounter with the Europeans was with Coronado in 1541; later Juan de Oñate. They figure prominently in the settlement of the West. Lewis & Clark write of them on their journey up the Missouri in July 1804. Although the Pawnee evaded the early rush of settlers from the east, construction of the railroad and the discovery of gold in Colorado put them in the direct path of western migration. To the emigrants, they were "a treacherous, hostile race." They suffered from continuing wars with the Lakota, Cheyenne, and other tribes of the Plains. As a consequence, they often served as scouts for the Army, including service for Colonel Edwin Sumner and the Cheyenne Expedition of 1857.

It is estimated that a quarter of the Pawnee also fell victim to the smallpox epidemic of 1837, but they fared better than the Mandan, Hidatsa, and Arikara. With treaties in 1833, 1848, and 1857 they had ceded all their lands to the government and were given a tract of land in Oklahoma that was subsequently allotted to them in severalty.

The Arikara branched off from the Pawnee, specifically the Skidi Pawnee, and continued to maintain close relations with them. Nester refers to them as their Pawnee cousins. The Pawnee were longtime enemies of the Osage and Cheyenne. Today the Pawnee Nation is located in Pawnee County in north central Oklahoma. At their peak they numbered about 10,000-15,000. They came into the twenty-first century with approximately 2,300 members on the tribal roll.

PAWNEE SOLDIER-SCOUTS

Frank Joshua North was born in New York state in 1840. His family moved Ohio and later to Omaha in Nebraska Territory in 1856, then west to Platte County near present-day Columbus, Nebraska. North work as a clerk in the trader's store at the nearby Pawnee Agency where he soon learned the Pawnee language. At one time or another before joining the army, Frank was a mail carrier, scout, surveyor, and interpreter. He and his brother Luther would very close over the years sharing many of the same experiences.

The Pawnee never went on the warpath against the settlers and were willing to form alliances with the U. S. army, particularly against their hereditary enemies the Sioux and Cheyenne. In 1864 Major General Curtis arranged for Frank to organize and lead a company of Pawnee Scouts against bands of Indians who were resisting the government. The next year Frank was commissioned a captain in the army and given command of the scouts. From 1864-1877 North, later promoted to major, and the Pawnee Soldier-Scouts served in Nebraska, Kansas, and Wyoming.

North and the Pawnee served under Major General Patrick Conner in the Powder River Expedition of 1865. Conor told his soldiers that the Indians north of the Platte "must be hunted like wolves." There was to be no parley. They were to be attacked and killed, "every male Indian over twelve years of age." His superior at the time, Maj. General Grenville M. Dodge, had ordered Connor to chance and eliminate as many Indians as possible. Neither Dodge or Connor had any use for Indians, whatever their stripe. It was a wonder that Connor accepted the services of the Pawnee scouts. On August 23, the expedition attacked a party of Sioux and Cheyenne and killed thirty-four. Later that month the scouts directed Connor and his men to what some reports say was a peaceful Arapaho village where they drove off a large herd of horses and mules. It was during this time that the Pawnee gave North the name "Pani Le-Shar" (Chief of the Pawnee). The Pawnee company was mustered out of service in 1866.

In March 1867 General Christopher Auger commissioned North to reform the Pawnee Soldier-Scouts and hire 200 warriors. During 1867 and 1868 they were assigned the task of protecting workers building the Union Pacific Railroad. On August 7, 1867, a party of Cheyenne warriors led by Spotted Wolf wrecked a Union Pacific train near Plum Creek station and killed at least one brakeman and engineer, but the accounts differ. They also took what goods and supplies that they could carry and burned the freight cars. (A telegraph repairman was shot, stabbed and scalped, but survived. The Indian who scalped him dropped the scalp as he rode away, and the repairmen was able to retrieve it and make his escape during the night The scalp was later placed in the Union Pacific museum in Omaha.)

North and a company of Pawnee soldier-scouts trailed the Cheyenne to their camp. Of 150 Cheyenne in the camp, including women and children. seven were killed outright when the Pawnee crept up on the camp in the early morning hours and began firing without giving warning. The fighting continued throughout the day. A number of Cheyenne were killed and wounded, and two were taken prisoner. Part of the goods from the train were also recovered. None of the Pawnee died in the attack. In fact, only one Pawnee was ever killed while serving with North. The death occurred as a result of a Brulé attack on a Pawnee village in the summer of 1868.

In the years that followed, the soldier-scouts served under Major General E. A. Carr at the Battle of Summit Springs in the Republican River Campaign of 1869 and under General George Crook in the Big Horn Expedition of 1876-1877. North retired in 1877, and the Pawnee Soldier-Scouts were retired. North died in 1885.

(Rail facilities at the mouth of Plum Creek on the Platte River was a frequent target of the Cheyenne and the Sioux. The site was first used as a Pony Express station, but it gave way to a trading post and later the town of Lexington, Nebraska, and a Union Pacific staging yard. Brulé warriors attacked the post for the first time in August 1866, but were driven off by the arrival of chief engineer Dodge of the Union Pacific, late of the U.S. Army, with about twenty construction workers. In September 1868, Sioux warriors wrecked a freight train by bending the rails. Although two men were killed in the wreck, the action proved to be little more than an mild inconvenience to the railroad.)

PAWOKTI

Originally, an independent tribe and a member of the Creek Confederacy of Upper Creeks, the Pawokti were likely of Muskhogean stock and related to the Alabama or Tawasa. They lived near the shores of the Gulf of Mexico west of the Choctawhatchee River in Florida. From 1717, with the establishment of Fort Toulouse, to 1799 they were on the Alabama River south of present Montgomery. Later, they were reported as an Alabama town, and their history is merged with that of the Alabama.

PAWTUCKET

The Pawtucket, Pentucket, or Wamesit tribe was also known as the Rumney Marsh Indians. Although the Pawtucket has been generally classified as a village of the Pennacook (the two names being used as synonymous with one another). The two tribes are generally treated separately.

The Pawtucket lived on the lower Merrimac with the Charles River as their southern boundary, including the modern city of Reserve, Massachusetts, not far from Boston. Pawtucket was a Praying [Indian] Village comprised of Indians from the Pennacook and Massachusett tribes. They were nearly destroyed about 1614 by war with the Tarratines (Abnaki), a related group that lived along the eastern coast of Maine. As a consequence, they moved their settlement first to Middlesex Fells and then to Medford

PAYANKATANK

The Payankatank lived on the Piankatank River about Turk's Ferry and Grimesby, Virginia.

PEANQUICHA

The Peanquicha lived on the Wabash River in present Union County, Ohio. Chevalier reported that the Peanquicha were routed by a combined force of Sioux and the Ayavois (Iowa) warriors and that they subsequently joined the Quicapous (Kickapoo) and some Mascoutins, Renards (Fox) and Metesigamias (Michigamea) to take their vengeance on the Ayavois, Paiute, or Osage. The Sioux were too strong to challenge. Presumably the year was c. 1702. He gives no other information.

PECHANGA LUISEÑO

The Pechanga or Temecula (Temeekuya or Temeekuyam) was one of six recognized tribes of Luiseños. The tribe inhabited the Temecula Valley of California. The Temecula were evicted from the rich Temecula Valley with a degree granted by the District Court of San Francisco in 1873. President Chester A. Arthur signed an executive order June 27, 1882 that established the Pechanga Indian Reservation. Subsequent land patents were issued in 1893, 1931 and 1971, each one increasing the size of the reservation. In 1891, 1,233 acres of reservation land was allotted to individual households in 20 and 10 acre plots. For more see Luiseño.

PECOS PUEBLO

Along with the Jemez, the Pecos Pueblo, more commonly found under the name Pecos, constituted the Jemez Group. They were of the Tiwa Pueblo of the Tanoan linguistic stock, now part of the Kiowa-Tanoan stock. Situated on the upper branch of the Pecos River southeast of Santa Fé, it was one of the largest and most important of all the Pueblos. Four successive mission churches were built on the site beginning in 1621. Roberts refers to the first as a "veritable cathedral," constructed of 300,000 adobe blocks by what amounted to the slave labor of the Puebloans under the unrelenting manic pressure of Fray Andrés Juárez. It was decimated by the effects of the Pueblo Revolt and by disease, the remnants of the Pecos joined the Jemez in 1838.

PEDEE

Swanton writes, "there is every reason to suppose" that the Pedee (also Pee Dee) spoke a dialect of the Siouan language. They inhabited the middle course of the Great Pee Dee River in Chesterfield and Marlboro counties in South Carolina and fought on the side of the British in the Yamasee War of 1715-1716. They were driven from the lands by the Catawba in 1744. By the late 1700s, they effectively ceased to exist as a tribe with the remnants absorbed into the Catawba or assimilated into the white colonies. Their name last appeared in a state document in 1808. The estimated population at the time was thirty. Today, Pee Dee Indian Tribe of South Carolina is headquartered in Marlboro County. The Pee Dee Indian Tribe of South Carolina (January 27, 2006) is headquartered in McColl; and the Pee Dee Indian Nation of Upper South Carolina (February 2005) is located in Little Rock. The Marlboro, Chesterfield, Darlington County Pee Dee Indian Tribe is headquartered in McColl but is not recognized by the State or the Federal government. See the Pee Dee Indians of Beaver Creek, following. The alternate spellings of the two tribal names are the same.

PEE DEE INDIANS OF BEAVER CREEK

The Pee Dee Indians of Beaver Creek were of Muskogean linguistic group as differentiated from the Siouan Pedee. The Beaver Creek Indians originally lived around the Great Pee Dee River. In 1738, the Pee Dee moved from Pee Dee Indian Old Town in Marion County to a reservation on the lands of James Coachman in Indian Field Swamp on the Edisto River in present-day Dorchester County and later moved upriver. Members of the tribe received land grants in that area for service during the American Revolutionary War in Captain John Alston's "Raccoon Company," a company of 50 Pee Dee Indian riflemen. Swanton makes no mention of a group of Indians on Beaver Creek related or not related to the those he identifies as the Pedee, and the state of South Carolina in its only summaries makes no attempt to differentiate between the two tribes. The Beaver Creek Indians are now a recognized <u>group</u> by the State of South Carolina, Pee Dee Indian Tribe of Beaver Creek.

PEHNAHTERKUH

The Pehnahterkuh (Penateka, Penande, Penetethka, or Pehnahner, meaning wasps or honey eaters) was one of the five major sub-tribes or bands of the Comanche. It was the largest band and possibly the first to move southward in pursuit of the bison. It would be the Pehnahterkuh that would play the most significant role in Texas history and the history of the Comanche nation. For more see Comanche.

COUNCIL HOUSE TRAGEDY AND BATTLE OF PLUM CREEK

All the principal chiefs of the Pehnahterkuh band of the Comanche except one assembled for a council of truce in San Antonio. The Indian representatives consisted of twelve war chiefs and Mook-war-ruh, a civil chief. They were accompanied by a few warriors, women, and children. When arrangements had been made with the three chiefs who had arrived some days earlier, the commanding officer in charge of the southern region of the Texas Rangers agreed to talk peace only on the condition that all white captives be returned.

The Texans believed that the Comanche held some two hundred white captives at the time, possibly a score or more with the Pehnahterkuh. But when the chiefs assembled in what was hereafter called the

Council House on March 19, 1840, they brought with them only one Mexican boy and one young white girl who had been severely ravaged and beaten, almost to the point of mutilation, and declared their price for the other captives in their control. Instead, the chiefs were told that they would be held prisoner until all the captives were returned. A fight broke out inside the one story building that carried outside. Thirty-three chiefs, women and children were killed; and thirty-two women and children, many wounded, were thrown into jail. Seven whites were killed and ten badly wounded.

One female Indian hostage was subsequently released to return to her people with terms—hostages for hostages. The Comanche, led by Buffalo Hump, responded to the new terms and what they saw as the vilest treachery at the Council House by torturing, killing, and mutilating all the captives except for one woman who stole a horse and escaped with her baby, leaving her small son behind. The Pehnahterkuh received only vocal support from the other Comanche bands in their war with the Texans. What followed was a war of raids in force that included a Comanche attack on Victoria and Linnville, Texas, followed by the Battle of Plum Creek on August 12, 1840, in which the Comanche were routed leaving eighty dead warriors and a few women on the ground. A large number of women and children were taken captive, most of whom eventually escaped. The Comanche were also forced to abandon the horses they captured and stores of goods and supplies taken in their raid on the warehouses at Linnville. The assembled Texas Rangers and militia volunteers were led by General Felix Houston and Ranger Captain Ben McCullock, aided by a dozen or more Tonkawa warriors who also shared the spoils. In making their escape, the Comanches found time to inflict a gruesome death on their captives.

Two months later in October Colonel John J. Moore rode west and north with a column of state militia and Texas Rangers in a punitive expedition guided by Lipan scouts. They surprised a large camp of Pehnahterkuh. Every man, woman and child was killed—one hundred and thirty by one count. Few escaped. The mercy and humanity shown at Plum Creek was not to be repeated. Only one Texan lost his life. The Pehnahterkuh got the message. For a time, the raids on the Texas frontier stopped. There was even talk of peace, but ever so slowly the raids and killings began again and continued until the "final solution" to the Indian problem some thirty years in the future.

PENNACOOK

The Pennacook was a separate and distinct tribe of the Algonquian linguistic family although some writers treat them as a sub-tribe of the Abenaki. Conversely, the Pawtucket has been generally classified as a village of the Pennacook (the two names being used as synonymous with one another). Nevertheless, the two tribes are generally treated separately.

With a large number of subdivisions or villages, the Pennacook inhabited northeastern Massachusetts, southern and central New Hampshire, and the southernmost parts of Maine. Two of the bands or villages, Nashua and Wachusset, joined the hostile tribes in King Philip's War (1675-1676), but the others remained friendly to the colonists. Nevertheless, some two hundred people from the friendly bands were seized and imprisoned. As a result, the majority abandoned their homelands and moved to Canada where they joined the Abnaki and others of St. Francis. Others settled at Scaticook in Rensselaer County, New York. Also see Pawtucket.

PENOBSCOT

The Penobscot were of the Algonquian linguistic stock, commonly referred to as the Eastern Abenaki. They were hunters, trappers, fishermen and gatherers about Penobscot Bay and the drainage area of the Penobscot River in Maine. Although they are generally considered as a sub-tribe of the Abnaki, they are often treated in the literature as a separate and distinct tribe affiliated with the Abenaki. They were closely related to the Maliseet and Passamaquoddy.

PENSACOLA

It is believed that the Pensacola were of Muskhogean stock and were closely related to the Choctaw. They inhabited the area around Pensacola Bay where they were first encountered in 1528 although their name was not recorded until 1677. The Pensacola went to war with the Mobile in 1686. When the Spanish set up their base at Pensacola, the Indians moved inland. Around 1725 they were located near the village of the Biloxi of Pearl River. There is no mention of them after 1764. It is likely that remnants, if any, were incorporated into the Choctaw.

PEORIA

The Peoria were one of the major tribes of the Illinois Cluster of Tribes. It is believed that the they lived in northeastern Iowa and later moved to the area around present Peoria, Illinois. The Peorias were later removed to the region at of the confluence of the Kansas (Kaw) and Missouri rivers. Fr. Van Quickenborne first met the Peoria in Indian Territory around 1835-1836. See the Illinois.

PEPICOKIA

The Pepicokia or Pepikokia of the Algonquian linguistic stock was one of the six major divisions of the Miami thought to have merged with the Indians of the Piankashaw division.

PEQUAWKET

The Pequawket was a subdivision of the Abnaki. They lived on Lovell's Pond and the headwaters of the Saco River of Maine and New Hampshire. The Pequawket village was situated around Fryeburg.

PEQUOT

The Pequot were of Algonquian linguistic stock and inhabited southern portion of modern Connecticut and Rhode Island. It is believed that they originally came from the upper Hudson Valley, probably the shores of Lake Champlain. One theory is that they may have been the Adirondack.

By the 1630s, the Pequot was arguably the largest and most influential tribe in southern New England with economic power to rival the Massachusetts Bay Colony. With what is called the Pequot War of 1637, the Pequot tribe was destroyed. Remnants spent the next twenty years under the authority of Mohegan overlords until they were released and resettled near the Mystic River in 1655. For more see Pequot War and King Philip's War.

PEQUOT WAR OR MASSACRE AT MYSTIC RIVER

The Pequot War of 1637 was not a war at all, but in essence a single event of mass murder led by the Puritans of Massachusetts Bay Colony and their allies the Mohegan with halting support by the Narragansett on the Pequots of southeastern Connecticut. The Puritans launched an attack that destroyed the Pequot village fortress at Mystic River. Four hundred men, women, and children were shot and hacked to death. (Some accounts suggest a death toll as high as 600.) In addition to the killings, many women and children were sold into slavery in the West Indies. Those that were not killed or sold were joined with the Niantic and placed under the control of Uncas. The Mohegan were led by sachem Uncas; the Narragansett, by Miantonomi.

The pretext for the carnage was the murder of several English ship captains by Indians whose identity remains unknown and the murder by the Pequot of a trader who Pequot believed had treated them dishonestly.

As in the case of the massacre of the Massachusetts at Wessagussett by the Plymouth Colony in 1623, the Pequot War changed the dynamics of the region. The Mohegans rose in power and prestige, and the Massachusetts Bay Colony's preeminent position as the economic power in the region became firmly established. The Narragansett, on the other hand, saw their power and prestige begin to ebb as they questioned the what and why of what was happening to the Pequot.

William Bradford, the governor of Plymouth, wrote, "It was a fearful sight to see them thus frying in the fire and the streams of blood quenching the same." Yet, Bradford and the other holy Puritans saw the massacre at Mystic River as the work of the Lord, a righteous victory given to them by God.

PIANKATANK

Piankatank, Payankatank or Peanketan was Powhatan subdivision and a member of the Powhatan Confederacy. They lived along the Piankatank River in Middlesex County, Virginia.

PIANKASHAW

The Piankashaw belonged to the Algonquian linguistic family and were one of the six major divisions of the Miami but were later recognized as an independent tribe. They lived apart from the Miami originally in Illinois and Indiana. It is believed that another of the six bands, the Pepicokia, was eventually absorbed into the Piankashaw.

In the late 1700s and the early 1800s, the Piankashaw and the Wea lived and worked closely together, often sharing the same villages. Although the Piankashaw played only a minor role in Ohio Country, but signed numerous treaties by which forfeited all claims to the land in what is modern-day Ohio. See the Wyandot. Jesuit missionaries began visiting the tribe in 1836 in Indian Territory.

PIANRIA

The Pianria lived in present Union County, Ohio.

PICURIS PUEBLO

The Picuris (Picurís) "Those Who Paint" was of the Tiwa Pueblo of the Tanoan linguistic family that was part of the Kiowa-Tanoan stock. The tribal name is also spelled as Pikuri, and they were known as Pikuria by the Spanish. With the Taos Pueblo, they comprised one of the three divisions of the Tiwa. Picuris Pueblo was the smallest of the Pueblo groups. They occupied the upper waters of the Rio Grande Riveri about sixty miles north of Santa Fe in the Sangre de Cristo range.

PIEGAN BLACKFEET

Piegan (Pikuni) was one of the three subdivisions or tribes of the Siksika (Blackfeet) nation that spoke a dialect of the basic Algonquian (Algonquian) language. They remained the farthest south of the three divisions. The Piegan or Pikuni, a corruption of the word apiku'ni, meaning "badly tanned robe," formed the largest of the three tribes. To fur traders they were known as the Muddy River Indians. Some writers further classify the Piegan as North Piegan, the larger group, and South Piegan.

The Piegan hunting ground ranged along the foothills from Rocky Mountain House to Heart Butte, Montana, and eastward onto the plains. By the mid-19th century they had moved farther south to an area around the Teton River and Marias River in Montana and the Milk River in Alberta but traveled as far north as Fort Edmonton and east to the present Alberta-Saskatchewan border. With its large size, the tribe eventually split into two groups, a northern and a southern group, the latter being the largest, though it was difficult to really differentiate between the two.

The Southern Piegan was given a reservation in Montana where they adopted the official title of Blackfeet Indians of Montana. At one time, the reservation covered the entire northern one-fourth of the state from the North Dakota border west to the Rocky Mountains. Considerably more land than the Piegans could possibly make use of, it was subsequently reduced to the western portion bordered on the south by Birch Creek and on the east by Cut Bank Creek with the international border to the north and the foothills of Rockies to the west. (The land to the east was ceded to the government in 1888; the western strip along the mountains in 1896.) The remaining land of just under a million and a half acres was still more than sufficient for a population of just over two thousand. The Northern Piegan, along with the Blood and Northern Blackfeet, signed Treaty No. 7 with the Canadian government on September 22, 1877, and settled on a reserve near the Porcupine Hills on Oldman River, west of Fort Macleod, where their name was spelled and they called themselves the Pikuni.

MARIAS MASSACRE

On the 23rd of January 1870, a force of four calvary companies, fifty-five mounted infantrymen, and a company of infantry led by Colonel E. M. Baker from Fort Ellis attacked the camp of peaceful Piegans belonging to chief Heavy Runner's band. The official account put the estimated number of Indians killed at one hundred and seventy-three, fifty-three women and children killed accidentally. The report put the number of women and children taken captive at one hundred and forty. Although the captives were later released, their homes had been destroyed and they were left homeless to roam the northern plains. The Indian agent, an Army officer named W. A. Pease, reported that only fifteen of the dead were men ages twelve to thirty-seven, ninety were women and fifty were children. One soldier died, and one suffered a broken leg. The attack made on the specific orders of General Phil Sheridan following a series of depredations committed by both Indians and whites over the preceding months. The target of the Baker's expedition, however, was to be the Piegan band of Medicine Chief. Not surprisingly, Indian and army accounts of what happed differ. The massacre brought an outcry from the eastern press and in Congress. As a result, a bill to transfer responsibility for Indian affairs from the Interior Department to the Army was killed.

It was the first and only time that the Blackfeet faced the U.S. Army. There was an unexpected result. The Blackfeet, "Raiders of the Northern Plains," were wholly and completed cowed by events. From that time on, except for occasional, isolated incidents, the Blackfeet tribes maintained peaceful relations with their white neighbors.

PIKAKWANARAT UTE

The Pikakwanarata was a subdivision of the Ute. Members were placed on the Uinta Reservation in 1873. For more see Ute.

PIMA

The Pima or "Akimel Au-Authm" (River People) originally comprised two divisions, Pima Bajo and Pima Alto. The Pima Bajo of Sonora Mexico is now known as the Nevome. The Pima are of the Piman linguistic division of the Uto-Aztecan stock. They originally inhabited the Salt River Valley of Arizona, thus becoming known as the Salt River Indians. The Pima believe they are the descendants of the Hohokam, who inhabited the valley in ancient times.

The Pima later spread into the Gila River valley as well. Generally a friendly tribe to both whites and their Indian neighbors, they welcomed the migration of the Maricopa in the early 1800s and formed a strong, mutually-supportive relationship with them. A reservation near Phoenix was established for them and the Pima in 1859, now known as Salt River Pima-Maricopa Indian Community. It was enlarged by an Executive Order by President Hayes in 1879 and again in 1882 and 1883.

PIMOCAG-NA

Pimocag-na was a sub-tribe of the Tongva of California that inhabited the area about Rancho de los Ybarrras. For more see Tongva.

PINAL COYOTERO

The Pinal Apache was a tribe of Western Division of the Apache nation that was generally grouped with the multiple bands of the Cibicue, the San Carlos, and the Tonto collectively called the Western Apaches. The Pinal and White Mountain Apache comprised the geographic division of the Apache called the Coyoteros, thus the name Penal Coyotero Apache. The Pinal lived in the vicinity of the Pinal Mountains, north of the Gila River in Arizona and ranged across the country from the San Francisco Mountains to the Gila. They were defeated by General Crook in 1873 and were ultimately placed on the San Carlos and Fort Apache agencies at the White Mountain Reservation where they are officially listed as Coyoteros. For more see Apache.

PINALEŃO

The Pinaleño (not to be confused with the Pinal Coyotero) were closely related to the Chiricahua Apaches. They lived about the Pinaleño Mountains, south of the Gila river in southeastern Arizona. They regularly conducted raids far into Sonora and Chihuahua, Mexico. Know officially known as the Pinal, they are under the San Carlos and Fort Apache agencies at the White Mountain Reservation.

PINEUG-NA

Pineug-na was a sub-tribe of the Tongva of California that inhabited the area about Santa Catalina Island. For more see Tongva.

PINNESHOW

Drake reports that the Pinneshow was a band of the Eastern Division of the Sioux that lived on the St. Peter's River, fifteen miles from its mouth.

PIRO PUELBO GROUP

The Piro were of the Tanoan linguistic family of the Kiowa-Tanoan stock. They comprised one of the eight groups of four linguistic families of Pueblo. They comprised two divisions. For more See Pueblo Peoples.

Rio Grande Valley from about San Marcial (Soccoro) north to within fifty miles of Albuquerque

Tompiros and Salineros east of the Rio Grande in the vicinity of the salt lagoons

817 PISCATAQUA

The Piscataqua was a subdivision or village of the Pennacook of New Hampshire. They lived on the Piscataqua River near Dover, just northwest of Portsmouth.

Confusion has arisen because the name Piscataway, reported as an alternate name for the Piscataqua, is the name given to the Conoy proper, two distinct and independent Algonquian tribes. For more see Pennacook, Conoy Peoples, and Conoy.

PISHQUITPAH

The Pishquitpah (Pish-quit-pahs) inhabited parts of the present state of Oregon where they encountered Lewis & Clark and the Corps of Discovery. The heads were not as flattened as others down river.

PISQUOSE

The Pisquose or Pisko was a sub-tribe of the Yakima that is generally referred to separately. They lived about the mouth of Toppenish Creek in Washington State. In the 1855 Yakima treaty at Camp Stevens, the Pisquose ceded all their lands to the government and settled on the Yakima Reservation. For more see Yakima.

PISSASEC

Pissasec was a member of the Powhatan Confederacy and inhabited parts of King George and Westmoreland counties of Virginia.

PIT INDIANS

Their common name was the Pit Indians. Their true name was Achomawi. They lived principally on a large camp site at the mouth of the Pit River in Oregon. They acquired the name because the members dug pits to trap both their game and their enemies. (Both the Klamath Lake Indians and Modoc have been called Pit Indians because of the construction of their shelters.) The Pit Indians acted as guides to the U.S. troops in their battle with the Snake and Piute.

PITHLAKO

The Pithlako has been assigned by some writers as was a member of the Creek Confederacy. No additional information is known.

PLAINS OJIBWA

The Plains Ojibwa or Bung, a Canadian tribe, emerged from the Northern Chippewa after 1780 having migrated to Manitoba, Saskatchewan, and North Dakota. See Chippewa.

PLAYANO SALINAS

The Playano was a division of the Salinas of the Hokan linguistic family. They lived along the coast of California.

POCASSET

The Pocasset was a sub-tribe of Wampanoag generally treated as a separate tribe. They lived on Mount Hope Bay near present Tiverton, Rhode Island. For more see Wampanoag.

POCUMTUC

The Pocumtuc belonged to the Algonquian linguistic family and occupied the counties of Franklin, Hampshire, and Hampden, Massachusetts and adjacent lands in Connecticut. There were two major divisions, the Pocomtuc proper in the valleys of the Deerfield and Connecticut rivers and the Neotuc that lived about Northhampton.

PODUNK

The Podunk was a subdivision or sub-tribe of the Wappinger and lived in the eastern part of Hartford County, Connecticut, east of Connecticut River. For more see Wappinger.

POHOGUE SHOSHONI

The Pohogue Shoshoni (Sagebrush people), also called the Fort Hall Indians, lived about the confluence of the Portneuf and Snake rivers with the Bannock. The Pohogue were one of the four subgroups of the Northern Shoshoni.

The Executive Order of President Grant of June 14, 1867, established the Fort Hall Reservation on the upper Snake River in southeastern Idaho for use by the Boise and Bruneau bands of Shoshoni and the Bannock in the southern part and for the Coeur d'Alene and others in the northern part. The reservation included within its limits the original Fort Hall army post. For more see the Shoshoni.

POHOY

The Pohoy or Poy or Posoy were closely connected to the Timucuan division of the Muskhogean linguistic stock. They lived on the south shore of Tampa Bay, Florida. They first appeared in the chronicles of De Soto in 1539 under the names Qçita or Ucita, referring to a province. It is reported that De Soto set up his headquarters in the town of the head chief in June of that year. They first appear under their own name in 1612. In 1675 there was reference to a Pohoy River. A few members of the tribe were placed in a mission south of St. Augustine in 1726 but later returned to their home lands.

POJOAQUE PUEBLO

The Pojoaque (Po-Suwae-Geh) Pueblo is of the northern Tewa group of the Tanoan linguistic stock. They lived on an eastern tributary of the Rio Grande about eighteen miles northwest of Santa Fe. The pueblo lived and died in the early historic period following the Pueblo Revolt and the reconquest by the Spanish and was reborn in the early 1700s. The pueblo was officially recognized as a tribal reservation by the federal government in 1936.

POLAKAKAI

Polakakai or Polacco is included in the listing of tribal names by Kappler, but no additional information is available.

POMEIOOC

The Pomeiooc is believed to be of the Algonquian linguistic group and has been described as a sub-tribe of the Secotan, but available information on its status is limited. The location of the village is unknown, but it is thought that it may have been located near the water possibly on Farr Creek in Hyde County, near present-day Engelhard, North Carolina. For more see Secotan.

POMO PEOPLES

The Pomo were of the Hokan linguistic family. They lived along the Pacific coast of California between Cleone above Fort Bragg on the north and what was Duncan's Point in northern Sonoma County on the south and inland to Clear Lake. A relatively large tribe of 8,000 in 1770, it remained strong with 1,143 members recorded in the 1930 census. The Pomo were comprised of seven major dialectic subdivisions that were culturally similar but politically independent.

MAJOR SUBDIVISIONS

Northeastern Pomo or Salt Pomo, on the headwaters of Stony Creek
Eastern Pomo, on the northern and southern affluents of Clear Lake
Southeastern Pomo, about Lower Lake
Northern Pomo, about Navarro River and Ukiah on Russian River**
Central Pomo, about the Gualala on the coast and Cloverdale on the Russian River
Southern Pomo or Gallinomero, inland all along the area between Cleone and Duncan's Point*
Southwestern Pomo or Gualala, along the coast at the southern end of the Pomo range*

*Treated separately.
**Two sub-tribes, Mato and Mitcom, treated separately.

A federal reservation of Pomo Indians of 364 acres is located in Mendocino County, near the town of Point Arena (Manchester-Point Arena Rancheria). Another (Middletown Rancheria) is located in Lake County about 30 miles east of Santa Rosa. It is also home to some Whap and Lake Miwok people. The Pomo people also live at the Pionoleville Rancheria in Mendocino County near the city of Ukiah and a number of other reservations located throughout the state.

CLEAR LAKE MASSACRE

Two white men, Charles Stone and Andrew Kelsey, had been killed for enslaving and abusing members of the tribe and raping the Indian women. The Clear Lake or Bloody Island Massacre in May 1850 (1849, 1852) resulted in the killing of some one hundred and thirty five Pomo Indians of the four hundred or so encamped near present-day Clear Lake, California. Sixty persons were killed at the village and another 75 on the nearby Russian River. Many of those killed that were women and children. Other accounts of the number killed range from seventy-five to two hundred. One report put the count at four hundred. Captain Nathaniel Lyon was in command of the military detachment that was sent to quell a Pomo uprising, along with the ever-present white volunteers The residents of the village attacked by Lyon, Badonnapoti, were not involved in the Stone-Kelsey affair.

MENDOCINO WAR

In the late 1850s, the Indians of Mendocino County on the northern California coast began killing cattle, in most cases just to survive, in other instances for revenge against those who had usurped their lands. Any dead cow, brought raids an Indian rancheria and the indiscriminate killing of men, women and children that erupted into open warfare and what has been called the Mendocino War of 1859. Hundreds of Indians were killed.

Following an investigation, the State Legislature issued a report on the Mendocino War of 1860 that declared, "We are unwilling to dignify, by the term "war", a slaughter of beings, who at least possess the human form, and who make no resistance, and make no attacks, either on the person or on the residence of the citizen." The report assigned the blame for the Indian troubles to the white men and declared that in four months of 1859, more Indians of Mendocino County had been killed than in a century of Spanish and Mexican rule. A Minority Report stated that the Indians were a cowardly lot and suggested that they be turned over to settlers as servants.

Killings and massacres of California Native Americans became so commonplace that many not only went unrecorded they went unnoticed.

POMPTON

The Pompton was a sub-tribe of the Unami division of the Delaware. They lived on Pompton Creek in New Jersey. For more see Unami and Delaware.

PONCA

The Ponca or Ponka were of the Dhegiha Siouan language group that included the Omaha, Osage, Kansas, and Quapaw. They inhabited the right bank of Lower Missouri at the mouth of the Niobrara in northcentral Nebraska. The Ponca came west and south as part of the Omaha before separating from them for a time and later rejoining them on the Lower Missouri. They began to appear under their own name about 1780.

In the treaty of 1858, the Ponca were forced to give up their lands for life on a reservation. In 1877 the great majority were forcibly removed to lands purchased from the Cherokee in Indian Territory. As a result of an investigation, some were allowed to remain on the old lands. For more see Omaha.

PONKAPOAG

The Ponkapoag (also, Ponkipog or Punkapog) were converted Christian Indians of the Massachusetts that emerged in the mid-1600s as a town of Praying Indians (the second Christian town). The town or Plantation as it was called was in the present-day cities of Canton and Stoughton, Massachusetts. In 1657 the town of Dorchester allotted 6,000 acres for the establishment of a village of Praying Indian south of the Great Blue Hills. The last of the tribal lands was sold in 1827. For more see Praying Indians.

POOSPATUCK

The Poospatuck or Poosepatuck were a division of the Montauk and lived on the southern coast of Long Island from Patchogue to Westhampton. Descendants of the Montauk are recognized as a tribe by the State of New York under the name Shinnecock. For more see Montauk.

POQUONOCK

The Poquonock was a subdivision or sub-tribe of the Wappinger and lived in the towns of Windsor, Windsor Locks, and Bloomfield, Hartford County, Connecticut. For more see Wappinger.

PORT GAMBLE S'KLALLAM

The Port Gamble S'Klallam was a member of the Northwest Indian Fisheries Commission in the Tribal Natural Resource Directory. The Port Gamble S'Klallam Reservation consists of 1,340 acres of Federal Trust land. For more see Clallam (S'Klallam).

PORT ORFORD

The Port Orford was a band or sub-tribe of Indians that lived west of the Cascade Mountains in Oregon. Port Orford is located along the Southern Coast of Oregon and is said to be the westernmost incorporated city in the contiguous United States. In April 1792, Captain George Vancouver had established Cape Orford near the present town. When potential settlers arrived June 9, 1851, they met by a band Indians that Adams describes as California Siwash Indians. Oregon Parks and Recreation identifies the Indians as Rogue Indians (which could be the Takelma of the upper reaches of the Rogue or Tututni of the lower reaches). Another reference (Frommer) refers to the "Rogue River (or TuTuNi) Indians" of the area, but not specifically the battle. The various names are juxtaposed throughout the literature. Having reviewed the literature and using Swanton as a base, this author's best guess is that the Port Orford Indians referred to in the government "definitions" were Indians of the Kaltsergheatunne village of the Tututini.

One point on which there is no confusion, what ensued was a protracted battle or skirmish between the Indians and the sailors at a point of land subsequently named Battle Rock. After a two-week standoff, the nine-man party was able to make its escape without any loss of life or serious injury. They left thirteen Indians dead. The first white family arrived in late 1852, and by 1855 a minor gold rush had hit the area. The first U.S.

POSO CREEK YOKUTS

The Poso Creek Group was one of the seven subdivisions of the Yokut Indians of California with villages on Poso Creek and the adjoining Kern River, on the White River, and in Linn's Valley. For more see Yokuts.

POSTITO

The Postito were generally thought to be of the Coahuiltecan group that inhabited the region west of San Antonio. The Postito may have been the same as the Pastates listed in Father Ortiz's memorial to the Spanish king. The Four Corners Institute lists the Postito in the Coahuiltecan linguistic family, but no additional information is provided.

There is also the distinct possibility that the Postito may be the same group called the Pastia. They are reported to have lived in the area generally south of San Antonio, especially between the Medina and San Antonio rivers and the great southward bend of the Nueces River in La Salle and McMullen counties to include the lower Frio River. It is generally believed that the Postito/Paste/ were supplanted by the Apache when they moved into the coastal plain of southern Texas. Remnants most likely entered the Spanish mission of San José y San Miguel de Aguayo of San Antonio that was established in 1720.

POTANO

The Potano, as the Utina, were of the Timucua Division of the Muskhogean linguistic family. They inhabited lands within present Alachua County, Florida. For more see the Utina.

POTAPACO

The Potapaco was one of the nine divisions of the Conoy and lived in the southern and central parts of Charles County, Maryland. For more see Conoy Peoples.

POTAWATOMI

The Potawatomi* are of the Algonquin linguistic stock and believed to have originally been one people with the Ojibwa and Ottawa. Their name comes from the Ojibwe word "potawatomink" meaning "people of the fire." Their Huron name had a similar meaning.

In 1600 the Potawatomi lived in the northern third of lower Michigan. Threatened by the Ontario tribes that were allied with the French (Neutrals, Tionontati, Ottawa, and Huron), the Potawatomi began a migration to the west side of Lake Michigan into northern Wisconsin in 1641. By 1665 all of the Potawatomi were living in northern Wisconsin east of Green Bay where they remained until 1687 when they moved south along the west shore of Lake Michigan reaching the south end by 1695. At about the same time, one band settled near the Jesuit mission on the St. Joseph River in southwest Michigan. Other groups settled about Detroit. By 1716 most Potawatomi villages were stretched between the present-day cities of Milwaukee and Detroit. In the 1760s they expanded into northern Indiana and central Illinois.

The Potawatomi Nation was comprised of three major bands or sub-tribes that inhabited the forests and fertile lands of Indiana, Michigan, and Illinois around DeKalb before being pushed across the Midwest, first into Iowa then into Kansas. In the 1700s the three groups were: 1) the Detroit Potawatomi in southeast Michigan; 2) the Prairie Potawatomi (the Mascoutin or Council Bluffs Band) in northern Illinois; and 3) the St. Joseph Potawatomi (Mission Band) in southwest Michigan. By 1800 the names and locations of these three groups had changed. The Potawatomi of the Woods inhabited southern Michigan and northern Indiana; the Forest or Michigan Potawatomi inhabited northern Wisconsin and upper Michigan; and the Potawatomi of the Prairie, northern Illinois and southern Wisconsin.

In Northern Indiana the Potawatomi lived along the border with Michigan near present-day South Bend, Indiana, in the area of the St. Joseph River and old Yellow River. (The St. Joseph River flows from Michigan into Indiana and runs through South Bend and along the Michigan border. The Yellow River, which no longer exists, joined the Kankakee River near the present town of Brems, Indiana, SW of South Bend.) The great majority of the Indians living in the area were converted to the Catholic faith. At the time all of Indiana was within the Catholic Diocese of Vincennes, established in October 1834. The history of Vincennes, Indiana, located in southwest Indiana on the border with Illinois, dates to the establishment of a fort there by French traders in 1702. Fr. Benjamin Marie Petit, a Sulpician missionary who had arrived in America from France in July 1836, was posted to serve the Potawatomi in Northern Indiana by Bishop Brute in November 1837. Catholic Potawatomies in Michigan were administered to by the Sisters of Charity. (The Catholic see was changed to Indianapolis in April 1898.)

The Potawatomi took the side of the British in the War of 1812. Of their brief alliance, see the infamous affair of Fort Dearborn below.

In a treaty concluded at the missionary station on the St. Joseph River at Lake Michigan in 1827, the Potawatomi ceded significant portions of the land previously set aside for their use in Michigan in return for a lump-sum payment and annuities in specie and goods. Five years later in October 1832 on the Tippecanoe River, the Potawatomi were forced to cede all their lands in the State of Indiana for cash, goods, and annuities and the erasure of the debts that they had been induced to incur through actions of the government A number of reservations were made from the cession for individual bands. Five thousand dollars in horses were delivered to the Potawatomi as part of the settlement for their use in the migration west. In the ten-year period from 1827 to 1837, the Potawatomi signed nineteen treaties. Their homelands now belonged to the whites. The treaty of February 11, 1837, signed in Washington, set the removal of the Potawatomi of Indiana, within two years, to "a tract of country, on the Osage river south-west of the Missouri river."

The forced removal of the Potawatomi comes down in history as the "Trail of Death." Fr. Petit said his last Mass for his flock and accompanied them from north-central Indiana near Rochester, across the Wabash, to Danville, Illinois and across the Illinois River to Quincy on the banks of the Mississippi. Crossing the Mississippi, they made they way through Missouri to Independence and into Western Territory (Kansas) and the town of Osawatomie, where they arrived on November 4, 1838, three months after leaving Indiana. Of the 859 Potawatomi who began the journey, forty-one died along the way and were buried in unmarked graves. Over seventy-five trail markers now dot the landscape across Indiana, Illinois and Missouri.

Father Benjamin Petit, stricken with a strep infection, placed the Potawatomi in the spiritual hands of Jesuit Father Christian Hoecken at the Sugar Creek Mission in Kansas and set out for St. Louis, accompanied by Abram Burnett (Nan-wesh-mah), a full-blood Potawatomi. Fr. Petit suffered the winter in St. Louis and died February 10, 1839. He was buried in St. Louis, but in 1856 Father Edward Sorin, founder of Notre Dame University, took Father Petit's body back to Indiana for its final resting place under the Log Chapel at St. Mary's Lake on the grounds of the new Notre Dame University. (Notre Dame was founded by Father Sorin of the Congregation of Holy Cross, C.S.C. in 1842 and received its charter in 1844.) Burnett carried Petit's chalice and personal effects to Bishop Brute at Vincennes. Father Petit's baptismal records and journals are now in the library of the University of Notre Dame.

The Potawatomi west of Lake Michigan surrendered their land around the lake in 1833 for a large tract of land in southwestern Iowa that they inhabited with a few Chippewa and Ottawa. A young Jesuit, Father Peter John De Smet, established Saint Joseph's Mission for the Potawatomi near present-day Council Bluffs, Iowa, in May 1838 and served for eighteen months. At the time the mission administered to 2,000 souls. When De Smet visited the mission for the first time after his departure in the fall of 1840, the mission served just fifty families. Not long thereafter the Jesuits moved with the remaining Potawatomi to Sugar Creek in Kansas Territory. (The old mission grounds became the staging site for the Mormons on their route west from Nauvoo.)

The land in Iowa was receded to the government in exchange for lands in Kansas east of the Potawatomi of the Woods. The first of the Potawatomi removed to Kansas began their migration in the mid-late 1830s, settling first in Miami County in 1837 and then in Linn County to the south in March 1839.

Several Potawatomi villages were in the vicinity of what is now the town of Osawatomie in Miami County, Kansas, about 45 miles southwest of Kansas City on the Missouri Pacific railway line. The town itself, was settled about 1854 by colonists sent by the New England Emigrant Aid Company and was platted in 1855. Its name was coined from parts of the names of the Potawatomies and the Osage who also had villages in the area.

Jesuit missionary Fr. Christian Hoecken, who was serving the Kickapoo near Fort Leavenworth, first visited the Potawatomi at their request in Kansas in January 1838. Jesuit missionaries continued to serve the Potawatomi in Kansas until the majority of the Indians removed to the Indian Territory (Oklahoma) in eighteen sixties. The Catholic Mission of St. Mary (also referred to the Sugar Creek Mission) was founded in 1839 by Fr. Peter Verhaegen at Sugar Creek, Kansas, in Linn County just west of Pleasanton.

Two schools were opened. The school for boys first opened in 1840, taught by the Jesuits; but it remained open only for a short while. A school for girls was constructed in July 1841 and trusted to the hands of the Catholic Sisters of the Society of the Sacred Heart from St. Charles, Missouri. A new school for boys was constructed in 1842.

Among the Sisters was Rose Philippine Duchesne who was canonized a saint in 1988 by Pope John Paul II. Sr. Duchesne was seventy-one year old when she moved to Kansas in June 1841. To the Indians, she was Quah-Kah-Ka-Num-Ad (the woman who prays always). Frail health forced back to St. Charles a year later where she spent the last decade of her life. The schools were closed in 1848. A Shrine to Sister Rose, who died November 18, 1852, stands at the Sugar Creek site. The State of Missouri named her first among the women on its Pioneer Roll of Fame.

In 1848 the Potawatomi were resettled (under the treaty of June 17, 1846) on lands west of present capital of Topeka, part of which is now in Wabaunsee County—named for the Potawatomi leader Wabansi. The New St. Mary's Mission was established at what is now St. Mary's, Kansas, near Topeka, with staff from the two religious orders. It was learned that an agreement had been made between the St. Louis University and the government to erect a school at the St. Mary's Mission, but the work of education had already begun by the Sisters. Five new boarding students were received at the Mission in the winter of 1848. It was the beginning St. Mary's College, the oldest educational institution in the state of Kansas. In

1849 a roof was put in place on a new church, the Immaculate Conception. The Baptists also established a mission and school to serve the Potawatomi.

In 1855 the Potawatomi population in Kansas was officially estimated at 3,700 of a total of some 4,000. Following Kansas statehood (January 29, 1861), the reservation was divided between the Citizen Band (formerly the Mission Band of Michigan and Indiana and including the Potawatomi of the Woods) that made up over half of the population of the Potawatomi Nation and the more traditional Prairie Band (formerly the Council Bluffs Band of Illinois and Wisconsin).

The Citizen Band chose U.S. citizenship and allotment. Excess land was sold to the Atchison, Topeka & Santa Fe Railroad. (Originally the land was to be sold to the Leavenworth, Pawnee & Western Railroad.) Selling off the remainder of their Kansas land, the Citizen Band removed to Indian Territory in 1870-1871 based at Shawnee, Oklahoma. Most of their land was lost to allotment in 1899. With the removal of the Citizen Band to Oklahoma, St. Mary's Mission no longer served significant numbers of Potawatomi by the 1870s and was closed.

The Prairie Band remained on a diminished Potawatomi Reservation in Kansas. Allotment in 1895 almost destroyed what was left of the band as a recognized entity. In 1915 members of the band of the Catholic faith dug the foundation for their own church at Mayetta, about 25 miles north of the capital of Topeka on the reservation lands. The white wooden church built on the hill was named Our Lady of the Snows.

Small groups of Potawatomi are now living in Wisconsin, Michigan, and Ontario, Canada. One of the founders of Davenport, Iowa, and railroad booster, Antoine Le Claire, was the son of a Frenchman and a Potawatomi maiden. It was from Davenport that the Mississippi and Missouri Railroad laid track that stretched west to Council Bluffs and on to the Sacramento Valley.

FORT DEARBORN MASSACRE**

Following the declaration war against the British in 1812, American General William Hull was ordered to launch an attack on Canada opposite the site of Fort Detroit. Chief Tecumseh of the Shawnee, leading a British coalition force of Indians from the Ohio country, attacked Hull's advance party. The attack combined with the surrender a few days earlier of the American post at Makinaw on the strait that linked Lake Michigan and Lake Huron so frightened Hull that he surrendered Detroit to the British. Hull also ordered the evacuation of Fort Dearborn at the mouth of the Chicago River on the western shore of Lake Michigan. They were to be brought to safety by an escort of thirty Miami scouts led by Billy Wells, a white man raised by the Miami. The entire settlement followed the garrison when they left the post on August 15. Less than two miles out from the fort, the party of sixty-six soldiers and militia, nine women and eighteen children under the command of Captain Nathan Heald was attacked by a Potawatomi force of some five hundred led by Chief Blackbird. Over half of the soldiers were killed; twelve of the children, who were beheaded; and two women, plus Billy Wells. At least two soldiers were wounded, including Heald. The fort was burned. British success at Detroit brought many holdouts into Tecumseh's growing confederacy. (The fort was rebuilt in 1816 and served until 1837 when it was abandoned. The fort itself stood until 1856.)

*Variations in the spelling of Potawatomi include: Potawatami, Potawatamie, Putawatimi, Pattawatima, Patawattimie, Pottawatami, Pottawatimie, Potowatomi, Potawattimie, Pottawattimie, Pattawatima, Putawatame, Pottowotomee, Pottawatamy, Poutawatamie, Pottowautomie

**Also see the Massacre at Fort William Henry under the Abenaki.

MISSOURI FRENCH-CANADIAN COLONY

There was a French-Canadian colony located at the site of an trading post where the Nishnabotna and Missouri rivers meet in Atchison County, Missouri, during the 1840s and 1850s. The French-Canadians lived there with their Indian wives, believed to be of the Potawatomi tribe, and their children. They were visited by Jesuit missionary Fr. Christian Hoecken. Records show a number of Baptisms in September and October 1843 in the towns of Nissinabotne, Irish Grove in Atchison County, and Savannah in Andrew County.

POTAWATOMI OF THE WOODS

Five bands of Potawatomi, called Potawatomi of the Woods, lived in the state of Indiana until 1840 when they removed to a tract of land on the Osage River in the state of Kansas. (The treaty was signed in 1837.) They ceded the land back to the government for a reserve between the Shawnee and Delaware in present Shawnee County, Kansas. The Prairie Potawatomi removed to lands to the east of the Potawatomi of the Woods in 1847-1848. (A part moved back to Wisconsin following the Civil War.) The Michigan Potawatomi removed to the same area in Kansas in 1850. By 1871 the major part of the Potawatomi of the Woods had removed to Oklahoma. For more see Potawatomi.

POTOASH

The Potoash of the northwest territory was enumerated by Lewis & Clark and referred to by Drake in connection with the Palish, but no additional information has become available.

POTOMAC

The Potomac or Potomack was a member tribe of the Powhatan Confederacy. They lived at the mouth of Potomac Creek on what is the present Marlborough Point where they fished both Accokeek Creek and the Potomac River. In 1662, leaders of colonial Virginia seized and imprisoned the chief of the Potomac. For more see Powhatan

POWHATAN

Powhatan proper was a member tribe of the Powhatan Confederacy and inhabited parts of Henrico County, Virginia. For more see Powhatan Confederacy.

POWHATAN CONFEDERACY

Wahunsonacock (1547-1618), whom the English gave the name Powhatan was the chief of the Pamunkey tribe. He built an empire of some thirty tribes in numerous villages that has come down in history as the Powhatan Confederacy. Estimates of the number of Indians with the confederacy range from 8,000 to 25,000. Some reports mistakenly identify it as the Powhatan Nation rather than a confederacy of distinct, independent tribes.

The confederated tribes all belonged to the Algonquian linguistic family. They inhabited present Maryland and Virginia in the region of the Chesapeake Bay from north of the Mattaponi River, a tributary of the York River, to the lands south of the James River. The principal village, Werowocomoco, was located on the Pamunkey River, land which later became part of Gloucester and Mathews Counties, Virginia.

TRIBES OF THE POWHATAN CONFEDERACY
Accohanoc
Accomac
Arrohattoc
Chesapeake

Chickahominy
Chiskiac
Cuttatawomen
Kecoughtan
Mattaponi
Moraughtacund
Mummapacune
Nansemond
Nantaughtacund
Onawmanient
Pamunkey
Paspehean
Pataunck
Piankatank
Pissasec
Potomac
Powhatan proper
Rappahannock*
Secacawoni
Tauxenent
Warrasqueoc
Weanoc
Weapemeoc
Werowocomoco
Wicocomoco
Youghtanund

*Some writers list the Rappahannock as independent of the Confederacy.

Powhatan was the father of Matoaka, who has come down through history as Pocahontas. He was early a friend of the English settlers in Jamestown (1607) but soon began to feel threatened by them. Peace between the Native Americans and the Europeans came with the marriage of Pocahontas to settler John Rolfe in 1614. With the death of Pocahontas in England in 1617 at the age of 22 and the death of Powhatan the following year, violence erupted again.

The new leader from 1618 to 1644, was Opechancanough, Powhatan's brother. Fearing the ever-increasing number of English on their lands and their unbridled arrogance, he planned a surprise attack in 1622 to wipe out all the settlers. The great majority were saved by an early warning given by one of Opechancanough's men who had been converted to Christianity. Still the Jamestown Massacre of 1622 resulted in the deaths of 347 men women and children. As the debate raged whether the Indians should be exterminated, the settlers retaliated with an all out war that lasted for almost a decade, taking retribution many times over, killing men and women indiscriminately and capturing the children to be worked as slaves. In one incident some two hundred Pamunkey were poisoned to death when they drank toasts at a peace parley. Another fifty were killed using traditional methods. The colonists also systematically destroyed and burned crops and villages and took over the land.

In 1644, Opechancanough called for one final attempt to force the English off the land. In a surprise attack, five hundred colonists were killed in what is called the Massacre of 1644. Opechancanough himself was captured and killed. The colonists were led personally by William Berkely, governor of Virginia. The resultant campaign reduced the Pamunkey and others to a tributary status, and English expansion mushroomed. A treaty made in 1646 severely restricted movement of the various tribes and confined them to small reservations. In addition Necotowance, who now served as head of the confederacy, was forced to pay a personal tribute to the governor. By the mid-1660s, the confederacy had all but dissolved, and in a treaty of 1677, "every Indian King and Queen" was forced to pay a tribute. An act of the Virginia assembly in 1669 had identified a total of 725 warriors in nineteen tribes

Five new counties were formed out of the land formerly inhabited by the Powhatan confederated tribes. By 1722, many of the tribes comprising the original confederacy were reported extinct.

PRAIRIE POTAWATOMI

Following a series of treaties, the last of which was the Treaty of Chicago of 1833, the Potawatomi that lived west of Lake Michigan that became known as the Prairie Potawatomi ceded their lands for a large tract of land in southwestern Iowa. A few Chippewa and Ottawa joined them. In a treaty of 1846 the land was ceded back to the government in exchange for a reserve in Shawnee County, Kansas, to the east of the Potawatomi of the Woods to which they resettled in 1847-1848. In 1850 both were joined by the Michigan Potawatomi. Part of the Prairie division moved back to Wisconsin following the Civil War. The remainder shared in the Kansas land in severalty. For more see Potawatomi and Potawatomi of the Woods.

PRAYING INDIANS

Rev. John Eliot labored among the Indians of the Massachusett tribe, beginning with the Indians of the villages at Nonantum about Newton and Neponset, on the Neponset River about Stoughton. He gathered a large part of his converted, Christian Indians into villages of "Praying Indians." It was through this work that he produced the "Eliot Bible" and other works that preserved a knowledge of the Massachusett language. The Indians of the Massachusetts were joined by others, particularly those from the Wampanoag. The principal Praying Villages are listed below. The first was Natick; the second, Punkapog. More can be found under those titles.

PRAYING VILLAGES
Cowate, at the Falls of Charles River
Natick, near the present Natick
Pequimmit, near Stoughton
Punkapog, near Stoughton
Titicut, possibly Wampanoag, Middleborough or Middleboro in Plymouth County

PROBABLE PRAYING VILLAGES
Magaehnak, six miles from Sudbury
Nemasket, Wampanoag, about Middleborough

PSHWANWAPAM

The Pshwanwapam (or Psch-wan-wap-pam), also called the Upper Yakima or Kittitas, belonged to the Shahaptian division of the Shapwailutan linguistic family. Closely related to he Yakima, they lived along the Yakima River, including the Kittitas Valley, in Washington State. They have also been described as a part of the greater Yakima Nation. For more see Yakima.

PUBUG-NA

Pubug-na was a sub-tribe of the Tongva of California that inhabited the area about Alamitos. For more see Tongva.

PUEBLO PEOPLES

During the historic period, pueblo (Spanish for "town") was the common name given to independent communities of village-dwelling Indians located on the mesas of New Mexico and eastern Arizona, including the Hopi of northeastern Arizona, the Zuni of western New Mexico, and the Rio Grande Pueblos. The people were descendants from the Anasazi who entered the Pueblo period about the year 750. Anasazi derives from a Navaho Indian word meaning "the ancient ones." The Pueblo period passed through several phases before reaching what is regarded as the historic period about 1600.

The Pueblo of the historic period were comprised of native peoples of different linguistic families. In addition to a common linguistic stock, these peoples can be divided between the eastern tribes of the aired Rio Grande Valley and the western tribes of the desert of western New Mexico and eastern Arizona. The latter group include the Zuni and Hopi. The relative isolation of the Hopi and Zuni enabled them to remain free of influence and pressures of the Anglo-Europeans and to preserve more of their ancestral heritages. Bernadett Charley Gallegos identified five different linguistic groups within three linguistic families or stocks, excluding the Hopi of Arizona.

KERESAN Linguistic Stock
    Keres Group

KIOWA-TANOAN Linguistic Stock
    Tewa Group
    Tiwa Group
    Towa Group

ZUNIAN Linguistic Stock
    Zuni Group

Swanton places the Pueblo peoples within eight groups of four linguistic families, including the Hopi. Excluding the Hopi and Zuni groups, Swanton lists over 150 named Pueblo towns or villages within the various groups. For many, the name is all that is known. David Roberts puts the count of separate pueblos at the time of Coronado in 1540 at 110, including the Hopi and Zuni but excluding the associated outlying villages, with a population of some 80,000. By August 1580 at the time of the Pueblo revolt, the number of pueblos was down to a little over forty. The population had been hafted and hafted again to less than 20,000.

KIOWA-TANOAN Linguistic Stock
    Tewa Group
        Northern Division: Nambe, Tesuque, San Ildefonso, San Juan, Santa Clara, Pojoaque, Hano
        Southern Division or Tano: include San Marcos, San Lázaro, San Cristóbal, Galisteo
    Tiwa Group: Isleta, Isleta del Sur (Mexicanized), Sandia, Taos, Picuris
    Jemez Group: Jemez, Pecos
    Piro Group: Senecu, Senecu del Sur (Mexicanized)

KERESAN Linguistic Stock
    Eastern Group: San Felipe, Santa Ana, Sia, Cochiti, Santo Domingo
    Western Group: Acoma, Laguna

ZUNIAN Linguistic Stock
    Zuni Group: Zuni

SHOSHONEAN Linguistic Stock of the Uto-Aztecan Linguistic Family
    Hopi Group: Walpi, Sichomovi, Mishongnovi, Shipaulovi, Shongopovi, Oraibi

Modern-day Pueblo Indians of the Rio Grande area speak Tanoan languages (including Tewa and Tiwa); and those of the Acoma and Laguna pueblos, in the high plateaus of west central New Mexico, speak Keresan. The Zuni continue their own language, unrelated to any of the others, as do the Hopi, whose language is related to Shoshonean and Ute. Today, in all , there are twenty active, breathing pueblos, nineteen in New Mexico and one in Arizona, the Hopi, with their several villages on three mesas in the northeastern corner of the state.

NEW MEXICO PUEBLOS OF TODAY

Acoma or Anacona*
Cochiti
Isleta*
Jemez
Laguna*
Nambe
Picuris
Pojoaque
Sandia*
San Felipe
San Ildefonso
San Juan
Santa Ana
Santa Clara
Santo Domingo
Taos
Tesuque
Zia
Zuñi*
19
Range west across New Mexico from the Rio Grande.

The Tewa Pueblo were associated with the Tanoan linguistic family that was part of the Kiowa-Tanoan stock. The Tewa comprised two main branches or divisions living in some one hundred villages and towns. The pueblos of the Northern Tewa stretched from near Santa Fe north to the mouth of the Rio Chama in northcentral New Mexico, including Hano. The Southern Tewa (or Tano) inhabited the lands from Santa Fe south to near the Golden River. With the Pueblo Revolt and the subsequent return of the Spanish twelve years later, most of the Southern Tewa had joined the Hopi by 1694. Remnants were decimated by a smallpox epidemic early in the nineteenth century. The Northern group also suffered but not as severely and remained a strong presence well into the twentieth century. The San Juan Pueblo, Santa Clara, and the San Ildefonso near present Santa Fe, among others, were of the Northern division.

The Tiwa Pueblo were also associated with the Tanoan linguistic family that was part of the Kiowa-Tanoan stock. The Tiwa formed three geographic divisions. One division occupied Taos and Picuris on the upper waters of the Rio Grande River; the second inhabited Sandia and Isleta, north and south of Albuquerque; and the third living in pueblos of Isleta de Sur (El Paso, Texas) and Senecu del Sur (Chihuahua, México). Swanton and others place Senecu del Sur in the Piro Group.

The Jemez Group (Towa under Gallegos classification) included the Jemez proper and the Pecos, now extinct.

Swanton identifies the Piro Pueblo of the Kiowa-Tanoan stock. as comprised of the Senecú and the Mexicanized Senecú del Sur.   Gallegos does not list the Piro nor the Senecú. Her listing includes the languages spoken by the nineteen villages of twenty-first century New Mexico. Others identify two divisions within the Piro. One inhabited the Rio Grande Valley from present San Marcial in Socorro County north to about fifty miles from Albuquerque adjoining the land of the Tiwa Pueblo. The second division (Tompiros and Salineros) occupied an area east of the Rio Grande River in the vicinity of the salt lagoons (salinas).

The Keresan or Keres linguistic stock was divided into two dialectic groups, the Eastern (Queres) and the Western (Sitsime or Kawaiko). They lived along the Rio Grande River in north central New Mexico, between the Rio de los Friholes and the Rio Jemez and along the Rio Jemez from the Pueblo of Sia (Zia) to its mouth. They include the Acoma (Western) and the Cochiti and Santa Ana (Eastern), among others.

The word "pueblo" is Spanish for town. Their towns were built with adjoining adobe walls in tiers like apartment buildings. Many geographical locations in the present state of New Mexico and elsewhere continue to be defined in terms of the pueblos, for example, Pueblo San Cristobal or Acoma Pueblo. The Puebloans were farmers unlike their neighbors who lived primarily by hunting, but the contrasting cultures created mutually-beneficial trade relationships. Their staple crops were corn, beans, and squash. The Puebloans were also renowned for their basket weaving and pottery and, later, their silverwork.

SPANISH NEW MEXICO

Coronado was the first of the Spanish explorers to enter the country above the Rio Grande and crisscrossed the landscape from 1540 to 1542. Other expeditions followed. Then in 1598 came Don Juan de Oñate who conquered the land and its peoples and declared them for Spain and for his Christian God. The future governor and captain-general of the Province of New Mexico brought with him priests and settlers along with soldiers. Exploratory forays were made to the coast and to Quivera (Kansas), but these men were not explorers. They established permanent settlements along the Rio Grande, force-fed their religion on the natives, and nearly destroyed an entire race.

Puebloan life as they new it was forever changed. Economically, the Spanish kept the Puebloans to their farms but destroyed their mutually-beneficial trade relations with their neighbors. Spiritually, the Spanish destroyed or forced underground the Puebloan's kachina religion. Physically, the Indians were pressed into service building a New Mexico in the Spanish mode, particularly the Christian missions and churches. Their treatment more often inhumane than not. Depredations were heaped upon them, all contrary to the express orders of the Spanish King and the authorities in New Spain (Mexico). Civil and religious authorities were equally responsible. Then in 1640 and again in 1671, the pueblos were hit with devastating smallpox epidemics, and in 1667 began five successive years of severe draught. By the mid-1670s, many of the pueblos and been abandoned, their remnants spread across the land.

At the time of Coronado's *entrada*, the population of the Pueblo Peoples numbered some 80,000. By 1680, that number had fallen to 17,000. The year 1680 brought the Pueblo Revolt that drove the Spanish from their lands. The Spanish reconquest of New Mexico came twelve years later in 1692 at the hand of Diego José de Vragas. For more see the Pueblo Revolt and the notes on the individual pueblos and Pueblo groups and subgroups. Also see the Anasazi.

PUEBLO REVOLT

Coronado was the first to explore the lands north of Spanish Mexico in 1540. In 1598 the Spanish, under Don Juan de Oñate, conquered all of what they called Nuevo México (New Mexico.) For the next eighty -two years, the Puebloan people suffered the effects of disease, starvation, and servitude. The population was decimated, both in body and spirit.

On August 10, 1680, the men of the Pueblos of northern New Mexico, for the first time united and rose in revolt against their Spanish suppressors. The revolt erupted like a volcano of molten ash spreading everywhere. In its wake, twenty-one Franciscans, who had gained the particular enmity of the Puebloans, died that first day. Soon, one-third of the European population of the region of the upper Rio Grande lay dead.

The Spanish capital of Santa Fe, founded in 1610 by Governor Pedro de Peralta, lay under siege beginning August 15, surrounded by upwards of 2,500 Indians. The siege was mounted by the Pecos and Tano warriors, the latter included the pueblos on the northern edge of the Galisteo Basin south of Santa Fe: San Marcos, San Lázaro, San Cristóbal, and the Galisteo Pueblo. Within days they were joined by the warriors of the northern pueblos.

The revolt had been organized by a Puebloan shaman named Popé from the San Juan Pueblo. Back in 1775, forty-seen "sorcerers," as the Spanish called them, were rounded up as trouble-makers. Three were hanged, one committed suicide, and 44 were flogged and imprisoned at Santa Fe. Popé was one of them. The Tewa massed together and marched on Santa Fe and demanded their release. Shaken the governor complied. On his release, Popé began plotting the revolt that would come five years later.

In a desperate move, the Spanish Governor, Don Antonio de Otermín led 100 soldiers who charged out of the gates on the morning of August 20 and attacked the surprised Indians. The governor recorded 300 killed plus prisoners. While the Indians licked their wounds and regrouped, Otermín took one thousand survivors, along with loyalists Indians and Indian prisoners, and fled south to El Paso. He had hoped to gather to him the troops in the south under the command of Lieutenant Governor Alonzo Garciá and march back north and retake the city. But, believing Otermín dead, Garciá had already departed with 1,500 refugees. Within days, the Puebloans had succeeded in driving the Spanish population of just under three thousand from their lands.

Otermín organized an abortive attempt at reconquest in November 1681. He reached no farther than Isleta Pueblo. He abandoned his efforts and returned to El Paso with 385 Isleta who had remained loyal. A second attempt at reconquest was mounted in 1689 by Domingo Jironza Petríz de Cruzate with eighty soldiers. Little is known of his efforts except that reaching the Zia Pueblo he fought a day-long battle that left fifty of his men wounded and 600 Zia men, women and children dead.

A Spanish army under the command of Diego de Vargas retook the Pueblos in a bloodless reconquest in the fall of 1692. He had arrived in Santa Fe September 13. With firm but gentle negotiations over the next several days and throughout the remainder of the year, all the Puebloans except one Hopi village, Oraibi, agreed to accept their Spanish overlords and Christianity. Vargas returned to El Paso to assemble settlers for a new Spanish colony to the north. In October 1693, he left El Paso at the head of a caravan of settlers, soldiers, and priests with wagons of supplies and driving a large of cattle and other livestock.

The new colonists made camp north of Santa Fe in December, but in his absence the atmosphere and mood of the people had changed. Believing false reports that he was returning to murder all of them. Many had gathered behind the walls at Santa Fe and prepared for war. All negotiations to dissuade them failed, and Indians launched their arrows and missiles from the parapets on December 29, 1693. The disciplined, well-armed soldiers succeeded in breaching the walls and capturing the town. Vargas had seventy warriors executed by firing squad. The women and children he sentenced to ten years of servitude.

Benevolence was overcome by anger, and the days of the first conquest were repeated.

Those that escaped took refuge on San Ildefonso Mesa (Black Mesa) where they were joined by Indians from other pueblos in the area. Puebloans also fled to two other refuge pueblos in the ensuing months, Old Koytiti and the Jemez Pueblo on the Peñol, as the Spanish called it. By September 1694 all three were reduced with the aid of Puebloan auxiliaries. Acoma also became a refuge, as did the Zuñi and Hopi pueblos farther west. At Acoma, Vargas allowed father time to bring the Indians to toe . Resistance had been costly to the Puebloans in terms of lives lost and prisoners taken. The year 1695 was relatively quiet. In April, Vargas founded a second Spanish town, Santa Cruz, north of Santa Fe. By that time there were 276 Spanish families in New Mexico, significantly less than the 500 he had hoped for.

Late spring of 1696 brought on second revolt, but one on a much smaller in scale. Five priests and twenty-one settlers were killed. Once more the rebels were tracked and captured or killed. By December 1696, what began as a bloodless reconquest was complete. During the years of reconquest, a number of Puebloans escaped to their fates. In July 1697, Vargas' successor as governor assumed responsibility for Spanish New Mexico. (Vargas returned in 1703 for a second term but died soon thereafter.)

The new governor faced a dispirited group of settlers, resentful Puebloans, shortages of food, and an even stronger, now mounted bands of eastern Apaches. Before long the mantel of power in the area would be grasped and held by the Comanches.

Of Note

The Spanish also introduced the mustang to the American Indians; and a new culture was born, the horse. Although the Pueblo were the first to experience the horse, they themselves made only limited use of the new resource. To others, the horse offered limitless possibilities, thus making the Puebloans a target for raids by neighboring Apaches, Navajos, and Comanches. When the Spanish were driven from the land, they left herds of livestock, including the horse, that the Pueblo allowed to run wild, thus the beginnings of the wide mustangs herds of the west. This new culture quickly spread throughout the Southwest and into the Plains and Prairies to the north and east.

Contemporary American Indian Art is being actively solicited by museums throughout the country. One standout artist is Roxanne Swentzell, born in Taos in 1962, who has popularized the Pueblo Clown or Kosha (or more properly, a *koshare*—a kachina clown).

PURISIMEÑO CHUMASH

The Purisimeño were one of the eight dialectic and geographical divisions of the Chumash of the Southern California coast. The Purisimeño Chumash lived on the coast between the Barbareño and Obispeño Chumash. For more see the Chumash.

PUYALLUP

The Puyallup lived near the mouth of the Puyallup River and the adjoining coast, including the Carr Inlet and the southern part of Vashon Island, in Washington State. They belonged to the coastal division of the Salisham linguistic family.

857 QUILEUTE

The Quileute or Qil-leh-ute (also spelled Qui-Leh-Ute), with the Hoh and Chimakum, constituted the Chimakuan linguistic family. They lived on the Quilayute River on the west coast of Washington Territory near Puget Sound. They were subsequently removed to the Quileute and Makah reservations.

QUABAOG

The Quabaog was a subdivision or village of the Nipmuc of the Algonquian linguistic family. They lived about the present city of Brookfield, Massachusetts.

QUABAUG

The Quabaug was a sub-tribe of the Nipmuc that was based in present Brookfield, Massachusetts. In 1657, at the age of eighty, Pokanoket sachem Massasoit took up residence with them until his death a few years later. In the records of the Massachusetts Bay Colony, Massasoit appears as the official leader of the Quabaug, reportedly a position originally established twenty years earlier which helps explain the close relationship that existed between the Quabaug and Pokanoket. For more see Nipmuc and Pokanoket.

QUAHATTIKA

The Quahattika was of the Piman division of the Tuo-Aztecan stock and closely related to the Pima, from which they may have been a branch. The lived in the desert of southern Arizona, fifty miles south of the Gila River.

QUANAKINA

The Quanakina was listed in Jefferson's *Notes on the State of Virginia*, taking his information from Bouquet (1764). A population of 200 warriors was reported; but no location was given. For more see "Aborigines," Appendix D.

QUANATAGUO

The Quanataguo were most likely part of the Coahuiltecan group of Texas. A single entry appears in the burial 1728 records of San Antonio de Valero Mission at San Antonio. There is a possibility that the Quantaguo may be the Anathagua listed in Father Ortiz's memorial to the Spanish king.

QUAPAW

The Quapaw (downstream people) were of the Dhegiha Siouan language group. The area about the mouth of the Arkansas River where it empties into the Mississippi is considered their traditional home, having migrated south from about the Ohio River. They were also known by a variety of names: Ima, the Bow Indians, Beaux Hommes, and Papikaha.

As for the Arkansas River, it was Father Jacques Marquette who first called the river Akansa in his journal of 1673. From its origin in the Rockies the Arkansas runs 1,450 miles through Colorado, Kansas, Oklahoma, and Arkansas to its juncture with the Mississippi at Napoleon. Hernando De Soto reportedly met the Quapaw on the Lower Mississippi River in 1540. The Quapaw village of Uzutiuhi appears as Atotchasi on Father Jacques Marquette's 1673 and has been treated separately in this work. First contact with the missionaries came in the early 1700s. Jesuit missionaries began visiting the Quapaw on a regular basis in 1847 after they had been removed to the Indian Territory.

The resettlement of the first group of some 6,000 Cherokees from Georgia west of the Mississippi onto Osage lands beside the Arkansas River was the cause of bitter conflict between the Cherokee immigrants or intruders, depending on one's point of view, and the Quapaw and Osage who called the lands home. Then Superintendent William Clark was charged to stop the fighting by acquiring as much of the Quapaw and Osage lands as possible for the Cherokee and other southern nations. The Quapaw were the first to agree. With a treaty signed on August 24, 1818, in St. Louis, the Quapaw ceded 30 million acres of land within the present states of Arkansas and Oklahoma for the kingly sum of $4,000 in goods and an annual stipend of $1,000. The Quapaw secession was part of the 51 million acres in Missouri and Arkansas for which Clark was able to extinguish Indian titles. In addition to the southern nations, the lands became home, at least temporarily, to the Delawares, Miamis, Weas, Potawatomis, Shawnees, and Wyandots forced from their lands north of the Ohio as a result of the treat concluded at St. Mary's near Lake Erie.

QUARAI PUEBLO

The Quarai Pueblo was belonged to the Tiwa group. It was situated east of the Manzano mountain chain in New Mexico where the mission church was built in 1630. Abandoned in the 1670s, the Quarai Pueblo, Grand Quivira Pueblo, and Abó Pueblo now comprise the Salinas Pueblo Missions National Monument.

QUATHLAHPOHTLE

The Quathlahpohtle was of the Columbia River country where they encountered Lewis & Clark. The "Quath lah pah tle" village was located within what is today the Ridgefield National Wildlife Refuge in Washington State. Lewis and Clark spent the night of March 29, 1806, near the village. They first visited the area on their journey to the Pacific on November 4, 1805. Headquartered in Ridgefield, Washington, the refuge is located on the shore of the Lower Columbia River, ten miles downstream from Portland, Oregon, and Vancouver, Washington. The explorers wrote that the Quathlahpohtle nation were numerous and that their village was located on the northeast side of the Columbia above the mouth of a small river the Indians called Châh-wâh-na-hi-ooks that Clark renamed the Lewis River.

QUATOGHIE

Drake reports that the Quatoghie was possibly another name for a band of the Wyandot that once lived on the south side of Lake Michigan and ceded their lands to English in 1707.

QUEET

The Queet belonged to the coastal division of the Salisham linguistic family and lived along the Queets River and its branches in Washington State. They were closely related to the Quinault to the south.

QUEISSEI

The Queissei or Quisi inhabited eastern Texas between the middle Trinity and the Adaes rivers. They were counted among the Nations for the North. They were very likely the Quisi listed by Father Ortiz in his memorial to the king of Spain sometime after February 14, 1747, cited by Bolton in "Missions on the San Gabriel." It is believed that the Quisi lived in east central or southeastern Texas, but there is no additional information could be found under either name. For more see Nations of the North.

QUI-NAI-ELT

The Qui-nai-elt or Quinaielt inhabited the area about the Qui-nai-elt river in Washington State and were closely linked to if not related to the Quileute of Washington. The tribe was one of the principals in the treaty of July 1, 1855, but little additional information is available. Signing was Tah-ho-lah, Head Chief.

QUIEETSO

The Quieetso lived on the Pacific coast north of the Columbia River and north of the Quiniilt in Washington State.

QUILOTES

The Quilotes was one of the four allied tribes of the Karankawan Tribes of Texas. For more see Karankawan Tribes.

QUINAULT

The Quinault, also spelled Quinalt and Qui-nai-elt (kwi'nail), inhabited Washington Territory around Puget Sound. In 1853 Isaac Stevens was named as the first Governor for the new territory formed out of the Oregon Territory. He saw as his first responsibility the removal of the native peoples to accommodate the influx of white settlers. Accordingly, he set about to execute of series of treaties with the indigenous people of the area that included the Quinault, Quileute, Chehalis, Cowlitz, and Chinook and others.

In all, five treaties were signed within his first two years: the Treaty of Medicine Creek, Treaty of Point Elliott, the Treaty of Point No Point, the Treaty of Neah Bay, and the Treaty of Olympia with the Qui-nai-elt and Qil-leh-ute. The first three were made around Puget Sound. Different tribes or bands were included in each treaty. In all cases, lands were ceded and reserves established. Some eight thousand Indians were affected, but they received little in compensation for their lands.

Out of sheer meanness because they held out for a more favorable reserves on the Chehalis River and at Shoalwater Bay and would not sign a proffered treaty that February, the Cowlitz, Chinook, Chehalis and Shoalwater Bay people have been denied treaty status and treaty rights to this day although they were eventually given reserves they wanted.

The harsh terms of the treaties have been cited as one of the root causes of the Indian wars of 1850s. Of equal or possibly greater significance was the aggressive behavior of the white settlers in appropriating large tracts of public lands for their personal use.

QUINIPISSA

The Quinipissa belonged to the southern division of the Muskhogean family and were closely related to the Choctaw. They lived along the west bank of the Mississippi in Louisiana some distance up river from New Orleans. They may have been related to the Acolapissa and/or the Napissa of Napochi, and they may have been the same as the Mugulasha who were destroyed by the Bayogoula in May 1700. They were first encountered by La Salle in 1682, but Iberville found no sign of them in 1699. Some writers believe that the Quinipissa were identical to the Mugulasha that were destroyed by the Bayogoula in 1700.

QUINNECHART

The Quinnechart lived on the Pacific coast north of the Columbia River and north of Calasthocles in Washington State.

QUINNIPIAC

The Quinnipiac was a subdivision or sub-tribe of the Wappinger and lived in the central part of New Haven County, Connecticut. For more see the Wappinger.

QUIOCOCHÀNOC

The Quiocochànoc was listed in Jefferson's *Notes on the State of Virginia*. They reportedly had a small population of warriors and lived in Surry County, Virginia, about the Upper Chipoak. For more see "Aborigines," Appendix D.

QUIUTCANUAHA

Quiutcanuaha is the name of a group of Indians identified in 1691 as living southwest of the Hasinai Indians of eastern Texas, but no additional information is known. Campbell notes that the Quiutcanuaha bear a resemblance to the Quanataguo and Anathagua of the Coahuiltecan group.

RAPPAHANNOCK

The Rappahannock lived at the mouth of a creek on the Rappahannock River in Richmond County, Virginia. Swanton and others include the Rappahannock as a member of the Powhatan Confederacy. A minority believe that they were non-aligned.

RARITAN

The Raritan was a sub-tribe of the Unami division of the Delaware. They lived in the Raritan River Valley of New Jersey and on the bank of the Delaware south to the falls at Trenton. They gave their name to the Raritan River that flows through New Brunswick in east central New Jersey. The Dutch spelled it Raretangh. During the Dutch Period between 1609 and 1664, Governor Kieft ordered soldiers to a Raritan village in 1642 in response to the theft of some hogs from a Dutch farm on Staten Island that belonged to a David de Vries. Several Indians were killed. The Raritan responded by attacking De Vries' farm and killing four farm hands. Rather than entering into a war with the Raritan, Kieft put a bounty on their heads. Soon thereafter an Indian from a tribe at odds with the Raritan came to collect bearing the hand of the chief of the Raritan on a stick.

RECKGAWAWANC

Reckgawawanc (also spelled Rechgawawanck) was a sub-tribe of the Unami division of the Delaware. They lived on Upper Manhattan Island and the adjacent parts of New York State west of the Bronx in Orange County. Also see the Wickquasgeck.

REPUBLICAN PAWNEE

The Republican Pawnee or Kitkehahki were one of the four subdivisions of the Pawnee and were themselves composed of two divisions. At one time they were thought to have composed of four: Kitkehahki proper, Little Kitkehahki, Black Heads, and Karikisu. The Black Heads have subsequently been identified as a society, and Karikisu has been identified as a ceremony associated with corn planting. They lived about the Republican River in Kansas. For more see Pawnee.

RINCON LUISEÑO

The Rincon near Valley Center was one of six recognized tribes of Luiseños. In 1875 President Ulysses S. Grant signed an Executive Order that established reservations for the Pala, La Jolla, and Rincon. In 1891 the Mission Indian Relief Act made the reservations permanent. For more see Luiseños.

ROANOKE

The Roanoke inhabited Roanoke Island on the Outer Banks of the Carolinas. During the colony's relatively brief existence, the Roanoke both traded with and fought the first English settlers to America. They also reportedly kept them alive. The first meeting was in summer of 1584. Two of the Roanoke, Manteo and Wanchese, traveled back to England. By 1590 the island was deserted.

ROCAMECA

The Rocameca was a subdivision of the Abnaki. They lived on the upper course of Androscoggin River. For more see Abenaki.

ROCKAWAY

The Rockaway or Reckowacky or Rechouwakie was a division of the Montauk and a member of the Algonquian linguistic group. They inhabited the area that is now Richmond Hill in southeastern Long Island, New York, in Newtown, Jamaica, and Hempstead townships. Burrows & Wallace place them with the Delaware. For more see Montauk Peoples and Delaware. Burrows & Wallace also write that the Rockaway spoke the Munsee dialect of the Delaware. The report in The Wave calls them a sub-tribe of the Canarsee that would put them in the Unami dialectic group.

Tradition says that the Rockaway peninsula was deeded away by Chief Tackapousha of the Rockaway. There are conflicting reports on the origin of the name. It may have been a corruption of either "Reckonwacky," a name given it by the Indians and meaning "place of our own people," or "Reckanawahaha," meaning "the place of laughing waters." According to at least one report, the term "Rockaway Indians" refers not to a tribe, but to the several individual Algonquin families who lived in a "Sandy Place."

ROUND HEADS

The Round Heads or Le Tetes do Boule (literally, like a ball) were a tribe of the Ohio country that lived near the headwaters of the Ottawa River in modern Union County, Ohio. Round Heads is also a name commonly given to the Huron. (On the west coast, the expression Round Heads was used to identify all Indians and others that did not follow the Chinookan practice of flattening their heads.

RYAWA

Drake reported the Ryawa that lived on the Paduca Fork of the Missouri (Platte River) but gives no other information. The North Platte River was known as the Padouca Fork as late as 1805. The Padouca is also spelled Paducah and Paduca.

S'HOMAMISH

The S'Homamish inhabited Puget Sound in Washington territory. In 1833 they visited Hudson's Bay fort and requested a missionary. They were a signatory to the Treaty with the Nisqually, Puyallup, and others of 1854, and in 1855-56 the S'Homamish were placed at Fox Island.

S'HOTLE-MA-MISH

The S'Hotle-Ma-Mish belonged to the Nisqually Branch of the coastal division of the Salisham linguistic family of Washington Territory about Puget Sound. They later became a subdivision of the Squaxin Island Tribe and lived about the Carr Inlet of Squaxin Island. For more see Squaxon.

SA-HEH-WA-MISH

The Sa-Heh-Wa-Mish belonged to the Nisqually Branch of the coastal division of the Salisham linguistic family of Washington Territory about Puget Sound. They later became a subdivision of the Squaxin Island Tribe and lived about the Hammersley Inlet of Squaxin Island. See the Squaxon.

SAH-KU-MEHU

The Sah-ku-mehu (Sah-Ku-Meh-Hu) was a subdivision of the Skagit of Washington. It was one of the tribes listed in the Treaty of Point Elliott in January 1855. The Sauk-Suiattle Indian Reservation is located in Skagit County, Washington, north of present Darrington, and the Sauk-Suiattle tribe is listed in the Tribal Natural Resource Directory of the Northwest Indian Fisheries Commission. For more see the Skagit.

SAHEHWAMISH

The Sahehwamish or Sa-Heh-Wamish belonged to the Nisqually group of the coastal division of the Salisham linguistic family. They lived on the innermost inlets of Puget Sound in Washington State.

SAINT REGIS

The Saint Regis (St. Regis) or Akwesasne, for the name of their village, was an independent community of Catholic Iroquois Indians primarily of Mohawk ancestry. They village was located along the shores of the St. Lawrence River at the mouth of the St. Regis River on the international boundary. Before the end of the eighteenth century, they had been relegated to a six square mile reserve in northern New York.

The St. Regis Mission was established about 1755 by French Jesuits as a branch of the mission and village of Kahnawake in order to relive the overcrowding at Kahnawake and to bring inhabitants closer to the their traditional homelands to the south. The Kahnawake mission on the Saint Lawrence River near Montreal was settled in 1667 by Iroquois converts to Christianity and French Catholic missionaries. Kahnawake was populated mostly by Mohawks, but there were also many Onondagas and Oneidas and few captured English colonists. The Mohawk language was spoken; and Mohawk customs, as modified by their new Catholic religion, were followed.

The St. Lawrence River missions were established to draw the Iroquois away from their traditional homelands and into a political alliance with New France. In 1747, the mission of Oswegatchie (known to the Mohawks as Sawekatsi) was established at what is now Ogdensburg, New York, that drew from the Onondaga, Cayuga, and Oneida. Akwesasne territory was situated halfway between Oswegatchie and Kahnawake or Caughnawaga.

(Another account is that two brothers, white captives, who had married into the Kahnawake, were encouraged if not forced to leave the village. The story goes that the brothers, their wives, and the wives parents moved south and founded Saint Regis about 1755 where they were subsequently joined by others from the Mohawk Valley; by a few Indians from a band of Abnaki that had sought sanctuary at Saint Regis during the French and Indian War in 1759; and by former inhabitants of the Oswegatchie mission, primarily Onondagas.)

With their French Catholic background, the Saint Regis allied themselves with the French against the British in the French and Indian War. Their non-Christianized brethren in the Iroquois league allied themselves with the English, led by the Mohawks of the Mohawk Valley. As a result they were excluded from league affairs and in effect ostracized—not an uncommon situation for Catholics in colonial America, Indian or white.

Their French mentors helped the Saint Regis Indians and the other Catholic Indian communities to establish their own league that became known as the Seven Indian Nations of Canada. With their French allies driven from northern territories, the league dissolved by the beginning of the nineteenth century. In the American War of Independence, the majority of the Catholic Iroquois sided with the English, but a minority allied themselves with the Americans. As a result, many of the inhabitants of Kahnawake moved south to Saint Regis to escape possible retribution from the British.

When the Mohawk of the Valley moved south to Grand River in Ontario following the American Revolution, the Saint Regis Indians claimed the Mohawk Valley lands in New York, but the claim was rejected by the state. Instead, under the terms of a treaty executed in 1796, the St. Regis were given a six-square mile tract of land in New York to relinquish all future claims. Subsequent treaties reduced the size of the tract and increased the annuity paid to the Indians.

Treaty of Paris in 1783 that officially ended the War of Independence set the U.S.-Canadian border at the 45th Parallel putting the Saint Regis on both sides of the line. By the mid-1830s, annuity payments from the state of New York to those on the Canadian side of the boundary were halted. In 1888, the Saint Regis were welcomed into the Iroquois League of Six Nations as full members replacing the original Mohawks who forfeited their membership when the tribe settled at Grand River.

The 1910 census put the Saint Regis Indian population at 1219, a significant number comparatively speaking. The Saint Regis Indians (Mohawks) rejected the Indian Reorganization Act of 1935. As a consequence, no significant organizational activity followed. The tribe also rejected administrative termination in 1953, and the relationship between the Saint Regis and the other members of the Iroquois League and the federal government has remained clouded. Also see Blessed Kateri Tekakwitha, the Lily of the Mohawks, in this work.

SAKONNET

The Sakonnet inhabited the colony of Rhode Island to the south of the Pocasset. In the last half of the seventeenth century, they were led by a female sachem, Awashonks. The village of Sakonnet was at the far eastern tip of the mainland at the mouth of the Sakonnet River, more a large channel or estuary, that ran along the east side of Aquidneck Island. The remnants of the Wampanoag settled with the Sakonnet

SALINAN

The Salinan was belonged to the large Hokan linguistic family. They inhabited the area generally around the headwaters of the Salinas River in California north to Santa Lucia Peak, to include the territory along the San Antonio River, Nacimiento Creek, and Chholame Creek and including the San Miguel Mission. There were three linguistic subdivisions: San Antonio Division, San Miguel Division, and the Playano. The estimated population of 2,000 in 1770 had been reduced to zero in 1930.

SALISH

The Salish belonged to the interior division of the Salishan linguistic family from which the name is derived. They were also known as Tushepaw (Tushepau) or Flathead, their English name. The name is also written Tush-she-pâh. They called themselves the Salish. The Salish inhabited western Montana north of the Gallatin River and west of Crazy Mountain and the Little Belt Ranges and around Helena; later they moved farther west around Flathead Lake; also in Idaho. A coastal division of the Salish lived along the Strait of Georgia coast and on the adjacent mainland around Puget Sound, with other groups in western Washington. The two divisions kept in contact.

The Salish enjoyed good relations with white men, beginning with Lewis and Clark in September 1805. The journal entries of September 4-6, 1805, suggest that the Salish may be the Welsh Indians of legend because of their light skin and the "Strangest language." The Tushepaw, as Lewis and Clark called them, supplied the Expedition with twelve horses to enable the Corps to cross Lolo Pass. The Salish and Nez Percé led the Lewis and Clark out of the Bitterroot Mountains and down the Clearwater and Snake rivers to the Columbia.

Although the Salish were called Flatheads (or Flat Heads), they did not practice the custom of flattening the skull of their children like the Chinook and other Columbia River tribes. They got the name because Salish were considered flat-headed compared to the heads of those Columbian tribes that considered their own purposely deformed skulls to be pointed. It is believed that the name Tushepau, used by Lewis and Clark, may come from the Shoshoni word tatasiba, literally, "the people with shaved heads." The Arapaho, Cheyenne, Crow, and Chippewa all gave the Salish a name meaning Flathead (Flat Head) in their respective languages. Use of the term became so common among whites and Indians alike that the names Salish and Flathead, when used to identify a particular tribe or nation, became synonymous. The suffix "ish" in their name, common with many of the names of the Northwest tribes, means "people."

The Salish acquired the horse around 1720 and became buffalo hunters on the plains of Montana but were driven up into the mountains of northwestern Montana by the more aggressive Blackfeet and other plains tribes who were also receiving guns from French traders in exchange for pelts. Around 1790, the Flathead were also hit with epidemics of smallpox and malaria that almost decimated the entire population. Their encounter with the Corps of Discovery was in the valley that is now called Ross or Ross's Hole, east of modern Sula, Montana.

Many of the Salish were converted to Christianity by Catholic missionaries in the 1840s. Following the War of 1812, several dozen Iroquois braves traveled west to Oregon country with fur traders of the North West Company. Several of the Iroquois joined the Flathead and introduced them to Christianity thus becoming the first apostles to the Indians. Of their number was a Christian Iroquois named Ignace la Mousse who lived with the Flathead for several years.. It was his influence that encouraged the Flatheads to ask that one of the Jesuit Black Robes from St. Louis be sent to them.

The first Flathead delegation in search of the Black Robes arrived at Florissant, Missouri, in 1831; the second in December 1835 was delivered on their behalf by Ignace la Mousse himself. Timing, however, was not right for the Jesuits, but the fact that Indians from the far Northwest were open to Christianity induced the Methodists to send missionaries to the far North country. They were followed by missionaries from the American Board of Commissioners of Foreign Missions. Both groups, however, bypassed the Flathead for the locations closer to white civilization. The Methodist established their mission in the Willamette valley; the American Board in the Walla Walla Valley with a second on the Snake River.

The Flatheads send a third delegation to St. Louis in 1837, but the party got only as far as Ash Hollow Creek, Nebraska, where it was ambushed by the Sioux. The fourth delegation stopped at Saint Joseph's Potawatomi Mission of Father De Smet at Council Bluffs, Iowa, on September 18, 1839, where they received letters of introduction to Jesuit authorities at Saint Louis. After a short delay, Father De Smet followed the delegates to St. Louis. He arrived February 20, 1840 having crossed Missouri on foot in the midst of winter. The entreaties to the Jesuit authorities gained them the promise that a Jesuit missionary would be sent to the Flathead that spring. Father De Smet, on site when the decision was to be made, was given the assignment.

In the spring of 1840, Father De Smet traveled to Westport, Missouri, where he joined one of the delegates, young Ignace, who had remained behind at the Kickapoo mission north of Fort Leavenworth. De Smet and Ignace accompanied the pack train of the American Fur Company northwest to the Green River rendezvous near present-day Daniel, Wyoming. On reaching the rendezvous June 30, two months after leaving Westport, they met up with the second member of the 1839 delegation, Pierre Gaucher, and an escort of nine Flathead braves. The entire party continued to the main Flathead camp of some sixteen hundred people at Pierre's Hole along the Snake River north of Jackson Hole in northwest Wyoming, arriving on July 12.

Several days later the camp was moved to the headwaters of the Missouri, and Father De Smet joined the braves on a buffalo hunt. Father De Smet was extremely pleased and gratified with the reception he received. In a short period of time, he preached and taught, and Baptized several hundred. He encountered none of the social problems resulting from the effects of whisky and the white man's greed. In his report to Florissant, he recommended that a permanent mission be established in the North Country.

Father De Smet left the Flathead camp August 27, 1840 with a twenty-man Flathead escort to guide and protect him on his return to St. Louis promising to return in the Spring. He released his escort at Fort Alexander at the junction of the Yellowstone and Rosebud rivers and proceeded on to St. Louis. Fr. De Smet returned August 30, 1841, almost a year to the day when he first departed. With him were two Jesuits priest, Father Nicolas Point and Father Gregory Mengarini, and three Jesuit brothers. On September 24, a mission was established in the Bitterroot Valley near the present-day city of Stevensville, Montana. Father De Smet christened it Saint Mary's Mission. It was to become the administrative center for the Jesuit's Rocky Mountain Mission system.

The Flathead took extremely well to Christianity, but the Flathead saw Black Robe and his Christian teaching as something more than a new, inspired religion. They saw Christianity if not as a weapon, then certainly a shield that would protect them from their Blackfeet enemies.

By the summer of 1846, the Flathead, who were led by their grand chief named Victor, grew so confident of the new power that they believed they now held that they invaded the lands of the Crow, who up to then had been allies. They were joined by some Nez Percé and a few Blackfeet. In the battle northeast of the Three Forks of the Missouri, nine Crow braves were killed. The Flathead suffered no casualties, and one Nez Percé died. Word of the new power the Flathead possessed spread; and on September 25, 1846, Father De Smet mediated a formal peace between the Flathead and Blackfeet at Fort Benton on September 25, 1846. and left on his long journey back to St. Louis on the 28th. The Flathead soon came to resent sharing the power of the Black Robe and eventually fell away from Christianity altogether. In 1849-1850 Saint Mary's Mission in the Bitterroot Mountains was closed and the buildings sold to a private party.

A treaty was executed between the United States and the Flathead, Kootenay, and Upper Pend d'Oreilles Indians July 16, 1855. The Flathead ceded all their lands in Montana and Idaho with the exception of land in Northwest Montana north of Missoula and southwest of Glacier National Park near Dixon that was established as a reserve and to which they were removed June 5, 1872.

DE SMET, FATHER PETER JOHN (PIERRE JEAN)

Peter John De Smet was born at Dendermonde, Belgium, January 30, 1801. He attended local schools until one day in 1821 he heard a lecture by a Jesuit priest who was recruiting missionaries for America. The next day Peter John volunteered. He arrived at Georgetown College in the District of Columbia on October 3 where he was formally enrolled into the Society of Jesus. On the last day of May of 1823 he arrived at the new Missouri Mission in Florissant, Missouri; and on September 23, 1837, Father De Smet was ordained a priest. His first mission assignment with the Indians came in 1838 with the Potawatomi in Iowa in 1838. That was followed by a mission to the Salish (Flathead) in 1840. Over the years Fr. De Smet met with, visited, and administered to about thirty different tribes and sub-tribes, the great majority of which were located in Oregon Territory and in the region of the Upper Missouri, to include the following:

Arikara	Kootenay
Assiniboin	Mandan
Blackfeet	Nez Percé
Brulé	Oglala
Chinook	Omaha
Clatsop	Otoe
	Pawnee
Coeur d'Alene (Skitswish)	Ponca
Colville	Potawatomi
Crow	Flathead (Salish)
Gros Ventre of the River (Hidatsa)	Santee
Hunkpapa	Sauk
Iowa	Two Kettles
Kalispel (Pend Oreille)	Yankton
Kickapoo	Yanktonai

Although Father De Smet was unable to administer to the Indians personally on a continuing basis after 1846, he served the Indians and the Jesuit missions from St. Louis, Washington, DC, and Europe, raising money, planning and organizing new missions, insuring that they were adequately supplied, and publicizing the cause of the American Indians with his numerous writings. Few men made as great an impact on Indian relations and the history of the Upper Missouri region and the Northwest territory as did Father De Smet, and few men in history have been so highly respected by such a diverse assemblage of persons on two continents.

Father De Smet died May 23, 1873, in his bed at St. Louis University. Ten days earlier he blessed the newest steamboat of his longtime friend Captain La Barge, the *De Smet*. His body was buried at the Jesuit novitiate at Florissant.

SALMON RIVER INDIANS

The Salmon River Indians of the coastal division of the Salishan linguistic family was a subdivision of the Tillamook who lived on the Salmon River in Oregon. For more see Tillamook.

SALUDA

It is believed that the Saluda of South Carolina was a band of the Shawnee and therefore of the Algonquian stock. The lived along the Saluda River but later removed to Conestogo in Pennsylvania.

SAMISH

The Samish (or Sam-ahmish) inhabited the region of Samish Bay and Samish Island in Washington State. They belonged to the coastal division of the Salishan linguistic group. Other villages were located on northwest portion of Fidalgo Island and on Guemes Island. They were removed to the Lummi Reservation.

SAMPIT UTE

The Sampit or Sanpet was a subdivision of the Ute and lived about Manti on San Pitch Creek and on the Sevier River in Utah. For more see Ute.

SAN ANTONIO SALINAS

The San Antonio Salinas were a division of the Salinan of the Hokan linguistic family. They lived below the San Miguel Salinas on the Salinas River in California, adjoining the Costanoan lands.

SAN FELIPE PUEBLO

San Felipe is of the Keresan linguistic stock. The pueblo is located about thirty miles from Albuquerque. For more see Pueblo.

SAN ILDEFONSO PUEBLO

The San Ildefonso Pueblo was of the Northern division of the Tewa Pueblo Group of the Tanoan linguistic family that is part of the Kiowa-Tanoan stock. They lived eighteen miles northwest of Santa Fe near the eastern bank of the Rio Grande. For more see Pueblo.

SAN JUAN PUEBLO

The San Juan Pueblo was of the Northern division of the Tewa Pueblo Group of the Tanoan linguistic family that is part of the Kiowa-Tanoan stock. They lived near the eastern bank of the Rio Grande twenty-five miles northwest of Santa Fe. For more see Pueblo.

Of Note

Spanish explorer Juan de Oñate y Salazar established the first Spanish settlement New Mexico in 1598 from his headquarters at the Yuque-Yunque Pueblo of Tewa Indians in the northern Rio Grande Valley near the junction of the Rio Grande and Chama rivers, just north of present Española. He renamed the pueblo the San Juan Pueblo (San Juan de los Caballeros for Saint John the Baptist). The capital for New Spain was established on the opposite bank of the Rio Grande and named San Gabriel de YuqueYunque. In 1607-1608, the inhabitants of San Gabriel moved to a new town being built to the south that they called Santa Fé (Holy Faith). In his march into northern New Mexico, Oñate founded El Camino Real (The Royal Road), the communication and trade link between Mexico City and Santa Fé that would serve the region for centuries. The San Juan Pueblo officially changed its name back to Ohkay Owingeh, "Place of the Strong People" in 2005.

SAN MANUEL

The San Manuel or Yuhaviatam "People of the Pines" belonged to the Shoshonean division of the Uto-Aztecan linguistic stock that included the Kitanemuk, Vanyume, Kawaiisu, and Alliklik. They were of the Serrano group that inhabited the deserts and valleys adjoining the San Bernardino Mountains of California. The 800-acre San Manuel reservation, named after tribal leader Santos Manuel, was established in 1891 in the foothills of the San Bernardino Mountain region north of the city

SAN MARCOS PUEBLO

The San Marcos Pueblo about fifteen miles south and southwest of Santa Fe was located in the Galisteo Basin in what is now Santa Fe County. San Marcos, of the Tano or southern Tewa, was established around 1300 and quickly grew into a major trading center with a population of several thousand people. Whether Coronado visited the pueblo in 1540 is unknown. The first recorded Spanish explorers to visit the area was the Rodríguez-Chamuscado Expedition of 1581. The Spanish called San Marcos *Malpartida* (Bad Parting) for the mineral deposits they found about three miles from the pueblo. With the establishment of the Franciscan mission, it was renamed San Marcos. By the time of the Pueblo Revolt in 1680, its population had been reduced to some six hundred souls that dispersed throughout the area. Nature reclaimed the site; and, except for the occasional squatters, the pueblo was never reoccupied.

SAN MIGUEL SALINAS

The San Miguel Salinas was a division of the Salinan of the Hokan linguistic family. They lived on the upper course of the Salinas River in California.

SANDIA PUEBLO

The Sandia was part of the Kiowa-Tanoan stock. The Sandia and the Isleta formed one of the three divisions of the Tiwa, inhabiting the area north and south of Albuquerque. For more see Pueblo.

SAGUENAY

Explorer and navigator Jacques Cartier returned to France following his first voyage to North America in 1534 with the name Saguenay for a fabulously rich and fertile kingdom "to the north" of present-day Quebec, but he had nothing more than the name and the stories. There were stories of spices and oranges and men who could fly. There were stories of gold and other treasures. The king sent him back to America the next year to find this fabulous kingdom, but his search was in vain. He found no kingdom, only more stories. Most writers hold with Saguenay was a mythical kingdom made up by the Hurons.

Some reports want to make the Saguenay be part of the Montagnais living about the mouth of the Saguenay River. The Saguenay joins the St. Lawrence from the East about a hundred-plus miles above Quebec. Others, who heard the Algonquian stories of white men with blond hair, rich in gold and furs, think Saguenay must have been an ancient Viking settlement. About mid-way between the St. Lawrence and Lac St-Jean is the present-day city of Saguenay.

SANKHIKAN

The Sankhikan or Sankieken (also Sanckhekin and Sonckhicon) belonged to the Algonquian linguistic group and was a sub-tribe of the Delaware. They lived in the area about present-day cities of Jersey City and Newark, New Jersey.

SANPOIL

The Sanpoil lived on the Sanpoil River and Nespelem Creek as well as on the Columbia River below Bid Bend in Washington State. They belonged to the inland division of the Salisham linguistic family.

SANS ARC

The Sans Arc or San Arc or Itazipacola or Itazipco ("Without Bow") was a tribe of the Western Division (Lakota) of the Sioux Nation. Sans Arc is used in both singular and plural. For more see Sioux and Lakota.

SANTA ANA PUEBLO

The Santa Ana belonged to the eastern dialectic group of Keresan or Keres linguistic stock. They were a member of the Northern Tewa division and lived along the Rio Grande River in north central New Mexico, between the Rio de los Friholes and the Rio Jemez and along the Rio Jemez from the Pueblo of Sia (Zia) to its mouth. For more see Pueblo.

SANTA CLARA PUEBLO

The San Clara Pueblo was of the Northern division of the Tewa Pueblo Group of the Tanoan linguistic family that is part of the Kiowa-Tanoan stock. They lived on the western bank of the Rio Grande about thirty miles north of Santa Fe. For more see Pueblo.

SANTA YNEZ CHUMASH

The Santa Ynez were one of the eight dialectic and geographical divisions of the Chumash of the Southern California coast. The Santa Ynez Chumash lived inland along the Santa Ynez River between the Barbareño and Cuyama. For more see the Chumash.

SANTEE OF SOUTH CAROLINA

It is believed that the Santee were of the Siouan stock. They lived along the middle course of the Santee River that originates in central South Carolina southeast of Columbus. They took part in the Yamasee War against the whites in 1715. A year later they were attacked by the combined force of Etiwas and Cusado as allies of the colonists. The greater part were captured and sent off as slaves to the West Indies.

Survivors were incorporated into the Catawba. Santee is also the name given to the tribes of the Eastern Division (Dakota) of the Sioux nation.

SANTIAM KALAPUYA

The Santiam belonged to the Calapooya dialectic division of the Kalapooian linguistic stock. The tribe lived along the Santiam River, a branch of the Willamette, near Lebanon. See Kalapuya Peoples.

SANTO DOMINGO PUEBLO

Santo Domingo is of the Keresan linguistic family. The Indians of the Santo Domingo of New Mexico are well-known for their fine jewelry. For more see Pueblo.

SAONE

Saone was a nickname given by the Oglala and Brulé to five tribes of their Lakota kinsmen: Miniconjou, San(s) Arc, Two Kettle(s), Hunkpapa, and the Blackfoot Sioux. Although it first appeared in Minnesota, the name did not come into general used until those of the Teton group had removed to the Upper Missouri, taking the name with them. It was still in common use in 1840 but disappeared by the end of the century. A tribe or band under the name Teton Saone was one of the ten separate Sioux tribes identified by Lewis and Clark. For more see Sioux and Lakota.

SAPONI

The Saponi belonged to the Siouan linguistic family. Earliest reports from the mid-1600s put the Saponi on the banks of the Rivana River in present Albermarle County, Virginia, subsequently southwest on Otter Creek southwest of Lynchburg, later to the junction of the Staunton and Dan Rivers where they occupied an island in Roanoke River in present Mecklenburg County. Leery of possible attack by the Iroquois, they moved further south around 1701 to the Wadkin River near present Salisbury, North Carolina.

Almost constantly on the move, they were next found just west of present Windsor (Bertie), North Carolina, and in the area of Gholsonville, Brunswick County. Many of these moves were in conjunction with the Tutelo. (With the treaty of Albany of 1722, the Iroquois agreed to desist in their incursions into Virginia.)

About 1740 the great majority of the Saponi and the Tutelo moved north to the upper waters of the Susquehanna in Pennsylvania where some remained until 1778. But in 1771 a large segment moved north and resettled near Ithaca, New York, in the territory of the Cayuga Iroquois. Of those that remained in Virginia and North Carolina, one band was adopted by the Cayuga while another was fused into the Tuscarora, Meherrin, and Machapunga, going north with them in 1802 as the sixth nation of the Iroquois Confederacy.

SARCEE

The Sarcee was of the Athabascan linguistic family. A Canadian tribe, members also lived about the upper plains of Montana in the region of the headwaters of the Missouri River where at one time they were neighbors of the Kiowa. It is believed that they had split from another northern tribe, possibly the Beaver. Their name originated from a Blackfoot word for "boldness" or "hardiness." The Sarcee and Gros Ventre were members of the Blackfeet Confederacy.

In addition to the death and destruction wrought by wars, the Sarcee tribe was hit by the smallpox epidemic in 1837 and scarlet fever in 1864. They moved to their reservation of some 280 sq. km. that adjoins the southwestern city limits of Calgary, Canada, following a 1877 treaty. In 1996 there were 1225 Sarcee.

SATSOP

The Satsop belonged to the coastal division of the Salisham linguistic stock, often classed with the Lower Chehalis of Washington State. They lived along the Satsop River, a branch of the Chehalis River. They were closely affiliated with the Lower Chehalis but spoke the dialect of the Upper Chehalis.

SATURIWA

The Saturiva belonged to the Mukhoean subdivision of the Timucua linguistic stock. They lived about the mouth of the St. Johns River in Florida and possibly on Cumberland Island. The first known encounter with the Europeans was Jean Ribault in 1562, but there may have been earlier contact. The first recorded record is in the chronicles of the French Huguenot settlement in Florida in 1564-1565. The French Fort Caroline was built on their lands. The name Saturiwa was the name of the chief during that period, who aided De Gourgues in his 1567 attack on the Spanish.

When the Spanish displaced the French, the Spanish allied themselves with the Utina (Timucua), probably in response to the 1567 attack. Later the Saturiwa was served by the Mission of San Juan del Puerto of Francisco de Pareja established by the Spanish. San Juan was the main mission for the province that included Vera Cruz, Arratobo, Potaya, San Matheo, San Pablo, Hicachirico (Little Town), Chinisca, and Carabay. The missions of San Diego de Salamototo, near Piscolata, and Nuestra Señora de Guadalupe, about ten miles from Saint Augustine were somewhat different. The Saturiwa, devastated by disease in 1617 and 1672, disappeared from history by the beginning of the eighteenth century.

SAUK

The Sauk (people of the yellow earth) or Sac belonged to the Algonquian linguistic stock and were of the same group as the Fox and Kickapoo. Oral history records that the tribe originated near the Saint Lawrence Seaway in Canada. Catholic missionaries were the first to encounter the Sac about Saginaw Bay (place of the Sauks) in upper Michigan. Midway into the seventeenth century, they were driven south by the Ottawa and the Neutrals into the upper part of Green Bay in Wisconsin on Lake Michigan and the lower course of the Fox River where they would become allied with the Fox. The Fox had also migrated from the south shore of Lake Superior in Michigan to the land around Lake Winnebago, Wisconsin, and the Fox River having been gently eased out by the Chippewa.

About 1733, the French drove the Sauk and the Fox into an undeclared confederation that would continue for the next century. The French drove the Sac and the Fox into northern Illinois, thus leaving Wisconsin to the Menominee, Chippewa, and Winnebago. The combined onslaught of the Sac and Fox, in turn, drove the Illinois Indians from their land between the Fox River west of Chicago and the Mississippi. During Jefferson's tenure as president from 1801-1809, the Sauk and Fox slowly and inexorably ceded acre after acre of land to the whites, first for rifles, knives, and hunting paraphernalia. More debt, which the white man encouraged, consumed more land. Finally they surrendered vast tracts of land both east and west of the Mississippi. Over 50 million acres in southern Wisconsin were ceded to the government with the treaty of 1804. The treaty laid the cornerstone for Black Hawk War thirty years later.

With the Treaty of November 3, 1804, negotiated with William Henry Harrison, then Governor of Indiana Territory, the Sauk and Fox were allowed to remain on the land until it was settled. The treaty could not become effective, however, until it was confirmed by the Fox and Sauk residing on the Des Moines River in Iowa and by the Sauls on the Rock River in Illinois, which did not occur until 1815 and 1816, respectively.

The Sacs and Foxes occupied the land between the Mississippi and the Rock River in northwest Illinois and across the Mississippi in northeast Iowa. (The Rock River generally runs from Rockford, Illinois, just south of the border with Wisconsin southwest to its mouth on the Mississippi at Rock Island south of Moline.) The Sauk built a grand city on the north bank of the Rock River at Rock Island that they named Saukenuk. The city prospered and grew to a population of some eleven thousand. The Fox for the most part clustered in small towns across the Mississippi in Iowa. In their new homes, the Sac and Fox came to fear the Osage and Sioux to the west more than the French or the English to the east. Another treaty executed in 1815 ceded vast tracts of lands west of the Mississippi and in Illinois north of Saukenuk and reinforced the provisions of treaty of 1804. The process was repeated again in 1825.

The Sac and Fox allied themselves with the English in the War of 1812 and were encouraged to make war on white settlers in Missouri Territory. Black Hawk led many of the raids against the Americans. In September 1813 a volunteer force of some 1,400 Missourians under the command of General Howard destroyed several of their villages and stores of corn putting an end to the attacks. When the war with Britain ended, some 1200 or 1500 Indians who lived along the Rock River and Des Moines River continued the war against the Americans. Peace was finally secured at a conference held at Portage de Sioux in the St. Charles District, Missouri, in June 1815. The Fox and Sac subsequently located north of the Missouri River and held the territory between the Missouri and the Mississippi Rivers as far north as the headwaters of the Des Moines and Iowa rivers.

Disagreements between the Sauk and the Fox over treaties caused one Sauk group to separate from the others and move south to the Missouri River where they became known as the Missouri Band. There they remained there until 1824 when they were removed to the northwest corner of Missouri (Platte Territory). In 1823, the Sacs and Foxes ceded all claims to the territory north of the Missouri between the Missouri and the Mississippi and on the west on a line from the mouth of the Kansas River north for 100 miles. In 1836 the two tribes ceded all rights to that portion of Missouri in the northwest corner known as the Platte Purchase that was added to the state that same year and included the present counties of Platte, Buchanan, Andrew, Holt, Nodaway, and Atchison, Missouri. In exchange, they received a reserve west of the Missouri River on the Kansas-Nebraska border. The Sac and Fox of Missouri continued to retain a small reservation in Kansas following allotment with the tribal headquarters located in the town of Reserve.

By 1828, the land was being sold, and settlers began to arrive. The Sauk were told to move west into the southeast of what would become the state of Iowa. The tribe split. The main body under Keokuk (Watchful Fox), a secondary chief, removed voluntarily to Iowa with the Fox. (The town of Keokuk, Iowa, on the Des Moines River at its mouth on the Mississippi takes its name from the Sauk chief.) Black Hawk's band at Rock Island held on until they were forced out.

In 1829 when Andrew Jackson became president, Black Hawk (a-La-Tai-Me-She-Kia-Kiak) was then sixty-two years old. He became chief in the late eighteenth century. Black Hawk, who was also called Black Sparrow Hawk, was born on the Rock River in 1767. (Some reports cite Wisconsin; others, Illinois). His family had emigrated earlier from near Montreal. He earned a reputation as a warrior by leading raids against the neighboring Osage and Cherokee.

Resentful of the American government for taking his lands, Black Hawk gathered a small force from among allies and crossed the Mississippi in 1831. He was confronted by troops under Maj. General Edmund P. Gaines who commanded at Rock Island and was forced to sign a treaty and return to Iowa. What followed was called the Black Hawk War. It culminated in the Battle of Bad Axe on the Mississippi on August 2.

Black Hawk's British Band as it was called was destroyed, and the remnants were removed to Iowa Territory where they joined the Fox. The two tribes remained in Iowa until 1842 when they ceded their lands for a reserve in Kansas just south of present-day capital of Topeka. (Several had to be tracked down by the Army.) Disagreements developed between the Fox and the Sauk, and some of the Fox joined the Kickapoo and later left with them for northern Mexico. Twelve years later in May 1854, four representatives of the Sauk and Fox were invited to Washington to hear plans for the transcontinental railroad. Before they left, they ceded four hundred square miles of land to the government for subsequent transfer to the railroads. Also see the Oto.

By 1859 the influx of white settlers into Kansas following the passage of the Kansas-Nebraska Act put additional pressure on the Sauk to cede part of their Kansas reserve and accept allotment without consulting the Fox, keeping the money. As early of 1851, small numbers of Fox had begun returning to Iowa; but with the treaty of 1859 some three hundred of those that remained broke with the Sauk and followed their kinsmen to Iowa where they purchased eighty acres along the Iowa River near the town of Tama for $1,000 or $12.50 an acre. The Fox in Iowa continued to increase their land holdings until they had acquired some 5,000 acres. They are the only federally recognized tribe in Iowa, where they prefer to be called the Mesquaki Indian Settlement. However, because of treaties that had been signed jointly with the Sauk, the official name is the Sac and Fox of the Mississippi in Iowa.

About one hundred Fox remained with the Sauk in Kansas. After the admission of Kansas to statehood in 1861, the call went up for the removal of all Indians. In 1867 the Fox and Sauk in Kansas signed their last treaty ceding all their lands in Kansas in exchange for a 750,000 acre reservation created for them in central Oklahoma from lands taken from the Creek, Cherokee, and Seminole for siding with the Confederacy. In 1869 a total of about 700 Sauk and Fox from Kansas left for Potawatomi, Lincoln, and Payne Counties east of Oklahoma City becoming the Sac and Fox Nation. The treaty also permitted the Sac and Fox of Missouri to join them if they so desired. In 1889, the Sauk accepted allotment. Afterward most of this was released to settlement in 1891. By the end of the twentieth century, all that remained was some one thousand acres of tribal lands near Stroud, Oklahoma. After allotment,

BLACK HAWK WAR

Black Hawk recrossed the Mississippi in April 1832 with a band of five to seven hundred warriors and that many again of women, children. At 65 years of age, he came to regain his homeland and plant his crops as his people always had. In so doing, he brought on the short-lived Black Hawk War that lasted from April though August and ranged inland along the Mississippi River from near Rock Island, Illinois, to near Prairie du Chien, Wisconsin. The Potawatomi living to the east were sympathetic, but wanted no part of a confrontation with the Chemokemons (as the word Americans came out in Black Hawk's broken English). A peace parley to take place on Potawatomi land ended in the deaths of several Indians. Attacks, raids, and reprisals took place across northern Illinois and southern Wisconsin that included ambushing troops ordered out by General Henry Atkinson who was in command at Fort Armstrong at Rock Island, but there were few deaths on either side.

(Abraham Lincoln enlisted in the Illinois state militia from Sangamon in answer to the governor's call for volunteers to meet Black Hawk's threat and was soon elected Captain. Lincoln and his men, though trampling about Illinois and southern Wisconsin, never met Black Hawk and his warriors in battle.)

By summer, Black Hawk was confronted by over two thousand soldiers and militia led by experienced officers. He was overtaken and defeated at the Battle of Wisconsin Heights on July 21, 1832, by forces under the command of Gen. James Henry and Col. Henry Dodge. Some seventy Indians were killed in the battle. The army suffered one man killed and seven or eight wounded. Black Hawk ordered a rear guard action in an attempt to divert the militia and took the main party of some five hundred beleaguered followers northwest to the Mississippi and the hoped-for safety beyond.

What they found was death at the Bad Axe River at its mouth on the Mississippi, thirty miles north of Prairie do Chien, Wisconsin, on August 1-2, 1832. The army of Chemokemons—"Americans" in the

Sauk dialect, was under the command of General Atkinson (White Beaver) and included Winnebago and Sioux scouts and Illinois militia under Generals Dodge, Henry, and Alexander.

The killing began the first day as the Indians were almost finished building their bark rafts with which to cross the river. Twenty-three Indians died that day canon and rifle shot from the steamer Warrior to which Black Hawk had sent a white flag of surrender.

The next day soldiers, militia, and their Indian allies struck in a surprise attack that sprang out of the nearby woods. Reports of the number of Indians killed range from 150 to 300, and the number of prisoners taken, mostly women and children, from fifty to "hundreds." Black Hawk himself wrote that about sixty were killed plus those who drowned in the Mississippi. Although many of the Indians died in the fighting, many more, especially the women and children, were murdered. Children were killed outright; the women raped and mutilated. It is believed that General Atkinson tried unsuccessfully to stop the slaughter. Col. Zachary Taylor's role, on the other hand, is unclear. The number of soldiers and militia that died was less than twenty.

From the account of Dr. James Lewis: "The slaughter on the eastern bank of the river continued for eight hours. The soldiers shot at anyone--man, woman, or child--who ran for cover or tried to swim across the river. They shot women who were swimming with children on their backs; they shot wounded swimmers who were almost certain to drown anyway. Other women and children were killed as they tried to surrender. The soldiers scalped most of the dead bodies. From the backs of some of the dead, they cut long strips of flesh for razor strops [*sic*]."

Black Hawk, his son Naapope, and Wabokishick (referred to as Prophet) escaped along with about twenty others and headed north to The Dalles on the Wisconsin (Wisconsin Dells). Accounts differ as to whether Black Hawk was run down and captured by Winnebagoes and turned over to the army or whether he surrendered at Fort Crawford at Prairie du Chen. But by August 8, he was in custody and taken to prison at Jefferson Barracks south of St. Louis. He was soon removed and paraded through the East before eventually being released by President Jackson on June 4, 1833. He returned to Rock where he dictated his autobiography to a government interpreter. Black Hawk lived to be eighty years old and died October 3, 1838, at the Sauk reservation along the banks of the Des Moines River near Eldon, Iowa, and was buried on the West bank of Mississippi. A sculpture dedicated to Black Hawk by American artist Lorado Taft stands on the bluff overlooking the Rock River in Oregon, Illinois.

SAULT CHIPPEWA

The Sault or Saulteaux were those of the Chippewa nation that inhabited the region around Sault Saint (Ste.) Marie in Upper Michigan and the juncture of Lake Superior and Lake Huron. The two lakes are linked by the Saint Mary's River. Because the level of Lake Superior is above that of Lake Huron, the stretch of river where the two join consists of rapids and cascades that fall some twenty feet. The word *sault* literally translates as "jump." It was the place where one "jumped into" or "put into" the St. Mary's River.

The native peoples gave the place the name "Gathering Place" (*Bahweiting*). It was the place where fur traders gathered beginning in the 1600s and began calling the wild area *Sault du Gastogne*. It was at Sault Saint Marie that settlers gathered to establish the first city in Michigan and the third European settlement in what became the United States. It was at that time in 1668 that the Jesuit missionary and explorer Fr. Jacques Marquette established the Mission of Sault Saint Marie and renamed the settlement in honor of the Virgin Mary. For more see the Chippewa.

SAVANNAH

The Indians that became known to the English colonists as the Savannah occupied the middle Savannah River in South Carolina. It was they that gave their name to the river. The Savannah have been identified as Yamasee, Yuchi, and Shawnee and as a separate and distinct tribe. Best evidence, however, suggests that they were Shawnee, a colony of the Shawnee of the Cumberland basin in Tennessee. As the Shawnee name implies, together they were the southern vanguard of the Algonquian linguistic stock.

To prove the association, some writers suggest that the name "Savannah" derives from a Muskogean word and that is a variant of the native name of the Shawnees, "Sawanno." Although a convenient argument, without any explanation as to how or why the form Shawnee in English took the form Savannah in contradiction to the applicable linguistic rules, the name Savannah must have derived from a source different from the Shawnee name for themselves. That source , it appears, comes from the denotation of the word itself. The word savanna is a topographical term, not a name, as in the savannas of Africa. *Random House* defines a savanna as a "grassland region with scattered trees, grading into either open plain or woodland, usually in subtropical or tropical regions." The term is not used anywhere else in the United States except as it is found in Georgia and South Carolina although the name has been given to towns in Tennessee and Illinois. From *Names in South Carolina*: "It therefore seems plausible that the term savannah was first applied by the Charleston settlers to grasslands along the Savannah River, then to Indians living in the area, and was eventually construed as a proper name identifying both the Indians and the river." Better evidence of the of the Shawnee connection was provided by William Bartram: "I was told by an old trader that the Savannuca and Shawanese speak the same language, or very near alike."

Swanton affirms the connection: "Shortly after 1674 the Hathawekela or that part of the Shawnee afterward so called, settled upon Savannah River, and in 1681 they proved of great assistance to the new colony of South Carolina by driving the tribe known as Westo, probably part of the Yuchi, from the middle Savannah" in what came to be known as the Westo War of 1680. (The identification of the Westo is also under some question.) It would appear that these Hathawekela came to be known as the Savannah. The Savannah, in turn, were attacked and enslaved by the Catawba. The dates reported in the literature vary, but sometime between 1730s and 1770s the Savannah removed to join their Shawnee brethren on the Cumberland. For more see the Shawnee. One account indicates that the Savannah settlement had been abandoned by 1722.

SAWOKLI

The Sawokli belonged to the Atcik-hata division of the Muskhogean linguistic stock. They are most commonly noted as living on the Chattahoochee River in the northwest part of present Barbour County, Alabama. They were a member of the Creek Confederacy of Lower Creeks.

SCATICOOK

The Scaticook or Scattakook or Schaghticoke, meaning "scattered," was a sub-tribe of the Mahican who lived in three villages in Duchess and Rensselaer Counties, New York, and in Litchfield County, Connecticut, on the Housatonic River about its junction with the Ten Mile River. Moravian missionaries established a sub-mission there in 1740. Present-day Scaticook, Connecticut, is located in the Township of Kent. The Schaghticoke Reservation, now inhabited by only a handful of descendants, is on the New York-Connecticut border.

SCOTON

The Scoton tribe was of southern Oregon. The name Scoton (var. spelled Scoten and Scotan) also appears in the literature as Shasta Scoton and Chasta Scoton. However, there is no evidence to suggest that the Scoton was either a branch of or a subdivision of the Shasta or Chasta (Chastacosta). Three bands of the Scoton signed the 1854 treaty along with the Chasta and others.

SE-AP-CAT

The Se-ap-cat was a sub-tribe of the Yakima that is sometimes referred to separately. In the 1855 Yakima treaty at Camp Stevens, the Se-ap-cat ceded all their lands to the government and settled on the Yakima Reservation. For more see Yakima.

SEATAUKET

The Seatauket or Seatalcat was a division of the Montauk and were a member of the Algonquian linguistic group that were generally treated separately. They lived on Long Island, New York. For more see Montauk and Delaware.

SECACAWONI

Secacawoni was a member of the Powhatan Confederacy and inhabited parts of Northumberland County, Virginia.

SECATOAG

The Secatoag or Secatogue was a division of the Montauk and a member of the Algonquian linguistic family. They lived on Long Island, New York, in Islip Township. For more see Montauk Peoples and Delaware.

SECONONDIHAGO

Little is known about the Seconondihago except for a reference that suggests that they may have been a subdivision or clan of the Susquehanna. For more see Susquehanna.

SECOTAN

The Secotan lived between Albermarle and Pamlico sounds in Benton County, North Carolina, in the 1580s at the time of the Roanoke Colony. The site of the village of the Secotan proper has been put near the present town of Bath, North Carolina. There are reports that the Secotan may have later merged with or were adopted by the Machapunga, but no date or other information is recorded. Swanton writes that Secotan may also have been a village of the Machapunga, which would appear to confirm the status of the Secotan relative to the Machapunga (Mattamuskeet). The name Secotaooc, with the "ooc" suffix referring to shellfish and a large body of water, may be only variation in the spelling, as well as the name Secotaoc.

The Secotan, enemies of the Tuscarora, were widely scatter throughout the region. Williard writes that the Secotan was comprised of five subgroups or villages: Roanoke, Pomeiooc, Dasemunkepeuc, Aquascogooc, and Tramaskecooc, in addition to the Secotan proper, which lay south of the Pamlico River. Reed appears to support the composition of the Secotan, at least in part, but treats Secotan and Secotaoc as two distinct towns.

SECOWOCOMOCO

The Secowocomoco was one of the nine divisions of the Conoy. They lived on the Wicomico River in St. Marys and Charles counties, Maryland. For more see Conoy Peoples.

SEECHELT

The Canadian Seechelt constituted a distinct dialectic group within the coastal division of the Salisham linguistic stock. They lived on Jervic and Seechelt Inlets, Nelaon Island, and the southern part of Texada Island, British Columbia.

SEKAMISH

The Sekamish was a subdivision of the Muckleshoot of Washington State. They lived on the upper White River. It is believed the Sekamish of Swanton may be the same as the Stkamish of Auburn, Washington, history. For more see Muckleshoot and Smalhkamish.

SEMATUSE

The Sematuse were of Salishan stock. They reportedly lived about the Big Blackfoot River, the area called "Big Camas" or "Camas Prairie," and Deer Lake in Montana. Some writers consider the Samatuse either mythical or that they preceded the Salish.

SEMIAHMOO

The Semiahmoo belonged to the coastal division of the Salisham linguistic family. They inhabited Semiahmoo Bay in northwest Washington State and southwest British Columbia. By 1909, no Semiahmoo were enumerated on the American side of the border.

SEMINOLE

The word Seminole is said to have derived from the Spanish word, *cimarrón*, meaning "wild" or "untamed," referring to the fact that they lived in wild, unoccupied areas. It has also been interpreted as "wanderers." It is also said to have derived from the Indian word, *seminolee*, meaning something that is "free," used as an adjective; others ascribe it to a Creek noun meaning "a runaway." The Seminole was a new nation composed of wanderers from the old, mostly Creeks and a number of escaped black slaves. The Creeks-turned-Seminoles were composed primarily of former Creeks from Alabama and Georgia who resisted the intrusion of white settlers into their lands. The big surge of migration began following the sale of the Florida to the United States. Holdouts and refugees from other tribes were also included in the new Indian nation. (Florida was acquired from Spain in 1821.)

Lower Creeks (Miccosukees) began migration into north Florida in the 1710s, and the First Creek settlements in Bay area of Florida were established around 1767. Black slaves also began arriving in Florida, first from the Carolinas and later Georgia and Alabama. Around 1804, the Indian who was to have the most dramatic impact on the relations between Native Americans and white settlers, Osceola, was born in Tallahassee, Alabama. He moved to Florida with his mother and great uncle around 1814. Two years before saw 1812 the beginning of the Creek War and the migration of the Upper Creeks (Muskogees) into Florida. In 1818 Thlonotasassa (Thlonoto-Sassa) was settled by approximately two hundred Seminoles.

Whites were determined to drive all Indians from Florida. The presence of fugitive slaves among their midst further fueled that determination. There were to be three Seminole wars. The first lasted from 1817 to 1818. With the Treaty of Moultrie Creek, the Seminole were removed from their Florida homelands and confined to a reservation on Florida's west coast that extended about thirty miles north of Tampa Bay and away from the coast line. Also established were six separate, small reservations in north Florida for six Apalachicola chiefs. Fort Brooke was established at Tampa Bay and ready for use in June of the following year to help insure peace between the settlers and the Indians. It would remain a part of Tampa Bay and west coast history for over fifty years.

The Seminoles of Florida were to be included in the execution of the Indians Removal Act of 1830. A small group of Seminoles was coerced into signing a removal treaty in 1832.* In 1834, 3,824 Indians were removed. The majority, however, declared the treaty illegitimate and refused to leave. Fighting broke out into the protracted Second Seminole War that lasted from 1835 to 1842 led Chief Osceola. As in the first war, fugitive slaves fought beside the Seminoles. Thousands of lives were lost in addition to the financial cost to the government of some forty to sixty million dollars—ten times the amount allotted for Indian removal. Osceola was captured in late 1837 and died soon thereafter at Fort Moultrie, South Carolina, on January 30, 1838.

Coacoochee assumed leadership and on July 3, 1841, he led his people on board a prison ship in Tampa. By March 1842, three thousand Seminoles had been moved west. One of the principal groups still resisting was the Ochlockonee band led by Pascofa. He finally surrendered in December 1842 and was put on board a boat to Port Leon on the St. Mark's River south of Tallahassee for the journey west, ending the Second Seminole War.

Still a few Seminoles remained in the impenetrable Everglades. They fought the Third Seminole War that lasted from 1855 to 1858 as the government attempted to drive them out. In the end, the Federal government paid the remaining Seminoles to move.

The opening of the Tamiami Trail that cuts through the Everglades in 1928 exposed once hidden Seminole villages to tourists and developers. The first state reservation in Florida was established in 1930, consisting of 99,200 acres of wilderness in the Ten Thousand Islands region, and in 1934 Big Cypress Reservation of 104,800 acres of swamp and marsh was set aside—over half receded to the government in 1951 for a drainage project. The Seminole Tribe of Florida was incorporated in 1957, and in 1962 the Miccosukee Tribe of Indians of Florida. It was not until 1985 the Tampa Seminole Reservation was established.

*With the treaty of Payne's Landing, Florida, the Ocklawaha River on May 9, 1832, the Seminole ceded all their lands in Florida. The treaty also required that the over four thousand Seminoles leave Florida for Indian Territory within three years. The Black Seminoles and any others with any African blood were to remain behind to be sold into slavery.

The names of individual Seminole towns, bands, and villages are listed here because so many frequently appear as distinct tribes in the literature, making them difficult to identity.

TOWNS, VILLAGES AND BANDS

Ahapopka
Ahosulga
Alachua
Alafiers
Alapaha
Alligator
Alouko
Apukasasocha
Asapalaga
Attapulgas
Beech Creek
Big Cypress Swamp
Big Hammock
Bowlegs' Town
Bucker Woman's Town
Burges Town
Calusahatchee
Capola
Catfish Lake
Chefixico's Old Town
Chetuckota
Chiaha
Chicuchatti
Choconikla
Chohalaboohhulka
Chokoukla
Coe Hadjo's Town
Cohowofooche
Cow Creek
Cuscowilla
Etanie
Etotulga
Fisheating Creek
Fowl Town
Hatchcalamocha Hiamonee

Hitchapuksassi
Hitchitipusy
Homosassa
John Hicks' Town
Jolee
Lochchiocha
Loksachumpa
McQueen's Village
Miami River
Mikasuki
Mosquito Indians
Mulatto Girl's Town
Negro Town
New Mikasuky
Notasulgar
Ochisialgi
Ochuceulga
Ochupocrassa
Ocilla
Oclackonayahe
Oclawaha
Ohathtokhouchy
Okehumpkee
Oktahatke
Oponays
Owassissas
Payne's Town
Pea Creek Band
Picolata
Pilaklikaha
Pilatka
Phillimees
PinderTown
Red Town
Sampala

Santa Fé
Sarasota
Seccherpoga
Seleuxa
Sitarky
Spanawatka
Suwanee
Talahassee
Talofa Okhase
Taluachapko-apopka
Tattowhehally
Toctoethla
Tohopekaliga
Toloawathla
Toponanaulka
Totstalahoeetska
Tuckagulga
Tuslalahockaka
Wacahoota
Wakasassa
Wasupa
Wechotookme
Weechitokha
Welika
Wewoka
Willanoucha
Withlacoochee
Withlacoocheetalofa
Withlako
Yalacasooche
Yalaka
Yolanar
Yumersee (Yamasee)

DUNLAWTON

An attack by Seminole Indians on December 26, 1835, initiated the Second Seminole War. The Indians climbed the lighthouse the Ponce Inlet Lighthouse, smashed all the glass in the lantern, set fire to the wooden stairs, and absconded with the lamp reflectors. Coácoochee (Wildcat), the son of the Seminole Leader King Philip, wore one of the reflectors as a headdress at the Battle of Dunlawton three weeks later. (The inlet where the Ponce Inlet Lighthouse stands has been known as one of the most treacherous in the southeast. Ponce Inlet was originally called Mosquito Inlet.)

In early January 1836, the Seminoles burned two neighboring plantations, Bulowville and Damietta. A company of Mosquito Roarers under Major Benjamin Putnam in pursuit of the Indians was defeated in the Battle of Dunlawton Plantation, a sugar plantation on the Halifax River, on January 17. The

Mosquito Roarers militia was organized by residents of Mosquito (later Volusia) County prior to the Second Seminole War. (Florida was admitted as 27th state March 3, 1845.)

HATCHEE-LUSTEE (SECOND SEMINOLE WAR)

The Army's 2nd Brigade, which included the Marines, and the Creeks under the command of Marine Commandant Col. Archibald Henderson engaged the Seminole in the Great Cypress Swamp across the Hatchee-Lustee Creek (Muskogee for "Black Creek") on January 28, 1837. The soldiers and marines were forced to swim across the deep 20-yard-wide stream or walk across the logs floating on the water.

The Battle of the Hatchee-Lustee was the Marines' largest battle of the war. Six Marines were killed or died of their wounds. The battle led to talks with the Seminole chiefs who agreed to an armistice that was signed March 6 and to be removed to a reservation. Two important leaders, Osceola and Sam Jones (Opoica of Arpeika, under var. spellings), did not sign the armistice and were violently opposed to relocation. They broke into the holding camp at Fort Brooke in early June and led away the 700 Seminoles who had surrendered. The war continued for another five years.

BLACK SEMINOLE REBELLION

Black Seminole Rebellion that lasted from 1835 to 1838 and resulted in the deaths of 400 whites. From 935-1,265 blacks participated, of which about four hundred were plantation slaves. In the end, five hundred emigrated West with Indians; some ninety plus were caught and reenslaved; and hundreds more were forced to surrender to slavery. The number of casualties is unknown.

SENECA

The Seneca, called "Keepers of the Western Door," inhabited a large region of western New York State. As a member of the federation of Iroquois-speaking Indian nations known as the League of Great Peace, they occupied the lands farthest to the west beyond the Finger Lakes up to and south of Lake Erie. The Seneca were also the largest by far of the Six Nations.

From their position to the west, the Seneca were the last to feel the pressure of settlers and speculators hungry for Indian lands. They came out on the loosing side in the American War for Independence, and their prestige and dominions took a sharp turn for the worse thereafter. Divided between sites on Buffalo Creek (the future Buffalo, New York) and on the Allegheny on the New York-Pennsylvania border, they watched as the white man siphoned off Iroquois lands. Their turn came in the Treaty of Big Tree on September 16, 1796, when the Morris family took all but 200,000 acres of the Seneca's four million acres for $100,000 or three cents an acre. They were left with ten scattered reservations, six of which contained 1,280 to 10,240 acres; two with 26,880 acres; an Allegheny reservation of 46,080 acres; and a Buffalo Creek reservation of 81,920 acres. The Onondaga and Cayuga, who had been guests of the Seneca, moved to the Mohawk reservation on Grand River.

The black gold prevalent on Seneca land became an item of trade among the Indians before the end of the eighteenth century. The Senecas found the oil floating on ponds and creeks. They would place a blanket over the water to soak up the oil and then ring it out into a container.

Although some Seneca remained in New York, the vast majority migrated west to the Ohio country at the end of the eighteenth century where they remained until February 1831. That year they signed a treaty by which they gave up a sizable portion of fertile Ohio grasslands for the unknown beyond the Mississippi as part of Jackson's great removal. They were bound for territory north of the country of the eastern Cherokees and east of the Neosho River.

The Ohio Senecas, along with some Delawares, began their trek west in November 1831—down the Miami River to Cincinnati and by steam boat to St. Louis. From St. Louis they traveled west by wagon making camp on Missouri's Cuivre River (near Troy, Missouri, in Lincoln County some 30 miles NW of St. Louis.

Some refused to ride the steamboat and went overland through Indiana. Worn by the their journey, they halted at Muncitown and had to beg food for survival. Finally a contingent of them were brought west to join the others on the banks of the Cuivre. The Senecas and Delawares were herded onto wagons to continue their journey west. The government hoped to get them to their new homes by Spring planting season. Many had already become sick, and the harsh winter followed by swollen creeks and rivers brought more sickness, deaths and depredations as Indians marched west across Missouri. On July 4, 1832 the Seneca and Delaware Indians of Ohio reached their designated home on the Elk River. It became the first Indian settlement in what would become the state of Oklahoma. It was the first of the Indian removals.

A few Indians continued to reside in Ohio, including Senecas and Shawnees at Lewistown; Shawnees at Hog Creek and Wapakoneta; and Ottawas at Branchard's Fork and Oquanoxa. Their voluntary exodus was to begin in the Spring of 1832. It was not until September that they were on their way. November 18 found them camped on the Missouri River. On the last day of November they passed through the town of Independence, Missouri. Twenty miles further west in Kansas was the future home of the Shawnees. Not only tired, sick, and cold, many were half drunk thanks to those whites ever ready to make a few cents selling the Indians whisky. Ottawa land was forty miles farther on, but they refused to continue. They would stay with the Shawnees, at least for while.

Joint owners of land in extreme southwestern Kansas, the Seneca ceded the land to the government in 1867. Together with the Tuscarora, some Wyandot, and remnants of the Erie, they were given a reservation in northeastern Oklahoma. For more see Iroquois League.

WYOMING, PENNSYLVANIA, MASSACRE*

The Wyoming Valley of Pennsylvania was the site of what has been called the Wyoming Massacre that occurred during the American Revolutionary War. A Tory force of some one hundred men and 600 Iroquois, led by the Seneca war chief Sayenqueraghta, was assembled at Fort Niagara by Major John Butler. (Some accounts put the number of warriors as high as 1,200.) On June 30, 1778, they killed or captured eight men and boys as they moved south into the Wyoming Valley near present-day Wilkes-Barre.

Butler then demanded and received the surrender of Wintermoot's Fort and Jenkins' Fort on July 2. The following day he demanded of Colonel Nathan Denison the surrender of all Continental forts in the area. Denison and Colonel Zebulon Butler (no relation) with a Connecticut militia force of nearly four hundred decided to attack rather than give in to Tory demands. The battle was fought July 3 on Abraham's Creek near Wintermoot's Fort. The number of Americans killed have been put between 227 and 301, including prisoners. The total number of Tory and Indian casualties was probably less than twenty. Formal surrender took place late the afternoon of July 4. Immediately thereafter, the looting began. A monument in the town of Wyoming marks the gravesite of the victims.

ONOQUAGA AND CHERRY VALLEY*

In October 1778 during the Revolutionary War, New York Governor George Clinton requested General Washington to have the Iroquois villages at Onaquaga and neighboring Unadilla destroyed because they were being used as bases of operation by the British and their Indian allies. Onoquaga was located in southern New York State just north of the border with Pennsylvania on the Susquehanna River. Continental soldiers and militia garrisoned at Cherry Valley, a settlement on the southern edge of the Mohawk Valley, under the command of Colonel Thomas Hartley, destroyed Onoquaga and the surrounding fields and killed the children that were hiding in the groves and fields. In retaliation, a combined force of British Loyalists led by Colonel John Butler and upwards of 300 Seneca warriors, as well as Mohawk Chief Joseph Brant, attacked the camp at Cherry Valley on November 11 and killed sixteen Continental soldiers and militia. The Seneca also killed and scalped thirty-two Indians and loyalist townspeople, including women and children.

*Major General Sullivan's expedition the summer of 1779 brought the war to the Iroquois. For more see Iroquois League.

Of Note

Handsome Lake (Ganioda'ya), a prophet and half-brother Chief Cornplanter was a recipient of a letter from Thomas Jefferson in 1802. Handsome Lake had been among those who had traveled to Washington to meet with the President.

SENECÚ DEL SUR PUEBLO

The Senecú de Sur (of the South) Pueblo, also known as San Antonio de Senecú, was of the Piro Group of the Kiowa-Tanoan stock. It was established in Texas by Piro Indians who formerly occupied the Senecú Pueblo of New Mexico. For more see Pueblo Peoples.

SENECÚ PUEBLO

Senecú (Senecu) Pueblo (pronounced Sen-eh-COO) was of the Piro Group (pronounced PEE-ro) of the Kiowa-Tanoan stock and inhabited an area south of Socorro, New Mexico. Swanton states that the Piro was comprised of the Senecú and the Mexicanized Senecú del Sur (of the South). Gallegos does not list the Piro nor the Senecú. Others identify two divisions within the Piro of New Mexico: one inhabiting the Rio Grande Valley from present San Marcial in Socorro County north to about fifty miles from Albuquerque adjoining the land of the Tiwa Pueblo, and the second division (Tompiros and Salineros) occupying an area east of the Rio Grande River in the vicinity of the salt lagoons (salinas). For more see Pueblo Peoples.

SENIJEXTEE

The Senijextee or Lake Indians belonged to inland division of the Salishan linguistic group and are generally considered identical to the Lahanna of Lewis and Clark. They inhabited both sides of the Columbia River from Kettle Falls to the Canadian border, the valley of the Kettle River, and an area near the mouth of the Kootenay River in Washington State and the region of Arrow Lakes, British Columbia— thus the name Lake Indians. It was a large area to be occupied by a population of only somewhere around five hundred persons in 1780. The Senijextee were subsequently placed on the Colville Reservation. For more see Kalispel-Pend d'Orielle.

SERRANO

The Serrano Indians were inhabitants of an area in the San Bernardino Range, the San Grbriel Mountains or Sierra Madre west to Mount San Antonio, and possibly in the lowlands south of the Sierra Madre in California. They belonged to the Shoshonean division of the Uto-Aztecan linguistic stock that included the Kitanemuk, Vanyume, Kawaiisu, and Alliklik.

SETAUKET

The Setauket was a division of the Montauk and a member of the Algonquian linguistic group. They lived on Long Island, New York, on the north shore from Stony Brook to the Wading River. For more see Montauk Peoples and Delaware.

SEUVARIT UTE

The Seuvarit or Sheberetch was a subdivision of the Ute and lived in the Castle Valley and on the headwaters of the San Rafael River in east central Utah. For more see Ute.

SEWEE

The Sewee were believed to be of Siouan stock. They inhabited the lower course of the Santee river and the coast west to the divide of the Ashley River around present Monks Corner in Berkeley County, South Carolina. It is believed that the Yamasee War ended Sewee identity as a separate tribe and that remnants were incorporated into the Catawba.

SHACKOCONIA

The Shackoconia was a sub-tribe of the Manahoac of Virginia or a member of the Manahoac Confederacy that lived on the south bank of the Rappahannock River in Spotsylvania County.

SHAKI

The Shaki tribe (not to be confused with the Shàki) was listed in Jefferson's *Notes on the State of Virginia*. Hutchins (1768) reported a population of 200 warriors living on the banks of the Wabash River near Fort Ouiatonon. For more see "Aborigines," Appendix D.

SHÀKI

The Shàki tribe (not to be confused with the Shaki) was listed in Jefferson's *Notes on the State of Virginia*. Croghan (1759), Bouquet (1764) and Hutchins (1768) reported population figures between 200-550 warriors. They lived near Puans Bay on Lake Michigan. For more see "Aborigines," Appendix D.

SHAKORI

The Shakori or Shoccoree belonged to the southern division of Siouan linguistic family of the East. A people continually on the move, they were closely associated with the Eco. They are generally associated with the areas about the Shocco and Big Shocco creeks in present Vance, Warren, and Franklin counties of North Carolina. See the Eno and Keyauwee. It is believed that they moved south into South Carolina with the Eco after 1716 and that they were subsequently absorbed into the Catawba. In a much earlier period, they may have lived near the Enoree River. The Shakori/Chicora have also been linked with the Sissipahaw.

SHALEE

The Shalee or Chalee (also Ootlashoots or Oat-lash-shoots) was a band of the Tushepaw or Salish. Under the various names, they appear in the Drake's Enumeration and in the Journals of Lewis and Clark. For more see the Salish.

SHALLALAH

The Shallalah encountered Lewis and Clark and the Corps of Discovery. Drake reports them living below the Columbia River in Oregon, next to the Cookkoo-oose. (Not to be confused with Shallalah Creek within the Cumberland Mountains of Kentucky.)

SHALLATTOO

The Shallattoo reportedly lived on the Columbia River, above the Skaddal in Washington State.

SHASTA

The Shasta or Chasta belonged to the Shantan Division of the Hokan stock. They lived along the Klamath River generally from the Indian and Thompson creeks to the mouth of Fall Creek; also the areas of the Scott River and the Shasta River in California and the north side of the Siskiyous in Oregon on the affluents of the Rogue River, the Stewart River and Little Butte Creek. They were often confused with the Chasta Costa/Chastacosta of the Athabascan linguistic stock. Treaty references to the single word "Chasta" with a "c" only further confuses the identity of the participants.

SHAWNEE

The Shawnee belonged to the Algonquian linguistic stock and came to inhabit the east-central lands of southern Ohio, West Virginia, and Kentucky. Compared to many of the woodlands tribes, the Shawnee was a relatively small tribe of wanderers comprised of five groups or divisions, all known to be warlike. Some reports put the Shawnee population at only twenty-five hundred people. For a small tribe, they produced a lot of history. Disease, war, and dispersals took their toll on the Shawnee in the seventeenth century.

DIVISIONS
Chillicothe
Hathawekela or Thawekila
Kispoko
Mekoche
Pekowi

At one time, there had been a sixth group, the Shauwonoa, as well as a number of additional clans that had been all but destroyed. The remnants merged into the other five groups and the still healthy clans. For a relatively small tribe, they spread themselves thin over a very wide area. As a result they became acquainted with many of the native peoples who inhabited the land east of the Mississippi.

During the mid-1600s, the Shawnee inhabited the area around the Cumberland and Ohio rivers. The Shawanoe were the earliest known occupants of Kentucky. It was the Shawnee who gave the state of its name. Kentuckee was Shawnoese for "head or long river." The Shawnee were defeated at the Battle of Sandy Point, Ohio, by the Iroquois and left Kentucky after 1673 and settled about the Illinois River and the Savannah in South Carolina; some the upper part of the Carolinas. By the mid-eighteenth century most regrouped in present Ohio, Pennsylvania, and Alabama. They also lived among other tribes, including the Creek, the Choctaw, the Delaware, and the tribes of present Illinois.

The Shawnee migrated northward into the Ohio country in the mid-1750s and occupied lands adjacent to the Wyandot on the Scioto, Mad, the Great Miami rivers, and the upper waters of the Maumee. The Shawnee-Wyandot alliance served the two tribes well over the coming years.

About the same time, the Shawnee of Ohio formed a loose confederacy with the Mingo and the Delaware based at Logstown. The Ohio League as it was called was a matter of self-protection from the French and the Ottawa to the north and northwest and the British and the Iroquois to the east and northeast. The period of 1750 to 1795, ending with the Battle of Fallen Timbers and the Treaty of Greenville, was one of war and preparations for war. George Rogers Clark led a force against them at Pickaway on the Grand Miami and defeated them with heavy losses. The principal war chief during much of the period was Blue Jacket, who was born about 1740 and rose quickly in the esteem of this fellow warriors.

With the Treaty of Fort Stanwix in 1768, the Six Nations ceded their claims to Kentucky and Western Pennsylvania and, in effect, replaced the 1763 Proclamation Line with a new boundary on the Ohio.

(In 1775 the Cherokee ceded most of their claims to Kentucky.) The Shawnee were given no say in the matter. To the outside world they had lost all claim to the land to the Iroquois. The Shawnee did not see it that way and would fight to defend their claim.

The Shawnee were determined to regain their lands. The colonists, under the guise of Lord Dunmore, Governor of Virginia, were determined to clear Kentucky of all Indians. What ensued was the War for Kentucky. The war was a singular success for the colonists, and the Shawnee were forced to sue for peace. The agreement opened the land to an influx of new settlers and land speculators. But not all the Shawnee accepted the agreement forcing a division in the tribe that gradually pulled the two sides apart from the summer of 1775 through the winter of 1776. Cornstalk and those who wanted only peace headed northeast among the Delaware on the Tuscarawas River. In early 1777 Blue Jacket and those who vowed to continue the fight established a new town to the northwest in the more inaccessible regions of the Ohio. Blue Jacket would find his greatest victory in the defeat of Arthur St. Clair in 1791.

With the beginning of the American Revolutionary War, the Shawnee hope to win back their lands in Kentucky with the aid of the British, as did almost all the Ohio Indians, but it would be to no avail. The Shawnee, whose homes were nearest the front lines, suffered repeated losses of their homes and possessions. At the conclusion of the war, the Shawnee were forced to concede the loss of Kentucky. With the Treaty of Paris in 1783, the British ceded the Ohio Territory to the United States. The Shawnee and other Ohio Indians were now forced to fight for their lands north of the Ohio—a fight they would ultimately loose.

A treaty was concluded with the Shawnee in January 1786 at Fort Finney at the Mouth of the Great Miami on the northwestern bank of the Ohio by which the Shawnee were forced to relinquish almost their entire traditional homeland in southern and eastern Ohio. The treaty clearly identified the lands that were allotted to them. Most of the Shawnee disavowed the treaty and called for war. They were joined by the Mingo and by several hundred Lakes Indians of the Potawatomi, Ojibwa, and Ottawa, but the first bloody blow was struck in October by some eight hundred Kentuckians and would continue to rage until the defeat of the Ohio Indians by General Anthony Wayne at Fallen Timbers, August 20, 1794. The Treaty of Greenville followed in 1795. Blue Jacket's defeats of Josiah Harmar in 1790 and Arthur St. Clair in 1791 meant little except as stories to tell the children and grandchildren. Blue Jacket died at his village on the Detroit River in early 1808.

The second war for Ohio began in the summer of 1809 primarily as a result of the Treaty of Fort Wayne by which then Governor William Henry Harrison grabbed large tracts of land from the Indians in Ohio led by Tecumseh who made his home on the Wabash. He too tried to assemble a great Indian confederacy to fight the white man. Tecumseh is generally acknowledged as one of the most striking and influential men of his generation. His twin brother, Tenskwatawa or the Prophet, led the confederacy in the Battle of Tippecanoe in November 1811 that ended in a Shawnee defeat although American forces suffered a greater number of casualties.

Tecumseh became a force in the War of 1812, particularly at Fort Meigs on the Maumee River in May 1813. He died in battle on the Thames River in Canada fighting with the British in early 1813. William Henry Harrison was again the victor. With the end of the War of 1812 and Tecumseh's death, the Indian war for the Ohio country was over.

WAR FOR KENTUCKY

The War for Kentucky or Lord Dunmore's War as it is called began with sporadic raids by settlers and Indians alike in the spring of 1774 that resulted in a relatively low number of casualties on both sides.

But the incidents brought Lord Dunmore, Governor of Virginia, to the decision to clear all of Kentucky of the Shawnee. Virginia had laid claim to the Kentucky lands early in the colonial period.

On his own authority, Dunmore called out the Virginia militia on June 10, 1774. In a two-pronged advance, Colonel Andrew Lewis moved in from Western Virginia with a thousand men. Dunmore moved to the northwest with a force of two thousand and established his base of operations at Pittsburgh. Chief Cornstalk of the Shawnee assembled a force of about one thousand warriors composed of Shawnee, Ottawa, Delaware, Wyandot, and Miami and crossed the Ohio to engage the Americans .

The fighting began in earnest with the Battle of Point Pleasant, Ohio, at the juncture of the Kanawha and the Ohio rivers, the future site of Fort Randolph. After a determined fight that lasted throughout the day on October 10, 1774, the weight of numbers and superior weaponry drove the Indian alliance from the field in a smashing victory by Lewis and his frontiersmen.

Cornstalk met with Lord Dunmore under a flag of truce at Camp Charlotte in present Hocking County. The Shawnee gave up their rights to hunt south of the Ohio River. The agreement opened the land to an influx of new settlers and land speculators. The agreement also caused a division in the ranks of the Shawnee, Cornstalk and the peace faction on one side and Blue Jacket and the war faction on the other.

The brief, but brutal, confrontation left a number of innocent casualties, among them the family of the friendly Mingo leader, Oneida chief Tachnedorus (or Tah-gah-ju-te), known as John Logan. One of the innocents was Logan's pregnant sister who was hung by her thumbs and horribly mutilated. He later sent a speech by letter to Dunmore. Logan spoke of the plight that had befallen all of America's Native Peoples.

> I appeal to any White man to say, if ever he entered Logan's cabin hungry, and he gave him not meat; if ever he came cold and naked, and he clothed them not. During the course of the last long and blood war Logan remained idle in his cabin, an advocate for peace. Such was my love for the Whites, that my countrymen pointed as they passed, and said, "Logan is the friend of White men. I had even thought to have lived with you, but for the injuries of one man. Colonel [Michael] Cresap, the last spring, in cold blood, and unprovoked, murdered all the relations of Logan, not even sparing my women and children. There runs not a drop of my blood in the veins of any living creature. This called on me for revenge. I have sought it: I have killed many: I have fully glutted my vengeance; for my country I rejoice at the beams of peace. But do not harbor a thought that mine is the joy of fear. Logan never felt fear. He will not run on his heel to save his life. Who is there to mourn for Logan" Not one.

Thomas Jefferson himself declared that Logan had been long "distinguished as a friend of the whites" and included the letter in his *Notes on the State of Virginia.*

BATTLE OF TIPPECANOE

A Native American tribal confederacy led by Tecumseh (1768? - 1813), chief of the Shawnee, and his brother Tenskwatawa, called the Prophet, demanded that white settlers leave the lands of the Indians in the Old Northwest territory. Maj. General William Henry Harrison, then Governor of the Indiana Territory (see Treaty of Greenville), gathered a force of 300 regular infantry and 650 militia, mostly mounted, with some Delaware scouts in a preemptive foray up the Wabash River in the autumn of 1811. Their destination was the Shawnee principal town of Prophetstown at the mouth of the Tippecanoe River. Tecumseh was away in the south attempting to build a Indian confederacy against the whites. In the meantime his brother had assembled a band of warriors at Prophetstown to await further direction from Tecumseh, but he had been told to avoid a confrontation.

After observing Harrison's movements, the Prophet ordered an attack on the camp about a mile from the town at dawn on November 7, 1811. After furious hand-to-hand fighting, a calvary charge drove the Indians from the field. The Americans, who outnumbered the Indians by a margin of two to one, lost 39 men killed and 151 wounded of whom 29 later died. (Another account puts the number of casualties as 49-50 killed and 129 wounded.) Although the number of Indian casualties could not be determined, the aggregate was considerably less. Following the battle, Harrison ordered the destruction of Prophetstown and Indians' winter store of food for the winter that had been left undefended as the Indians hastened to make their escape.

Harrison had cited earlier, undefined Indian attacks on white settlers in the Ohio country as his reason for marching into Indian territory, but subsequent events and Harrison's own words lent credence to the charge that he was only looking for an excuse. The Indian's battle for their homelands in the Northwest Territory was effectively over, but the Battle of Tippecanoe put the Tecumseh and his allies squarely on the side of the British in the forthcoming War of 1812.

BATTLE ON THE THAMES RIVER

With the advance of an American force of thirty-five hundred regulars and militia under Maj. General Henry Harrison during the War of 1812, the British commandant at Detroit, Colonel Henry A. Proctor took his force of about 800 soldiers and retreated north down the Thames River into Canada despite pleadings of Tecumseh to stand and fight. Tecumseh, with 500 warriors, followed reluctantly. Proctor finally stopped and took up a defensive position on the river, north of Lake Erie near Chatham, Ontario; but his force was routed by the sustained attacks by Harrison's mounted calvary on October 5, 1813. Tecumseh was left dead on the field, a leader with the countenance all men respected, Indian and White alike. The battle also left twelve British soldiers and twenty-two wounded. The Indian lost thirty-three killed, in addition to those that died during the retreat. The battle was a stirring victory for the Americans in the war with Britain and destroyed the Indian threat in the Northwest. (Shortly after the battle, Harrison resigned his commission because of a falling out with the War Department. The vacated rank of major general went to Andrew Jackson.)

REMOVAL WEST

The first permanent white settlement in what became the state of Missouri was Cape Girardeau in the southeast corner of the state. It was founded by Louis Lorimier in 1795, an Indian trader who had been in the area as early since 1787 after working his trade in Ohio and Indiana. In 1793 a considerable number of Shawnee and a few Delaware from Ohio and Indians accepted an offer from Spanish officials of a large grant of land in southeast Missouri as an inducement to emigrate west across the Mississippi. Lorimier wanted the easterners in Missouri as protection against the Osage who were considered less civilized than the Woodland tribes of the East.

With the Treaty of Greenville in 1795, the Shawnee were forced from their homes on the Miami. Part settled upon the Auglaize River in northwestern Ohio; others joined the Delaware on the upper west fork of the White River in present-day Hamilton, Madison, and Delaware Counties in central Indiana; but the majority removed to Missouri.

In Missouri, they settled along Apple Creek and other small tributaries of the Mississippi and by 1812 had located along the Whitewater River as well as the Mississippi itself. About the same time a medicine man and prophet Tenskwatawa stirred up the Shawnee at White River against the whites precipitating an attack by Gen. William Henry Harrison on November 7, 1811. The Indians were almost totally destroyed by Battle of Tippecanoe. More battles followed until the death of Tecumseh, Tenskwatawa's brother. The displacement caused by continual wars with the Americans led to the establishment of what became known as the Lewistown Band of Shawnee after its leader, Quah-tah-wah-peeyah, who the Americans called Colonel Lewis. The Lewistown Band was granted a reserve in western Ohio in 1817 that they shared with an independent band of mixed Seneca and Cayuga Indians. The group became known as the Mixed Band of Seneca and Shawnee around 1831 when they were forced to move west. They negotiated a treaty to exchange their Ohio lands for a reservation in Indian Territory. In 1867, the two groups separated, the Shawnee became the Eastern Shawnees because they were the eastern-most tribe of Shawnees in the territory.

From Charloe on the left bank of the Auglaize River in Paulding County on the western border of Ohio, about 400 Indians under their chief Oquanoxa moved had west to Missouri in 1820. In an agreement reached in 1825, the Shawnee-Delaware lands in southeastern Missouri that had been received from the Spanish government was exchanged for lands at the confluence of the Kansas (Kaw) and Missouri rivers. The Shawnee received a tract of land of some 1,600,000 acres west of Missouri in what would become Kansas Territory. The reservation was from the Missouri River on the east to the Republican River just west of Manhattan about 130 miles on the west and from the Kansas River on the north to about 30 miles south into Miami County. The reservation included parts of present-day Shawnee, Geary, Morris, Waubaunsee, Franklin, Wyandotte, and Miami counties and all of Douglas and Johnson counties. The Delaware reservation north of the Kansas River was about the same size. In 1825 it was the first Indian Territory. (Kansas Territory was the beginning of what was often referred to as the Great American Desert—land no whites wanted.)

The Shawnee began the move to lands of the Kansas reservation in 1828. The Shawnee concentrated south of the Kaw River in what is now southern Wyandotte and northern Johnson counties. They initially settled in the vicinity of Turner, Kansas, in Wyandotte County. Cyprian Chouteau established a trading post about a miles upstream that did a lucrative business with both the Shawnee and the Delaware.

The treaty that provided for the removal of the last group of Shawnees from Ohio was negotiated in Washington in 1831. Joseph Parks who was appointed the interpreter to the assembled Shawnee chiefs. In 1831-1832 the Ohio Shawnees were marched to Kansas in what was their "Trail of Tears." Many died enroute. Parks, variously called Chief and Captain, was a full-blooded Shawnee, mixed blood, or white and captured by Indians a very early age. He was born in 1794 probably in present-day Michigan and raised as a white man by Army General Lewis Cass. For the next several years after the treaty was signed, he remained in Washington as an agent for the Shawnee Nation.

In 1820 a part of the Missouri Shawnee had moved southwest into the fertile lands of eastern Texas. In 1839, the new Republic of Texas cleared out what it called the "rats' nest" of East Texas; and the Shawnee, their homes and crops burned, were driven north into Indian Territory.

SCHOOLS AND MISSIONS

In 1830 Isaac McCoy, a Baptist missionary and surveyor, was hired by the secretary of war to survey a boundary for the Delaware Indians to the north of the Shawnee. The following year he established a Baptist mission for the Shawnee and Delaware Indians with Johnston Lykins and his son-in-law near present-day 53rd and Walmer streets in Johnson County. McCoy also transcribed the Shawnee language and began the production of the *Shawnee Sun (Siwinowe Kesibwi)*, the first native language newspaper and the first printed in Kansas. The mission closed in 1855. (Lykins went on to become the first official mayor of Kansas City.) Between 1834 and 1835, The Society of Friends or Quakers, left Ohio to be able to continue to serve the Shawnee at their new reservation. Construction began in 1836 on the Friends mission near what is today 61st and Hemlock. The mission operated continually until 1871.

In July 1830, a group of Shawnee Indians headed by Chief Fish, a white chief, requested the services of Christian missionaries. The Missionary Society of the Methodist Episcopal Church was established by the Missouri Conference on September 16, 1830, in St. Louis. Their first act of business was to appoint Rev. Thomas Johnson missionary to the Shawnee Indians. Johnson was born in the Shenandoah Valley of Virginia in 1802 and emigrated to Missouri where he married Sarah Davis at Clarksville, Missouri, in 1830. Later that year, Johnson and his new bride arrived at a site near present-day Turner, three miles west of Westport inside Kansas Indian Territory. There he established the first Shawnee Methodist Mission and School in a two-story log building to serve both the Shawnee and the Delaware Indians. (His brother William was appointed missionary to the Kansa Indians. When Joseph Parks returned to Kansas he joined the Methodist church and became actively involved in the Rev. Johnson's mission work and the school.

In 1834 Johnson received the first printing press in Kansas and used it in his educational program. Three years later, he shifted the emphasis of the school to vocational training and enrollment surpassed 35. Johnson taught English and arithmetic to both sexes; home arts to the girls; and agriculture, wagon-making, and crafts to the boys.

In 1838 he recommended to the Methodist missionary society the establishment of a central manual labor school for the benefit of all tribes. The War Department, which administered Indian affairs at the time, agreed to finance it but stipulated that the school be located on Indian lands outside the State of Missouri. (The Indian Bureau of the Interior Department took over the management of Indian affairs in 1849. The Indian Bureau was established with an act of Congress signed into law by President James Monroe on May 25, 1824.)

Johnson chose a location on Shawnee lands southeast of Turner where a branch of the Santa Fe Trail passed through the Shawnee lands. Construction began in January 1839. The Shawnee Methodist Mission and Indian Manual Labor School opened in October 1839 as a boarding school. To the dismay of the Quakers, Johnson used slaves to construct the mission buildings. Indian laborers plowed and enclosed some 400 acres of land that were planted in orchards and gardens that yielded rich harvests, including sufficient grain to feed the herds of livestock.

Indian children of many displaced tribes attended the school to learn basic academics, manual arts, and agriculture. In addition to the Shawnee and Delaware, the school served the children of the Kansa, the Munsee, the Ottawa, the Chippewa, the Otoe, the Osage, the Cherokee, the Peoria, the Kickapoo, the Potawatomi, the Wea, the Gros Ventre, the Omaha, and the Wyandot. In February 1840, sixty students were enrolled. In 1847 Dr. Johnson began a shift toward academic instruction and the institution was renamed the Fort Leavenworth Indian Manual Training School. He established a classical department beginning in August 1848 known as Western Academy that offered courses in Latin and Greek, as well as in English. The academy was directed by Rev. Nathan Scarritt and was opened to both Indian and white children. It was moved to Westport in 1854 where it operated as a private institution that continued to serve Indian children from well-to-do families like William Bent.

In 1854, the Shawnees granted portions of the mission lands and its improvements to the missionary society of the Methodist Episcopal Church, South, on the condition that the church pay the Shawnee $10,000 to use for the education of their children. The next year the Indian Bureau agreed to pay the society $5,000 annually and credit the $10,000 that was due the Shawnees at the rate of $1,000 per year if it would board, clothe, and educate a certain number of Shawnee children at the school. The school was renamed the Shawnee Manual Labor School but continued to educate children from other tribes. The Shawnees became dissatisfied with the arrangement, and over the next several years there various claims of mismanagement. In September 1862, the Shawnee Mission closed and the contract between the Government and the Methodist Episcopal Church ended. Union troops occupied the mission during the Civil War. At the height of its activity, the mission covered some 2,240 with sixteen buildings, including the three large brick structures, which still stand on a

12-acre historic site. School enrollment had reached nearly one hundred and fifty students ranging in age from five to twenty-three. The mission had operated continuously from 1830 to 1862.

KANSAS REMOVAL

In 1845 three bands, the Hathawekela, Kispokotha, and Piqua, that became known as the Absentee Shawnee moved from Kansas to the Canadian River country in Oklahoma. Nine years later in 1854 the Kansas Territory was officially established, and Kansas was ordered cleared of Indians. Encroachment on reservation land had already begun, and in May 1854 Parks returned to Washington where he signed the treaty ceding all but 200,000 acres of the 1,600,000 Shawnee reservation back to the government in exchange for a reservation in Oklahoma. Their Kansas land that was quickly consumed by eager pioneers flocking west. The Shawnee took the remaining land, bounded by the Kansas-Missouri border and the Kansas River, in severalty—200 acres to each individual. By 1870 most of the Shawnee had sold their parcels in Kansas and migrated to Oklahoma. Within three years, Kansas Territory had been substantially cleared of Indians. In 1867 the Shawnee that had been living with the Seneca also removed to Oklahoma where they became known as the Eastern Shawnee. A good number of Shawnee were incorporated into the Cherokee of Oklahoma.

There are presently three federally recognized Shawnee entities: Absentee-Shawnee Tribe of Indians of Oklahoma, Eastern Shawnee Tribe of Oklahoma, and Shawnee Tribe, Oklahoma.

Of Note

—Although a proslavery advocate, 62-year-old Rev. Johnson pledged an oath of allegiance to the Union. As a consequence he was killed by guerrillas who fired through the front door of his Missouri farmhouse. He died January 2, 1865, and was buried in the cemetery of his Shawnee Methodist Mission. Johnson County, Kansas, named in his honor, was organized in 1855 out of a part of the original Shawnee reservation land. Johnson's heirs acquired title to the mission property in 1865.

—When Joseph Park returned to Kansas, he settled on an 1,280 acre farm where he built a two-story brick house in 1845 that stood until 1905 when it was torn down to make room for tennis courts for a local private high school (Pembroke Hill). He also joined the Town of Westport Lodge of the Masons. He was the only slavemaster in the Kansas Territory besides the Rev. Johnson. Parks died at the age 65 on April 3, 1859, and was buried in the Indian cemetery near what is now 59th Terrace east of Nieman Road in the city of Shawnee, Kansas. A historical plaque affixed to the oldest building in the old Town of Westport credits him with the title of Captain and of being of mixed white and Indian blood.

—For the years 1832 and 1833 there were four Methodist Indian missions in Kansas, comprising the Indian Missionary District. In 1833 and 1834 it was called the North Indian Mission District.

—On November 24, 1854, Andrew H. Reeder, a Free Stater and first Territorial Governor of Kansas, moved his offices from Fort Leavenworth to the Shawnee Mission. In the summer of 1855 he relocated to Pawnee, Kansas, adjoining the Fort Riley Military Reservation, where he convened the first Territorial Legislature. The proslavery party, in turn, convened what has been called the "bogus legislature" back at the Shawnee Mission and adopted a proslavery constitution.

SHEASTUKLE

The Sheastukle lived on the Pacific coast south of the Columbia River in Oregon near the present-day town of Yachats, west of Corvallis in Lincoln County. Drake places the Sheastukle on the coast in reference to the Youitz but gives no information on the Youitz.

SHEHEKE

The Sheheke tribe, as Lewis and Clark called the people, was encountered by the Corps of Discovery living along the Missouri River. No additional information is available.

SHINNECOCK

The Shinnecock, the People of the Shore or People of the Stony Shore, was a division of the Montauk and a member of the Algonquian linguistic group. They lived along the coast of Eastern Long Island from Shinnecock Bay to Montauk Point. Shinnecock is the name under which the Montauk are recognized by the State of New York. For more see Montauk

SHIPAULOVI HOPI

Shipaulovi was Hopi village on the Second or Middle Mesa of Arizona. See Hopi.

SHIVWITS

The Shivwits, used in both the singular and the plural, was a band of Southern Paiute. They inhabited the Shivwits Plateau. In the early 1900s, the Shivwits, having refused to go to the Uintah Reservation that was established by President Lincoln in 1861, accepted tracts of reserve land in southern Utah—along with the Kaibab, Cedar City, Indian Peaks, Kanosh, and Koosharem bands. For more see Paiute and Southern Paiute.

SHOALWATER

The Shoalwater inhabited Washington Territory around Shoalwater Bay. No additional information is available.

SHOHOPANAITI

The Shohopanaiti or Connonwood Bannock was a subdivision of the Bannock of Idaho, but not well defined. For more see the Bannock.

SHOSHOKO

The Shoshoko (also Shoshokie and Root Diggers) belonged to the Shoshoni-Comanche dialectic group of the Shoshonean Division of the Uto-Aztecan linguistic family, but the Shoshoko was not a separate, independent tribe as far as can be determined. Other than their linguistic connection, nothing has been established with any certitude. Catlin writes of "the Shoshokies or root diggers" in the same sentence that he writes of the "Shoshonees," implying two separate entities. His description might suggest members of the Bannock tribe of "Diggers." Irving writes of the "Shoshokoes, or Root Diggers" as a branch of the great Snake tribe (Northern Shoshoni). The National Forest Service (Ogden) speaks of the local "Shoshone tribe" referred to by white pioneers as "root diggers;" the National Park Service (Yellowstone) of "root diggers - a Shoshone group of the Yellowstone Plateau." Clark writes of the "Shoshokoe" of Utah and Nevada. Curtis paints the Root Digger camp as that of the Yakima. Others write of the Southern Paiute "Diggers" of roots in Utah. Those writers dealing with the Native Americans of California write of the "Root Diggers" without any correlation to one of the better known tribes.

It can be stated with a fair degree of confidence that the Shoshoko root diggers were a poor people, unpretentious, and peaceful that lived in Northern Utah and Southern Idaho, possibly ranging into Montana. Best guess is that they were American Indians better known as the Western Shoshoni or Bannock. It should be noted that all the groups referred to except the Yakima and the vast majority of the Indians of California were related and are often confused. For more on the various writes, see the Notes and Sources.

SHOSHONI

The Shoshoni (also Shoshone) belonged to the Shoshoni-Comanche dialectic group of the Shoshonean Division of the Uto-Aztecan linguistic family. They inhabited parts of Montana, Idaho, Nevada, Wyoming, Utah, and California. The appellation "Snake" has also been applied to the Shoshoni, but not to all groups equally.

At their height, the Shoshoni numbered about fifteen thousand souls and ranged across a wide geographical area that included many distinct life styles. As a result, their classification has been anything but precise or consistent. There are almost as many classifications today as chroniclers. They are classified by location, region, drainage area, the food they eat, and by their respective chiefs or headmen. As a consequence, a single subgroup or band may appear in up to five different categories, giving the appearance of multiple bands. Also, many subgroups are treated as major groups or divisions rather than as a subgroup, and classifications by location offer their own unique problems. Additional confusion arises because of similarities in the language between several subgroups of Shoshoni and members of the Bannock and the Northern Paiute tribes.

The Shoshoni signed the Fort Laramie Treaty of 1851 along with the other tribes of the Upper Plains. For the most part, the Shoshoni peacefully acceded to white demands and served courageously and valiantly for the army in the government's attempt to bring other tribes into line. During the building the transcontinental railroad east from Sacramento, the Central Pacific Railroad negotiated special treaties with the Paiute and Shoshoni granting rights to ride the trains "whenever they saw fit."

Swanton reports the Shoshoni as falling within one of two major groups or divisions, Northern Shoshoni and Western Shoshoni, whereas the later literature generally places the Shoshoni in one three major groups of divisions with a number of major subgroups that are often treated separately. This approach, which is outlined here, appears to help simply the classification process.

EASTERN SHOSHONI

Also known as the Wyoming Shoshoni, Wind River Shoshoni, Eastern Snakes. The smallest of the three major divisions, the Eastern Shoshoni, which are generally associated with the state of Wyoming, inhabited the mountains and plains from the Wind River to Fort Bridger and astride the Oregon Trail. As a group they are also identified as Chief Washakie's Band (Washikee). Under the earlier classification, the Eastern Shoshoni were included among the Northern Shoshoni. At some point in time, a number of the bands of the Northern Shoshoni moved beyond the mountain plateaus and into the Plains and adopted much of the Plains culture. It was this group that has been separately identified as the Eastern Shoshoni.

They claimed the lands near Elk Mountains at the northern tip of the Medicine Bow Mountains. They had to give way to the Lakota who moved west in overwhelming numbers. Enemies they were, the Lakota, the Snake, and the Crow of the Plains, but it was said that they were honorable enemies in which they probed each other's lands to steal horses and out of a sense of adventure and to prove their manhood and fighting skills—not like their relations with the white man.

The Eastern Shoshoni have been subdivided between Plains and Mountains and also by the food they eat, Buffalo, Sheep, and Doves, but not to be confused with the Sheepeaters. (See below)

The Eastern Shoshoni and the Bannock Indians (not the Bannock Creek Shoshoni of the Northern-Northwest division) signed the Treaty of Fort Bridger on July 3, 1868, by which they ceded all rights to their lands in Idaho and Wyoming, except for the land that became the Wind River Reservation in Fremont County in the northwest Wyoming.

The reservation subsequently became home to the Eastern Shoshoni and the Northern Arapaho. The tribal governments of the two tribes continue to operate separately.

Many of the Eastern Shoshoni served as scouts for the army. Some three hundred Snake and Crow scouts fought with General George Crook in the 1870s to subdue Crazy Horse and the last of the Lakota and Northern Cheyenne who remained outside the reservation system.

WESTERN SHOSHONI

The Western Shoshoni, the most numerous of the three major divisions, who are generally associated with the state of Nevada, inhabited several hundred villages in central and western Idaho, northwestern Utah, central and northeastern Nevada, Oregon, and the lands in California about Death Valley and Panamint Valley. They were generally grouped by area, for example, the Spring, Snake, and Antelope valleys, Humboldt River, and Grouse Creek. Eleven different bands are generally reported within the Western division. Three of the bands or subgroups have been routinely treated separately.

A number of bands who lived along the Owyhee River of southeastern Oregon, southwestern Idaho, and the Humbolt River of northeastern Nevada were placed on the Duck Valley Reservation in southwest Idaho and northern Nevada that was established April 16, 1877. Paiute from the lower Weiser country of Idaho and other Northern Paiute families joined the Shoshoni on the reservation. Paddy Cap's Band of Northern Paiute arrived in 1884.

Gosiute (or Goshute, Goshuite)

The Gosiute inhabited the area west and southwest of the Great Salt Lake and about the present-day town of Ibapah, Utah, of northern Utah and eastern Nevada. About 900 in number at their peak, they lived in the valleys and mountains west and southwest of Great Salt Lake. Remnants are located in and around Ibapah, Utah.

Sheepeaters (or Sheep Eaters, Tukuarika, Tukuadüka)

The Sheepeaters inhabited an area extending from what is now Yellowstone National Park to the middle course of the Salmon River. For more see Tukuarika Shoshoni.

Panamint or Koso

The Panamint inhabited parts of eastern California. For more see Koso Shoshoni.

NORTHERN SHOSHONI

The Northern Shoshoni are generally associated with the state of Idaho but ranged into Montana, Utah, and Nevada. The Northern group, under the earlier classification, included the Eastern Shoshoni. References in the literature to the Shoshoni, without further explanation or qualification, generally refer to the Northern Shoshoni, and references to the Northern Shoshoni, without any further description, generally refer to the Indians of the Lemhi subgroup. The Northern and Eastern Shoshoni were the horse and buffalo divisions, and their members lived predominantly in tepees.

The Northern Shoshoni suffered extensively from the emigrants traveling the western trails that crossed their lands; from the Mormon farmers and ranchers, who kept pushing farther and farther north; and from the prospectors and suppliers for Montana gold and responded with raids on farms and ranches and attacks on miners and travelers. The Northern Shoshoni have been divided into four subgroups that are quite frequently treated as major divisions of the Shoshoni.

<u>Pohogue Shoshoni</u>

The Pohogue Shoshoni (Sagebrush people), also called the Fort Hall Indians, lived about the confluence of the Portneuf and Snake rivers with the Bannock. For more see the Pohogue Shoshoni.

<u>Lemhi</u>

The Lemhi lived in the area from the Beaverhead country of southwest Montana to the Salmon River, in western Idaho, and along the Boise and Bruneau rivers. For more see Lemhi Shoshoni.

<u>Agaideka</u>

The Agaideka or Salmon Eaters lived about the principal spawning grounds of the Salmon River. For more see Agaideka Shoshoni.

<u>Northwestern Shoshoni</u>

The Northwestern Shoshoni are generally associated with the state of Utah. The three subgroups lived in the valleys of northern Utah, especially the Weber and Cashe valleys and along the eastern and northern shores of the Great Salt Lake. The Northwestern Shoshoni, many of whom also adopted the Plains Culture, have also been identified as the Southern Shoshoni and the Diggers—the name Southern leading to a great deal of confusion. Other names by which they are known are Mormon Snake, Cache Valley Shoshoni, and Salt Lake Diggers. Following the Bear Creek Massacre, remnants of Chief Bear Hunter's band under Sagwitch and the chiefs of nine other Northwestern Shoshoni bands signed the Treaty of Box Elder at Brigham City, Utah, on July 30, 1863. In accordance with the treaty, they were to receive their annuities at Corinne, Utah, near the mouth of the Bear River. They were later settled on the Fort Hall Reservation in Idaho.

Northwestern Subgroups

- Weber Ute Band or, more properly, Salt Lake Valley Band from the Weber Valley. Also, Chief Little Soldier's Band. They lived in the Ogden, Weber, and Salt Lake valleys.

- Chief Pocatello's Band or Bannock Creek Shoshoni (Kamduka) from Grouse Creek—not to be confused with the Bannock Indians. For more see Bannock Creek Shoshoni.

- Chief Bear Hunter's Band from Bear Creek and Bear River. Chief Bear Hunter was the principal war chief of the Northwestern Shoshoni and was killed at the Bear River Massacre.

BEAR RIVER MASSACRE

In 1862 Shoshoni under Chief Bear Hunter had been making scattered attacks against Mormon settlements in the Great Salt Lake basin that had started spreading north encroaching into Indian territory and also on emigrants traveling the Oregon Trail.

Colonel Patrick Edward Connor, drove north out of California with two to three hundred California Volunteers from Camp Douglas in Salt Lake City and marched on the winter camp of Chief Bear Hunter's band on Beaver Creek at its confluence with the Bear River, some twelve miles west of the Mormon village of Franklin in Cache Valley and about 140 miles north of Bear Lake in Idaho on January 29, 1863.

What ensued was nothing less than a massacre of two hundred and fifty Indians, including ninety women and children. Twenty-three soldiers were killed and fourteen wounded (accounts vary). Bear Hunter was captured and tortured, then killed with a red-hot bayonet thrust into his brain through his ear. Survivors were tortured, butchered, and raped. Connor was later promoted to general. It has been written that Bear Creek was "one of the largest, most brutal, and…least-known massacres of Indians in American History," wholly overshadowed by news of the Civil War. Remnants of Chief Bear Hunter's band under Sagwitch and other chiefs of Northwestern Shoshoni bands signed the Treaty of Box Elder six months later.

CAVERNS BATTLEGROUND

On September 26-27, 1867, a battle raged between U.S. troops and Shoshoni, Paiute, and Pit Indians who had taken refuge in a series of caverns located at the top of a rocky slope in present Modoc County. Over a third of the command was killed or wounded in the battle. Six soldiers were buried at the foot of the slope.

SACAGAWEA

Sacagawea or Sacajawea (Bird Woman) was the young Shoshoni woman who accompanied Lewis and Clark on their journey across the Northern Plains and the Continental Divide to the Pacific with her husband, French Canadian trapper Toussaint Charbonneau, who was hired as an interpreter, and her infant son Jean Baptist or Pompey. The fortitude of seventeen-year old mother (Clark thought she might only be sixteen), who Clark insisted on calling Janey, proved a strength and an inspiration to the men of the Corps of Discovery as she carried her newborn infant on her back uncomplaining throughout the journey. The expedition encountered the Lemhi at the headwaters of the Missouri in western Montana. Without her the Corps would have had no access to the Shoshoni, the Shoshoni horses, and Shoshoni guides that were critical to the success of the expedition.

For his services, Charbonneau received his horse, his teepee, and five hundred and one-third dollars (Clark writes "500$ 33 1/3 cents") from the U.S. Government. (Charbonneau's name was spelled a number of different ways by Lewis & Clark; most frequently, Chabono.) Sacagawea received nothing. In a letter to Charbonneau dated August 20, 1806, Captain Clark paid tribute to Sacagawea and what she meant to the party, "Your woman who accompanied you that long dangerous and [fatiguing] route to the Pacific Ocean and back [deserved] a greater reward for her attention and services on that rout than we had in our power to give her." (Ambrose, *Undaunted Courage*, 389, 389n.)

SHOTO

The Shoto was a subdivision or sub-tribe of the Multnomah of Oregon generally treated separately. They belonged to the Clackamas division of the Chinookan linguistic family. They lived on the north side of Columbia River, a short distance from it and nearly opposite the mouth of the Willamette. For more see Mulnomah.

SHUMAN

It is believed that the Shuman belong to the Uto-Aztecan linguistic stock. They are more commonly known as the Jumano or Humano. They lived along the Rio Grande between the mouth of the Concho and the El Paso rivers and extended west as far as the Casa Grandes in Chihuahua.

There were two division, the Shuman or Jumano proper to the east along the Rio Grande and the Suma, a large group that moved into the plains of western Texas and New Mexico and divided into two sub-groups, one around El Paso and the other in the region of Casa Grandes. Sauer interprets Suma as a synonym rather than as a separate tribe or sub-tribe.

A mission was established at Casa Grandes in 1664. The northern division had effectively disappeared by the beginning of the twentieth century. The western division of the Suma became allied with the Apache and Jocomo against the Piman tribes to the west, particularly the Opata but, according to some reports, they were later destroyed by the Apache.

SHUMOPOVI

Shumopovi or Shongopovi was a Hopi village on the Second or Middle Mesa. For more see Hopi.

SHYIK

The Shyik was a sub-tribe of the Yakima. The Shyik signed the 1855 Yakima treaty at Camp Stevens by which they ceded all their lands to the government and settled on the Yakima Reservation. For more see Yakima.

SIBAG-NA

Sibag-na was a sub-tribe of the Tongva of California that inhabited the area about San Gabriel. For more see Tongva.

SICAOG

The Sicaog was a subdivision or sub-tribe of the Wappinger and lived in Hartford and West Hartford, Connecticut. For more see Wappinger.

SICAUNIE

The Sicaunie are referred to by Schoolcraft ("they bury their dead"), but no other information is available except that they were probably related to the Tacullie. They are believed to be of the Athapascan linguistic family that lived in Canada.

SICHOMOVI

The Sichomovi or Sichumovi was a Hopi village located on the First or East Mesa. See Hopi.

SICONESSE

The Siconesse was a sub-tribe of the Unalachtigo division of the Delaware. They lived on the eastern bank of the Delaware River near Salem, Delaware. For more see Unalachtigo and Delaware.

SIKSIKA BLACKFEET

The Siksika (meaning black foot, black feet, or black soles) were one of the three divisions or tribes of the Blackfeet and constituted the Blackfeet proper. The names Siksika and Blackfeet were often used interchangeably. Of the three divisions, the Siksika remained the farthest north and were commonly called, simply, the Northern Blackfeet. The Siksika, with the Bloods and the Northern Piegans, signed Treaty No. 7 with the Canadian government September 22, 1877, and swore allegiance to the Queen Mother. The treaty established a reserve for the Siksika at Blackfoot Crossing near Calgary. For more see Blackfeet.

SILETZ

The Siletz belonged to the Salishan linguistic stock. They lived along the Siletz River in Lincoln County, Oregon.

SIMILKAMEEN OKANAGON

The Similkameen was one of the two major divisions of the Okanagon. The were comprised of the Upper Similkameen, Ashnola, and Lower Similkameen, each with a number of villages. For more see Okanagon.

SINAGUA

The Sinagua (seen aug wah) were an ancient civilization that lived in central Arizona between the Little Colorado River and the Salt River, including the Verde Valley and portions of the Mogollon Rim. They have also been referred as the Western Anasazi. It is believed that they may have begun to emerge from Yuman origins about the 7th century, although many accounts do not pick them up until about 1060. Changes in life style over the years reflect a growing relationship with their neighbors, the Mogollon, Hohokam, Anasazi, and Patayan. Between the 12th and 14th centuries, they built cliff dwellings, among which is the famous five-story, 20-room, misnamed Montezuma Castle, 27 miles east of Sedona. Continued migration took a part of the people to the Zuni lands and the Rio Grande Valley, but the majority found their way to the Hopi Mesas. The Sinagua migrations appear to be incorporated in Hopi oral history. As a distinct cultural entity, the Sinagua disappeared from the archaeological record after the 15th century.

SINKAIETK

The Sinkaietk belonged to the interior group of the Salishan linguistic family. They lived along the Okanagan River from its mouth to near the mouth of the Similkameen in Washington State. Also called the Lower Okanagon, they are sometimes classified with the Okanagon.

SINKAKAIUS

The Sinkakaius belonged to the inland division of the Salishan linguistic family. They inhabited the area between the Columbia River and the Grand Coulee in Washington. Swanton reports that they were composed largely of people from the Moses-Columbia Band of the Sinkiuse-Columbia and from the Tukoratum Band of the Sinkaietk.

SINKYONE

The Sinkyone were of the southern California group of the Athapascan family. They lived along the South Fork of the Eel River and its branches and the adjacent coast generally between Four Mile Creek and Usal Lagoon.

SINTSINK

The Sintsink was a subdivision or sub-tribe of the Wappinger and lived between Hudson, Croton, and Pocantico rivers of New York State. For more see Wappinger.

SIOUX

The Sioux are popularly referred to the Sioux Nation or Saone. The tribes and bands that comprise the Sioux are of the Siouan linguistic stock. They know themselves as the Dakota, meaning friend or ally. The name Sioux came from a French corruption of the Chippewa (Ojibwe) name Natawesiwak (Nadouesse, Nadowe-is-siw, Nadowessie, or Nadouessioux), meaning just the opposite—Adders, i.e., enemies, a name also applied by the Ojibwe to the Iroquois. The French took the last syllable and came up Sioux, and the name stuck, becoming an all-encompassing term. Some Sioux descendants accept the name as almost traditional; others see it as a label imposed upon them. Other than the Chippewa, the Sioux was the largest and most significant Native American tribe north of Mexico.

Archaeological evidence indicates that the Dakota occupied what is now western Ontario and eastern Manitoba prior to 1200 AD and western Manitoba and eastern Saskatchewan prior to 900 AD. Other writers report that the Sioux came originally from the South but give nothing to support that argument except for the fact that there are a number of the tribes of the Siouan linguistic stock that inhabited the central Carolinas, Virginia, and Mississippi—the majority of which are now extinct. They included the Biloxi, the Cape Fear Indians, the Cheraw, the Eno, the Keyauwee, the Lumbee, and the Mahahoac, among others—the principal survivor being the Catawba of South Carolina.

From Canada the majority of the Sioux migrated west-southwest and settled in Minnesota. It is reasonable to conclude that some groups continued south in the mid-Atlantic region. They established themselves on the headwaters of the Mississippi and the drainage basin of the Red River of the North in present northwestern Minnesota during the sixteenth century. Modern recorded history considers the area the original homeland of the Sioux. It was there that the French first contacted them in 1659. They were first mentioned historically by the Jesuits in 1640.

Other members of the Siouan linguistic family included the Missouri, Iowa, Oto, Kansa, Omaha, Ponca, Osage, and Winnebago. All except the Winnebago lived west of the Mississippi in southern Minnesota, northwestern Wisconsin on or near the Mississippi and adjoining parts of Iowa.

Although recognized as fierce and aggressive fighters, the Sioux of the 1700s found themselves pushed out of their original homeland by the Cree and Chippewa newly armed with European weapons. The move south and west began in the mid-1670s. By the late seventeenth century, the modern historical structure of the Sioux Nation was in place consisting of three divisions, from east to west: Dakota, Nakota, and Lakota. It was during this period that the name for the Eastern Sioux or Dakota began to be used for the Sioux nation as a whole.

Sioux Divisions and Subgroups
DAKOTA (Eastern or Santee or Isanti)
Mdewakantunwan
Wahpekute
Wahpetunwan
Sissetunwan
NAKOTA (Middle or Yankton or Ihanktun)
Yankton or Ihanktunwan
Yanktonai or Ihaktunwananna

LAKOTA (Western or Teton or Titunwan)
Oglala
Brulé
Hunkpapa*
Miniconjou*
Oohenonpa or Two Kettles*
Sans Arcs or Itazipacola*
Blackfoot or Sihasapa or Siksika*
*Saone

With the new structure emerged three distinct dialects, the differences being the initial consonant sound, and changes in habits and customs. The culture of the Santee was similar to the Ojibwa and Winnebago. The Yankton Sioux were influenced by the Mandan and the Arikara, and were semi-sedimentary planters of corn. The Teton Sioux, the largest of the three divisions, were the hunters and the more aggressive. Of the three dialects, the Nakota is now almost extinct.

To some writers, the four subgroups of Dakota; two subgroups of Nakota; and the combined seven subgroups of Lakota constituted the Oceti Sakowin meaning "Seven Fires" or "Seven Council Fires," a socio-political and kinship alliance of the Sioux Nation. Joseph Marshall, however, defines Oceti Sakowin as consisting of the seven subgroups of Lakota.

LEWIS AND CLARK identified ten separate Sioux tribes or bands
Mindawarcarton, or Keenkesah
Sistasoone, or Sisatone
Tetons Minnakenozzo
Tetons of the Burnt Woods
Tetons Okandandas
Tetons Saone
Wahpatone, or Wahpetunwan
Wahpatoota, or Leaf Beds
Yanktons
Yanktons of the Plains, or Big Devils (Yanktonai)

MIGRATION

The Oglala (Ogallala) of the Teton Sioux led the advance westward from the upper reaches of Minnesota. They became the first to cross the Missouri, the first to the Black Hills, and the first to the Platte River. They crossed the Mississippi, drove the Arikara from the Upper Missouri, crossed the Missouri, and invaded the Black Hills country. With them almost step-for-step were the Brulé. They too acquired soon guns, ammunition, and metal weapons from the French. From the Arikara, they acquired the horse. The Middle Sioux or Nakota followed, but only part way. The Eastern Sioux or remained relatively undisturbed, protected by topography and proximity to the Algonquian.

The Teton and Yankton divisions inhabited all of South Dakota, most of North Dakota, over half of Nebraska, just north of Omaha above the latitude of 43 degrees, into the eastern third of Wyoming, the southeast corner of Montana, and the western fringe of Minnesota along the Dakota borders—generally from the Mississippi to the Rockies. The Sioux became masters of the Upper Plains, but it was not uncommon to find them as far south as Kansas and Missouri. With their migration west, the Sioux drove out the Crow, the Kiowa, the Omaha, and others before them, and it was they who pressed the Comanche and others as the Cree had pressed them.

FREEDOM TO SUBJUGATION

The twenty-five year period between 1850 and 1875 was marked by deepening tensions between Indians and whites. The first sign of the escalating conflict was the significant increased traffic along the Oregon Trail. The conflict deepened with the building of the railroads, the wanton destruction of the buffalo herds, the discovery of gold in the Black Hills and Montana, and white incursions on Indian land. They led to skirmishes, depredations, random killings, and military expeditions from Minnesota to Powder River and from the Upper Missouri to the Platte. All the pent-up hatred and animosity rose to the surface with the massacre of twenty-nine men led by a high-spirited but foolish young lieutenant named John L. Grattan in the summer of 1854—over a cow. There was only one survivor from the unit, and he was mortally wounded. The incident began what has been generally regarded as the First Sioux War that lasted for two years and the first of a continuing series of events that would spawn a generation and lead to Red Cloud's War of 1866-1868, the Great Sioux War from 1876 to 1877, and finally to the total subjugation of the Dakota Nation.

BATTLE AT KILLDEER MOUNTAIN

What amounted to full-scale war erupted in southern Nebraska along the Platte River Trail as emigrants flooded the region and the along what became known as the Bozeman Trail from Fort Laramie to Virginia City, Montana, that ran through the Powder River hunting lands of the Oglala. On July 28, 1864, General Alfred Sully moved from his cantonment at Fort Rice north to Fort Berthold where he engaged some sixteen hundred warriors of the Lakota and Santee at Killdeer Mountain taking more than a hundred lives. There was no count made of the wounded. Skirmishes continued through August.

GREAT SIOUX WAR

Sitting Bull, chief of the Hunkpapa, had taken his people into the Yellowstone country west of the Black Hills where they might be free to live in the old ways and avoid reservation control. There were joined by large numbers of Brulé and Oglala Sioux as well as members of the Northern Cheyenne and Northern Arapaho. In 1871 and 1872 they discovered surveyors laying out a route for the Northern Pacific Railroad from Lake Superior through Duluth and Brainerd, Minnesota, and across the Missouri to Bismarck. With each encounter, under the lead of Sitting Bull of the Hunkpapa and Crazy Horse, War Chief of the Oglala, the Lakota and their Cheyenne allies drove them away. Over time the encounters became more frequent and more intense. The first overt action was the Battle of Arrow Creek in the summer of 1872. One year later, on August 11, 1873, the Battle of the Yellowstone, near its junction with the Rosebud, erupted on the northern plains. As many as fifteen hundred warriors who challenged the army's advance were forced to withdraw after fierce fighting by a force of some 450 men led by Lt. Colonel George Armstrong Custer. Custer's force was part of the Yellowstone Expedition under the command by Colonel David S. Stanley that had been ordered out from Fort Rice and Fort Lincoln, just south and southwest of present-day Bismarck by General Phil Sheridan as part of the solution to "the Indian problem" and to protect the railroad survey parties.

Although the army achieved a tactical victory, the army and the railroad were put on notice that construction of the Northern Pacific would face stiff, determined opposition. The Northern Pacific stalled on the on the east bank of the Missouri. But it was not fear of an Indian attack that brought work to a standstill; it was the machinations of Wall Street and the economic Panic of 1873. It would be six years before work would resume. (In 1872, the Northern Pacific Railroad, who was to receive 25,600 acres for each mile of track, laid claim to Dakota land that had been granted by treaty to the Sisseton-Wahpeton Sioux. The government extinguished Sioux title and turned the land over to the railroad by the simple expediency of a vote of Congress, paying the Sioux ten cents an acre to make it legal. A 1875 ruling by the Supreme Court held that railroad land grants did not apply to those lands that the Indians were left free to occupy pursuant to treaty.)

From the Yellowstone, Lakota attention was drawn to the Black Hills where gold had been discovered. A trickle of prospectors soon turned to a flood of prospectors and settlers. The government wanted the Black Hills and was willing to buy, rent or steal to get them. The increasing violence and frustration led to the Great Sioux War that began with an attack on the Sioux and Cheyenne camp of He Dog of the Oglala on the Powder River on the morning of March 17, 1876, by General Joseph J. Reynolds and did not end until the spring of 1877. The 374-man force was part of the command of General George Crook out of Fort Laramie. On this occasion, it was the Sioux and Cheyenne that achieved a tactical victory forcing the attackers to withdraw, but a strategic victory for the army. The number of dead and wounded on both sides were light, but the soldiers drove off the entire herd of Indian ponies and burned or otherwise destroyed the entire camp, including tents, food stuffs and vital supplies, and all personal and household goods, leaving the Indian families with little but the clothes on their backs.

The Sioux War came to be marked in the public consciousness by the defeat of Custer in the valley of the Little Big Horn, but the Battle of the Little Big Horn was just one battle in the much larger war. It was a war against the government in the truest sense, but it also pitted Indian against Indian. The anti-government Indians were comprised primarily of Oglala, Miniconjou, and Hunkpapa Lakota and the Northern Cheyenne, joined by bands from the Brulé and San Acrs, the Northern Arapaho, the Santee, and Yanktonai. The pro-government Indians included the Crow, the Arikara, the Shoshoni, the Ute, the Pawnee, the Bannock, and the Nez Percé. The Crow, the Shoshoni, and the Arikara had warred with the Sioux and the Northern Cheyenne for years; and the Bannock and the Nez Percé had had their own wars with the government and lost. As time moved on, the Lakota themselves became divided between the agency Indians of Red Cloud and Spotted Tail and the "wild" Indians of Sitting Bull, Crazy Horse, and Dull Knife.

Sitting Bull called for an assembly of tribes to discuss the increasing encroachment of the white man on Lakota lands and to develop a strategy for dealing with it. In the late spring of 1876, they came together on Ash (Reno) Creek near its confluence with the Little Big Horn River (to the Sioux, the Greasy Grass River) near present-day Hardin, Montana, It was the largest concentration of Sioux ever to assemble—some seven thousand persons that included a thousand warriors, both young and old, and ten thousand horses. Represented were the Hunkpapa, Sicangu, Itazipacola, Miniconjou, Oglala, and a small band of Ihanktunwan Dakota and the Sahiyela (Northern Cheyenne). Many had come from the Red Cloud and Spotted Tail agencies.

While the assembly at Ash Creek was coming together, one thousand soldiers, calvary and infantry under the command of Brig. General George Crook, were on the march with a small army of three hundred Crow and Shoshoni scouts had come together to the south and were moving north. Warned by outriders of the coming of the soldiers, Crazy Horse issued a call for warriors to join him by invoking an ancient ritual known as "Gathering the Warriors." Without having to say a word, some six hundred Lakota and Northern Cheyenne answered his call to stop the soldiers and protect the Ash Creek encampment and followed him as he raced south fifty miles through the night. At the end of their seven-hour ride, the first shots of the Battle of the Rosebud were fired at dawn on the morning of June 17, 1876. The battle ended in what was effectively a draw. With his supply of ammunition almost exhausted, Crazy Horse ordered a withdraw even though the fighting was going in their favor. The Indians lost ten men killed and many more wounded. They left the soldiers with neither the will nor the energy to pursue. The soldiers turned back south down the trail from which that they had come. The events on the Rosebud were soon overshadowed by a second battle eight days hence.

In the meantime, the large herd of horses had depleted the available grass on Ask Creek, and the encampment was moved to the banks of the Greasy Grass River. The Indians expected to remain encamped together for another three days before separating, each to his own homeland. Some had already departed; others fearing reprisals from the army headed south to the agencies.

A week later, soldiers of U.S. 7th Calvary Regiment under the command of Lieutenant Colonel George Armstrong Custer mounted two, unsuccessful attacks on the Indian encampment on the Greasy Grass River on June 25, 1876. A third contingent under the command of Captain Frederick Benteen was sent to scout the surrounding bluffs. The first attack of some 175 soldiers and Indian scouts was led by Major Marcus A. Reno. The attack was repulsed, and the soldiers were driven back with losses behind make-shift defensive works where he was joined by Benteen. The Indians were content to keep Reno and his men holed up until the next day, the 26th, when they withdrew and broke camp. The second attack a short time later was led by Custer. His force consisted of five troops or companies totaling about 210 men, including soldiers, scouts, and civilians. Outnumbered more than three to one, Custer and his men were destroyed to the last man in what history records as the Battle of the Little Big Horn.* Sitting Bull and Gall (Hunkpapa) and Crazy Horse and He Dog (Oglala), among others, led the fight for the Lakota; Dull

Knife and Two Moons for the Northern Cheyenne. The number of casualties in the 7th Calvary's two-day encounter with the Sioux and their allies included 263 killed and another 60 wounded.

The Powder River Expedition was formed in 1876 under the command of Maj. Gen. George Crook and headed out from Fort Fetterman on November 14 to bring the anti-treaty Indians led by led by Crazy Horse to terms. Final preparations were made at Cantonment Reno for the push north into Yellowstone country. Crook's command numbered more than 1,750 officers and men of the calvary, infantry and artillery, supported by a civilian packtrain. These times also pitted Indian against Indian. The anti-government Indians came mostly from the Lakota and the Northern Cheyenne, with some support from the Santee and Yanktonai Sioux and the Arapaho. The pro-government Indians serving as scouts and auxiliaries were recruited from the Crow, the Arikara, the Shoshoni, the Ute, the Pawnee, the Bannock and the Nez Percé. Primary support came from the Crow and Shoshoni. Crook's command that totaled more than twenty-one hundred included nearly 400 Indian auxiliaries—well-regarded, compact fighting units. Ninety-one additional Indians, mostly Shoshoni, joined the command in route, bringing the Indian contingent to more than 350 and the total force to more than twenty-one hundred.

Early in the campaign, striking at a target of opportunity, Colonel Ronald Mackenzie all but destroyed Dull Knife's Northern Cheyenne. The Sioux were on their own, and their strength was waning. By this time, too, Crazy Horse had become an embittered man; his resistance total and unbridled; and his attitude towards the moderates, dictatorial and coercive. Meanwhile the units of the Powder River Expedition received new orders. The Sioux were left to face the ambitious and talented Colonel Nelson A. Miles.

Colonel Miles directed the campaign in the north with a dogged determination throughout the winter and early spring of 1876-1877. The Sioux began to fall one at a time until.. An attack by a company of the Third Calvary destroyed a Lakota camp of ten lodges at Crow Creek near Deadwood on March 23, 1877. The attack demonstrated in dramatic fashion that Lakota had only two choices—death or the agency. There was to be no softening of the fight. The troopers continued on a search and destroy mission through April before returning to Camp Robinson.

Following the surrender of the majority of the Cheyenne in the spring of 1877, those who wished to continue the fight joined Lame Deer's Miniconjous on a tributary of the Rosebud. About the same time, 1,200 - 1,300 Miniconjous from other bands and San(s) Arcs surrendered to General Crook at Camp Sheridan on April 14. A week later the last band of Cheyenne surrendered at the Red Cloud agency.

For the Oglala there was no place left to turn. Men and women, old and young alike were tired—tired of running, of hiding, of burying the dead. Although some young braves wanted to continue the fight, there were not enough men to fight and protect and care for the weak and the helpless. On May 6, Crazy Horse brought almost nine hundred Oglalas peacefully into Camp Robinson (Red Cloud Agency). That same week Sitting Bull found sanctuary in Canada, and on May 7 Colonel Miles attacked the camp of Lame Deer's Miniconjou. Lame Dear and Iron Star were killed, and on May 14 the Miles arrived at the Rosebud with his prisoners.. The Great Sioux War was over. Those few that remained free roamed the Upper Plains for a time, completely destitute, before going into one of the agencies to surrender.

U.S. Army losses in the Great Sioux War were 283 killed and 125 wounded. Losses for civilian auxiliaries, government Indian scouts, and private citizens are unknown. The economic cost of the war has been reported as in excess of two and one-quarter million dollars. Losses by the Sioux and their allies have not been determined.

Crazy Horse was killed by a soldier on September 5, 1877, while trying to escape from the guardhouse at Camp Robinson to which he was to be confined before being sent to one of the distant detention centers.

(Born in the Black Hills about 1840, Crazy Horse or Tasunke Witko was of the Hunkpitila (Hunkpatila) band of the Oglala. His battlefield exploits at the Battle of Rose Bud, the Fetterman Fight, and the Battle of Little Big Horn earned him claim to the title of "the greatest Lakota warrior.") Spotted Tail was killed in 1881.

When Sitting Bull returned from Canada in 1883, he found that the railroad had been completed across Sioux lands and that the buffalo had disappeared from the Yellowstone. He joined Buffalo Bill's Wild West Show in 1885. Five years later Indian agents in the employ of the army killed Sitting Bull on December 15, 1890, near present-day Fort Yates, North Dakota. Some believe that his death was nothing less than the assassination of a divisive chief—allegedly, one of several. That same year, that same month, the final chapter in the struggles of the Native Americans to remain free was closed at Wounded Knee (see Lakota).

TREATIES AND RESERVATIONS

An early Indian conference of Indian tribes was held in May 1815 at Portage de Sioux, Missouri. The conference was an ambitious attempt on the part of William Clark and Auguste Chouteau to establish peace among the Indian tribes as well as peace between Indians and whites following the end of the War of 1812 that pit one tribe against another. The result was a series of treaties of peace and friendship executed between May and September with the Sioux, Fox, Sauk, Osage, Kickapoo, and Maka. One of the few executed between the government and the American Indians that did not call for their removal or cession of lands. (The town got its name as a result of the war between the Missouri and the Sioux who evaded the lands of the Missouri to their south. To avoid an ambush set up by the Missouri at the mouth of the Missouri River, the Sioux crossed the Mississippi River just north of the confluence of the two rivers at the site of the town named in their honor and carried their canoes to the Missouri River. The Sioux escaped with their spoils of war.)

The treaty at Portage de Sioux was the second treaty to which the Sioux were a part. The first, in 1805 but never ratified, ceded to the government for nine square miles of land near the confluence of the Mississippi and St. Peter's rivers on the upper Mississippi, to include the falls of St. Anthony. In all the Sioux executed a total of twenty-nine treaties between 1805 and 1882. In addition there was an additional sixty-plus treaties executed with the various bands or tribes. Several were never ratified by Congress; others were amended prior to ratification. There were two of particular note, in addition to those that were in effect treaties of surrender.

The "Great Council" Treaty was signed in September 1851 at Horse Creek some miles east of Fort Laramie. Tribes represented included the Snake from the mountains, the Crow and others from the Yellowstone, the Oglala, most of the Brulé, plus the of Cheyenne and Arapaho. First of all, it was to be a peace treaty among the Indian nations. From that standpoint, it was little more than a piece of paper. The Sioux would continued their ongoing war against the Crow, the Pawnee, and others. The treaty also defined the territories of the respective tribes and gave the government right to build roads and military posts on Indians lands. In return the tribes were to received annuities in the form of goods and supplies for ten years (as amended by Congress) totaling fifty thousand dollars divided amongst them in proportion to their populations. The Sioux openly repudiated the treaty and disdained the annual annuity of goods, a fact the agents kept from their superiors in Washington, keeping the goods for themselves.

The second was the Treaty of Fort Laramie concluded in April 1868 that decreed that the reservations were to be the permanent homes of the tribes and denied to them the right to occupy territory outside of the reservations. What that provision meant in real terms was the loss to the Sioux of their primary food source. The Brulé were hit the hardest by the provisions of the treaty because their proximity to the Platte Trail laid them open to the diseases introduced by the emigrant migration to Oregon and California.

Smallpox, cholera, measles and other white-man diseases nearly destroyed them. The treaty closed the Bozeman Trail and called for the abandonment of the military posts established to protect emigrants along the trail. It also specified, as had treaties dating from the close of the French and Indian War, those lands considered to be unceded Indian territory that no white person would be permitted to settle upon or occupy any portion of or pass through without first obtaining the consent of the Indians.

The Sioux reservations, several much diminished in size from when they were first established, are now located in Minnesota, Montana, Nebraska, North Dakota, and South Dakota. With eight reservations, South Dakota has by far the largest concentration of Sioux. The principal reservations are the Pine River Reservation, Rosebud Reservation, Lower Brulé Reservation, Cheyenne River Reservation; and Standing Rock Reservation—all along the western shore of the Missouri River. The Pine Ridge Reservation is by far the largest, single reservation. It is the home to the Oglala Lakota Nation. Portions of the Standing Rock Reservation (home to both the Lakota Oyate and the Dakota) is located in the southeast corner of North Dakota. Among the smaller and lesser-known reservations are the Crow Creek Reservation, the Yankton Sioux Reservation, and the Santee Sioux Reservation in Nebraska. The Lake Traverse Reservation and Flandreau Sioux Reservation are also in South Dakota. The Fort Peck Reservation, on lands originally established for the Assiniboin, is located in northeast Montana.

*The Custer Battlefield National Monument in Montana was renamed the Little Bighorn National Monument in 1991. Interspersed throughout the site are small, white marble markers denoting the place where soldiers of the 7th Calvary fell. A few have names, most do not. The markers for the unknown read, "U.S. Soldier 7th Calvary fell here June 25, 1876." To those markers, a dozen-plus red granite stones have been added since 1999 for those American Indians killed that day. One reads, "Hevovetaso, Little Whirlwind, a Cheyenne Warrior fell here on June 26, 1876, while defending the Cheyenne way of life." In 2003 a separate Indian sculpture was dedicated at the site as a reminder not only of the events of that June day but also of the of the fragile state of Native American culture in the white man's world—then and now.

SISATONE

The Sisatone or Sistatoone reportedly lived along the upper portions of Red River of the North, Lake Winnipec, and the St. Peter's River. The Sistasoone was identified by Lewis and Clark as one of the ten separate Sioux tribes or bands. They are very likely the same tribe as that identified as the Sissetunwan, Sisseton or Sisitonwan—People of the Fish Ground. For more see Sioux and Dakota.

SISITCANOG-NA

The Sisitcanog-na was a sub-tribe of the Tongva of California that inhabited the area about Pear Orchard. For more see Tongva.

SISSIPAHAW

It is believed that the Sissipahaw were of the Siouan linguistic family. Their principal settlements were about the present Saxapahaw on the Haw River in southern Alamance County, North Carolina. One opinion is that they were a branch of the Shakori. They joined the other tribes in the region in the Yamasee war of 1715. It is more likely that remnants joined the Catawba.

SIUSLAW

The Siuslaw inhabited parts of Oregon coast about the Siuslaw River. They belonged to the Siuslawan division of the Yakonan linguistic stock. Their lives and history were parallel with that of the Coos. For more see the Coos.

SIWANOY

The Siwanoy or Sinanoy was a subdivision or sub-tribe of the Wappinger and lived in Westchester County and part of Fairfield County, Connecticut, between the Bronx and Five Mile River. For more see

SK-KAHL-MISH

The Sk-kahl-mish were one of the coastal Salish peoples that inhabited western Washington. They were included in the Treaty of Point Elliott (Muckl-te-oh) of 1855.

SK-TAH-LE-JUM

The Sk-tah-le-jum (Sk-Tah-Le-Jum) were participants in the January 22, 1855 treaty at Point Elliott, but no additional information is known.

SKACKAMAXON

The Skackamaxon was a sub-tribe of the Unalachtigo division of the Delaware. They lived in the area about the present Kensington near Philadelphia, Pennsylvania. For more see Unalachtigo and Delaware.

SKADDAL

In 1806 Lewis and Clark reported the Skaddal tribe living in 1806 on Cataract (Klikitat) river, twenty-fives miles north of Big Narrows in the present Washington State. They have been mentioned by other writers under the name Saddals. They have classified as a division of the Pisquow that lived about Boston Creek and Kahchass Lake at the head of the Yakima River and later at the entrance to Selah Creek. Pisquow was another name for the Wenatchee (Wina't:ca). The Wenatchee/Pisquow should not be confused with the Pisquose (Pisko) division of the Yakima. For more see Yakima, Pisquose, Wenatchee.

SKAGIT

The Skagit lived along the Skagit and Stillaguamish rivers in Washington State, except around the mouths of the two rivers. They were of the coastal division of the Salishan linguistic stock. Swanton lists twelve subdivisions that include the Sauk on Sauk River above the confluence of the Suiattle River, including a settlement on Sauk Prairie above present Darrington, Washington, and the Stillaguamish on Stillaguamish River from Arlington north, including villages at Arlington and Trafton. The Skagit River flows into Puget Sound. He makes no reference to the Upper Skagit. See the Upper Skagit in this work.

SKAI-WHA-MISH

The Skai-wha-mish (Skai-Wha-Mish) were participants in the January 22, 1865 treaty at Point Elliott, but no additional information is known.

SKARU'RE

The Skaru're (hemp gathers) or Tuscarora proper was one of the three tribes or subdivisions of the Tuscarora confederacy.

SKEETSOMISH

Lewis and Clark reported that the Skeetsomish or Skeets-so-mish lived at the falls of the Flat Head River (renamed the Clark River), a tributary of the Columbia. The Skeetsomish were a band or division of the Skitswish that was comprised of three major divisions. For more see Skitswish.

SKIDI PAWNEE

Skidi or Skiri Pawnee were one of the four subdivisions of the Pawnee. They were also called the Loos, Loup, and Wolf Indians. They lived about the Platte River in Nebraska. For more see Pawnee.

SKILLOOT

The Skilloot or Skiloot belonged to the Clackamas division of the Chinookan linguistic family and inhabited both sides of the Columbia River above and below the Cowlitz River in Washington State and Oregon. Their 1780 population was estimated at three thousand. Lewis and Clark put their population at 2,500 in 1806; but Lane put the population in 1850 at just two hundred. The Skilloot have since entirely disappeared.

SKINPAH

The Skinpah, Skin-pah, Skinpah or Skin belonged to the Shahaptian division of the Shapwailutan linguistic stock and a sub-tribe of the Yakima. They inhabited the area on the Columbia River in Washington from The Dalles north some seventy-five miles. In the 1855 Yakima treaty at Camp Stevens, the Skinpah ceded all their lands to the government and settled on the Yakima Reservation. For more see Yakima.

SKITSWISH

The Skitswich, more popularly known as the Coeur d'Alêne, belonged to the inland division of the Salishan family. They lived on the headwaters of the Spokane River in Idaho from above Spokane Falls to its sources. The Skitswich was comprised of three divisions: The St. Joe River Division, the Coeur d'Alene River Division, and the Coeur d'Alene Lake and Spokane River Division. The Skitswich were also known as Q'ma'shpal and Pointed Hearts (a derivative of the French translation of Coeur d'Alene). In the spring of 1842, Jesuit John Paul De Smet visited the Coeur d'Alene on the Spokane River and that summer directed Father Nicholas Point to establish the Mission of the Sacred Heart located at the southern end of Lake Coeur d'Alene, just about a mile up the St. Joe River.

SKOKOMISH

The Skokomish was the principal division of the Twana of Washington State. They lived about Annas Bay and the drainage area of the Skokomish River. In some writings, the name Skokomish is used to refer to the whole of the Twana. For more see Twana.

SKOPAMISH MUCKLESHOOT

The Skopamish or Skopamich was a subdivision of the Muckleshoot of Washington State. They lived on the upper Green River. For more see Muckleshoot and Smalhkamish.

SMALHKAMISH

The Smalhkamish or Smulkamish was a subdivision of the Muckleshoot. They belonged to the Nisqually dialectic group of the coastal division of the Salishan linguistic family. They lived in Washington State on the upper White River about present Auburn. In the valley around Auburn also lived the Skopamich or Skopamish and Stkamish until white settlers arrived in the 1850s. All three Indian sub-tribes were participants in the January 22, 1865 treaty at Point Elliott. For more see Muckleshoot.

SNOHOMISH

The Snohomish belonged to the Nisqually dialectic group of the coastal division of the Salishan linguistic family. The lived along the lower course of the Snohomish River in Washington State and at the southern end of Whidbey Island.

SNOQALMIE

The Snoqalmie lived along the Snoqualmie River and Skykomishh River in Washington State. They belonged to the Nisqually Branch of the coastal division of the Salishan linguistic family.

SOACATINO

The Soacatino (also spelled Socatino) or Xactin was of the Caddo, but has not been identified with a specific group or tribe. They inhabited northwestern Louisiana and northeastern Texas where they encountered member of De Soto's party.

SOBAIPURI

They Sobaipuri belonged to the Piman division of the Uto-Aztecan linguistic stock and inhabited the main and tributary valleys of the San Pedro and Santa Cruz Rivers in Arizona, primarily between the mouth of the San Pedro and the ruins of Casa Grande. They are believed to have been a part of the Papago. They may be the same as the Soba Papago of Arizona, referred to by Swanton.

SOBOBA LUISEÑO

The Soboba was one of six recognized tribes of Luiseño. The Soboba reservation that was established in 1883 is located at the edge of the City of San Jacinto. For more see Luiseño.

SOCOWOCOMOCO

The Socowocomoco was one of the nine divisions of the Conoy and lived on the Wicomico River in St. Marys and Charles counties of Maryland.

SOKOKI

The Algonquin-speaking Sokoki was a subdivision of the Abnaki or Wabanaki but have been treated separately in the literature. They lived on the Saco River and in the adjacent parts of Cumberland and York counties in Maine. In the late 1600s, one group removed to St. Francois du Lac in Quebec where they joined with other. For more see Abenaki and

SOKULK

According to Lewis & Clark, the Sokulk (So-kulk Perced noses) lived at the mouth of the Kimoenim (Ki moo e nim) or Snake River. There has been some debate over the proper identification of the Sokulk. They are generally believed to be of the Wanapam tribe of Washington State; others believe the Yakima. For more see Wanapam.

SONAG-NA

Sonag-na was a sub-tribe of the Tongva of California that inhabited the area about Mr. White's Farm. For more see Tongva.

SOUIKILA

The Souikila was listed in Jefferson's *Notes on the State of Virginia*. Bouquet (1764) reported a population of 200 warriors, but no location was given. For more see "Aborigines," Appendix D.

SOUTHERN GROUP OF THE VALLEY YOKUTS

The Southern Group of the Valley Division was one of the seven subdivisions of the Yokuts Group of Indians of California. They inhabited villages on the Kern River, the lower Tule River, on the Deep and Outside Channels of the Kaweah River, Wahtoke Creek, Cameron channel, and Tulare Lake. For more see Yokuts.

SOUTHERN PAIUTE

The Southern Paiute or Digger Indians, also called the Ute-Southern Paiute, belonged to the Ute-Chemehuevi group of the Shoshonean branch of the Uto-Aztecan stock. Some reports refer to the language as being of the Southern Numic group. They called themselves Nüma signifying "people." They occupied western Utah, northwestern Arizona, southeastern Nevada, and parts of southeastern California. For more see the Paiute.

SOUTIES

Hodge listed the Souties as a band or village of the Chippewa.

SOYENNOM

Drake reported that the Soyennom was either another name for or a band of the Chopummish (Nez Percé) and that they lived on the north side of the east fork of Lewis's River. He also stated that they numbered four hundred braves in 1820.

SPOKAN

The Spokan or Spokane were part of the island division of the Salishan linguistic stock and inhabited a large region bordering on the Spokane and Little Spokane rivers. There were three subdivisions: the Lower Spokane, the Upper Spokan, and the Middle Spokan. The Lower Spokan lived about the lower Spokane River at its mouth, a part of which subsequently became the Spokane Indian Reserve. The Upper Spokan or Little Spokan as they were called lived in the valley of the Little Spokan River and east of the Lower Spokan into the boarders of Idaho. The Middle Spokan, also called the Southern or South Spokan, occupied the lower Hangmans Creek.

Lewis & Clark and the Corps of Discovery was their first encounter with Europeans. The Lower Spokan, the majority of the Middle Spokan, and a few of the Upper Spokan were placed under the Colville Agency. The remainder were placed on the Flathead Reservation in Montana.

SPOKANE WAR

The short-lived Spokan War lasted from May through early October 1858. On May 6, 1858, Col. Edward J. Steptoe led a detachment of 150 regular army troops and volunteers from Ft. Walla Walla to gather additional information on complaints of depredations committed by the Cayuse, Spokanes, and Coeur d'Alenes on the ever-increasing influx of gold seekers, traders, and whisky peddlers onto their lands. He had not prepared to fight a major engagement. Combined elements from among the Palouses, Sinkiuses and a few Cayuse led by the Spokane attacked and routed Steptoe's command in southern Spokane country, killing eight and chasing the soldiers back to Fort Walla Walla. The Indian raids continued throughout the summer. In response, Colonel George Wright took out a well-organized force of regular army troops of the Ninth U.S. Infantry northeast from Walla Walla to punish the raiders. At Four Lakes near present-day Spokane, Washington, on September 1 and Spokane Plains four days later, Colonel Wright attacked and utterly defeated a combined force of northern Indians, including those that had attacked Colonel Steptoe plus Coeur d'Alenes and a few braves from other bands. Wright ordered several Indians hanged on the spot, permitted his troop to kill almost a thousand horses, and took a number of Indians back to Fort Walla Walla as prisoners. Four of the prisoners were eventually hanged, three for murder and one for inciting a war.

On October 9, Wright assembled the chiefs of the Walla Walla and the Cayuse and warned that any future murders would be dealt with severely.

SQUANNAROO

The Squannaroo reportedly lived on the Cataract River below the Skaddal in Washington State.

SQUAXON

The Squaxon (Squakson, Squaxin, Squawksin, or Squalin) belonged to the Nisqually Branch of the coastal division of the Salisham linguistic family. They lived about North Bay, Puget Sound, in Washington Territory. They are now one of the sub-tribes of what become the Squaxin Island Tribe. Others include the Noo-Seh-Chatl, Steh Chass, Squi-Aitl, Sawamish/T'Peeksin, Sa-Heh-Wa-Mish, and S'Hotle-Ma-Mish. They lived along several inlets of southern Puget Sound.

The Squaxin signed the Treaty of Medicine Creek on December 26 along with the Nisqually and Puyallup. It was the first in Washington Territory. The tribes ceded 4,000 square miles or 2,560,000 acres, extending from the Cascades on the east to the Black Hills on the west, and from Mt. St. Helens to the Skookumchuck and Chehalis Rivers on the south and Wilke's Portage Vashon Island and the divide between the Puyallup and White Rivers on the North. In exchange, three small reserves were established. One small island, four and a half miles long and a half mile wide was reserved as the main area. The island was named after the Squawksin of Case Inlet and became known as Squaxin Island. By 1862, the island housed only fifty persons. Today there are no year-around residents of the island, but it remains a bond between its first inhabitants.

SQUIAITL

The Squiaitl or Squi-Aitl belonged to the Nisqually Branch of the coastal division of the Salisham linguistic family of Washington Territory about Puget Sound. They would later become a subdivision of the Squaxin Island Tribe and lived about Eld Inlet of Squaxin Island. For more see the Squawksin.

SQUINAMISH

The Squinamish or Squin-Ah-Mish or Squin-Ah-Nush inhabited western Washington. They were included in the Treaty of Point Elliott, 1855.

ST. JOE RIVER SKITSWISH

The St. Joe River was one of the three divisions of the Skitswish. They joined the Palouse, Spokane, and Coeur d'Alene in what was called the Coeur d'Alene War. For more see Skitswish and Coeur d'Alene.

STADACONAN

The Stadaconan of Canada were of the Iroquoian linguistic stock and inhabited the village of Stadacona, the site of present-day Quebec. They are generally believed to have been a branch of the Huron-Iroquois race, the general consensus being that they were of the early Hurons, most often referred to separately. The Stadaconan were first encountered by French explorer and navigator Jacques Cartier during his second voyage in 1535. By Samuel de Champlain's first voyage in 1603, they had disappeared. For more see the Huron.

STEGARAKI

The Stegaraki was a sub-tribe of the Manahoac of Virginia or a member of the Manahoac Confederacy that lived in Orange County on the Rapidan River.

STEH CHASS

The Steh Chass belonged to the Nisqually Branch of the coastal division of the Salisham linguistic family of Washington Territory about Puget Sound. They later become a subdivision of the Squaxin Island Tribe and lived about Budd Inlet of Squaxin Island. For more see Squawksin.

STEILACOOM

The Steilacoom (also spelled Shilacum) was an independent group of Indians that spoke a separate sub-dialect of the Puget Sound Salish language. They lived in five bands in the area around Chambers Creek (or the Steilacoom River) and the Segwallitchu River in the Tacoma Basin southwest of what is now the city of Tacoma. The area was also the home of the Nisqually Indians. The region was one of the earliest in the Puget Sound region to be occupied by white settlers. As a consequence, Fort Steilacoom was constructed in 1849 near the present town of Lakewood (called the Prairie in the beginning).

The tribe was a signatory to the treaty Medicine Creek Treaty that placed them on reservations established for the Puyallup, Nisqually and Squaxin. Angered by the one-sided nature of the treaty Indians attacked several white settlers on October 29, 1855. During the "Indian War" of 1855-56, the Fort Steilacoom served as headquarters for the 9th U.S. Infantry. Future generals McClellan, Pickett, Sheridan, and Grant served at the post in the years prior to the beginning of the American Civil War.

BANDS
Steilacoom proper, six sites on Chambers Creek
Sastuck, three sites on Clover Creek
Spanaway, Spanaway Lake
Tlithlow, Murray Creek
Segwallitchu, two sites on the Segwallitchu River

STILLAGUAMISH

The Stillaguamish of the coastal division of the Salishan linguistic stock was a subdivision of the Skagit. They lived about the Stillaguamish River from Arlington north in Washington territory. For more see Skagit.

ST-KAH-MISH

The St-kah-mish were one of the coastal Salish peoples that inhabited western Washington. They were included in the Treaty of Point Elliott of 1855.

STOCKBRIDGE INDIANS

The Stockbridge belonged to the Algonquian linguistic group. Some writers treat the them as a distinct and independent tribe, but they are generally considered a subgroup of the Housatonic and other sub-tribes of the Mahicans that lived in the Housatonic Valley and were gathered together into the Stockbridge mission in 1736. The name was subsequently applied to all Mahicans or, more precisely, those remnants placed on a reservation in Shawano County, Wisconsin. For more see the Mahicans.

STOLUCK-WHA-MISH

The Stoluck-wha-mish inhabited western Washington Territory. They were included in the Treaty of Point Elliott of 1855.

STONEY-NAKODA

The Stoney-Nakoda (îyârhe Nakodabi) or "Rocky Mountain Sioux," are culturally and linguistically allied to the Assiniboin of the Plains, but they speak the northern dialect of the Dakota language. Also called the Stonies, Stone Indians, and the Sioux of the Rocks. Tradition has it that their forefathers lived along the foothills of the Rocky Mountain since anyone could remember.

The first written record is from the Jesuit Missionaries who noted that the Stoney-Assiniboin separated from the Dakota/Lakota nation sometime before 1640. It is thought that they may have migrated westward with the Cree. They were encountered in Alberta around 1750. Another Jesuit, Father De Smet reported in 1840 that the Rocky Mountain Stoney separated from the Plains Assiniboin about 1790. However, it is believed that he may have referring to groups such as the Bearspaw band, who tradition has fleeing westward to escape smallpox.

STONO

The Stono was a subdivision or sub-tribe of the Cusabo proper (North). They lived about the Stono River or Intercoastal Canal entrance to Charleston Harbor in South Carolina. For more see the Cusabo and Coosa.

SUANG-NA

Suang-na was a sub-tribe of the Tongva of California that inhabited the area about Suanga. For more see Tongva.

SUGEREE

It is believed that the Sugeree were of the Siouan linguistic stock and lived in the area along Sugar Creek in York County, South Carolina, and Mecklenburg County, North Carolina. Their identity as a tribe was lost following the Yamasee War, and remnants were incorporated into the Catawba.

SUHTAI

The Suhtai or Sutaio belonged to the Algonquian linguistic family. They were closely related to the Cheyenne and lived near them in the area of the Minnesota River. After warring between themselves, the two tribes eventually made peace. The Sutaio migrated southwest across the Missouri River probably sometime before the Cheyenne. The Sutaio became nomadic hunters and ranged the plains west of the Missouri, thus acquiring the name Kites, for wanderers. because they were constantly moving about. The Suhtai and Cheyenne frequently crossed paths and at times lived side by side. By 1830s the Suhtai had been wholly incorporated into the Cheyenne proper or Tsistsistas as a separate band among those that became known as the Northern Cheyenne. The Suhtai are frequently referred to as the Chousa band of the Cheyenne from the name of their village.

It is reported that it was the Suhtai that introduced the Cheyenne to the buffalo and the Sacred Buffalo Hat ceremony. The Sutaio that choose not to join the Cheyenne moved north beyond the Missouri and were not heard of again. The Suhtai were the Staitan of the journals of the Lewis and Clark expedition, the name a contraction of Sutai-hitän, They were also the Staetan listed by Drake, who reported that they resembled the Kiawas (Kiowa). For more see Cheyenne.

SUMA

The Suma was of the Uto-Aztecan linguistic stock. They may have been a separate tribe or represented the western division of the Shuman of Texas and New Mexico or just a synonym for Shuman. Suma is a known tribe of Mexico. For more see Shuman.

SUQUÁMISH

The Suquámish belonged to the Nisqually branch of the coastal division of the Salishan linguistic stock with close connections to the Dwámish. Seattle (1786-1866), was the chief of both tribes. He was buried in the tribal cemetery at Suquamish, Washington. The tribe inhabited the west side of Puget Sound in Washington and claimed the lands from Applegate Cove to Gig Harbor. The Suquámish were established on the Port Madison Indian Reservation located on the Kitsap Peninsula in Washington State, situated on the waterfront across the Puget Sound.

SURRUQUE

The Surruque was of the Timucuan linguistic group that inhabited Florida near present Cape Canaveral. It is believed that they joined the Timucua/Utina.

SUSQUEHANNA

The Susquehanna (or Susquehannah) belonged to the Iroquoian linguistic family. They had several very common, popular names including the Adastse, Conestoga, and Minqua. The Huron called the tribe Andastoquehronnon, a word the French abridged to Andaste or Andastoque. The Dutch called them Minqua or White Minqua. The earliest recorded encounter with Europeans occurred in 1608 with the meeting of Captain John Smith, and it was they who welcomed the first settlers to Pennsylvania with food and gifts.

Under the various names, they inhabited the region north of Chesapeake Bay and the valley of the Susquehannah River in Pennsylvania, New York, and Maryland; the headwaters of the Allegheny in northeast Pennsylvania; and the valley of the Delaware River (South River to the Dutch). The various names have led to considerable confusion, for example, some reports identify the Andaste as a sub-tribe of the Susquehannock (Susquehanna).

Swanton suggests that the Susquehanna may originally have been the name of a confederacy of tribes rather than a single tribe. It has been suggested that the Wyoming about what is now the present state of Wyoming were of the Wyoming Valley in Pennsylvania (a twenty-five mile stretch of the north branch of the Susquehanna River) and at one time a member of Susquehanna group or Susquehanna confederacy; another suggested member was the Wysox that lived on a creek flowing into the Susquehanna. (The name Wyoming was derived from a corruption of Maugh-way-wame, a Delaware Indian name for The Large Plains. Having been driven west, the Delaware settled in the valley around 1758. They later moved on to the Ohio Valley. During the American Revolutionary War, Wilkes-Barre, Pennsylvania, was renamed

Fort Wyoming. The town of Wyoming is located about mid-way between Wilkes-Barre and Scranton, east-southeast of the county of Wyoming. The Borough of Wyomissing was located about Reading, in Berks County.)

The literature also contains references to the Turtle, Fox, and Wolf families or clans in reference to the Susquehanna. The same names were found among the other tribes of the region. References in the literature to the Ohongeeoquena, Unquehiett, Kaiquariegahaga, Usququhaga, and Seconondihago nations may have also been clans or sachems.

During the Dutch Period from 1609 to 1664, they were the principal traders with the settlers of New Sweden who had encroached on Dutch territory to the south in 1637. In March 1638, Peter Minuit, a former manager of the Dutch West India Company at New Netherland, led a party of soldiers and settlers from Sweden to the New Word to establish a colony on a tributary of Delaware River in the name of the King of Sweden. The West India Company had purchased land from the "Minquaon" on the east bank of the Delaware (in New Jersey) and built Fort Nassau in 1624 at the mouth of the Schuykill (Schuy Kill "Hidden River").

Minuit proceeded to buy the lands on the western shore of the Delaware below the Schuykill that was more convenient for trade with the Susquehanna. He established a garrison post called Fort Christina near the tributary of the Delaware called Minquas Kill. Minuit died on the journey back to Stockholm to pick up supplies and recruit new settlers. The outpost, however, continued to flourish for the next seventeen years and became a sizable Swedish colony—a colony within a colony. The colony of New Salem ultimately extended one hundred miles up the Delaware and encompassed parts of the future states of Delaware and Maryland and the southeast corner of Pennsylvania, to include the sites of the modern cities of Philadelphia and Trenton. The colony was destroyed in 1655 by Peter Stuyvesant, the director-general of Dutch New Netherland..

On September 15, 1655, a large assemblage of Algonquin Indians of the Lower Hudson, the Raritan, and Long Island attacked New Amsterdam; Pavonia (Jersey City); and Staten Island in what has been called the Peach War—a misnomer. The attack is generally attributed to the Wappinger or Esopus. The traditional story has it that the war took its name because a Dutch settler, Hendrick van Dyck, killed an Indian for stealing peaches from his orchard. The killing of the Indian for stealing peaches may or may not have been true, but the alleged event did not precipitate the Indian raids throughout New Netherland in September 1655.

Shorto writes that the attackers seemed to come from everywhere and included the Maqua (Mohawk) and the Mahikander (Mahican) as well as the Indians of the North River (Hudson). The raids were organized and led by a chief of the Susquehanna of the South River region, and the attacks were the direct result of the capture and dismantling of New Sweden by Stuyvesant. Stuyvesant had taken away their livelihood—their prosperous trading arrangements with the Swedes; and they retaliated. The Indians also destroyed farms and burned crops. Shorto writes that six hundred Indians alone struck at the southern tip of Manhattan.

It was a brief war that took forty to fifty European lives and another 50 to 100 captured—mostly women and children, who were later ransomed. (One writer identifies the Algonquin tribe as the Esopus; another writer gives the date as October 5, 1655, and only speaks of the Algonquin in the generic. Alfieri runs the Peach War into the Esopus Indian Wars, 1655-1664.)

The Susquehanna were bitter enemies of the Iroquois and may also have warred with the Mahican who inhabited the Hudson River valley. The last of the Iroquois wars ended around 1677. The Susquehanna to the south, who lived at the head of Chesapeake Bay, were involved with a number of other tribes of Virginia and Maryland in the Rebellion of 1676 in colonial Virginia known as Bacon's Rebellion. Driven from the headwaters of the Bay by the Seneca, the Susquehannah took sanctuary at the fort of the Piscataway on Matapoint Creek, east of the Potomac. They numbered, perhaps, some one hundred warriors. For more see Bacon's Rebellion and Conoy.

By the early 1700s the Susquehanna had been dispersed. Some were absorbed by the Iroquois; others were taken in by the Meherrin of New York. Remnants who returned to their home lands were murdered by fanatic settlers or found their homeland taken by other tribes to escape the Europeans. Their language is considered to have become extinct about 1763.

CONESTOGA MASSACRE

In mid-December 1763 a small, peaceful community under the name Conestoga near Lancaster was attacked and burned by a band of frontiersmen from Paxton, Pennsylvania, known as the Paxton Boys, but who referred to themselves as Hickory Boys. Six Indians at home at the time were massacred and their bodies mutilated. Fourteen others were taken into protective custody only to be dragged out and butchered—men, women, and children. Some of the Paxton Boys had discovered the tortured bodies of squatters for the Susquehanna Company killed at Wyoming in October and sought revenge, but for the most part the Paxton boys sought a land purged of all Indians.

(The deaths of the squatters were in retaliation for the death of Delaware leader Teedyuscung who was killed in the blaze the past April when his house was set on fire. The same peopled burned the entire Indian village was burned to the ground. And so it went. Through it all, the Conestoga at Lancaster were innocent.)

The murders of Lancaster County, that have come down in history as the Conestoga Massacre, appalled even the most hardened hearts. One of those killed, the Seneca Shehaes or Sheehays, was believed to have been present for the negotiation of a 1701 treaty with William Penn. So sickened by what had happened, Benjamin Franklin wrote a pamphlet in January titled, *A Narrative of the Late Massacres in Lancaster County, of a Number of Indians, Friends of This Province.*

SWALLAH

Swallah belonged to the coastal division of the Salishan linguistic family. Swallah villages were located on Orcas, San Juan, and Waldron islands in Washington State.

SWINOMISH

The Swinomish belonged to the coastal division of the Salishan linguistic family. The lived about the mouth of the Skagit River along the northern part of Whidbey Island that lay between Skagit Bay and Padilla Bay in northwest Washington Territory . Because of their location, the some writers have been identified them as a subdivision of the Skagit. Swanton, on the other hand, identifies the Skagit on Whidbey Island as a subdivision of the Swinomish. Other subdivisions of the Swinomish: Ho'baks, Kikia'los, Skwada'bah, Swinomish proper.

T'PEEKSIN

The T'Peeksin or Sawamish belonged to the Nisqually Branch of the coastal division of the Salisham linguistic family of western Washington about Puget Sound. They would later become a subdivision of the Squaxin Island Tribe and lived about Totten Inlet of Squaxin Island. They were a signatory to the Treaty with the Nisqually, Puyallup and others of 1854. See the Squawksin.

TABEGUACHE UTE

The Tabeguache or Tabaquache or Uncompahgre, the names used interchangeably. It was a subdivision of the Northern Ute and lived in and about Los Pinos in southwest Colorado. Chief Ouray of the Tabeguache (1833-1880), whose father was half Jicarilla Apache, led the Southern Ute Tribe during the mid 1800s. For more see Ute.

TACKIE

The Tackie was a member of the of the Southern Caddoan group. They are mentioned by Glover, but no additional information is known. For more see Caddo Peoples.

TACSTACURU

The Tacstacuru (also spelled Tacatacura) of Florida lived on Cumberland Island, formerly Tacstacuru Island. Their first encounter with Europeans was Frenchman Jean Riboult in 1562. They were forced to leave Cumberland Island in 1675 when it was occupied by the Yamasee. By the 1700s they were incorporated into other Timucua tribes.

TACULLIE

The Tacullie are referred to be Schoolcraft (they burn their dead), but no additional information has become available except that they probably related to the Sicaunie. They are believed to be of the Athapascan linguistic family that they lived in Canada.

TADIVA

The Tadiva was one of the six or seven allied tribes of the southwestern or Hasinai Division of the Caddo Indians or Hasinai Confederacy. For more see Hasinai Confederacy and Caddo Peoples.

TAENSA

The Taensa were one of the three tribes of the Natchez division of the Muskhogean stock. They inhabited the western end of Lake St. Joseph in Tensa Parish, Louisiana. They were encountered by both De Soto and La Salle.

When Iberville's brother Bienville (Jean-Baptiste LeMoyne de) explored west of the Mississippi into the Red River basin that comprises the present-day New Iberia, Lafayette and Morgan City in late 1699 and the spring of 1670, he was accompanied by six Taensa and one Ouachita guide. The Taensa, however, deserted the party after only a few days. Bienville traveled as far as Yatasi before returning to Biloxi.

Threatened by the Yazoo and Chickasaw, they abandoned their village and settled in the village of the Tayogoula in 1706 whom they later either destroyed or drove away. Following intermittent moves, they settled in Mobile in 1715. After Mobile was surrendered to the English in 1763, the Taensa moved to the Red River near the Apalachee. After some forty years, they sold their lands and moved to Bayou Boeuf and later farther south to the head of Grand Lake. By the early 1800s the Taensa were extinct as a tribe.

TAHNEEMUH

The Tahneemuh (liver eaters) was one of the sub-tribes or bands of the Comanche. For more see Comanche.

TAHSAGROUDIE

The Tahsagroudie lived about modern Detroit, Michigan, in 1723. Drake believed that they were probably the Tsonothouans, which were also listed in his enumeration.

TAIDNAPAM

The Taidnapam were also called the Upper Cowlitz. The tribe belonged to the Shahaptian division of the Shapwailutan linguistic family and lived on the headwaters of the Cowlitz River in an area possibly extending to the headwaters of the Lewis River in Washington.

TAKELMA

The Takelma, commonly called the Rogue River Indians. With the Latgawa, they constituted the Takilma linguistic stock, possibly related to the Salishan (Shastam) stock of northern California. With the Salishan, Yakonan, and Kusan linguistic families, they constitute the group of Indians classified as the Siletz.

The Takelma lived on the middle course of the Rogue River in Oregon from above the Illinois River to near Grant's Pass and on its northern tributaries from the upper course of Cow Creek and south almost to the border with California. Because of the location they were also commonly called the Upper Rogue River Indians.

In December 1851 gold was found in the Rogue River valley. Its discovery and the influx of prospectors eventually led to the Rogue River wars that took place between 1850 and 1856. With the treaty of 1853 (Treaty with the Rogue River), the Takelma ceded all their rights, titles, interests, and claims to the lands of the Oregon Territory and were assigned to an Indian reserve—Table Rock, until such time as "a suitable selection shall be made by the direction of the President...for their permanent residence and buildings erected thereon, and provision made for their removal. reservation."

ROGUE RIVER WARS

The troubles between whites and Indians between the years 1852 and 1856 were precipitated primarily by the discovery of gold and resulted in what has been called the Rogue River Wars.

Gold was discovered in the Rogue River valley in present-day southwest Oregon in December 1851. Miners and gold-seekers, mostly single men, crossed over from California. Relations between whites and Indians in western Oregon was tense, but it was nothing compared to the explosive situation created in the south as the Indians were pushed from their homes.

The First Rogue River War that consisted of a number of random killings in the years 1853. Table Rock Treaty was negotiated between the government and several groups of Rogue River Indians September 10, 1853. At best it was a temporary fix. By 1855, the number and frequency of Indians raids and killings began to increase. The depredations coupled with deteriorating economic conditions made the valley ripe for a new Indian war.

What is commonly referred to as the Rogue River War, or the Second Rogue River War, raged from October 1855 to mid-1856 and involved the all the tribes of the Rogue River Valley of southern Oregon. On October 8, 1855, a mob from the mining town of Jacksonville led by James Lupton, southwest Oregon's first representative to the territorial legislature, attacked and killed twenty-eight or more Indians camped near the Table Rock Reservation at the mouth of Butte Creek. (Other accounts put the number killed at 23 with many wounded.) Several of the volunteers were wounded. Lupton was killed. Most of the Indian dead were women, children, and old men.

The real issue was not retribution, nor criminal prosecution, nor land. The issue was jobs. As the mines dried up, unemployed miners took up the work of killing Indians as paid volunteers. The war was *created* as a dole for the unemployed or, as some call it, a pork-barrel war. Tecumtum (Chief John) of the Etch-ka-taw-wah band of the Takelma led the Indian resistance.

Some of the Indians fell back to Fort Lane for protection. (In January they were removed to the Grand Ronde Reservation in northwestern Oregon.) The others, who chose to fight fled to the coastal mountains as the attacks on Indian camps continued throughout the winter of 1855-56. In the spring, the Indians brought the war to the whites down the Rogue River to the coast. Regular soldiers marched in from the south as volunteer militia came down from the north. The last battles of the war were fought at Big Meadows in late May 1856 followed by Big Bend on the Rogue River shortly thereafter. In June the last of the Indians of the Rogue River Valley surrendered and were sent to the Coast Reservation on Oregon's central coast (later the Siletz Reservation). They were forced to walk the 125 miles to their new home. By the fall of 1856, the Takelma, Latgawa, Tututni, Coos, Coquille, and Umpqua of southwest Oregon had been removed to the Coast Reservation.

TAKKUTH-KUTCHIN

The Takkuth-kutchin tribe of Canada belonged to the Kutchin group of the northern division of the Athapascan linguistic family. They lived along upper course of the Porcupine River. Others in the group were the Tatlit-kutchin (Peel River); Nakotcho-kutchin (lower course of the Mackensie); and Katcha-kutchin (Alaska). They are included in this section because they are sometimes mentioned in connection with the tribes of the United States.

TALI

The Tali lived about the great bend of the Tennessee River in Tennessee and northern Alabama, but they may have been a part of the Creek. They had an early encounter with men of De Soto's

TALLEWHEANA

The Tallewheana was a band of the Seminole that lived on the east side of the Flint River, near the Cheraw.

TALTUSHTUNTUDE

The Taltushtuntude lived on Galice Creek in Oregon. They belonged to the Athapascan linguistic stock.

TAMA'LI

The Tama'li Indians were reported in the journals of early Spanish explorers as among the southern group of Georgia Indians. A member of the Creek Confederacy of Lower Creeks, their village of Tamatle was situated on the lower Chattahoochee River. They were also known as Tamali, Tomatola, or Tama. There were also two Cherokee villages of the same name located on the Valley and Little Tennessee Rivers.

TAMAROA

The Tamaroa were one of the major tribes of the Illinois Cluster of Tribes. They lived about the mouths of the Illinois and the Missouri rivers on both sides of the Mississippi. See the Illinois.

TAMATHLI

Th Tamathli were of the Atsik-hata group of the Creek Confederation. They inhabited southwestern Georgia and neighboring parts of Florida. It is believed that they were the Toa or Toalli of De Soto's chronicles. The Tamathli migrated in Florida and were established in a mission named La Purificatrión de la Tama in the Apalachee country in 1675. There was also the record of a Nuestra Señora de la Candelaria dela Tama. The Tomathli suffered with the Apalachee in the attack by Moore in 1704. They went into another mission near St. Augustine that was attacked by the Creeks in 1725. Those that survived moved to a new mission and came down in history as the New Tamathli (1738) or northern division. The southern division was called the Old Tamathli. The word "division" is an exaggeration as groups numbered only in the tens. It is believed that they were absorbed into the Seminole.

TANAINA

The Tanaina belonged to the Athapascan linguistic group of Alaska. They lived about the drainage of Cook Inlet north of Seldovia and the north half of Iliamna Lake, as well as its drainage, including Clark Lake. They are also known under the older name Kinai, which was used by Drake. The Tanaina is included in this section in order to avoid possible confusion arising from its inclusion in Drake's enumeration of tribes. It is the only Alaskan tribe listed.

TANCAGUE

The Tancague was counted among the Nations for the North, but little additional information has been found. Bolton writes that they were listed in a memorial of Father Ortiz to the king of Spain, after February 14, 1747. For more see Nations of the North.

TANGIPAHOA

The Tangipahoa were part of the southern division of the Muskhogean stock and inhabited the area about the present Tangipahoa River in Tangipahoa Parish in Louisiana. There is a record La Salle's visit to a town called Tangibao on the eastern side of the Mississippi in 1682 near the supposed site of the Quinipissa. It is likely that the Tangipahoa were absorbed in to the Acolapissa.

TANICO

The Tanico tribe is cited in Bolton, "Missions on the San Gabriel," as living near the Mississippi, but no additional information has become available.

TANIMA

The Tanima (Danemme, Teneme, Tiniema) was one of the sub-tribes or bands of the Comanche of Texas. They ranged widely over northern Texas but are often linked with the area that lies between the upper Brazos and Red rivers that they shared with the Nokoni and Tenawa, with whom they are frequently confused. They also camped with the Penateka to the south between the Brazos and Colorado rivers. For more see Comanche.

TANKITEKE

The Tankiteke was a subdivision or sub-tribe of the Wappinger and lived mainly in Fairfield County, Connecticut, between Five Mile River and Fairfield and extending inland to Danbury and even into Putnam and Duchess Counties, New York. For more see Wappinger.

TANO PUEBLO

The Tano were of the Southern Tewa group of the Tanoan linguistic family that is part of the Kiowa-Tanoan stock. The Tano lived in the area from near Santa Fe to near the Golden River. As a result of the aftereffects of the Pueblo Revolt, most of the Southern Tewa joined the Hopi after 1694. For more see Pueblo Peoples.

TANXNITANIA

The Tanxnitania was a sub-tribe of the Manahoac of Virginia or possibly a member of the Manahoac Confederacy. They lived on the north side of the upper Rappahannock River in Fauquier County.

TAOS PUEBLO

The Taos Pueblo was of the Tiwa group of the Tanoan linguistic family that was part of the Kiowa-Tanoan stock. With the inhabitants of Picuris, they comprised one of the three divisions of the Tiwa that occupied the upper waters of the Rio Grande River. The imposing pueblo lies at the foothills of New Mexico's highest peaks at an elevation of 7,200 feet on land of just under 100,000 acres.

In 1970, 48,000 acres of mountain land that included the sacred Blue Lake of the Taos Pueblo was returned to the pueblo. The land had been taken by the government for National Forest Lands in 1906. For more see Pueblo Peoples.

TAOS REVOLT OF 1847

Having marched into Santa Fe without firing a shot in August, General Stephen Watts Kearney established the first civilian government in the territory of New Mexico under the U.S. flag. On September 22, before heading west to California, Kearney placed Colonel Sterling Price in command of military forces and appointed trader and rancher Charles Bent New Mexico's first governor. Resentment to American presence in New Mexico remained high. Incited by Mexican insurgents, the Indians of the Taos Pueblo revolted and vowed to kill all Americans. Agitation began in the final months of 1846, and on January 19, 1847, Governor Bent was murdered in his in his Taos home. Also killed that evening were the sheriff of Taos and several others. The revolt spread to Turley's Mill near Arroyo Hondo where Simeon Turley and several other Americans were killed. Frey Martinez provided sanctuary for several Americans who sought refuge at his house.

From Santa Fé, Colonel Price led his men towards Taos and ordered Captain Burgwin's company of calvary up from Albuquerque. Price defeated rebels held up at Santa Cruz de la Cañada. Those that escaped fled to Embudo and tried to make another stand before they were forced to retreat again. Price reached Taos (San Fernando de Taos) on February 3. Price's force of about 320 soldiers, with about 60 volunteers assembled by Ceran St. Vrain, Bent's trading partner, surrounded Pueblo de Taos and laid down a artillery barrage that had only limited effect on the thick adobe walls. The next day Price ordered a frontal attack of infantry and artillery that finally breached the walls that opened the town to the soldiers. An estimated 150-200 Puebloans and Mexican insurgents were killed. The Taos Pueblo Church, where the rebels made their final stand, was destroyed. Price reported the loss of seven, including Captain John Burgwin, and 45 wounded. By February 5, the revolt had come to an end. Of the suspected leaders of the revolt, one was killed in his cell, and another was tried and convicted of treason and hanged. Twenty-one hangings followed for the succeeding six months. (See the Treaty of Guadalupe-Hidalgo.)

The event has also been referred to as the "Second Pueblo Revolt" and the "Pueblo Revolt Against the Americans." Other references are made to the "Siege of the Pueblo de Taos."

TAOVAYA

The Taovaya (also Taovayase) may have been a member of the Wichita Group from Kansas and southern Nebraska forced south into southern Oklahoma and north central Texas in the eighteenth century. They lived along the lower Canadian River near the Tawakoni and Yscani when first contacted by the French trader and explorer Sieur Bernard de La Harpe in 1719. Migrating into Texas, they settled along the Red River near Spanish Fort. They were counted among the Nations of the North or Norteños (northerners). Under the provision of a 1835 treaty with the United States, the Taovaya and related Wichita Indians were settled in Indian Territory.

TAPAGE PAWNEE

The Tapage or Pitahauerat Pawnee were one of the four subdivisions of the Pawnee. They were comprised of two bands or villages, the Pitahauerat proper and the Kawarakis. They lived about the Platte River in Nebraska. For more see Pawnee.

TAPOSA

It is believed that the Taposa belonged to the Muskhogean stock. Their best known location was along the Yazoo River in Mississippi. A small tribe, they were first mentioned by Iberville. They are often included with the Chakchiuma.

TAPOUARO

The Tapouaro was one of the minor tribes of the Illinois Cluster of Tribes for which there is only passing mention. For more see Illinois Cluster.

TAPPAN

The Tappan was a sub-tribe of the Unami division of the Delaware. They lived on the western bank of the Hudson River in Rockland County, New York, and in Bergan County, New Jersey.

TATLIT-KUTCHIN

The Tatlit-kutchin tribe of Canada belonged to the Kutchin group of the northern division of the Athapascan linguistic family. They lived along the Peel River and the adjoining part of the Mackenzie River. Others in the group were the Takkuth-kutchin (upper course of the Porcupine River); Nakotcho-kutchin (lower course of the Mackensie); and Katcha-kutchin (Alaska). They are included in this section because they are frequently mentioned in connection with the tribes of the United States.

TATSANOTTINE

The Tatsanottine or Copper Indians of Canada (not to be confused with Copper River Indians) belonged to the Athapascan (Athapascal) linguistic stock and were later classified with the Chipewyan. The Tatsanottine lived along the northern shores and eastern bays of Great Slave Lake. They were noted for their possession of copper ore that came from a mountain near the Coppermine River.

TAUKAWAYS

Drake reported that the Taukaways lived about the sources of Trinity, Brazos, De Dios, and Colorado Rivers. No other information is available.

TAUXENENT

The Tauxenent tribe was a member of the Powhatan Confederacy and inhabited parts of Fairfax County, Virginia.

TAWAKONI

The Tawakoni (known by several names) were of the Caddoan linguistic stock. Swanton writes that they may have been a member of the Wichita Group or, and if not more likely, an independent tribe. In either case, the Tawakoni have been treated separately in the literature. They lived along the Canadian River north of the Wichita in present Oklahoma, near the Taovaya and Yscani when they were first contacted by the French trader and explorer Sieur Bernard de La Harpe in 1719.

They migrated south and west into Texas and in 1772 settled in two groups. The first group settled on the Brazos River at what became Tehuacana Creek east-northeast of Waco. The second group settled on the Trinity River near present Palestine. In 1779 the two groups rejoined on the Brazos, but by 1824 they had separated again when the second group moved back on the Trinity. In 1855 the Tawakoni were placed on a reservation near Fort Belknap on the Brazos. In 1859 they officially joined the Wichita on the Wichita Reservation in Oklahoma. For more see Nations of the North.

Texas writings note that the creek, originally called Tohawacony Creek, took its name from the Tawakoni who lived about the area. In other writings they are referred to as the Tehuacanas Indians. The Tawakoni were of the signatories to the treaty with the Republic of Texas at Tehuacana Creek October 9, 1844. (An Indian Council had been held at the site March 28, 1843.) The name Tah-wah-karro is also used in the treaty.

They were also a party to the treaty of May 15, 1846, at Council Springs near the Brazos River in Robinson County under the name Tahwacarro. It is believed that they were also the Towacanno or Towash listed by Drake as living on the Brazos River. The Tawakoni should not be confused with the Tonkawa who inhabited central Texas generally between the Cibolo Creek and the Trinity River.

Of Note

The Tawakoni, under the spelling Towaconies, were mistakenly identified as the Indians killed in the Wichita Agency Massacre. See the Tonkawa.

TAWASA

The Tawasa was an independent tribe with a town was near present-day Montgomery, Alabama. De Soto reportedly stayed at the Tawasa village in 1540. The Tawasa subsequently moved to an area near Ft. Toulouse in northern Alabama near the Apalachicola River and became a member of the Creek Confederacy (Upper Creeks). It is believed that by the mid-1700s, part have joined the Alabama and followed them into Louisiana and Texas. Following the Creek war, those that remained joined the Creeks and the Alabama. Some likely ended up in Florida.

TAWEHASH

The Tawehash were of the Caddoan linguistic stock and closely related to the Wichita, Tawakoni, Waco, and Yscani. They inhabited the area along the Canadian River in present Oklahoma north of the headwaters of the Washita. They were first encountered in 1718 by La Harpe. They later moved south and were found settled on the Red River in 1759 where they were defeated by a Spanish force sent against them. They remained along the Red River until they eventually united with the Wichita and disappeared from history as a distinct tribe. Their descendants remained with the Wichita when they were removed to Indian Territory.

TCI-HE-NDE MIMBRE

The Tci-he-nde Mimbre or Mimbreño (Spanish for Willows) or Chihenne (Chi-hen-ne) was one of the three major bands or sub-tribes of the Chiricahua Apache and played a major role in the Apache wars. They have also been commonly referred to as Warm Springs Apache, Ojo Caliente, and simply as the Mimbre. They took their popular name from the Mimbres Mountains of southwestern New Mexico. The Ojo Caliente (Warm Springs) in southwestern New Mexico at the foot of the San Mateo mountains was revered as a sacred place by the Tci-he-nde. (It should not to be confused with the city of Ojo Caliente in north central New Mexico west of Taos.) They were also called Coppermine Apaches because the occupied the area of the Santa Rita mines in southwestern New Mexico, The principal leader of the Mimbre was Mangas Coloradas (1810-1874). He was followed by his son Mangus; Beduiat (Victorio); and chiefs Nana and Loco. Victorio was the principal leader of the second Apache war. Mangus, one of the last holdouts, surrendered in 1886 and died in 1901. Old Nana as he was called died in 1896; Loco in 1905.

From their base in the mountains, they roamed from the east side of the Rio Grande in New Mexico to the San Francisco river in Arizona, a favorite haunt being near Lake Guzman, west of El Paso, in Chihuahua. In habits they were similar to the other Apaches. They made their livelihood by raiding settlements in New Mexico, Arizona and Mexico. They made peace with the Mexicans from time to time, and before 1870 were supplied with rations by the military post at Janos, Chihuahua. In 1875 they were placed on the Mescalero reservation and the Hot Springs (Chiricahua) agency in New Mexico. They are now divided between the Mescalero reservation and the Fort Apache agency in Arizona. For more see Apache and Chiricahua Apache.

TEGNINATEO

The Tegninateo was a sub-tribe of the Manahoac of Virginia or a tribe of the Manahoac Confederacy. They lived in Culpepper County at the headwaters of the Rappahannock River.

TEGNINATI

The Tegninati was one of the Mannahoac tribes. They lived on the Potomac River in Virginia, in Culpepper County.

TEJAS

There was no single tribe of Indians called the Tejas, but the Caddoan groups of East Texas used the word to refer to the allied tribes. It is believed that the Teyas were absorbed by larger Lipan bands, one of which migrated into southern New Mexico west of the Rio Grande and was subsequently absorbed by the Mescalero Apaches. See the Caddo.

The word texas and its variants (tejas, tayshas, texias, thecas?, techan, teysas, techas?) had wide usage among the Indians of East Texas before the days of the Spanish explorers. Reportedly, with the word texias or techas?, "friends," the coastal Indians welcomed the Spanish of the first DeLeon-Massanet expedition in the early seventeen hundred. The Spanish applied the name to the Indians themselves and to what became the state of Texas. Somewhat later the name was used to identify tribes allied against the Apaches. The word has also be interpreted as a form of greeting used by the Hasinai. The state motto of Texas is "Friendship."

TELMOCRESSE

The Telmocresse was a band of the Seminole that lived on the west side Chattahoochee River, fifteen miles from the fork.

TENAWA

The Tenawa, known by several names, including Tahnahwah, Tenahwit, Denavi, Tanewa, Tannewish, Tannewa, Tenawit, Tenhua, was one of the sub-tribes or bands of the Comanche. It is believed that they were an offshoot of the Yamparika Comanches who migrated from Western Comancheria to Eastern Comancheria. They lived in the area that lies between the upper Brazos and Red rivers. The name means "those who stay downstream." They are sometimes confused in the writings with the Tanima band of Comanche. For more see Comanche and Tanima.

TENINO

The Tenino was a division of the Shahaptian branch of the Shapwailutan linguistic stock. They lived along the north bank of the Columbia River near the mouths of the Umatilla and Deschutes rivers and Olive Creek in Oregon; also on the John Day River. The Tukspush division on the John Day River were commonly referred to as the John Day Indians. They were mentioned by Lewis and Clark in 1805. For more see Tukspush.

The Tenino and Taih (Tyigh) were separate, independent tribes rather than bands of the Walla Walla as referred to in the Treaty with the Tribes of Middle Oregon (1855). The Tenino ceded all their lands for the Yakima Reservation in Washington. The Warm Springs tribe is made up of the Tenino, Upper Deschutes (Tygh), Lower Deschutes (Wyam), and John Day (Dock-spus) bands. The Wasco tribe is made up of The Dalles (Ki-gal-twal-la) and Dog River bands. Together with several Paiute bands from southeastern Oregon they comprise the Confederated Tribes of the Warm Springs Reservation of Oregon located on 640,000 acres in north central Oregon.

TEQUESTA

Tequesta or Tekesta was one of the small tribes to inhabit Florida. The Tequestas passed into history by the 1800s. Generally by 1763 when Florida passed from the Spanish into the hands of the English the original aboriginal life in Florida had all but disappeared. Remnants removed to Cuba. The former town of Tekesta is the site of modern Miami.

MIAMI STONE CIRCLE

The Miami Circle was an important part of the town of Tekesta that preceded present-day Miami. In August 1998, excavations for a parking garage exposed a circle of holes chiseled into the limestone bedrock. Also found were pottery shards, stone axe heads, and other artifacts that were put on display at the Historical Museum of Southern Florida's exhibit called "First Arrivals."

TESUQUE PUEBLO

The Tesuque (Te-soo´-ka) Pueblo was of the Northern division of the Tewa Pueblo Group of the Tanoan linguistic family that is part of the Kiowa-Tanoan stock. They lived eight miles north of Santa Fe. For more see Pueblo Peoples.

TEWA PUEBLO GROUP

The Tewa were of the Tanoan linguistic family of the Kiowa-Tanoan stock. It was one of the eight groups of four linguistic families of Pueblo. The Tewa comprised two divisions, the Northern Tewa from near Santa Fe to the mouth of the Rio Chama and the Southern Teas (Tano) from Santa Fe to the near Golden. For more see Pueblo Peoples.

TÉXAS

The Téxas that inhabited the area along the Neches and the Angelina rivers that ran parallel with one another about ten miles apart west of Nacogdoches. Vigotes was the chief of Téxas during the late Spanish period when a mission was established at Nacogdoches. Téxas was one of the tribes that were commonly referred to as the eastern tribes that inhabited the territory between the Adaes and the Middle Trinity rivers. The Vidais, Quitseis, and Tonkawaswere were others.

TEYA

The Teya were first encountered during the Coronado expedition in 1540-42. They lived in the eastern part of the Texas Panhandle adjoining Oklahoma. Most writers identify them as Plains Apaches.

THLINGCHADINNE

The Thlingchadinne of Canada belonged to the Athapascan linguistic family. They lived between Great Bear Lake and Great Slave Lake, but not as far as the Mackenzie River. They were comprised of four divisions: Lintchanre, Takfwelottine, Tsantieottine, and Tseottine. They are frequently mentioned in connection with the Indians of the United States.

THREE FIRES CONFEDERACY

Three Fires Confederacy or Three Brothers Federation or Brothers of Three Fires was a loose confederation of the Ottawa, Chippewa (Ojibwe), and Potawatomi. The three Algonquian tribes inhabited the valley of St. Joseph River (originally Sau-wau-see-bee "Fate of the Sisters) of Michigan, presently St. Joseph County. The confederacy was also known as the People of the Tree Fires and Three Files Council. (In his listing of Great Lakes/Ohio Country tribes, Calloway lists the Anishinabeg separately from the Chippewa and identifies them as one of the tribes of the Three Fires Confederacy along with the Ottawa and Potawatomi and makes no reference to the fact that Anishinabeg is generally considered another name for the Chippewa. Elsewhere he replaces the name Anishinabegs with the name Ojibwas in naming the members of the confederacy.)

Tradition includes a fourth tribe of the St. Joseph valley, Mus-quah-tas. Aside from the single reference by Ms. Silliman, no additional information has become available. She writes that the tribe was almost exterminated when it challenged the Ottawa. See Musquash.

Of Note

The Chippewa called the river Sau-wau-see-bee "Fate-of-the-Sisters"; Pottawatomies, Sauwk Wauwk or Sil Buck; Ottawas, Sau-gan-see-pe. The Iroquois League called it the River of The Illinois after 1630 and called Lake Michigan, The Lake of The Illinois.

TIBAHAG-NA

The Tibahag-na was a sub-tribe of the Tongva of California that inhabited the area about Serritos. For more see Tongva.

TIGUA PUEBLO

The Isleta del Sur Pueblo (Ysleta del Sur or Ysleta of the South) was located just south of modern-day El Paso, Texas. It, was the home of the Tigua (Tiguex, Tiwa, Tihua) Indians. The pueblo was established in 1682 by refugees from Isleta Pueblo southwest of present-day Albuquerque on the Rio Grande and the Indians of the Quivera Pueblo located in the Manzano Mountains southeast of Albuquerque. Quivera had been abandoned because of persistent drought and repeated raids by the Apaches. From Isleta came about three 385 loyal Isleta and Tigua who fled south in December 1681 with Governor Otermín following his abortive attempt at reconquest. For more see Pueblo Peoples, Quivera Pueblo and Isleta Pueblo.

Of Note

Today the Ysleta del Sur, the only pueblo still in Texas, occupies about twenty-six acres of trust land that was established in 1968. The tribe hosted the 65th annual Tekakwitha Conference, July 28 - August 1, 2004.

TIKABAHCHEE

The Tikabahchee was one of the sub-tribes of the Creek of Alabama that is sometimes treated separately.

TILKUNI

The Tilkuni was a subdivision of the Tenino. They lived between the present White and Warm Springs Reservations in Oregon. For more see Tenino.

TILLAMOOK

The Tillamook proper was one of the four subdivisions of the Tillamook group of tribes. They lived in several villages on Tillamook Bay and the streams flowing into it. Lewis & Clark enumerated eleven villages, all under the name Killamuck. Swanton refers to five. For more see Tillamook Group.

LEWIS & CLARK JOURNALS (Swanton*)
Chishucks*
Chucktin*
Kahunkle
Kilherhursh*
Kilherner*
Killawat
Lickawis
Towerquotten*
Ulseah

TILLAMOOK GROUP

The Tillamook Group of tribes were of the coastal division of the Salishan linguistic stock and inhabited lands along the coast from Nehalem to the Salmon River in Oregon where they were encountered by the Corps of Discovery. They are generally described as the most powerful tribe or group along the Oregon coast. The four subdivisions are often treated separately in the literature.

SUBDIVISIONS

Nehalem
Nestucca
Salmon River

Tillamook proper

TIMUCUA

The Timucua (or Timuca) were the Timucua proper of the Timucuan Division of the Muskhogean linguistic family and the leading tribe and gave their name to the whole that is also identified as the Utina. The inhabited large parts of Florida and Georgia. It is difficult differentiate between the Timucua division as a whole and the Timucua proper in the historical accounts found in the literature. For more see the Utina.

TIONONTATI

Tionontati or Tionontates, more popularly known as the Tobacco Indians, the Petuns, and Gens du Petun or "Tobacco Nation," were related to the Huron to the extent that some references give them the designation of Huron. The Tionontati was of Iroquoian linguistic stock and inhabited the eastern Great Lakes on Lake Huron in Canada. Remnants later appeared in Wisconsin integrated into the Wyandot. (Petun was a Native American name for tobacco.) Agriculturists, the tribe received its name because it raised tobacco as a "cash" crop for barter with other tribes and with the Europeans, the Hurons serving as the middle-man.

The Tionontati's first encounter with Europeans was with Samuel de Champlain in 1616. The Hurons told the Tionontati that the French were sorcerers (*nipissings*) in order to protect their position as middle-men in the tobacco trade. For more see Dinondadies, Huron, and Wyandot.

TIOPANE

The Tiopane (Sayupane) was one of the four allied tribes of the Karankawan of Texas. It is believed that they lived along the San Antonio River in the general vicinity of present Karnes County. For more see Karankawan Tribes.

TIOU

The Tiou belonged to the Tunica linguistic family. The earliest reports have them situated near the upper course of the Yazoo River in Mississippi. Later they lived first near then among the Natchez. They are included in with the Natchez in all population figures. It is not uncommon to find the name misspelled Sioux thus confusing them with the Dakota.

TIRANS

The Tirans was a sub-tribe of the Unalachtigo division of the Delaware. They lived on the northern shore of Delaware Bay about Cape May and possibly in Cumberland County. For more see Unalachtigo and Delaware.

TIWA PUEBLO

The Tiwa Pueblo was one of the eight groups among the four linguistic families of Pueblo. They belonged to the Tanoan linguistic family of the Kiowa-Tanoan stock. They were composed of three divisions.
    Taos and Picuris (the most northerly of the New Mexican Pueblos), on the upper Rio Grande
    Sandia and Isleta, north and south of present Albuquerque, respectively
    Isleta de Sur and Senecu del Sur near El Pasco, Texas and Chihuahua, Mexico. For more see Pueblo Peoples.

Tiwa is also the name of a Wichita band.

TOCKWOGH

The Tockwogh was a division of the Nanticoke. They lived along the Sassafras River (originally called Toghwogh because the Indians made bread from the sassafras root from along the shores) in Kent and Cecil counties in Maryland, along the Eastern Shore. They were of the Algonquian linguistic family, but spoke a different dialect from others in the region. The Tockwogh allied themselves with the Susquehannock.

TOCOBAGA

The Tocobaga were one of the larger tribes of the Timucuan subdivision of the Muskhogean linguistic stock. They inhabited the area around Old Tampa Bay and were said to number 1,000 in 1650, but they disappeared from the records soon thereafter and were not listed as participating in the Timucua revolt of 1656. They may have united with the Calusa or other Timucuan tribes. It is also possible that they may be the Tompacuas who appear somewhat later in Apalachee country or they may have been the Indians under the name Macapiras or Amacapiras who entered the San Buenaventura mission in 1726. For more see the Utina.

TOHOME

The Tohome belonged to the southern branch of the Muskhogean linguistic group and were closely related to the Mobile. They lived about McInosh's Bluff on the west bank of the Tombigbee River, above its junction with the Alabama River when first encountered by whites, but there is evidence they may have lived on a creek once known as the Oke Thome (Ctoma) that flows into the Alabama River below Montgomery.

In reports dated in the mid-1550s, the Tombigbee River is called the River of the Tome. Iberville learned of the tribe in April 1700 and visited them in 1702, but he did not venture beyond the Naniaba River. Their history thereafter follows that of the Mobile. There is little mention of the Tohome after 1762. It is believed that the remnants of both tribes were absorbed into the Choctaw.

TOLOWA

The Tolowa inhabited the area about Crescent Bay, Lake Earl, and the Smith River in California. Although closely related to the Athapascan of Oregon, they constituted one of the divisions of the California people of the Athapascan stock. Some two hundred Tolowa Iwere savagely killed at their Yontoket village in 1853 by citizens of Crescent City. In the little reported incident, children were reportedly thrown into the fire along with the Indians' ceremonial robes and regalia. The following year hundreds more were murdered after the Tolowa stole a white man's horse. (Some reports put the number of Indians killed at 450.)

TONAWANDA

Tonawanda was band of Seneca division of Iroquois. They lived on Tonawanda Creek in Niagara County, New York. The Big Tree Treaty of 1797 assigned them 46,080 acres, more substantial than several of the other allotments, but by 1856 their lands had been reduced to a little over 7,500 acres.

TONGVA

The Tongva or Gabrielino, meaning "People of the Earth," inhabited the Los Angeles basin of California throughout the area of what is now Los Angeles and Orange Counties. They also inhabited the islands of Santa Catalina, San Nicholas, San Clemente, and Santa Barbara in some thirty-plus sites. They belonged to the California branch of the Shoshonean Division of the Uto-Aztecan linguistic family. The name Gabrielino became quite common because of the Indians close association with the Spanish Mission of San Gabriel that was established in 1771, from which the name was derived. The Tongva also joined the Missions San Fernando and San Juan Capistrano. (Swanton uses the name Gabrielino but makes no direct reference to the Tongva.)

Their first contact with Europeans was their meeting with Juan Rodriquez Cabrillo in 1542 off what is now San Pedro. The Tongva was comprised of a number of tribes, sub-tribes, or villages throughout the area. Swanton lists thirty-four villages. There was an estimated population of five thousand in 1770 living in the drainage area of the San Gabriel River, the territory about Los Angeles south to include half of present Orange County, and on Santa Catalina Island and possibly San Clemente. By the 1950s they were nearly extinct, but they have managed to maintain their native bloodline and their traditions into the twenty-first century with a population of less than one thousand.

TONKAWA

The Tonkawa proper from Tonkaweya was the largest and most important and only surviving tribe of the four Tonkawan Tribes that made up the distinct Tonkawan linguistic family. They were encountered by the Spanish early in the sixteenth century.

The Tonkawa inhabited central Texas generally between the Cibolo Creek and the Trinity River. They should not be confused with the Tawakoni of the Caddoan stock that at one time lived along the Canadian River north of the Washita in Oklahoma.* The distinction becomes more difficult following the migration of the Tawakoni south into central Texas on the Trinity and Brazos rivers.

Out in pursuit of Comanche following the destruction of the San Saba Mission and the killing the priests near San Antonio, Spanish troops with Lipan and Coahuiltecan auxiliaries, came upon an encampment of Tonkawa in September 1759. The soldiers attacked the unsuspecting village. According to the official report, possibly exaggerated, some three hundred warriors were killed and 150 women and children taken. In March 1778, a treaty was made with the Tonkawa at Bucareli by which the tribe would regularly be visited by a trader.

A hundred years later, some one hundred and fifty Tonkawa men, women and children of the at the Wichita Agency in Indian Territory were massacred by a combined force of pro-Union Indians. The survivors wandered aimlessly for a time before being taken in at Fort Belknap in Young County, Texas. Belknap was abandoned and replaced by Fort Griffin, which opened in 1867. Remnants of the Tonkawa in 1884 were placed on a reservation in Oklahoma, near the Ponca. For more see the Tonkawan Tribes.

WICHITA AGENCY MASSACRE OR TONKAWA MASSACRE

The answers as to why are skewed depending on one's perspective. Whether the raid was a military action or a personal vendetta is unknown. Both factors most likely entered into the matter. In late October 1862, there was a raid on the Wichita Agency in Indian Territory that supervised the Tonkawa reservation. The date is variously reported as October 23, 24, and 25.

The agency was located near present-day Anadarko in Caddo County, Oklahoma. Four white men, presumably Confederate Indian agents, soldiers, or sympathizers, were killed and the agency buildings were ransacked and burned. The raiders then attacked the nearby Tonkawa village. About 150 of the 390 Tonkawa men, women and children of the agency were massacred, including Plácido, a major chief of the Tonkawa. (William Jones puts the numbers at 137 of 309.) According to reports, the agency was to be protected by members of the Choctaw Battalion stationed at a Confederate cantonment designated as Camp McIntosh, but they were apparently unaware of what had transpired until it was too late. The survivors fled to Fort Arbuckle for safety. The Confederate government did not attempt to re-establish the Wichita Agency, and the Tonkawa returned to the open plains until taken in at Fort Belknap, Texas, where they remained until the end of the Civil War.

There was almost as much uncertainty about who as there was about why. It is generally believed that the principals were one hundred or so pro-Union Delaware and Shawnee warriors from Kansas led by the Delaware Ben Simon and that they were joined by warriors from local Caddo tribes, including the Keechi band of Wichitas. Other participants are believed to be warriors from the local Kickapoo, Kiowa and Comanche tribes, all of whom resented the Tonkawas' continued service as scouts for the Confederacy. Complicating the issue of why was the fact that the Tonkawa also had a reputation of cannibalism.

*In a report in the of the incident by S. S. Scott, to Maj. Gen. Holmes, Commander of the Trans-Mississippi Department, dated November 2, 1862, Scott mistakenly identifies the Indians attacked and killed as the Towaconies [Tawakoni], but correctly identifies Plácido, the Tonkawa chief who was killed. (*O.R.*, Ser. I, Vol. 13, ar19, 920-921)

TONKAWAN TRIBES

The four principal Tonkawan Tribes constituted a distinct linguistic family with affinity for the Coahuiltecan, Karankawan, and Tunican language groups. They lived in central Texas from Cibolo Creek to within a few miles of the Trinity River.

TRIBES	
Tonkawa proper	Tenu
Yojuane	Tetzino
Mayeye	Tishin
Ervipiame	Tusolivi
	Ujuiap

POSSIBLE TRIBES	ASSOCIATED TRIBES
Sana	Nonapho
Emet	Sijame
Cava	Simaomo
Toho	Muruam (but probably Caohuiltecan)
Tohaha	Pulacuam (but probably Caohuiltecan)
Quiutcanuaha	Choyapin (but probably Caohuiltecan)

TONTO

The Tonto Apaches were composed of two divisions or subgroups: the Northern Tonto Group and the Southern Tonto Group. The Tonto were of the Western Division of the Apache nation grouped with the multiple bands of the Cibicue, the San Carlos or Gileños Apache, and the White Mountains, collectively called Western Apaches. They inhabited the Toto Basin of Arizona north of the Salt River with the Middle Verde River on the west. Swanton places them in the San Carlos Group that includes the Cibicue and White Mountains, but not the Gileños.

The name Tonto was misapplied by early writers to nearly all the Indians of two linguistic families, the Apache and the Yuma, that ranged between the White Mountains of Arizona and the Colorado river. The Toto Basin, the drainage of the Tonto Creek with the Mazatzal and Superstition mountains on the west and south and the Mogollon Rim to the north, covered some 1,500 square miles.

TONTO WAR

Brigadier General George Crook undertook to pacify the region and halt the depredations in what has been called the Tonto War. It began November 16, 1872 and ended in April of 1873 with key battles at Salt River Cave and Turret Peak that brought the Western Apache group to terms. In the campaign Crook employed native scouts for the first time who were instrumental in his success. The scouts were an elite fighting force comprised of friendly Apaches, Yavapais, Walapais, Paiutes, and Maricopas. Crook also used his trademark pack mules rather than wagons to carry supplies. Up into early December 1872, the scouts did most of the fighting. In December the soldiers of the 5th Calvary and 23rd Infantry that had replaced the 3rd Calvary and 21st Infantry began to assert themselves. The war, such as it was, ended in the fight at the Tontos' Turret Peak hideout in the mountains. Chief Cha-lipun (Tcà-libáhn or Brown Hat) of the Southern Tonto, surrendered April 6. Northern Tonto Chief Delshay in the northeastern part of the basin surrendered April 25 and was sent to Camp Verde. It was the government's first military victory over the Apaches. (Crook was still wearing his Lt. Colonel insignia at the time.)

Most of the captured Tontos along with those that had previously turned themselves in were placed on the San Carlos Reservation with the Pinal and Arivaipa of the Gileño Apaches. The uneasy relations between the two groups was inflamed by a corrupt agent from Tucson who held the position on an interim basis pending the arrival of the permanent agent. In his few months at San Carlos, he caused the death of an army lieutenant that, in turn, led three thoroughly incorrigible Tonto chiefs to bolt the reservation. At the same time Delshay struck out from Camp Verde. The renegades were eventually caught and killed in Crook's second Tonto War of the spring and early summer of 1874. Delshay was found and killed in late August by another Tonto chief, or possibly a White Mountain chief, named Des-a-lin, who wanted to co-operate with the whites. Des-a-lin also brought in seventy-six of Delshay's people and another thirty-nine of his own people into the reservation.

The new agent at San Carlos arrived August 8. John Philip Clum, twenty-two years old and no experience dealing with Indians, became one of the most remarkable agents to ever serve the Bureau of Indian Affairs. He was recommended by the Dutch Reformed Church that President Grant had given the responsibility for the Apaches. He quickly earned the trust and respect of the Indians while completely reorganizing the life and affairs of the reservation. He immediately put the Indians to work improving their living conditions. He filled their days with productive work that contained the deadly disease of idleness, and at the same time significantly improved their health and welfare. His efforts were not appreciated by either the army or war profiteers, and particularly not by those who would settle for nothing less than extermination.

OATMAN MASSACRE

Oatman Massacre refers to the murder of all but three members of the Oatman family at what came to be known as Oatman Flat, about a hundred miles east of Yuma, Arizona. Royce Oatman left Independence, Missouri, in August 1850, with his wife and seven children as part of a wagon train. The other members of the train decided to remain in Arizona, and in February 1851 the Oatmans set off for California on their own and were attacked by a band of Tonto Apaches. All the members of Oatman family were killed with the exception of two daughters, Olive, 16, and Mary Ann, 10, who were taken captive. A son, Lorenzo, 14, who the Indians thought to be dead, also survived. When he regained consciousness, he made his way back to the Pima Villages where some of the members of the wagon train had remained. After a little over a year, the two girls were sold to the Mohaves, and shortly thereafter, the youngest died. Through the combined efforts of her brother Lorenzo, a concerned carpenter named Henry Grinnell, a friendly Indian, and the commander of Fort Yuma, Colonel Burke, Olive regained her freedom in the February 1856 and was united with her brother.

TOYBIPET

Toybipet was a sub-tribe of the Tongva of California that inhabited the area about San Jose. For more see Tongva.

TRAMASKECOOC

The Tramaskecoocre is believed to be of the Algonquian linguistic group and has been described as a sub-tribe of the Secotan, but available information on its status is limited. The village is presumed to have been located on Buck Ridge just East of Gum Neck, North Carolina. For more see Secotan.

TREMENTINA

Trementina (or Tremintina or Nementina) "turpentine" was a band of Plains Apache, possibly an early band of the Lipan. And it is very likely that they were the same as, or at least very closely related to, the Limita. The name was also sometimes equated with Chipayne. Their range, as reported, was generally the same as the Limita, that is, eastern New Mexico and the adjoining parts of Texas (Panhandle) south of the Canadian, disappearing from recorded history in the mid-1700s at the time of the Comanche invasion. For more see Lipan, Chipayne, Limita.

TSANCHIFIN KALAPUYA

Tsanchifin was a subdivision of the Calapooya of Oregon and a member of the Central Division of the Kalapooian linguistic stock who lived along the McKenzie River. For more see Kalapuya Peoples.

TSILTADEN

The Tsiltaden or Chilion Apache was a band of the Chiricahua Apache generally considered to be a part of the Pinaleños. They are now under the San Carlos Agency, Arizona. For more see Apache.

TUACANE

The Tuacane (Tuacanas or Tahuacanes to the Spanish) lived in the area of east Texas between the middle Trinity and Adaes rivers. They were also known as the Tawakeno. For more see Nations of the North.

TÜBATULABAL

The Tübatulabal constituted one of the major divisions of the Shoshonean branch of the Uto-Aztecan linguistic stock. Their popular name was the Kern River Indians. The lived in the area of the upper part of the valley of the Kern River and the South Fork in California. They were first encountered by Father Garcés in 1775. By 1846 white settlers had established themselves in the South Fork Valley, and in 1857 the Kern River gold rush began in Palagewan territory. A few of the Tübatulabal joined the Owens Valley Paiute in hostilities against the whites while at the same time a group of Koso settled in the area, intermarrying with the Tübatulabal but principally with the Kawiisu. Some forty Tübatulabal and Palagewan were massacred near Kernville by American soldiers. The remnants of the Tübatulabal and Palagewan were allotted land in the South Fork Valley and the Kern Valley in 1893.

TUKABAHCHEE

The Tukabahchee was a sub-tribe or subdivision of the Muskogee and one of the four foundation groups of the Creek Confederacy. The other three foundation tribes were the Coweta, Kasihta and Coosa. For more see Creek Confederacy.

TUKSPUSH

The Tukspush was a division of the Tenino generally treated separately. They lived on the John Day River in Oregon and were commonly referred to as the John Day Indians. The treaty of 1855 referred to the John Day Indians as the Dock-Spus and a band of the Walla Walla. For more see Tenino.

TUKUARIKA SHOSHONI

The Tukuarika (Tukuaduka or Tukudeka), also known as Sheep Eaters, was a subdivision of the Western Shoshoni, but they have been generally treated as if a separate, independent tribe. They inhabited the lands from the present Yellowstone National Park to the middle course of the Salmon River in Idaho. The name Sheepeater (Tukudeka in the Shoshone language) came because of their proficiency in hunting the Big Horn Sheep that inhabited the Salmon River country of Idaho. The Lemhi Indian Reservation established February 12, 1875, by President Ulysses S. Grant provided specifically for the Shoshoni, the Bannock, and the Tukuarika.. For more see the Shoshoni.

SHEEPEATER CAMPAIGN (WAR)

Sheepeater were a mix of Bannocks, Western Shoshonis, and Weiser Shoshonis (Northern) Indians. The Sheepeater Campaign was a short-lived campaign 1879 offshoot of the Nez Percé War that took place generally in Middle Fork County, Idaho. Gold had been discovered in the area about ten years earlier bringing with it an influx of white and Chinese prospectors onto Indian lands. Violence erupted with the killing of five Chinese miners in February 1879. Whites blamed the killings on the Sheepeaters.

Three contingents of regular army troops from Boise, Camp Howard near Grangeville, and the Umatilla Reservation, and twenty Cayuse and Umatilla scouts, were ordered out by General O.O. Howard. to pursue the Sheepeaters and bring them to Boise. A few minor skirmishes and light casualties on both sides ended on September 25 with the surrender of 51 natives, mostly women and children, who were taken back as prisoners. The campaign's principal claim is that it was Idaho's Last Indian War.

TULALIP

The Tulalip tribe belonged to the Nisqually dialectic group of the coastal division of the Salishan linguistic group. They lived about Tulalip Bay in Washington State. Swanton makes only two minor references to the Tulalip in his remarks on the Snohomish, but not as a subdivision of the Snohomish. Washington State Native American Tribes describes the Tulalip as members of the Snohomish tribe. The plural, Tulalip Tribes, is listed as one of the Washington Tribes.

The Tulalip tribe listed individually as a member of the Northwest Indian Fisheries Commission. The Tulalip Tribes of the Tulalip Reservation, Washington, organized under the Indian Reorganization Act of 1934, is recognized as a single entity by the BIA (2002). The Tulalip Reservation consists of 22,000 acres, over 50 percent of which is in federal trust status, in the mid-Puget Sound area.

The reservation was established by the Treaty of Point Elliott (January 22, 1855) and enlarged by Executive Order of December 23, 1873. It was to provide a permanent home for the Snohomish, Snoqualmie, Skagit, Suiattle, Samish and Stillaguamish tribes and allied bands then living in the region.

TULE-KAWEAH YOKUTS

The Tule-Kaweah Indians were one of the seven subdivisions of the Yokuts Group of Indians of California with villages on the Tule River, Dear Creek, Kaweah River, and Rattlesnake Creek. For more see Yokuts.

TUM-WATERS

The Tum-Waters inhabited Oregon Territory. Several bands of the Tum-Waters were signatories to the Treaty with the Kalapuya and others of 1855, but little additional information is available. They were placed on the Grand Ronde Reservation in Oregon.

TUMPANOGOT UTE

The Tumpanogot or Timpaiavat was a subdivision of the Northern Ute and lived about Utah Lake in Utah. For more see Ute.

TUNAHE

The Tunahe (Tuna'xe) or Tunaha has been reported as an extinct Salishan tribe from central Montana and also as a Plains subdivision of the Kutenai that inhabited west-central Montana.

TUNICA

The Tunica were of the Tunica group of the Tunican stock that included the Chitimacha and Atakapa. A peaceful, agricultural people, they lived on the south side of the lower course of the Yazoo in Mississippi about twelve miles from its mouth and in parts of Arkansas. They were first encountered by Hernando de Soto west of the Mississippi. The tribal name appears as Tanik-wa on Father Jacques Marquette's 1673 map. Other variations of the name are Tamisa, Tonka, and Tonica. Delanglez places them in the Arkansas Group (No. 46).

A missionary priest from Canada, Father Davion, joined them in 1699 only to flee three years later. At their request he returned and remained with them for fifteen years, leaving in 1719 or 1720. In 1706 they left the Yazoo and moved to the Houma town near the mouth of the Red River on the opposite bank. It is reported that the Tunic turned on their hosts and killed more than half of them and continued to live in the region. The Tunica were strong friends and allies of the French. Because of that friendship, they were attacked by the Natchez and their allies in 1731. Both sides suffered heavy loses.

Between 1784 and 1803 the Tunica moved up the Red River to present Marksville, Louisiana, on the land of the Avoyel. Just before this move, the Tunica had joined the Avoyel and Ofo and some Choctaw in an attack against a British expedition ascending the Mississippi. Into the 1900s, there had been reports of descendants of the Tunica living among the Choctaw in Oklahoma; near Beaumont, Texas; and among the Atakapa. The 155-acre Tunica-Biloxi Reservation established in northwestern Avoyelles Parish, just south of Marksville is home to both the Tunica and Biloxi who united for political reasons in 1920. The tribe was incorporated in 1976. The site of the reservation had served as a communal land for Native Americans since the 1780s when Bernardo de Gálvez, Spanish governor of Louisiana, granted it to the Tunica Tribe. Although the two tribes were on friendly terms with one another, they spoke to completely different languages. As a result, both tribes shifted to the use of the French language in order to communicate. The U.S. government formally recognized the Tunica-Biloxi Indian Tribe of Louisiana as a separate tribal entity in 1981.

Tunica County, Mississippi, was named for the Tunica that established a settlement in the southwest corner of the county. The county claims to be the site of De Soto's discovery of the Mississippi River. An honor also claimed by Coahoma County to the south and Memphis, Tennessee, to the north. Coahoma County claims that Quizquiz was a Tunica village in the southwestern corner of Coahoma County and the capital of a rich province of thousands of Tunica Indians conquered by De Soto. The flat land of Tunica County is dotted with a series of Indian mounds from an ancient civilization that dates to around 700 A.D.*

*Now coming into use by some are the abbreviations C.E. (Common Era) for A.D. (Anno Domini, in the Year of Our Lord) and B.C.E. (Before the Common Era) for B.C. (Before Christ).

TUNXIS

The Tunxis (used in the singular and plural) was a subdivision or sub-tribe of the Wappinger and lived in the southwestern part of Hartford County, Connecticut. They allied with the Narragansett against the Mohegan and with King Philip against the English. For more see Wappinger.

TUPS

According to Bolton, "Missions on the San Gabriel," the Tups was a sub-tribe or one of the allied tribes of the Karankawa that lived on the lower Colorado River and Gulf coast. For more see Karankawan Tribes.

TUSCARORA

The Tuscarora was a confederacy of three tribes: Ka'te'nu'a'ka' (People of the submerged pine tree); Akawantca'ka; and Skaru're (hemp gathers) or Tuscarora proper. They inhabited Roanoke, Tar, Pamlico, and Neuse rivers in North Carolina. After the Tuscarora Wars of 1711-13, remnants wandered about and eventually settled in upper New York State where they were adopted by the Oneida as a full member of the Six (formerly five) Nation Iroquois-speaking League of Great Peace in 1722. One band under Chief Tom Blunt or Blount remained neutral in the wars and remained in Carolina until they also moved north in 1766 and 1802. The majority of the Tuscarora fought beside the colonists in the War of Revolution. For more see the Iroquois League.

TUSCARORA WARS

By 1700 growing numbers of white farmers were moving onto Indian lands of Colonial America. The Tuscarora Wars of 1711-13 were the result of the deteriorating relationship. In the following years, the Indians that were not killed in battle or forced off their homelands often succumbed to the white man's diseases.

In 1710, a group of German and Swiss settlers established a settlement on the Neuse River that emptied into Pamlico Sound in North Carolina, in an ancestral lands of the Tuscarora. New Bern rapidly became a prosperous community, but the native people became enraged by encroachment on their lands. They also believed that they were being unfairly treated in their trade dealings.

On September 22, 1711, the Tuscarora under Chief Hencock attacked New Bern and other settlements on the Trent and Pamlico rivers in North Carolina. Some one hundred and thirty settlers were killed, and their homes and crops destroyed. Colonel John Barnwell with about thirty white men and some five hundred friendly Indians moved out against Hencock and others who had allied themselves with him. There was a great loss of life on both sides. To prevent further blood shed, Hencock and Barnwell agreed to peace terms, and Barnwell withdrew, ending the First Tuscarora War. But as he withdrew, Barnwell and his men captured a number of Indians and sold them off as slaves, thus bringing on what is referred to as the Second Tuscarora War. (Some writers treat is all as one.)

It was not until March 20-23, 1713, that the settlers regained control. Captain James Moore of South Carolina, with the aid of some nine hundred Yamasee warriors, defeated the Tuscarora at their village of Neoheroka and killed nearly a thousand. Some of the captured Tuscarora were sold into slavery to help defray war costs. The remainder were forced out of the Carolinas and eventually ended up in Pennsylvania and New York.

TUSKEGEE

It is believed that the Tuskegee were of the southern Muskhogean stock and related to the Alabama. Early Spaniards passed through their towns. In the late 1600s, part of them were located on the Chattahoochee River. Others were on the upper Tennessee River near Long Island. Apparently the Tuskegee formalized the division after the turn of the century with the group on the Tennessee eventually becoming absorbed in the Cherokee. The first group moved to the area between the Coosa and Tallapoosa rivers that history traditionally gives as the home of the Tuskegee. It is this group that subsequently became a member of the Creek Confederacy of Upper Creeks and were removed with the Creeks to Indian Territory where they maintained their own identity.

TUTELO

The Tutelo (also spelled Totero or Tutero) belonged to the Siouan linguistic stock. They were first encountered about present Salem, Virginia, first named Totero Town in 1671. The Big Sandy River, where they lived for a time, was recorded on old maps as the Tuterro (Tutelo) River. They later moved to an island in the Roanoke River. By 1701 they were found in the area of the headwaters of the Yadkin. The Tutelo tribe was closely allied with the Saponi, and both tribes later joined the Occaneechi farther south. At the time of Bacon's revolt, in which the Occaneechi became embroiled, all three tribes moved south to North Carolina. Around 1716, they returned to Virginia where they settled about Fort Christanna in Brunswick County.

In 1771 the Tutelo settled in a village on Cayuga Inlet that was destroyed in 1779 by Maj. General John Sullivan in 1779 in the course of the Revolutionary War. They were joined by the Nahyssan, Occaneechi, and Saponi and were later adopted by the Cayuga but continued to retain their own identity. Members of the tribe also ventured into New York, Pennsylvania, and Canada.

TUTSEEWA

The Tutseewa reportedly lived on an unidentified river west of the Rocky Mountains that was a branch of the Columbia River.

TUTUTNI

The Tututni belonged to the Athapascan linguistic family, closely related to the Mishikhwutmetunne. They inhabited the lower Rogue River and the adjoining coast, north and south, in Oregon. They were also referred to as the Lower Rogue River Indians.

TWANA

The Twana or Toanho inhabited both sides of Hoods Canal in Washington State. The name signified the "portage" between the upper end of Hoods Canal and the headwaters of Puget Sound. They were a single dialectic group of the coastal division of the Salishan linguistic stock. They were also known as the Skokomish, their principal subdivision.

First European contact occurred in 1792 and resulted in a devastating smallpox epidemic. There were nine Twana communities, the largest being known as the Skokomish, or "big river people." Descendants lived on the Skokomish Reservation and have become known as members of the Skokomish Tribe.

TWO KETTLES

The Two Kettles (also Two Kettle) or Two Boils Kettles or Oohenonpa or Oohenumpa was a tribe or subdivision of the Lakota. For more see the Sioux and Lakota.

TYIGH

The Tyigh, Tysch, or Taih (also Tiah) or Upper De Chutes or De Chutes (Deschutes) was part of the Tenino branch of the Shahaptian division of the Shapwailutan linguistic stock. They lived about the Tygh and White rivers in Oregon. The Tenino and Tyigh were separate, independent tribes rather than bands of the Walla Walla as referred to in the Treaty with the Tribes of Middle Oregon of 1855. They have also been identified as a band of the Chinook. They gave their name to the Tygh Valley, Tygh Ridge and Tygh Creek. Fremont's Journals referred to the Taih Prairie. For more see the Tenino.

UFALLAH

The Ufallah was the name given by Drake to a band of Indians that lived twelve miles above Fort Gaines on the Chattahoochee River in Georgia that would classify them as Lower Creek. (Drake called them Seminoles.) The fort, named for Gen. Edmund Pendleton Gaines, was established in 1814 and is now the seat of Clay County, Florida. It is situated astride the border with Alabama and just north of Florida. For more see Creek and Seminole.

UGALJACHMUTZI

The Ugaljachmutzi tribe is thought to belong to the Athapascan family. They may have been related to the Tanaina or Kinai. They lived about Prince William's Sound on the northwest coast.

UINTA UTE

The Uinta (Uintah) or Yoovte was a subdivision of the Northern Ute. They lived in northeastern Utah. For more see Ute.

UMATILLA

The Umatilla belonged to the Shahaptian division of the Shapwailutan linguistic family. They lived about the Umatilla River in Oregon and about the banks of the Columbia River near the mouth of the Umatilla.

KENNEWICK MAN

The terms "Kennewick Man" or the "Ancient One" refer to the human skeletal remains that were found in July 1996 below the surface of Lake Wallula, a section of the Columbia River pooled behind McNary Dam in Kennewick, Washington. The bones are of a man believed to have lived 9,200 years ago. He was found on federal lands in Eastern Washington in 1996. A controversy has evolved between American Indians, the federal government, and scientists on the disposition of the bones. Indian claimants include the Umatilla, Yakama, Colville and Nez Percé tribes. Anthropologists speculate that the Ancient One could reveal who first settled the Americas. The Burke Museum of the University of Washington, Seattle, was selected as the most suitable repository for the bones until final disposition rights are determined.

UMPQUA

The Umpqua, commonly called Upper Umpqua, belonged to the Athapascan linguistic stock and lived along the upper Umpqua River in Oregon east of the Kuitsh or Lower Umpqua. In 1852 gold was found along the Umpqua River in west-central Oregon near the settlement of Scottsburg. The Umpqua on Cow Creek division is often treated separately. (They are listed separately in this work.) Other possible subdivisions include a people called Palakahu that was more likely an Ahtapascan or Yakonan tribe and also the Skoton and Chasta that Swanton reports may have actually been parts of the Chatacosta or Tututni

UNALACHTIGO

The Unalachtigo was of the Algonquian linguistic stock and one of the three main divisions of the Delaware. The Unalachtigo had a number of sub-tribes or subdivisions that inhabited the southern portion of New Jersey. Swanton assigns first contact with the Swedes on the Delaware River in 1637 to the Unalachtigo. For more see Delaware.

SUBDIVISIONS	Nantuxet
Amimenipaty	Naraticon
Asomoche	Neshamini
Chikohoki	Okahoki
Eriwonec	Passayonk
Hopokohacking	Skackamaxon
Kahansuk	Siconesse
Manta	Tirans
Memankitonna	Yacomanshaghking

UNAMI

The Unami was of the Algonquian linguistic stock and one of the three main divisions of the Delaware and one of the two dialects. The Unami had a number of sub-tribes or subdivisions that inhabited the intermediate territory in New Jersey between the Munsee to the north and the Unalachtigo to the south. Swanton assigns first contact with the Henry Hudson in 1609 to the Unami and Munsee. See Delaware and Manhattan.

SUBDIVISIONS	Meletecunk
Aquackanonk	Mosilian
Assunpink	Navasink
Axion	Pompton
Calcefar	Raritan
Canarsee	Reckgawawanc
Gachwechnagechga	Tappan
Hackensack	Waoranec
Haverstraw	

UNKECHAUG

The Unkechaug was of the Algonquian linguistic stock, and the Poosepatuck was a part of the Unkechaug. After a time the two names became synonymous. The Unkechaug, a distinct and independent tribe, occupied the South Shore of Long Island, New York. Later, they and other smaller tribes on Long Island were subjugated more or less by the more warlike Montauk. As a consequence, it is not uncommon in the literature to find the Unkechaug referred to as a sub-tribe or subdivision of the Montauk. And, because of the similarities in the spelling of their names, there is also considerable confusion between the Unkechaug of Long Island and the Passamaquoddy of Maine also known as the Unquechauge.

UNQUEHIETT

Little is known about the Unquehiett except for a reference that suggests that they may have been a subdivision or clan of the Susquehanna. For more see Susquehanna.

UPPER CREEK

The Upper Creeks were located on the Coosa (Abihka) and Tallapoosa rivers with two sub-branches corresponding with the two rivers. For more see Creek Confederacy.

UPPER PEND D'OREILLES

The several bands of the Upper Pend d'Oreilles or Upper Kalispel, a division of the Kalispel, inhabited Idaho and Montana from the Flathead Lake and Flathead River to near Thompson Falls on the Clark Fork of the Pend Oreille River, south towards present Missoula and northward to the border with Canada, including the Little Bitterroot.

UPPER SKAGIT

The ancestors of the Upper Skagit people of today belonged to the coastal division of the Salishan linguistic stock. The Upper Skagit was comprised of ten villages on the Upper Skagit River and Sauk River in Washington State and was a signatory to the Point Elliott Treaty of 1855. No reference has been found in Swanton of an Upper Skagit tribe or reference to the ancestors of the Upper Skagit people of today. Swanton treats only of the Skagit living on the Skagit and Stillaguamish rivers with reference to a Skagit subdivision of the Swinomish.

It is believed, but only conjecture at this point, that the name of the original tribe may have been Bsigwigwilts that was referred to in the Treaty of Point Elliott as the "Mee-see-qua-quilch" (also spelled Me-Sek-Wi-Guilse). The premise is based on the fact that the Federal courts have determined the Bsigwigwilts tribe was the predecessor of the Upper Skagit. Court documents noted that in the proceedings of the Indian Claims Commission, the Bsigwigwilts tribe was referred to as the "Mee-see-qua-quilch," but no other reference to the Bsigwigwilts tribe or the Mee-see-qua-quilch tribe has been found. The signer of the treaty is listed only as Sd'zek-du-num, Me-sek-wi-guilse sub-chief.

The Upper Skagit people received federal recognition in the early 1970s, and land was put into trust for the tribe in 1984. The present Upper Skagit Reservation covers an 84-acre parcel of land east of Sedro Woolley in Skagit County plus another fifteen acres in the general area.

USQUQUHAGA

Little is known about the Usququhaga except for a reference that suggests that they may have been a subdivision or clan of the Susquehanna. For more see Susquehanna.

UTE

The Ute belonged to the Shoshonean Division of the Uto-Aztecan linguistic stock and were closely related to the Paiute, Kawaiisu, and Chemehuevi. They inhabited central and western Colorado and eastern Utah including the Utah Valley and the valley of the Salt Lake and into the upper drainage area of the San Juan River in New Mexico. And by 1500 AD they were well-established in the region Four Corners area. The name 'Ute,' from which the name of the state of Utah was derived, means "high land" or "land of the sun." The Ute also ranged into Nevada and Wyoming.

The Ute are generally divided into Southern Ute and Northern Ute, comprised of three and twelve subdivisions, respectively. Within each there were a number of bands. Each of the fourteen is listed separately in this work. Swanton also refers to five tribes or sub-tribes connected to the Ute but of uncertain status. He also lists four other bands

SOUTHERN
Capote
Moache
Weeminuche (Mountain Ute)
NORTHERN
Elk Mountain
Kaviawach (White River)
Kosunat
Pahvant
Pavogowunsin
Pikakwanarat
Sampit
Seuvarit
Tabeguache (Uncompahgre)
Tumpanogot Ute
Uinta Ute (Yoovte)
Yampa Ute

UNCERTAIN
Sogup, in or near New Mexico
Yubuincariri, west of the Green River in Utah
Kwiumpu
Nauwanatat
Unkapanukint.

Beginning the 1670s the Ute began to filter south in small groups into the rugged high country of the upper Rio Grande and the valley of the San Juan River drawn by the metal weapons, guns, and horses of the Spaniards. Within a short time the Ute were well equipped. In 1675 the Ute made their first peace treaty with the Spanish. Supplied with Spanish weapons and horses, the Ute turned on their former ally, the Navaho; then on the Plains Apache. By the time the Spanish retook the province of New Mexico in 1692 after the Pueblo Revolt, the Ute were well entrenched above Taos.

Around 1700, the Ute brought some of their northern kinsmen from Wyoming, the Comanche, to join in raids, first on the Spanish and Pueblo and then Navaho and Plains Apache. After a while the Comanche separated from the Ute moving farther into the plains and struck out on their own against the Plains Apache. The Ute, who generally remained to the west in the mountains, and Comanche later became enemies. The Ute signed their first treaty with the government in 1849. As the Mormons took more and more Ute land for their own, the Northern Utes struck with a series of raids against isolated Mormon settlements between 1853 and 1854—sometimes referred to as the Walker War.

An executive order issued October 3, 1861, set aside the Uintah Valley for the Uinta while the remainder of their land was simply taken. The process was repeated frequently thereafter for other bands and divisions under various treaties and executive orders. In 1869 the Northern Utes were forcibly removed to the Uintah Valley Reservation. They were joined by the White River Utes and Tabeguache from Colorado in 1881 following the Ute War of 1879.

Today the Northern Ute live on the Uintah-Ouray Reservation near Fort Duchesne in northeastern Utah. The Southern Ute live on a reservation in the southwestern corner of Colorado near Ignacio. The reservation originally comprised 56 million acres, approximately the western third of the present state of Colorado. That prime land was not to be theirs for long. A series of treaties subsequently reduced the reservation to a strip of arid, desolate land 15 miles wide and 110 miles long. The reservation of the

Mountain Ute, descendants of the Weminuche band who moved to the western end of the Southern Ute Reservation in 1897, is located near Towaoc, Colorado, and includes small sections of Utah and New Mexico.

UTE WAR

After reporting on the Civil War, writer and newspaperman Nathan C. Meeker convinced Horace Greeley to support the establishment of a utopian community in Colorado in the spring of 1870. Called Union Colony of Colorado, it was later renamed Greeley, Colorado. After Greeley's death, Meeker was forced to give up publication of his Greeley newspaper. In March 1878, Meeker was appointed Indian agent to the 700 Utes at the White River Indian Agency in northwestern Colorado. His wife and daughter also lived and worked at the agency. Meeker immediately began trying to convert the Indians from their hunting lifestyle based on the horse to a sedentary life of farming. Resentment among the Utes continued to mount until it came to a head in September 1879 when Meeker plowed up the racetrack where the Utes raced their ponies. In less than a year, Meeker not only threatened the Utes' traditional culture and lifestyle, he threatened the practice of their religion. What made Meeker's policies all the worse was the fact that they came on the heals of decades of changes wrought by the influx of new settlers, the destruction of the buffalo herds, the discovery of gold, construction of the transcontinental railroad, and the demand for Colorado statehood.

Chief Ouray of the Tabeguache band, the leader of the Southern Utes, tried to mediate the situation. Ute Jack saw no solution short of war. On the 10th of September, Meeker notified the Indian Bureau that he feared for his life. The bureau immediately notified the War Department. On September 16, 1879, Major T. T. Thornburgh received his orders and on the 21st departed Fort Steele with about 200 men from E Company, 3d Cavalry; D and F Companies, 5th Cavalry; and B Company from his own 4th Infantry. Included in the column as it left Rawlins, Wyoming, were thirty-three supply wagons and 220 pack mules—rations for thirty days and forage for fifteen days. Thornburgh set up a supply base at Fortification Creek on the 24th where he left the infantry company and continued on to the agency.

On September 29, Major Thornburgh and his men were attacked in Red Canyon about 20 miles north of Meeker by 300 to 400 Ute warriors and were forced to hold up to await reinforcements. It was the beginning of the Ute War. By the end of the day, twelve troopers had been killed, including Major Thornburgh, and 43 wounded. Captain J. Scott Payne of the 5th Cavalry assumed command. Earlier, in the summer of 1879, a detachment of Negro cavalrymen—D Company, 9th Cavalry, under Captain Dodge had been sent to nearby Hot Sulphur Springs as a precautionary measure. Dodge and his men rode to assistance of the besieged troopers on October 1, but quickly found themselves bottled up as well. A relief force of 500 men from Fort D. A. Russell, near Rawlins, under the command General Wesley Merritt, left on October 2 and , riding hard, arrived at the Milk Creek battle site on the fifth·, breaking the siege.

With the soldiers holed up at Mill Creek, the Utes, led by war chief Ute Jack, attacked the agency and killed Meeker and seven to ten other male employees. Five women and children, including Meeker's wife and daughter, were taken captive and held for about three weeks before being released, thanks to the intervention of Chipeta, the wife of the Chief Ouray. The incident has come down in history as the Meeker Massacre.

The army had also ordered the 4th Cavalry, under Colonel Ranald S. Mackenzie, from Fort Clark in the Department of Texas, as well as the 9th Cavalry, under Colonel Hatch from Forts Garland and Union troops from the Department of the Missouri to the scene. With the three converging columns, Colonel Merritt's combined force totaled over 1,500 men. In the face of overwhelming force, the Utes fled into the mountains. On November 10, 1879, twenty chiefs of the White River Utes, including Chiefs Douglas and Ute Jack, accepted the terms of surrender.

Chief Ouray, the great compromiser, died August 24, 1880, the year the Ute agreement was signed. In 1881 Tabeguache and White River Utes removed to the Uintah Reservation in Utah. The army moved out from what would become the town of Meeker in 1883. (The town was established in 1885 near the site of the agency.)

Hostilities erupted again in 1887, but resulted in few casualties. A number of Utes had moved off the reservations and set up camps near their traditional homelands in Colorado. One group was camped at the forks of the White River. Only a few old men and several women and children were in camp when a posse of settlers rode in and opened fire wounding four as Indians fled. Another posse struck a camp on Yellowjacket Pass. One Indian boy was killed before the posse withdrew. The Governor ordered out the militia who were aching to clear out the Indians for good. At the mouth of Wolf Creek near Rangely, the militia caught up with the Indians as they retreated back towards the reservation. On the morning of August 25, Major Leslie's force of scouts and soldiers of the First Colorado Cavalry surrounded the Ute camp and opened fire without warning. The braves returned the fire and held off the soldiers as the women, children, and old men fled toward the reservation. The defenders followed, leaving all their property behind. Thus ended the hostilities of 1887

UTINA

The Utina or Timucua were of the Timucuan Division of the Muskhogean linguistic family. The name Utina was probably taken from the name of the chief, whereas the name Timucua was taken from the linguistic group. The Utina was composed of three sub-tribes: Timucua proper, Potano, Hostaqua, and Tocobaga. It appears that they were a very close net group, and whatever affected one affected all.

With over one hundred and fifty towns and villages, the Utina inhabited a wide area of Florida from the Suwannee River in the west to the St. Johns River in the east and inland from Tampa Bay. Their first contact with Europeans came from Ponce de Leon's first expedition in 1513.

At one time (1650) the Utina numbered some 13,000, including 3,000 Potano; 8,000 for the Timucua proper and their allies, including a population of somewhat more than 1,500 for the Utina tribe by itself; 1,000 Hostaqua; and 1,000 Tocobaga. The population continued to decline as a result of a series of epidemics in the sixteen hundreds and continuing attacks from the Creek and Yuchi to the north. The destiny of the Timucua was effectively sealed following the full-scale Timucuan Rebellion against the Spanish in 1656 in the Timucua mission province of Florida's interior

After eight months of turmoil, the political and geographical makeup of the region was transformed by forced resettlement. The Timucua were concentrated in the missions around St. Augustine and between St. Augustine and Apalachee. By the mid-eighteenth century, the Utica had been either killed or enslaved, and the Timucua name had passed into history. Some suggest an earlier date. Remnants may have been absorbed into the Seminole.

UZUTIUHI

Uzutiuhi was a Quapaw village located on the south side of the lower course of the Arkansas River not far from Arkansas Post. The name of the "tribe" appears as Atotchasi on Father Jacques Marquette's 1673 map. Delanglez places the tribe in his Arkansas Group (No. 41). Variations in the spelling of the name include Southoui, Atotchasi, Atotiosi, Otochassi, and Otochiahi.

VANYUME

The Vanyume were of the Shoshonean Division of the Uto-Aztecan linguistic family that included the Kitanemuk, Serrano, Kawaiisu, and Alliklik. They lived along the Mohave River in California. Their closest relation was with the Kitanemuk.

VARNERTOWN INDIANS

The Varnertown Indians are descendents of the historical tribes of Charleston and Berkeley Counties including Catawba, Cherokee, Edisto and Etiwan.

VENTUREÑO CHUMASH

The Ventureño were one of the eight dialectic and geographical divisions of the Chumash of the Southern California coast. The Ventureño lived about present Ventura on the coast and from the Ventura River to the southeast, and the drainage areas of the Ventura River, Calleguas Creek, and the Santa Clara River inland. For more see the Chumash.

VERMILION

The Vermilion Indians lived on the Vermilion River in east central Illinois. Their connection—under the name Vermilion Indians—is uncertain; but best evidence indicates that the Vermilion were a band of the Kickapoo, who dominated the area. There were two bands of Kickapoo in Illinois, the Vermilion Band and the Prairie Band. The Kickapoo had lived in the area since they were driven south by the Iroquois.

Other evidence suggested that the Vermilion Indians may have been a band or village the Piankashaw or even the Illinois. The latter appears very doubtful. The Miami themselves called the Vermilion River itself 'Piauk-e-shaw.' The Kickapoo that ceded the large tract of land now known as Vermilion County to the government in July 30 and August 30, 1819. For more see Kickapoo.

VIDAI

The Vidai was one of the tribes of east Texas living between Adaes and the middle Trinity rivers near present Bidais Creek that flows into the Trinity River between Walker and Madison counties. They were counted among the Nations for the North, but no reference was found in the Texas journals under that spelling. For more see Nations of the North.

VIEUX DÉSERT

Vieux Désert (Vieux De Sert) or Lac Vieux Désert was a band of the Lake Superior Chippewa Indians. In 1864 they were confined to the area around the present-day town of Watersmeet, the home of the present community. The Lac Vieux Désert is one of twelve Lake Superior bands and one of the three located in Michigan. The other two are the L'Anse Band and Ontonogan Band that are now united as the Keweenaw Bay Chippewa Indian Community). The other nine bands are located in northern Wisconsin and Minnesota. For more see Chippewa.

WABANAKI CONFEDERACY

The Wabanaki or Eastern Confederacy was comprised of five aligned tribes of the northeast formed primarily in defense against the Five Nations of the Iroquois League. The five tribes were the Abenaki, from whence the name was derived; the Penobscot, if considered a separate tribe; the Maliseet; the Passamaquoddy; and the Micmac. They remained politically separate, each with their own identity, but generally spoke with one voice on matters of politics, war, and trade. The year 1862 is given as the date that the confederation officially disbanded in 1862, but the five tribes continued to maintain close ties with one another. For more see the Wampanoag.

WABASH

The Wabash was a band of the Miami that lived about the Little St. Joseph River that flows into the Maumee River at Fort Wayne. The name Wabash, however, came to refer to the all Miami Indians in general. On Father Jacques Marquette's 1673 map, the name was written Wabous-quigou. A variation was Wabouquigou. (The Wabash Confederacy was a loose confederation of tribes of the Wabash River valley.) For more see Miami.

John Baptist de Coigne was a recipient of one of Thomas Jefferson addresses to the Indians of which there were five. Some sources identify de Coigne as the Chief of the Wabash and the Illinois Indians; others put with the Kickapoo. Jefferson's correspondence refers to "our friends," the "Piorias, Piankenshaws, Kickaous, and Wyanttanons."

1164 WACCAMAW

The Waccamaw lived along the Waccamaw River and the lower course of the Pee Dee River in South Carolina. They are believed to be of the Siouan linguistic stock. Many were killed by the colonists in 1720 and others in a raid by the Cherokee and Natchez in 1755. Remnants may have incorporated into the Catawba or the Croatan of North Carolina.

WACO

The Waco most likely belonged to the Wichita Group of the Caddoan linguistic stock and were closely related to the Tawakoni and may, in fact, have been a part of the Tawakoni at one time before separating. The best guess is that the Waco originated in present Oklahoma with the Wichita, but first appeared near along the Brazos River near present-day Waco, Texas. One report puts them migrating southwest at the same time as the Tawakoni about 1700. Their early relationship with the Tawakoni and Wichita is supported by the fact that they ultimately merged with the two tribes. However, another opinion holds that they were descendants of the Shuman of Texas; still another that they were identical to the Yscani.

There are a few scattered references in the literature, including the letters of George Catlin, of a tribe identified as the Wico that was closely associated with the Wichita, the Comanche, and the Kiowa and is believed to be the Waco; however the evidence is all circumstantial.

WAHEPKUTE

The Wahepkute meaning "Shooters among the Leaves" was a tribe of the Santee or Eastern Division of the Sioux. For more see Sioux.

WAHKIAKUM

The Wahkiakum or Wahkiaku was a band of the Chinook Indians. They lived in two villages at the mouth of the Elochoman River on the northwest coast of Oregon, where they were encountered by Lewis & Clark. The explorers also encountered the Cathlamet tribe in the same general area. The present-day town Cathlamet is the county seat of Wahkiakum County in Washington State. For more see Chinook.

WAHOWPUM

The Wahowpum was a relatively small tribe of the Shahaptian linguistic family. The village was about four miles east and on the opposite side of the river from today's Blalock, Oregon, where the Wahowpum encountered Lewis and Clark.

WAHPACOOTA

The Wahpacoota was known as the Wahpatoota, or Leaf Beds, by Lewis and Clark. They listed them as one of the ten separate Sioux tribes or bands and described them as living on both sides of the St. Peter's River below the Yellow Wood River with a population of about 150 men. For more see Sioux.

WAHPETUNWAN

The Wahpetunwan, "Dwellers among the Leaves," was one of the four subgroups of the Eastern or Santee Division of the Sioux. They were also known as the Wahpeton or Wahpetonwan.

Lewis and Clark knew them as the Wahpatone or Otaharton and listed them as one of the ten separate Sioux tribes or bands. They reported that the Wahpatone lived above the mouth of the St. Peter's River and had a population of about 200 men. The Wahpetunwan, under the name Wahpeton, later joined the Sisseton band to form the Sissetonp-Wahpeton Sioux Tribe on the Lake Traverse Reservation. For more see Sioux and Dakota.

WAIAM

The Waiam or Wiam was a subdivision of the Tenino. They lived near the mouth of the Deschutes River in Oregon. For more see Tenino

WAILAKI

The Wailaki were of the southern California division of the Athapascan linguistic stock. They lived along the Eel River near the Big Bend and on Kekawaka Creek, and along the North Folk.

WAKOKAI

The Wakokai (or Wokokai) was a sub-tribe or division of the Muskogee and a member of the Creek Confederacy.

WALAPAI

The Walapai belonged to the Yuma branch of the Hokan linguistic stock. They lived along the middle course of the Colorado River between Sacramento Wash and National Canyon. It is believe that their first encounter with Europeans was with Hernando de Alarcon in 1540.

WALLA WALLA

The Walla Walla (Wallawalla, also with a hyphen) belonged to the Shahaptian Division of the Shapwailutan linguistic stock and were closely related to the Nez Percé. The lived along the lower Wallawalla River in Washington State and near the junction of the Colorado River and the Snake River in Washington and Oregon.

Indians identified as bands of the Walla Walla in The Treaty with the Tribes of Middle Oregon of 1855— the Upper De Chutes (Dechutes River); Lower De Chutes; Tenino; and the Dock-Spus or John Day's River band—were actually separate, independent tribes or bands of other tribes.

The Walla Walla were removed to the Umatilla Reservation that was established in 1855, where now with the Cayuse and Umatilla people they comprise the Confederated Tribes of the Umatilla Indian Reservation at Pendleton, Oregon, organized in 1949. With the Wasco and the Northern Paiute, bands of the Walla Walla, who lived along the tributaries of the Columbia, now called the Warm Springs Indians, comprise the Confederated Tribes of Warm Springs, Oregon, established in 1938.

WALLOWA

The Wallowa or Willewah was the most important of the several bands of the Nez Percé. The lived in the Wallowa valley in Oregon. For more see Nez Percé.

WALPAPI

The Walpapi, commonly called the Snake or Snake People, were a subdivision of the Northern Paiute that inhabited Oregon, but they should not be confused with the Northern Shoshoni (the Snake Indians) nor with the Southern Paiute (the Snake Diggers). For more see the Northern Paiute.

WALPI HOPI

Walpi was a Hopi village or town on the First or East Mesa. For more see Hopi.

WAMPANOAG

The Wampanoag or Pokanoket was a tribe of the Algonquian linguistic stock and spoke the N-dialect. A large tribe comprised of a number of bands and villages, they inhabited the coast line of modern Massachusetts, the head of Narragansett Bay, Martha's Vineyard and adjacent islands, and parts of Rhode Island, near present Warren, prior to the arrival of the colonists at Plymouth in November 1620.

They lived by farming, fishing, and hunting. Late in the second decade of the 1600s, from 1616 to 1619, the tribe was devastated by disease, possibly bubonic plague picked up from cod fishermen in and around modern Maine and Newfoundland that spread south along the coast to the eastern shore of Narragansett Bay. (By 1600 European cod fishing vessels had become common off the coast of New England while inland waterways became home to fur traders, and trade with the Indians had become routine.) The fight for survival brought on by the ravages of disease threw tribe against tribe in bloody wars. The Wampanoag were allied with the Massachusetts to the north and the Nauset on Cape Code.

Massasoit, the sachem of the Pokanoket, became the principal leader of the Wampanoag. It was he who welcomed the Pilgrims from the Mayflower. Without his help, the Pilgrims literally would not have survived their first year. It was his warning to the colonists, whether real or contrived, that led to the Massacre at Wessagusett in the winter of 1623 and Massasoit's ascension to the position of leader of the Indians in the entire area about Cape Cod and land to its north. He was no longer just the sachem of the Pokanoket. It was following the massacre at Wessagusett that the Wampanoag nation as we know it came into existence. For more on the massacre, see the Massachusett.

By 1624, Massasoit (later called Usamequin) began selling Wampanoag land to the Plymouth colonists, exclusively, as he had agreed in his treaty of peace. First, in November 1624, was the site of the future township of Rehoboth; in 1650, 196 square miles of modern Bridgewater; in 1652, Dartmouth; the following year, the land at the head of Narragansett Bay. In his last official act for the Pokanoket on September 21, 1657, he endorsed the sale of Hog Island in Narraganset Bay to Rhode Islander Richard Smith that his son Wamsutta negotiated in 1654.

Massasoit died in 1660 at the Quabaug village at Brookfield where he had taken up permanent residence in 1657. William Bradford, the governor of Plymouth, died about the same time. He and Massasoit had maintained an uneasy truce. With their deaths, the truce began to unravel. Massasoit's son Wamsutta, who the colonists dubbed Alexander at his request, became chief. With the steady depletion of the fur trade, the native tribes were forced to sell their land to purchase the English goods that they had come to depend upon. With the colonists hungry for land, they wanted the exclusive rights to Wampanoag land. The Plymouth Court was anxious to exert its control over the Indians and ordered the Wamsutta brought before the court. Enroute under guard, he fell sick and returned to home to Mount Hope. Within a week in the summer of 1662 he was dead. The mysterious circumstances of his death undercut the thin fabric of trust that remained between the Indians and the colonists.

In August 1662, the position of supreme sachem fell to Wamsutta's twenty-four year old brother, Metacom or Metacomet, who the colonists gave the name Philip. Because Metacom did not hesitate to speak up and refused to be cowed by the Plymouth Court, the colonists dubbed him "King Philip," and the name stuck.

Over the next several years, the Wampanoag were swindled out of their lands, forced to give up their weapons, and in 1672 Philip was forced to sign a treaty by which they he agreed to pay an annual tribute to Plymouth. Philip was determined to seek retribution. He begged, borrowed, and mortgaged everything he could get his hands on to buy guns and ammunition. At the same time, he forged alliances with the Cape tribes whose people were being captured and enslaved or sold as slaves abroad. Some escaped to Canada and to sanctuary with the Indians on the Hudson River valley. Events came to a head with the murder of Philip's former interpreter, a Christian Indian by the name of Sassamon, in the spring of 1675. Sassamon had warned Plymouth officials in January that Philip was planning to wage war. Three Indians, one of whom was a senior counselor to Philip, were tried for the murder by a Plymouth court, found guilty, and executed—two on June 8; the third one month later.

All-out war to drive the English out erupted in late June 1675 in what became known as King Philip's War. It lasted fourteen months. Philip was killed, and the confederacy broken.

The principal villages of the Wampanoan are listed below. Descendants of the Wampanoaglive in southeastern Massachusetts. In 1990, 2175 people claimed to be of Wampanoag descent. For more see King Philip's War and Herring Pond Indians. See King Philip's War.

VILLAGES

Acushnet	Miacomit
Agawam	Munponset
Assameekg	Namasket
Assawompset	Nashamoiess
Assonet	Nashanekammuck
Betty's Neck	Nukkehkummees
Chaubaqueduck	Nunnepoag
Coaxet	Ohkonkemme Pachade
Cohannet	Pocasset
Cooxissett	Quittaub
Cowsumpsit	Saconnet
Gayhead	Saltwater Pond
Herring Pond	Sanchecantacket
Jones River	Seconchqut
Kitteaumut	Shawomet
Loquasquscit	Shimmoah
Mattakeset	Talhanio
Mattapoiset	Toikiming
	Wauchimoqut

PLYMOUTH COLONY

On November 11, 1620, the *Mayflower* anchored at Provincetown Harbor. Indians and future colonists first encountered each other for the first time from a distance on November 15. On their second exploring expedition to find a permanent settlement site, the colonists looted the Indian wigwam homes, their graves, and their storage bins of native corns, but with at least a modest degree of conscience. During the second week of December, an expedition was attacked by about thirty Indians. No one was injured on either side as the Indians scattered into the woods. The expedition continued and a few days later the explorers came upon a suitable site for their new home, Plymouth Harbor or Patuxet, almost due west across the cape from where the *Mayflower* was anchored at Provincetown. By the end of December, the *Mayflower* was anchored at Plymouth Harbor, and the settlers began construction of their homes and common buildings. At the same time, more lives were lost to accidents, disease, and the elements.

By spring only fifty-two of the original one hundred and two colonists were still alive. Their first face to face encounter with the Native Americans occurred March 16 when a single Indian walked into the settlement. His name was Somerset, and he was an English-speaking sachem from Pemaquid Point in Maine, near Mohegan Island. He told them of Chief Massasoit and Pokanoket, about forty miles southwest at the head of Narragansett Bay, and of the Nausets, from whom the settlers had stolen the corn and whose graves they had disturbed. Massasoit arrived a few days later, and on March 22 the Pokanoket and settlers negotiated a treaty of peace and cooperation. On April 5, the Mayflower sailed back to England. Historian Nathaniel Philbrick writes, "During the winter of 1621, the survival of the English settlement had been in balance. Massasoit's decision to offer them assistance had saved the Pilgrims' lives in the short term."

Massasoit's attitude was remarkable given the cold blooded murder of his people in the spring of 1620 by sailors from an unnamed English ship in Narragansett Bay. The sailors invited a large number of Pokanoket aboard their ship where they were systematically shot and killed them. Englishman Thomas Dermer who returned to the area from Virginia that summer suffered the consequences. His party was attacked on Martha's Vineyard by warriors led by a sachem named Epenow, and all his men were killed except one. Dermer himself was wounded and died soon thereafter in Virginia. Epenow had been captured in 1611 with five or six others and taken to England. (Several other Indians had been killed at the time.) Lying to his captors about his knowledge of the whereabouts of gold, Epenow was taken back to the Cape Cod where he jumped ship and escaped.

KING PHILIP'S WAR

Metacom or Metacomet, known in history as King Philip, was the second son of the famous chief of the Wampanoag (Pokanoket), Massasoit. The war that has come down in history as King Philip' War or Metacom's War lasted fourteen months. It was also known as the Wampanoag Rebellion and as the Wabanaki (for Eastern tribes) Rebellion. Beginning in 1672, Philip began making his plans for war, establishing stores of guns and ammunition and organizing a confederation of native peoples to drive the English settlers from their lands.

Joining Philip and the Pokanokets were the Nipmucks; the Nemaskets; the Sakonnets—at the beginning; and, reluctantly, the Pocassets. For their part, the English drove the Narragansett to Philip's side with a precipitous attack. In the cold of December 1675, a colonial army one thousand-men strong attacked the principal Narragansett village, actually a fort that housed some three thousand inhabitants. The warriors that were not killed were driven from the fort where they took up positions and fired back into the fort until driven off. The English proceeded to torch the fort and everything in sight, including the hundreds of wigwams with women and children hunkered down behind their stores of food inside. No count was ever made of the native dead at what has been called the Great Swamp Fight. Later estimates put the count of men, women, and children shot or burned to death at between 350 and 600. The English suffered roughly twenty percent casualties with some 200 men killed or wounded.

Those Indians who had remained neutrals soon became belligerents as they came to realize that the issue was race and greed, not local politics. Allied with the English were the Massachusetts, the Mohegans, the remnants of the Pequots, the Niantics, and the Mohawk. Philip established his headquarters at Mount Hope, modern Bristol, Rhode Island.

The war began with vandalism and stealing on June 20, 1675. Two unoccupied houses in a village north of Mount Hope were ransacked and burned to the ground. The next day Plymouth ordered the militia assembled and asked Massachusetts Bay for assistance. The depredations continued over the next two days, but the Indians scrupulously avoided spilling human blood. First flood was drawn by an Englishman on June 23. On the twenty-fourth, the attacks, ambushes, and killings replaced vandalism. The war quickly spread across Rhode Island, Massachusetts, Connecticut, and farther north into New Hampshire and the coastal regions of Maine.

The first full-fledged battle was the Peace Field Fight. Although many shots were fired, there were no English deaths and one known death of the Indians. Such a fortunate turn of events would not be repeated. Soon the Pokanokets were a fighting force in name only as the Nipmucks assumed the lead role. As for Philip, although the war bore his name and the name of his people, he was a spectator, running from place to place always just a step of his pursuers. Irrelevant to the war, Philip was still a symbol of native defiance. Over the ensuing months, towns and fields throughout New England placed their mark in the history of King Philip's War: Brookfield; Deerfield where sixty-four Englishmen were buried; Northfield; and Turner Falls. But it was at Schaghticoke in western Connecticut in February 1676 that a native army sent from Canada by the French to join Philip was attacked and routed by the Mohawk. The victory may very well have determined the ultimate outcome of the war that has been described as the greatest Indian war in American history pitting Indian against Indian; Algonquian against Iroquois.

Other battle names included the Pocasset Swamp Fight; the Nipsachuck Swamp Fight; and Pierce's Massacre where 55 English and ten of their "loyal" Indians were killed in the fighting. Nine more English were captured and taken away where they were tortured and killed. At Clark's Garrison just south of Plymouth that had been used by the citizens of Plymouth as a sanctuary, eleven died and the structures were burned to the ground on March 12, 1676. There was also the lot that befell the peaceable Praying Indians who were rounded up and put out to Deer Island in Boston harbor where hundreds suffered from the elements and died of starvation and disease. As time went on a number of the Praying Indians went onto the side of the English and proved quite effective. The Nipmucs were the first to sue for peace.

Benjamin Church finally received approval to put together a small company of Englishmen and volunteer Sakonnets who made a complete turn-about. During two months of patrols, Church's men captured nearly eight hundred dispirited Indians. In the second week of August 1676, Philip was finally run to ground at the tip of Mount Hope where he was killed by a Pacasset warrior in Church's company. In September, Church and company captured Philip's war chief, Annawon, at his camp east of Providence. Although a few remnants continued to resist, King Philip's War had come to an end. The odds against the Indians were overwhelming. They not only had to fight and defeat the English army on the field of battle, they had to fight hunger, disease, and nature itself. They lacked food and ammunition and were further encumbered by the need to protect and feed their women and children. Most importantly, they had to fight their own kind.

The bloody war left one in ten soldiers on both sides injured or killed, resulting in an estimated five thousand deaths—three quarters Native Americans. Hundreds more were sold into slavery in the West Indies—estimates are generally of at least a thousand, over half from Plymouth Colony. Those rejected in the Indies were shipped off to Africa where they were left to their own fate. For the most part, English captives were treated relatively well by their native masters. There was no known incident of a female captive being raped, and captives ate what the Indians ate. Those that died received proper burials. The war, however, brought out the worst in men and society. Atrocities occurred on both sides, but some of the English seemed particularly pleased with their efforts in that direction. Indian heads were severed and put on display as a matter of course; bodies were torn, quartered, and burned; and body parts were distributed as tokens of victory.

The confederacy was shattered; the power of the Native Americans in the Northeast was broken forever; Mount Hope was purged of people. (The land on Mount Hope Peninsula went up for sale in 1680.) It took several years for the Plymouth and the other New England colonies to recover from the damage done to property and the burden of debts. It is believed that a third of all towns and settlements were totally destroyed. Not long after the last shots were fired, the first royal governor was appointed over New England, and in 1692 Plymouth Colony was merged into Massachusetts Bay. The effects of the war were felt all the way south along the Atlantic coast and into the Chesapeake colonies.

MOUNT HOPE RESERVE

In 1640, less than twenty years after they first arrived on shore, officials of Plymouth Colony established Mount Hope Indian Reserve. The reserve included the entire Mount Hope Peninsula, that juts out between Mount Hope Bay on the east and Narragansett Bay on the west, including the territory on the east shore of Mount Hope Bay known as Pocasset. The area would one day include the site of present-day Bristol, Rhode Island.

WANAPAM

The Wanapam or Wanapum belonged to the Shahaptian division of the Shapwailutan linguistic stock. In the Sahaptin language, Wanapam or Wanaláma referred to "people of the river." The tribe was comprised of two branches, the Wanapam proper and the Chamnapum, and were closely associated with the Palouse. The Wanapam inhabited the area at the bend of the Columbia River between Priest Rapids and a point below the mouth of the Umatilla River, and extending east of the Columbia and north of Pasco in Washington State. Lewis and Clark spent two days with the Wanapum and their chief, Cutssahnem. Clark wrote extensively of their houses and clothing and the physical characteristics of the people. The present-day Wanapam community is based at Priest Rapids, Washington.

WANDO

The Wando was a subdivision or sub-tribe of the Cusabo proper (North). They lived on the Cooper River of South Carolina. For more see Cusabo and Coosa.

WANGUNK

The Wangunk or Wongunk was a subdivision or sachemship of the Wappinger of New York State. They lived on both sides of Connecticut River generally from present-day Hartford to Haddam, Connecticut. Mattabesec was the largest and most important village of the Wangunk. For more see Wappinger and Mattabesic.

WAORANEC

The Waoranec was a sub-tribe of the Unami division of the Delaware. They lived near Esopus Creek in Ulster County, New York. For more see Unami and Delaware.

WAPPING

The Wapping or Wappinger proper was the principal tribe of the Wappinger Confederacy. They lived about Poughkeepsie in Duchess County, New York. For more see Wappinger Confederacy.

WAPPINGER CONFEDERACY

The Wappinger was large nation of tribes or subdivisions of Algonquian stock that occupied the land on the east bank of Hudson River from Poughkeepsie to Manhattan Island and the country extending east beyond the Connecticut River. The name itself is loosely translated as "easterner" as was the Abnaki of Maine (also used for the Delaware) and the Wampanoag of Massachusetts. Their totem was the Wolf or Loup in French.

Swanton identified seventeen subdivisions or sachemships as he calls them of the Wappinger. Others refer to them collectively as a confederacy. PageWise names seven sub-tribes or subdivisions of Swanton's seventeen; AccessGeneology, nine—the seven of PageWise plus the Mattabesec and the Manhatan. See the list below. Regardless of their classification, each tribe functioned as an independent, autonomous unit. They came together only in the event of a wide-scale war.

The first European contact with the Wappinger was Giovanni de Verranzano in 1524. Their next contact was with Henry Hudson in 1609. The Wappinger suffered from encounters with the Dutch, especially in Kieft's War of 1643-1645, and from the Mahicans. The Wappinger likely took part in the Peach War of September 1655 and the Esopus Indian Wars from 1658 to 1664. The Wappinger signed large tracts of land between 1683 and 1685.

The Wappinger were decimated by the Indian wars with the Dutch, and by 1730 what had been a nation of some eight thousand was reduced to a few hundred. They fled to Pennsylvania in 1745 but returned in 1746 for a peace settlement. Their ranks were further reduced by disease and alcohol. Those that survived fought alongside the colonists in the War of Independence. Some were absorbed into the Stockbridge. By the nineteenth century, the remnants were located on a reservation in Wisconsin. For more, see Kieft's War in the Wecquaesgeek; also Susquehanna and Esopus. (Alfieri runs the Peach War into the Esopus Indian Wars, 1655-1664.)

SUBDIVISIONS OR SACHEMSHIPS
—or CONFEDERACY OF TRIBES

Hammonasset, S
Kitchawank, S, PW, AG
Manhatan, AG
Massaco, S
Mattabesec, AG
Menunkatuck, S
Nochpeem, S, PW, AG
Paugusset, S
Podunk, S
Poquonock, S

Quinnipiac, S
Sicaog, S
Sintsink, S, PW, AG
Siwanoy, S, PW, AG
Tankiteke, S, PW, AG
Tunxis, S
Wangunk, S
Wappinger proper, S, PW, AG
Wecquaesgeek, S, PW, AG

"S"	Swanton
"PW"	PageWise
"AG"	AccessGeneology

WAPPO

The Wappo was of the Yukian linguistic family. They inhabited the area around the headwaters of the Napa River and Pope and Putah creeks in California; also a portion of the Russian River.

WAPPOO

The Wappoo was a subdivision or sub-tribe of the Cusabo of South Carolina. For more see the Cusabo.

WARANAWONKONG

The Waranawonkong was a sub-tribe of the Munsee division of the Delaware and one of the five tribes of the Esopus group. They inhabited the area around Esopus, Wallkill, and Shawangunk creeks, in Ulster County, New York.

WARRASQUEOC

The Warrasqueoc tribe was a member of the Powhatan Confederacy and inhabited parts of Isle of Wright County, Virginia.

WASCO

The Wasco belonged to the upper branch of the Chinookan linguistic stock. The Wasco bands on the Columbia River were the eastern-most group of Chinookan-speaking Indians. They lived in the vicinity of The Dalles in present Wasco County, Oregon. One band, the Wascopum, is treated separately in the literature. It is not uncommon to see the names Wasco and the Wascopum in the same sentence as if they were two separate and distinct tribes. The Wasco were one of the original member tribes of the Confederated Tribes of Warm Springs, Oregon, formally organized in 1938.

The Tenino and Taih (Tyigh) were separate, independent tribes rather than bands of the Walla Walla as referred to in the Treaty with the Tribes of Middle Oregon (1855). The Tenino ceded all their lands for the Yakima Reservation in Washington. The Warm Springs tribe is made up of the Tenino, Upper Deschutes

(Tygh), Lower Deschutes (Wyam), and John Day (Dock-spus) bands. The Wasco tribe is made up of The Dalles (Ki-gal-twal-la) and Dog River bands. Together with several Paiute bands from southeastern Oregon they comprise the Confederated Tribes of the Warm Springs Reservation of Oregon located on 640,000 acres in north central Oregon.

WASCOPUM

The Wascopum was a band of the Wasco that lived at the present-day site of The Dalles, Oregon, in Wasco County. The Wascopum are generally treated separately in the literature. In the Treaty with the Tribes of Middle Oregon, 1855, they were identified as one of the "three principal bands." The name has mistakenly been written as Wyampum. (Wyam is another name for the Celilo Falls.) The modern city of The Dalles was actually named Wascopum in the mid-1850s. A Methodist mission was established at The Dalles in 1838. It was later abandoned and in early 1848 the militia of the Provisional Territorial Government occupied the site calling it Fort Wascopam (also called Fort Lee for Major Henry A.G. Lee, militia commander and peace commissioner).

Of Note

The name The Dalles is derived from the French word *dalle*, meaning flagstone. It was applied to the narrows of the Columbia River just above the present city by French fur traders. The word *dalles* was used to signify the river rapids flowing swiftly through a narrow channel over flat, basaltic rocks. The name La Grande Dalle de la Columbia became established in the early decades of the 1800s. Lewis and Clark camped at the site in 1806 and named it Rockfort Camp. The Indians called it Win-quatt, meaning a place encircled by rock cliffs.

WASHA

The Washa belonged to the Chitimachan branch of the Tunican linguistic family. They lived along Bayou La Fourche (or Lafourche) that was referred to by Iberville as the River of the Washas. They may also lived about present-day city of Labadieville in Assumption Parish, Louisiana. They were closely related to the Chawasha. Iberville's brother Bienville resettled them on the south side of the Mississippi River just above New Orleans in 1715. In 1739 they were living with the Chawasha at Les Allemands. They seemed to have passed into history as a distinct tribe by the 1800s. See the Chawasha.

WASHO

The Washo have generally been placed in the Hokan linguistic family; others have them linguistically related to the Chumash; others have them related to some of the California tribes; and still others classify them as distinct. They lived about the Truckee River, the Carson River, the borders of Lake Tahoe, and the Sierra valley in Nevada. They were defeated by the Northern Paiute tribes in 1860-1862 in a fight over the site of Carson City. Later they lived a parasitic lifestyle between Reno and a point south of Carson City.

WASSAMASAW

The Wassamasaw was an inland tribe of Edisto Island in South Carolina that was related to the coastal Edisto. Descendants comprise the state recognized Wassamasaw Tribe of Varnertown, South Carolina.

WATEPANETO

Drake reported that the Watepaneto lived on the Padouca Fork (North Platte River), but no additional information has become available.

WATEREE

The Wateree have been placed in the Siouan linguistic family. They inhabited the area on the Wateree River below present Camden, South Carolina, and were one of the more powerful tribes of South Carolina. They sold the neck of land between the Congaree and Wateree rivers to a trader n 1744, and about that time they joined the Catawba.

WATLALA

The Watlala, or more popularly Cascade Indians, inhabited the north side of the Columbia River from the Cascades of the Columbia to Skamania and the mouth of the Willamette River, possibly as far as Cape Horn in Washington State and Oregon. One subdivision occupied the south side of the river. The Watlala belonged to the Clackamas group of Chinookan linguistic stock. Lewis and Clark put the population at the time at under three thousand. They later lived on the Dog (now Hood) River about halfway between the Cascades and The Dalles, in Wasco County, Oregon. By the 1950s they were grouped with the Wishram and Wasco.

It is generally believed that the Watlala were comprised of six subdivisions, but there is also some thought that one or more may be separate tribes.

SUBDIVISIONS
Cathlakaheckit, at the Cascades
Cathlathlala, just below the Cascades
Clahclellah, near the foot of the Cascades
Neerchokioon, on the south side of the Columbia River above Souvies Island
Washougal, near Quicksand River
Yehuh, just above the Cascades

WAUYUKMA

The Wauyukma inhabited the Snake River below the mouth of the Palouse in Washington State. They belonged to the Shahaptian division of the Shapwailutan linguistic group and were closely related to the Palouse.

WAWARSINK

The Wawarsink (Waoranecker, Warwarsing) was a sub-tribe of the Munsee division of the Delaware and one of the five tribes of the Esopus group. They lived at or near the junction of the Warwarsing and Rondout creeks in New York State.

WAWENOC

The Wawenoc was a subdivision of the Abnaki. They lived on seacoast of Sagadahoc, Lincoln and Knox counties. For more see Abenaki.

WAWYACHTONOC

The Wawyachtonoc were a subdivision of the Mahican and lived in what became Duchess and Columbia counties in New York east to the Housatonic River in Connecticut. See the Mahican Group.

WAXHAW

The Waxhaw inhabited Lancaster County, South Carolina, and Union and Mecklenburg counties in North Carolina. Evidence indicates that they were possibly of Siouan linguistic stock. Because they deformed the heads of their children, they are also called Flatheads. They also referred to as the Wisacky. Some reports consider them part of the Catawba, but that seems unlikely given subsequent events. Following the Yamasee War, they refused to make peace with the English and were attacked by the Catawba, and many were killed. Of those who escaped, some joined the Cheraw; and one small band joined the Yamasee and fled to Florida.

WEA

The Wea, for which there are a number of variations in the spelling of the name, belonged to the Algonquian linguistic family. Some writers believe that the Wea were one of the six sub-tribes of the Miami and subsequently separated from them. Others believed that the Wea comprised a distinct and independent tribe misclassified as a subdivision of the Miami. Some reports refer to the Wea *as* the Miami. For their part, the Wea state that they had always been independent; however, there were relatively few wholly independent tribal entities. Early history finds the Wea at Greenbay, an Island to the west side of Great Lake Michigan, and in and around the modern city of Detroit. Pressured by the Iroquois and whites, they migrated to the area of present-day Chicago prior to 1688. Over the years, they were pushed from the Old Northwest Territory of the eighteenth century to modern upper Indiana. By 1700 a large group had settled in the western part of the state in the valley of the Wabash from around the Lafayette to Vincennes and as far east as around Thorntown. A much smaller group settled in present Ohio around Greenville and in Darke County; others moved farther west to Illinois around Kaskaskia and Fort de Chartres. The Indian removal of 1830s placed them at the confluence of the Kansas (Kaw) and Missouri rivers.

Civil Chief Christmas Noel Winriscah Dagenette (1799-1848) led many his people west in a series of three trips between 1836-1846. Of the 350 persons that completed the trip over one hundred and fifty died from starvation, disease, and despair within the first year. (Christmas Dagenette was buried near Louisburg, Kansas.) Others fled into the wilderness of southern Indiana and Ohio to avoid removal. They coalesced around Chief Jacco Tackeketah Godfroy (1777-1854). He died and was buried in Indiana. Survivors settled throughout Indiana, Michigan and Ohio.

Because of their small numbers, the Wea, Peoria, Kaskaskia, and Piankashaw in Kansas were banded together and, with the Treaty of 1854, became known as the Confederated Peoria Tribes. At that time, the Wea as a separate entity was considered extinct. Later the confederacy became known as the Peoria Indian Tribe of Oklahoma.

WEANOC

Weanoc was a member of the Powhatan Confederacy and inhabited parts of Charles City County, Virginia.

WEAPEMEOC

The Weapemeoc were of the Algonquian linguistic stock of North Carolina and closely related to the Powhatan, the Chowan, the Machapunga, and Pamlico. There were four subdivisions that inhabited present Chowan County in North Carolina north to Albermarle Sound and along its North Shore. They first appeared in the chronicles of the Raleigh Colony of 1585-1586. Later they were often spoken of under the name of one of their subdivisions: Pasquotank, Perquiman, Poteskeet, and Yeopim, the latter most prominently. The ending "oc" may be a variation of the common suffix "ooc" referring to shellfish and a large body of water.

WEBING

The Webing lived on the Mississippi River below the Shaki on the Wabash River. In the mid-1700s they were estimated to have had a population of some 200 warriors.

WECQUAESGEEK WAPPINGER

The Wecquaesgeek was a subdivision or sub-tribe of the Wappinger and lived between the Hudson, Bronx, and Pocantico rivers. For more see Wappinger.

PAVONIA MASSACRE

Pavonia was the name of a Dutch colony in New Jersey. There was no tribe or sub-tribe of Delaware or Wappinger Indians of the name Pavonia as suggested by some reports in the literature.

On November 22, 1630, Michiel Reyniersz Pauw of the West India Company bought a tract of land on the west side of the Hudson River in New Jersey at what is now the site of the cities of Hoboken and Jersey City from the Delaware Indians (Lenni Lenape) to establish a colony that he named Pavonia, the Latinized form of his last name. It was the first permanent settlement in what became the state of New Jersey.

The colony was the site of the Pavonia Massacre February 25, 1643. The Mohawk, allies of the Dutch, had attacked a band of Wecquaesgeek Wappinger Indians (other reports call them the Tappans) and drove them to seek shelter at Pavonia. There Dutch soldiers from New Amsterdam under the command of Hendrick van Dyck, systematically and brutally executed some eighty men, women, and children. (Another attack occurred almost at the same time Corlaer's or Corlear's Hook , at what is today the Lower East Side of Manhattan.) Dutch Governor Keift and the soldiers considered their actions a deed of valor. In retaliation, the Wappinger were joined by Mahican, Delaware in a war against the Dutch that became known as Governor Keifts' War or the Wappinger War (1643 to 1645).

An anti-war group, whether for political or humanitarian reasons, published and anti-Keift pamphlet called "Broad Advice" that described the horrors of the night at Pavonia: "[I]nfants were torn from their mother's breasts, and hacked to pieces in the presence of their parents, and the pieces thrown into the fire and in the water, and other sucklings, being bound to small boards, were cut, stuck, and pieced, and miserably massacred in a manner to move a heart to stone….Some came to our people in the country with their hands, some with the legs cut off, and some holding their entrails in their arms, and others had such horrible cuts and gashes, that worse than they were could never happen."

Because the purpose of the pamphlet was political in nature, many of the facts were exaggerated; but to what extent is unknown. Nonetheless, there was no question that the most savage of atrocities were committed. Ordered home, the ship on which Governor Keift was sailing ran aground on the coast of Wales and smashed against the rocks—for many observers it was due punishment dealt by the hand of God.

WEEMINUCHE UTES

The Weeminuche under a variety of spellings or Mountain Ute were a subdivision of the Southern Ute that inhabited southeastern Utah and southwest Colorado. For more see Ute.

WEKISA

Drake reported that the Wakes as a band of the Seminole that lived on the west side Chattahoochee River, four miles above the Cheskitaloas.

WELSH INDIANS

Legend says that the ancestors of the Welsh Indians emigrated to American shores in the year 1170. They were reportedly in a party of explorers and settlers led by Madog ab Owen Gwynedd, Prince of Wales. The story continues that they later settled on the west side of the Mississippi River. These accounts were given by General Bowles, a Creek or Cherokee Indian, who visited London and by others. An observer of the Plains Indians noted that the round, earth lodges used by the Mandan and some of tribes of the area bore a similarity to those found in Wales. From that point, some have drawn the conclusion that the legendary Welsh Indians were absorbed into the Mandan. In the writings of Col. Henry Bouquet, on the other hand, the Welsh Indians are said to be a large tribe of some 10,000 fighting men in over a hundred villages known as the Notoweases.

The Salish enjoyed good relations with white men, beginning with Lewis and Clark in September 1805. In their journal entries of September 4-6, 1805, Lewis and Clark suggest that the Tushepaw nation (Salish) or Flatheads may be the Welsh Indians of legend because of their light skin and the "Strangest language."* Joseph Whitehouse (April 2, 1806) wrote rather hesitantly of the possible existence of a Welsh Indian Nation. He wrote that those referred to as Welsh may possibly be the Clackamas (Clark-a-mus). Whitehouse also made reference to the description of the Welsh given by others of being light-skinned Indians, some with beards. Another member of the Expedition, John Ordway (September 4, 1805) wrote that they had encountered Indians whose language was so strange that perhaps they were the Welsh.

*George Catlin makes the same points about the Mandans as did John Evans who had visited the Mandans prior to Lewis and Clark. Evans was a Welshman who had come to the United States with the express purpose of locating the mythical Welsh Indians, went to work for trader James Mackay, and explored the Upper Missouri.

WENATCHEE

The Wenatchee (Wina't-ca) also known as Chelan and as the Pisquow belonged to the inland division of the Salishan linguistic family. They are closely related to the Sinkiuse-Columbia. They inhabited the area around the Methow and Wenatchee rivers and Chelan Lake. The Wenatchee/Pisquow should not be confused with the Pisquow (Pisko) division of the Yakima. They were comprised of five major divisions and four minor divisions.

MAJOR	MINOR
Sinia'lkumuk	Camiltpaw
Sinkumchi/muk	Shanwappom
Sinpusko'isok	Siapkat
Sintia'thumuk	Skaddal
Stske'tamihu	

In the 1855 Yakima treaty at Camp Stevens, they ceded all their lands to the government and settled on the Yakima Reservation. For more see Yakima and Skaddal.

WENATSHAPAM

The Wenatshapam was a sub-tribe of the Yakima. In the 1855 Yakima treaty at Camp Stevens, the Wenatshapam ceded all their lands to the government and settled on the Yakima Reservation. For more see Yakima.

WENROHRONON

The Wenrohronon (shortened to Wenro in at least one report) belonged to the Iroquoian linguistic stock and were closely affiliated with the Neutrals. The lived about present town of Cuba in Allegany County, New York, were they were allied with the Neutrals. Cuba was the site of an oil spring that the Indians referred to as the place of floating scum. As a consequence, the Wenrohronon were referred to the "People of the Floating Scum. In 1639 they took refuge with the Huron and the Neutrals and thus shared the fate of the Neutrals. For more see Neutrals.

WEROWOCOMOCO

The Werowocomoco was a member of the Powhatan Confederacy and inhabited parts of Gloucester County, Virginia.

WESTERN INDIAN CONFEDERACY

The Western Indian Confederacy was comprised of a number of aligned tribes of the Ohio Country, the Great Lakes Region, and adjoining lands in Canada determined to establish the Ohio River as the boundary between Indians and whites. In the negotiations with U.S. commissioners conducted August 13, 1793, at the foot of the Miami Rapids (present-day Maumee, Ohio), sixteen signatories declared, "We shall be persuaded that you mean to do us justice if you agree, that the Ohio, shall remain the boundary line between us, if you will not consent thereto, our meeting will be altogether unnecessary. This is the great point which we hoped would have been explained, before you left your homes, as our message last Fall was principally directed to obtain that information." The commissioners answered "that it was now impossible to make the River Ohio the boundary" and that negotiations were at an end. What followed was the August 20, 1794, Battle of Fallen Timbers that resulted in the utter defeat the Indians of the Western Confederacy by General Anthony Wayne.

WESTERN OREGON TRIBES

Title 25 of the U.S. Code was amended August 13, 1954. The statute terminated federal supervision over the tribes of western Oregon. Significant for the purposes of this work was the definition of the word "tribe" as used in the statute. By defining the term, the statute provided the names of the tribes, bands, and groups of Indians located west of the Cascade Mountains in Oregon that might not otherwise have been available.

Confederated Tribes of the Grand Ronde
Community
Confederated Tribes of Siletz Indians
Alsea
Applegate Creek
Calapooya
Chaftan
Chempho
Chetco
Chetlessington
Chinook
Clackamas
Clatskanie
Clatsop
Clowwewalla
Coos
Cow Creek
Euchees
Galic Creek
Grave
Joshua
Karok
Kathlamet
Kusotony
Kwatami or Sixes
Lakmiut
Long Tom Creek
Lower Coquille
Lower Umpqua
Maddy
Mackanotin

Mary's River
Multnomah
Munsel Creek
Naltunne
Nehalem
Nestucca
Northern Molalla
Port Orford
Pudding River
Rogue River
Salmon River
Santiam
Scoton
Shasta
Shasta Costa
Siletz
Siuslaw
Skiloot
Southern Molalla
Takelma
Tillamook
Tolowa
Tualatin
Tututui
Upper Coquille
Upper Umpqua
Willamette Tumwater
Yamhill
Yaquina
Yoncalla

WESTO

Swanton identifies the Westo as Yuchi. He suggests that the name may have given to them by the Cusabo; yet he admits that identification is not without question. Not surprisingly, therefore, it is quite common to find the Westo treated as a separate and distinct tribe in the literature. Eric Brown describes the Westo as a wondering tribe that had their original homeland in the Northeast and that they were driven from their lands by the Five Nations of the Iroquois. Brown notes that they were also known as the Rickahocan or Chichimeco. The name Rickahocan is a slight variation on the spelling of Rickohokan that Swanton notes was used by Hewitt (Hodge, 1907) for the Yuchi. Swanton suggests that Rickohokan may have been an early name for part of the Yuchi. In other words, the two positions are not necessarily self-exclusive. It is not uncommon for sub-tribes or individual bands or segments of a given Indian population to attain such a level of independent action that they are deemed to be separate and distinct entities. The question, however, may never be resolved.

The Westo established an early alliance with the English in Virginia and Carolinas. As a consequence they were one of the first to obtain firearms which they used effectively to dominate and enslave natives throughout the region, trading human flesh instead of furs for goods. Exceptionally hard hit by their attacks were the Cusabo. Their dominance of the region continued until the Westo themselves became dominated by the Savannah Yamasee. According to Brown, the lands vacated by the Westo were quickly filled by a number of small "bands, including the Appalachees, the Yuchis, and the Chickasaws, settled near the fall line." For more see the Yuchi.

WETEPAHATO

The Wetepahato reportedly lived with the Kiowa on the Padouca Fork of Platte River (North Platte).

WHILKUT

The Whilkut belonged to the Hupa group of the Athapascan linguistic stock. They lived on the upper part of Redwood Creek above the Mad River and the vicinity of Iaquo Butte in California.

WHITE MOUNTAIN COYOTERO

The White Mountain Coyotero was a tribe of Western Division of the Apache nation that was generally grouped with the multiple bands of the Cibicue, the San Carlos, and the Tonto and collectively called the Western Apaches. The White Mountain and Pinal Apache comprised the geographic division of the Apache called the Coyoteros, thus White Mountain Coyotero Apache. They lived in eastern Arizona.

The White Mountain name is now applied to all the Apaches of the Fort Apache agency, Arizona. They include the Aravaipa, Tsiltaden or Chilion, Chiricahua, Coyotero (White Mountain and Pimal), Mimbreño and Mogollon. For more see Apache.

WHITE SALMON

The White Salmon belonged to the upper branch of the Chinookan linguistic stock. They lived in the area of The Dalles in present Wasco County, Oregon.

The White Salmon River was named by Lewis and Clark when they observed the river teeming with salmon whose color had turned white after spawning.

WHONKENTI

The Whonkenti lived between the Potomac and Rappahanoc rivers in Fauquier County, Virginia.

WHONKENTIA

The Whonkentia was a sub-tribe of the Manahoac of Virginia or a member of the Manahoac Confederacy that lived in Fauquier County near the headwaters of the Rappahannock.

WICHITA

The Wichita or Black Pawnee were one of the major tribes of the Caddoan linguistic family and lived about the Arkansas River and on the Canadian River in present Oklahoma and in Texas. Their relative position with respect to the larger Caddoan group and subordinate tribes or divisions and the many names assigned to the Wichita has considerable confusion down through recorded history and into the present time. The Wichita lived in dome-shaped grass houses and subsisted on farming and hunting, especially corn, tobacco, and melons.

Some writers classify the Tawakoni, Waco, Tawehash or Taovaya, and Yscani as sub-tribes or subdivisions of the Wichita although most accounts treat them as separate, independent tribes. Others include in that list the Akwits or Akwesh, Kirikiris, Isis Yscani, Tokane Yscani, and Itaz which were more likely bands.

Still others refer to the Kirishkitsu or Kichai, Asidahetsh and Kishkat. Among their many names are variations on the word Panis, in both French and English. In Texas, they had a slightly darker complexion than the native people of the state and were distinguished by their elaborate tattoos (Freckled Panis). The name Panis, in turn, causes much confusion with the Pawnee tribe, generally farther north.

The name Wichita (Ousita) was first found in the early seventeenth century in historical records of French traders; but the Coronado expedition through present Kansas in 1541 visited a tribe that Coronado called Quivira, who have been identified by archeological and historical studies as Wichitas. They were pushed and pulled by the migrating Comanche until they left Kansas for Oklahoma, putting them in conflict with the Hasinai to the south and the Osage to the east. By 1719 they were settled in Oklahoma where they were encountered by the French trader Jean Baptiste Bénard de La Harpe.

By the nineteenth century the name came to be used to refer to several confederated bands who had similar traditions and culture becoming prominent middlemen in the trade between the Comanches on the plains and Louisiana merchants. Several bands continued the southward march into Texas on the Red, Wichita, and Brazos rivers.

Survivors of wars with the governments of the Spain, Texas, and the United States and inter-tribal wars joined remnants of other bands of the Wichita "confederacy" or kinsmen on the Washita River in 1859. With the outbreak of the Civil War broke, they fled north into Kansas. After the war, the Wichita, Waco, Tawakoni, and Kichai, and other associated tribes were relocated to the Wichita Reservation near present Anadarko, Oklahoma. The reservation was opened to allotment in 1891.

WICKQUASGECK

The Wickquasgeck or Wiechquaesgeck, was a sub-tribe of the Delaware. The tribe was also referred to the New York Algonquin. They inhabited northern Manhattan, the Bronx, and Winchester, New York.

In 1626 a small number of Wickquasgeck approached the Dutch at New Amsterdam to trade furs. They were robbed and murdered. One twelve-year-old boy escaped. Fifteen years later he killed a prominent Dutch settler in retribution, Claes Swits. In response, Governor Willem Kieft, ignoring the common will of the citizens of New Amsterdam, embarked on Kieft's War that was characterized by a series of murderous attacks committed by both sides that continued from 1643 into 1645. The war served to unite the tribes of the Lower Hudson Valley. Much of the war was fought in and around the present-day city of Westchester.

The bloodiest day of the war occurred the night of February 25, 1643. Two parties of soldiers massed for an attack on the natives. They moved on a camp at Corlaer's Hook (Lower East Side of Manhattan) and another camp in the area of plantation called Pavonia (Jersey City) where the Wickquasgeck and the Tappan had gathered to escape the Mohawk from the north. Afterwards, the soldiers bragged of having killed eighty Indians—men, women, and children—and considered it a deed of valor.

On August 30, 1645 chiefs and sachems of Hackinsack, Tappan, Rechgawawanck, Nyack, and Aepjen of the Wickquasgeck met with Kieft and other settlers in front of the Fort at New Amsterdam and made their marks pledging peace.

In the midst of the Esopus Indian Wars, on March 6, 1660, the Hackensack, Nyack, Haverstraw, Wecquaesgeek (Weschester), and Western Long Island Indians accepted a peace treaty with the Dutch that isolated the Esopus.

The Wickquasgeck Trail or Wickquasgeck Road as it is also referred to ran the length of the Manhattan south-to-north into the Bronx. It was the route followed by the Manhattan to reach the Wickquasgeck to the north;

thus the name. The Dutch named the southern portions of the trail Gentlemen's Street or High Street or simply Highway. The English called it Broadway. The trail rejoins today's Broadway at the northern end.

WICOCOMOCO

The Wicocomoco was a subdivision of the Powhatan and inhabited parts of Northumberland County, Virginia.

WIDYUNUU

The Widyunuu (or Widyu Yapa, awl people) was one of the sub-tribes or bands of the Comanche. For more see Comanche.

WIEKAGJOY

The Wiekagjoy was a subdivision of the Mahican. They lived along the eastern bank of the Hudson River near Hudson, New York. See the Mahican Group.

WIGHCOCÒMICO

The Wighcocòmico lived in Northumberland County, Virginia, on the Wicocomico River.

WIGHCOMOCO

The Wighcomoco lived on the eastern shore of Chesapeake Bay about the Wighcomoco River (now Pocomoke).

WIMBEE

The Wimbee was of the Muskogean linguistic group and a subdivision or sub-tribe of the Cusabo proper (South). They lived between the upper and the lower Coosawhatchie River and about the lower Ashepoo River in Hampton and Jasper counties of South Carolina. For more see Cusabo and Coosa.

WIMINUCHE UTE

The Wiminuche was a subdivision of the Ute that inhabited southwest Colorado around the valley of the San Juan River and its tributaries.

WINIBIGOSHISH

Winibigoshish or Winnebegoshishiwininewak was a band of Chippewa that lived on Lake Winnibigashish, Minnesota, that is sometime referred to an independent tribe.

WINNEBAGO

The Winnebago, Puans, or Ho-Chunk, their name for themselves, belonged to the Chiwere division of the Siouan linguistic family. Other tribes in the division were the Oto, Iowa, and Missouri. Their traditional homeland was on the south side of Green Bay and inland to Lake Winnebago in Wisconsin. (Lake Michigan was originally called Lake of the Puans.) The also occupied lands in Iowa, South Dakota, Minnesota, Nebraska and Illinois, claiming title to more than ten million acres. The name Winnebago (Ouinepegi), meaning "People of Filthy (or Stinky) Waters," was given to them by the Sauk and Fox. The remained the official name until 1993, when their original name Ho-Chunk was reclaimed.. Jean Nicolet, sent by Governor Champlain, was the first white man first to visit the Ho-Chunk in 1634. In his journal, George Rogers Clark called them the Meadow Indians.

The Winnebago, along with the Menominee and Chippewa, drove the Sac and Fox out of Wisconsin, leaving them the dominant tribe in the western part of Wisconsin along the Mississippi River into the first decade of the 1830s although a part of their lands were taken to make a home for the Oneida of New York. They were hit by a smallpox epidemic in 1836 that nearly devastated the tribe. With the influx of white settlers into southern Wisconsin, the Ho-Chunk ceded their lands to the government in 1837 and in 1840 were removed to northeastern Iowa. Some refused to move until 1848 when they were moved to the Long Prairie Reservation in northern Minnesota territory between the Sioux and the Ojibwe. They moved again in 1853 to Crow River and in 1856 to Blue Earth. By 1859, their reservation was reduced from eighteen square miles to nine, and in 1863, following the Dakota revolt, they were moved to the Crow Creek Reservation in South Dakota.

They were eventually able to exchange the South Dakota reservation for lands cut from the Omaha reservation in Nebraska and are now known as the Winnebago Tribe of Nebraska. Throughout all the moves, some remained in or returned to Wisconsin; others, Minnesota.

WINNEFELLY KALAPUYA

Winnefelly (Winefelly) were of the Central Division of the Kalapooian linguistic stock and lived along the Mohawk and McKenzie rivers and the Coast Fork of the Willamette Rivers. For more see Kalapuya Peoples.

WINTU

The Wintu or Wintun belonged to the Penutian family and was one of the three divisions of the Wintum, the northern division. They are sometimes referred to in the literature as synonymous with the Wintum group as a whole. They lived in the valleys of the upper Acramento and upper Trinity rivers north of Cottonwood Creek and from Cow Creek on the east to the South Fork of the Trinity on the west coast of California.

HAYFORK MASSACRE

In May 1852, Indians killed a white man named John Anderson and stole his cattle near the town of Weaverville in northern California's Trinity County. Why John Anderson and whether it was a single, isolated incident is unknown. A posse led by Sheriff Dixon tracked the Indians and set up camp at Hayfork Creek, a short distance downstream from the Indian camp. The pose surrounded the Wintu camp at night. At dawn, they launched a surprise attack and killed everyone in sight except one woman and two children who were taken prisoner to be sold. One hundred and fifty Wintu were killed that May morning in what has been called the Hayfork Massacre. Other names are the Bridge Gulch Massacre, the Natural Bridge Massacre, and the Weaverville Massacre. (Other accounts put the death toll at 152 and 153.)

WINTUN

The Wintum linguistic family (or Copehan) is part of the Penutian linguistic stock. They inhabited the west side of the Sacramento Valley from the Sacramento River to the coast range and about Cottonwood Creek and Afton and Stonyford in California. The Wintun comprised three divisions: Wintu (northern), Nomlaki (central), and Patwin (southern). There were an estimated 12,000 peoples of the Wintum, Wintu, and Wappo in 1770. By 1930, there were just 512.

WINYAW

The Winyaw lived about Winyaw Bay, Black River, and the lower course of the Pee Dee River in South Carolina. They have been placed in the Siouan linguistic family. The Winyaw disappeared from history after 1720. Remnants likely joined the Waccamaw.

WISCONSIN

The principal tribes of the early period of Wisconsin history were the Potawatomi, Oneida, Menominee, Ho-Chunk (Winnebago), Sauk, Fox, and Ojibwa (Chippewa). The first French form of the name Wisconsin was *Misconsing*. That is the name written on Father Jacques Marquette's 1673 map. Over time, the French word gradually developed into Oisconsin and then finally into its present form.

Evidence to the contrary, it appears reasonable to assign Marquette's "Misconsing" to the Menominee tribe. Variations of the name are Missi-ousing and Miskonsing. One of the subdivisions of the Menominee was the Wi'skos Se'peon Wini'niwuk, "Wisconsin River people." The name Wisconsin derives from wi'skos "muskrat."

WISHRAM

The Wishram or Wish-ham belonged to the Chinookan stock and spoke the same dialect as the Pisquouse. They inhabited the land on the north side of the Columbia River in present Klickitat County, Washington. They were encountered by the Corps of Discovery in 1806 where they were referred to as the E-che-loot. They have also been referred to as the Upper Chinook.

The Wishram were very likely a member of the Yakima Confederation. In the 1855 Yakima treaty at Camp Stevens, the Wishram ceded all their lands to the government and settled on the Yakima Reservation. For more see Yakima. For more see Yakima.

WIWOHKA

The Wiwohka was a sub-tribe or division of the Muskogee and a member of the Creek Confederacy. They lived near the mouth of Hatchet Creek in Coosa County and on Weoka Creek in Elmore County in Alabama.

WIYOT

There has been considerable debate among ethnologists as to the linguistic connection of the Wiyot or Sulatelik. They have been judged as an independent Wishoskan stock and, in conjunction with the Yuork, as constituting the Ritwan. They lived along the lower Mad River, Humboldt Bay, and the lower Eel River in California.

HUMBOLDT BAY MASSACRES

On February 26, 1860, local white settlers, without any apparent provocation, attacked four villages of friendly Wiyot Indians around Humboldt Bay in Humboldt County in the Northern Californian. They slaughtered and horribly butchered one hundred and eighty-eight, mostly women and children. Some accounts put the number killed considerably higher. One village was located at Gunther's or Indian Island in Humboldt Bay, opposite Eureka; the others on the Eel and Mad rivers.

Miners discovered the land in 1849, and by 1860, over half of the Indians had perished from disease or cold-blooded slaughter. Fort Humboldt was established in 1853 and operated until 1866. The 450 remaining Wiyot people were relocated to the Klamath reservation, north of their homeland.

Of Note

When the atrocities were condemned by famed author and poet Francis Bret Harte, best known under the name Bret Harte for his accounts of pioneering life in California, he was forced to leave Arcata (Union or Uniontown), at the time a mining camp on Humboldt Bay where he had lived since 1857. He moved to San

Francisco where he found work on the *Golden Era*, first as compositor then as a writer. In May of 1864, he joined others in starting *The Californian* and a short time later was made editor of the new *Overland Monthly*.

WOCCON

The Woccon belonged to the Siouan linguistic stock and were closely related to the Catawba. They lived between the Neuse River and one of its affluents, possibly about present Goldsboro (Waye), North Carolina. They were not mentioned until 1701 when some of their words were recorded. One opinion has it that they may have been a division of the Waccamaw of South Carolina who ranged across into North Carolina from the headwaters of the Waccamaw River. The Woccon took the Indian side in the Tuscarora War and likely became extinct as a tribe thereafter with the remnants joining the Catawba or other eastern

WYAHTINAW

The Wyahtinaw reportedly lived on the Wabash River, 30 miles from the Vermilion (Kickapoo) Indians; but their connection is unknown. They may have been a band or village of the Piankashaw.

WYAM

The Wyam or Lower De Chutes was a signatory to the Treaty with the Tribes of Middle Oregon (1855) in which it was referred to as a band of the Walla-Walla. Whether it was a band or the Walla Walla or an separate, independent tribe as was the Taih (Tyigh) or Upper De Chutes is uncertain. For more see the Tenino.

WYANDOT

In earlier times the Wyandot were known as the Huron, a Eastern Woodland tribe of Iroquoian linguistic stock, agriculturist in their culture, inhabitants of the St. Lawrence Valley and the present-day Canadian province of Ontario. Following attacks by the Iroquois and a long course of wanderings from place to place, part of the Huron moved west and south to present Sandusky, Ohio, and Detroit, Michigan, by the late seventeenth century. It was the French that gave them the Huron name (Fr. huré w/ suffix -on). See Huron in this work.

"The Wyandotts had resided on the soil of Ohio [near Sandusky] long before the French or English visited the country. Forty-six years ago, I took a census of them when they numbered 2300 souls. In 1841 and 2, I was, as the commissioner of the United States, negotiating with them a treaty of cession and emigration, when it was found, by actual and accurate count, that, in a little less than 50 years, they had been reduced to the number of 800; none had emigrated—all that was left were the subjects of my negotiation. I had been their agent a great part of my life; and after being separated from them for 11 years by the power of the Executive, it fell to my lot, under the appointment of my honored and lamented friend and chief, President Harrison, to sign and seal the compact with their chiefs for their final removal from their cherished homes and graves of their ancestors, to which, of all their race, I had ever known, they were the most tenderly attached, to the country southwest of Missouri. (Missouri River)" —Indian Agent, Col. John. Johnston

A treaty was concluded with the Wyandot and others at Fort M'Intosh in January 1785 that granted to the Wyandot and Delaware Nations exclusive rights to lands along the Miami or Ome River and the south shore of Lake Erie to the mouth of Cayahoga. The 1789 treaty signed at Fort Harmar confirmed the boundaries of the 1785 treaty but stipulated that the lands could not be sold or otherwise disposed of to any other party except to the United States government itself.

The most significant of all the early treaties for the Woodland tribes was the Treaty of Greenville. Parties to the treaty included all tribes living northwest of the Ohio River: Wyandot, the Delaware, the Shawnee, the Ottawa, the Chippewa, the Potawatomi, the Miami, the Eel River, the Wea, the Kickapoo, the

Piankashaw, and the Kaskaskia. The treaty established, in great particulars, the boundary between the lands of the whites and the lands of the Indians. The treaty also allowed for the cession of sixteen separate parcels of land to the government for the construction of military posts and other facilities and allowed for the passage of citizens across the Indian lands. With those exceptions, the United States relinquished all claims "to all other Indian lands northward of the river Ohio, eastward of the Mississippi, and westward and southward of the Great Lakes and the waters, uniting them, according to the boundary line agreed on by the United States and the King of Great Britain, in the treaty of peace made between them in the year 1783." It would all come to naught.

In the Treaty of 1817, the Wyandot, Seneca, Delaware, Shawnee, Potawatomi, Ottawa, and Chippewa ceded much of their land in the East to the government, and the Wyandots were relocated to the lands at the confluence of the Kansas (Kaw) and Missouri rivers.

KANSAS TERRITORY

The Kansa Indians were the first recorded owners of what became Wyandotte County, Kansas, from the Louisiana Purchase of 1803. The Kansa migrated west from the land of the Wabash up the Missouri to the land about the mouth the Kaw River. There they stayed until 1825.

In a treaty with the Kansa of June 3, 1825, the government acquired all their lands. In return, the Kansa were placed on a reservation. On October 3, 1818, the Delaware Indians on the White River in east central Indiana (near present Muncie) ceded their lands in Indiana for lands in the West yet to be described. In the interim they joined other members of the Delaware who lived on the Whitewater River in southeast Missouri. A supplementary article to the 1818 treaty was executed in 1829 by which the reservation in Missouri was given up in exchange for land at the fork of the Missouri and Kansas (Kaw) rivers that extended far up the Kansas where they immediately settled themselves.

In the meantime the Wyandot Indians had been forced to remove from Ohio to Kansas in July of 1843 and were given a tract of 148,000 acres on the Neosho River in eastern Kansas Territory. They had expected to purchase and settle on a portion of the Shawnee Reserve south of the Kansas River near the town of Westport, Missouri. When they arrived, the Shawnee were unwilling to go through with the agreement. As a result the Wyandot were forced to camp on the narrow strip of government land that lay between the Missouri border and the Kansas River that was nothing but swampy lowland. Over sixty of their number, some ten percent, died of disease and exposure. The Wyandots began a cemetery across the Kansas River on the land of the Delaware Reserve (established in 1829). The location was on the crest of a hill about one-half mile west of the confluence of the Kansas and Missouri Rivers, overlooking the broad sweep of the Missouri River valley. The cemetery became known as the Huron Indian Cemetery.

The land on the Neosho was examined, but the Wyandot would not accept it because it was too far from civilization. The Wyandot were the most Anglicized of all the North American Tribes. Connelley wrote that no member of the Wyandots that came to Kansas was more than one-quarter Indian. (In 1832 they had looked at the lands of the Platte Purchase in what became northwest Missouri.) With the issue of their reservation being unresolved, The Wyandots took matters into their own hand and signed an agreement with the Delaware on December 14, 1843, to purchase the eastern portion of the Delaware Reserve of thirty-six sections for the sum of $46,080. (Some writings report the amount as $48,000.) The Delaware gave the Wyandot another three sections in appreciation for Wyandot assistance back in Ohio. The Wyandot acquired all the land between the Kansas and Missouri rivers west, The transaction, which was approved by the government July 25, 1848, was called the Wyandot Purchase. A small settlement was established between the riverfront and the cemetery that became known as the town of Wyandot or Wyandot City—present Kansas City, Kansas, and Armstrong Float.

When they moved into Kansas, the Wyandot brought with them the first mission founded by the Methodist Episcopal Church. He had been established in Upper Sandusky, Ohio, by John Steward, a free Negro, in 1816. It became the Washington Avenue Methodist Episcopal Church of Kansas City, Kansas.

The move began in 1848, and in 1850 the Wyandots began to press the government on the question of citizenship and the individual ownership of tribal lands. With the influx of white settlers following passage of the Kansas-Nebraska Act in 1854, the issue increased in importance. In Washington on January 31, 1855, the Wyandot Tribal Council signed a treaty dissolving their tribal government thereby allowing all competent Wyandots who wished to do so to become U.S. citizens. In addition, the treaty ceded the lands from the Wyandot Purchase to the government to be surveyed, subdivided into allotments, and reconveyed by patent to the individual members of the tribe.

In the fall of 1856, the Quindaro Town Company was formed by an alliance of Wyandots and several individuals from the free-state town of Lawrence with ties to the New England Emigrant Aid Company. Quindaro became a profitable and safe port of entry for free-state settlers into Kansas. (The river ports of Atchison and Leavenworth were in the hands of pro-slavery groups at the time. Several of the wealthy Wyandots were slave owners themselves.) The site was comprised of 693 acres of land in the Wyandotte Reserve bordering the Missouri River. The new town was named in honor of Nancy Brown Guthrie (1820-1886), whose Wyandot name was Seh Quindaro; also written Nancy Quindaro. She was only one-eighth Indian. The competing town of Wyandot, the future Kansas City, Kansas, was formed nearby and absorbed Quindaro.

In 1867 the government concluded a treaty allowing the Indian Party Wyandots to purchase 20,000 acres from the Seneca in Indian Territory and resume tribal status. The treaty recognized the Indian Party council as the only legal Wyandot tribal council, and initially barred Citizen Class Wyandots and their descendents from tribal membership. The treaty was ratified in 1868, but its implementation was delayed for several years. The move to the Wyandot Reserve in Indian Territory was completed in 1872.

WYCOME

Drake reported that the Wycome lived on the Susquehanna River in 1648 with bands of the Oneida.

WYNIAW

Drake reported that the Wyniaw was a small tribe that was living in North Carolina in 1701.

WYNOOCHEE

The Wynoochee belonged to the coastal division of the Salishan linguistic stock and were closely related to the Chehalis. They lived on the Wynoochee, an affluent of the Chehalis River in Washington State. They were closely affiliated with the Lower Chehalis whose dialect they spoke.

WYOMING

It has been suggested that the Wyoming Indians about the present state of Wyoming were at one time a member of Susquehanna group or confederacy from the Wyoming Valley of Pennsylvania.

The state of Wyoming was reportedly named after the Wyoming Valley in Pennsylvania following the popularity of the lengthy, two-part 1809 poem "Gertrude of Wyoming" by Thomas Campbell. The second stanza reads, in part:

"Delightful Wyoming! beneath thy skies,
The happy shepherd swains had nought to do
But feed their flocks on green declivities,
Or skim perchance thy lake with light canoe…"

WYSOX

The Wysox lived about a creek that flows into the Susquehanna at the present Wysox. The Wysox may have been a subdivision of the Susquehanna, but no other reference has been found.

XARAMANE

The Xaramane of Texas was among the Nations of the North, but no additional information has been uncovered. For more see Nations of the North.

YACHATS

The Yachats or Yahute belonged to the relatively small Yakonan linguistic stock. They inhabited the Oregon coast about twenty-five miles south of the present-day city Newport in Lincoln County on the Yachats River. They are commonly written of as a distinct and independent tribe, but the evidence suggests that the Indians of Yachats actually constituted one of the southern bands of the Alsea, a short distance to the north. The literature contains a number of reference to the Yachats under several different names but provides very little information on the Indians themselves. Two of those names, Youitts and Youitz, came from Lewis & Clark and Drake, respectively. Drake refers to the Youitz in placing the location of the Sheastukle, but gives no information on the Youitz itself; nor does his list the Youitz in his enumeration of tribes. In writings discussing the Alsea and the tribes of the Yakonan stock, there is little or no mention of the Yachats. The Yachats village was apparently hit extremely hard by disease and became extinct sometime prior to the establishment of the Alsea-Sub Agency in 1860.

YACOMANSHAGHKING

The Yacomanshaghking was a sub-tribe of the Unalachtigo division of the Delaware. They lived in the area about present Camden, New Jersey. For more see Unalachtigo and Delaware.

YACOVANE

The Yacovane was among the Nations of the North of Texas, but no additional information has been uncovered. For more see Nations of the North.

YADKIN

The Yadkin were of the Siouan linguistic stock and lived along the Yadkin River in North Carolina. Although their record in history is short lived, there are a number of entities in North Carolina to which their name is connected.

YAHI

The Yahi were of the southernmost group of the Yanan Division of the Hokan linguistic family. They lived along Mill and Deer creeks in California.

YAHUSKIN

The Yahuskin were one of the principal sub-tribes or sub-divisions of the Northern Paiute. The other major group was the Walpapi. Collectively they were known, expecially to the the Indians of Oregon, as the Snake Indians. They belonged to the Shoshonean branch of the Uto-Aztecan linguistic family and lived about Silver Lake. The Northern Paiute ranged over a large area of southeastern Oregon. See the Paiute and Northern Paiute.

YAKIMA

The Yakima or Yakama belonged to the Shahaptian division of the Shapwailutan linguistic family. The spelling of "Yakama" was reintroduced in 1994 in a return to the original spelling. They lived along the lower course of the Yakima River in Washington Territory. The Yakima consisted of ten subdivisions, but it had been suggested that the name may at one time have referred a confederacy of distinct, independent tribes under the Yakima name. There is also at least one report that refers to the Yakima under the name Lohim. Their first encounter with the white man was the Lewis & Clark expedition near the confluence of the Yakima and Columbia rivers in 1805. The explorers wrote of them under the name Cutsahnin.

<u>Subdivisions</u>
Atanum-lema, on Atanum Creek
Nakci'sh-hlama, on Naches River (possibly Pshwa'nwapam)
Pisko, about the mouth of Toppenish Creek
Se'tas-lema, on Satus Creek
Si'hlama, on Yakima River above the mouth of Toppenish Creek
Si'la-hlama, on Yakima River between Wenas and Umtanum Creeks
Si'mokoe-hlama, on Simcoe Creek
Tkai'waicjash-hlama, on Cowiche Creek
Topinish, on Toppenish Creek
Waptailmin, at or below Union Gap

With the 1855 treaty at Camp Stevens (June 9, 1855), the Yakima ceded all their lands (some 11.5 million acres) to the government. In return the Yakima and other interior tribes were placed on a government reserve designated the Yakima Reservation in south-central Washington state east of the Cascade Mountains and south of Yakima and the Yakima River.

There were a total of fourteen parties to the 1855 treaty, including distinct, individual tribes and a number of tribal bands. For the purposes of the treaty they were considered one nation called Yakama, some related and some unrelated. The treaty listed the Yakama, Palouse, Pisquouse, Wenatshapam, Klikatat, Klinquit, Kow-was-say-ee, Li-ay-was, Skin-pah, Wish-ham, Shyiks, Ochechotes, Kah milt-pah, and Se-ap-cat. Several of the tribes never recognized the treaty. The 1855 treaty was ratified by Congress four years later on March 8, 1859. It was late 1860 before the provisions of the treaty were put into effect.

While the treaty languished in Congress, what has been called the Yakima War broke out in 1855 and continued through most of 1857 although some accounts merge the Yakima War into the Spokane War that ended in September 1858. In 1860 the Yakima and other tribes were moved onto the reservation. Allotment followed, and much of the land ended up in the hand of developers and speculators. The Confederated Tribes of the Yakama Nation of which there are 14 members was established in 1933. For more see Lohim, Pshwanwapam, and Cayuse.

YAKIMA WAR

Resentment had been building against the increasing white encroachment onto Indian lands. Then, just two weeks after the 1855 treaty was signed Governor Stevens threw the Indian lands open for white settlers less than two weeks after the treaty was signed. The Yakima, Cayuse and others condemned the declaration and demanded that all whites leave their lands. The hostile tribes came together under the under leadership of Yakima chief Kamiakin in late 1855 in open rebellion. It was to be a war of extermination. There followed a number of raids and skirmishes between the Indians and members of the Washington territorial militia ending with what has been described at the Grande Ronde Massacre perpetrated on Walla Walla Indians by troops of the Washington Territorial Army under the command of Colonel B. F. Shaw near present-day Elgin, Oregon, on July 17, 1856.

Shaw estimated that forty Indians were killed (twenty-seven bodies were counted at one site) and many more wounded, many of whom were women, children, and old people. In addition, Indian goods were destroyed and about two hundred horses captures, many of which were killed. Account differ, but it possibly five soldiers were killed and four wounded. Regular army command did not see the events in the same light as the volunteers. On August 2, 1856, General Wood, commander of the Department of the Pacific, issued an order effectively closing Indian country from the white man. Sporadic deaths and depredations continued on both sides until the fall of 1857. It was about that time that what became known as the Spokane War broke out. In the end, Kamiakan escaped to Canada. Other leaders were apprehended and executed. Not ten years later it was the Nez Percé War.

YAMACRAW

The Yamacraw were a sub-tribe or band of the Yamasee but have been treated separately in the literature. Swanton suggests that the name very likely derived from the name of Spanish mission in Florida, Nombre de Dios de Amacarisse, where a number of the Yamasee lived for a time. Following the Yamasee, this small band settled with Apalachicola until about 1730 when they settled along the banks of the Savannah River. It was there that Governor Oglethorpe encountered them when he first visited what would become site for the city of Savannah. He found a gentle group of Indians led by a kindly old chief named Tomochichi. They had made their home just above the site later chosen for the city.

YAMASEE

The Yamasee spoke a Muskhogean dialect, closely related to the Hitchiti. They inhabited lands in northern Florida and southern Georgia. First encounter with the Europeans dates to the arrival of De Soto and the Spanish in 1540. Apparently their was little contact between the two races until the early 1600s as the Yamasee began to look to the Spanish missionaries, who reportedly also brokered a peace between the Yamasee, the Apalachee, Chatot, and Lower Creeks. Relations with the Spanish were on generally good terms until the 1680s. By 1675 there had been three Yamasee missions on the Atlantic coast.

What caused the relations between the two races to deteriorate to the point they did is unknown, but the Yamasee moved north into South Carolina. It does not seem logical that the Spanish would have driven them north after all the time and effort they had committed to bringing them within the fold. It may have been that some aspect of their new Christian religion, as practiced by the Spanish, caused a rift that could not be reconciled. In their new homelands, they lived on the west bank of the Savannah River near its mouth.

Relations with their neighbors in the north started out relatively well where they supplied eighty-seven warriors in the expedition against the Tuscarora in North Carolina led by John Barnwell. But after time conflict developed between the Yamasee and the colonists that came to a head with the formation of a Yamasee-led confederacy of local tribes that included the Catawba and the Lower Creeks and the beginning of the Yamasee War in the spring of 1715. Over the years, the Yamasee had grown dependent on European goods and ended up wallowing in debt at the same time that their fields and hunting lands were being absorbed by the white settlers. Fur (deerskin) traders enslaved Yamasee women and children when the Yamasee could not pay.

The Yamasee War, with attacks on the white settlements in South Carolina, resulted in the deaths of several hundred colonists; homes burned; and livestock slaughtered. Settlers fled the outlying areas for the relative safety of Charleston; others fled the region altogether. Total obliteration of English settlements in South Carolina appeared in the offing until the Cherokee were bribed to join the colonists. The Yamasee and their allies were defeated by the combined force of the colonists, their Indians allies, and the volunteers from Virginia at Saltketchers on the Combahee River in January 1716 that brought the Yamasee War to an end.

The Yamasee retreated south through Georgia and into their ancestral lands in northern Florida where they allied themselves with the Spanish The Yamasee population was decimated when their village at St. Augustine was attacked and destroyed by the English and their allies in 1727. (Although it takes a stretch of the imagination, there are reports that continue the Yamasee War up through the destruction of St. Augustine.) Continuing wars with the Creeks and others, in addition to intra-tribal friction, effectively resulted in the demise of the Yamasee nation. Many of those not killed in wars were captured. Others were incorporated into Hitchiti and Seminole and moved with them to Indian Territory; still others removed to Georgia where again they were well received. For a brief time, the Savannah Yamasee band of Georgia was a member of the Creek Confederacy of Upper Creeks. Whether they were the Savannah Indians who helped drive out the Westo is open to question. The Christian Yamasee fled with the Spanish in 1763 after the territory was transferred to the British. By the beginning of the 1800s, the Yamasee as a tribe had passed into history. The Oklawaha band of Seminole is believed to have been descended from the Yamasee. For more see the Savannah.

YAMEL KALAPUYA

The Yamel or Yamhill belonged to the northern division of the Kalapooian linguistic stock and lived about the Yamhill River, a tributary of the Willamette River in northwestern Oregon, and named for the tribe. The area was prime destination of settlers crossing the Oregon Trail.

YAMPA UTE

The Yampa was a subdivision of the Northern Ute that lived about the Green River and the Colorado River in eastern Utah. For more see Ute.

YAMPARIKA

The Yamparika (or Yamparack, Yapparethka, Yamparock, root eaters—yap root) were one of the five major sub-tribes or bands of the Comanche. For more see Comanche.

YANA

The Yana were of the Hokan linguistic family. The three dialectic divisions lived in an about the Pit River and Cedar Creek; about Cow Creek and Bear Creek; and about the Battle, Payne, and Antelope creeks in California.

YANG-NA

The Yang-na was a sub-tribe of the Tongva of California that inhabited the area about Los Angeles. For more see Tongva.

YANKTON

The Yankton (Ihanktonwan) and Yanktonai constituted the Middle Division (Nakota) of the Sioux Nation. For more see Sioux and Nakota.

YANKTONAI

Yanktonai (Ihanktonwana) and Yankton constituted the Middle Division (Nakota) of the Sioux Nation. For more see Sioux, Nakota, and Assiniboin.

YAQUINA

The Yaquina was of the Yakonan linguistic group and lived along both sides of the Yaquina River and about Yaquina Bay in Oregon.

YATASI

The Yatasi or Yattassee belonged to the Caddo division of the Caddoan linguistic group. They were one of the four principal divisions of the Natchitoches Confederacy of Louisiana. The tribe inhabited the area near Shreveport on the Red River. For more see Natchitoches Confederacy and Caddo Peoples.

YATASI, UPPER

The Upper Yatasi belonged to the Caddo division of the Caddoan linguistic group. They separated from Yatasi proper and joined the Kadohadacho Confederacy of Texas.

YAVAPAI

The Yavapai belonged to the Yuman branch of the Hokan linguistic stock or simply Yuma stock. They lived in western Arizona from the Pinal and Mazatzal Mountains to the vicinity of the Colorado River and from the Williams and Santa Maria rivers to the vicinity of the Gila River. They were popularly called Mojave-Apache of Western Arizona. Although neighbors to the Apache, they were not related, and the name Apache-Mojave was a misnomer. Nevertheless, they were later absorbed into Apache following conquest by the Apache. In May 1873, they were removed to the Verde River Agency and two years later placed on the San Carlos Apache Agency. In 1903 they were assigned to the Camp McDowell

YAZOO

It is believed that the Yazoo belonged to the Tunican linguistic stock. They lived along the south side of the Yazoo River in Mississippi about twelve miles above its mouth and into Arkansas. They were mentioned by La Salle in 1682. A French post was built near their main village in 1718, and Jesuit missionary Father Seuel settled near them in 1727. In 1729 they joined the Natchez in the revolt against the French, killing Father Seuel. The inhabitants of the post were massacred. The Natchez uprising was one of the very few incidents of violence against the French not instigated by the British. Generally the French got along quite well with all the native people they encountered. Thereafter, Yazoo history followed that of the Koroa with whom they were very closely related. In the end, they were absorbed by the Chickasaw or the Choctaw.

YEHAH

Drake placed the Yehah above what was at that time the rapids of the Columbia River as it passed through the gorge in the Cascade Mountain Range in Washington State, about 100 miles from the coast. The rapids or cascades of the Columbia River gave name to the mountain range through which it passes. The river begins is march through the gorge from the east at Hood River, Oregon. By 1938 the rapids had disappeared under the waters of Lake Bonneville that formed behind Bonneville Dam.

YELETPOO

The Yeletpoo was reportedly a band of the Chopunnish (Nez Percé) that lived on the Weancum River.

YOKUTS

Yokut or Mariposan belonged to the Penutian linguistic family. They inhabited the San Joaquin Valley from the mouth of the San Joaquin River to the foot of Tehachapi and the adjacent lower foothills of the Sierra Nevada from the Fresno River south in present California. Father Garcés (1775-1776) gave them the name Noche. The estimated population of the Yokuts in 1770 total nearly 18,000 divided among seven groups with several dialects. The 1930 census returned a population of 1,145.

SUBDIVISIONS
Buena Vista
Poso Creek
Tule-Kaweah
Kings River
Northern Group of the Foothills Division
Northern Group of the Valley
Southern Group of the Valley

YONCALLA KALAPUYA

The Yoncalla (Yonkalla) or Upper Kalapuya were of the Kalapooian linguistic family and lived on Elk and Calapooya creeks, tributaries of the Umpqua River in Oregon.

YOSEMITE

The Yosemite were of the Miwok family and descendents of the Ahwahneeche of pre-history. They lived in numerous camps within the Yosemite (Ah-wah'-nee) Valley and later the area around Mono Lake in California where they were ultimately absorbed by the Mono Paiutes. There were two divisions or clans within the Yosemite, Coyote and Grizzly Bear. When Californians diverted water to serve Southern California, their fresh water streams dried up and Mono Lake became extremely salty. As a result the Indians were forced to adapt to a completely different lifestyle. The Yosemite figured prominently in the Mariposa War.

MARIPOSA WAR

The Yosemite had committed random raids on the white settlements on the Mariposa River in 1850. The war began with an attack on a white settlement on the Fresno River. The Indians destroyed everything they could not use and take with them. The number of whites killed was not reported. A Mariposa Battalion of two hundred men was formed that was led by a scout named James Savage.

The militia tracked the Indians until they came upon a village with at least three different tribes of about six hundred, including 150 Chochillas (Chowchilla Yokuts). The Indians fled into the mountains substantially unscathed, but their village, food stuffs, and possessions were destroyed. The war continued with a scorched earth policy, destroying huts and food stores. Some tribes came in and surrendered; others held out for a time. The Chochilla held out until the death of their chief José Rey.

YOUGHTANUND

The Youghtanund was a subdivision of the Powhatan. They lived about the Pamunkey River of Virginia.

YOUICONE

The Youicone lived on the Pacific coast north of the mouth of Columbia River in Washington State.

YREKA SHASTA

It is reported that the ancestors of the Shasta (Susti'ka) lived about the present site of Yreka, California. Swanton refers to the Yreka Shasta separately but only indirectly as giving names to other tribes, e.g. the alternate Modoc name Pxánai is identified as the name used by the Yreka Shasta. He also mentions that the Yreka Indians spoke a dialect of Shasta; or it might be said the Shasta spoke a dialect of the Yreka Shasta, but he does not list a Shasta village or subdivision at Yreka. Presently, there is a Shasta community at Yreka that has applied for official recognition. For more see Shasta.

YSCANI

The Yscani or Yscanes were reportedly a member of the Wichita Group. They lived along the lower Canadian River near the Tawakoni and Taovaya when first contacted by the French trader and explorer Sieur Bernard de La Harpe in 1719 before migrating into east Texas west of Nacogdoches where they were counted among the Nations for the North by the Spanish. The name was not heard of after 1794. There has been speculation that the Waco may be the Yscani under another name. For more see Nations of the North.

YUCHI

The Yuchi come down in history under several different names and spellings, among them are Uchee, Euchee or Westo. Swanton identifies the Westo as Yuchi, quite possibly a name given to them by the Cusabo; yet he admits that identification is not without question. It is quite common to find the Westo treated as a separate and distinct tribe in the literature. The Yuchi constituted a linguistic stock, the Uchean, distinct from all others but resembling the Muskhogean and Siouan. Their earliest known location was in Eastern Tennessee along the Hiwassee River. It is believed that they also settled as far north as the Green River in Kentucky, east into South Carolina along the Savannah River, and south to the area about Columbus, Georgia, commonly identified as the Westo. A part settled in West Florida, in Walton County, possibly as early as the 1600s but certainly by the middle of the eighteenth century. The Euchee Valley in Florida is a small area south of Defuniak Springs in the northwest.

The Yuchi fought along side the Yamasee and other tribes against the white settlers in the Yamasee War of 1715 but with the whites and against the Red Sticks faction of the Creeks in the Creek War of 1814. They joined the Creek Confederacy (Upper Creeks) in the mid-1700s.

With the Indian Removal of the 1830s, part of the Yuchi joined the Seminole south in Florida; others joined the Creek in the movement West and later fought on the side of the Union in the American Civil War. For a time, there was an Euchee Boarding School located in Sapulpa, Oklahoma. Currently, the Yuchi are officially recognized as members of the Muscogee Creek Nation, but otherwise maintain their own tribal culture. For more see the Westo, the Creek and the Creek War.

Of Note

Major Timpoochee Barnard, under the command of General Floyd, led the Yuchi at the 1814 Battle of Callabee Creek. Floyd's command consisted mostly Georgia militia. Floyd entered Red Stick territory via Fort Mitchell (close to the Chattahoochee River, a little south of present day Columbus, GA). Andrew

Jackson was not present. Reportedly, the battle could easily have turned into a major victory for the Creeks who had almost cut off the artillery from Floyd's main camp and that it was a Yuchi counter charge lead that saved the American force from being routed. Floyd retired to Fort Mitchell after the engagement. Later Barnard participated in operations in Florida. Patty Car was took over command of the Yuchi contingents. Barnard did not remove to Oklahoma, but died in the Chattahoochee Valley and was buried in the military cemetery at Fort Mitchell.

YUI

The Yui was one of the Timucuan tribes that inhabited mainland Florida inland from Cumberland Island and parts of southeastern Georgia. They were Christianized by the Spanish in the early seventeenth century and disappeared soon thereafter. See Utina.

YUKI

The Yuki were of independent stock. They lived in the land drained by the Eel River above the North Fork in California. The Yuki were comprised of seven subdivisions and a large number of villages and settlements.

SUBDIVISIONS
Huititno'm, on the South Fork of Middle Eel River
Onkolukomno'm, on the South Eel River
Sukshaltatano'm, on the North Fork of Middle Eel River
Ta'no'm, with a number of subdivisions, on Eel River proper
Ukomno'm, about Round Valley Middle Fork
Utitno'm, about the forks of the Middle and South Eel Rivers
Witukomno'm, on the branches of Middle Eel River
There were two settlement at either end of Eden Valley: K'ilikuno'm, in the north or lower end of the valley, and Witukomno'm, near the head of the valley.

EDEN VALLEY MASSACRE

The *Alta California*, published in San Francisco, reported on a massacre of Native Americans carried out by one Captain Jarboe in September 1859: "The attacking party rushed upon them, blowing out their brains and splitting their heads open with tomahawks. Little children in baskets, and even babes, had their heads smashed to pieces or cut open. Mothers and infants shared the same phenomenon.... Many of the fugitives were chased or shot as they ran.... The children, scarcely able to run, toddled toward the squaws for protection, crying with fright, but were overtaken, slaughtered like wild animals and thrown into piles."

On April 12, 1860 the state legislature approved $9,347.39 for "payment of the indebtedness incurred by the expedition against the Indians in the County of Mendocino organized under the command of Captain W. S. Jarboe in 1859." California's governor wrote a letter to Jarboe congratulating him for doing "all that was anticipated" and giving his "sincere thanks for the manner in which it [the campaign] was conducted."

Jarboe had reported to the Governor, "I fought them twenty--three times, killed two hundred and eighty-three warriors--the number of wounded was not known--took two hundred and ninety-two prisoners: sent them to the reservation. In the several engagements I had four men severely wounded, as well as myself."

The following is an extract from the *Bulletin* of San Francisco on the points raised by Jarboe:

> The pretext upon which these butcheries were perpetrated is that nineteen settlers had been killed, and six hundred head of stock stolen. Now, we have the testimony of Major Johnson and

Lieutenant Dillon that not one white settler had lost his life in that region at the hands of Indians during the past year--except a person who was killed in revenge for outraging an Indian woman. In fact, all these tales of Indian hostilities, when sifted, are proved to be arrant fabrications. As to the stock said to have been appropriated by the starving savages, (far less savage than their persecutors), what does it amount to? Six hundred head taken by nine thousand Indians--driven from their lands and fisheries, and starving literally to death--were worth, at the outside, $12,000. Let the State pay it, or double or treble the sum, and call upon the Federal Government to refund the amount. For such a purpose the liberality and the justice of the Government need not be doubted. Jarboe reports the total expense of his expeditions at $11,143--which is the smallest amount of blood money we ever heard demanded, in proportion to the murders committed. ...In the slaughter of this hecotomb of victims, it is said that five of the butchers were severely wounded--one of them was Jarboe himself. He has been in Sacramento nearly all winter, and his wounds have never before been heard of.

YUMA

The Yuma, called by several names, was one of the principal tribes of the Yuman linguistic stock, to which it gave its name. The Yuma inhabited of southwestern Arizona on both sides of the Colorado River above Cocopa, about fifty miles upstream from its mouth. Initially hostile to the intrusion of whites onto their land, they were defeated by General Heintzelman in 1853. Fort Yuma was built about in the middle of their territory. References to the Yuma tribes refer to the Yuman language group of the Hokan linguistic family that include the Havasupai and Tonto of Arizona and the Esselen of California with a connection to the Zuñi of New Mexico.

YUMA MASSACRE

As part of the ongoing battle of Native Americans against the Spanish intrusion into their lives, a band of Yuma Indians living along the Colorado River attacked a party of Spanish soldiers on July 17, 1781. The soldiers and their families were en route to duty in California along the trail that had been established in the spring of 1774 by Juan Baultista de Anza from presidio Tubac, south of present Tucson, to the Mission San Gabriel Arcángel at Los Angeles in Southern California. Thirty soldiers and four Franciscan missionaries were killed, and the women and children were taken captive. The attack and massacre closed the road from Northern New Spain into California for nearly forty years.

YUMA-APACHE

Yuma-Apache Indians of Western Arizona were of Yuma stock, not related to the Apaches. Following the wars with the Apache, however, remnants were later were absorbed into the Apache.

YUROK

The Yurok were originally combined with the Wiyot into the Ritwan family with two distinct dialects but subsequently classified as part of the Algonquian family of the eastern United States. (The classification has not been universally accepted.) There was no connection to Yurok Tsulu-la (Chilula). The Yurok lived on the lower Klamath River in California and along the coast to the north and south in some fifty villages.

ZIA PUEBLO

The Indians of the Zia or Sia Pueblo in New Mexico were of the Keresan or Keres linguistic stock. They lived in five villages along the Rio Jemez above its mouth, north of Albuquerque. Following Otermín's ill-fated efforts of reconquest in 1683 following the Pueblo Revolt, a second attempt was mounted in 1689 by Domingo Jironza Petríz de Cruzate with eighty soldiers. Little is known of his movements except that on reaching the Zia Pueblo he fought a day-long, pitched battle that left fifty of his men wounded and six hundred Zia men, women and children dead, in what is often categorized as a massacre. Over the years, the population was further decimated by disease and repeated attacks by Apaches and Navajos. From a pre-contact population that numbered in the thousands, the Zia were reduced to ninety-seven people souls by 1891. Today, eight hundred descendants live on a reservation of 122,000 acres. For more see Pueblo Peoples.

ZUÑI

The Zuñi or Zuñi Pueblo or Ashiwi were descendants of two tribes, one from the north that was joined by one from the southwest or west from the lands about the lower Colorado River. They were related to or resembled the Yuman and Piman in culture. Other writers believe that the Zuñi were descendents of the Anasazi. Although the Zuñi formed their own linguistic stock (Zunian), they are believed to be related to the Indians of the other Pueblos of New Mexico who together were subjected to Spanish exploration, subjugation, and settlement and in 1670 to raids by the Apache and Navaho.

The central Zuñi settlement with its outlying villages was located along the north bank of the upper Zuni River in present Valencia County of New Mexico and into eastern Arizona. Swanton lists twenty villages. The Zuni took part in the Pueblo rebellion of 1680 and were reconquered in 1692 while inhabiting the Taaiyalone Mesa. They fled once more to their mesa stronghold after killing a missionary priest in 1703, returning to their village two years later. The government subsequently built a school and irrigated the land around their village.

American Indian Tribes in the Civil War

"For all, the Civil War proved a calamity of far-reaching, long-lasting significance."[109] Estimates of upwards of some 20,000 Native Americans served in the Union and Confederate armies during the Civil War, participating on a large scale in the battles of the trans-Mississippi west that included Pea Ridge and the First Battle of Newtonia, Missouri; but they also made their presence felt at Fredericksburg, Second Manassas, Antietam, Spotsylvania, Cold Harbor, and in the Federal assaults on Petersburg.

In total numbers, the Cherokee, Creek, Choctaw, Chickasaw, and Seminole (the Five Civilized Tribes) were the principal Indian tribes taking an active part in the American Civil War. They were the tribes whose roots lay in the heart of the Confederacy. Their support was divided but with the majority, except for the Seminole, going to the Confederacy. Other tribes to become involved in the clash between North and South included the Quapaw, Osage, Shawnee, Delaware, Yuchi, Ottawa, and members of the Powhatan Confederacy and Iroquois League, especially the Seneca and Oneida; also the Pamunkey and Lumbee, Kickapoo, Potawatomi, and Ojibwa. These tribes for the most part sided with the Union. Siding with the Confederacy were the Tonkawa and other tribes of Texas, who were enemies of the Comanche and Kiowa. There were also small bands and single individuals who joined one side or another.

Trans-Mississippi Tribes

FIVE CIVILIZED TRIBES. By the outbreak of the Civil War, the vast majority of the Five Civilized Tribes had been moved west to Indian Territory. Slaves and slavery were not at issue. Only a few Indians owned slaves, and the relationship between Indian and black slave was entirely different from that of a white slave master and a black slave. The issues separating the two sides were intertribal and intra-tribal relationships, the position of mixed-blood Indians, the relationships between the tribes and the federal and state governments, and, as always, pride and egos. Behind it all was Indian lands, what lands were still held in the Southeast and their new lands in Indian Territory. Confederate recruiting agents were active among the Indians during the early days of the war, but for the most part the full-blood leaders favored the Union or preferred to remain neutral. The mix-bloods favored the South.

Creek

The Creeks split their loyalties. Opoeithleyohola, the old chief of the Creek tribe, supported the Federal government. Opothleyahola, was also spelled Opothle Yohola, Opothleyoholo, and Hu-pui-hilth Yahola, and Hopoeitheyohola. He was also known by his nickname, "Old Gouge." Opoeithleyohola was a Muscogee Creek and a highly-regarded spokesman of the Upper Creeks who fought against the United States during the first two Seminole Wars.

Supporters of the Confederacy were led by the two sons of ex-chief William McIntosh. The animosity between the two groups dated back long before the war. William McIntosh, a mix-blood planter and Brig. Gen. who served under Andrew Jackson, was killed in 1825 by for his part in the Treaty of Indian Springs. David N. McIntosh, 22 years younger than his brother, was commissioned a colonel of a Creek regiment; his brother "Chitty" McIntosh a lieutenant-colonel of a Creek battalion. (Colonel James McQueen McIntosh, CSA was no relation to the Indian McIntoshes.)

---

109 Robert M. Utley, *The Indian Frontier of the American West*, 73.

In the fall of 1861, Colonel Douglas H. Cooper was appointed commander the Confederate department of Indian operations. Cooper at onetime was the U.S. Agent to the Choctaws in Indian Territory. Cooper used all his guile to bring Opoeithleyohola, who owned a large plantation in Indian Territory with slaves, into the Southern camp. Failing that, he made it his personal mission to destroy Opoeithleyohola and drive him from the country.

Three successive battles were fought In November and December 1861:

1ˢᵗ Round Mountain, November 19.
   Also known as the Battle of Round Mountains and Round Mounds

2ⁿᵈ Chusto Talasah (caving canks), December 9.
   Also known as the Battle of Bird Creek or High Shoal

3ʳᵈ Chustenahlah (shoal in a stream), December 26.
   Also known as Shoal Creek.

Cooper's brigade of Native Americans included six Companies of the 1st Choctaw-Chickasaw Mounted Rifles and detachments from the Choctaw Battalion, the 1st Creek Regiment, and the 1st Cherokee Mounted Rifle Regiment plus a separate detachment of Creeks

The Creeks loyal to Opoeithleyohola and the Federal government (Lockapoka Creeks and Muscogee Creeks) and the allied tribes of Seminoles were defeated and driven into sanctuary at Fort Row in Kansas in the midst of winter where many of the survivors died of disease, starvation, and the effects of weather.

At Fort Row they were joined by other pro-Union Creeks and Seminoles that made the trek from Indian Territory to Kansas. Only about 7,000 of the original 9,000 made it to relative safety in Kansas in a bitter trek known as the "Trail of Blood on Ice." Some of the Indians were settled near Fort Belmont where conditions were somewhat better than at Fort Row, but disease, exposure starvation continued to take their toll. Chief Opothleyahola's fighting days were over. He died in a Creek refugee camp near the Sac and Fox Agency at Quenemo in Osage County, Kansas, and was buried beside his daughter near Fort Belmont.

Seminole

The pro-Union Seminoles were led by Chief Halleck Tustenuggee and Chief Billy Bowlegs (Holato Mico). Chief Billy Bowlegs led his people in the Third Seminole War (1855-1858) before finally agreeing to take them to Indian Territory. After the opening of the Civil War, he fought to protect his new home from the Confederates and aligned his followers with Opothleyahola's Upper Creeks. He fought a delaying action as the survivors from Chustenahlah made their way towards Kansas pursued by three hundred Cherokees under Col. Stand Watie resulting in more deaths.

Billy Bowlegs enlisted in the Union Army as a captain in May 1862 in the Union Army's First Indian Home Guards where he spent his last years. He saw action in a number of battles, including Rhea Mills, and Cane Hill where he received an official commendation for his action by the brigade commander. He died in 1864 of smallpox and was buried in the Fort Gibson National Cemetery. Indian Agent G. C. Snow remarked on his passing, "His loss is very much regretted, as he was an influential man among (the Seminoles) and I believe generally beloved by all." The town of Bowlegs, Oklahoma, in Seminole County, is named in his honor. A small number of Osage joined the Confederacy.

Choctaw and Chickasaw

In 1855 agent Cooper successfully negotiated a treaty that defined the boundaries between the Choctaw and Chickasaw, and in 1856 he moved his office to Fort Washita where he organized a militia unit from among the two tribes. With the outbreak of the Civil War, Colonel William H. Emory removed his U.S. troops to Fort Leavenworth and abandoned Fort Washita to Cooper and his militia. Cooper was commissioned a Colonel of the Choctaw and Chickasaw Mounted Rifles CSA and later promoted to Brigadier General. In April 1865, the Choctaw and Chickasaw Nations surrendered and signed treaties of peace.

Cherokee

Chief John Ross of the Cherokee at first chose neutrality even to the point of issuing a proclamation enjoining his people to remain neutral. The majority of the full-blooded Cherokees, called Pin Indians, were opposed to the South, but the Union loss at Wilson's Creek in Missouri and the death of Union General Nathaniel Lyon, made them come to believe, with some coaxing, that the Confederacy would be victorious.* In September 1861, the Cherokees signed a treaty with Confederate States that stipulated that the Indian troops would be used for home protection and would not be taken out of the Indian Territory. Those fine words were short lived.

As a result of Ross's treaty with the Confederacy, a regiment of Cherokee Mounted Rifles was formed, commanded by John Drew who was commissioned a colonel. William P. Ross was commissioned a lieutenant-colonel. Stand Watie, a leader of the minority Treaty Party, raised a regiment of half-breeds and commissioned a colonel in the Confederacy under the command of General McCulloch's. Altogether, the Indians mustered one battalion and parts of four regiments for a total of about 3,500 men.

Following the Battle of Pea Ridge, Drew's Mounted Rifles defected to the Union forces in Kansas, where they joined the Indian Home Guard, and in the summer of 1862, Federal troops captured Ross. Ross was paroled and spent the remainder of the war in Philadelphia and in Washington, DC, where he died proclaiming Cherokee loyalty to the Union. With Ross's absence, Stand Watie was chosen principal chief of the Cherokee Nation, and immediately drafted all Cherokee males aged 18-50 into Confederate military service. What ensued was a Cherokee Civil War within a Civil War.

Watie, a more than capable calvary field commander in the trans-Mississippi west, was promoted to brigadier general in May 1864, and given command of the Indian Cavalry Brigade, composed of the 1st and 2nd Cherokee Cavalry and battalions of Creek, Osage and Seminole. Watie was the last to surrender at the conclusion of the war, on June 23 at Doaksville in Indian Territory—two months after Gen. Robert E. Lee and a month after Gen. E. Kirby Smith, commander of all troops west of the Mississippi. Following the Civil War, Watie was blamed for the loss of many Cherokee lives because with his support of the Confederacy. At the same time an argument over compensation and property rights tore at the heart of the Cherokee nation. Watie moved his family to Breebs Town on the Canadian River and went into the tobacco business. When Congress passed a new federal excise tax on tobacco and spirits, Watie refused to pay and took his case to court. He lost the case in a landmark decision that established the legal precedent that an act of Congress could supercede provisions of a treaty. Watie went into bankruptcy and field penniless in 1871.

*The liberal mix-blood Indians ridiculed the conservative full-blood Indians who favored the North. They labeled them "pin" Indians, a form of derision. Monaghan writes, "…a name said to have originated from the clandestine meetings of Keetoowah [a popular secret society dedicated to the preservation of tribal customs] in the hills, like Washington Irvings's mythical little men who bowled above thunder clouds in the Catskills. More likely the name referred not to ninepins, but to the order's insignia—a poor man's pins fixed in a cross on coat lapel or hunting shirt."

Yuchi

Part of the Yuchi joined the Seminole in south Florida; others joined the Creek in their move West and later fought on the side of the Union.

Union Recruits from the Five Civilized Nations

In January, 1862, William Dole, U.S. Commissioner of Indian Affairs, asked Native American agents to "engage forthwith all the vigorous and able-bodied Indians in their respective agencies." The request resulted in the assembly of the 1st and 2nd Indian Home Guard that included Delaware, Creek, Seminole, Kickapoo, Seneca, Osage, Shawnee, Choctaw and Chickasaw. The Cherokee, Creek, and Seminole that remained loyal to the Union were organized into a brigade composed of three Kansas regiments of one thousand men each.

> First Indian Regiment: Creeks and Seminoles
> Second Indian Regiment: Cherokee, Osage, Delaware, Quapaw, Shawnee
> Third Indian Regiment: Cherokees formed after the battle at Locust Grove

Also organized were the 1st, 2nd, 3rd, 4th, and 5th Indian Home Guards; the latter occupied Fort Gibson.

The majority of the offices of each regiment were white. Active in organizing the Indian regiments was William A. Phillips of Kansas who commanded the Indian brigade from its inception to the close of the war. He had taken part in the action at Locust Grove. The Indian brigade fought in the battles of Newtonia, Missouri; Maysville, Arkansas; Prairie Grove, Arkansas; and Honey Springs and Perryville in Indian Territory in addition to a number of minor skirmishes. In each instance, they acquitted themselves well.

Confederacy Recruits from the Five Civilized Nations

The Confederacy also organized three regiments of Indians from the Choctaw, Chickasaw, Cherokee, Creek, and Seminole.
> 1st Choctaw-Chickasaw Mounted Rifles, Maj. Mitchell Laflore
> Choctaw Battalion, Capt. Alfred Wade
> 1st Creek Regiment, Col. Daniel N. McIntosh
> 1st Cherokee Mounted Rifle Regiment, Col. John Drew

Influential in recruiting in Indian Territory were the former U.S. Indian Agents like Cooper, who for the most part were secessionists. The tribes were also influenced by their kinsmen in neighboring Arkansas and Texas. Indian troops from Texas participated in several engagements in attempts to capture Federal supply trains from Fort Scott to Fort Gibson and Fort Smith but were repeatedly driven off by Union artillery fire that had a devastating physiological impact on the Indian troops.

Battle for Fort Gibson

Fort Gibson, established in 1824, was reactivated in 1863 and served as the Union Army's key post in Indian Territory. It also became a haven for thousands of pro-Union refugees. Confederate forces wanted Fort Gibson, and skirmishing between Union and Confederate troops was a common occurrence. The Union commander in the area, Maj. Gen. James G. Blunt, correctly surmised that Confederate forces, mostly Native American troops under the command of Brig. Gen. Douglas H. Cooper, were about to concentrate and would then attack Fort Gibson in force.

Advancing from Fort Smith, Arkansas. Blunt began crossing the swollen Arkansas River on July 15, 1863, and, by midnight on July 16-17, he had a force of 3,000 men, composed of whites, Native Americans, and African Americans, marching toward Brig. Gen. Douglas H. Cooper at Honey Springs, eighteen miles below Fort Gibson. General Blunt, with his black soldiers from the First Kansas Colored Infantry, "pin" Indians made up of the 1st, 2nd, and 3rd Indian Home Guard Regiments, and a battalion of volunteers from Colorado, struck Southern forces made up of Texas Confederates and Cooper's Indians. McIntosh's Creeks retreated, and the Cherokees, without their leader Stand Watie, gave way, as did the Chickasaw.

Skirmishing on the morning of the 17th erupted into full-scale fighting by mid-afternoon. The Confederates were soundly defeated, and with that defeat went all hope of   taking Fort Gibson. Afterwards, Union forces controlled all of the Indian Territory, north of the Arkansas River. Union soldiers suffered an estimated 79 casualties in the battle; the Confederates, six hundred and thirty-seven.

Battle of Locust Grove

In the spring and early summer of 1862 the Federal government sent an expedition of five thousand men under Colonel William Weer of 10th Kansas Infantry to drive out the Confederate forces out of Indian Territory and restore the refugees to their homes. He was joined by Captain Green and Colonel Jewell of the 6th Kansas Calvary. The Confederate soldiers and Indian allies were defeated at Locust Grove, near Grand Saline, Cherokee Nation, on July 2. On the 16th, the Kansans captured Tahlequah, a captain of the Cherokee Nation; and on the July 19, they captured Fort Gibson, the principal Confederate supply base in Indian Territory. All Confederate forces were driven south of the Arkansas River.

Battle of Pea Ridge

Watie's and Drew's Cherokees, under of the command of Brig. Gen. Albert Pike, participated in the Battle of Pea Ridge or Elkhorn Tavern, Arkansas, March 6-8, 1862. Pike, Brig. Gens. Sterling Price, and Ben McCullock were under the overall command of Maj. Gen. Earl Van Dorn. Pike's Cherokees were accused of participating in the scalping and mutilation of the fallen Union soldiers. General Pike issued an order denouncing the outrage and sent a copy to Brig. Gen. Samuel R. Curtis, the Union commander at Pea Ridge. Pike claimed that the guilty Indians were in McCulloch's command. Southern forces included three regiments of Indians, two Cherokee and one Creek. Total casualties number about 1,300 for each side. Among those killed, which was one of the largest single engagements west of the Mississippi, were McCulloch and Brig. Gen. James McQueen McIntosh. As a result of the battle, the Confederates were forced to withdraw leaving the field to the Federals. The Battle of Pea Ridge also closed the second struggle for Missouri. (Curtis was promoted to Maj. General for his performance at Pea Ridge.)

Battle of Newtonia (First)

At the First Battle of Newtonia, Native American Indians were engaged on both sides and played a significant role in the outcome of the battle. Col. Douglas Cooper commanded the Native American forces of the Confederacy in the Battle of Newtonia, Missouri, in early October. Following the Confederate victory at Newtonia, Cooper and his Indian forces withdrew to Indian Territory. Brig. Gen. James G. Blunt, with troops from Fort Scoot in Kansas, pursued and overtook Indians at Old Fort Wayne, Indian Territory, and scattered them on October 22. (Hindman, commander of the CS District of Arkansas that included Missouri and Indian Territory, had appointed Cooper to replace Albert Pike as commander of the Indians.)

Poison Spring Massacre and the Camden Expedition

In the spring of 1864, the Choctaw, under the overall command of Maj. Gen. John S. Marmaduke fought in several battles against Maj. Gen. Frederick Steele in his Camden Expedition, dishonoring themselves, along with their fellow white soldiers, in the massacre of black troopers of the 1st Kansas Colored Infantry at the Battle of Poison Spring, Arkansas, April 19, 1864. One hundred and seventeen died and 65 were wounded. The death toll was aggravated by the brutal killing and mutilation of captured and wounded Blacks left on the field. Understandably, the accounts of the battle and the killings of black soldiers differ widely. Some accounts ignore the killings altogether. In "Cut to Pieces...," Mark K. Christ writes: "The springs of American history have all too often been poisoned by racism, so perhaps it was foreordained that troops on two sides, of different colors and nationalities (Choctaws were present, too), would come to this place to enact rituals of hate."

Battle of Cabin Creek

Gen. Richard M. Gano four hundred Texans with Stand Watie's Indians attacked an encamped Federal wagon train at Military Crossing Of Cabin Creek, Indian Territory, September 18, 1864. Maj. Henry Hopkins was forced to retreat towards Fort Scott leaving wagons and stores to the Confederate Indians who went on a rampage of wanton destruction and killed and mutilated prisoners.

Battle for Western Arkansas

Union Maj. Gen. James G. Blunt defeated a battalion of Col. Daniel N. McIntosh's Creeks on August 24, 1863, in western Arkansas then marched through Choctaw country in Indian Territory. He detached Cap. Samuel Crowford to hunt down all organized bands from the Five Civilized Tribes fighting for the Confederacy. Blunt himself marched into Fort Smith, Arkansas, without firing a shot.

Battle of Pleasant Bluff

Brig. Gen Stand Watie's Indian calvary brigade captured the Union steamboat JR Williams at Pleasant Bluff, Arkansas, on June 10, 1864. It was loaded with supplies valued at $120,000.

Battle of Cabin Creek

General Richard M. Gano's four hundred Texans and Stand Watie's Indian calvary brigade attacked an encamped Federal wagon train at the Military Crossing of Cabin Creek. Hopkins was forced to retreat towards Fort Scott leaving wagons and stores to the Confederates that included 129 supply wagons and over seven hundred head of stock. They also capted 120 prisoners and inflicting 200 casualties. There were reports of wanton destruction of materials and the killing and mutilation of prisoners by the Indians.

Verdigris River Massacre

On May 15, 1863, a small detachment of Confederate soldiers that was marching north towards the Arkansas River in Kansas were stopped and challenged by a small party of Osage Indians from the nearby reservation. The soldiers killed one Indian, and the rest escaped back to their main camp. They returned with a force of two hundred fighting men and killed the entire Confederate detachment in a running fight along and on a sand-bar in the Verdigris River, a tributary of the Arkansas west of Chanute. All the bodies were decapitated and mutilated. It is possible that two other soldiers were shot while trying to swim across the river and were either killed by gunfire or drowned in the river. They may have escaped.

Troop G, Ninth Kansas Calvary, consisting of 100 men under the command of Capt. Willoughby Doudna was stationed at Humboldt in southeastern Kansas about 40 miles west of Fort Scott. Afterwards the Indians reported to Capt. Doudna who investigated the scene.

On investigation of papers taken from the dead, it was learned that the entire party consisted of commissioned officers under the command of a colonel and operating under orders issued by General Kirby Smith. Only one soldier was identified by name, Capt. Harrison. Their mission was to meet and treat with the Indians of the West and Southwest to bring them into the war on the side of the Confederacy, with the settlements in the state of Kansas being a particular target. A small number of Osage did join the Confederacy.

Humbolt Raid

Humbolt, Kansas, is located about forty miles west of Fort Scott. General Lane had detached 200 men with General James G. Blunt in command to seek out the marauders who had raided Humbolt. Blunt found the raiders at Quapaw Agency on September 8, 1861, and killed several including John Mathews, Indian trader and Osage squawman, who had orders from Ben McCulloch in Arkansas to enroll Quapaw Indians in the Confederate cause.

Delaware Scouts

The Delaware Nation maintained close ties with the U.S. government following or in spite of their removal to Indian Territory in Kansas. Before the war, the Delaware were used as guides and scouts for westward wagon trains, scientific explorations of the West, and in the Rocky Mountain fur trade. Both before and after the Civil War, the Delaware scouted for the government in the wars with the Plains Indians. Recruited by Maj. Gen. John Charles Frémont, the Delaware turned their talents to providing intelligence for the Union army in the west. The painting, *Scouts for the National Army in the West* by Henry Lovie, appeared in the December 6, 1861, issue of *Frank Leslie's Illustrated*. It is believed that the Delaware from Kansas, led by Ben Simon, participated in the Wichita Agency Massacre of the Tonkawa, who served as scouts for the Confederacy, in October 1862. Whether the event was precipitated by the war is uncertain. For more the Tonkawa in the main listing.

Displaced Tribes

To the south the Wichita, Waco, Tawakoni, and Kichai, and other associated Caddo groups fled to southern and eastern Kansas from Oklahoma to avoid the conflict of the Civil War. After the war in 1867, they were relocated to the Wichita Reservation near present Anadarko, Oklahoma. Union troops occupied the Shawnee mission on the Kansas-Missouri border during the Civil War, and Indian traders in southern Kansas moved farther north to be closer to Fort Leavenworth for protection but making it harder for the Indians to do business.

Plains Indians

Throughout the period of the Civil War, the Indian situation took a back seat to more pressing issues at the Federal level. The Plains Indians took advantage of the respite and wrought havoc along the frontier. What ensued was a period of bloody guerilla warfare between whites and Indians across the Plains from Minnesota to Texas.

George Bent

Among the individual Indians to become embroiled in the conflict was George Bent, half-breed Southern Cheyenne, the son of William Bent of Bent's Fort fame, joined the Confederate army during the Civil War and fought beside the Cherokee and the Choctaw. He was captured in Battle of Corinth and released September 1, 1862, on the entreaties of Robert Campbell, a trader and merchant with whom William Bent conducted much of his business. He was released to the custody of his brother Robert who happened to be in St. Louis to purchase goods. George was with Black Kettle's band at Sand Creek that November where he was wounded. Bent's partner, St. Vrain, supplied Union forces in the southwest throughout the Civil War.

Sand Creek Massacre

Another massacre is listed by the Civil War Site Preservation Committee for the National Park Service (CWSAC Ref. #: CO001). It is presented as a Union victory led by Col. John Chivington. The location was northwestern Colorado. The victims, whose numbers vary according to the telling, totaled about two hundred killed and mutilated—the vast majority women and children. They were mostly Cheyenne with a few Arapaho Indians led by the Cheyenne Chief Black Kettle. The date was November 29-30, 1864. The name was Sand Creek. It only relation to the American Civil War, in the opinion of this writer, is that it occurred during the war years, 1861-1865. Sand Creek was a conscious act of extermination, nothing more nor less, and it had a profound effect on White-Indian relations for the next two decades.

Eastern Tribes

PAMUNKEY AND LUMBEE

In Virginia and North Carolina, the Pamunkey and Lumbee joined the ranks of the Union. The Pamunkey served as civilian and naval pilots for Union warships and transports. The Lumbee fought as guerillas. One man in particular, Henry Berry Lowry, became a folk hero to the Lumbee people for his fighting skills as well as for his leadership in the battle for Native Americans civil rights.

IROQUOIS LEAGUE

The Seneca and Oneida were the most active members of the Iroquois Nation in the war. Members joined Company K, 5th Pennsylvania Volunteer Infantry. (Calvary?) Captain John O'Farrell

POWHATAN CONFEDERACY

Members of the Powhatan Confederacy in the mid-Atlantic states served as land guides, river pilots, and spies for the Army of the Potomac.

PEQUOT

There are reports of a number of Pequot from New England that served in the 31st U.S. Colored Infantry of the Army of the Potomac, as well as other colored regiments. No distinction was made when a Native American joined the U.S. Colored Troops. Well into the twentieth century, the word "colored" included not only African Americans.

Confederate Department Of Texas

The Comanche and the Kiowa were bitter enemies of the Texans. Put on a personal level, there was an imbibing hatred between the races. Any party or Indian tribe, e.g. the Tonkawa, for one was against the other. The Department of Texas also encompassed New Mexico and Arizona. Nor did the Texans or the Confederacy have any use for the Apaches and the Navajo. In correspondence dated May 4, 1862, Brig. Gen. Henry H. Sibley suggested that it would be good policy "to encourage private enterprises" against the Navajo and the Apaches "and to legalize the enslaving of them." (*O.R.*, Ser. 1, Vol. 9, ar9, 512)

However, a law passed by the Confederate States legislature reflects the sensitivity of the South to the treatment of friendly Indians:

> If any person shall send, make, or carry, or deliver any talk, speech, message, or letter to any Indian nation, tribe, band, chief, or individual, with intent to make such nation, tribe, band, chief, or Indian dissatisfied with their relations with the Confederate States or uneasy or discontented, the person so offending shall, on conviction, be punished by fine not exceeding $10,000 nor less than $2,000, and by imprisonment not less than two nor more than ten years, and the intent above mentioned shall be conclusively inferred from knowledge of the contents of any such talk, speech, message, or letter in writing. (Section 29, act of Congress regulating intercourse with the Indians and to preserve peace on the frontiers, approved April 8, 1862, *O.R.*, Ser. 1, Vol. 13, ar19, 41)

Far West Tribes

To the west, open season on Indians continued unabated, most notorious was the massacre of Shoshoni at Bear Creed in January 1863, but all overshadowed by the events of the Civil War.

AT WAR'S END

It was a full-blooded Seneca Indian, Colonel Ely Samuel Parker, who wrote up the official copy of articles of surrender in ink from the pencil draft written by General Grant and agreed to by General Lee at Appomattox Court House on April 9, 1865. (Parker's subsequent promotion to Brigadier General was backdated to April 9, 1865.) Parker, a trained lawyer, who was barred from practicing law and who at one time was rejected for army service because of his race, served as General Ulysses S. Grant's military secretary. As the staff and other officers in the room were introduced, Lee was visibly surprised to see Parker who he at first thought was a Negro because of his dark, sunburnt skin. It has been reported that, addressing Parker, Lee uttered the words, "I am glad to see one real American here," to which Parker replied, "We are all Americans." Neither Horace Porter, *Campaigning with Grant*, nor Brooks D. Simpson, *Ulysses S. Grant*, refer to any such conversation. In fact, Porter, who was present at the surrender, writes, "Lee did not utter a word...."

Parker was born in 1828 in Genesee City, New York, the son of a Seneca chief and was raised and educated in two cultures. He was a trained attorney, a self-taught civil engineer, a captain of engineers with the Rochester regiment of the New York State Militia, and a sachem in his tribe. Parker, a good friend of James A. Rawlins of Galena and Grant's future Chief of Staff, first met then-Captain Grant when he supervised the building of the Galena, Illinois, courthouse and post office. Grant helped Parker secure a commission, and in September 1863 he joined Grant's staff as Assistant Adjutant. With the Army of the Potomac, he was generally referred to as "the Indian," "Grant's Indian," or "Big Indian." How he came to Grant's attention is uncertain, but in 1863, with Grant's support, he was commissioned as officer in the U.S. Army and assigned Brig. Gen. John E. Smith's staff, after which he later joined Grant's personal staff. His commission as a brigadier general was backdated to April 9, 1865. After the war, Parker's military fame advanced his career. At the same time he remained Grant's friend and secretary. Grant was the best man at the marriage of Parker and Minnie Sackett, a white woman.

In 1869 amid considerable controversy, President Grant appointed commissioner of Indian Affairs. Political infighting, corrupt officials, self-righteous religious leaders led to his political downfall. An investigation by the House of Representatives found nothing, but he was never able to shed the stigma associated with the affair, and what was left of his business interests were shattered in the financial panic of 1873. Until his August 1895, Parker lived hand-to-mouth. His widow received nothing but a copy of the document Lee signed at Appomattox thirty years earlier.

Camp Napoleon Compact

Some twenty Confederate and Prairie tribes were brought together May 26, 1865 at Cottonwood Grove on the Washita River (now Verden, Grady-Caddo County line, Oklahoma) to agree to the provisions of what has been called the Camp Napoleon Compact. Among the Plains Indians attending were the Caddo, Cheyenne, Arapaho, Lipan Apache, Osage.

Ostensibly, the compact, put together by the Confederate Commissioner to the Indians and later governor of Texas, committed all tribes to united action against possible Union demands for land reparations from the Confederate tribes for their part in the Civil War. With the war effectively over, the real issue of interest of interest to Texans was the negotiation of ransoms for captives of the Plains Indians.

American Indians in Military Service

Thanks mainly to Hollywood, many people are familiar with the story of the Navaho Code Talkers of the Second World War in the Pacific Theater. The Marine Corps' Navajo Code Talker Program was established in September 1942 from a recommendation made by Philip Johnston, the son of a missionary to the Navajo tribe who was fluent in the language. He believed that the use of Navajo as a code language in voice transmission over both radio and wire would guarantee communications security. Following a highly successful demonstration to senior Marine Corps officers that February, the recruitment of 200 Navajos was approved for the program. Twenty-nine recruits entered the first code talkers training class at Camp Pendleton, California. Code words were established for those military terms that had no counterpart in the Navajo language, and letter-substitution codes were devised that would enable them to spell-out any unfamiliar English word. By August 1943, a total of 191 Navajos had joined the Marine Corps specifically for the program that was receiving nothing but praise from field commanders.

The movie *Windtalkers* (Metro-Goldwyn-Mayer, 2002) dramatized the dedication of the code talkers as it portrayed the personal relationships between the code talkers and their fellow Marines. It should be noted that an undetermined number of Navajos, as well as members of other tribes, also served in the Marines in other capacities.

Often overlooked in the telling are the members of other American Indian tribes who served as code talkers in both the First and Second World War. In France during World War I, two Indian officers the 142nd Infantry Regiment, 36th Division, were selected to supervise a communications system staffed by eighteen Choctaw Indians. Soldiers from other tribes, including the Cheyenne, Comanche, Cherokee, Osage and Yankton Sioux also were enlisted to communicate as code talkers.

In North Africa during the Second World War, eight Soldiers from the Meskwaki (Fox) tribe in Iowa served as code talkers in the 168th Infantry Regiment, 34th Division. In Europe, the U.S. Army's 4th Signal Company, 4th Infantry Division, was assigned seventeen Comanche code talkers. They served in battle from Normandy to Berlin. Two code talkers were assigned to each of the three regiments of the 4th Infantry Division. Others were assigned to division headquarters. Although several were wounded, they all survived the war. The Germans never broke the Indian "code," and the soldiers became known as "code talkers."

American Indians did more than talk. They fought, and they died. With the turn of the nineteenth century, Native American loyalties fell solidly behind the government of the United States beginning with then Colonel Theodore Roosevelt's Rough Riders who recruited Indians for action in Cuba in the Spanish-American War in 1898. They next saw action in America's defense as Indian Scouts accompanying Gen. John J. Pershing's expedition to Mexico in pursuit of Pancho Villa in 1916. (The Scouts, established by the U.S. Army in 1866, were deactivated in 1947 when the last member retired from military service.)

Some 600 Indians from Oklahoma, most from the Choctaw and Cherokee tribes, were proud members in the 142nd Infantry of the 36th Texas-Oklahoma National Guard Division that saw action in France. They were just the beginning. An estimated 12,000 American Indians served in the military during World War I although they were not as yet recognized as U.S. citizens. Full citizenship did not come to

American Indians until 1924 with passage of the Snyder Act. Before the United States entered the war, a number of Native Americans joined Canada's 107th Regiment in order to fight.

Less than twenty-five years later as the United States found itself embroiled in a second world conflict, more than 44,000 American Indians, inductees and volunteers, put on the American uniform between 1941 and 1945 and served honorably in both European and the Pacific. General history books on the First and Second World Wars for the most part give short rift to the participation of American Indians. That could be as both good and bad—good because it could signify that American Indians were included in the mainstream of American life, if that were true.

American Indians were back in uniform again the in Korea in the early fifties and in Vietnam in the sixties and seventies. An estimated 42,000, mostly volunteers, served in Vietnam. The twenty-first century saw Native Americans wherever American troops were stationed.

Nine American Indians received the nation's highest award, the Medal of Honor, for service in the 20th century—five for heroism during the Second World War and three for their efforts beyond the call of duty in Korea. On March 3, 2008, Master Sergeant Woodrow Wilson Keeble, the last, was awarded the Medal of Honor posthumously for risking his life to save his fellow soldiers during the final allied offensive of the Korean War. Keeble was the first full-blooded Sioux Indian to receive the nation's highest honor. A veteran of World War II in addition to his service during the Korean War, he was one of the most decorated soldiers in North Dakota history.

Keeble was born May 16, 1917, in Waubay, South Dakota, on the Sisseton-Wahpeton Sioux Reservation, which extended into North Dakota where he spent most of his life and where he attended an Indian school. In 1942 Keeble joined the North Dakota National Guard and that same year found himself in the fighting on Guadalcanal in the South Pacific. It was there that he earned the first of four Purple Hearts and his first Bronze Star. He went on to earn the Distinguished Service Cross and the Silver Star for his actions throughout his tour in Korea. Keeble was honorably discharged March 1, 1953. After his discharge, Keeble was a unyielding champion for veterans and their causes until his death in 1982.

It was not only Native American men that served their country, over eight hundred Native American women served in the various branches of the military in the wars of the twentieth century. Over the years, American Indian men and women have demonstrated their skills, their dedication, their professionalism, and most importantly their patriotism to a nation whose population, for the most part, held them in low esteem.

Indian men and women also graduated from the nation's military academies. Joseph J. "Jocko" Clark, a Cherokee, was the first Native American to graduate from the U.S. Naval Academy at Annapolis. He rose to the rank of Rear Admiral and commanded the Navy's 7th Fleet during the Korean War. Among the other general-grade officers that fought in Korea were Colonel, later Brigadier General, Otwa Autry of the Creek Nation and Major General Hal L. Muldrow Jr., a Choctaw, who commanded the 45th Infantry Division Artillery.

For many of the personal stories of Native American men and women who served in the military, see the Notes and Sources.

Master List of American Indian Tribal Names — Popular and Common Names and Synonyms

Following is the master list of Indian tribal names and spelling variations that have been found in the literature to identify particular tribes or groups. Although the list is quite extensive (over 4,700), there undoubtedly are hundreds more that might be included, particularly those hidden in the records and journals of early explorers and missionaries prior to 1700 in the northeast and along the Canadian border. To the right of the name, in capital letters, is the corresponding primary name used in the alphabetical enumeration of tribes in the body of this text. Each primary name appears once in both columns in order to maintain consistency. The word or words in parentheses to the right of the name identify the source or originator of the name or to provide additional information.

A da ka' do ho (Hidatsa)	ARIKARA	Achomawi	ACHOMAWI
A'-a'tam or A'-a'tam a'kimult	PIMA	Acolapissa	ACOLAPISSA
A'-mu-kwi-kwe (Zuñi)	HOPI	Acoma Pueblo	ACOMA PUEBLO
A'-uya (Tonkawa)	KICKAPOO	Acopseles	ACOPSELES
Â'dal-k'ato'igo (Kiowa)	NEZ PERCÉ	Acoste	KOASATI
A'kimmash (Atfalati Kalapouya)	CLACKAMAS	Acquintanacsuak	ACQUINTANACSUAK
A'latskné-I	CLATSKANIE	Acuera	ACUERA
A-ar-ke or E-ar'-ke (Apache)	HOPI	Acurag-na	ACURAG-NA
A-gutch-a-ninne-wug (Chippewa)	HIDATSA	Acuyé	PECOS PUEBLO
A-ko-t'as'-ka-ro'-re (Mohawk)	TUSCARORA	Adaes	ADAES
A-ko-tca-ka-ne (Mohawk)	DELAWARE	Adai	ADAES
A-me-she' (Crow)	HIDATSA	Adders, Big (Ojibwe)	IROQUOIS
A-pa-o-pa (Atsina)	NEZ PERCÉ	Adders, Little (Ojibwe)	SIOUX
A-pu-pe (Crow)	NEZ PERCÉ	Addle-Heads (misinterprepation of	MENOMINEE
A-rach-bo-cu (Hidatsa)	MANDAN	Folles Avoines)	
A-re-tear-o-pan-ga (Hidatsa)	ATSINA	Adero	ADERO
A-shu'-e-ka-pe (Crow)	SALISH	Adirondak	ADIRONDAK
A-t'as-ka-lo'-le (Oneida)	TUSCARORA	Adwanuqdji (Ilmawi)	ATSUGEWI
Ä-tagúi (Kiowa)	LIPAN	Affagoula	AFFAGOULA
A-too-ha-pe (Hidatsa)	SALISH	Afúlakin (Kalauya)	WASCO
A-was-she-tan-qua (Hidatsa)	CHEYENNE	Agaid ika	AGAIDEKA SHOSHONI
Aä'ninena	ATSINA	Agaideka	AGAIDEKA SHOSHONI
Aanishinabe	CHIPPEWA	Agaidika	AGAIDEKA SHOSHONI
Aays	EYEISH	Agawam	PAWTUCKET
Abanaki	ABENAKI	Agawom	AGAWOM
Ab-boin-ug (Chippewa)	DAKOTA	Agua Dulce	FRESH WATER INDIANS
Ab-boin-ug, Boinug (Chippewa)	SIOUX	Aguaje	SKIDI PAWNEE
Abenaki and Abenakis	ABENAKI	Ah'alakat (Pima)	CHEMEHUEVI
Abenakic (Hutchins)	ABENAKI	Ah-hi'tä-pe	BLACKFEET
Abenakis (mistakenly; see Abenaki)	DELAWARE	Ah-mo-kái (Zuni)	HOPI
Abenaquis (Bouquet)	ABENAKI	Ah-pen-ope-say or A-pan-to'-pse	ARIKARA
Abenaquis (mistakenly; see Abenaki)	DELAWARE	(Crow)	
Abenquis	ABENAKI	Aha'lpam (Atfalati Kalapuya)	SANTIAM KALAPUYA
Abihka	ABIHKA	Ahaharway	AMAHAMI
Abinga	WAPPINGER	Ahantchuyuk Kalapuya	AHANTCHUYUK
	CONFEDERACY	Ahiahichi	ALLIKLIK
Abnaki	ABENAKI	Ahiahichi	EYEISH
Abnaki (mistakenly; see Abenaki)	DELAWARE	Ahihinin (Arapaho)	PAWNEE
Abo Pueblo	ABO PUEBLO	Ahnahway	AMAHAMI
Abotireitsu	ABOTIREITSU	Ahtena	AHTENA
Absaraka	CROW	Ahuádje (Havasupai)	APACHE
Absaroka	CROW	Ahwahaway	AMAHAMI
Absároke or Absarokee	CROW	Ähyä'to (Kiowa)	ARAPAHO
Acapatos	ATSINA	Ai-a'-ta (Panamint)	APACHE
Accocesaw	ACCOCESAW	Ai-yah-kin-nee (Navaho)	HOPI
Accohanoc	ACCOHANOC	Aiaich	EYEISH
Accomac	ACCOMAC	Aígspaluma (Nez Percé)	MODOC
Accomàck	ACCOMAC		

Aígspaluma, Aígspalo or Aíspalu (Nez Percé)	KLAMATH
Aijados	TAOVAYA
AinaiIoni	HAINAI
Aionai	AIONAI
Aionai	HAINAI
Aiouez	IOWA
Aiouways	IOWA
Ais	AIS
Aix	EYEISH
Aix	SAHEHWAMISH
Ajoue	IOWA
Ak-ba-su'-pai (Walapai form)	HAVASUPAI
Ak-min'-e-shu'-me (Crow)	KALISPEL
Akaitchi	AKAITCHI
Akansa (Illinois)	QUAPAW
Akawantca'ka	AKAWANTCA'KA
Akenuq'la'lam (Kutenai)	OKANAGON
Akênuq'la'lam (Kutenai)	OKANAGON
Akhrakouaehronon (Jesuit)	SUSQUEHANNA
Akimel Au-Authm	PIMA
Ako-me	ARAPAHO
Akochakanen (Iroquois)	MAHICAN GROUP
Akokisa	AKOKISA
Akokisa	ATÁKAPA
Akura-nga	ACURAG-NA
Akwesasne	SAINT REGIS
Ala'dshush (Nestucca)	CHINOOK
Alabama	ALABAMA
Aláhó (Kiowa)	KANSA
Alakema'yuk (Atfalati)	LOWER CREEK
Albivi	ALBIVI
Alemousiski (Abnaki)	ARMOUCHIQUOIS
Aleupkig-na	ALEUPKIG-NA
Algonkian	ALGONQUIN GROUP
Algonkin	ALGONQUIN
Algonquin	ALGONQUIN
Algonquin	ALGONQUIN GROUP
Algonquin Group	ALGONQUIN GROUP
Aliatan (Ute)	SHOSHONI, NORTHERN
Alibamo	ALABAMA
Alibamou	ALABAMA
Alibamu	ALABAMA
Aliche	EYEISH
Allakaweah	ALLAKAWEAH
Allebome (Lewis & Clark)	COMANCHE
Alliance Indians	BLACKFEET CONFEDERACY
Allibama	ALABAMA
Alligewi or Alleghanys (a people referred in Delaware tradition)	CHEROKEE
Alliklik	ALLIKLIK
Alliniwek	ILLINOIS CLUSTER OF TRIBES
Alnânbai	ABENAKI
Alnôbak	ABENAKI
Alsé	ALSEA
Alsea	ALSEA
Alsee	ALSEA
Alsi	ALSEA
Alsi-ya	ALSEA
Altamaha	ALTAMAHA
Amacano	AMACANO
Amacapiras	MACAPIRAS
Amahami	AMAHAMI
Amalecite	MALISEET
Amaliste	AMELISTE
Amaseconti	AMASECONTI
Amatiha	METEHARTA
Amayes	JEMEZ PUEBLO
Ameias	JEMEZ PUEBLO
Amejes	JEMEZ PUEBLO
Ameliste	AMELISTE
Amgútsuish (Shasta)	UMPQUA
Amimenipaty	AMIMENIPATY
Amolélish (Kalapuya)	MOLALLA
Amonokoa	AMONOKOA
Ámpzänkni (Klamath)	WASCO
An-ish-in-aub-ag	CHIPPEWA
Anacona	ACOMA PUEBLO
Anadaca or Ana-Da-Ca	ANADARKO
Anadarko	ANADARKO
Anagonges (Iroquois)	ABENAKI
Anahami	AMAHAMI
Anahaway	AMAHAMI
Anahou (French, Caddo)	OSAGE
Anakwan-ki (Cherokee)	DELAWARE
Ananis	BILOXI
Anasazi	ANASAZI
Anasitch	ANASITCH
Anatagu	ANATHAGUA
Anathagua	ANATHAGUA
Anathagua	QUANATAGUO
Anaxis	BILOXI
Anchose	ANCHOSE
Andaste (very common substitution)	SUSQUEHANNA
Andastoque	SUSQUEHANNA
Andastoquehronnon	SUSQUEHANNA
Andatahouats (Huron)	OTTAWA
Anduico	ANADARKO
Andusta	EDISTO
Ani'-Gu'sa (Cherokee)	MUSKOGEE
Ani'-Kitu'hwagi (Algonquian)	CHEROKEE
Ani'-Na'Tsi (Cherokee)	NATCHEZ
Ani'-Shala'li (Cherokee)	TUSCARORA
Ani'-Suwa'li (Cherokee)	CHERAW
Ani'-Tsa'ta (Cherokee)	CHOCTAW
Ani'-Tsi'ksu	CHICKASAW
Ani'-Ut'tsi or Ani'-Yu'tsi (Cherokee)	YUCHI
Ani'-Yun'-wiya	CHEROKEE
Anikituaghi	CHEROKEE
Anikituhwagi	CHEROKEE
Ani'Sawanu'gi (Cherokee)	SHAWNEE
Ani'ta'gua (Cherokee)	CATAWBA
Ani-yun-wi-ya	CHEROKEE
Anípörspi (Calapooya)	NEZ PERCÉ
Anishinaabe	CHIPPEWA
Anishinabe	CHIPPEWA
Anishinabeg	CHIPPEWA
Anishinabek	CHIPPEWA
Anisnabe (also Anishnabe)	ALGONQUIN GROUP
Aniyunwiya	CHEROKEE
Annocchy (early French)	BILOXI
Anniyaya	CHEROKEE
Ano's-anyotskano (Kichai)	ARAPAHO
Antelope	KWAHADA
Apache	APACHE
Apache-Mojave and Apache Mohaves	YAVAPAI
Apáches	YAVAPAI
Apalachee	APALACHEE
Apalachicola	APALACHICOLA
Apapax	APAPAX
Apayxam	APAPAX
Apenakis	ABENAKI
Apenakis (mistakenly; see Abenaki)	DELAWARE
Api'nefu (Kalapuya, other)	CHEPENAFA KALAPUYA
Apineus	WAPPINGER CONFEDERACY
Appalachicola	APALACHICOLA
Appalousa	OPELOUSA
Applegate Creek Indians	DAKUBETEDE
Applegate River Indians	DAKUBETEDE
Applegate River People	TAKELMA
Appomatotox	APPOMATOTOX
Appomattoc	APPOMATOTOX
Apsaalooke	CROW
Aqiu	PECOS PUEBLO
Aqokúlo	CHIMAKUM

Aquackanonk	AQUACKANONK
Aquannaque	ABENAKI
Aquascogooc	AQUASCOGOOC
Aquelou Pissas (Le Page du Pratz)	ACOLAPISSA
Áqusta (Naltunnetunne)	TOLOWA
Ara	KAROK
Arapaha	ARAPAHO
Arapaho	ARAPAHO
Arapahoe	ARAPAHO
Aravaipa Apache	ARAVAIPA
Archithinue	BLACKFEET
Arickara	ARIKARA
Arickaree	ARIKARA
Arikara	ARIKARA
Arivaipa	GILEŇOS
Arivipa	GILEŇOS
Arkansaw or Arkansas (Illinois)	QUAPAW
Arkanza	QUAPAW
Armouchiquois	ARMOUCHIQUOIS
Arosaguntacook	AROSAGUNTACOOK
Arrapahoe	ARAPAHO
Arrenamuse	ARRENAMUSE
Arrohattoc	ARROHATTOC
Arrowhàtoc	ARROHATTOC
As-a-ka-shi (Crow)	MANDAN
Asakiwaki	SAUK
Asán'ka	KOOTENAY
Asay or Osay	HOPI
Ascani	YSCANI
Aseney	KADOHADACHO CONFEDERACY
Ash-o-chi-mi	WAPPO
Ashepoo	ASHEPOO
Ashiwi or A'shiwi	ZUŇI
Ashnuhumsh (Kalapuya)	SNOHOMISH
Asinai (possibly)	KADOHADACHO CONFEDERACY
Asinay	KADOHADACHO CONFEDERACY
Asinay (possibly)	TEJAS
Askwalli (Calopooya)	NISQUALLY
Asomoche	ASOMOCHE
Assinaboes	ASSINIBOIN
Assinais	KADOHADACHO CONFEDERACY
Assinay	HAINAI
Assiniboin	ASSINIBOIN
Assiniboin of the Forest	ASSINIBOIN
Assiniboine	ASSINIBOIN
Assinneboin	ASSINIBOIN
Assinnipoual	ASSINIBOIN
Assista Ectaeronnons (Huron)	MASCOUTIN
Assistaectaronon (Huron)	MASCOUTIN
Assistaeronon (Huron)	MASCOUTIN
Assistagueronon (Huron)	MASCOUTIN
Assistagueronou (Huron)	MASCOUTIN
Assitaehronon (Huron)	MASCOUTIN
Assitagueronon	MASCOUTIN
Assony	NASONI
Assunpink	ASSUNPINK
Asucsag-na	ASUCSAG-NA
Asuksa	ASUCSAG-NA
At'-ta-wits (Comanche)	KADOHADACHO CONFEDERACY
At-pasha-shliha (Koasati)	HITCHITI
Atai or Atais	ADAES
Atákapa (Choctaw)	ATÁKAPA
Atanum	ATANUM
Atanumlema	ATANUM
Atasacneus	ATASACNEUS
Atasi	ATASI
Atayos	ADAES
Atcháshti ame'nmei or Atchashti ámim (Atfalati Kalapuya)	CHASTACOSTA

Atchatchakangouen or Miami Proper	ATCHATCHAKANGOUEN
Atchatchakangouen or Miami Proper	MIAMI
Atchihwa' (Yavapai)	MARICOPA
Atchixe'lish (Calapooya)	CHEHALIS
Atcik-hata	HITCHITI
Atfalati Kalapuya	ATFALATI KALAPUYA
Athabasca	CREE
Atiasnogue	ATIASNOGUE
Atlashimih	CARRIER
Atokúwe (Kiowa)	APACHE
Atotchasi (Marquette)	UZUTIUHI
Atotiosi (Jolliet)	UZUTIUHI
Atra'kwae'ronnons	SUSQUEHANNA
Atsina	ATSINA
Atsistarhonon (Huron)	POTAWATOMI
Atsugewi	ATSUGEWI
Attacapa	ATÁKAPA
Attakapa	ATÁKAPA
Attamuskeet	MACHAPUNGA
Attiemospicayes	THLINGCHADINNE
Attikamigue	ATTIKAMIGUE
Attimospiquaies (La Potherie)	THLINGCHADINNE
Attistae	MASCOUTIN
Attiwandaronk	NEUTRALS
Aucocisco	AUCOCISCO
Aughquaga	AUGHQUAGA
Aughquàgah	AUGHQUAGA
Auölasús (Pima)	SOUTHERN PAIUTE
Auricara	ARIKARA
Avogel	AVOYEL
Avoyel	AVOYEL
Awahi (Caddo & Wichita)	PAWNEE
Awahu (Arikara)	PAWNEE
Awásko ammim (Kalapuya)	WASCO
Awátch or Awatche (Ute)	APACHE
Aweatsiwaenhronon (Huron)	WINNEBAGO
Awena'tchela (Klickitat)	WENATCHEE
Awi-adshi (Molalla)	KLICKITAT
Awig-na	AWIG-NA
Awó (Tonkawa)	PAWNEE
Awo-pa-pa (Pima)	MARICOPA
Axion	AXION
Axshissayé-rúnu (Wyandot)	CHIPPEWA
Axwe'lapc (Chinook & Quinalult)	KWALHIOQUA
Ayankeld, living at	YONCALLA KALAPUYA
Ayatchinini (Chippewa)	BLACKFEET
Ayatchiyiniw (Cree)	BLACKFEET
Ayauais	IOWA
Ayavois	IOWA
Ayiches	EYEISH
Ayiches	ALLIKLIK
Aynais	HAINAI
Aynay	HAINAI
Ayoes	IOWA
Ayonai	HAINAI
Ayouas	IOWA
Ayutan	AYUTAN
Ba-akush (Caddo)	DAKOTA
Ba-akush' (Caddo)	SIOUX
Ba-akush' (Caddo)	DAKOTA
Ba-qa-o (Puyallup)	MAKAH
Ba-ra-shup'-gi-o (Crow)	DAKOTA
Ba-ra-shup'-gi-o (Crow)	SIOUX
Báachinena	ARAPAHO, NORTHERN
Backhook or Back Hook	BACKHOOK
Bad Hearts	KIOWA APACHE
Bágowits (Southern Ute)	NAVAJO
Báhakosin (Caddo)	CHEYENNE
Bahkanapül	TÜBATULABAL
Bahwetego-weninnewug (Chippewa)	ATSINA
Bakau	MITOM POMO
Bald Heads	COMANCHE
Ban-at-teels	BANNOCK
Banabeouiks	WINNEBAGO

445

Baniatho (Arapho)	CHEROKEE
Bannack	BANNOCK
Bannock	BANNOCK
Bannock Creek Shoshoni	BANNOCK CREEK SHOSHONI
Banumints (Chemehuevi)	SERRANO
Barbareño Chumash	BARBAREÑO CHUMASH
Bashabas	ABENAKI
Basket People	COLVILLE
Batem-da-kai-ee	KATO
Bawichtigouek (Jesuit)	CHIPPEWA
Bay Indians	WINNEBAGO
Bay River Indians	BEAR RIVER INDIANS OF NORTH CAROLINA
Bayogoula	BAYOUGOULA
Bayougoula	BAYOUGOULA
Be'-zai (Navaho)	JICARILLA
Be'shiltcha (Kiowa Apache)	KIOWA
Bean People	PAPAGO
Bear Hunter's Band, Chief	SHOSHONI, NORTHERN > NORTHWESTERN
Bear River Indians of California	BEAR RIVER INDIANS OF CALIFORNIA
Bear River Indians of North Carolina	BEAR RIVER INDIANS OF NORTH CAROLINA
Beaux Hommes	BLACKFEET
Beaux Hommes	QUAPAW
Beaver Indians	BEAVER INDIANS
Bedae	BIDAI
Bedies	BIDAI
Bedonkohe (sub-group)	NDE-NDA-I CHIRICAHUA
Bedzaqetcha (Tsattine)	CHIPPEWA
Bedzietcho (Kawchodinne)	CHIPPEWA
Belantse-Eta	ATSINA
Belantse-Etea	ATSINA
Belantse-Etoa	ATSINA
Beothuk	BEOTHUK
Beothunk	BEOTHUK
Beshde'ke (Dakota)	FOX
Betidee (Kiowa Apache)	ARAPAHO
Bidai	BIDAI
Bidia	BIDAI
Bierni'n (Sandia)	KERESAN PUEBLOS
Big Bellies (Big Belly)	ATSINA
Big Devils	YANKTONAI SIOUX
Big Sandy Indians	TUTELO
Big-bellied Indians	ATSINA
Bik-ta'-she (Crow)	SHOSHONI, NORTHERN
Bilocchy	BILOXI
Biloxi	BILOXI
Birch Bay Indians	SEMIAHMOO
Bird People or Bird-people)	CROW
Black Arms	CHEYENNE
Black Hook	BACKHOOK
Black Minqua	HONNIASONT
Black Panis	WICHITA
Black Pawnee	WICHITA
Blackfeet	BLACKFEET
Blackfeet Confederacy	BLACKFEET CONFEDERACY
Blackfeet Indians of Montana	PIEGAN BLACKFEET
Blackfoot or Black foot	SIKSIKA BLACKFEET
Blackfoot Sioux	BLACKFOOT SIOUX
Blancs Ý Barbus	MENOMINEE
Blanes Barbus	MENOMINEE
Blewmouth	BLEWMOUTH
Blood Indians (also Bloody Indians)	KAINAI BLACKFEET
Blue Clouds (Dakota)	ARAPAHO
Blue Muds	NEZ PERCÉ
Bo'dalk iñago (Kiowa)	COMANCHE
Bo'teaced (Nez Percé)	COLUMBIA
Bodega Miwok	BODEGA MIWOK
Bohicket or Bohickett	BOHICKET

Bohickott	BOHICKET
Boinup (Chippewa)	DAKOTA
Bois Brûlé	BRULÉ
Bois Fort	BURT WOODS CHIPPEWA
Bokeaí (Sandia Tiwa)	HOPI
Bone Indians	OSAGE
Borrados (Spanish)	SHUMAN
Bot-k'in'ago	ATSINA
Botshenin	BOTSHENIN
Botshenins	OCCANEECHI
Bow Indians	QUAPAW
Bread People	PASCAGOULA
Broken Arrow	SANS ARC
Brotherton	BROTHERTON
Brothertown	BROTHERTON
Brulé or Brulé Sioux	BRULÉ
Bruleé or Brule	BRULÉ
Bsigwigwilts Tribe	UPPER SKAGIT
Buena Vista Yokuts	BUENA VISTA YOKUTS
Buffalo People of the Suhtai Tribe	NORTHERN CHEYENNE
Buffalo Eaters	KOTSOTEKA
Buffalo Eaters	SHOSHONI, EASTERN
Buffalo-eaters	BANNOCK
Buhk'hérk (Isleta Tiwa)	HOPI
Bukín (Isleta)	HOPI
Buldam	MITOM POMO
Bungees (traders)	CHIPPEWA
Burt Woods Chippewa	BURT WOODS CHIPPEWA
Ca'-tha (Arapaho)	COMANCHE
Cabellos realzados (Spanish)	CHIPPEWA
Cache Valley Indians	SHOSHONI, NORTHERN > NORTHWESTERN
Cacores	SHAKORI
Cacores (a misprint)	SHAKORI
Cacta'-qwût-ne'tûnne (Naltunne)	UMPQUA
Caddo Peoples	CADDO PEOPLES
Caddoe	CADDO PEOPLES
Cadoe	CADDO PEOPLES
Cafitaciqui	COFITACHEQUI
Cah'parahihu (Shasta)	HUPA
Cahinnio	CAHINNIO
Cahokia	CAHOKIA
Cahueg-na	CAHUEG-NA
Cahuila	CAHUILLA
Cahuilla	CAHUILLA
Caigua or Caihua	KIOWA
Caiwa	KIOWA
Cajuenche	KOHUANA
Calamox	TILLAMOOK GROUP
Calapooia	CALAPOOYA KALAPUYA
Calapooia	KALAPUYA PEOPLES
Calapooya	KALAPUYA PEOPLES
Calapooya Kalapuya	CALAPOOYA KALAPUYA
Calasthocle	CALASTHOCLE
Calcefar	CALCEFAR
Calispel	KALISPEL
Callapnowah	KALAPUYA PEOPLES
Callimix	CALLIMIX
Caluça	OKELOUSA
Calusa	CALUSA
Camanche	COMANCHE
Camas People	KALISPEL
Campers/Dwellers of the End	YANKTON SIOUX
Canal Builders	HOHOKAM
Canarsee	CANARSEE
Canawaghauna	CANAWAGHAUNA
Canawese	CONOY PEOPLES
Cancepne	CANCEPNE
Cancepu	CANCEPNE
Cances (Caddo, "deceivers")	LIPAN
Cances	KANSA
Cancey or Kantsi (Caddo, also applied to others)	KIOWA APACHE
Cancy or Canecy	APACHE

Cannon-gageh-ronnons (Mohawk)	ABENAKI
Canoe Indians	MAHICAN GROUP
Canosi	CATAWBA
Cansa	KANSA
Canses	KANSA
Canton Indians	IROQUOIS LEAGUE
Caoco	COAQUE
Caouita	CAOUITA
Caparaz	CAPARAZ
Cape Fear Indians	CAPE FEAR INDIANS
Cape Flattery Indians	MAKAH
Cape Indians	NAUSET
Cape People	MAKAH
Capiché	CAPICHÉ
Capinans	CAPINANS or BILOXI or PASCAGOULA
Capoque	COAQUE
Capoques	COAQUE
Capote Ute	CAPOTE UTE
Carancaquaca	KARANKAWA
Caree	CAREE
Carlana	APACHE
Carmeneth (Crow)	BLACKFEET
Carnarsie	CANARSEE
Carrier	CARRIER
Cascade Indians (popular name)	WATLALA
Cascangue	CASCANGUE
Cascangue	ICAFUI
Cascangue	ICAFUI
Caschotethka	KOTSOTEKA
Casco (local)	AUCOCISCO
Caso	CASO
Casor	CUSSO
Casqui	KASKINAMPO
Casquin	KASKINAMPO
Castahan	CASTAHANA
Castahana	CASTAHANA
Castors des Prairies	SARCEE
Cat People	ERIE
Cataha	KIOWA
Cataka	KIOWA
Catawba	CATAWBA
Cathlacomatup	CATHLACOMATUP
Cathlacumup	CATHLACUMUP
Cathlahpotle	CATHLAPOTLE
Cathlakaheckit	CATHLAKAHECKIT
Cathlamat	CATHLAMET
Cathlamet	CATHLAMET
Cathlanaquiah	CATHLANAQUIAH
Cathlapootle	CATHLAPOTLE
Cathlapotle	CATHLAPOTLE
Cathlapotle (Lewis & Clark)	CHINOOK
Cathlasko	CATHLASKO
Cathlath	CATHLATH
Cathlathlala	CATHLATHLALA
Cats	SHAWNEE
Catskill	CATSKILL
Cattanahaw	CATTANAHAW
Caughnawaga	KANAWAKE
Caughnewaga	CAUGHNEWAGA
Caumuche	COMANCHE
Cavuga	CAYUGA
Cawina	KOHUANA
Caxo	CASO
Caygua	KIOWA
Cayuga	CAYUGA
Cayusa	CAYUSE
Cayuse	CAYUSE
Cecilville Indians	CECILVILLE INDIANS
Cenepisa (La Salle)	ACOLAPISSA
Cenis	HAINAI
Cetguanes	YUMA
Chabanakongkomun	CHABANAKONGKOMUN
Chacato	CHATOT

Chacktaw	CHOCTAW
Chactaw	CHOCTAW
Chactoo	CHATOT
Chafan	TSANCHIFIN KALAPUYA
Chaftan	CHAFTAN
Chaguyenne	CHEYENNE
Chah'-ra-rat (Pawnee)	SIOUX
Chah'-ra-rat (Pawnee)	DAKOTA
Chah'-shm (Santo Domingo Keres)	APACHE
Chahiksichahiks	PAWNEE
Chakankni Molalla	CHAKANKNI MOLALLA
Chakchiuma	CHAKCHIUMA
Chaktaw	CHOCTAW
Chala	CHALA
Chalee	SHALEE
Chamnapum	CHAMNAPUM
Chaouanou (Nicholas Perot)	SHAWNEE
Charaw	CHERAW
Chasta	SHASTA
Chasta (erroneously)	CHASTACOSTA
Chasta Costa	CHASTACOSTA
Chasta Scoton	SCOTON
Chastacosta	CHASTACOSTA
Chatot	CHATOT
Chats	SHAWNEE
Chauchila	CHOWCHILLA YOKUT
Chaudière	COLVILLE
Chauhagueronon (Huron)	MONTAGNAIS-NASKAPI
Chaui	GRAND PAWNEE
Chaushila	CHOWCHILLA YOKUT
Chavanon	SHAWNEE
Chawasha	CHAWASHA
Chaye	CHOYE
Chayenne	CHEYENNE
Che-wai-rae or Che-wae-rae	OTO
Checlukimaukes (OIA)	LOWER CREEK
Cheegee	CHEEGEE
Cheehaylas (Catlin)	CHEHALIS
Chehalis (also Chehali)	CHEHALIS
Chehaw	CHIAHA
Chelan	WENATCHEE
Chelemela Kalapuya	CHELEMELA KALAPUYA
Chelokee (Creek)	CHEROKEE
Chemapho	CHEMAPOHO KALAPUYA
Chemapoho Kalapuya	CHEMAPOHO KALAPUYA
Chemegué Caujála	SOUTHERN PAIUTE
Chemehuevi	CHEMEHUEVI
Chepalis	COPALIS
Chepenafa Kalapuya	CHEPENAFA KALAPUYA
Chepoussa	CHEPOUSSA
Cheraw	CHERAW
Charitica	COMANCHE
Cherechos (Onate)	KERESAN PUEBLOS
Cheroenhaka	NOTTAWAY
Cherokee	CHEROKEE
Chesapeak	CHESAPEAKE
Chesapeake	CHESAPEAKE
Cheskitalowa	CHESKITALOWA
Chetco	CHETCO
Chetlessington	CHETLESSINGTON
Cheveux-releves (French)	CHIPPEWA
Chewelah	CHEWELAH
Cheyenne	CHEYENNE
Cheyenne	SUHTAI
Cheyenne Sioux	CHEYENNE (DOG SOLDIERS)
Chiaha	CHIAHA
Chiakanessou	CHIAKANESSOU
Chicago	CHICAGO
Chichnee	CHICORA
Chichimeco	YUCHI
Chichimici	CHICHIMICI
Chickahominie	CHICKAHOMINY
Chickahominy	CHICKAHOMINY

Chickamauga	CHICKAMAUGA	Chu-mai-a (Pomo)	YUKI
Chickanee	WATEREE	Chugnut	CHUGNUT
Chickasaw	CHICKASAW	Chumash	CHUMASH
Chickeles	CHEHALIS	Ci-cta'qwût-me'tûnne or Ci-cta'qwût	UMPQUA
Chickesaw	CHICKASAW	(Tututni; Chastacosta)	
Chicktaghick or Chicktaghik	ILLINOIS CLUSTER OF	Ci-sta'-qwût-mê tunne	KUITSH
(Iroquois)	TRIBES	(Mishikwutmetunne)	
Chickoree	CHICORA	Cibicue Apache	CIBICUE
Chicora	CHICORA	Cibola	ZUÑI
Chien Indians (Fr. for Dog)	CHEYENNE	Cicuye	PECOS PUEBLO
Chigtuas	TIWA PUEBLO	Cimarron (Drake)	SEMINOLE
Chiheeleesh	CHIHEELEESH	Cintu-aluka (Teton Dakota)	COMANCHE
Chihenne	TCI-HE-NDE/	Circee	SARCEE
	CHIRICAHUA	Ciriés	SARCEE
Chikahomini	CHICKAHOMINY	Clack-A-Mas	CLACKAMAS
Chikamauga	CHICKAMAUGA	Clackamas	CLACKAMAS
Chikohoki	CHIKOHOKI	Clackamus	CLACKAMAS
Chilakee (De Soto)	CHEROKEE	Clackstar	CLATSKANIE
Children of the Middle Waters	OSAGE	Clah-clel-lah (Lewis & Clark)	CLAHCLELLAH
Chilion	TSILTADEN	Clahclellah	CLAHCLELLAH
Chillate	CHILLATE	Clallam	CLALLAM
Chilluckittequaw	CHILLUCKITTEQUAW	Clamcoets	KARANKAWAN TRIBES
Chilpaines	CHIPAYNE	Classet (Nootka)	MAKAH
Chiltz	CHEHALIS	Clatsanie	CLATSKANIE
Chilucan	CHILUCAN	Clatskanie	CLATSKANIE
Chilula	CHILULA	Clatsop	CLATSOP
Chilwitz	CHEHALIS	Clickatat	LAGUNA PUEBLO
Chimakum	CHIMAKUM	Clockamus	CLACKAMAS
Chimariko	CHIMARIKO	Clowwewalla	CLOWWEWALLA
Chimbuiha Molalla	CHIMBUIHA MOLALLA	Club Indians	YUMA
Chimnapum	CHIMNAPUM	Coahuiltecan Tribes	COAHUILTECAN TRIBES
Chine	CHINE	Coapite	COAPITE
Chinko	CHINKO	Coaque	COAQUE
Chinook	CHINOOK	Coast Yuki	COAST YUKI
Chipaindes	CHIPAYNE	Cochaug	CORCHAUG MONTAUK
Chipawa	CHIPPEWA	Cochecho (Indian name for Dover)	PISCATAQUA
Chipayne	CHIPAYNE	Cochita	COCHITI PUEBLO
Chipewyan	CHIPEWYAN	Cochiti Pueblo	COCHITI PUEBLO
Chippanchikchik	CHIPPANCHIKCHIK	Coco	COAQUE
Chippawa	CHIPPEWA	Cocomaricopa	MARICOPA
Chippewa	CHIPPEWA	Coconino (Zuñi)	HAVASUPAI
Chippewa	VIEUX DÉSERT	Cocopa	COCOPA
Chippeway	CHIPPEWA	Cocopah	COCOPA
Chiricahua Apache	CHIRICAHUA	Cocos	COAQUE
Chirumas	YUMA	Coeur d'Alêne or Coeur d'Alene	SKITSWISH
Chishyë (Laguna)	APACHE	Coeur d'Alêne Skitswish	COEUR D'ALÊNE
Chisca	KASKINAMPO		SKITSWISH
Chisca or Chiska (Muskogee)	YUCHI	Cofitachequi	COFITACHEQUI
Chiskiac	CHISKIAC	Cofitachequi (De Soto)	KASIHTA
Chitimacha	CHITIMACHA	Cofitachiqui	COFITACHEQUI
Chitimicha	CHITIMACHA	Cohakies	CAHOKIA
Cho-bah-ah-bish	CHO-BAH-AH-BISH	Coharie	COHARIE
Cho-pun-nish (Lewis & Clark)	NEZ PERCÉ	Cohokia	CAHOKIA
Chochilla	CHOWCHILLA YOKUT	Cohpáp (Pima)	MARICOPA
Chock-Katit (Arikara)	BLACKFEET	Cohunnewago	COHUNNEWAGO
Chocktaw	CHOCTAW	Coiracoentanon	COIRACOENTANON
Choctaw	CHOCTAW	Colapissa	ACOLAPISSA
Chokishg-na	CHOKISHG-NA	Colapissas or Coulapissas	ACOLAPISSA
Chokonen	CHIRICAHUA	Coluchike	COFITACHEQUI
Chonque (Quapaw)	MOSOPELEA	Columbia	COLUMBIA
Chopunnish (Lewis & Clark)	NEZ PERCÉ	Colville	COLVILLE
Choula	CHOULA	Comanche	COMANCHE
Chouman (French)	SHUMAN	Comantz	COMANCHE
Chousa	SUHTAI	Combahee	COMBAHEE
Chowan	CHOWANOC	Comeya (used in Handbook of AI)	KAMIA
Chowanoc	CHOWANOC	Conawaghruna	CANAWAGHAUNA
Chowanok	CHOWANOC	Concepue	CANCEPNE
Chowchilla Yokut	CHOWCHILLA YOKUT	Conchatta	KOASATI
Chowig-na	CHOWIG-NA	ConCow Maidu	CONCOW MAIDU
Choye	CHOYE	ConCow or Concow	CONCOW MAIDU
Christanoes	CREE	Conejero	CONEJERO
Christenaux	CREE	Conestoga	SUSQUEHANNA
Christian	MUNSEE	Conexero	CONEJERO
Christinaux	CREE		

Confederate Indians or Confederates	FIVE NATIONS OF THE IROQUOIS
Congaree	CONGAREE
Connonwood Bannock	SHOHOPANAITI
Conoie	CONOY
Conoy	CONOY
Conoy Peoples	CONOY PEOPLES
Cookkoo-oose	COOKKOO-OOSE
Coopspellar	COOPSPELLAR
Coos	COOS
Coosa	COOSA
Coosan	COOS
Coosaw	COOSA
Coosawda	KOASATI
Cooshatta	KOASATI
Copalis	COPALIS
Copanes	KOPANO
Copper Indians	TATSANOTTINE
Coppermine Apache	TCI-HE-NDE/ CHIRICAHUA
Coquille	MISHIKHWUTMETUNNE
Corsaboy	CUSABO
Coranine	COREE
Corchaug Montauk	CORCHAUG MONTAUK
Coree	COREE
Corn Eaters	ARIKARA
Coshattie	KOASATI
Cosnino (Zuñi)	HAVASUPAI
Cosshatte	KOASATI
Costanoan	COSTANOAN
Coste	KOASATI
Costehe	KOASATI
Couexi	CUSSO
Coupe-gorges	DAKOTA
Coupe-gorges (French from sign language)	SIOUX
Coushatta	KOASATI
Couteaux Jaunes	TATSANOTTINE
Cow Creek Umpqua	COW CREEK UMPQUA
Ców-ang-a-chem	SERRANO
Coweset	NIPMUC
Coweta	COWETA
Coweta	KAWITA
Cowlitz	COWLITZ
Coyotero Apache	COYOTERO
Crane People	ATCHATCHAKANGOUEN
Crane People	MIAMI
Cree	CREE
Creek	UPPER CREEK
Creek	LOWER CREEK
Creek	MUSKOGEE
Creek Confederacy	CREEK CONFEDERACY
Cri	CREE
Cris	CREE
Croatan	KEYAUWEE
Croatan	CROATAN
Croatan	HATTERAS
Croatoan	CROATAN
Crow	CROW
Cruzados (Oñate)	YAVAPAI
Cuabajái (Mohave)	SERRANO
Cuartelejo	APACHE
Cucamog-na	CUCAMOG-NA
Cuchan or Cuchano (own name)	YUMA
Cupeño	CUPEÑO
Cusabo	CUSABO
Cussaboy	CUSSO
Cussabee	CUSABO
Cussah	COOSA
Cusseta	KASIHTA
Cusso	CUSSO
Cut People or Cut Arms	CHEYENNE
Cut-throats	DAKOTA
Cutifaciqui	COFITACHEQUI

Cuthead or Cut Head (a band of Yanktoni)	YANKTONAI SIOUX
Cutrafichiqui	COFITACHEQUI
Cuts-sáh-nem	YAKIMA
Cutsahnim (Clark)	YAKIMA
Cuttatawoman	CUTTATAWOMEN
Cuttatawomen	CUTTATAWOMEN
Cuyama Chumash	CUYAMA CHUMASH
Cwareuuooc	CWAREUUOOC
Dä'sha-I (Wichita)	KADOHADACHO CONFEDERACY
Da-da'ze ni'-ka-ci'-ga (Kansa)	SOUTHERN PAIUTE
Dacábimo (Hopi)	NAVAJO
Dacota	DAKOTA
Dacotah	DAKOTA
Dagelma	TAKELMA
Dahcota	SIOUX/DAKOTA
Dahcotah	SIOUX/DAKOTA
Dakelh	CARRIER
Dakota	SIOUX
Dakota	DAKOTA
Dakubetede	DAKUBETEDE
Dalles, The	WASCOPUN
Danemme	TANIMA
Dárazhazh (Kiowa Apache)	PAWNEE
Dasemunkepeuc	DASEMUNKEPEUC
Datse-a (Kiowa Apache)	COMANCHE
Datumpa'ta (Hidatsa)	KIOWA
Dávaxo (Apache)	NAVAJO
De Chutes (Dechutes River)	TYIGH
De Chutes, Lower	WYAM
De Chutes, Upper	TYIGH
De la Rivière Grosventre	HIDATSA
De-d'á tené (Tutuni)	MISHIKHWUTMETUNNE
De-wa-ka-nha (Mohawk)	CHIPPEWA
Deadose	DEADOSE
Dehaui	TAHNEEMUH
Delaware	DELAWARE
Delawart	DELAWARE
Deleware	DELAWARE
Denavi	TENAWA
Deschutes	TYIGH
Destroyers	PEQUOT
Detsanyuka	NOKONI
Detseka'yaa (Caddo)	ARAPAHO
Diegueño	DIEGUEÑO
Digger Indians	SHOSHONI, NORTHERN
Digger Indians	SOUTHERN PAIUTE
Diggers	BANNOCK
Diggers	SHOSHOKO
Diggers	SHOSHONI, NORTHERN > NORTHWESTERN
Díhit or Li-hit or Ríhit	PONCA
Dil-shay's (Apache)	YUMA
Dil-zha	YAVAPAI
Dilwishne (Sinkyone)	WIYOT
Diné or Dinë	NAVAJO
Dineh	NAVAJO
Dinondadies	DINONDADIES
Djëné (Laguna)	NAVAJO
Do'gu'at (Kiowa)	WICHITA
Do'kana (Comanche)	WICHITA
Dock-Spus (for John Day Indians)	TUKSPUSH
Docota	DAKOTA
Doeg(s)	NANTICOKE
Dog Eaters (Comanche & Shoshoni)	ARAPAHO
Dog Indians (confusion w/ Fr. Chien)	CHEYENNE
Dog People	MOSOPELEA
Dog-Ribs	THLINGCHADINNE
Dotame	DOTAME
Dotami	DOTAME
Doustioni or Doustione	DOUSTIONI
Drinkers of the Dew (Zuni)	KERESAN PUEBLOS
Dshipowe-hága (Caughnawaga)	CHIPPEWA

449

Dudley Indians	CHABANAKONGKOMUN
Dulcinoe	DOUSTIONI
Duwamish	DUWÁMISH
Duwámish	DUWÁMISH
Dwa-ka-ne (Onondaga)	CHIPPEWA
Dwellers among the Leaves	WAHPETUNWAN SIOUX
Dwellers at the End	YANKTONAI SIOUX
Dzitsi'stas	CHEYENNE
E-che-loot (Lewis & Clark)	WISHRAM
E-nag h-magh	TIWA PUEBLO
E-nyaé-va Pai	YAVAPAI
E-pa	HUALAPAI
E-pa	WALAPAI
E-tah-leh (Hidatsa)	ARAPAHO
E-tans-ke-pa-se-qua (Hidatsa)	ASSINIBOIN
E-tans-ke-pa-se-qua (Hidatsa)	STONEY-NAKODA
E-wu-h-a'-wu-si (Arapaho)	SHOSHONI, NORTHERN
Earring People	KALISPEL
Eastern Abenaki	PENOBSCOT
Eastern Mono	EASTERN MONO
Eastern Mono (combined within)	MONO
Eastern Shoshoni	SHOSHONI EASTERN
Eastern Sioux	DAKOTA
Easterners (mistakenly; see Abenaki)	DELAWARE
Easterners (those living at the east/ at the sunrise)	ABENAKI
Ecasqui	KASKINAMPO
Echeloot	ECHELOOT
Echeloot (Lewis & Clark)	WISHRAM
Echelute	ECHELOOT
Echemin	MALISEET
Echemin (Drake)	ETCHEMIN
Echota	CHEROKEE
Edisto	EDISTO
Eeh-tahtah-oh Comanche	EEH-TAHTAH-OH COMANCHE
Eel River	EEL RIVER
Ekpimi (Ilmawi)	SHASTA
Elk Mountain Ute	ELK MOUNTAIN UTE
Eloot	ECHELOOT
Elwha Clallam	ELWHA KLALLAM
Elwha Klallam	ELWHA KLALLAM
Eeges	JEMEZ PUEBLO
Emigdiano Chumash	EMIGDIANO CHUMASH
Emusa	EMUSA
Eneesher	ENESHER
Enesher	ENESHER
Eneshur	ENESHER
Eneshure	ENESHER
Enneshuh	ENESHER
Eno	ENO
Eno River Tribe	ENO
Enquisaco	ENQUISACO
Entari ronnon (Wyandot)	CHEROKEE
Equinipichas	ACOLAPISSA
Erawika (Pawnee)	KADOHADACHO CONFEDERACY
Erie	ERIE
Eries (Jesuit Relations)	SHAWNEE
Eriwonec	ERIWONEC
Esaugh	CATAWBA
Esaw	CATAWBA
Escamacu	ESCAMACU
Eskeloot	ECHELOOT
Eskiaeronnon (Huron)	CHIPPEWA
Esophus	ESOPUS
Esopus	ESOPUS
Espachomy	ESOPUS
Espeminkia	ESPEMINKIA
Esquimaux	ESQUIMAUX
Esselen	ESSELEN
Essequeta (Kiowa & Comanche, misapplied)	KIOWA APACHE
Etali	CHEROKEE

Etchemin	ETCHEMIN
Etchemin	MALISEET
Etechemin	ETCHEMIN
Etiwa	ETIWAW
Etiwan	ETIWAW
Etiwaw	ETIWAW
Etnémitane	UMPQUA
Etocale	OCALE
Etohussewakke	ETOHUSSEWAKKE
Euchee (Creek)	YUCHI
Eufaula	EUFAULA
Euqchan	YUMA
Eutaw	ETIWAW
Excamacu	EXCAMACU
Eyaníni diné (Navaho)	HOPI
Eyeish	EYEISH
Fall Indians	ATSINA
Fall Indians	CLOWWEWALLA
Fall Indians	FALL INDIANS
Faraon	FARAON
Faraon	MESCALERO
Fernandeño	FERNANDEÑO
Fire Indians	MASCOUTIN
Fire Nation or Fire-Nation (Huron)	MASCOUTIN
Fire Nation	POTAWATOMIE
Fisheaters	[PACIFIC COAST INDIANS, ESP. OREGON]
Five Civilized Nations	FIVE CIVILIZED NATIONS
Five Nations	IROQUOIS LEAGUE
Fkabcs-de-Chien	THLINGCHADINNE
Flat Heads (Flatheads)	CHOCTAW
Flatbows or Flat Bows for Lower Kutenai	KOOTENAY
Flathead or Flat Head (when used to identify a tribe or nation v. the practice of deforming heads, refers to Salish)	SALISH
Flatheads	WAXHAW
Flatheads (commonly used for those tribes that adopted the practice of deforming heads)	CHINOOK
Flatheads (trans. of Si ni'-te-li)	TILLAMOOK GROUP
Floating Scum, People of the	WENROHRONON
Follavoine (MauriceBlondeau)	MENOMINEE
Folles Avoines (Mad Oats)	MENOMINEE
Fon du Lac Loucheux	TATLIT-KUTCHIN
Fort Hall Indians (prior to reservation days)	POHOGUE SHOSHONI
Fox	FOX
Foxes	FOX
Freckled Panis	WICHITA
Fremont	FREMONT
French Chaouanons	FRENCH CHAOUANONS
French Prairie Indians	AHANTCHUYUK
Fresh Water Indians	FRESH WATER INDIANS
Friendly Village (on Doug's Bearch, Lewis & Clark)	CHINOOK
Fus-hatchee	FUS-HATCHEE
Gä-quä'-go-o-no	ERIE
Gabrieleño	TONGVA
Gabrielino	STONO
Gachwechnagechga	GACHWECHNAGECHGA
Gahe'wa (Wichita & Kichai)	KIOWA
Gaitchim	JUANEÑO
Galic Creek Indians	TALTUSHTUNTUDE
Galice Creeks	GRAVE CREEK UMPQUA
Gallinomero Pomo	GALLINOMERO POMO
Ganawese	CONOY PEOPLES
Ganniataratich (Mohawk)	NANTICOKE
Garroteros	YUMA
Gáta'-ka (Pawnee) or Gattacka	KIOWA APACHE
Gatacka	KIOWA

Gatsalghi (Kiowa Apache)	CHEYENNE
Geghdageghroano (Iroquois)	ILLINOIS CLUSTER OF TRIBES
Gemes	JEMEZ PUEBLO
Genigueches	SERRANO
Gens des Serpent	SHOSHONI, NORTHERN
Gens des Vach[es] (Lewis & Clark)	ARAPAHO
Gens du fond du lac	TATLIT-KUTCHIN
Gens du Petun	TIONONTATI
Gens du Serpent (FR. Snake Indians)	SHOSHONI, NORTHERN
Gentlemen Indians	WACO
Geote	GEOTE
Ghecham	LUISEÑO PEOPLES
Gi-aucth-in-in-e-wig (Chippewa)	HIDATSA
Gig Harbor	GIG HARBOR
Gikidanum (selectively)	SERRANO
Gila Apache	GILA
Gila'q!ulawas	KWALHIOQUA
Gila'xicatck (Chinook)	WATLALA
Gileños Apache	GILEÑOS
Gillamooks	TILLAMOOK GROUP
Ginä's (Wichita)	KIOWA APACHE
Ginebigônini (Chippewa)	SHOSHONI, NORTHERN
Gita'q!emas (Clatsop)	CLACKAMAS
Gitanemuk (selectively)	SERRANO
Gíts'aji (Kansa)	KICHAI
Gohún	YAVAPAI
Good Canoemen	MOHEGAN
Good River People [St. John River]	MALISEET
Gorretas	MANSO
Goship	GOSIUTE SHOSHONI
Goshiute	GOSIUTE SHOSHONI
Goshute	GOSIUTE SHOSHONI
Goshuite	GOSIUTE SHOSHONI
Gosiute	GOSIUTE SHOSHONI
Gosute	GOSIUTE SHOSHONI
Gowanus	GOWANUS
Gran Quivira Pueblo	GRAN QUIVIRA PUEBLO
Grand Pawnee	GRAND PAWNEE
Grande Eaux	GRANDE EAUX
Granite People	ONEIDA
Gras	GRIGRA
Grasshopper Indians	UTE
Grave	GRAVE CREEK UMPQUA
Grave Creek Umpqua	GRAVE CREEK UMPQUA
Gray Village of the Natchez	GRIGRA
Greem Wood Omdoam	NEZ PERCÉ
Griga	GRIGRA
Grigra	GRIGRA
Gris	GRIGRA
Gros or Gross Ventre...	ATSINA or HIDATSA
Gros Ventre of the Missouri	HIDATSA
Gros Ventre of the Plains	ATSINA
Gros Ventre of the Prairies	ATSINA
Gros Ventre of the River	HIDATSA
Gros Ventres de la Rivière	HIDATSA
Gros Ventres des Plaines	ATSINA
Grosventre	ATSINA
Grosventre	HIDATSA
Grousevauntare	HIDATSA
Gu'ta'k (Omaha & Ponca)	KIOWA APACHE
Guacata	GUACATA
Guaes (Coronado)	KANSA
Gualala Pomo	GUALALA POMO
Guale	GUALE
Gualiba	HUALAPAI
Gualiba (Yavapai)	WALAPAI
Guapo	WAPPO
Guasámas (Clackamas)	CATHLAMET
Guasco	GUASCO
Guatari (Spanish spelling)	WATEREE
Guerriers de pierre	ASSINIBOIN
Guerriers de pierre (French)	STONEY-NAKODA
Guibisnuches	WEEMINUCHE UTES
Guichita (Spanish form)	WICHITA
Guichyana	YUMA
Guiguimuches	WEEMINUCHE UTES
Guithlamethl (Clackamas)	CATHLAMET
Guyandot	WYANDOT
Guyandotte	WYANDOT
Gyai'-ko (Kiowa)	COMANCHE
H'-doum-dei-kih (Kiowa)	KADOHADACHO CONFEDERACY
H'iwana (Taos)	APACHE
H'lilush (Nestucca)	TUTUTNI
Ha'-mish or Hae'-mish (Kersean)	JEMEZ PUEBLO
Há-lum-mi	LUMMI
Ha-ma-kaba-mitc kwa-dig (Mohave)	APACHE
Hacanac	HACANAC
Hackensack	HACKENSACK
Hackinsack	HACKENSACK
Hahatonwan (Dakota)	CHIPPEWA
Hahatonway (Hidatsa)	CHIPPEWA
Hahderuka (Mandan)	CROW
Haï'luntchi (Molalla)	CAYUSE
Hai-ai'-nima (Yakima)	SANPOIL
Haideroka (Hidatsa)	CROW
Hainai	HAINAI
Háish	EYEISH
Halchidhoma	HALCHIDHOMA
Haldokehewuk	CECILVILLE INDIANS
Halyikwamai	HALYIKWAMAI
Hammonasset	HAMMONASSET
Hand Cutters (English translation of Ute name)	SIOUX
Hand Cutters (Ute)	DAKOTA
Hanging Ears	KALISPEL
Hanis	HANIS
Hannakallal	HANNAKALLAL
Hano Pueblo	HANO PUEBLO
Har-dil-zhays	YAVAPAI
Harahey (Coronado)	PAWNEE
Harasg-na	HARASG-NA
Hare Indians	KAWCHOTTINE
Hasinai	TEJAS
Hasinai	HASINAI CONFEDERACY
Hasinai Confederacy	HASINAI CONFEDERACY
Hassanameisit	HASSANAMISCO
Hassanamisco	HASSANAMISCO
Hassinunga	HASSINUNGA
Hat Creek Indians (popular name)	ATSUGEWI
Hathawekela	SHAWNEE
Hati'hski'rû'nû (Huron)	WINNEBAGO
Hatilshe'	YUMA
Hatindia8ointen (Huron)	WYANDOT
Hatiwa¹nta-runh (Tuscarora)	NEUTRALS
Hatteras	HATTERAS
Haudenosaunee	IROQUOIS
Havasupai	HAVASUPAI
Haverstraw	HAVERSTRAW
Hawálapai	WALAPAI
Hawalapai or Hawálapai	HUALAPAI
Haynokes	ENO
Hellwits	HELLWITS
Hemp Gathers	TUSCARORA
Henne'sh (Arapaho)	CHOCTAW
Herring Pond	HERRING POND
Hewaktokto (Dakota)	HIDATSA
Hiaways	KIOWA APACHE
Hich'hu (Chimariko)	HUPA
Hidasta of North Dakota	HIDATSA
Hidatsa	HIDATSA
Hierbipiames	HIERBIPIAMES
Hietan	HIETAN
Hietan or Ietan (Lewis & Clark, Drake, Dr. Sibley)	COMANCHE
Hígabu (Omaha & Ponca)	KICKAPOO

Higgahaidahu (Nestucca)	TILLAMOOK GROUP
Hihighenimmo	HIHIGHENIMMO
Hikanagi (Shawnee)	MAHICAN GROUP
Hilibi	HILIBI
Hinásso (Arapaho)	WICHITA
Hini	HAINAI
Hiokuö'k (Isleta Tiwa)	PECOS PUEBLO
Hiaways	KIOWA APACHE
His-tu-I'ta-ni-o	ATSINA
Hisca	HISCA
Hitänwo'iv (Cheyenne)	ARAPAHO
Hitasi'na or Itasi'na	CHEYENNE
Hitchiti	HITCHITI
Hitchittee	HITCHITI
Hitúnena (Arapaho)	ATSINA
Ho-Chunk or Ho Chunk	WINNEBAGO
Ho-kan-di-ka	SHOSHONI, NORTHERN > NORTHWESTERN
Ho'-ma-ha (Winnebago)	OMAHA
Ho-ni'-itani-o (Cheyenne)	PAWNEE
Hochelagan	HOCHELAGAN
Hochelaguian	HOCHELAGAN
Hodinonhsyo:ni	FIVE NATIONS OF THE IROQUOIS
Hogapä'goni (Shoshoni)	SOUTHERN PAIUTE
Hogologe (Delaware)	YUCHI
Hoh	HOH
Hoh'ees	HOIS
Hohay (Parkman)	ASSINIBOIN
Hohe (Dakota and Cheyenne)	ASSINIBOIN
Hohe (Dakota)	STONEY-NAKODA
Hohokam	HOHOKAM
Hois (Fehrenbach, minority opinion)	PEHNAHTERKUH
Hois	HOIS
Holiwahali	HOLIWAHALI
Holiwahali	HULIWAHLI
Honecha	WACO
Honey-eaters	BANNOCK
Honniasont	HONNIASONT
Hood River Indians	CHILLUCKITTEQUAW
Hook	BACKHOOK
Hoopa	HUPA
Hopi	HOPI
Hopia and Hopi[a]	HOPI
Hopokohacking	HOPOKOHACKING
Horse People	COMANCHE
Hostaqua	HOSTAQUA
Hotanka (Dakota)	WINNEBAGO
Hotcangara	WINNEBAGO
Hoti'nestako' (Onondaga)	SAUK
Houechas	WACO
Houma	HOUMA
Houmas	HOUMA
Hounena (Arapaho)	CROW
Housatonic	HOUSATONIC
Housatonic	STOCKBRIDGE INDIANS
Houtg-na	HOUTG-NA
How-mox-tox-sow-es (Hidasa?)	MANDAN
Hoxsuwitan (Cheyenne)	WICHITA
Hu-ta'-ci (Comanche)	LIPAN
Hu-úmùi (Cheyenne)	OMAHA
Hua'amú'u (Havasupai)	NAVAJO
Huaco	WACO
Hualapai	HUALAPAI
Hualupai	HAVASUPAI
Huanchané	WACO
Huchnom	HUCHNOM
Huecos	WACO
Hughchee	YUCHI
Huhamog-na	HUHAMOG-NA
Húkwats (Paiute)	YUMA
Huliwahli	HULIWAHLI
Hum-a-luh	SKAGIT
Humanasm Jumanas, Xumanas (Spanish)	SHUMAN
Humano	SHUMAN
Humboldt Bay Indians	WIYOT
Humptulip	HUMPTULIP
Hunkpapa	HUNKPAPA
Hunkpatina (Swanton; to others, two distinct groups)	YANKTONAI
Hupa	HUPA
Hupene	JUPE
Huron	WYANDOT
Huron	ROUND HEADS
Huron	HURON
Hútañga	KANSA
Hutucg-na	HUTUCG-NA
I tsi sí pi sa (Hidatsa)	BLACKFEET
I'-ka-du (Osage)	KICKAPOO
I'-na-cpe (Quapaw)	NEZ PERCÉ
I'-um O'-otam (Pima)	KAMIA
I'hl-dëné (Jicarilla)	NAVAJO
I-on-i	AIONAI
I-sonsh'-pu-she (Crow)	CHEYENNE
Iätä-go (Kiowa)	UTE
Iaway	IOWA
Ibaja or Iguaja (Timucua)	GUALE
Ibitoupa	IBITOUPA
Icafui	ICAFUI
Idahi	WALPAPI
Idahi (Kiowa Apache)	COMANCHE
Ietan	UTE
Igihua'-a (Havasupai)	APACHE
Ihanktum	NAKOTA
Ihanktunwan	YANKTON SIOUX
Ihanktunwanna	YANKTONAI SIOUX
Ikanafáskalgi (Creek)	SEMINOLE
Ikankúksalgi	SEMINOLE
Ila'xluit	WISHRAM
Ilga't (Nestucca)	CHEHALIS
Ilinois or Illini	ILLINOIS CLUSTER OF TRIBES
Illiniwek	ILLINOIS CLUSTER OF TRIBES
Illinois	ILLINOIS
Illinois Cluster of Tribes	ILLINOIS CLUSTER OF TRIBES
Ima (Caddo)	QUAPAW
Indá (Jicarilla)	COMANCHE
Indé or Indeh or Inde	APACHE
Ing-wë-pi'-ra-di-vi-he-ma (San Ildefonso Tewa)	KERESAN PUEBLOS
Inie	HAINAI
Innu	MONTAGNAIS-NASKAPI
Inuna-ina	ARAPAHO
Inya'vapé	YAVAPAI
Iones	KADOHADACHO CONFEDERACY
Ioni	HAINAI
Ioni	IONI
Iowa	IOWA
Ioway (also in the plural, Ioways)	IOWA
Ipa's People	LIPAN
Ipa-N'de	LIPAN
Ipataragüites	SHUMAN
Ipoilq (Yakima)	SANPOIL
Iroquois	IROQUOIS
Iroquois	IROQUOIS LEAGUE
Iroquois League	IROQUOIS LEAGUE
Irusitsu	IRUSITSU
Isanthcag-na	ISANTHCAG-NA
Isanti	DAKOTA
Isashbahátse (Crow)	SARCEE
Iscani	YSCANI
Ish-te-pit'-e (Crow)	BLACKFEET

Ishak	ATÁKAPA	Kahansuk	KAHANSUK
Ishpow	ASHEPOO	Kahnawá:ke and Kanawaké	KANAWAKE
Island Chumash	ISLAND CHUMASH	Kahosadi Shasta	KAHOSADI SHASTA
Isle-de-Pierre	COLUMBIA	Kai Po-mo	KATO
Isle-river	EEL RIVER	Kaibab	KAIBAB
Isleta del Sur Pueblo	TIGUA PUEBLO	Kainah	KAINAI BLACKFEET
Isleta Pueblo	ISLETA PUEBLO	Kainai Blackfeet	KAINAI BLACKFEET
Isonkuafli	OKANAGON	Kaiquariegahaga	KAIQUARIEGAHAGA
Issa (possibly an early independent band)	CATAWBA	Kaispa (Sarsi)	DAKOTA
		Kaispa (Sarsi)	SIOUX
Issappo (Siksika)	CROW	Kait-ka (Umpqua)	CALAPOOYA KALAPUYA
Isti seminole	SEMINOLE	Kaiwa	KIOWA
Iswa (possibly an early independent band)	CATAWBA	Kakasky	KASKASKIA
		Kakinonba	ACCOCESAW
Ita ha'tski (Hidatsa)	DAKOTA	Kakinonba (Marquette)	KASKINAMPO
Ita ha'tski (Hidatsa)	SIOUX	Kalapooia	KALAPUYA PEOPLES
Ita-Iddi (Hidatsa)	ARAPAHO	Kalapuya Peoples	KALAPUYA PEOPLES
Itah-Ischipahji (Hidatsa)	CHEYENNE	Kalispel	KALISPEL
Itawan	ETIWAW	Kalispell	KALISPEL
Itazipacola	SANS ARC	Kalu-xnádshu (Tonkawa)	KADOHADACHO CONFEDERACY
Itazipco or Itazipco Sioux	SANS ARC		
Itazipco Sioux	ITAZIPCO SIOUX	Kamdüka	BANNOCK CREEK SHOSHONI
Ithalé teni (Umpqua)	MISHIKHWUTMETUNNE		
Ithkyemamits	ITHKYEMAMITS	Kamia	KAMIA
Ivap'I (Shasta)	KAROK	Kammatwa Shasta	KAMMATWA SHASTA
Iwai	IWAI	Kamu'inu	NEZ PERCÉ
Jaguallapai	HUALAPAI	Kan'ka (Winnebago)	PONCA
Jaguallapai	WALAPAI	Kan-hatki	KAN-HATKI
Jallicumay	HALYIKWAMAI	Kanastóge	SUSQUEHANNA
Jameco	JAMECO	Kanawake	KANAWAKE
Jarosoma (Pima)	APACHE	Kanawha	CONOY PEOPLES
Jeaga	JEAGA	Kanawha or Pkanawha (Erroneous)	KASKINAMPO
Jece	AIS	Kanenavish (Lewis & Clark)	ARAPAHO
Jelan	JELAN	Kangitoka (Yankton Dakota)	CROW
Jemez Pueblo	JEMEZ PUEBLO	Kanienkehaka	KANAWAKE
Jicarilla Apache	JICARILLA	Kaninahoish (Chippewa)	ARAPAHO
John Day Indians	TUKSPUSH	Kanit' (Arikara)	MANDAN
Joshua	JOSHUA	Kank.'utla'atlam (Kutenai)	OKANAGON
Joso (Tewa)	HOPI	Kansa	KANSA
Juaneño	JUANEÑO	Kanza	KANSA
Jum-pys	YAVAPAI	Karankawa	KARANKAWA
Jumane	WICHITA	Karankawa proper	KARANKAWA
Jumano	SHUMAN	Karankawan Tribes	KARANKAWAN TRIBES
Jumpers	CHIPPEWA	Kariko (Comanche)	TONKAWA
Jupe Comanche	JUPE	Karok	KAROK
K'á-pätop (Kiowa)	KIOWA APACHE	Kasahá ú nu (Yuchi)	CHICKASAW
K'cu-qwic'tunne (Naltunne)	SIUSLAW	Kashinampo	KASKINAMPO
K'inähi-piäko (Kiowa)	TONKAWA	Kasihta	KASIHTA
K'o-so-o (San Ildefonso Tewa)	HOPI	Kaskaias	KIOWA APACHE
K'odalpa-Kinago (Kiowa)	SIOUX	Kaskaias (possibly)	KIOWA APACHE
K'odalpa-Kiñago (Kiowa)	DAKOTA	Kaskaskia and Kas-kas-ki-a	KASKASKIA
K'ok'-o-ro-t'u'-yu	PECOS PUEBLO	Kaskinampo	KASKINAMPO
K'qlo-qwec tunne (Chastacosta)	SIUSLAW	Kaskinonba	KASKINAMPO
Ka'-xi (Winnebago)	CROW	Kasquinampo	KASKINAMPO
Ka'i gwu	KIOWA	Kasseye'I (Tonkawa)	KADOHADACHO CONFEDERACY
Ka'nan-in (Arapaho)	ARIKARA		
Ka'neaheawastsik (Cree)	CHEYENNE	Katee (Sarsi)	BLACKFEET
Ka'nina (Zuñi)	HAVASUPAI	Kathlamet	CATHLAMET
Ka'te'nu'a'ka'	KA'TE'NU'A'KA'	Kathlaminimin	KATHLAMINIMIN
Ka-ka-I-thi (Arapaho)	SALISH	Katlagakya	WATLALA
Ka-ko'-is-tsi'-a-ta'-ni-o (Cheyenne)	SALISH	Kato	KATO
Ka-lox-la'-tce (Choctaw)	KADOHADACHO CONFEDERACY	Katskill	CATSKILL
		Katteka (Drake)	PADOUCA
Ka-ta-ka	KIOWA	Kattera	TUTELO
Ka-Ta-Ka	KIOWA APACHE	Katuku (Shasta)	CHASTACOSTA
Ka-waikah	LAGUNA PUEBLO	Kaus	COOS
Ka-wi'-na-han (Arapaho)	BLACKFEET	Kaviawach Ute	KAVIAWACH UTE
Kachkaskia	KASKASKIA	Kaw	KANSA
Kadapaus	KADAPAUS	Kawaiisu	KAWAIISU
Kádiko (Kiowa)	TONKAWA	Kawaik	LAGUNA PUEBLO
Kadohadacho	KADOHADACHO	Kawaiko (Western Group)	KERESAN PUEBLOS
Kadohadacho Confederacy	KADOHADACHO CONFEDERACY	Kawchottine	KAWCHOTTINE
		Kaweah	CAHUILLA
Kah milt-pah	KAH MILT-PAH	Kawia	CAHUILLA

Kawita	KAWITA
Kayamaici	KAYAMAICI
Ke-at	KOSO SHOSHONI
Kealedji	KEALEDJI
Kebiks	MONTAGNAIS-NASKAPI
Kecoughtan	KECOUGHTAN
Keeche	KICHAI
Keechi (also, Keechis)	KICHAI (or BAND OF WICHITA)
Keechy	KICHAI
Keenkesah	MINDAWARCARTON SIOUX
Keepers of the Western Door	SENECA
Keetoowah	CHEROKEE
Keew-ahomony (Saponi)	TUSCARORA
Kenake'n (Tobacco Klickitat)	OKANAGON
Kennebecs	ABENAKI
Keresan Pueblos	KERESAN PUEBLOS
Kern River Indians	TÜBATULABAL
Kern River Shoshoneans	TÜBATULABAL
Kettle Falls Indians	COLVILLE
Keyauwee	KEYAUWEE
Keyche	KICHAI
Keychie (Caddo)	KEYCHIE (CADDO)
Khecham	LUISEÑO PEOPLES
Khoso (Santa Clara)	HOPI
Ki'-ei-ku'-eue (Omaha)	WICHITA
Ki'-tchesh (Caddo)	KICHAI
Ki-ci'-tcac (Omaha)	KICHAI
Ki-gal-twal-la	WASCOPUN
Kiawa	KIAWA (SC)
Kiawah	KIAWA (SC)
Kiawaw	KIAWA (SC)
Kichai	KICHAI
Kickabou and ...boua (Jesuit Relations)	KICKAPOO
Kickapoo	KICKAPOO
Kickapou	KICKAPOO
Kiétsash (Wichita)	KICHAI
Kigene	KIGENE
Kighetawkigh Roanu (Iroquois)	ILLINOIS CLUSTER OF TRIBES
Kihnatsa (Hidatsa)	CROW
Kij	STONO
Kik-Ial-Lus or KikIalLus	KIKIA'LOS
Kikapo	KICKAPOO
Kikia'los	KIKIA'LOS
Kikiallu	KIKIA'LOS
Kikiallus or Kik-i-allus	KIKIA'LOS
Kikima	HALYIKWAMAI
Kikiyalus	KIKIA'LOS
Kikonino (Zuñi)	HAVASUPAI
Kiksadi Tlingit	KIKSADI TLINGIT
Kilamox	TILLAMOOK
Kilatika	KILATIKA
Killamook	TILLAMOOK GROUP
Killamuck	TILLAMOOK
Killasthokle	KILLASTHOKLE
Killawat	KILLAWAT
Kinebikowininiwak (Algonquian)	SHOSHONI, NORTHERN
Kings River Yokuts	KINGS RIVER YOKUTS
Kinipissa (Tonti)	ACOLAPISSA
Kinkipar	KINKIPAR
Kinway Ga'taqka	KIOWA
Kinya-inde (Mescalero)	JICARILLA
Kiowa	KIOWA
Kiowa (generally in older literature)	KIOWA APACHE
Kiowa Apache	KIOWA APACHE
Kioway	KIOWA APACHE
Kirikiris or Kirikurus	WICHITA
Kirishkitsu	KICHAI
Kiristinon	CREE
Kiruhikwak (Shasta)	YUROK
Kipikavvi	POTAWATOMI
Kipikawi	POTAMATOMI
Kipikuskwi	POTAWATOMI
Kishakevira (Karok)	HUPA
Kisínahis (Kichai)	KIOWA APACHE
Kitanemuk	KITANEMUK
Kitchawank	KITCHAWANK
Kitchigamich (Jesuit Relations)	KITCHIGAMICH
Kitchigamick (Wisconsin Dictionary)	KITCHIGAMICH
Kite	SUHTAI
Kitikitish	WICHITA
Kititanum and Kikitamkar	KITANEMUK
Kitkehahki	REPUBLICAN PAWNEE
Kitsai	KICHAI
KitsaiKeechy	KICHAI
Kittitas	PSHWANWAPAM
Kituhwa	CHEROKEE
Kizh	KIAWA
Kizh	STONO
Kkpayttchare ottiné (Chipewyan)	KAWCHOTTINE
Klallam	CLALLAM
Klamath	KLAMATH
Klatskanai	CLATSKANIE
Klick-a-Tack (Catlin)	KLICKITAT
Klickitat	KLICKITAT
Klinquit	KLINQUIT
Knisteneau (and ...eaux)	CREE
Ko'm-maidüm (Maidu)	ACHOMAWI
Ko'mpabi'anta (Kiowa)	KIOWA
Ko-mun'-i-tup'-i-o (Siksika)	NEZ PERCÉ
Ko-toh'-spi-tup'-I-o (Siksika)	SALISH
Koasati	KOASATI
Koh-mahts	COMANCHE
Kohaldje (Mohave)	SOUTHERN PAIUTE
Kohani	KOHAN*I
Kohátk	QUAHATTIKA
Kohenins	YAVAPAI
Kohuana	KOHUANA
Kokeni'k'ke (Kutenai)	OKANAGON
Kokenu'k'ke (Kutenai)	OKANAGON
Kokokiwak (Fox)	CROW
Kolapissas (Gravier)	ACOLAPISSA
Kolomi	KOLOMI
Koluschan	KIKSADI TLINGIT
Kom'-bo (Maidu)	YANA
Komanci	COMANCHE
Komseka-Ki'nahyup (Kiowa)	ARAPAHO
Konagen	KONAGEN
Konkau	CONCOW MAIDU
Konkoné or Komkomé	TONKAWA
Konkow and Konkow Maidu	CONCOW MAIDU
Konomihu	KONOMIHU
Konomihu	KONOMIHU
Konza	KANSA
Kool-sa-ti-ka-ra (Buffalo Eaters)	SHOSHONI EASTERN
Kootenai	KOOTENAY
Kootenay	KOOTENAY
Koots-cha	SAN FELIPE PUEBLO
Kop-tagúi (Kiowa)	JICARILLA
Kopanes	KOPANO
Kopano	KOPANO
Koroa	KOROA
Kosati	KOASATI
Kosho (Hano Tewa)	HOPI
Koskinempo	KASKINAMPO
Koso	KOSO SHOSHONI
Kosunat Ute	KOSUNAT UTE
Kotsai	KOTSOTEKA
Kotsoteka Comanche	KOTSOTEKA
Kowassati	KOASATI
Kow-was-say-ee	KOWASAYEE
Kowasayee	KOWASAYEE
Kris	CREE
Kristenaux	CREE
Kristinaux	CREE
Kû-lis'-kite hitc'lûm (Alsea)	TALTUSHTUNTUDE

454

Ku-û'-sha (Wyandot)	MUSKOGEE	Lanos	MANSO
Ku-we-ve-ka pai-ya	YAVAPAI	Lar-ti-e-lo (Lewis & Clark)	SPOKAN
Kuhtsoo-ehkuh	KOTSOTEKA	Larapihu (Pawnee)	ARAPAHO
Kúikni (Klamath)	MOLALLA	Lassik	LASSIK
Kuitare-I (Comanche)	PAWNEE	Latagawa	LATGAWA
Kuitsh	KUITSH	Latgawa	LATGAWA
Kuitsh (rel. Lower Umpqua)	UMPQUA	Láti-u or La'tiwe	MOLALLA
Kukwil' (Alsea)	MISHIKHWUTMETUNNE	Le Tetes do Boule	ROUND HEADS
Kul-hul-atsi (Creeks)	KADOHADACHO	Le Tetes do Boule (Round Heads)	HURON
	CONFEDERACY	Le Vieux Désert	VIEUX DÉSERT
Kúlua (Choctaw)	KOROA	Leaf or Sioux of the Broad Leaf	SIOUX
Kumeyaay	DIEGUEÑO	Leapers	CHIPPEWA
Kún (Apache; also to Tulkpaia)	YUMA	Lêcle'cuks (Wasco)	SPOKAN
Kun na-nar-wesh (Lewis & Clark)	ARAPAHO	Lemhi	LEMHI SHOSHONI
Kunis'tunne (Chastacosta)	ALSEA	Lemita	LIMITA
Kûnis'tûnne (Chastocosta)	ALSEA	Lenape	DELAWARE
Kunú-háyanu (Caddo)	POTAWATOMI	Lenni Lenape	DELAWARE
Kúsa	COOS	Lenope	DELAWARE
Kusco	COOSA	Lepan	LIPAN
Kusotony	KUSOTONY	Les Puans	WINNEBAGO
Kussah	COOSA	les renards	FOX
Kusso or Kussoe	COOSA	Lesser Campers	YANKTONAI SIOUX
Kusso-Natchez	EDISTO	Lezar	LEZAR
Kutaki (Fox)	CHIPPEWA	Li-ay-wa	LI-AY-WA
Kutenai	KOOTENAY	Liaywa	LIAYWA
Kutenay	KOOTENAY	Limita	LIMITA
Kutsshundika (Buffalo-eaters)	BANNOCK	Linnelinopie	DELAWARE
Kutzadika'a	KUTZADIKA'A	Lintcanre	THLINGCHADINNE
Kutzadika'a People	KUTZADIKA'A	Linway	LINWAY
Kutzadika'a People	MONO	Lipan Apache	LIPAN
Kúuspelu (Nez Percé)	KOOTENAY	Lipanes or Lipanese	LIPAN
Kwahada Comanche	KWAHADA	Little Algonkin	LITTLE ALGONKIN
Kwahadi	KWAHADA	Little Lake or Littlelake	MITOM POMO
Kwahari	KWAHADA	Little Taensa	AVOYEL
Kwaharior	KWAHADA	Lohim	LOHIM
Kwaiailk	KWAIAILK	Lohim	YAKIMA
Kwalhioqua	KWALHIOQUA	Lokota	LAKOTA
Kwapa	QUAPAW	Long Island, New York, Indian Tribes	LONG ISLAND, NEW
Kwatami	KWATAMI		YORK, INDIAN TRIBES
Kwe-net-che-chat	MAKAH	Long Tom Creek (or River) Indians	CHELEMELA KALAPUYA
Kwerhar-rehnuh	KWAHADA	Long-haired Indians	CROW
kwi'nail	QUI-NAI-ELT	Long-isle	EEL RIVER
Kwi'nail	QUINAULT	Long-Wha or Long-wha	LONGWHA
Kwillu'chini (Chinook)	CATHLAMET	Longwha	LONGWHA
Kwitcyán^a	YUMA	Loos Indians	SKIDI PAWNEE
Kwokwoos	COOS	Lopas	TOLOWA
Kwoshonipu (Shasta)	CHIMARIKO	Los Angeles Mission (Nuestra Senora	PECOS PUEBLO
Kwowahtewug (Ottawa)	MANDAN	de los Angeles de Porciuncula)	
Kwu'da	KIOWA	Los Mecos (Mexican)	COMANCHE
Kwu-the-ni (Kwalhioqua)	KWAIAILK	Loup (Fr. Wolf)	DELAWARE
Kyaukw (Alsea)	TILLAMOOK GROUP	Loup (Fr. Wolf)	MAHICAN GROUP
Kyu'-kutc hítclûm (Alsea)	TAKELMA	Loup Indians	SKIDI PAWNEE
L'Anse	L'ANSE	Lower Chehalis	CHEHALIS
La Jolla Luiseño	LA JOLLA LUISEÑO	Lower Coquille Indians	MILUK
La Plais	COMANCHE	Lower Creek	LOWER CREEK
La Purisima de Zuñi (mission name)	ZUÑI	Lower Creeks	SEMINOLE
La'-ri'hta (Pawnee)	COMANCHE	Lower De Chutes (Deschutes River)	WYAM
La-la-cas	MODOC	Lower Elwha Klallan	ELWHA KLALLAM
Lac Courte Oreille	LAC COURTE OREILLE	Lower Okanagon	SINKAIETK
Lac Vieux Désert	VIEUX DÉSERT	Lower Pend d'Oreilles	LOWER PEND D'OREILLES
Lacame	LACANE	Lower Rogue River Indians	TUTUTNI
Lacane	LACANE	Lower Umpqua	KUITSH
Lacane	NACANISH	Lowland Cree (subdivision of Plains	CREE
Lacopsele	LACOPSELE	Cree)	
Lacota	LAKOTA	Lowland Takelma	TAKELMA
Lagoons	TOLOWA	Ltsxe'als (Nestucca)	NISQUALLY
Laguna Pueblo	LAGUNA PUEBLO	Luckiamute Kalapuya	LUCKIAMUTE KALAPUYA
Lahanna	SENIJEXTEE	Luckkarso	LUCKKARSO
Lake Indians	SENIJEXTEE	Luiseño Peoples	LUISEÑO PEOPLES
Lakhota	LAKOTA	Lúk'-a-tatt (Puyallup)	KLICKITAT
Lakmiut	LOWER CREEK	Lukawi	LUKAWI
Lakmiut	LUCKIAMUTE KALAPUYA	Lukton	LUKTON
Lakota	LAKOTA	Lumbee	LUMBEE
Laleshiknom (Yuki)	KATO	Lummi	LUMMI

Lutwáwi or Lutuami (Pit River Indians; Ilmawi)	MODOC
Lyich	TYIGH
Ma tera (Catawba)	CHEROKEE
Ma'-mo a-ya-di or Ma'-mo ha-ya (Biloxi)	ALABAMA
Ma'-seip'-kih (Kiowa)	KADOHADACHO CONFEDERACY
Ma-buc-sho-roch-pan-ga (Hidasta)	SHOSHONI, NORTHERN
Maastoetsjkwe	HOPI
Mabila	MOBILE
Mac qua noot na	MIKONOTUNNE
Macapiras	MACAPIRAS
Machapunga	MACHAPUNGA
Machapunga	MACHEPUNGO
Machecou	MACHECOU
Machecoux	MACHECOU
Machepungo	MACHEPUNGO
Macheye	MAYEYE
Machias	PASSAMAQUODDY
Machikoutench	MASCOUTIN
Machkouten	MASCOUTIN
Machkoutench	MASCOUTIN
Machkouteng	MASCOUTIN
Macono	NACAO
Macousin	MASCOUTIN
Macquaejeet (Micmac)	BEOTHUK
Mactcingeha wai (Omaha & Ponca)	UTE
Mad Oats (Folles Avoines)	MENOMINEE
Maddy (band)	CHEMAPOHO KALAPUYA
Maeykan	MAHICAN
Maghay (La Salle)	MAYEYE
Maha (Lewis & Clark)	OMAHA
Mahaha	AMAHAMI
Mahahoac	MANHAHOAC
Mahán (Isleta)	COMANCHE
Máhana (Taos)	COMANCHE
Máhane (Umpqua)	KLICKITAT
Maharineck	MEHERRIN
Mahars (Lewis & Clark)	OMAHA
Maheye	MAYEYE
Mahican	MAHICAN
Mahican Group	MAHICAN GROUP
Mahigan	MAHICAN
Mahikander	MAHICAN
Mahinganak	MAHICAN
Mahock	MANHAHOAC
Mahocks	MANAHOAC
Mahpiyato (Dakota)	ARAPAHO
Mai-dec-kiz-ne (Navaho)	JEMEZ PUEBLO
Maidu	MAIDU
Maiduan	MAIDU
Maiece	MAYEYE
Maieye	MAYEYE
Maikan	MAHICAN
Maishan Apaches	KIOWA APACHES
Makadewana-ssidox (Chippewa)	BLACKFEET
Makah	MAKAH
Malecite	MALISEET
Maliseet	MALISEET
Maliseet (mistakenly)	ARMOUCHIQUOIS
Maliset	MALISEET
Malisit	MALISEET
Malleye	MAYEYE
Mämakata'wana-si'tä'-ak (Fox)	BLACKFEET
Mamekoting	MAMEKOTING
Manahoac	MANAHOAC
Manakin	MONACAN
Manamoyick	MANAMOYICK
Mandan	MANDAN
Maneaters	TONKAWA
Manetaws (APS Indian Manuscripts Collection)	HIDATSA
Mangoags	TUTELO

Mangoak (Algonquian)	NOTTAWAY
Manhahoac	MANHAHOAC
Manhansick	MANHASSET
Manhasset	MANHASSET
Manhatan	MANHATAN
Manhatesen	MANHATAN
Manhattan	MANHATAN
Manhigan (Dutch)	MAHICAN
Manhotes	MANHATAN
Manitaries	HIDATSA
Mannahoak	MANAHOAC
Manrhoat (La Salle, possibly)	KIOWA
Manso	MANSO
Manta	MANTA
Mantona	MENTO
Maqua (also, Maquas used in sing.)	MOHAWK
Maqua (Dutch)	ONEIDA
Maquies	MAYEYE
Mar-an-sho-bish-ko (Crow)	DAKOTA
Mar-an-sho-bish-ko (Crow)	SIOUX
Marachite	MALISEET
Marechite	MALISEET
Maricopa	MARICOPA
Mariposan or Maripossan	YOKUTS
Marsapeague	MARSAPEAGUE
Marsapequa	MASSAPEQUA
Marshewtooc	MARSHEWTOOC
Marshpee	MASHPEE WAMPANOAG
Mary's (or Marys) River Indians or Mary's (or Marys) River Band	CHEPENAFA KALAPUYA
Mascouteins Nadouessi	LAKOTA
Mascouten	MASCOUTIN
Mascoutin	MASCOUTIN
Masequetooc	MASEQUETOOC
Mashkoutenec	MASCOUTIN
Mashpee Wampanoag	MASHPEE WAMPANOAG
Mashppe	MASHPEE WAMPANOAG
Mashukhara (Karok)	SHASTA
Maskókî	MUSKOGEE
Maskouten	MASCOUTIN
Maskoutens-Nadouessians	LAKOTA
Maskoutin	MASCOUTIN
Massachuse	MASSACHUSETT
Massachusett	MASSACHUSETT
Massaco	MASSACO
Massapequa	MASSAPEQUA
Massasoit	WAMPANOAG
Massawomeck (John Smith, var.)	SHAWNEE
Massawomekes (John Smith)	SHAWNEE
Massawomes (John Smith, var.)	SHAWNEE
Massipee	MASHPEE WAMPANOAG
Mastutc'kwe	HOPI
Mat-che-naw-to-waig (Ottawa)	IROQUOIS LEAGUE
Mat-hat-e-vátch (Yuma)	CHEMEHUEVI
Mataveke-Paya (Yavapai)	HUALAPAI
Matáveke-Paya (Yavapai)	WALAPAI
Mathkoutench	MASCOUTIN
Mathlanob	MATHLANOB
Mathora	MENTO
Mathorha	MENTO
Matinecoc	PRAIRIE POTAWATOMI
Matinecock	MATINECOCK
Mato Pomo	MATO POMO
Matokatági (Shawnee)	OTO
Matootonha	MANDAN
Matora	MENTO
Matoua	MENTO
Matoutenta	OTO
Mattabesec	MATTABESIC
Mattabesic	MATTABESIC
Mattamuskeet	MACHAPUNGA
Mattapanient	MATTAPANIENT
Mattapoment	MATTAPANIENT
Mattaponi	MATTAPONI

Mattole	MATTOLE
Matu-es'-wi skitchi-nú-ûk (Malecite)	MICMAC
Maug-na	MAUG-NA
Mauilla	MOBILE
Mauvais Monde des Pleds-Noirs	SARCEE
Mauvila (De Soto)	MOBILE
Mavila	MOBILE
Mawatani	MANDAN
Mawhickon	MAHICAN
Maye or Mayes (sing.)	MAYEYE
Mayeye	MAYEYE
McKenzie	TSANCHIFIN KALAPUYA
Mdewahaton	MDEWAHATON
Mdewahatonwan	MDEWAHATON
Mdewakanton Sioux	MDEWAKANTON SIOUX
Mdewakanton	MDEWAHATON
Mdewkanton	MDEWAHATON
Me-Sek-Wi-Guilse	UPPER SKAGIT
Me-tum'mah	MITOM POMO
Meadow Indians	WINNEBAGO
Meamie	MIAMI
Mechkentowoon	MECHKENTOWOON
Medawah-Kanton	MDEWAKANTON SIOUX
Mee-see-qua-guilch	UPPER SKAGIT
Meghty (La Salle)	MAYEYE
Meherrin	MEHERRIN
Meidoo	MAIDU
Mekusuky (Oklahoma Village)	MIKASUKI
Meletecunk	MELETECUNK
Meli'lema	TENINO
Melukitz	MELUKITZ
Memankitonna	MEMANKITONNA
Membreño	CHIRICAHUA
Mengakonkia	MENGAKONKIA
Mengwe (Algonquian)	NOTTAWAY
Menominee	MENOMINEE
Menominee	WISCONSIN
Menominie	MENOMINEE
Menomonee	MENOMINEE
Menomonie	MENOMINEE
Mento	MENTO
Menton	MENTO
Mentou	MENTO
Menunkatuck	MENUNKATUCK
Meotac	MONTAUK PEOPLES
Meracock	MERRICK
Merikoke	MERRICK
Meroke	MERRICK
Merrick	MERRICK
Merrimac	PENNACOOK
Mescalero Apache	MESCALERO
Meshkwa kihug (own name)	FOX
Meskwaki	FOX
Mespat	MESPAT
Mesquaki	FOX
Mesquaki	SAUK
Messasagu	MESSASAGU
Metaharta	METEHARTA
Metchegamia	MICHIGAMEA
Meteharta	METEHARTA
Methow	METHOW
Metoac	MONTAUK PEOPLES
Métutahanke	MANDAN
Mewuk	MIWOK
Meyemma	CHIMARIKO
Mfskigula	PASCAGOULA
Mi'kmaq	MICMAC
Mi'kyashe (Crow)	SHOSHONI, NORTHERN
Mi-Çlauq'-tcu-wûn'ti (Alesa)	KLICKITAT
Miame	MIAMI
Miami	MIAMI
Miami proper	MIAMI
Miami proper	ATCHATCHAKANGOUEN

Mical	MICAL
Miccosukee	MIKASUKI
Miccosukee (mistakenly)	MUSKOGEE
Miccosukee	SEMINOLE
Miccosukee Creek (Catlin)	MIKASUKI
Michigamia	MICHIGAMEA
Michigan	MICHIGAMEA
Michigan Potawatomi	MICHIGAN POTAWATOMI
Michmac	MICMAC
Michopdo (village of Northwestern Divison)	MAIDU
Micmac	MICMAC
Micmaq	MICMAC
Middle Columbia Salish	COLUMBIA
Middle Missouri Tradition People	MIDDLE MISSOURI TRADITION PEOPLE
Middle Oregon Tribes (w/ Wasco, Taih, Wyam, Tenino et al.)	WALLA WALLA
Migmac	MICMAC
Miká-ati (Hidasta)	SHOSHONI, NORTHERN
Mikadeshitchisi (Kiowa Apache)	NEZ PERCÉ
Mikasuki	MIKASUKI
MikMak	MICMAC
Mikmaq	MICMAC
Mi'kmaw	MICMAC
Mi'kmawi'simk	MICMAC
Mikonotuni	MIKONOTUNNE
Mikonotunne	MIKONOTUNNE
Miluk	MILUK
Mimbreño (also Mimbreno)	TCI-HE-NDE MIMBRE
Mimgo	MINGO
Minassiniu	MUNSEE
Minataree (Catlin)	HIDATSA
Mindawarcarton Sioux	MINDAWARCARTON SIOUX
Mineami	MIAMI
Minetaree	HIDATSA
Mingo	MINGO
Mingwe	MINGO
Mingwe (Lenape/Delaware)	IROQUOIS LEAGUE
Miniconjou	MINICONJOU
Miniconju	MINICONJOU
Minishupsko (Crow)	SIOUX
Minishúpsko (Crow)	DAKOTA
Minisink	MINISINK
Minisink	MUNSEE
Minitaree	ATSINA
Minitari of the River (Mandan)	HIDATSA
Minnakenozzo Sioux	MINNAKENOZZO SIOUX
Minneconjou	MINICONJOU
Minnetaree	ATSINA
Minnetaree of Fort de Prarie	ATSINA
Minnetaree of the Plains or ...of the Prairies	ATSINA
Minnetarre	HIDATSA
Minnetarre of North Dakota	HIDATSA
Minnetwees Metaharta	METEHARTA
Minnicongew (Parkman)	MINICONJOU
Minqua (Algonquian and Dutch) very common substitution; also Minquas used as sing.	SUSQUEHANNA
Minquaon (Dutch)	SUSQUEHANNA
Minsi	MINISINK
Minsi	MUNSEE
Mintache	MISSOURI
Miscòthin	MISCÒTHIN
Miscousing	WISCONSIN
Mishi	MISHIKHWUTMETUNNE
Mishikhwutmetunne	MISHIKHWUTMETUNNE
Mishongnovi	MISHONGNOVI
Miskigúla (Biloxi)	PASCAGOULA
Miskito	MOSQUITO

Miskitu	MOSQUITO	Monozi (Maidu)	NORTHERN PAIUTE
Miskonsing	WISCONSIN	Montagnais	CREE
Missaquogue	NISSEQUOGE	Montagnais-Naskapi	MONTAGNAIS-NASKAPI
Missi-ousing	WISCONSIN	Montagne	CREE
Missiassik	MISSIASSIK	Montaineers	CREE
Mississauga Chippewa	MISSISSAUGA CHIPPEWA	Montauk	MONTAUK
Mississippi Chippewa	MISSISSIPPI CHIPPEWA	Montauk Peoples	MONTAUK PEOPLES
Missouri	MISSOURI	Montesano	MONTESANO
Missouria	MISSOURI	Monthey	MUNSEE
Mitchigamea	MICHIGAMEA	Moosehead Lake Indians	PENOBSCOT
Mitchigamia	MONTAUK	Moosehead Lake Indians	MOOSEHEAD LAKE
Mitchigamie	MICHIGAMEA		INDIANS
Mitom Pomo	MITOM POMO	Moratok	MORATOK
Mitsitá (Kansa)	WICHITA	Moratuooc	MORATUOOC
Mitutanka	MANDAN	Moraughtacund	MORAUGHTACUND
Miúxsen (Cheyenne)	TONKAWA	Moraughtacuttd	MORAUGHTACUND
Miwok	MIWOK	Mormon Snakes	SHOSHONI, NORTHERN
Mkatewetitéta (Shawnee)	BLACKFEET		> NORTHWESTERN
Mniconju	MINICONJOU	Moshome (Keresan)	NAVAJO
Mo-no'ni-o (Cheyenne)	MANDAN	Mosilian	MOSILIAN
Moache Ute	MOACHE UTE	Mosopelea	MOSOPELEA
Moadoc	MODOC	Mosquis	HOPI
Moassones (Penobscot)	ABENAKI	Mosquito	MOSQUITO
Mobile	MOBILE	Motútatak (Fox)	OTO
Mochomes	DELAWARE	Mountain Comanche	APACHE
Mococo	MOCOCO	Mountain Diggers	SOUTHERN PAIUTE
Moctobi (or Moctoby)	MOCTOBI or BILOXI or	Mountain Lemhi	LEMHI SHOSHONI
	PASCAGOULA	Mountain Ute	WEEMINUCHE UTES
Modoc	MODOC	Mow-way (a Chief, misapplied as a	KOTSOTEKA
Mogollon Apache	MOGOLLON	tribe or band)	
Mogoulacha	MOGOULACHA	Moyawance	MOYAWANCE
Moh-tau-hai'-ta-ni-o (Cheyenne)	UTE	Muache	MOACHE UTE
Mohave	MOJAVE	Muckleshoot	MUCKLESHOOT
Mohawk	MOHAWK	Mucoco	MOCOCO
Mohawk	MOHAWK RIVER	Muddy Creek	CHEMAPOHO KALAPUYA
	KALAPUYA	Muddy River Indians	PIEGAN BLACKFEET
Mohawk River Kalapuya	MOHAWK RIVER	Mugulasha	MOGOULACHA
	KALAPUYA	Mugulasha	QUINIPISSA
Moheakunnuk	MOHEGAN	Muhhekanew	MOHEGAN
Mohegan	MOHEGAN	Muhhuhwau	MUHHUHWAU
Mo-hee-con-neuh	MOHEGAN	Muhhuhwau	ORONDOC
Mohican	MAHICAN GROUP	Mukanti Molalla	MUKANTI MOLALLA
Mohiccon	MOHEGAN	Mukkudda Ozitunnug (Ottawa)	BLACKFEET
Mohock	MANHAHOAC	Muklasa	MUKLASA
Mohock	MOHAWK	Muleye	MAYEYE
Móhtawas (Comanche)	KANSA	Mulluk	MILUK
Moingonan	MOINGWENA	Multnomach	MULTNOMAH
Moingwena	MOINGWENA	Multnomah	MULTNOMAH
Moiseyu	MOISEYU	Multnomash	MULTNOMAH
Mojave	MOJAVE	Mummapacune	MUMMAPACUNE
Moki or Moki (Keresan?)	HOPI	Mûn-an'-ne-qu' tûnne	KLICKITAT
Molala	MOLALLA	(Naltunnetunne)	
Molale	MOLALLA	Muncey	MUNSEE
Molalla	MOLALLA	Muncie or Munci	MUNSEE
Molel	MOLALLA	Mundock	MUNSEE
Mollalah	MOLALLA	Munsee	MUNSEE
Monacan	MONACAN	Munsel Creek	MUNSEL CREEK
Monache	MONO	Munsie or Munsi	MUNSEE
Monachi (Yokuts)	NORTHERN PAIUTE	Mus-quah-ta	MUS-QUAH-TA
Monachie	KUTZADIKA'A	Muscaoutin	MASCOUTIN
Monasiccapano	SAPONI	Muscogee	MUSKOGEE
Monasukapanough	SAPONI	Muscogee	CREEK CONFEDERACY
Moncy	MUNSEE	Muscogulge	MUSKOGEE
Moneton	MONETON	Muscuitine	MASCOUTIN
Mono	KUTZADIKA'A	Musketoon	MASCOUTIN
Mono	MONO	Muskogee	MUSKOGEE
Mono Lake Kutzadika'a	KUTZADIKA'A	Muskogee	CREEK CONFEDERACY
Mono Lake Kutzadika'a	MONO	Muskrats	MALISEET
Mono Lake Paiute	MONO	Musquaki	MUSQUAKI
Mono Lake Paiutes	KUTZADIKA'A	Mûtsíana-taníu (Cheyenne)	KIOWA APACHE
Mono-Paviotso	PAIUTE	Mutsum	COSTANOAN
Mono-Paviotso	NORTHERN PAIUTE	Muxtsuhintan (Cheyenne)	APACHE
Monomoyick	MONOMOYICK	Mvskoke	MUSKOGEE
Monozi	PAIUTE	Mynonàmi	MYNONÀMI

N'de or Nde	APACHE
N'poch-le	SANPOIL
N'Quentl-ma-mish	N'QUENTL-MA-MISH
Na-as (Catlin)	NISKAH
Na'-to-wo-na (Cheyenne)	DAKOTA
Na'la'ni (Navaho & Comanche)	KIOWA
Na'lani (Navaho)	COMANCHE
Na'nita (Kichai)	COMANCHE
Na'taa (Wichita)	COMANCHE
Na'to-wo-na (Cheyenne)	SIOUX
Na-izha'ñ	LIPAN
Na-teté tûnne (Naltunne)	TAKELMA
Naabuggindebaig (Chippewa)	CHOCTAW
Naadawensiw (Ojibwe)	SIOUX
Naamkeek	PAWTUCKET
Naansi	NAANSI
Naas Indians or Naas River Indians	NISKAH
Nabedache	NABEDACHE
Nabeyeyxa	NABEYEYXA
Nabijos	NAVAJO
Nabiltsee	HUPA
Nabiti	NACOGDOCHE
Nabiti	NAMIDISH
Nacachao	HAINAI
Nacachau	NACACHAU
Nacachua	HAINAI
Nacadocheeto	NACANISH
Nacaha	HAINAI
Nacan	NABEDACHE
Nacanish	NABEDACHE
Nacanish	NACANISH
Nacao	NACACHAU
Nacao	NACAO
Nacaug-na	NACAUG-NA
Nacha	NECHE
Nachitos	NATCHITOCHES CONFEDERACY
Nachittoos	NATCHITOCHES CONFEDERACY
Nachtichoukas	NATCHITOCHES CONFEDERACY
Nacitos	NATCHITOCHES CONFEDERACY
Nacodissy	NACANISH
Nacodochito	NACANISH
Nacogdoche	NACOGDOCHE
Nacoho	NACACHAU
Nacomone	NACAO
Naconee	NOKONI
Naconicho	NABEDACHE
Nacono	NACONO
Nacota	NAKOTA
Nacotchtank	NACOTCHTANK
Nactythos (d'Iberville)	NATCHITOCHES CONFEDERACY
Nadaco	ANADARKO
Nadamin	NADAMIN
Nadchito (Bienville)	NATCHITOCHES CONFEDERACY
Nadíisha-déna	KIOWA APACHE
Nadona (NW Algonquians)	IROQUOIS LEAGUE
Nadooessis of the Plains	LAKOTA
Nadouesse	SIOUX
Nadouessioux (Ojibwe/Algonquian)	SIOUX
Nadouessioux Maskouten (Algonquian)	IOWA
Nadouessioux (Ojibwe/Algonquian)	SIOUX
Nadowa (Algonquian)	WYANDOT
Nadowe-is-siw	SIOUX
Nadowessie	SIOUX
Nadsoo	NANATSOHO
Naesha	NECHE
Nagodoche	NACANISH

Naguidis	NAGUIDIS
Nah'-Chee	NATCHEZ
Naheeshandeenah	KIOWA APACHE
Nahmah-er-nuh Comanche	NAHMAH-ER-NUH
Nahyssan	NAHYSSAN
Nai-te-zi (Navajo)	ZUÑI
Naishandina	KIOWA APACHE
Nakahanawan	NAKANAWAN
Nakanawan	NAKANAWAN
Nakasa	NAKASA
Nakasé	NAKASA
Nákasine'na	ARAPAHO, NORTHERN
Naked Indians (language confusion)	MIAMI
Naketosh	NATCHITOCHES CONFEDERACY
Nakoda	ASSINIBOIN
Nakoni	NOKONI
Nakota (call themselves)	ASSINIBOIN
Nakota	NAKOTA
Naks'-at (Pima and Papago)	MOJAVE
Naltunne	NALTUNNE
Nambe Pueblo	NAMBE PUEBLO
Namidish	NACOGDOCHE
Namidish	NAMIDISH
Nanatsoho	NANATSOHO
Nandacao	ANADARKO
Nandakoe	NANDAKOE
Naniaba Choctaw	NANIABA CHOCTAW
Nanoniks-kare'niki (Kichai)	CHEYENNE
Nansamond	NANSEMOND
Nansemond	NANSEMOND
Nantaughtacund	NANTAUGHTACUND
Nanticocs	NANTICOKE
Nanticoke	NANTICOKE
Nantikoke	NANTICOKE
Nantuxet	NANTUXET
Naouydiche	GUASCO
Napgitache	NATCHITOCHES CONFEDERACY
Napochi	NAPOCHI
Naquitoches (Belle-Isle)	NATCHITOCHES CONFEDERACY
Nar-a-tah (Waco)	COMANCHE
Nar-wah-ro (Wichita)	DELAWARE
Narankamigdok epitsik arenanbak	ABENAKI
Naraticon	NARATICON
Narcotah	NARCOTAH
Narragansett	NARRAGANSETT
Narsh-tiz-a (Apache)	ZUÑI
Nasahossoz	NACANISH
Nascapee	MONTAGNAIS-NASKAPI
Nascha	NECHE
Nashaway	NASHUA
Nashi'tosh	NATCHITOCHES CONFEDERACY
Nashteíse (Apache)	PIMA
Nashtezhe (Naajo)	ZUÑI
Nashua	NASHUA
Nashuay	NASHUA
Nasitti	NATCHITOCHES CONFEDERACY
Nasoni	NASONI
Nasoni, Upper	NASONI, UPPER
Nasoni, Upper	NASONI, UPPER
Nasoui	NASONI
Nassonite	NASONI
Násuia kwe (Zuni)	UTE
Nasumi	NASUMI
Nataché	NAKASA
Natao	ADAES
Natawesiwak (Ojibwe/Algonquian)	SIOUX
Natchés	NAKASA
Natches	NATCHEZ
Natchez	NATCHEZ

459

Natchitoches	NATCHITOCHES CONFEDERACY	Nespelem	NESPELIM
Natchitoches	NATCHITOCHES	Nespelim	NESPELIM
Natchitoches Confederacy	NATCHITOCHES CONFEDERACY	Nesta	NECHE
		Nestucca Tillamook	NESTUCCA TILLAMOOK
Natchitoches, Upper	NATCHITOCHES, UPPER	Netela	JUANEÑO
Nateotetain	NATEOTETAIN	Netsepoye	BLACKFEET
Natick	NATICK	Neuse Indians	NEUSIOK
Natinnoh-hoi	HUPA	Neusiok	NEUSIOK
Natio Luporum	ABENAKI	Neutral Nation	NEUTRALS
Nation of Fire (Huron)	MASCOUTIN	Neutrals	NEUTRALS
Nation of the Willows	HAVASUPAI	Neuustooc	NEUUSTOOC
Nations of the North	NATIONS OF THE NORTH	New River Indians	KAMIA
Natni or Natnihina (Arapaho)	DAKOTA	New York Algonquin	WICKQUASGECK
Natságana (Caughawaga)	ABENAKI	Newichwannock (Indian name for Dover)	PISCATAQUA
Natsoho	NANATSOHO	Nez Percé	NEZ PERCÉ
Natsshostanno	NATSSHOSTANNO	Nez Percé (traders' nickname)	IOWA
Natsvto	NANATSOHO	Nhíkana (Shawnee)	MAHICAN GROUP
Natsytos	NATCHITOCHES CONFEDERACY	NI'chihine'na (Arapaho)	KIOWA
		Ni'ckitc hitclûm (Alsea)	DAKUBETEDE
Natsytos (d'Iberville)	NATCHITOCHES CONFEDERACY	Ni'ekeni	BEAR RIVER INDIANS OF CALIFORNIA
Nauche	NATCHEZ	Ni'ris-hari's-ki'riki (Wichita)	KADOHADACHO CONFEDERACY
Naudi	NAUDI		
Naugdoche	NACANISH	Ni-he-ta-te-tup'i-o (Siksika)	KALISPEL
Nausegooc	NAUSEGOOC	Nia'rhari's-kurikiwa'ahuski (Wichita)	ARAPAHO
Nauset	NAUSET	Niantic	NIANTIC
Navaho	NAVAJO	Niantic, Eastern	NIANTIC, EASTERN
Navajo	NAVAJO	Niantic, Western	NIANTIC, WESTERN
Navasink	NAVASINK	Nicariaga	NICARIAGA
Navóne (Comanche)	LIPAN	Niciatl	SEECHELT
Nawidish	NACOGDOCHE	Nicoleño	NICOLEÑO
Nawkohnee	NOKONI	Niere'rikwats-kuni'ki (Wichita)	CHEYENNE
Nawkoni	NOKONI	Nimiipuu	NEZ PERCÉ
Náwunena	ARAPAHO, SOUTHERN	Nimipu	NEZ PERCÉ
Nawuitoches	NATCHITOCHES CONFEDERACY	Nipegon	WINNEBAGO
		Nipissin	NIPISSIN
Nawyehkuh	NOKONI	Nipissing	NIPISSIN
Nazone	NASONI	Nipmuc	NIPMUC
Nda kun-dadéhe (Lipan)	KARANKAWAN TRIBES	Nipmuck	NIPMUC
Ndaton8atendi (Huron)	POTAWATOMI	Nipnet	NIPMUC
Nde-nda-i	NDE-NDA-I CHIRICAHUA	Nipnuck	NIPMUC
Nednhis (sub-group)	NDE-NDA-I CHIRICAHUA	Nishinam Maidu	NISHINAM MAIDU
Ne'me ne or Nimenim or Numa	COMANCHE	Niskah	NISKAH
Né-a-ya-og (Cree)	CHIPPEWA	Nisohone	NASONI
Ne-e-no-il-no	MONTAGNAIS-NASKAPI	Nisqualli	NISQUALLY
Ne-gá-tce (Winnebago)	CHIPPEWA	Nisqualli or Nesqually	NISQUALLY
Nebadache	NEBADACHE	Nisqually	NISQUALLY
Nebagindibe (Chippewa)	SALISH	Nissequoge	NISSEQUOGE
Nechacokee	NECHACOKEE	Niútachi	MISSOURI
Nechacolee	NECHACOLEE	No-ochi or Notch	UTE
Nechaui	NECHAUI	Nó-si or Nó-zi	YANA
Nechavi	NECHAUI	Noam-kekhl (Wintum)	YUKI
Neche	NECHE	Nocao	NACACHAU
Nechegansett	PENNACOOK	Noche (Garcés, 1775-1776)	YOKUTS
Nednhi (sub-band)	NDE-NDA-I/CHIRICAHUA	Nochpeem	NOCHPEEM
Neekeetoo	NEEKEETOO	Nocodosh	NACANISH
Neepmuck	NIPMUC	Nocono	NACAO
Neepnet	NIPMUC	Nocony	NOKONI
Nehalem Tillamook	NEHALEM TILLAMOOK	Nogatl	NOGATL
Nehantic	NIANTIC	Noisy Pawnee (Gov. William Clark)	TAPAGE PAWNEE
Neihahat	NEIHAHAT	Nokoni	NOKONI
Neipnett	NIPMUC	Nokonmi (Yuki)	POMO PEOPLES
Nemaha	HASSINUNGA	Nom-kewel	NOMLAKI
Nementina	TREMENTINA	Nom-laka	NOMLAKI
Némeréxka (Comanche)	TONKAWA	Nomalaki	NOMALAKI
Nenetgo	DELAWARE	Nome Lackee	NOMLAKI
Neponset	NEPONSET	Nomelaki	NOMLAKI
Nerm	COMANCHE	Nomi Lackee	NOMLAKI
Nermernuh	COMANCHE	Nomlaki	NOMLAKI
Nesaquake	NESAQUAKE	Nongatl	NOGATL
Nesaquake	NISSEQUOGE	Noo-Seh-Chatl	NOO-SEH-CHATL
Neshamini	NESHAMINI	Noo-Wha-Ha	NOO-WHA-HA
Nesilextci'n or .n.selixtci'n	SANPOIL	Nook-wa-chah-mish	NOOK-WA-CHAH-MISH

Nooksack	NOOKSACK
Nooksak or Nootsak	NOOKSACK
Nootsak; also used for others	COLUMBIA
Noquet	NOQUET
Norridgewock	NORRIDGEWOCK
Norteños or Nortenos	NATIONS OF THE NORTH
Norteños	PIRO PUELBO GROUP
Northeastern Maidu	MAIDU
Northern Cheyenne	NORTHERN CHEYENNE
Northern Group of the Foothills Yokuts	NORTHERN GROUP OF THE FOOTHILLS YOKUTS
Northern Molalla (U.S. Code)	MOLALLA
Northern Paiute	NORTHERN PAIUTE
Northern Paiute Indians of Mono Lake	KUTZADIKA'A
Northern Paiute of Oregon	WALPAPI
Northern Pawnee	ARIKARA
Northwest Indians Fisheries Commission (NWIFC)	NORTHWEST INDIANS FISHERIES COMMISSION (NWIFC)
Northwestern Maidu	MAIDU
Northwestern Shoshoni	SHOSHONI, NORTHERN > NORTHWESTERN
Nota-á (Navaho)	UTE
Notchitoches	NATCHITOCHES CONFEDERACY
Nothern Group of the Valley Yokuts	NOTHERN GROUP OF THE VALLEY YOKUTS
Nottaway	NOTTAWAY
Nouga (Eskimo)	KAWCHOTTINE
Nouista	NECHE
Nouket	NOQUET
Nouquet	NOQUET
Nsekau's or Ns tiwat (Nestucca)	CLACKAMAS
Nsietshawas	TILLAMOOK GROUP
Ntlakyapamuk	NTLAKYAPAMUK
Ntlakyapamuk	OKANAGON
Nu-sklaim	CLALLAM
Nu-so-lupsh (for Upper Cowlitz & Upper Chehalis)	COWLITZ
Nu-so-lupsh (Sound Indians)	KWAIAILK
Nuciu	UTE
Nuestra Senora de Guadalupe de Zuñi (mision name)	ZUÑI
Nuh-lum-mi	LUMMI
Nuklésh (Skagit)	LUMMI
Nuktusem or Nktusem (Salish)	DAKOTA
Nuktusem or Nktusem (Salish)	SIOUX
Num-ee-muss (Yuork)	HUPA
Nüma	SOUTHERN PAIUTE
Numakaki	MANDAN
Numni	NUMNI
Nutaa (Chukchansi Yokuts)	NORTHERN PAIUTE
Nwa-ka (Tuscarora)	CHIPPEWA
Nyack	NYACK
Nyavapai	YAVAPAI
O-dug-am-eeg (Chippewa)	FOX
O-e'-tun'-i-o (Cheyenne)	CROW
O-no'-ni-o (Cheyenne)	ARIKARA
O-o'ho-mo-i'-o (Cheyenne)	DAKOTA
O-o-ho-mo-i'-o (Cheyenne)	SIOUX
Oat-lash-shoots	SHALEE
Obispeño Chumash	OBISPEÑO CHUMASH
Obwahnug (Chippewa)	DAKOTA
Obwahnug, Wanak (Chippewa)	SIOUX
Ocale	OCALE
Ocaneechi	OCCANEECHI
Occaneechee	OCCANEECHI
Occaneechi	OCCANEECHI
Ochechote	OCHECHOTE
Ochee	YUCHI
Ochesee (Hitchiti)	MUSKOGEE
Ochesee or Ocheese	YUCHI
Ocheti shakowin "the seven council fires"	DAKOTA
Ocheti shakowin (Dakota)	SIOUX
Ochie'tari-ronnon (Wyandot)	CHEROKEE
Ocona	OCONEE
Oconee	OCONEE
Oconee	KAWITA
Oconi	OCONEE
Odawa	OTTAWA
Ofo or Ofogoula	MOSOPELEA
Ogillallah (Parkman)	OGLALA
Oglala	OGLALA
Ogoize (Kalispel)	BANNOCK
Ohio Iroquois	MINGO
Ohio Seneca	MINGO
Ohio-based Shawnee	MINGO
Ohongeeoquena	OHONGEEOQUENA
Ojibwa	CHIPPEWA
Ojibway	CHIPPEWA
Ojibbeway	CHIPPEWA
Ojibwe	CHIPPEWA
Okahoki	OKAHOKI
Okanagon	OKANAGON
Okandanda Sioux	OKANDANDA SIOUX
Okangan	OKANAGON
Okatiokinans	OKATIOKINANS
Oke-Choy-atte	ALABAMA
Okehai	OKEHAI
Okelousa	OKELOUSA
Okena.qai'n	OKANAGON
Okena.qai'n (Ntlakyapamuk)	OKANAGON
Okinagan	OKANAGON
Okinagon	OKANAGON
Okmulgee	OKMULGEE
Okwanuchu	OKWANUCHU
Omaha	OMAHA
Omahaw	OMAHA
Omanomini (Chippewa)	MENOMINEE
Onagungees or Onnogonges (Iroquois)	ABENAKI
Onatheaqua	ONATHEAQUA
Onaumanient	ONAWMANIENT
Onawmanient	ONAWMANIENT
Ondatawawat (Huron)	OTTAWA
Onechechaug	PATCHOAG MONTAUK
Oneida and O-nei-da	ONEIDA
Oneota	ONEOTA
Oneyda	ONEIDA
Ongwanosionni'	IROQUOIS LEAGUE
Oni-häº (Cheyenne)	OMAHA
Onneiout (Fr. derivation of Huron)	ONEIDA
Onnontiogg	CHEROKEE
Onodaga	ONONDAGA
Onondaga	ONONDAGA
Onondagoes	ONONDAGA
Ontario	ONTARIO
Ontonagon	ONTONAGON
Ontponea	ONTPONEA
Ontponie	ONTPONEA
Ontwagana	SHAWNEE
Onyota'a:ká (own name)	ONEIDA
Oohenonpa	TWO KETTLES
Oohenumpa	TWO KETTLES
Oohenunpa	TWO KETTLES
Oohy (Pima)	HUALAPAI
Oohy (Pima)	WALAPAI
Oop (Papago)	APACHE
Oop or Oohp (Pima)	NAVAJO
Ootlashoots	SHALEE
Op or Awp (Pima)	APACHE
Opelousa	OPELOUSA
Openagoes	PASSAMAQUODDY
Openaji	ABENAKI

461

Openaji (mistakenly; see Abenaki)	DELAWARE
Openaki	ABENAKI
Openaki (mistakenly; see Abenaki)	DELAWARE
Oquagas (used in the plural, the name referred to the inhabitants of the cluster of four separate towns)	ONEIDA
Oraibi	ORAIBI
Orcoquisac	ORCOQUISAC
Orista	EDISTO
Orleans Indians	KAROK
Orondoc	ORONDOC
Orondock	ORONDOC
Orunges	MAHICAN GROUP
Osa'kiwug	SAUK
Osage	OSAGE
Osaoe	OSAGE
Osaw	OZAW
Oshahak (Fox)	DAKOTA
Oshahak (Fox)	SIOUX
Oshawanoag (Ottawa)	SHAWNEE
Osochi	OSOCHI
Ossipe	MOSOPELEA
Ossipee	OSSIPEE
Ostiagahoroones (Iroquois)	CHIPPEWA
Oswegatchi	OSWEGATCHI
Otä's-itä'niuw (Cheyenne)	KADOHADACHO CONFEDERACY
Otaharton	WAHPETUNWAN SIOUX
Otayáchgo (Mahican & Delaware)	NANTICOKE
Otcenake' or Otcena.qui'n (Salish)	OKANAGON
Otcenake' or Otcena.qai'n	OKANAGON
Oto	OTO
Otochassi	UZUTIUHI
Otochiahi.	UZUTIUHI
Otoe	OTO
Otogamie (Jefferson Notes, Query XI)	FOX
Ottawa	OTTAWA
Otto	OTO
Ottowa	OTTAWA
Ottoway	OTTAWA
Ouachanon	OUACHANON
Ouachita	OUACHITA
Ouade	GUALE
Ouanakina	OUANAKINA
Ouanchita	OUACHITA
Ouchage	OSAGE
Oudataouatouat (Wyandot)	ILLINOIS CLUSTER OF TRIBES
Ouendat	WYANDOT
Ouesperie	MOSOPELEA
Ouiatanon	WEA
Ouiàtonon	OUIÀTONON
Ouichita	WICHITA
Ouinepegi	WINNEBAGO
Ouisconsin	MENOMINEE
Ouisconsing	OUISCONSING
Ouisconsing	WISCONSIN
Quizqui	KASKINAMPO
Quizquiz	KASKINAMPO
Ouma or Oumas	HOUMA
Ousasoy	OUSASOY
Ousita	WICHITA
Outagami or Outagamie (original name)	FOX
Outimac	OUTIMAC
Outitchakouk (Jesuits)	KICKAPOO
Ouyas	WEA
Ouyas-tanons	WEA
Ouyatanon	WEA
Ovedsita	OVEDSITA
Owaragees (Iroquois)	PENNACOOK
Owassissas	OWASSISSAS
Owenagunges (Iroquois)	ABENAKI
Owens Valley Paiute	OWENS VALLEY PAIUTE
Owhillapsh (erroneous)	KWALHIOQUA
Oyadagahroenes (Iroquois)	CATAWBA
Oyata'ge'ronon (Iroquois)	CHEROKEE
Ozage	OSAGE
Ozaw	OZAW
Ozette	OZETTE
Ozimie	OZIMIE
P'a-qu-lah (Jemez)	PECOS PUEBLO
P'e'-a-ku' (Keresan)	PECOS PUEBLO
P'ónin (Isleta)	APACHE
Pa Ka'-san-tse (Osage)	NEZ PERCÉ
Pa O-bde'ca (Yankton Dakota)	SALISH
Pa s falaya	CHOCTAW
Pa'gonotch	SOUTHERN PAIUTE
Pabierni'n (Isleta)	KERESAN PUEBLOS
Pacer Band of Apache	KIOWA APACHE
Padani	ARIKARA
Padani	PAWNEE
Padduca	KIOWA APACHE
Padouca	PADOUCA
Padouca (from Penateka band by early French and Spanish)	COMANCHE
Padouca (misassigned by some writers)	KIOWA
Padouca (from *padu-kesh* meaning "enemy people" by early French)	APACHE
Padowaga	PADOWAGA
Padowaga? (Drake)	SENECA
Paego (Keresan)	PECOS PUEBLO
Páei wasábe (Ponda & Omaha)	WICHITA
Paequiu or Paequiuala (Keresan)	PECOS PUEBLO
Paganavo (Shoshoni & Comanche)	CHEYENNE
Págowitch (Southern Ute)	NAVAJO
Paguate	PAGUATE
Pah Utahs	SOUTHERN PAIUTE
Pah Ute or Pah-Ute	PAIUTE
Pah-kee (Shoshoni)	BLACKFEET
Pah-rú-sá-páh (Chemehuevi)	SOUTHERN PAIUTE
Pahkanapîl	TÜBATULABAL
Pahmap	PAHMAP
Pahodja	IOWA
Pahucah	PADOUCA
Pahvant Ute	PAHVANT UTE
Paifan amim or Päifan amím (Luckiamute Kalapuya)	ALSEA
Pailsh	PAILSH
Painyá (Havasupai)	PIMA
Paiute	PAIUTE
Paiutes of Mono Lake	KUTZADIKA'A
Pakana	PAKANA
Pala Luiseño	PALA LUISEÑO
Palache	APALACHEE
Palache	PALACHE
Pallotepellow (Lewis & Clark)	PALOUSE
Paloos	PALOUSE
Paloos	VENTUREÑO CHUMASH
Palouse	PALOUSE
Pamacocack	PAMACOCACK
Pambizimina (Shoshoni)	SIOUX
Pambizimina (Shoshoni)	DAKOTA
Pamlico	PAMLICO
Pampe Chyimina (Ute)	SIOUX
Pámpe Chyimina (Ute)	DAKOTA
Pamptecough	PAMPTECOUGH
Pamunkee	PAMUNKEY
Pamunkey	PAMUNKEY
Pamunkie	PAMUNKEY
Panaca	PANACA
Panackee	BANNOCK
Panai'ti	BANNOCK
Panamint (common name)	KOSO
Panana or Pana or Panamaha	PAWNEE
Panauuaiooc	PANAWICKY
Panawicky	PANAWICKY

Paneassa	WICHITA
Pani (as were the Pawnee)	ARIKARA
Pani Mahas or Panias Mahars	PAWNEE
Pani or Panies	PAWNEE
Pania	PAWNEE
Pania Luup (Wolf Indians)	PAWNEE
Panimahaor	PAWNEE
Panis	PAWNEE
Panis blanc	WICHITA
Panis blancs	WICHITA
Panis noir	WICHITA
Panis piques	WICHITA
Panis piqués or picks	WICHITA
Panis-maha or Panishmaha	SKIDI PAWNEE
Pannack	BANNOCK
Panyi Waewe (Iowa, Oto, & Missouri)	WICHITA
Paoneneheo (Cheyenne)	PAWNEE
Paouichtigouin (Jesuit)	CHIPPEWA
Papago	PAPAGO
Papikaha (Marquette, 1673)	QUAPAW
Papitsinima (Comanche)	SIOUX
Papitsinima (Comanche)	DAKOTA
Papshpun'lema (Yakima)	KALISPEL
Papspê'lu (Nez Percé)	COLUMBIA
Par-is-ca-oh-pan-ga (Hidatsa)	CROW
Paraje	PARAJE
Parkeenaum	PARKEENAUM
Pascagoula	PASCAGOULA
Pascataqua	PISCATAQUA
Pascataway	CONOY
Pascataway	PISCATAQUA
Pasecg-na	PASECG-NA
Pashóhan (Pawnee)	IOWA
Pasinog-na	PASINOG-NA
Paspageghe	PASPEHEAN
Paspahegh	PASPEHEAN
Paspehean	PASPEHEAN
Pasquotank	WEAPEMEOC
Passamaquoddy	PASSAMAQUODDY
Passayonk	PASSAYONK
Pastate	PASTATE
Pastate	POSTITO
Pastia	PASTIA
Pastia	PASTATE
Pastia	POSTITO
Pataquilla	PATAQUILLA
Pataraabuay	SHUMAN
Patarabueyes	SHUMAN
Pataunck	PATAUNCK
Patawatomi	POTAWATOMI
Patawattimie	POTAWATOMI
Patchoag	POOSPATUCK
Patchoag Montauk	PATCHOAG MONTAUK
Patchogue	PATCHOAG MONTAUK
Patchogue	PATCHOGUE
Patchogue	POOSPATUCK
Patchogue (a village)	MONTAUK PEOPLES
Pathague	UNKECHAUG
Patiri	PATIRI
Patoka (Osage)	COMANCHE
Patôuvomek	PATÔUVOMEK
Patshenin	BOTSHENIN
Patshenins	OCCANEECHI
Pattawatima	POTAWATOMI
Pattwin	PATWIN
Patuxent	PATUXENT
Patwin	PATWIN
Pauch	CROW
Paugusset	PAUGUSSET
Pauma Luiseño	PAUMA LUISEÑO
Paunies	PAWNEE
Paviotso	NORTHERN PAIUTE
Pavogowunsin Ute	PAVOGOWUNSIN UTE
Pawistucienemuck	PAWISTUCIENEMUCK

Pawnee	PAWNEE
Pawnee of the Platte	PAWNEE
Pawnee Pact	WICHITA
Pawnee Pict or Pick (no connection to Pawnee of the Platte; an adapation of early French, Panis piqués)	WICHITA
Pawokti	PAWOKTI
Pawtucket	PAWTUCKET
Paxuado ameti (Yavapai)	HUALAPAI
Páxuádo ámeti (Yavapai)	WALAPAI
Payankatank	PAYANKATANK
Payankatank	PIANKATANK
Payankatonk	PIANKATANK
Páyi (Kansa)	PAWNEE
Pe ga'-hdo-ke (Kansa)	NEZ PERCÉ
Pe-warea	PEORIA
Peadea	PEDEE, also PEE DEE INDIANS OF BEAVER CREEK
Peahko (Santa Ana)	PECOS PUEBLO
Peakuní (Laguna)	PECOS PUEBLO
Peanketan	PIANKATANK
Peanquicha	PEANQUICHA
Peaux-de-Lièvres	KAWCHOTTINE
Pecan (Drake)	NIPMUC
Pechanga Luiseño	PECHANGA LUISEÑO
Pecos	PECOS PUEBLO
Pecos Pueblo	PECOS PUEBLO
Pedee	PEDEE, also PEE DEE INDIANS OF BEAVER CREEK
Peedee	PEDEE, also PEE DEE INDIANS OF BEAVER CREEK
Pee Dee	PEDEE
Pee Dee Indians of Beaver Creek	PEE DEE INDIANS OF BEAVER CREEK
Peel River Kutchin	TATLIT-KUTCHIN
Pegan	CHABANAKONGKOMUN
Pehnahner	PEHNAHTERKUH
Pehnahterkuh	PEHNAHTERKUH
Peigan	PIEGAN BLACKFEET
Peki'neni (Fox)	POTAWATOMI
Pelloatpallah	PALOUSE
Pelollpellow	NEZ PERCÉ
Pelone	APACHE
Penacook	PENNACOOK
Penande	PEHNAHTERKUH
Penateka	PEHNAHTERKUH
Pend d'Oreilles	KALISPEL
Penetethka	PEHNAHTERKUH
Pennacook	PENNACOOK
Pennacook (improperly used)	PAWTUCKET
Penobscot	PENOBSCOT
Penobscots (mistakenly)	ARMOUCHIQUOIS
Penointikara (Honey-eaters)	BANNOCK
Pensacola	PENSACOLA
Pentagouet	PENOBSCOT
Pentucket	PAWTUCKET
Penxaye	APACHE
People at the Landing	CAYUGA
People of Filthy (or Stinky) Water	WINNEBAGO
People of Nekelim or Nehalem	TILLAMOOK GROUP
People of the Dawn	PASSAMAQUODDY
People of the Dust	GOSIUTE SHOSHONI
People of the Earth Lodges	MANDAN
People of the Fish Ground or Marsh	SISATONE SIOUX
People of the Flint	KANAWAKE
People of the Flint	MOHAWK
People of the Great Hill	SENECA
People at the Long House	FIVE NATIONS OF THE IROQUOIS
People of the Mountain	ONONDAGA

People of the Northern Lights	ABENAKI
People of the Pines	SAN MANUEL
People of the River	WANAPAM
People of the Round Earth	NAMBE PUEBLO
People of the Standing Stone	ONEIDA
Peoria and Pe-o-ri-a	PEORIA
Pepicokia	PEPICOKIA
Pepikokia	PEPICOKIA
Pequawket	PEQUAWKET
Pequot	PEQUOT
Pequot of Massachusetts (Catlin)	MOHEGAN
Perquiman	WEAPEMEOC
Petsikla (Yurok)	KAROK
Petun	TANCAGUE
Petun	TIONONTATI
Pex'-ge (Navaho)	JICARILLA
Pezhi'-wokeyotila (Teton Dakota)	SHOSHONI, NORTHERN
Pharoah, Pharaones or Pharoaha	FARAON
Pheasant People	MANDAN
Phillips's Indians (for King Phillip)	WAMPANOAG
Pi'-ke-e-wai-I-ne (Picuria)	JICARILLA
Pi-ci'-kse-ni-tup'I-o (Siksika)	SHOSHONI, NORTHERN
Pi-ta'-da	PAWNEE
Pianguichia	PIANKESHAW
Piankashaw and Pi-an-ke-shaw	PIANKESHAW
Piankatank	PIANKATANK
Piankenshaw	PIANKESHAW
Piankeshaw	PIANKESHAW
Piankisha	PIANKESHAW
Piankishaw	PIANKESHAW
Pianria	PIANRIA
Picks	WICHITA
Picuris Pueblo	PICURIS PUEBLO
Pidees	PEDEE, also PEE DEE INDIANS OF BEAVER CREEK
Piegan	PIEGAN BLACKFEET
Piegan Blackfeet	PIEGAN BLACKFEET
Pierced Noses	NEZ PERCÉ
Pierced Noses (traders)	IOWA
Pikakwanarat Ute	PIKAKWANARAT UTE
Pikuni	PIEGAN BLACKFEET
Pikuria	PICURIS PUEBLO
Pima	PIMA
Pima Alto	PIMA
Pimocag-na	PIMOCAG-NA
Pinal (NOT the Pinal Coyotero)	PINALEŃO
Pinal Coyotero Apache	PINAL COYOTERO
Pinaleńo (in error)	PINAL COYOTERO
Pinaleńo Apache	PINALEŃO
Pinataqua	CONOY
Pineifu (Kalapuya, other)	CHEPENAFA KALAPUYA
Pineug-na	PINEUG-NA
Pinneshow	PINNESHOW
Pioche	PANACA
Pioria	PEORIA
Pipatsje	MARICOPA
Piro Puelbo Group	PIRO PUELBO GROUP
Piscataqua	PISCATAQUA
Piscataqua	CONOY
Piscataqua	PAWTUCKET
Piscataway	PISCATAQUA
Piscataway (village name)	CONOY
Piscattaway	CONOY
Pishakulk (Yakima)	SIOUX
Pishakulk (Yakima)	DAKOTA
Pishquitpah	PISHQUITPAH
Pisko	PISQUOSE
Pisquose	PISQUOSE
Pisquow	WENATCHEE
Pisquouse (Salish)	WENATCHEE
Pissasec	PISSASEC
Pit Indians	PIT INDIANS
Pit River Indians	ACHOMAWI

Pitahauerat Pawnee	TAPAGE PAWNEE
Pitanisha (Yokut)	TŰBATULABAL
Pitchinávo (Comanche)	WICHITA
Pithlako	PITHLAKO
Pkíwi-léni (Shawnee)	MIAMI
Plains Appache	PADOUCA
Plains Cree (River Cree and Lowland Cree)	CREE
Plains Dwellers	LAKOTA
Plains-hunting Sherry-dika	SHOSHONI, NORTHERN
Plains Ojibwa	PLAINS OJIBWA
Plats-Côtes-de-Chien	THLINGCHADINNE
Playano Salinas	PLAYANO SALINAS
Playsanos	STONO
Playsanos (all California	KIAWA
Po'-ge-hdo-ke (Dakota)	NEZ PERCÉ
Po'-o-mas (Cheyenne)	BLACKFEET
Po-suwae-geh	POJOAQUE PUEBLO
Póanïn (Sandia & Isleta)	APACHE
Pocasset	POCASSET
Pocatello's Band, Chief	BANNOCK CREEK SHOSHONI
Pocomtuc	POCUMTUC
Pocumtuc	POCUMTUC
Pocomtuck	POCUMTUC
Pocutuc	POCUMTUC
Podunk	PODUNK
Pohoc	BACKHOOK
Pohogue	POHOGUE SHOSHONI
Pohoy	POHOY
Pointed Hearts	SKITSWISH
Pojoaque Pueblo	POJOAQUE PUEBLO
Pokanoket	WAMPANOAG
Polacco	POLAKAKAI
Polakakai	POLAKAKAI
Poloma	APACHE
Polu'ksalgi (Creek)	BILOXI
Pomeiooc	POMEIOOC
Pomo Peoples	POMO PEOPLES
Pompton	POMPTON
Ponca	PONCA
Poncakanet	WAMPANOAG
Poncar or Poncarar	PONCA
Poncha	PONCA
Ponka	PONCA
Ponkapoag	PONKAPOAG
Ponkipog	PONKAPOAG
Poosepatuck	POOSPATUCK
Poosepatuck	UNKECHAUG
Poospatuck	POOSPATUCK
Pooy	POHOY
Poquonock	POQUONOCK
Porcupine Indians	MICMAC
Port Gamble S'Klallam	PORT GAMBLE S'KLALLAM
Port Orford	PORT ORFORD
Port Townsend Indians	CHIMAKUM
Poso Creek Yokuts	POSO CREEK YOKUTS
Posoy	POHOY
Postito	POSTITO
Postito	PASTATE
Potano	POTANO
Potapaco	POTAPACO
Potawatomi	POTAWATOMI
Potawatomi of the Woods	POTAWATOMI OF THE WOODS
Potawatami	POTAWATOMI
Potawatamie	POTAWATOMI
Potawatomi	POTAWATOMI
Potawattimie	POTAWATOMI
Poteskeet	WEAPEMEOC
Potoash	POTOASH
Potomac	POTOMAC

Potomac or Potomack	POTOMAC
Pottawatami or Pottawatamy	POTAWATOMI
Pattawatima or Pottawatimie	POTAWATOMI
Pottawatomie	POTAWATOMI
Pottawattimie	POTAWATOMI
Pottowautomie	POTAWATOMI
Pottowotomee	POTAWATOMI
Poualak or Pounak (Fr. For Aab-boin-ug)	DAKOTA
Poualak or Pounak (French for Ab-boin-ug)	SIOUX
Poutawatamie	POTAWATOMI
Pouteotamie	POTAWATOMI
Powhatan	POWHATAN
Powhatan Confederacy	POWHATAN CONFEDERACY
Prairie Apache	JICARILLA
Prairie Apaches	KIOWA APACHE
Prairie Indians	LAKOTA
Prairie Potawatomi	PRAIRIE POTAWATOMI
Praying Indians	NATICK
Praying Indians	PRAYING INDIANS
Prickled Panis	WICHITA
Psch-wan-wap-pam	PSHWANWAPAM
Pshwanwapam	PSHWANWAPAM
Puans	WINNEBAGO
Puants	WINNEBAGO
Pubug-na	PUBUG-NA
Pudding River Indians	AHANTCHUYUK
Pueblo de Las Humanas	GRAN QUIVIRA PUEBLO
Pueblo Peoples	PUEBLO PEOPLES
Puk-tis (Pawnee)	OMAHA
Pun-nush	BANNOCK
Puncah (Catlin)	PONCA
Puncha (Catlin)	PONCA
Punkapog	PONKAPOAG
Purisimeño Chumash	PURISIMEÑO CHUMASH
Putawatame	POTAWATOMI
Putawatimi	POTAWATOMI
Puyallup	PUYALLUP
Pwiya'lap	PUYALLUP
Pxánai (Yreka Shasta)	MODOC
Q'ma'shpal (Yakima for camas)	SKITSWISH
Qçita	POHOY
Qil-leh-ute	QUILEUTE
Qtlumi	LUMMI
Quabaog	QUABAOG
Quabaug	QUABAUG
Quahada (Quahadi)	KWAHADA
Quahattika	QUAHATTIKA
Quaitso	QUEET
Quaitso; also Queets	QUEET
Qualia	CHEROKEE
Quallyamish	NISQUALLY
Quamash (Camas root/Camassia quamash, diatary staple)	SKITSWISH
Quanakina	QUANAKINA
Quanataguo	QUANATAGUO
Quanataguo	ANATHAGUA
Quapaw	QUAPAW
Quapaw (Village of)	UZUTIUHI
Quarai Pueblo	QUARAI PUEBLO
Quasmigdo	BIDAI
Quataquoi	KIOWA APACHE
Quathlahpohtle	QUATHLAHPOHTLE
Quatoghie	QUATOGHIE
Quatokeronon (Huron)	SAUK
Quazula (Jemez)	UTE
Quechan	YUMA
Queet	QUEET
Queissei	QUEISSEI
Queitsei	QUEISSEI
Quelancouchis	KARANKAWAN TRIBES
Quemáya (Garcés, 1775-1776)	KAMIA

Queres (Eastern Group)	KERESAN PUEBLOS
Qui-nai-elt	QUI-NAI-ELT
Qui-nai-elt	QUINAULT
Qui-nite-"l or Qui-Nite-'L	QUI-NAI-ELT
Quicapou	KICKAPOO
Quicasquiri	WICHITA
Quichais	KICHAI
Quichuan	KIOWA
Quidehai(s)	KICHAI
Quieetso	QUIEETSO
Quieunontati	TIONONTATI
Quigyuma	HALYIKWAMAI
Quil-Ley-Yute	QUILEUTE
Quileute	QUILEUTE
Quilotes	QUILOTES
Quinaielt	QUI-NAI-ELT
Quinalt	QUI-NAI-ELT
Quinalt	QUINAULT
Quinapisa	QUINIPISSA
Quinault	QUINAULT
Quinipissa	QUINIPISSA
Quinnechart	QUINNECHART
Quinnipiac	QUINNIPIAC
Quiocochànoc	QUIOCOCHÀNOC
Quirasquiris (French form)	WICHITA
Quisi	QUEISSEI
Quitsei(s)	KICHAI
Quiutcanuaha	QUIUTCANUAHA
Quivira (Coronado)	WICHITA
Quiyuga	CAYUGA
Quniaielt	QUINAULT
Quoddy	PASSAMAQUODDY
Quoissei	QUEISSEI
Quokim	KOHUANA
Qwû'lh-hwai-pùm	KLICKITAT
Rabbitskins	KAWCHOTTINE
Rahowacah	MONACAN
Rapid Indians	ATSINA
Rappahannock	RAPPAHANNOCK
Rappahanoc	RAPPAHANNOCK
Raritan	RARITAN
Rasaouakoueton	MASCOUTIN
Reatkin	YADKIN
Recares	ARIKARA
Rechaweygh	ROCKAWAY
Rechgawawanck	RECKGAWAWANC
Rechouwakie	ROCKAWAY
Rechquaakie	ROCKAWAY
Reckgawawanc	RECKGAWAWANC
Reckowacky	ROCKAWAY
Red Crawfish [People]	CHAKCHIUMA
Red Man or Red Men (Europeans applied to all Indians)	BEOTHUK
Red Paint People	TCI-HE-NDE/ CHIRICAHUA
Red Sticks (Weatherford Band in Creek War)	MUSKOGEE
Red Talkers (Sioux)	CHEYENNE
Red-knife Indians	TATSANOTTINE
Redwood Indians (popular name)	WHILKUT
Redwoods (popular name)	HUCHNOM
Rees	ARIKARA
Renards	FOX
Republican Pawnee	REPUBLICAN PAWNEE
Ricara	ARIKARA
Riccarree	ARIKARA
Rice Men	MENOMINEE
Richahecrian	YUCHI
Rickahocan	YUCHI
Rickohockan	YUCHI
Rikara	ARIKARA
Rincon Luiseño	RINCON LUISEÑO
River Cree (subdivision of Plains Cree)	CREE
River Indians	MAHICAN GROUP

River Indians (as are the Mahican)	MOHEGAN
River People	ACHOMAWI
River People	PIMA
Roanoke	ROANOKE
Robber Indians	BANNOCK
Rocameca	ROCAMECA
Rockaway	ROCKAWAY
Rogue River Indians	TUTUTNI
Rogue River Indians (most common)	TAKELMA
Root Diggers or Root-Diggers	SHOSHOKO
Root Diggers	YAKIMA
Root Diggers	[CALIFORNIA INDIANS] see SHOSHOKO
Round Head	HURON
Round Heads	ROUND HEADS
Round Town People	YUCHI
Rsársaavinâ (Pima)	SOBAIPURI
Ryawa	RYAWA
S'chkoé or S'chkoeishin (Kalispel) Shåktci homma	BLACKFEET
S'Homamish	S'HOMAMISH
S'Homanish?	SUQUÁMISH
S'Hotle-Ma-Mish	S'HOTLE-MA-MISH
S'Klallam	CLALLAM
S'quies'tshi (Salish)	ARIKARA
Sa'pani (Shoshoni)	ATSINA
Sa'u'ú (Havasupai)	ZUŃI
Sa-ákl (Nestucca)	YAQUINA
Sa-áptin (Okanagon)	NEZ PERCÉ
Sa-Heh-Wa-Mish	SA-HEH-WA-MISH
Sa-Heh-Wamish	SAHEHWAMISH
Sa-to-tin	TATLIT-KUTCHIN
Saawano	SHAWNEE
Saawanwa	SHAWNEE
Sac	SAUK
Sachdagugh-roonaw (Iroquois)	PAMUNKEY
Sachdagugh-roonaw (Iroquois)	POWHATAN
Sack	SAUK
Sádalsómte-k'íago (Kiowa)	KIOWA APACHE
Saddals	SKADDAL
Sagaree	SUGEREE
Sage'wabsh	SAHEHWAMISH
Saguenay	SAGUENAY
Sah-Ku-Me-Hu	SAH-KU-MEHU
Sah-ku-mehu	SAH-KU-MEHU
Saha'ntia (Kutenai)	BLACKFEET
Sáhagi (Shawnee)	DAKOTA
Sahaptin	NEZ PERCÉ
Sahehwamish	SAHEHWAMISH
Sahiyela	NORTHERN CHEYENNE
Saia (Hupa)	NOGATL
Saidoka (Shoshoni)	MODOC
Saikiné (Apache)	PIMA
Saikinné (Apache)	PAPAGO
Saint Helena	ESCAMACU
Saint Regis	SAINT REGIS
Saish	SALISH
Sak'o'ta (Kiowa)	CHEYENNE
Sakonnet	SAKONNET
Salameco	CHIAHA
Saliman	SALINAN
Salinan	SALINAN
Salish	SALISH
Salishan	SALISH
Salmon Eaters	AGAIDEKA SHOSHONI
Salmon River Indians	SALMON RIVER INDIANS
Sälsxuyilp (Okanagon)	COLVILLE
Salt Lake Diggers	SHOSHONI, NORTHERN > NORTHWESTERN
Salt Lake Valley Indians	SHOSHONI, NORTHERN > NORTHWESTERN
Salt River Indians	PIMA
Saluda	SALUDA
Sam-ahmish	SAMISH

Samish	SAMISH
Sampit Ute	SAMPIT UTE
Samwamwa	SHAWNEE
San Antonio de Senecú	SENECÚ DEL SUR PUEBLO
San Antonio Salinas	SAN ANTONIO SALINAS
San Carlos Apache	GILEŃOS
San Felipe Pueblo	SAN FELIPE PUEBLO
San Ildefonso Pueblo	SAN ILDEFONSO PUEBLO
San Juan Pueblo	SAN JUAN PUEBLO
San Manuel	SAN MANUEL
San Marcos Pueblo	SAN MARCOS PUEBLO
San Miguel Salinas	SAN MIGUEL SALINAS
Sán'ka	KOOTENAY
Sanakíwa (Cheyenne)	CHOCTAW
Sanckhekin	SANKHIKAN
Sandbanks	HATTERAS
Sandhill Men (Ni om a-he' tan iu)	CHEYENNE
Sandia Pueblo	SANDIA PUEBLO
Sanish	ARIKARA
Sankhikan	SANKHIKAN
Sänko (Kiowa)	COMANCHE
Sanpoil	SANPOIL
Sans Arc	SANS ARC
Santa Ana Pueblo	SANTA ANA PUEBLO
Santa Barbara Indians	CHUMASH
Santa Clara Pueblo	SANTA CLARA PUEBLO
Santa Ynez Chumash	SANTA YNEZ CHUMASH
Santee	DAKOTA
Santee of South Carolina	SANTEE OF SOUTH CAROLINA
Santiam Kalapuya	SANTIAM KALAPUYA
Santo Domingo Pueblo	SANTO DOMINGO PUEBLO
Sanyona	SAONE SIOUX
Saone Sioux	SAONE SIOUX
Sápa wichasha (Dakota)	UTE
Sapona	SAPONI
Saponi	SAPONI
Sapooni	SAPONI
Sapsuckers	CROW
Saptin	NEZ PERCÉ
Sara	CHERAW
Saraw	CHERAW
Saray (Tiwa)	ZUŃI
Sarcee	SARCEE
Saria Tuhka or Sata Teicha or Särētīka or Sarh Rikka or Sarritecha	COMANCHE
Sarí (Isleta & Sandi)	ZUŃI
Sarrowhawk	CROW
Sarsis or Sarsi	SARCEE
Säshkiá-a-rúnû (Wyandot)	MIAMI
Satana (Five Nations)	SHAWNEE
Satoeronnon (Huron)	SAUK
Satsop	SATSOP
Sattee	SANTEE OF SOUTH CAROLINA
Saturiwa	SATURIWA
Sau'hto (Caddo)	COMANCHE
Sauk	SAUK
Sauk-Suiattle	SAH-KU-MEHU
Sauke	SAUK
Sault Chippewa	SAULT CHIPPEWA
Saulteaux	SAULT CHIPPEWA
Saura	CHERAW
Savannah	SAVANNAH
Savannuca	SAVANNAH
Sawamish	T'PEEKSIN
Sawketakix	BLACKFEET
Sawokli	SAWOKLI
Sáxlatks (Molala)	WASCO
Scachcook	SCATICOOK
Scachkook	SCATICOOK
Scantacooks	SCATICOOK
Scantecook	SCATICOOK

Scanticook	SCATICOOK	Shahań (Osage, Kansa & Oto)	DAKOTA
Scarred Arms	CHEYENNE	Shahan (Osage, Kansa, Oto)	SIOUX
Scatacogue	SCATICOOK	Shake-kah-quah (Wichita)	KICKAPOO
Scatacook	SCATICOOK	Shaki	SHAKI
Scatecook	SCATICOOK	Shàki	SHÀKI
Scaticook	SCATICOOK	Shakori	SHAKORI
Scaticouk	SCATICOOK	Shalee	SHALEE
Scattacook	SCATICOOK	Shallalah	SHALLALAH
Scattakook	SCATICOOK	Shallatto	SHALLATTOO
Scatticook	SCATICOOK	Shallattoo	SHALLATTOO
Schachooke	SCATICOOK	Shalsaé'ulk (Skinkiuse)	KOOTENAY
Schackhook	SCATICOOK	Shanaki (Caddo)	CHEROKEE
Schackhooke	SCATICOOK	Shanana (Kiowa Apache)	SIOUX
Schackok	SCATICOOK	Shánana (Kiowa Apache)	DAKOTA
Schaghook	SCATICOOK	Shannakiak (Fox)	CHEROKEE
Schaghticoke	SCATICOOK	Shanwappoms (Lew & Clark)	YAKIMA
Schahi (Hidatsa)	CREE	Shar'ha (Arikara & Peoria)	CHEYENNE
Sciatoga (most likely; some suggest Nez Percé)	CAYUSE	Shara or People on this Side (Lewis & Clark)	CHEYENNE
Scioux des Fond Du Lac Superior	SIOUX	Sharha	CHEYENNE
Scioux of the West	LAKOTA	Shasta	SHASTA
Scioux of the Woods	SIOUX	Shasta Costa	CHASTACOSTA
Scotan	SCOTON	Shasta Scoton	SCOTON
Scoten	SCOTON	Shateras	TUTELO
Scoton	SCOTON	Shati	KOASATI
Scotuks	PASSAMAQUODDY	Shawala (Teton Dakota)	SHAWNEE
Se-ap-cat	SE-AP-CAT	Shawanee	SHAWNEE
Seaux or ...uex (Lewis & Clark)	SIOUX	Shawano (...oe)	SHAWNEE
Seaside People	MOHEGAN	Shawanoese	SHAWNEE
Seatalcat	SEATAUKET	Shawash (Yuki)	ACHOMAWI
Seatauket	SEATAUKET	Shawnaese	SHAWNEE
Seattacook	SCATICOOK	Shawnee	SHAWNEE
Secacaonic	SECACAWONI	Shawonee	SHAWNEE
Secacawoni	SECACAWONI	Sheastukle	SHEASTUKLE
Secatoag	SECATOAG	Shebit	SHIVWITS
Secatogue	SECATOAG	Sheep Eaters or Sheepeaters	TUKUARIKA SHOSHONI
Seconondihago	SECONONDIHAGO	Sheetsomish	SKEETSOMISH
Secotan	SECOTAN	Sheheke	SHEHEKE
Secowocomoco	SECOWOCOMOCO	Sherry-dika Snakes	SHOSHONI, NORTHERN
Seechelt	SEECHELT	Shi e ah la or Shieya (Sioux)	CREE
Seen aug wah	SINAGUA	Shi'ini (Mescalero)	LIPAN
Seeoux (Lewis & Clark)	SIOUX	Shi'wanish (Tenino; also for Cayuse)	NEZ PERCÉ
Seewee	SEWEE		
Sekamish	SEKAMISH	Shienne (used by Catlin & Parkman)	CHEYENNE
Selakampóm (Comecrudo)	COMANCHE	Shígapo or Shikapu (Apache)	KICKAPOO
Sematuse	SEMATUSE	Shilacum	STEILACOOM
Semiahmoo	SEMIAHMOO	Shinnecock	SHINNECOCK
Seminole	SEMINOLE	Shinnecock	MONTAUK PEOPLES
Seminolies (Stuart)	SEMINOLE	Shipaulovi	SHIPAULOVI
Seneca and Sen-e-ca	SENECA	Shis-Inday	APACHE
Senecú del Sur Pueblo	SENECÚ DEL SUR PUEBLO	Shishinówutz-hitä'neo (Cheyenne)	COMANCHE
Senecú Pueblo	SENECÚ PUEBLO	Shista-kwusta	CHASTACOSTA
Seneka	SENECA	Shivwits	SHIVWITS
Senijextee	SENIJEXTEE	Sho-sho-kos (used by mountain men)	SHOSHOKO
Sennake	SENECA	Shoalwater	SHOALWATER
Sennecaa	SENECA	Shoccoree	SHAKORI
Senoxami'naex (Okanagon)	SPOKAN	Shoe Indians	AMAHAMI
Senoxma'n (Upper Kutenai)	SPOKAN	Shohta	SUHTAI
Sentutu (Upper Kutenai)	SPOKAN	Shohopanaiti	SHOHOPANAITI
Sera or Sara	CHERAW	Shonack (Beothuk)	MICMAC
Seretee	SANTEE OF SOUTH CAROLINA	Shooters among the Leaves	WAHEPKUTE
		Shoshokie (Catlin)	SHOSHOKO
Serrano	SERRANO	Shoshokoe (Irving)	SHOSHOKO
Seta Koxniname (Hopi)	HUALAPAI	Shoshone	SHOSHONI
Setá Kóxniname (Hopi)	WALAPAI	Shoshoni	SHOSHONI
Setauket	SETAUKET	Shota	SUHTAI
Seuvarit Ute	SEUVARIT UTE	Shotawininiwug (for the Ojibwa, used to designate the Hebrew race)	SUHTAI
Sewanakie	MONTAUK PEOPLES		
Sewee	SEWEE	Shoto	SHOTO
Sha hi ye na or Sha hi' e la (Sioux)	CHEYENNE	Shoudamunk (Beothuk)	MONTAGNAIS-NASKAPI
Sha-ho (Pawnee)	CHEYENNE	Shuman	SHUMAN
Shachcook	SCATICOOK	Shumopovi	SHUMOPOVI
Shackoconia	SHACKOCONIA	Shyik	SHYIK
Shahala (Chinook)	WATLALA		

Si ni'-te-li (Mishikwutmetunne & Alsea)	TILLAMOOK GROUP
Si ni'-te-li tunne (Naltunne)	ALSEA
Si ni'të-li tunne (Naltunne, meaning "flatheads")	ALSEA
Si-ha'-sa-pa (Yankton Dakota)	BLACKFEET
Si-ke-na (Apache)	MARICOPA
Si-ke-na (Apache)	PAPAGO
Si-ke-na (Apache)	PIMA
Sia	ZIA PUEBLO
Siatoga (most likely; some suggest Nez Percé)	CAYUSE
Siaux (Lewis & Clark)	SIOUX
Sibag-na	SIBAG-NA
Sicä'be (Kansa)	BLACKFEET
Sicangu	BRULÉ
Sicaog	SICAOG
Sicaunie	SICAUNIE
Sichomovi	SICHOMOVI
Sichumovi	SICHOMOVI
Siciatl	SEECHELT
Sickenames	PEQUOT
Siconesse	SICONESSE
Sierra Blanca Apache	WHITE MOUNTAIN COYOTERO
Siete Ciudades de Cibola (Seven Cities of Cibola)	ZUŇI
Sieoux (Lewis & Clark)	SIOUX
Sihapa	BLACKFOOT SIOUX
Sihasapa	BLACKFOOT SIOUX
Sihasapa	SIHASAPA
Sik'-a-pu (Comanche)	KICKAPOO
Siksika	BLACKFOOT SIOUX
Siksika or Siksiká	SIKSIKÁ BLACKFEET
Siksika Blackfeet	SIKSIKÁ BLACKFEET
Siletz	SILETZ
Similkameen Okanagon	SIMILKAMEEN OKANAGON
Siminoli	SEMINOLE
Sin-te'-had wi-ca-sa (Yankton Dakota)	SHOSHONI, NORTHERN
Sinagua	SINAGUA
Sinanoy	SIWANOY
Sinkaietk	SINKAIETK
Sinkakaius	SINKAKAIUS
Sinkiuse	PALOUSE
Sinkiuse	COLUMBIA
Sinkiuse-Columbia	COLUMBIA
Sinkyone	SINKYONE
Sinneken (Dutch for all the Iroquois living west of Mohawk)	ONEIDA
Sinneken (later, exclusively)	SENECA
Sintsink	SINTSINK
Sioune	SAONE SIOUX
Sioux	SIOUX
Sioux	DAKOTA
Sioux des prairies	LAKOTA
Sioux nomades	LAKOTA
Sioux occidentaux	LAKOTA
Sioux of the Des Moyan	SIOUX
Sioux of the East	DAKOTA
Sioux of the Lakes	SIOUX
Sioux of the Meadows	LAKOTA
Sioux of the Plains	LAKOTA
Sioux of the River St Peter's	SIOUX
Sioux of the Rocks	STONEY-NAKODA
Sioux of the Rocks	ASSINIBOIN
Sioux of the Woods	SIOUX
Sis'qûn-me'tûnne (Chetco)	YAQUINA
Sisatone Sioux	SISATONE SIOUX
Sisitcanog-na	SISITCANOG-NA
Sisitonwan	SISATONE SIOUX
Sisízhanin (Atsina)	SHOSHONI, NORTHERN
Sisseton	SISATONE SIOUX

Sissetunwan	SISATONE SIOUX
Sissetuwan	SISATONE SIOUX
Sissipahaw	SISSIPAHAW
Sistatoone	SISATONE SIOUX
Sitka	KIKSADI TLINGIT
Sitsime (Western Group)	KERESAN PUEBLOS
Siuslaw	SIUSLAW
Siwanoy	SIWANOY
Six Nations (after Tuscarora)	IROQUOIS LEAGUE
Sixes	KWATAMI
Sk-kahl-mish	SK-KAHL-MISH
Sk-tah-le-jum	SK-TAH-LE-JUM
Skacewanilom (Iroquois)	ABENAKI
Skachcook	SCATICOOK
Skachkook	SCATICOOK
Skackamaxon	SKACKAMAXON
Skaddal	SKADDAL
Skagit	SKAGIT
Skai-wha-mish	SKAI-WHA-MISH
Skalzi	KOOTENAY
Skaniadaradighroonas (Iroquois)	NANTICOKE
Skaru're	SKARU'RE
Skatacook	SCATICOOK
Skaxshurunu (Wyandot)	FOX
Skeetsomish	SKEETSOMISH
Skelsá-ulk (Salish)	KOOTENAY
Skidi Pawnee	SKIDI PAWNEE
Skilloot	SKILLOOT
Skiloot	SKILLOOT
Skin	SKINPAH
Skin-pah	SKINPAH
Skinpah	SKINPAH
Skiri Pawnee	SKIDI PAWNEE
Skitswish	SKITSWISH
Skiuse	CAYUSE
Sklallam or Skallan	CLALLAM
Sko'-ki ha-ya (Biloxi)	MUSKOGEE
Skokomish	SKOKOMISH
Skokomish	TWANA
Skopamish	MUCKLESHOOT
Skopamish Muckleshoot	SKOPAMISH MUCKLESHOOT
Skope-ahmish	MUCKLESHOOT
Sku'tani (Dakota)	ATSINA
Skuäisheni (Salish)	BLACKFEET
Skuakfsagi (Shawnee)	FOX
Skunnemoke (a chief)	ATÁKAPA
Skuyèlpi (Salish)	COLVILLE
Skwalliahmish	NISQUALLY
Slender Bows	KOOTENAY
Smalhkamish	SMALHKAMISH
Small Robes [band]	PIEGAN BLACKFEET
Snake	WALPAPI
Snake (only for the Northern Paiute of Oregon)	NORTHERN PAIUTE
Snake or Snake Indians (most common, but also used for others)	SHOSHONI, NORTHERN
Snake Diggers	SOUTHERN PAIUTE
Snake People	WALPAPI
Snakes or Snake Men (Cheyenne, Kiowa, Arapaho)	COMANCHE
Sno-h--mish	SNOHOMISH
Snóa (Okanagon)	SHOSHONI, NORTHERN
Snobomish	COLUMBIA
Snohomish	SNOHOMISH
Snolqualmoo	SNOQALMIE
Snoqalmie	SNOQALMIE
Snoqualmie	SNOQALMIE
Snoqualmoo	SNOQALMIE
So So nes	SHOSHONI
Soacatino	SOACATINO
Soba Papago	SOBAIPURI
Sobaipuri	SOBAIPURI
Soboba Luiseño	SOBOBA LUISEÑO

Tá-ashi (Comanche)	APACHE
Ta-cáb-ci-nyu-muh (Hopi)	NAVAJO
Ta-ih	TYIGH
Tă-Kuth-Kutchin	TAKKUTH-KUTCHIN
Tá-qta (Quapaw)	CHOCTAW
Ta-qu'-qûe-ce (Chetco)	TUTUTNI
Ta-wa-ka-ro	TAWAKONI
Tăa Ashiwani	ZUÑI
Tabaquache	TABEGUACHE UTE
Tabeguache Ute	TABEGUACHE UTE
Tabkepáya (Yavapai)	WALAPAI
Tachi(es) or Tachie(s) (Sibley)	HAINAI
Tackie	TACKIE
Tacstacuru	TACSTACURU
Taculli	CARRIER
Tacullie	TACULLIE
Tadirighrones (Iroquois)	CATAWBA
Tadiva	TADIVA
Taensa	TAENSA
Taenso	TAENSA
Taguacana	TAWAKONI
Taguaya	TAOVAYA
Taguayos	TAOVAYA
Tagúi (Kiowa)	APACHE
Tagúi (Kiowa)	KIOWA APACHE
Tágukerésh (Pecos)	APACHE
Tagukerish (Pecos, all Apaches)	KIOWA APACHE
Táh'ba (Yavapai)	PAPAGO
Tah-wa-carro	TAWAKONI
Tah-wah-karro	TAWAKONI
Tahensa	TAENSA
Tahnahwah	TENAWA
Tahneemuh	TAHNEEMUH
Tahogalewi (Delaware)	YUCHI
Tahsagroudie	TAHSAGROUDIE
Tahuacane	TAWAKONI
Tahuacarro	TAWAKONI
Tahuayases	TAOVAYA
Tahwacarro	TAWAKONI
Taidnapam	TAIDNAPAM
Taigh	TYIGH
Taih	TYIGH
Takahli	CARRIER
Takelma	TAKELMA
Takensa	TAENSA
Takulli	CARRIER
Tálemaya (Umpqua)	TUTUTNI
Tali	TALI
Tallahassee	APALACHEE
Tallewheana	TALLEWHEANA
Talligewi (Delaware)	CHEROKEE
Taltushtuntude	TALTUSHTUNTUDE
Talwa lako	APALACHICOLA
Tama	TAMA'LI
Tama	TAMATHLI
Tama'li	TAMA'LI
Tamahita (eastern Siouans)	YUCHI
Tamali	TAMA'LI
Tamaroa	TAMAROA
Tamarois	TAMAROA
Tamathli	TAMATHLI
Tamatle	TAMA'LI
Tamisa	TUNICA
Tamos	PECOS PUEBLO
Tan-nah-shis-en	JICARILLA
Tanaina	TANAINA
Tancague	TANCAGUE
Tancaro	TAWAKONI
Taneks aya	BILOXI
Tanewa	TENAWA
Tangipahoa	TANGIPAHOA
Tani'bänen (Arapaho)	KADOHADACHO CONFEDERACY
Tanico	TANICO
Tanik-wa (Marquette)	TUNICA
Tanima	TAHNEEMUH
Tanima Comanche	TANIMA
Tanish	ARIKARA
Tankiteke	TANKITEKE
Tankupi	CALAPOOYA KALAPUYA
Tannewa	TENAWA
Tannewish	TENAWA
Tano	TEWA PUEBLO GROUP
Tano Pueblo	TANO PUEBLO
Tanxnitania	TANXNITANIA
Taos Pueblo	TAOS PUEBLO
Taouaizes	TAOVAYA
Taovaya	TAOVAYA
Taovayas	TAOVAYA
Tapage Pawnee	TAPAGE PAWNEE
Tapanash (general name used by Mooney, 1928)	SKINPAH
Taposa	TAPOSA
Tapouaro	TAPOUARO
Tappan	TAPPAN
Taros	YAVAPAI
Tarrateens (tribes of southern New England)	ABENAKI
Tarratines (Puritans)	ABENAKI
Tasámewé (Hopi)	NAVAJO
Tascaloosa	MOBILE
Tashash (Wichita)	KADOHADACHO CONFEDERACY
Tashi'ne (Mescalero)	JICARILLA
Tashin (Comanche)	APACHE
Tashin (Comanche, all Apaches)	KIOWA APACHE
Tassenocogoula (Mobilian)	AVOYEL
Tatasiba (Shoshone)	SALISH
Tatlit-kutchin	TATLIT-KUTCHIN
Tatsanottine	TATSANOTTINE
Taukaways	TAUKAWAYS
Taux	NANTICOKE
Tauxenent	TAUXENENT
Tauxitanians	TANXNITANIA
Tawa	OTTAWA
Tawakana	TAWAKONI
Tawakaro	TAWAKONI
Tawakoni	TAWAKONI
Tawasa	TAWASA
Tawatawas	MIAMI
Tawehash	TAWEHASH
Tawehash	TAOVAYA
Taxkahe (Arapaho)	APACHE
Tazwachguáns (Mahican & Delaware)	NANTICOKE
Tca-ka' ne (Mohawk)	DELAWARE
Tca-qtá a-ya-dí (Biloxi)	CHOCTAW
Tca-qtá ha-ya (Biloxi)	CHOCTAW
Tca-tá (Kansa)	CHOCTAW
Tcashtalálgi (Creek)	POTAWATOMI
Tch yákon amin (Luckiamute Kalapuya)	YAQUINA
Tcha yaxo amim (Luckiamute Kalapuya)	ALSEA
Tcha yáxo amin (Luckiamute Kalapouya)	ALSEA
Tchaktchán (Arapaho)	CHICKASAW
Tchaxsúkush (Caddo)	NEZ PERCÉ
Tchiáxsokush (Caddo)	PONCA
Tchihogasat (Havasupai)	MARICOPA
Tchíkasa (Creek)	CHICKASAW
Tci-he-nde Mimbre	TCI-HE-NDE/ CHIRICAHUA
Tcingawúptuh (Hopi)	UTE
Tcunoíyana (Yana)	ATSUGEWI
Tcutzwa'ut or Tcitxua'ut	OKANAGON
Tcutzwa'ut, Teitxua'ut, Twawa'nemux (Ntlakyapamuk)	OKANAGON

Te'liémnim (Isleta)	NAVAJO
Te'pda'	KIOWA
Te-ne-mis	TENAWA
Teáxtkni or Telknikni (Klamath)	TYIGH
Tebas, Tigua, Tiguex, Tihuas	TIWA PUEBLO
Teeton	BRULÉ
Tegninateo	TEGNINATEO
Tegninati	TEGNINATI
Teguayos	TAOVAYA
Tehacane	TAWAKONI
Tehachapi	KAWAIISU
Tehayesatlu (Nestucca)	ALSEA
Tehayesátlu (Nestucca)	ALSEA
Tehuacana	TAWAKONI
Tei-ka-sa (Kansa)	CHICKASAW
Tejano	COAHUILTECAN TRIBES
Tejas	TEJAS
Tékapu (Huron)	KICKAPOO
Tekesta	TEQUESTA
Telamateno (Delaware)	WYANDOT
Telmocresse	TELMOCRESSE
Temecula or Temecula Indians	PECHANGA LUISEÑO
Temeekuya or Temeekuyam	PECHANGA LUISEÑO
Tenahwit	TENAWA
Tenawa Comanche	TENAWA
Tenawit	TENAWA
Teneme	TANIMA
Tenewa	TANIMA COMANCHE
Tenhua	TENAWA
Tenino	TENINO
Tenisaw	TAENSA
Tenyé (Laguna)	NAVAJO
Tenza	TAENSA
Teo'ko or Tsu'qos (Kutenai)	SARCEE
Tepki'nägo	KIOWA
Tequesta	TEQUESTA
Tesuque Pueblo	TESUQUE PUEBLO
Tet-sugeh	TESUQUE PUEBLO
Tete Pelée	COMANCHE
Têtes Plates (French)	CHOCTAW
Teton	LAKOTA
Tetongues (Lewis & Clark)	BRULÉ
Tetons Minnakenozzo (Lewis & Clark)	MINNAKENOZZO
Tetons of the Burnt Woods (Lewis & Clark)	BRULÉ
Tetons Okandandas (Lewis & Clark)	OKANDANDA
Tetons Saone (Lewis & Clark)	SAONE
Tevawish	TAHNEEMUH
Tewa Pueblo Group	TEWA PUEBLO GROUP
Tewohomony (Saponi)	TUSCARORA
Tex-pas (Maricopa)	PIMA
Téxas	TÉXAS
Texas (Sibley)	HAINAI
Texpamais (Maricopa)	PAPAGO
Teya	TEYA
Tha'ká-hine'na (Arapaho)	KIOWA APACHE
Thah-a-I-nin (Arapaho)	APACHE
Thastchetci' (Onondaga)	WYANDOT
The Dalles	WASCOPUN
Theloël or Thécoël	NATCHEZ
Thlála'h(Clackama)	CHINOOK
Thlingchadinne	THLINGCHADINNE
Thoig'a-rik-kab (Shoshoni)	NEZ PERCÉ
Three Canes (mistranslation of Fr.)	TAWAKONI
Three Fires Confederacy	THREE FIRES CONFEDERACY
Thy	TYIGH
Ti'attluxa (Wasco Chinook)	COLUMBIA
Ti'wan (pl. Tiwesh')	TIWA PUEBLO
Ti-ka'-ja (Quapaw)	CHICKASAW
Tibahag-na	TIBAHAG-NA
Tideing Indians (Lewis & Clark)	KIOWA
Tidewater People (as was neighboring division of Delaware)	NANTICOKE
Tidewater People (as was the Nanticoke)	DELAWARE
Tigh	TYIGH
Tigua Pueblo	TIGUA PUEBLO
Tiguex Indians (for Tigua)	TIGUA PUEBLO
Tihokahana (Yavapai)	PIMA
Tihua Indians (for Tigua)	TIGUA PUEBLO
Tikabahchee	TIKABAHCHEE
Tilkuni	TILKUNI
Tillamook	TILLAMOOK
Tillamook Group	TILLAMOOK GROUP
Timpaiavat	TUMPANOGOT UTE
Timuca	TUMUCUA PROPER
Timucua	TUMUCUA PROPER
Timucua	UTINA (TUMUCUA)
Tiñ'tlama'eka (Kutenai)	ASSINIBOIN
Tin-ne-áh	APACHE
Tinde	JICARILLA
Tindé	APACHE
Tiniema	TANIMA
Tinnä'-ash (Wichita)	APACHE
Tinza	TAENSA
Tionontates	TIONONTATI
Tionontati	TANCAGUE
Tionontati	TIONONTATI
Tiopane	TIOPANE
Tiou	TIOU
Tipai	KAMIA
Tiqui-Liapais	WALAPAI
Tiqui-Llapai	HUALAPAI
Tirans	TIRANS
Tirapihu (Pawnee)	ARAPAHO
Tisaiqdji (Ilmawi)	YANA
Titenai	LAKOTA
Titonwon	LAKOTA
Titskan wátitch	TONKAWA
Titunwan	LAKOTA
Tiu'tlama'eka (Kutenai)	STONEY-NAKODA
Tiwa, misapplied	WICHITA
Tiwa Indians (for Tigua)	TIGUA PUEBLO
Tiwa Pueblo	TIWA PUEBLO
Tkulhiyogoa'ikc (Chinook)	KWALHIOQUA
Tla'asath (Nootka)	MAKAH
Tla'lem	CLALLAM
Tlakäï'tät anim (Kalapuya)	KLICKITAT
Tlakimish	CLACKAMAS
Tlakluit	WISHRAM
Tlalliguamayas	HALYIKWAMAI
Tlatskanai	CLATSKANIE
Tlokeang	KATO
To-che-wah-coo (Arikara)	FOX
Toags	NANTICOKE
Toanho	TWANA
Toavayases	TAOVAYA
Toaya	TAOVAYA
Tobacco Huron	TIONONTATI
Tobacco Indians, Tobacco Nation	TIONONTATI
Tobikhars	KIAWA
Tobikhars	STONO
Tobohar	STONO
Toboso	TAOVAYA
Tocaninambiches	ARAPAHO
Tockwogh	TOCKWOGH
Tocobaga	TOCOBAGA
Toholo	CHOWCHILLA YOKUT
Tohome	TOHOME
Tohono O'odham	PAPAGO
Tolameco	CHIAHA
Tolowa	TOLOWA
Tomathle	TAMATHLI
Tomatola	TAMA'LI
Tonawanda	TONAWANDA

Tongva	TONGVA	Tu'hu tane (Umpqua)	CLACKAMAS
Tonica	TUNICA	Tu-a'd-hu	TWANA
Tonica	THREE FIRES CONFEDERACY	Tu-sa-be' (Tesuque)	JICARILLA
		Tu-tsän-nde (Mescalero)	LIPAN
Tonka	TUNICA	Tuacana	TAWAKONI
Tonkawa	TONKAWA	Tuacane	TUACANE
Tonkawan Tribes	TONKAWAN TRIBES	Tualatin	ATFALATI KALAPUYA
Tonkaway	TONKAWA	Tübatulabal	TÜBATULABAL
Tońkońko (Kiowa)	BLACKFEET	Tuhu'vti-omokat (Comanche)	BLACKFEET
Tóno-oohtam	PAPAGO	Tuk-pa'-ha-ya-di (Biloxi)	ATÁKAPA
Tonto Apache	TONTO	Tukabahchee	TUKABAHCHEE
Took-a-ri-ka	TUKUARIKA SHOSHONI	Tükahum (Isleta Tiwa)	PIRO PUELBO GROUP
Tootootna	TUTUTNI	Tukspush	TUKSPUSH
Topin-keua (Zuñi)	HOPI	Tukuadüka	TUKUARIKA SHOSHONI
Totero	TUTELO	Tukuarika	TUKUARIKA SHOSHONI
Touacara	TAWAKONI	Tukudeka	TUKUARIKA SHOSHONI
Toucara	TAWAKONI	Tul'bush (Wailaki)	MATTOLE
Toustchipa (most likely, some suggest Kutenai)	SALISH (FLATHEAD)	Tulalip	TULALIP
		Tule-Kaweah Yokuts	TULE-KAWEAH YOKUTS
Towacanno	TAWAKONI	Tum-Waters	TUM-WATERS
Towaconi		Tumangamalum (Luiseño)	STONO
Towakoni	TAWAKONI	Tumangamalum (Luiseño)	KIAWA
Towash	TAWAKONI	Tumpanogot Ute	TUMPANOGOT UTE
Toweash	TAWEHASH	Tumwater Indians	CLOWWEWALLA
Towash	TAOVAYA	Tuna'xe	TUNAHE
Too--ee-ahge (variation of Túxquet)	WICHITA	Tunaha	TUNAHE
Toybipet	TOYBIPET	Tunahe	TUNAHE
Tpe-tliet-Kouttchin	TATLIT-KUTCHIN	Tunaxa	TUNAHE
Tramaskecooc	TRAMASKECOOC	Tunica	TUNICA
Trementina	TREMENTINA	Tunxis	TUNXIS
Tremintina	TREMENTINA	Tups	TUPS
Trinity	HUPA	Tusayan	HOPI
Trinity Indians	HUPA	Tuscarora	TUSCARORA
Ts'û-qûs-li'-qwut-me tunne (Naltunne)	DAKUBETEDE	Tush-she-pâh	SALISH
Tsä Shnádsh amín (Luckiamute Kalapuya)	SILETZ	Tushepau	SALISH
		Tushepaw	SALISH
Tsaba'kosh or Ba-akush' (Caddo)	SIOUX	Tuskarora and Tus-ka-to-ra	TUSCARORA
Tsaba-kosh (Caddo)	DAKOTA	Tuskegee	TUSKEGEE
Tsah-tû (Creek)	CHOCTAW	Tutelo	TUTELO
Tsaisuma (Maidu)	WASHO	Tuterro or Tutero	TUTELO
Tsalagi (own name, orginally from Choctaw)	CHEROKEE	Tutseewa	TUTSEEWA
		Tututni	TAKELMA
Tsan Ámpkua amím (Luckiamute Kalapuya)	UMPQUA	Tututni	TUTUTNI
		Tututni	PORT ORFORD
Tsana-uta amin (Luckiamute)	SIUSLAW	Túxquet	WICHITA
Tsanchifin Kalapuya	TSANCHIFIN KALAPUYA	Tuyetchiske (Comanche)	SIOUX
Tsänh-alokual amím (Luckiamute)	CALAPOOYA KALAPUYA	Tuyetchíske (Comanche)	DAKOTA
Tsankupi	CALAPOOYA KALAPUYA	Twana	TWANA
Tsawa/neumux	OKANAGON	Twana; also for others	COLUMBIA
Tsch-tsi-uetin-euerno	MONTAGNAIS-NASKAPI	Twightwees (Iroquois)	MIAMI
Tse Amínema (Luckiamute Kalapuya)	TYIGH	Two Boils Kettle	TWO KETTLES
		Two Kettle	TWO KETTLES
Tse Skua'lli ami'm (Luckamiut Kalapooian)	NISQUALLY	Two Kettles	TWO KETTLES
		Tygh	TYIGH
Tse-sa do hpa ka (Hidasta)	PAWNEE	Tyigh	TYIGH
Tshishé (Laguna)	APACHE	Tzi-na-ma-a	MOJAVE
Tsi'-ka-ce (Osage_	CHICKASAW	U'-aha (Pawnee)	OMAHA
Tsi'kwob.c (Snohomish)	WENATCHEE	U-ka'-she (Crow)	MANDAN
Tsiltaden Apache	TSILTADEN	Uala-to-hua	JEMEZ PUEBLO
Tsinúk	CHINOOK	Uchee or Uche	YUCHI
Tsistsistas (Cheyenne proper)	CHEYENNE	Ucita	POHOY
Tsoka-ne-nde	CHIRICAHUA	Udawak (Penobscot)	OTTAWA
Tso-Ottinè	SARCEE	Ufallah	UFALLAH
Tsononthouan (Fr. Hennepin as rpt. by Drake)	SENECA	Ugaljachmutzi	UGALJACHMUTZI
		Uh-kos-is-co	AUCOCISCO
Tsoyaha	YUCHI	Uinta	SHOHOPANAITI
Tsuhárukats (Pawnee)	NEZ PERCÉ	Uinta Ute	UINTA UTE
Tsulu, people of; also Tsulu-la	CHILULA	Uintah	UINTA UTE
Tsútpeli	NEZ PERCÉ	Ukase (Fox)	KANSA
Tsúùtínà	SARCEE	Ukhotno'm	COAST YUKI
Tu'-ba-na (Taos)	TEWA PUEBLO GROUP	Ukie	YUKI
Tu'-ven (Isleta & Sandia)	TEWA PUEBLO GROUP	Ukua'-yata (Huron)	OTTAWA
Tu'-wa	JEMEZ PUEBLO	Ulno Mequaegit (Micmac)	BEOTHUK
		Uma Pi Ma	UMATILLA

Umatilla	UMATILLA	Vidai	VIDAI
Umpqua	UMPQUA	Vidshi itíkapa (Tonto)	PAPAGO
Umpqua on Cow Creek	COW CREEK UMPQUA	Vieux De Sert or Vieux Désert	VIEUX DÉSERT
Umpwua	KUITSH	Villiage Farmer People	CROW
Un=chee	YUCHI	Wa-ju'-xdea (Quapaw)	MISSOURI
Unalachtigo	DELAWARE	Wa-nuk'-e-ye'-na (Arapaho)	HIDATSA
Unalachtigo	UNALACHTIGO	Wa-otc (Winnebago)	IOWA
Unami	UNAMI	Wa-sa-sa-o-no (Iroquois)	SIOUX
Unchachaug	PASSAMAQUODDY	Wä-sä-sa-o-no (Iroquois)	DAKOTA
Unchagogs	UNKECHAUG	Wa-yä-tä-no'-ke	MIAMI
Unchechauge	PASSAMAQUODDY	Wa-zi'-ya-ta Pa-da'-nin (Yankton)	ARIKARA
Uncompahgre	TABEGUACHE UTE	Waas	WEA
Uncpapa	HUNKPAPA	Wáatenihts (Atsina)	UTE
Undatomátendi (Huron)	POTAWATOMI	Wabanaki (Huron)	ABENAKI
Unechtgo	DELAWARE	Wabanaki (mistakenly; see Abenaki)	DELAWARE
Ungiayó-rono	SEMINOLE	Wabanaki (at their choice)	MICMAC AND MALISEE
Unkecha	UNKECHAUG		COLLECTIVELY
Unkechaug	UNKECHAUG	Wabash	WABASH
Unkpapa	HUNKPAPA	Wabenaki	ABENAKI
Unkus or Uncas Indians	MOHEGAN	Wabinga	WAPPINGER
Unquache	PASSAMAQUODDY		CONFEDERACY
Unquachock	PASSAMAQUODDY	Wabingie or Wapingei	WAPPINGER
Unquachog or Unchachaug	PASSAMAQUODDY		CONFEDERACY
Unquechauge	PASSAMAQUODDY	Wabouquigou	WABASH
Unquehiett	UNQUEHIETT	Wabous-quigou	WABASH
Upland Indians	MOHEGAN	Waccamaw	WACCAMAW
Upper Chehalis	KWAIAILK	Waclalah	WATLALA
Upper Chinook	WISHRAM	Waco	WACO
Upper Coquille	MISHIKHWUTMETUNNE	Wacoe	WACO
Upper Cowlitz	TAIDNAPAM	Wacútada (Omaha & Ponca)	OTO
Upper Creek	UPPER CREEK	Waçuxea (Osage)	MISSOURI
Upper De Chutes (Dechutes River)	TYIGH	Wadótata (Kansa)	OTO
Upper Kalapuya	YONCALLA KALAPUYA	Waganha's (Iroquois)	OTTAWA
Upper Pend d'Oreilles	UPPER PEND D'OREILLES	Waggamaw	WACCAMAW
Upper Porcupine River Kutchin	TATLIT-KUTCHIN	Wah-ho'-na-hah	POTAWATOMI
Upper Rogue River Indians	TAKELMA	Wah-kah-towah (Assiniboin)	CHIPPEWA
Upper Skagit	UPPER SKAGIT	Wahepkute	WAHEPKUTE
Upper Umpqua	UMPQUA	Wáhiúeaxá (Omaha)	POTAWATOMI
Upper Yakima	PSHWANWAPAM	Wáhiúyaha (Kansa)	POTAWATOMI
Upsaroka	CROW	Wahkiaku	WAHKIAKUM
Uragees	MAHICAN GROUP	Wahkiakum	WAHKIAKUM
Us-suc-car-shay (Crow)	MANDAN	Wahnookt (Cowlitz)	KLICKITAT
Uscamu	ESCAMACU	Wahoppum	WAHOWPUM
Ush-ke-we-ah (Crow)	BANNOCK	Wahowpum	WAHOWPUM
Ushaxtáno (name given to the	ILLINOIS CLUSTER OF	Wahowpun	WAHOWPUM
Illinois River)	TRIBES	Wahpacoota Sioux	WAHPACOOTA SIOUX
Usherys	CATAWBA	Wahpakoota	WAHPETUNWAN SIOUX
Ushpee	MOSOPELEA	Wahpatone	WAHPETUNWAN SIOUX
Usququhaga	USQUQUHAGA	Wahpeton	WAHPETUNWAN SIOUX
Ussagene'wi (Penobscot)	MONTAGNAIS-NASKAPI	Wahpetonwan	WAHPETUNWAN SIOUX
Ussaghenick (Malecite)	MONTAGNAIS-NASKAPI	Wahpetunwan Sioux	WAHPETUNWAN SIOUX
Usseta (var. of Cusseta by Bartram)	KASIHTA	Waiam	WAIAM
Ussinnewudj (Ottawa)	SARCEE	Waiilatpu or Waiilatpus	CAYUSE
Usuchee	YUCHI	Waiki lako (Muskogee)	OKMULGEE
Utah	UTE	Wailaki	WAILAKI
Utáseta (Cheyenne)	KADOHADACHO	Wailetpu	CAYUSE
	CONFEDERACY	Wakiacum	WAHKIAKUM
Utce-cí-nyu-muh or Utsaamu	APACHE	Wákidohka-numak (Mandan)	SHOSHONI, NORTHERN
(Hopi)		Wakina (Dodge Expedition)	ARIKARA
Utcena'qai'n (Salish)	OKANAGON	Wakokai	WAKOKAI
Ute	UTE	Wäkushég (Potawatomij)	FOX
Ute Diggers	SOUTHERN PAIUTE	Wálamskni (Klamath)	CHASTACOSTA
Utina	UTINA	Wálamswach (Medoc)	CHASTACOSTA
Utsúshuat (Wyandot)	QUAPAW	Walapai	HUALAPAI
Uwatayo-rono (Wyandot)	CHEROKEE	Walapai	WALAPAI
Uxul (Tonkawa)	LIPAN	Walatoa	JEMEZ PUEBLO
Uzutiuhi	UZUTIUHI	Walla Walla	WALLA WALLA
Uzutiuhi (village)	QUAPAW	Wallapai	HUALAPAI
Vanyume	VANYUME	Wallawalla (also Wallwalla)	WALLA WALLA
Varnertown Indians	VARNERTOWN INDIANS	Wallowa	WALLOWA
Ventureño Chumash	VENTUREÑO CHUMASH	Walpapi	WALPAPI
Vermilion	KICKAPOO	Walpi Hopi	WALPI HOPI
Vermillion	VERMILLION	Walula	WALLA WALLA
Vi'täpätui (Sutaio)	KIOWA	Walumskni (Klamath)	LATGAWA

Wam-pa-no	WAPPINGER CONFEDERACY
Wamakava (Havasupai)	MOJAVE
Wamakava (Havasupai; also to Mohave)	YUMA
Wamenuches	WEEMINUCHE UTES
Wamesit	PAWTUCKET
Wampanoag	WAMPANOAG
Wampono	WAPPINGER CONFEDERACY
Wanak (Chippewa)	DAKOTA
Wanaláma	WANAPAM
Wanapam	WANAPAM
Wanapum	WANAPAM
Wando	WANDO
Wangunk	WANGUNK
Waoranec	WAORANEC
Waoranecker	WAWARSINK
Wapanachki	ABENAKI
Wapanachki (mistakenly; see Abenaki)	DELAWARE
Wapanoo	WAPPINGER CONFEDERACY
Wapato Lake Indians	ATFALATI KALAPUYA
Wapinger	WAPPINGER CONFEDERACY
Wapingo	WAPPINGER CONFEDERACY
Wappato (Cree or Chippewa)	MULTNOMAH
Wappenger	WAPPINGER CONFEDERACY
Wappeno or Wappenoo	WAPPINGER CONFEDERACY
Wappinck or Wappinx	WAPPINGER CONFEDERACY
Wapping	WAPPING
Wapping or Waping	WAPPINGER CONFEDERACY
Wappinger (mistakenly; see Wappinger)	DELAWARE
Wappinger Confederacy	WAPPINGER CONFEDERACY
Wappinter	WAPPINGER CONFEDERACY
Wappo	WAPPO (CA)
Wappoo	WAPPOO (SC)
Waptai'lmin	YAKIMA
War-Ree-Ka (more properly, Warrarica)	SHOSHONI, SOUTHERN
Warananconguins	WAPPINGER CONFEDERACY
Waranawonkong	WARANAWONKONG
Warm Springs	WALLA WALLA
Warm Springs Indians (official designation)	TENINO
Warm Springs People/Apache	TCI-HE-NDE/ CHIRICAHUA
Warrarica	SHOSHONI, SOUTHERN
Warrasqeak	WARRASQUEOC
Warrasqueoc	WARRASQUEOC
Warwarsing	WAWARSINK
Wasawsee	OSAGE
Wasco	WASCO
Washa	WASHA
Washakee's Band, Chief	SHOSHONI, EASTERN
Washaki's Band, Chief	SHOSHONI, EASTERN
Washakie Shoshoni	SHOSHONI, EASTERN
Washo	WASHO
Wassamasaw	WASSAMASAW
Watanon	WEA
Watawawininiwok (Chippewa)	OTTAWA
Wateknasi (Yokut)	TÜBATULABAL
Wateni'the (Arapaho)	BLACKFEET
Watepaneto	WATEPANETO
Water Falls People	ATSINA
Water-dwelling Snakes (more properly, Warrarica)	SHOSHONI, SOUTHERN
Wateree	WATEREE
Watlala	WATLALA
Watohtata (Dakota)	OTO
Wattasson	AMAHAMI
Wattersoon	AMAHAMI
Watútata (Osage)	OTO
Waupenocky	ABENAKI
Waupenocky (mistakenly; see Abenaki)	DELAWARE
Wauyukma	WAUYUKMA
Wawáh (Mono)	WINTUN
Wawáh (Paiute; also used for all Sacramento River tribes)	MAIDU
Wawarsink	WAWARSINK
Wawenoc	WAWENOC
Wawenok	ABENAKI
Wawping	WAPPINGER CONFEDERACY
Wawyachtonoc	WAWYACHTONOC
Waxhaw	WAXHAW
Wazhazhe (own name)	OSAGE
Wdowo (Abnaki)	OTTAWA
We-messouret	MISSOURI
Wea	WEA
Weah-Wea-Weau	WEA
Weanoc	WEANOC
Weapemeoc	WEAPEMEOC
Weatano	WEA
Weber Ute	SHOSHONI, NORTHERN > NORTHWESTERN
Webing	WEBING
Wecquaesgeek	WICKQUASGECK
Wecquaesgeek Wappinger	WECQUAESGEEK WAPPINGER
Wee-hee-skeu or People on this Side (Lewis & Clark)	CHEYENNE
Weea	WEA
Wee-ah	WEA
Weeminuche Utes	WEEMINUCHE UTES
Weenee	WINYAW
Weepers	STONEY-NAKODA
Weepers	ASSINIBOIN
Weisers (Boise/Weiser River)	SHOSHONI, NORTHERN
Weitchpec (Hupa & Karok)	YUROK
Wekisa	WEKISA
Welch or Welch Indians	WELSH INDIANS
Welsh or Welsh Indians	WELSH INDIANS
Welsh Indians (Catlin; Evans)	MANDAN
Welsh Indians (Lewis & Clark)	SALISH
Weminutc	WEEMINUCHE UTES
Wenatchee	WENATCHEE
Wenatshapam	WENATSHAPAM
Wendat	HURON
Wenoc	WEANOC
Wenro	WENROHRONON
Wenrohronon	WENROHRONON
Werowocomico	WEROWOCOMOCO
Werowocomoco	WEROWOCOMOCO
Wes'anikaciga (Omaha & Ponca)	SHOSHONI, NORTHERN
West Schious	LAKOTA
Westenhuck	HOUSATONIC
Western Mono	MONO
Western Oregon Tribes	WESTERN OREGON TRIBES
Westo (Cusabo)	YUCHI
Westoe	YUCHI
Weta Sioux (APS Indian Manuscripts Collection)	AMAHAMI
Wetc.naqei'n (Skitswish)	OKANAGON

474

Wetepahato	WETEPAHATO
Wetitsaán (Arikara)	HIDATSA
Whe-el-po (Lewis & Clark)	COLVILLE
Whilkut	WHILKUT
Whirlpool People	WEA
White Indians or White Indians with Beards	MENOMINEE
White Minqua (Dutch)	SUSQUEHANNA
White Mountain Coyotero Apache	WHITE MOUNTAIN COYOTERO
White Panis	WICHITA
White River	KAVIAWACH UTE
White Salmon	WHITE SALMON
White Salmon (River) Indians	CHILLUCKITTEQUAW
Whiwunai (Sandia Tiwa)	HOPI
Whonkenti	WHONKENTI
Whonkentia	WHONKENTIA
Wi'lfa Ampa'fa ami'm (Luckiamute-Kalapuya)	TWANA
Wi'skos Se'peon Wini'niwuk	MENOMINEE
Wi'tapahatu (Dakota & sim. to Cheyenne)	KIOWA
Wiam	WAIAM
Wiandot	WYANDOT
Wiatanons	WEA
Wicheta	WICHITA
Wichita	WICHITA
Wickquacoingh	WICKQUASGECK
Wickquasgeck	WICKQUASGECK
Wicoa	WICKQUASGECK
Wicocomico	WICOCOMOCO
Wicocomoco	WICOCOMOCO
Widshi ití'kapa (Tonto-Yuma)	PIMA
Widshi itíkapa (Tonto)	MARICOPA
Widyu Yapa	WIDYUNUU
Widyunuu	WIDYUNUU
Wiechquaesgeck	WICKQUASGECK
Wiekagjoy	WIEKAGJOY
Wighcocòmico	WIGHCOCÒMICO
Wighcocomoce	WICOCOMICO
Wighcomoco	WIGHCOMOCO
Wighcomoco	WEROWOCOMOCO
Wild Coyotes (Zuni)	NAVAJO
Wild Oat Indians	MENOMINEE
Wild Rice Men (Fr. Folles Avoines)	MENOMINEE
Wili idahapa (Tulkepaya)	MOJAVE
Willamette Falls Indians	CLOWWEWALLA
Willamette Indians	CLOWWEWALLA
Willamette Tumwater	CLOWWEWALLA
Willapa (erroneous)	KWALHIOQUA
Willetpo	WALLOWA
Wimbee	WIMBEE
Wimbehee	WIMBEE
Wiminuche	WEEMINUCHE UTES
Wiminuche Ute	WIMINUCHE UTE
Wimonuntci	WEEMINUCHE UTES
Wïna't:ca (Wasco)	WENATCHEE
Winatara for Minnetaree	ATSINA or HIDATSA
Winatarie for Minnetaree	ATSINA or HIDATSA
Winatchi	WENATCHEE
Wind People	KANSA
Winebago	WINNEBAGO
Winefelly	WINEFELLY KALAPUYA
Winefelly Kalapuya	WINEFELLY KALAPUYA
Winetaree for Minnetaree	ATSINA or HIDATSA
Winibigoshish	WINIBIGOSHISH
Winnebago	WINNEBAGO
Winnebaygo	WINNEBAGO
Winnebegoshishiwininewak	WINIBIGOSHISH
Winnerago	WINNEBAGO
Wintu	WINTU
Wintun	WINTUN
Wintun	WINTU
Winyah	WINYAW
Winyaw	WINYAW
Wisacky	WAXHAW
Wisconsin	MENOMINEE
Wisconsin	WISCONSIN
Wish-ham	WISHRAM
Wishosk	WIYOT
Wishram	WISHRAM
Witchetaw	WICHITA
Witishaxtánu (Huron)	ILLINOIS CLUSTER OF TRIBES
Witsúne (Comanche)	KADOHADACHO CONFEDERACY
Wiwohka	WIWOHKA
Wiyot	WIYOT
W'Nahk'-Chee	NATCHEZ
Woccon	WOCCON
Wobanaki	ABENAKI
Wóhesh (Wichita)	PAWNEE
Wolf Indians	PAWNEE
Wolf Nation	ABENAKI
Wolf Pawnee	SKIDI PAWNEE
Wolf People or Wolf Indinans	PAWNEE
Wollawalla	WALLA WALLA
Wong'-ge (Santa Clara & Ildefonso)	JEMEZ PUEBLO
Wongunk	WANGUNK
Woodland Cree	CREE
Woraxa (Iowa, Missouri & Oto)	POTAWATOMI
Woráxe (Winnebago)	POTAWATOMI
Wula'stegwi'ak	MALISEET
Wulx (Takelma)	SHASTA
Wusi (Alsea name for Alsea River)	ALSEA
Wyahtinaw	WYAHTINAW
Wyam	WYAM
Wyandot	HURON
Wyandot	WYANDOT
Wyandott	WYANDOT
Wyandotte	WYANDOT
Wycome	WYCOME
Wylacki	WAILAKI
Wyniaw	WYNIAW
Wynoochee	WYNOOCHEE
Wyoming	WYOMING
Wyoming Shoshoni	SHOSHONI, EASTERN
Wysox	WYSOX
Xa-he'-ta-ño' (Cheyenne)	APACHE
Xactin	SOACATINO
Xaramane	XARAMANE
Xaray (Tiwa)	ZUÑI
Xátukwiwa (Shasta)	WINTUN
Xawálapáiy	WALAPAI
Xyaka or Xualla (Spanish & Portuguese w/ "X" for "Sh"	CHERAW
Ya'-ide'sta (Umpqua)	MOLALLA
Yaªgala' (Takelma)	UMPQUA
Yabipai Cajuala	SOUTHERN PAIUTE
Yabipai Jabesua	HAVASUPAI
Yabipai Lipan	LIPAN
Yabipais Nabajay	NAVAJO
Yabipais Natagé	KIOWA APACHE
Yachats	YACHATS
Yacomanshaghking	YACOMANSHAGHKING
Yacovane	YACOVANE
Yadkin	YADKIN
Yahach	YACHATS
Yahatc	YACHATS
Yahats	YACHATS
Yahaut	YACHATS
Yahi	YAHI
Yahooskin	YAHUSKIN
Yahuch	YACHATS
Yahuskin	YAHUSKIN
Yahute	YACHATS
Yakama	YAKIMA
Yakima	YAKIMA

Yákokon kápai (Tokawa; incl. Coahuiltecan)	KARANKAWAN TRIBES
Yam Hill	YAMEL KALAPUYA
Yam-pa-ri-cot	YAMPARIKA
Yamacraw (Yamasee whose name came from that of a Florida mission)	YAMACRAW
Yamasee	YAMASEE
Yamassee	YAMASEE
Yamecah	JAMECO
Yamel Kalapuya	YAMEL KALAPUYA
Yamhill	YAMEL KALAPUYA
Yamiscaron	YAMASEE
Yampa Ute	YAMPA UTE
Yampah or Yä'mpaini (Shoshoni)	COMANCHE
Yampaos	YAVAPAI
Yamparack	YAMPARIKA
Yamparika Comanche	YAMPARIKA
Yamparock	YAMPARIKA
Yana	YANA
Yang-na	YANG-NA
Yanimna	TAHNEEMUH
Yankton Sioux	YANKTON SIOUX
Yanktonai Sioux	YANKTONAI SIOUX
Yanktons of the Plains	YANKTONAI SIOUX
Yapparethka	YAMPARIKA
Yaqa' yik	YACHATS
Yaqui	YAQUINA
Yaquina	YAQUINA
Yatasi	YATASI
Yatasi, Upper	YATASI, UPPER
Yatchee-thinyoowuc (Cree)	CHIPEWYAN
Yatchitoches (Lewis & Clark)	NATCHITOCHES CONFEDERACY
Yátilatlávi (Tonto)	NAVAJO
Yattassee	YATASI
Yattken	YADKIN
Yava Supai	HAVASUPAI
Yavapai	YAVAPAI
Yawhick	YACHATS
Yaxka'-a (Wyandot)	CROW
Yayecha	EYEISH
Yazoo	YAZOO
Ybaha or Yguaja (Timucua)	GUALE
Ycha-yamel-amin (Atfalati Kalapuya)	YAMEL KALAPUYA
Yeahtentanee	WEA
Yehah	YEHAH
Yeletpoo	YELETPOO
Yellow-knife Indians	TATSANOTTINE
Yemassee	YAMASEE
Yeopim	WEAPEMEOC
Yoa	YAMASEE
Yoetahá or Yutahá (Apache)	NAVAJO
Yokuts	YOKUTS
Yokuts, Buena Vista	BUENA VISTA YOKUTS
Yokuts, Kings River Group	KINGS RIVER YOKUTS
Yokuts, Northern Group of the Foothills Division	NORTHERN GROUP OF THE FOOTHILLS YOKUTS
Yokuts, Nothern Group of the Valley Division	NORTHERN GROUP OF THE VALLEY YOKUTS
Yokuts, Poso Creek	POSO CREEK YOKUTS
Yokuts, Southern Group of the Valley Division	SOUTHERN GROUP OF THE VALLEY YOKUTS
Yokuts, Tule-Kaweah	TULE-KAWEAH YOKUTS
Yoncalla Kalapuya	YONCALLA KALAPUYA
Yonkalla	YONCALLA KALAPUYA
Yoovte	UINTA UTE
Yoron	TUNICA
Yosemite	YOSEMITE
Yosemite-Mono Lake Paiutes	KUTZADIKA'A
Yotche-eme (Hopi)	APACHE
Youghtanund	YOUGHTANUND

Youicone	YOUICONE
Youitts (Lewis & Clark, recorded by) Youitz (Drake)	YACHATS YACHATS
Yreka Shasta	YREKA SHASTA
Yscane	YSCANI
Yscani	YSCANI
Ysleta del Sur	TIGUA PUEBLO
Ysleta of the South	TIGUA PUEBLO
Ysleta Pueblo	ISLETA PUEBLO
Yu-i'-ta (Panamint)	NAVAJO
Yuchi	YUCHI
Yuhaviatam	SAN MANUEL
Yui	YUI
Yuk'hiti ishak	ATÁKAPA
Yuki	YUKI
Yum	KAMIA
Yuma	YUMA
Yuma-Apache	YUMA-APACHE
Yupaha (Timucua)	GUALE
Yupini	JUPE
Yurok	TOLOWA
Yurok	YUROK
Yussaha (Wyandot)	SIOUX
Yussáha (Wyandot)	DAKOTA
Yustaga	HOSTAQUA
Yutaletan	UTE
Yutara'ye-ru'nu (Huron)	KICKAPOO
Yute	UTE
Yutilapá (Yavapai)	NAVAJO
Yutilatláwi (Tonto)	NAVAJO
Yûukama	YAKIMA
Yxcani	YSCANI
Za'-ke (Santee and Yankton)	SAUK
Zaratenumanke (Mandan)	PAWNEE
Ze-gar-kin-a (Apache)	ZUÑI
Zia	ZIA PUEBLO
Zia Pueblo	ZIA PUEBLO
Zuñi	ZUÑI
Zuni or Zuñi Pueblo	ZUÑI
Zuzéca wicása (Teton Dakota)	SHOSHONI, NORTHERN

Drake's Indians of North America

An Alphabetical Enumeration of the Indian Tribes and Nations

Samuel G. Drake, *The Aboriginal Races of North America: Biographical Sketches of Eminent Individuals, An Historical Account of the Different Tribes from First Discovery of the Continent to Present Period* (popular title, *Drake's Indians of North America*), 15th Edition, Rev. (New York: Hurst & Company, 1880), pp. 9-16.

Drake[1]	Atlas[2]		
Abekas	Abihka	Athapascow	
Abenakies	Abnaki	[Athapuskow]	Cree
Absoroka	Crow	Atnas	Shuswap #
Accokesaw	Accocesaw	Attacapas	Attacapa
Acomak	Accomac (Nanticoke or Powhaten)	Attapulgas	Seminole
		Attikamigues	Attikamigues (D)
Adaize	Adaes	Aucosisco	Aucocisco
Adirondaks	Adirondak	Aughquaga	Aughquagah
Affagoula	Affagoula	Ayauais	Iowa
Agawom	Wampanoag	Ayutans	Ayutans (D)
Ahwahaway	Amahami	Bayogoula	Bayogoula
Ajoues	Iowa	Bedies [Bidai]	Attacapa
Alansar	Clowwewalla or Fall Indians	Big-Devils [Big Devils]	Yanktonai Sioux
Algonkin	Algonkin or Algonquin #	Biloxi	Biloxi
Aliatan	Shoshoni, Northern	Blackfeet	Blackfeet or Siksika
Aliche	Eyeish	Blanche,	
Allakaweah	Allakaweah	Bearded or White	Menominee
Allibama	Alibama	Blue-Mud	Nez Percé
Amalistes	Ameliste	Brotherton	Brotherton Indians
Anasaguntakook		Caddo	Caddo
[Arosaguntacook]	Abnaki	Cadodache	Kadohadacho
Andaste	Susquehanna	Caiwa, or Kaiwa	Kaiwa
Apache	Lipan Apache	Calasthocle	Quinault
Apalachicola	Apalachicola	Callimix	Callimix (D)
Appalousa	Opelousa	Camanches	Comanche
Aquanuschioni	Iroquois	Canarsee	Canarsee
Arapahas	Arapaho	Cances	Lipan Apache
Armouchiquois,		Canibas [or Kenneth]	Abnaki
or Marachite	Armouchiquois	Carankoua	Karankawa
Arrenamuse	Arrenamuse (D)	Caree	Caree (D)
Assinnaboin	Assiniboin	Carriers	Carriers #
Atenas	Shuswap #	Castahana	Castahana (D)
		Cataka	Kiowa

Catawba	Catawba	Clatsops	Clatsop
Cathlacumups	Cathlacumup (Multnomah)	Cneis [Cenis]	Hainai
Cathlakahikit	Cathlakaheckit	Cohakies	Cahokia
Cathlakamaps	Cathlacomatup (Multnomah)	Colapissas	Acolopissa
Cathlamat	Cathlamet	Conchattas	Koasati
Cathlanamenamen	Kathlaminimin (Multonomah)	Congarees	Congaree
Cathlanaquiah	Cathlanaquiah (Multnomah)	Conoys	Conoy
Cathlapootle	Cathlapotle	Cookkoo-oose	Anasitch (Coos)
Cathlapooya	Calapooya Kalapuya	Coopspellar	Coopspellar (D)
Cathlasko	Cathlasko (D)	Coosadas [Coosawda]	Koasati
Cathlath	Cathlath (D)	Copper [Copper Indians]	Tatsanottine #
Cathlathlala @	Cathlathlala (Watlala)	Corees	Coree
Cattanahaw	Cattanahaw (D)	Coronkawa	Karankawa
Caughnewaga	Caughnewaga #	Cowlitsick	Cowlitz
Chactoo	Chatot (Chacatos)	Creeks	Creek
Chaouanons	Shawnee	Creess	Cree
Cheegee	Cheegee (Cherokee)	Crows	Crow
Chehaws	Chiaha	Cutsahnim	
Chepeyan	Chipewyan #	[Cuts-sáh--nem]	Yakima
Cherokee	Cherokee	Dahcota, or Docota	Dakota (collective or division uk)
Cheskitalowa	Cheskitalowa (D)	Delaware	Delaware
Chickasaw @	Chickasaw	Dinondadies	Dinondadies (Tionantati) #
Chien	Cheyenne	Doegs	Nanticoke
Chiheeleesh	Chiheeleesh (D)	Dogribs [Dog-Ribs]	Thlingechadinne #
Chikahomini	Chickahominy	Dogs	Mosopelea
Chikamauga	Chickamauga	Dotame	Dotame
Chillates	Chillates (D)	Eamuse. See Emusa	Emusa (Yamasee)
Chillukittequau	Chilluckitequaw	Echemins	Etchemin
Chiltz	Chehalis	Edistos	Edisto (Cusado)
Chimnahpum	Chimakum	Emuas	Emusa (Yamasee)
Chinnook	Chinook	Eneshures	Enesher
Chippanchikchiks @	Chippanchikchiks (D)	Eries	Erie
Chippewas	Chippewa	Esaws	Catawba
Chitimicha	Chitimacha	Eskeloots	Echeloot
Choktaw	Choctaw	Esquimaux	Esquimaux #
Chopunnish	Nez Percé	Etohussewakkes	Etohussewakkes (D)
Chowan	Chowan	Facullies	Carrier, Northern #
Chowanok	Chowanoc	Fall	Clowwewalla
Christenaux	Cree #	Five Nations	Five Nations of the Iroquois
Clahclellah	Clahclellah	Flat-Heads [Flatheads]	Chinook
Clakstar	Clatskanie	Folles Avoines	Menominee
Clamoctomich		Fond du Lac	Chippewa
[Clamoitomish]	Chinook	Fowl-Towns [Fowl towns]	Seminole (descriptive term)
Clanimatas	Claninnata (Multnomah)	Fox	Fox
Clannarminimuns	Kathlaminimin (Multnomah)	Ganawese	Conoy
Clarkames @	Clatsop	Gayhead [Gay Head]	Wampanoag

Grand River	Mohawk et al. #	Kiskakons	Staitan
Gros Ventres [Gros		Kites @	Staitan
Ventres of the Prairie	Atsina	Knistenaux [Kristinaux]	Cree #
Hallibees	Hilibi (Muskogee)	Konagens	Konagens (D)
Hannakallal	Hannakallal	Kook-koo-oose	
Hare-Foot @		[Cook-koo-oose]	Coos
[Hare Indians]	Kawchottine #	Kuskarawaoks	Nanticoke
Hassanamesits	Nipnuck	Lahanna	Senijextee
Hellwits	Hellwits	Lapanne. See Apaches	Lipan Apache
Herring Pond	Herring Pond (Wampanoag)	Lartielo [Lar-ti-e-lo]	Spokan
Hietans [Ietan,		Leaf	Sioux
more properly Ute]	Hietan (Comanche)	Leech River	Chippewa
Hihighenimmo @	Hihighenimmo (D)	Lenna Lenape	
Hini	Hainai (Hasinai Confederacy or Caddo)	[Lenni Lenape]	Delaware
		Lipanis	Lipan Apache
Hitchittees	Hitchiti	Loucheux	
Hohilpos	Salish	[Louchieux proper]	Takkuth-kutchin #
Humas	Huma	Lukawis	Lukawis (D)
Hurons	Huron	Lukkarso	Luckkarso
Illinois	Illinois	Luktons	Luktons (D)
Inies, or Tachies [Hainai]	Hainai (Hasinai Confederacy of Caddo)	Machapungas	Machapunga
		Mandans	Mandan
Ioways	Iowa	Mangoags, or Tuteloes	Nottaway
Iroquois	Iroquois	Manhattans	Manhattan
Isatis [Isanti]	Sioux, Dakota/Eastern Division	Mannahoaks	Manahoac
Ithkyemamits	Ithkyemamits	Marachites	Maliseet
Jelan	Jelan (D)	Marsapeagues	Marsapeague
Kadapaus	Kadapaus (Catawba)	Marshpees	Mashpee (Wampanoag)
Kahunkles [Kahunkle]	Tillamook	Mascoutins	Mascoutin
Kaloosas	Calusa	Massachucsetts	Massachusett
Kanenavish	Arapaho	Massawomes	
Kanhawas	Karankawa	[Massawineck or	
Kansas	Kansa	Massawomeck]	Shawnee
Kaskaskias	Kaskaskia	Mathlanobs	Mathlanobs (D)
Kaskayas	Pawnee	Mayes [Maye]	Mayeye
Katteka	Padouca	Menominies	Menominee
Keekatsa [Kihnatsa]	Crow	Messassagnes	Mississauga # (Chippewa)
Keyche	Keychie (Caddo)	Miamis	Miami
Kiawa	Kiawa	Mikasaukies	Mikasuki
Kigene	Kigene (D)	Mikmaks	Micmac #
Kikapoo	Kickapoo	Miksuksealton	Salish
Killamuk [Killamook]	Tillamook	Mindawarcarton @	Mindawarcarton (Sioux)
Killawat	Killawat (D)	Minetares	
Killaxthocles	Killasthokle	[Minnetaree of the River]	Hidatsa
Kimoenims		Mingoes	Mingo
[Cho-pun-nish]	Nez Perce	Minsi	Minisink
Kinai	Tanaina (AK)		

Missouries	Missouri	Otagamies [Outagamie]	Fox
Mitchigamies	Michigamea	Otoes	Oto
Mohawks	Mohawk	Ottawas	Ottawa
Mohegans	Mohegan	Ouiatanons	Wea
Monacans	Monacan	Oumas	Huma
Mongoulatches	Mogoulacha	Owassissas	Owassissas (Seminole)
Montagnes	Montagnais-Naskapi #	Ozas	Ozaw
Montauks	Montauk	Ozimie	Ozimie (D)
Moratoks	Moratok	Pacana	Pakana (Muscogee)
Mosquitos	Mosquito (CA)	Padouca	Comanche
Multnomahs	Multnomah	Padowaga	Padowaga (D)
Munseys	Munsee	Pailsh	Pailsh (D)
Muskogees	Muskogee	Palache	Palache (D)
Nabedaches	Nabedache	Pamlico	Pamlico
Nabijos	Navajo	Panca	Ponca
Nandakoe	Nandakoe (Caddo)	Panis	Wichita
Nantikokes	Nanticoke	Pascagoula	Pascagoula
Narcotah	Narcotah	Pascataway [Piscataway]	Conoy
Narragansets	Narrangansett	Passamaquoddie	Passamaquoddy
Nashuays	Nashua	Paunee	Pawnee
Natchez	Natchez	Pawistucienemuck	Pawistucienemuck (D)
Natchitoches	Natchitoches	Pawtuckets	Pawtucket (Pennacook)
Nateotetains	Nateotetains (D)	Pecans [Pegan]	Chabanakongkomun (Nipmuc)
Natiks	Natick (Massachusett)	Pelloatpallah	Palouse
Nechacoke	Nechacokee (Multnomah)	Pennakooks	Pennacook
Neekeetoo	Neekeetoo (D)	Penobscots @	Penobscot
Nemalquinner	Clowwewalla	Peorias	Peoria
Niantiks	Niantic	Pequakets	Pequawket
Nicariagas	Nicariagas (D)	Pequots	Pequot
Nipissins	Nipissin	Phillimees	Seminole
Nipmuks	Nipmuc	Piankashaws	Piankashaw
Norridgeworks	Norridgewock	Piankatank	Piankatank
Nottoways	Nottaway	Pinneshow	Pinneshow (D)
Nyacks or Manhattans	Manhattan	Pishquitpah	Pishquitpah
Oakmulges	Okmulgee	Potoash	Potoash
Ocameches	Occaneechi	Pottowattomie	Potawatomi
Ochees	Yuchi	Powhatans	Powhatan & Powhatan Confederacy
Oconas	Oconee		
Ojibwas	Chippewa	Puans [Les Puans]	Winnebego
Okatiokinans	Okatiokinans (D)	Quabaogs	Quabaog (Nipmuc)
Omahas	Omaha	Quapaw	Quapaw
Oneidas	Oneida	Quathlahpohtles	Quathlahpohtle
Onondagas	Onondaga	Quatoghie	Quatoghie (D)
Ootlashoots		Quesadas [Coosawda]	Koasati
[Oat-lash-shoots; Shalees]	Shalee (Salish)	Quieetsos	Quieetsos (D)
Osages	Osage	Quiniilts	Quinault
		Quinnechart	Quinnechart (D)

Quinnipissa	Quinipissa	Skunnemoke	Atákapa
Quoddies.		Smokshop [Smackshop]	Chilluckittequaw
See Passamaquoddie	Passamaquoddy	Snake. See Aliatans, or	
Rapids	Atsina	Shoshonees.	Shoshoni, Northern
Red Stick	Muscogee	Sokokie [Sokoki]	Sokoki (Abenaki)
Redground		Sokulk	Sokulk
[Red Town]	Seminole	Souriquois	Micmac #
Redknife [Red-knife]	Tatsanottine #	Souties	Souties
Red-Wing [Red Wing]	Sioux, Dakota/Eastern Division	Soyennom	Soyennom (D)
Ricaree	Arikara	Spokain	Spokan
River [River Indians]	Mahican or Mohegan	Squannaroo	Squannaroo (D)
Round-Heads	Huron	St. John's @	Maliseet
Ryawas	Ryawas (D)	Staetans	Suhtai or Sutaio
Sachdagughs		Stockbridge, Mass.	Stockbridge Indians
[Sachdagugh-roonaw]	Powhatan	Stockbridge, New	Stockbridge Indians
Sankhikans	Sankhikan	Susquehannok	Susquehanna
Santees	Sioux, Dakota/Eastern Division	Sussees	Sarcee
Saponies	Saponi	Symerons	Seminole
Satanas	Shawnee	Tacullies	Taculli (Carriers) #
Sauk, or Sac	Sauk	Tahsagroudie	Tahsagroudie (D)
Sauteurs, or Fall Indians	Chippewa	Tahuacana [Tehuacana]	Tawakoni
Savannah	Savannah	Tallahasse	Tallahasse
Scattakooks	Scattakook	Tallewheana	Tallewheana (D)
Seminoles	Seminole	Tamaronas	Tamaroa (Illinois Cluster of Tribes)
Senecas	Seneca		
Sepones	Saponi	Tamatles [Tamatle]	Toma'li (Creek, Lower)
Serranna	Serrano	Tarratines [Tarrateens]	Abnaki
Sewees	Sewee	Tattowhehallys	Seminole
Shallalah	Shallalah	Taukaways	Taukaways (D)
Shallattoos	Shallattoos (D)	Tawakenoe [Tawakeno]	Tuacane
Shanwappone		Tawaws	Tawasa
[Shanwappoms]	Yakima	Telmocresse	Telmocresse (D)
Shawane	Shawnee	Tenisaw	Taensa
Sheastukle	Sheastukle (D)	Tetons	Lakota Sioux (Western Division)
Shinikooks	Shinnecock (Montauk)	Tionontaties	Tionontati #
Shoshonee	Shoshoni	Tockwoghs	Tockwogh (Nanticoke)
Shoto	Shoto (Multnomah)	Tonicas	Tunica
Sicaunies	Sicauni	Tonkahans	Tonkawa
Sioux	Sioux	Tonkawa	Tonkawa
Sisatones	Sisatones (D)	Toteros [Tuterro]	Tutelo
Sitimacha	Chitimacha	Totuskeys. See Moratoks	Moratok
Sitka	Kiksadi (Tlingit) (AK)	Towacanno, or Towoash	Tawakoni
Six Nations %	Six Nations of the Iroquois	Tsononthouans	Tsononthouans (D)
Skaddals	Skaddal (Wenatchee)	Tukabatche	Tukabahchee (Muskogee)
Skeetsomish	Skeetsomish (Skitswish)	Tunica	Tunica
Skilloot	Skilloot	Tunxis	Tunxis
		Tuscarora	Tuscarora

Tushepahas, and Ootlashoots	Salish	Wollawalla	Walla Walla
Tuteloes. See Mangoaks, or Mangoags	Tutelo	Wyandots	Wyandot
		Wycomes	Wycomes (D)
		Wyniaws	Wyniaws (D)
Tutseewa	Tutseewa (D)	Yamacraw	Yamasee
Twightwees	Miami	Yamasee	Yamasee
Uchee	Yuchi	Yamperack	Yamparika (Comanche)
Ufallah	Ufallah (D)	Yanktons	Yankton Sioux (Nakota)
Ugaljachmutzi	Ugaljachmutzi	Yattassee	Yatasi
Ulseah	Tillamook	Yazoos	Yazoo
Unalachtgo [Unalachtigo]	Nanticoke	Yeahtentanee	Wea
Unamies	Unami	Yehah	Yehah (D)
Unchagogs	Unkechaug	Yeletpoo	Yeletpoo (D)
Upsaroka	Crow	Youicone	Youicone (D)
Waakicum	Wahkiakum (Cathlamet)		
Wabinga	Wappinger		
Waco	Waco		
Wahowpum	Wahowpum		
Wahpacoota	Wahpacoota (Sioux, Dakota/ Eastern Division)		
Wahpatone @	Wahpetunwan (Sioux, Dakota/ Eastern Division)		
Wamesits	Pawtucket		
Wampanoag	Wampanoag		
Wappings	Wappinger		
Warananconguins	Wapping		
Washaws	Washa		
Watanons, or Weas. See Oulatinons.	Wea		
Watepaneto	Watepaneto (D)		
Waterees	Wateree		
Wawenoks	Abnaki		
Waxsaw	Waxhaw		
Weas, or Waas	Wea		
Wekisa	Wekisa (D)		
Welch	Welsh (Salish)		
Westoes	Yuchi		
Wetepahato	Wetepahato (D)		
Wheelpo [Whe-el-po]	Colville		
Whirlpools [Whirlpool People]	Wea		
White [White Indians]	Menominee		
Wighcomoco	Wighcomoco		
Willewahs	Wallowa (Nez Percé)		
Winnebago	Winnebago		
Wokkon	Woccon		
Wolf	Abnaki, Delaware, Pawnee, et al.		

Aborigines
(from *Notes on the State of Virginia*)

In the fall of 1781, Thomas Jefferson compiled his response to series of questions (queries) from a French diplomat, François de Barbé Marbois, that he subsequently published under the title "Notes on the State of Virginia." His responses drew on material beyond the confines of the boundaries claimed by the state of Virginia. (During the colonial period, Virginia encompassed modern West Virginia and a vast areas beyond, north, west and south.)

Query XI concerned local Aborigines, "A description of the Indians established in that state?" The response was in the form of a narrative and series of tables listing the names of 119 tribes with their respective populations ("warriors") and locations. Jefferson included tribes both within the then limits of the United Colonies and those "Northward and Westward" beyond. He placed a number of the local tribes within three major group: Monacan (5); Mannahoac (8); and Powhatans. To prepare his response, Jefferson relied on data from four principal sources: George Croghan (1759); French trader, whose list was appended to the report of Colonel Boquet's Expedition (1764); Captain Thomas Hutchins (1768); and John Dodge, American trader (1779).

Following is an alphabetical list of the 119 tribal names compiled from the tables provided in Query XI with their common or popular name or spelling, if known, in parentheses. Also indicated in parentheses are the tribal names that have not been identified beyond the reference in the Notes and supporting documents; those names corresponding to an as yet unidentified subgroup of a known tribe; and those for which a probable connection to a known tribe has been established but not confirmed.

---

[1]Name of Tribe, Band or Subgroup as it appears in Drake, of which there are 464, with the popular spelling in [ ] if applicable. The notations ", or" and "See…" were taken from the original. Any brief notes related to location or association have been omitted.
[2]Identified Tribal Name as it appears in this work with parent group in ( ) if applicable.

[ ]	Popular Spelling
( )	Parent Tribe
#	Canadian Tribe. Others: AK-Alaska; CA-Central America; M-Mexico
@	Out of alphabetical sequence in original
%	Five Nations of the Iroquois plus Shawnee instead of Tursarora
D	The names (57) are very likely variations in the spelling of the names of tribes, bands or villages that have not yet been identified.

Abenakics (Abnaki)
Accohanocs (Accohanoc)
Accomàcks (Accomac)
Ajoues (Iowa)
Algonquins (Algonquin)
Alibamous (Alabama)
Amelistes (*)
Appamàttocs (Appomatotox)
Arkanzas (Quapaw)
Arrowhàtocs (Arrohattoc)
Assinaboes (Assiniboin)
Aughquàgahs (*)
Blancs or [Ý] Barbus
(Menominee)
Canses (Kanza)
Caouitas (*)
Catawbas (Catawba)
Cavùgas (Cayuga)
Chacktaws (Choctaw)
Chalas (*)
Cherokees (Cherokee)
Chèsapeaks (Chesapeake)
Chiakanessou (*)
Chickahòminies
(Chickahominy)
Chickasaws (Chickasaw)
Chippawas (Chippewa)
Chìskiacs (Chiskiac)
Christinaux or Kris (Cree)
Cohunnewagoes (*)
Connasedagoes (Conestoga)
Conoies (Conoy)
Cuttatawomans
(Cuttatawomen)
Delawares or Linnelinopies
(Delaware)
Folle avoine (Menominee)
Grandes eaux (*)
Hassinungaes (Hassinunga)
Illinois (Illinois)
Kaskaskias (Kaskaskia)
Kecoughtáns (Kecoughtan)

Kickapous (Kickapoo)
Les Puans (Winnebago)
Lezar (*)
Linways (*)
Little Algonkins (*)
Lower Creeks (Lower Creek)
Machecous (*)
Màscoutens (Mascoutin)
Màttapomènts (Mattapanient)
Messasagues (*)
Miamis (Miami)
Michmacs (Micmac)
Mìmgoes (Mingo)
Mineamis (Miami)
Miscòthins (*)
Missouris (Missouri)
Mohìccons (Mohegan)
Mohocks (Mohawk)
Moràughtacuttds
(Moraughtcund)
Munsies (Munsee)
Musquakies (*)
Mynonàmies (*)
Nansamònds (Nansemond)
Nantaughtacunds
(Mantaughtacund)
Nánticocs (Nanticoke)
Natchez (Natchez)
Nipissins (*)
Onaumanìents (Onawanient)
Onèidas (Oneida)
Onondagoes (Onondaga)
Ontponies (Ontponea)
Orondocs (*)
Osages (Osage)
Oswegatchies (*)
Otogamies or Foxes (Fox)
Ottawas (Ottawa)
Ouanakina (*)
Ouiàtonons (*)
Ouisconsings (*)
Ousasoys. Grand Tuc. (*)

Outimacs (*)
Padoucas (Padouca)
Pamùnkies (Pamunkey)
Panis. Freckled (? Wichita)
Panis. White (? Pawnee)
Paspahèghes (Paspahean)
Patôuvomekes (*)
Payankatanks (*)
Piankishas (Piankeshaw)
Piorias (Peoria)
Pissasecs (Pissasec)
Pouteòtamies (Potawatomie)
Powhatàns (Powhatan)
Quiocochànocs (*)
Rappahànocs (Rappahannock)
Round heads (Huron)
Sapòonies (Saponi)
Secacaonics (Secacawoni)
Senecas (Seneca)
Shakies (*)
Shàkies (*)
Shàwanees (Shawnee)
Sioux (Sioux)
Sioux of the Meadows (Lakota)
Sioux of the Woods (# Sioux)
Sioux, Eastern (Dakota)
Souikilas (*)
Tegninaties (*)
Tauxenents (Tauxenent)
Tauxitanians (Tanxnitania)
Tuscaròras (Tuscarora)
Twightwees (Miami)
Upper Creeks (Upper Creek)
Vermillions (*)
Wàrrasqeaks (Warrasqueoc)
Webings (*)
Wènocs (Weanoc)
Wèrowocomicos
(Werowocomoco)
Whonkenties (*)
Wighcocòmicoes (*)
Wyandots (Wyandot)

119

Notes:
Cross-entries made for all spelling variations.
*Unable to identify. Record established. (31)
#Unable to identify subgroup. (1)
?Probable connection. Record established. (2)

Sources:

Thomas Jefferson, "Notes on the State of Virginia" (1781-1782), *Thomas Jefferson, Writings*. Merrill D. Peterson, ed. (New York: Library of America, 1984) , Query XI, pp. 218-232.

"Capt. Croghan to Gen. John Stanwix (Pittsburgh, July 15, 1759)," from the Ohio Valley-Great Lakes Ethnohistory Archives (Bloomington, IN: Glenn Black Laboratory of Archaeology, 1996-2000), 191-193, at http://www.gbl.indiana.edu/archives/miamis12/M59-60_5a.html [July 22, 2006].

William Smith, "Names of Different Indian Nations in North America, with Their Numbers of Fighting Men...," Appendix V, Historical account of Bouquet's expedition against the Ohio Indians, in 1764 (Cincinnati, OH: Roger Clarke Co., 1907), 153-156, available from Historic Pittsburgh (Pittsburgh, PA: University of Pittsburgh, n.d.) at http://digital.library.pitt.edu/cgi-bin/t/text/text-idx?idno=00hc07093m ;view=toc;c=pitttext [July 25, 2006].

"Virginia Indians" (Richmond, VA: Virginia Tourism Commission, 2006) at http://www.virginia.org/ site/features.asp?FeatureID=188 [July 22, 2006].

Inez Ramsey, "Virginia's Indians, Past & Present" (VA: James Madison University, n.d.) at http://falcon. jmu.edu/~ramseyil/vaindians.htm [July 22, 2006].

Thomas Jefferson, "Aborigines: A description of the Indians established in that state?," *Notes on the State of Virginia* , Query XI, from the Electronic Text Center, University of Virginia Library (Charlottesville, VA, 2006), 219-233, at http://etext.lib.virginia.edu/etcbin/toccer-new2?id =JefVirg.sgm&images= images/ modeng&data=/texts/english/modeng/parsed&tag=public&part=11&division=div1 [January 8, 2007].

American Indian and Alaskan Native Populations by State

2000 Census

	State/Category	AIAN - One Race	% AIAN
1.	California	333,346	13.5%
2.	Oklahoma	273,230	11.0%
3.	Arizona	255,879	10.3%
4.	New Mexico	173,483	7.0%
5.	Texas	118,362	4.8%
6.	North Carolina	99,551	4.0%
7.	Alaska	98,043	4.0%
8.	Washington	93,301	3.8%
9.	New York	82,461	3.3%
10.	South Dakota	62,283	2.5%
11.	Michigan	58,479	2.4%
12.	Montana	56,068	2.3%
13.	Minnesota	54,967	2.2%
14.	Florida	53,541	2.2%
15.	Wisconsin	47,228	1.9%
16.	Oregon	45,211	1.8%
17.	Colorado	44,241	1.8%
18.	North Dakota	31,329	1.3%
19.	Illinois	31,006	1.3%
20.	Utah	29,684	1.2%
21.	Nevada	26,420	1.1%
22.	Louisiana	25,477	1.0%
23.	Missouri	25,076	1.0%
24.	Kansas	24,936	1.0%
25.	Ohio	24,486	1.0%
26.	Alabama	22,430	0.9%
27.	Georgia	21,737	0.9%
28.	Virginia	21,172	0.9%
29.	New Jersey	19,492	0.8%
30.	Pennsylvania	18,348	0.7%

31.	Arkansas	17,808	0.7%
32.	Idaho	17,645	0.7%
33.	Indiana	15,815	0.6%
34.	Maryland	15,423	0.6%
35.	Tennessee	15,152	0.6%
36.	Massachusetts	15,015	0.6%
37.	Nebraska	14,896	0.6%
38.	South Carolina	13,718	0.6%
39.	Puerto Rico	13,336	0.5%
40.	Mississippi	11,652	0.5%
41.	Wyoming	11,133	0.4%
42.	Connecticut	9,639	0.4%
43.	Iowa	8,989	0.4%
44.	Kentucky	8,616	0.3%
45.	Maine	7,098	0.3%
46.	Rhode Island	5,121	0.2%
47.	West Virginia	3,606	0.1%
48.	Hawaii	3,535	0.1%
49.	New Hampshire	2,964	0.1%
50.	Delaware	2,731	0.1%
51.	Vermont	2,420	0.1%
52.	District of Columbia	1,713	0.1%

Total AIAN Population (One Race)   **2,489,292**   0.9%

less Puerto Rico   13,336

AIAN in 50 States & DC   **2,475,956**   0.9% of U.S. Population

Living on Reservations & Off-Reservation Trust Lands   *910,527*   *36.8%*   *of AIAN Alone, one or more tribes*
(PCT2)

AIAN Alone or Combined w/ Another Race   **4,119,301**   1.5% of U.S. Population

Living on Reservations & Trust Lands   *1,047,770*   *25.4%*   *of AIAN Alone, one or more tribes,*
  (PCT3)   *or Combined*

AIAN Combined w/ Another Race Only   **1,643,345**   *39.9%*   *of Total*

Living on Reservations & Trust Lands   *137,243*

Total United States Population   **281,421,906**   100.0%

White   211,460,626   75.1%

Black or African American   34,658,190   12.3%

Asian	10,242,998	3.6%
Hawaiian or Other Pacific Islanders	398,835	0.1%
Some Other Race	15,359,073	5.5%
Total Two or More Races	6,826,228	2.4%
Two or More Races excluding AIAN	5,182,883	1.8%
Hispanic or Latino	35,305,818	12.5%

Source: U.S. Census Bureau Publications, Census 2000.

"Table 1. Population by Race and Hispanic or Latino Origin, for the United States, Regions, Divisions, and States, and for Puerto Rico: 2000" (April 2, 2001)taken from Census 2000 Redistricting Data (P.L. 94-171) Summary File for states and Census 2000 Redistricting Summary File for Puerto Rico, Tables PL1 and PL2.

PCT2. AMERICAN INDIAN AND ALASKA NATIVE ALONE WITH ONE OR MORE TRIBES REPORTED FOR SELECTED TRIBES [47] — Universe: People who are American Indian and Alaska Native alone - total tribes tallied for people with one or more tribes, and people with no tribe reported. Data Set: Census 2000 Summary File 1 (SF 1) 100-Percent Data.(651 locations)

PCT3. AMERICAN INDIAN AND ALASKA NATIVE ALONE OR IN COMBINATION WITH ONE OR MORE OTHER RACES AND WITH ONE OR MORE TRIBES REPORTED FOR SELECTED TRIBES [47] — Universe: People who are American Indian and Alaska Native alone or in combination with one or more other races - total tribes tallied for people with one or more tribes, and people with no tribe reported. Data Set: Census 2000 Summary File 1 (SF 1)100-Percent Data.

See also *American Indian, Alaska Native Tables from the Statistical Abstract of the United States: 2004-2005*; *The American Indian and Alaska Native Population: 2000 Census 2000 Brief*, C2KBR/01-15, esp. Table 2, American Indian and Alaska Native Population for the United States, Regions, and States, and for Puerto Rico: 1990 and 2000, (February 2002), p. 5.

American Indian Reservations and Resident Populations within the Contiguous 48 States

The table beginning on the following page was constructed from the following tables issued by the Bureau of the Census for the 2000 Census. The full tables are available in printed form and on the Bureau's American FactFinder web site:

< http://factfinder.census.gov/home/saff/main.html?_lang=en >

PCT1: People who are American Indian and Alaska Native alone - total tribes tallied for people with one tribe only; and people with no tribe reported: Total tribes tallied.

PCT2: People who are American Indian and Alaska Native alone - total tribes tallied for people with one or more tribes; and people with no tribe reported: Total tribes tallied.

PCT3: People who are American Indian and Alaska Native alone or in combination with one or more other races - total tribes tallied for people with one or more tribes; and people with no tribe reported: Total tribes tallied.

PCT4: People who are American Indian or Alaska Native alone or in combination with one or more other races: Total.

PCT7: Total population: Total.

Reservations & Trust Lands	PCT1	PCT2	PCT3	PCT4	PCT7
Acoma Pueblo and Off-Reservation Trust Land, NM	2721	2725	2741	2739	2802
Agua Caliente Reservation, CA	172	180	290	283	21358
Alabama-Coushatta Reservation, TX	463	463	463	463	480
Allegany Reservation, NY	1291	1303	1394	1388	6804
Alturas Rancheria, CA	2	2	2	2	2
Augustine Reservation, CA	0	0	0	0	0
Bad River Reservation, WI	1096	1096	1124	1124	1411
Barona Reservation, CA	354	360	393	390	536
Battle Mountain Reservation, NV	112	112	113	113	124
Bay Mills Reservation and Off-Reservation Trust Land, MI	660	660	687	687	812
Benton Paiute Reservation, CA	39	39	44	44	50
Berry Creek Rancheria and Off-Reservation Trust Land, CA	110	110	111	111	138
Big Bend Rancheria, CA	0	0	0	0	0
Big Cypress Reservation, FL	110	110	110	110	142

Big Lagoon Rancheria, CA	19	19	20	20	24
Big Pine Reservation, CA	274	300	329	314	462
Big Sandy Rancheria, CA	76	78	85	84	98
Big Valley Rancheria, CA	187	189	195	194	225
Bishop Reservation, CA	903	997	1079	1026	1441
Blackfeet Reservation and Off-Reservation Trust Land, MT	8382	8632	8811	8684	10100
Blue Lake Rancheria, CA	33	33	43	41	78
Bois Forte Reservation, MN	455	473	479	470	657
Bridgeport Reservation, CA	21	23	26	25	43
Brighton Reservation, FL	448	450	486	485	566
Burns Paiute Colony and Off-Reservation Trust Land, OR	148	148	154	154	171
Cabazon Reservation, CA	15	15	18	18	806
Cahuilla Reservation, CA	106	106	116	116	154
Campbell Ranch, NV	204	210	223	220	446
Campo Reservation, CA	245	245	258	258	351
Capitan Grande Reservation, CA	0	0	0	0	0
Carson Colony, NV	207	275	299	265	286
Catawba Reservation, SC	359	365	414	411	494
Cattaraugus Reservation, NY	2121	2129	2151	2147	2412
Cedarville Rancheria, CA	22	22	23	23	26
Celilo Village, OR	39	39	42	42	44
Chehalis Reservation, WA	387	389	426	424	691
Chemehuevi Reservation, CA	146	152	167	164	345
Cheyenne River Reservation and Off-Reservation Trust Land, SD	6242	6256	6354	6346	8470
Chicken Ranch Rancheria, CA	0	0	0	0	11
Chitimacha Reservation, LA	282	288	292	289	409
Cochiti Pueblo, NM	691	699	716	712	1502
Coconut Creek Reservation, FL	0	0	0	0	0
Cocopah Reservation, AZ	519	519	532	532	1025
Coeur d'Alene Reservation, ID	1244	1258	1335	1327	6551
Cold Springs Rancheria, CA	176	178	189	188	193
Colorado River Reservation, AZ--CA	2204	2380	2614	2517	9201
Colusa Rancheria, CA	59	59	64	64	77
Colville Reservation and Off-Reservation Trust Land, WA	4506	4550	4804	4775	7587
Coos, Lower Umpqua, and Siuslaw Reservation and Off-Reservation Trust Land, OR	10	10	10	10	25
Coquille Reservation and Off-Reservation Trust Land, OR	125	131	148	145	258
Cortina Rancheria, CA	18	18	18	18	19
Coushatta Reservation, LA	20	20	20	20	25

Cow Creek Reservation, OR	5	5	7	7	22
Coyote Valley Reservation, CA	84	84	96	96	104
Crow Reservation and Off-Reservation Trust Land, MT	5107	5223	5334	5275	6894
Crow Creek Reservation, SD	1935	1937	1973	1972	2225
Cuyapaipe Reservation, CA	0	0	0	0	0
Dresslerville Colony, NV	243	331	337	292	315
Dry Creek Rancheria, CA	35	37	43	42	53
Duck Valley Reservation, NV--ID	991	1005	1024	1017	1265
Duckwater Reservation, NV	116	116	118	118	149
Eastern Cherokee Reservation, NC	6657	6673	6907	6898	8092
Elko Colony, NV	616	638	663	649	729
Elk Valley Rancheria, CA	39	41	44	43	77
Ely Reservation, NV	84	90	108	105	133
Enterprise Rancheria, CA	1	1	1	1	1
Fallon Paiute-Shoshone Colony, NV	102	108	117	114	123
Fallon Paiute-Shoshone Reservation and Off-Reservation Trust Land, NV	529	539	557	552	620
Flandreau Reservation, SD	326	326	353	353	408
Flathead Reservation, MT	6813	7185	8106	7883	26172
Fond du Lac Reservation and Off-Reservation Trust Land, MN--WI	1353	1353	1492	1492	3728
Forest County Potawatomi Community and Off-Reservation Trust Land, WI	466	498	505	489	531
Fort Apache Reservation, AZ	11666	11738	11891	11854	12429
Fort Belknap Reservation and Off-Reservation Trust Land, MT	2647	2933	2952	2809	2959
Fort Berthold Reservation, ND	3975	3997	4102	4091	5915
Fort Bidwell Reservation, CA	98	104	105	102	108
Fort Hall Reservation and Off-Reservation Trust Land, ID	3638	3658	3734	3724	5762
Fort Independence Reservation, CA	40	42	49	48	86
Fort McDermitt Reservation, NV--OR	300	302	302	301	309
Fort McDowell Reservation, AZ	723	787	803	771	824
Fort Mojave Reservation and Off-Reservation Trust Land, AZ--CA--NV	549	569	602	592	1043
Fort Peck Reservation and Off-Reservation Trust Land, MT	6339	6443	6629	6577	10321
Fort Pierce Reservation, FL	0	0	0	0	2
Fort Yuma Reservation, CA--AZ	1335	1369	1474	1455	2376
Gila River Reservation, AZ	10298	10408	10633	10578	11257
Goshute Reservation, NV--UT	97	97	97	97	105
Grand Portage Reservation and Off-Reservation Trust Land, MN	322	322	354	354	557
Grand Ronde Community and Off-Reservation Trust Land, OR	30	30	33	33	55

Grand Traverse Reservation and Off-Reservation Trust Land, MI	429	444	473	465	545
Greenville Rancheria, CA	5	5	5	5	22
Grindstone Rancheria, CA	139	143	148	146	162
Guidiville Rancheria and Off-Reservation Trust Land, CA	1	1	1	1	2
Hannahville Community and Off-Reservation Trust Land, MI	328	332	342	340	395
Havasupai Reservation, AZ	452	454	454	453	503
Ho-Chunk Reservation and Off-Reservation Trust Land, WI--MN	819	835	861	853	960
Hoh Reservation, WA	81	81	86	86	102
Hollywood Reservation, FL	537	539	560	559	2051
Hoopa Valley Reservation, CA	2220	2240	2294	2282	2633
Hopi Reservation and Off-Reservation Trust Land, AZ	6374	6772	6835	6633	6946
Hopland Rancheria and Off-Reservation Trust Land, CA	33	33	33	33	45
Houlton Maliseet Trust Land, ME	111	111	112	112	136
Hualapai Reservation and Off-Reservation Trust Land, AZ	1232	1274	1285	1261	1353
Huron Potawatomi Reservation, MI	9	9	9	9	11
Immokalee Reservation, FL	142	142	147	147	175
Inaja and Cosmit Reservation, CA	0	0	0	0	0
Indian Township Reservation, ME	564	564	597	597	676
Iowa Reservation and Off-Reservation Trust Land, KS--NE	99	99	99	99	168
Isabella Reservation and Off-Reservation Trust Land, MI	1393	1417	1716	1699	25838
Isleta Pueblo, NM	2656	2694	2876	2856	3166
Jackson Rancheria, CA	0	0	0	0	2
Jamestown S'Klallam Reservation and Off-Reservation Trust Land, WA	2	2	3	3	16
Jamul Indian Village, CA	1	1	1	1	1
Jemez Pueblo, NM	1941	1941	1943	1943	1958
Jicarilla Apache Reservation, NM	2415	2535	2576	2514	2755
Kaibab Reservation, AZ	131	131	138	137	196
Kalispel Reservation, WA	178	182	183	181	206
Karuk Reservation and Off-Reservation Trust Land, CA	226	226	248	248	333
Kickapoo (KS) Reservation, KS	707	721	777	766	4419
Kickapoo (TX) Reservation, TX	406	406	406	406	420
Klamath Reservation, OR	4	4	4	4	9
Kootenai Reservation, ID	71	71	72	72	75
Lac Courte Oreilles Reservation and Off-Reservation Trust Land, WI	2146	2154	2183	2179	2900
Lac du Flambeau Reservation, WI	1744	1812	1835	1797	2995

Lac Vieux Desert Reservation, MI	113	113	114	114	135
Laguna Pueblo and Off-Reservation Trust Land, NM	3667	3671	3721	3719	3815
La Jolla Reservation, CA	288	300	320	314	390
Lake Traverse Reservation, SD--ND	3442	3464	3604	3593	10408
L'Anse Reservation and Off-Reservation Trust Land, MI	891	901	1089	1078	3672
La Posta Reservation, CA	15	15	15	15	18
Las Vegas Colony, NV	95	105	109	103	108
Laytonville Rancheria, CA	160	160	171	171	188
Leech Lake Reservation and Off-Reservation Trust Land, MN	4547	4575	4865	4850	10205
Likely Rancheria, CA	0	0	0	0	0
Little River Reservation, MI	0	0	0	0	2
Little Traverse Bay Reservation, MI	0	0	0	0	0
Lone Pine Reservation, CA	126	136	140	135	212
Lookout Rancheria, CA	4	4	4	4	7
Los Coyotes Reservation, CA	56	56	59	59	70
Lovelock Colony, NV	86	86	95	95	103
Lower Brule Reservation and Off-Reservation Trust Land, SD	1236	1238	1247	1246	1353
Lower Elwha Reservation and Off-Reservation Trust Land, WA	245	251	279	274	315
Lower Sioux Reservation, MN	294	294	303	303	335
Lummi Reservation, WA	2090	2139	2269	2240	4193
Makah Reservation, WA	1081	1085	1149	1147	1356
Manchester-Point Arena Rancheria, CA	149	153	181	178	197
Manzanita Reservation, CA	56	56	56	56	69
Maricopa (Ak Chin) Reservation, AZ	650	654	665	663	742
Mashantucket Pequot Reservation and Off-Reservation Trust Land, CT	227	227	250	250	325
Menominee Reservation and Off-Reservation Trust Land, WI	3065	3075	3094	3088	3225
Mesa Grande Reservation, CA	59	61	65	64	75
Mescalero Reservation, NM	2866	2910	2969	2946	3156
Miccosukee Reservation, FL	0	0	0	0	0
Middletown Rancheria, CA	51	51	51	51	73
Mille Lacs Reservation and Off-Reservation Trust Land, MN	1171	1171	1225	1225	4704
Minnesota Chippewa Trust Land, MN	64	64	64	64	78
Mississippi Choctaw Reservation and Off-Reservation Trust Land, MS	4893	4911	4965	4956	5190
Moapa River Reservation, NV	159	171	174	168	206
Mohegan Reservation, CT	0	0	0	0	2
Montgomery Creek Rancheria, CA	3	3	5	5	5
Mooretown Rancheria, CA	115	117	134	133	166

Morongo Reservation, CA	531	555	593	581	954
Muckleshoot Reservation and Off-Reservation Trust Land, WA	1032	1034	1096	1095	3606
Nambe Pueblo and Off-Reservation Trust Land, NM	455	455	511	511	1764
Narragansett Reservation, RI	9	9	9	9	60
Navajo Nation Reservation and Off-Reservation Trust Land, AZ--NM--UT	172996	174980	176253	175228	180462
Nez Perce Reservation, ID	2075	2127	2405	2375	17959
Nisqually Reservation, WA	355	359	395	392	588
Nooksack Reservation and Off-Reservation Trust Land, WA	368	378	441	436	547
Northern Cheyenne Reservation and Off-Reservation Trust Land, MT--SD	3960	4098	4180	4106	4470
North Fork Rancheria, CA	5	5	5	5	9
Northwestern Shoshoni Reservation, UT	0	0	0	0	0
Oil Springs Reservation, NY	0	0	1	1	11
Omaha Reservation, NE--IA	2275	2329	2396	2365	5194
Oneida (NY) Reservation, NY	14	14	14	14	26
Oneida (WI) Reservation and Off-Reservation Trust Land, WI	3238	3338	3657	3602	21321
Onondaga Reservation, NY	763	763	803	803	1473
Ontonagon Reservation, MI	0	0	0	0	0
Osage Reservation, OK	6024	6796	9836	9209	44437
Paiute (UT) Reservation, UT	250	250	254	254	270
Pala Reservation, CA	684	702	728	719	1573
Pascua Yaqui Reservation, AZ	2979	3025	3094	3070	3315
Passamaquoddy Trust Land, ME	0	0	0	0	0
Pauma and Yuima Reservation, CA	157	159	165	164	186
Pechanga Reservation, CA	346	346	353	353	467
Penobscot Reservation and Off-Reservation Trust Land, ME	477	477	478	478	584
Picayune Rancheria, CA	15	15	15	15	20
Picuris Pueblo, NM	165	167	186	185	1801
Pine Ridge Reservation and Off-Reservation Trust Land, SD--NE	14268	14340	14521	14484	15521
Pinoleville Rancheria, CA	91	93	97	96	136
Pit River Trust Land, CA	7	7	7	7	9
Pleasant Point Reservation, ME	567	567	578	578	640
Poarch Creek Reservation and Off-Reservation Trust Land, AL--FL	130	132	146	145	211
Pojoaque Pueblo, NM	262	266	288	285	2712
Port Gamble Reservation, WA	505	505	514	514	699
Port Madison Reservation, WA	494	500	644	640	6536
Prairie Band Potawatomi Reservation, KS	517	519	555	554	1238

Prairie Island Indian Community and Off-Reservation Trust Land, MN	165	167	167	166	199
Puyallup Reservation and Off-Reservation Trust Land, WA	1303	1351	1987	1940	41341
Pyramid Lake Reservation, NV	1200	1242	1285	1264	1734
Quartz Valley Reservation, CA	42	46	51	49	126
Quileute Reservation, WA	307	307	324	324	371
Quinault Reservation, WA	1051	1051	1069	1069	1370
Ramona Village, CA	0	0	0	0	0
Red Cliff Reservation and Off-Reservation Trust Land, WI	927	929	938	937	1078
Redding Rancheria, CA	29	29	33	33	45
Red Lake Reservation, MN	5067	5075	5091	5087	5162
Redwood Valley Rancheria Reservation, CA	105	107	113	112	263
Reno-Sparks Colony, NV	723	937	955	845	881
Resighini Rancheria, CA	36	36	36	36	36
Rincon Reservation, CA	409	413	441	439	1495
Roaring Creek Rancheria, CA	9	9	9	9	9
Robinson Rancheria and Off-Reservation Trust Land, CA	128	128	128	128	153
Rocky Boy's Reservation and Off-Reservation Trust Land, MT	2549	2607	2627	2598	2676
Rohnerville Rancheria, CA	60	64	69	67	98
Rosebud Reservation and Off-Reservation Trust Land, SD	9023	9057	9182	9165	10469
Round Valley Reservation and Off-Reservation Trust Land, CA	214	224	238	233	300
Rumsey Rancheria, CA	21	21	26	26	36
Sac and Fox/Meskwaki Reservation and Off-Reservation Trust Land, IA	624	640	661	650	761
Sac and Fox Reservation and Off-Reservation Trust Land, NE--KS	49	49	51	51	217
St. Croix Reservation and Off-Reservation Trust Land, WI	561	561	577	577	641
St. Regis Mohawk Reservation, NY	2629	2629	2636	2636	2699
Salt River Reservation, AZ	3250	3482	4146	4029	6405
San Carlos Reservation, AZ	8890	8952	9102	9065	9385
Sandia Pueblo, NM	490	510	537	525	4414
Sandy Lake Reservation, MN	66	66	66	66	70
San Felipe Pueblo, NM	2462	2468	2486	2483	3185
San Ildefonso Pueblo, NM	528	528	544	544	1524
San Juan Pueblo, NM	1328	1328	1383	1383	6748
San Manuel Reservation, CA	41	41	44	44	74
San Pasqual Reservation, CA	339	343	386	384	752
Santa Ana Pueblo, NM	473	473	476	476	487
Santa Clara Pueblo, NM	1312	1346	1432	1414	10658

Santa Rosa Rancheria, CA	426	426	457	457	517
Santa Rosa Reservation, CA	52	54	54	53	65
Santa Ynez Reservation, CA	83	83	94	94	122
Santa Ysabel Reservation, CA	225	225	226	226	250
Santee Reservation, NE	562	564	570	569	878
Santo Domingo Pueblo, NM	3084	3086	3093	3092	3166
Sauk-Suiattle Reservation, WA	35	35	37	37	45
Sault Ste. Marie Reservation and Off-Reservation Trust Land, MI	1030	1034	1161	1159	1676
Seminole Trust Land, FL	0	0	0	0	0
Shakopee Mdewakanton Sioux Community and Off-Reservation Trust Land, MN	214	214	244	244	338
Sherwood Valley Rancheria, CA	130	132	139	138	179
Shingle Springs Rancheria, CA	18	18	39	36	57
Shoalwater Bay Reservation and Off-Reservation Trust Land, WA	44	44	44	44	70
Siletz Reservation and Off-Reservation Trust Land, OR	181	183	266	265	308
Skokomish Reservation, WA	509	511	520	519	730
Skull Valley Reservation, UT	30	30	30	30	31
Smith River Rancheria, CA	41	41	41	41	62
Soboba Reservation, CA	428	438	445	440	522
Sokaogon Chippewa Community and Off-Reservation Trust Land, WI	328	336	340	336	392
Southern Ute Reservation, CO	1401	1465	1676	1642	11159
South Fork Reservation and Off-Reservation Trust Land, NV	116	116	118	118	123
Spirit Lake Reservation, ND	3288	3346	3399	3368	4435
Spokane Reservation, WA	1530	1536	1598	1595	2004
Squaxin Island Reservation and Off-Reservation Trust Land, WA	300	306	331	327	405
Standing Rock Reservation, SD--ND	5960	5968	6060	6054	8250
Stewart Community, NV	137	163	172	157	196
Stewarts Point Rancheria, CA	55	55	55	55	57
Stillaguamish Reservation, WA	76	76	76	76	102
Stockbridge-Munsee Community, WI	753	785	823	807	1527
Sulphur Bank Rancheria, CA	53	53	54	54	69
Summit Lake Reservation, NV	11	11	11	11	15
Susanville Rancheria, CA	191	249	271	242	298
Swinomish Reservation, WA	616	618	658	655	2664
Sycuan Reservation, CA	21	21	22	22	33
Table Bluff Reservation and Off-Reservation Trust Land, CA	67	71	73	71	97
Table Mountain Rancheria, CA	1	1	1	1	11
Tampa Reservation, FL	0	0	0	0	0

Taos Pueblo and Off-Reservation Trust Land, NM	1316	1346	1415	1399	4492
Tesuque Pueblo and Off-Reservation Trust Land, NM	344	366	374	363	806
Tohono O'odham Reservation and Off-Reservation Trust Land, AZ	9673	9763	9843	9794	10787
Tonawanda Reservation, NY	210	210	220	220	543
Tonto Apache Reservation, AZ	113	117	118	116	132
Torres-Martinez Reservation, CA	186	204	221	212	4146
Trinidad Rancheria and Off-Reservation Trust Land, CA	59	59	59	59	73
Tulalip Reservation, WA	2040	2058	2277	2265	9246
Tule River Reservation, CA	492	498	506	503	566
Tunica-Biloxi Reservation, LA	56	56	64	64	89
Tuolumne Rancheria and Off-Reservation Trust Land, CA	129	131	137	136	168
Turtle Mountain Reservation and Off-Reservation Trust Land, MT--ND--SD	7997	8021	8055	8043	8331
Tuscarora Reservation, NY	311	311	328	328	1138
Twenty-Nine Palms Reservation, CA	0	0	0	0	0
Uintah and Ouray Reservation and Off-Reservation Trust Land, UT	2654	2906	3285	3137	19182
Umatilla Reservation, OR	1414	1440	1512	1499	2927
Upper Lake Rancheria, CA	45	45	47	47	82
Upper Sioux Reservation, MN	47	47	47	47	57
Upper Skagit Reservation, WA	180	180	192	192	238
Ute Mountain Reservation and Off-Reservation Trust Land, CO--NM--UT	1563	1655	1681	1635	1687
Viejas Reservation, CA	145	147	160	159	394
Walker River Reservation, NV	659	675	700	691	853
Wampanoag-Aquinnah Trust Land, MA	66	66	79	79	91
Warm Springs Reservation and Off-Reservation Trust Land, OR	3009	3067	3134	3105	3314
Wells Colony, NV	39	39	44	44	54
White Earth Reservation and Off-Reservation Trust Land, MN	3371	3385	4036	4029	9192
Wind River Reservation and Off-Reservation Trust Land, WY	6492	6596	6928	6864	23250
Winnebago Reservation and Off-Reservation Trust Land, NE--IA	1441	1453	1474	1467	2588
Winnemucca Colony, NV	44	44	47	47	62
Woodfords Community, CA	111	217	255	192	219
XL Ranch, CA	11	11	11	11	14
Yakama Reservation and Off-Reservation Trust Land, WA	7121	7701	8509	8193	31799
Yankton Reservation, SD	2623	2643	2742	2732	6500
Yavapai-Apache Nation Reservation, AZ	634	666	689	673	743
Yavapai-Prescott Reservation, AZ	110	124	163	156	182
Yerington Colony, NV	124	124	132	132	139

Yomba Reservation, NV	89	89	89	89	96
Ysleta Del Sur Pueblo and Off-Reservation Trust Land, TX	300	300	306	306	421
Yurok Reservation, CA	498	500	541	538	1103
Zia Pueblo and Off-Reservation Trust Land, NM	645	645	646	646	646
Zuni Reservation and Off-Reservation Trust Land, NM--AZ	7413	7439	7479	7466	7758
Kickapoo (KS)/Sac and Fox joint use area, KS	0	0	0	0	0
Menominee/Stockbridge-Munsee joint use area, WI	275	277	277	276	295
San Felipe/Santa Ana joint use area, NM	0	0	0	0	0
San Felipe/Santo Domingo joint use area, NM	0	0	0	0	0
Caddo-Wichita-Delaware OTSA, OK	1826	1896	2345	2299	14638
Cherokee OTSA, OK	74236	77854	107248	104482	462327
Cheyenne-Arapaho OTSA, OK	7077	7732	10753	10310	157869
Chickasaw OTSA, OK	21599	24296	34330	32372	277416
Choctaw OTSA, OK	28426	30622	41700	39984	224472
Citizen Potawatomi Nation-Absentee Shawnee OTSA, OK	6427	7042	11157	10617	106624
Creek OTSA, OK	49406	53200	80177	77253	704565
Eastern Shawnee OTSA, OK	98	104	142	138	661
Iowa OTSA, OK	345	381	543	519	6148
Kaw OTSA, OK	522	588	836	793	6123
Kickapoo OTSA, OK	1688	1788	2425	2345	18544
Kiowa-Comanche-Apache-Fort Sill Apache OTSA, OK	9310	10040	13540	13045	193260
Miami OTSA, OK	55	59	81	78	271
Modoc OTSA, OK	55	61	76	73	228
Otoe-Missouria OTSA, OK	373	375	408	407	778
Ottawa OTSA, OK	892	930	1251	1216	6204
Pawnee OTSA, OK	1948	2078	2783	2678	16509
Peoria OTSA, OK	659	707	1029	996	4840
Ponca OTSA, OK	766	834	936	900	2284
Quapaw OTSA, OK	1124	1244	1800	1700	7455
Sac and Fox OTSA, OK	5101	5570	7574	7232	55690
Seminole OTSA, OK	3554	4295	5428	4975	22792
Seneca-Cayuga OTSA, OK	495	513	699	681	3997
Tonkawa OTSA, OK	369	383	507	495	4119
Wyandotte OTSA, OK	361	373	468	460	1678
Creek-Seminole joint use area OTSA, OK	367	441	553	510	2102
Kaw-Ponca joint use area OTSA, OK	1650	1780	2640	2534	27821
Kiowa-Comanche-Apache-Ft Sill Apache-Caddo-Wichita-Delaware joint use area OTSA, OK	4073	4286	4849	4724	11855
Miami-Peoria joint use area OTSA, OK	777	839	1156	1121	4341

Aroostook Band of Micmac TDSA, ME	285	287	344	343	9756
Cayuga Nation TDSA, NY	21	25	58	56	10707
Ione Band of Miwok TDSA, CA	4	4	4	4	8
Jena Band of Choctaw TDSA, LA	445	477	827	792	59984
Mechoopda TDSA, CA	132	142	237	229	3198
Pokagon Band of Potawatomi TDSA, IN--MI	455	477	878	851	35415
Samish TDSA, WA	312	324	672	653	33265
Golden Hill (state) Reservation, CT	0	0	0	0	0
Hassanamisco (state) Reservation, MA	2	2	2	2	2
Mattaponi (state) Reservation, VA	46	46	46	46	58
MOWA Choctaw (state) Reservation, AL	93	101	102	98	124
Pamunkey (state) Reservation, VA	38	38	39	39	58
Paucatuck Eastern Pequot (state) Reservation, CT	21	21	21	21	26
Poospatuck (state) Reservation, NY	216	216	231	231	283
Rankokus (state) Reservation, NJ	0	0	0	0	0
Schaghticoke (state) Reservation, CT	3	3	3	3	9
Shinnecock (state) Reservation, NY	459	459	460	460	504
Tama (state) Reservation, GA	55	55	55	55	57
Adais Caddo SDAISA, LA	398	444	650	612	39080
Apache Choctaw SDAISA, LA	781	2875	3475	2237	23459
Cherokees of Southeast Alabama SDAISA, AL	348	384	886	850	120294
Cherokee Tribe of Northeast Alabama SDAISA, AL	0	0	6	6	173
Chickahominy SDAISA, VA	514	514	558	558	3313
Clifton Choctaw SDAISA, LA	166	168	183	181	476
Coharie SDAISA, NC	1410	1448	1980	1946	123761
Eastern Chickahominy SDAISA, VA	30	30	31	31	104
Echota Cherokee SDAISA, AL	1923	1959	3234	3182	65068
Four Winds Cherokee SDAISA, LA	913	973	1761	1687	79657
Haliwa-Saponi SDAISA, NC	2455	2461	2602	2596	8272
Indians of Person County SDAISA, NC	73	73	81	81	1919
Lumbee SDAISA, NC	58052	58424	62615	62327	474100
MaChis Lower Creek SDAISA, AL	325	333	615	602	24198
Meherrin SDAISA, NC	190	196	239	236	7867
Nanticoke Indian Tribe SDAISA, DE	393	395	519	517	22683
Nanticoke Lenni Lenape SDAISA, NJ	341	361	546	532	12316
Ramapough SDAISA, NJ	239	239	284	284	892
Star Muskogee Creek SDAISA, AL	85	87	202	197	7331
United Houma Nation SDAISA, LA	10892	11146	15547	15305	839880
Waccamaw Siouan SDAISA, NC	1427	1435	1482	1478	2329

Reservations & Trust Lands	*AIAN Locations*	PCT1	PCT2	PCT3	PCT4	PCT7
Total	651	822,441	851,721	982,620	962,658	5,310,930
Alaska	208	59,102	60,714	67,095	66,075	184,028
Hawaii	61	23,658	23,658	23,658	23,658	23,658
Continental 48 States	382	739,681	767,349	891,867	872,925	5,103,244

OTSA: Oklahoma Tribal Statistical Area (Census Bureau geographic area for Oklahoma tribes formerly having a reservation)

SDAISA: State Designated American Indian Statistical Area

Indian Entities within the Continental United States Recognized and Eligible to Receive Services from the United States Bureau of Indian Affairs

1. Absentee-Shawnee Tribe of Indians of Oklahoma
2. Agua Caliente Band of Cahuilla Indians of the Agua Caliente Indian Reservation, California
3. Ak Chin Indian Community of the Maricopa (Ak Chin) Indian Reservation, Arizona
4. Alabama-Coushatta Tribes of Texas Alabama-Quassarte Tribal Town, Oklahoma
5. Alturas Indian Rancheria, California
6. Apache Tribe of Oklahoma
7. Arapahoe Tribe of the Wind River Reservation, Wyoming
8. Aroostook Band of Micmac Indians of Maine
9. Assiniboine and Sioux Tribes of the Fort Peck Indian Reservation, Montana
10. Augustine Band of Cahuilla Mission Indians of the Augustine Reservation, California
11. Bad River Band of the Lake Superior Tribe of Chippewa Indians of the Bad River Reservation, Wisconsin
12. Bay Mills Indian Community, Michigan
13. Bear River Band of the Rohnerville Rancheria, California
14. Berry Creek Rancheria of Maidu Indians of California
15. Big Lagoon Rancheria, California
16. Big Pine Band of Owens Valley Paiute Shoshone Indians of the Big Pine Reservation, California
17. Big Sandy Rancheria of Mono Indians of California
18. Big Valley Band of Pomo Indians of the Big Valley Rancheria, California
19. Blackfeet Tribe of the Blackfeet Indian Reservation of Montana
20. Blue Lake Rancheria, California
21. Bridgeport Paiute Indian Colony of California
22. Buena Vista Rancheria of Me-Wuk Indians of California
23. Burns Paiute Tribe of the Burns Paiute Indian Colony of Oregon
24. Cabazon Band of Mission Indians, California
    (previously listed as the Cabazon Band of Cahuilla Mission Indians of the Cabazon reservation)
25. Cachil DeHe Band of Wintun Indians of the Colusa Indian Community of the Colusa Rancheria, California
26. Caddo Nation of Oklahoma (formerly the Caddo Indian Tribe of Oklahoma)
27. Cahuilla Band of Mission Indians of the Cahuilla Reservation, California
28. Cahto Indian Tribe of the Laytonville Rancheria, California
29. California Valley Miwok Tribe, California (formerly the Sheep Ranch Rancheria of Me-Wuk Indians of California)
30. Campo Band of Diegueno Mission Indians of the Campo Indian Reservation, California
31. Capitan Grande Band of Diegueno Mission Indians of California: Barona Group of Capitan Grande Band of Mission Indians of the arona Reservation, California
32. Viejas (Baron Long) Group of Capitan Grande Band of Mission Indians of the Viejas Reservation, California
33. Catawba Indian Nation (aka Catawba Tribe of South Carolina)
34. Cayuga Nation of New York
35. Cedarville Rancheria, California
36. Chemehuevi Indian Tribe of the Chemehuevi Reservation, California
37. Cher-Ae Heights Indian Community of the Trinidad Rancheria, California
38. Cherokee Nation, Oklahoma
39. Cheyenne-Arapaho Tribes of Oklahoma
40. Cheyenne River Sioux Tribe of the Cheyenne River Reservation, South Dakota
41. Chickasaw Nation, Oklahoma
42. Chicken Ranch Rancheria of Me-Wuk Indians of California
43. Chippewa-Cree Indians of the Rocky Boy's Reservation, Montana
44. Chitimacha Tribe of Louisiana
45. Choctaw Nation of Oklahoma
46. Citizen Potawatomi Nation, Oklahoma
47. Cloverdale Rancheria of Pomo Indians of California
48. Cocopah Tribe of Arizona

49. Coeur D'Alene Tribe of the Coeur D'Alene Reservation, Idaho
50. Cold Springs Rancheria of Mono Indians of California
51. Colorado River Indian Tribes of the Colorado River Indian Reservation, Arizona and California
52. Comanche Nation, Oklahoma
53. Confederated Salish & Kootenai Tribes of the Flathead Reservation, Montana
54. Confederated Tribes of the Chehalis Reservation, Washington
55. Confederated Tribes of the Colville Reservation, Washington
56. Confederated Tribes of the Coos, Lower Umpqua and Siuslaw Indians of Oregon
57. Confederated Tribes of the Goshute Reservation, Nevada and Utah
58. Confederated Tribes of the Grand Ronde Community of Oregon
59. Confederated Tribes of the Siletz Reservation, Oregon
60. Confederated Tribes of the Umatilla Reservation, Oregon
61. Confederated Tribes of the Warm Springs Reservation of Oregon
62. Confederated Tribes and Bands of the Yakama Nation, Washington
63. Coquille Tribe of Oregon
64. Cortina Indian Rancheria of Wintun Indians of California
65. Coushatta Tribe of Louisiana
66. Cow Creek Band of Umpqua Indians of Oregon
67. Cowlitz Indian Tribe, Washington
68. Coyote Valley Band of Pomo Indians of California
69. Crow Tribe of Montana
70. Crow Creek Sioux Tribe of the Crow Creek Reservation, South Dakota

71. Death Valley Timbi-Sha Shoshone Band of California
72. Delaware Nation, Oklahoma
73. Dry Creek Rancheria of Pomo Indians of California
74. Duckwater Shoshone Tribe of the Duckwater Reservation, Nevada

75. Eastern Band of Cherokee Indians of North Carolina
76. Eastern Shawnee Tribe of Oklahoma
77. Elem Indian Colony of Pomo Indians of the Sulphur Bank Rancheria, California
78. Elk Valley Rancheria, California
79. Ely Shoshone Tribe of Nevada
80. Enterprise Rancheria of Maidu Indians of California
81. Ewiiaapaayp Band of Kumeyaay Indians, California (formerly the Cuyapaipe Community of Diegueno Mission Indians of the Cuyapaipe Reservation)

82. Federated Indians of Graton Rancheria, California (formerly the Graton Rancheria)
83. Flandreau Santee Sioux Tribe of South Dakota
84. Forest County Potawatomi Community, Wisconsin
85. Fort Belknap Indian Community of the Fort Belknap Reservation of Montana
86. Fort Bidwell Indian Community of the Fort Bidwell Reservation of California
87. Fort Independence Indian Community of Paiute Indians of the Fort Independence Reservation, California
88. Fort McDermitt Paiute and Shoshone Tribes of the Fort McDermitt Indian Reservation, Nevada and Oregon
89. Fort McDowell Yavapai Nation, Arizona
90. Fort Mojave Indian Tribe of Arizona, California & Nevada
91. Fort Sill Apache Tribe of Oklahoma

92. Gila River Indian Community of the Gila River Indian Reservation, Arizona
93. Grand Traverse Band of Ottawa and Chippewa Indians, Michigan
94. Greenville Rancheria of Maidu Indians of California
95. Grindstone Indian Rancheria of Wintun-Wailaki Indians of California
96. Guidiville Rancheria of California

97. Habematolel Pomo of Upper Lake, California (formerly the Upper Lake Band of Pomo Indians of Upper Lake Rancheria of California)
98. Hannahville Indian Community, Michigan
99. Havasupai Tribe of the Havasupai Reservation, Arizona
100. Ho-Chunk Nation of Wisconsin
101. Hoh Indian Tribe of the Hoh Indian Reservation, Washington
102. Hoopa Valley Tribe, California
103. Hopi Tribe of Arizona
104. Hopland Band of Pomo Indians of the Hopland Rancheria, California
105. Houlton Band of Maliseet Indians of Maine
106. Hualapai Indian Tribe of the Hualapai Indian Reservation, Arizona
107. Huron Potawatomi, Inc., Michigan

108. Inaja Band of Diegueno Mission Indians of the Inaja and Cosmit Reservation, California
109. Ione Band of Miwok Indians of California
110. Iowa Tribe of Kansas and Nebraska
111. Iowa Tribe of Oklahoma

112. Jackson Rancheria of Me-Wuk Indians of California
113. Jamestown S'Klallam Tribe of Washington
114. Jamul Indian Village of California
115. Jena Band of Choctaw Indians, Louisiana
116. Jicarilla Apache Nation, New Mexico

117. Kaibab Band of Paiute Indians of the Kaibab Indian Reservation, Arizona
118. Kalispel Indian Community of the Kalispel Reservation, Washington
119. Karuk Tribe of California
120. Kashia Band of Pomo Indians of the Stewarts Point Rancheria, California
121. Kaw Nation, Oklahoma
122. Keweenaw Bay Indian Community, Michigan
123. Kialegee Tribal Town, Oklahoma
124. Kickapoo Tribe of Indians of the Kickapoo Reservation in Kansas
125. Kickapoo Tribe of Oklahoma
126. Kickapoo Traditional Tribe of Texas
127. Kiowa Indian Tribe of Oklahoma
128. Klamath Tribes, Oregon (formerly the Klamath Indian Tribe of Oregon)
129. Kootenai Tribe of Idaho

130. La Jolla Band of Luiseno Mission Indians of the La Jolla Reservation, California
131. La Posta Band of Diegueno Mission Indians of the La Posta Indian Reservation, California
132. Lac Courte Oreilles Band of Lake Superior Chippewa Indians of Wisconsin
133. Lac du Flambeau Band of Lake Superior Chippewa Indians of the Lac du Flambeau Reservation of Wisconsin
134. Lac Vieux Desert Band of Lake Superior Chippewa Indians, Michigan
135. Las Vegas Tribe of Paiute Indians of the Las Vegas Indian Colony, Nevada
136. Little River Band of Ottawa Indians, Michigan
137. Little Traverse Bay Bands of Odawa Indians, Michigan
138. Lower Lake Rancheria, California
139. Los Coyotes Band of Cahuilla & Cupeno Indians of the Los Coyotes Reservation, California (formerly the Los Coyotes Band of Cahuilla Mission Indians of the Los Coyotes Reservation)
140. Lovelock Paiute Tribe of the Lovelock Indian Colony, Nevada
141. Lower Brule Sioux Tribe of the Lower Brule Reservation, South Dakota
142. Lower Elwha Tribal Community of the Lower Elwha Reservation, Washington
143. Lower Sioux Indian Community in the State of Minnesota
144. Lummi Tribe of the Lummi Reservation, Washington
145. Lytton Rancheria of California

146. Makah Indian Tribe of the Makah Indian Reservation, Washington
147. Manchester Band of Pomo Indians of the Manchester-Point Arena Rancheria, California
148. Manzanita Band of Diegueno Mission Indians of the Manzanita Reservation, California
149. Mashantucket Pequot Tribe of Connecticut
150. Match-e-be-nash-she-wish Band of Pottawatomi Indians of Michigan
151. Mechoopda Indian Tribe of Chico Rancheria, California
152. Menominee Indian Tribe of Wisconsin
153. Mesa Grande Band of Diegueno Mission Indians of the Mesa Grande Reservation, California
154. Mescalero Apache Tribe of the Mescalero Reservation, New Mexico
155. Miami Tribe of Oklahoma
156. Miccosukee Tribe of Indians of Florida
157. Middletown Rancheria of Pomo Indians of California
158. Minnesota Chippewa Tribe, Minnesota (Six component reservations: Bois Forte Band (Nett Lake); Fond du Lac Band; Grand Portage Band; Leech Lake Band; Mille Lacs Band; White Earth Band)
159. Mississippi Band of Choctaw Indians, Mississippi
160. Moapa Band of Paiute Indians of the Moapa River Indian Reservation, Nevada
161. Modoc Tribe of Oklahoma
162. Mohegan Indian Tribe of Connecticut
163. Mooretown Rancheria of Maidu Indians of California
164. Morongo Band of Cahuilla Mission Indians of the Morongo Reservation, California
165. Muckleshoot Indian Tribe of the Muckleshoot Reservation, Washington
166. Muscogee (Creek) Nation, Oklahoma

167. Narragansett Indian Tribe of Rhode Island

168. Navajo Nation, Arizona, New Mexico & Utah
169. Nez Perce Tribe of Idaho
170. Nisqually Indian Tribe of the Nisqually Reservation, Washington
171. Nooksack Indian Tribe of Washington
172. Northern Cheyenne Tribe of the Northern Cheyenne Indian Reservation, Montana
173. Northfork Rancheria of Mono Indians of California
174. Northwestern Band of Shoshoni Nation of Utah (Washakie)

175. Oglala Sioux Tribe of the Pine Ridge Reservation, South Dakota
176. Omaha Tribe of Nebraska
177. Oneida Nation of New York
178. Oneida Tribe of Indians of Wisconsin
179. Onondaga Nation of New York
180. Osage Tribe, Oklahoma
181. Ottawa Tribe of Oklahoma
182. Otoe-Missouria Tribe of Indians, Oklahoma

183. Paiute Indian Tribe of Utah (Cedar City Band of Paiutes, Kanosh Band of Paiutes, Koosharem Band of Paiutes, Indian Peaks Band of Paiutes, and Shivwits Band of Paiutes)
184. Paiute-Shoshone Indians of the Bishop Community of the Bishop Colony, California
185. Paiute-Shoshone Tribe of the Fallon Reservation and Colony, Nevada
186. Paiute-Shoshone Indians of the Lone Pine Community of the Lone Pine Reservation, California
187. Pala Band of Luiseno Mission Indians of the Pala Reservation, California
188. Pascua Yaqui Tribe of Arizona
189. Paskenta Band of Nomlaki Indians of California
190. Passamaquoddy Tribe of Maine
191. Pauma Band of Luiseno Mission Indians of the Pauma & Yuima Reservation, California
192. Pawnee Nation of Oklahoma
193. Pechanga Band of Luiseno Mission Indians of the Pechanga Reservation, California
194. Penobscot Tribe of Maine
195. Peoria Tribe of Indians of Oklahoma
196. Picayune Rancheria of Chukchansi Indians of California
197. Pinoleville Rancheria of Pomo Indians of California
198. Pit River Tribe, California (includes XL Ranch, Big Bend, Likely, Lookout, Montgomery Creek and Roaring Creek Rancherias)
199. Poarch Band of Creek Indians of Alabama
200. Pokagon Band of Potawatomi Indians, Michigan and Indiana
201. Ponca Tribe of Indians of Oklahoma
202. Ponca Tribe of Nebraska
203. Port Gamble Indian Community of the Port Gamble Reservation, Washington
204. Potter Valley Tribe, California (formerly the Potter Valley Rancheria of Pomo Indians of California)
205. Prairie Band of Potawatomi Nation, Kansas
206. Prairie Island Indian Community in the State of Minnesota
207. Pueblo of Acoma, New Mexico
208. Pueblo of Cochiti, New Mexico
209. Pueblo of Jemez, New Mexico
210. Pueblo of Isleta, New Mexico
211. Pueblo of Laguna, New Mexico
212. Pueblo of Nambe, New Mexico
213. Pueblo of Picuris, New Mexico
214. Pueblo of Pojoaque, New Mexico
215. Pueblo of San Felipe, New Mexico
216. Pueblo of San Juan, New Mexico
217. Pueblo of San Ildefonso, New Mexico
218. Pueblo of Sandia, New Mexico
219. Pueblo of Santa Ana, New Mexico
220. Pueblo of Santa Clara, New Mexico
221. Pueblo of Santo Domingo, New Mexico
222. Pueblo of Taos, New Mexico
223. Pueblo of Tesuque, New Mexico
224. Pueblo of Zia, New Mexico
225. Puyallup Tribe of the Puyallup Reservation, Washington
226. Pyramid Lake Paiute Tribe of the Pyramid Lake Reservation, Nevada

227. Quapaw Tribe of Indians, Oklahoma
228. Quartz Valley Indian Community of the Quartz Valley Reservation of California
229. Quechan Tribe of the Fort Yuma Indian Reservation, California & Arizona
230. Quileute Tribe of the Quileute Reservation, Washington

231. Quinault Tribe of the Quinault Reservation, Washington

232. Ramona Band or Village of Cahuilla Mission Indians of California
233. Red Cliff Band of Lake Superior Chippewa Indians of Wisconsin
234. Red Lake Band of Chippewa Indians, Minnesota
235. Redding Rancheria, California
236. Redwood Valley Rancheria of Pomo Indians of California
237. Reno-Sparks Indian Colony, Nevada
238. Resighini Rancheria, California
239. Rincon Band of Luiseno Mission Indians of the Rincon Reservation, California
240. Robinson Rancheria of Pomo Indians of California
241. Rosebud Sioux Tribe of the Rosebud Indian Reservation, South Dakota
242. Round Valley Indian Tribes of the Round Valley Reservation, California
243. Rumsey Indian Rancheria of Wintun Indians of California

244. Sac & Fox Tribe of the Mississippi in Iowa
245. Sac & Fox Nation of Missouri in Kansas and Nebraska
246. Sac & Fox Nation, Oklahoma
247. Saginaw Chippewa Indian Tribe of Michigan
248. St. Croix Chippewa Indians of Wisconsin
249. St. Regis Band of Mohawk Indians of New York
250. Salt River Pima-Maricopa Indian Community of the Salt River Reservation, Arizona
251. Samish Indian Tribe, Washington
252. San Carlos Apache Tribe of the San Carlos Reservation, Arizona
253. San Juan Southern Paiute Tribe of Arizona
254. San Manual Band of Serrano Mission Indians of the San Manual Reservation, California
255. San Pasqual Band of Diegueno Mission Indians of California
256. Santa Rosa Indian Community of the Santa Rosa Rancheria, California
257. Santa Rosa Band of Cahuilla Mission Indians of the Santa Rosa Reservation, California
258. Santa Ynez Band of Chumash Mission Indians of the Santa Ynez Reservation, California
259. Santa Ysabel Band of Diegueno Mission Indians of the Santa Ysabel Reservation, California
260. Santee Sioux Nation, Nebraska (formerly the Santee Sioux Tribe of the Santee Reservation of Nebraska)
261. Sauk-Suiattle Indian Tribe of Washington
262. Sault Ste. Marie Tribe of Chippewa Indians of Michigan
263. Scotts Valley Band of Pomo Indians of California
264. Seminole Nation of Oklahoma
265. Seminole Tribe of Florida, Dania, Big Cypress, Brighton, Hollywood & Tampa Reservations
266. Seneca Nation of New York
267. Seneca-Cayuga Tribe of Oklahoma
268. Shakopee Mdewakanton Sioux Community of Minnesota
269. Shawnee Tribe, Oklahoma
270. Sherwood Valley Rancheria of Pomo Indians of California
271. Shingle Springs Band of Miwok Indians, Shingle Springs Rancheria (Verona Tract), California
272. Shoalwater Bay Tribe of the Shoalwater Bay Indian Reservation, Washington
273. Shoshone Tribe of the Wind River Reservation, Wyoming
274. Shoshone-Bannock Tribes of the Fort Hall Reservation of Idaho
275. Shoshone-Paiute Tribes of the Duck Valley Reservation, Nevada
276. Sisseton-Wahpeton Oyate of the Lake Traverse Reservation, South Dakota (formerly the Sisseton-Wahpeton Sioux Tribe of the Lake Traverse Reservation)
277. Skokomish Indian Tribe of the Skokomish Reservation, Washington
278. Skull Valley Band of Goshute Indians of Utah
279. Smith River Rancheria, California
280. Snoqualmie Tribe, Washington
281. Soboba Band of Luiseno Indians, California
282. Sokaogon Chippewa Community, Wisconsin
283. Southern Ute Indian Tribe of the Southern Ute Reservation, Colorado
284. Spirit Lake Tribe, North Dakota
285. Spokane Tribe of the Spokane Reservation, Washington
286. Squaxin Island Tribe of the Squaxin Island Reservation, Washington
287. Standing Rock Sioux Tribe of North & South Dakota
288. Stockbridge Munsee Community, Wisconsin
289. Stillaguamish Tribe of Washington
290. Summit Lake Paiute Tribe of Nevada
291. Suquamish Indian Tribe of the Port Madison Reservation, Washington
292. Susanville Indian Rancheria, California
293. Swinomish Indians of the Swinomish Reservation, Washington
294. Sycuan Band of the Kumeyaay Nation formerly the Sycuan Band of Diegueno Mission Indians of California)

295.   Table Mountain Rancheria of California
296.   Te-Moak Tribe of Western Shoshone Indians of Nevada (Four constituent bands: Battle Mountain Band; Elko Band; South Fork Band and Wells Band)
297.   Thlopthlocco Tribal Town, Oklahoma
298.   Three Affiliated Tribes of the Fort Berthold Reservation, North Dakota
299.   Tohono O'odham Nation of Arizona
300.   Tonawanda Band of Seneca Indians of New York
301.   Tonkawa Tribe of Indians of Oklahoma
302.   Tonto Apache Tribe of Arizona
303.   Torres Martinez Desert Cahuilla Indians, California (formerly the Torres-Martinez Band of Cahuilla Mission Indians of California)
304.   Tule River Indian Tribe of the Tule River Reservation, California
305.   Tulalip Tribes of the Tulalip Reservation, Washington
306.   Tunica-Biloxi Indian Tribe of Louisiana
307.   Tuolumne Band of Me-Wuk Indians of the Tuolumne Rancheria of California
308.   Turtle Mountain Band of Chippewa Indians of North Dakota
309.   Tuscarora Nation of New York
310.   Twenty-Nine Palms Band of Mission Indians of California

311.   United Auburn Indian Community of the Auburn Rancheria of California
312.   United Keetoowah Band of Cherokee Indians in Oklahoma
313.   Upper Sioux Community, Minnesota
314.   Upper Skagit Indian Tribe of Washington
315.   Ute Indian Tribe of the Uintah & Ouray Reservation, Utah
316.   Ute Mountain Tribe of the Ute Mountain Reservation, Colorado, New Mexico & Utah
317.   Utu Utu Gwaitu Paiute Tribe of the Benton Paiute Reservation, California

318.   Walker River Paiute Tribe of the Walker River Reservation, Nevada
319.   Wampanoag Tribe of Gay Head (Aquinnah) of Massachusetts
320.   Washoe Tribe of Nevada & California (Carson Colony, Dresslerville Colony, Woodfords Community, Stewart Community, & Washoe Ranches)
321.   White Mountain Apache Tribe of the Fort Apache Reservation, Arizona
322.   Wichita and Affiliated Tribes (Wichita, Keechi, Waco & Tawakonie), Oklahoma
323.   Winnebago Tribe of Nebraska
324.   Winnemucca Indian Colony of Nevada
325.   Wiyot Tribe, California (formerly the Table Bluff Reservation—Wiyot Tribe)
326.   Wyandotte Nation, Oklahoma (formerly the Wyandotte Tribe of Oklahoma)

327.   Yankton Sioux Tribe of South Dakota
328.   Yavapai-Apache Nation of the Camp Verde Indian Reservation, Arizona
329.   Yavapai-Prescott Tribe of the Yavapai Reservation, Arizona
330.   Yerington Paiute Tribe of the Yerington Colony & Campbell Ranch, Nevada
331.   Yomba Shoshone Tribe of the Yomba Reservation, Nevada
332.   Ysleta Del Sur Pueblo of Texas
333.   Yurok Tribe of the Yurok Reservation, California

334.   Zuni Tribe of the Zuni Reservation, New Mexico

Source: Transcribed from "Indian Entities Recognized and Eligible to Receive Services from the United States Bureau of Indian Affairs; Notice." *Federal Register* (Washington, DC: Department of the Interior, Bureau of Indian Affairs, November 25, 2005), vol. 70, no. 226, 71194-71198.

Notes and Sources

American Indian Tribes of the Continental U.S.

Kwebekwe

(An Anisnabe (Algonquin) word meaning "Welcome Stranger!" It was from Kwebekwe that the city of Quebec derived it's name.)

Where authors, book titles, and publication data are given here in a more convenient, abbreviated form, full details on the may be found in the Bibliography.

Two texts deserve special mention.: John R. Swanton, *The Indian Tribes of North American* and Charles J. Kappler, *Indian Affairs: Laws and Treaties.* Special mention should also be made of several online documents and Internet web sites that were invaluable in compiling data for this work. They are all highly recommended to the reader to further one's knowledge and understanding of the subject.

"A Century of Lawmaking for a New Nation: U.S. Congressional Documents and Debates, 1774-1785" (Washington, DC: Library of Congress, 2003) at http://memory.loc.gov/ammem/amlaw/lawhome.html.

American Journey documents made available by the Wisconsin Historical Society at http://www.americanjourneys.org/texts.asp.

"Executive Orders of the Presidents, Federal Register (Washington, DC: National Archives and Records Administration, n.d.) at http://www.archives.gov/federal-register/executive-orders/.

"Federal and State Laws" (Mountain View, CA: FindLaw, 1994-2006) at http://www.findlaw.com/casecode/index.html.

Felix S. Cohen, *Handbook of Federal Indian Law* (Washington: United States Government Printing Office, 1941. 1945 - 4th Printing) available online through the efforts of Marilyn K. Nicely, University of Oklahoma Law Center (Norman, mod. 2005) at http://thorpe.ou.edu/cohen.html. Esp. helpful, "Introductory Materials and Tribal Index of Materials on Indian Law."

"Index of Treaties Entered Into By The Various North American Indian Tribes, Bands, and Nations" (Tulsa, OK: University of Tulsa Law School, 2006) at http://www.utulsa.edu/law/classes/rice/Treaties/001_Treaty_Index.htm.

"Indian Affairs: Laws and Treaties, Compiled and Edited by Charles J. Kappler" (Stillwater, OK: Oklahoma State University Library, n.a.) at http://digital.library.okstate.edu/kappler/.

"Search the United States Code" (Washington, DC: U.S. House of Representatives, n.d.) at http://uscode.house.gov/search/criteria.shtml.

"Statutes at Large," American Memory (Washington, DC: Library of Congress, n.d.) at http://memory.loc.gov/ammem/amlaw/lwsl.html.

"Supreme Court Cases" (Mountain View, CA: FindLaw, 1994-2006) at http://www.findlaw.com/casecode/supreme.html.

"Treaties Between the United States and Native Americans," Avalon Project (New Haven, CN: Yale Law School, 1996-2006) at http://www.yale.edu/lawweb/avalon/ntreaty/chr1794.htm.

"U.S. Supreme Court Multimedia," OYEZ Project (Chicago: Northwestern University, Jerry Goldman, 1996-2005) at http://www.oyez.org/oyez/frontpage.

The following notes and sources correspond to the Annotated Tribal Listing of the main section of this text, referenced here by Record Number.

Abenaki

Swanton, 13-15, 48; Nathaniel Philbrick, *Mayflower*, 264, 332, 338; Colin G. Calloway, *The Western Abenakis of Vermont, 1600-1800: War, Migration; the Survival of an Indian People*; Daniel K. Richter, *Facing East from Indian Country*, 65, 158, 160, 165, 172, 173. Also, "The Great Council Fire, An Abenaki Perspective" (Pleasant Point, ME: Passamaquoddy Tribe, 2003, mod. 04/12/06) at http://www.wabanaki.com/wampum.htm [April 25, 2006].

Henry R. Schoolcraft, *The Indian In His Wigwam: Characteristics of The Red Race of America From Original Notes and Manuscripts* (New York: Dewitt & Davenport,1848) made available from Three Rivers, Hudson-Mohawk-Schoharie (Berry Enterprises, 1998-2003) at http://www.threerivershms.com/indianwigwam.htm [July 28, 2006].

"The Squaw Sachem and Her Red Men... (Winchester, MA, n.d.) at http://www.winchestermass.org/sachem_6.html and http://www.winchestermass.org/sachem_notes.html [August 12, 2006]; "FAQ: Faye W., Wincot Tribe" (AAANativeArts, 1999-2006) at http://www.aaanativearts.com [August 20, 2006].

"Names of Different Indian Nations In North-America, With the Numbers of Their Fighting Men," Historical Account of Bouquet's Expedition Against the Ohio Indians, in 1764 ((Cincinnati, OH: Robert Clarke, & Co., 1868), Appendix V (prepared by unknown French trader), made available from Glen Black Laboratory of Archaeology (Bloomington, IN: University of Indiana, 1996-2000) at http://www.gbl.indiana.edu/archives/dockett_317/317_84a.html; "The Western Border: Indian Occupants-Border Warfare-Treaties-Facts And Incidents," History of Union County [Ohio] (Chicago: W. H. Beers & Co., 1883), ch. II, 223, made available by Allen L. Potts (Heritage Pursuit, last updated June 21, 2006) at http://www.heritagepursuit.com/Union/Unp3c2.htm [August 27, 2006].

Colin G. Calloway, "Gray Lock (fl. 1723-1744), Abenaki war chief," *American National Biography* (New York: Oxford University Press, 2000) at http://www.libarts.ucok.edu/history/faculty/roberson/course/1483/suppl/chpV/GrayLock.htm; "Program 10: The Frontier Wars," The Story of Maine (Maine Public Broadcasting Network) at http://www.mpbc.org/homestom/p10abenaki.html; On the French & Indian Wars, see "Treaty of Utrecht" (Port-Toulouse, Isle Royale, 2004) at http://www.porttoulouse.com/html/the_treaty_of_utrecht.html; J.K. Hiller, "Treaty of Utrecht" (Memorial University of Newfoundland, 1996-2000) at http://www.heritage.nf.ca/exploration/utrecht.html [October 25, 2006].

On the Massacre at Fort William Henry, see David R. Starbuck, *Massacre at Fort William Henry*; Edward P. Hamilton, *The French and Indian Wars: The Story of Battles and Forts in the Wilderness* (New York: Doubleday, 1962). Also, "Fort William Henry 'Massacre,' August 1757," U-S-History (Online Highways, 2002-2005) at http://www.u-s-history.com/pages/h1175.html; "Massacre at Fort William Henry," Bone Trauma (Gainesville, FL: University of Florida, 2006) at http://plaza.ufl.edu/gator59/page2.htm; "The Massacre at Fort William Henry' (SparkNotes, 2006) at http://www.sparknotes.com/history/american/frenchindian/section5.rhtml; Jessica Baker Roche, "The Siege and Massacre at Fort William Henry during the French and Indian War" (Lehigh University: R. B. Roche, 1999) at http://www.lehigh.edu/~ineng/jbr/jbr-history.htm [November 9, 2006]

Abihka

Swanton, 153, 157, 161, 222, 228; Kenneth W. McIntosh, "Creek (Muskogee)," *Encyclopedia of North American Indians* (New York: Houghton Mifflin Company, n.a.) at http://college.hmco.com/history/readerscomp/naind/html/na_009100_creek.htm [March 11, 2006].

Abo Pueblo

Author Correspondence: Amy G. Johnson, Curatorial Assistant, Indian Pueblo Cultural Center, Albuquerque, New Mexico, March 10, 2006.

Accocesaw

Henry R. Schoolcraft, *The Indian In His Wigwam: Characteristics of The Red Race of America From Original Notes and Manuscripts* (Buffalo: Derby & Hewson; Auburn: Derby, Miller & Co., 1848) made available from Three Rivers (Berry Enterprises, 1998-2003) at http://www.fortklock.com/indianwigwamAA.htm [July 27, 2006].

Accohanoc

Swanton, 66-71.

Accomac

Swanton, 66-71. Henry R. Schoolcraft, *The Indian In His Wigwam: Characteristics of The Red Race of America From Original Notes and Manuscripts* (Buffalo: Derby & Hewson; Auburn: Derby, Miller & Co., 1848) made available from Three Rivers (Berry Enterprises, 1998-2003) at http://www.fortklock.com/indianwigwamAA.htm [July 27, 2006].

Achomawi

Swanton, 479-480. Also, Phillip M. White, "California Indians and Their Reservations" (San Diego State University, 2006) at http://infodome.sdsu.edu/research/guides/calindians/calinddict.shtml?print; "Achomawi," Four Directions Institute (Four Directions Press, 2004) at http://www.fourdir.com/achomawi.htm [February 28, 2006].

Acolapissa

Swanton, 195-196.

Acoma Pueblo

Swanton, 332-334, 339-340; David Roberts, *Pueblo Revolt*, 77-79, 84-88, 88-90, 90-96; David Zax, "Ancient Citadel," *Smithsonian*, May 2008, 56-60; Catherine Watson, "Power of the Pueblo," *Kansas City Star*, February 4, 2007, H1. Also, "New Mexico's Colonial Past" (Washington, DC: Library of Congress, n.a.) at http://memory.loc.gov/ammem/today/sep21.html; "Cuartocentennial of the Colonization of New Mexico" (University Park, NM: New Mexico State University, 2005) at http://web.nmsu.edu/~publhist/ccconc-1.html [April 30, 2006]. "Acoma "Sky City" (NetChannel Inc., 2006) at http://www.acomazuni.com/acoma.cfm and James Abarr, "Legendary Walls," *Albuquerque Journal*, September 14, 1997, available from online edition at http://www.abqjournal.com/venue/day/heritage_acoma.htm [October 24, 2006].

Acopseles

Herbert E. Bolton, "The Founding of the Missions on the San Gabriel River, 1745-1749," *Southwestern Historical Quarterly*, vol. 17, no. 4, 323-378, SHQ Online at http://www.tsha.utexas.edu/publications/journals/shq/online/v017/n4/article_1.html [May 24, 2006].

Acquintanacsuak

Swanton, 57-59.

Acuera

Swanton, 120.

Adaes

Swanton, 196-197, 201, 309. Also, Herbert E. Bolton, "The Founding of the Missions on the San Gabriel River, 1745-1749," *Southwestern Historical Quarterly*, vol. 17, no. 4, 323-378, SHQ Online at http://www.tsha.utexas.edu/publications/journals/shq/online/v017/n4/article_1.html [May 24, 2006].

Margery H. Krieger, "Adaes Indians," Handbook of Texas Online (Austin, TX: Texas State Historical Association and University of Texas, 2001) at http://www.tsha.utexas.edu/handbook/online/articles/AA/bma5.html; "Colonial Natchitoches" (Natchitoches, LA: Neocom Technologies, 1998-2006) at http://www.explorenatchitoches.com/colonial.php?task=view&articleID=75 [May 26, 2006].

Adero

Mildred P. Mayhall, *The Kiowas*, 25. Also, Anna Lewis, "La Harpe's First Expedition in Oklahoma, 1718-1719," *Chronicles of Oklahoma*, December 1924, vol. 2, no. 4, 331-349, available from the Oklahoma State University Digital Library at http://digital.library.okstate.edu/chronicles/v002/v002p331.html [June 6, 2006].

Adirondak

Henry R. Schoolcraft, *The Indian In His Wigwam Characteristics of The Red Race of America From Original Notes and Manuscripts* (New York: Dewitt & Davenport,1848) made available from Three Rivers, Hudson-Mohawk-Schoharie (Berry Enterprises, 1998-2003) at http://www.threerivershms.com/indianwigwam.htm; Stephen B. Sulavik, "Adirondack: Of Indians and Mountains, 1535-1838" (Purple Mountain Press, 2005) at http://www.catskill.net/purple/sulavik.htm [July 28, 2006].

Affagoula

Henry R. Schoolcraft, *The Indian In His Wigwam: Characteristics of The Red Race of America From Original Notes and Manuscripts* (New York: Dewitt & Davenport,1848) made available from Three Rivers, Hudson-Mohawk-Schoharie (Berry Enterprises, 1998-2003) at http://www.threerivershms.com/indianwigwam.htm [July 28, 2006].

Agawom

Swanton, 25. Eben Norton Horsford, "The Indian Names of Boston, and Their Meaning," New England Historic Genealogical Society, November 4, 1885 (Cambridge, MA: John Wilson and Son. University Press, 1886) available from Wellesley College Library Digital Collections (Wellesley, MA: Wellesley College, 2005-2006) at http://aurora.wellesley.edu/horsford/horsford-text.html; "Mashantucket Pequot Research Library Connecticut Tribes and Bands Mentioned In Historical and Contemporary Sources" (Mashantucket Pequot Museum & Research Center, 2005) at http://www.pequotmuseum.org/uploaded_images/8564D213-7519-4055-B791-ADD058B62EA7/Connecticut%20Indian%20Tribes%20Part%201[July 28, 2006].

Ahantchuyuk Kalapuya

Swanton, 452.

Ahtena

Swanton, 529-530.

Aionai

Charles J. Kappler, ed., *Indian Affairs: Laws and Treaties*, vol. I, Laws (Washington, DC: Government Printing Office, 1904).

Ais

Gloria Jahoda, *Trail of Tears*, 244.

Akaitchi

Stephenie Flora, "Northwest Indians" (The Oregon Territory and Its Pioneers, 1998-2005) at http://www.oregonpioneers.com/tribe.htm [August 28, 2006].

Akawantca'ka
Swanton 85-88.

Akokisa
Swanton, 197-199.

Alabama
Swanton, 153-156; T. R. Fehrenbach, *Comanches*, 227.

Algonquin
Swanton, 544-545. Also, "Algonquin Indian Tribe," Kipawa Discussion Board (Multimedia Pandora, 1996-2005) at http://www.kipawa. com/algonqui.htm; Norm Léveillée, "Algonquin Indian Tribe" (Woonsocket, RI, 1997-2006) at http://www.leveillee.net/ancestry/algonquin/ algonquinpeople.htm [April 14, 2006].

Algonquin Group
Swanton, 65, 66, 74, 77, 78, 80, 82, 83, 246, 392. Also, Edwin G. Burrows & Mike Wallace, *Gotham*, 13, 86. Also see Laura Redish, Director, "Native Languages of the Americas: Algonquin" (St. Paul, MN: Native Languages of the Americas, n.d.) at http://www.native-languages.org/ algonquin.htm [September 10, 2006].

Allakaweah
"Indian A Tribes," Indian Genealogy (Access Genealogy, 2004-2006) at http://www.accessgenealogy.com/native/tribes/nations/tribesa.htm [July 28, 2006]. Source: *Handbook of American Indians*, 1906.

Alliklik
Swanton, 480, 497.

Alsea
Swanton, 452-453, 469. Also, Jay Schamber, "Paddling Through Alsi' History" (Oregon Websites and Watersheds Project, 1996-2006) at http://www.orww.org/Reports/S/007J/0912/Kingfisher/Alsi_history.htm; "Alsea Bay and River History" (Waldport, OR: Port of Alsea, 2001-2003) at http://www.portofalsea.com/Port_Information/History/history.html; Joanne Kittel and Suzanne Curtis, "The Yachats Indians, Origins of the Yachats Name, and the Reservation Years (Confederated Tribes of the Coos, Lower Umpqua, and Siuslaw Indians, and the Confederated Tribes of the Siletz Indians of Oregon, 1996) available from Soft Solutions (2004) at http://www.yachats.info/history/title.htm [October 21, 2006].

Altamaha
Swanton, 114-116.

Amacano
Swanton, 122, 128, 129.

Amahami
See Hidatsa.

Anasazi
David Roberts, *The Pueblo Revolt*, 1, 33-35, 35-36, 38-39, 109. Also, Philip Kopper, *The Smithsonian Book of North American Indians Before the Coming of the Europeans*, 234-236, 238, 241, 245; Jay W. Sharp, "The Anasazi" (San Diego, CA: DeseretUSA, 2002) at http://www. desertusa.com/ind1/du_peo_ana.html; "Anasazi," Native Americans (n.a.) at http://www.crystalinks.com/anasazi.html; Bijal P. Trivedi," Ancient Timbers Reveal Secrets of Anasazi Builders," *National Geographic* (September 28, 2001) available at http://news.nationalgeographic.com/ news/2001/09/0928_TVchaco.html [September 9, 2006].

Anasitch
"Kusan Family" (Native American Nations, 2000-2006) at http://www.nanations.com/linguistic/kusan_family.htm; "Anasitch [Language]" (Babylon, 1997-2005) at http://www.babylon.com/definition/Anasitch/All; John Madsen, "Linguistic Classification of American Indians, Greenland, Canada, USA, Mexico," (2000) at http://hjem.tele2adsl.dk/johnmadsen/Indian/indian0.html#IV [August 4, 2006].

Anathagua
Herbert E. Bolton, "The Founding of the Missions on the San Gabriel River, 1745-1749," *Southwestern Historical Quarterly*, vol. 17, no. 4, 323-378, SHQ Online at http://www.tsha.utexas.edu/publications/journals/shq/online/v017/n4/article_1.html; Thomas N. Campbell, "Anathagua Indians," Handbook of Texas Online (Austin, TX: Texas State Historical Association and University of Texas, 2001)' at http://www.tsha.utexas.edu/handbook/online/articles/PP/bmp40.html; Thomas N. Campbell, "Quanataguo Indians," Handbook of Texas Online (Austin, TX: Texas State Historical Association and University of Texas, 2001) at http://www.tsha.utexas.edu/handbook/online/articles/ QQ/bmq1.html; "Coahuiltecan Tribes," Four Corners Institute(Four Directions Press, 2005) at http://www.fourdir.com/coahuiltecan_tribes. htm [May 26, 2006].

Anchose
Herbert E. Bolton, "The Founding of the Missions on the San Gabriel River, 1745-1749," *Southwestern Historical Quarterly*, vol. 17, no. 4, 323-378, SHQ Online at http://www.tsha.utexas.edu/publications/journals/shq/online/v017/n4/article_1.html [May 24, 2006].

Apache
James L. Haley, *Apaches*, esp. 6-7, note 207n18; Swanton, 327-330; T. R. Fehrenbach, *Comanches*, *passim*; Donald J. Berthrong, *The Southern Cheyennes*, 91; John Upton Terrell, *The Plains Apache*, esp. 3-23; Helen Hunt Jackson, *A Century of Dishonor*, 324-335; Swanton 327-330; Kristie C. Woferman, *The Osage in Missouri*, 26; Daniel J. Boorstin, The Americans: *The Democratic Experience*, 38; George Crook, "The Apache Problem," *Journal of the Military Service Institute of the United States* (1886), vol. xxvii, 268, "the greed and rapacity"; Greenville Goodwin, "The Social divisions and economic life of the western Apache," *American Anthropology* (1935), vol. 37, 55-64. See also Peter Aleshire, *Cochise*, esp. 42, 47, 48, 130-138, 148, 152, 185-186, 192, 227, 273-278, 285-288; "a place" taken from p. 227.

Thomas Edwin Farish, *The History of Arizona*, vol. vii, chp. 2, taken from Books of the Southwest, University of Arizona Library, History of Arizona, vol. VII, at http://digital.library.arizona.edu/southwest/hav7/body.1_div.1.html; Jeffrey D. Carlisle, "Apache Indians," Handbook of Texas Online (Austin, TX: Texas State Historical Association and University of Texas, 2001) at http://www.tsha.utexas.edu/handbook/online... /articles/ view/AA/bma33.html; Pam Eck and Diane Dwenger, eds. "Apache, Pueblo, Zuni Indians," *Southwest Native Americans, Study of Native Americans* (Indianapolis, IN: Indiana University-Purdue University Indianapolis, April 1998) at http://inkido.indiana.edu/w310work/romac... /indians.htm et al.; Glenn Welker, Inde (Apache) Literature, Indigenous Peoples' Literature (Baltimore, MD: American Indian Heritage Foundation, 2003) at http://www.indians.org/welker/apache.htm et al., esp. "Tehuacana Creek Treaty" at http://www.indians.org/welker... /liptrea1.htm; "Geronimo" at http://www.indians.org/welker/geronimo.htm; and "Cochise" at http://www.indians.org/welker/cochise.htm [September 8, 2006].

Tara Rose Zitzmann, "Chiricahua" (Mankato, MN: Minnesota State University, n.d.) at http://www.mnsu.edu/emuseum/cultural/ ...northamerica/ chiricahua.html and Jicarilla Apache Nation (Dulce, NM, n.d.) at http://www.jicarillaonline.com/ and "White Mountain Apache Tribe" (Fort Apache, AZ, n.d.) at http://www.wmat.nsn.us/ [July 23, 2007]. "Yavapai-Apache" (Camp Verde, AZ: Yavapai-Apache Nation, n.d.) at http:// www.yavapai-apache-nation.com/; Bernadette Adley-SantaMaria, "White Mountain Apache Language: Issues in Language Shift, Textbook Development, and Native Speaker-University Collaboration" (Flagstaff, AZ: Northern Arizona University, 2003) at http://jan.ucc.nau.edu/~jar/ TIL_12.html; "The Man-Made Environment: The People" (Anchorage, AK: UAA-ISER, 1998-2004) at http://www.alaskool.org/resources/regional/yukon_reg_profile/people.html [March 8, 2006].

On the Gadsden Purchase, see Howard Roberts Lamar, *The Far Southwest, 1846-1912*, 416-417, 423; James M. McPherson, *Battle Cry of Freedom*, 108; Eugene W. Hollow, *The Southwest, Old and New*, 188-189, 192. See full account in Paul Neff Garber, *The Gadsden Treaty* (Philadelphia: Press of the University of Pennsylvania, 1923). For Shaman (Shamanism), see Norman Bancroft-Hunt and Werner Forman, *People of the Toten*, 69, 70, 76-86, 97, 104, 106; T. R. Fehrenbach, *Comanches*, 50-51. See the Movie, *Geronimo*, with Chuck Conners, 1962; Made-for-TV movie, "Geronimo," with Joseph Running Fox as Gerónimo, August Schellenberg as Cochise, and Harrison Lowe as Nana, 1993.

<u>American Indian Boarding Schools</u>
Judith A. Boughter, *Betraying the Omaha Nation, 179-1916*, 78, 79-80, 83, 85-87—"to tell them" taken from p. 83. Also, Mary Annette Pember, "Bitter Legacy of American Indians boarding schools," *Rise-up* (Kansas City: The Kansas City Star Company), August 1-7, 2008, 14-15; "History of American Indian Boarding Schools" (Allentown, PA: Native American Heritage Programs, 2002-2008) at http://www. lenapeprograms.info/Teacher/bording_schools.htm; Bibliography of Indian Boarding Schools: Approximately 1875 to 1940" (Tempe: Arizona State University Libraries, 2008) at http://www.asu.edu/lib/archives/boardingschools.htm; Kay Marie Porterfield, "Brainwashing and Boarding Schools: Undoing the Shameful Legacy" (2003) at http://www.kporterfield.com/aicttw/articles/boardingschool.html; Charla Bear, "American Indian Boarding Schools Haunt Many" (Washington, D.C.: NPR, 2008) at http://www.npr.org/templates/story/story.php... ?storyId=16516865 [August 6, 2008]. For an interesting aside on Haskell Indian Nations University, see Raymond Schmidt, "Fords of the Prairie: Haskell Indian School Football, 1919-1920," *Journal of Short History* (College Football Historical Society), Fall 2001, vol. 28, no. 3, 403-426, at Eric Adler, "For Haskell Indian Nations University football team, it's a matter of pride," *The Kansas City Star*, October 26, 2007. Also see Tom Swift, *Chief Bender's Burden: The Silent Struggle of a Baseball Star* (Lincoln: University of Nebraska Press, 2008)

Apalachee
Gloria Jahoda, *Trail of Tears*, 244; Swanton, 122-125. Also, "History" (Tallahassee: FL: City of Tallahassee, 2005-2006) at http://www.talgov. com/gov/facts/history.cfm; "Florida's Historic Places: Tallahassee," Exploring Florida (Tampa, FL: University of South Florida, 2002) at http:// fcit.coedu.usf.edu/florida/lessons/tallahassee/tallahassee.htm [September 11, 2006]. Theodore Calvin Pease and Raymond C. Werner, *The French Foundations*, 1680-1693 (Springfield, IL: Illinois State Historical Library, 1934), s.v. "Index: Apalachee [Palache]," made available from *American Memory* (Library of Congress, n.d.) at http://memory.loc.gov/master/gc/gcmisc/gcfr/0006/04290407.txt [August 11, 2006].

Apalachicola
Swanton, 104-105; Gloria Jahoda, *Trail of Tears*, 245.

Apapax
Swanton, 309-311; Herbert E. Bolton, "The Founding of the Missions on the San Gabriel River, 1745-1749," *Southwestern Historical Quarterly*, vol. 17, no. 4, 323-378, SHQ Online at http://www.tsha.utexas.edu/publications/journals/shq/online/v017/n4/article_1.html [May 24, 2006].

Appomatotox
Edmond S. Morgan, *American Slavery, American Freedom*, 255; Swanton, 66-71.

Aquascogooc
Fred Willard, "Trade Items as Transfer of Money," November 2002, made available by the Lost Colony Center for Science and Research (Eastern Carolina University) at http://lost-colony.com/trade.html [June 12, 2006].

Arapaho
Dee Brown, *Hear That Lonesome Whistle Blow*, 78, 85, 87-88, 204, 205, 207; T. R. Fehrenbach, *Comanches*, 76; William Y. Chalfant, *Cheyennes and Horse Soldiers*, 87, 90, 243, 303-305, 306, 307; William R. Nester, *The Arikara War*, 15-16; Swanton, 384-386; Mildred P. Mayhall, *The*

Kiowas, 4, 7, 14, 19, 32, 51, 61, 87, 128-129, 173. 190-191, 239, 247. See also Hugh Lenox Scott, "The Early History and Names of the Arapaho" (NaNations, 2000-2006) at http://www.nanations.com/early_arapaho.htm [August 9, 2006].

Arikara

William R. Nester, *The Arikara War*, esp. 145, 160-181, 210-212; Gloria Jahoda, *Trail of Tears*, 174, 178, 184, 186; Dee Brown, *Hear That Lonesome Whistle Blow*, 262; John C. Ewers, ed., *Edwin Thompson Denig's Five Indian Tribes of the Upper Missouri*, 41-62; George E. Hyde, Red Cloud's Folk: A History of the Oglala Sioux, 14-16, 17-19, 24, 27, 36-38; Stephen E. Ambrose, *Undaunted Courage*, 178-185, 189-190, 389-390, 450-451; Bernard De Voto, ed., *The Journals of Lewis and Clark*, 33, 34, 45n3, 47-52, 60-62, 69-70, 214-215, 302, 452, 456-461; Mildred P. Mayhall, *The Kiowas*, 7, 12, 19, 27, 30, 36, 72n100, 86, 87, 108. Jean Baptiste Trudeau lived among the Arikara 1794-1795 and penned the first description of them. See also "Intertribal Trade" (UM Regional Learning Project, 2003-2006) at http://www.trailtribes.org/kniferiver/ intertribal-trade.htm [September 6, 2006].

On Fur Traders and Fur Trading Companies, see William R. Nester, *The Arikara War*, 106-126, 201-210; David Dary, *The Oregon Trail*:
-NWC, 14-15, 18, 21-22, 28, 30-31, 32, 33, 47, 48, 183.
-AFC, 17-19, 71, 83, 159, 194, 217-218, 246, 260.
-HBC, 13-15, 48, 50-55, 60-63, 74, 77, 105, 105, 109-110, 118, 126, 129, 144, 146, 150, 177, 182, 195, 226, 288.
-Sublette, Milton, 94.
-Sublette, William, 54, 57-59, 65, 82, 86-87, 102, 144, 194.

Also see O. Ned Eddins, "Historical Facts On The American And Canadian Fur Trade" (Afton, WY, 2006) at http://www.thefurtrapper.com/... fur_trade.htm [March 29, 2006]. Also by Eddins, "History of the North American Fur Trade" at http://www.thefurtrapper.com/rendezvous.htm [September 12, 2006]; "Fort William (Fort Laramie)" (Malachite's Big Hole, 2006) at http://home.att.net/~mman/FortWilliam.htm [March 29, 2006]; Alexander M. Stewart. John S. Allen, ed., "René Menard 1605-1661" (Stewart, 1934; Allen, 1997. Last revised 21 August 1999) at http://www.bikexprt.com/menard/index.htm#table ... [August 27, 2006]. For the Yellowstone Expedition, see William R. Nester, *The Arikara War*, 198-200, 203-205.

Armouchiquois

"Indian A Tribes," Indian Genealogy (Access Genealogy, 2004-2006) at http://www.accessgenealogy.com/native/tribes/nations/tribesa.htm [July 28, 2006]. Source: *Handbook of American Indians*, 1906. See related site: http://www.accessgenealogy.com/native/tribes/atribe.htm. Also see "Maine History" (Davistown, ME: Davistown Museum, n.d.) at http://www.davistownmuseum.org/bibMEprimary.htm; Peter Landry, "Chief Henri Membertou" (1998-2000) at http://www.blupete.com/Hist/BiosNS/1600-00/Membertou.htm; also "The Micmac of Megumaagee" at http://www.blupete.com/Hist/Gloss/Indians.htm; "Timeline of Native American Culture," Story of Maine (Main Public Broadcasting Network) at http://www.mpbc.org/homestom/timelines/natamtimeline.html; Thomas Grassman, "Panounias (Panoniac)" (Dictionary of Canadian Biography) at http://www.biographi.ca/EN/ShowBioPrintable.asp?BioId=34567 [September 11, 2006].

Arrenamuse
Samuel G. Drake, *The Aboriginal Races of North America...*, 9-16.

Arrohattoc
Swanton, 66-71.

Assiniboin
Swanton, 387-388; Gloria Jahoda, *Trail of Tears*, 174, 178, 187; John C. Ewers, ed., *Edwin Thompson Denig's Five Indian Tribes of the Upper Missouri*, 63-98; John C. Ewers, *The Blackfeet*, 185-187, 260-261. De Smet quote taken from Robert C. Carriker, *Father Peter John De Smet*, 89-90. See the painting by George Catlin, *Wi-jun-jon, Pigeon's Egg Head (The Light) Going and Returning From Washington*, Assiniboine/Nakoda, 1837-1839. George Catlin was a nineteenth century American artist and author who spent his life describing life of the American Indian in words and paintings. He wrote numerous books on Indian life and culture. The majority of his paintings are parts of the Smithsonian's American Art Museum. Also, "Assiniboine," *L'Encyclopédie Canadienne* (Fondation Historica du Canada, 2004) at http://www.canadianencyclopedia.ca/index.cfm?PgNm=TCE&Params=A1ARTA0000355 [September 8, 2006]..

Atákapa
Swanton, 186 (joined by Houma), 193 (of the Tunica group), 197-199, 205 (allied w/ French), 208 (Opelousa alliance), 210 (intermarriage), 307 (Akokisa), 308 (Bidai), 314 (Deadose). Hugh Singleton, "Atakapa Ishak Indians of Southwest Louisiana," (Lutherana Online, n.d.) at http://www.lutheransonline.com/servlet/lo_ProcServ/dbpage=page&mode=display&gid=0001200000105715906897842 [May 25, 2006].

"Attakapas," *Encyclopedia Louisiana* (1998-2001) at http://www.enlou.com/places/attakapas.htm [August 21, 2006]; "Index to Volume IX," *Southwestern Historical Quarterly* Online (Austin, TX) vol 9, no. 1, at http://www.tsha.utexas.edu/publications/journals/shq/online... /v009/n1/ front_3.html [March 10, 2006]; R. E. Moore, "The Atakapan Indian Groups: The Bidai, Akokisa, Han, Deadoses, Patiris" (R. Edward. Moore and Texarch Associates, 1998, 2000) at http://www.texasindians.com/ [December 5, 2006].

Also, Powell in *7th Annual Rpt. B.A.E.* (1891), 56; Julia Kathryn Garrett, "Letter 12, Natchitoches May 8th, 1809," Dr. John Sibley and the Louisiana-Texas Frontier, 1803-1814, vol. 47, no. 3, *Southwestern Historical Quarterly* Online (Texas State Historical Association, 2004), n69, at http://www.tsha.utexas.edu/publications/journals/shq/online/v047/n3/contrib_DIVL5843.html and A. K. Christian, "Mirabeau Buonaparte Lamar", vol. 24, No.1,at http://www.tsha.utexas.edu/publications/journals/shq/online/v024/n1/contrib_DIVL669.html [August 1, 2006].

Atákapa, Eastern
See Atákapa.

Atasacneus

Herbert E. Bolton, "The Founding of the Missions on the San Gabriel River, 1745-1749," *Southwestern Historical Quarterly*, vol. 17, no. 4, 323-378, SHQ Online at http://www.tsha.utexas.edu/publications/journals/shq/online/v017/n4/article_1.html [May 24, 2006].

Atasi

Swanton, 156, 161.

Atfalati Kalapuya

Swanton, 453-454, 476.

Atiasnogue

Herbert E. Bolton, "The Founding of the Missions on the San Gabriel River, 1745-1749," *Southwestern Historical Quarterly*, vol. 17, no. 4, 323-378, SHQ Online at http://www.tsha.utexas.edu/publications/journals/shq/online/v017/n4/article_1.html [May 24, 2006].

Atsina

John C. Ewers, *The Blackfeet*, esp. 242-243; Keith Algier, *The Crow and the Eagle: A Tribal History from Lewis & Clark to Custer*, 14, 15, 113 (smallpox), 201 (1866 Treaty), 225 (1868 Treaty), 249 and 255 (agency). On Atsina standing within the Blackeet Confederacy, Algier, esp. 73, 183-184. Also, Swanton, 389-390; Gloria Jahoda, *Trail of Tears*, 175; Stephen E. Ambrose, *Undaunted Courage*, 274, 377, 378; Bernard De Voto, ed., *The Journals of Lewis and Clark*, 84, 120, 192-193, 196, 198, 214, 383, 395, 434-435, 437.

Atsugewi

Swanton, 480-481.

Attikamigue

Samuel G. Drake, *The Aboriginal Races of North America...*, 9-16.

Aucocisco

"Indian A Tribes," Indian Genealogy (Access Genealogy, 2004-2006) at http://www.accessgenealogy.com/native/tribes/nations/tribesa.htm [July 28, 2006]. Source: *Handbook of American Indians*, 1906.

Aughquaga

"Letters of Francis Parkman to Pierre Margry," *American Memory* (Washington, DC: Library of Congress, 22 Sep. 2004 et al.), 558, 558, at http://memory.loc.gov/master/gc/gcmisc/gcfr/0002/05650558.txt and http://memory.loc.gov/master/gc/gcmisc/gcfr/0002/05660559.txt; William Stone, *The Life and Times of Sir William Johnson, Bart.* (Albany: J. Munsell, 1865), vol. II, ch. 2, 1757, made available from Three Rivers (Berry Enterprises, 1998-2003) at http://www.fortklock.com/SWJ%20vol2ch2.htm [August 31, 2006]. Also, Samuel G. Drake, *The Aboriginal Races of North America...*, 9-16

Avoyel

Swanton, 199-200.

Ayutan

Samuel G. Drake, *The Aboriginal Races of North America...*, 9-16.

Backhook

"South Carolina – Indians, Native Americans – Indian Tribes" (Columbia, SC: SCIway.net, 2007) at http://www.sciway.net/hist/indians/tribes.html; "Native American Words and Definitions" (Jelsoft Enterprises Ltd., 2000-2007) at http://www.occultcorpus.com/forum/showthread.php?p=5180 [October 21, 2007].

Bannock

Merrill D. Beal, *"I Will Fight No More Forever": Chief Joseph and the Nez Percé War*, 78, 143, 165. Swanton, 398-399. See also "Massacre Rocks" (Idaho State University, n.d.) at http://www.isu.edu/~trinmich/Massacre.html; "Massacre Rocks State Park" (Pioneer Country Travel Council of Southeastern Idaho, 1996-2006) at http://www.seidaho.org/massacrerock.html [September 10, 2006].

David Comer, "Shoshone-Bannock Indians History/Links" (2002) at http://www.rootsweb.com/~idreserv/fhhist.html; Oliver O. Howard, "Outbreak of the Piute and Bannock War," *Overland Monthly and Out West* (June 1887), vol. 9, no. 54, 587-592, available from the collection, Making of America Journal Articles, available from the University of Michigan Library at http://name.umdl.umich.edu/ahj1472.2-09.054 [October 27, 2006].

Sarah Winnemucca Hopkins, *The Bannock War, Life Among the Piutes: Their Wrongs and Claims* (1883), chp. vii, available at http://www.yosemite.ca.us/library/life_among_the_piutes/bannock_war.html [October 28, 2006]. Firsthand account. Puts the number of warriors at 450. In another instance, she notes the presence of 1500-2000 Indians; another time, six hundred camps. Also, "Bannock War of 1878" (n.a.) at http://members.aol.com/thays46945/bnkw.htm [October 27, 2006]. "Indian strength was about eight hundred or more." Sources cited: Frederick A. Mark, *The Bannock Indian War of 1878* and Robert M. Utley & Wilcomb E. Washburn, *Indian Wars*; Peter Cozzens, ed. *Eyewitnesses to the Indian Wars, 1865-1890: The Wars for the Pacific Northwest* (Mechanicsburg, PA: Stackpole Books, 2002). Robert H. Rudy and John A. Brown, *The Cayuse Indians*, 283-286, refer to the 1878 Bannock War as the Snake-Paiute War.

William Thompson, *The Great Bannock War, Reminiscences of a Pioneer*, Chapter XV at http://www.books-about-california.com/Pages/ Reminiscences_of_a_Pioneer/Reminiscences_Chapter_15.html [October 27, 2006]. Puts count at "a thousand to twelve hundred plumed and mounted warriors." John Pike, "Rogue River War" (Global Security, 2000-2006) at http://www.globalsecurity.org/military/ops/bannock-war. htm [October 28, 2006]. Puts total hostiles at "2000 in all." Also, Eric Mayer, "The Northwest Tribes" (Emazine, n.d.) at http://www.emayzine. com/lectures/nwtribes.htm; Ralph Zuljan, "Bannock War 1878" (OnWar, n.d.) at http://www.onwar.com/aced/nation/uni/usa/fbannock1878. htm [October 27, 2006]. Reports massacre. AllExperts at http://experts.about.com/e/b/ba/bannock_war.htm cites Zuljan.

"History" (Fort Hall, ID: Shoshone-Bannock Tribes, 2006) at http://www.shoshonebannocktribes.com/; "Bannock Indians" (Washington, DC: National Geographic, 1996-2006) at http://www.nationalgeographic.com/lewisandclark/record_tribes_001_11_7.html; Cain Allen, "Family of Bannock Indians, 1872," The Oregon History Project (Oregon Historical Society, 2002-2005) at http://www.ohs.org/education/oregonhistory/ historical_records/dspDocument.cfm?doc_ID=62F22F79-F524-BDE2-23F017D4416EEFBB [October 29, 2006].

Bannock Creek Shoshoni
Swanton, 403-404.

Barbareño Chumash
Swanton, 484-487.

Bayougoula
Swanton, 200-201; David Graham, "Pierre LeMoyne Sieur d'Iberville and the Establishment of Biloxi," from David Hawkwind (1995-1996) at http://www.datasync.com/~davidg59/biloxi1.html [September 9, 2006].

Bear River Indians of California
Swanton, 481, 515.

Bear River Indians of North Carolina
Swanton, 74, 81, 83, 481.

Beaver Indians
Swanton, 552; "Beaver (Native Group)," *L'Encyclopédie Canadienne* (Fondation Historica du Canada, 2004) at http://www.canadianencyclopedia.ca/index.cfm?PgNm=TCE&Params=A1ARTA0000614 [September 9, 2006].

Beothuk
Swanton, 548-549; Daniel K. Richter, *Facing East from Indian Country*, 15, 27.

Bidai
Swanton, 197, 308, 324; Kevin Ladd, "El Orcoquisac," Handbook of Texas Online (Austin, TX: Texas State Historical Association and University of Texas, 1999-2003) at http://www.tsha.utexas.edu/handbook/online/articles/EE/hve49.html [March 10, 2006]. In comparison, the following form of the citation was adapted from the *Chicago Manual of Style*, 15th ed.: Handbook of Texas Online, s.v. "EL ORCOQUISAC," http://www. tsha.utexas.edu/handbook/online/articles/EE/hve49.html [March 10, 2006].

Biloxi
Swanton, 174-176, 191; David Graham, "Pierre LeMoyne Sieur d'Iberville and the Establishment of Biloxi," from David Hawkwind (1995-1996) at http://www.datasync.com/~davidg59/biloxi1.html [September 9, 2006].

Blackfeet
John C. Ewers, *The Blackfeet: Raiders on the Northwestern Plains*, esp. 185-193, 214-221, 248-253; Keith Algier, *The Crow and the Eagle: A Tribal History from Lewis & Clark to Custer*, 14-15, 51, 53, 57, 58, 73-75, 98, 100, 102, 106, 112-113, 116, 117, 121, 130, 135, 136, 139, 165, 173, 182-183; on Atsina standing within the Blackeet Confederacy, see Algier, esp. 73, 183-184. Also Swanton, 395-398; Gloria Jahoda, *Trail of Tears*, 174, 187; William R. Nester, *The Arikara War*, 16, 36, 73, 76, 118, 151, 153, 165-66, 201, 207; Dee Brown, *Hear That Lonesome Whistle Blow*, 262; Stephen E. Ambrose, *Undaunted Courage*, 232, 273-276, 366-368; Bernard De Voto, ed., *The Journals of Lewis and Clark*, 112, 120n4, 122, 161, 383, 395, 427, 435-440, 453; Robert C. Carriker, *Father Peter John De Smet*, 48, 54, 60, 77, 81, 88, 91-93, 101-103, 173, 179, 180, 203.

Hugh A. Dempsey, "Blackfoot (Siksika)," *L'Encyclopédie Canadienne* (Fondation Historica du Canada, 2004) at http://www.canadianencyclopedia.ca/index.cfm?PgNm=TCE&Params=A1ARTA0000801; the Blood at ...A1ARTA0000831; the Piegan at ...A1ARTA0006187; and Blackfoot Nation at ...A1ARTA0000802 [September 9, 2006].

Blewmouth
"The Province of Georgia in 1740: Economic Progress and Indians," Learning Page(Washington, DC: Library of Congress, 2003) at http:// lcweb2.loc.gov/learn/features/timeline/colonial/georgia/province.html [October 6, 2007]. Taken from a pamphlet titled "A State of The Province of Georgia, Attested upon Oath, in the Court of Savannah, Nov. 10, 1740. Also, *Diary Of The First Earl Of Egmont (Viscount Peecival). Vol. III. 1739—1747* (London: His Majesty's Stationery Office, 1923), p. 30, available from the Historical Manuscripts Commissioners at http://fax.libs. uga.edu/DA501xE31m/1f/diary_of_viscount_percival_vol_3.txt [October 6, 2007].

Bodega Miwok
Swanton, 502-507.

Brotherton
Alan Taylor, *The Divided Ground*, 146-147, 173, 184, 296, 319-322, 381; Gloria Jahoda, *Trail of Tears*, 96, 101. Swanton writes of the Brotherton, esp. 28, 30, 31, 42, 43, 47, but does not treat them separately.

Brulé
For Fort Laramie, the Grattan Massacre, and the Battle of Blue Water Creek, see Robert M. Utley, *The Lance and the Shield*, 45; George Bird Grinnell, *The Fighting Cheyenne*, 104-108; William Y. Chalfant, *Cheyennes and Horse Soldiers*, 28-32; R. Eli Paul, *Blue Water Creek and the First Sioux War, 1854-1856*. Also David Dary, *The Oregon Trail*, 259-261; Shirley Christian, *Before Louis and Clark*, 378, 392, 396, 403, 409-411, 429, 481n (apparent error in one of original sources used to set the month cited for plunder of Fort John); Merrill J. Mattes, *Fort Laramie Park History, 1834-1977* (U.S. Department of the Interior, National Park Service, Rocky Mountain Regional Office, September 1980); Frank McLynn, *Wagons West*, 68-69. Also see Joseph M. Marshall, III, *The Journey of Crazy Horse*, 39-42, and for "Woman Killer" at the Sicangu Encampment 63-69, 91-92. In general, references to the American Fur Company after 1834 s/b to either B. Pratte & Company; Pratte, Chouteau & Company; or P. Chouteau Jr. & Company. On the Wazhazha band, see Kingsley M. Bray, *Crazy Horse: A Lakota Life.*, 21, 31, 34, 46, 104, 128, 310, 395, 453n13. On p. 34, Bray refers to "lodges of Brules and Wazhazhas" as if two separate enntities.

Burt Woods Chippewa
"Boozhoo" (Nett Lake, MN: Bois Forte Band of Chippewa, 2005) at http://www.boisforte.com/ [April 8, 2006].

Caddo Peoples
Swanton, 201, 205, 212, 214, 269, 289, 299, 300, 309, 315, 316, 319, 320, 324, 325, 326; Gloria Jahoda, *Trail of Tears*, 288; T. R. Fehrenback, *Comanches*, 227, 314; Samuel G. Drake, *The Aboriginal Races of North America...*, 9-16; Carter Elkins and Cecile Elkins, *Caddo Indians: Where We Come From.*

Timothy K. Perttula, "Caddo Indians," Handbook of Texas Online (Austin, TX: Texas State Historical Association and University of Texas, 1999-2003) at http://www.tsha.utexas.edu/handbook/online/articles/view/CC/bmcaj.html [September 9, 2006]; William B. Glover, "A History of the Caddo Indians," *Louisiana Historical Quarterly* (October 1935), vol. 18, no. 4, made available by Computing and Information Services (College Station, TX: Texas A&M University, 2006) at http://ops.tamu.edu/x075bb/caddo/Indians.html [August 3, 2006]

"Caddoan Family" (Native American Nations, 2000-2006) at http://www.nanations.com/linguistic/caddoan_family.htm; Julia Kathryn Garrett, "Doctor John Sibley and the Lousiana-Texas Frontier, 1803-1814," *Southwestern Historical Quarterly*, vol. 49, n. 4, made available by the Texas State Historical Association (Austin, TX: University of Texas, 2004) at http://www.tsha.utexas.edu/publications/journals/shq/online/v049/n4/contrib_DIVL8836.html [August 16, 2006]. "Arkansas Indians" (Fayetteville, AR: Arkansas Archeological Survey, 2003) at http://www.uark.edu/campus-resources/archinfo/ArkansasIndianTribes.pdf [September 16, 2007].

Cahinnio
Swanton, 317-320.

Cahokia
Swanton, 241-242; Frederick Webb Hodge, ed., "Cahokia," *Handbook of American Indians North of Mexico* (Washington, DC: Smithsonian Institution, Bureau of American Ethnology Bulletin 30, 1910) made available by Jim Fay, Prairie Nations (University of Illinois School of Library and Information Sciences, 2006) at http://www.prairienet.org/prairienations/cahokia.htm [August 3, 2006].

On the Cahokia of the Mississippian Period, see Biloine Whiting Young and Melvin J Fowler, *Cahokia, the Great Native American Metropolis* (Urbana: University of Illinois Press, 1999) and Emmett Berg , "The Lost City of Cahokia," *Humanities* (September/October 2004), vol. 25, no. 5, from FreeRepublic (Fresno, CA, posted 01/17/2006) at http://www.freerepublic.com/focus/f-news/1559848/posts [October 2, 2007].

Cahuilla
Swanton, 357, 481-482; Harry C. James, The Cahuilla Indians (Banning, Calif.: Malki Museum Press, 1969); Lowell John Bean, Mukat's People: The Cahuilla Indians of Southern California (Berkeley: University of California Press, 1972); Also, "Cahuilla Indinas" (Hot Springs Reservation, AR: Manataka American Indian Council, 2007) at http://www.manataka.org/page550.html [September 23, 2007].

Calapooya Kalapuya
Swanton, 454, 463, 468.

Calasthocle
Swanton, 435, 436.

Callimix
Samuel G. Drake, *The Aboriginal Races of North America...*, 9-16.

Calusa
Gloria Jahoda, *Trail of Tears*, 244; Swanton, 125-128.

Canarsee
Swanton, 48-55.

Canawaghauna
"Names of Different Indian Nations In North-America, With the Numbers of Their Fighting Men," Historical Account of Bouquet's Expedition

Against the Ohio Indians, in 1764 (Cincinnati, OH: Robert Clarke, & Co., 1868), Appendix V (prepared by unknown French trader), made available from Glen Black Laboratory of Archaeology (Bloomington, IN: University of Indiana, 1996-2000) at http://www.gbl.indiana.edu/archives/dockett_317/317_84a.html [August 27, 2006].

Cancepne
Herbert E. Bolton, "The Founding of the Missions on the San Gabriel River, 1745-1749," *Southwestern Historical Quarterly*, vol. 17, no. 4, 323-378, SHQ Online at http://www.tsha.utexas.edu/publications/journals/shq/online/v017/n4/article_1.html; Thomas N. Campbell, "Cancepne Indians," Handbook of Texas Online (Austin, TX: Texas State Historical Association and University of Texas, 2001) at http://www.tsha.utexas.edu/handbook/online/articles/CC/bmc22.html [May 25, 2006].

Caparaz
Swanton, 122, 123, 128, 129.

Cape Fear Indians
Swanton, 75, 97.

Capiché
Swanton, 205-206.

Capinans
Swanton, 137, 174-175, 176. Also see Biloxi.

Capote Ute
Swanton, 373-374.

Caree
Samuel G. Drake, *The Aboriginal Races of North America...*, 9-16.

Carrier
Swanton, 549-550.

Henry Rowe Schoolcraft, *Personal Memoirs Of A Residence of Thirty Years With The Indian Tribes On The American Frontiers* (BookRags, 2000-2006), 143, at http://www.bookrags.com/ebooks/11119/143.html; "Athapascan Family" (Native American Nations, 2000-2006) at http://www.nanations.com/linguistic/athapascan_family.htm; John Wesley Powell, *Indian Linguistic Families Of America, North Of Mexico* (Seventh Annual Report of the Bureau of Ethnology to the Secretary of the Smithsonian Institution, 1885-1886, Washington, DC: GPO, 1891) available from Project Gutenberg Literary Archive Foundation (2003-2006) at http://www.gutenberg.org/etext/17286 [August 16, 2006]. Also at http://www.sakoman.net/pg/html/17286.htm. Also, "Dakelh," First Nations in British Columbia (?Encyclopedia, 2005) at http://www.tocatch.info/en/Carrier_tribe.htm [August 16, 2006].

Cascangue
Swanton, 132

Caso
Herbert E. Bolton, "The Founding of the Missions on the San Gabriel River, 1745-1749," *Southwestern Historical Quarterly*, vol. 17, no. 4, 323-378, SHQ Online at http://www.tsha.utexas.edu/publications/journals/shq/online/v017/n4/article_1.html; Thomas N. Campbell, "Caso Indians," Handbook of Texas Online (Austin, TX: Texas State Historical Association and University of Texas, 2001) at http://www.tsha.utexas.edu/handbook/online/articles/CC/bmc34.html [May 25, 2006].

Castahana
Samuel G. Drake, *The Aboriginal Races of North America...*, 9-16.

Catawba
Gloria Jahoda, *Trail of Tears*, 288; Swanton, 76, 79, 81, 90-92, 93, 96, 97, 99, 101. Also, "The Early Peoples of North Carolina," North Carolina Handbook (New York: Holt, Reinhart and Winston, n.d.) at http://go.hrw.com/resources/go_ss/samples/SN9SAMPL.PDF [September 9, 2006].

"South Carolina – Indians, Native Americans – Catawba" (SCIway, 2006) at http://www.sciway.net/hist/indians/catawba.html; Gene Waddell, "Cofitachiqui," Carologue (Autumn 2000) made available by Gene Waddell (Charleston, SC: College of Charleston, 2006), vol. 16, no. 3, 8-15 at \http://www.cofc.edu/~waddelle/CofitachiquiRev2.html; Steven Pony Hill, "Patriot Chiefs and Loyal Braves: Chapter I, 'A Very Large Nation' – The Colonial Period" (©2005) at http://sciway3.net/clark/freemoors/CHAPTER1colonial.htm; Almon Wheeler Lauber, "Processes of Enslavement: Trade," Indian Slavery in Colonial Times Within the Present Limits of the United States, Ch. VII (New York: Columbia University, 1913), 168-195, made available by Dinsmore Documentation (Westfield, MA, 2002) at http://www.dinsdoc.com/lauber-1-7.htm [August 5, 2006].

Orlando M. McPherson, "Indians of North Carolina: Letter from the Secretary of the Interior, Transmitting, in Response to a Senate Resolution of June 30, 1914, a Report on the Condition and Tribal Rights of the Indians of Robeson and Adjoining Counties of North Carolina," September 19, 1914, made available from Documenting the American South (Chapel Hill, NC: University Library, University of North Carolina, 2004, updated March 28, 2005) at http://docsouth.unc.edu/nc/mcpherson/mcpherson.html [August 5, 2006].

Cathlacumup
Swanton, 467; "Chinookan Devastation: 'Marsh Miasms'" (Vancouver, WA: Center for Columbia River History, 2004-2005) at http://www.ccrh.org/comm/slough/chinook5.htm.

Cathlakaheckit
"Chinookan Indian Tribes" (Access Genealogy, 2004-2006) at http://www.accessgenealogy.com/native/tribes/chinook/chinookhistory.htm [August 2, 2006]. Source: *Handbook of American Indians, 1906.*

Cathlamet
Swnaton, 414; "Wahkiakum County" (Wahkiakum County, WA, 2006) at http://www.co.wahkiakum.wa.us/aboutus.htm [August 30, 2006].

Cathlanaquiah
Swanton, 467; "Chinookan Devastation: 'Marsh Miasms'" (Vancouver, WA: Center for Columbia River History, 2004-2005) at http://www.ccrh.org/comm/slough/chinook5.htm [August 2, 2006].

Cathlapotle
Swanton, 414-415.

Cathlasko
Samuel G. Drake, *The Aboriginal Races of North America...*, 9-16.

Cathlath
Samuel G. Drake, *The Aboriginal Races of North America...*, 9-16.

Catskill
Swanton, 48-55.

Cattanahaw
Samuel G. Drake, *The Aboriginal Races of North America...*, 9-16.

Caughnewaga
Swanton, 37. Also, Henry Howe, "Seneca County," Historical Collections of Ohio" (1888), vol. II, 572 available from Learning Center (Ancestry.com, n.d.) at http://freepages.genealogy.rootsweb.com/~henryhowesbook/seneca.html; "John Gilmary Shea Papers, Folder Listing" (Washington, DC: Georgetown University Libraries Special Collections, 2004), Box: 10 Fold: 1, Mohawk, 1700?, at http://www.library. georgetown.edu/dept/speccoll/fl/f269}4.htm; Elias Boudinot, *A Star in the West...* (Trenton, NJ, 1815), 115, available from Oliver's Bookshelf (2002) at http://olivercowdery.com/texts/boud1816.htm; Duane Ganser, "Chairman Letter," Fall 2003 Newsletter (Westlake, OH: Ohio Decoy Collectors and Carvers Association, 2006) at http://www.odcca.org/Fall%202003%20Newsletter.htm; "Light Infantry" (My Military Pages, n.d.) at http://mymilitaryhistorypages.bravehost.com/LightInfantryUnits.htm [August 3, 2006].

Cayuga
Edwin G. Burrows & Mike Wallace, *Gotham*, 13; Gloria Jahoda, *Trail of Tears*, 90; Swanton, 40, 44, 57, 72, 73.

Cayuse
Robert H. Rudy and John A. Brown, *The Cayuse Indians: Imperial Tribesmen of Old Oregon*, generally; on the 1855 treaty, 189-204 w/ the quote"knee deep in blood" taken from p. 203. Also see Merrill D. Beal, *"I Will Fight No More Forever": Chief Joseph and the Nez Percé War*, 24-26; David Dary, *The Oregon Trail*, 63, 178-183, 183-186, 192, 205; Swanton, 454-455.

For the Whitman Massacre and the Cayuse War, see Rudy and Brown: murders, 109-127; war and search for culprits, 128-161; trial and execution, 162-171, 303-305. "So we die to save our people," quoted from Herbert Howe Bancroft, *History of Oregon, Vol. II, 1848-1893*, 95, on p. 162-162. Also see Helen Hunt Jackson, *A Century of Dishonor*, 407-410. Hunt's account is taken from an article published in the *Army and Navy Journal*, November 1, 1879. The author is unnamed. See also Angie Debo, *A History of the Indians of the United States*, 150-156. Robert C. Carriker, *Father Peter John DeSmet*, 140 (mentions only the massacre); Frank McLynn, *Wagons West*, 425-426; *Oregon Spectator*, July 27, 1850.

Cecilville Indians
Swanton, 514.

Chaftan
25 U.S.14, Subchapter XXX, §692.

Chakchiuma
Swanton, 176, 185, 187, 192.

Chala
"Names of Different Indian Nations In North-America, With the Numbers of Their Fighting Men," *Historical Account of Bouquet's Expedition Against the Ohio Indians, in 1764* (Cincinnati, OH: Robert Clarke, & Co., 1868), Appendix V (prepared by unk French trader), made available from Glen Black Laboratory of Archaeology (Bloomington, IN: University of Indiana, 1996-2000) at

http://www.gbl.indiana.edu/archives/dockett_317/317_84a.html; "The Western Border: Indian Occupants-Border Warfare-Treaties-Facts And Incidents," *History of Union County* [Ohio] (Chicago: W. H. Beers & Co., 1883), ch. II, 223, made available by Allen L. Potts (Heritage Pursuit, last updated June 21, 2006) at http://www.heritagepursuit.com/Union/Unp3c2.htm [August 27, 2006].

Chalaoklowa Chickasaw
"SC – Indians, Native Americans – Chaloklowa Chickasaw" (2007 SCIway.net, 2007) at http://www.sciway.net/hist/indians/chaloklowa-chickasaw-indians.html; "South Carolina Indian Tribes and Groups" (Columbia, SC: State of South Carolina, n.d.) at http://www.state.sc.us/cma/pdfs/s_c_tribes_and_groups.pdf [October 20, 2007].

Chato
Swanton, 617, 621.

Chatot
Swanton, 128, 129.

Chawasha
Swanton, 201-202.

Cheegee
Swanton, 218, 230-231; "Native Americans," *Migration and Settlement* (Bowling Green, KY: Western Kentucky, 2005) at Universityhttp://www.wku.edu/library/museum/education/frontieronline/frontiermigration.htm [August 3, 2006].

Chehalis
Swanton 415-416, 418; Bernard De Voto, ed., *The Journals of Lewis and Clark*, 297-298. Also, "Confederated Tribes of the Chehalis" (Oakville, WA: The Confederated Tribes of the Chehalis, n.d.) at http://www.chehalistribe.org/index.htm and http://www.chehalistribe.org/about.htm [June 22, 2006]; Dan Van Mechelen, "History of the Quinault Reservation," (Rod Van Mechelen, 2004-2006) at http://www.vanmechelen.net/quinres... .html; "Lewis & Clark" (National Geographic, 1996-2006) at http://www.nationalgeographic.com/lewisandclark/record_tribes_082_14_2.html [August 3, 006].

Chelemela Kalapuya
Swanton, 456; U.S. Code Title 25, Chapter 14, Subchapter XXX, § 692 Definitions.

Chemapoho Kalapuya
Swanton, 452; U.S. Code Title 25, Chapter 14, Subchapter XXX, § 692 Definitions.

Chemehuevi
Swanton, 357, 383, 482-483, 496; Thomas Edwin Farish, *The History of Arizona*, vol. vii, chp. 18.

Chepenafa Kalapuya
Swanton, 452, 456.

Cheraw
Swanton, 76-77.

Cherokee
Swanton, 215-224; Helen Hunt Jackson, *A Century of Dishonor*, 257-297; H. W. Brands, *Andrew Jackson*, 69, 80-81, 83-86, 86-88, 216-217, 314-315, 435-436, 488-493, 535-536; Edmond S. Morgan, *American Slavery, American Freedom*, 48; Grace Steele Woodward, *The Cherokees*; T. R. Fehrenback, *Comanches*, 227; Arthur M. Schlesinger, Jr., *The Age of Jackson*, 350; Gloria Jahoda, *Trail of Tears*, 20-30, 48, 50, 209-242, 290; Dee Brown, *Hear That Lonesome Whistle Blow*, 83. It is interesting to note that Schlesinger makes brief mention of the case of *Worcester v. Georgia* but makes no mention of the passage and implementation of the Indian Removal Act. Also, Thomas Jefferson, "To the Chiefs of the Cherokee Nation," Washington, January 10, 1806, *Writings* (New York: Library of America, 1984), 561-563. In his Second Annual Message to Congress, December 6, 1830, Andrew Jackson informed the Congress of his progress with the removal plan and stated that was moving ahead smoothly, and explained how it benefited everyone involved. (Brands, 489-491). Daniel K. Richter, *Facing East from Indian Country*, 5, 163-165, 169-171, 186-187, 213-215, 218-221, 242, 249; Landon Y. Jones, *William Clark and the Shaping of the West*, 297, 304-305.

"Indian removal, 1814-1858," Africans in America, Part 4: 1831-1865 (Boston: WGBH, 2004) at ttp://www.pbs.org/wgbh/aia/part4/4p2959.html; "Indian Treaties and the Removal Act of 1830" (Washington, DC: Bureau of Public Affairs, U.S. Department of State, 2004) at http://www.state.gov/r/pa/ho/time/dwe/16338.htm; Gary E. Moulton, ed., "Chief Ross To the Senate and House of Representatives [Protesting the Treaty of New Etocha, Red Clay Council Ground, Cherokee Nation]," September 28, 1836, The Papers of Chief John Ross, vol. 1, 1807-1839, (Norman: University of Oklahoma Press, 1985) at http://www.pbs.org/wgbh/aia/part4/4h3083t.html; "History and Culture" (Cherokee, NC, 2005) at http://www.cherokee-nc.com/history_main.php? [September 7, 2006].

Donnis D. Whitfield, *The Fraud of New Echota* (1835), available from Chickamauga Cherokee of Alabama (2001-2005) at http://cca2000.4t.com/fraudofnewechota.htm;Barbara "Shining Woman" Warren, "History of The Cherokee tsa-la-gi Language" (Sugar Land, TX: Powersource, n.a.) at http://www.powersource.com/cocinc/language/history.htm [April 29, 2006].

"Cherokee Nation of Oklahoma" (Tahlequah, OK: Cherokee Nation, 1998-2000) at http://www.cherokee.org/; Eastern Band of the Cherokee (Cherokee, NC, 2002) at http://www.cherokee-nc.com/; "Indian Land Cessions in the American Southeast," (TNGenNet Inc, 2001-2003;

updated August 06, 2004) at http://www.tngenweb.org/cessions/...; Elan Michaels "Welcome To My Tsa-la-gi (Cherokee) Page" (Midi-Trail of Tears, 1999) at http://www.simplyangel.com/tsalagi.htm; Jennifer Paxton, "Raven's Tsalagi Resources" (San Marcos, CA: Cal State San Marcos) at http://public.csusm.edu/raven/cherokee.dir/chrfram.html [June 24, 2006]. Also, "History" (Tahlequak, OK: Cherokee Nation, 1998-2006) at http://www.cherokee.org/home.aspx?section=culture&culture=history [June 30, 2006].

For Indian Removal Act of 1830 and the Trail of Tears, see Daniel K. Richter, *Facing East from Indian Country*, 226-227, 233-236, 242, 246, 249-250; Gloria Jahoda, *Trail of Tears*, esp. x, 39-48 w/ text on pp. 39-41; H. W. Brands, *Andrew Jackson*, 435-436, 488-493, 535-536. Also, "Indian removal, 1814-1858," Africans in America, Part 4: 1831-1865 (Boston: WGBH, 2004) at http://www.pbs.org/wgbh/aia/part4/4p2959 .html; Vincent Ferraro, "The Removal Act, 28 May 1830" (South Hadley, MA: Mount Holyoke College, 2004) at http://www.mtholyoke.edu / acad/intrel/removal.htm; Vernellia R. Randall, "Indian Removal Act (1830)" (Dayton, OH: University of Dayton School of Law, 1997-2001) at http://academic.udayton.edu/race/02rights/native10.htm [September 8, 2006].

SUPREME COURT CASES INVOLVING THE CHEROKEE NATION
Cherokee Nation v. Journeycake (provides an excellent history of the Cherokee treaties with the U.S.)
155 U.S. 196 (1894)
Docket Number: 619
November 19, 1894
available at FindLaw (Mountain View, CA,1994-2003) at
http://caselaw.lp.findlaw.com/scripts/getcase.pl?court=us&vol=155&invol=196.

Cherokee Nation v. State of Georgia
30 U.S. 1 (5 Pet. 1831)
Worcester v. Georgia
31 U.S. 515 (1832)
Decided: March 3, 1832
Worcester [Samuel A.] v. State of Georgia 31 U.S. 515 (1832), (Mountain View, CA: FindLaw, 1994-2003) at
http://caselaw.lp.findlaw.com/cgi-bin/getcase.pl?court=US&vol=31&invol=515. See also *Butler, Plaintiff in Error v. The State of Georgia*.
Stephens v. Cherokee Nation
174 U.S. 445 (1899)
http://caselaw.lp.findlaw.com/scripts/getcase.pl?court=us&vol=174&invol=445
Cherokee Nation v. Hitchcock
187 U.S. 294 (1902)
http://caselaw.lp.findlaw.com/scripts/getcase.pl?court=us&vol=187&invol=294
Delaware Indians v. Cherokee Nation
193 U.S. 127 (1904)
http://caselaw.lp.findlaw.com/scripts/getcase.pl?court=us&vol=193&invol=127
U.S. v. Cherokee Nation
202 U.S. 101 (1906)
http://caselaw.lp.findlaw.com/scripts/getcase.pl?court=us&vol=202&invol=101
Cherokee Nation v. Whitmire
223 U.S. 108 (1912)
http://caselaw.lp.findlaw.com/scripts/getcase.pl?court=us&vol=223&invol=108
Cherokee Nation v. United States
270 U.S. 476 (1926)
http://caselaw.lp.findlaw.com/scripts/getcase.pl?court=us&vol=270&invol=476
United States v. Cherokee Nation of Oklahoma
480 U.S. 700 (1987)
http://caselaw.lp.findlaw.com/scripts/getcase.pl?court=us&vol=480&invol=700.

Chesapeake
Edmond S. Morgan, *American Slavery, American Freedom*, 71, 72; Swanton, 66-71. Also, Fred Willard, "Trade Items as Transfer of Money," November 2002 (Eastern Carolina University, n.d.) at http://lost-colony.com/trade.html [June 12, 2006].

Cheskitalowa
Samuel G. Drake, *The Aboriginal Races of North America...*, 9-16.

Chetco
Swanton, 456-457.

Chetlessington
Title 25, Chapter 14, Subchapter XXX, §692 of the U.S. Code.

Chewelah
Swanton, 399-400.

Cheyenne
George Bird Grinnell, *The Cheyenne Indians* and *The Fighting Cheyenne*; Donald J. Berthrong, *The Southern Cheyenne*; quotes taken from pp. 113-114 and 126, 151, 388. Also William Y. Chalfant, *Cheyennes and Horse Soldiers*, esp. xiii-xiv, xx, 53, 53n, 59; Utley's quote from xiv; "two

cultures" from p. xx; "chastisement" from p. 59. See also Charles M. Robinson III, *A Good Year to Die*, ix-x, 7, 291-305, 328-329, 331, 341; Mari Sandoz, *Cheyenne Autumn*, generally; Jerome A. Greene, *Morning Star Dawn: The Powder River Expedition and the Northern Cheyennes, 1876*, exp. 42, 78, 85, 92, 103, 118, 139-140, 162-163, 186; George E. Hyde, *Red Cloud's War: A History of the Oglala Sioux*, esp. 287-288; Dee Brown, *Bury My Heart at Wounded Knee*, 67-102 and 148-176 (Southern); 105-118; 126-140 and 276-306 (Northern); Dee Brown, *Hear That Lonesome Whistle Blow*, 78, 85, 87-89, 204, 205, 207; Helen Hunt Jackson, *A Century of Dishonor*, 66-102, 343-358; Thomas F. Doran, "Kansas Sixty Years Ago," *Kansas Historical Collections*, 1919-1922 (Topeka: Kansas State Historical Society, 1923), vol. xv, 491-492, 492n4; Swanton, esp. 278-280, 285, 299, 385, 386, 390. On the Chien (Cheyenne) River, see Bernard De Voto, ed., *The Journals of Lewis and Clark*, 45-46, 450. For Bent's Fort, see Nicholas J. Santoro, *William Bent and Bent's Fort* (unpublished, 2008). "The Cheyenne Language" (Cheyenne Indian, 2002) at http://www.cheyenneindian.com/cheyenne_language.htm [December 19, 2006]. On the "Strong Hearts" see Francis Parkman, *The Oregon Trail*, 299., and for an extensive discussion of the warrior societies, see Grinnell, *The Cheyenne Indians*, vol. II, 48-79.

For the Beecher's Island Fight, see Dee Brown, *Hear That Lonesome Whistle Blow*, 87-88; William Y. Chalfant, *Cheyennes and Horse Soldiers*, 290; George Bird Grinell, *The Fighting Cheyennes*, 277-291; Mari Sandoz, *Cheyenne Autumn*, 188; Scout John Hurst and Scout Sigmund Shlesinger, "Battle of the Arikaree" (The Beecher Island Fight)," *Kansas Historical Collections* 1919-1922 (Topeka: Kansas State Historical Society, 1923), vol. xv, 530-547. For the Battle of Washita, see George Bird Grinell, *The Fighting Cheyennes*, 298-309; Mildred P. Mayhall, *The Kiowas*, 249-256; Dee Brown, *Hear That Lonesome Whistle Blow*, 88.

For Sand Creek Massacre, see George Bird Grinell, *The Fighting Cheyennes*, 149-180; William Y. Chalfant, *Cheyennes and Horse Soldiers*, 288; David Haward Bain, *Empire Express*, 185-191; David Lavender, *Bent's Fort*, 359; George Bird Grinnell, "Bent's Old Fort and Its Builders," 66; Halaas, *Halfbreed*, 139, 155, 159; Dee Brown, *Bury My Heart at Wounded Knee*, 87, 91. Fehrenbach, *Comanches*, 326, 460-462; "Inglorious war" from 462. Also, Dee Cordry, "True Heart: The Story of Edmund Guerrier" (n.a.) at http://www.ionet.net/~okhombre/edmund.html [July 11, 2006]. For the Julesburg Raid and the Sioux raid on the survey party, see George Bird Grinell, *The Fighting Cheyennes*, 182-188; David Haward Bain, *Empire Express*, 346-347, 353-354, 374-375.

For the Sappa Creek Fight (Massacre at Cheyenne Hole), see Mari Sandoz, *Cheyenne Autumn*, 55, 83-95. Also, Thomas R. Buecker, "Massacre at Cheyenne Hole: Lieutenant Austin Henely and the Sappa Creek Controversy," *Montana: The Magazine of Western History* (Autumn 2001) available from ProQuest Information and Learning Company at http://www.findarticles.com/p/articles/mi_qa3951/is_200110/ai_n8961581 [September 26, 2006]. And, A review of John H. Monnett, *Massacre at Cheyenne Hole: Lieutenant Austin Henely and the Sappa Creek Controversy* (Boulder: University Press of Colorado, 1999); Evelyn M. Ward, "The Battle Between Buffalo Hunters and Indians" made available by Kansas State Library (Phillips County, KS, 2006) at http://skyways.lib.ks.us/genweb/phillips/plindianbattle.html [September 26, 2006]. Article first published in *Sherman County Historical Society Newsletter*, vol. 26, no. 4 (April 2002); William Y. Chalfant, Cheyennes at Dark Water Creek (Norman: University of Oklahoma Press). See review at http://www.oupress.com/bookdetail.asp?isbn=0-8061-2875-5 [September 26, 2006].

For the battles of Summit Springs and Adobe Walls, see George Bird Grinell, *The Fighting Cheyennes*, 310-318, 319-327, respectively.

Chiaha
Swanton, 105-107; Gloria Jahoda, *Trail of Tears*, 245.

Chicago
Kristie C. Woferman, *The Osage in Missouri*, 27; Violette, *History of Missouri*, 9-10; Shirley Christian, *Before Lewis and Clark*, 49; William Duncan Strong, *The Indian Tribes of the Chicago Region, with Special Reference to the Illinois and the Potawatomi*, Anthropology Leaflet 24 (Chicago: Field Museum of Natural History, 1926); A.T. Andreas, *History of Chicago, From the Earliest Period to the Present Time* (Chicago: A.T. Andreas, 1884).

"A Place Called Che-Cau-Gou" (Chicago Public Library) at http://www.chipublib.org/digital/lake/CFDChecaugou.html; "The Chicago Portage National Historic Site" (I&M Canal National Heritage Corridor Civic Center Authority, 2006) at http://www.civiccenterauthority.org/... pages/ portsite.htm and "Chicago Portage National Historic Site Forest Preserve District of Cook County" (CLONK, 1997, 2003) at http://users.rcn. com/clonk/CCFPD/ChicagoPortageHistoricSite.html [September 10, 2007]. The latter based on a publication of the Forest Preserve District of Cook County, Illinois.

Chichimici
Edmond S. Morgan, *American Slavery, American Freedom*, 29.

Chickahominy
Edmond S. Morgan, *American Slavery, American Freedom*, 57, 74, 372; Swanton, 66-71.

Chickamauga
Swanton, 218; Donnis D. Whitfield, *The Fraud of New Echota* (1835), available from Chickamauga Cherokee of Alabama (2001-2005) at http:// cca2000.4t.com/fraudofnewechota.htm [April 29, 2006].

Chickasaw
Arrell M. Gibson, *The Chickasaws*; H. B. Cushman, *History of the Choctaw, Chickasaw and Natchez*; Gloria Jahoda, *Trail of Tears*, 161-172; quote from 162; Swanton, 177-180. Also, "Our History" (Ada, OK: Chickasaw Nation, 2005) at http://www.chickasaw.net/heritage/250_299.htm [June 30, 2006] and N. K. Rogers, *History Of Chattahoochee County, Georgia* (Columbus, GA: Columbus Office Supply, 1933), made available online by Joy Fisher (2004) at http://ftp.rootsweb.com/pub/usgenweb/ga/chattahoochee/... history/other/gms443chapteri.txt [October 6, 2007]. See esp. Peter A. Brannon, "Indian History," Chapter I.

"Secret Journal on Negotiations of the Chickasaw Treaty of 1818," The Avalon Project: Treaties Between the United States and Native Americans (New Haven, CN: Yale Law School, 1996-2004) at http://www.yale.edu/lawweb/avalon/ntreaty/nt005.htm; "Refusal of the Chickasaws and Choctaws to Cede Their Lands in Mississippi : 1826," The Avalon Project: Treaties Between the United States and Native Americans (New Haven, CN: Yale Law School, 1996-2004) at http://www.yale.edu/lawweb/avalon/ntreaty/nt007.htm; "Indian removal, 1814 - 1858," Africans in America, Part 4: 1831-1865 (Boston: WGBH, 2004) at http://www.pbs.org/wgbh/aia/part4/4p2959.html [September 7, 2006].

Chicora
Swanton, 84, 99, 100. Also see Shakori.

Chiheeleesh
Samuel G. Drake, *The Aboriginal Races of North America...*, 9-16.

Chillate
Samuel G. Drake, *The Aboriginal Races of North America...*, 9-16.

Chilluckittequaw
Swanton, 416-417.

Chilucan
Swanton, 129.

Chilula
Swanton, 483, 492.

Chimakum
Swanton, 414, 417, 419, 435.

Chimariko
Swanton, 483, 495, 497, 507.

Chimnapum
Stephenie Flora, "Northwest Indians" (The Oregon Territory And Its Pioneers, 1998-2005) at http://www.oregonpioneers.com/tribe.htm [August 28, 2006]. Also, "Captain Clark: October 18, 1805," In the Footsteps of Lewis and Clark (San Francisco, CA: Sierra Club, n.d.) at http://www.sierraclub.org/lewisandclark/journal/index.asp?source=Clark&date=10/18/1805; Eugene S. Hunn, "Review of Linguistic Information," *Cultural Affiliation Report* (Washington, DC: National Park Service, updated 2005) at http://www.cr.nps.gov/archeology/kennewick/HUNN.HTM; Noah Brooks, "First Across the Continent: The Story of The Exploring Expedition of Lewis and Clark in 1804-5-6" (American History Company) at http://www.americanhistory.com/history/FirstAcross/fatc14.html [August 30, 2006].

Chine
Swanton, 122, 123, 128, 129.

Chinook
Stephen E. Ambrose, *Undaunted Courage*, 300-302, 308-310, 319-321, 329-331; Bernard De Voto, ed., *The Journals of Lewis and Clark*, 288-290, 297-299, 301-302, 305-306, 329-330, 332-334; Swanton, 417-419, 467. Also see "Information on the Chinookan Indians Recorded by Members of the Lewis and Clark Expedition 1805-06," *The Lewis and Clark Journey of Discovery* (Washington, DC: National Park Service, 1996-2006) at http://www.nps.gov/archive/jeff/LewisClark2/TheJourney/NativeAmericans/Chinookan.htm [August 30, 2006].

Chipayne
John I. Kessell, "Pecos, the Plains, and the Provincias Internas, 1704-1794," *Kiva, Cross and Crown: The Pecos Indians and New Mexico, 1540-1840*, Chapter VIII (Washington, DC: National Park Service, 1979), available online at http://www.cr.nps.gov/history/online_books/kcc/chap8a.htm [October 4, 2006].

Chipewyan
Swanton, 551-552.

Chippanchikchik
Samuel G. Drake, *The Aboriginal Races of North America...*, 9-16.

Chippewa
Swanton, 260-264; Gloria Jahoda, *Trail of Tears*, 41, 92-93, 288; G. Elmore Reaman, *The Trail of the Iroquois Indians*, 3-4; Edmund Jefferson Danziger, Jr., *The Chippewas of Lake Superior*; William W. Warren, *The History of the Ojibway People*.

"A History of the Anishinabek Nation" (North Bay, ON: Nipissing First Nation, Union of Ontario Indians, 2004) at http://www.anishinabek.ca/uoi/history.htm; Charles A. Bishop, "Ojibwa," *L'Encyclopédie Canadienne* (Fondation Historica du Canada, 2004) at http://www.canadianencyclopedia.ca/index.cfm?PgNm=TCE&Params=A1ARTA0005903; "Anishinabe," MSU EMuseum (Mankato: Minnesota State University, 2003) at http://www.mnsu.edu/emuseum/history/mncultures/anishinabe.html; "Objibwe," (Mankato: Minnesota

State University, 2003) at http://www.geo.msu.edu/geo333/ojibwe.html; Rose Edwards (Wauwaushkaesh (wah-wah-ski-see) Little Deer), "Rose's Native Stuff" (Keweenaw Bay Indian Community, WI, 1995-2003) at http://www.edwards1.com/rose/native/ [September 8, 2006].

Frederick Webb Hodge, ed., "Chippewa," *Handbook of American Indians* North of Mexico, (Washington, DC: Smithsonian Institution, Bureau of American Ethnology Bulletin 30. GPO, 1910) available at http://www.prairienet.org/prairienations/chippewa.htm [August 15, 2006]; "The Ojibway Story" (Turtle Island Production, 2003) at http://www.turtle-island.com/ojibway.html [August 27, 2006]; "Ojibwa - Language, Culture, Bands and First Nations of Ojibwe People," *Cambridge Encyclopedia* (Net Industries, 2007), vol. 55, at http://encyclopedia.stateuniversity.com... /pages/16275/Ojibwa.html [October 19, 2007]. Tara Rose Zitzmann, "Saulteaux," (Mankato, MN: Minnesota State University, n.d.) at http://www.mnsu.edu/emuseum/cultural/northamerica/saulteaux.html, from "Ojibwa," *The New Encyclopedia Britannica* (1998); "Saulteaux First Nation" (Cochin, SK) at http://www.sicc.sk.ca/bands/bsault.html; "Saulteaux" (Aboriginal Communities, 2007) at http://www.aboriginalcanada. gc.ca/acp/community/site.nsf/en/fn347.html [October 19, 2007].

Chiricahua Apache
See Apache (R49), esp. James L. Haley, *Apaches: A History and Culture Portrait*, 9, 49 87, 94, 191-207.

Chiskiac
Swanton, 66-71; "Colonel George Reade" (Polly's Family First Americans) at http://www.fortunecity.com/millennium/dogdayz/129/first/greade. html. Notes that Col. Reade acquired 2000 acres on the Piankatank River, vacating the Chiskiack, possibly Gloucester County. Also see "A Warner Family Line" at http://www.geocities.com/awoodlief/warner.html [August 12, 2006].

Chitimacha
Swanton, 193, 197, 201, 202-204; Audrey B. Westerman, "Louisiana State Recognized Tribes of Lafourche and Terrebonne Parishes," (Lafourche Heritage Society Seminar, August 4, 2001) and Terry Galliano, "A Cultural History of Lafourche Parish [The Chitimacha Indians]" (Nicholls State College, 1965) made available from Biloxi-Chitimacha-Choctaw of Louisiana (n.d.) at http://www.biloxi-chitimacha.com/history.htm [August 15, 2006].

Choctaw
H. B. Cushman, *History of the Choctaw, Chickasaw and Natchez*; Swanton, esp. 180-185; Gloria Jahoda, *Trail of Tears*, 18, 74-88; Thomas Jefferson, "To the Brothers of the Choctaw," December 17, 1803, *Writings* (New York: Library of America, 1984), 558-560; Landon Y. Jones, *William Clark and the Shaping of the West*, 304-305.

Clara Sue Kidwell, *Choctaws and Missionaries in Mississippi, 1818-1918*; "History" (Durant, OK: Choctaw Nation of Oklahoma, 2000-2005) at http://www.choctawnation.com/History/?CFID=430880&CFTOKEN=61655267 [June 30, 2006]. "Indian removal, 1814-1858," Africans in America, Part 4: 1831-1865 (Boston: WGBH, 2004) at http://www.pbs.org/wgbh/aia/part4/4p2959.html; "Refusal of the Chickasaws and Choctaws to Cede Their Lands in Mississippi : 1826," The Avalon Project: Treaties Between the United States and Native Americans (New Haven, CN: Yale Law School, 1996-2004) at http://www.yale.edu/lawweb/avalon/ntreaty/nt007.htm [September 7, 2006].

Choula
Swanton, 186-187.

Chowanoc
Swanton, 77-78.

Maurice A. Mook, "Algonkian Ethnohistory of the Carolina Sound, Part 2: Late Sixteenth Century Towns and Tribes," courtesy of the Washington Academy of Science (Carolina Algonkian Project, 2001-2005) at http://homepages.rootsweb.com/~jmack/algonqin/mook2.htm [June 8, 2006]. Original source: Maurice A. Mook, "Algonquian Ethnohistory of the Carolina Sound," American University. *Journal of the Washington Academy of Sciences*, vol. 34, no. 6 (June 15, 1944), 181-196, 213-228.

Chowchilla Yokut
Swanton, 523-526; H. W. Brands, *The Age of Gold*, 311-312, 313.

Choye
Swanton, 205-206.

Chugnut
Alan Taylor, *The Divided Ground*, 42.

Chumash
Swanton, 484-487. "Chumash," Los Angeles Almanac (Given Place Publishing Co., 1998-2005) available online at http://www.laalmanac.com/history/hi05.htm [March 11, 2006]; Luistxo Fernandez, "Chumash: Barbareño Chumash" (GeoNative, n.a.) at http://www.geocities.com/Athens/9479/chumash.html [May 7, 2006].

"The Chumash People of California" (Santa Barbara, CA: Santa Barbara Museum of Natural History, n.d.) at http://www.sbnature.org/research/anthro/chumash/intro.htm; George Stammerjohan, "History of Fort Tejon" (Fort Tejon Memorial Association, updated 2004) at http://www.forttejon.org/history.html; "Native Tribes, Groups, Language Families and Dialects of California in 1770," California PreHistory (Coyote Press, 2001-2005) at http://www.californiaprehistory.com/tribmap.html; "Classification of Native Americans: United States and Canada" (Chamas Enterprises, 2006) at http://pedia.nodeworks.com/C/CL/CLA/Classification_of_Native_Americans [May 7, 2006].

Cibicue Apache

Charles Collins, Apache Nightmare: The Battle at Cibecue Creek; "Nochaydelklinne" (The High Chaparral, 2006) at http://www.thehighchaparral.com/historic7.htm; "Cibecue Creek Battlefield," Survey of Historic Sites... (Washington, DC: National Park Service, 2005) at http://www.cr.nps.gov/history/online_books/soldier/sitec1.htm; "Cibecue Battlefield" (Fort Tour Systems, n.d.) at http://www.forttours.com/pages/cibecue.asp [December 2, 2006].

Clackamas

Swanton, 419, 457, 459; Patricia Kohnen, "The Clackamas Chinook People" (Clakamas County, OR, 2006) at http://www.usgennet.org/alhnorus/ahorclak/clackamas.html [August 11, 2006].

Clahclellah

Stephenie Flora, "Northwest Indian Tribes" (The Oregon Territory and Its Pioneers, n.d.) at http://www.oregonpioneers.com/tribe.htm [August 3, 2006].

Clallam

Swanton, 417, 419-420; Gina Beckwith, Marie Hebert, and Tallis Woodward, "Land & People & Lifestyle: Culture & History" (Port Gamble, WA: Port Gamble S'Klallam Tribe, 2005) at http://www.pgst.nsn.us/; John Ryan, "Native American Literacy," KPLU Public Radio, April 12, 2004 (Seattle: WA: The Learning Curve) at http://www.learningcurveonline.org/reports/kplu11a.asp [June 22, 2006].

Clatskanie

Swanton, 458; "Clatskanie's History" (Clatskanie, OR: Clatskanie Chamber of Commerce, n.d.) at http://www.clatskanie.com/chamber/history.htm; "Clatskanie Indians" (Washington, DC: National Geographic, 1996-2006) at http://www.nationalgeographic.com/lewisandclark/record_tribes_085_13_23.html [August 30, 2006].

Clatsop

Stephen E. Ambrose, *Undaunted Courage*, 308-311, 313-315, 319, 321-324, 329-331. Bernard De Voto, ed., *The Journals of Lewis and Clark*, 289, 292-293, 295-299, 301-302, 304-306, 319-320, 332-334; Swanton, 425, 458.

Clowwewalla

Swanton, 458-459; Stephenie Flora, "Northwest Indian Tribes" (The Oregon Territory and Its Pioneers, n.d.) at http://www.oregonpioneers.com/tribe.htm [August 11, 2006].

"Clark, William. Estimate of the Western Indians," American Indian Manuscripts (American Philosophical Association Library), Item 2433, D. 4p. and 1p. Map, at http://www.amphilsoc.org/library/guides/indians/info/noea.htm; "Northwest Native Americans" (Portland, OR: Oregon State Travel Guide, n.d.) at http://www.oregonmaiden.com/Native-Americans-of-Oregon.html [August 3, 2006]. Lyn Topinka, "April 3, 1806: Five Volcanoes and the Willamette River," The Volcanoes of Lewis and Clark (Washington, DC: U.S. Geological Survey, 2004) at http://vulcan.wr.usgs.gov/LivingWith/Historical/LewisClark/volcanoes_lewis_clark_april_03_1806.html [December 6, 2006].

Coahuiltecan Tribes

Swanton, 308, 309-311; "Coahuiltecan Tribes," Four Corners Institute (Four Directions Press, 2005) at http://www.fourdir.com/coahuiltecan_tribes.htm [May 26, 2006].

Coaque

Herbert E. Bolton, "The Founding of the Missions on the San Gabriel River, 1745-1749," *Southwestern Historical Quarterly*, vol. 17, no. 4, 323-378, SHQ Online at http://www.tsha.utexas.edu/publications/journals/shq/online/v017/n4/article_1.html [May 24, 2006].

Coast Yuki

Swanton, 527-528.

Cocopa

Swanton, 349.

Coeur d'Alêne Skitswish

Robert C. Carriker, *Father Peter John De Smet*, 59,77, 80, 83, 84, 153-159, 207, 232. Swanton, 411-412.

Cofitachequi

Swanton, 111, 165; Daniel K. Richter, *Facing East from Indian Country*, 23-24, 34-35, 38-39. Also see Gene Waddell, "Cofitachiqui," *Carologue* (Autumn 2000), vol. 16, no. 3, 8-15. Revised December 8, 2006, with addition of notes and bibliography and made available by the College of Charleston (Charleston, SC, 2006) at www.cofc.edu/~waddelle/CofitachiquiRev2.html [August 5, 2006]. Also available from Informational Web Site on the Catawba Indian People (Albuquerque, NM, last updated: 07/31/2007) at http://www.catawba-people.com/cofitachiqui.htm [September 11, 2007].

Coharie

"History of the Coharie Indians" (Clinton, NC: Coharie Intra-Tribal Council, Inc., n.d.) at http://www.geocities.com/coharieindian.../coharies.html; Sylvia Pate and Leslie S. Stewart, *Economic Development Assessment for the Coharie Tribe* (Pembroke and Chapel Hill, NC: University of North Carolina Office of Economic Development, Kenan Institute, July 2003) available at http://www.kenan-flagler.unc.edu/assets/documents/ED_Coharie.pdf [November 3, 2007].

Columbia
Swanton, 420-421, 429.

Colville
Swanton, 400, 421-422, 431, 440.

Comanche
T. R. Fehrenbach, *Comanches*. See "...the true lords of the Southwestern Frontier" on p. 213. "The tragedy..." is taken from p. 410. Also see Donald J. Berthrong, *The Southern Cheyennes*, 83-84, 90-91 etc.; Daniel J. Boorstin, The Americans: *The Democratic Experience*, 34; William Y. Chalfant, *Cheyennes and Horse Soldiers*, 242, 283; Swanton, esp. 312-314. See painting by George Catlin, *Comanche Village* (1834).

Courtney Bouchie, "Comanche" (Mankato, MN: Minnesota State University MSU EMuseum, 2003) at http://www.mnsu.edu/emuseum/cultural/northamerica/comanche.html; Darren McCathern, "Maruawe! Welcome To — Numuukahni / Comanche Lodge" (Antelope Productions, 2004) at http://www.comanchelodge.com/; Edward S. Curtis, The North American Indian, vol. 19, The Indians of Oklahoma-Part 2, a Comprehensive History-All Other: Comanche (Hobe Sound, FL: Curtis Collection, n.d.). See "Notes from..." online at http://www.curtis-collection.com/tribalindex.html [September 7, 2006].; "Welcome to Comancheria," Comanche Lodge (Antelope Productions, 2006) at http://www.comanchelodge.com/comancheria.html [May 14, 2006].

Barbara Goodin, *A Comanche History* (Lawton, OK: The Comanche Language and Cultural Preservation Committee, n.d.) at http://www.comanchelanguage.org/history.htm; R. E. Moore, "The Texas Comanches" (Texarch Associates,1998, 2000) at http://www. texasindians.com/comanche.htm; Carol A. Lipscomb, "Comanche Indians," *Handbook of Texas Online* (Austin, TX: Texas State Historical Association and University of Texas, 2001) at http://www.tsha.utexas.edu/handbook/online/articles/CC/bmc72_print.html [August 23, 2006].

For the Red River War, see T. R. Fejrembach, *Comanches*, 531-550; James L. Haley, *Apaches*, 321, 394n; Mildred P. Mayhall, *The Kiowas*, 294-298, 300; Jerome A. Greene, *Morning Star Dawn*, 88, 191, 228-229n3, 234n12. Also, James L. Haley, "Red River War," *Handbook of Texas Online* (Austin, TX: Texas State Historical Association and University of Texas, 2001) at http://www.tsha.utexas.edu/handbook/online/articles/RR/qdr2.html [November 14, 2006]; Bob Izzard, "Red River War" (Mobeetie, TX: Old Mobeetie Texas Association, 2005) at http://www.mobeetie.com/pages/rrwar.htm [January 4, 2007]. " Red River War: Battles of the Red River War," Texzs Beyond Hisstory (Austin, TX: University of Texas, 2001) at http://www.texasbeyondhistory.net/redriver/battles.html [September 24, 2007].

ConCow Maidu
Swanton, 499-501; "History of the ConCow Maidu" (Oroville, CA: Konkow Valley Band of Maidu) at http://www.maidu.com/maidu/ maiduculture/ firstcontactto1863.html; "Nome Cult Trail: History of the 1863 Relocation" (Covelo, CA: Round Valley Indian Tribal Council, 1998-2001) at http://www.covelo.net/tribes/pages/nomecult/tribes_nome_cult_history.shtml [May 22, 2006]. Also "The Maidu Indians [ConCow Maidu]" (Penn Valley Area Chamber of Commerce, 2006-2007) at http://www.pennvalleycoc.org/html/the_maidu_indians.html, paraphrased from A. L. Kroeber, *Handbook of the Indians of California*. Bureau of American Ethnology Bulletin 78 (Smithsonian Institute, 1925) [March 1, 2007].

Conejero
H. Allen Anderson, "Conejero," *Handbook of Texas Online* (Austin, TX: Texas State Historical Association and University of Texas, 2001) at http://www.tsha.utexas.edu/handbook/online/articles/CC/bmc82.html [October 5, 2006].

Congaree
Swanton, 93; "South Carolina – Indians, Native Americans – Congaree " (SCIway, 2006) at http://www.sciway.net/hist/indians/congaree.html; "South Carolina Tribes and Their Locations," *Human Interactions* (Burlington, VT: University of Vermont,2006) at http://www.uvm.edu/~efjoseph/nr260/human%20interactions.html [August 4,2006].

Conoy [Proper]
Swanton, 57-59.

Conoy Peoples
Swanton, 57-59.

Cookkoo-oose
"Kusan Family" (Native American Nations, 2000-2006) at http://www.nanations.com/linguistic/kusan_family.htm [August 4, 2006].

Coopspellar
Samuel G. Drake, *The Aboriginal Races of North America...*, 9-16; Allen "Doc" Wesselius, "A Lasting Legacy: The Lewis and Clark Place Names of the Pacific Northwest," Columbia Magazine, Spring 2001 (Columbia Legacy © Wade Norton) at http://home.comcast.net/~wadenorton/columbia_legacy.htm [August 26, 2006].

Coos
Swanton, 452. "Tribal Overview" (Confederated Tribes of the Coos, Lower Umpqua, Siuslaw, n.a.) at http://www.ctclusi.org/; "A brief history," Coos, Lower Umpqua and Siuslaw Indians, The Confederated Tribes (Online Highways, 1995-2005) at http://www.ohwy.com/or/c/cootribe.htm; "Kusan Family" (Native American Nations, 2000-2006) at http://www.nanations.com/linguistic/kusan_family.htm [August 4, 2006]; Steve Greif, "Historical and Genealogical Research Sources for Oregon's South Coast" (Coos County Historical Society, 2006) at http://www.cooshistory.org/micro.html [August 10, 2006].

Coosa

Swanton, 93, 94, 95, 96, 161. "The Vanquishing of The Coosam 1671" at http://www.motherbedford.com/USMHWeb05.htm [June 24, 2006]; Gene Waddell, "Indians of the South Carolina Low Country, 1562-1751," (Columbia, SC: University of South Carolina, 1980), 244-259 at http://www.cofc.edu/~waddelle/IndiansContents.htm and http://www.cofc.edu/~waddelle/Sources9.pdf [August 5, 2006].

Copalis

Swanton, 422.

Coree

Swanton, 78, 81, 82, 86.

Costanoan

Swanton, 487-488.

Cow Creek Umpqua

Swanton, 474-475. "Story" (Roseburg, OR: Cow Creek Band of Umpqua Tribe of Indians, 1997-2006) at http://www.cowcreek.com/story/index.html [June 10, 2006].

Coweta

Swanton, 134n2, 162, 166. N. K. Rogers, *History Of Chattahoochee County, Georgia* (Columbus, GA: Columbus Office Supply, 1933), made available online by Joy Fisher (2004) at http://ftp.rootsweb.com/pub/usgenweb/ga/chattahoochee/... history/other/gms443chapteri.txt [October 6, 2007]. See esp. Peter A. Brannon, "Indian History," Chapter I.

Cowlitz

Swanton, 416, 422-423, 426; Bernard De Voto, ed., *The Journals of Lewis and Clark*, 297-298.

Coyotero Apache

Swanton, 327-330; Thomas Edwin Farish, "The Indians of Arizona," vol. VII, Chp. I (San Francisco: Filmer Brothers Electrotype Company 1918) available online from Books of the Southwest, University of Arizona Library at http://southwest.library.arizona.edu/hav7/body.1_div.1.html [April 4, 2006].

Cree

Swanton, 390, 554-556; John C. Ewers, ed., *Edwin Thompson Denig's Five Indian Tribes of the Upper Missouri*, 99-136. Also, George Catlin, *North American Indians* (Penguin ed.), 17, 20, 36-37, 47, 52, 437, 490; "Cree," *L'Encyclopédie Canadienne* (Fondation Historica du Canada, 2004) at http://www.canadianencyclopedia.ca/index.cfm?PgNm=TCE&Params=A1ARTA0002005; Tom Ojo, "Native Tribe Listing" (Canada: Heritage Bank Consulting, 27 Apr 2006) at http://users.rttinc.com/~asiniwachi/wnt.html [August 9, 2006]. Also see Catlin's *Cree Knisteneaux*, a full-length portrait of a young woman with a child on her back.

Creek Confederacy

Gloria Jahoda, *Trail of Tears*, 2-17, 143-159, 245; T. R. Fehrenback, *Comanches*, 227; Swanton, 107-108, 156-157, 160-169; H. W. Brands, *Andrew Jackson*, 238, 307, 310, 315, 319, 435, 436, 441, 519 and Creek War, 196-200, 215-222, 231-235; Drake, *Indians of North America*, 363-369.

Carol Middleton, "Bartram Among The Creeks" (Creek Stories, n.d.) at http://homepages.rootsweb.com/~cmamcrk4/brtrmck1.html [August 20, 2007Originally published James & Johnson (Philadelphia, 1791): William Bartram, *Travels Through North & South Carolina, Georgia...*, pt. iii, chap. viii. The full text of Bartram's Travels is now available in an electronic edition from the University of North Carolina (Chapel Hill, 2001) at http://docsouth.unc.edu/nc/bartram/menu.html [August 20, 2007]. Also, N. K. Rogers, *History Of Chattahoochee County, Georgia* (Columbus, GA: Columbus Office Supply, 1933), made available online by Joy Fisher (2004) at http://ftp.rootsweb.com/pub/usgenweb/ga/chattahoochee/... history/other/gms443chapteri.txt [October 6, 2007]. See esp. Peter A. Brannon, "Indian History," Chapter I.

"Indian removal, 1814-1858," *Africans in America*, Part 4: 1831-1865 (Boston: WGBH, 2004) at http://www.pbs.org/wgbh/aia/part4/4p2959.html; Benson J. Lossing, *Pictorial Field-book of the War of 1812* (1869), Chapter XXXIV, War Against the Creek Indians available from Bill Carr (2001) at http://freepages.history.rootsweb.com/~wcarr1/Lossing2/Chap34.html [September 7, 2006].

"From the Teton River [SD] to the Marias River [MT]," Lewis & Clark Expedition (Bolling Green: University of Kentucky, n.d.) at http://www.uky.edu/AS/ModernStudies/HumSocSci/lc94/Section2/Phase2/Ethnographic/General.html [August 10, 2006]; "Creek Treaties Related to Georgia" (Athens, GA: University of Georgia Institute of Government, 2006) at http://www.cviog.uga.edu/Projects/gainfo/crtreaty.htm [October 24, 2006].

For the Creek War, see W. H. Brands, *Andrew Jackson*, 172-173, 193-200, 205-222, 216-219, 231-235, 334; *American Military History*, 1607-1953 (Washington, DC: Department of the Army, July 1956), 138-139. Walter Lord, *The Dawn's Early Light*, 46-47, 325, 341. Also, James E. Medley, "IV. *Andrew Jackson's Iron Will in the Creek War, 1813-1814*," Studies in Battle Command (Leavenworth, KS: Command and General Staff College, n.d.) at http://www.au.af.mil/au/awc/awcgate/army/csi-battles.htm#IV; "The Creek War, 1813-1814: Just Around the Bend" (Daviston, AL: Horseshoe Bend National Military Park, n.d.) at http://www.nps.gov/hobe/home/creekwar.htm; J. Tyler, "Yuchis at Callabee Creek" (Stone Mountain, GA, 17 Dec 2003 2:14:14) and Josh Wilks, "Walton County" (n.a.) at http://www.drwebman.com/euchee/

yuchimail/; William C. Bell, contr. by, "Halbert & Ball: The Creek War of 1813 and 1814" (James and Marcia Foley, 2002) at http://www. marciesalaskaweb.com/creekwar.htm; Thomas G. Rodgers, "Night Attack at Calabee Creek" (n.a.) at http://www.hsgng.org/pages/nightatt.htm; Steve Canerossi, "Ft. Mims Massacre, Baldwin County, Alabama, August 30, 1813" (n.a.) at http://www.canerossi.us/ftmims/massacre.htm [July 2-3, 2006] and Tom Kanon, "Brief History of Tennessee in the War of 1812" (Nashville, TN: Tennessee State Library and Archives, n.d.) at http://www.state.tn.us/TSLA/history/military/tn1812.htm [November 5, 2006].

For the Fort Mims Massacre, see W. H. Brands, *Andrew Jackson*, 193-195. Also see "The Creek War" (Washington, DC: National Park Service, n.d.) at http://www.nps.gov/archive/hobe/home/creekwar.htm; Steve Canerossi, "The Fort Mims Massacre 1813" (The Dupuy Institute. On War, n.d.) at http://www.onwar.com/aced/nation/uni/usa/ffortmims1813.htm [November 6, 2006]. For the Battle of Tallushatchee, see W. H. Brands, Andrew Jackson, 198, 211.

For Creeks in the American Civil War, see ChristineSchultz White and Benton R. White, *.Now The Wolf Has Come: The Creek Nation in the CivilWar;* "Reestablishment of the Department of Kansas: Participant in the Civil War " (Native American Nations, 2000-2007) at http://www. nanations.com/civilwar/reestablish-dept-kansas.htm [August 20, 2007]. From *The American Indian as Participant in the Civil War*, 1919.

Croatan
Swanton, 80, 81, 90, 101; Ralph Lane, "The Colony At Roanoke, 1586" (National Center Historical Documents) at http://www.nationalcenter. org/ColonyofRoanoke.html; Darren Smith, "What Happened To Virginia Dare?" (New York: About, Inc., part of the New York Times Company, 2006) at http://usparks.about.com/cs/parkhistory/a/virginiadare.htm; Fred Willard, "Cultural Anthropology of Indian Villages" (East Carolina University) at http://www.lost-colony.com/cultural.html; Lawrence Keech, "Migration from Croatan," Washington Daily News, Washington, NC, May 30, 2002, available from The Lost Colony Center for Science and Research at http://www.lost-colony.com/migration.html; "Letter from the Secretary of the Interior, Transmitting, in Response to a Senate Resolution of June 30, 1914, a Report on the Condition and Tribal Rights of the Indians of Robeson and Adjoining Counties of North Carolina," September 19, 1914 (University of North Carolina) at http:// docsouth.unc.edu/nc/mcpherson/mcpherson.xml [June 10, 2006].

Crow
Keith Algier, *The Crow and the Eagle: A Tribal History from Lewis & Clark to Custer, generally*; Sapsuckers from p.190; "wipe them out" from p. 227, 233n80. *Edwin Thompson Denig's Five Indian Tribes of the Upper Missouri*, 137-204; Gloria Jahoda, *Trail of Tears*, 174; Dee Brown, *Hear That Lonesome Whistle Blow*, 215; William R. Nester, *The Arikara War*, 15; Stanton, esp. 390-391; Joseph M. Marshall, *Journey of Crazy Horse*, esp. 19, 32, 33, 35, 75-76, 99-100, 178-181; John C. Ewers, ed., Philip Kopper, *The Smithsonian Book of North American Indians Before the Coming of the Europeans*, 184. In 1805, Francois LaRocque, a Canadian trader, traveled with the Crow and wrote the first report on the customs of that tribe. See " Big Horn Basin," Wyoming Tails and Trails (G. B. Dobson , 2004) at http://www.wyomingtalesandtrails.com/... bighorn. html; "Northern Pacific Railroad" (American Western History Museums, 1999) at http://www.linecamp.com/museums/americanwest/... western_clubs... /northern_pacific_railroad/northern_pacific_railroad.html [September 25, 2008].

Also see "Vocabularies of the languages of various Indian tribes [1817-1819]," American Indian Manuscripts (American Philosophical Association Library), Item 3004, D, at http://www.amphilsoc.org/library/guides/indians/info/pl.htm; "Vocabulary of the language of the Upsaroka nation commonly called the Crows [1817-1819]," Item 815, D, at http://www.amphilsoc.org/library/guides/indians/info/chi.htm; "Curly" (Spartacus Educational, 2006) at http://www.spartacus.schoolnet.co.uk/WWcurly.htm; John Madsen, "Indian Tribes and Their Language Affiliations" (2006) at http://greatdreams.com/nalang.htm [August 19, 2006]. Also, David I. Bushnell, *Villages of the Algonquian, Siouan, and Caddoan Tribes West of the Mississippi* (1976) available from Access Genealogy (1996-2006) at http://www.accessgenealogy.com/scripts/data/... database.cgi?file =Data&report=SingleArticle&ArticleID=001735.

Cupeño
Swanton, 488.

Cusabo
Swanton, esp. 94-96; Paul R. Sarrett, Jr. "The Cusabo," SCGenWeb, August 11, 1998 (Victoria Proctor, 2003) at http://sciway3.net/proctor/state/natam/cusabo.html [June 24, 2006].

Cuttatawomen
Swanton, 66-71.

Cuyama Chumash
Swanton, 484-487.

Cwareuuooc
Fred Willard, "Trade Items as Transfer of Money," November 2002, made available by the Lost Colony Center for Science and Research (Eastern
Carolina University) at http://lost-colony.com/trade.html [June 12, 2006].

Dakota
Paul N. Beck, *Inkpaduta, Dakota Leader*; David Dary, *The Oregon Trail*, 284-285; Robert C. Carriker, *Father Peter John De Smet: Jesuit in the West*, 174; Benjamin Capps, *The Indians*, 170-179. Also, Frederick L. Johnson, "Red Wing at the Time of the Grand Excursion" (Red Wing, MN: Goodhue County Historical Society, n.d.) at http://www.goodhuehistory.mus.mn.us/GrandExcursionPartI.html; "Our Mdewakanton History" (Welch, MN: Prairie Island Indian Community, n.d.) at http://www.prairieisland.org/History.htm [August 13, 2006]. For more on Spirit Lake Massacre, "Spirit Lake Massacre Iowa's bloodiest" (Des Moines: Essential Iowa, 2006-2008) at http://www.essentialiowa.com/Spiritlake... massacre.html; "Spirit Lake Massacre" (Des Moines: Iowa National Guard, n.d.) at http://www.iowanationalguard.com/Museum/IA_History/...

SpiritLakeMassacre.htm " Abbie Gardner Cabin Background and History" (Des Moines: State Historical Society of Iowa, n.d.) at http://www.iowahistory.org/sites/gardner_cabin/background_history.htm [October 16, 2008]

Dakubetede
Swanton, 459.

Dasemunkepeuc
"Virginia Records Timeline: 1553-1743," American Memory (Washington, DC: Library of Congress) at http://memory.loc.gov/ammem/collections/jefferson_papers/mtjvatm.html; Fred Willard, "Trade Items as Transfer of Money," November 2002, made available by The Lost Colony Center for Science and Research (Eastern Carolina University) at http://lost-colony.com/trade.html; "Section V, The Lost Colony of 1587," A Teacher's Heritage Education Handbook, Part II (Washington, DC: National Park Service: Fort Raleigh National Historic Site, Manteo, NC) at http://www.nps.gov/fora/teacher2.htm; Shawn Miles, "The Lost City" (Athens, OH: Ohio University, n.d.) at http://www.ohiou.edu/~glass/vol/1/15.htm; Marjorie Hudson, "Among the Tuscarora: The Strange and Mysterious Death of John Lawson, Gentleman, Explorer, and Writer," North Carolina Literary Review, 1992 (J. Y. Joyner Library, East Carolina University, 2003-2004) at http://digital.lib.ecu.edu/exhibits/lawson/htmlFiles/TUSC.html; Paul Hulton and David Beers Quinn, "33. Arrival of the English in Virginia, "American Drawings of John White, 1577-1590 (University of North Carolina Press, 1964), available from Virtual Jamestown at http://www.virtualjamestown.org/images/white_debry_html/white.html [June 12, 2006].

Michael Leroy Oberg, "Between 'Savage Man' and 'Most Faithful Englishman' Manteo and the Early Anglo-Indian Exchange, 1584-1590" (Carolina Algonkian Project, 2001) at http://homepages.rootsweb.com/~jmack/algonqin/oberg1.htm; Fred Willard and Barbara Midgette. Edited by E. Thomas Shields, Jr. and Charles Ewen, "The Roanoke Sagas and Sixteenth Century Fortifications in North Carolina," (East Carolina University) at http://www.lost-colony.com/sagas.html [June 12, 2006].

Deadose
Swanton, 197, 308, 314, 324.

Delaware
Swanton, 48-55; Edwin G. Burrows & Mike Wallace, Gotham, 5-13, 23-24, 37-39, 67-69, 86; the name Delaware appears only on p. 316; Helen Hunt Jackson, A Century of Dishonor, 317-324. T. R. Fehrenback, Comanches, 227; Eugene Morrow Violette, History of Missouri, 47, 69, 72, 207; Daniel J. Boorstin, The Americans: The Democratic Experience, 256; Gloria Jahoda, Trail of Tears, 59, 297-298; Dee Brown, Hear That Lonesome Whistle Blow, 37-38, 47. The valuation of Kansas tribal land is taken from Brown, p. 47. Also see, Walter A. Schroeder, "Populating Missouri, 1804-1821," Missouri Historical Review (Columbia: State Historical Society of Missouri, July 2003), xcvii, 4, 263-294; Helen Hunt Jackson, A Century of Dishonor, 32-65, 317-324; Russell Shorto, The Island in the Center of the World, 32, 42; "Wyandot and Shawnee Indian Lands in Wyandotte County, Kansas," Kansas Historical Collections (Topeka: Kansas State Historical Society,1919-1922), vol. xv, 103-105; Frederick E. Hoxie, ed. Encyclopedia of North American Indians, 157-159; Angie Debo, A History of the Indians of the United States, 124, 126, 127, 150, 152, 154, 264. Manypenny,"When I made those treaties" quoted in Judith A. Boughter, Betraying the Omaha Nation, 1790-1916, 119-120.

Larry "Joe" Brooks, "Delaware Tribe of Indians" (Bartlesville, OK: Delaware Tribal Headquarters, n.d.) at http://www.delawaretribeofindians.nsn.us/; Tuomi J. Forrest, "William Penn, Visionary Proprietor," American Studies (Richmond: University of Virginia, 2004) at http://xroads.virginia.edu/~cap/PENN/pnhome.html; J. Alfieri et allis, The Lenapes: A Study of Hudson Valley Indians (Poughkeepsie, NY: Marist College, n.d.) at http://www.ulster.net/~hrmm/halfmoon/lenape/effects.htm; Susan Ditmire, "Native People of New Jersey" (2000, updated 2006) at http://www.usgennet.org/usa/nj/state/Lenape.htm; [May 6, 2006].

Anne Schillingsburg Woodruff and F. Alan Palmer, "The Unalachtigo of New Jersey: 'The Original People of Cumberland County'" (Cumberland County, NJ: Cumberland County Library) at http://www.co.cumberland.nj.us/facts/history/unalachtigo/unalachtigo.html; Bob Barnett, "The Lenape or Delaware Indians" (West Jersey, updated 2003) at http://westjersey.org/wj_len.htm; "Rockaway..."place of waters bright," The Wave (Rockaway, NY, n.d.) at http://www.rockawave.com/common/history/history.html;Art Mattson,"The Rockaway Indians One Millennium Ago" (February 2001) available from Lynbrook Historical and Preservation Society at http://members.aol.com/lynhistory/lhps/lyn-hs03.htm; American Indians of Long Island, NY" (New York: Richmond Hill Historical Society, with recognition to Author/Illustrator William Krooss, "A Peek at Richmond Hill Through the Keyhole of Time") at http://www.richmondhillhistory.org/indians.html; "The Indians of Long Island," Long Island: Our Story, Chapter 2 (New York: Newsday, n.d.) http://www.newsday.com/community/guide/lihistory/ny-history-chap2cov,0,7847609.storygallery [May 9, 2006].

"Delaware Indian Tribe" (Kansas Genealogy, 2002-2006) at http://www.kansasgenealogy.com/indians/delaware_indian_tribe.htm [August 10, 2006]; "Delaware Indians" (Columbus, OH: Ohio Historical Society, 2006) at http://www.ohiohistorycentral.org/entry.php?rec=584 [October 7, 2006]; David G. Vanderstel, "Native Americans of Indiana: Resistance and Removal" (Fishers, IN: Conner Prairie, 2006) at http://www.connerprairie.org/HistoryOnline/indnam.html [September 29, 2006].

For the Battle of Bushy Run, see Niles Anderson, The Battle of Bushy Run (Harrisburg, PA: Pennsylvania History & Museum, 1988). Ref. Jane Ockershausen, "Broken Promises, Broken Dreams: North America's Forgotten Conflict at Bushy Run Battlefield," Pennsylvania Heritage (Summer 1997), vol. xxii, no. 3.

For the Gnadenhütten Massacre and the Moravian Missions, see Helen Hunt Jackson, A Century of Dishonor, 317-324; Daniel K. Richter, Facing East from Indian Country, 221-222; Swanton 47, 54. Also, "Records of Moravian Missions Among American Indians - Collection 153," Billy Graham Center Archives (Wheaton, IL: Wheaton College, n.d.) at http://www.wheaton.edu/bgc/archives... /GUIDES/153.htm; Vernon H. Nelson, "Introduction: The Moravian Mission Among the Indians of North America" (Bethlehem, PA: Moravian Church, n.d.) at http://microformguides.gale.com/Data/Introductions/32430FM.htm [October 7, 2006]. Originally published December 1969.

Diegueño
Swanton, 488-489, 499. Also "Kumeyaay Nation" (Kumeyaay Information Village, 2004-2006) at http://www.kumeyaay.info/ [April 3, 2006].

Dinondadies
Swanton, 604-605. Also, The History of Wyandot County, Ohio (Chicago: Leggett, Conaway & Co., 1884), 233, 234, made available by Allen L. Potts (Salt Lake City, UT: Heritage Pursuit, The Place For Historians And Genealogists, 2006) at http://www.heritagepursuit.com/Wyandot/ WyCh2.htm; William W. Campbell, "Annals of Tryon County; or, the Border Warfare of New York,During the Revolution" (New York: J. & J. Harper, 1831) available from Three Rivers (Berry Enterprises, 1998-2003) at http://www.threerivershms.com/tryonintro.htm; "Huron Indians" (CPOV, 2005) at http://christ.relately.com/wiki/Huron_Indians [August 4, 2006].

Dotame
Frederick Webb Hodge, ed., "Comanche," *Handbook of American Indians North of Mexico*, (Washington, DC: Smithsonian Institution, Bureau of American Ethnology Bulletin 30. GPO, 1910) available from Access Genealogy (2004-2006) at http://www.accessgenealogy.com/native tribes/comanche/comanchehist.htm; Ted & Carole Miller, Nebraska History & Record of Pioneer Days, vol. VI, no 1 (2000, 2001) at http:// www.rootsweb.com/~neresour/OLLibrary/Journals/HPR/Vol06/nhrv06p4.html [August 4, 2006].

Doustioni
Swanton, 205-206; *History of Natchitoches Parish: Biographical and Historical Memoirs of Northwest Louisiana* (Southern Publishing Company, 1890) available from Greg English (Louisiana 101, 2000) at http://www.louisiana101.com/rr_natchitoches.html [August 25, 2006].

Duwámish
Swanton, 423.

Eastern Mono
Swanton, 376.

Echeloot
Noah Brooks, *First Across the Continent: The Story of The Exploring Expedition of Lewis and Clark in 1804-5-6* (New York: Charles Scribner's Sons, 1902), 208, 210, 212, 222, 258, available from Nonprofit Library for Genealogy & History-Related Research (WebRoots, 2001-2004) at http:// www.webroots.org/library/usatrav/fatclc05.html [August 25, 2006].

Edisto
Swanton, 94, 96. "South Carolina – Indians, Native Americans – Kusso-Natchez" (Columbia, SC: SCIway. net, 2007) at http://www.sciway. net/hist/indians/kusso_natchez.html [October 21, 2007].

Eel River
"Eel River," Ohio's Historic Indians: Tribes (Columbus: Ohio Historical Society, 1998-2004) at ttp://www.ohiohistorycentral.org/entry.php?rec... =585 [September 9, 2006]. Re: Isle River, see Hodge, *Handbook of American Indians*, Part 1, 419.

Elk Mountain Ute
Swanton, 373.

Elwha Klallam
Swanton, 419; "Lower Elwha Klallam Tribe," NWIFC Member Tribes (Olympia, WA: Northwest Indian Fisheries Commission, n.d.) at http://www.nwifc.wa.gov/tribes/tribe.asp?tribe=elwha; "Culture History" (Port Angeles, WA: Lower Elwha Klallam Tribe , n.d.) at http://www. elwha.org/Culture-History.htm [September 10, 2006].

Emigdiano Chumash
Swanton, 484-487; Hampton Sides, *Blood and Thunder*, 324. Also see" Tejon Indian Reservation" (Washington, DC: National Park Service, November 17, 2004) at http://www.cr.nps.gov/history/online_books/5views/5views1h92.htm [March 6, 2007].

Emusa
Swanton, 116. Samuel G. Drake, *The Aboriginal Races of North America...*, 9-16.

Enesher
Bernard De Voto, ed., *The Journals of Lewis and Clark*, 323, 354-355, 356-362; Lyn Topinka , "The Volcanoes of Lewis and Clark: May 4 - June, 1806, To The Rockies - Snake River to Long Camp" (USGS, 2004) at http://vulcan.wr.usgs.gov/LivingWith/Historical/LewisClark/ volcanoes_ lewis_clark_may_04_1806.html [August 26, 2006].

Eno
Swanton, 79, 80, 83, 84, 96, 99; "Cultural History of the Eno River " and "Eno Indian Tribe" (Eno River Media, 2003-2006) at http://ermp. tv/eno-river-tribe.php [August 18, 2006].

Erie
Swanton, 230-231, 300; "Iroquois Indians" (Ohio Historical Society, 2005) at http://www.ohiohistorycentral.org/entry.php?rec=597 ; "The "Erie" Indians - A Name From Long Ago" (Erie, PA: School District of Erie, 2006) athttp://esd.iu5.org/lessonplans/erie/indians.htm; "The Erie Indians, Avon, Ohio" (Avon, OH, n.d.) at http://www.centuryinter.net/tjs11/hist/erind.htm; "Erie tale reveals demise of local Indians"

(Lakewood, OH: Lakewood Public Library, n.d.) at http://www.lkwdpl.org/lore/lore96.htm [September 9, 2006]. Originally published in *Lakewood Sun Post*, July 19, 1990.

Esopus
Washington Irving, *The Life and Times of Washington* (1871), 408; Swanton, 48-55. Also, Richard Frisbie, *A History of Ulster County under the Dominion of the Dutch* (Saugerties, NY: Hope Farm Press, 1995) at http://www.hopefarm.com/indians3.htm; J. Alfieri et allis, "The Lenapes: A Study of Hudson Valley Indians" (Poughkeepsie, NY: Marist College, n.d.) at http://www.ulster.net/~hrmm/halfmoon/lenape/effects.htm [September 10, 2006].

"Mohonk Preserve in the Shawangunk Mountains, New York" (NY: Adventures Great and Small, 1996-2001) at http://www.great-adventures.com/destinations/usa/new_york/mohonk.html; Deborah Champlain, "Northeast Tribes: Native American History for March" (Rhode Island: Northeast Wigwam, 1998-2000) at http://www.newigwam.com/histdtes.html [temporarily offline].

"Eastern Woodland Tribes of First Contact: Virginia, Maryland, Delaware & New Jersey" (Pamunkey Indian Women's Circle, 2003-2006) at http://www.ewebtribe.com/NACulture/easterntribes.htm [March 8, 2006]; Anonymous, "Delaware History," February 25, 2000 available from Red History, Inc. (PHP-Nuke, 2004) at http://www.rednation.net/modules.php?name=News&file=article&sid=928 [May 4, 2006].

Esquimaux
Henry Livingston, "For the New-York Magazine. Of the Esquimaux Indians, at Hudson's Bay. With a Copperplate Engraving," New-York Magazine (May 1792), vol. III, no. V, 259-61, available at http://www.iment.com/maida/familytree/henry/writing/prose/esquimaux.htm; Joseph Noad, "Lecture On The Aborigines Of Newfoundland Delivered Before The Mechanics' Institute, At St. John's, Newfoundland, On Monday, 17th January, 1859" made available from Project Gutenberg (February 21, 2005), EBook #15126 at http://www2.cddc.vt.edu/gutenberg/1/5/1/2/15126/15126-8.txt; "The Manners Of The Esquimaux Indians," Old and Sold Antiques Digest (From "The Description given by Mr. [William] Wales of the Esquimaux Indians.") available at http://www.oldandsold.com/articles31n/lore-53.shtml; Benjamin Kohlmeister and George Kmoch, *Journal Of A Voyage From Okkak, On The Coast Of Labrador, To Ungava Bay, Westward Of Cape Chudleigh* made available by Hans Rollmann (Religion, Society, and Culture in Newfoundland Labrador, 1999-2006) at http://www.mun.ca/rels/morav/texts/ungava/ungava.html [August 5, 2006].

Esselen
Swanton, 490.

Etchemin
Swanton, 13-15, 16, 17, 578-579, 580, 591, 694; Jay Gould, *History of Delaware County, New York* (1856), Ch. II, made available by Delaware County, New York, Genealogy and History Site (Joyce Riedinger, Trustee, 1996-2003) at http://www.dcnyhistory.org/books/gould2.html; Reuel Robinson, History of Camden and Rockport, Maine, (Camden Publishing Co., 1907), Ch. III, made available by the Davistown Museum (Liberty, ME, n.d.) at http://www.davistownmuseum.org/InfoAboriginals.html [August 4, 2006].

Etohussewakke
Samuel G. Drake, *The Aboriginal Races of North America...*, 9-16.

Eufaula
Swanton, 134, 152, 157, 162, 166.

Eyeish
Swanton, 314-315; Frederick Webb Hodge, ed., *Handbook of American Indians* North of Mexico, 448-449; Jean Delanglez, "The Jolliet Lost Map of the Mississippi," Mid-America, An Historical Review (Chicago, IL: Loyola University, April 1946), vol. 28 (New Series, vol. 17), no. 2, 67-143, esp. 108-109. Author Correspondence: Mike Klein, Senior Reference Librarian, Geography and Map Division, Library of Congress, Washington, DC, June 8, 2006.

"The Illinois Country, 1673-1787," Illinois Periodicals Online (Northern Illinois University Libraries) at http://www.lib.niu.edu/ipo/2004/iht1120419.html; Lloyd Arnold Brown, "Early maps of the Ohio Valley : a selection of maps, plans, and views made by Indians and colonials from 1673 to 1783" (Pittsburgh: University of Pittsburgh Press, 1959) available from Historic Pittsburgh at http://digital.library.pitt.edu/cgi-bin/t/text/text-idx?c=pitttext;view=toc;idno=00afh9610m [June 7, 2006].

Fall Indians
Samuel G. Drake, *The Aboriginal Races of North America...*, 9-16; "Saskatchewan Historical Time Line" (Saskatchewan Gen Web, 2004) at http://www.rootsweb.com/~cansk/Saskatchewan/Timeline-Sk.html [July 25, 2006].

Faraon
Glenn Welker, "Inde (Apache) Literature" (Indigenous Peoples' Literature, n.d.) at http://www.indians.org/welker/apache.htm; "Faraon Apache Indian History and "Mescarlero Apache Indian History," from Frederick Webb Hodge, *Handbook of American Indians North of Mexico* (1906) available from Access Genealogy (2004-2006) at http://www.accessgenealogy.com/native/tribes/apache/faraon.htm and http://www.accessgenealogy.com/native/tribes/apache/mescarlero.htm [October 5, 2006].

Fernandeño
Swanton, 490.

Five Civilized Nations
Grant Foreman, *The Five Civilized Tribes*; "History" (Muskogee, OK: Five Civilized Tribes Museum, 2003) at http://www.fivetribes.org/... history. html [June 30, 2006]; "The Five Civilized Tribes" (Native Americans.com, 2007) at http://www.nativeamericans.com/Five... CivilizedTribes.htm [September 22, 2007].

Fox
Swanton, 250-252. R. David Edmunds and Joseph L. Peyser, *The Fox Wars: The Mesquakie Challenge to New France*; *Jesuit Relations (1669-1671)*, vol. 54, 205, 207, available from the OhioValley-Great Lakes Ethnohistory Archives: The Miami Collection (Bloomington, IN: Glenn Black Laboratory of Archaeology and Trustees of Indiana University, 1996, updated October 26, 2000) at http://www.gbl.indiana.edu... /archives/ miamis/M69-79_1b.html [April 1, 2006]. Linda Pingel, "A Little Outagamie County History" (Outagamie County, WI, 2003) at http:// outagamiebios.tripod.com/; Thomas Henry Ryan, "History of Outagamie County, Wisconsin" (Appleton, WI: Fox Valley Memory, 2003-2006) at http://www.foxvalleymemory.org/Ryans/Textfiles/part10r.html and http://www.foxvalleymemory.org/Ryans/Textfiles/part18r.html; Jane M. Woolsey, Wisconsin Indians (Outgamie County, WI, Historical Society) at http://www.foxvalleyhistory.org/documents/ Introduction. pdf#search='Indians%20Outagamie' [August 11, 2006]. "Kitchigamick Indians," Dictionary of Wisconsin History" (Madison, WI: Wisconsin Historical Society, 1996-2007) at http://www.wisconsinhistory.org/dictionary/index.asp?action=view&term_id=280& and ...id=343& [November 2, 2007]. Also see sources under the Sauk.

Fremont
David B. Madsen, Exploring the Fremont (Salt Lake City: Utah Museum of Natural History/University of Utah, 1989); "Great Basin Human History" (Washington, DC: Department of the Interior, National Park Service) at http://www.nps.gov/grba/EdPages/RAG/Unit%206. pdf#search='numic%20language' [March 27, 2006].

French Chaouanons
Swanton, 225-229.

Fresh Water Indians
Swanton, 130-131.

Fus-hatchee
Swanton, 157, 163.

Gallinomero Pomo
Swanton, 509-512.

Geote
Herbert E. Bolton, "The Founding of the Missions on the San Gabriel River, 1745-1749," *Southwestern Historical Quarterly*, vol. 17, no. 4, 323-378, SHQ Online at http://www.tsha.utexas.edu/publications/journals/shq/online/v017/n4/article_1.html [May 24, 2006].

Gig Harbor
"Peninsula Pioneers" (Gig Harbor, WA: Gig Harbor Peninsula Historical Society & Museum, n.d.) at http://www.gigharbormuseum.org/ onlinexh-B.html; Paul Sukovsky, "Tribes Fight to Keep Native Culture Alive," Canku Ota (Many Paths), August 24, 2002, no. 68 (Paul C. Barry, 1999-2002) at http://www.turtletrack.org/Issues02/Co08242002/CO_08242002_Washington_Tribes.htm [May 18, 2006].

Gila Apache
James L. Haley, *Apaches: A History and Culture Portrait*, 9, 191, 219, 221; "The Apache, "Indians of Arizona, Books of the Southwest (University of Arizona Online), Chapter I, pp. 5, 16 available at http://southwest.library.arizona.edu/hav7/body.1_div.1.html [March 3, 2006].

Gileños Apache
James L. Haley, Apache, 6-7, 9-11, 254-261, 266, 371, 449; Swanton, 327-330.. "The Apache," Indians of Arizona, Books of the Southwest (University of Arizona Online), Chapter I, 16 available at http://southwest.library.arizona.edu/hav7/body.1_div.1.html [March 3; May 16, 2006].

For Camp Grant Massacre, see James L. Haley, *Apaches*, 254. 261-262n, 259-261, 270, 275, 277, 364, 393, 397; Helen Hunt Jackson, A Century of Dishonor, 324-335.

Gosiute Shoshoni
Swanton 372-373, 375, 407-408. Also see sources under Shoshoni.

Gowanus
Henry R. Stiles, "From the Discovery of Manhattan Island to the Incorporation of the Village of Breuckelen, 1909-1946," *A History of the City of Brooklyn Including the Old Town and Village of Brooklyn, the Town of Bushwick, and the Village and City of Williamsburg*, in Three Volumes, vol. I, Chp. 1, 23-24 (Brooklyn, NY: by subscription, 1867) available from Cassidy (n.a.) at http://www.panix.com/~cassidy/stilesv1/v1c1/TOC2.html [May 13, 2006].

Gran Quivira Pueblo
Author Correspondence: Amy G. Johnson, Curatorial Assistant, Indian Pueblo Cultural Center, Albuquerque, New Mexico, March 10, 2006; David Roberts, *The Pueblo Revolt*, 1007-109. Also, "Gran Quivira: A Blending of Cultures in a Pueblo Indian Village: The Coming of the Spaniards" (Washington, DC: National Park Service, n.d.)

at http://www.cr.nps.gov/nr/twhp/wwwlps/lessons/66gran/66facts2.htm; also Salinas Pueblo Missions National Monument: Gran Quivira Ruins at http://www.nps.gov/archive/sapu/quivira.htm [October 24, 2006].

Grave Creek Umpqua
M. Constance Guardino III and Marilyn A. Riedel, compiled by, *Sovereigns of Themselves: A Liberating History of Oregon and Its Coast*, vol. VII, Abridged Online Edition (Maracon Productions, January 2006) at http://www2.wi.net/~census/lesson40.html; "Mount Shasta Annotated Bibliography, Chapter 3, Chastacosta Tribe" (Weed, CA: College of the Siskiyousat, 2006) at http://www.siskiyous.edu/shasta/bib/B3.htm [July 10, 2006].

Grigra
Swanton, 185, 189.

Guacata
Swanton, 121, 131.

Gualala Pomo
Swanton, 509-512.

Guale
Swanton, 108-111.

Hacanac
Swanton, 316, 323; John R. Swanton, *Source Material on the History and Ethnology of the Caddo Indians* (Smithsonian Institution, Bureau of American Ethnology Bulletin 132, Washington: GPO, 1942). Also, Thomas N. Campbell, "Hacanac Indians," Handbook of Texas Online (Austin, TX: Texas State Historical Association and University of Texas, 2002) at http://www.tsha.utexas.edu/handbook/online/articles/view/HH/bmh1.html [September 9, 2006].

Hackensack
Swanton, 48-55; Edwin G. Burrows & Mike Wallace, *Gotham*, 5. Deborah Champlain, "Northeast Tribes: Native American History for March" (Rhode Island: Northeast Wigwam, 1998-2000) at http://www.newigwam.com/histdtes.htm [subsequently offline].

Hainai
Swanton, 315-317. Also, "A Table exhibiting the different Tribes of Indians within the Geographical limits of the province of Texas, with their probable Number of Warriors and Residence," prepared by David Dickson, U.S. Consulate, San Antonio, July 1, 1827," Dispatches from U.S. Consuls in Texas made available by Rena McWilliams (Refugio County, TX: TXGenWeb, 2005-2006) at http://www.rootsweb.com/~txrefugi/ConsulateLT06.htm; Isaac Joslin Cox, "The Louisiana-Texas Frontier," *The Quarterly of the Texas State Historical Association* [*Southwestern Historical Quarterly*], vol. x, no. 1, July 1906, available online from Texas State Historical Association (Austin, TX: University of Texas, 2006) at http://www.tsha.utexas.edu/publications/journals/shq/online/v010/n1/issue.html [August 16, 2006].

Halchidhoma
Swanton, 349-350.

Halyikwamai
Swanton, 350-351.

Hanis
Swanton, 459.

Hannakallal
The *Journals of Lewis and Clark* includes an Appendix, "Estimate of the Western Indians, that gives the names of the Indian tribes of the area, their general location, the number of lodges, and their estimate of the population." The Appendix can be found on pp. 471-476 of the Nicholas Biddle edition (Dayton, 1840). Also, "Lewis & Clark: A Journey" is available from the University of Cincinnati Digital Press (Cincinnati, OH, n.d.) at http://www.ucdp.uc.edu/lewisandclark/biddle/volume2_pt3.pdf [August 7, 2006]. See Items Nos. 27 and 28, pp. 473-474. Access the Digital Library at http://www.ucdp.uc.edu.

Hano Pueblo
Swanton, 340-341.

Hasinai Confederacy
Swanton, 315-317, 320, 326. Also, generally, Herbert Eugene Bolton, *The Hasinais: Southern Caddoans as Seen by the Earliest Europeans*.

Russell M. Magnaghi, "Hasinai Indians," *Handbook of Texas Online* (Austin, TX: Texas State Historical Association and University of Texas, 2001) at http://www.tsha.utexas.edu/handbook/online/articles/view/HH/bmh8.html [September 10, 2006].

Hassanamisco
Swanton, 22-23.

Hassinunga
Swanton, 61-62.

Hatteras
Swanton, 80, 81; Fred Willard, "Disappearing Indians" (East Lake, NC: The Lost Colony Center for Science and Research, November, 2001) at http://www.lost-colony.com/disappearing.html [September 10, 2006].

Havasupai
Swanton, 351; Thomas Edwin Farish, *The History of Arizona*, vol. vii, chps. 5, 6; Jeffrey Scott, "Hualupai Indians" (AZ, updated June 27, 2002) at http://jeff.scott.tripod.com/hualpai.html [August 31, 2006].

Haverstraw
Swanton, 48-55. Deborah Champlain, "Northeast Tribes: Native American History for March" (Rhode Island: Northeast Wigwam, 1998-2000) at http://www.newigwam.com/histdtes.html [temporarily offline].

Hellwits
"A 1940 Journey Across Oregon: Rainier to Astoria" (Salem OR: Oregon State Archives, n.d.) at http://arcweb.sos.state.or.us/exhibits/across/rainier.html; "Clatskanie and Clatskanie River, Oregon" (U.S. Army Corps of Engineers, 2003) at http://englishriverwebsite.com/LewisClarkColumbiaRiver/Regions/Places/clatskanie_river.html [August 8, 2006].

Herring Pond
"Herring River Watershed" (State of Massachusetts) at http://www.mass.gov/dcr/stewardship/acec/acecs/l-herriv.htm; "1693 List of "Praying Indians' in Herring Pond Congregation" (Plymouth, MA: Plymouth Hall Museum, Updated 14 July, 1998) at http://www.pilgrimhall.org/natamdocs.htm#1693%20list; "Alphabetical Roster of Individuals in Earle Report" (Thomas L. Doughtonat, 1997) at http://www.twodogssouthwestgallery.com; From *Earle Report* (Mass. Senate Report #96 of 1861) or Report to the Governor and Council Concerning the Indians of the Commonwealth Under the Act of April 6, 1859 (Boston: William White, 1861) by John Milton Earle. A similar study was conducted in 1849, Briggs Report, which is available at http://geocities.com/quinnips/briggs/briggs2.html; Simeon L. Deyo, "Town of Harwich by Josiah Paine," *History of Barnstable County, Massachusetts* (New York: H. W. Blake & Co, 1890), Ch. XXV, pp. 825-890 available from Cape Cod History (2004) at http://www.capecodhistory.us/Deyo/Harwich-Deyo.htm; Theodore Walker, Jr., *A History of Red-Black Solidarity: Reflection on William Loren Katz's Black Indians: A Hidden Heritage* (New York: Athenaeum, 1986)" made available by Theodore Walker, Jr. (update: 24 March 1997) at http://faculty.smu.edu/twalker/1992.htm; Lincoln Newton Kinnicutt, *Indian Names of Places in Plymouth, Middleborough, Lakeville and Carver Plymouth County Massachusetts* (1909) available from Access Genealogy (1999-2005) at http://www.accessgenealogy.com/massachusetts/indianames/page7.htm [August 8, 2006].

Hidatsa
Dee Brown, *Hear That Lonesome Whistle Blow*, 262; Stephen E. Ambrose, *Undaunted Courage*, 182, 183, 187-189, 207-209, 228-229, 230; Bernard De Voto, ed., *The Journals of Lewis and Clark*, 54, 57-59, 65, 68, 71, 75, 77, 83-84, 88-90, 112, 114, 117, 146, 148, 171, 177n4, 201, 203, 208, 214-216, 236, 302, 419-421, 451-461 passim, 466; Swanton 275-276; George Catlin, *North American Indians* (Penguin ed.), 185-192. 193-201;Gloria Jahoda, *Trail of Tears*, 178. Also, Washington Matthews, *Ethnography and Philology of The Hidatsa Indians* (Washington, DC: Government Printing Office, 1877), Department of the Interior, United States Geological and Geographical Survey Misc. Pub. No. 7 at http://delta.ulib.org/ulib/data/moa/3d1/407/bdb/944/eec/5/data.txt [November 1, 2007].

"Information on the Mandan and Hidatsa Indians Recorded by Members of the Lewis and Clark Expedition, Oct. 27, 1804-April 6, 1805," The Lewis and Clark Journey of Discovery (Washington, DC: National Park Service, n.d.) at http://www.nps.gov/archive/jeff/LewisClark2... / TheJourney/NativeAmericans/MandanandHidatsa.htm; "Hidatsa Indians" (Washington, DC: National Geographic, 1996-2006) at http://www.nationalgeographic.com/lewisandclark/record_tribes_007_5_2.html and "Amahami Indians" at http://www.nationalgeographic.com... / lewisandclark/record_tribes_021_5.html [August 30, 2006]. And, "Indian Tribes 1880- A-B-C," Indian Genealogy (Access Genealogy, 2004-2006) at http://www.accessgenealogy.com/native/tribes/nations/page1.htm [July 28, 2006]. Source: *Handbook of American Indians, 1906*; Frank..., "Hidatsa" (2007) at http://www.franksrealm.com/sivu-indians-hidatsa.html [November 1, 2007].

Hierbipiames
Herbert E. Bolton, "The Founding of the Missions on the San Gabriel River, 1745-1749," *Southwestern Historical Quarterly*, vol. 17, no. 4, 323-378, SHQ Online at http://www.tsha.utexas.edu/publications/journals/shq/online/v017/n4/article_1.html [May 24, 2006].

Hietan
Bernard De Vito, ed., *The Journals of Lewis & Clark*, 475; Swanton, 373.

Journal of Anthony Glass: Trading Journey to Texas 1808, made available by Sons of Dewitt Colony Texas (Wallace L. McKeehan, 1997-2002) at http://www.tamu.edu/ccbn/dewitt/glassanthony.htm; Julia Kathryn Garrett, "Dr. John Sibley and the Louisiana-Texas Frontier, 1803-1814," *Southwestern Historical Quarterly*, vol. 47, no. 3, made available from the Texas State Historical Society (Austin, TX, 2004) at http://www.tsha.utexas.edu/publications/journals/shq/online/v047/n3/contrib_DIVL5843.html; "Rebecca Scott's notes from: 'Voyages of Captains Lewis and Clarke in the years 1804, 1805, and 1806'" available from the Oklahoma Alliance for Geographical Information (Norman, OK: University of Oklahoma, n.d.), pp. 192-195 at http://www.ou.edu/okage/lodgepole/lewisandclark4.html; "Comanche et al." (Red Wolf's American Indian Genealogy Heritage, n.d.) at http://www.angelfire.com/la/brantley/; Thomas J. Nuttall, "Nuttall's Journal," *North American Review* (1823) made available by Historic Arkansas (1999-2003) at http://stellar-one.com/arkansas_history/0010.htm [August 8,2006]. Based on Nuttall's travels in Arkansas in 1819.

Hihighenimmo
Samuel G. Drake, *The Aboriginal Races of North America...*, 9-16; "Hub of the West" from Discovering Lewis & Clark (VIAs Inc., 2003) at http://www.lewis-clark.org/content/content-article.asp?ArticleID=2273 [August 26, 2006].

Hilibi
Swanton, 157, 162.

Hisca
Herbert E. Bolton, "The Founding of the Missions on the San Gabriel River, 1745-1749," *Southwestern Historical Quarterly*, vol. 17, no. 4, 323-378, SHQ Online at http://www.tsha.utexas.edu/publications/journals/shq/online/v017/n4/article_1.html [May 24, 2006].

Hitchiti
Swanton, 111, 131-132, 157; "Languages of Georgia Indians," *New Georgia Encyclopedia* (Athens, GA: Georgia Humanities Council and the University of Georgia Press, 2004-2006) at http://www.georgiaencyclopedia.org/nge/Article.jsp?id=h-2752; Jerry Wilkinson, "History of the Seminoles" (Keys Historeum, n.d.) at http://www.keyshistory.org/seminolespage1.html [August 6, 2006].

Hochelagan
Daniel K. Richter, *Facing East from Indian Country*, 16, 28, 30, 32, 40. Edwin O. Wood "Chapter II, Hochelaga," *History of Genesee County, Michigan, Her People, Industries and Institutions* (Online edition by Holice, Deb & Clayton, 2002) at http://www.usgennet.org/usa/mi/... county/lapeer/gen/ch2/hochelaga4.html; Claude Bélanger, "Hochelaga," *Quebec History Encyclopedia* (Montreal, Marianopolis College, 2004) at http://faculty.marianopolis.edu/c.belanger/quebechistory/encyclopedia/Hochelaga.htm [October 1, 2007].

Hoh
Swanton, 424.

Hohokam
Swanton, 360-363, 369-370, writes of the Hokan linguistic group but makes no reference to the Hohokam; David Roberts, *Pueblo Revolt*, 33-35.

"The Hohokam: The Land and the People" (City of Phoenix, 2006) at http://www.ci.phoenix.az.us/PUEBLO/exmain.html; "Hohokam Irrigation," Dr. Michael Tang's Science, Technology and Culture Course, Fall Semester, 1998 (Denver: University of Colorado at Denver, 1998) at http://carbon.cudenver.edu/stc-link/hohokam/Hohokam.htm; "The Hohokam, Farmers of the Desert" (DesertUSA, 1996-2006) at http://www.desertusa.com/ind1/ind_new/ind8.html; Warrick Bell and Catherine Lavender, "Hohokam Chronology" (WestWeb, 1999) at http://www.library.csi.cuny.edu/westweb/ancient/hohokam/chronol.html [March 17, 2006].

Hois Comanche
T. R. Fehrenbach, *Comanches*, esp. 142-144.

Holiwahali
Swanton, 162.

Honniasont
Swanton, 55.

Hopi
Swanton 351-353; David Roberts, *Pueblo Revolt*, 48, 49, 65, 68, 78, 90, 104, 166, 180-181, 226, 232, 235; on Awatoni, see 180, 226, 232-239; "Hopi Indian Reservation" (St. Johns, AZ: Carizona, 1997/98/99) at http://www.arizonalodging.com/nativeland/hopi.html; Thomas Edwin Farish, *The History of Arizona*, vol. vii, chp. 2, taken from Books of the Southwest, University of Arizona Library, History of Arizona, vol. VII, at http://digital.library.arizona.edu/southwest/hav7/body.1_div.1.html [September 8, 2006].

Hostaqua
Swanton, 135.

Houma
Swanton, 185-186; "Colonial Louisiana" (Baton Rouge: Louisiana State Museum, 2002) at http://lsm.crt.state.la.us/cabildo/cab3.htm; Richard E. Condrey, "Discover Louisiana's Environmental Past..." (Baton Rouge: Louisiana State University, n.d.) at http://www.leeric.lsu.edu/le/cover/lead015.htm [July 26, 2006].

David Graham, "Pierre LeMoyne Sieur d'Iberville and the Establishment of Biloxi," from David Hawkwind (1995-1996) at http://www.datasync.com/~davidg59/biloxi1.html; "Pierre Le Moyne, Sieur de Iberville, 1661-1706," *Encyclopedia Louisiana* (1998, updated November 28, 2001) at http://www.enlou.com/people/ibervillep-bio.htm [September 9, 2006].

On La Salle, "Henri Tonti Letters," *Mid-America, An American Review* (Chicago, IL: Loyola University, 1939), available from the Ohio Valley-Great Lakes Ethnohistory Archives: The Miami Collection (Bloomington, IN: Glenn Black Laboratory of Archaeology and Trustees of Indiana University, 1996, updated October 26, 2000) at http://www.gbl.indiana.edu/archives/miamis4/M17-03_8c.html; Erin Fuller, "A Newsletter for the Black River Watershed Project" (Paw Paw, MI: Black River Watershed, March 2004) 5th ed. at http://www.vbco.org/downloads/304_newsletter1.pdf ; "Indian Tribes of St. Joseph Valley" (St. Joseph County, MI: Denise Frederick, 1998) at http://members.tripod.com/~tfred/chap1.html [July 4, 2006].

Hualapai

Swanton, 365-366; Thomas Edwin Farish, *The History of Arizona*, vol. vii, chp. 7. Also, "Southwest Indian People—The Hualapai" (Mesa, AZ: Southwest Indian Relief Council, 2001) at http://www.swirc.org/people/coloradoriver/hualapai.html; John Crossley, "Hualapai Indian Reservation" (American Southwest, 1994-2004) at http://www.americansouthwest.net/arizona/grand_canyon/hualapai_reservation.html [September 8, 2006].

Huchnom

Swanton, 492.

Huliwahli

Swanton, 162.

Humptulip

Swanton, 424.

Hunkpapa

For Images of American Indians on U.S. Currency, see *Walter Breen's Complete Encyclopedia of U.S. and Colonial Coins* and *Who Was Who in Native American History* and the *Encyclopedia of Native American Biography*.

Hupa

Swanton, 492-493.

Huron

William E. Connelley, "Religious Conceptions of the Modern Hurons," *Kansas Historical Collections* (Topeka: Kansas State Historical Society,1919-1922), vol. xv, 92-102; Edwin G. Burrows & Mike Wallace, *Gotham*, 13, 86; G. Elmore Reaman, *The Trail of the Iroquois Indians*, 3-8, 33; Swanton, 44, 235, 245, 605; Bernie Arbic, *City of the Rapids: Sault Ste. Marie's Heritage* (Sault Ste. Marie, MI: Pricella Press, 2006).

Claude Bélanger, "Hurons," *Quebec History* (Marianopolis College, 2004) at http://www2.marianopolis.edu/quebechistory/encyclopedia/HuronIndiansEC.htm; Edward Channing. "French Colonists, Missionaries, and Explorers," A Short History of the United States for School Use (1908), ch. 4, made available from American History Company (1996-2006) at http://www.americanhistory.com/history/ShortHistory/shorthistory2.html [August 24, 2006].

Ibitoupa

Swanton, 186-187.

Icafui

Swanton, 132.

Illinois

Gilbert Imlay, A Topographical Description of the Western Territory of North America..., 3rd ed. (London, 1797), 364-365, made available from Glen Black Laboratory of Archaeology (Bloomington, IN: University of Indiana, 1997-2000) at http://www.gbl.indiana.edu/archives/dockett_317/317_33.html [August 11, 2006].

Dorothy Libby, "An Anthropological Report on the Piankashaw Indians: Piankashaw Locations, ca. 1776- ca. 1783," pp. 90-99, available from the OhioValley-Great Lakes Ethnohistory Archives: The Miami Collection (Bloomington, IN: Glenn Black Laboratory of Archaeology and Trustees of Indiana University, 1997-2000), at http://www.gbl.indiana.edu/archives/dockett_99/d99toc.html [October 24, 2006]; *Johnson v. M'Intosh*, 21 U.S. 543 (1823); Eric Kades, "History and Interpretation of the Great Case of *Johnson v. M'Intosh*," *Law and History Review*, vol. 19, no. 1, Spring 2001 (Urbana: Board of Trustees of the University of Illinois, 2001) at http://www.historycooperative.org/journals/lhr/19.1/kades.html. [December 12, 2006].

Illinois Cluster of Tribes

Swanton, 212, 241-242; Kristie C. Woferman, *The Osage in Missouri*, 27. Also see "Rock River (Winnebago, Ogle, Lee, Whiteside, Henry, and Rock Island Counties, Illinois)" at http://pages.ripco.net/~jwn/rock.html; Scott K. Williams, Florissant, Missouri (2002), "Tribes of the Region of First Contact (1673)," American Indian History From Prehistory to the Nineteenth Century Relating to St. Louis and the Surrounding States of Missouri and Illinois (R. K. Ross, Missouri State History ALHN, 2001-2003) at http://www.usgennet.org/usa/mo/county/stlouis/native/1stcontact.htm#Illini%20Confederacy [September 8, 2006] And, "Missouri Indian Tribes" (AccessGenealogy and Authors, 2000-2004) at http://www.accessgenealogy.com/native/tribes/siouan/missourihist.htm (Source: *Handbook of American Indians*, 1906).

Ioni

"Ioni, Texas," *Handbook of Texas Online* (Austin, TX: Texas State Historical Association and University of Texas, 2001)at http://www.tsha.utexas.edu/handbook/online/articles/II/hvi14.html and Mark Odintz, "Ioni Texas," Handbook of Texas Online (Texas State Historical Association, updated June 1, 2001) at http://www.tsha.utexas.edu/handbook/online/articles/II/hri9.html; Glenn Welker. "Tehuacana Creek Treaty, October 9, 1844" (updated September 30, 3003) at http://www.indians.org/welker/liptrea1.htm; "Ioni Creek," Place Names (Buttle & Tuttle, 2000-2006) at http://www.placenames.com/us/p1360018 and "Ioni Creek," USGS National Mapping Information (Reston, VA: Department of the Interior U.S. Geological Survey, built June 14, 2006) at http://geonames.usgs.gov/pls/gnis/web_query.GetDetail?tab=Y&id=1338487 [June 14, 2006].

Iowa
William S. Belko, "A Founding Missourian," 108; Eugene Morrow Violette, *History of Missouri*, 72; Swanton, esp. 265; James H. Knipmeyer, "Denis Julier: Midwestern Fur Trader," *Missouri Historical Review* (Columbia: State Historical Society of Missouri, April 2001), xcv, 3, 245-263; Martha Blaine, *The Ioway Indians*. See painting by George Catlin, *Shon-ta-yi-ga, Little Wolf, a Famous Warrior*, Iowa (1844).

B. F. Gue, "History of Iowa," (1902) (Iowa History Project, 2002-2006) at http://iagenweb.org/history/hoi/HOI2.html [July 27, 2006]; Lance Foster, "Baxoje, the Ioway Nation" (Ioway Cultural Institute, 2001-2004) at http://ioway.nativeweb.org/; Roger Pyle and John Matthews, "Doniphan County," *Cutler's History of Kansas* (Kansas Collection Books, April 1999) at http://www.kancoll.org/books/cutler/doniphan/doniphan-co-p1.html [September 6, 2006].

Iroquois League
Alan Taylor, *The Divided Ground*, esp. 3-11, 19, 22-23, 78-108, 165, 167, 168, 171-172, 173, 178, 184, 189, 199, 284, 288-293, 308; Joseph T. Glatthaar and James Kirby Martin, *Forgotten Allies*, 11, 15, 17, 314; quote taken from p. 11. Also, Robert C. Carriker, *Father Peter John De Smet: Jesuit in the West*, 18-20, 96; Bruce Lancaster, *The American Revolution*, 306-310, 316-319; Willard Stern Randal, *George Washington*, 360-363; Edmond S. Morgan, *American Slavery, American Freedom*, 49n13, 58; Swanton, esp. 33-40; G. Elmore Reaman, *The Trail of the Iroquois Indians*, esp. 3-10, 25-27, 30-34; Edwin G. Burrows & Mike Wallace, *Gotham*, 13, 23n4, 86; John Sugden, *Blue Jacket: Warrior of the Shawnees*, 37-38; Henry Wadsworth Longfellow, "The Song of Hiawatha (1855)," *Favorite Poems of Henry Wadsworth Longfellow* (New York: Doubleday, 1947), 149-295; George Catlin, *North American Indians* (Penguin ed.), 369-370.

Benison J. Lossing, *Our Country*, vol. 1, chp. II (1905) available at http://www.angelfire.com/ca6/minuteman/chapter002.htm; "George Washington - Message to the Senate of September 17, 1789 Regarding Treaties with Native Americans," The Avalon Project: Treaties Between the United States and Native Americans (New Haven, CN: Yale Law School, 1996-2004) at http://www.yale.edu/lawweb/avalon... /presiden/ messages/gw006.htm; "Indian Land Cessions in the American Southeast," (TNGenNet Inc, 2001-2003; updated August 06, 2004) at http:// www.tngenweb.org/cessions/ ...; "West Virginia County Histories: Barbour County History," County Commissioners' Association of West Virginia (Morgantown, WV : West Virginia University Department of Political Science, n.d.) at http://www.polsci.wvu.edu/wv/history.html [September 8, 2006].

W. J. McKnight, "A Pioneer Outline History of Northwestern Pennsylvania" (J. Lippincott Co., 1905), 22-47, available from Accessible Archives) at http://www.accessible.com/amcnty/PA/Northwest/Northwest02.htm; William L. Stone, "The Life and Times of Sir William Johnson, Bart.," vol. II (Albany: J. Munsell, 78 State Street, 1865), Ch. II, 17 July 1757, available from Three Rivers (Berry Enterprises, 1998-2003) at http:// www.threerivershms.com/SWJ%20vol2ch2.htm [August 1, 2006].

For the Western Expedition of Colonial America, see Alan Taylor, *The Divided Ground*, 97-102; Bruce Llancaster, *The American Revolution*, 306-310, 319; John Ferling, *A Leap in the Dark*, 220; Morris Bishop, "The End of theIroquois," *American Heritage* (October 1969) vol. 20, no. 6, available at http://www.americanheritage.com/articles/magazine/ah/1969/6/1969_6_28_print.shtml [October 31, 2006].

On the Jay Treaty, see esp. Alan Taylor, *The Divided Ground*, 287, 294. For more on the Covenant Chain, see Daniel K. Richter, *Facing East from Indian Country*, 147-150, 153-157, 160, 166-168, 179-180, 184, 193, 209-210. On the Treaty of Camp Charlotte, also see Richter, 214.

Irusitsu
Swanton, 514.

Island Chumash
Swanton, 484-487.

Isleta Pueblo
David Roberts, *Pueblo Revolt*, 108, 131, 135-136, 173, 183, 232; "Pueblo of Isleta" (Isleta, NM, n.d.) at http://www.isletapueblo.com/ [October 26, 2006].

Ithkyemamits
Stephenie Flora, "Northwest Indian Tribes" (The Oregon Territory and Its Pioneers, 1998-2006) at http://www.oregonpioneers.com/tribe.htm; "Chinookan Family History" (Access Genealogy, 2004-2006) at http://www.accessgenealogy.com/native/tribes/chinook/chinookanfamilyhist. htm
[August 8, 2006]. Source: *Handbook of American Indians*, 1906.

Jameco
Swanton, 54. Liz Goff, "How We Got Here: A Look At The Birth Of A Business Community," (New York: Queens Press, 2001) at http://www.queenspress.com/anniversary2001-birthofabusiness.htm; "About Jamaica, Queens, New York City, NY" (Jamaica, NY: Cultural Collaborative, Jamaida, n.d.) at http://www.go2ccj.org/jamaica.htm [May 12, 2006].

Jeaga
Swanton, 132-133.

Jelan
Samuel G. Drake, *The Aboriginal Races of North America...*, 9-16.

Jemez Pueblo
Swanton, 330-332; David Roberts, 110-111; William Whatley, "History of The Pueblo of Jemez" (n.a., 1993) at http://www.jemezpueblo.org/history.htm [March 2,2006]; Bernadett Charley Gallegos, "New Mexico Pueblos" (n.a., 1999-2004) at http://members.aol.com/chloe5/pueblos.html [April 30, 2006].

Jicarilla Apache
James L. Haley, *Apaches: A History and Culture Portrait*, 9, 30, 49-50, 184-186; Swanton, 370-372; "Bent's Old Fort and its Builders," Kansas State Historical Society, 85, 91.

Joshua
Swanton, 472-473.

Juaneño
Swanton, 494.

Ka'te'nu'a'ka'
Swanton 85-88.

Kadapaus
David Williamson, "Archaeologists, students at UNC, discover two Indian settlements key in US history" (Chapel Hill: University of North Carolina, 2003) at http://www.eurekalert.org/pub_releases/2003-06/uonc-asa062603.php; also at http://research.unc.edu/endeavors/fall2003/catawba.html [August 9, 2006].

Kadohadacho
Swanton, 317-320.

Kadohadacho Confederacy
Swanton, 317-320.

Kaibab
Swanton, 383. Steward, 1933.

Kainai Blackfeet
John C. Ewers, *The Blackfeet: Raiders on the Northwestern Plains, esp.260-261*; Swanton, 395-398.

Kaiquariegahaga
Swanton, 56.

Kalapuya Peoples
Swanton, 452, 454, 463; Frank McLynn, *Wagons West*, 176; Henry B. Zenk, "Kalapuyans," *Handbook of North American Indians* (Washington, DC: Smithsonian Institution, 1990), vol. 7, 547-553.

Janice Weide and Jane Kirby, "Kalapuya of the Willamette Valley," Salem Online History (Salem, OR: Salem Public Library, 2005) at http://www.salemhistory.net/people/native_americans.htm; "Kalapuyan," taken from Michael Johnson, The Native American Tribes of North America,176 (Eugene: University of Oregon, 1997) at http://logos.uoregon.edu/explore/oregon/kalapuyan.html; Margaret Robertson, "The Kalapuya" from Kevin Matthews, "Message - The Kalapuya of the Upper Willamette Valley," Neighbors and Nature Forum (1999-2002) at http://neighbors.designcommunity.com/notes/1347.html; Oscar Johnson, "The Kalapuya of Clackamas County," Smoke Signals (Grande Ronde Tribe, Spring 1999) at http://www.usgennet.org/alhnorus/ahorclak/kalapuyas.html; "The Ancient Lands of the Confederated Tribes of Grand Ronde and Neighboring Tribal Affiliations" OR: Confederated Tribes of Grand Ronde, n.d.) at http://www.grandronde.org/cultural/ancient.htm [May 18, 2006].

Don Macnaughtan, "American Indian Languages of Western Oregon" (Eugene, OR: Lane Community College Library, 1999) at http://www.lanecc.edu/it/hdrefs/Follow%2520directions%2520at:%2520http://expresslane.lanecc.edu/library/don/orelang.htm; With the Treaty of Calapooia Creek, Oregon (November 29, 1854), the Umpqua and Kalapooian tribes of the Umpqua Valley ceded their lands; and with the Treaty at Dayton, Oregon (January 22, 1855), the Calapooya and other tribes of the Willamette Valley ceded their lands.

"Kalapuya-Amin (Land of the Kalapuya) " (Oregon Websites and Watersheds Project, 1996-2006) at http://www.orww.org/Kalapuya-Amin_2006/index.html [October 21, 2006].

Kalispel
Swanton, 399-400.

Kamia
Swanton 494-495.

Kan-hatki
Swanton, 157, 163.

Kanawake
Joseph T. Glatthaar and James Kirby Martin, *Forgotten Allies*, 38, 96-97; Swanton, 34, 37; "Kahnawake History" (Kahnawake, Quebec: Mohawk Council of Kahnawá:ke) at http://www.kahnawake.com/history.asp; T. J. Cambell, "Auriesville," Catholic Encyclopedia, vol. II (Robert Appleton Company. 1907). Online Edition Copyright © 2005 by K. Knight at http://www.newadvent.org/cathen/02111b.htm [April 28, 2006].

Kansa
Swanton, esp. 293-294; Father Nicholas Point, *Souvenirs des Montagnes Rocheuses* (My Rocky Mountain Memories); Eugene Morrow Violette, *History of Missouri*, 72; William Y. Chapfant, *Cheyennes and Horse Soldiers*, 77n; William E. Unrau, *The Kansa Indians* (Norman: University of Oklahoma Press, 1971) with quotes taken from 89, 93, 133, 140, 214; Kristie C. Woferman, *The Osage in Missouri*, 26, 35; Perl W. Morgan, ed.. *History of Wyandotte County Kansas and Its People*, 2 Vols. (Chicago, The Lewis publishing company, 1911), chp. 2. See George Catlin's "Meach-o shin-gaw, The Little White Plume, A Kansa Warrier," Chief White Plume, circa 1830.

Berlin B. Chapman, "Charles Curtis and the Kaw Reservation," *Kansas Historical Quarterly* (Topeka, KS: Kansas State Historical Society, November 1947), vol. 14, no. 4, pp. 337 to 351, available at http://www.kshs.org/publicat/khq/1947/47_4_chapman.htm; "Kaw Mission, State Historical Site" (Topeka, KS, 2004) at http://www.kshs.org/places/kaw/history.htm [September 7, 2006].

The Kansas Indians (Topeka: Kansas State Library, n.d.) at http://skyways.lib.ks.us/kansas/kansas/genweb/archives/wyandott/history/1911/volume1/17.html [May 22, 2006]; "Alphabetical Listing of the Tribes of Kansas," Blue Skyways (Topeka: Kansas State Library) at http://skyways.lib.ks.us/genweb/nativeam/Text%20index.htm [August 27, 2006]; Marvin H. Garfield, "The Indian Question in Congress and in Kansas," *Kansas Historical Quarterly* (Topeka: Kansas State Historical Society), February 1933, vol. 2, no. 1, 29-44, available online through the efforts of Lynn Nelson and Tod Roberts at https://www.kshs.org/publicat/khq/1933/33_1_garfield.htm [May 30, 2006]; Piyush Patel, "The Kaw Nation," *Six Tribes* (Tonkawa, OK: Northern Oklahoma College for Standing Bear Native American Foundation, Ponca, OK, 2001-2006) at http://12.13.112.169/acs/acs/orderentry.asp?TyE_0qa53VXJ-QiKtwIpVgaa [June 7, 2006]; "Lands of the Kansas Indian Tribe" (Kansas Genealogy, 2002-2006) at http://www.kansasgenealogy.com/indians/lands_of_the_kansas_indian_tribe.htm [September 29, 2006].

Karankawa
Swanton, 320-321.

Henry Schoolcraft, "Karankawan Family," *Thirty Years with Indians* ...(Native American Nations, 2000-2006) at http://www.nanations.com/linguistic/karankawan_family.htm; Frank Wagner, "Beranger, Jean," *Handbook of Texas Online* (Austin, TX: Texas State Historical Association and University of Texas, 2002) at http://www.tsha.utexas.edu/handbook/online/articles/BB/fbeam.html; "Port Aransas and the 1700's" (Port Aransas, TX, n.d.) at http://www.angelfire.com/journal2/port/3.html; Wallace L. McKeehan, "New Spain," College Station, TX: Texas A&M University, Sons of Dewitt Colony Texas, 1997-2002) at http://www.tamu.edu/ccbn/ccbn/dewitt/Spain.htm [August 21, 2006].

Karankawan Tribes
Swanton, 320-321; T. R. Fehrenback, *Comanches*, 227.

R. Edward Moore, "The Karankawa Indians" (Texarch Associates,1998, 2000) at http://www.texasindians.com/karank.htm [March 10, 2006]. Also from Johnson County, Texas, at http://www.historictexas.net/jackson/history/indians.htm [September 10, 2006].

Carol A. Lipscomb, "Karankawa Indians," *Handbook of Texas Online* (Austin, TX: Texas State Historical Association and University of Texas, 2004)at http://www.tsha.utexas.edu/handbook/online/articles/KK/bmk5.html; "The Karankawa Indians" (n.a.) at http://www.thisoldappliance.com/indians.html; "The Karankawa Indians," *The Conquistadors* (Oregon Public Broadcasting and PBS Online, 2000) at http://www.pbs.org/opb/conquistadors/namerica/adventure1/b2.htm; C. David Pomeroy, Jr., "Indians of Pasadena," The Early Years (Pasadena, TX, 2005) at http://www.earlytexashistory.com/Pasadena/indians.html; "Karankawa Indian Tribe History" (Access Genealogy, 2004-2006) at http://www.accessgenealogy.com/native/tribes/karankawa/karankawahist.htm [August 9, 2006]. Source: *Handbook of American Indians*, 1906.

Karok
Swanton, 495-496.

Kasihta
Swanton, 111, 163. Also, N. K. Rogers, *History Of Chattahoochee County, Georgia* (Columbus, GA: Columbus Office Supply, 1933), made available online by Joy Fisher (2004) at http://ftp.rootsweb.com/pub/usgenweb/ga/chattahoochee/... history/other/gms443chapteri.txt [October 6, 2007]. See esp. Peter A. Brannon, "Indian History," Chapter I.

Kaskaskia
Swanton, 212, 241-242, 300.

Kaskinampo
Swanton, 158, 212, 224-225; Conoy, 57. Also see Jean Delanglez, "The Jolliet Lost Map of the Mississippi," *Mid-America, An Historical Review* (Chicago, IL: Loyola University, April 1946), vol. 28 (New Series, vol. 17), no. 2, 67-143, esp. 113.

Henri Tonti Letters, *Mid-America, An American Review* (Chicago, IL: Loyola University, 1939), vol. 21, 231, n43, available from the Ohio Valley-Great Lakes Ethnohistory Archives: The Miami Collection (Bloomington, IN: Glenn Black Laboratory of Archaeology and Trustees of Indiana University, 1996, updated October 26, 2000) at http://www.gbl.indiana.edu/archives/miamis4/M17-03_8c.html [July 2, 2006].

"Comparative Table," American Memory (Washington, DC: Library of Congress, n.d.) at http://memory.loc.gov/master/gc/gcmisc/gcfr... /0016/03510000.txt and at http://memory.loc.gov/master/rbc/rbfr/0010/03600000.txt [June 7, 2006]; "Native Americans , Artifacts and Explorers" (Clarksdale, MS: Coahoma County Tourism Commission, n.d.) at http://www.clarksdaletourism.com/HTML/indians.htm; "Historical Markers in Coahoma County" (Clarksdale, MS: Coahoma County, n.d.) at http://www.ssrc.msstate.edu/grr/coahm.htm; and "Tennessee American Indian Migrations" (Knoxville, TN: Tennessee American Indian Migrations Project, 2007) at http://www.tnaim.org/index.php [September 17, 2007].

"Kaskinampo," Four Directions Institute (Four Directions Press, 2005) at http://www.fourdir.com/kaskinampo.htm; also "Coushatta" at http://www.fourdir.com/coushatta.htm [July 2, 2006]. The latter states that they were joined by the Kaskinampo in 1701. The former states that the Kaskinampo moved onto the lower end of Pine Island in 1701 and joined the Coushatta in 1800. The results were the same.

Kathlaminimin
Swanton, 467; "Chinookan Devastation: 'Marsh Miasms'" (Vancouver, WA: Center for Columbia River History, 2004-2005) at http://www.ccrh.org/comm/slough/chinook5.htm [August 2, 2006].

Kato
Swanton, 496.

Kawaiisu
Swanton, 496. For the Keysville Massacre, see "Keysville Massacre, April 19, 1863," Kern County Historical Society, *Quarterly* (November 1952) available at http://vredenburgh.org/tehachapi/data/mclaughlin.htm; Larry M. Vredenburgh, "Kawaiisu Indians of Tehachapi" (Historic and Geologic Resources of South Central California, n.d.) at http://vredenburgh.org/tehachapi/data/indians.htm [November 20, 2006]. Re. The 1856 incident, see John Gorenfeld, "The Tule River War" (Weider History Group, 2006) at http://www.historynet.com/wars_conflicts/american_indian_wars/3037981.html?showAll=y&c=y; "History"(Kern County, California, 2006) at http://www.usacitiesonline.com/cakerncounty.htm [November 20, 2006].

Kawchottine
Swanton, 574.

Kawita
""Vaudreuil to Maurepas, March 15, 1747," Archives Nationales, pp. 8-10, available from the Ohio Valley-Great Lakes Ethnohistory Archives: The Miami Collection (Bloomington, IN: Glenn Black Laboratory of Archaeology and Trustees of Indiana University, 1996, updated November 2000) at http://www.gbl.indiana.edu/archives/miamis9/M46-48_9a.html; Kawita Band of Creeks: HB470 and HB782, Rev. Section 1. Section 41-9-708, Code of Alabama 1975, Alabama Legislature at http://www.legislature.state.al.us/searchableinstruments/2004RS/Bills/HB470.htm and http://www.legislature.state.al.us/searchableinstruments/2005RS/Bills/HB782.htm; Crane, Verner W. Crane, "The Southern Frontier in Queen Anne's War," American Historical Review 24 (April 1919), 379-95. HTML by Dinsmore Documentation: Classics of American Colonial History (May 8, 2002) at http://dinsdoc.com/crane-1.htm [June 14, 2006].

Kayamaici
Swanton, 315-317.

Kealedji
Swanton, 157, 163.

Kecoughtan
Swanton, 66-71.

Keresan Pueblos
Swanton, 332-334, 339-340.

Keyauwee
Swanton, 66, 76, 77, 79, 80-81, 96.

Kiawa
Swanton 96, 107.

Kichai
Swanton, 300, 306, 321-322; George Bird Grinnell, *The Fighting Cheyennes*, 128; Herbert E. Bolton, "The Spanish Abandonment and Re-occupation of East Texas, 1773-1779," *Southwestern Historical Quarterly*, vol. 9, no. 2, n64, from SHQ Online at http://www.tsha.utexas.edu/publications/journals/shq/online/v009/n2/article_1_print.html [May 24, 2006].

Kickapoo
Eugene Morrow Violette, *History of Missouri*, 72; Gloria Jahoda, *Trail of Tears*, 288-289; Dee Brown, *Hear That Lonesome Whistle Blow*, 37. Also see Walter A. Schroeder, "Populating Missouri, 1804-1821," *Missouri Historical Review* (Columbia: State Historical Society of Missouri, July 2003) xcvii, 4, 263-294; T. R. Fehrenback, *Comanches*, 227; Swanton, esp. 252-254. Robert C. Carriker, *Father Peter John De Smet*, 18, 169-170. See painting by George Catlin, *Cock Turkey, Kickapoo*, (date n.a.)

Joseph B. Herring, "The Kickapoo Indians: Illinois' Earliest Pioneers," Illinois Periodicals Online (Northern Illinois University Libraries) at http://www.lib.niu.edu/ipo/1999/iht0619915.html [October 24, 2006]; George A. Root, ed. "No-ko-aht's Talk: A Kickapoo Chief's Account of a Tribal Journey From Kansas to Mexico and Return in the Sixties," *Kansas Historical Quarterly* (February 1932), vol. 1, no. 2), 153-159, made available from Kansas State Historical Society (Topeka, KS, 2006) at http://www.kshs.org/publicat/khq/1932/32_2_root.htm [August 12, 2006].

Kigene
Samuel G. Drake, *The Aboriginal Races of North America...*, 9-16.

Kikia'los
Swanton, 446; Senator Haugen, "Senate Resolution 8672" (Olympia: Washington State Senate, p. 2002) available at http://www.leg.wa.gov/pub/billinfo/2003-04/senate/8650-8674/8672.pdf#search='Indians%20KikIalLus' [May 17, 2006].

Kiksadi Tlingit
Swanton, 540-543; "Culture and History" (Sitka, AK: Sitka Convention & Visitors Bureau, 2005) at http://www.sitka.org/culture.html; Anna Maxwell, "The Hoonah Indians Visit Sitka," Overland Monthly and Out West Magazine (September 1891), 243-246, from Making of America Journal Articles (Ann Arbor, MI: University of Michigan, n.d.) at http://www.hti.umich.edu/cgi/t/text/pageviewer-idx?c=moajrnl;cc=moajrnl;rgn=full%20text;idno=ahj1472.2-18.105;didno=ahj1472.2-18.105;node =ahj1472.2-18.105%3A2;view=image;seq=0249 [August 15, 2006].

Kilatika
Swanton, 237-240.

Killasthokle
Swanton, 418.

Killawat
Samuel G. Drake, *The Aboriginal Races of North America...*, 9-16.

Kiowa
Mildred P. Mahyall, *The Kiowas*; T. R. Fehrenbach, *Comanches*, 78, 116, 135, 245-247; William Y. Chalfant, *Cheyennes and Horse Soldiers*, 242, 283; Swanton, esp. 294-296. Also, Glenn Welker, "Kiowa Literature" (1998) at http://www.indians.org/welker/kiowa.htm; Virginia Haase, "Kiowa" (Mankato: Minnesota State University, 2003) at http://www.mnsu.edu/emuseum/cultural/northamerica/kiowa.html; "Kiowa," Texas Before History (Austin: University of Texas, 2005) at http://www.texasbeyondhistory.net/plateaus/peoples/kiowa.html; Mildred P. Mayhall, "Kiowa Indians," *Handbook of Texas Online* (Austin, TX: Texas State Historical Association and University of Texas, 2001) at http://www.tsha. utexas.edu/handbook/online/articles/view/KK/bmk10.html [September 9, 2006]. George Catlin, *North American Indians* (Penguin ed.), to Kiowa, 334, 337, 338, 339; to Kioway, 296, 339, 340, 341.

On the Buffalo War, see James L. Haley, The Buffalo War; also "The Buffalo War" (Washington, DC: Public Broadcasting Service) at http://www.pbs.org/buffalowar/ and "Buffalo Management 'Montana-Style'" (Buffalo FieldCampaign, 1996-2006) at http://home.earthlink.net/~the_heyoka/menu.html [April 8, 2006].

Kiowa Apache
Swanton, 296-297; William R. Nester, *The Arikara War*, 15, 16, 17; T. R. Fehrenbach, *Comanches*, 464-465 etc.; John Upton Terrell, The Plains Apache, 18-19, 24-26. Also see J. Gilbert McAllister and H. Allen Anderson, "Kiowa Apache Indians," *Handbook of Texas Online* (Austin, TX: Texas State Historical Association and University of Texas, 2001) at http://www.tsha.utexas.edu/handbook/online/articles/view/KK/bmk11. html [September 9, 2006].

Kitanemuk
Swanton, 496-497.

Kitchigamich
Reuben Gold Thwaites, ed., "Kitchigamich," *The Jesuit Relations and Allied Documents*, vols. 54, 58, available from Creighton University (Omaha, NE) at http://puffin.creighton.edu/jesuit/relations/relations_59.html [November 4, 2007]; John Gilmary Shea, "The Indian Tribes of Wisconsin," *Collections of the State Historical Society of Wisconsin*, vol. 3. See "Kitchigamick Indians," Dictionary of Wisconsin History" (Madison, WI: Wisconsin Historical Society, 1996-2007) at http://www.wisconsinhistory.org/dictionary/index.asp?action=view&term_id=344& [November 2, 2007].

Klamath
Swanton, 459-461. For the Dokdokwas massacre, see Hamilton Sides, *Blood and Thunder*, 78-81, 85-88; quotes taken from 86, 88. "Perfect Butchery" is also to be found in David Roberts, *A Newer World: Kit Carson, John C. Fremont and the Claiming of the American West* (New York: Simon & Schuster, 2000), 141-162.

Klickitat
Swanton, 424-425; George Catlin, *North American Indians* (Penguin ed.), 385.

Koasati
Swanton, 157-159; T. R. Fehrenback, *Comanches*, 227; Jonathan B Hook, *The Alabama-Coushatta Indians* (College Station: Texas A & M University Press, 1997). Also, Grant Foreman, "Area History" *Chronicles of Oklahoma*, vol. 2, no. 1, March, 1924 (Muskogee, OK: Three Forks

Harbor, 2004) at http://www.threeforksharbor.org/area-history.html [August 3, 2006]. The Three Forks of the Arkansas is the junction of the Verdigris, Grand and Arkansas rivers, about four miles northeast of present Muskogee, Oklahoma.

Julia Kathryn Garrett, "Doctor John Sibley and the Louisiana-Texas Frontier, 1803-1814," *Southwestern Historical Quarterly*, vol. 45, n. 3, made available by the Texas State Historical Association (Austin, TX: University of Texas, 2004) at http://www.tsha.utexas.edu/publications/journals/shq/online/v045/n3/contrib_DIVL8836.html; Howard N. Martin, "Alabama-Coushatta Indians," *Handbook of Texas Online* (Austin, TX: Texas State Historical Association and University of Texas, 1999-2004) at hhttp://www.tsha.utexas.edu/handbook/online/articles/view/AA/bma19.html [August 3, 2006].

Kohuana
Swanton, 353-354.

Kolomi
Swanton, 159, 163.

Konagen
Samuel G. Drake, *The Aboriginal Races of North America...*, 9-16.

"Timeline of Russian-American Relations 18-20th Centuries" (Moscow, Russia: Embassy of the United States) at http://moscow.usembassy.gov/links/print_history.php; Alexander von Humboldt, *Personal Narrative of Travels to the Equinoctial Regions of America During The Year 1799-1804*, vol. 2, 259, available from BookRags at http://www.bookrags.com/ebooks/7014/259.html [August 26, 2006].

Konomihu
Swanton, 497.

Kootenay
Swanton, 392-393. George P. Sanger, ed., *Statutes at Large, Treaties, and Proclamations of the United States of America from December 5, 1859 to March 3, 1863*, vol. XII, 975-979/1443; "Kootenay," *L'Encyclopédie Canadienne* (Fondation Historica du Canada, 2004) at http://www.canadianencyclopedia.ca/index.cfm?PgNm=TCE&Params=A1ARTA0004367 [September 8, 2006].

Kopano
Swanton, 321.

Koroa
Swanton, 187-188.

Koso Shoshoni
Swanton, 405, 497. Also see sources under Shoshoni.

Kuitsh
Swanton, 461-462.

Kusotony
Title 25, Chapter 14, Subchapter XXX, §692 of the U.S. Code.

Kutzadika'a
Thomas C. Fletcher, "Kuzedika'a People" (Lee Vining, CA: Mono Lake Committee, 1996-2006) at http://www.monolake.org/naturalhistory/kutzadikaa.htm; Erik Gauger, "Mono Lake, An Economy of Ecology," Great Basin (Notes from the Road: Travels in City and Country, 2006) at http://www.notesfromtheroad.com/greatbasin/greatbasinmonolake.htm [June 15, 2006].

Kwaiailk
Swanton, 426.

Kwalhioqua
Swanton, 413.

Kwatami
Swanton, 452, 456, 516. "From Southern Oregon Settlers to Siletz Reservation Agent Fairchild," The Oregon History Project (Portland: Oregon Historical Society, 2002) at http://www.ohs.org/education/oregonhistory/historical_records/dspDocument.cfm?doc_ID=00072778-F1A5-1DBE-BB3880B05272FE9F [April 3, 2006].

L'Anse
Robert N. Van Alstine, "Keweenaw Bay Indian Community" (n.a.) at http://www.itcmi.org/thehistorytribal4.html; "Keweenaw Bay Indian Community" (Baraga, MI, updated 2006) at http://www.kbic-nsn.gov/ [April 7, 2006].

La Jolla Luiseño
Phillip M. White, "California Indians and Their Reservations" (San Diego: San Diego State University, updated 2006) at

http://infodome.sdsu.edu/research/guides/calindians/calinddictdl.shtml?print#l; James Mooney, "Mission Indians (of California), Catholic Encyclopedia, vol. X (New York: Robert Appleton Company, 1908; Online Edition, K. Knight, 2003) at http://www.newadvent.org/cathen/10369a.htm [April 3, 2006].

Lac Courte Oreille
Swanton 261.

Lacane

Thomas N. Campbell, "Lacane Indians," *Handbook of Texas Online* (Austin, TX: Texas State Historical Association and University of Texas, 2001) at http://www.tsha.utexas.edu/handbook/online/articles/view/LL/bml1.html [September 9, 2006].

Lacopsele

Herbert E. Bolton, "The Founding of the Missions on the San Gabriel River, 1745-1749," *Southwestern Historical Quarterly*, vol. 17, no. 4, 323-378, SHQ Online at http://www.tsha.utexas.edu/publications/journals/shq/online/v017/n4/article_1.html [May 24, 2006].

Laguna Pueblo

Swanton 332-334, 339-340. "Laguna Pueblo," *New Mexico Magazine*, April 2006 (Santa Fe, NM), vol. 84, no. 4, available at http://www.nmmagazine.com/NMGUIDE/laguna.html [April 7, 2006].

Lakota

Jacob Lindley's Account of the Quaker Expedition to Detroit 1793," Clark Historical Library (Mount Pleasant, MI: Central Michigan University,
modified: 05/05/2006) at http://clarke.cmich.edu/detroit/lindleyquakerexp.htm; "Hutchins: A Comparison of the Number of Fighting Men " (1764), available from the Ohio Valley-Great Lakes Ethnohistory Archives: The Miami Collection (Bloomington, IN: Glenn Black Laboratory of Archaeology and Trustees of Indiana University, 1996-2001) at http://www.gbl.indiana.edu/archives/miamis15/M64_1a.html; "Lakota Archive" (Bornali Halder, 2002) at http://www.lakotaarchives.com/sitemap.html; "The Teton Sioux (Lakota)" (Arcata, CA: Humbolt State University, n.d.) at http://www.humboldt.edu/~wrd1/legacyte.htm [July 21, 2006].

For the Fight for the Powder River Country, see Robert M. Utley, *The Lance and the Shield*, 71, 75, 77-78, 82-83; David Dary, *The Oregon Trail*, 291, 292, 297-299, 300, 302. For the Fetterman Fight, see Joseph M. Marshall, III, *The Journey of Crazy Horse*, 144-151, 188-189; George Bird Grinell, *The Fighting Cheyennes*, 230-244.

For Hayfield and Wagon Box Fights, see Joseph M. Marshall, *The Journey of Crazy Horse*, 153; David Haward Bain, *Empire Express*, 385-386; Robert M. Utley, *The Lance and the Shield*, 75; David Dary, *The Oregon Trail*, 300. Also see Jerome A. Greene, "Hayfield Fight: A Reappraisal of a Neglected Action," *Montana Magazine* (Autumn 1972), 30-43; and Roy E. Appleman, "The Wagon Box Fight," *Great Western Indian Fights* (Lincoln: University of Nebraska Press, 1960).

For Wounded Knee, see Dee Brown, *Bury My Heart at Wounded Knee*, esp. 439-446; quote taken from p. 444; Robert M. Utley, *The Lance and the Shield*, 308-309, 311; Kevin Fedarko, "'This Ride Is About Our Future,'" *Parade* (New York: Parade Publications, May 16, 2004), pp. 4-7 plus cover; Thomas H. Tibbles, "Wounded Knee: An Eyewitness Remembers," *Omaha World Herald*, January 11, 1976 (Tibbles' account first appeared in the *Omaha World-Herald* on December 30, 1890, the day following the disaster.) Also, Richard W. Hill, Sr., "Wounded Knee, A Wound That Won't Heal: Did the Army Attempt To Coverup the Massacre of Prisoners of War?" (1999) at http://www.dickshovel.com/hill.html [September 9, 2006]. See Wounded Knee Reparations Hearings (1938); *U.S. v. Con. Wounded Knee Cases* (1974).

On the White Buffalo, see Robert M. Utley, *The Lance and the Shield* 1-2, 8, 30-31, 76; "The Seven Sacred Rites" (Lakota Teaching Project, n.d.) at http://mreid.com/lakota/rit.htm [September 8, 2006]. Broken Arrow tribe from Keith Algier, *The Crow and the Eagle: A Tribal History from Lewis & Clark to Custer*, 73.

Lassik
Swanton, 498.

Latgawa
Swanton, 462, 469; Stephenie Flora, "Northwest Indian Tribes" (The Oregon Territory and Its Pioneers, n.d.) at http://www.oregonpioneers.com/tribe.htm [August 3, 2006].

Liaywa
Stephenie Flora, "Northwest Indians" (The Oregon Territory And Its Pioneers, 1998-2005) at http://www.oregonpioneers.com/tribe.htm [August 28, 2006].

Limita
H. Allen Anderson, "Limita Indians," *Handbook of Texas Online* (Austin, TX: Texas State Historical Association and University of Texas, 2001) at http://www.tsha.utexas.edu/handbook/online/articles/LL/bml2.html [October 4, 2006].

Lipan Apache
Swanton, esp. 322-323. James L. Haley, *Apaches*, esp. 9, 24, 27-28, 34-36, 39, 40, 185, 240, 321; T. R. Fehrenbach, *Comanches*, 138-139, 228,428.; Lipan Apache Band of Texas (Moulton, TX, n.d.) at http://hometown.aol.com/lipanapachetx/lipan.html; "Lipan Apache Nation," (El Mesteno Magazine, 1997-2006) at http://el-mesteno.com/stories/0012lipan.html [October 4, 2006].

Lohim

Swanton, 379, 462. Kathyrn Lee, "Indians of Eastern Oregon" (Washington, D.C.: National Park Service, last updated 11/02) at http://www. nps.gov/archive/joda/lee/lee1-2.htm [December 30, 2007]. From Wilbur A. Davis, *Survey of Historic and Prehistoric Resources in the John Day Fossil Beds National Monument* (May 1977), Appendix I. "Northern Paiute" (Four Directions Press, 2007) at http://www.fourdir.com/ northern%20paiute.htm [December 30, 2007].

Long Island, New York, Indian Tribes

"Treaty with the New York Indians, January 15, 1838, Buffalo Creek, New York; Long Island Indians and The Early Settlers" (Long Island, NY: Long Island Genealogy, n.d.) at http://www.longislandgenealogy.com/indians.html [Jun e 25, 2006].

Lower Pend d'Oreilles

Swanton, 399-400.

Luckiamute Kalapuya

Swanton, 454, 463.

Luckkarso

Swanton, 472 ; *Lewis, Meriwether, 1774-1809 and Clark, William, 1770-1838. History of the Expedition Under the Command of Captains Lewis and Clark, to the Sources of the Missouri...* 2 Vols. (Philadelphia: Bradford and Inskeep, 1814) from the University of Cincinnati Digital Press (Cincinnati, OH, n.d.) at http://www.ucdp.uc.edu/lewisandclark/biddle/volume2_pt3.pdf [August 7, 2006]. See Vol. 2, 473-473, Items Nos. 27 and 28. Also, "The People Lost" (Oyate noni) at http://members.ij.net/theshop/tribes/data.html [August 8, 2006].

Luiseño Peoples

Swanton, 498-499. "The People" (Temecula, CA: Pechanga Band of Luiseño Indians, 2006) at http://www.pechanga-nsn.gov/page?pageId=8 [April 2, 2006].

For the Pauma Massacre, see Leland E. Bibb, "William Marshall, 'The Wickedest Man in California,' A Reappraisal," *Journal of San Diego History* (San Diego Historical Society, Winter 1976), vol. 22, no.1 at ttp://www.sandiegohistory.org/journal/76winter/marshall.htm and Richard Griswold del Castillo, "The U.S.-Mexican War in San Diego, 1846-1847: Loyalty and Resistance," *Journal of San Diego History* (2003), vol. 49, no. 1, at http://www.sandiegohistory.org/journal/v49-1/war.htm; For the Garra Revolt, see Richard F. Pourade, "Garra Uprising," *The History of San Diego*, Chapter 9, available from the San Diego Historical Society at http://www.sandiegohistory.org/books/pourade/silver/silverchapter10. htm#garra [November 20, 2006].

Lukawi

Samuel G. Drake, *The Aboriginal Races of North America...*, 9-16.

Lukton

Samuel G. Drake, *The Aboriginal Races of North America...*, 9-16.

Lumbee

"Lumbee Tribe" (Pembroke, NC: Lumbee Tribe of North Carolina, 2000-2004) at http://www.lumbeetribe.com/ ... [September 10, 2006].

Lummi

Swanton, 427. "Lhaq'Tmish – The People of the Sea" (Bellingham, WA: Lummi Nation, 2004) at http://www.lummi-nsn.org/ [September 10, 2006].

Macapiras

Swanton, 122, 133.

Machapunga

Swanton, 81.

Machecou

Shirley Christian, *Before Lewis and Clark*, 142; Thomas Jefferson, Query XI, *Notes on the State of Virginia* (1781).

Machepungo

Swanton, 62, 73, 74, 78, 80, 81, 86, 88; Edmond S. Morgan, *American Slavery, American Freedom*, 52n25.

Mahican Group

Russell Shorto, *The Island in the Center of the World*, 46-47, 51, 87, 102, 139; J. Fenimore Cooper, *The Last of the Mohicans or A Narrative of 1757* (Chicago: Rand, McNally & Company, 1826); Swanton, 41-42, 254, 255, 257-258; Edwin G. Burrows & Mike Wallace, *Gotham*, 13, 23; Gloria Jahoda, *Trail of Tears*, 96, 101; "From the Mohican's Land to Mohicanland" (Mohican Press, 1997-2006) at http://www.mohicanpress. com/mo11002.html; also "The Mohicans...Children of the Delaware at http://www.mohicanpress.com/mo08014.html [April 18, 2006].

Maidu

Swanton, 499-502. Also see "Konkow Valley Band of Maidu" (Oroville, CA: Konkow Valley Band of Maidu, updated 2005) at http://www. maidu.com/maidu/index.html; Raymond G. Gordon, Jr., ed. "Maidu, Northwest," *Ethnologies: Languages of the World*, Fifteenth edition. (Dallas,

TX: SIL International, 2006) available from SIL online edition (2006) at http://www.ethnologue.com/show_language.asp?code=mjd [May 21, 2006].

For the Maidu Massacre, see H. W. Brands, *The Age of Gold*, 32-34; Kevin Starr, *California, A History*, 65-70; Larry McMurtry, *Oh What a Slaughter*, who references David Roberts, *A Newer World: Kit Carson, John C. Fremont and the Claiming of the American West* (New York: Simon & Schuster, 2000). Also, Edward D. Castillo, "Short Overview of California Indian History," (Sacramento: California Native American Heritage Commission, 1998) at http://www.ceres.ca.gov/nahc/califindian.html [March 1, 2007]. Hampton Sides in *Blood and Thunder* makes to mention of the incident

Maidu, Northeastern
Swanton, 499-502.

Maidu, Northwestern
Swanton, 499-502.

Makah
Swanton, 427-428, 433, 587, 588; Mildred P. Mayhall, *The Kiowas*, 27.

Maliseet
Swanton, 15, 16, 17, 578-579, 580, 591. "Native Languages of the Americas: Maliseet (Malecite, Malecites, Malisit)" (St. Paul MN: Native Languages of the Americas, n.a.) at http://www.native-languages.org/maliseet.htm [April 11, 2006].

"About Us" (Littleton, ME: Houlton Band of Maliseet Indians, n.d.) at http://www.maliseets.com/; "Maliseet Tobique Reservation" (Edmundston, CA: Université de Moncton, n.d.) at http://www.cuslm.ca/madvic/emaleci.htm; Krista Wright, "Woodstock First Nation's History" (Woodstock First Nation, n.d.) at http://www.woodstockfirstnation.com/wfnhistory.htm [August 5, 2006].

Mamekoting
Swanton, 48-55.

Manahoac
Swanton, 61-62.

Manamoyick
Nathaniel Philbrick, *Mayflower*, 137-138; "Orleans, Barstable County" (MA Department of Housing and Community Development) at http://www.mass.gov/dhcd/iprofile/224.pdf [July 17, 2006]; Caleb Johnson, "Biography of Tisquantum (Squanto)" (MayflowerHistory.com, 1994-2006) at http://www.Mayflowerhistory.com/History/BiographyTisquantum.php [July 17, 2006].

Mandan
Gloria Jahoda, *Trail of Tears*, 173-187; Stephen E. Ambrose, *Undaunted Courage*, 178-181, 182-201; Bernard De Voto, ed., *The Journals of Lewis and Clark*, 3, 50-86 passim, 92-93, 214, 215, 216, 450-461 passim, 466; Swanton 276-278; Thomas Jefferson, "To the Wolf and People of the Mandan Nation," December 30, 1806, Writings (New York: Library of America, 1984), 564-566; George Catlin, *North American Indians* (Penguin ed.), esp. 73-97, 181-184; "polite and friendly" from p. 89; "peculiar" from p. 181. On their ancestors being White and the connection to the Welsh Indians, see Catlin, pp. 89-90, 181-184, esp. the Appendix, "Extinction of the Mandans," with an extended section on "The Welsh Colony," 486-497. Also, "La Vérendrye History" (La Vérendrye Trail Association, 1997-2000) at http://laverendryetrail.mb.ca/history.html [September 6, 2006]. See painting by George Catlin, *Four Bears (Ma-to-toh-pe), Chief of the Mandan*, 1832.

Manhahoac
Swanton, 61-62, 63, 64, 70, 73, 74.

Manhasset
Edwin G. Burrows & Mike Wallace, *Gotham*, 37.

Manhatan
Swanton 44-48 (Wappinger); 48-55 (Delaware); Edwin G. Burrows & Mike Wallace, *Gotham*, 23-24; Russell Shorto, *The Island in the Center of the World*, 33, 34, 36, 49-50, 51, 54, 58, 65, 75-81, 87, 88, 108, 114-117, 120, 123-127, 163, 225, 277-283; 337n163; Alanson Skinner, *The Indians of Manhattan Island and Vicinity* (New York: American Museum of Natural History, 1909) available from Get NY! at http://www.adsny.com/nyindian/nyindian.html...[April 12, 2006].

Andrew Meyers, *New York City and the American Dream* (New York: Columbia University Continuing Education, n.d.) at http://www.ecfs.org/Projects/Fieldston57/sphsmeyersnyc/SPHS_NYC_EncounterDBQ.html; "A Virtual Tour of New Netherlands," (Albany, NY: New Netherland Project, 2001-2002) at http://www.nnp.org/newvtour/regions/Hudson/tribes.html; J. Alfieri et allis, "The Lenapes: A Study of Hudson Valley Indians" (Poughkeepsie, NY: Marist College, n.d.) at http://www.ulster.net/~hrmm/halfmoon/lenape/effects.htm; "The Hudson River" (Yonkers, NY: Beczak Environmental Education Center, n.d.) at http://www.beczak.org/home_page.htm; "Origin of the Word Manhattan" (New York: *Gotham* Center, New York City History , 2004) at http://www.Gothamcenter.org/discussions/viewthread.cfm?ID=126&ForumID=33; East Harlem History" (New York: East Harlem.com, 1999-2004) at http://www.upper-manhattan.com/history.htm [May 8, 2006].

Nicholas Visscher, Novi Belgii Novaque Angliae, 1656. Visscher's 1656 map is the best known map of New Netherland. It is largely based on a map published by Joannes Janssonius in 1651, which in turn borrowed heavily from the Blaeu map of 1635. The map is available from the State University of New York at http://www.sunysb.edu/libmap/Visscher. htm [May 8, 2006].

Manso
Swanton, 325, 334.

Maricopa
Swanton, 354-356; Thomas Edwin Farish, *The History of Arizona*, vol. vii, chp. 13.

Marsapeague
"History of Queens County" (New York: W.W. Munsell & Co., 1882), 144-192, available from Borough of Brooklyn, New York (n.d.) at http://www.bklyn-genealogy-info.com/Queens/history/hempstead.html; Steve Wick, "Untangling a Myth Europeans apparently mistook Indian place names for tribal labels," Long Island, Our Story (Newsday, Inc., 2006) at http://www.newsday.com/community/guide/lihistory/ny-history-hs207a,0,6043583.story [August 14, 2006].

Marshewtooc
Fred Willard, "Trade Items as Transfer of Money," November 2002, made available by the Lost Colony Center for Science and Research (Eastern Carolina University) at http://lost-colony.com/trade.html [June 12, 2006].

Mascoutin
Swanton, 247, 254; Gloria Jahoda, *Trail of Tears*, 288; Reuben Gold Thwaites, ed., "Kitchigamich," *The Jesuit Relations and Allied Documents*, vols. 54, 58, available from Creighton University (Omaha, NE) at http://puffin.creighton.edu/jesuit/relations/relations_59.html [November 4, 2007]; Jon Gilmary Shea, "Indian Tribes of Wisconsin" (1857) published in 1904 by the State Historical Society of Wisconsin (Madison) from the Collections of the State Historical Society of Wisconsin edited by Lyman Copeland Draper and made available to Waupaca County, Wisconsin, by Paula Vaugh (© 1999-2007) at http://www.rootsweb.com/~wiwaupac/NatAm/Ind1.htm [November 4, 2007]. Also see "Illinois," Frederick Webb Hodge, *Handbook of American Indians North of Mexico*,; "American Indian Tribes of Illinois" (Illinois State Museum, 2002-2004) at http://www.museum.state.il.us... /muslink/nat_amer/post/; "Mascoutens Indians," Catholic Encyclopedia at http://www.newadvent.org/... cathen/09768b.htm; "Mascouten Indian Tribe History" (Access Genealogy, 2004-2006) at http://www.accessgenealogy.com/native/tribes/... pottawatomie/mascoutenshist.htm [October 11, 2006];"Timeline of Wisconsin history, 1700-1749" (Madison, WI: Wisconsin Historical Society, 1996-2007) at http://www.wisconsinhistory.org/dictionary/index.asp?action=view&term_id=10477&search_term=timeline [November 5, 2007].

David Schweingruber, "Indian Statue in Muscatine, Iowa," *Sociology of Monuments* (Ames, IA: Iowa State University), September 15, 2004, available online at www.iastate.edu/~f2004.soc.134/134lecture10(sep15).pdf; James W. Loewen "Muscatine, Iowa, Honors Red Men Who Can't Join...," *Lies My Teacher Told Me* (The New Press, February, 1995), online from University of Vermont (1997-2006) at http://www.uvm.edu... /~jloewen/slideshowdisplay.php?slide=5 [November 4, 2007]. Red Men quote from "The Improved Order of Red Men" (Waco, TX, 1998-2007) at http://www.redmen.org/ [November 5, 2007]. The Red Men claim dependency from the patriotic colonial societies that patterned themselves after the governing structure of the Iroquois Confederacy and adopted " the customs and terminology of Native Americans as a basic part of the fraternity."

Masequetooc
Fred Willard, "Trade Items as Transfer of Money," November 2002, made available by the Lost Colony Center for Science and Research (Eastern Carolina University) at http://lost-colony.com/trade.html [June 12, 2006].

Mashpee Wampanoag
Nathaniel Philbrick, *Mayflower*, 349, 353 (for Mashpee Revolt). Also see "History" (Mashpee, MA: Mashpee Wampanoag Tribal Council, n.d.) at http://www.mashpeewampanoagtribe.com/History.htm; "Mashpee," Massachusetts Pathways (Maxm Consulting, 1996) at http://www.oneweb.com/mashtown/guide/pathways.html [September 3, 2006]; "Mashpee Yesteryear" (Mashpee, MA, 2001) at http://www.mashpeeyesteryear.net/; Sean Gonsalves, "Tribe Strives to Pass on Wampanoag Culture," Canku Ota Online Newsletter, (June 29, 2002), no. 64 (Paul C. Barry, 1999-2002) at http://www.turtletrack.org/Issues02/Co06292002/CO_06292002_Mashpee_Wampanoag.htm [November 9, 2006].

On William Apess, see esp. Daniel K. Richter, *Facing East from Indian Country*, 237-253, 298n3; Nathan Philbrick, Mayflower, 353. Also see Thompson Gale, "William Apess," *Encyclopedia of World Biography* (Thompson Corporation, 2005-2006) available from BookRags at http://www.bookrags.com/biography/william-apess/ and Gordon Sayre, "William Apess," abridged, *The Literary Encyclopedia*, (The Literary Dictionary Company Limited, 2001) at http://www.litencyc.com/php/speople.php?rec=true&UID=127 [October 11, 2007]. In addition, Paul P. Reuben, "Chapter 3: William Apes " PAL: Perspectives in American Literature- A Research and Reference Guide (Turlock, CA: California State University, Stanislaus, n.d.) at http://web.csustan.edu/english/reuben/pal/chap3/apess.html, including Aaron Garcia, " William Apes or William Apess (Pequot) (1798-1839): A Brief Biography" [October 12, 2007].

Massachusett
Swanton, 19-20, 23, 24, 27; Nathaniel Philbrick, *Mayflower*, 49, 116, 130-131, 140-141, 146-155; "Massachuset Indian Chiefs and Leaders" (AccessGenealogy, 2000-2004) at http://www.accessgenealogy.com/native/tribes/massachuset/massachusetchief.htm [July 27, 2006]. Sources: Drake's *Indians of North America*; *Handbook of American Indians*, 1906.

Massapequa
Edwin G. Burrows & Mike Wallace, *Gotham*, 5, 8, 37, 59, 67, 100, 144, 147, 219, 254, 329, 391, 718, 751, 854.

Mathlanob
Samuel G. Drake, *The Aboriginal Races of North America...*, 9-16.

Mato Pomo
Swanton, 510.

Mattabesic
Swanton, 33, 46; Ruttenber, *Indian Tribes of the Hudson River* (1872); "Wappinger Towns and Villages" (AccessGenealogy, 200-2005) at http://www.accessgenealogy.com/native/tribes/delaware/wappingertowns.htm#Manhattan. Source: *Handbook of American Indians*, 1906. Also, S. Clark Pickens, "Windsor Indian History" (Windsor, CN) at http://members.tripod.com/SCPickens/indians.html [September 9, 2006].

Mattapanient
Swanton, 57-59.

Mattaponi
Swanton, 66-71.

Mattole
Swanton, 501-502.

Mayeye
Thomas N. Campbell, "Mayeye Indians," *Handbook of Texas Online* (Austin, TX: Texas State Historical Association and University of Texas, 2001) at http://www.tsha.utexas.edu/handbook/online/articles/MM/bmm22.html [May 24, 2006].

Mdewahaton
"Shakopee Mdewakanton" (Prior Lake: MN: Shakopee Mdewakanton Sioux Community, 2006) at http://www.shakopeedakota.org/ and "Mendota Mdewakanton" (Mendota, MN: Mendota Mdewakanton Dakota Community, 1998-2006) at http://www.mendotadakota.org/ [April 6, 2006].

Mdewakanton Sioux
Barbara Feezor Buttes, "Shakopee Mdewakanton Sioux Community Enrollment Problems and the Minnesota Mdewakanton Sioux Identity" (Maquah Publications) at http://www.maquah.net/press/Buttes_letter.html [September 11, 2006]. Published in the *Native American Press / Ojibwe News*, September 27, 2002.

Meherrin
Swanton, 62-63, 65,73, 82

Mengakonkia
Swanton, 237-240.

Menominee
David R. M. Beck, *The Struggle for Self-Determination: History of the Menominee Indians*; Swanton, 254-255; Gloria Jahoda, *Trail of Tears*, 92-93, 98-99, 288. See painting by George Catlin, *Ko-Man-I-O-Haw, Little Whale, a Brave* (date n.a.)

Mento
Jean Delanglez, "The Jolliet Lost Map of the Mississippi," *Mid-America, An Historical Review* (Chicago, IL: Loyola University, April 1946), vol. 28 (New Series, vol. 17), no. 2, 67-143, esp. 109, 134-135. Also, Henri Tonti Letters, *Mid-America, An American Review* (Chicago, IL: Loyola University, 1939), vol. 21, 229, n36, available from the Ohio Valley-Great Lakes Ethnohistory Archives: The Miami Collection (Bloomington, IN: Glenn Black Laboratory of Archaeology and Trustees of Indiana University, 1996, updated October 26, 2000) at http://www.gbl.indiana.edu/archives/miamis4/M17-03_8c.html [July 2, 2006].

Mescalero Apache
Swanton, 327-330; James L. Haley, *Apaches*, 9, 30, 31, 49, 81, 185, 187-188; C. L. Sonnichsen, *The Mescalero Apaches*; O.R., ser. 1, vol. 15, bk. 21, 580, and ser. 1, vol. 26/1, bk. 41, 629.

Mespat
David Hartman and Barry Lewis, "History," A Walk through Queens (New York: Educational Broadcasting Corporation, 2004) at http://www.thirteen.org/queens/history.html; Eric P. Robinson, "Maspeth" (New York: Chamber of Commerce of the Borough of Queens, 2006) athttp://www.queenschamber.org/QueensInfo/NeighborhoodPages/maspeth.html [May 12, 2006].

Meteharta
See Hidatsa.

Methow
Swanton, 428.

Miami
Swanton, 237-240; Eugene Morrow Violette, *History of Missouri*, 69; Washington Irving, *Life and Times of Washington*, 691; Bert Anson, *The Miami Indians*. For Fallen Timbers, see Alan Taylor, *The Divided Ground*, 281, 287-288; Richard Brookhiser, *Founding Father*, 88. For St. Clair's Defeat, see Taylor, 249, 259, 267, 277. Also see "Harmar's Defeat," at http://www.ohiohistorycentral.org/entry.php?rec=505 and "St. Clair's Defeat," at ...rec=557, respectively, from Ohio History Central (Columbus: Ohio Historical Society, 2006) [November 7, 2006]. Also,

Richard Battin, "Early America's Bloodiest Battle" (Tampa Bay, FL: Archiving Early America, n.d.) at http://www.earlyamerica.com/review/summer/battle.html [November 7, 2006].

"Miami Indians," Ohio's Historic Indians: Tribes (Columbus: Ohio Historical Society, 2006) at http://www.ohiohistorycentral.org/entry.php?rec=606; Pamela J. Bennett, ed., "Finding Our Way Home: The Great Lakes Woodland People," *The Indiana Historian* (September 2001), no. 7052, p.12, available at http://www.statelib.lib.in.us/www/ihb/amerindians/findourwayhome.pdf [September 7, 2006].

Chas. Whittlesey, "Early Maps of the Lake Country," *Early History of Cleveland, Ohio...*, (Cleveland, OH: Fairbanks, Benedict & Co., 1867), 81-85, at http://web.ulib.csuohio.edu/ebooks/whittlesey/Chapter3.html [July 22, 2006]; James Mooney, "Miami Indians," *The Catholic Encyclopedia Online* (K. Knight, 2005) at http://www.newadvent.org/cathen/10271a.htm [August 21, 2006].

For the Treaty of Greenville, see Department of the Army, *American Military History*, 111-114, 121-122; Richard Norton Smith, Patriarch: George Washington and the New American Nation (Boston: Houghton Mifflin Company, 1993), 218-219; John R. Alden, *George Washington, A Biography* (New York: Wings Books), 258-259. "Treaty of Greeneville (1795)," Ohio's Historic Indians (Columbus: Ohio Historical Society, 1998-2004) at http://www.ohiohistorycentral.org/entry.php?rec=1418 and related; "Michikinikwa (Little Turtle)," Fallen Timbers Battlefield Archeological Project (Tiffin, OH: Heidelberg College, n.d.) at http://www.heidelberg.edu/FallenTimbers/FTbio-LittleTurtle.html; "Little Turtle - War Chief" (Summit Webs Internet Solutions, 2000-2003) at http://littleturtle.net/warchief.shtml and related [September 10, 2006]; Marcy Kaptur, Representative (9th District), "Fallen Timbers Battlefield," Ohio: Local Legacies (Washington, DC: Library of Congress Bicentennial, 2000) at http://lcweb.loc.gov/bicentennial/propage/OH/oh-9_h_kaptur5.html [September 10, 2006].

Allen L. Potts "Northwest Territory," *The History Of Union County Ohio*, (Salt Lake City, Utah: Heritage Pursuit, updated April 28, 2004) at http://www.heritagepursuit.com/Union/UnPIch1.htm; "Ohio Map [circa 1822]," Ohio Memory Project (Columbus, OH: Ohio Historical Society, 2003) at http://worlddmc.ohiolink.edu/OMP/NewDetails?oid=1980862&fieldname=xml&results=10&sort=title&searchstatus=1&hits=3&searchmark=0&searchstring=Ohio+Map+1822&searchtype=kw&format=list&count=2; "Village of Riverlea History" (Riverlea, OH, 2003) at http://www.riverleaohio.com/residentinformation/aboutus/history/treatyofgreenville.htm [September 10, 2006]. Site includes full text of treaty and photograph of segment of boundary line.

Mical
Swanton, 428.

Michigamea
Swanton, 212, 213, 241-242. "Historic Diaries: Marquette and Jolliet," (Madison: Wisconsin Historical Society, 1996-2006) at http://www.wisconsinhistory.org/diary/001395.asp; Meredith and Jim Fay, "'Michigamea' entry from Hodge's *Handbook* (Prairie Nations, supported by University of Illinois School of Library and Information Sciences) at http://www.prairienet.org/prairienations/mich.htm [June 17, 2006].

Michigan Potawatomi
Swanton, 297-298, 302

Micmac
Swanton, 579-581; Daniel K. Richter, *Facing East from Indian Country*, 26-27, 37, 40, 65. Also, "Brief Synopsis of the History of the Aroostook Band of Micmacs" (Presque Isle, ME: Aroostook Band of Micmacs , 2003-2006) at http://www.micmac-nsn.gov/html/history.html; Laura Redish, dir., "Native Languages of the Americas: Mi'kmaq—Mi'kmawi'simk, Mi'kmaw, Micmac, Mikmaq" (St. Paul MN: Native Languages of the Americas, n.d.) at http://www.native-languages.org/mikmaq.htm; Deborah Champlain, "Northeast Tribes: The Micmac" (Rhode Island: Northeast Wigwam, 1998-2000) at http://www.newigwam.com/hmicmac.html [September 9, 2006].

Mikasuki
Swanton, 107 and 129 (Chiaha branch); 133-134; "accompanied," 301. "Miccosukee Seminole Nation" (Miccosukee Seminole Nation.com (MSN), 2000-2006) at http://www.miccosukeeseminolenation.com/; Aimee Reist and John Nemmers, "Seminole Indians Miccosukee Tribe" (Florida State University, 1998) at http://www.fsu.edu/~speccoll/miccosuk/micccont.htm; Laura Redish, Director, "Miccosukee Indian Language (Mikasuki, Hitchiti)" (Native Languages of the Americas website © 1998-2007) at http://www.native-languages.org/mikasuki.htm; Jerry Wilkinson, "History of the Seminoles," *Keys Historeum* (Historical Preservation Society of the Upper Keys) at http://www.keyshistory.org/seminolespage1.html [October 17-18, 2007].

Mikonotunne
Swanton, 472-473.

Miluk
Swanton, 459, 463.

Mindawarcarton Sioux
John Freeman et al., "no. 2971. Clark, William," *American Indian Manuscripts*, (American Philosophical Society, 1999) at http://www.amphilsoc.org/library/guides/indians/info/pl.htm [August 10, 2006].

A. T. Andreas, *History of the State of Nebraska* (Chicago: The Western Historical Company, 1882), Part 5, "Lewis and Clark Expedition," available from Kansas Collection Books, produced by Gary Martens and Laurie Saikin, at http://www.kancoll.org/books/andreas_ne/history/erlyhst-p5.html; "Naming of Minneapolis," Early History (Minneapolis, MN: Minneapolis Public Library) at http://www.mplib.org/history/eh4.asp [September 21, 2006].

Mingo

Deborah Johnson, "Mingo Indians" (Elkins, WV: Allegheny Regional Family History Society, mod. March 14, 2004) at http://www.swcp.com/~dhickman/notes/mingo.html; "Mingo Indians," the Pages of Shades–Native Americans (n.a.) at http://www.angelfire.com/realm/shades/nativeamericans/mingo.htm [September 8, 2006], reportedly taken in part from "West Virginia," Microsoft Encarta Online Encyclopedia 2001 (Seattle, WA: Microsoft Corporation, 1997-2001).

"West Virginia County Histories: Barbour County History," County Commissioners' Association of West Virginia (Morgantown, WV : West Virginia University Department of Political Science, n.d.) at http://www.polsci.wvu.edu/wv/history.html; "Mingo Indians," Ohio's Historic Indians (Columbus: Ohio Historical Society, 1998-2004) at http://www.ohiohistorycentral.org/entry.php?rec=608 [September 8, 2006].

Minisink

Swanton, 48-55. Also, Laura Redish, dir., "Munsee Delaware: Minsi, Muncee, Muncey" (St. Paul MN: Native Languages of the Americas) at http://www.native-languages.org/munsee.htm; Morton L. Montgomery, *History of Berks County* (1886), Ch. III, pp. 56-64, available from Accessible Archives (n.a.) at http://www.accessible.com/amcnty/PA/berks/Berks3.htm; "Ramapough Mountain" (New Jersey Department of State, 1996-2001) at http://www.state.nj.us/state/american_indian/mo/; "A Brief History of Oakland, New Jersey" (Oakland, NJ, n.d.) at http://www.oakland-nj.org/history.html; "Semi-Centennial, The Borough of South Bethlehem, Pennsylvania Souvenir History" (Bethlehem Area Public Library), 8-9, at http://www.bapl.org/lochist/comlife/landm/semcent/sbsc008-009.html; "Delaware Indian Tribe" (Kansas Genealogy, 2002-2006) at http://www.kansasgenealogy.com/indians/delaware_indian_tribe.htm; Daniel C. Hyde, "What Indians lived in Potter County?," *Potter County History* (Potter County, PA, 1996-2005) at http://www.eg.bucknell.edu/~hyde/potter/history3.html [August 10, 2006].

Mishikhwutmetunne

Swanton, 463-464.

Mishongnovi

Swanton, 352.

Mississauga Chippewa

Alan Taylor, *The Divided Ground*, 109, 120-121, 128-133, 263, 330, 340-344, 346-347, 350, 398-399. Also, "The Mississaugas of the New Credit [River] First Nation, Past & Present" (Hagersville, Ontario: Mississaugas of the New Credit First Nation) at http://www.newcreditfirstnation.com/past2.htm#indians; "Treaty Made November 15, 1923 Between His Majesty The King And The Mississauga Indians Of Rice Lake, Mud Lake, Scugog Lake And Alderville" (Treaty Policy Directorage, 2004-2006) at http://www.ainc-inac.gc.ca/pr/trts/trmis_e.html; "Home of the Mississauga Ojibway" (Curve Lake First Nation, 2001) at http://click.nativeamericans.com/curvelakefn.com [August 23, 2006].

Mississippi Chippewa

"Historical Narrative" (Sandy Lake Band of Ojibwe, 2005) at http://www.sandylakeojibwe.org/hist2.htm; also, "Struggle for Recognition" at http://www.sandylakeojibwe.org/recog.htm; Paul Peter Buffalo, "Early Life at Leech Lake" (Duluth, MN: University of Minnesota Duluth, 1997-2006) at http://www.d.umn.edu/cla/faculty/troufs/Buffalo/PB01.html [August 10, 2006].

MISSISSIPPI RIVER

Jean Delanglez, "The Jolliet Lost Map of the Mississippi," *Mid-America, An Historical Review*, April 1946, vol. 28 (new vol. 17), no. 2, 67-144;
Ray Samuel, Leonard V. Huber, and Warren C. Ogden, *Tales of the Mississippi* (New York: Hastings House, 1955), 1-9; Nicolas de La Salle; William C. Foster, ed.; Johanna S. Warren, translator, *The La Salle Expedition on the Mississippi River: A Lost Manuscript of Nicolas de La Salle, 1682* (Austin, TX: Texas State Historical Association, 2004).

Charles Hudson, *De Soto Working Paper #1: The Uses of Evidence in Reconstructing the Route of the Hernando De Soto Expedition* (Tuscaloosa, AL: Alabama De Soto Commission, University of Alabama State Museum of Natural History, 1987) made available online by the University of Alabama at Tuscaloosa at http://www.as.ua.edu/ant/Mabila/De%20Soto%20Working%20Paper%201%20-%20Hudson.pdf [September 16, 2007]. John Gilmary Shea, *Discovery And Exploration of the Mississippi Valley: With the Original Narratives of Marquette, Allouez, Membré Hennepin, And Anastase Douay* (Albany, NY: Joseph Mcdonough, 2nd ed. 1903).

Muriel H. Wright, "The Naming Of The Mississippi River," *Chronicles of Oklahoma* (Oklahoma City, OK: Oklahoma Historical Society, December 1928), vol. 6, no. 4, available online from OSU Library Electronic Publishing Center (Stillwater, OK, 2001), 529-531, at http://digital.library.okstate.edu/... chronicles/v006/v006p529.html; "The Mississippi River" (Minneapolis-St. Paul, MN: 2007 Twin Cities Tours.) at http://www.twincitiestours.com/info_mississippi_river.html [September 6, 2007].

"Pierre LeMoyne Sieur d'Iberville and the Establishment of Biloxi" (davidg59@datasync.com) at http://www.datasync.com/~davidg... 59/biloxi1.html [September 10, 2007]. From *Pierre LeMoyne d'Iberville's Journals* produced as Richebourg Gaillard McWilliams, ed., *Iberville's Gulf Journals* (Tuscaloosa, AL: University of Alabama Press, 1981).

Luys Hernandez De Biedma, "Relation Of The Conquest Of Florida: Account of the Island of Florida" (1544). Transcription by Jon Muller as translated from the original by Buckingham Smith, made available by Southern Illinois University (Carbondale, IL: Board of Trustees, Southern Illinois University, 2007) at http://www.siu.edu/~anthro/muller/Biedma/Biedma_frame.html [September 11, 2007]. Taken from Edward G. Bourne, ed., *Narratives of the career of Hernando de Soto*, Vol. II (New York: A. S. Barnes, 1904), 3-40. Reprinted by Bourne from Buckingham Smith, *Narratives of the Career of Hernando de Soto in the Conquest of Florida* (New York: Bradford Club, 1866), 230-261. The original Spanish text was first published by Buckingham Smith in *Coleccion de Varios Documentos para la Historia de la Florida y Tierras Adyacentes*. Tomo I. (London, 1857), 47-65.

"Mississippi" and "Louisiana," *Catholic Encyclopedia*, Vols. X and IX (New York: Robert Appleton Company, 1911), New Advent Edition (Kevin Knight, 2007) at http://www.newadvent.org/cathen/10394a.htm and http://www.newadvent.org/cathen/09378a.htm; Lawrence A. Clayton, Vernon James Knight, Jr., Edward C. Moore, translation by John E. Worth *The De Soto Chronicles Volume I: The Expedition of Hernando De Soto to North America 1539-1543* (1994) available from the National Park Service (Washington, DC, 2003) at http://www.nps.gov/archive/... deso/chronicles/Volume1/toc.htm, with Rangel, Elvas, Biedma and Inca Indian Proper Names tabulated by John R. Swanton, originally published in the *Final Report of the De Soto Expedition Commission* (Smithsonian Institution Press, 1939), 499-502, [September 14, 2007]; Donald E. Sheppard , "The Final Report of the United States De Soto Expedition Commission [...to locate Hernando de Soto's Conquest Trail]" (Florida History, n.d.) at http://www.floridahistory.com/inset99.html [September 6, 2007]. Also, Christopher Morris, "Finding Louisiana: La Salle's Encounter with the Mississippi River Delta plain" (Falls Church VA: Society for the History of Discoveries 1999-2007) at http://www.sochistdisc.org/2004_articles/morris.htm and "Life & Times of La Salle" (Austin, TX: Texas Historical Commission, n.d.) at http://www.thc.state.tx.us/La Salle/laslife.html [September 10, 2007].

"History of Tunica" (Tunica, MS: Tunica Chamber of Commerce, 2005) at http://www.tunicachamber.com/Content/Economic%20...Development/Culture%20and%20Living.htm; "Native Americans , Artifacts and Explorers" (Clarksdale, MS: Coahoma County Tourism Commission, n.d.) at http://www.clarksdaletourism.com/HTML/indians.htm; "Historical Markers in Coahoma County" (Clarksdale, MS: Coahoma County, n.d.) at http://www.ssrc.msstate.edu/grr/coahm.htm; "Tennessee American Indian Migrations" (Knoxville, TN: Tennessee American Indian Migrations Project, 2007) at http://www.tnaim.org/index.php [September 17, 2007].

Missouri

Swanton, esp. 269-271; Jean Delanglez, "The Jolliet Lost Map of the Mississippi," *Mid-America, An Historical Review* (Chicago, IL: Loyola University, April 1946), vol. 28 (New Series, vol. 17), no. 2, 67-143; Eugene Morrow Violette, *History of Missouri*, 9-10, 41n1, 66; Gloria Jahoda, *Trail of Tears*, 297; Dee Brown, *Hear That Lonesome Whistle Blow*, 37; Kristie C. Woferman, *The Osage in Missouri*, 18-23, 25-27; William E. Unrau, The Kansa Indians, 61-65; Steven E. Ambrose, *Undaunted Courage*, 155-156; "Lewis & Clark: Nebraska bluffs site of national event," *Great Fall Tribune*, July 31, 2004; David Hendee, "Otoe-Missouria welcomed home," *Omaha World Herald*, July 31, 2004; Kim Roberts-Gudeman, "Park adds symbolic sculpture," *Omaha World Herald*, August 3, 2004.

See also he'na (Dewey Dailey), "Brief History of the Otoe-Missouria Tribe" (Broken Claw, current update November 22, 2003.) at http://www.brokenclaw.com/genealogy/hist_otoe-mis.html; "Utz Site," National Historic Landmarks (Washington, DC: National Park Service, n.d.) at http://tps.cr.nps.gov/nhl/detail.cfm?ResourceId=295&ResourceType=Site [July 2, 2006]; Broken Claw (Xra-Sa'ge-Gi-xu'ge), "History of the Otoe-Missouria," (n.d.) at http://native.brokenclaw.net/otoe/hist_otoe-mis.html [September 10, 2006]. Dan Hechenberger ,"Etienne de Véniard sieur de Bourgmont: Timeline," The Lewis and Clark Journey of Discovery, (Washington, DC: National Park Service, n.d.) at http://www.nps.gov/jeff/LewisClark2/TheBicentennial/Symposium2002/Papers/Hechenberger_Dan.htm, compiled from Frank Norall, *Bourgmont* [October 13, 2007].

Mitom Pomo

Swanton, 510. Also, Susan M. Hector, et al., "A Charmstone Discovery in the Redwood Forests of Mendocino County, California" (Sacramento, CA: California Department of Forestry and Fire Protection, November 30, 2005) available from Indiana University (Bloomington, 2006) at http://www.indiana.edu/~e472/cdf/charmstone/; Phillip M. White and Natalie Pastor, "California Indians and Their Reservations" (San Diego, DA: San Diego State University, updated 2006) at http://infodome.sdsu.edu/research/guides/calindians/calinddictqs.shtml; "Round Valley Indian Tribes" (Covelo, CA: Round Valley Indian Tribal Council, 1998-2001) at http://www.covelo.net/tribes/pages/tribes.shtml; "California's Two-Year Tribal College" (Davis, CA: D-Q University, 2006-2006) at http://www.dqu.cc.ca.us/; "Big River - A History - The Story of Two Villages: Buldam and Mendocino" (Mendocino, CA: Stanford Inn) at http://www.stanfordinn.com/history.html [May 22, 2006].

Miwok

Swanton, 502-507. Also see "Member Tribes" (Jackson, CA: Alliance of California Tribes, 2001) at http://www.allianceofcatribes.org/jackson.htm [May 7, 2006]. Also, "Coast Miwok" (CA: Federated Indians of Graton Rancheria, 2004) at http://www.gratonrancheria.com/timeline.htm; "The Miwok - Mount Diablo's Earliest Inhabitants" (Walnut Creek, CA; Mount Diablo Interpretative Association, n.d.) at http://www.mdia.org/chnamd.htm; "Mission San Rafael Arcangel," The California Missions On-Line Project (Cucamonga, CA: Cucamonga School District, 2005) at http://www.cuca.k12.ca.us/lessons/missions/Rafael/SanRafaelArcangel.html#founding [June 5, 2006]. For the Miwok Revolt, see Kevin Starr, California, 47; Swanton, 503. Also see Diana Tumminia, "California Indians Memorial" (Sacramento, CA: CSU at Sacramento, n.d.) at http://www.csus.edu/indiv/t/tumminia/MEMORIAL.HTM [June 5, 2006].

Mobile

Swanton, 136, 154, 159-160, 171, 172, 180; Gloria Jahoda, *Trail of Tears*, 4; Daniel K. Richter, *Facing East from Indian County*, 24-25, 34.

Mococo

Swanton, 134.

Moctobi

Swanton, 175, 188, 191. Also see Biloxi.

Modoc

Keith A. Murray, *The Modocs and Their War*; Robert M. Utley, *The Indian Frontier of the American West*, 171-172; Swanton, 452, 461, 464-466, 507; H. W. Brands, *The Age of Gold*, 481; Kevin Starr, *California*, 100; Drake, *Indians of North America*, 707-174; "California State Historical Landmarks in Modoc County" (California Resources Agency, 1996-2004) at http://ceres.ca.gov/geo_area/counties/Modoc/landmarks.html [June 19, 2006].

Mogoulacha
Swanton, 192, 200, 204, 208; "Tonti Letters" available from the Ohio Valley-Great Lakes Ethnohistory Archives: The Miami Collection (Bloomington, IN: Glenn Black Laboratory of Archaeology and Trustees of Indiana University, 1996, updated October 26, 2000), 225, n12, at http://www.gbl.indiana.edu/archives/miamis4/M17-03_8b.html [August 24, 2006]. From John Delanglez, "Tonti, Henri de," *Mid-America* (1939), vol. 21, 209-238.

Mohawk
Alan Taylor, *The Divided Ground*, esp. 4, 120-130, 254-255, 331-344; Joseph T. Glatthaar and James Kirby Martin, *Forgotten Allies*, esp. 7, 10, 17-18, 77, 87, 103, 104, 106; Edwin G. Burrows & Mike Wallace, *Gotham*, 13, 86; Russell Shorto, The *Island in the Center of the World*, 46-47, 65, 75-81, 162-163; Jill Wendholt Silva, "A Brave New England: Driving western Massachusetts' Mohawk Trail...," *Kansas City Star*, August 8, 2004, G1. Also see the Iroquois in Swanton, pp. 33-40, esp. 34 (not listed in Index) and in Swanton, 24, 32, 41-42 on war with Mahican. Also, Book Report: Win. M. Beauchamp, S.T.D., ed. *Moravian Journals in Central New York 1745-66* from *Schoharie County Historical Review*, Spring 2001 (Schoharie, NY: Schoharie County Historical Society, n.d.) at http://www.schohariehistory.net/Review/Spring01/BookReport.htm; "Raid of Deerfield, Massachusetts in Queen Anne's War" America's Story from America's Library (Washington, D. C.: Library of Congress, n.d.) at http://www.americaslibrary.gov/cgi-bin/page.cgi/jb/colonial/deerfld_1 [September 8, 2006].

For Kateri Tekakwitha, see Daniel K. Richter, *Facing East from Indian Country*, 79-90; Melanie Gleaves-Hirsch, "Two Kateri Statues Safely Weather The Storm," *The Post-Standard* (Syracuse, NY), September 14, 1998. Also, Terry H. Jones, "Kateri Tekakwitha" (St. Louis: Catholic Community Forum/Liturgical Publications of St. Louis, n.d.) at http://www.catholic-forum.com/saints/saintk01.htm; Norm Léveillée, "Kaia'tanó:ron—Kateri Tekakwitha" (West Greenwich, RI, 2004) at http://www.normlev.net/kateri/; Blanche M. Kelly, "Blessed Kateri Tekakwitha," *Catholic Encyclopedia Online Edition* (New York: K. Knight, 2003), xiv, at http://www.newadvent.org/cathen/14471a.htm [September 9, 2006].

Mohawk River Kalapuya
Swanton 463. Don Macnaughtan, "American Indian Languages of Western Oregon" (Eugene, OR: Lane Community College Library, 1999) at http://www.lanecc.edu/it/hdrefs/Follow%2520directions%2520at:%2520http://expresslane.lanecc.edu/library/don/orelang.htm [March 19, 2006].

Mohegan
Swanton, 29-30; Nathaniel Philbrick, *Mayflower*, 178, 179-180, 182, 356; George Catlin, *North American Indians* (Penguin ed.), 369-370; A"Heritage" (Uncasville, CT: Mohegan Tribe, 2004) at http://www.mohegan.nsn.us/heritage/ [July 17, 2006].

Moingwena
Swanton, 241-242.

Moiseyu
Swanton, 278-280; follows Mooney (1928). William Y. Chalfant, *Cheyennes and Horse Soldiers*, 301, 310; George Bird Grinnell, *The Cheyenne Indians*, 88-90; "Native American Tribal Arts & Architecture," Native American Arts Classification Manual (Albuquerque, NM: Bunting Visual Resource Library, University of New Mexico, 2005) at http://www.unm.edu/~bbmsl/plainsart.htm [June 17, 2006}.

Mojave
Swanton 356-357; Thomas Edwin Farish, *The History of Arizona*, vol. vii, chp. 13; "California: Mohave" (Mesa, AZ: Southwest Indian Relief Council, 2005-2006) at http://www.swirc.org/res_mohave.cfm?ep=7&ec=4 and "Arizona: Colorado River" at http://www.swirc.org/res_coloradoriver.cfm?ep=7&ec=1; Fort Mojave Indian Tribe, "Mojave National Preserve" (Washington, DC: National Park Service, n.d.) at http://www.nps.gov/moja/mojahtm1.htm [September 9, 2006].

Molalla
Swanton, 452, 455, 466; U.S. Code Title 25, Chapter 14, Subchapter XXX, § 692 Definitions; Laura Redish, dir. "Molale (Molalla)" (St. Paul, MN: Native Languages of the Americas, n.d.) at http://www.native-languages.org/molale.htm [June 17, 2006].

Monacan
Swanton, 63-64, 72, 73; Edmond S. Morgan, *American Slavery, American Freedom*, 72.

Moneton
Swanton, 61, 74.

Mono
Swanton, 376; *2004 Yosemite National Park Annual Report for Undertakings Reviewed for Section 106 of The National Historic Preservation Act* (Washington, DC: Department of the Interior, National Park Service, 2004). Also see Paiute in this work.

Also, Mary Ann Resendes, "Western Mono Indians," *Historical Accounts of the Central Sierra* (Shaver Lake, CA: Central Sierra Historical Society, n.a.) at http://www.sierrahistorical.org/archives/monoindians.html [March 23, 2006]; Thomas C. Fletcher, "Kuzedika'a People" (Mono Lake Committee, 1996-2006) at http://www.monolake.org/naturalhistory/kutzadikaa.htm; Frances Spivy-Weber et al. "Mono Lake" (Playa del Rey, CA: Mono Lake Committee, n.a.) at http://www.livinglakes.org/mono/; Phillip M. White, "Mono, Western (Monache)," California Indians and Their Reservations (San Diego, CA: San Diego State University, 2006) at http://infodome.sdsu.edu/research/guides/calindians/calinddictmp.shtml#monowest; Ajay Sampat et al. "Mono Basin Paiutes: Mono Lake and Owens Valley Native Americans" (San Dimas, CA: San Dimas High School, 2000-2001) at http://www.bonita.k12.ca.us/schools/sandimas/teachers/mono/pages2000/Projects/NativeAmericans/report.htm; James May, "Mono Lake Kutzadika," Indian Country Today, August 9, 2000 (Canastota, NY: ICT, 1998-2006) at http://www.indiancountry.com/content.cfm?id=713 [March 26, 2006].

"An Act To authorize the Secretary of the Interior to exchange certain lands and water rights in Inyo and Mono Counties, California, with the city of Los Angeles, and for other purposes," Chapter 114, April 20, 1937. | [H. R. 5299.] 50 Stat., 70, Charles J. Kappler, *Indian Affairs: Laws and Treaties*, vol. 5 (Washington, DC: Government Printing Office, 1941) from Oklahoma State University Library at http://digital.library.okstate.edu/kappler/Vol5/html_files/v5p0512c.html [September 11, 2006]; "Executive Order of President Woodrow Wilson reserving tract in Mono County for small band," July 22, 1915, vol. IV, p. 1016 (see previous).

For the "Numic Language," see The Linguist (Eastern Michigan University & Wayne State University, n.a.) at http://listserv.linguistlist.org/cgi-bin/wa?S2=linguist&q=Numic&s=&f=&a=&b=; William Bright and John McLaughlin, "Inyo Redux" (Eureka, CA: Northern California Indians Development Council, n.a.) at http://www.ncidc.org/bright/inyo_redux.doc; Ulrich Lueders, "Timbisha (Panamint): McLaughlin" (Linguist, November 14, 2005) at http://www.sfs.nphil.uni-tuebingen.de/linguist/issues/16/16-3285.html; James L. Armagost and John E. McLaughlin, "Taps and Spirants in Numic Languages," vol. 34, nos. 1-4,1992 (Anthropological Linguistics, 1996) at http://www.indiana.edu/~anthling/v34-1-4.html; "The Shoshone Interpretive Project" (Blue Earth Alliance) at http://www.blueearth.org/projects/shoshone/; "Great Basin Human History" (Washington, DC: Department of the Interior, National Park Service) at http://www.nps.gov/grba/EdPages/RAG/Unit%206.pdf#search='numic%20language' [March 27, 2006].

Monomoyick
Warren Sears Nickerson, "Indinan Nations and Tribes" (Book of Cape Cod Native American Genealogies) at http://wolfwalker2003.home.comcast.net/wamp5.htm [September 3, 2006].

Montagnais-Naskapi
Swanton, 581-583; Daniel K. Richter, *Facing East from Indian Country*, 12-15, 27, 40, 65.

Montauk Peoples
Swanton, 42-43, 44; Burrows & Wallace, *Gotham*, 5-13; Russell Shorto, *The Island in the Center of the World*, 117-118.

"American Indians of Long Island, NY" (New York: Richmond Hill Historical Society, with recognition to Author/Illustrator William Krooss, "A Peek at Richmond Hill Through the Keyhole of Time") at http://www.richmondhillhistory.org/indians.html; "The Indians of Long Island," Long Island: Our Story, Chapter 2 (New York: Newsday, n.d.) http://www.newsday.com/community/guide/lihistory/ny-history-chap2cov,0,7847609.storygallery [May 9, 2006]. "Metoac (Montauk)," Four Directions Institute (Four Directions Press, 2005) at http://www.fourdir.com/metoac.htm w/ links to "Meotac/Montauk/Sewanakie" (Shades) at http://www.angelfire.com/realm/shades/nativeamericans/meotac.htm [June 21, 2006].

Montesano
Paul Sukovsky, "Tribes Fight to Keep Native Culture Alive," Canku Ota (Many Paths), August 24, 2002, no. 68 (Paul C. Barry, 1999-2002) at http://www.turtletrack.org/Issues02/Co08242002/CO_08242002_Washington_Tribes.htm [May 18, 2006].

Moosehead Lake Indians
Swanton, 16.

Moratok
Swanton, 82.

Moratuooc
Fred Willard, "Trade Items as Transfer of Money," November 2002, made available by the Lost Colony Center for Science and Research (Eastern
Carolina University) at http://lost-colony.com/trade.html [June 12, 2006].

Moraughtacund
Swanton, 66-71.

Mosopelea
Swanton, 190, 207, 231-232, 194.

Mosquito
Christopher Buyers, "Mosquitos: Brief History" (2002-2004) at http://www.4dw.net/royalark/Nicaragua/mosquito.htm; "Jamaica/Nicaragua Campaign Request for Arms &ca" (Great Britain: On-Line Institute for Advanced Loyalist Studies, 2006) at http://www.royalprovincial.com/history/battles/moslet1.shtml; "Stephen Kemble Papers, 1780 April 9-1793 October 13" (Ann Arbor, MI: William L. Clements Library University of Michigan, n.d.) at http://www.clements.umich.edu/Webguides/HK/Kemble.html [August 11, 2006].

Moyawance
Swanton, 57-59.

Muckleshoot
Swanton, 428-429; "People" (Auburn, WA: Muckleshoot Indian Tribe, n.d.) at http://www.muckleshoot.nsn.us/people.htm; Don Healy, "The Muckleshoot Nation" (Trenton, NJ) at http://users.aol.com/Donh523/navapage/muckle.htm; "Arburn, Billed as 'the loveliest village of the plain'" (Seattle: WA: Seattle Post-Intelligencer, 1996-2006) at http://seattlepi.nwsource.com/webtowns/article.asp?WTID=61&ID=103133 [June 22, 2006].

Muhhuhwau
Warren Sears Nickerson, "Indian Nations and Tribes" (Book of Cape Cod Native American Genealogies) at http://wolfwalker2003.home.comcast.net/wamp5.htm [September 3, 2006].

Muklasa
Swanton, 157, 160.

Multnomah
Swanton, 466-467; Kathy Tucker, "Owl Sculpture, Sauvie Island," Oregon History Project (Oregon Historical Society, 2002) at http://www.ohs.org/education/oregonhistory/historical_records/dspDocument.cfm?doc_ID=00078713-DD99-1DBE-BB3880B05272FE9F ; "The City on Willamette Falls" (Oregon City, OR, n.d.) at http://www.endoftheoregontrail.org/road2oregon/sa27ORcity.html; "Peoples of the Slough: Wapato Indians" (Center for Columbia River History, n.d.) at http://www.ccrh.org/comm/slough/chinook.htm; Stephenie Flora, "Northwest Indians: Myths and Legends" (Oregon Pioneers, n.d.) at http://www.oregonpioneers.com/myths.htm; "The Volcanoes of Lewis and Clark, April 4 - 5, 1806, Back on the Columbia - The Willamette Valley" (Vancouver, WA: U.S. Geological Survey, n.d.) at http://vulcan.wr.usgs.gov/LivingWith/Historical/LewisClark/volcanoes_lewis_clark_april_04_1806.html; Noah Brooks, "From Tidewater to the Sea," *First Across the Continent: The Story of The Exploring Expedition of Lewis and Clark in 1804-5-6* (New York: Charles Scribner's Sons, 1902) made available from Nonprofit Library for Genealogy & History-Related Research(WebRoots, 2001-2004), ch. xvii, 220-265, at http://www.webroots.org/library/usatrav/fatclc05.html; Lyn Topinka, "Sauvie Island, Oregon" (English River, 2006) at http://www.iinet.com/~englishriver/LewisClarkColumbiaRiver/Regions/Places/sauvie_island.html [August 22, 2006].

Mummapacune
Swanton, 66-71.

Munsee
Swanton, 48-55; Gloria Jahoda, *Trail of Tears*, 96, 288.; Paul Wallace Gates, "A Fragment of Kansas Land History: The Disposal of the Christian Indian Tract, *Kansas Historical Quarterly*" (Topeka, KS: Kansas State Historical Society, August 1937), vol. 6, no. 3, pp. 227 to 240; William E. Unrau, The Kansa Indians, 186.

"Mohonk Preserve in the Shawangunk Mountains, New York" (NY: Adventures Great and Small, 1996-2001) at http://www.great-adventures.com/destinations/usa/new_york/mohonk.html [September 8, 2006]. Also for Delaware: "New Jersey Indian Tribes" (Access Genealogy.com, 2004-2006) at http://63.247.83.241/native/newjersey/ [May 4, 2006].

Mus-quah-ta
Sue I. Silliman, *St Joseph in Homespun, A Centennial Souvenir* (Three Rivers, MI: Three Rivers Publishing Company, 1931, reprinted as originally published), 2.

Muskogee
Swanton, 107-108, 116-117, 156-159, 160-168; "Red Stick Heritage," (Okmulgee, OK: Muscogee Red Stick Society, n.d.) at http://creekcombatveterans.org/ [August 13, 2006]; Thomas Foster, "[Muskogee Cussetuh Indians]" (Highland Heights, KY: Northern Kentucky University) at http://www.nku.edu/~fosterh1/news.htm [September 8, 2006]. See Creek Confederacy.

Naansi
Swanton, 315-317.

Nabeyeyxa
Swanton, 315-317.

Nacono
Swanton, 315-317.

Nacotchtank
Swanton, 57-59.

Nadamin
Swanton, 315-317.

Naguidis
Herbert E. Bolton, "The Founding of the Missions on the San Gabriel River, 1745-1749," *Southwestern Historical Quarterly*, vol. 17, no. 4, 323-378, SHQ Online at http://www.tsha.utexas.edu/publications/journals/shq/online/v017/n4/article_1.html [May 24, 2006].

Nahyssan
Swanton, 64.

Nakanawan
Thomas N. Campbell, "Nakanawan Indians," *Handbook of Texas Online* (Austin, TX: Texas State Historical Association and University of Texas, 2001) at http://www.tsha.utexas.edu/handbook/online/articles/view/NN/bmn13.html [September 9, 2006].

Nakasa
Swanton, 205-206.

Nakota
Swanton, 282, 388.

"About the Wiciyela Sioux," (Rapid City, SD: American Indian Relief Council, updated Apr. 27, 2006) at http://www.airc.org/res_crowcreek.cfm?ep=8&ec=1; Japkeerat, "The Native American Tribe of the Sioux," Vlife VLibrary (Vydharthi) at http://vyharthi.netfirms.com/Essays/nativesioux.htm; "About the Yankton, Yanktonai, and Assiniboine Sioux" (Sioux Falls, SD: Sioux Nation Relief Fund, 2005) at http://www.snrfprograms.org/res_sd_yankton.htm; A. T. Andreas, History of the State of Nebraska (Chicago: The Western Historical Company, 1882), Part 5, "Lewis and Clark Expedition," available from Kansas Collection Books, produced by Gary Martens and Laurie Saikin, at http://www.kancoll.org/books/andreas_ne/history/erlyhst-p5.html; Judi Schiller and Richard Schiller, "Whitestone Hill: A Place in History" (1996) at http://www.emily.net/~schiller/whitston.html; Phil Konstantin, "June 27, 1879: The Drifting Goose Reserve...Mag-a-bo-das, or Drifting Goose, band of the Yanktonais Sioux Indians" (On this Day in History) at http://nativenewsonline.org/history/hist0627.html [August 1, 2006]. Also, "Yanktonai Indian Tribe History" (Access Genealogy, 2004-2006) at http://www.accessgenealogy.com/native/tribes/siouan/ yanktonaihist.htm [August 1, 2006]. Source: Hodge's *Handbook of American Indians*, 1906.

Naltunne
Swanton, 467, 452 (Alsea), 459 (Dakubetede), 469 (Takelma).

Nambe Pueblo
Swanton, 340-341. "New Mesico Pueblos" (Santa Fe: Tahoe Digital, 2005) at http://www.santa-feonline.com/pueblos.htm; "Pueblos, Tribes, & Reservations" (Santa Fe: New Mexico Tourism Department, 2005) at http://www.newmexico.org/go/loc/cities/page/cities-pueblos.html [April 7, 2006].

Namidish
Swanton, 315-317. Margery H. Krieger, "Namidish Indians," *Handbook of Texas Online* (Austin, TX: Texas State Historical Association and University of Texas, 2001) at http://www.tsha.utexas.edu/handbook/online/articles/view/NN/bmn3.html [September 10, 2006].

Nanatsoho
Swanton, 317-320; Thomas N. Campbell, "Nanatsoho Indians," *Handbook of Texas Online* (Austin, TX: Texas State Historical Association and University of Texas, 2001) at http://www.tsha.utexas.edu/handbook/online/articles/view/NN/bmn14.html [September 9, 2006].

Naniaba Choctaw
Swanton 160, 172.

Nantaughtacund
Swanton, 66-71.

Nanticoke
Swanton, 59-61; Edmond S. Morgan, *American Slavery, American Freedom*, 250-251, 250n2.

"Our Beginning" (Bridgeton, NJ: Nanticoke Lenni-Lenape Indians of New Jersey, n.d.) at http://www.nanticoke-lenape.org/ [September 10, 2006]; "The Nanticoke Lenni-Lenape Indians of New Jersey" (Bridgeton, NJ, n.a.) at http://www.jersey.net/~standingbear/home9.htm [May 6, 2006]. Also, "Tribe History" (Millsboro, DE: Nanticoke Indian Association, 2003-2004) at http://www.nanticokeindians.org/history.cfm; "The History of the Nantikoke" (Ed WindDancer, 2005) at http://www.edwinddancer.com/history.html [August 10, 2006].

For Bacon's Rebellion, see Edmond S. Morgan, *American Slavery, American Freedom*, 250-270, esp. 250-251, 250n2, 255, 259, 269-270; quote taken from p. 255; Daniel K. Richter, *Facing East from Indian Country*, 105-108. Also, Nathaniel Bacon, "Bacon's Rebellion: The Declaration (1676)" available from History Matters at http://historymatters.gmu.edu/d/5800; Susan McCulley. Rev. Jen Loux, "Bacon's Rebellion," Jamestown Historic Briefs (Washington, DC: National Park Service, n.d.) at http://www.nps.gov/archive/colo/Jthanout/BacRebel.html [October 27, 2006].

Napochi
Swanton, 165, 168-169, 195, 208.

Narcotah
"Sauk and Foxes" (Access Genealogy, 2004-2006) at http://www.accessgenealogy.com/scripts/data/database.cgi?file= Data&report=SingleArticle&ArticleID=0017311 [August 11, 2006]. Source: Bushnell's, *Villages of the Algonquian, Siouan, and Caddoan Tribes West of the Mississippi* (1976).

Narragansett
Swanton, 19, 27-28, 29, 31, 32, 43; Nathaniel Philbrick, *Mayflower*, 49, 96, 106, 113, 120, 126-127, 130-131, 136, 172, 179-82, 194, 206. 280-281; "Historical Perspective of the Narragansett Indian Tribe" (Charlestown, RI: Narragansett Indian Tribe, n.d.) at http://www.narragansett-tribe.org/history.htm [July 17, 2006].

Nashua
Swanton, 17-18, 22-23, 29, 31.

Nasoni

Swanton 315-317, 317-319; Thomas N. Campbell, "Nasoni Indians," *The Handbook of Texas Online* at http://www.tsha.utexas.edu/handbook/online/articles/view/NN/bmn17.html [September 9, 2006].

Nasoni, Upper

Swanton, 317-320.

Nasoni, Upper

Swanton, 317-319.

Natchez

H. B. Cushman, *History of the Choctaw, Chickasaw and Natchez*; Swanton, 82, 97, 153,188-190, 204, 215. For the Natchez War, see Swanton, 176, 178, 189-190, 192, 194, 201, 204, 206, 317, 318, 320; Drake, *Indians of North America*, 380-385. Also, George Sabo, III, Review of Daniel H. Usner, Jr., *American Indians in the Lower Mississippi Valley: Social and Economic Histories* (Lincoln: University of Nebraska Press, 1998), *William and Mary Quarterly* (2001), vol. lvii, no. 3, available at http://www.wm.edu/oieahc/wmq/Jul01/UsnerJuly2001.pdf#search='Natchez%20Revolt' [November 10, 2006].

Natchitoches

Swanton, 196, 204, 206, 317, 318, 320.

Natchitoches Confederacy

Swanton, 201, 204, 205-207, 212, 309, 315, 316. Thomas N. Campbell, "Natchitoch Indians," *Handbook of Texas Online* (Austin, TX: Texas State Historical Association and University of Texas, 2001) at http://www.tsha.utexas.edu/handbook/online/articles/view/NN/bmn18.html [September 9, 2006].

Natchitoches, Upper

Swanton, 317-320.

Nateotetain

Samuel G. Drake, *The Aboriginal Races of North America...*, 9-16; Henry Rowe Schoolcraft, *Personal Memoirs Of A Residence Of Thirty Years With The Indian Tribes on the American Frontiers* (BookRags, Inc., 2000-2006), 143, at http://www.bookrags.com/ebooks/11119/143.html; Tom Ojo, "Native Tribe Listing" (Canada: Heritage Bank Consulting, 27 Apr 2006) at http://users.rttinc.com/~asiniwachi/wnt.html [August 9, 2006].

Natick

Swanton, 19-20; "Official Tribal Website" (Praying Indians of Natick and Ponkapoag, 2004-2006) at http://natickprayingindians.org/; "1651-2001, 350th Anniversary of Natick, Massachusetts and the Natick Praying Indians" (Miller Microcomputer Services, 1997-2006) at http://www.millermicro.com/natprayind.html [August 23, 2006].

Nations of the North

Elizabeth Cooper, "Presidio San Sabá," *Texas Beyond History* (Austin, TX: University of Texas at Austin, 2003) at http://www.texasbeyondhistory.net/presidio/; "Presidio de San Sabá" (Menard, TX: Presidio de San Saba Restoration Corporation, n.d.) at http://www.presidiodesansaba.com; Herbert E. Bolton, "The Spanish Abandonment and Re-occupation of East Texas, 1773-1779," *Southwestern Historical Quarterly*, vol. 9, no. 2, 67-137, esp. n64, SHQ Online at http://www.tsha.utexas.edu/publications/journals/shq/online/v009/n2/article_1_print.html; J. Marvin Hunter, "San Saba Mission Rises From Its Ruins," Contents of Volume, *Frontier Times Magazine Online*, vol. 14, no. 11, August 1937 (2004) at http://www.frontiertimesmagazine.com/0837.html; Don Antonio Bonilla, "A Brief Compendium of the Events which have Occurred in the Province of Texas from its Conquest, or Reduction, to the Present Date," *Southwestern Historical Quarterly* (November 10, 1772), vol. 8, no. 1, 9-78 SHQ Online at http://www.tsha.utexas.edu/publications/journals/shq/online/v008/n1/article_5.html [May 24, 2006]. "upon the Mission of San Sabas" "attacked the Presidio of San Savas" Also, Herbert E. Bolton, "The Founding of the Missions on the San Gabriel River, 1745-1749," *Southwestern Historical Quarterly*, vol. 17, no. 4, 323-378, SHQ Online at http://www.tsha.utexas.edu/publications/journals/shq/online/v017/n4/article_1.html [May 24, 2006].

Natsshostanno

Swanton, 315-317.

Naudi

Herbert E. Bolton, "The Founding of the Missions on the San Gabriel River, 1745-1749," *Southwestern Historical Quarterly*, vol. 17, no. 4, 323-378, SHQ Online at http://www.tsha.utexas.edu/publications/journals/shq/online/v017/n4/article_1.html [May 24, 2006].

Nausegooc

Fred Willard, "Trade Items as Transfer of Money," November 2002, made available by the Lost Colony Center for Science and Research (Eastern Carolina University) at http://lost-colony.com/trade.html [June 12, 2006].

Nauset

Swanton, 19, 21-22, 24, 26, 27; Nathaniel Philbrick, *Mayflower*, 49, 61-64, 66-67, 94, 111-113, 119.

Navajo

Ruth M. Underhill, *The Navajos*. Hampton Sides, *Blood and Thunder*, esp. 152-154, 219-222, 273-274, 336-369, 400-402; Swanton, 334-336; John Upton Terrell, *The Plains Apache*, 2, 14; T. R. Fehrenbach, *Comanches*, 386, 460. Also see Thomas Edwin Farish, *The History of Arizona* (Phoenix, 1915-1918), vol. 1, chp. 13; vol. vii, chps. 3, 4, available online from the Arizona Board of Regents in the University of Arizona's Books of the Southwest series at http://southwest.library.arizona.edu...

Ted Rushton, "Dine' (Navajo Nation)," Utah Division of Indian Affairs (State of Utah, 2003) at http://dced.utah.gov/indian/Today/dine.html; "Navajo History: Dinétah (Homeland)," Of Stones and Stories: Pueblitos of Dinétah (Santa Fe, NM: Bureau of Land Management, n.a.) at http://www.nm.blm.gov/features/dinetah/navajo_history.html; "New Mexico's Colonial Past" (Washington, DC: Library of Congress, n.a.) at http://memory.loc.gov/ammem/today/sep21.html; "The Long Walk," Indigenous Voices of the Colorado Plateau (ABOR, NAU, 2005) at http://www.nau.edu/library/speccoll/exhibits/indigenous_voices/navajo/longwalk.html; "Barboncito," San Juan Heritage (San Juan, NM: San Juan School District, 2003) at http://dine.sanjuan.k12.ut.us/heritage/people/dine/biographies/barboncito.htm; "Cuartocentennial of the Colonization of New Mexico" (University Park, NM: New Mexico State University, 2005) at http://web.nmsu.edu/~publhist/ccconc-1.html and ...ccjune30.html [April 30, 2006].

"Navajo Nation" (Window Rock, AZ, 2004) at www.navajo.org/; William M. Edwardy, "The Navajo Indians." *Harper's Weekly* (July 5, 1890), 30, 530, available from Electronic Text Center (Charlottesville: University of Virginia Library, 2002) at http://wyllie.lib.virginia.edu:8086/perl/toccer-new?id=EdwNava.sgm&images=images/modeng&data=/texts/english/modeng/parsed&tag=public&part=1&division=div1; Harrison Lapahie Jr., "Navajo Timeline" (2000-2004) at http://www.lapahie.com/Timeline_Mexican_1821_1847.cfm [August 11, 2006].

Nde-nda-i

See Apache (R49) and Chiricahua (R192)

Nebadache

See Natchitoches Confederacy (R640)

Nechacokee

Joseph D. Myers, "Blue Lake: Unhappy Hunting Ground: Once Powerful Naechacokee Indian Tribe Became Extinct in early 19th Century with the coming of White Man and Disease," *Oregonian* (November 3, 1946), made available from Center for Columbia River History (Washington State University Vancouver and Portland State University, n.d.) at http://www.ccrh.org/comm/slough/primary/nechakocee.htm [August 25, 2006].

Neche

Swanton, 315-317; Thomas N. Campbell, "Neche Indians," *The Handbook of Texas Online* (Austin, TX: Texas State Historical Society, 2001) at http://www.tsha.utexas.edu/handbook/online/articles/view/NN/bmn20.html [September 9, 2006].

Neekeetoo

Samuel G. Drake, *The Aboriginal Races of North America...*, 9-16.

Nehalem Tillamook

Swanton, 471-472.

Neihahat

Swanton, 315-317.

Nespelim

Swanton, 429, 437-439.

Nestucca Tillamook

Swanton, 471-472. "Native Americans of the Oregon Coast" (Lynn Ewing, 2000) at http://www.chenowith.k12.or.us/TECH/SUBJECT/SOCIAL/natam_or/coastal.html [April 7, 2006].

Neusiok

Swanton, 82; C. Wingate Reed, *Beaufort County: Two Centuries of Its History* (1962), 1-2, 7, 66, 67 made available online by the North Carolina History and Fiction Digital Library (Greenville, NC: Joyner Library, East Carolina University, n.d.) at http://digital.lib.ecu.edu/historyfiction/document/reb/entire.html [June 12, 2006].

Neutrals

Swanton, 33, 43-44, 48, 232, 235, 240, 243, 586.

Neuustooc

Fred Willard, "Trade Items as Transfer of Money," November 2002, made available by the Lost Colony Center for Science and Research (Eastern Carolina University) at http://lost-colony.com/trade.html [June 12, 2006].

Nez Percé

Swanton, 265, 301, 393, 400-403, 413, 429, 433, 455, 467; Merrill D. Beal, *"I Will Fight No More Forever": Chief Joseph and the Nez Percé War*, quotes from p. 229 ("fight no more") and p. 302 ("true magnanimity"). "In 11 weeks" taken from Department of the Army, *American Military History* 1607-1953, 287. The DA gives the date of surrender as October 4 although Chief Joseph officially presented his rifle to Colonel Miles on the

5th when he gave his formal speech of surrender. See also, Helen Hunt Jackson, *A Century of Dishonor*, 103-135; Drake, *Indians of North America*, 714-715; Bernard De Voto, ed., *The Journals of Lewis and Clark*, 246-248, 260, 323, 338-339, 360, 362-364, 369, 381-385, 389, 394-396, 401-402, 405, 407-409, 415, 417; Gerome A. Greene, *Nez Perce Summer, 1877: The U.S. Army and the Nee-Me-Poo Crisis*; Dawn Borman, "Fort marked on tribe's trail of woe," *Kansas City Star*, November 20, 2004, B8.

Niantic
Nathaniel Philbrick, *Mayflower*, 213, 302, 303, 304, 319; Swanton, 31; "History of Niantic/East Lyme" (Savage Systems, 2002) at http://niantic.com/hist.htm; "Niantic," Four Directions Institute (Four Directions Press) at http://www.fourdir.com/niantic.htm [July 17, 2006].

Niantic, Eastern
Swanton, 19, 24, 27, 28-29, 30-31.

Niantic, Western
Swanton, 19, 24, 27, 30-31, 32

Nicariaga
Samuel G. Drake, *The Aboriginal Races of North America...*, 9-16; "Mackinac State Historic Parks" (MI: Mackinac Island State Park Commission, 2004) at http://www.mackinacparks.com/ [August 26, 2006].

Nicoleño
Swanton, 507.

Nipissin
Bouquet (1764).

Nipmuc
Swanton, 22-23, 27, 29, 31; Nathaniel Philbrick, *Mayflower*, 195, 219, 256, 258, 259-262, 264, 265, 280-281, 283, 286-295, 307, 309, 315, 332; map, 166-167; Samuel G. Drake, *The Aboriginal Races of North America...*, 9-16.

"The Nipmuck Indians" (Grafton, MA: Grafton Roots, 2000) at http://www.grafton.k12.ma.us/VirtualHistoryTour/Background/GroupBreAngela/Nipmucks.cfm; "The Nipmuc People, Their Territory & Language" (Thompson, CT: N.I.A.C., Inc., 1994-2006) at http://www.nativetech.org/Nipmuc/placenames/territory.html. Also see Robert Folz, "Sign indicating that Lake Chargoggacoggmanchauggauggagoggchaubunagungamaugg in Webster, Massachusetts, USA is the Home of the Nipmuck Indians" (Visuals Unlimited) at http://www.visualsunlimited.com/checkauth.jsp?key=nipmuck&type=and; "Greetings from... Lake Chargoggagoggmanchauggagoggchaubunagungamau" (DaleyBlog, 2004) at http://www.daleyblog.com/weblog/archives/2004/11/; Cheryll Toney Holley, "A Brief Look at Nipmuc History" (2001) at http://www.nipmucnation.homestead.com/files/Nipmuc_History.txt [August 20, 2006]. "Nipmuc Place Names of New England" (Thompson, CT: N.I.A.C., Inc., 1994 - 2006) at http://www.nativetech.org/Nipmuc/placenames/mainmass.html [August 26, 2006].

Nishinam Maidu
Swanton, 499-502.

Niskah
Swanton, 538, 586-587, 606; George Catlin, *North American Indians* (Penguin ed.), 385; J. Halcombe, *Stranger Than Fiction* (London: Society For Promoting Christian Knowedge, 1873, 3rd ed), 77, 136, 141, available from Boston University Theology Library (Boston, 2007) at http://digilib.bu.edu/dspace/bitstream/2144/778/3/strangerthanfict00halcrich.txt [November 19, 2007]. Also see William Downie, *Hunting For Gold: Reminiscences Of Personal Experience And Research In The Early Days Of The Pacific Coast From Alaska To Panama* (1893); 1971 facsimile edition published by American West Publishing Company (Palo Alto, California).

Nisqually
Swanton, 429-430. "Lakewood Heritage" (Lakewood, WA: Chamber of Commerce, n.d.) at http://www.lakewood-wa.com/html/history.html; "South Puget Sound Indians-What happened in the Indian War?" (Tumwater, WA: City of Tumwater, n.d.) at http://www.ci.tumwater.wa.us/ResearchCenter/Indians-page%207.htm; "146 years later, executed chief's reputation restored," *Kansas City Star* (December 12, 2004), A12.

Nogatl
Swanton, 507; Owen C. Coy, "The Indian Wars in the Van Duzen and Eel River Watershed Area," The Humboldt Bay Region 1850 -- 1875: A Study in the American Colonization of California (Los Angeles: California State Historical Association, 1929) at http://www.humboldt1.com/~cbender/Carlotta/history/IndianWars.htm [November 20, 2006].

Nomalaki
Paula Giese, "Federally Recognized California Tribes" (1996-1997) at http://www.kstrom.net/isk/maps/ca/california.html; Jeff Elliott, "The Dark Legacy of Nome Cult," *Albion Monitor*, September 2, 1995 (Occidental CA: Monitor Publishing) at http://www.monitor.net/monitor/9-2-95/history.html [May 22, 2006].

Nomlaki
Swanton, 519-520, 520-521.

Mike Barkley, "The Nomi Lackee Monument -- Northern California's Trail of Tears" (Manteca, CA, 2001) at http://www.mjbarkl.com/nomi. htm; Dottie Smith, "Shasta County History" (Redding, CA, 1996-2000) at http://www.cagenweb.com/shasta/shasthis.htm; Phillip M. White and Natalie Pastor, "California Indians and Their Reservations" (San Diego: San Diego State University, 2006) at http://infodome.sdsu.edu/ research/guides/calindians/calinddictmp.shtml; "Forced Relocation" ()at http://www.1849.org/ggg/relocation.html; "Nome Lackee Indian Reservation," A History of American Indians in California: Historic Sites (Washington, DC: Department of the Interior, National Park Service, 2004) at http://www.cr.nps.gov/history/online_books/5views/5views1h55.htm [April 8, 2006].

Nooksack
"About the Tribe" (Demming WA: Nooksack Tribe, 2003) at
http://www.npaihb.org/profiles/tribal_profiles/Washington/Nooksack%20Tribal%20Profile.htm#HISTORY [September 10, 2006].

Noquet
"Indian Treaties: Their Ongoing Importance to Michigan Residents, Treaty of Cedar Point, 1836" (Central Michigan University Clark Historical Library, 1999) at http://clarke.cmich.edu/cedarpoint1836.htm [September 10, 2006]. Text of Treaty with the Menominee, September 3, 1836; Roy Cole, "Pre-conquest Peoples of the Great Lakes Region" at http://www4.gvsu.edu/coler/GPY345/Ppoint/IndiansGLR.ppt [September 10, 2006].

Norridgewock
Swanton, 13, 15.

Northern Cheyenne
For the Battle of Slim Buttes, see Jerome A. Greene, *Morning Star Dawn*, 7-8. On the tragic march of the Cheyenne to their homelands to the north see George Bird Grinnell's account from first-hand sources in *The Fighting Cheyennes*, 398-427. Greene covers the subject briefly on pages 192-195.

Northwest Indians Fisheries Commission (NWIFC)
"Member Tribes - Map & Information" (Olympia, WA: NWIFC, n.d.) at http://www.nwifc.wa.gov/tribes/index.asp [June 22, 2006].

Nottaway
Swanton, 62, 65.

Ntlakyapamuk
Swanton, 430, 432, 588-591.

Numni
"Tribes / Nations" (Wolf's Retreat, n.a.) http://www.realduesouth.net/WolfsRetreat/tribes.htm [April 6, 2006].

Nyack
Deborah Champlain, "Northeast Tribes: Native American History for March" (Rhode Island: Northeast Wigwam, 1998-2000) at http://www.newigwam.com/histdtes.html [subsequently offline].

Obispeño Chumash
Swanton, 484-487.

Ocale
Swanton, 134-135.

Occaneechi
Swanton, 65-66, 73, 74, 79, 80, 81, 83; Edmond S. Morgan, *American Slavery, American Freedom*, 259-262; Jason O. Watson, "VA-U60 Occaneechi Indians," Commonwealth of Virginia Historical Markers (2004-2006) at http://www.historical-markers.org/distance/index. cgi?mid=153_5348 [August 18, 2006].

Oconee
Swanton, 104, 112, 123, 130, 135, 142; Gloria Jahoda, *Trail of Tears*, 245.

Oglala
For Battle at Platte River Bridge Station, see George Bird Grinell, *The Fighting Cheyennes*, 216-229; Dee Brown, *Bury My Heart at Wounded Knee*, 98-98, 106, and "History of the Fort Caspar Area" (City of Casper, WY, 2005) at http://www.casperwy.gov/Content/leisure/fort/... Outreach. asp [November 1, 2006]. Also, Doris Soule, "Lieutenant Casper Collins: Fighting the Odds at Platte Bridge," Wild West (December 1996) made available online by History Net at http://www.thehistorynet.com/we/bl-casper-collins/; "Indian Wars" (Wyoming Tales and Trails) at http:// www.wyomingtalesandtrails.com/custer.html; and "Fort Caspar, 'Platte Bridge Station'" (Mills, WY: Historic America, 2000-2002.) at http://www.historic-america.com/ftcasper.html [July 8, 2006].

Ohongeeoquena
Swanton, 56.

Okanagon
Swanton, 430-433.

Okatiokinans
Samuel G. Drake, *The Aboriginal Races of North America...*, 9-16.

Okehai
Swanton, 163.

Okelousa
Swanton, 190, 202, 207.

Okmulgee
Swanton, 112-113, 157.

Okwanuchu
Swanton, 507.

Omaha
Alice C. Fletcher. & Francis La Flesche, *The Oneida Tribe*. A short narrative of tribal history beginning with the Omaha tribe's first encounter with the white race can be found in Vol. II , 611-640; Judith A. Boughter, *Betraying the Omaha Nation*, esp. 113-115, 118, 134-140; "Magna Carta" quoted on 114; "premature" from 137. Also see Eugene Morrow Violette, *History of Missouri*, 173-175; Dee Brown, *Hear That Lonesome Whistle Blow*, 7, 37; William E. Unrau, *The Kansa Indians*, 12-13; George E. Hyde, *Red Cloud's Folk: A History of the Oglala Sioux*, 9-10, 14-15, 23-24; Stephen E. Ambrose, *Undaunted Courage*, 125, 155, 160, 172-174; Swanton, 213, 259, 264, 265, 268, 271, 284, 285, 286-287, 291, 293; Bernard De Vito, ed., *The Journals of Lewis & Clark*, 18, 470, 472. Pat Navaille, "Pipestone National Monument" (Washington, DC: National Park Service, 2000) at http://www.nps.gov/pipe/history.htm [September 8, 2006].

Onatheaqua
Swanton, 135.

Onawmanient
Swanton, 66-71.

Oneida
Joseph T. Glatthaar; James Kirby Martin, *Forgotten Allies: The Oneida Indians and the American Revolution* (New York: Hill and Wang, 2006), esp. pp. 7, 87-89, 298, 300, 301, 303, 309, 314, 310, 320; "Oneidas emerged" from p. 303. Also, Edwin G. Burrows & Mike Wallace, *Gotham*, 13; Swanton, 40, 57, 87, 252, 256, 257; Gloria Jahoda, *Trail of Tears*, 99-10. For Battle of Oriske, see Alan Taylor, *The Divided Ground*, 91. For Hamilton-Oneida Academy, see Ron Chernow, *Alexander Hamilton* (New York: Penguin Press, 2004), 337-338.

Onondaga
Joseph T. Glatthaar and James Kirby Martin, *Forgotten Allies*, esp.17-18, 133-134; Edwin G. Burrows & Mike Wallace, *Gotham*, 13; Swanton, 33-40; Benison J. Lossing, *Our Country*, vol. 1, chp. II (1905) available at http://www.angelfire.com/ca6/minuteman/chapter002.htm [September 8, 2006].

Ontario
"A History of the Anishinabek Nation" (North Bay, ON; Nipissing First Nation, Union of Ontario Indians, 2004) at http://www.anishinabek.ca/uoi/history.htm [September 8, 2006].

Ontponea
Swanton, 61-62.

Opelousa
Swanton, 197, 202, 207-208.

Oraibi
Swanton 351-353.

Orcoquisac
"El Orcoquisac," *Handbook of Texas Online* (Austin, TX: Texas State Historical Association and University of Texas, 2001) at http://www.tsha.utexas.edu/handbook/online/articles/EE/hve49.html [March 10, 2006]; "Early History of East Texas" (Kountze, TX: Big Thicket Directory..., 2000) at http://www.bigthicketdirectory.com/farmcorner/june31959.html [September 10, 2006].

Orondoc
Warren Sears Nickerson, "Indinan Nations and Tribes," Book of Cape Cod Native American Genealogies, at http://wolfwalker2003.home.comcast.net/wamp5.htm [September 3, 2006].

Osage
Eugene Morrow Violette, *History of Missouri*, 8-10, 47-48, 66-72, 105n1; quote from p. 71. Shirley Christian, *Before Lewis and Clark*, passim, esp. 43-50, 65, 91-92, 97-99, 101, 103-104, 202; Chouteau quote from p. 101; on Fort Osage and Treaty of 1808, 156-160; on Osage extermination, 64, 93-94, 156. Margot Ford McMillen, ed., "Les Indiens Osages: French Publicity for the Traveling Osages," *Missouri Historical Review* (Columbia: State Historical Society of Missouri, July 2003), xcvii, 4, 295-309; Kristie C. Woferman, *The Osage in Missouri*; W. L.

Bartles, "Massacre of Confederates by Osage Indians in 1863," *Kansas Historical Collection* (Topeka: Kansas State Historical Society, 1904), viii, 62; George Bird Grinnell, *The Fighting Cheyennes*, 62, 81, 102, 102n12, 128, 301; Stephen E. Ambrose, *Undaunted Courage*, 126-127, 200-201, 332-333, 440-447; Judith A. Boughter, *Betraying the Omaha Nation, 1790-1916*; Swanton, esp. 271-273; Terri Baumgardner, "Tracing the Ancient Paths," *Star Magazine* (*Kansas City Star*, April 16, 2006), 26-31; Walter A. Schroeder, "Populating Missouri, 1804-1821," *Missouri Historical Review* (Columbia: State Historical Society of Missouri, July 2003), vol. xcvii, no. 4, 276; William R. Nester, *The Arikara War*, 55-57; W. S. Fitzpatrick, comp., *Treaties and Laws of the Osage Nation, as Passed to November 26, 1890* (Wilmington DE: Scholarly Resources, 1973, 1895 reprint), 1, 11, 18; Donald Jackson, ed., *Missouri Historical Society Bulletin*, vol. 20, no. 3 (April 1964), 182-192; William E. Unrau, *The Kansa Indians* (Norman: University of Oklahoma Press, 1971), 12-13, 60-65; and Swanton, 312-313. Also, Catholic Church Sacramental Records: "Baptismal Register of the Osage Nation (Osages)" and "Baptisms performed at Chouteau's Trading Post, 1827."

George E. Tinker. Angelic Saulsberry, ed., *The Osage: A Historical Sketch*, (Little Rock, AR: University of Arkansas at Little Rock Sequoyah Research Center, American Native Press Archives, 2006) at http://anpa.ualr.edu/digital_library/Osage_Sketch/osage_sketch.htm[-]#Table%20 of%20Contents [February 20, 2007]. William H. Thomas, *Journal of a Voyage from St. Louis, Louisiana, to the Mandan Village, Undertaken by the St. Louis Missouri Fur Company* (June 28, 1809) at http://alt.xmission.com/~drudy/mtman/html/thomas.html; Diane Good, "A Moment in Time" (Topeka, KS: Kansas State Historical Society, March 2002) at http://www.kshs.org/features/feat302.htm; Grant Foreman, "The Three Forks," *Chronicles of Oklahoma* (Oklahoma Historical Society, n.d.), vol. 2, no. 1, March 1924, pp.37-43, at http://digital.library.okstate.edu/chronicles/v002/v002p037.html; Larry Hancks, "The Emigrant Tribes: Wyandot, Delaware & Shawnee, A Chronology: July 10, 1713" (Kansas City, KS: Wyandot Nation of Kansas, 1995) at http://www.wyandot.org/emigrant.htm [September 6, 2006].

Dan Hechenberger ,"Etienne de Véniard sieur de Bourgmont: Timeline," The Lewis and Clark Journey of Discovery, (Washington, DC: National Park Service, n.d.) at http://www.nps.gov/jeff/LewisClark2/TheBicentennial/Symposium2002/Papers/Hechenberger_Dan.htm, compiled from Frank Norall, *Bourgmont* [October 13, 2007]. Also, Tim A. Nigh, "Before Lewis and Clark," *Missouri Conservationist* (Jefferson City: Missouri Conservation Commission, August 1995), vol. 56, no. 8, at http://www.mdc.mo.gov/conmag/1995/08/04.html; *Kansas Historical Quarterly* Removal of the Osages from Kansas Part One by Berlin B. Chapman August, 1938 (vol. 7, no. 3), pages 287 to 305 http://www.kshs.org/publicat/khq/1938/38_3_chapman.htm; and Berlin B. Chapman, "Removal of the Osages from Kansas," *Kansas Historical Review* (Topeka: Kansas State Historical Society, August 1938), vol. 7, no. 3, 287-305, at http://www.kancoll.org/khq/1938/38_3_chapman.htm and November 1938, vol. 7, no. 4, 399-410, at http://www.kshs.org/publicat/khq/1938/38_4_chapman.htm [September 10, 2006].

The Journals of de Bourgmont: Bourgmont Diary Entries, June 25 - November 5, 1724 (Nebraska Studies, n.d.) at http://www.nebraskastudies.org/0300/frameset_reset.html?http://www.nebraskastudies.org/0300/stories/0301_0112_00.html\; "Etienne Véniard de Bourgmont's *Exact Description of Louisiana*," *The Bulletin* (Missouri Historical Society, October 1958), vol. 15, 3-19, available from American Journeys AJ-093 (Madison: Wisconsin Historical Society, 2003) at http://www.americanjourneys.org/aj-093/summary/index.asp and http://content.wisconsinhistory.org/cdm4/document.php?CISOROOT=/aj&CISOPTR=265 [July 6, 2006].

Osochi
Swanton, 157, 169.

Oto
Swanton, 287-289; Gloria Jahoda, *Trail of Tears*, 292; Dee Brown, *Hear That Lonesome Whistle Blow*, 29, 32, 34, 35, 38, 53; Stephen E. Ambrose, *Undaunted Courage*, 155-160, 204-205, 334n, 335. Also see the sources cited under the Missouri.

Ottawa
Swanton, esp. 244-246; Kristie C. Woferman, *The Osage in Missouri*, 18-19; Joseph B. King, "Ottawa Indians in Kansas and Oklahoma," *Kansas Historical Collections* (Topeka: Kansas State Historical Society, October 1913), vol. xiii, 1913-1914, 373-378. Also see "Ottawa Indians," Ohio's Historic Indians: Tribes (Columbus: Ohio Historical Society, 2006) at http://www.ohiohistorycentral.org/entry.php?rec=614; John Gilmary Shea, *Discovery and Exploration of the Mississippi Valley...* (New York: Redfield,1853) available online and in print from Making of America Series (Ann Arbor: University of Michigan, n.d.) at http://www.hti.umich.edu/cgi/t/text/text-idx?c=moa;idno=AJA2729.0001.001 [September 7, 2006].

On Pontiac's Rebellion, see Daniel K. Richter, *Facing East from Indian Country*, 193-201; H. W. Brands, *Andrew Jackson*, 5-9; Robert Middlekauff, *The Glorious Cause*, 55-56; Howard Peckham, *Pontiac and the Indian Uprising*, generally.

On Father Jacques Marquette, see Jean Delanglez, "The Jolliet Lost Map of the Mississippi," *Mid-America, An Historical Review* (Chicago, IL: Loyola University, April 1946), vol. 28 (New Series, vol. 17), no. 2, 67-143. Also see Reuben Gold Thwaites, ed., "Lower Canada, Illinois, Ottawas 1667—1669," *The Jesuit Relations and Allied Documents*, vol. 59, available from Creighton University (Omaha, NE) at http://puffin.creighton.edu/jesuit/relations/relations_59.html [September 8, 2006].

Ouachanon
"Western Border: Indian Occupants-Border Warfare-Treaties-Facts and Incidents," *The History of Union County, Ohio*. Chapter II (Chicago: W. H. Beers & Co., 1883), 223-224, made available from Heritage Pursuit (Union County, OH, n.d.) at http://www.heritagepursuit.com/Union/Unp3c2.htm [July 20, 2006].

Ouachita
Swanton, 205-206, 208.

Ovedsita
Herbert E. Bolton, "The Spanish Abandonment and Re-occupation of East Texas, 1773-1779", vol. 9, no. 2, *Southwestern Historical Quarterly* Online, 67-137, n64, at http://www.tsha.utexas.edu/publications/journals/shq/online/v009/n2/article_1_print.html [March 9, 2006].

Owens Valley Paiute
Swanton, 375-381.

Ozaw
"Treaty with the Creeks 1796," *Indian Affairs: Laws and Treaties*, vol. II; Gilbert Imlay, A Topographical Description of the Western Territory of North America..., 3rd ed. (London, 1797), 364-365, made available from Glen Black Laboratory of Archaeology (Bloomington, IN: University of Indiana, 1997-2000) at http://www.gbl.indiana.edu/archives/dockett_317/317_33.html; "Native Americans," Migration and Settlement (Bowling Green, KY: Western Kentucky, 2005) at University at http://www.wku.edu/library/museum/education/ frontieronline/ frontiermigration.htm [August 3, 2006].

Ozette
Swanton, 428, 433.

Ozimie
Samuel G. Drake, *The Aboriginal Races of North America...*, 9-16.

Padouca
William E. Unrau, *The Kansa Indians*, 60-65; Swanton, 312-313; *The Journals of de Bourgmont: Bourgmont Diary Entries, June 25 - November 5, 1724* (Nebraska Studies, n.d.) at http://www.nebraskastudies.org/0300/frameset_reset.html?http://www.nebraskastudies.org/0300/ stories/0301_0112_00.html [September 10, 2006].

Padowaga
Samuel G. Drake, *The Aboriginal Races of North America...*, 9-16.

Paguate
"Paguate Village" (Laguna, NM: Pueblo of Laguna, 2003-2006) at http://www.lagunapueblo.org/ [April 7, 2006].

Pahvant Ute
Swanton, 373. Also see Jay M. Haymond, "Sevier Lake," Utah History Encyclopedia (Salt Lake City: Media Solutions, University of Utah, 1996-1998, updated 2004) at http://www.media.utah.edu/UHE/s/SEVIERLAKE.html—originally published by the University of Utah Press, 1994.

"Ute Indians - Northern" at http://www.media.utah.edu/UHE/u/UTES%2CNORTHERN.html; "Gunnison Massacre Site," Great Basin Heritage Route (Ely, NV: Great Basin Heritage Area Partnership, 2006) at http://www.greatbasinheritage.org/gunnison.htm [April 1, 2006].

For the Gunnison Massacre, see David Haward Bain, *Empire Express*, 50 (deaths attributed to "Utah Indians"); Irving Stone, Men to Match My Mountains, 185-186 (to "rampaging Paiutes"); Donald Worster, *A River Running Wild*, 178 (to Paiutes). Also, Robert Kant Fielding, "A Brief Summary of the Gunnison Massacre: Utah Territory, October 26, 1853" (Delta, UT: Millard County, 1998...) at http://www.millardcounty.com/massacre.html; "What was the Gunnison Massacre?" (Brigham Young University) at http://ldsfaq.byu.edu/view.asp?q=394;"Chapter XVII. Utah As a Territory. 1849-1853," *Hubert Howe Bancroft's History of Utah, 1540-1886*," pp. 439-472, made available by Utah Lighthouse Ministry (Salt Lake City, UT) at http://www.utlm.org/onlinebooks/bancroftshistoryofutah_chapter17.htm%3FFACTNet; "Gunnison Massacre Site, Utah" (Washington, DC: National Park Service, last updated Aug. 19, 2005) at http://www.cr.nps.gov/history/online_books/soldier-brave/sitec17.htm [June 13, 2006].

Pailsh
Samuel G. Drake, *The Aboriginal Races of North America...*, 9-16.

Paiute
Swanton, 375-383; Frank McLynn, *Wagons West*, 439; Dee Brown, *Hear That Lonesome Whistle Blow*, 101-102, 150. Thomas Edwin Farish, *The History of Arizona*, vol. vii, chp. 18; Robert H. Rudy and John A. Brown, *The Cayuse Indians*, 4-5n4, 283.

Sarah Winnemucca Hopkins, "Life Among the Piutes: Their Wrongs and Claims (self-published, 1883)" available from the Yosemite Online Library (Dan Anderson, 1997-2005) at http://www.yosemite.ca.us/library/life_among_the_piutes/; "California Indian Languages: Uto-Aztecan Tribes" (Sacramento, CA: California Department of Parks & Recreation, 2004) at http://www.parks.ca.gov/?page_id=23735; "Northern Paiute," Four Directions Institute (Four Directions Press, 2004) at http://www.fourdir.com/northern%20paiute.htm; "Southern Paiute," Four Directions Institute (Four Directions Press, 2005) at http://www.fourdir.com/southern_paiute.htm; "Aztec Tanoan & Uto Aztecan Languages," North American Indian Nations (Wontolla's Reservation, 1998-2006) at http://wontolla.homepage.t-online.de/wontolla/14e-uto.html; "History" (Cedarville, CA: Cedarville Rancheria, Northern Paiute Tribe, n.d.) at http://www.citlink.net/~cedranch/; "Native Americans in Utah" (State of Utah, 2006) at http://historytogo.utah.gov/utah_chapters/american_indians/nativeamericansinutah.html; Sarah Dirkse, "Paiute" (Mankato, Minnesota: Minnesota State University, n.a.) at http://www.mnsu.edu/emuseum/cultural/northamerica/paiute.html [March 27, 2006].

Scottie Johnson, "California Intermountain: Paiute Indians," *Historic American Cultures* (Spokane Valley, WA: Central Valley School District, Evergreen Middle School, Kohler's Classroom, 2005) at http://www.cvsd.org/evergreen/classrooms/akohler/StudentPages/ScottieJ/Culture.htm [March 27, 2006]; "History & Culture" (Warm Springs, OR: Confederated Tribes of Warm Springs, 1999-2005) at http://www.warmsprings.com/Warmsprings/Tribal_Community/History__Culture/ [May 15, 2006].

For the Mountain Meadows Massacre see Irving Stone, *Men to Match My Mountains*, 182-185, 349-350; Sally Denton, *American Massacre: The Tragedy at Mountain Meadows*, September 1857; Hampton Sides, *Blood and Thunder*, 320-323, 327, citing Maj. James H. Carleton, *Special Report on the Massacre at Mountain Meadows* (1859). Also, "What Happened at Mountain Meadows?," *American Heritage* (October 2001), vol. 52, no. 7 available at http://www.americanheritage.com/articles/magazine/ah/2001/7/2001_7_76.shtml [February 27, 2006]; Scott Renshaw, "Burying the Hatchet: Documentary filmmaker looks for human angle of Mountain Meadows Massacre," Salt Lake City Weekly (February 20, 2003) available at http://www.slweekly.com/editorial/2003/arts_2003-02-20.cfm [February 27, 2006].

For the Paiute War, see Elizabeth R. Gibson, "Pah Ute War" (Richland, WA, Last updated: 11/8/98)at http://members.aol.com/Gibson0817/pahute.htm; Thompson and West, " Indians And Their Wars In Nevada," *History of Nevada 1881, With Illustrations And Biographical Sketches Of Its Prominent Men And Pioneers*. Chapter XXI. (n.a.), 158-165, available from *The Nevada Observer* (December 9, 2005) at http://www.nevadaobserver.com/Indians%20and%20Their%20Wars%20in%20Nevada%20Part%202%20(1881).htm [November 21, 2006].

For the Massacre in Carson Valley, see Larry Carpenter, "Stories of the Central Overland and California Pony Express" at http://www.xphomestation.com/tales.html#MASSACRE: "May 12, 1860: Massacre in Carson Valley," The Contra Costa Gazette and "Massacre in Carson Valley," Martinez, Morning May 12, 1860. History of Utah, 1540-1886, Chapter 2 at http://www.answers.com/topic/history-of-utah-1540-1886-chapter-2 [November 20, 2006].

Northern Paiute
Swanton, 375-381.

Southern Paiute
Swanton 381-383; H. W. Brands, *The Age of Gold*, 164-165.

Pakana
Swanton, 170, 204, 210, 323; "Louisiana: Louis Judice Sr." (Zoom Information Inc., 2006) at http://www.zoominfo.com/people/judice_louis_932308039.aspx; "Pacana (Pakanas) Indians" (Illinois Historical Collections, n.d.) at http://memory.loc.gov/master/gc/gcmisc/gcfr/0004/06680582.txt and http://memory.loc.gov/master/gc/gcmisc/gcfr/0005/07280672.txt [August 11, 2006].

Palache
Samuel G. Drake, *The Aboriginal Races of North America...*, 9-16.

Palouse
Swanton, 403, 433-434.

Pamacocack
Swanton, 57-59.

Pamlico
Swanton, 83; "Native Languages of the Americas: Lumbee (Croatan, Croatoan, Pamlico, Carolina Algonquian)" (n.a.) at http://www.native-languages.org/lumbee.htm; C. Wingate Reed, *Beaufort County: Two Centuries of Its History* (1962), 1-2, 7, 66, 67 made available online by the North Carolina History and Fiction Digital Library (Greenville, NC: Joyner Library, East Carolina University, n.d.) at http://digital.lib.ecu.edu/historyfiction/document/reb/entire.html [June 12, 2006].

Pamptecough
C. Wingate Reed, "Beaufort County: Two Centuries of Its History" (1962), 1-2, 7, 66, 67 made available online by the North Carolina History and Fiction Digital Library (Greenville, NC: Joyner Library, East Carolina University, n.d.) at http://digital.lib.ecu.edu/historyfiction/document/reb/entire.html [June 12, 2006].

Pamunkey
Edmond S. Morgan, *American Slavery, American Freedom*, 49, 121, 149, 258, 263, 268; Swanton, 66-71.

Panawicky
Fred Willard, "Migration Patterns of Coastal N.C. Indians"; "Disappearing Indians"; "Cultural Anthropology of Indian Villages"; and "Trade Items as Transfer of Money," available from The Lost Colony Center for Science and Research (East Carolina University) at http://www.lost-colony.com/migrationpatterns.html; http://www.lost-colony.com/disappearing.html; http://www.lost-colony.com/cultural.html; and http://lost-colony.com/trade.html [June 12, 2006].

Papago
Swanton, 357-360; Thomas Edwin Farish, *The History of Arizona*, vol. vii, chp. 17; David Roberts, *Pueblo Revolt*, 33-35; "Tohono O'odham Nation," Southeast Desert (St. Johns, AZ: CArizona, 1997/98/99) at http://www.arizonalodging.com/nativeland/tohono.html; "Tohono O'odham Nation" (Sells, AZ: Inter Tribal Council of Arizona, 2003) at http://www.itcaonline.com/tribes_tohono.html [June 24, 2006].

Paraje
"Paraje Village" (Laguna, NM: Pueblo of Laguna, 2003-2006) at http://www.lagunapueblo.org/ [April 7, 2006].

Pascagoula
Swanton, 137, 175, 176, 188, 190-191-, 208, 323-324.

Paspehean
Edmond S. Morgan, *American Slavery, American Freedom*, 74, 81; Swanton, 66-71.

Passamaquoddy
Swanton, 15-16; Associated Press, "Ceremony honors first French colonists," *Kansas City Star*, June 27, 2004, A5.

"Quest for Qonasqamkuk" et allis. (Pleasant Point, ME: Passamaquoddy Tribe, 2003, mod. 04/12/06) at http://www.wabanaki.com/index.html; "The Passamaquoddy Tribe" (Eastport, ME: Old Sow Publishing, 1997-2001) at http://www.quoddyloop.com/pssmqddy.htm [September 9, 2006]. "The Border Dispute: How the Maine-New Brunswick border was finalized" (C. Gagnon, 2005-2005) at http://www.upperstjohn.com/history/northeastborder.htm; "Sipayik Nation" (ME: ICQ Inc., 2002) at http://www.sipayik.com/ [April 27, 2006].

Pastate
Herbert E. Bolton, "The Founding of the Missions on the San Gabriel River, 1745-1749," *Southwestern Historical Quarterly*, vol. 17, no. 4, 323-378, SHQ Online at http://www.tsha.utexas.edu/publications/journals/shq/online/v017/n4/article_1.html; Thomas N. Campbell, "Pastate Indians," *Handbook of Texas Online* (Austin, TX: Texas State Historical Association and University of Texas, 2001) at http://www.tsha.utexas.edu/handbook/online/articles/PP/bmp40.html [May 26, 2006].

Pataunck
Swanton, 66-71.

Patiri
Swanton, 308, 324.

Patuxent
Swanton, 57-59.

Patwin
Swanton, 507-509.

Pauma Luiseño
"The Pauma Band of Mission Indians" (Irvine: University of California at Irvine, 2006) at http://www.ics.uci.edu/~aisi/97_aisics/people/ctoledo/luiseno1.html [April 3, 2006].

Pawistucienemuck
Samuel G. Drake, *The Aboriginal Races of North America...*, 9-16.

Pawnee
Swanton, 289-291; William R. Nester, *The Arikara War*, 15, 56, 98, 184, 207, 211; William Y. Chalfant, esp. 27, 32, 36, 39, 107-109, 111; Robert M. Utley, *The Lance and the Shield*, 16; Bernard De Voto, *The Journals of Lewis and Clark*, 10, 11, 12, 465, 474; H. W. Brands, *The Age of Gold*, 139, 164 (Brands quotes Eleazar Ingalls, p. 139); George E. Hyde, *The Pawnee Indians*; William E. Connelley, "The Prairie Band of Pottawatomie Indians (Reservation, Jackson County, Kansas)," *Kansas Historical Collections*, 1915-1918 (Topeka: Kansas State Historical Society, 1918), vol. 14, 488-569,; William E. Connelley, ed., "Letters Concerning the Presbyterian Mission in the Pawnee Country," *Kansas Historical Collections*, 1915-1918, 570-784.

Guy Rowley Moore, " Pawnee Traditions And Customs," *Chronicles of Oklahoma*, June 1939, vol.17, no. 2, 151-169, available from the Oklahoma State University Digital Library at http://digital.library.okstate.edu/Chronicles/v017/v017p151.html [November 13, 2007]. Also, Kristie C. Woferman, *The Osage in Missouri*, 30. "The Panis/Pawnee Indians" (Maison Quesnel, n.d.) at http://www.members.tripod.com... / quesnelhouse/id122.htm; "The Visit of a Pawnee Chief," Journeying and Wintering" (Columbia, SC: University of South Carolina Libraries, 2005) at http://www.sc.edu/library/spcoll/amlit/l&c/journeying.html [May 22, 2006]; W. H. G. Kingston, *In the Rocky Mountains* (New York: Thomas Nelson & Sons, 1906, first pub. 1878), Ch. II, made available from Athelstane E-Texts (2002-2005) at http://www.athelstane.co.uk/ kingston/inrokmts/irkmt02.htm [August 9, 2006].

For the Pawnee Soldier-Scouts and Plum Creek, see David Haward Bain, *Empire Express*, 285-286, 355-356, 386-89, 399, 525, 547-548; Connor quote from 230. Also, Stephen E. Ambrose, *Nothing Like in the World*, 222-223; "Major Frank Joshua North" (Lincoln: Nebraska Department of Education, n.d.) at http://www.nde.state.ne.us/SS/notables/north.html; "The North Brothers" (Lincoln: Nebraska State Historical Society, 2004) at http://www.nebraskahistory.org/publish/markers/texts/north_brothers.htm [November 11, 2006].

Pawokti
Swanton, 135, 154, 157.

Pawtucket
Swanton, 18. "Brief Historical Background" (Reserve, MA: Revere Society for Cultural & Historic Preservation) at http://www.revere.org/history_fr.htm; Katie M, "Worcester History from 1657 to 1786" (Worchester, MA, n.d.) at http://www.geocities. com/sssbonus/KatieWH.html; "The Nipmuc People, Their Territory & Language" (Thompson, CT: N.I.A.C., Inc., 1994-2006) at http:// www.nativetech.org/Nipmuc/placenames/territory.html; "The Squaw Sachem and Her Red Men... (Winchester, MA, n.d.) at http://www. winchestermass.org/sachem_6.html and http://www.winchestermass.org/sachem_notes.html; Wilson Waters, "History of Chelmsford, an

excerpt" (Chelmsford, MA, n.d.) at http://www.chelmhist.org/INDIANS.htm; "About Medford" (Medford, MA: Medford Historical Society, n.d.) at http://www.medfordhistorical.org/peculiarplantation.php [August 12, 2006].

Edward W. Pride, *Tewksbury: A Short History* (Cambridge: Tewksbury Village Improvement Association and Riverside Press, 1888) available from Tewksbury Historical Society (2002) at http://www.tewksbury.com/pride.html; "Soldiers in King Philip's War" (USGenNet Safe-Site, 2001), pt. 2, ch. 27, at http://www.usgennet.org/usa/topic/newengland/philip/21-end/ch27pt2.html and pt. 3, ch. 21, at http://www.usgennet.org/usa/topic/newengland/philip/21-end/ch21pt3.html; William James Sidis, "Wonalancet, the 'Pleasant-Breathing,'" Passaconaway in the White Mountains (Sidis Archives, n.d.), ch. 3, at http://www.sidis.net/PASSChap3.htm; Bonnie May, "Tribal Wamesit Indian History" (Wamesit, NH and Tewksbury, Wamesit, MA, n.d.) at http://home1.gte.net/vze79mi8/index.htm...; John H. Goodale, "History of Nashua, New Hampshire…," pt. 2, 144, made available by Janice Brown for Genealogy and History of New Hampshire at http://www.nh.searchroots.com/documents/Hillsborough/History_Nashua_NH_2.txt; Sumner Hunnewell, "The Battle at Moore's Brook, Scarborough, Maine, June 29, 1677," The Maine Genealogist (May and August, 2003) available from Hampton Library (Hampton, NH, 2003) at http://www.hampton.lib.nh.us/hampton/history/military/mooresbrook.htm [August 20, 2006].

Peanquicha
"Western Border: Indian Occupants-Border Warfare-Treaties-Facts and Incidents," The History of Union County, Ohio. Chapter II (Chicago: W. H. Beers & Co., 1883), 223-224, made available from Heritage Pursuit (Union County, OH, n.d.) at http://www.heritagepursuit.com/Union/Unp3c2.htm [July 20, 2006].

"Extract, Memoir on Louisiana, ca. 1702" made available from Glen Black Laboratory of Archaeology (Bloomington, IN: University of Indiana, 1997-2001) at http://www.gbl.indiana.edu/archives/miamis4/M17-03_25a.html [August 24, 2006]. From Chevalier de Beaurain, English Translation of Margry, vol. 6, 93-110.

Pechanga Luiseño
"History" (Temecula, CA: Pechanga Band of Luiseño Indians, 2006) at http://www.pechanga-nsn.gov/page?pageId=11[April 2, 2006].

Pecos Pueblo
Swanton, 336-337.

Pedee
Swanton, 97. "South Carolina – Indians, Native Americans – The Pee Dee" South Carolina Information Highway (2007 SCIway.net, 2007) at http://www.sciway.net/hist/indians/peedee.html; "South Carolina Indian Tribes and Groups" (Columbia, SC: State of South Carolina, n.d.) at http://www.state.sc.us/cma/pdfs/s_c_tribes_and_groups.pdf [October 20, 2007].

Pee Dee Indians of Beaver Creek
"Native Americans – Pee Dee Indian Nation of Beaver Creek," South Carolina Information Highway (2007 SCIway.net, 2007) at http://www.sciway.net/hist/indians/beaver-creek-pee-dee-indians-sc.html; "South Carolina Indian Tribes and Groups" (Columbia, SC: State of South Carolina, n.d.) at http://www.state.sc.us/cma/pdfs/s_c_tribes_and_groups.pdf [October 20, 2007]. Sonja Gleaton, "The Great Spirit...never forgets," *The Times and Democrat*, n.d. (Orangeburg, SC, 2007) at http://www.timesanddemocrat.com/articles/2007/03/11/features/doc45...f480082152b218049844.prt; J. Michelle Schohn, "History" (SC: Pee Dee Indian Nation, n.d.) at http://www.peedeeindiannation.com/page2.html [October 22, 2007].

Pehnahterkuh Comanche
For the Council House Tragedy, see T. R. Fehrenbach, *Comanches*, 322-333, 334-348. Also, Wallace L. McKeehan, "The Council House Fight" and the Comanche Attack on Linnville: The Battle of Plum Creek (Sons of Dewitt County Texas, 1997-2005) at http://www.tamu.edu/ccbn/dewitt/plumcreek.htm; "Raiding Comanches soundly defeated at Plum Creek," *Handbook of Texas Online* (Austin, TX: Texas State Historical Association and the University of Texas, 2006) at http://www.tsha.utexas.edu/daybyday/08-12-001.html; "Comanche War" (Austin: Texas State Library & Archives Association, 2005) at http://www.tsl.state.tx.us/exhibits/indian/war/page2.html [November 11, 2006].

Pennacook
Swanton, 13, 15, 16, 17-18, 19, 20, 23. Edward W. Pride, *Tewksbury: A Short History* (Cambridge: Tewksbury Village Improvement Association and Riverside Press, 1888) available from Tewksbury Historical Society (2002) at http://www.tewksbury.com/pride.html [August 20, 2006].

Penobscot
Swanton, 16-17; Deborah Champlain, "Penobscot: Where the Rocks Spread Out" (Rhode Island: Northeast Wigwam, 1998-2000) at http://www.newigwam.com/hpenobscot.html [subsequently offline].

Pensacola
Swanton, 136-137, 159, 191.

Peoria
Swanton, 241-242.

Pepicokia
Swanton, 237-240.

Pequawket
Swanton, 13-15.

Pequot
Swanton, 31-33; Nathaniel Philbrick, *Mayflower*, 353, 356; Laurence M. Hauptman and James D. Wherry, *The Pequots in Southern New England: The Fall and Rise of an American Indian Nation*. For the Pequot War, see Nathaniel Philbrick, *Mayflower*, 178-179, 231, 241, 253, 277; Brandford quote from 178. Also see Swanton, 32. Also, Major John Mason, "A Brief History of the Pequot War" available Daynes Family (New London, CT, updated 2006) at http://www.daynesfamilytree.com/Mason'sNarrative.htm [April 12, 2006].

Piankatank
Swanton, 66-71. Charles A. Grymes, "'Indians' of Virginia - The Real First Families of Virginia" (Virginia Places, 1998) at http://www.virginiaplaces.org/nativeamerican/; Deane Winegar, "Longstreet Highroad Guide to the Chesapeake Bay" (Decater, GA: Lenz Design, 2001-2002) at http://www.sherpaguides.com/chesapeake_bay/middle_peninsulas/middle_peninsula.html [August 12, 2006]. First published in the Print Media, 2000.

Piankeshaw
Swanton, 54, 237-240, 242, 297, 300, 302. Gloria Jahoda, *Trail of Tears*, 288, 292; Charles J. Kappler, ed., *Indian Affairs: Laws and Treaties* (Washington, DC, 1903), vol. II; Francis Paul Prucha, *Atlas of American Indian Affairs* (Lincoln, NE: University of Nebraska Press, 1990).

"Piankeshaw Indians," Ohio's Historic Indians (Columbus: Ohio Historical Society, 1998-2004) at http://www.ohiohistorycentral.org/entry.php?rec=617; Dorothy Libby, *An Anthropological Report on the Piankashaw Indians: Piankashaw Locations, ca. 1776- ca. 1783*, available from the OhioValley-Great Lakes Ethnohistory Archives: The Miami Collection (Bloomington, IN: Glenn Black Laboratory of Archaeology and Trustees of Indiana University, 1996, updated October 6, 2000), 90-99, at http://www.gbl.indiana.edu/archives/dockett_99/99_6a.html [August 11, 2006].

Pianria
"Western Border: Indian Occupants-Border Warfare-Treaties-Facts and Incidents," *The History of Union County, Ohio*. Chapter II (Chicago: W. H. Beers & Co., 1883), 223-224, made available from Heritage Pursuit (Union County, OH, n.d.) at http://www.heritagepursuit.com/Union/Unp3c2.htm [July 20, 2006].

Wm. M. Darlington, "Indian Nations and Their Numbers of Fighting Men," Appendix V of:
Smith, Col. James, *An Account of the Remarkable Occurrences in the Life and Travels of Col. James Smith* (Cincinnati, 1907), 153-155, made available from Glen Black Laboratory of Archaeology (Bloomington, IN: University of Indiana, 1997-2001) at http://www.gbl.indiana.edu/archives/miamis15/M64_5a.html [August 12, 2006].

Picuris Pueblo
Swanton, 344-346; T. Harmon Parkhurst, Indian Tales from Picurís Pueblo (Santa Fe, NM: Ancient City Press, 1989). "Pikuri" (Peñasco, NM: Picuris Pueblo, n.d.) at http://www.laplaza.org/penasco/picuris/picuris.html; "San Lorenzo Mission"; "Los Matachines" at .../sanlorenzo.html and .../matachines.html; "Dances and Feast Days" (Guilford, CT: Insiders' Guide, Globe Pequot Press, n.a.) at http://www.insiders.com/santafe/main-cultures3.htm [April 7, 2006].

Piegan Blackfeet
John C. Ewers, *The Blackfeet: Raiders on the Northwestern Plains*; Swanton, 393, 395-398. For the Marias Massacre, see Ewers, 246-253; Robert M. Utley, *The Indian Frontier of the American West*, 133.

Pima
Swanton, 360-363. Thomas Edwin Farish, *The History of Arizona*, vol. vii, chps. 14, 15, 16. "History & Culture" (Phoenix, AZ: Salt River Pima-Maricopa Indian Community, 2001-2006); "Native American" (Clarkdale, AZ, n.a.) at http://www.wildapache.net/NativeAmericanSite/ [April 3, 2006].

Pinal Coyotero Apache
Swanton 327-330; James L. Haley, *Apaches*, 247, 258-259, 260, 261, 272, 284, 295, 307.

Pinaleño Apache
Swanton, 365.

Pinneshow
Samuel G. Drake, *The Aboriginal Races of North America...*, 9-16.

Piro Pueblo Group
Swanton, 334, 337-339, 340.

Piscataqua
Swanton, 17-18 (Pennacook); 57-59 (Conoy).

"The Many Names of Dover" (Dover, NH: Dover Public Library) at http://www.dover.lib.nh.us/DoverHistory/many_names_of_dover.htm; Richie, "I is for Indian: Indian Princess Mary" (Towson, MD: Towson University, 2006) at http://www.towson.edu/csme/mctp/StudentProjects/FamousMarylanders/page9.htm; "The Beginning, Progress, and Conclusion of Bacon's Rebellion in Virginia, In the Years 1675 and 1676" (Washington, DC: Peter Force, 1835) made available from *Thomas Jefferson Papers, Series 8: Virginia Records, 1606-1737*, at http://memory.loc.gov/ammem/collections/jefferson_papers/tm.html [August 11, 2006].

Anonymous, "On Bacon's Rebellion in Virginia (1676)" available from Annals of American History (Encyclopædia Britannica, Inc.) at http://america.eb.com/america/print?articleId=385083; "Pennacook/Merrimac/St. Francois Indians (Accominta, Agawam, Morattigan, Nashua, Natticook, Naumkeag, Newichawawock, Pennacook, Pentucket, Piscataqua, Souhegan, Squamscot, Wachusett, Wamesit, Weshacum, Winnecowet, and Winnipesaukee)" (Shades - Design by ChrisTime, n.d.) at http://www.angelfire.com/realm/shades/nativeamericans/pennacook. htm [August 11, 2006]. This site refers to First Nations histories at http://www.dickshovel.com/penna.html.

Pishquitpah

"Information on the Yakima and Walla Walla Indians," The Lewis and Clark Journey of Discovery (Washington, DC: National Park Service), [Lewis] Friday April 25th 1806, at http://www.nps.gov/jeff/LewisClark2/TheJourney/NativeAmericans/Yakima.htm; Noah Brooks, "First Across the Continent: The Story of The Exploring Expedition of Lewis and Clark in 1804-5-6" (New York: Charles Scribner's Sons, 1902) made available by WebRoots.org (WebRoots, Inc., 2001-2004), 2nd printing of 1901 ed., ch. xx, 270, at http://www.webroots.org/library/usatrav/fatclc06.html [August 12, 2006].

Pisquose

Swanton, 450.

Pissasec

Swanton, 66-71.

Pit Indians

H. W. Brands, *The Age of Gold*, 188; Swanton, 479-480; Lake County Museum Native American Room (Lakeview, OR: Lake County Museum, 2005) at http://www.lakecountymuseum.com/nativeamericanroom.html [June 19, 2006].

Plains Ojibwa

Swanton, 260-264.

Playano Salinas

Swanton, 512.

Pocasset

Nathaniel Philbrick, *Mayflower*, 199, 206, 244, 246, 251, 253, 254, 256, 316; map 166-167.

Pocumtuc

Swanton, 23-24.

Pohoy

Swanton, 137.

Pojoaque Pueblo

Swanton, 340-344.

Polakakai

Charles J. Kappler, "Revised Spelling of Names of Indian Tribes and Bands," *Indian Affairs: Laws & Treaties*, Appendix I, vol. I, Laws (Washington, DC: Government Printing Office, 1904) available from Oklahoma State University at http://digital.library.okstate.edu/kappler/Vol1/HTML_files/APP1021.html [April 7, 2006].

Pomeiooc

Fred Willard, "Trade Items as Transfer of Money," November 2002, made available by the Lost Colony Center for Science and Research (Eastern Carolina University) at http://lost-colony.com/trade.html [June 12, 2006].

Pomo Peoples

Swanton, 509-512; Kevin Starr, 99.

Phillip M. White, "California Indians and Their Reservations" (San Diego, CA: San Diego State University, updated 2006) at http://infodome.sdsu.edu/research/guides/calindians/calinddictmp.shtml; Paula Giese, "Pomo People: Brief History' (1996-1997) at http://www.kstrom.net/isk/art/basket/pomohist.html [May 7, 2006].

For the Clear Lake Massacre, see Kevin Starr, *California*, 99. Also, "Bloody Island, Lake County," A History of American Indians in California (Washington, DC: National Park Service, Modified: Nov 17, 2004) at http://www.cr.nps.gov/history/online_books/5views/5views1h8.htm; Chris and David Long, "Clear Lake Massacre or the Bloody Island Massacre" (2006) at http://www.chrisanddavid.com/clearlakemassacre/index.shtml; Chris Gray, "Effects of the California Gold Rush on Native Americans" (Rossville, KS, 2004) at http://www.kawvalley.k12.ks.us/schools/rjh/marneyg/03-04_Plains-Projects/Gray_04_goldrush.htm [July 7, 2006].

For the Mendocino War, see Chronology of California History: The Gold Rush, 1848 to 1869 at http://www.notfrisco.com/almanac/timeline/goldrush.html; "California and the Indian Wars: The Mendocino War of 1859-1860" (California State Military Museum, n.d.) at http://www.militarymuseum.org/Mendocino%20War.html [November 20, 2006].

Ponca
Swanton, esp. 291; William E. Unrau, *The Kansa Indians*, 12-13; Helen Hunt Jackson, *A Century of Dishonor*, 186-217, 359-374.

Ponkapoag
"Ponkapoag Indians of Massachusetts" (Brockton, MA: Ponkapoag Tribal Council, n.d.) at http://home.comcast.net/~dalresearch/ponka.htm; "Canton's Native Americans: The Ponkapoag Tribe" (Canton, MA: Canton Historical Society) at http://www.canton.org/native/ [September 12, 2006].

Port Gamble S'Klallam
"Port Gamble Tribe," NWIFC Member Tribes (Olympia, WA: Northwest Indian Fisheries Commission, n.d.) at http://www.nwifc.wa.gov/tribes/members/tribe.asp?tribe=port_gamble; Tribal Council, "The Port Gamble S'Klallam Tribe" (Kingston, WA: Port Gamble S'Klallam Tribe, n.d.) at http://home.earthlink.net/~gregoryaa/skybird/gamble/ [September 10, 2006].

Port Orford
Swanton, 472; Title 25, Chapter 14, Subchapter XXX, §692 of the U.S. Code.

"Oregon History- Indian Wars," *Blue Book* (Salem, OR: Office of the Secretary of State, n.d.) at http://bluebook.state.or.us/cultural/history/history14.htm; "The Battle of Battle Rock" (Port Orford, OR: City of Port Orford) at http://www.portorford.org/visit/History/Founding.html; Janine M. Bork, *History of the Pacific Northwest: Oregon and Washington 1889*, (Union County, OR, 2000 - 2003), vol. I, ch. xliii (1851), 389-396, at http://www.usgennet.org/usa/or/county/union1/1889vol1/1889volumepage389-396.htm; J. D. Adams, "The History of Battle Rock" (Northwest Travel Tips, 2001-2006) at http://www.travel-to-oregon-tips.com/port-orford.html, refers to the "local Indians, California Siwashes." [July 11, 2006].

"Humbug Mountain State Park" (Salem, OR: Oregon Parks and Recreation, 2006) at http://www.oregonstateparks.org/images/pdf/humbug_full.pdf#search='Indians%20Port%20Orford'; "Southern Oregon Coast," Frommer's Oregon, 5th ed. (Wiley Publishing, 2000-2005) at http://www.frommers.com/destinations/print-narrative.cfm?destID=2760&catID=27600 10001 [July 12, 2006].

Postito
Thomas N. Campbell, "Pastate Indians," *Handbook of Texas Online* (Austin, TX: Texas State Historical Association and University of Texas, 2001) at http://www.tsha.utexas.edu/handbook/online/articles/PP/bmp40.html; "Coahuiltecan Tribes," Four Corners Institute (Four Directions Press, 2005) at http://www.fourdir.com/coahuiltecan_tribes.htm [May 26, 2006]. Also see Campbell's "Pastia Indians" at the *Handbook of Texas Online* at http://www.tsha.utexas.edu/handbook/online/articles/PP/bmp42.html [December 13, 2006]. Also, see "Pasita" of the Tamaulipec group of Mexico in Swanton, 631, 635.

Potano
Swanton, 137-138, 150.

Potapaco
Swanton, 57-59.

Potawatomi
Swanton, 247-250; 297-298, 302 (Potawatomie of the Woods). Gloria Jahoda, *Trail of Tears*, 190-200; Dee Brown, *Hear That Lonesome Whistle Blow*, 14, 47. Robert C. Carriker, Father Peter John DeSmet, xvi, 30, 41; Barbara O. Korner, "Philippine Duchesne: A Model of Action," *Missouri Historical Review* (Columbia: State Historical Society of Missouri, July 1992), lxxxvi, 4, 341-362. Benjamin Marie Petit, *The Trail of Death Letters* (Indiana Historical Society, 1941; reprinted 2003 in *Potawatomi Trail of Death*).

Richard D. and Lucena A. Taylor, "The Pottawatomie Indians of Elkhart and South Bend," An American Trek (2005-2006) at http://www.richarddeantaylor.com/htm/pottawatomie.htm [August 17, 2006]; David A. Baerreis, "The Band Affiliation of Potawatomi Treaty Signatories," available from the OhioValley-Great Lakes Ethnohistory Archives: The Miami Collection (Bloomington, IN: Glenn Black Laboratory of Archaeology and Trustees of Indiana University, 1996-2003), 41-46, at http://www.gbl.indiana.edu/Pot2/TS_5a.html; also Geographic Locations at http://www.gbl.indiana.edu/Pot/PIL147.html [August 23, 2006].

Smokey McKinney, "William Elsey Connelley's 'Prairie Band of Pottawatomie Indians,'" (Topeka, KS: Kansas State Historical Society, 1997) at http://www.kansasheritage.org/PBP/books/kshsroll/c_intro.html; Arthur J. Hope, *The Story of Notre Dame: Notre Dame—One Hundred Years* (University of Notre Dame Press, 1999) available at http://www.archives.nd.edu/hope/hope.htm; Diane Good, "A Moment in Time" (Topeka, KS: Kansas State Historical Society, March 2002) at http://www.kshs.org/features/feat302.htm; Rebecca Martin, "A Moment in Time" (Topeka, KS: Kansas State Historical Society, May 1995) at http://www.kshs.org/features/feat595.htm; James Mooney, "Catholic Indian Missions of the United States," *Catholic Encyclopedia*, (K. Knight, 2004), vol. x, at http://www.newadvent.org/cathen/10384a.htm [June 7, 2006]. Also, W. Willard, "Potawatomi Trail of Death" (Rochester, IN: Fulton County Historical Society, updated Sep 1, 2007) at http://www.potawatomi-tda.org/ [September 28, 2007].

Mark G. Thiel, Archivist, "Christianity and Native America," Special Collections/ University Archives (Milwaukee, Wisconsin: Marquette University, 2003) at http://www.mu.edu/library/collections/archives/indians.html; Jeanne Kun, "I Can Only Adore the Designs of God": The Life of St. Rose Philippine Duchesne (The Word Among Us, 2002) at http://www.wau.org/about/authors/kun1.html; Rev. Thomas H. Kinsella, "The History of Our Cradle Land," A Centenary of Catholicity in Kansas, 1822-1922 (Kansas City: Casey Printing Co, 1921) available from the Kansas State Library Blue Shyways (1998) at http://skyways.lib.ks.us/genweb/miami/kinsella/kinsel04.html [June 7, 2006].

For the Fort Dearborn Massacre, see W. H. Brands, *Andrew Jackson*, 178. Also, "The Fort Dearborn Massacre," War of 1812 (Canada: Galafilm, 2006) at http://www.galafilm.com/1812/e/events/ftdearborn.html; Nelly Kinzie Gordon, ed., *The Fort Dearborn Massacre* (1912), 17-23, 44-77, available from Hillsdale College (Hillsdale, MI: 2005) at http://www.hillsdale.edu/personal/stewart/war/America/1812/North/1812 -Dearborn-Helm.htm and ...Dearborn-Kinzie.htm [November 6, 2006].

For the Missouri French-Canadian Colony, see *Jesuit Services to Indians, Addendum 1: Some Examples of Jesuit Service to the Indian Nations and Work in the State of Missouri within the Boundaries of the Present Diocese of Kansas City-St. Joseph by County* (Kansas City: Diocese of Kansas City-St. Joseph, n.d.).

Potawatomi of the Woods
Swanton, 297-298, 302

Potoash
Samuel G. Drake, *The Aboriginal Races of North America...*, 9-16; "Sauvie Island" (Portland, OR: MFPCA, n.d.) at http://vgaetz.home.mindspring.com/sauvie.html [August 14, 2006].

"Clark, William. Estimate of the Western Indians," American Indian Manuscripts (American Philosophical Association Library), Item 2433, D. 4p. and 1p. Map, at http://www.amphilsoc.org/library/guides/indians/info/noea.htm; also Lewis, Meriwether, and William Clark, Codex N: *Clark's journal* [Aug. 15-Sept. 26, 1806], Item 2990, D. 1, at http://www.amphilsoc.org/library/guides/indians/info/pl.htm [August 9, 2006].

Potomac
Edmond S. Morgan, *American Slavery, American Freedom*, 250, 250n2; Swanton, 66-71.

Powhatan
Swanton, 66-71; Edmond S. Morgan, *American Slavery, American Freedom*, 331; Daniel K. Richter, *Facing East from Indian Country*, 69-78.

Powhatan Confederacy
Edmond S. Morgan, *American Slavery, American Freedom*, 49, 57, 72, 97-100, 104, 121, 149, 230, 231, 231n45; Swanton, esp. 66-71; Drake, *Indians of North America*, 355-359.

"Powhatan," Historical Information (Gloucester, VA, updated 05/22/2006) at http://www.co.gloucester.va.us/powha1.htm; "Chief Powhatan" (Association for the Preservation of Virginia Antiquities,1997-1998) at http://www.apva.org/ngex/chief.html; "The Powhatan Indians" (BayDreaming, 2003) at http://www.baydreaming.com/powhatan.htm; "Uncovering Werowocomoco," William and Mary News, October 23, 2003 (College of William & Mary, 2006) at http://powhatan.wm.edu/pressReleases/index.htm [September 4, 2006]. See Werowocomoco Research Project at http://powhatan.wm.edu/.

Cynthia L. Swope, "Military Actions of the Powhatan Confederacy" (Within the Vines, 2003-2004) at http://www.cynthiaswope.com/withinthevines/jamestown/natamer/militaryactions.html; "Virginia State History," State History Guide (SHG Resources, 2003) at http://www.shgresources.com/va/history/ [July 8, 2006].

Prairie Potawatomi
Swanton, 297-298, 302. "History" (Mayetta, KS: Prairie Band Potawatomi Nation, n.d.) at http://www.pbpindiantribe.com/history.htm [November 30, 2006].

Praying Indians
Swanton, 19-20, 25; Drake, *Indians of North America*, 175-184. Nathaniel Philbrick, *Mayflower*, Praying Indians, 191-192, 211, 219, 221, 222, 261, 262, 263, 296-297, 309, 311 and Nemasket village, 105, 106, 113, 115, 119.

Bill Taylor, "Praying Indians of Titicut" (Middleborough, MA: Taunton River Assn., n.d.)at http://www.tauntonriver.org/prayindian.htm [September 12, 2006]; "First People of Tennessee And the American Southeast" (TNGenNet, 2002-2003) at http://www.tngennet.org/tnfirst/tribes-list.html; Indian A Tribes," Indian Genealogy (Access Genealogy, 2004-2006) at http://www.accessgenealogy.com/native/tribes/nations/tribesa.htm [July 28, 2006]. Source: Hodge, *Handbook of American Indians*, 1906.

Pshwanwapam
Swanton, 424, 434. Jennifer Cochran, "About the County" (Kittitas County, WA, 2007) at http://www.co.kittitas.wa.us/about/history.asp [December 30, 2007].

Pueblo Peoples
David Roberts, *The Pueblo Revolt*, esp. 28-29, 31-35, 116, 124; T. R. Fehrenbach, *Comanches*, 85-86; Philip Kopper, *The Smithsonian Book of North American Indians Before the Coming of the Europeans*, 82, 91, 236, 238-240, 245, 279; Swanton, 317, 324, 333, 335, 383, 339-340, 343, 346; Alice Thorson, "Bring in the Clowns" and Alice Thorson and Neil Nakahodo, "Anatomy of a Kosha," *Kansas City Star*, September 18, 2005, I-1, I-8, respectively.

"The Ancestral Pueblos (Anasazi)" (Dolores, CO: Anasazi Heritage Center, Bureau of Land Management, 2004) at http://www.co.blm.gov/ahc/anasazi.htm; Indian Pueblo Cultural Center (Albuquerque, NM: Institute for Pueblo Indian Studies, n.a.) at http://www.indianpueblo.org/index.cfm?module=ipcc&pn=1; Alan Petersen, "ART221 Art of the Southwest" (Flagstaff: AZ: Coconino Community College, 2000-2003) at http://www.coco.cc.az.us/apetersen/_art221/spanish1.htm [March 9, 2006].

For *Pueblo Revolt*, see David Roberts, *Pueblo Revolt*, esp. 9-27, 125-126, 135-136, 165, 192. Also, Charles Wilson Hackett, "The Revolt of the Pueblo Indians of New Mexico in 1680", *Southwestern Historical Quarterly* Online, vol. 15, no. 2, 93-147 at http://www.tsha.utexas.edu/publications/journals/shq/online/v015/n2/article_1_print.html [April 5, 2006].

Purisimeño Chumash
Swanton, 484-487.

Puyallup
Swanton, 422, 429, 434.

Quabaog
Swanton, 23. Also, "Soldiers in King Philip's War" (USGenNet, 2001), ch. 17, pt. 4, at http://www.usgennet.org/usa/topic/newengland/philip/11-20/ch17pt4.html; also ch. 17, pt. 1, at http://www.usgennet.org/usa/topic/newengland/philip/11-20/ch17pt1.html; Thomas Wheeler, "Wheeler's Narrative [Expedition to Quabaug in 1675]," *Granite State Magazine* (January 1906), vol. 1, no.1, available online from publisher (Manchester, NH, 2005) at http://granite-state-magazine.blogspot.com/2005_02_01_granite-state-magazine_archive.html [August 13, 2006].

Quabaug
Nathaniel Philbrick, *Mayflower*, 195.

Quahattika
Swanton, 363-364.

Quanataguo
Swanton, 309-311; Thomas N. Campbell, "Quanataguo Indians," *Handbook of Texas Online* (Austin, TX: Texas State Historical Association and University of Texas, 2001) at http://www.tsha.utexas.edu/handbook/online/articles/QQ/bmq1.html [May 26, 2006].

Quapaw
Swanton, 213-215; William E. Unrau, *The Kansa Indians*, 12-13; Jean Delanglez, "The Jolliet Lost Map of the Mississippi," *Mid-America, An Historical Review* (Chicago, IL: Loyola University, April 1946), vol. 28 (New Series, vol. 17), no. 2, 67-143, esp. 109, 134-135. See also Landon Y. Jones, *William Clark and the Shaping of the West*, 243, 247-248. "Arkansas Indians" (Fayetteville, AR: Arkansas Archeological Survey, 2003) at http://www.uark.edu/campus-resources/archinfo/ArkansasIndianTribes.pdf [September 16, 2007].

Quarai Pueblo
Author Correspondence: Amy G. Johnson, Curatorial Assistant, Indian Pueblo Cultural Center, Albuquerque, New Mexico, March 10, 2006.

Quathlahpohtle
"Information on the Chinookan Indians," The Lewis and Clark Journey of Discovery (Washington, DC: National Park Service, n.d.) at http://www.nps.gov/jeff/LewisClark2/TheJourney/NativeAmericans/Chinookan.htm; Lyn Topinka, "Lewis and Clark and the Lewis River ..." (English River Website, 2006) at http://englishriverwebsite.com/LewisClarkColumbiaRiver/Regions/Places/lewis_river.html; Meriwether Lewis and William Clark, "*The Journals of Lewis and Clark*" (Pearson Education, 2000-2006), April 3, 1806, at http://www.infoplease.com/t/hist/lewis-clark-journal/day690.html [August 13, 2006].

Quatoghie
Samuel G. Drake, *The Aboriginal Races of North America...*, 9-16.

Queet
Swanton, 434-435.

Queissei
Herbert E. Bolton, "The Founding of the Missions on the San Gabriel River, 1745-1749," *Southwestern Historical Quarterly*, vol. 17, no. 4, 323-378, SHQ Online at http://www.tsha.utexas.edu/publications/journals/shq/online/v017/n4/article_1.html [May 24, 2006].

Quieetso
Samuel G. Drake, *The Aboriginal Races of North America...*, 9-16.

Quileute
Swanton, 417, 424, 435; Robert Brockstedt Lane and Barbara Lane, "The Treaties of Puget Sound 1854-1855," The Fourth World Documentation
Project (Olympia, WA: Center for World Indigenous Studies, 1999) at http://www.cwis.org/fwdp/Americas/wwpugsnd.txt [September 8, 2006].

Quinault
Swanton, 435-436; Robert Brockstedt Lane and Barbara Lane, "The Treaties of Puget Sound 1854-1855," The Fourth World Documentation
Project (Olympia, WA: Center for World Indigenous Studies, 1999) at http://www.cwis.org/fwdp/Americas/wwpugsnd.txt [September 8, 2006].

Quinipissa
Swanton, 208-209.

Quinnechart
Samuel G. Drake, *The Aboriginal Races of North America...*, 9-16.

Quiutcanuaha
Swanton, 309-311; Thomas N. Campbell, "Quanataguo Indians," *Handbook of Texas Online* (Austin, TX: Texas State Historical Association and University of Texas, 2001) at http://www.tsha.utexas.edu/handbook/online/articles/QQ/bmq1.html [May 26, 2006].

Rappahannock
Swanton, 66-71.

Raritan
Russell Shorto, *The Island in the Center of the World*, 119-120; Edwin G. Burrows & Mike Wallace, *Gotham*, 5; Swanton, 48-55.

Reckgawawanc
Swanton, 48-55, esp. 49; Edwin G. Burrows & Mike Wallace, *Gotham*, 5.

Rincon Luiseño
"Directory of Indigenous Education Resources, West Region" (WestEd, 2006) at http://www.wested.org/lcd/IndigenousEdDir/CA/RSRC_CA.html [April 3, 2006].

Roanoke
Swanton, 80, 81. Edmond S. Morgan, *American Slavery, American Freedom*, 26-27, 33-34, 36-42, 57n.

Rockaway
Edwin G. Burrows & Mike Wallace, *Gotham*, 5, 8; Eric P. Robinson, "Far Rockaway" (New York: Chamber of Commerce of the Borough of Queens, 2006) at http://www.queenschamber.org/QueensInfo/NeighborhoodPages/farrockaway.html [May 9, 2006].

Round Heads
The History of Union County. Chapter II, Western Border: Indian Occupants-Border Warfare-Treaties-Facts and Incidents (Chicago: W. H. Beers & Co., 1883), 223-224, made available by Heritage Pursuit (Union County, OH, n.d.) at http://www.heritagepursuit.com/Union/Unp3c2.htm [July 20, 2006].

Ryawa
Samuel G. Drake, *The Aboriginal Races of North America...*, 9-16.

S'Homamish
Dr. Bruce Haulman, "Vashon-Maury Timeline" (2003) at http://www.vashonhistory.com/vashontimeline.htm; "Native American Studies" (Orono, ME: University of Maine Folger Library, 2004) at http://www.library.umaine.edu/class/Fernandez/nas2984.htm [May 18, 2006].

Sah-ku-mehu
"The Many Faces of Totem Poles" Coupeville, WA: Island County Historical Museum, n.d.) at http://www.islandhistory.org/research2.htm; "Sauk-Suiattle Web Page" (Darrington, WA: Sauk-Suiattle Indian Tribe, n.d.) at http://www.sauk-suiattle.com/.; "Sauk-Suiattle Tribe," NWIFC Member Tribes (Olympia, WA: Northwest Indian Fisheries Commission, n.d.) at http://www.nwifc.wa.gov/tribes/members/tribe.asp?tribe=Sauk [September 10, 2006].

Sahehwamish
Swanton, 436-437.

Saint Regis
Alan Taylor, *The Divided Ground*, 158, 225, 268, 307, 344-46; Swanton, 39, 40. "Tribal History" (Akwesasne, NY: Saint Regis Mohawk Tribe, 2004) at http://www.stregismohawktribe.com/his.htm; Darren Bonaparte, "St. Regis Mission Established 250 Years Ago This Year," *People's Voice*, March 25, 2005, available from The Wampum Chronicles (n.a.) at http://www.wampumchronicles.com/missionestablished.html [April 25, 2006].

Sakonnet
Swanton, 26, 27; Nathaniel Philbrick, *Mayflower*, 220, 233, 235, 236, 246, 247-251, 312-314, 316-319, 321-344, 348, 349-350.

Salinan
Swanton, 512.

Salish
Norman Bancroft-Hunt, *People of the Totem: The Indians of the Pacific Northwest*, 11; Bernard De Voto, ed., *The Journals of Lewis and Clark*, 209, 233-237, 249, 260, 321, 333-334, 336-337, 399, 411, 424, 436, 437n; Swanton, 393-395; Stephen E. Ambrose, *Undaunted Courage*, 284-286; Rober C. Carriker, *Father Peter John De Smet: Jesuit in the West*, esp. 18-21, 29-31, 34-40, 45-49, 100-103, 138-140, 157-159.

"Information on the Salish Indians Recorded by Members of the Lewis and Clark Expedition 1805" (Washington, DC: National Park Service, n.d.) at http://www.nps.gov/jeff/lewisclark2/TheJourney/NativeAmericans/Salish.htm; Stephenie Flora, "Northwest Indian Tribes" (The Oregon Territory and Its Pioneers, 1998-2006) at http://www.oregonpioneers.com/tribe.htm [August 6, 2006].

For Fr. De Smet, see Robert C. Carriker, *Father Peter John De Smet: Jesuit in the West*; David Dary, *The Oregon Trail*, 63-64, 72-73, 74, 76, 79, 248, 250, 302; Robert M. Utley, *The Lance and the Shield*, 76-81, 237, 341n5, 349-350n3; Irving Stone, *Men to Match My Mountains*, 27-28; Jonathan Wright, God's Soldiers, 261-262.

Published Works by Father Pierre Jean De Smet
The Indian Missions in the United States of America Under the Care of the Missouri Province of the Society of Jesus (Philadelphia: King and Baird, 1841); *Letters and Sketches with a narrative of a Year's Residence among the Indian Tribes of the Rocky Mountains* (Philadelphia: M. Fithian, 1843); *Oregon Missions and Travels over the Rocky Mountains in 1845-46* (New York: E. Dunigan, 1847); *New Indian Sketches* (New York: D. & J. Sadleir & Co., 1863); *Western Missions and Missionaries: A Series of Letters* (New York: J.B. Kirker, late E. Dunigan and Brother, 1863).

Salmon River Indians
Swanton, 471-472.

Saluda
Swanton, 56, 97-98, 99.

Samish
Swanton, 427, 437.

San Antonio Salinas
Swanton, 512.

San Manuel
"Tribal Overview" (CA: San Manuel Band of Mission Indians, 2006) at http://www.sanmanuel-nsn.gov/ [April 3, 2006].

San Marcos Pueblo
David Roberts, *The Pueblo Revolt*, 9-10,15-16, 22, 40-41, 44, 50, 199. Also, Michael Padilla, "The Secrets of San Marcos Pueblo" (Albuquerque, NM: University of New Mexico, n.d.) at http://www.unm.edu/~quantum/quantum_fall_1999/san_marcos.html; "Notice of Inventory Completion: American Museum of Natural History" (Washington, DC: National Park Service) at http://www.cr.nps.gov/nagpra/fed_notices/nagpradir/nic0830. html and http://www.cr.nps.gov/nagpra/fed_notices/nagpradir/ nic0829.pdf#search='San%20Marcos%20Pueblo' [October 18, 2006].

Homer E. Milford, "The Settlement of the Los Cerrillos Area, 1643-1880s" (n.a.) at http://www.cerrilloshills.org/mines/real08.htm; "Period of Spanish Exploration, 1540-1598" at http://www.cerrilloshills.org/mines/real06.htm [October 18, 2006]. Originally published by the New Mexico Abandoned Mine Land Bureau: Reports 1994-2 and 1996-1.

San Miguel Salinas
Swanton, 512.

Saguenay
Daniel K. Richter, *Facing East from Indian Country*, 29, 30, 32. Also, Manon Hamel, " Royaume du Saguenay" (FOTW Flags of the World, 2007) at http://www.crwflags.com/fotw/flags/ca-qc-sa.html; James Mooney, "Montagnais Indians," *Catholic Encyclopedia*, Vol. X (New York: Robert Appleton Company, 1911), New Advent Edition (Kevin Knight, 2007) at http://www.newadvent.org/cathen... /10512a.htm [October 1, 2007].

Sankhikan
James B. Jones, Jr., "Susquehanna Indian Tribe History " (Southern History, 2005) at http://www.southernhistory.net/index.php?name=News... &file=article&sid=9472&theme=Printer; "Sonckhicon (or Sanckhekin)," Primary Source Microfilm Guide (Gale, Inc., 2002) at http://... microformguides.gale.com/Data/Index/203000s.htm; "The Mohawks," *History of the Mohawk Valley: Gateway to the West 1614-1925*. Chapter 5 (NY: Schenectady County Public Library, 2006) at http://www.schenectadyhistory.org/resources/mvgw/history/005.html [August 14, 2005].

Sanpoil
Swanton, 431, 437-438.

Santa Clara Pueblo
Swanton, 340-341.

Santa Ynez Chumash
Swanton, 484-487.

Santee of South Carolina
Swanton, 98, 103.

Santiam Kalapuya
Swanton, 467-468.

Saone Sioux
George E. Hyde, *Red Cloud's Folk: A History of the Oglala Sioux*, 12-13.

Saponi

Swanton, 71-73; "Saponi History" (Chapel Hill, NC: Ibiblio, n.d.) at http://www.ibiblio.org/dig/html/split/report47b.html [August 15, 2006]; Brenda Collins Dillon and Rachel McCraw, "Searching for Saponi Town" (Jelsoft Enterprises Ltd., 2000-2006), posted 01-11-2004 and 03-12-2004, respectively, at http://www.saponitown.com/forum/showthread.php?s=d60cef23191770e55886c7ed37c32dcc&threadid=846 [August 18, 2006]. From, in part, Samuel James Ervin, Jr., *A Colonial History of Rowan County North Carolina*.

Sarcee

Swanton, 555, 591-593; Eung-Do Cook, "Sarsis," *L'Encyclopédie Canadienne* (Fondation Historica du Canada, 2004) at http://www.canadianencyclopedia.ca/index.cfm?PgNm=TCE&Params=A1ARTA0007149 [September 9, 2006].

Satsop

Swanton, 439-440.

Saturiwa

Swanton, 138-139.

Sauk

William T. Hagan, *The Sac and Fox Indians*; Eugene Morrow Violette, *History of Missouri*, 67, 68, 69, 70-71, 71n1; Shirley Christian, *Before Lewis and Clark*, 124-125; Gloria Jahoda, *Trail of Tears*, 92-93, 109-142, esp. 92-93, 110; Dee Brown, *Hear That Lonesome Whistle Blow*, 38. On the Sauk and Fox in Missouri, see also Walter A. Schroeder, "Populating Missouri, 1804-1821 (Columbia: *Missouri Historical Review*, July 2003), vol. xcvii, no. 4, 276, and Margot Ford McMillen, ed., "Les Indiens Osages: French Publicity for the Traveling Osages (MHR), vol. xcvii, no. 4, 296, 298-299, 305; Stephen E. Ambrose, *Undaunted Courage*, 444-447. Also see W. S. Fitzpatrick, comp., *Treaties and Laws of the Osage Nation, as Passed to November 26, 1890* (1895; reprint, Wilmington DE: Scholarly Resources, 1973), 1, 11, 18; James H. Knipmeyer, "Denis Julier: Midwestern Fur Trader," *Missouri Historical Review* (Columbia: State Historical Society of Missouri, April 2001), vol. xcv, no. 3, 245-263; Swanton, esp. 256-257.

"The Sac and Fox Nation" (Digital-Cowboy.Com, 1998-2000) at http://www.cowboy.net/native/sacnfox.html; "Rock River (Winnebago, Ogle, Lee, Whiteside, Henry, and Rock Island Counties, Illinois)" at http://pages.ripco.net/~jwn/rock.html; Roger Pyle and John Matthews, "Doniphan County," *Cutler's History of Kansas* (Kansas Collection Books, April 1999) at http://www.kancoll.org/books/cutler/doniphan/doniphan-co-p1.html [September 6, 2006].

For the Black Hawk War, see Ward H. Lamon, *The Life of Abraham Lincoln*, 98-116; Landon Y. Jones, *William Clark and the Shaping of the West*, 310-315, 319-320; Gloria Jahoda, *Trail of Tears*, 109-142. Also see "Battle at Bad Axe" (Washington, DC: U.S. Army Corps of Engineers St. Paul District, updated 2000) at http://www.mvp.usace.army.mil/history/bad%5Faxe/; Peter Shrake, "The Battle of Bad Axe," *Sauk County Historical Society Newsletter*, August 2001 (Baraboo, WI: SCHS, n.d.) at http://www.saukcounty.com/schs/history-battle.htm; James Lewis, *The Black Hawk War of 1832* (Northern Illinois University Abraham Lincoln Historical Digitization Project, 2000) at http://lincoln.lib.niu.edu/ blackhawk/ and http://lincoln.lib.niu.edu/blackhawk/page2c.html; C. V. Porter, "The Black Hawk War: Second Battle of the Bad Axe," *De Soto Chronicle*, February 5, 1887 available at http://www.geocities.com/old_lead/badax01.htm; "The Massacre at Bad Axe: Black Hawk's Account" (Madison: Wisconsin Historical Society, 1996-2006) at http://www.wisconsinhistory.org/teachers/lessons/secondary/bh_badaxe.asp[May 12, 2006]. Also, Mark Grimsley, "Interrogating the Project of Military History" (Columbus, OH: Ohio State University, 1996-2005, rev. October 31, 2006) at http://people.cohums.ohio-state.edu/grimsley1/ dialogue/postcolonialism/resistance_77.htm; Reuben Gold Thwaites, *The Black Hawk War* (1832), History Central (MultiEducator, 2000) at http://www.historycentral.com/documents/Blackhawk.html [November 3, 2006].

Sault Chippewa

Swanton. 260; Bernie Arbic, *City of the Rapids: Sault Ste. Marie's Heritage* (Sault Ste. Marie, MI, 2006); "Our Local History" (Sault Ste Marie, MI: Convention & Visitors Bureau, 2003) at http://www.saultstemarie.com/our-local-history-9/ and http://www.saultstemarie.com/sault-ste.-marie-in-the-1600--1700s-10/ [September 9, 2006].

Savannah

Daniel K. Richter, *Facing East from Indian Country*, 162; Claude Henry Neuffer, ed., *Names in South Carolina* (Columbia, SC: University of South Carolina, Winter, 1976), vol. 23, 20-21, available from the College of Arts and Sciences Institute for Southern Studies (Columbia, SC: University of South Carolina, 2002-2005), Winter, 1976, vol. 23, 20-22, at http://src1.cas.sc.edu/dept2/iss/SCNames/index.php?action... =showPage&book=3&volume=23&page=21;.Eric Browne,"Westo Indians" (Athens, GA: Georgia Humanities Council and the University of Georgia Press, 2004-2007) at http://www.georgiaencyclopedia.org/nge/Article.jsp?id=h-575; and "How the Colony Grew, Chapter 5," *History of Georgia, Colonial to 1900*, (n.d.) maintained by Tim Stowell, (Chattanooga, TN, 2002-2004) at http://www.usgennet.org/usa/ga/state1/history... /hist-5.htm; " English Conquest of Georgia" (WebRing, Ind., 2007) at http://www.lostworlds.org/gbo_english_conquest.html [October 5, 2007]. The last item originally published by John E. Worth at SpanishFlorida.net (1998-2003). Also, Terry Gray, "Commonwealths: Raiders; More Raiders" (Palomar College, 2001) at http://daphne.palomar.edu/marguello_students/Fall_2003/005387152/commonwealths_files/frame.htm; "Shawnee," Indian Tribes and Nations 8 (Indian Tribes and Nations : History, 2005) at http://www.axel-jacob.de/nations8.html [October 5, 2007]. For Bartram quote, see *Bartram's Travels* (Philadelphia, 1791), chap. viii, 466.

Sawokli

Swanton, 157, 170-171.

Scaticook

Swanton, 41-42. Charles F. Sedgwick, *General History of the Town of Sharon, Litchfield County, Conn. from Its First Settlement*, Chapter VI

(Amenia, NY: Charles Walsh, Printer and Publisher, 1877) available from Sharon, CT, at http://www.100megsfree3.com/litchfield/towns... /sharon/sharon-ch6.htm; "Pre-Settlement Inhabitants/Native American Presence, Town of Sharon" (Sharon, CT: Sharon Historical Society, updated 2005) at http://www.sharonhist.org/Sharonhistory.htm [April 18, 2006].

"Scattakook Indians," Massachusetts Archives Collection, 1629-1799, (Massachusetts Archives) at http://www.sec.state.ma.us/Archives... Search/RevolutionarySearch.asp?Action=S; Warren Sears Nickerson, "Indian Nations and Tribes," *Warren Sears Nickerson's Book of Cape Cod Native American Genealogies* (WIP) at http://wolfwalker2003.home.comcast.net/wamp5.htmhttp://www.sec.state.ma.us/ArchivesSearch... / RevolutionarySearch.asp [August 14, 2006].

Scoton
Palmer to Manypenny, 12 January 1854, in United States, Office of Indian Affairs, *Letters Received by the Office of Indian Affairs, 1824-1880*, National Archives Microcopy 234, Roll 608, NADP Document D22 and Ambrose to Palmer, 10 October, 1855, in United States, Office of Indian
Affairs, *Letters Received by the Office of Indian Affairs, 1824-1880*, National Archives Microcopy 234, Roll 608 (excerpt), NADP Document D31, available at http://www.csusm.edu/nadp/d22.htm#3 and #1 [May 18, 2006].

Secacawoni
Swanton, 66-71.

Seconondihago
Swanton, 56.

Secotan
Swanton, 81. Fred Willard, "Cultural Anthropology of Indian Villages" (East Carolina University) at http://www.lost-colony.com/cultural.html [June 10, 2006]; C. Wingate Reed, "Beaufort County: Two Centuries of Its History" (1962), 1-2, 7, 66, 67 made available online by the North Carolina History and Fiction Digital Library (Greenville, NC: Joyner Library, East Carolina University, n.d.) at http://digital.lib.ecu.edu/historyfiction/document/reb/entire.html; Fred Willard, "Trade Items as Transfer of Money," November 2002, made available by the Lost Colony Center for Science and Research (Eastern Carolina University) at http://lost-colony.com/trade.html [June 12, 2006].

Secowocomoco
Swanton, 57-59.

Seechelt
Swanton, 593.

Sekamish
Leonard Forsman and Dennis Lewarch of Larson, "Archaeology of the White River Valley," *White River Journal* (April 2001) made available by the White River Valley Museum (Auburn, WA, 2002, updated January 27, 2003) at http://www.wrvmuseum.org/journal/journal_0401.htm [June 22, 2006].

Sematuse
Swanton, 394-395.

Semiahmoo
Swanton, 440.

Seminole
Swanton, esp. 139-143; Fowl Towns, 132. Gloria Jahoda, *Trail of Tears*, 5, 243-262, 264-278; Daniel J. Boorstin, *The Americans: The Democratic Experience*, 278; T. R. Fehrenback, *Comanches*, 227; Mark F. Boyd, "The Seminole War: Its Background and Onset," *Florida Historical Quarterly* (July 1951), 30.

"Seminoles, A People Who Never Surrendered" (Seminole, OK: Seminole Nation, I. T., 2001-2006) at http://www.seminolenation-indianterritory.org/; "Indian removal, 1814-1858," Africans in America, Part 4: 1831-1865 (Boston: WGBH, 2004) at http://www.pbs.org/wgbh/aia/part4/4p2959.html; Donald L. Chamberlin, "Fort Brooke: Frontier Outpost, 1824-42," available from the University of South Florida (Tampa, FL, n.d.) at http://www.lib.usf.edu/ldsu/digitalcollections/T06/journal/v07n1_85/v07n1_85_05.pdf#search=Chamberlin%20Frontier%20Outpost%20182442' [September 7, 2006].

Exploring Florida (Tampa FL: College of Education, University of South Florida, 2002) at http://fcit.coedu.usf.edu/florida/lessons/tallahassee/tallahassee.htm and http://fcit.coedu.usf.edu/Florida/docs/j/jacks04.htm [August 6, 2006]; J. B. Bird, "The Seminoles," Rebellion (Austin, TX: University of Texas, 2005) at http://www.johnhorse.com/trail/00/bg/15.htm and http://www.johnhorse.com/trail/00/bg/03.1.htm [August 15, 2006].

For the Battle of Dunlawton, see Drake, *Indians of North America*, 425-426; Patrick L. Cooney, "Territorial Period To Statehood, 1821-1844,"Discovering Jacksonville and the Surrounding Area: Historical Tours, chp. 8 (Vernon Johns Society, n.d.) at http://www.vernonjohns.org/nonracists/jxsemwar.html and "Volusia County," Florida Historical Markers Program (Florida Department of State, 2006) at http://dhr.dos.state.fl.us/preservation/markers/markers.cfm?ID=volusia; For the Battle of Hatchee-Lustee, see Drake, *Indians of North America*, 478-477; Don Burzynski, "Gone to Fight the Indians," Army Times, February 17, 2006, available at http://www.armytimes.com/story.php?f=1-292308-1540303.php [October 30, 2006].

On the Black Seminole Rebellion, see J. B. Bird, "The largest slave rebellion in U.S. history" (Austin, TX: Rebellion: John Horse and the Black Seminoles, 2001-2005) at http://www.johnhorse.com/highlights/essays/largest.htm and "Le Vieux Carré et Paul Morphy" (Paul Morphy, n.d.) at http://sbchess.sinfree.net/vieuxcaree2.html [September 10, 2006].

Seneca

Swanton, 33-40, 55, 87, 228, 231, 237, 298, 300, 302; Alan Taylor, *The Divided Ground*, 133-136, 246-253, 313-316. Daniel J. Boorstin, *The Americans: The Democratic Experience*, 41-42; Edwin G. Burrows & Mike Wallace, *Gotham*, 13, 146; Gloria Jahoda *Trail of Tears*, 59-67, 68, 72; Washington Irving, Life and Times of Washington, 691; Thomas Jefferson, "To Brother Handsome Lake," Washington, November 3, 1802, Writings (New York: Library of America, 1984), 555-557; Samuel G. Drake, *The Aboriginal Races of North America...*, 9-16. For battles of Onoquaga and Cherry Valley, see Alan Taylor, *The Divided Ground*, 76, 93-94.

David Minor, "1677" (Eagles Byte, 2000) at http://home.eznet.net/~dminor/NYNY1675.html et al [September 7, 2006]; "Tribal History" Seneca Indians, 2000-2001) at http://www.senecaindians.com/seneca_tribal.htm [August 23, 2006].

"Onoquaga and Otsiningo" (1997-2001 Iroquois Studies Association, 1997-2001) at http://www.tier.net/~isa/onoq-ots.htm; Jack Brubaker, "Down the Susquehanna to the Chesapeake," published by Penn State University Press (Penn State University, 2002) at http://www.psupress.org/Justataste/samplechapters/justataste_brubaker5.html [October 31, 2006].

For the Wyoming, Pennsylvania, Massacre, see Alan Taylor, *The Divided Ground*, 93, 98, 138; William Sterne Randall, *George Washington*, 360; The Battle of Wyoming and Hartley's Expedition (Pennsylvania Historical and Museum Commission) at http://www.phmc.state.pa.us/ppet/wyoming/page1.asp?secid=31... [August 25, 2006].

Senecú del Sur Pueblo

John H. McNeely, "San Antonio de Senecú" *Handbook of Texas Online* (Austin, TX: Texas State Historical Association and University of Texas, 2001) at http://www.tsha.utexas.edu/handbook/online/articles/SS/uqs7.html [March 2, 2006].

Senecú Pueblo

Paul Harden, "El Camino Real de Tierra Adentero - Part 1," *El Defensor Chieftain*, November 5, 2005 (Socorro, NM, 1999-2004), available online at http://www.dchieftain.com/news/55968-11-05-05.html [March 2, 2006].

Senijextee

Swanton, 440; Lake," Four Directions Institute (Four Directions Press, 2005) at http://www.fourdir.com/lake.htm; James Mooney, "Lake Indians," *Catholic Encyclopedia* (K. Knight, 2006), vol. viii, at http://www.newadvent.org/cathen/08751a.htm [August 10, 2006].

Serrano

Swanton, 480, 497, 498, 512-513, 517.

Sewee

Swanton, 98, 99.

Shackoconia

Swanton, 61-62.

Shakori

Swanton, 83-84.

Shallalah

Samuel G. Drake, *The Aboriginal Races of North America...*, 9-16. "Lewis, Meriwether and Clark, Codex L: *Lewis' journal* [May 21, 1806-Aug. 8, 1806 (incomplete)]. D. 1," and "3008. Lewis, Meriwether, and William Clark. Codex M: *Clark's journal* [June 7-Aug. 14, 1806]. D. 1," American Indian Manuscripts (American Philosophical Association Library), Item 3007, D. 4p. and 1p. Map, at http://www.amphilsoc.org/... library/guides/indians/info/pl.htm [August 15, 2006].

Shallattoo

Samuel G. Drake, *The Aboriginal Races of North America...*, 9-16.

Shasta

Swanton, 468, 495, 497, 507, 514; Definitions in the U.S. Code.

M. Constance Guardino III and Rev. Marilyn A. Riedel, compiled by, "Sovereigns Of Themselves: A Liberating History of Oregon and Its Coast," *Oregon History, Abridged Online Edition* (Maracon Productions, 2006), vol. viii, at http://www2.wi.net/~census/lesson41.html; Palmer to Manypenny, 12 January 1854, in United States, Office of Indian Affairs, Letters Received by the Office of Indian Affairs, 1824-1880, National Archives Microcopy 234, Roll 608, NADP Document D22, p. 3, at http://www.csusm.edu/nadp/d22.htm [June 21, 2006]; Ambrose to Palmer, 10 October, 1855, in United States, Office of Indian Affairs, Letters Received by the Office of Indian Affairs, 1824-1880, National Archives Microcopy 234, Roll 608 (excerpt), NADP Document D31, at http://www.csusm.edu/nadp/d31.htm [June 21, 2006].

Shawnee

For an excellent compact history of the Shawnee, see Colin G. Calloway, *The Shawnees and the War for America*. Also see, Eugene Morrow Violette, *History of Missouri*, 47, 69, 72, 207; Gloria Jahoda, *Trail of Tears*, 27-36; Dee Brown, *Hear That Lonesome Whistle Blow*, 37. Also see Walter A. Schroeder, "Populating Missouri, 1804-1821," *Missouri Historical Review* (Columbia: State Historical Society of Missouri, July 2003), xcvii, 4, 263-294; T. R. Fehrenback, *Comanches*, 227; H. W. Brands, *Andrew Jackson*, 164-169, 176-178, 201-204; Swanton, esp. 225-229.

"Wyandot and Shawnee Indian Lands in Wyandotte County, Kansas," *Kansas Historical Collections* (Topeka: Kansas State Historical Society, n.d.), vol. xv, 1919-1922, 103-180; Wilda Sandy, "Biography of Chief Joseph Parks,1794-1859, Indian chief" (1999); "Shawnee Mission, State Historical Site" (Topeka, KS: Kansas State Historical Society, 2004) at http://www.kshs.org/places/shawnee/history.htm; Indian Agent, Col. John. Johnston, Vocabularies of the Shawnoese and Wyandott Languages, etc (1958) available from Wyandot Nation of Kansas (Kansas City, KS, n.d.) at http://www.wyandot.org/lang1.html; Ronald Branson, "Acquisition of Our Territory -- Story of Clark's Conquest: Supplementary Matter: Sketch of George Rogers Clark" (State of Indiana County History, 2000-2002) at http://www.countyhistory.com/history/037.htm; Bennison J. Lossing, "PreColumbian Civilization," Our Country, vol. 1 (1905) available from LoveToKnow, Inc. (2002-2003) at http://www.publicbookshelf.com/public_html/Our_Country_Vol_1/precolumbi_c.html; "Colonial Period Indian Land Cessions in the American Southeast and Related Documents," (TNGenNet Inc, 2001; updated May 24, 2002) at http://www.tngenweb.org/cessions/colonial.html and http://www.tngenweb.org/cessions/colonial2.html [September 7, 2006].

"Excerpts from Colden," available from the OhioValley-Great Lakes Ethnohistory Archives: The Miami Collection (Bloomington, IN: Glenn Black Laboratory of Archaeology and Trustees of Indiana University, 1996, updated January 12, 2001), 65, at http://www.gbl.indiana.edu/ archives/miamis3/M82-99_25a.html; "History of Hardin County [Ohio]"(Chicago: Warner, Beers & Co., 1883) made available by Allen L. Potts (Heritage Pursuit, 2006), 237, at http://www.heritagepursuit.com/Hardin/HarChapII.htm; James B. Jones, Jr., "Susquehanna Indian Tribe History" (Southern History, 2005) at http://www.southernhistory.net/index.php?name=News&file=article &sid=9472&theme=Printer; "A. J. Morrison, "The Virginia Indian Trade to 1673," *William and Mary College Quarterly Historical Magazine* (October 1921), sr. 2, 1, 217-36 from Classics of American Colonial History (Dinsmore Documentation, 2003) at http://www.dinsdoc.com /morrison-1.htm; "What Happened: The Second Voyage to Discover the Bay" (Mariners' Museum, 2002) at http://www.mariner.org/ chesapeakebay/colonial/col011.html [August 14, 2006].

"Shawnee Mission, Kansas" (Washington, DC: National Park Service, 2005) at http://www.cr.nps.gov/history/online_books/soldier/siteb10.htm; Bob Holdgreve, "Window to the Past," Delphos Historical Society (Delphos Herald Newspaper, 1999), Part 3, at http://www.delphos-ohio.com/history/Holdgreve/indians.htm; "Centennial History of Argentine; Kansas City, KS 1880-1980" (Kansas State Library) at http://skyways.lib.ks.us/genweb/wyandott/argentine/03.htm; Henry Harvey, "History of the Shawnee Indians from the Year 1681 to 1854 Inclusive" (Manataka American Indian Council) at http://www.manataka.org/page1943.html [September 29, 2006]. Originally published Cincinnati: Ephraim Morgan & Sons, 1855.

"Brief Historical Summary of the Eastern Shawnee Tribe of Oklahoma" (Eastern Shawnee Tribe of Oklahoma) at http://www.easternshawnee.org/history.htm; "The Shawnee in Johnson County: Pioneer Settlers, Traders, Developers" (Overland Park, KS: Johnson County Public Library, 2006) at http://www.jocohistory.com/people/7no2shawnee.asp [September 29, 2006].

On the War for Kentucky, see Daniel K. Richter, *Facing East from Indian Country*, 213-216, 222. Logan's letter beginning "I appeal to any white man..." taken from Richter, 213-214. Also see Landon Y. Jones, *William Clark and the Shaping of the West*, esp. 25-45; Willard Sterne Randall, *Thomas Jefferson, A Life*, 190-191, 238; Thomas Jefferson, *Writings*. Merrill D. Peterson, ed. (New York: Library of America, 1984), 188-189. For the Battle of Tippecanoe, see Department of the Army, *American Military History*, 121-122; W. H. Brands, *Andrew Jackson*, 176-177. For the Battle on the Thames River, see Alan Taylor, *The Divided Ground*, 131, 132, 399-403; W. H. Brands, *Andrew Jackson*, 202-204.

Sheastukle

Samuel G. Drake, *The Aboriginal Races of North America...*, 9-16.

Shinnecock

Bevy Deer Jensen, "History" (Southhampton, NY: Shinnecook Indian Nation, n.a.) at http://www.shinnecocknation.com/history.asp [April 18, 2006].

Shipaulovi

Swanton, 352.

Shivwits

Swanton, 382. "Shivwits Band of Paiutes" (Washington County, UT: Cynthia B. Alldredge, 2000, 2006) at http://www.lofthouse.com/USA/Utah/washington/shivwit.html [April 6, 2006].

Shohopanaiti

Swanton, 398.

Shoshoko

George Catlin, *North American Indians* (Penguin ed.), 386, 481-482. Swanton on the Bannock, 398; on Western Shoshoni, 405-410; on Shoshonean people, 413. Washington Irving, *The Adventures of Captain Bonneville*, Chapters 29 and 30 at http://www.xmission.com/drudy/... mtman/html/bville/chap__.html [November 14, 2007]. Edward S. Curtis, *Camp of the Root Diggers -Yakima* (1909) made available from First People of America at http://www.firstpeople.us... /tipi/camp-of-the-root-diggers.html and Edward S. Curtis, *The North American Indian* (2003) available from Northwestern University Library at http://digital.library.northwestern.edu/curtis/; Jarvis Clark, "The Clark Story" (Milton-Freewater, OR: Frazier Farmstead Museum, n.d.) at http://museum.bmi.net/Pioneer%20Trails/clark_story.htm [November 14, 2007].

"Western Shoshone," *World Culture Encyclopedia-North America* (Advameg Inc., 2007) at www.everyculture.com/North-America/ Western-Shoshone.html [November 15, 2007]: " ETHNONYMS: Diggers, Root-Diggers, Shoshocoes, Walkers." "Beus Canyon Trail" (Washington, DC: Department of Agriculture, Ogden Ranger District, 2003) at http://www.fs.fed.us/wcnf/unit... /ogden/beus.htm [November 15, 2007], excerpt: "The local Shoshone Tribe utilized edible plants as well as roots found along this trail. ...These Native Americans were referred to by the white pioneers as "root diggers." "Indians of The Yellowstone Plateau" (Washington, DC: National Park Service, Yellowstone National Park, 2003) at http://www.windowsintowonderland.org/history/teachers/indians.htm [November 15, 2007]. William Secrest, *When the Great Spirit Died: The Destruction of the California Indians 1850-1860* (Quill Driver Books/Word Dancer Press, 2005) the following excerpt taken from http://www.quilldriverbooks.com/when_great_spirit/excerpt_intro.htm [November 15, 2007], "'Root Diggers' was the epithet used by the early pioneers to describe the California Indians, and they were, in truth, a simple people living close to the earth. They did not build spectacular dwellings...[nor have did they have the] elaborate traditions and ceremonies of the Plains and Eastern tribes."

Also, William Perkins, *Three Years in California: William Perkins' Journal of Life at Sonora, 1849-1852* at http://www.duendedrama.com... / pdf/ffperkins'%20journal%20excerpt.pdf; "Yakima Indians," (A&E Television Networks, 1996-2007) at http://www.history.com... /encyclopedia. do?articleId=226236 [November 15, 2007]. Excerpt from article from Funk & Wagnalls' *New Encyclopedia*. © 2006 World Almanac Education Group (A WRC Media Company). "Paiute" (World Encyclopedia, 2005) at http://www.encyclopedia.com/doc/1O142-Paiute.html; "Paiute" (Native Americans.com, 2007) at http://www.nativeamericans.com/Paiute.htm; "Utah State University Student Folklore Genre Collection" (Logan: Utah State University Libraries, 2007) at http://library.usu.edu/Folklo/folkarchive/etiological.htm [November 15, 2007].

Shoshoni
Brigham D. Madsen, *The Northern Shoshoni*; Swanton, 403-410; Dee Brown, *Hear That Lonesome Whistle Blow*, 101, 150; Stephen E. Ambrose, *Undaunted Courage*, 209, 210, 230, 268-283; Bernard De Voto, ed., *The Journals of Lewis and Clark*, 75, 77n2, *passim* 185-245, 367-368, 383, 407; Joseph M. Marshall, *The Journey of Crazy Horse*, xii, 19, 76, 97, 118, 165-166, 241; Dee Brown, Bury My Heart at *Wounded Knee*, 288; Robert M. Utley, *The Lance and the Shield*, 139-141, 145. F. W. Lander, "Letters From Nevada Indian Agents - 1860, " *Nevada Observer*, July 24, 2006, at ttp://www.nevadaobserver.com/Reading%20Room%20Documents/Letters%20from%20Nevada%20Indian%20Agents%20 1860.htm [January 9, 2008].

David Dominick, "The Sheepeaters," *Annals of Wyoming* (Cheyenne, WY: Wyoming State Historical Society, 1995-2007), 36:2:131-168, at www.windriverhistory.org/exhibits/sheepeaters/Resources/Dominick.pdf; "Northern Shoshoni Intertribal Trade and Fur Trade," *Idaho State Historical Series*, No. 490 (Boise, ID, 1978) at www.idahohistory.net/Reference Series/0490.pdf [January 10, 2008].

"The Shoshoni, 13-30 August 1805, Louisiana Expansion" (St. Louis: University of Missouri - St. Louis, n.d.) at http://www.umsl.edu/~econed... /louisiana/Am_Indians/12-Shoshoni/12-shoshoni.html; "Shoshoni and Northern Paiute Indians In Idaho," Reference Series (Boise, ID: Idaho State Historical Society, November 1970), No. 484, at http://www.idahohistory.net/Reference%20Series/0484.pdf; "Northern Shoshoni Intertribal Trade and Fur Trade," Reference Series (Boise, ID: Idaho State Historical Society, 1978), No. 490, at http://www.idahohistory.net. ... Reference%20Series/0490.pdf; Kenneth Briggs, "Lords of the Southern Plains" (OpEdNews, 2002-2007) at http://www.opednews.com... / articles/life_a_kenneth__070620_lords_of_the_souther.htm [January 3, 2008].

Ottmar Ederer, "Uto-Aztecan Language Family" (Wontolla's Reservation, 1998-2006) at http://wontolla.homepage.t-online.de/wontolla/14e-uto.html; Sam Silverhawk, "Wind River Indian Reservation" (Fort Washakie , WY, 1997-2000) at http://www.easternshoshone.net... / EasternShoshoneHistory2.html.; White Moon Raven, "Plateau and Great Basin Tribes about 1700" (Raven's Roost, n.d.) at http://www. whitemoonraven.com/maps/plateau.html [January 3, 2008]. Ft. Washakie serves as the headquarters of the Wind River Indian Reservation. It was created in 1858 and covers 2.2 million acres. The reservation, home to more than 8,000 Shoshone and Arapaho, is the only Indian reservation in Wyoming. Originally named Camp Brown, it was renamed to honor Chief Washakie of the Shoshone and is the only U.S. fort named to honor an American Indian. Chief Washakie's gravesite is located in the local military cemetery. The gravesite of Sacajawea is located in another cemetery nearby.

"The Shoshone Interpretive Project" (Blue Earth Alliance) at http://www.blueearth.org/projects/shoshone/ [March 27, 2006]. "Shoshone-Bannock of the Fort Hall Reservation" (Pocatello, ID: Idaho State University, n.d.) at http://challenge.isu.edu/multicultural/NativeAm/... ShoBan/ forthall.htm; "History" (Fort Hall, ID: Shoshone-Bannock Tribes, 2006) at http://www.shoshonebannocktribes.com/fhbc.html;"The Shoshone Homelands" (n.a.) at http://www.onewest.net/~tillman/shoshone/lifestyles.htm; "Shoshone Indians" (2003) at http://www.shoshoneindian. com/ [January 4, 2008]. Also, J. P. Dunn, Jr., *Massacres Of The Mountains: A History Of The Indian Wars In The Far West* (New York: Harper & Brothers, 1886), 283-314, at http://www.olivercowdery.com/smithhome/1880s-1890s/1886Dunn.htm (transcribed 2007); Mae Parry, "The Northwestern Shoshone: Utah's Native Americans," Chp. 2 (Salt Lake City, UT: Utah History to Go, 2007) at http://historytogo.utah.gov/ people/ethnic_cultures/the_history_of_utahs_american_indians/chapter2.html; *History of Utah Tribes: Shoshoni, Ute, Goshute* (State of Utah: Division of Indian Affairs, 2007) at http://indian.utah.gov/history_of_utah_tribes/index.html); Brigham D. Madsen, "History of Shoshone Indians," *Utah History Encyclopedia* (Online Utah, n.d.) at **h**ttp://www.onlineutah.com/shoshonehistory.shtml; "Shoshoni Indians" (Intellectual Reserve, 2002) at http://www.familysearch.org/Eng/Library/fhlcatalog/printing/subjectdetailsprint.asp?subject=314003... &first=1;"Shoshoni Indians" (Access Genealogy, 2004-2008) at http://www.accessgenealogy.com/native/tribes/shoshoni/shoshoniindianhist.htm; Danny L. Noss, "Western Shoshoni Indians in Nevada" (Ely Nevada: White Pine Historical and Archaeology Society, 1998-2004) at http://www.webpanda.com/ white_pine_county/ethnic/shoshone.htm [January 3, 2008].

For the Bear Creek Massacre, see David Haward Bain, *Empire Express*, 229-231 w/ Alvin Josephy quoted on 728n23; David Dary, *The Oregon Trail*, 288-289; Brigham D. Madsen, *The Shoshoni Frontier and the Bear River Massacre*; Robert M. Utley, *The Indian Frontier of the American West*, 71; Brigham D. Madsen, "Bear River Massacre, Utah, " *Utah History Encyclopedia* (Boise: Online Utah.com) at http://www.onlineutah. com/bearrivermassacre.shtml, respectively [October 4, 2008].

For Sacagawea, see Stephen E. Ambrose, *Undaunted Courage*, 389, 389n. "Your woman" quoted in Ambrose from Donald Jackson, ed., *Letters of the Lewis and Clark Expedition, with Related Documents: 1783-1854*, 2nd ed. (Urbana, IL: University of Illinois Press, 1978), 315, and Harold P. Howard, *Sacajawea*. Also, Bernard De Voto, ed., *The Journals of Lewis and Clark*, 63n5, 64n7, 77n2, 80, 92-94, 96, 113, 120, 203, 391-400, 451, 457-458 et al.

Shoto
Swanton, 467; "Chinookan Devastation: 'Marsh Miasms'" (Vancouver, WA: Center for Columbia River History, 2004-2005) at http://www.ccrh.org/comm/slough/chinook5.htm [August 2, 2006].

Shuman
Swanton, 324-325, 624, 634.

Shumopovi
Swanton, 352.

Sicaunie
Henry Rowe Schoolcraft, *Personal Memoirs Of A Residence Of Thirty Years With The Indian Tribes On The American Frontiers*, from Book Rags (2000-2006), 143, at http://www.bookrags.com/ebooks/11119/143.html [August 15, 2006]. Also from FullBooks at http://www.fullbooks.com/Personal-Memoirs-Of-A-Residence-Of-Thirty4.html.

Sichomovi
Swanton, 351-352.

Siksika Blackfeet
John C. Ewers, *The Blackfeet: Raiders on the Northwestern Plains*; Swanton, 395-398.

Siletz
Swanton, 468.

Similkameen Okanagon
Swanton, 430-433.

Sinagua
"The Sinagua" (DesertUSA, 1996-2006) at http://www.desertusa.com/ind1/du_peo_sin.html [October 31, 2006].

Sinkaietk
Swanton, 440-441.

Sinkakaius
Swanton, 441.

Sinkyone
Swanton, 481, 498, 507, 514-515.

Sioux
Charles M. Robinson, *A Good Year to Die: The Story of the Great Sioux War*; Dee Brown, *Bury My Heart at Wounded Knee*, 291-198, 425-427, 428-431, 437-438; Dee Brown, *Hear That Lonesome Whistle Blow*, 29-30, 78, 85, 87, 88, 93, 204-209, 214-215, 216, 217, 258; Eugene Morrow Violette, *History of Missouri*, 41n1; George E. Hyde, Red Cloud's Folk: A History of the Oglala Sioux, esp. 3-42, 134-163, 249-250, 291-293, 297-298; Gloria Jahoda, *Trail of Tears*, 174; Helen Hunt Jackson, *A Century of Dishonor*, 136-185; James P. Ronda, Lewis and Clark Among the Indians, 33; John C. Ewers, ed., *Edwin Thompson Denig's Five Indian Tribes of the Upper Missouri*, 3-40; Robert C. Carriker, Father Peter John De Smet: *Jesuit in the West*, 174, 176, 179, 185, 198, 207, 219-225; Robert M. Utley, *The Lance and the Shield: The Life and Times of Sitting Bull*, esp. 87, 147-164, 230-233, 299-305, 310-31, 351n1; Swanton, esp. 280-284; T. R. Fehrenbach, *Comanches*, 458-459. Also, Joseph Marshall, III, *The Journey of Crazy Horse*; R. Eli Paul, *Blue Water Creek and the First Sioux War, 1854-1856*. Also see the paintings by George Catlin, *One Horn (Miniconjou)* and *Black Rock* (1832). Also *Sioux and Buffalo* by Black Lance; Kingsley M. Bray, *Crazy Horse*, esp. re: Crazy Horse during the winter and spring of 1876-1877, 248, 252, 253-254, 261-264.

Barbara Benge, "Lakota Page: The Great Sioux Nation" (2002) at http://members.aol.com/bbbenge/page6.html; "Dakota," *Canadian Encyclopedia Online* (Historical Foundation of Canada, 2004) at http://www.canadianencyclopedia.ca/index.cfm?PgNm=TCE&Params... =A1ARTA0002108; "Dakota-Lakota-Nakota Human Rights Advocacy Coalition" (Rosebud Sioux Indian Reservation, SD: Dakota/Lakota/ Nakota Human Rights Advocacy Coalition (DLN), 2004) at http://www.dlncoalition.org/home.htm; David Melmer "At Rosebud a proud buffalo nation carries on," *Indian Country Today*, 2004 from AAA Native Arts (2001-2004) at http://medicine-woman-writer.aaanativearts.com/ article688.html; James Mooney, "Sioux Indians," *Catholic Encyclopedia Online Edition* (New York: K. Knight, 2003) , vol. xiv, at http://www.newadvent.org/cathen/14017a.htm; James V. Fenelon, "From Peripheral Domination to Internal Colonialism: Socio-Political Change of the Lakota on Standing Rock," *Journal of World-Systems Research* (Spring 1997), 3, 2, 259-320 available at http://jwsr.ucr.edu/archive/vol3/v3n2a3.php [September 6, 2006].

"Lewis and Clark and Native Americans, Part I," Classroom Resources (Washington, DC: Public Broadcasting Service (PBS, 1995-2004), L5, at http://www.pbs.org/lewisandclark/class/l05.html; Raymond A. Bucko, S.J., "Lakota na Dakota Wowapi Oti Kin" (Omaha, NE: Department of Sociology and Anthropology, Creighton University, 2003) at http://puffin.creighton.edu/lakota/; John E. Koontz, "Etymology: What is the origin of the word Sioux?" (2001-2003) at http://spot.colorado.edu/~koontz/faq/etymology.htm [September 18, 2006].

William Glenn Robertson, et. Al., "Atlas of the Sioux Wars" (Leavenworth, KS: U.S. Army Command and General Staff College, modified: Thursday, April 06, 2006) at http://www-cgsc.army.mil/carl/resources/csi/sioux/sioux.asp [July 21, 2006]; "Clark, William. A list of the names of the different nations and tribes of Indians ... expressive of the names, languages, numbers, trade, water courses ...[Jan. 1805]," American Indian Manuscripts (American Philosophical Association Library), Item 2971, D. 2, at http://www.amphilsoc.org/library/guides/indians/info/pl.htm [August 19, 2006]. Entry made August 31, 1804. See Paul Allen, ed., *History of the Expedition...*, vol. I (1814).

"Expedition of Lewis & Clark," Part 5. Early History, *Andreas' History of the State of Nebraska* (Chicago, IL: Western Historical Company, A. T. Andreas, Proprietor, 1882) made available from the Kansas Collection Books (n.d.) at http://www.kancoll.org/books/andreas_ne... /history/ erlyhst-p5.html [August 19, 2006]; "Black Hills: Lands Taken from the Indian Groups" (University of Illinois at Chicago College of Education, 2006) at http://www.uic.edu/educ/bctpi/historyGIS/blackhills_1wk/bhselfserve/landcessions/index.html [November 1, 2006].

For the Battle of the Yellowstone, Robert M. Utley, *The Lance and the Shield*, 112-114, 119, 145; Kingsley M. Bray, *Crazy Horse*, 167-169. For Battle of the Rosebud, see Joseph M. Marshall, III, *The Journey of Crazy Horse*, 217-222; Robert M. Utley, *The Lance and the Shield*, 140-142, 145, 298; Kingsley M. Bray, *Crazy Horse*, 204-214;George Bird Grinell, *The Fighting Cheyennes*, 328-344. For the Greasy Grass Fight, see Joseph H. Marshall, *The Journey of Crazy Horse*, xii, xiii-xiv, 47, 226-229, 230-233, 235, 236, 238, 252, 255, 272, 274, 282, 283-285, 286; Robert M. Utley, *The Lance and the Shield*, 74, 147-164 (casualties, 160), 168, 194, 202, 231, 238, 239, 243, 246, 251, 263, 270, 275, 298, 361-364; Kingsley M. Bray, *Crazy Horse*, 215-234, 287;George Bird Grinell, *The Fighting Cheyennes*, 345-358; Swanton, 280. Also, "Custer's Last Stand, Battle of the Little Big Horn" (American Western History Museums, 2006) at http://www.linecamp.com/museums/americanwest/... western_places/ little_big_horn_custers_last_stand/little_big_horn_custers_last_stand.html; "The Battle of the Little Bighorn, 1876," Eye Witness to History (Ibis Communications, n.d.) at http://www.eyewitnesstohistory.com/custer.htm; "Little Bighorn Battlefield" at http://www.nps.gov/libi and "The Battle of Little Bighorn" (Washington, DC: National Park Service, 2006) at http://www.nps.gov/archive/libi/battle.html [November 7, 2006].

Sisatone Sioux
Samuel G. Drake, *The Aboriginal Races of North America...*, 9-16.

Sissipahaw
Swanton, 83, 84-85, 100.

Siuslaw
Swanton 468-469.

Siwanoy
Edwin G. Burrows & Mike Wallace, *Gotham*, 5.

991 Sk-kahl-mish
Janet Enzmann, "Excerpts from Current Exhibit" (Coupeville, WA: [Whidbey] Island County Historical Society, 2006) at http://www.islandhistory.org/LibraryArchives.htm [June 22, 2006].

Skaddal
Swanton, 448-449, 450.

Skagit
Swanton, 441-442.

Skaru're
Swanton 85-88.

Skeetsomish
"Lewis and Clark Expedition, Phase 5 / Date 2: May 5-May 14, 1806," made available from Modern Studies Curriculum (Lexington, KY: University of Kentucky, n.d.) at http://www.uky.edu/AS/ModernStudies/HumSocSci/lc94/Section2/Phase5/Dates/Date2.html; "May 06, 1806, Meriwether Lewis" (Third Millennium Online, n.d.) at http://www.3rd1000.com/history/corp/journals/1806/05/050606.htm [August 15, 2005]. See esp. editorial notes within journal text.

Skidi Pawnee
"Information on the Oto Indians Recorded by Members of the Lewis and Clark Expedition 1804," Lewis and Clark Journey of Discovery (Washington, DC: National Park Service, n.d.) at http://www.nps.gov/jeff/LewisClark2/TheJourney/NativeAmericans/Oto.htm [July 20, 2006].

Skilloot
Swanton, 442, 469; "Peoples of the Slough: Wapato Indians" (Center for Columbia River History, n.d.) at http://www.ccrh.org/comm/slough/ chinook.htm [August 22, 2006].

Skinpah
Swanton, 442-443.

Skitswish

Swanton, 411-412; "May 06, 1806, Meriwether Lewis" (Third Millennium Online, n.d.) at http://www.3rd1000.com/history/corp/journals/1806/05/050606.htm [August 15, 2005]. See esp. editorial notes within journal text.

Skokomish

Swanton, 447.

Smalhkamish

Swanton, 428.

Snohomish

Swanton, 443; "Native Americans attack settlers along White River between Kent and Auburn on October 28, 1855," Rivers In Time Project (Seattle, WA: History Ink, 2006), Essay 2008, at http://www.historylink.org/essays/output.cfm?file_id=2008 [October 7, 2006].

Snoqalmie

Swanton, 443-444.

Soacatino

Swanton 325.

Sobaipuri

Swanton, 357-360; Thomas Edwin Farish, *The History of Arizona*, vol. vii, chp. 17.

Soboba Luiseño

"Culture and History" (San Jacinto CA: Soboba Band of Luiseño Indians) at http://www.soboba-nsn.gov/cultureandhistory.html [April 2,2006].

Socowocomoco

Swanton, 57-59.

Sokoki

Swanton, 13-15; Russell Shorto, *The Island in the Center of the World*, 51.

Sokulk

Bernard De Voto, ed., *The Journals of Lewis and Clark*, 250-255, 323. Also, Eugene S. Hunn, "Kennewick Man," Archaeology Program (Washington, DC: National Park Service, updated: 11/02/2005) at http://www.cr.nps.gov/archeology/kennewick/Hunn.htm [August 9, 2006]. This report is a little confusing as to what Dr. Hunn is actually trying to say.

Stephenie Flora, "Northwest Indian Tribes" (The Oregon Territory and Its Pioneers, 1998-2006) at http://www.oregonpioneers.com/tribe.htm; "Salmon Fishing by Wanapum (Sokulk) Indians" (Olympia, WA: Legislative Information Center, Washington State Legislature, n.d.) at http://apps.leg.wa.gov/rcw/default.aspx?cite=77.12.453; George Gibbs, "Indian Tribes of Washington Territory" (Wellpinit, WA: Wellprint School District, 2004) at http://www.wellpinit.wednet.edu/sal-hist/gibbs_toc.php [August 9, 2006]. Article originally published in *the United States Geographical and Geological Survey of the Rocky Mountain Region* (Washington, DC, 1877).

Lynn Waterman , "Through The Rockies to the Pacific," *Louisiana Purchase*, Chapter XV (2001) at http://www.usgennet.org/usa/topic/...preservation/history/louis/chpt15.htm; "Upper Columbia River Indians: October - November 1805, January – April 1806," The Louisiana Expansion (St. Louis: University of Missouri St. Louis, n.d.) at http://www.umsl.edu/~econed/louisiana/Am_Indians/13-Columbia/13-columbia.html [August 9, 2006].

"Wilderness Notebooks: Columbia River Gorge" (San Francisco, CA: Sierra Club, n.d.) at http://www.sierraclub.org/lewisandclark/... notebooks/columbiagorge2.asp; "Lewis and Clark Meet the Yakima Indians, from the Journal of William Clark" (n.a.) at http://rickgriffis.tripod.com/entry.html [August 10, 2006]. (Yakima)

Souties

Frederick Webb Hodge, ed., "Chippewa," *Handbook of American Indians North of Mexico*, (Washington, DC: Smithsonian Institution, Bureau of American Ethnology Bulletin 30. GPO, 1910) available at http://www.prairienet.org/prairienations/chippewa.htm [August 15, 2006].

Soyennom

Samuel G. Drake, *The Aboriginal Races of North America...*, 9-16.

Spokan

Swanton, 444-445; Robert H. Rudy and John A. Brown, *The Spokane Indians: Children of the Sun*; Robert H. Rudy and John A. Brown, The Cayuse Indians, 124, 131, 141, 144, 147, 149, 201, 224, 236, 237, 242, 256, 258, 283; on the Spokane War, 256-258.

Squannaroo

Samuel G. Drake, *The Aboriginal Races of North America...*, 9-16.

Squaxon

Swanton, 445; Theresa M. Henderson, "General Information" (Shelton WA: Squaxin Indian Tribe) at http://www.squaxinisland.org/frames. html [June 22, 2006].

Stadaconan

Daniel K. Richter, *Facing East from Indian Country*, 28-32, 34, 36-38, 39, 42.

Stegaraki

Swanton, 61-62.

Steilacoom

"Steilacoom Tribe of Indians" (Steilacoom, WA: Steilacoom Tribal Council, updated February 19, 2003) at http://members.shaw.ca/nyjack/steilacoom/the_tribe_today.htm; "Lakewood Heritage" (Lakewood, WA: Chamber of Commerce, n.d.) at http://www.lakewood-wa.com/html/history.html; "Historic Fort Steilacoom" (Lakewood, WA: Fort Steilacoom, 2006) at http://www. fortsteilacoom.com/ [June 22, 2006]; "Steilacoom Indians," American Memory: American Indians of the Pacific Northwest (Washington, DC: Library of Congress w/ University of Washington Libraries, 2000.) at http://lcweb2.loc.gov/cgi-bin/query/S?ammem/aipn:@field(SUBJ+@ od1(Steilacoom+Indians)) [September 10, 2006].

Stillaguamish

Swanton, 442. "Stillaguamish Tribe," NWIFC Member Tribes (Olympia, WA: Northwest Indian Fisheries Commission, n.d.) at http://www.nwifc.wa.gov/tribes/tribe.asp?tribe=stillaguamish [June 22, 2006].

Stockbridge Indians

Swanton, 42, 254, 255, 257-258.

Stoney-Nakoda

Swanton, 387-388, 545; "Stoney-Nakoda," *L'Encyclopédie Canadienne* (Fondation Historica du Canada, 2004) at http://www.canadianencyclopedia.ca/index.cfm?PgNm=TCE&Params=A1ARTA0007731 [September 9, 2006].

Stono

Swanton, 94, 95.

Sugeree

Swanton, 85, 100, 102, 103.

Suhtai

Donald J. Berthrong, *The Southern Cheyennes*, 9-10, 15, 27, 361; William Y. Chalfant, *Cheyennes and Horse Soldiers*, 301-302, 310; George Bird Grinnell, *The Cheyenne Indians*, **I**, 2, 2n1, 9-11, 58, 86-88, 90, 91, 95-96; **II**, 56, 192, 285, 337, 339, 344Swanton, 278, 279, 280, 284, 285; George Bird Grinnell, *The Fighting Cheyennes*; Samuel G. Drake, *The Aboriginal Races of North America...*, 9-16.

Trenholm et al., "Platte County 1812-1981" (Cheyenne: WY: Catholic Diocese of Cheyenne) at http://www.dioceseofcheyenne.org/history ... / Whtld_Platte_Cnty_1812-1981Trenholm&.html; Meriwether Lewis and William Clark, *History of the Expedition under the Command of Captains Lewis and Clark, vol. I.: To The Sources Of The Missouri, Thence Across The Rocky Mountains And Down The River Columbia To The Pacific Ocean. Performed During The Years 1804-5-6*. Paul Allen, ed. (Philadelphia: Bradford and Inskeep; New York: Abm. H. Inskeep, 1814) made available online by Project Gutenberg, (Salt Lake City, UT: Project Gutenberg Literary Archive Foundation 2003-2006) at http://www.gutenberg.org/ files/16565/16565.txt [June 15, 2006]. Also, "Cheyenne" (n.a.) at http://www.franksrealm.com/sivu-indians-cheyenne.html [October 13, 2006].

Suma

Stanton, 324-325.

Suquámish

Swanton, 445; Chief Seattle, "Yonder sky that has wept tears of compassion...", Seattle Sunday Star, Seattle, Washington Territory, October 29, 1887, reprint of 1854 speech; "Suquamish Tribe" (Suquamish, WA: Suquamish Tribe, n.d.) at http://www.suquamish.nsn.us/ [September 8, 2006].

Surruque

Swanton, 143.

Susquehanna

Swanton, 40, 55, 56-57, 58, 66, 70; Helen Hunt Jackson, *A Century of Dishonor*, 298-317; Edmond S. Morgan, *American Slavery, American Freedom*, 250-258, 328; Russell Shorto, *The Island in the Center of the World*, 182, 184, 279-281. Reference to the Minquas and Mahikanders in the events of September 1655 was taken from a quote appearing on page 280. Sorto (346) gives the source, which is listed as on page 279, as Charles T.Gehring, trans., *Delaware Papers: Dutch Period ,1648-1664* (Baltimore: Genealogical Publishing, 1977), 35.

David Minor, "1677" (Eagles Byte, 2000) at http://home.eznet.net/~dminor/NYNY1675.html; "The Wea Indian Tribe" (Lafayette, IN, 1999-1001) at http://www.angelfire.com/in3/weatribe/11dodgediary.html\; "Andaste ou Andastoque" (n.a.) at http://www.netrover.com/~t310735/ Nouv-Fr/Tribus/andaste.html; John F. Meginness, "Aboriginal Occupation," Chapter I, and "Appearance of the Painted Savage," Chapter II,"

History of Lycoming County Pennsylvania (1892) available from the Lycoming County Genealogy Project (Lycoming County, PA, 2001) at http://www.usgennet.org/usa/pa/county/lycoming/history/lyco-history-01.html [September 10, 2006].

"SUSQUEHANNOCK: an extinct language of USA," *Ethnologue: Languages of the World*, 14th Edition (SIL International, 2004) at http://www.ethnologue.com/show_language.asp?code=SQN; Chuck DeSocio, "Captain John Smith Visits Cecil County," *Cecil County Magazine* (North East, MD, n.d.) at http://www.ccmagazine.org/features/smith.htm; Larry D. Smith, "The Land Of The Susquehannock" (2001) at http://www.motherbedford.com/Indian5.htm; Broken Claw (Xra-Sa'ge-Gi-xu'ge), "Where are the Susquehannock?" (n.d.) at http://native.brokenclaw.net/articles/susquehannock.html [September 10, 2006]; "Pennsylvania History: Pennsylvania On The Eve Of Colonization" (Pennsylvania General Assembly) at http://www.legis.state.pa.us/WU01/VC/visitor_info/pa_history/whole_pa_history.htm [August 25, 2006].

For the Conestoga Massacre, see Alan Taylor, *The Divided Ground*, 32-33; H. W. Brands, *The First American*, 350-354; Daniel K. Richter, *Facing East from Indian Country*, 199-200, 201-208

Swallah
Swanton, 445-446.

Swinomish
Swanton, 446; "Swinomish Tribe," NWIFC Member Tribes (Olympia, WA: Northwest Indian Fisheries Commission, n.d.) at http://www.nwifc.wa.gov/tribes/tribe.asp?tribe=swinomish [September 10, 2006].

T'Peeksin
"Native American Studies" (Orono, ME: University of Maine Folger Library, 2004) at http://www.library.umaine.edu/class/Fernandez/nas2984.htm [May 18, 2006].

Tacstacuru
Swanton, 144.

Tacullie
Henry Rowe Schoolcraft, "Personal Memoirs Of A Residence Of Thirty Years With The Indian Tribes On The American Frontiers" from Book Rags (2000-2006), 143, at http://www.bookrags.com/ebooks/11119/143.html [August 15, 2006]. Also from FullBooks at http://www.fullbooks.com/Personal-Memoirs-Of-A-Residence-Of-Thirty4.html.

Tadiva
Swanton, 315-317.

Taensa
Swanton, 188, 209-210; Thomas N. Campbell, "Taensa Indians," *Handbook of Texas Online* (Austin, TX: Texas State Historical Association and University of Texas, 2001) at http://www.tsha.utexas.edu/handbook/online/articles/TT/bmt4.html [August 17, 2006].

Tahsagroudie
Samuel G. Drake, *The Aboriginal Races of North America...*, 9-16.

Taidnapam
Swanton, 422, 425.

Takelma
Swanton, 469-470; Merrill D. Beal, *"I Will Fight No More Forever": Chief Joseph and the Nez Percé War*, 24-26; David Dary, *The Oregon Trail*, 252. Also, James Mooney, "Siletz Indians," *The Catholic Encyclopedia*, vol. XIII, Online Ed. (K. Knight, 2005) at http://www.newadvent.org/cathen/13791a.htm; "Oregon History- Indian Wars," *2005-2006 Oregon Blue Book* (Portland, OR: Office of the Secretary of State, 2005) at http://bluebook.state.or.us/cultural/history/history14.htm [March 8, 2006].

For the Rogue River Wars, see David Dary, *Oregon Trail*, 252-253. Also, "Rogue River War: Speech by Dr. A. G. Henry of Yamhill" (December 30, 1855) available from Corvallis Community Pages (Corvallis, OR) at http://www.corvalliscommunitypages.com/Americas/US/Oregon/OregonNotCorvallis/rogueriverwarall.htm; "A Brief Interpretive History of the Rogue River War and the Coast, Alsea, and Siletz Reservations to 1894," Native American Documents Project (San Marcos, CA: California State University, 2000, updated 2004) at http://www.csusm.edu/nadp/subject.htm [May 24, 2006]; Huber Howe Bancroft, *The Works of Hubert Howe Bancroft, History of Oregon*, vol. 30, Part II, Chapter XII, Rogue River War, 1853-1854; Chapter XV, Further Indian Wars, 1855-1866; Chapter XVI, *Extermination of the Indians, 1856-1857* (San Francisco, CA: History Company, 1888), 31; 369; 397, respectively, available from 1st Hand History (Roseburg, OR, 2001-2005) at http://www.1st-hand-history.org/Hhb/30/3__.jpg [July 7, 2006].

A. G. Walling, History of Southern Oregon, Indian Wars, Chapter XX (Portland, OR, 1884) available from 1st Hand History (Roseburg, OR, 2001-2005) at http://www.1st-hand-history.org/Hso/177.jpg ...[November 15, 2006].

Takkuth-kutchin
Swanton, 575, 585, 602, 603.

Tali
Swanton, 229.

Tallewheana
Samuel G. Drake, *The Aboriginal Races of North America...*, 9-16.

Taltushtuntude
Swanton, 459, 470.

Tama'li
William W. Baden, "Historical Background, "Tomotley: An Eighteenth Century Cherokee Village (TVA, 1983) available from Indiana University-Purdue University (Fort Wayne, IN, 2004-2006), ch. 2, at http://users.ipfw.edu/baden/anthro/Tellico/tomotley/ and http://users.ipfw.edu/baden/anthro/Tellico/tomotley/c2.html [August 17, 2006].

Tamaroa
Swanton, 241-242.

Tamathli
Swanton, 113-114, 115.

Tanain
Swanton, 538-539; "Previous Classifications" (NodeWorks - Encyclopedia) at http://pedia.nodeworks.com/N/NA/NAT/Native_American_languages/Previous_classifications [August 9, 2006].

Tancague
Herbert E. Bolton, "The Founding of the Missions on the San Gabriel River, 1745-1749," *Southwestern Historical Quarterly*, vol. 17, no. 4, 323-378, SHQ Online at http://www.tsha.utexas.edu/publications/journals/shq/online/v017/n4/article_1.html[May 24, 2006].

Tangipahoa
Swanton, 195, 196, 210-211.

Tanico
Herbert E. Bolton, "The Founding of the Missions on the San Gabriel River, 1745-1749," *Southwestern Historical Quarterly*, vol. 17, no. 4, 323-378, SHQ Online at http://www.tsha.utexas.edu/publications/journals/shq/online/v017/n4/article_1.html [May 24, 2006].

Tanima Comanche
Thomas N. Campbell, "Tanima Indians," *Handbook of Texas Online* (Austin, TX: Texas State Historical Association and University of Texas, 2001) at http://www.tsha.utexas.edu/handbook/online/articles/TT/bmt13.html [June 24, 2006].

Tanxnitania
Swanton, 61-62.

Taos Pueblo
Hampton Sides, *Blood and Thunder*, 167-184, 215, 336. Also, L. Bradford Prince, "Taos," *Spanish Mission Churches of New Mexico* (Cedar Rapids, IA: The Torch Press, 1915), chp. 21, 245-262, made available by Books of the Southwest (Tucson, AZ: University of Arizona Library, n.d.) at http://southwest.library.arizona.edu/spmc/body.1_div.21.html [October 30, 2006]. "A Brief History of Taos: United States Sovereignty in Taos " (Taos, NM: LaPlaza Telecommunity, 1995-2002) at http://www.laplaza.org/comm/about_taos/history/sovereignty.html [October 30, 2006].

Taovaya
Edward B. Jelks, "Taovaya Indians," *Handbook of Texas Online* (Austin, TX: Texas State Historical Association and University of Texas, 2001) at http://www.tsha.utexas.edu/handbook/online/articles/view/TT/bmt17.html [May 24, 2006].

Taposa
Swanton, 177, 187, 192.

Tappan
Swanton, 48-55; Edwin G. Burrows & Mike Wallace, *Gotham*, 5.

Tatlit-kutchin
Swanton, 575, 585, 602, 603.

Tatsanottine
Swanton, 603-604.

Taukaways
Samuel G. Drake, *The Aboriginal Races of North America...*, 9-16.

Tauxenent
Swanton, 66-71.

Tawakoni
Swanton 303, 305; T. R. Fehrenback, *Comanches*, 197; Mildred P. Mayhall, *The Kiowas*, 25; Samuel G. Drake, *The Aboriginal Races of North*

America..., 9-16. Also see Anna Lewis, "La Harpe's First Expedition in Oklahoma, 1718-1719," *Chronicles of Oklahoma*, December 1924, vol. 2, no. 4, 331-349, available from the Oklahoma State University Digital Library at http://digital.library.okstate.edu/chronicles/v002/v002p331. html; Margery H. Krieger, "Tawakoni Indians," *Handbook of Texas Online* (Austin, TX: Texas State Historical Association and University of Texas, 2001) at http://www.tsha.utexas.edu/handbook/online/articles/view/TT/bmt22.html [September 9, 2006].

"Interview with Mr. C. S. Bradley, White Pioneer, Groesbeck, Texas" (Washington, DC: WPA, Federal Writers' Project, 1936-1940), District 8, File no. 240, at http://lcweb2.loc.gov/wpa/33010808.html; "Texas Indians and Texas Place-Names" (Texas Historical Commission, n.d.) at http://www.thc.state.tx.us/triviafun/trvindian.html [August 16, 2006].

Tawasa
Swanton, 144-145, 154, 155, 157; "Tawasa," Four Directions Institute (Four Directions Press, 2005) at http://www.fourdir.com/tawasa. htm; "Apalachicola Reserve, Florida" (National Estuarine Research Reserve System, 2004) at http://nerrs.noaa.gov/Apalachicola/History.html [October 15, 2006].

Tawehash
Swanton, 303-304.

1082 Tci-he-nde Mimbre Apache
See Apache (R49) and Chiricahua (R192)

Tegninateo
Swanton, 61-62.

Tejas
George Klos, "Indians" *Handbook of Texas Online* (Austin, TX: Texas State Historical Association and University of Texas, 1999-2003)at http://www.tsha.utexas.edu/handbook/online/articles/II/bzi4.html and Donald E. Chipman, "Spanish Texas" at http://www.tsha.utexas.edu/handbook/online/articles/SS/nps1.html; Mattie Austin Hatcher, "Description of the Tejas or Asinai Indians, 1691-1722," *Southwestern Historical Quarterly*, vol. 31, no. 1, 50-62, available at http://www.tsha.utexas.edu/publications/journals/shq/online/v031/n1/article_7.html [September 9, 2006]

Telmocresse
Samuel G. Drake, *The Aboriginal Races of North America...*, 9-16.

Tenawa Comanche
Thomas N. Campbell, "Tenawa Indians," *Handbook of Texas Online* (Austin, TX: Texas State Historical Association and University of Texas, 2001) at http://www.tsha.utexas.edu/handbook/online/articles/TT/bmt33.html [June 24, 2006].

Tenino
Swanton, 470-471, 473, 474; Stephenie Flora, "Northwest Indians" (The Oregon Territory And Its Pioneers, 1998-2005) at http://www.oregonpioneers.com/tribe.htm [August 28, 2006]; "The Confederated Tribes of the Warm Springs Reservation of Oregon" (Columbia River Inter-Tribal Fish Commission, 2007) at http://www.critfc.org/text/warmsprings.html [December 24, 2007].

Tequesta
Swanton,145-146; Gloria Jahoda, *Trail of Tears*, 244.

Tewa Pueblo Group
Swanton, 340-344.

Téxas
Herbert E. Bolton, "The Spanish Abandonment and Re-occupation of East Texas, 1773-1779", vol. 9, no. 2, *Southwestern Historical Quarterly* Online, 67-137 at http://www.tsha.utexas.edu/publications/journals/shq/online/v009/n2/article_1_print.html [March 9, 2006].

Teya
H. Allen Anderson, "Teya Indians" *Handbook of Texas Online* (Austin, TX: Texas State Historical Association and University of Texas, 2001) at http://www.tsha.utexas.edu/handbook/online/articles/view/TT/bmt43.html [September 10, 2006].

Thlingchadinne
Swanton, 604.

Three Fires Confederacy
Sue I. Silliman, *St Joseph in Homespun, A Centennial Souvenir* (Three Rivers, MI: Three Rivers Publishing Company, 1931, reprinted as originally published), 1, 2-5, 26; Colin G. Calloway, *The Shawnees and the War for America*, xvii, xviii, 34. Also see "Brief History of Michigan: Michigan," Michigan Manual 2001-2002 (Lansing, MI: State Legislature, n.d.), ch. 1, 3-26, at http://www.legislature.mi.gov/... (dye51sfyuclhscffutiyvd55)/documents/publications/manual/2001-2002/2001-mm-0003-0026-History.pdf; "People of the Three Fires," (Michigan: © Rose Edwards, 1997-2004) at http://www.rootsweb.com/~minatam/; Bob Owens & Scott Null, "A Brief History of the Native American and European Names of the Saint Joseph-River" (Friends of the St. Joe River Association, n.d.) at http://www.fotsjr.org/... river/history.htm; "Geologic History of the DRS" (Cook Lake, MI: M E A N D R S: Dowagiac River System, updated, April 2000) at http://www.meandrs.org/history.html; "Hannaville Potawatomie Tribal Profile" (Sault Ste. Marie, MI: Inter-Tribal Council of Michigan, n.d.) at http://www.itcmi.org/thehistorytribal1.html [July 9, 2006].

Tigua Pueblo
Bill Wright, "Tigua Indians," *Handbook of Texas Online* (Austin, TX: Texas State Historical Association and University of Texas, 2001) at http://www.tsha.utexas.edu/handbook/online/articles/TT/bmt45.html [March 2, 2006]; R. Edward Moore, "The Tigua Indians of Texas" (New Braunfels, TX: R E. Moore and Texarch Associates, 2000) at http://www.texasindians.com/tigua.htm [March 2, 2006].

Tikabahchee
Brenda Jean Bova, "Southeastern US Tribes" (Armada, MI: Golden Gate Services, 1998-2005) at http://www.genealogyforum.com/ gfaol/ resource/NA/gfna0002.htm; also "South Western United States" at http://www.genealogyforum.com/gfaol/resource/NA/naswus.htm [June 24, 2006]; "Tribes / Nations" (Wolf's Retreat, n.d.) at http://www.realduesouth.net/WolfsRetreat/tribes.htm [June 24, 2006].

Tillamook
Swanton, 471-472; Bernard De Vito, ed., *The Journals of Lewis & Clark*, 300-302, 304, 306, 332-334. Also, "Clark, William. Estimate of the Western Indians," American Indian Manuscripts (American Philosophical Association Library), Item 2433, D. 4p. and 1p. Map, at http://www.amphilsoc.org/library/guides/indians/info/noea.htm [August 9, 2006].

Tillamook Group
Swanton, 471-472.

Timucua Proper
See Utina.

Tionontati
Swanton 233, 235, 236, 258, 307, 604-605; G. Elmore Reaman, *The Trail of the Iroquois Indians*, 8.

John S. Allen, "René Menard 1605-1661, Comments, reviews and corrections" (1997, rev. 1999) at http://www.bikexprt.com/menard/comments.htm; "Iroquois Wars of the 17th Century" (Madison: Wisconsin Historical Society, 1996-2006) at http://www.wisconsinhistory.org/turningpoints/tp-005/?action=more_essay; Charles Garrad, "'Petun' and the Petuns" (Kansas City, KS: Wyandot Nation of Kansas, 1996-2006) at http://www.wyandot.org/rb10.htm [August 4, 2006].

Tiopane
Thomas N. Campbell, "Tiopane Indians," *Handbook of Texas Online* (Austin, TX: Texas State Historical Association and University of Texas, 2001) at http://www.tsha.utexas.edu/handbook/online/articles/TT/bmt51.html [June 24, 2006].

Tiou
Swanton, 177, 185, 188, 189, 192-193.

Tiwa Pueblo
Swanton, 344-346.

Tockwogh
"History Timeline for the North Sassafras Parish and Cecil County, Maryland" (Towson, MD: BCPL, 2006) at http://www.bcpl.net/~ellen/timeline.html; "Indians in Maryland, an Overview," Maryland Online Encyclopedia (Maryland Historical Society et al., 2004-2005) at http://www.mdoe.org/indiansoverview.html; Chesapeake Bay (Mariners' Museum, 2002) at http://www.mariner.org/chesapeakebay/colonial/col011.html; William Henry Egle, "History of the Counties of Dauphin and Lebanon" (Accessible Archives), 3-13, at http://www.accessible.com/amcnty/PA/DauphinLebanon/Dauphin01.htm [August 18, 2006].

Tocobaga
Swanton, 146, 150, 151.

Tohome
Swanton, 160, 170-171.

Tolowa
Fergus M. Bordewich, *Killing the White Man's Indian* (New York: Anchor Books,1996), 50-51. (Bordewich is also the author of *Bound for Canaan: The Epic Story of the Underground Railroad, America's First Civil Rights Movement*, Harper Collins, 2005); Swanton, 515-516;"Tolowa People," The Indians of the Coast (CND Marketing Group/CND Marketing and Design, 2002/2003) at http://members.tripod.com/~boyett/ind.html; Charles R. Smith, "An Introduction to California's Native People: American Period" (Aptos, CA: Cabrillo College, n.d.) at http://www.cabrillo.edu/~crsmith/anth6_americanperiod.html [May 26, 2006]. For the Yontoket Massacre, see "Indians in Northern California: A Case Study of Federal, State, and Vigilante Intervention, 1850 - 1860" (Arcata, CA: Humboldt State University, n.d.) at http://www.humboldt.edu/~go1/kellogg/northerncalifornia.html [July 8, 2006].

Tonawanda
Swanton, 37. Alan Taylor, *The Divided Ground*, 314. Israel Chapin, Jr. Treaty of September 16, 1797.

Tongva
Swanton, 490-491; "Gabrieleno/Tongva" (San Gabriel, CA: Gabrielino/Tongva Tribal Council of San Gabriel, n.a.) at http://www.tongva.com/; "Tongva (Gabrielinos)," Los Angeles Almanac, available from Francis F. Steen, Communication Studies, University of California Los Angeles at http://cogweb.ucla.edu/Chumash/Tongva.html; "California Region United States" (Armada, MI: Golden Gate Services, 1998 - 2005) at

http://www.genealogyforum.rootsweb.com/gfaol/resource/NA/nacaus.htm [March 11, 2006].

"La Puente Valley" (Los Angles, CA: County of Los Angeles Public Library, 2001) at http://www.colapublib.org/history/lapuente/faq.html#q7 [June 6, 2006].

Tonkawa
T. R. Fehrenback, *Comanches*, 205-206, 227; Swanton, 301, 303, 304, 308, 321, 323, 326, 327, 330.

For Wichita Agency Massacre or Tonkawa Massacre, see *Report of the Commissioner of Indian Affairs, 1859* (Washington, 1860), p. 329; Annie Heloise Abel, *American Indian as Participant in the Civil War* (Cleveland: Arthur H. Clark Company, 1919), p. 153. Also, Thomas F. Schilz, "PLÁCIDO," Handbook of Texas Online (Austin, TX: Texas State Historical Association in partnership with the University of Texas Libraries at the University of Texas at Austin, 2002) at http://www.tsha.utexas.edu/handbook/online/articles/PP/fpl1.html and William K. Jones, "Notes On The History And Material Culture of the Tonkawa Indians," *Anthropology* (Washington, DC: Smithsonian Institution, 1969), vol. 2, no. 5, at http://www.sil.si.edu/SmithsonianContributions/Anthropology/text/SCtA-0002.5.txt [September 23, 2007].

"Records of the Central Superintendency of Indian Affairs, 1813 - 1878" (Topeka, KS: Kansas State Historical Society, 2007) at http://www.kshs.org/research/collections/documents/businessrecords/business_records_findingaids/central_superintendency_nara.htm; C. Ross Hume, "Historic Sites Around Anadarko," *Chronicles of Oklahoma*, December 1938, vol. 16, no. 4, pp. 410-424, from the Electronic Publishing Center (Stillwater, OK: Oklahoma State University, 2007) at http://digital.library.okstate.edu/chronicles/v016/v016p410.html; Patricia Adkins-Rochette, "Tonkawa Massacre and the Tonkawa Tribe" (Duncan, OK, 2004-2007) at http://www.bourlandcivilwar.com/TonkawaMassacre.htm. From *Bourland [Benjamin Bourland family]in North Texas and Indian Territory During the Civil War: Fort Cobb, Fort Arbuckle & the Wichita Mountains.* [September 21, 2007].

Tonkawan Tribes
Swanton, 308, 309, 326-327.

Tonto Apache
Swanton, 327-330, 365; James L. Haley, *Apaches*, 284-293, 342n1, 353. For the Oatman Massacre, see Brian McGinty, *The Oatman Massacre*. Also, Thomas Edwin Farish, History of Arizona, vol. I (Phoenix, AZ, 1915), chp. xv., 257-262, available from Books of the Southwest, University of Arizona Library (Arizona Board of Regents, n.d.) at http://southwest.library.arizona.edu/hav1/body.1_div.15.html [November 10, 2006].

Tramaskecooc
Fred Willard, "Trade Items as Transfer of Money," November 2002, made available by the Lost Colony Center for Science and Research (Eastern Carolina University) at http://lost-colony.com/trade.html [June 12, 2006].

Trementina
H. Allen Anderson, "Trementina Indians," *Handbook of Texas Online* (Austin, TX: Texas State Historical Association and University of Texas, 2001) at http://www.tsha.utexas.edu/handbook/online/articles/TT/bmt77.html [October 4, 2006].

Tsanchifin Kalapuya
Swanton, 454.

Tuacane
Julia Kathryn Garrett, "Doctor John Sibley and the Lousiana-Texas Frontier, 1803-1814," *Southwestern Historical Quarterly*, vol. 47, n. 1, and vol. 47, no. 1, made available by the Texas State Historical Association (Austin, TX: University of Texas, 2004) at http://www.tsha.utexas.edu/publications/journals/shq/online/v047/n1/contrib_DIVL1027.html and http://www.tsha.utexas.edu/publications/journals/shq/online/v049/n4/contrib_DIVL8836.html [August 17, 2006].

Tübatulabal
Swanton, 516-517.

Tukabahchee
Swanton, 119, 163, 172, 174. Marszalek, "Creek," Native Americans (Buffalo Grove, IL: Twin Groves Middle School, 1998-2006) at http://www.twingroves.district96.k12.il.us/NativeAmericans/Creek.html; "Muskogee," Four Directions Institute (Four Directions Press, 2005) at http://www.fourdir.com/muskogee.htm [June 24, 2006].

Tukuarika Shoshoni
Swanton, 404, 405. David Dominick, *The Sheepeaters* (Wind River History, n.a.) at http://www.windriverhistory.org/exhibits/sheepeaters... / Resources/Dominick.pdf. For the Sheeteaters Campaign (War) see Carrey, Johnny Carrey & Cort Conley, *The Middle Fork and the Sheepeater War*; Robert H. Rudy and John A. Brown, *The Cayuse Indians*, 286-287. Also, "Middle Fork of the Salmon River - Sheepeater Campaign" (Orbitz Away, 1999-2007) at http://gorp.away.com/gorp/resource/us_river/id/she_midd.htm [December 30, 2007]

Tulalip
Swanton, 443; "Tulalip Tribe," NWIFC Member Tribes (Olympia, WA: Northwest Indian Fisheries Commission, n.d.) at http://www.nwifc.wa.gov/tribes/tribe.asp?tribe=tulalip; Tulalip Tribes (Tulalip, WA: Tulalip Tribes of Washington, n.d.) at http://www.tulaliptribes-nsn.gov/; Rich Street and Sandra Schugren, "Tulalip," Washington State Native American Tribes (TribalQuest, n.d.) at http://ttt.pugetsoundcenter.org/projects/1998/web/tribal/tribesofwa.htm [September 10, 2006].

Tum-Waters
"Letter from Anson Dart to the Bureau of Indian Affairs in 1851. Adapted from McChesney, et. al. *The Rolls of Certain Indian Tribes in Washington and Oregon*, available at http://www.ccrh.org/comm/slough/primary/ansondrt.htm [May 16, 2006].

Tunahe
Swanton, 392, 394, 398.

Tunica
Swanton, 186, 188, 192, 193-194, 199, 200, 207, 215, 232; Jean Delanglez, "The Jolliet Lost Map of the Mississippi, "*Mid-America, An Historical Review* (Chicago, IL: Loyola University, April 1946), vol. 28 (New Series, vol. 17), no. 2, 67-143, esp. 109, 134-135; Veronica E. Velarde Tiller, ed. "Louisiana," *Federal and State Indian Reservations and Trust Areas* (Washington, DC: EDA, 1974), 349-352, available online at http://www. eda.gov/ImageCache/EDAPublic/documents/pfddocs/20louisiana_2epdf/vi/20louisiana.pdf [July 17, 2007], subsequently published under the title *Tiller's Guide to Indian Country: Economic Profiles of American Indian Reservations* (1996). Jeffrey P. Brain, "On the Tunica Trail," 3rd ed. (Baton Rouge, LA: Department of Culture, Recreation and Tourism, 1994) made available by Louisiana Division of Archaeology (Baton Rouge, LA) at http://www.crt.state.la.us/archaeology/TUNICA/TUNICA.HTM; "Establishment of the French in Louisiana," American Memory (Washington, DC: Library of Congress, n.d.) at http://lcweb2.loc.gov/master/rbc/rbfr/0009/00470035.txt; "Historical Memoirs of Louisiana" at http://memory.loc.gov/master/rbc/rbfr/0011/01140096.txt [August 18, 2006].

"Mississippi," *New Catholic Dictionary* at http://www.catholic-forum.com/saints/ncd05510.htm; Robert Carlton Clark, "Louis Juciiereau De Saint-Denis And The Reestablishment Of The Tejas Missions," *Southwestern Historical Quarterly* made available from Texas State Historical Association(Austin, TX: University of Texas, 2006), vol. 6, no. 1, 1-26, at http://www.tsha.utexas.edu/publications/journals/shq/online/... v006/n1/article_3.html; "Henri Tonti Letters," available from the OhioValley-Great Lakes Ethnohistory Archives: The Miami Collection (Bloomington, IN: Glenn Black Laboratory of Archaeology and Trustees of Indiana University, 1996-2000), 229-235, at http://www.gbl. indiana.edu/archives/miamis4/M17-03_8c.html [August 18, 2006]. From Henri de Tonti in John Delanglez, Mid-America (1939), vol. 21, 209-238. Also, Phil Konstantin, "May 1st to 8th in American Indian History," (1996-1998) at http://members.tripod.com/~PHILKON/May1.html [orig site, August 18, 2006; July 17, 2007]; "Tunica-Biloxi Tribe of Louisiana" (Marksville, LA, n..d.) at http://www.tunica.org/ [July 17, 2007].

"Indian Burial Mounds" (Austin: University of Texas, n.d.) at http://www.lib.utexas.edu/maps/national_parks/mississippi_burial_mounds97. pdf and "History of Tunica" (Tunica, MS: Tunica Chamber of Commerce, 2005) at http://www.tunicachamber.com/Content/Economic%20... Development/Culture%20and%20Living.htm [September 17, 2007].

Tunxis
Swanton, 24, 44-48.

Tups
Herbert E. Bolton, "The Founding of the Missions on the San Gabriel River, 1745-1749," *Southwestern Historical Quarterly*, vol. 17, no. 4, 323-378, SHQ Online at http://www.tsha.utexas.edu/publications/journals/shq/online/v017/n4/article_1.html [May 24, 2006].

Tuscarora
Swanton, 85-88; John Lawson, "Account of the Indians of North-Carolina," made available by George Howard (Restoration Systems, n.d.) at http://www.georgehoward.net/lawsontext5.htm [August 18, 2006]. Also see "Colonial North Carolina: The Tuscarora War," U-S-History (Florence, OR: Online Highways, 2002) at http://www.u-s-history.com/pages/h627.html [September 9, 2006].

Tuskegee
Swanton, 157, 172-173.

Tutelo
Swanton, esp. 44, 64, 66, 72, 73-74.

"Indians A.D. 1600–1800," First People: The Early Indians of Virginia (Virginia Department of Historic Resources, n.d.), page 3 of 4, at http://www.dhr.state.va.us/arch_NET/timeline/contact_indian_3.htm; also p. 48, from Knowledgerush (1999-2004) at http://www. knowledgerush.com/paginated_txt/nvycr10/nvycr10_s1_p48_pages.html; John Lawson, "A New Voyage to Carolina..." (London, 1709) available from Trading Ford Historic District Preservation Association (Salisbury, NC, 2001) at http://www.tradingford.com/lawson/lawson. html; "A Brief History of Salem, Virginia" (Salem Museum Historical Society, 2004) at http://www.salemmuseum.org/hist_brief.html; "Senate Bill 480: Title V--Monacan Indian Nation," (United States Senate, 109th Congress, March 1, 2005) at http://www.washingtonwatchdog.org/ documents/cong_bills/109/s/s109_480is.html [August 18, 2006].

Linda and George, "Searching for Saponi Town" (Jelsoft Enterprises Ltd., 2000-2006), posted 06-04-2003 and 06-04-2003, respectively, at http://www.saponitown.com/forum/showthread.php?s=71550cac41729b53bd74f653d865ffcd&threadid=653 [August 18, 2006]. From, in part, A.Gwynn Henderson et al., *Indian Occupation and Use In Northern and Eastern Kentucky During the Contact Period, 1540-1795, An Initial Investigation* (University of Kentucky), p. 130.

Tutseewa
Samuel G. Drake, *The Aboriginal Races of North America...*, 9-16.

Tututni
Swanton, 472-473.

Twana

Swanton, 445, 447. "Culture and History of the Skokomish Tribe" (Skokomish Nation, WA: Skokomish Tribal Nation, 2004) at http://www.skokomish.org [September 10, 2006].

Tyigh

Swanton, 471, 473-474.

Ufallah

Samuel G. Drake, *The Aboriginal Races of North America…*, 9-16.

Ugaljachmutzi

John Wesley Powell, *Indian Linguistic Families…*, 17, 121; Samuel G. Drake, *The Aboriginal Races of North America…*, 9-16. Also, "Athapascan Family" (Native American Nations, 2000-2006) at http://www.nanations.com/linguistic/athapascan_family.htm [August 19, 2006]. Originally from Gallatin in Schoolcraft, Ind. Tribes, III, 402, 1853. "Indians, North America," Online Encyclopedia (Net Industries, 2004) at http://encyclopedia.jrank.org/I27_INV/INDIANS_NORTH_AMERICAN.html [October 16, 2006]. Originally appearing in Volume V14, Page 454.

Umatilla

Swanton, 474. On the Kennewick Man, see "Kennewick man ruling – politics or science?," New Scientist, February 2004. Also, F. P. McManamon, "Kennewick Man," National Park Service Archaeology and Ethnography Program (Washington, DC: Department of the Interior, 2004) at http://www.cr.nps.gov/aad/kennewick/; Andy Perdue, "Kennewick Man Virtual Interpretive Center" (Kennewick, Pasco, and Richmond, WA: Tri-City Hearld, 2004) at http://www.kennewick-man.com/ [September 10, 2006].

Umpqua

Swanton, 474-475; David Dary, *The Oregon Trail*, 252.

Unalachtigo

Swanton, 48-55.

Unami

Swanton, 48-55.

Unkechaug

Swanton, 15-16, 42-43.

"Long Island Indians and The Early Settlers" (Long Island, NY: Long Island Genealogy, n.d.) at http://www.longislandgenealogy.com/indians.html; Bernice Forrest Guillaume, "Poosepatuck (Unkechaug Nation)" (Shinnecock Lodge 360, Suffolk Country Council # 404, 2002-2004) at http://www.shinnecock360.org/Resources/Unkechaug%20History.PDF; "Poospatuk Reservation: Looking for an Upturn After Years of Turmoil," Long Island Our Story (Long Island, NY: Newsday, 2006) at http://www.newsday.com/community/guide/lihistory/ny-historytown-hist008i,0,7245128.story [June 25, 2006].

Ottmar Ederer, "North American Indian Nations" (Sünching, Germany: Wontolla's Reservation, 1998-2005) at http://wontolla.homepage.t-online.de/wontolla/14etribe.html [June 25, 2006]. Ederer, for one, gives the following name alternatives for Unkechaug: Unchachaug, Unquaches, Unquachock, and UNCHECHAUGE [June 25, 2006].

Unquehiett

Swanton, 56.

Upper Pend d'Oreilles

Swanton, 399-400. George P. Sanger, ed., *Statutes at Large, Treaties, and Proclamations of the United States of America from December 5, 1859 to March 3, 1863*, vol. XII, 975-979/1443.

Upper Skagit

Swanton, 441, 446. "History" (Sedro Wolley, WA: Upper Skagit Tribe) at ttp://www.northregionems.com/native/Upper%20Skagit%20Tribe.htm; "Upper Skagit Tribe," NWIFC Member Tribes (Olympia, WA: Northwest Indian Fisheries Commission, n.d.) at http://www.nwifc.wa.gov/tribes/tribe.asp?tribe=skagit [May 17, 2006].

Usququhaga

Swanton, 56.

Ute

Swanton, 373-375; John Upton Terrell, *The Plains Apache*, 131-136, 150, 172. Also see "An Introduction to Ute Tribal History" (Ignacio, CO: Southern Ute Indian Tribe, 2006) at http://www.southern-ute.nsn.us/history/intro.html [November 16, 2006]; "Colorado Ute Legacy " (Ignacio, CO: Southern Ute Indian Tribe, 2000) at http://www.utelegacy.org/; "Ute" (Land Use History of North America: Colorado Plateau, n.d.) at http://www.cpluhna.nau.edu/People/ute_indians.htm [September 8, 2006].

John D. Grahame and Thomas D. Sisk, eds., *Canyons, cultures and environmental change: An introduction to the land-use history of the*

Colorado Plateau (2002) at http://www.cpluhna.nau.edu/People/ute_indians.htm; Robert S. McPherson, "Ute Indians - Southern" and "Ute Indians - Northern," *Utah History Encyclopedia* (Salt Lake City: Media Solutions, University of Utah, 1996-1998, updated 2004) City: University of at http://www.media.utah.edu/UHE/u/UTES%2CSOUTHERN.html and http://www.media.utah.edu/UHE/u/UTES%2CNORTHERN. html; "Southern Ute Tribal History" (Ignacio, CO: Southern Ute Indian Tribe, n.a.) at http://www.southern-ute.nsn.us/history/index.html; http://www.southern-ute.nsn.us/history/ouray.html [April 5, 2006].

For the Ute War, see Drake, *Indians of North America*, 715-717. Also, Russell D. Santala, "The Ute Campaign of 1879: A Study in the Use of the Military Instrument" (Combat Studies Institute, 1994) available from the Command and General Staff College (Leavenworth, KS, 2006) at http://www-cgsc.army.mil/carl/resources/csi/santala/santala.asp [November 16, 2006]. And, "The Last Major Indian Uprising" (Meeker, CO: Historical Society, n.d.) at http://www.meekercolorado.com/HSociety.htm; "History: Meeker Colorado" (Meeker, CO: Meeker Chamber of Commerce, 2001-2006) at http://www.meekerchamber.com/historical.htm; Steve Porter, "Idealist who founded Greeley died in Meeker Massacre" (Fort Collins, CO: Poudre Magazine, n.d.) at http://www.poudremagazine.com/areahistory.cfm [November 16, 2006].

Utina (or Timucua)
Swanton, 114, 43, 144, 147-152; Gloria Jahoda, *Trail of Tears*, 244. "About Orlando Fine Arts!" (Orlando, FL: Orlando/Orange County Convention and Visitors Bureau, n.d.) at http://www.hotelkingdom.com/aboutorlandoarts.htm[September 9, 2006].

Uzutiuhi
Jean Delanglez, "The Jolliet Lost Map of the Mississippi," *Mid-America, An Historical Review* (Chicago, IL: Loyola University, April 1946), vol. 28 (New Series, vol. 17), no. 2, 67-143, esp. 109, 134-135.

Vanyume
Swanton, 480, 497, 517.

Vrnertown Indians
"SC – Native Americans – Wassamasaw Tribe of Varnertown" (Columbia, SC: SCIway.net, 2007) at http://www.sciway.net/hist/indians/ wassamasaw-varnertown-indians-sc.html [October 21, 2007].

Ventureño Chumash
Swanton, 484-487.

Vermillion
Dorothy Libby, *An Anthropological Report on the Piankashaw Indians: Piankashaw Locations, ca. 1776- ca. 1783*, pp. 90-99, available from the OhioValley-Great Lakes Ethnohistory Archives: The Miami Collection (Bloomington, IN: Glenn Black Laboratory of Archaeology and Trustees of Indiana University, 1997-2000), at http://www.gbl.indiana.edu/archives/dockett_99/d99toc.html [October 24, 2006].

Gilbert Imlay, *A Topographical Description of the Western Territory of North America...*, 3rd ed. (London, 1797), 364-365, made available from Glen Black Laboratory of Archaeology (Bloomington, IN: University of Indiana, 1997-2000) at http://www.gbl.indiana.edu/archives/ dockett_317/317_33.html... [August 11, 2006].

"The Vermilion River Basin," Critical Trends Assessment Program (Springfield: Illinois Department of Natural Resources, 2000) at http://dnr.state.il.us/orep/c2000/assessments/vermilion/page3.htm; "Local Area History," Danville, Illinois (Community Profile Network, 2001) at http://www.allarounddanville.com/home/localhistory.htm; *History of Vermillion County Illinois*, Chapter IV (1911) made available by Jody Fisher at http://ftp.rootsweb.com/pub/usgenweb/il/vermilion/history1911/chapter4.txt [October 24, 2006].

Vieux Désert
Robert N. Van Alstine, "Lac Vieux Desert Band of Lake Superior Chippewa Indians" (Watersmeet, MI: Lac Vieux Desert Band of Chippewa Indian Community, July 11, 2001) at http://www.itcmi.org/thehistorytribal5.html [April 5, 2006].

Wabash
"The Miami Nation" (Huntington, IN; Historic Forks of the Wabash, n.d.) at http://www.historicforks.org/miami/index.html [June 26, 2006].

David A. Baerreis, *The Band Affiliation of Potawatomi Treaty Signatories*, pp. 11-20, available from the OhioValley-Great Lakes Ethnohistory Archives: The Miami Collection (Bloomington, IN: Glenn Black Laboratory of Archaeology and Trustees of Indiana University, 1996-2003) at http://www.gbl.indiana.edu/Pot2/TS_2a.html; Dorothy Libby, *An Anthropological Report on the Piankashaw Indians: Piankashaw Locations, ca. 1776- ca. 1783*, pp. 90-99, available from the OhioValley-Great Lakes Ethnohistory Archives: The Miami Collection (Bloomington, IN: Glenn Black Laboratory of Archaeology and Trustees of Indiana University, 1997-2000), at http://www.gbl.indiana.edu/archives/dockett_99/ d99toc.html [October 24, 2006]. "The History of Wabash Indiana" (Wabash, IN: Wabash Carnegie Public Library, 2004) at http://www.wabash. lib.in.us/historyofwabash.html; "The Indians and Wells County" (Bluffton, IN: Wells County Historical Society, 1998) at http://www.parlorcity. com/pbender/indianswellsco.html; John R. Williams, "Lawrence County History," taken from *Atlas of Lawrence County* (W. R. Brink & Co, 1875) at http://www.lawrencecountyillinois.com/history/lchist.html [July 5, 2006].

Thomas Jefferson, "To Brother John Baptist de Coigne," Charlottesville, June 1781, Writings (New York: Library of America, 1984), 551-554. Re: de Coigne, see "Tribe Listing," Indian Records and Information (Raven's Roost, n.d.) at http://www.whitemoonraven.com/native/records. html and A. A. Liscomb and A. L. Bergh, eds., *The Writings of Thomas Jefferson* (Bloomington: Glen Black Laboratory of Archaeology, 1997-2000), vol. 16, 377-386, at http://www.gbl.indiana.edu/archives/dockett_317/317_30a.html [July 19, 2006].

Waccamaw
Swanton, 75, 88, 90, 97, 100-101, 103.

Waco
Swanton, 304-305; T. R. Fehrenback, *Comanches*, 197.

As to the Wico, George Catlin, *North American Indians* (Penguin ed.), 334, 339, 340, 341, and from 350 but omitted from Penguin ed. See Catlin online edition from http://www.pdflibrary.com/Samples/AMERICAN_INDIANS/1582182728.pdf, and from American Mountain Men Association Library of Western Fur Trade Historical Source Documents at http://www.xmission.com/~drudy/mtman/html/catlin/ [November 19, 2007]. See also, "Indian Tribes of North America (esp. in relationship to Jackson Era)" from Hal Morris, *A History Resource, and an Experiment in Hypertext Style* (2001) at http://www.jmisc.net/indians.htm; Quinn Gardner, "President Roosevelt Creates a Refuge: A Re-Telling" (Lawton, OK, n.d.) at http://www.sirinet.net/~project/President... Roosevelt.html [November 19, 2007]. A search of for "Wico" in the files of Oklahoma State University Electronic Publishing Center proved negative (http://libgooglem.library.okstate.edu/search?q=Wico&site=... EPC& btnG.=EPC+Search&sort=date%3AD%3AL%3Ad1&output=xml_no_dtd&lr=lang_en&oe=UTF-8&ie=UTF-8&client=EPC&proxystyle... sheet.=EPC [November 19, 2007]). Fehrenback in *Comanches* makes no reference to a Wico or the Waco.

Wahkiakum
"Wahkiakum Indians" (Washington, DC: National Geographic, 1996-2006) at http://www.nationalgeographic.com/lewisandclark/record_tribes_094_14_12.html; "A Bit of History" (Cathlamet, WA: Lower Columbia Economic Development Council, 2005-2006) at http://lowercolumbiaedc.org/tourism.shtml; Anna Zerzyke, "Indians," The Story of Rainier, 1805-1925 (Rainier, OR, 1924-1925), Article V, restored by Eleanor H. Abraham (Rainier, Oregon, February 24, 1999) available at http://www.columbia-center.org/shpubliclibrary/webs/Story_of_Rainier/V_Indians.htm [August 30, 2006].

Wahowpum
David L. Nicandri, "The Columbia Country and the Dissolution of Meriwether Lewis
Speculation and Interpretation," *Oregon Historical Quarterly* (Oregon Historical Society), Spring 2005, vol. 106, no. 1, available from the History Cooperative at http://www.historycooperative.org/journals/ohq/106.1/nicandri.html#FOOT23 [August 19, 2006]; Stephenie Flora, "Northwest Indians" (The Oregon Territory And Its Pioneers, 1998-2005) at http://www.oregonpioneers.com/tribe.htm [August 28, 2006].

Wahpacoota Sioux
"The Shakopee Mdewakanton Sioux Community Enrollment Problems and the Minnesota Mdewakanton Sioux Identity," Native American Press /Ojibwe News, September 27, 2002(Maquah Publications) at http://www.maquah.net/press/Buttes_letter.html [August 19, 2006].

Wailaki
Swanton, 517-518.

Wakokai
Swanton, 163, 173.

Walapai
Swanton, 365-366.

Walla Walla
Swanton, 447-448; Robert H. Rudy and John A. Brown, *The Cayuse Indians*, 5 (Deschutes) , 8, 14, 22, 33, 48, 61, 78, 98, 125, 138, 141, 156, 180, 182, 210, 211, 237, 268, 293; Stephen E. Ambrose, *Undaunted Courage*, 298-299, 348-349; "History & Culture" (Warm Springs, OR: Confederated Tribes of Warm Springs, 1999-2005) at http://www.warmsprings.com/Warmsprings/Tribal_Community/History__Culture/; "Our History & Culture" (Pendleton, OR: Confederated Tribes of the Umatilla Indian Reservation, n.d.) at http://www.umatilla.nsn.us/history.html [May 16, 2006].

Walpapi
Robert H. Rudy and John A. Brown, *The Cayuse Indians*, 4-5n4; T. R. Fehrenbach, *Comanches*, 135; Swanton, 375, 475.

Walpi Hopi
Swanton, 352.

Wampanoag
Swanton, 24-27; Nathaniel Philbrick, *Mayflower*, xiii-xiv, xvi, 48-49, 51-52. 53-54, 119, 155, 195-196, 201-205-215, 216-220, 349, 250, 353, 356; quote taken from 119. Also, Drake, *Indians of North America*, 81-92, 99-100.

"Northeast Tribes Wampanoag," Northeast Wigwam (RI: Deborah Champlain, 1998-2000) at http://www.newigwam.com/hwampanoag.html; "Wampanoag: History, Culture" (Plymouth, MA: America's Homepage, 1997) at http://pilgrims.net/native_americans/ [September 9, 2006].

"The People and the Land: The Wampanoag of Southern New England" (MSN Groups: Native American) at http://groups.msn.com/Traditions/nativeamerican.msnw?action=get_message&mview=0&ID_Message=15869&LastModified=46754379742 88732720; "King Philip. More Names Than We Thought?," *Colonial Gazette* (Interactive Communications, 1998, 1999,2000-2006) at http://www.*Mayflower*families.com/enquirer/philip_a_new_name.htm [July 27, 2006].

Charles E. Banks, "Annals of Gay Head," The History of Martha's Vineyard (1911), vol. II, 3-8, available by Chris Baer (Vineyard Haven, MA:

Historical Records of Dukes County) at http://history.vineyard.net/dukes/bnk2gh_3.htm; "Wampanoag Cultural Survival: The Dynamics of a Living Culture" (Fortune Family Web, n.d.) at http://www.fortunefamily.org/fortuneallengenealogy/indians.html; "New England Indians," (MyFamily.com Inc., 1998-2006), Chs. 11-14, at http://freepages.genealogy.rootsweb.com/~massasoit/ccod03.htm; Wampanoag" (Native American Artifacts) at http://www.jelcwcm.com/Life/Arrows.htm [August 8, 2006].

For King Philip's War, see Nathaniel Philbrick, *Mayflower*, xiv-xvi, 216, 229-348; Daniel K. Richter, *Facing East from Indian Country*, 90-105; Swanton, 24-27; Edwin G. Burrows & Mike Wallace, *Gotham*, 86; Drake, *Indians of North America*, 208-257. Also, King Philip's War" (Plymouth, MA: Pilgrim Hall Museum, 1998) at http://www.pilgrimhall.org/philipwar.htm [September 10, 2006]; Joseph Dow, History of Hampton: Indian Wars, 1675-1763, King Philip's War, 1675-1675 (Hampton, NH: Hampton Library, 1999) ch. 13, pt. 1, at ttp://www.hampton.lib.nh.us/HAMPTON/history/dow/chap13/dow13_1.htm [August 11, 2006].

Wanapam
Stephen E. Ambrose, *Undaunted Courage*, 298; Swanton, 448.

"Wanapum Indians (Wanapam, Sokulks)," from National Geographic Society (1998-2006) at http://www.nationalgeographic.com/lewisand...clark/record_tribes_069_13_31.html; "Selected Resources on Columbia Basin Native Americans" (Portland State University, updated 30Sep 2002) at http://www.lib.pdx.edu/resources/pathfinders/basinmap.html; David M. Buerge, "Chief Seattle and Chief Joseph: From Indians to Icons" (University of Washington, 1998-2005) at http://content.lib.washington.edu/aipnw/buerge2.html; Andrew H. Fisher, "Tangled Nets: Treaty Rights and Tribal Identities at Celilo Falls," *Oregon Historical Quarterly* (Summer 2004), vol. 105, no. 2, available from the Historical Cooperative (University of Illinois et al., 2005) at http://www.historycooperative.org/journals/ohq/105.2/fisher.html [August 9, 2006]. Also, "Wanapum Heritage Center" (Beverly, WA, 2007) at http://www.wanapum.org/ [December 23, 2007].

Wangunk
Swanton, 33, 44-48, esp. 46.

Wappinger Confederacy
Edwin G. Burrows & Mike Wallace, *Gotham*, 23; Russell Shorto, *The Island at the Center of the World*, 279-281; Swanton, 44-48.

"Who were the Wappinger Indians?" (Austin, TX: PageWise, 2002) at http://ndnd.essortment.com/wappingerindian_rmqo.htm; J. Alfieri et allis, "The Lenapes: A Study of Hudson Valley Indians" (Poughkeepsie, NY: Marist College, n.d.) at http://www.ulster.net/~hrmm/halfmoon / lenape/effects.htm; Meghan McCaffrey, "The Wappingers Tribe in the Hudson Valley" (Poughkeepsie, NY; Marist College) at http://www.marist.edu/summerscholars/97/natives.htm [April 15, 2006].

"On This Day in History: September 15, 1655" (Native News Online) at http://nativenewsonline.org/history/hist0915.html [September 8, 2006]. The Esopus attacked settlers at New Amsterdam in a retaliatory raid for the killing of an Indian woman for stealing peaches; thus the "The Peach War."

"Mashantucket Pequot Research Library Connecticut Tribes and Bands Mentioned In Historical and Contemporary Sources" (Mashantucket Pequot Museum & Research Center, 2005) at http://www.pequotmuseum.org/uploaded_images/8564D213-7519-4055-B791-ADD058B62EA7/ConnecticutIndianTribesPart1.htm; William W. Campbell, "The Life and Writings of Dewitt Clinton: The Iroquois. Address Delivered Before The New York Historical Society, Dec. 6, 1811" made available from Rochester History Resources (Rochester, NY: University of Rochester, 1999) at http://www.history.rochester.edu/canal/bib/campbell/Chap07.html [August 19. 2006].

Wappo
Swanton, 518-519.

Waranawonkong
Swanton, 48-55.

Warrasqueoc
Swanton, 66-71.

Wasco
Swanton, 475; "History & Culture" (Warm Springs, OR: Confederated Tribes of Warm Springs, 1999-2005) at http://www.warmsprings.com/Warmsprings/Tribal_Community/History__Culture/ [May 15, 2006]; "The Confederated Tribes of the Warm Springs Reservation of Oregon" (Columbia River Inter-Tribal Fish Commission, 2007) at http://www.critfc.org/text/warmsprings.html [December 24, 2007].

Wascopun
Robert H. Rudy and John A. Brown, *The Cayuse Indians*, 84, 85, 121. R. Gibson, "The Dalles, Oregon" (2007) at http://hometown.aol.com/Gibson0817/dalles.htm [Lynn Ewing, "A History of Wasco County-The Dalles" (School Districts of Wasco County, Oregon, 2007) at http://www.wasco-history.r9esd.k12.or.us/comm/td.html and Elizabeth December 22, 2007]; Lewis L. McArthur, *Oregon Geographic Names*, 6th ed., 594.

Washa
Swanton, 137, 200, 201, 202, 207, 211-212.

Washo
Swanton, 383-384.

Wassamasaw
Bo Petersen, "Edistow Indians see their history erode," (Columbia, SC: The State.com, September 23, 2007) at http://www.thestate.com/regional-news/story/181370.html; "SC – Native Americans – Wassamasaw Tribe of Varnertown" (Columbia, SC: SCIway.net, 2007) at http://www.sciway.net/hist/indians/wassamasaw-varnertown-indians-sc.html [October 21, 2007].

Watepaneto
Samuel G. Drake, *The Aboriginal Races of North America...*, 9-16.

Wateree
Swanton, 88, 101-102; "Forest Acres, South Carolina History" (POW Publishing, n.d.) at http://www.powpublishing.com/ForestAcresSouthCarolina.html; Jean Prather, The Indians of South Carolina (November 18, 1998) available from Old96District (n.d.) at http://homepages.rootsweb.com/~scroots/sc14487.htm [August 20, 2006].

Watlala
Swanton, 476; "Northwest Native Americans" (Portland, OR: Oregon State Travel Guide, n.d.) at http://www.oregonmaiden.com/Native-Americans-of-Oregon.html [August 3, 2006].

Wauyukma
Swanton, 448.

Wawarsink
Swanton, 48-55.

Waxhaw
Stanton,102.

Wea
Swanton, 239, 242, 297, 300, 305; "Wea Indian Tribe" (Clinton, IN: Wea Indian Tribe of Indiana, 2005) at http://www.weaindiantribe.com/... [September 7, 2006]; Erminie Wheeler-Voegelin, et al., *An Anthropological Report on the History of the Miamis, Weas, and Eel River Indians* (Bloomington, IN: Glen Black Laboratory of Archaeology University of Indiana, 1997-2000), vol. 1, ch. 3, 146-150, at http://www.gbl.indiana.edu/archives/dockett_317a/317a_4h.html; Ronald Branson, "The Danger Period -- Indian[a] History: Distribution and Territorial Claims of the Indians" (Indiana County History Preservation Society, 2000-2006) at http://www.countyhistory.com/history/087.htm; Preston M. Smith, "The Expedition to Fort Chartres" (42nd Royal Highlanders, Inc., 2004) at http://www.42ndrhr.org/chartres.php [August 11, 2006].

Weanoc
Swanton, 66-71.

Weapemeoc
Swanton, 88-89. Fred Willard, "Trade Items as Transfer of Money," November 2002, made available by the Lost Colony Center for Science and Research (Eastern Carolina University) at http://lost-colony.com/trade.html [June 12, 2006].

Wecquaesgeek Wappinger
For the Pavonia Massacre, see Swanton 44-48, 48-55; Russell Shorto, The Island at the Center of the World, 123-124, 125, 172, 177, 241. Also, "Pavonia," A Virtual Tour of New Netherland (New York: New Netherland Project, 2001-2003) at http://www.nnp.org/newvtour/regions/Hudson/pavonia.html; Alfieri, J., Berardis et al., "The Effects of Contact on the Lenape," *The Lenapes: A Study of Hudson Valley Indians* (Poughkeepsie, NY: Marist College, n.a.) at http://www.ulster.net/~hrmm/halfmoon/lenape/effects.htm [April 15, 2006].

James Sullivan, ed., "The History of New York State, Book II, Chapter II, Part IV" (Lewis Historical Publishing Company, Inc., 1927), Online Edition (USGenNet Safe-Site, 2004) at http://www.usgennet.org/usa/ny/state/his/bk2/ch2/pt4.html [April 15, 2006]. Gives number of victims as eight; identifies them as Tappan.

"History of Jersey City" (Jersey City, NJ; City of Jersey City, 2004) at http://www.cityofjerseycity.com/history.html, taken from John M. Kelly, Rita M. Murphy, and William J. Roehrenbeck, "1660-1960 Jersey City Tercentenary Celebration" (1960) [April 15, 2006]. Typographical error: starting date s/b 1643 v. 1634. Number of victims not recorded.

"New Netherlands" (Frederick H. Kunchick, Jr., 2000) at http://www.usgennet.org/usa/nj/state1/new_netherland.htm [April 15, 2006]. Tappan Indians attacked February 27, by 80 soldiers.

Wekisa
Samuel G. Drake, *The Aboriginal Races of North America...*, 9-16.

Welsh Indians
Shirley Christian, Before Lewis and Clark, 147; George Catlin, *North American Indians*, 89-90, 181-184, esp. 491-497. "Welch Indians," *The Geneva Gazette* (Geneva, NY, August 18, 1819), vol. xi, no. 11, taken from the *St. Louis Enquirer* made available from Uncle Dale's Readings in Early Mormon History: Newspapers of New York (2006) at http://www.sidneyrigdon.com/dbroadhu/NY/miscNYSg.htm; George Burder, ed., *The Welch Indians, or, A collection of papers respecting a people whose ....*, Early Canadian Online (Canadiana, 2005-2006) at http://www.canadiana.org... /mtq?id=1f1cbf0ef4&doc=16615 and http://www.canadiana.org/ECO/SearchResults?id=f60ee1b9429a12f7&query=Ameri

ca%20--%20Discovery%20and%20exploration%20--%20Welsh.&range=subject&bool=exact&subset=all; "The Welch Nations," Were the Many Families Here in Ancient America? (Orbit, 2002) at http://www.cyberspaceorbit.com/welsh.html; "Mandan Indians" (Bowen Family Web History, 2000-2004) at http://freepages.family.rootsweb.com/~bowen/mandans.html.

The Journals of Lewis at Clark, available from American Studies (University of Virginia, 2002) at http://xroads.virginia.edu/~HYPER/... JOURNALS/toc.html; "Lewis & Clark" (Washington, DC: National Geographic, 1996-2006) at http://www.nationalgeographic.com... / lewisandclark/record_tribes_022_12_16.html; "Lewis and Clark Expedition: Phase 4a: August 21-November 7, 1805, From the Great Divide [MT] to the Pacific Ocean [WA]" available from Modern Studies (Lexington, KY: University of Kentucky, n.d.) at http://www.uky.edu/AS/ ModernStudies/HumSocSci/lc94/Section4/Phase4a/Ethnographic/General.html; James Richard From, "Lewis & Clark: Encounters with Indians" (The Third Millennium Online) at http://www.3rd1000.com/history/corp/journals/070703/070703.htm; "A List of Indian Nations, their places of abode & Chief Hunting (1759)," from "Accounts of the Western Indians," in Stevens, et al. *The Papers of Col. Henry Bouquet*, Series 21655, 1943, 85-88, available from the OhioValley-Great Lakes Ethnohistory Archives: The Miami Collection (Bloomington, IN: Glenn Black Laboratory of Archaeology and Trustees of Indiana University, 1996-2000) at http://www.gbl.indiana.edu/archives/miamis12/M59-60_2a.html; "Information on the Salish Indians Recorded by Members of the Lewis and Clark Expedition1805," The Lewis and Clark Journey of Discovery (Washington, DC: National Park Service, n.d.) at http://www.nps.gov/jeff/LewisClark2/TheJourney/NativeAmericans/Salish.htm; "American Indian Resources: Manuscript Holdings: Deland, Charles Edmund (H69-5)" (Pierre SD: South Dakota State Historical Society, 2006) at http:// www.sdhistory.org/arc/arc_indm.htm [August 20, 2006].

Wenatchee
Swanton, 448-449.

Wenrohronon
Swanton, 48, 57.

Werowocomoco
Swanton, 66-71.

Western Indian Confederacy
Daniel K. Richter, *Facing East from Indian Country*, 224-225. Quotes taken from"EGOTIATIONS between the Western Indian Confederacy & U.S. Commissioners on the issue of the Ohio River as the boundary of Indian lands, August 1793" (National Humanities Center for use in a Professional Development Seminar, n.d.) at http://nationalhumanitiescenter.org/pds/livingrev/expansion/text6/negotiations.pdf. Taken fromE. A. Cruikshank, ed., *The Correspondence of Lieut. Governor John Graves Simcoe*,1 vol. I-II, (Toronto: Ontario Historical Society, 1923-1924). Also, David Swader, "Abstract: A Common Dish: The Ohio Indian Confederacy aand the Struggle for the Upper Ohio Valley, 1783-1795" (Youngstown, OH: Youngstown State University, 1999) at http://www.ohiolink.edu/etd/view.cgi?acc_num=ysu997988207 [October 4, 2007].

Western Oregon Tribes
U.S. Code: Title 25 (Indians), USC Chapter 14 (Miscellaneous), Subchapter XXX (Western Oregon Indians: Termination of Federal Supervision), § 692 Definitions. Source: August 13, 1954, Ch. 733, § 2, 68 Stat. 724, available at http://www.washingtonwatchdog.org... documents/usc/ttl25/ch14/subchXXX/sec692.html [December 11, 2006]; "U.S. Code: Title 25, Chapter 14" (Washington, DC: U.S. Hose of Representatives, Office of the Law Revision Counsel, January 19, 2004) at http://uscode.house.gov/download/pls/25C14.txt; "Index of Available Documents: Title 25" (Oklahoma City, OK: Oklahoma State Courts Network, n.d.) at http://www.oscn.net/applications/OCISWeb... /index. asp?level=1&ftdb=FDSTUS25 [July 7, 2006]; "Termination of Federal Supervision Over the Property of the Western Oregon Tribes and Bands of Indians of Oregon, and the Individual Members Thereof," Fed. Reg. vol. 21,1956, pp. 1499-1500," compiled and published in *Indian Affairs: Laws and Treaties*, vol. VII, Laws (Washington, DC: Government Printing Office), produced by the Oklahoma State University Library at http:// digital.library.okstate.edu/kappler/ [July 10, 2006].

Westo
See sources under the Yuchi. Also, Eric E. Bowne, "Westo Indians" (Athens, GA: Georgia Humanities Council and the University of Georgia Press, 2004-2007) at http://www.georgiaencyclopedia.org/nge/Article.jsp?id=h-575 [October 5, 2007]; Eric E. Bowne, "The Rise and Fall of the Westo Indians," *Early Georgia*, vol. 28, no. 1 (2000); Eric E. Bowne, *The Westo Indians: Slave Traders of the Early Colonial South* (Tuscaloosa: University of Alabama Press, 2005); John E. Worth, *The Struggle for the Georgia Coast: An Eighteenth-Century Spanish Retrospective on Guale and Mocama* (New York: American Museum of Natural History, 1995; distributed by University of Georgia Press). Daniel K. Richter, *Facing East from Indian Country*, 162.

Wetepahato
Samuel G. Drake, *The Aboriginal Races of North America...*, 9-16.

Whilkut
Swanton, 483, 492, 519.

White Salmon
Albert J. Thompson, "Memories of White Salmon and Its Pioneers, *Washington Historical Quarterly*, Washington University State Historical Society, Seattle, WA, vol. XIV, no. 4, April 1923, pp. 108-126, available from Jeffrey L. Elmer at http://homepages.rootsweb.com/~westklic/ mwspione.html; Camilla Thomson Donnell, "Early Days at White Salmon and the Dalles," *Pacific Northwest Quarterly*, University of Washington, Seattle, WA, vol. 4, no. 2 (April 1913), pp. 105-115, available from Jeffrey L. Elmer at http://homepages.rootsweb.com/~westklic/edays.html [June 26, 2006].

Whonkentia
Swanton, 61-62.

Wichita
Swanton, esp. 305-306; Earl H. Elam, "Wichita Indians," *Handbook of Texas Online* (Austin, TX: Texas State Historical Association and University of Texas, 1999-2003) at http://www.tsha.utexas.edu/handbook/online/articles/view/WW/bmw3.html; Le Page Du Pratz, *History of Louisiana*, Part 6 of 8, available from Full Books at http://www.fullbooks.com/History-of-Louisisana6.html [May 17, 2006]. Also, Guy Rowley Moore, " Pawnee Traditions And Customs," *Chronicles of Oklahoma*, June 1939, vol.17, no. 2, 151-169, available from the Oklahoma State University Digital Library at http://digital.library.okstate.edu/Chronicles/v017/v017p151.html [November 13, 2007].

Wickquasgeck
Russell Shorto, *The Island in the Center of the World*, 60, 111, 112, 119, 123-124, 164, 194, 196; Edwin G. Burrows & Mike Wallace, *Gotham*, 5. Deborah Champlain, "Northeast Tribes: Native American History for March" (Rhode Island: Northeast Wigwam, 1998-2000) at http://www.newigwam.com/histdtes.html [September 10, 2006].

Wicocomoco
Swanton, 67, 71; Al Byrd, "Wicocomico Indian Nation" (2001-2007) at http://www.wicocomico-indian-nation.com/pages/genocide.html [September 28, 2007].

Wighcomoco
Gail M. Walczyk, "Indians of the Lower Eastern Shore" (Nassawadox, VA: Ghotes of Virginia, 2004) at http://www.esva.net/ghotes/history/indians.htm [August 21, 2006].

Wimbee
"South Carolina – Indians, Native Americans – Wimbee" (2007 SCIway.net, South Carolina Information Highway) at http://www.sciway.net/hist/indians/wimbee.html; Judith Van Noate, North American Indians - A Guide To Research, A Bibliographic Essay (Charlotte, NC: Murrey Atkins Library UNC Charlotte, 2000) at http://www.cabrillo.edu/~crsmith/research.html [October 18, 2007].

Wiminuche Ute
Swanton, 374.

Winibigoshish
Swanton, 263.

Winnebago
Gloria Jahoda, *Trail of Tears*, 36, 92-93, 96; Helen Hunt Jackson, *A Century of Dishonor*, 218-256; Swanton, esp. 258-259.

"Ho-Chunk History" (Milwaukee, WI: Milwaukee Public Museum) at http://www.mpm.edu/wirp/ICW-150.html; "Heritage of the Ho-Chunk people" (Ho-Chuunk Nation, 2006) at http://www.ho-chunknation.com/heritage/heritage.htm...; "The Clark Chronicle #41 for air week of August 26th," The Chronicles of George Rogers Clark (Louisville, KY: WFPL, n.d.) at http://www.wfpl.org/grc/41.htm; I. A. Lapham, Levi Blossom, & George Dousman, "Indians of Wisconsin" (Madison, WI: University of Wisconsin, n.d.) at http://www.library.wisc.edu/etext/WIReader... /WER0142.html; *Historical Account of Bouquet's Expedition Against the Ohio Indians, in 1764* made available from Glen Black Laboratory of Archaeology (Bloomington, IN: University of Indiana, 1996-2000) at http://www.gbl.indiana.edu/archives/dockett_317/317_84a.html [August 12, 2006].

Clifford E. Kraft, "Origins of the French and English Names for the Bay of Green Bay," Wisconsin's French Connections (Green Bay, WI: University of Wisconsin Green Bay, n.d.) at http://www.uwgb.edu/wisfrench/library/articles/kraft.htm; Wm. M. Darlington, "Indian Nations and Their Numbers of Fighting Men," Appendix V of: Smith, Col. James, An Account of the Remarkable Occurrences in the Life and Travels of Col. James Smith (Cincinnati, 1907), 153-155, made available from Glen Black Laboratory of Archaeology (Bloomington, IN: University of Indiana, 1997-2001) at http://www.gbl.indiana.edu/archives/miamis15/M64_5a.html [August 12, 2006]; "Indian Occupants-Border Warfare-Treaties-Facts and Incidents," History of Union County (Union County, OH, n.d.), ch. II at http://www.heritagepursuit.com/Union/Unp3c2.htm; "Lake Michigan: History, Facts & Figures" (St. Joseph, MI: Southwest Michigan Business & Tourism Directory, n.d.) at http://www.swmidirectory.org/History_of_Lake_Michigan.html [August 12, 2006].

Wintu
Swanton 519-520. For the Hayford Massacre, see "The Bridge Gulch Massacre" (Trinity County, CA, n.d.) at http://www.trinitycounty.com/stnf-nb.htm [July 8, 2006]. Also see John Carr, Pioneer Days.

Wintun
Swanton, 507-509, 519-520, 520-521.

Winyaw
Swanton, 97, 101, 102-103.

Wisconsin
Swanton, 250-259, esp. 254; Nancy Oestreich Lurie, *Wisconsin Indians* (Madison: Wisconsin Historical Society Press, 2002 rev. ed.)

Frances Scharko, "American Indians in Early Wisconsin" (Wisconsin Mosaic, 2000) at http://www.scils.rutgers.edu/~dalbello/FLVA/voices/839/voices/amind/; Rose Arnold, *Wisconsin Indians: History and Culture* (Madison, WI: Legislative Reference Bureau, August 2001) at http://www.legis.state.wi.us/lrb/pubs/ttp/ttp-8-2001.html [June 27, 2006].

Wishram
Swanton, 449-450.

Wiwohka
Swanton, 164, 174.

Wiyot
Swanton, 521-522. For the Humboldt Bay Massacres, see Chronology of California History: The Gold Rush, 1848 to 1869 at http://www.notfrisco.com/almanac/timeline/goldrush.html; Owen C. Coy, "The Indian Wars in the Van Duzen and Eel River Watershed Area, "The Humboldt Bay Region 1850 -- 1875: A Study in the American Colonization of California (Los Angeles: California State Historical Association, 1929) at http://www.humboldt1.com/~cbender/Carlotta/history/IndianWars.htm; Robert F. Heizer, ed. *The Destruction Of California Indians* (Lincoln, NA: University of Nebraska Press & Bison Books, 1993) available at http://virtual.yosemite.cc.ca.us/smithaj/destruction_of_california_indian.htm [November 20, 2006].

Woccon
Swanton, 89-90, 100-101.

Wyahtinaw
Dorothy Libby, "An Anthropological Report on the Piankashaw Indians: Piankashaw Locations, ca. 1776- ca. 1783," pp. 90-99, available from the OhioValley-Great Lakes Ethnohistory Archives: The Miami Collection (Bloomington, IN: Glenn Black Laboratory of Archaeology and Trustees of Indiana University, 1997-2000), at http://www.gbl.indiana.edu/archives/dockett_99/d99toc.html [October 24, 2006]; Gilbert Imlay, *A Topographical Description of the Western Territory of North America...* (London, 1797, 3rd ed.), 364-365, made available from Glen Black Laboratory of Archaeology (Bloomington, IN: University of Indiana, 1997-2000) at ttp://www.gbl.indiana.edu/archives/dockett_317/317_33.html [August 11, 2006].

Wyam
"History & Culture" (Warm Springs, OR: Confederated Tribes of Warm Springs, 1999-2005) at http://www.warmsprings.com/Warmsprings/Tribal_Community/History__Culture/ [May 15, 2006].

Wyandot
Swanton, esp. 233-236; Gloria Jahoda, *Trail of Tears*, 280-285; Dee Brown, *Hear That Lonesome Whistle Blow*, 214; Alan W. Farley, "Annals of Quindaro: A Kansas Ghost Town." The *Kansas Historical Quarterly*, vol. XXII, no. 4 (Winter, 1956): 305-320; Grant W. Harringrton, *Historic Spots or Mile-Stones in the progress of Wyandotte County*, Kansas (Merriam, Kansas: The Mission Press, 1935); William E. Connelley, *Huron Place: The Burial Ground of the Wyandot Nation, in Wyandotte County, Kansas* (Kansas City: City of Kansas City, Kansas, 1991). An annotated transcript of Connelley's 1896 survey and notes. Also, William E. Connelley, "Kansas City, Kansas: Its Place in the History of the State," *Kansas Historical Collections* (Topeka: Kansas State Historical Society, April 4, 1918), vol. xv, 1919-1922, 181-191; "Wyandot and Shawnee Indian Lands in Wyandotte County, Kansas," *Kansas Historical Collections* (Topeka: Kansas State Historical Society, n.d.), vol. xv, 1919-1922, 103-180.

Chief Leaford Bearskin, "Wyandottes belong in KCK," *Kansas City Star*, July 18, 2004, p. B10. Excerpt: "The Wyandottes are part of Kansas City, Kan. We started Kansas City, and if we had been white, there would most likely be statues of us in the streets and the parks across the city. ...To us, the street signs are our statues, because we platted the streets, and we name them after our great leaders. We named the city Wyandot [now Kansas City, Kansas], and it was the largest city on the frontier. ...The Wyandotte Nation operated the only ferry across the river in the area, and ran shops, businesses, farms, churches and schools."

"Quindaro and Western University," (Kansas City, KS, Unified Government, n.d.) at http://www3.wycokck.org/static/planning.zoning/HISTORY2004/quindaro.pdf; Indian Agent, Col. John. Johnston, Vocabularies of the Shawnoese and Wyandott Languages, etc (1958) available from Wyandot Nation of Kansas (Kansas City, KS, n.d.) at http://www.wyandot.org/lang1.html; Larry Hancks, "The Emigrant Tribes: Wyandot, Delaware & Shawnee, A Chronology" (Kansas City, KS: Wyandot Nation of Kansas, 1995) at http://www.wyandot.org/emigrant.htm [September 7, 2006].

The History of Wyandot County, Ohio (Chicago: Leggett, Conaway & Co., 1884) made available by Allen L. Potts (Salt Lake City, UT: Heritage Pursuit, The Place For Historians And Genealogists, 2006) at http://www.heritagepursuit.com/Wyandot/WyCh2.htm [August 4, 2006].

Wycome
Samuel G. Drake, *The Aboriginal Races of North America...*, 9-16.

Wyniaw
Samuel G. Drake, *The Aboriginal Races of North America...*, 9-16.

Wynoochee
Swanton, 415, 450.

Wyoming
Swanton, 56; Thomas Campbell, "Gertrude of Wyoming" (1809) available online from Poem Hunter at http://www.poemhunter.com/p/m/ poem.asp?poet=3042&poem=17250 [August 26, 2006].

Wysox
Swanton, 56.

Xaramane
Herbert E. Bolton, "The Spanish Abandonment and Re-occupation of East Texas, 1773-1779", vol. 9, no. 2, *Southwestern Historical Quarterly* Online, 67-137, n64, at http://www.tsha.utexas.edu/publications/journals/shq/online/v009/n2/article_1_print.html [March 9, 2006].

Yachats
Joanne Kittel and Suzanne Curtis, "The Yachats Indians, Origins of the Yachats Name, and the Reservation Years" (Confederated Tribes of the Coos, Lower Umpqua, and Siuslaw Indians, and the Confederated Tribes of the Siletz Indians of Oregon, 1996) available from Soft Solutions (2004) at http://www.yachats.info/history/title.htm; M. Constance Guardino III and Marilyn A. Riedel, "Sovereigns of Themselves: A Liberating History of Oregon and Its Coast," vol. IV, Abridged Online Edition (Maracon Productions, 2006) at http://users.wi.net/~census/lesson37.html; "History" (City of Yachats, OR, n.d.) at http://www.ci.yachats.or.us/Yachats%20History.htm; Lynn Ewing, "Native Americans of Oregon" (2000) at http://www.chenowith.k12.or.us/tech/subject/social/natam_or.html [October 20, 2006].

Yadkin
Swanton, 90.

Yahi
Swanton, 522.

Yahuskin
Robert H. Rudy and John A. Brown, *The Cayuse Indians*, 4-5n4; Swanton, 476; Lynn Ewing, "Native Americans of Oregon" (2000) at http://www.chenowith.k12.or.us/tech/subject/social/natam_or.html [October 20, 2006]. Also, John Robbins, Notices (April 9, 2003) reported in *Federal Register*, vol. 68, no. 85, Friday, May 2, 2003, 23492.

Yakima
Swanton, 413, 425, 433, 450-451, 462, 471; Merrill D. Beal, *"I Will Fight No More Forever": Chief Joseph and the Nez Percé War*, 24-26; "Yakama Indian Nation" (Online Highways, 1995-2005) at http://www.ohwy.com/wa/y/yakamana.htm [December 29, 2007]; "The Confederated Tribes and Bands of the Yakama Nation" (Columbia River Inter-Tribal Fish Commission) at http://www.critfc.org/text/yakama.html [June 14, 2006].

For the Yakima War, see Rose M. Smith, *Guide to the Cayuse, Yakima, and Rogue River Wars Papers 1847-1858*"(Eugene, OR: University of Oregon Libraries, 2004) at http://nwda-db.wsulibs.wsu.edu/documents/retrieve.asp?docname=orubx%5F047.xml [July 7, 2006]; Robert H. Rudy and John A. Brown, *The Cayuse Indians*, 225-255; "Washington Wars," Indian Wars and Conflicts (n.a.) at http://www.washingtonwars. net... /washington_wars.htm [September 8, 2006].

Yamacraw
David H. Connolly, Jr., "Oglethorpe and the Georgia Indians: A Change of Heart," Topics in Georgia History (Savannah, GA: Amstrong Atlantic State University, 2003) at http://www.sip.armstrong.edu/Indians/Essay.html; F. D. Lee and J. L. Agnew, *Historical Record of the City of Savannah* (Savannah, 1868), ch. 2, made available from Chatham County (USGenNet, 2003-2006) at http://www.usgennet.org/usa/ga/county/ chatham/history/1868-2.htm [August 14, 2006].

Yamasee
Swanton, 114-116, 152, 157, 174; Gloria Jahoda, *Trail of Tears*, 244-245. Also see Steven J. Oatis, *A Colonial Complex: South Carolina's Frontiers in the Era of the Yamasee War, 1680–1730*. Also, "Colonial South Carolina: The Yamasee War, 1715-1718," U-S-History (Florence, OR: Online Highways, 2002) at http://www.u-s-history.com/pages/h1169.html [September 9, 2006].

Yamel Kalapuya
Swanton 476-477.

Yana
Swanton, 522-523.

Yaquina
Swanton, 477-478.

Yatasi
Swanton, 205-206; *History of Natchitoches Parish: Biographical and Historical Memoirs of Northwest Louisiana* (Southern Publishing Company, 1890) available from Greg English (Louisiana 101, 2000) at http://www.louisiana101.com/rr_natchitoches.html [August 25, 2006].

Yatasi, Upper
Swanton, 317-320.

Yavapai

Timothy Braatz, *Surviving Conquest: A History of the Yavapai Peoples*; Swanton, 351, 357, 365, 367-369.

Yazoo

Swanton, 187, 188, 194-195, 201, 209, 215, 232.

Yehah

Samuel G. Drake, *The Aboriginal Races of North America...*, 9-16.

Yeletpoo

Samuel G. Drake, *The Aboriginal Races of North America...*, 9-16.

Yokuts

Swanton, 523-526; H. W. Brands, *The Age of Gold*, 316.

Yoncalla Kalapuya

Swanton, 478.

Yosemite

H. W. Brands, *The Age of Gold*, 313-315, 315-317; for the Mariposa War, see esp. 307-315..

John W. Bingaman, "Yosemite Indians," *Guardians of the Yosemite*, Chp. XX (1961) available from Yosemite Online Library (Yosemite National Park, CA, 1997-2006) at http://www.yosemite.ca.us/library/guardians_of_the_yosemite/yosemite_indians.html; A. L. Kroeber, "Indians of Yosemite," *Handbook of Yosemite National Park* (1921) available from Yosemite Online Library (Yosemite National Park, CA, 1997-2006) at http://www.yosemite.ca.us/library/handbook_of_yosemite_national_park/indians.html; "History of Yosemite" (Ace & Friends, 1993-2006.) from Yosemite Gold at http://www.yosemitegold.com/yosemite/history.html; "Last Survivors of the Yosemite Indians" (Madera County, CA, 2000) at http://www.cagenweb.com/madera/YosemiteIndians.htm [June 27, 2006]. Also see Galen Clark, Indians of the Yosemite Valley and Vicinity: Their History, Customs and Traditions (1904) available from Project Gutenberg Literary Archive Foundation (2003-2006) at http://www.gutenberg.org/etext/16572 [September 17, 2006] and http://www.yosemite.ca.us/library/indians_of_the_yosemite/indians_of_the_yosemite.pdf [November 8, 2008].

Youghtanund

Swanton, 66-71.

Youicone

Samuel G. Drake, *The Aboriginal Races of North America...*, 9-16.

Yreka Shasta

Swanton, 460, 464, 514; "Shasta Indian Tribe History," from Frederick Webb Hodge, *Handbook of American Indians North of Mexico* (1906) available from Access Genealogy (2004-2006) at http://www.accessgenealogy.com/native/tribes/shastan/shastaindiantribe.htm; "Shasta Indians Seek To Clarify Its Jurisdiction" (CA: Klamath Basin, 2001-2006) at http://www.klamathbasincrisis.org/tribes/shastaclarify031206.htm [June 27, 2006].

Yscani

Swanton, 303, 305, 307. And, Margery H. Krieger, "Yscani Indians," *Handbook of Texas Online* (Austin, TX: Texas State Historical Association and University of Texas, 2001) at http://www.tsha.utexas.edu/handbook/online/articles/view/YY/bmy16.html [May 24, 2006].

Herbert E. Bolton, "The Founding of Mission Rosario: A Chapter in the History of the Gulf Coast," *Southwestern Historical Quarterly* (Austin, TX: Texas State Historical Association, October 1906), x, 2, available online at http://www.tsha.utexas.edu/publications/journals/shq/online/v010/n2/issue.html [June 27, 2006]; Herbert E. Bolton, "The Spanish Abandonment and Re-occupation of East Texas, 1773-1778," *Southwestern Historical Quarterly* (Austin, TX: Texas State Historical Association, October 1905), ix, 2, available online at http://www.tsha.utexas.edu/publications/journals/shq/online/v009/n2/issue.html [March 10, 2006].

Yuchi

Swanton, 104, 116-120, 140, 152, 157, 307; Gloria Jahoda, *Trail of Tears*, 245; Chapman J. Milling, *Red Carolinians*, 179-87; Barbara A. Leitch, *A Concise Dictionary of Indian Tribes of North America*, 536-38; Daniel K. Richter, *Facing East from Indian Country*, 162.

Also, J. Tyler, "Yuchis at Callabee Creek" (Stone Mountain, GA, December 17, 2003) at http://www.euchee.com/yuchimail; Josh Wilks, "Yuchi/Euchee of Walton County" (February 26, 2004.) at http://www.drwebman.com/euchee/yuchimail/ [July 2, 2006] and "South Carolina – Indians, Native Americans – Yuchi" (Columbia: South Carolina Information Highway, 2007) at http://www.sciway.net/hist/indians/yuchi.html; Phil Lea, "Who Were the Mysterious Yuchi Indians of Tennessee and the Southeast?" (Benton, TN, n.d.) at http://www.euchee.com/yuchi [August 20, 2007].

Yui

Swanton, 152-153.

Yuki

Swanton, 526-527; 527-528. For the Eden Valley Massacre, see "Federal Effort To Transfer Indian Affairs To The State Of California,

1860," *Congressional Globe*, 36th Congress, 1st Session, 2365— 2369: Senate Debate, May 26, 1860 available from the University of California at Irvine (1995-2006) at http://eee.uci.edu/clients/tcthorne/anthro/1860debate.htm [November 8, 2006].

Yuma

Swanton, 349, 354, 356, 365, 369-370; Thomas Edwin Farish, *The History of Arizona*, vol. vii, chp. 13. For the Yuma Massacre, see Kevin Starr, *California*, 39, 41-42.

Yuma-Apache

Swanton, 369.

Yurok

Swanton, 521, 528-529.

Zia Pueblo

David Roberts, *Pueblo Revolt*, 154-156, 165. James Stephenson and Matilda Coxe Stevenson, *Sia* (Washington, DC: U.S. Bureau of Ethnology, 1894).

Zuñi

Swanton, 340, 346-348; "The Zuni - A Mysterious People" (Legends of America, 2003-2006) at http://www.legendsofamerica.com/NA-Zuni. html; T. J. Ferguson, "Zuni," from John D. Grahame and Thomas D. Sisk, eds., *Canyons, Cultures and Environmental Change: An Introduction to the Land-use History of the Colorado Plateau* (CP-LUHNA, 2002.) http://www.cpluhna.nau.edu/People/zuni.htm [September 8, 2006].

Appendix A (American Indian Tribes in the Civil War)

Clarissa W. Cofer, *The Cherokee Nation in the Civil War* (Norman: University of Oklahoma Press, 2007); Christine Schultz White and Benton R. White, *Now The Wolf Has Come: The Creek Nation in the Civil War* (College Station, TX: Texas A & M University Press, 1996); Jay Monaghan, *Civil War on the Western Border 1854-1865*, 195, 223, 224, 225-227, 239-251, 279, 290, 299, 308-309, 341-343; Gloria Jahoda, *The Trail of Tears*, 150, 151, 153-portrait, 154, 158, 275-276. Also, Eugene Morrow Violette, *History of Missouri*, 370-372; W. L. Bartles, "Massacre of Confederates by Osage Indians in 1863," *Kansas Historical Collection* (Topeka: Kansas State Historical Society, 1904), viii, 62 (address delivered before the Kansas State Historical Society, December 2, 1902); *A State Divided: Missouri and the Civil War* (Jefferson City, MO: Missouri Department of Natural Resources, Division of Parks and Historic Preservation, n.d.), 3; Russell Weigley, *A Great Civil War*, 103-104, 108; *O.R.*, ser. 1, vol. 1, pt. 1, 8-10; ser. 1, vol. 22, pt. 2, 286; James M. McPherson, *Battle Cry of Freedom: The Civil War Era* (New York: Oxford University Press, 1988), 404-405, 668.

W. David Baird , ed.. *A Creek Warrior for the Confederacy: The Autobiography of Chief G.W. Grayson* (Norman, University of Oklahoma Press, 1988); Patricia L . Fault, ed., *Historical Times Illustrated Encyclopedia of the Civil War* (New York: Harper and Row, 1986); W. Craig Gaines, *The Confederate Cherokees: John Drew's Regiment of Mounted Rifles* (Baton Rouge: Louisiana State University Press, 1989); Laurence M. Hauptman, *Between Two Fires: American Indians in the Civil War*; Michelle Starr, "Muskogee Autumn," *Civil War Times Illustrated* (Harrisburg, PA), March 1983; Gary E. Moulton, *John Ross, Cherokee Chief* (Athens: University of Georgia Press, 1978); Anna Lewis, "Camp Napoleon," *Chronicles of Oklahoma* (Oklahoma City, 1931), vol. ix, 359-364; Annie Heloise Abel, *American Indian Under Reconstruction*, 138-140.

On Colonel Parker, see Horace Porter, *Campaigning with Grant* (Lincoln: University of Nebraska Press, Bison Edition, 2000), 33, 34, 200, 207, 208, 476, 480, 481, 484; Brooks D. Simpson, *Ulysses S. Grant: Triumph Over Adversity, 1822-1865* (Boston: Houghton Mifflin, 2000); James M. McPherson, *Battle Cry of Freedom*, 849. For Horace Porter, "The Surrender at Appomattox Courthouse," *Battle and Leaders* (1887), IV, 739-40, "Surrender at Appomattox," EyeWitness to History (Ibis Communications, Inc., 1997) at http://www.eyewitnesstohistory.com/appomatx. htm and Porter's account at Mark H. Dunkelman, "Lieutenant Colonel Horace C. Porter: Eyewitness to the Surrender at Appomattox" (Weider History Group, 2007) at http://www.historynet.com/magazines/civil_.war_... times/3033991.html [September 22, 2007]. Originally published in the May 2000 issue of *Civil War Times Magazine*. See the quote at Jeffrey R Gudzune, "We Are All Americans: Ely S. Parker--Two Worlds, One Man" (Vancouver, British Columbia: Suite101.com Media Inc., n.d.), November 13, 2006, at http://nativeamericanfirstnationshistory. suite101.com... /article.cfm/cherokee_nation___the_confederacy and "Ely Samuel Parker" (Native Americans.com, 2007) at http://www. nativeamericans.com... /ElySamuelParker.htm [September 22, 2007].

"The Battle of Newtonia (First), September 30, 1862, in Newtonia, Missouri" (Genealogy Inc, 1999) at http://www.mycivilwar.com/battles... /620930.htm [July 15, 2007]. Also, "Engagements and Battles in MO during the War of the Rebellion 1861-1865 Index" (Union, MO: Missouri Commandery, Military Order of the Loyal Legion of the United States, 1997/1998) at http://home.usmo.com/~momollus/BATTLES. HTM, linked from new home address at http://suvcw.org/mollus/mo.htm [March 15, 2007]; "Reestablishment of the Department of Kansas: Participant in the Civil War " (Native American Nations, 2000-2007) at http://www.nanations.com/civilwar/reestablish-dept-kansas.htm [August 20, 2007]. From *The American Indian as Participant in the Civil War*, 1919; Wiley Britton, "Battles and Leaders of the Civil War" (Shotgun's Home of the American Civil War, last updated 02/16/02) at http://www.civilwarhome.com/unionconfedindians.htm [August 15, 2007].

See also "First Kansas Colored Infantry Flag" (Topeka: Kansas Historical Society, 2007) at http://www.kshs.org/cool2/coolflg1.htm; "We are all Americans," Native Americans (American.net, 1996-2003) at http://www.nativeamericans.com/CivilWar.htm [August 23, 2007]. Also, "Second Kansas Colored Infantry Flag" at http://www.kshs.org/cool/coolflag2ndks.htm; "Arkansas in the Civil War: 'Cut to Pieces and Gone to Hell': The Poison Spring Massacre" (HarpWeek, 1998-2007) at http://www.lincolnandthecivilwar.com/Activities/Arkansas/HubPages/04Articles... / Poison07.htm [August 25, 2007]. From Mark K. Christ, ed., *"All Cut to Pieces and Gone to Hell": The Civil War, Race Relations, and the Battle of Poison Spring*. (Little Rock, Ark.: August House Publishers, Inc., 2003).

"The Camden Expedition in Arkansas" (Washington, DC: The Civil War Preservation Trust, n.d.) at info@civilwar.org; "The Battle of Poison Spring: Steele's Camden Expedition in the Red River Campaign" (Little Rock: Civil War Round Table of Arkansas, 1997) at http://www.civilwarbuff.org/bluff_city.html; "Poison Spring State Park" (Little Rock: Arkansas Department of Parks and Tourism, 2007) at http://www.arkansasstateparks.com/poisonspring; "Red River Campaign" (Georgia's Blue and Gray Trail, added 11/01/2006) at http://blueandgraytrail.com/event/Red_River_Campaign; Martin Kelly, "Battle of Chustenahlah" (About, Inc., A part of The New York Times Company, 2007) at http://americanhistory.about.com/od/civilwarbattles/p/cwbattle_chust.htm; "The Battle of Chustenahlah" (Genealogy Inc, 1999) at http://www.mycivilwar.com/battles/611226.htm [August 25, 2007].

"Opothleyahola (c. 1798-1863)" (Centreville, VA: The Latin Library Ad Fontes Academy, n.d.) at http://www.thelatinlibrary.com/chron/...civilwarnotes/opothleyahola.html; Rienzi and Zollicoffer," December 26 1861 (Thursday)" (Civil War Circuit, updated 12/21/97) at http://www.civilweek.com/1861/dec2261.htm [August 18, 2007]. Includes copy of letter to Hopoeithleyohola from U.S. Commissioner of Indian Affairs on behalf of President Lincoln and the government, September 10, 1861.

"Chusto-Talasah: Caving Banks, Civil War Oklahoma" (AmericanCivilWar.com, n.d.) at http://americancivilwar.com/statepic/ok/ok002.html; Ross and David Schmitz, "Chusto-Talasah: Caving Banks" (Paths of the Civil War.com, n.d.) at http://www.pathsofthecivilwar.com/Pastfinder.../PCWsummary.asp?locationID=OK002. "The Battle of Round Mountain" (Genealogy Inc, 1999-2007.) at http://www.mycivilwar.com/...battles/611119.htm; "Douglas Hancock Cooper" (CivilWarAlbum.com, 1998-2007) at http://www.civilwaralbum.com/washita/Cooper.htm; CSWAC Battle Summaries (Washington, DC: National Park Service, n.d.) at http://www.nps.gov/history/hps/abpp/battles... [August 18, 2007].

Jeffrey R Gudzune, "Cherokee & the Confederacy: The South, the West, and a Second Civil War" ((Vancouver, British Columbia: Suite101.com Media Inc., n.d.), October 30, 2006, at http://nativeamericanfirstnationshistory.suite101.com/article.cfm/cherokee_nation___the_confederacy; Gordon Berg, "American Indian Sharpshooters at the Battle of the Crater" (Weider History Group, 2007) at http://www.historynet.com/wars_...conflicts/american_civil_war/7460182.html?page=2&c=y. Originally published in the June 2007 issue of *Civil War Times Magazine*. [September 20, 2007].

"Sand Creek," CWSAC Battle Summaries (Washington, DC: National Park Service, n.d.) at http://www.nps.gov/history/hps/abpp/battles... / co001.htm, and at http://americanhistory.about.com/od/civilwarbattles/p/cwbattle_sandc.htm [August 15, 2007].

Note

Tribal information presented on Access Genealogy web sites (http://www.accessgenealogy.com/native/tribes/...) was extracted from one or more of the following manuscripts:

Frederick W. Hodge, *Handbook of American Indians North of Mexico* (1906)
David I. Bushnell, *Villages of the Algonquian, Siouan, and Caddoan Tribes West of the Mississippi* (1922)
Samuel G. Drake, *Drakes Indians of North America* (1880)
Henry R. Schoolcraft, *History of the Indian Tribes of the United States* (1857)
John R. Swanton, *The Indian Tribes of North America* (1953)

Appendix B (American Indian in the Military Service)

David M. Kennedy, *Freedom from Fear: The American People in Depression and War* (New York: Oxford University Press, 1999), 829-830; Alison R. Bernstein, *American Indians and World War II: Toward a New Era in Indian Affairs*; Jere Bishop Franco, *Crossing the Pond: The Native American Effort in World War II*; Gerald Thompson, *The Army and the Navajo*. Also, "Navajo Code Talkers in World War II" (Quantico, VA: US Marine Corps History Division, July 2006) at http://hqinet001.hqmc.usmc.mil/HD/Historical /Frequently_Requested/Navajo_Code_Talkers.htm [February 22, 2007]. "Army Code Talkers," American Indians in the U.S. Army (Washington, DC: U.S. Army, October 25, 2005) at http://www.army.mil/americanindians/codetalkers_05.html [March 8, 2007]. "20th Century Warriors: Native American Participation in the United States Military"; "American Indians in World War II"; "American Indian Medal of Honor Recipients"; "Native American Women Veterans" ; and "Native Americans in the Korean War" (Washington, DC: Department of Defense, n.d.) at http://www.defenselink.mil/specials/nativeamerican... [November 2, 2007]. Also see Thomas A. Britten, *American Indians in World War I: At Home and At War*. And, David La Vere, "North Carolina's American Indians in World War II," *North Carolina's Shining Hour: Images and Voices from World War II* (Raleigh, NC: Our State Books) made available by the North Carolina Museum of History, Office of Archives and History, N.C. Department of Cultural Resources (2006). Also see *Tar Heel Junior Historian* 45:1 (fall 2005); Carrie McLeroy, "First Sioux to Receive Medal of Honor," Military News, February 22, 2008 (Washington, D.C.: United States Army, 2008) at http://www.army.mil/-news/2008/02/22/7566-first-sioux-to-receive-medal-of-honor/ [March 5, 2008].

Selected Bibliography

ISSUE SPECIFIC

Abel, Annie H., ed. *Chardon's Journal of Fort Clark 1834-1839.* Pierre, SD: Department of History of the State of South Dakota, 1932.

Abel, Annie Heloise. *The American Indian and the End of the Confederacy, 1963-1866.* Lincoln: University of Nebraska Press, 1993.

_____. *The American Indian as Slaveholder and Secessionist.* Lincoln: University of Nebraska Press, 1992.

_____. *The American Indian in the Civil War, 1862-1865.* Lincoln: University of Nebraska Press, 1992.

_____. *The American Indian Under Reconstruction.* Cleveland: Arthur H. Clark, 1925.

Acrey, Bill P. *Navajo History: The Land and the People.* Shiprock, NM: Central Consolidated School District No. 22, 1988.

Adams, Richard Calmit. *The Delaware Indians, A Brief History.* Saugerties, NY: Hope Farm Press (originally published by GPO, 1909), 1995.

Alden T. Vaughan, Gen. Ed. *Early American Indian Documents: Treaties and Laws, 1607–1789,* 20 Vols. Washington, DC: University Publications of America, 1979-.

Aleshire, Peter. *Cochise: The Life and Times of the Great Apache Chief.* New York: Wiley, 2001.

_____. *The Fox and the Whirlwind: General George Crook and Geronimo.* New York: Wiley, 2000.

Algier, Keith. *The Crow and the Eagle: A Tribal History from Lewis & Clark to Custer.* Caldwell, ID: Caxton Printers, 1993.

Anderson, Gary Clayton. *The Conquest of Texas: Ethnic Cleansing in the Promised Land, 1820-1875.* Norman: University of Oklahoma Press, 2005.

Andrist, Ralph K. *The Long Death: The Last Days of the Plains Indians.* Norman: University of Oklahoma Press, 2000.

Anson, Bert. *The Miami Indians.* Norman: University of Oklahoma Press, 2000.

Appleman, Roy E. *Great Western Indian Fights.* New York: Doubleday & Co, 1960.

Armer, Laura Adams. *In Navajo Land.* New York: David McKay Co., 1962.

Aten, Lawrence E. *Indians of the Upper Texas Coast.* New York: Academic Press, 1983.

Axtell, James. *The Indians' New South: Cultural Change in the Colonial Southeast.* Baton Rouge, LA: University of Louisiana Press, 1997.

Bailey, L.B. *A History of the Navajo Wars, 1846-1868.* Pasadena, CA: Westernlore Publications, 1978.

Baird, W. David. *The Quapaw Indians: A History of the Downstream People.* Norman: University of Oklahoma Press, 1980.

Bancroft-Hunt, Norman. *People of the Totem: The Indians of the Pacific Northwest.* Norman: University of Oklahoma Press (London: Orbis, 1979), 1988.

Banks, Dennis with Richard Erdoes. Ojibwa Warrior: Dennis Banks and the Rise of the American Indian Movement. Norman: University of Oklahoma Press, 2004.

Banner, Stuart. *How the Indians Lost Their Land: Law and Power on the Frontier.* Cambridge, MA: Harvard University Press (Belknap), 2005.

Barbour, Barton H. *Fort Union and the Upper Missouri Fur Trade.* Norman: University of Oklahoma Press, 2000.

Barrett, S. M., ed. *Geronimo: His Own Story.* New York: Dutton, 1970 (orig. 1906).

Bartram, William. *Travels Through North & South Carolina, Georgia, East & West Florida, the Cherokee Country, the Extensive Territories of the Muscogulges, or Creek Confederacy, and the Country of the Chactaws; Containing An Account of the Soil and Natural Productions of Those Regions, Together with Observations on the Manners of the Indians.* Philadelphia: James & Johnson, 1791.

Beal, Merrill D. *"I Will Fight No More Forever": Chief Joseph and the Nez Perce War.* Seattle: University of Washington Press, 1963(1982 imprint).

Bean, Lowell J. *Mukat's People: The Cahuilla Indians of Southern California.* Berkeley, CA: University of California Press, 1974.

Beck, David R. M. *The Struggle for Self-Determination: History of the Menominee Indians.* Lincoln: University of Nebraska Press, 2007.

Beck, Paul N. *Inkpaduta: Dakota Leader.* Norman: University of Oklahoma Press, 2008.

Beckham, Stephen Dow. *The Indians of Western Oregon: This Land was Theirs.* Coos Bay, OR: Arago Books, 1977.

Bennett, Pamela J., ed. "Finding Our Way Home: The Great Lakes Woodland People," *Indiana Historian.* Indianapolis: Indiana Historical Bureau, September 2001.

Bernstein, Alison R. *American Indians and World War II: Toward a New Era in Indian Affairs.* Norman: University of Oklahoma Press, 1999.

Berthrong, Donald J. *The Southern Cheyennes.* Norman: University of Oklahoma Press, 1963.

Blaine, Martha. *The Ioway Indians*. Norman: University of Oklahoma Press, 1979.

Blair, Emma H., trans. and ed. *The Indian Tribes of the Upper Mississippi Valley and Region of the Great lakes as Described by Nicolas Perrot*. Cleveland: Arthur H. Clark Co., 1912.

Bolton, Herbert Eugene. Russell M. Magnaghi, ed. *The Hasinais: Southern Caddoans as Seen by the Earliest Europeans*. Norman: Universityof Oklahoma Press, 2002.

Boughter, Judith A. *Betraying the Omaha Nation, 1790-1916*. Norman: University of Oklahoma Press, 1998.

Braatz, Timothy. *Surviving Conquest: A History of the Yavapai Peoples*. Lincoln: University of Nebraska Press, 2007.

Bray, Kingsley M. *Crazy Horse: A Lakota Life*. Norman: University of Oklahoma Press, 2006.

Brinton, Daniel Garrison. *The Lenâpé and Their Legends*. New York: AMS Press, 1969.

Britten, Thomas A. *American Indians in World War I: At Home and At War*. Albuquerque: University of New Mexico Press, 1999, c1997.

Brown, Dee. *Bury My Heart at Wounded Knee: An Indian History of the American West*. New York: Holt, Rinehart & Winston, 1970.

_____. *Showdown at Little Big Horn*. Lincoln: University of Nebraska Press, 2004.

Brown, John P. *Old Frontiers: The Story of the Cherokee Indians from Earliest Times to the Date of Their Removal to the West, 1838*. Kingsport, TN: Southern Publishers, 1938.

Brown, Joseph Epes, ed. *The Sacred Pipe: Black Elk's Account of the Seven Rites of the Oglala Sioux*. Norman: University of Oklahoma Press,

Brumwell, Stephen. *White Devil: A True Story of War, Savagery; Bengeance in Colonial America*. New York: Da Capo, 2006.

Buecker, Thomas R. *Fort Robinson and the American West, 1874-1899*. Norman: University of Oklahoma Press, 2003.

Bureau of Indian Affairs, Department of the Interior. *Indian Entities Recognized and Eligible To Receive Services From the United States Bureau of Indian Affairs*. Washington, DC: *Federal Register* / Vol. 67, No. 134 / 46328-46333, July 12, 2002.

Bushnell, David I., Jr. *Villages of the Algonquian, Siouan; Caddoan Tribes West of the Mississippi*. St. Clair Shores, MI: Scholarly Press, 1976 (Washington, DC: GPO, 1922).

Calloway, Colin G. *The Shawnees And The War For America*. New York: Viking Penguin, 2007.

_____. *The Western Abenakis of Vermont, 1600-1800: War, Migration; The Survival of an Indian People*. Norman: University of Oklahoma Press, 1994.

Capps, Benjamin. *The Indians (Old West Series)*. New York: Time-Life Books, 1973.

Carrey, Johnny & Conley, Cort. *The Middle Fork and the Sheepeater War*. Cambridge, ID: Backeddy Books, 1980.

Carrington, Frances C. *My Army Life and the Fort Phil Kearney Massacre, With an Account of the Celebration of "Wyoming Opened"*. Lincoln: University of Nebraska Press, 2004 (first pub. 1910).

Carter, Cecile Elkins. *Caddo Indians: Where We Come From*. Norman: University of Oklahoma Press, 2001.

Census Bureau Geography Division. *The American Indians and Alaska Natives in the United States Wall Map*. Washington, DC, October 1, 2002 (rev. 2004).

Catlin, George. *Letters and Notes on the Manners, Customs, Conditions of the North American Indians Written During Eight Years' Travel 1832-1839) Amongst the Wildest Tribes of Indians of North America*. Minneapolis: Ross and Haines, 1965.

_____. Edited by Peter Matthiessen under the title *North American Indians*. New York: Penguin Books, 1989.

Caton, John D. *The Last of the Illinois and a Sketch of the Pottawattomies*. Chicago: Rand McNally, 1870.

Chalfant, William Y. *Cheyennes and Horse Soldiers: The 1857 Expedition and the Battle of Solomon's Fork*. Norman: University of Oklahoma Press, 1989.

Champagne, Duane, ed. *Chronology of Native North American History from Pre-Columbia Times to Present*. Detroit: Gale Research, 1994.

Champerlain, Kathleen P. *Victorio: Apache Warrior and Chief*. Norman: University of Oklahoma Press, 2007.

Cheek, Lawrence W. *The Navajo Long Walk*. Tucson, AZ: Rio Nuevo Publishers (Look West Series), 2004.

Clark, Galen. *Indians of the Yosemite Valley and Vicinity, Their History, Customs and Traditions* (Yosemite Valley, CA,1904).

Clifton, James A. *The Pokagons, 1683-1983: Catholic Potawatomi Indians of the St. Joseph River Valley*. Lanham: University Press of America,

_____. *The Prairie People: Continuity and Change in Potawatomi Indian Culture, 1665-1965*. Lawrence: Regents Press of Kansas, 1977.

Collins, Charles. *Apache Nightmare: The Battle at Cibecue Creek*. Norman: University of Oklahoma Press, 1999.

Connell, Evan S. *Son of the Morning Star: Custer and the Little Bighorn*. New York: History Book Club, .

Corwin, Hugh. *The Kiowa Indians: Their History and Life Stories*. Lawton, OK: s.n., 1958.

Cozzens, Peter, ed. *Eyewitnesses to the Indian Wars, 1865-1890*, 5 Vols.. Mechanicsburg, PA: Stackpole Books, 2001-2005.

Curtis, Edward S. *The North American Indian*, 20 Vols. New York: Johnson Reprint Corp, 1970 (1907-30).

Cushman, H. B. and Angie Debo, ed. *History of the Choctaw, Chickasaw and Natchez Indians*. Norman: University of Oklahoma Press, 1999.

Danziger, Edmund Jefferson, Jr. *The Chippewas of Lake Superior*. Norman: University of Oklahoma Press, 1990.

Debo, Angie. *Geronimo: The Man, His Time, His Place*. Norman: University of Oklahoma Press, 1982.

_____. *The Rise and Fall of the Choctaw Republic*. Norman: University of Oklahoma Press, 1934.

_____. *A History of the Indians of the United States*. Norman: University of Oklahoma Press, 1970.

Deloria, Philip J. *Playing Indian*. New Haven, CT: Yale University Press, 1998.

Deloria, Vine, Jr. *Custer Died for Your Sins: An Indian Manifesto*. Norman: University of Oklahoma Press, 1988.

_____, ed. *The Indian Reorganization Act: Congress and Bills*. Norman: University of Oklahoma Press, 2002.

_____. Raymond J. DeMallie. *Documents of American Indian Diplomacy: Treaties, Agreements; Conventions, 1775-1979*. Norman: University of Oklahoma Press, 1999.

Denig, Edwin Thomson. J.N.B. Hewitt, ed. *The Assiniboine*. Norman: University of Oklahoma Press, 2000.

Densmore, Frances. *Dakota and Ojibwe People in Minnesota*. St. Paul: Minnesota State Historical Society, 1977.

Denton, Sally. *American Massacre: The Tragedy at Mountain Meadows*, September 1857. New York: Alfred A. Knopf, 2003.

Diuguid, Lewis W. "A History Ignored," *Kansas City Star*, January 13, 2006, p. B7. Kansas City: The Kansas City Star, 2006.

Dixon, David. *Never Come to Peace Again: Pontiac's Uprising and the Fate of the British Empire in North America*. Norman: University of Oklahoma Press, 2005.

Douthit, Nathan. *Uncertain Encounters: Indians and Whites at Peace and War in Southern Oregon, 1820s-1860s*. Corvallis: Oregon State University Press, 2002.

Dowd, Gregory Evans. *War under Heaven: Pontiac, the Indian Nations; the British Empire*. Baltimore: Johns Hopkins University Press, 2002.

Drake, Samuel Gardner. Additions by H. L. Williams. *The Book of the Indians of North America: Comprising Details in the Lives of about Five Hundred Chiefs and Others, the Most Dist...* New York: Hurst & Co., 1880, 15th ed. Rev. (First ed., Boston: Josiah Drake, 1832, under title *Indian Biography*; 1833 ed. under current title; 2001 POD ed. Avail.) Avail. UMK MNL SpecColl Snyder.

Drysdale, Vera Louise, ed. *The Gift of the Sacred Pipe: Black Elk's Account of the Seven Rites of the Oglala Sioux*. Norman: University of Oklahoma Press, 1995.

Eby, Cecil. *That Disgraceful Affair, The Black Hawk War*. New York: Norton, 1973.

Edmunds, R. David. *The Otoe-Missouria People*. Phoenix: Indian Tribal Series, 1976.

_____. *The Potawatomis: Keepers of the Fire*. Norman: University of Oklahoma Press, 1978.

_____ and Joseph L. Peyser. *The Fox Wars: The Mesquakie Challenge to New France*. Norman: University of Oklahoma Press, 1993.

Ehle, John. *The Trail of Tears: The Rise and Fall of the Cherokee Nation*. New York: Doubleday & Co., 1988.

Elizabeth A. H. John,. *Storms Brewed in Other Men's Worlds: The Confrontation of Indians, Spanish; French in the Southwest, 1540-1795*. College Station, TX: Texas A&M University Press, 1975.

Elmore, Reaman G. *The Trail of the Iroquois Indians: How the Iroquois Nation Saved Canada for the British Empire*. New York: Barnes & Noble, 1967.

Ernest Wallace and E. Adamson Hoebel. *The Comanches: Lords of the South Plains*. Norman: University of Oklahoma Press, 1987.

Ethridge, Robbie. *Creek Country: The Creek Indians and Their World*. Chapel Hill, NC: University of North Carolina Press, 2003.

Everett, Dianna. *The Texas Cherokees: A People between Two Fires, 1819-1840*. Norman: University of Oklahoma Press, 1995.

Ewers, John C. *The Blackfeet: Raiders on the Northwestern Plains*. Norman: University of Oklahoma Press, 1958.

Ewers, John C., ed. *Edwin Thompson Denig's Five Indian Tribes of the Upper Missouri: Sioux, Arickaras, Assiniboines, Crees, Crows*. Norman: University of Oklahoma Press, 1961 (written mid-1850s).

Farish, Thomas Edwin. *The History of Arizona: Indians of Arizona, Vol. VII*. Phoenix, AZ: Thomas Edwin Farish, Arizona Historian, 1918.

Fay, George E., ed. *Treaties Between the Potawatomi Tribe of Indians and the United States of America, 1789 - 1867*. Greeley, CO: University of Northern Colorado, 1971.

Fehrenbach, T. R. *Comanches: The Destruction of a People*. New York: Alfred A. Knopf, 1974.

Fletcher, Alice C. & Francis La Flesche. *The Oneida Tribe*, 2 Vols. Lincoln: University of Nebraska Press, 1992 (Bison Book). Reproduced from the Twenty-Seventh Annual Report of the Bureau of American Ethnology to the Secretary of the Smithsonian Institution, 1906-1906 (Washington: Government Printing Office, 1911).

Flynn, A. J. *The American Indian as a Product of Environment, with special reference to the Pueblos*. Boston: Little, Brown; Company, 1907.

Foley, Thomas W. *Father Francis M. Craft, Missionary to the Sioux*. Lincoln: University of Nebraska Press, 2002.

Foreman, Grant. *Indian Removal*. Norman: University of Oklahoma Press, 1953.

_____. *The Five Civilized Tribes*. Norman: University of Oklahoma Press, 1934.

_____. *The Last Trek of the Indians*. Chicago: University of Chicago Press, 1946.

Foster, Morris W. *Being Comanche: A Social History of an American Indian Community.* Tucson, AZ: University of Arizona Press, 1991.

Franco, Jere Bishop. *Crossing the Pond: The Native American Effort in World War II.* Denton, TX: University of North Texas Press, 1999.

Frazer, Robert W. *Forts of the West: Military Forts and Presidios and Posts Commonly Called Forts West of the Mississippi River to 1898.* Norman: University of Oklahoma Press, 1965.

Gallay, Alan. *The Indian Slave Trade: The Rise of the English Empire in the American South, 1670-1717.* New Haven, CT: Yale University Press, 2002.

Garroutte, Eva Marie. *Real Indians: Identity and the Survival of Native America.* Berkeley, CA: University of California Press, 2003.

Gates, Paul Wallace. "A Fragment of Kansas Land History: The Disposal of the Christian Indian Tract," *Kansas Historical Quarterly*, August 1937, vol. 6, no. 3, pp. 227 to 240. Topeka: Kansas Historical Society, 1937.

_____, ed. *The Rape of Indian Lands.* New York: Arno Press, 1979. (Series: Management of public lands in the United States)

Gibson, Arrell M. *The Chickasaws.* Norman: University of Oklahoma Press, 1972.

Gipson, Lawrence Henry. Translated from the German of the original manuscript by Harry E. Stocker. *The Moravian Indian Mission on White*

River: Diaries and Letters, May 5, 1799, to November 12, 1806. Indianapolis: Indiana Historical Bureau, 1938.

Glatthaar, Joseph T. and James Kirby Martin, *Forgotten Allies: The Oneida Indians and the American Revolution .* New York: Hill and Wang, 2006.

Goetzmann, William H. *Exploration and Empire: The Explorer and the Scientist in the Winning of the American West.* New York: History Book Club, 2006. (First Copyright 1996)

Grant, Bruce. *Concise Encyclopedia of the American Indian.* New York: Random House, 1958, 1960.

Greene, Jerome A. *Morning Star Dawn: The Powder River Expedition and the Northern Cheyennes,1876.* Norman: University of Oklahoma Press, 2003.

_____, ed. *Lakota and Cheyenne: Indian Views of the Great Sioux War, 1876-1877.* Norman: University of Oklahoma Press, 2000.

_____. Foreword by Alvin M. Josephy, Jr. *Nez Perce Summer, 1877: The U.S. Army and the Nee-Me-Poo Crisis.* Helena: Montana Historical Society Press, 2000.

Gregory A. Waselkov. *A Conquering Spirit: Fort Mims and the Redstick War of 1813-1814.* Tuscaloosa, Alabama: University of Alabama Press, 2006.

Griffin-Pierce, Trudy. *Native Peoples of the Southwest.* Albuquerque, NM: University of New Mexico Press, 2000.

Grinnell, George Bird. "Bent's Old Fort and Its Builders," *Kansas Historical Quarterly, Kansas Historical Collections, 1919-1922,* vol. 15, 28-91. Topeka: Kansas State Historical Society, 1922.

_____. *The Cheyenne Indians*, 2 Vols. Lincoln: University of Nebraska Press (Bison Book), 1972. Reproduced from the first edition published by the Yale University Press (New Haven, CN, 1923).

_____. *The Fighting Cheyennes.* Norman: University of Oklahoma Press, 1956. First published Charles Scribner's Sons (New York, 1915).

_____. *Two Great Scouts and Their Pawnee Battalion: The Experiences of Frank J. North and Luther H. North.* Cleveland: Arthur H. Clark Co., 1928.

Haefeli, Evan; Kevin Sweeney. *Captors and Captive: The 1704 French and Indian Raid on Deerfield.* Amherst: University of Massachusetts Press, 2003.

Hagan, William T. *Quanah Parker, Comanche Chief.* Norman: University of Oklahoma Press, 1995.

_____. *Taking Indian Lands: The Cherokee (Jerome) Commission, 1889-1893.* Norman: University of Oklahoma Press, 2003.

_____. *The Sac and Fox Indians.* Norman: University of Oklahoma Press, 1958.

_____. *United States-Comanche Relations: The Reservation Years.* Norman: University of Oklahoma Press, 1990 (originally published New Haven: Yale University Press, 1976).

Halaas, David Fridtjof and Andrew E. Masich. *Halfbreed: The Remarkable True Story of George Bent: Caught Between the Worlds of the Indian and the White Man.* New York: Da Capo, 2004.

Haley, James L. *Apaches: A History and Cultural Portrait.* Norman: University of Oklahoma Press, 1997.

_____. *Buffalo War: The History of the Red River Indian Uprising of 1874.* Garden City, NY: Doubleday & Co., 1976.

Hampton, Bruce. *Children of Grace: The Nez Perce War of 1877.* Lincoln: University of Nebraska Press, 2002.

Hardorff, Richard G. *Indian Views of the Custer Fight: A Source Book.* Norman: University of Oklahoma Press, 2005.

Harmon, Alexandra. *Indians in the Making: Ethnic Relations and Indian Identities around Puget Sound.* Berkeley: University of California Press, 1998.

Harmon, George D. *Sixty Years of Indian Affairs.* Chapel Hill: University of North Carolina Press, 1941.

Harrington, M. R. (Mark Raymond). *The Indians of New Jersey: Dickon Among the Lenapes.* New Brunswick, N.J: Rutgers University Press, 1963.

Hatch, Thom. *The Blue, The Gray, & The Red: Indian Campaigns of the Civil War.* Mechanicsburg, PA: Stackpole Books, 2003.

Hatley, Tom. *The Dividing Paths: Cherokees and South Carolinians through the Era of Revolution.* New York: Oxford University Press, 1993.

Hauptman, Laurence M. *Between Two Fires: American Indians in the Civil War.* New York: The Free Press (Simon and Schuster), 1995.

Hauptman, Laurence M. and James D. Wherry. *The Pequots in Southern New England: The Fall and Rise of an American Indian Nation.* Norman: University of Oklahoma Press, 1993.

Healy, Donald T. and Peter J. Orenski. *Native American Flags.* Norman: University of Oklahoma Press, 2003.

Heckewelder, John Gottlieb. *Account of the History, Manners; Customs of the Indian Nations Who Once Inhabited Pennsylvania and the Neighboring States.* New York: Arno Press, 1971 (orig. 1876).

Heckewelder, John Gottlieb Ernestus. *A Narrative of the Mission of the United Brethren Among the Delaware and Mohegan Indians, from Its Commencement, in the Year 1740, to the Close of the Year 1808.* New York: Arno Press, 1820 (1971).

Heizer, Robert F. , ed. Edward D. Castillo, "The Impact of Euro-American Exploration and Settlement," *Handbook of American Indians: California.* Vol. 8., 109. Washington, DC: Smithsonian Institution, 1978.

Heizer, Robert F., ed. *The Destruction Of California Indians.* Lincoln: University of Nebraska Press & Bison Books, 1993.

Hodge, Frederick Webb, ed. *Handbook of American Indians North of Mexico: Smithsonian Institution, Bureau of American Ethnology, Bulletin 30.* Washington, DC: Government Printing Office, 1910.

Holiday, John and Robert S. McPherson. *A Navajo Legacy: The Life and Teachings of John Holiday.* Norman: University of Oklahoma Press,

Hoover, Herbert T. *The Sioux and Other Native American Cultures of the Dakotas: An Annotated Bibliography.* Westport, CT: Greenwood Press, 1993.

Horsman, Reginald. *Expansion and American Indian Policy, 1783-1812.* Norman: University of Oklahoma Press, 1992.

Howard, Harold P. *Sacajawea.* Norman: University of Oklahoma Press, 1979.

Hoxie, Frederick E., ed. *Encyclopedia of North American Indians.* Boston: Houghton Mifflin, 1996.

Hughes, J. D. *American Indians in Colorado.* Boulder, CO: Pruett Publishing, 1987.

Hyde, George E. *Red Cloud's Folk: A History of the Oglala Sioux.* Norman: University of Oklahoma Press, 1976 (first ed. 1937).

_____. *The Pawnee Indians.* Norman: University of Oklahoma Press, 1988.

_____. Savoie Lottinville, ed. *Life of George Bent: Written from His Letters.* Norman: University of Oklahoma Press, 1987.

Hyslop, Stephen G. *Bound for Santa Fe: The Road to New Mexico and the American Conquest, 1806-1848.* Norman: University of Oklahoma Press, 2002.

"Indians of North America, "Supplement to *National Geographic*, December 1972, p. 739A, Vol. 142, No. 6.

Irwin, Lee. *The Dream Seekers: Native American Visionary Traditions of the Great Plains.* Norman: University of Oklahoma Press, 1996.

Jackson, Helen Hunt. *A Century of Dishonor: A Sketch of the United States Government's Dealings with some of the Indian Tribes.* Williamstown, MA: Corner House Publishers, 1973.

Jahoda, Gloria. *Trail of Tears: The Story of the American Indian Removals 1813-1855.* New York: Wings Books, 1995 ed. (New York: Holt, Rhinehart and Winston, 1975).

Janetski, J. C. *The Ute of Utah Lake.* Salt Lake City: University of Utah Press, 1990.

Jefferson, Thomas. *Notes on the State of Virginia* (1781-1782). Merrill D. Peterson, ed. *Thomas Jefferson: Writings.* New York: Library of America, 1984.

Johnson, F. Roy. *The Algonquians: Indians of That Part of the New World First Visited by the English.* Murfreesboro, NC: Johnson Publishing Company, 1972.

Johnson, Michael. *The Native American Tribes of North America: A Concise Encyclopedia.* New York: Macmillan, 1994.

Johnson, Terry C. *Black Sun: The Battle of Summit Springs, 1869.* New York: Mass Market Paperback, March 1991.

Jonathan B Taylor; Joseph P Kalt. *American Indians on Reservations: A databook of socioeconomic change between the 1990 and 2000 Censuses.* Cambridge, MA: Harvard Project on American Indian Economic Development, Malcolm Wiener Center for Social Policy, John F. Kennedy School of Government, Harvard University, 2005.

Jones, David S. *Rationalizing Epidemics: Meanings and Use of American Indian Mortality since 1600.* Cambridge, MA: Harvard University Press, 2004.

Josephy, Alvin M., Jr. *Now That the Buffalo's Gone: A Study of Today's American Indians.* Norman: University of Oklahoma Press, 1984.

Kappler, Charles J., ed. *Indian Affairs: Laws and Treaties,* 5 Vols. Washington, DC: Government Printing Office, 1972.

Kavanagh, Thomas W. *Comanche Political History: An Ethnohistorical Perspective, 1706-1875.* Lincoln: University of Nebraska Press, 1995.

Keenan, Jerry. *The Great Sioux Uprising: Rebellioin on the Plains, August-September 1862.* New York: Da Capo, .

Kidwell, Clara Sue. *Choctaws and Missionaries in Mississippi, 1818-1918.* Norman: University of Oklahoma Press, 1997.

Knaut; rew L. *The Pueblo Revolt of 1680: Conquest and Resistance in Seventeenth-Century New Mexico.* Norman: University of Oklahoma Press, 1997.

Kopper, Philip. *The Smithsonian Book of North American Indians Before the Coming of the Europeans.* Washington, DC: Smithsonian Books,

Kraft, Herbert C. *The Lenape: Archaeology, History and Ethnography.* Newark, NJ: New Jersey Historical Society, 1986.

Kraft, Louis. *Gatewood & Geronimo.* Albuquerque: University of New Mexico Press, 2000.

Kreuzer, Terese Loeb. "A holiday on the mesa," *Kansas City Star,* December 9, 2007, G1.

Kroeber, A.L. *Handbook of the Indians of California.* Washington, DC: Bureau of American Ethnology Bulletin 78, 1925.

Kroeber, Alfred L. *Native Tribes Map.* Berkeley, CA: University of California Press, 1966.

La Flesche, Francis. *The Osage and the Invisible World: From the Works of Francis La Flesche.* Norman: University of Oklahoma Press, 1995.

Landes, Ruth. *The Prairie Potawatomi: Tradition and Ritual in the Twentieth Century.* Madison: University of Wisconsin Press, 1970.

Lane, Joseph. *Report of the United States Office of Indian Affairs for 1850.* Washington, DC: Department of the Interior, 1850.

Larson, Robert W. *Gall: Lakota War Chief.* Norman: University of Oklahoma Press, 2007.

_____. *Red Cloud: Warrior-Statesman of the Lakota Sioux.* Norman: University of Oklahoma Press, 1999.

Lauber, Almon Wheeler. *Indian Slavery in Colonial Times Within the Present Limits of the United States.* New York: Columbia University Press, 1913.

Lavender, David. *Bent's Fort.* Garden City, NY: Doubleday & Co., 1954.

_____. *Let Me Be Free: The Nez Perce Tragedy.* Norman: University of Oklahoma Press, 1999.

Leitch, Barbara A. *A Concise Dictionary of Indian Tribes of North America.* Algonac, MI: Reference Publications, 1979.

Lemons, Nova A. *Pioneers of Chickasaw Nation, Indian Territory.* Miami, OK: Timbercreek Ltd., 1991.

Leutenegger, Benedict and Marion A. Habig. *The Zacatecan Missionaries in Texas, 1716-1834.* Austin, TX: Texas Historical Survey Committee, 1973.

Lewis, Bonnie Sue. *Creating Christian Indians: Native Clergy in the Presbyterian Church.* Norman: University of Oklahoma Press, 2003.

Lowie, Robert H. *The Crow Indians.* Lincoln: University of Nebraska Press (Bison Books), 2004 (first pub. 1935).

Madsen, Brigham D. *The Northern Shoshoni.* Caldwell, Idaho: Caxton Printers, 1980.

_____. *The Shoshoni Frontier and the Bear River Massacre.* Salt Lake City: University of Utah Press, 1985.

Mahon, John K. *The History of the Second Seminole War by John Bemrose.* Gainesville: University of Florida Press, 1966.

Malinowski, Sharon and Anna Sheets, eds. *The Gale Encyclopedia of Native American Tribes.* Detroit, MI: Gale, 1998.

Mandelbaum, David G. *The Plains Cree.* Regina: University of Regina, 1979.

Manypenny, George W. *Our Indian Wards.* New York: Da Capo Press, 1972 (orig. 1880).

Marken, Jack W. and Herbert T. Hoover. *Bibliography of the Sioux.* Metuchen, NJ: Scarecrow Press, 1980.

Marquis, Thomas Guthrie. *The War Chief of the Ottawas: A Chronicle of the Pontiac War.* Toronto: Glasgow, Brook & Company, 1915. George M. Wrong and H. H. Langton, eds. *Chronicles of Canada,* Volume 15 of 32. eText No. 15522 produced by Gardner Buchanan (April 2, 2005).

Marshall, Joseph M., III. *The Journey of Crazy Horse: A Lakota History.* New York: Viking, 2004.

Mason, W. Dale. *Indian Gaming: Tribal Sovereignty and American Politics.* Norman: University of Oklahoma Press, 2000.

Mathews, John Joseph. *The Osages.* Norman: University of Oklahoma Press, 1961.

_____. *Wah'Kon-Tah: The Osage the the White Man's Road.* Norman: University of Oklahoma Press, 1932.

Mayhall, Mildred P. *The Kiowas.* Norman: University of Oklahoma Press, 1962 (2nd ed. 1971).

McChristian, Douglas. *Fort Bowie, Arizona: Combat Post of the Southwest, 18858-1894.* Norman: University of Oklahoma Press, 2005.

McDonald, Daniel. *Removal of the Pottawattomie Indians from Northern Indiana: Embracing also a Brief Statement of the Indian Policy of the Government; Other Historical Matter Relating to the Indian Question.* Plymouth, IN: McDonald & Co., Printers, 1899.

McGinty, Brian. *The Oadman Massacre: A Tale of Desert Captivity and Survival.* Norman: University of Oklahoma Press, 2006.

McMurtry, Larry. *Oh What a Slaughter: Massacres in the American West: 1846-1890.* New York: Simon & Schuster, 2005.

McNitt, Frank. *Navajo Wars; Military Campaigns, Slave Raids and Reprisals.* Albuquerque, NM: University of New Mexico Press, 1972.

McPherson, Robert S. *Navajo Land, Navajo Culture: The Utah Experience in the Twentieth Century.* Norman: University of Oklahoma Press, 2002.

McReynolds, Edwin C. *The Seminoles.* Norman: University of Oklahoma Press, 1957.

Merrell, James H. *The Indians' New World: Catawbas and Their Neighbors from European Contact through the Era of Removal.* Chapel Hill, NC: University of North Carolina Press, 1989.

Michno, Gregory F. *Encyclopedia of Indian Wars: Western Battles and Skirmishes, 1850-1890.* Missoula, MN: Mountain Press Publishing, 2003.

Milling, Chapman J. *Red Carolinians.* Columbia: University of South Carolina Press, 1969.

Monnett, John H. *Massacre at Cheyenne Hole: Lieutenant Austin Henely and the Sappa Creek Controversy.* Boulder: University Press of Colorado, 2004.

_____. *Tell Them We Are Going Home.* Norman: University of Oklahoma Press, 2004.

Mooney, James. *The Aboriginal Population of America North of Mexico*, Misc. Coll., Vol. 80, No. 7. Washington, DC: Smithsonian Institution, 1928.

Moore, William Haas. *Chiefs, Agents; Soldiers.* Albuquerque, NM: University of New Mexico Press, 1994.

Morgan, Lewis H. *The League of the Ho-de-no-sau-nee [Iroquois].* New York: Corinth Books, 1962.

Murray, Keith A. *The Modocs and Their War.* Norman: University of Oklahoma Press, 1985.

Muth, Marcia. *Kachinas: A Selected Bibliography.* Santa Fe, N.M.: Sunstone Press, 1984.

Nabokov, Peter and Lawrence Loendorf. *Restoring a Presence: American Indians and Yellowstone Park.* Norman: University of Oklahoma Press, 2004.

Nerburn, Kent. *Chief Joseph and the Flight of the Nez Perce: The Untold Story of an American Tragedy.* San Francisco: Harper, 2005.

Nester, William R. *The Arikara War: The First Plains Indian War, 1823.* Missoula, MO: Mountain Press, 2001.

New Jersey State Museum. *From Lenape Territory to Royal Province: New Jersey, 1600-1750.* Trenton, NJ: State of New Jersey, 1971.

Newcomb, William Wilmon. *The Culture and Acculturation of the Delaware Indians.* Ann Arbor: University of Michigan, 1956.

Nichols, Roger L. *American Indians in U.S. History.* Norman: University of Oklahoma Press, 2005.

Norgren, Jill. *The Cherokee Cases: Two Landmark Federal Decision in the Fight for Sovereignty.* Norman: University of Oklahoma Press, 2004.

Nye, Wilbur Sturtevant. *Bad Medicine and Good: Tales of the Kiowas.* Norman: University of Oklahoma Press, 1962.

O'Beirne, H. F. *Leaders and Leading Men of the Indian Territory, Vol. 1, Choctaws and Chickasaws.* Conway, AR: Oldbuck Press (Chicago: American Publishers' Association, 1891), 1993 (facsimile reprint).

O'Bryan, Aileen. *The Diné: Origin Myths of the Navaho Indians*, Bureau of American Ethnology of the Smithsonian Institution Bulletin 163. Washington, DC: Smithsonian Institution, 1956. (available on line at http://www.harvestfields.netfirms.com/NativeTribal/06bk/om01.htm).

O'Connell, Barry, ed. *On Our Own Ground: The Complete Writings of William Apess, A Pequot.* Amherst, MA: University of Massachusetts Press, 1992.

O'Nell, Theresa DeLeane. *Disciplined Hearts: History, Identity; Depression in an American Indian Community.* Berkeley: University of California Press, 1996.

Oatis, Steven J. *A Colonial Complex: South Carolina's Frontiers in the Era of the Yamasee War, 1680–1730.* Lincoln: University of Nebraska Press, 2004.

Ogunwole, Stella U. *The American Indian and Alaska Native Population: 2000.* Washington, DC: U.S. Census Bureau, Department of Commerce (Census 2000 Brief), February 2002.

Ortiz, Alphonso, vol. ed. *Handbook of North American Indians*, Vol. 9, Southwest. Washington, DC: Smithsonian Institution, 1979.

Osborn, William M. *The Wild Frontier: Atrocities During the American-Indian War from Jamestown to Wounded Knee.* New York: Random House, 2001.

Overly, James W. *A Nation of Statesmen: The Political Culture of the Stockbridge-Munsee Mohicans, 1815-1972.* Norman: University of Oklahoma Press, 2005.

Palsano, Edna L. *We, the First Americans.* Washington, DC: U.S. Bureau of the Census, 1993. (available online at http://www.census.gov/apsd/wepeople/we-5.pdf.

Paul, R. Eli. *Blue Water Creek and the First Sioux War, 1854-1856.* Norman: University of Oklahoma Press, 2004.

Payne, John Howard and Grant Foreman, eds. *Indian Justice: A Cherokee Murder Trial at Tahlequah in 1840.* Norman: University of Oklahoma Press, 2002.

Pearson, J. Diane. *The Nez Perces in the Indian Territory: Nimiipuu Survival.* Norman: University of Oklahoma Press, 2008.

Peckham, Howard. *Pontiac and the Indian Uprising.* Princeton, NJ: Princeton University Press, 1947.

Perdue, Theda and Michael D. Green, eds. *The Cherokee Removal: A Brief History With Documents.* New York: St. Martin's Press, 1995.

Peroff, Nicholas C. *Menominee Drums: Tribal Termination and Restoration, 1954-1974.* Norman: University of Oklahoma Press, 2006.

Petit, Benjamin Marie (1811-1839). *The Trail of Death: Letters of Benjamin Marie Petit.* Indianapolis: Indiana Historical Society, 1941.

Philbrick, Nathaniel. *Mayflower: A Story of Courage, Community; War.* New York: Viking, 2006.

Phillipa, Paul Chrisler. *The Fur Trade.* Norman: University of Oklahoma Press, 1961.

Piker, Joshua. *Okfuskee: A Creek Indian Town in Colonial America.* Cambridge, MA: Harvard University Press, 2004.

Powell, John Wesley, 1834-1902. *Indian Linguistic Families Of America, North Of Mexico, Seventh Annual Report of the Bureau of Ethnology to the Secretary of the Smithsonian Institution, 1885-1886.* Washington, DC: Government Printing Office, 1891.

Powell, Suzanne I. *The Potawatomi.* New York: F. Watts, 1997.

Pratt, Richard Henry and Robert M. Utley, eds. *Battlefield and Classroom: Four Decades with the American Indian, 1867-1904.* Norman: University of Oklahoma Press, 2004.

Prins, Harald. *The Mi'kmaq: Resistance, Accommodation; Cultural Survival.* Fort Worth, TX: Harcourt Brace College Publishers, 1996.

Prucha, Francis Paul. *American Indian Policy in the Formative Years: The Indian Trade and Intercourse Acts, 1790-1834.* Lincoln, NE: University of Nebraska Press, 1970.

Prucha, Francis Paul. *Atlas of American Indian Affairs.* Lincoln: University of Nebraska Press, 1990.

Prucha, Francis Paul. *The Indians in American Society: From the Revolutionary War to the Present.* Berkley: University of California Press, 1953.

Rawls, James J. *Indians of California: The Chaning Image.* Norman: University of Oklahoma Press, 1986.

Remini, Robert V. *Andrew Jackson and His Indian Wars.* New York: Viking, 2002.

Reyhner, Jon and Jeanne Eder. *American Indian Education: A History.* Norman: University of Oklahoma Press, 2004.

Richardson, Rupert N. *The Comanche Barrier to South Plains Settlement.* Millwood, NY: Kraus (originally published Glendale, California: Clark, 1933), 1973.

Richter, Daniel K. *Facing East from Indian Country: A Native History of Early America.* Cambridge, MA: Harvard University Press, 2001 (First Harvard Press paperback edition, 2003).

Robert H. Lowie. *The Crow Indians.* Lincoln: University of Nebraska Press, 2004 (first published in 1935).

Robertone, Patricia E. *Grave Undertaking: An Archaeology of Roger Williams and the Narragansett Indians.* Washington, DC: Smithsonian, 2001

Roberts, David. *A Newer World: Kit Carson, John C. Fremont and the Claiming of the American West.* New York: Simon & Schuster, 2000.

_____. *Once They Moved Like the Wind: Cochise, Gerónimo: The Apache Wars.* New York: Simon & Schuster, 1994.

_____. *The Pueblo Revolt: The Secret Rebellion That Drove the Spaniards Out of the Southwest.* New York: Simon & Schuster, 2004.

Robinson III, Charles M. *A Good Year to Die: The Story of the Great Sioux War.* New York: Random House, 1995.

Ronda, James P. *Lewis and Clark Among the Indians.* Lincoln: University of Nebraska Press, 1994.

Roundtree , Helen C. *The Powhatan Indians of Virginia: Their Traditional Culture.* Norman: University of Oklahoma Press, 1992.

Royce, Charles C., comp. *Indian Land Cessions in the United States: 18th Annual Report of the Bureau of American Ethnology -- 1896-'97.* Washington, DC: Government Printing Office, 1897.

Ruby, Robert H. *The Chinook Indians: Traders of the Lower Columbia River.* Norman: University of Oklahoma Press, 1976.

Rudy, Robert H. and John A. Brown. *A Guide to the Indian Tribes of the Pacific Northwest.* Norman: University of Oklahoma Press, 1992.

_____. *The Cayuse Indians: Imperial Tribesmen of Old Oregon.* Norman: University of Oklahoma Press, 1972.

_____. *The Spokane Indians: Children of the Sun.* Norman: University of Oklahoma Press, 2006.

Sandoz, Mari. *Cheyenne Autumn.* Lincoln: University of Nebraska Press, 1992..

Sanger, George P., ed. *Statutes at Large, Treaties; Proclamations of the United States of America from December 5, 1859 to March 3, 1863,* Vol. XII. Boston: Little, Brown and Company, 1863.

Satz, Ronald N. *American Indian Policy in the Jackson Era.* Norman: University of Oklahoma Press, 2002.

Schoolcraft, Henry R. *History of the Indian Tribes of the United States.* San Francisco: Historical American Indian Press (Philadelphia: J. B. Lippincott & Co., 1857), 1975.

Schoolcraft, Henry R. *The American Indians: Their History, Conditions; Prospects.* Rochester, NY: Wanzer Foot and Co., 1851.

Schwartz, E. A. *The Rogue River Indian War and Its Aftermath, 1850-1980.* Norman: University of Oklahoma Press, 1997.

Seton, Julia M. *American Indian Arts: A Way of Life.* New York: Ronald Press, 1962.

Shuck-Hall, Sheri Marie. *Journey to the West: The Alabama and Coushatta Indians.* Norman: University of Oklahoma Press, 2008.

Sides, Hampton. *Blood and Thunder: An Epic of the American West.* New York: Doubleday, 2006.

Simpson, James H. Frank NcNitt, ed. *Navaho Expedition: Journal of a Military Reconnaissance from Santa Fe, New Mexico to the Navaho County, made in 1849 by Lieutenant James H. Simpson.* Norman: University of Oklahoma Press, 2003.

Skinner, Alanson. *Exploration of Aboriginal Sites at Throgs Neck and Clasons Point, New York City, New York.* New York: Museum of the American Indian, Heye Foundation, 1919.

Skinner, Alanson and Arthur C. Parker. *The Algonkian Occupation of New York.* Rochester, NY: Lewis H. Morgan Chapter, 1923.

Smith, Sherry L. *Reimagining Indians: Native Americans Through Anglo Eyes, 1880-1940.* New York: Oxford University Press, 2000.

Sonnichsen, C. L. *The Mescalero Apaches.* Norman: University of Oklahoma Press, 1979 (2nd ed.).

Speck, Frank Gouldsmith. Edited with an introduction by Edward S. Rogers. *A Northern Algonquian Source Book.* New York: Garland Publishing, 1985.

Stanley, Lori A. *The Indian Path of Life: the Life History of Truman Washington Dailey of the Otoe-Missouria Tribe: A doctoral dissertation submitted to the University of Missouri.* Columbia: University of Missouri, 1993.

Steele, Ian K. *Betrayals: Fort William Henry and the Massacre.* New York: Oxford University Press, 1990.

Stern, Kenneth S. Loud Hawk: *The United States versus the American Indian Movement.* Norman: University of Oklahoma Press, 1994.

Steward, Omer C. Henry T. Lewis and M. Kat Anderson, eds. *Forgotten Fires: Native Americans and the Transient Wilderness.* Norman: University of Oklahoma Press, 2002.

Stewart, Omer C. *Peyote Religion: A History.* Norman: University of Oklahoma Press, 1993.

Sturtevant, William C., gen. ed. *Handbook of North American Indians.* Washington, DC: Smithsonian Institution, 1978-.

Sugden, John. *Blue Jacket: Warrior of the Shawnees.* Lincoln: University of Nebraska Press, 2000.

Swanton, John R. *Source Material on the History and Ethnology of the Caddo Indians: Smithsonian Institution, Bureau of American Ethnology Bulletin 132.* Washington, DC: Government Printing Office, 1942.

_____. *The Indian Tribes of North America: Smithsonian Institution Bureau of American Ethnology Bulletin 145.* Washington, DC: Government Printing Office, 1953. (Reprint available from Baltimore: Genealogical Printing Company, 2003.)

Sweeney, Edwin R. *Cochise: Chiricahua Apache Chief.* Norman: University of Oklahoma Press, 1995.

_____, ed. *Making Peace with Cochise: The 1872 Journal of Captain Joseph Alton Sladen.* Norman: University of Oklahoma Press, 2008.

Tanner, Henel Nornbeck. *Atlas of Great Lakes Indian History.* Norman: University of Oklahoma Press, 1987.

Tate, Michale L. *Indians and Emigrants: Encounters on the Overland Trails.* Norman: University of Oklahoma Press, 2006.

Taylor, Alan. *The Divided Ground: Indians, Settlers; the Northern Borderland of the American Revolution.* New York: Alfred A. Knopf, 2006.

Tebbel, John and Keith Jennison. *The American Indian Wars.* New York: Harper, 1960.

Terrell, John Upton. *The Plains Apache.* New York: Thomas Y. Crowell Company, 1975.

Thompson, Gerald. *The Army and the Navajo.* Tucson, AZ: University of Arizona Press, 1976.

Townsend, Camilla. *Pocahontas and the Powhatan Dilemma: An American Portrait.* New York: Hill and Wang, 2004.

Trafzer, Clifford E. *As Long As The Grass Shall Grow and Rivers Flow: A History of Native Americans.* Belmont, CA: Thomson/Wadsworth, 2000.

Trudeau, Jean Baptiste. Trans. by Mrs. H. T. Beauregard. *Journal of Jean Baptiste Truteau on the Upper Missouri, June 7, 1749-March 26, 1795.* New York: American History Review, 19:299-333, 1914.

Tuner, Geoffrey. *Indians of North America.* Poole, Dorset, England: Blandford Press, 1979.

Tuttle, Edmund B. *Three Years On the Plains: Observations of Indians, 1867-1870.* Norman: University of Oklahoma Press, 2002.

Thwaites, Reuben Gold, ed., *The Jesuit Relations and Allied Documents: Travels and Explorations of the Jesuit Missionaries in New France 1610—1791.* Cleveland, OH: The Burrows Brothers Co., 1899.

U.S. War Department. *The War of Rebellion: A Compilation of the Official Records of the Union and Confederate Armies* (abr. *O.R.*), 4 series, 70 vols. in 128 pts. Washington, DC: Government Printing Office, 1880-1901.

Udall, Stewart L. *The Quiet Crisis.* New York: Holt, Rinehart and Winston, 1963.

Underhill, Ruth M. *The Navajos.* Norman: University of Oklahoma Press, 1983 (rev. ed.).

Unrau, William E. *The Kansa Indians: A History of the Wind People, 1673-1873.* Norman: University of Oklahoma Press, 1971.

Utley, Robert M. *The Indian Frontier of the American West 1846-1890.* Albuquerque: University of New Mexico Press, 1984.

_____. *The Lance and the Shield: The Life and Times of Sitting Bull.* New York: Henry Holt and Company, 1993.

_____. *The Last Days of the Sioux Nation.* New Haven, CT: Yale University Press, 2004 (2nd ed.).

Utter, Jack. *American Indians: Today's Questions.* Lake Ann, MI: National Woodlands Publishing, 1993.

Vaughan, Alden T., ed. *New England Encounters: Indians and Euroamericans, ca. 1600-1850.* Boston: Northeastern University Press, 1999.

Viola, Herman. Little *Bighorn Remembered: The Untold Indian Story of Custer's Last Stand.* New York: Times Books, 1999.

Vogel, Virgil. *American Indian Medicine.* Norman: University of Oklahoma Press, 1990.

Voget, Fred W. *The Shoshoni-Crow Sun Dance.* Norman: University of Oklahoma Press, 1998.

Waldman, Carl. Maps and Illustrations by Molly Braun. *Atlas of the North American Indian.* New York: Facts on File, 1985.

Wallace, Anthony F. C. *Jefferson and the Indians: The Tragic Fate of the First Americans.* Cambridge, MA: Harvard University Press, 1999.

_____. *The Long, Bitter Trail: Andrew Jackson and the Indians.* New York: Hill and Wang, 1993.

Wallace, Ernest and E. Adamson Hoebel. *The Comanches.* Norman: University of Oklahoma Press, 1952.

Warren, Stephen. *The Shawnees and Their Neighbors, 1795-1870.* Urbana: University of Illinois Press, 2005.

Warren, William W. Intro. by W. Roger Buffalohead. *History of the Ojibway People.* St. Paul: Minnesota Historical Society Press, 1984. Reprint. Originally published: *History of the Ojibways, Based Upon Traditions and Oral Statements* (St. Paul, 1885)

Webber, Bert. *Indians Along the Oregon Trail: The Tribes of Nebraska, Wyoming, Idaho, Oregon and Washington.* Medford, OR: Webb Research Group, 1989.

Weslager, C. A. *The Delaware Indian Westward Migration: With Texts of Two Manuscripts, 1821-22, Responding to General Lewis Cass's Inquiries About Lenape Culture and Language.* Wallingford, PA: Middle Atlantic Press, 1978.

Weslager, C. A. *The Delaware Indians: A History.* New Brunswick, NJ: Rutgers University Press, 1972.

White, Christine Schultz and Benton R. White. *Now The Wolf Has Come: The Creek Nation in the Civil War.* College Station: Texas A. & M University Press, 1996.

White, Jon Manchip. *Everyday Life of the North American Indian.* London: B.T. Batsford, 1979.

Whitman, William. *The Oto (A doctoral dissertation submitted to Columbia University).* New York: Columbia University, 1937.

Wilkins, David E. and Tsianina Lomawaima. *Uneven Ground: American Indian Sovereignty and Federal Law.* Norman: University of Oklahoma Press, 2002.

Wilkins, Thurman. *Cherokee Tragedy.* New York: Macmillan, 1970.

Williams, Glenn F. *The Year of the Hangman: George Washington's Campaign Against the Iroquois.* Yardley, PA: Westholme, 2005.

Williamson, Margaret Holmes. *Powhatan Lords of Life and Death: Commands and Consent in Seventeenth Century Virginia.* Lincoln: University of Nebraska Press, 2003.

Wilson, James. *The Earth Shall Weep: A History of Native America.* New York: Atlantic Monthly Press, 1998.

Woferman, Kristie C. *The Osage in Missouri.* Columbia: University of Missouri Press, 1997.

Woodward, Grace Steele. *The Cherokees.* Norman: University of Oklahoma Press, 1982.

Wooster, Robert. *Nelson A. Miles and the Twilight of the Frontier Army.* Lincoln: University of Nebraska Press, 1993.

Worcester, Donald. *The Apaches: Eagles of the Southwest.* Norman: University of Oklahoma Press, 1992.

Wray, Jacilee, ed. *Native Peoples of the Olympic Peninsula: Who We Are.* Norman: University of Oklahoma Press, 2002. (Olympic Peninsula Intertribal Cultural Advisory Committee).

Yellowtail, Thomas. *Yellowtail, Crow Medicine Man and Sun Dance Chief:* An Autobiography As Told to Michael Oren Fitzgerald. Norman: University of Oklahoma Press, 1994.

Zesch, Scott. *Captured: A True Story of Abduction by Indians on the Texas Frontier.* New York: St. Martin's Press, 2004.

OTHER RELAVENT WORKS

Alvord, Clarence W. *The Mississippi Valley in British politics: A Study of the Trade, Land, Speculation: Experiments in Imperialism Culminating in the American Revolution.* New York: Russell & Russell, 1959.

Ambrose, Stephen E. *Nothing Like in the World: The Men Who Build the Transcontinental Railroad, 1863-1869.* New York: Simon & Schuster, 2000.

_____. *Undaunted Courage: Meriwether Lewis, Thomas Jefferson; the Opening of the American West.* New York: Simon & Schuster, 1996.

Arbic, Bernie. *City of the Rapids: Sault Ste. Marie's Heritage.* Allegan, MI: Pricilla Press, 2006.

Axelrod, Alan. *America's Wars.* New York: Wiley, John & Sons, 2000.

Bain, David Haward. *Empire Express: Building the First Transcontinental Railroad.* New York: Viking, 1999.

Barry, Louise. *The Beginning of the West: Annals of the Kansas Gateway to the American West, 1540-1854.* Topeka: Kansas State Historical Society, 1972.

Belko, William S. "A Founding Missourian: Duff Green and Missouri's Formative Years, 1816-1825," Part 1, *Missouri Historical Review*, Vol. xcviii, No. 2, 93-114. Columbia: State Historical Society of Missouri, January 2004.

Bolton, Herbert Eugene. *Texas in the Middle Eighteenth Century: Studies in Spanish Colonial History and Administration* (Rrpt., Austin: University of Texas Press, 1970). Berkeley, CA: University of California Press, 1915.

Boorstin, Daniel J. *The Americans: The Democratic Experience.* New York: Random House, 1973.

Brands, H. W. *Andrew Jackson: His Live and Times.* New York: Doubleday & Co, 2005.

Brands, H. W. *The Age of Gold: The California Gold Rush and the New American Dream.* New York: Doubleday & Co., 2002.

Brookhiser, Richard. *Founding Father.* New York: The Free Press, 1996.

Brown, Dee. *Hear That Lonesome Whistle Blow: The Epic Story of the Transcontinental Railroad.* New York: Henry Holt and Company Owl Book (Holt, Rinehart and Winston, 1977), 2001.

Burrows, Edwin G. and Mike Wallace. *Gotham: A History of New York City to 1898.* New York: Oxford University Press, 1999.

Carriker, Robert C. *Father Peter John De Smet: Jesuit in the West.* Norman: University of Oklahoma Press, 1995.

Castañeda, Carlos E. *Our Catholic Heritage in Texas,* 7 Vols.,. New York: Arno Press (orig. published Austin: Von Boeckmann-Jones, 1936-1958.

Castillo, Richard Griswold del. *The Treaty of Guadalupe Hildalgo.* Norman: University of Oklahoma Press, 1992.

Chaffin, Tom. *Pathfinder: John Charles Fremont and the Course of American Empire.* New York: Hill and Wang, .

Chittenden, Hiram Martin and Alfred Talbot, Richardson, eds. Life, Letters; Travels of Father Pierre Jean De Smet, 4 Vols.. New York: F. P. Harper, 1905.

Christian, Shirley. *Before Louis & Clark: The Story of the Chouteaus, the French Dynasty that Ruled America's Frontier.* New York: Farrar, Straus, 2004.

Clay, John V. *Spain, Mexico and the Lower Trinity: An Early History of the Texas Gulf Coast.* Baltimore: Gateway Press, 1987.

Connelley, William E. *A Standard History of Kansas and Kansans,* 5 Vols. Chicago: Lewis Publishing Company, 1918.

Cutler, William G. *History of the State of Kansas.* Chicago: A. T. Andreas, 1883.

Dary, David. *The Oregon Trail: An American Saga.* New York: Alfred A. Knopf, 2004.

_____. *The Santa Fe Trail: Its History, Legends, Lore.* New York: Alfred A. Knopf, 2000.

De Voto, Bernard. *The Year of Decision, 1846.* New York: Truman Talley Books (St. Martin's Griffin), 1943.

De Voto, Bernard, ed. *The Journals of Lewis and Clark.* Boston: Houghton Mifdflin, 1953 (ren. 1981, pub. 1997).

Department of the Army. *American Military History 1607-1953.* Washington, DC: Government Printing Office, 1956.

Ellis, Joseph J. *American Sphinx, The Character of Thomas Jefferson.* New York: Alfred A. Knopf, 1997.

Ferling, John. *A Leap in the Dark: The Struggle to Create the American Republic.* New York: Oxford University Press, 2003.

Freehling, William W. *The Road to Disunion: Sessionists at Bay 1776-1854.* New York: Oxford University Press, 1990.

Friedenburg, Daniel M. *Life, Liberty; the Pursuit of Land: The Plunder of Early America.* New York: Prometheus Books, 1992.

Galloway, Patricia K., ed. *La Salle and His Legacy : Frenchmen and Indians in the Lower Mississippi Valley.* Jackson: University Press of Mississippi, 1982.

Gray, Lucile M. *The Story of Illinois.* Fenton: McRoberts Publishing Inc., 1977.

Hart, Albert Bushnell, ed.,. *The American Nation: A History from Original Sources,* Vol. 17. New York: Harper & Brothers, 1906.

Holiday, J. S. *Rush for Riches: Gold Fever and the Making of California.* Berkeley, CA: University of California Press, 1999.

Hollow, Eugene W. *The Southwest, Old and New.* New York: Alfred A. Knopf, 1961.

Jones, Landon Y. *William Clark and the Shaping of the West.* New York: Hill and Wang, 2004.

Kinnaird, Lawrence Kinnaird. *The Frontiers of New Spain: Nicolas de Lafora's Description.* Berkeley, CA: University of California Press Quivira Society, 1958.

La Harpe, Jean-Baptiste Bénard de. Translated By Joan Cain and Virginia Koenig. *The Historical Journal of the Establishment of the French in Louisiana.* Lafayette: University of Southwestern Louisiana, 1971.

Lamar, Howard Roberts. *The Far Southwest, 1846-1912, A Territorial History.* New Haven, CT: Yale University Press, 1966 (rev. ed., Albuquerque: University of New Mexico Press, 2000).

Lamon, Ward H. *The Life of Abraham Lincoln.* Lincoln: University of Nebraska Press, 1999 (orig. ed., 1872).

Lancaster, Bruce. *The American Heritage History of the American Revolution.* New York: American Heritage/Bonanza Books, 1984.

_____. *The American Revolution.* New York: Bonanza Books, 1984 (Originally published by American Heritage 1971).

Lavender, David. *Westward Vision: The Story of the Oregon Trail.* Lincoln: University of Nebraska Press, 1985 (first ed. 1963).

Lord, Walter. *The Dawn's Early Light.* New York: W. W. Norton, 1972.

Maier, Pauline. *American Scripture: Making the Declaration of Independence.* New York: Alfred A. Knopf, 1997.

McCormac, Eugene Irving. *James K. Polk, A Political Biography.* New York: Russell & Russell (Berkley: University of California Press, 1922), 1965.

McLynn, Frank. *Wagons West: The Epic Story of America's Overland Trails.* New York: Grove Press, 2002.

607

McWilliams, Richebourg Gaillard. *Iberville's Gulf Journals*. Birmingham: University of Alabama Press, 1981.

Miller, Nathan. *Theodore Roosevelt, A Life*. New York: William Morrow, 1992.

Morgan, Dale. *Jedediah Smith and the Opening of the West*. Indianapolis: Bobbs-Merrill Co., 1953.

Morgan, Edmund S. *American Slavery, American Freedom: The Ordeal of Colonial Virginia*. New York: History Book Club (first pub. W. W. Norton, 1975), 2005.

Moulton, Gary E., ed. *The Journals of the Lewis and Clark Expedition*, 13 Vols.. Lincoln: University of Nebraska Press, 1983–2004 (core 7-Vol. Set, 1986-1993).

_____, ed. *The Lewis and Clark Journals: An American Epic of Discovery*. Lincoln: University of Nebraska Press, 2003 (abridged).

Norall, Frank. *Bourgmont: Explorer of the Missouri, 1698-1725*. Lincoln: University of Nebraska Press, 1988.

O'Rourke, Thomas P. *The Franciscan Missions in Texas* (Ph.D. dissertation, Catholic University of America, 1927; pub. as Vol. 5 of the Catholic University of America Studies in American Church History. New York: AMS Press, 1974.

Opie, John. *Ogallala: Water for a Dry Land*. Lincoln: University of Nebraska Press, 1993.

Parkman, Francis. Illustrated by James Daugherty. *The Oregon Trail*. New York: Farrar &Rinehart, 1931

Pickett, Albert J. *History of Alabama*. Birmingham: Webb Book Co., 1900.

Randall, Willard Sterne. *George Washington, A Life*. New York: Henry Holt and Company, 1997.

_____. *Thomas Jefferson, A Life*. New York: Henry Holt and Company, 1993.

Rosen, Fred. *Gold: The Story of the 1848 Gold Rush and How It Shaped a Nation*. New York: Thunder's Mouth Press, 2005.

Schlesinger, Arthur M., Jr. *The Age of Jackson*. New York: Book-of-the-Month Club (Boston: Little, Brown and Company, 1945), 1989.

Seale, William. *The President's House: A History*. Washington, DC: White House Historical Association, 1986.

Shea, John Gilmary. *Discovery and Exploration of the Mississippi Valley with the Original Narratives of Marquette, Allouez, Membré, Hennepin; Anastase Douay*. New York: Redfield, 1853.

Shorto, Russell. *The Island in the Center of the World: The Epic Story of Dutch Manhattan & the Forgotten Colony that Shaped America*. New York: Doubleday & Co., 2004.

Silliman, Sue I. *St. Joseph in Homespun*. Three Rivers, MI: Three Rivers Publishing, 1931 (reprinted as originally published).

Starr, Kevin. *California, A History*. New York: Modern Library, 2005.

Wallace, Anthony F. C. *Jefferson and the Indians: The Tragic Fate of the First Americans*. New York: Belknap/Harvard University Press, 1999.

Worster, Donald. *A River Running West: The Life of John Wesley Powel*. New York: Oxford University Press, 2001.

Violette, Eugene Morrow. *History of Missouri*. New York: D. C. Heath & Co., 1918.

Wright, Jonathan. *God's Soldiers: A History of the Jesuits*. New York: Doubleday Image ed., 2004.

Selected Index

This Index will direct the reader to people and topics included in this work, exclusive of tribal names. For varioius tribal names the reader is referred to the Master List in Appendix B and the narratives in the main section.

Acknowledgements

I would like to recognize the kind and generous assistance of Theresa Gipson, Special Collections, Nichols Library of the University of Missouri-Kansas City and Amy Johnson, Indian Pueblo Cultural Center, Albuquerque, New Mexico. Many thanks also to Mike Klein, Senior Reference Librarian, Geography and Map Division, Library of Congress. Additional thanks to all those individuals and organizations that assisted in providing references and illustrations that made preparation of this Atlas possible, especially Pamela J. Bennett, Director of the Indiana Historical Bureau, and Holly Reed, National Archives, Still Picture Reference, Washington, DC.

Printed in the United States
144799LV00001B/55/P